AN ENCYCLOPAEDIA OF WORLD HINDI LITERATURE

By the same author :

Concise Oxford Companion to Hindi Literature
An Encyclopaedia of Indian Literature
World Perspectives on Swami Dayanand Saraswati

AN ENCYCLOPAEDIA
OF
WORLD HINDI LITERATURE

GANGA RAM GARG
M.A., Ph.D.

Foreword by :
DR. PRABHAKAR MACHWE

CONCEPT PUBLISHING COMPANY, NEW DELHI

First Published 1986

Ganga Ram Garg (*b.* 1924-)

Published by
Naurang Rai
Concept Publishing Company
H-13, Bali Nagar
NEW DELHI-110015 (India)

Printed at
Bimal Printers,
221/2A, Padam Nagar,
DELHI-110007

OM

Quod tuomst meumst, omne meum est autem tuom
—PLAUTUS, *Trinumus* Act ii, sc. 2.

[What is thine is mine, and all mine is thine.]

TO

My Eldest Son

VED PRAKASH GARG, M. Sc., Ph.D.

&

My Grandson

AYUSHMAN

Foreword

Dr. Ganga Ram Garg, ex-Vice-Chancellor of Gurukula Kangri Vishwavidyalaya (Hardwar) and author of the *Sankshipta Oxford Hindi Sahitya Parichayak* (Concise Oxford Companion to Hindi Literature), *Encyclopaedia of Indian Literature* (Sanskrit, Pali. Prakrit, Apabhransh), *World Perspectives on Swami Dayananda Saraswati* and the present *Encyclopaedia of World Hindi Literature* is a very meticulous, hard-working and thorough bibliographer, literary critic and compiler of obscure and untapped information. It requires not only painstaking perseverance, but also single-mindedness of purpose and crystal-clear sincerity. Dr. Garg is trained in the Vedic-Sanskrit tradition and yet is fully acquainted with western methodology in such monumental editing works. All his works have been very favourably reviewed in Indian and foreign magazines and journals and have been well appreciated by eminent scholars. In fact, the first time I met him, it was George Orwell and his Ideas, that he was doing research on, which he did more than two decades ago. He is a fine scholar of both Hindi and English, with a grounding in Sanskrit. He knows all the literary dialects of Hindi. So he is ideally suited to undertake such a mighty task, a gigantic encyclopaedic dictionary of authors and works in Hindi.

It is never possible to be perfect and all-exhaustive in such matters. One has to be choosey. What I saw, from the Hindi entries here, is that he has gone in details about well-known authors like Tulsidas, Kabir, Bhushan, Bihari, Premchand or Prasad, and also works by great authors are fully introduced ; yet if every small or big living writer expects that he or she should get the same amount of space or the same adjectives for his work (Tulsidas had said : 'Who does not like one's own creation?'), it will be unfair to the compiler and to the literature of that language. Sense of proportion has to be maintained, and however modern critics may extol and raise to the skies any ordinary penpusher belonging to their own coterie, or his temporarily-shocking work, the cruel sieve of time will decide. That is the ultimate acid test. Such works as the present volume are not compiled every day. They have to last for decades as Standard Reference Works. So if he appears scanty and sketchy in the case of X or Y, it is not because he does not like that author but because, in comparison of Titans, pigmies are pigmies.

This work gives wealth of details and I learnt many things from its entries about many old and mediaeval authors which I did not notice earlier. To cover the entire literature, even if important, of Khari Boli, Braj, Avadhi, Bhojpuri, Maithili, Rajasthani and other languages which made modern Hindi, is an uphill task. In addition to this, there are articles on folk-poets and folk-literature. Writers of non-Hindi speaking areas have also been well-presented. There are articles on writers and scholars of foreign countries, *e.g.*, Mauritius, Fiji, Guyana, Soviet Russia, America, France, England, Germany, Italy, Czechoslovakia, Japan, Hungary and other countries. I congratulate Dr. Garg on the production of such a volume.

Dr. Garg's style is pithy, compact and to the point. He does not waste nor mince his words ; he does not unnecessarily shower adjectives and superlatives too. So let there be greater power to his pen. Let such individual efforts be blessed by institutions. Only such dedication can result into some desired *magnum opus*. Dr. Garg now stays at Vanaprastha Ashram, Jwalapur (Hardwar). This beautiful path, which he is carving out from the *Vana* or jungle of the lack of information about Indian language literatures, surely it will guide many more further travellers. The woods no doubt are dark and deep. But all of us have to think and re-assure every one that all the promises are not yet kept ! I see much promise in such Herculean task. A pioneering attempt indeed, vast in its compass and monumental ! I congratulate him on achieving what once I was dreaming to do.

(DR.) PRABHAKAR MACHWE

Bharatiya Bhasha Parishad,
36-A Shakespeare Sarani,
Calcutta-17.
6.11.1985.

by the councillors. The words of doubt are [illegible] and [illegible] [illegible] have to them [illegible] every one that all [illegible] [illegible] not [illegible] I see much promise in such [illegible] [illegible] A [illegible] indeed, within its [illegible] [illegible] Bhasa Academy [illegible] [illegible] to do.

(Dr.) [illegible]

[illegible] Bhasha Parisad,
[illegible] Shakespeare Sarani,
Calcutta-17
[illegible] 1985

Preface

The present work, *An Encyclopaedia of World Hindi Literature* is the second volume of my *An Encyclopaedia of Indian Literature* (Sanskrit, Pali, Prakrit & Apabhransh; 1982; revised and enlarged edition under print) and is in a way a larger version of my *Concise Oxford Companion to Hindi Literature* (Oxford, 1963). The work embraces articles on important poets, dramatists, fiction writers, critics, scholars, linguists and their important works of Khari Boli, Braj, Avadhi, Maithili, Rajasthani, Bhojpuri, Magahi, Garhwali, Kumaoni, Bundelkhandi, Malwi, Kannauji, Chhattisgarhi, Haryanavi, Chambiyali, Kului, Brajbuli, Brajboli, Brajavali, etc. as also articles on folk-literature of the regions where the above languages and dialects are spoken. There are also articles on Hindi writers of non-Hindi areas, such as Tamil Nadu, Andhra, Kerala, Karnataka, Bengal, Assam, Orissa, Maharashtra, Gujarat, Jammu & Kashmir, Panjab, etc It also contains articles on creative writers and scholars of foreign countries like Mauritius, Fiji, Surinam, Nepal, Burma, Trinidad, Guyana, Russia, America, England, Japan, France, Germany, Italy, Canada, Belgium, Hungary, Holland, Sweden, Romania, Poland, Czechoslovakia, Thailand, Kenya, South Africa, Sri Lanka, Pakistan, Finland, Portugal, Hongkong, Korea, etc. Some names have been included, who have promoted the cause of Hindi in non-Hindi speaking areas or countries.

In the case of an eminent writer, some biographical details (with brief appreciation) have been given, while in the case of others, emphasis is given to the important works written by them. Only very important works have been treated separately. In non-Hindi speaking areas, writers, who have published stray writings or have done research, have been included ; this is by way of promotion to the cause of Hindi.

Hindi literature, both creative and critical, is quite vast. It is quite possible that names of some writers, especially of the modern ones, may be missing but as it is a question of what to select and what to deselect, a point on which not two persons would agree, differences in discretion in this regard are inevitable. But if my attention is drawn to such writers, I would try to make amends in the next edition, which is expected to come out soon. As at present, they may please not take it as a reflection on their merit. It is, however, to be understood that the present work is not a catalogue of authors and works published so far.

The work is mainly compilation, though it has taken me over a decade to give it a finale. In preparing such a work, a large number of works have been consulted. I am especially indebted to the following works : *Hindi Sahitya ka Brihat Itihas* (especially vols. 15 and 16 for non-Hindi speaking Hindi writers and Hindi folk-literature respectively), published by the Nagari Pracharini Sabha, Kashi, *Hindi Sahitya ka Itihas* by Ram Chandra Shukla, *Hindi Sahitya ka Itihas* by Nagendra and Suresh Chand Gupta, Histories of Hindi Literature by Ram Awadh Dwivedi, K.B. Jindal and R.L. Handa, my own Hindi book : *Concise Oxford Companion to Hindi Literature, History of Maithili Literature* by Jayakanta Mishra, *History of Rajasthani Literature* by H.L. Maheshwari, *Rajasthani Bhasha aur Sahitya* by Motilal Maneriya, *Braj Sahitya ka Itihas* by Satyendra, histories of literatures of the above dialects, *Dwitiya Mahayuddhotar Hindi Sahitya ka Itihas* by Lakshmi Sagar Varshney, *Modern Hindi Fiction* and *Hindi Kavita : Adhunik Ayam* by Ram Darash Mishra, *Hindi Drama and Stage* by Birendra Narayan, *Literary Criticism in Hindi* by Ram Chandra Prasad, *Bharatiya Sahitya Kosh* by Nagendra, *Divangat Hindi Sevi* by Kshem

Chandra Suman, *Haryana ki Lokdharmi Natya Parampara* by Purnachand Sharma, *HIndi ke Europiya Vidwan* by Murlidhar Shrivastav, *A Bibliography of Studies on Hindi Language and Linguistics* by Narindar K. Aggarwal, *Comparative Indian Literature* (Macmillan ; vol. I, 1984 ; vol. II, 1985), Reports of three Vishwa Hindi Sammelans, several issues of 'Indian Literature', 'Gagananchal', 'Vishwa Hindi Darshan', and hundreds of other works, magazines, catalogues, etc.

Dr. Prabhakar Machwe, an eminent poet, writer and scholar, has been kind enough to write a Foreword, which he did after going through the Script ; his suggestions have greatly improved the quality of the work. For this, I am thankful to Dr. Machwe.

For information on foreign writers, I wrote more than 100 letters to Universities and Institutes the world over and some of them duly responded as also provided details of the writers in their countries. Some of them suggested names to be approached direct for fuller details. In this connection, Dr. R. Stuart McGregor, Faculty of Oriental Studies, University of Cambridge, England, Professor Yevgeni Petrovich Chelyshev, Institute of Oriental Studies, U.S.S.R. Academy of Sciences, Moscow, Dr. Michael C. Shapiro, Department of Asian Languages and Literature, University of Washington, U.S.A., Dr. K. Koga, Head of the Department of Hindi, Osaka University of Foreign Studies, Osaka, Japan, Director, Mahatma Gandhi Institute, Moka, Mauritius and Mr. Narindar K. Aggarwal, Professor of Library Administration, University of Illinois, Urabana, U.S.A. have been quite helpful. I am grateful to Embassies in India of German Democratic Republic, Belgium, Romania, Italy, Japan, Hungary, Czechoslovakia, U.S.S.R., France and Max Mueller Bhavan, which have provided me with the correct spellings of Hindi scholars in their countries and my thanks go to them. Despite repeated reminders, I could get no information from some foreign writers and as such material about them is not available or if available, it is based on second-hand information.

Dr. Maan Singh, ex-Professor and Head of the Department of Sanskrit, Gurukula Kangri Vishwavidyalaya, Hardwar has gone through a portion of the Typescript and his suggestions have been quite helpful. Shri K.C. Dutt, Librarian, Sahitya Akademi, New Delhi and Shri Jagdish Vidyalankar, Librarian, Gurukula Kangri, have offered me all the facilities that they could. I owc my thanks to all of them.

Titles of some pioneer and important works have been translated into English ; a total translation of all the titles was not even necessary. Articles on Hindi journalists, on literature in Hindi translated from other languages, as also on Hindi literature on science and social subjects, have not been included for fear of crossing the limitations of the Encyclopaedia.

My second son, Dr. Surya Prakash Vidyalankar, Department of Hindi, Shambhu Dayal Post-graduate College, Ghaziabad and his wife, Dr. Bina Garg, Department of Hindi, V.M.L. Post-graduate College, Ghaziabad have supplied me with books from their College Libraries and have also assisted me in preparation of this work. My eldest son, Dr. Ved Prakash Garg, his wife, Mrs. Indu Garg, M.A. and his mother, Mrs. Shanti Garg have helped me in preparation of the press copy. Dr. Satya Prakash, my youngest son, and his wife, Mrs. Neeharika, M.A. have also assisted me in one way or the other. I also take this opportunity of blessing my maternal grand-children : Deepali, Deepankur, Rakhi, Varun and Tarun for the little things they did for me. I am presenting this work to my eldest son, and grandson, Ayushman (son of Dr. Surya Prakash Vidyalankar).

Shri Naurang Rai, Publisher and his sons : Shri Ashok, Arvind and Alok have done all they could for the expeditious printing of the work. The Press and the proofreaders also deserve thanks for the co-operation in the preparation of the Encyclopaedia. Despite concerted efforts, proof mistakes, sometimes emerging on the border of howlers, may still be there, for which I express regrets.

No one is more conscious than myself about the shortcomings of this Volume but I hope the reader would ignore them keeping in mind that the work, designed on such a broad spectrum, is the first of its kind. Slips on an untrodden path may be many but I hope through this Volume, the non-Hindi world would form a good idea of the richness of Hindi literature. At the same time, the Encyclopaedia should serve the purpose of a handy reference tool.

II/20 Vanaprastha Ashram, GANGA RAM GARG
Jwalapur (Hardwar) 249407 (India)
November 16, 1985.

Hints to the Reader

1. Articles on most of the Indian and authors of Indian origin have been given beginning with their Christian names as they are known as such in India, but for the convenience of foreign and other readers, a complete Author Index beginning with their surnames has been given at the end.

2. Phonetic spellings have been observed and Tulsidas and Jay Shankar Prasad are written as 'Tulsidas' and 'Jay Shankar Prasad' and not as 'Tulasidasa' and 'Jaya Shankara Prasada'. Exception has, however, been made in the case of some Sanskrit words. Since 'SH' is commonly used for Hindi 'श' and 'ष', 'SH' has been used for both. Similarly, the distinction between 'V' and 'W' is not uniformly kept in Hindi circles : some preferring 'V', while others preferring 'W' ; invariably 'V' is used for 'व', though in some words where 'W' is very common, particularly in geographical names as also in such names : Agrawal, Shekhawat etc. 'W' has been used. The reader is, however, advised to look for 'V' and 'W' as both of them are correct. Similarly some write 'गुप्त' as 'Gupta' and some 'Gupt'; there are other words of this type and both the forms are correct. For 'ड़' 'd' has been used, though exception has been made in commonly-spelt names: 'Arora', 'Sarak', etc. The reader may, however, find some inconsistency here and there.

3. In Hindi, it has become a common practice to join two words, especially proper names : Ram Chandra is written as Ramchandra. This practice has been followed, except, for the sake of uniformity in commonly-accepted alphabetical order, the titles of the entries have been given in two words as : Ram

Chandra. Where, however, it does not affect the alphabetical order and where the names are too long and too short, the two words have been joined.

4. Names of foreign Hindi authors, country-wise are given in an Appendix at the end.

Contents

A

ABDUR RAHIM KHANKHANA (1553-1626). Poet, who wrote under the nom de plume of 'Rahim'. Son of Bairamkhan, who was the guardian of Akbar in his minority, Rahim himself rendered great service to Akbar in various capacities. He was not only a successful general and administrator, but was a scholar and poet too. A scholar of Arabic, Sanskrit, Persian, he was familiar with all the Hindi dialects. He continued to live in the reign of Jahangir but was deprived by the latter of all the *Jagirs*; hence the last days of his life were passed in abject poverty.

Rahim was so generous that he had been compared to 'Karna' of the *Mahabharat*. He was a close friend of Tulsidas (q v.) and it is said that he completed the second half of a couplet sent to him by the latter. It is also said that once he offered a sum of rupees 36 lacs to the poet, Gang (q.v.). Himself a poet, Rahim was a patron of letters and had a galaxy of scholars and poets around him. He exerted a great influence on the cultural life of his times, for his friends included both Hindus and Muslims, and likewise his works present a fine blend of what is best in both the communities.

Rahim's Hindi works are : *Rahim Satsai* (q.v.) or *Dohavali*, *Barvai Nayika-Bhed* (q v.), *Shringar Sortha* (verses on *Shringar* in *Sortha* metre), *Madanashtak* (eight verses on love in *Malini* metre), *Ras-Panchadhyayi* (*Krishna's Ras-Lila* in five chapters), *Nagar Shobha* (The City's Splendour), etc. The *Nagar Shobha* contains description of women of various professions and regions. His complete works have appeared in *Rahim Ratnavali*. He is also known to have written a book on astrology in Persian mixed with Sanskrit.

Rahim is primarily known for his *Dohas*, which are a veritable treasure-house of his rich and noble experience. His didactic verses have great poetic excellence. He tried his hand at *Doha*, *Sortha*, *Barvai*, *Kavitta*, etc. and composed poems in Braj and Avadhi with remarkable success. Of the *Barvai* metre, he is regarded as the originator.

ABHA BAI (AMBHA BAI ; 1771-1853). Rajasthani saint-poetess of Didwana, who was initiated in the religious order in 1797 by Temdas, the disciple of Dariyav (q.v.). A follower of Ram Snehi Sampraday, Ren, her poems, extolling God and Guru in a simple manner, include *Guru Mahima*, *Shishya Sampraday*, *Kakka Battisi*, stray verses and *Padas*.

ABHAY DEV. Malayalam-speaking modern Hindi scholar, who wrote *Hindi-Malayalam Kosh*, a popular dictionary. He also edited 'Vishwabharati', a literary magazine from Kottayam.

ABHAY RAM SANADHYA. Poet of the Riti school, who, at the instance of Maharaja Anup Singh of Bikaner, composed his *Anup Shringar* in 1697. The Maharaja also conferred upon him the title of 'Kaviray'.

ABHAY VILAS. See *Sandu Prithwiraj*.

ABHAYANAND AVASTHI. Modern Hindi poet of Fiji, whose chief work is *Qismat*.

ABHIMANYU UNNUTH 'SHABNAM' (1937-). Fiction writer of Mauritius, who is Editor at the Mahatma Gandhi Institute, Mauritius. His chief novels are : *Aur Nadi Bahti Rahi* (And the River Continued Flowing ; 1970), *Jam Gaya Suraj* (The Sun Froze), *Lal Pasina* (The Red Sweat ; 1973), *Ek Bigha Pyar* (One Bigha of Love), *Sephali*, *Apni hi Talash* (Quest for Oneself), *Khamoshi ke Chitkar* (The Cries of Silence ; 1976), *Chun Chun Chunav* (The Selection out of the Select), *Par Pagdandi Nahin Marti* (But the Track does not End ; 1983), *Gandhiji Bole The* (Gandhiji Spake) and *Apni-apni Sima*. *Vah Bich ka Admi* (That Middle Man) and *Insan aur Machine* (The Man and the Machine) are his short story collections, while *Nagphani men Uljhi Sansen* (1977) and *Cactus ke Dant* (The Teeth of Cactus) are his collections of poems. He also edited a poetical anthology : *Mauritius ki Hindi Kavita* (1976). His drama *Virodh* was staged in Lucknow ; his another drama is *Tin Drishya*. Abhimanyu holds a prominent place among modern Hindi fiction writers.

ABODH BAHUGUNA. Poet, who is noted for his collection of poems : *Dagdha Hriday*. He has also edited *Dhunyal* (1954), a collection of Garhwali folk-songs.

ABRAHAM, C.G. (fl. early 20th cent.). Malayalam-speaking Hindi teacher, who propagated Hindi in Trivandrum.

ABU RAS. See *Palhan*

ACHALDAS KHICHI RI VACHNIKA. Poem in Dingal dialect by Shivdas Gadan, which is a small narrative work in rhyming prose and verse, the number of verses and prose-sets being 119.

It describes the invasion by Sultan Hoshang Ghori of Mandu on Achaldas Khichi, son of Bhoj of Gagrongarh, Khichi's fight against the invaders till death and the brave ladies performing '*Jauhar*' in the fort. The poet, a contemporary of Khichi and probably his court-poet, composed this work some time after the happenings, around 1430—35. The *Vachnika*, being free from the Apabhransh impact, is a milestone in the bardic poetry. It contains passages of charming prose and is a pioneer work in this respect.

ACHALO BANIYO. Modern Dingal song-writer, whose *Gits* describe the battle of Rana Khetsi of Mewar (1364-82) with Hada Lalsingh of Bundi.

ACHCHUNNI, V.V. Malayalam-speaking modern Hindi writer, who tr. Malayalam short stories as also Nandnar's Malayalam novel into Hindi under the title : *Anjane Log* ; the translation appeared serially in the 'Yug-Prabhat', a literary magazine.

ACHYUTANAND DATT (1903-43). Maithili writer, who tr. the *Mahabharata* (1931), *Raghuvansha* (1933), *Ritusamhara* and *Bhamini-Vilasa* into Maithili from the original Sanskrit. He also composed *Krishna-Charitra* (1940-44). His two narrative poems (composed earlier) : *Karna* and *Kans-Vadh* have been published in 1979.

ADAMS, REV. M.T. Christian missionary in Benares, whose *Hindi Bhasha ka Vyakaran* (A Hindi Grammar, for the instruction of the young in the form of easy questions and answers ; Calcutta, 1827) was the first grammar written in Hindi, by a European ; it was prescribed for several years in schools. Adams also compiled an *Anglo-Hindui Abhidhan* (Calcutta, 1829 ; 2nd ed. 1838), which is the first ever English-Hindi Dictionary written in Hindi. Adams was the first European to use the word 'Hindi'.

ADARSH. Modern Hindi poet of Jammu-Kashmir, whose chief poetical collection is *Ek Ayas Anayas*.

ADARSH KUMARI YASHPAL. Modern Braj scholar ; her chief work is *Braj ki Lok-Kathayen*.

ADESHWAR RAO, P. Telugu-speaking Hindi poet, who is noted for his *Antaral* (1969), a selection of his poems. Along with Sundar Reddy and Iqbal, he edited *Hindi tatha Dravid Bhashaon ke Samanrupi Bhinnarthi Shabda* (identical words with varied meanings in Hindi and Dravid languages ; 1974).

ADHA KISNA I. See *Kisna Adha I.*

ADHA KISNA II. See *Kishanji.*

ADHE ADHURE (Incomplete Personalities). Drama (1969) by Mohan Rakesh (q.v.). It deals with 'a disintegrating middle-class family, which revolves around Savitri, the wife of an unsuccessful man. She has three children, representing the self-centred generation of today. The wife wants to save the sinking family but is disillusioned. Her search for a complete man remains unsuccessful. In fact, she meets a couple of men who turn out to be the alter egos of her husband. In the end, the veil of self-deception is removed. Both the husband and the wife are found to be destined to live a condemned life in a social prison with no exit. Alienated from each other but at the same time staying together as broken images with unresolved conflicts and tensions, these characters hover on the middle-class level of existentialism.'

ADILSHAH, IBRAHIM (fl. 1550). Ruler of Bijapur in South India, who patronized many a Dakkhini poet. He himself was a poet of no mean order and his work *Naurasa* in Dakkhini has come to light only recently.

ADINARAYAN MURTI, K. Telugu-speaking modern Hindi writer, who is noted for his biography : *Dakshin ke Vidyasagar*.

ADINATH 'DAMODAR'. Maithili poet, who was noted for his lyrics. He was a contemporary of Maharaja Maheshwar Singh (1850-60). He also composed hymns on devotional and pseudo-philosophical subjects.

ADURAM (fl. early 19th cent.). Rajasthani saint-poet of Ram Snehi Sampraday, Sinthal, whose *Vani* consists of stray verses in popular metres.

ADYA NATH JHA 'NIRANKUSH'. Modern Maithili poet, who is known for his lyrics.

AGAR CHAND NAHTA ((1910-). Scholar of Rajasthan, whose chief works are *Bikaner Jain Lekh Sangrah* (ed.), *Historical Material in Rajasthani Literature* (1978) and *Rajasthan*

Sahitya ki Gauravpurna Parampara. He has also published Rajasthani proverbs, literary articles and has espoused the cause of Rajasthani.

AGNIDUT. Modern poet, whose chief works are: *Apang Surya ki Yatra* (The Journey of the Maimed Sun ; 1979), *Tuta Hua Cactus* and *Ek Mukti Aur.*

AGNIPUSHPA. Maithili poet, whose first collection of poems is *Sahasrabahu* (1982).

AGRADAS (fl. 1575). Poet of the Ram-cult, who was preceptor of Nabhadas, the author of the *Bhaktamal* (q.v.). Though Agradas's Guru, Krishnadas Payahari was a member of the *Ashtachhap* and was thus a worshipper of Krishna, Agradas had his leanings towards Ram. Agradas was a resident of Galta in Rajasthan and established his separate *Gaddi* at Raiwasa near Sikar (Rajasthan). As propounder of the *Madhur-Bhav* in Ram-bhakti, his sect is popularly called 'Rasik'. He composed also stray verses in his devotion to Ram-Sita. His works are : *Hitopadesh Upakhyan Bavni*, *Dhyan Manjari*, *Ram Dhyan Manjari* and *Kundaliya*, which are of considerable literary merit and are marked by the art and delicacy of expression which go with devotion. On the model of *Krishna-Lila*, he attempted a description which subsequently came to be known as *Ram-Lila.* The first work, which is his best, is written in the *Kundaliya* metre and is popularly known as the *Kundaliya Ramayan,* though no attempt has been made in it to deal with the story of Ram. As the title : *Hitopadesh Upakhyan Bavni* implies, it should contain 52 verses as against 68 ; the additional 16 seem to have been added by later redactors. *Ram Dhyan Manjari* in 69 verses describes Ram, his brothers and the splendour of Ayodhya.

AGRAWAL, V.S. See *Vasudev Sharan Agrawal.*

AGYACHAND BHANDARI. Rajasthani writer, who is noted for his *Panna Dhay* (1963), a historical drama, *Des Bhagat Bhamasa* (historical one-act plays) and *Badla ri Ag* (social one-act plays).

AGYEY (1911-). Celebrated modern poet, novelist, short story writer and critic, whose full name is Sachchidanand Hiranand Vatsyayan 'Agyey'. He was born at Kasya in the district of Deoria of Uttar Pradesh. After taking B.Sc. degree from Lahore, he joined M.A. (English) but as he was associated with the revolutionary movement, he was sent to jail. He has travelled widely. His works are as under :—

Poetry : *Bhagnadut* (The Vanquished Messenger), *Chinta* (Pensiveness), *Ityalam* (This is Enough), *Hari Ghas par Kshan Bhar* (For a Moment on the Green Grass ; 1949), *Bavra Aheri* (The Rabid Hunter ; 1954), *Indradhanu Raunde Huye Ye* (These Trampled Rainbows ; 1957), *Ari O'Karuna Prabhamay* (1959), *Angan ke Par Dwar* (The Door across the Courtyard ; 1961), *Sunahle Shaival* (The Golden Plants ; 1965), *Purva* (1965), *Kitne Navon Men Kitni Bar* (How Many Times in How Many Boats ; 1967), *Kyonki Main Use Janta Hun* (Because I Know Him ; 1969), *Sagar Mudra* (The Ocean Moods ; 1970), *Pahle Main Sannata Bunta Hun* (At First I Weave Listlessness ; 1974), *Mahavriksha ke Niche* (1977) , *Nadi ki Bank par Chhaya* (The Shadow on the Bend of the River ; collection of poems ; 1981), *Sarjna ke Kshan* and *Uttar Priyadarshi* (1967 ; *Gitinatya*). Agyey's poetry is cool, detached and reflective and sometimes remote and abstract. He also brought out in 1943 an anthology called *Tar Saptak* (The Sharp Septet), which included select poems of seven poets. This anthology ushered a new era of poetry called 'Prayogvadi Kavita' (Experimental Poetry) of which Agyey is acclaimed as the precursor.

Novel : *Shekhar-ek-Jivni* (q.v. ; 2 Pts. ; an autobiographical narration), *Nadi ke Dwip* (q.v. ; a love story) and *Apne-apne Ajnabi* (q.v. ; 1961) ; the last existentialist work describes the psychological states of two women who are besieged in a house buried in snow.

Short Story Collection : *Vipathga* (The Woman who treads the wrong Path ; 1937), *Parampara* (Tradition ; 1944), *Kothri ki Bat* (Affairs of the Chamber ; 1945), *Sharanarthi* (The Refugee ; 1948), *Jaydol* (1951), *Amar Vallari* (Perennial Creeper), *Ye Tere Pratirup* (These are your Images), *Kadiyan aur anya Kahaniyan*, *Jigyasa aur anya Kahaniyan*, *Meri Priya Kahaniyan* (My Favourite Stories), *Chhoda Hua Rasta* (Deserted Path ; 1st part of his complete short stories ; 1975) and *Lautati Pagdandiyan* (Returning Tracks ; 1975 ; second part of his complete short stories). His short stories depict the conflict of the individual and his environment. His important short stories are : 'Devi Singh', 'Seb aur Dev' (The Apple and the Angel), 'Shatru' (The Enemy), 'Pathar ka Dhiraj' (The Patience of the Plateau), 'Kalakar ki Mukti' (The Emancipation of the Artist), 'Roz' (Every Day ; the name was later changed to 'Gangrene'), 'The Letter Box', 'Hajamat ka Sabun' (The Shaving Soap), 'Khitin Babu', 'Sharan Data' (The Shelter-Giver), 'Badla' (Revenge), 'Muslim-Muslim Bhai Bhai' (Muslims are Brothers), 'Bedian' (The Chains), 'Police ki Siti' (The Whistle of the Police), 'Chhaya' (The Shadow), 'Holybon ki Battakhen' (The Ducks of Holybon), etc.

Essays : *Trishanku* (1945), *Atmanepada* (1960), *Hindi*

Sahitya : Ek Adhunik Paridrishya (Hindi Literature : A Modern View), *Sab Rang* (All Types ; under the pseudonym of Kuttichatan), *Alaval* (Water Basin ; 1971). *Bhavanti* (tr. into English ; 1972). *Likhi Kagad Kore* (Wrote on Blank Papers ; 1972), *Antara* (1975) *Shashvati* (The Earth ; 1979), *Pashyanti* (1980), *Kahan Hai Dwarka* (Where is Dwarka ; 1982 ; 12 critical essays on art, literature and life). *Aparoksh*, *Atmaparak*, *Kavi-drishti* (1983), *Kendra aur Paridhi* (1984), *Adyatan* and *Dhar aur Kinare*.

Travelogue : *Are Yayavar Rahega Yad* (O, you would Remember the Traveller ; 1935) and *Ek Bund Sahasa Uchhli* (A Drop Suddenly Rebounded ; 1960).

Works Edited : *Adhunik Hindi Sahitya* (Modern Hindi Literature), *Tar Saptak* (The Sharp Septet ; 1943), *Dusra Saptak* (The Second Septet ; 1951), *Tisra Saptak* (The Third Septet ; 1959), *Chautha Saptak* (The Fourth Septet ; 1979), *Pushkarini* (Lotus Pool), *Rupambara* (The Beautiful Cloud ; anthologies) and *Naye Ekanki* (New One-act Plays ; 1952). He has been the editor of '*Sainik*'. '*Vishal Bharat*', '*Arati*', '*Dinaman*', '*Pratik*' and '*Navabharat Times*'.

Agyey is credited with bringing modernity to Hindi literature.

AHMED (b. 1604). Sufi poet, who is remembered for his *Dohas* and *Savaiyas*. He is said to have been the author of *Rasa-Vinod*, a work of erotic import, written in the Sufi style ; the work is also named *Koksar*, *Gun Sagar* and *Samudrik*. Ahmed is also called Tahir or Tahar.

AHMED ALI SHAH. Assamese-speaking modern Hindi writer, who is noted for his essays.

AHMED BAKHSH (fl. end of 19th cent.). Folk-poet of Haryana, who composed and staged the *Sangs* : *Ramayan*, *Jaymal-Fatta*, *Gugga*, *Chauhan*, *Sorath*, *Chundrakiran*, *Navalde* and *Kanslila*. His *Sangs* were staged in an *Akhara* of Thaneshwar (Haryana) and were very popular. The *Sangs* those days were staged from early dawn to almost midday.

AHMEDABAD RA JHAGDA RA KAVITTA. See *Khidiya Bakhta*.

AHMEDULLAH 'DAKSHAN' (fl. 1717-22). Muslim Riti poet, who was a native of Vahriyabad. He made a tour of the whole of India and made a pilgrimage to Mecca. He composed *Dakshan-Vilas*, a work on *Rasa* and *Nayak-Nayika-Bhed*. In the beginning of his work, he made an obeisance to Saraswati and Ganesh.

AI ANAND VILAS. See *Bhavanidas Vyas.*

AIDAN GADAN (fl. latter half of 17th cent.). Rajasthani poet, whose *Shri Bhavani Shankar ro Gun Shiv Puran* narrates all the popular legends concerning Shiv.

AIJI (JIJI DEVI ; d. 1504). Rajasthani saint-poetess and propounder of the Ai Panth, who was said to have been the daughter of Vika, a Rajput of Dabi *Gotra.* She was believed to be the Shakti or Durga Incarnate and her followers, Ai Panthis, refrain from all sorts of intoxicants and meat-eating. The followers of this Panth are of Sirvi caste, who inhabit Pali and Jodhpur regions and certain parts of Madhya Pradesh. Jiji Devi herself entrusted her *Gaddi* to her disciple Goyand in 1500. See *Bhavanidas Vyas, Tarachand Vyas, Lumba Baba.*

AI MATA RI VEL. See *Lumba Baba.*

AI UGRA PRAKASH. See *Tarachand Vyas.*

AINJAN BARHAT. Rajasthani poet, who was a contemporary of Barhat Narharidas (1591-1676) and belonged to the village Rupavas (Jodhpur). Having heard his poem, *Kavitta Solanki Jivraj Ji Ra,* the widows of Thakur Jivraj of Rupnagar (Kishengarh) performed *Sati* six months after the death of their husband. He also wrote reprehensive verses on Rathore Mohkam Singh, a Jagirdar in Mewar.

AITI GRETISH LINGVA. Assamese-speaking modern Hindi writer, who is noted for memoirs and reportage.

AIYYAR, K.A.S. Malayalam-speaking modern Hindi writer, who has tr. the Malayalam *Mahabharata* into Hindi prose.

AJAB KUNVARI (1523-83). Poetess of the Krishna-cult (Vallabh Sect), who was a daughter-in-law of Rana Udaysingh of Udaipur. Some of her *Padas* are available.

AJATSHATRU. Drama (1922) by Jayshankar Prasad (q.v.).

Bimbsar, the king of Magadh, has two queens : Chhalna and Vasvi ; it is through the machinations of the former queen that her son Ajatshatru is installed king, while Bimbsar is forced to lead a monastic life according to the Buddhist tenets. Vasvi, the second queen, wants that the revenue derived from the Kashi province (the territory she brought in her dowry) be reserved for Bimbsar and this proves to be the bone of contention between the Koshal and Magadh kingdoms. After several political intrigues and conspiracies there is a war, in which the rulers of Magadh, Koshal and to some extent Vatsa and Avanti are involved. Vasvi is able to arrange marriage of Ajatshatru and Vajira, the princess of Koshal. When a son is born to Ajatshatru, he realizes the affection of a father ; he then presents himself before Bimbsar and a reconciliation follows.

The influence of the Buddha is present in the background and directs the course of action. The action is disconnected and the hero does not show much firmness of mind.

AJAY KUMAR PATTNAIK. Oriya-speaking modern Hindi writer, who has made in Hindi a comparative study of Pre-Independence Hindi and Oriya novels (*Hindi-Oriya Upanyas Sahitya*).

AJAY RAJ PATNI (fl. 1336). Jain poet, who composed *Neminath Charit*, a poem, describing the life of Neminath and Rajul.

AJIT KUMAR (1933-). Poet, whose chief works are : *Akele Kanth ki Pukar* (The Call of a Lone Throat ; 1958), *Ankit Hone Do* (Let it be Marked) and *Ye Phul Nahin* (These are not Flowers ; 1970). He and Bachchan have edited an anthology : *Athven Dashak ki Pratinidhi Shreshth Kavitayen* (Representative Poems of the Eighth Decade ; 1982). His critical works are : *Kavita ka Jivit Sansar* and *Acharya Shukla : Vichar Kosh*, while *Dur Van Men* (1983) is reminiscences.

AJIT SINGH, MAHARAJA (1678-1724). Rajasthani poet of Jodhpur, who, besides being a warrior, wrote *Gun Sar*, *Bhav Virhi* (both collections of verses on miscellaneous topics), *Durga Path Bhasha* (said to be a prose rendering of the Pingal *Durga Saptashati*, but no longer extant) and *Gaj-Uddhar Granth* (in 670 verses ; q.v.). The poet has a broad canvas and treats of mythological, religious, didactic, historical and secular subjects in his works.

AJITSINGHJI RI DAVAVAIT. See *Dwarkadas Dadhvadiya*.

AKBAR (r. 1556-1605). Mughal Emperor of India, whose verses in Hindi are extant.

AKHA (AKSHAYDAS ; 1573-1658). Greatest Gujarati saint-poet, whose works in Hindi are : *Sant-Priya*, *Brahma-Lila*, *Kundliyan*, *Jhulna*, *Bhajan*. *Jakdi*, *Ek-Laksha Ramaini*, *Amrit Kala*, *Pada*, *Dhuvasa*, *Sakhiyan*, *Kaya*, *Shodh*, *Anastha Nirupan* and *Panchadashi Tatparya* (the last work no longer extant) ; some scholars are of the opinion that *Kaya Shodh* and *Anastha*

Nirupan are inclined towards Gujarati. A Vedantist by views, Akha's works lay emphasis on self-realization by a person.

AKHAIRAM (fl. *c.* 1750). Saint-poet, who was a disciple of Charan Das (q. v.) of Shuk Sampraday. He composed *Akhaisar*, *Vichar Charitra*, *Kshetralila*, *Ganga Mahatam*, *Gyansabda*, *Sabda*, etc. At the instance of Pratap Singh, the Maharaja of Jaipur, he came to live in Jaipur.

AKHARAVAT. Poem in Avadhi by Malik Muhammad Jayasi (q.v. ; fl. 1493-1543), the greatest Hindi Sufi poet ; it gives an exposition of certain spiritual tenets in alphabetical arrangement.

AKHILESH TRIVEDI. Brajabhasha poet, whose chief work is *Ganga-Lahari* (The Wavelets of the Ganges ; 1947).

AKHIRI KALAM (The Last Sermon). Poem in Avadhi by Malik Muhammad Jayasi (fl. 1493-1543 ; q.v.), the greatest Hindi Sufi poet. Written in Persian characters it gives a brief account of the human soul in this life as also up to the Doomsday.

AKHO BHANAUT BARHAT (fl. between 1550—1650). Dingal poet and author of *Devidas Jaitawat ri Veli*, who had also written stray verses including Dingal *Gits* on contemporary heroes and events.

AKSHAR ANANYA (fl. 1653). Saint-poet and a scholar of Vedanta. He was Dewan of Prithwichand, the ruler of Datiya state and was the author of several works on Yoga and Vedanta, *viz.*, *Rajayoga*, *Vigyana-Yoga*, *Siddhant-Bodh*, *Vivek-Dipika*, *Brahma-Gyan* and *Ananya-Prakash* ; he also tr. *Durga-Saptashati* into Hindi verse. He initiated Raja Chhatrasal of Panna.

AKSHAY KUMAR JAIN. Modern writer, whose chief works are : *Yuga-Purush Ram*, *Yad Rahi Baten* and *Jay Gomteshwar*. He was editor of 'Navbharat Times'.

AKSHAY SINGH RATANU. Modern Rajasthani poet of Jaipur, whose poems in traditional Charan style are available. He has also paid poetic homage to the modern heroes, including those who sacrificed their lives in fighting against the Chinese attack on India.

AKSHAY UPADHYAY. Poet, whose *Chak par Rakhi Dharti* (The Earth Placed on a Potter's Wheel ; 1981) reveals suppressed anger at the injustice in society.

AKSHAYVAR SINGH. Modern Hindi poet of Fiji, who is noted for his stray poems.

ALAHDAD (fl. 18th cent.). Rajasthani saint-poet of Laldasi Sampraday, whose 20 *Padas* deal with the chanting of 'Ram'.

ALAKH NIRANJAN. Modern Maithili writer, whose *Bisaral Bat* and *Iho Biti Gel* are short story collections. He has also written essays dealing with the problems of art and life.

ALAM-SHEIKH (fl. 1683-1703). Alam was originally a Brahmin Hindi poet, but falling in love with a Muslim woman, named Sheikh, a dyer by trade, he embraced Islam. He was for a long time in the service of prince Muazzam, later Emperor Bahadur Shah (r. 1707-1712). Sheikh also wrote verses which have inextricably got mingled with those of Alam ; *Alam Keli* is the joint collection of amorous verses of both the husband and wife, though there are still a number of stray verses not contained in this work. The poetry embodies pangs of love, joys of union and sorrows of parting and is a sincere expression of emotions.

From recent researches, it appears that Alam joined the *Durbar* of Guru Govind Singh around 1688, along with his wife Sheikh and that Alam wrote that Govind Singh's munificence and liberality was greater than that of Raja Bhoj. Alam translated the main story of 'Madhavanal Kamkandala' into Hindi, the basis of which was the Sanskrit manuscript, ascribed to one Jodh and that in translating the above romance, Alam freely borrowed from the stories narrated in 'Four Hundred and Four Tales' of the *Dasham Granth*. *Shyam-Snehi* is a joint work of Alam and Sheikh. Alam was also the author of *Sudama-Charit* (The Story of Sudama) ; besides, he wrote a large number of *Kavittas*, *Chhands*, etc., which have been compiled in *Alam-ki Kavita*, *Alam Kavitta* and *Alam Sangrah*. Some scholars take him as a contemporary of Emperor Akbar.

ALAM GANJ. See *Santdas Barah-Hazari*.

ALBELI ALI (fl. 1718-43). Poet, who was a follower of Vishnuswami Sect and a disciple of Vanshiali. His *Samay-Prabandh-Padavali* runs into 313 Padas ; his Sanskrit work is *Shristotra*. His *Padas* are full of alliteration and word-music.

ALHAKHAND (The Lay of Alha). Work in Bundhelkhandi by Jagnik (q.v. ; fl. 1173), which is no longer extant. Different versions of songs based on this work are popular in several part of northern India and these have been collected under the title *Alhakhand* by Charles Elliot and George Grierson. Its Kannauji and Bhojpuri versions have since been printed. The work is also called *Parmal Raso.*

The poem describes the heroic exploits of two chieftains : Alha and Udal (Uday Singh) of Chandela king Parmal (Parmardidev) of Mahoba against Prithwiraj Chauhan of Delhi. Parmal was supported by Jaychand, a king of Kannauj, and his son.

Parmal is incompetent and the affairs of the state are managed by his clever wife, Malhan, the military power being maintained by Alha and Udal, the two Rajput heroes of the Banfar clan, and Talhan Syed, the commander-in-chief of the forces. The chief events of the poem are : the *Swayamvar* of Sanyogita ; the battle between Karing Ray and the Banfars ; the episode of the Naulakha Har (a celebrated necklace) ; the marriages of Alha and Udal, Malakhan and Brahma ; Alha and Udal's story at Kanauj and their exploits there ; their return to Mahoba and a series of battles fought against Prithwiraj who had attacked Mahoba ; an episode relating to Bela, Prithwiraj's daughther who was married to Brahma, son of Parmal, and the ultimate war between the warriors of Mahoba and Delhi resulting in a complete annihilation of the former after a heroic struggle.

Alhakhanda, in its existing form, may contain some of the original verses of Jagnik, which have great literary value, but it is a popular lay having an appeal only for the common people. Even now, the songs of *Alha* are recited to the accompaniment of music of the tambourine in rainy season in the Hindi-speaking areas of northern India. It is difficult to ascertain what portion forms part of the original poem but the language of the existing *Alhakhand* is not of the 12th century but of recent times and is highly variable, for it includes names of modern weapons like pistols, rifles, bayonets, etc.

ALI BAKHSH (fl. 1854-99). Sangi of Rewari (Haryana), whose *Sangs* were popular in Haryana, Meerut and Marwar. The *Sangs,* he composed and staged are : *Raja Nal ka Bagdav, Nal ka Ifsana-Ajaib, Padmavat, Krishna-Lila, Nihalde, Chandraval, Gulbakavali, Maharaj Shivdan Singh ka Barahmasa* and *Alwar ka Sifatnama.* His *Sangs* used to be literary and were accompanied with dance.

ALI MUHAMMAD LONE. Modern Kashmiri dramatist, who has tr. into Hindi his own Kashmiri drama *Suyya.*

ALI MUHIB KHAN 'PRITAM'. Poet of Agra, who was the author of *Khat-mal Baisi* (1730 ; q.v.).

ALLEN, W.S. Scholar, who is noted for his article : 'Notes on the Rajasthani Verb'.

ALLUJI KAVIYA (1468-*c.* 1568). Noted amongst the Charan Bhakta-poets of Rajasthan, his stray verses numbering about 85 and some Dingal *Gits* are available. They are in praise of Ram, Krishna, Gorakhnath, Jambhoji and others. Emotional intensity and devotion make his verses most appealing. Alluji Kaviya is one of the fourteen Charan Bhakta-poets mentioned in the *Bhaktamal* (q.v.) of Nabhadas, but details of his life and activities are not available.

ALOK SHARMA. Poet, whose *Samudra ka Ekant* (1981) is a collection of his poems, revealing discrepancies in the social system.

ALURI BAIRAGI CHAUDHARI (1925-78). Telugu-speaking Hindi poet of Hyderabad, whose *Badli ki Rat* and *Palayan* (The Escape ; 1951) are selections of his poems, influenced by Marxism. He also published *Adhunik Telugu Kavita*, a selection of modern Telugu poetry, in Hindi.

AMAN SINGH GOTIYA. Writer, whose chief work is a romantic drama, *Madan-Manjari* (Cupid's Creeper ; 1884).

AMANAT ALI. See *Indar Sabha*.

AMAR. See *Chandra Nath Mishra 'Amar'*.

AMAR DEPAVAT. Modern Rajasthani poet, who is noted for his patriotic and heroic poems.

AMARJIT KANVAL, MRS. Modern Hindi poetess of Fiji, whose chief work is : *Bhot Hot Hi*. She is the only poetess, whose songs in casettes are popular in the Pacific Ocean Islands.

AMAR KANT (1925-). Progressive writer, whose chief works are : *Zindagi aur Jonk* (The Life and Leech ; 1958), *Desh ke Log* (The Countrymen), *Mitra-Milan tatha anya Kahaniyan*, *Maut ka Nagar* (short story collections), *Akash Pakshi* (The Sky Bird ; 1967), *Kale Ujale Din* (Dark-Bright Days ; 1969), *Parai Dal ka Panchhi* (Bird of another's Branch), *Kantile Rah ke Phul* (The Flowers of a Thorny Path), *Sukh Jivi* (The Hedonists ; 1982), *Bich ki Divar* and *Sukha Patta* (Dry Leaf) (novels).

His chief short stories are : 'Zindagi aur Jonk', 'Nirvasit' (The Exiled), 'Dopahar ka Bhojan' (Midday Meal), 'Maut ka Nagar' (The City of Death), 'Hatyare' (The Murderers), 'Communist', etc.

AMAR KOSH. Hindi rendering in verse by an unknown poet of Jammu, which was done in the beginning of the 19th century.

AMAR NATH JHA (1897-1955). Maithili critic, who was Vice-Chancellor of Allahabad University (1938-47). His *Govind Das*, a critical work, has been published (1981) in the Mithilak Bibhuti Series. He also tr. *Bihari Satsai* into English, which was later on read by Girija Kumar Mathur.

AMAR SINGH, MAHARANA (r. 1496-1519). Rajasthani ruler, whose stray verses in different popular metres are available.

AMAR SINGH RAMAN. Modern Hindi writer and poet of Surinam, whose chief works are : *Surinam ki Kahani* and *Phuon ke Panchhi* (poems). He has composed songs for children and also wrote two dramas : *Shri Krishna-Sudama* and *Mahalakshmi Puja.* He uses Devnagari Script in his poems, while other poets and writers of Surinam use the Roman Script.

AMAR SINGH RANPATIYA. Modern Chambiyali scholar, who is famous for his articles on folk-songs and folk-literature.

AMBADATT SHARMA DANGWAL. Garhwali scholar, who is noted for his *Garhwali Kahavat Sangrah* (Collection of Garhwali Sayings ; 1931).

AMBA PRASAD 'SUMAN' (1916-). Linguist, whose chief works are : *Krishak-Jivan Sambandhi Brajabhasha Shabdavali* (2 Pts. ; Brajabhasha Terminology relating to Agricultural life), *Hindi Bhasha : Atit aur Vartman* (1965) and *Hindi Bhasha aur Uska Vyakaranik Vivechan.*

AMBA RAM. Gujarati Brahmin, who is said to have composed and staged *Sangs* at Saharanpur in 1819.

AMBA SHANKAR NAGAR (1925-). Gujarati-speaking modern Hindi scholar, who is Professor and Head of the Department of Hindi at the Gujarat Vishwavidyalaya. His chief works are *Gujarat ki Hindi Seva* (Contribution of Gujarat to Hindi), *Gujarat ke Santon ki Hindi Vani* (Hindi writings of Gujarat Saints ; ed.), *Gujarat ke Hindi Gaurav Granth* (ed.), *Dayaram Satsai* (ed.), *Hindi Kavita : Badalte Swar* (ed.), etc.

AMBDEV SURI. See *Samara Ras.*

AMBDIPUDI HANUMAYYA. Telugu-speaking modern Hindi writer, who has tr. the Telugu novels of Vishwanath Satyanarayan into Hindi as *Ekvira*, *Hahahuhu* and *Samudra ki Vela.*

AMBIKA DATT VYAS (1858-1900). Poet and writer, who was influenced by Bharatendu Harishchandra (q.v.). He started writing Brajbhasha poems at the age of 11 and the following year was conferred at the instance of Bharatendu, the title of 'Sukavi' (a fine poet). Vyas brought out two magazines : 'Piyush Pravah' and 'Vaishnav Patrika', which he himself edited.

Best known among his works are *Lalit Natika* (glimpses of the life-story of Krishna) and *Gau Sankat Natak* (advocating a ban on cow-slaughter). His other chief works are *Avtar-Mimansa* (on religion), *Bihari-Vihar* (based on Bihari's *Dohas*), *Pavas-Pachasa* (fifty poems of old style), *Gadya-Kavya-Mimansa* (a prose work), *Bharat Saubhagya Nataka*, *Kaliyuga aur Ghi* (farce), *Ashcharya Vrittant* (novel), *Sukavi Satsai* (700 verses), *Katha Kusum*, *Nij Vrittant* (autobiography) and *Rasili Kajri.* He composed some poems in Khari Boli as well. He also wrote a novel in Sanskrit, *Shivaraja-Vijaya*, which is considered a classic in that language.

AMBIKA PRASAD BAJPAI. Modern scholar, whose chief works are : *Dwij Dev aur unka Kavya* and a psychological study in Hindi of *Ramcharitmanas.*

AMBIKA PRASAD BHATT 'AMBIKESH' (1904-62). Poet of Rewa, who was poet of the courts of Rewa and Orchha. *Jyoti* (The Light ; 1941) is a collection of his poems.

'AMBIKESH', AMBIKA PRASAD BHATT. See *Ambika Prasad Bhatt 'Ambikesh'.*

AMINOVA, SVETLANA MIRONOVNA (1936-). Soviet Hindi scholar, who did doctorate in 1971 on the novels of Agyey (q.v.). Her field of specialization is the psychological element in the Hindi novel.

AMIR ALI 'MIR', SYED (1873-1937). Poet, who was born at Devri in Sagar district of Madhya Pradesh. His works on patriotism, Rashtrabhasha, etc. are extant. 'Surya', 'Sandhya', 'Ulahana Panchak', 'Janmashtmi', etc. are his poems and despite his being a Muslim, he wrote on Hindu festivals and customs.

AMIR DAS, SADHU (c. 1775-1868). Hindi writer of Punjab, whose *Shrikrishna Sahityasindhu* (1833) and *Sabhamandan* (1827) are Riti works. His other chief works are : *Vrijraj Vilas* (*Satsai*), *Vrij Chandroday* (on prosody) and *Sher Singh Prakash.*

AMIYA DIN (1443-1513). Rajasthani poet, who was one of the saints of the Vishnoi tradition (see *Jambhoji*). He composed stray verses on miscellaneous topics.

AMRIT (fl. around 1750). Poet, who composed a version of *Madhavanal Kamkandala* (q.v.).

AMRIT KESHAV NAIK (fl. 1850-1900). Marathi-speaking Hindi writer, whose short stories were published in various magazines.

AMRIT LAL CHAKRAVARTI (1863-1936). Bengali-speaking Hindi writer, whose *Sati Sukhdevi* (1902) is considered the first Hindi novel, written by a Bengali.

AMRIT LAL CHATURVEDI (1898-). Poet of Agra, whose Brajbhasha works are : *Shyam-Sandesau* (The Message of Krishna ; 1950 ; in the tradition of *Bhramargit*) and *Ghalib Amrit* (tr. of Ghalib's poems into Brajbhasha).

AMRIT LAL MATHUR (1898-1954). Rajasthani poet, who was born at the village Kuchera in the then Jodhpur State. His father, Gopal Lal, was a highly religious man and was a poet. Amrit Lal Mathur composed poems in Brajbhasha, Rajasthani and Khari Boli. His poetry is permeated with Ram-bhakti. His chief works are : *Raghav-Yash*, *Git Ramayan*, *Yamak Ramayan*, *Ram Premamrit*, *Amrit Satsai*, *Gangalahari*, etc.

AMRIT LAL NAGAR (1916-). Novelist, who was born in Agra ; originally his ancestors belonged to Gujarat. His chief works are : *Mahakal* (Great Famine ; 1947), *Bund aur Samudra* (The Drop and the Ocean ; q.v. ; 1956 ; on the relations between individual and society); *Shataranj ke Mohre* (The Pieces of Chess , 1959), *Suhag ke Nupur* (The Nuptial Anklets ; on the story of the famous Tamil epic, *Shilappadikaram* ; 1960), *Seth Bankemal*, *Ve Kothevaliyan* (Those Prostitutes), *Amrit aur Vish* (The Nectar and Poison ; q.v. ; 1966 ; one of the finest novels, which provides interesting glimpses of the social life and people's hopes and problems in independent India), *Sat Ghunghat-vala Mukhra* (A Face with Seven Veils ; 1968), *Ekada Naimisharaneya* (Once in the Naimisha Forest ; 1972 ;

based on the mythological story), *Manas ka Hans* (1972 ; on the life of Tulsidas) and *Nachyo Bahut Gopal* (Suffered Too Much, O Krishan ; 1978 ; about Harijans), *Khanjan Nayan* (The Eyes of the Wag-tail ; 1981 ; on Surdas, the saint-poet), *Bikhre Tinke* (The Scattered Straws ; 1982 ; on blackmail, sexual scandals, bribery, political corruption, etc.), *Ghadar ke Phul*, *Agnigarbha* (all novels), *Panchvan Dasta aur Sat Kahaniyan* (Fifth Platoon and Seven Stories), *Sikandar Har Gaya* (Alexander was Defeated ; both short story collections). *Chandan Van* (The Sandal Forest). *Chadhat na Dujo Rang* (on Surdas's conversion to Bhakti cult ; 1982), *Utar Chadhav* (The Rise and Fall), *Yugavtar*, *Nukkad Par* (On Street Corner) (dramas), *Bharat-Putra Naurangi Lal*, *Kripaya Bayen Chaliye* (Please Keep to your Left), *Nawabi-Masnad* (The Nawab's Bolster) and *Fidaye Lucknow* (satirical writings).

Nagar's important short stories are : 'Do Asthayen' (Two Beliefs), 'Gharib ki Hay' (The Curse of the Poor), 'Gorakh-Dhandha', 'Nirdhan' (The Poor Man), 'Qayamat ka Din' (The Doomsday), etc.

AMRIT MADHAV GHATAGE. Author of *Phonemic and Morphemic Frequencies in Hindi* (1964).

AMRIT RAY (1698-1753). Saint-poet of Maharashtra, who was very popular in singing *Kirtans.* He belonged to Aurangabad and was in service of a Mughal Subedar. He had a good knowledge of Sanskrit, Marathi and Hindi. In Marathi, he perhaps was the first poet to compose long poems. In Hindi also, he composed long poems. His poetry is characterized by sweetness.

AMRIT RAY (fl. 1679). One of the court-poets of Guru Govind Singh (q.v.) ; he was a resident of Lahore. It is said that he was so much enamoured of Lahore that he never willingly agreed to leave it, but at the instance of the Guru, he reached Anandpur and wrote *Guru-Vilas*, which is a collection of *Kavittas* and *Savaiyas*. He, however, depicted an attractive picture of Lahore and its surroundings in his *Chitra-Vilas*.

AMRIT RAI (1921-). Writer, whose chief works are : *Qalam ka Sipahi* : *Premchand* (Premchand, the Soldier of the Pen ; a biography of his father, Premchand, which offers an intimate insight into the man), *Nayi Samiksha* (New Criticism, a critical work), *Nagphani ka Desh* (The Country of Cactus, 1956), *Hathi ke Dant* (The Tusks of the Elephant), *Bij* (Seed ; 1959), *Sukh-Dukh* (Weal and Woe ; 1969), *Matiyali* (Muddy), *Samar Gatha*, *Jungle*, *Dhuvan* (Smoke), *Agni Diksha*, *Adi Vidrohi* (The

First Rebel) and *Dard ki Lakir* (novels), *Ek Sanvli Larki* (A Tawny Girl), *Meri Priya Kahaniyan* (My Favourite Short Stories), *Sargam* (short story collections), *Chindiyon ki Ek Jhalar* (A Frill of Fragments), *Shatabdi* (Centenary) and *Aj Abhi* (dramas). In his novels and criticism, he has tried to project socialist point of view. 'Savani Sama' (The Romance of the Rains) is of one his prominent short stories. He has tr. into Hindi some outstanding works from foreign languages and has written a critical work : *Adhunik Bhavbodh ki Sangya*.

AMRITA BHARATI (1937-). Poetess, whose chief works are *Main Tat par Hun* (I am on the Bank ; 1971), *Aj ya Kal ya Sau Baras Bad* (Today or Tomorrow or After Hundred Years), *Mitti par Sath-Sath* (Side by Side on Earth ; 1976) and *Mein Nahin Likhi Kavita.* She edits a literary magazine, 'Pashyanti'.

AMRITKAR (*c.* 1400-82). Maithili poet, who wrote under the patronage of Maharaja Shiv Singh and Maharaja Bhairav Singh of Oinivar dynasty. Vidyapati paid a tribute to Amritkar in one of his poems-praising his many qualities of statesmanship, generosity and scholarship. It seems that he was a dramatist (he wrote a drama on the story of Ratnavali), a poet and also a patron of poets.

ANAMIKA. Poetess, whose *Ghalat Pate ki Chitthi* (Letter at a Wrong Address ; 1979) is her first collection of poems ; her subjects, in the Persianized lyrical strain, are the Moon, moonshine, home, members of her family and love. She has also published a collection of short stories : *Pratinayak*.

ANAMIKA. See *Suryakant Tripathi 'Nirala'*.

ANAND. Old Rajasthani poet, who and Karmanand, have jointly composed poems in the sense that the first line of a couplet, composed by one, poses a question and the second line, composed by the other, answers it. In the *Shabdanushasan* or the Grammar of Hemchandra, there is a couplet of this sort with the name 'Anand' (401/3). Muni Karmanand has been remembered with reverence in *Ram Rasau*, composed about 1593 by Madhaudas Dadhvadiya. A devotional Dingal *Git* by Karmanand is also found, but it is not certain that the two Karmanands are identical.

ANANDGHAN (fl. early 16th cent.). Poet of the Krishna-cult (Chaitanya Sect), who got a temple built at Nandgaon near Vrindavan. His *Padas* are still sung at the Nandgaon Temple.

ANANDGHAN (1623-88). Gujarati-speaking Jain mystic poet, whose *Anandghan Bahotara* is a famous Hindi work, which contains 108 *Padas*, treating of moral and spiritual subjects.

ANANDGHAN. See *Ghananand.*

ANAND JHA (fl. early 20th cent.). Maithili dramatist, whose chief work : *Sita-Svayamvar* is based on an episode in the life of Ram. He wrote a drama on the poet, Vidyapati as also Maheshvanis, entitled *Mahesh Shatak.*

ANAND MISHRA (1933-74). Poet, whose chief works are : *Chanderi ka Jauhar* (Self-immolation of ladies of Chanderi ; 1957) and *Himalaya ke Ansu* (The Tears of the Himalayas).

ANAND MISHRA. Maithili scholar, who has edited *Kriti Rajkamalak* and *Varna-Ratnakar* (both in collaboration ; 1980).

ANAND PRAKASH DIKSHIT (1925-). Critic, whose chief works are : *Rasa-Siddhant : Swarup aur Vishleshan* (research ; Theory of Rasa : Nature and Analysis), *Tulsidas : Vastu aur Shilpa* (Tulsidas : Plot and Art), *Vidyapati : Path evam Alochana* (Vidyapati : Text and Criticism), *Saundarya Tattwa* (tr. from Bengali), *Kabirdas : Chintan aur Sarjan*, *Marathi Santon ki Hindi Vani*, *Maithilisharan Gupta*, *Hindi Riti Parampara*, *Sahitya Siddhant aur Shodh* (Literary Principles and Research), *Sumitranandan Pant* and *Alochana : Swarup aur Prakriya* (Criticism : Nature and Procedure). He has also critically ed. the text of *Belikrisan Rukmani-Ri* and *Haricharan Das Granthavali.* He is the Head of the Department of Hindi, Poona University.

ANAND PRAKASH JAIN (1927-). Writer, whose chief works are : *Kathputli ke Dhage* (The Threads of Puppet ; 1958), *Kunal ki Ankhen* (The Eyes of Kunal ; historical novel), *Tisra Netra* (The Third Eye), *Athvin Bhanvar* (Eighth Circumambulation of Fire ; regional novel), *Tambe ke Paise* (Copper Coins ; 1971 ; all novels), *Iti aur Has*, *Kal ke Pankh* (Wings of Time), *Atit ke Kampan* (Vibrations of the Past), *Sanshay ka Yuga* (short story collections) and *Masterji* (drama). 'Lipstick' is his chief story.

ANAND RAGHUNANDAN (Blissful Ramchandra). Drama by Vishwanath Singh (1789-1856 ; q.v.), which is regarded as the first Hindi drama. Written on the pattern of Sanskrit plays, it has 7 Acts and as its title suggests, portrays the life of Ram. Characters of different regions use their own dialects and one of the characters goes to the length of using a mixed Hindi-English verse, possibly designed to create humour. Its style is more poetic than dramatic and is sharply slanted towards the *Raslila* tradition. It is quite likely that the play had been staged.

ANAND RAM (fl. 16th cent.). Poet of the Ram-cult, who belonged to Hissar and came into contact with Tulsidas (q.v.) during the latter's visit to Kurukshetra. Anandram's devotional fervour turned him into a good poet. *Vachan-Vinod* (Wits in Discourse) and *Kok Manjari* are supposed to have been written by him; the manuscripts of these works are available in the Anoop Sanskrit Pustakalaya, Bikaner.

ANAND RAO DUBE. Modern Malwi poet, whose poems: *Ramaji raigya ne rel Jati Ri* and *Barsat Ai Gi Re* have greatly influenced budding Malwi poets.

ANAND SHANKAR MADHAVAN. Malayalam-speaking modern Hindi writer, whose *Anamantrit Mehman* (The Uninvited Guest) is an original novel. Madhavan has mainly lived in Bihar.

ANANDVARDHAN RAMCHANDRA RATNAPARKHI (1919—79). Marathi-speaking Hindi poet, who composed more than 50 poems, which are collected in *Namaskar* and *Vihag*. He was strongly influenced by the Chhayavadi Hindi poets. His other poems on various subjects are collected in *Rashmihas* and *Sandhyarav* (1956). He was born at Halikher in Bidar region of Andhra Pradesh and was educated at Gurukula Kangri, Hardwar.

ANAND VIJAY NATIKA. Kirtaniya form of Maithili drama in 4 Acts by Ram Das Jha (q.v.).

On hearing of Radha's beauty from his friend Anandkand, Madhav is eager to see her. Radha, along with her friends, Vichakshana and Vachal meets Anandkand, who deceives them by posing an astrologer and asks them to collect flowers for the worship of Shiv. While the girls are engaged in gathering flowers in the garden, Madhav and Anandkand make their appearance. Thus there is birth of love in Radha's heart. Both Madhav and Radha are shown as love-lorn. Ultimately, through her friends, Radha approaches Madhav and they are united. There are two versions of the text available at present.

ANANDAN, S.K. (1939-). Dogri-speaking Hindi poet, whose works are: *Dekhti Akash Ankhen* (Eyes Watching the Sky),

Sima ka Panchhi, *Nauka ka Itihas* (all poetical collections) ; he has also written some prose works and has edited several magazines.

ANANDI PRASAD SHRIVASTAV (1899-1953 ?). Writer, who was noted for his drama, *Achhut* (The Untouchable ; 1930). He was born in Fatehpur of Uttar Pradesh.

ANANDI RAMNATHAN. Tamil-speaking modern Hindi writer, who along with Yugjit Navalpuri has tr. into Hindi from the original Tamil the poems of Subrahmaniya Bharati under the title : *Bharati ki Kavitayen* (The poems of Bharati). He also tr. U. Ve. Saminad Ayyar's biography into Hindi as *Meri Jivni* (My Biography).

ANANT BIHARILAL DAS 'INDU'. Modern Hindi poet of Nepal, whose chief work is *Ragmayi*. He is famous for his lyrics.

ANANT CHAUDHARI. Author of *Hindi Vyakaran ka Itihas* (1972) and *Nagari Lipi aur Hindi Vartani* (1973).

ANANT DAS (fl. 16th cent.). Bengali or Oriya Vaishnav poet, who also composed *Padas* in Brajbuli. Some of his *Padas* are available in *Padakalpataru* (q.v.).

ANANT DAS (fl. latter half of 17th cent.). Rajasthani saint-poet, who was in the tradition of Dadu Sampraday. He wrote brief biographies in verse, known as *Parchi* : *Namdevji Ki*, *Kabirji Ki*, *Raidasji Ki*, *Pipaji Ki*, *Angadji Ki*, *Trilcochanji Ki*, *Ranka Banka Ki*, *Seu Samman Ki* and *Dhanna Ki*. His language is Rajasthani mixed Braj.

ANANT GOPAL SHEWDE (1911-79). Marathi-speaking modern Hindi novelist, who was born at Sausar in Chhindwara district of Madhya Pradesh. His chief works are : *Isai Bala*, *Jwalamukhi*, *Bhagna Mandir*, *Purnima*, *Mrigjal*, *Nishagit*, *Mangala*, *Kora Kaghaz*, *Adhura Sapna* and *Indradhanush* ; out of these *Amrit Kumbh*, *Jwalamukhi* and *Bhagna Mandir* are on nationalist themes, while the rest of them are social. *Tisri Bhukh* is a collection of his essays. He was Secretary of the First World Hindi Conference held at Nagpur in 1975.

ANANT KAMALNATH 'PANKAJ'. Telugu-speaking modern Hindi writer, who has tr. into Hindi as *Billi ki Ankhen*, a novel of Triveni, a Kannada writer.

ANANT KUMAR 'PASHAN'. Poet, whose chief poetical collection is *Amaltas* (1984).

ANANT MAHARAJ (fl. 16th cent.). Saint-poet of Maharashtra, who originally belonged to Ahmednagar but had settled at Pratishthan or Paithan. It appears that he was a disciple of Eknath (q.v.). A good number of *Padas* and *Chaupais* composed by him in Hindi are available.

ANANT PHANDI (fl. 18th cent.). Marathi folk-poet (*Shahir*), who also made some compositions in Hindi.

ANANYA ALI (*b. c.* 1683). Poet of the Krishna-cult (Radhavallabh Sect), whose original name was Bhagvandas. After he was initiated by Govindlal Goswami, he came to Vrindavan in 1702 and composed poems till death. He wrote 79 works, which are available at the Hitashram, Vrindavan. The total number of *Padas* in all his works is about 6,000.

ANBHAI VANI. See *Ramcharan.*

'ANCHAL'. See *Rameshwar Shukla 'Anchal'.*

ANDHA YUGA (The Blind Age). Poetic drama (1954) by Dharm Vir Bharati (q.v.), which describes the scepticism and suffocation of the modern age through the medium of the story from the last day of the Mahabharat War. The characters of Dhritarashtra, Gandhari, Ashwatthama, Krishna, Yuyutsu, etc. have been delineated to prove that not only the age of the blind Dhritarashtra but the modern age also suffers from delusion. *The Andha Yuga* is an important landmark in the development of Hindi drama.

ANDHERE BAND KAMRE (The Dark Closed Rooms). Novel (1961) by Mohan Rakesh (q.v.).

Describing the hollowness of Delhi's cultural, political and family life, the main story is concerned with Harbans and his fashionable wife Nilima, who smokes and drinks. Throughout the novel, both of them suffer from jealousy and meet and part many a time. Nilima, an ambitious lady, wants prominence in society through artistic pursuits like painting and dancing. Harbans also likes this but feels jealous when she goes about meeting artists freely. Harbans suffers within himself so much that he goes to a foreign country. Suffering there from homesickness, he writes repeatedly to Nilima to come to him. Cancelling her dance programme in Mysore, she reaches London, where they again live together but like strangers. Against Harbans's wish, she goes to Paris with an Indian dance party, but after her programme is over, she stays with Uba Nu, a noble-minded Burmese artist. This hurts the sentiments of

Harbans and they come back to India. On their return to Delhi, Nilima arranges a dance programme, which proves a flop, for which she blames her husband, who, she alleges, had made a poor planning of the show. The tension grows between them and Nilima goes away from Harbans presumably for ever, but in the loneliness of the night, Harbans sees that she has come back and is preparing tea. Here ends the story.

ANGAD VISHTI. See *Sanya Jhula.*

ANI RAY (fl. 17th cent.). One of the court-poets of Guru Govind Singh (q.v.), whose *Jang-Nama Guru Govind Singh* (The Battle Accounts of Guru Govind Singh) in fine Brajbhasha consists of about 70 *Chhands* and describes some of the battles which the Guru fought and won ; many *Chhands* are thrilling for their spirit of nationalism and love of freedom.

ANIL KUMAR ADYALIKAR (1924-79). Marathi-speaking Hindi poet, dramatist and writer. His poems are obsessed with economic disparities but end with an optimistic strain. His *Pranay Angar* is a collection of seven one-act plays, while *Utsav Priya* is his poetical work.

ANIRUDDHA PRASAD 'VIMAL'. Poet, whose *Andheri Ghatiyon ke Bich* (1983) is a poetical collection.

ANITA AULAK. Modern Hindi writer ; her chief short story collection is *Uska Apna Ap.*

ANJANEY SHARMA, VEMURI. Telugu-speaking modern Hindi writer, wko has tr. Telugu short stories into Hindi. He has also written a novel : *House Surgeon.*

ANMINI AMAL, N. Malayalam-speaking modern Hindi scholar, who is the author of *Hindi-Malayalam Kosh.*

ANNAJI INAMDAR (fl. 1850-1900). Marathi-speaking Hindi dramatist, whose chief work *Gopichand* contains 13 scenes.

ANNALS AND ANTIQUITIES OF RAJASTHAN. See *Tod, Colonel.*

ANNAPUREDDY SHRIRAMREDDY. Telugu-speaking Hindi poet, who is noted for his *Suman Man*, a collection of songs. His other works are : *Pant Kavya men Saundarya Yojna* and *Kaliyon ke Dwar par Aliyon ka Gunjan* (The Buzzing of Black Bees at the door of Buds ; 1974).

ANNAPURNA DAI. Modern Maithili writer, who is noted for her short story, *Sasuk Sneh.*

ANNAPURNA VERMA. Modern writer, whose chief psychological novel is *Parat-dar-Parat* (Layer after Layer).

ANNARAM 'SUDAMA'. Rajasthani poet and writer, who is a retired Headmaster of Udairamsar (Bikaner). His chief works are: *Pirol men Kutti Byai* (1969; poems portraying the corrupt life resulting from the materialist outlook), *Vyatha Katha ar Duji Kavitavan* (1982; a collection of his satirical poems), *Maikati Kaya Mullakati Dharti* (1966; novel on the tragic story of an old woman, Sugani, deserted by her husband), *Andhi ar Astha* (novel on the story of a poor Brahmin), *Mevai ra Runkh* (1977; a novel on the Emergency excesses), *Dankigata Manavi* (1981; on a Bania widow, who like her father, is a cruel money-lender), *Andhai nai Ankhyan* (1971; short stories), *Badhti Anval* (a drama on Panchayat election) and *Dur Disavar* (1975; a travelogue). Several of his publications have earned awards.

ANNAVADHUT (fl. 18th cent.). Kannada poet, who composed *Padas* in Kannada under the pseudonym of 'Vitthal Vyas'. Besides, he composed *Padas* in Hindi and Sanskrit as well.

ANSARI, D.M., MRS. German-speaking scholar, who, along with M. Ahmed Ansari, has published *Gesprachesbuch Deutsch-Hindi* (1981) on German-Hindi Conversation. She has also published *Chrestomathic der Hindi Prosader 20 Jahrhunderts*, an anthology of 20th century Hindi prose and *Hindi Vyakaran.*

ANSU (Tears). Long poem (1926) by Jay Shankar Prasad (q.v.). A perfect expression in poetry of those moods which bring tear to the eyes, it depicts pangs of separation by imagery, which is touched here and there with mystic associations. Its greatly-revised version appeared in 1933. It has been tr. into English by Jaykishan Das

ANUBHAV PRAKASH. See *Bananath.*

ANUBHAVANAND (fl. 2nd part of 17th cent.). Saint-poet of Gujarat, whose original name was Bhavan. His Hindi works are trs. of *Shiva Gita*, *Shridhari Gita* and *Brahma-Samhita* and composition of *Chaturiyas* and *Vishnupadas.* His language betrays the influence of Arabic and Persian.

ANUBHAVANAND ANAND. Modern Hindi poet of Fiji, who is noted for his stray poems.

ANUP. Modern Malwi writer, who is known for his farces and short stories.

ANUP CHAND BHAYANI. Gujarati-speaking modern Hindi scholar, whose *Madhyakalin Hindi Gujarati Sahitya ki Pravritiyon ka Tulnatmak Adhyayan* is a research work.

ANUP LAL MANDAL, the late (b. 1900). Novelist of Bihar, whose chief works are : *Gharibi ke Din* (The Days of Poverty), *Rup-lekha*, *Jyotirmayi* (Lustrous), *Savita*, *Ayaron ki Dunia* (The World of Lascivious People), *Samaj ki Vedi Par* (On the Altar of Society), *Mimansa*, *Das Bigha Zamin* (The Ten Bighas of Land), *Bujhane-na Paye* (Let It Not be Extinguished), *Ve Abhage* (Those Unfortunate) and *Badi Ma* (The Grandmother).

ANUP MISHRA. Modern Maithili poet, whose chief work is *Narad Vivah*.

ANUP SHARMA (1899-1960). Poet, whose chief works are : *Pheri Milibo* (1938), *Siddharth* (1937 ; on the life of Gautam Buddha) and *Varddhaman* (an epic on the life-story of *Mahavir* ; 1951).

ANUP SHRI ACHARYA. Writer, whose *Khoya Hua Sach* (The Lost Truth ; 1982) is a novel, recreating the past of the people of Orchha.

ANURAG BANSURI (The Love Flute). Poem by Nur Muhammad (b. 1745), a Sufi poet, which is remarkable for its Sanskritized diction and sustained allegorical interest.

ANVITA ABBI. Scholar, whose chief work is : *Reduplication in Hindi : A Generative Semantic Study* (Ph.D., Cornell, 1975).

ANWITA AGRAWAL. Modern writer ; her chief short story collection is *Mutthi Bhar Pahchan* (1969).

APNE-APNE AJNABI (To Each His Stranger). An existentialist novelette (1961) by Agyey (q.v.).

It is a psychological novel in which are depicted the mental states of two women characters, the aged Selma suffering from cancer and Yoke, the young tourist, who are trapped in a house buried under snow. The novel has been tr. into English.

APPASAHAB SANADI 'SHAIL'. Kannada-speaking Hindi poet, whose poems are chiefly collected in the first part of the *Shail aur Sagar* (The Mountain and the Ocean ; 1963). His other poems are : *Tuti Arsi* (The Broken Mirror-set Ring), *Nirav Halchal*, etc. *Adi Anant* (1970) is a collection of his five long short stories. His language is simple but idiomatic.

ARADI, EVA. Modern Hungarian Hindi scholar, who has tr. Prem Chand's *Nirmala* and 12 short stories into Hungarian in 1980. She has also prepared a *Hungarian-Hindi Vartalap Pustika*, which is expected to be published very soon.

ARBAKOV, MIKHAIL KIRILLOVICH (1927—). Soviet Hindi scholar who is a senior editor in Progressive Publishing House in Moscow. He has edited 'Sankshipta Vishwa Itihas', 'Mitron ke Swar' and poems of Pushkin and Lermontov.

ARCHANA VERMA. Poetess, whose first collection of poems is *Kuchh Der Tak* (1981) ; *Sthagit* (Postponed ; 1981) is her short story collection.

ARCHER, W.G. English Bhojpuri scholar, who, along with Sankata Prasad, published *Bhojpuri Gramya-Git* (Bhojpuri rural songs ; 1943), a collection mainly of marriage songs. Archer's other works are : *The Blue Grove*, *The Dove and the Leopard* (Calcutta, 1948) and *The Vertical Man* (London, 1947).

ARDHA KATHANAK. See *Banarsidas*.

ARIGPUDI, RAMESH CHAUDHARI. See *Ramesh Chaudhari, Arigpudi*.

ARISINGH. Maharana of Mewar, whose *Rasik-Chaman* (1768) in Pingal is a Riti work.

ARJUN ARVIND. Writer, who is noted for his collection of essays : *Mujhe Mere Mitron se Bachao* (Save Me from My Friends ; 1980).

ARJUN BHAGAT (1849—1919). Hindi poet of Gujarat, who was born near Ankleshwar. He composed *Bhajans* ; his language betrays the influence of Urdu.

ARJUN CHAUBE KASHYAP (1916—1978). Dramatist, who was born in Gaya (Bihar). His chief one-act play collections are : *Bargad ka Ped* (The Banyan Tree), *Rajnigandha* (The Night-fragrant Flower), *Kavipriya* (The Poet's Beloved) and *Tutati Kadi* (The Breaking Link). He also edited a number of magazines.

ARJUN DAS (fl. early 19th cent.). Rajasthani saint-poet of Ram Snehi Sampraday, Khedapa, whose *Janma Lila* and *Purva Janma* are significant poems from the socio-historical point of view.

ARJUN DAS KESRI. Modern writer, whose chief work is *Lorikayan.*

ARJUN DEV, GURU (1563—1606). The fifth Guru of the Sikhs, who compiled in 1604 the *Granth Sahib* (q.v.) or *Adi Granth*, which contains, apart from the hymns of Nanak and other Sikh Gurus, hymns of pre-Nanak saints. Many of the hymns are in Hindi.

ARJUN DEV CHARAN. Rajasthani writer, whose *Do Natak Aj Ka* (1979) contains two experimental stage-plays : *Sankario* and *Gavari*, which are untraditional both in style and substance.

ARJUN NATH RAINA. Kashmiri-speaking modern Hindi writer, whose *Kesar ke Phul* (The Flowers of Saffron) is a short story collection, giving glimpses of Kashmiri life.

ARNOLD, SIR EDWIN. Translator of Shakespeare's *The Merchant of Venice* into Hindi Prose (1888).

ARNOT, STANFORD (d. 1844). Author of *On the Origin and Structure of the Hindustani Tongue or General Language of British India* (London, 1828), *A New Self-Instructing Grammar of the Hindustani Tongue* (1831 ; rev. and enlarged ed. by Duncan Forbes in 1844 after the death of the author) and *The Native Press of India* (1829).

ARSI PRASAD SINGH (1911-). Poet, who was born at Airot, Rosda in the Darbhanga district of Bihar. His chief works are : *Kalapi* (Cuckoo ; 1938), *Kaleje ke Tukre* (The Most Loved Ones), *Arsi*, *Sanchayita* (a collection ; 1942), *Jivan aur Yauvan* (The Life and Youth ; 1944), *Nayi Disha* (New Directions ; 1944), *Panchjanya* (Krishna's Conch ; 1945), *Shatdal* and *Prem-Git* (Love Songs) ; *Panch-Pallav* (The Five Sprouts) and *Khota Sikka* (The Counterfeit Coin) are his short story collections. In Maithili, he has published two small volumes of poems : *Matik Dip* (1957) and *Pujak Phul* (1969) ; *Suryamukhi* (1981) is the selection of his Maithili poems.

ARUN KUMAR JHA 'ARUN'. Maithili poet, whose *Vidyapati Rahasya* (1982), in 18 parts, is a narration of many events based on Vidyapati's life.

ARUNA KAPUR. Poetess, whose chief work, *Tutate Andhere* (1979), a poetical collection, contains sentimental poems. Her other collection of poems is : *Akaron ke Dansh.*

ARUNA SITESH. Modern fiction writer, whose chief works are : *Lakshman Rekha, Koi Ek Adhurapan, Vahi Sapne* and *Chand bhi Akela Hai.*

ARVIND DESAI. Gujarati-speaking modern Hindi scholar of Surat, whose *Bharatendu aur Narmad : Ek Tulnatmak Adhyayan* is a research work.

ARVIND KUMAR AKKU. Maithili poet, whose *Kahi Ta Gabi Sunabi* (1981) is a collection of songs, while *Tal Mutthi* (1982) is a social play on the educated young generation.

ARVINDAKSHAN, A. Malayalam-speaking modern Hindi scholar, whose research work is : *Mahadevi ke Rekhachitra.*

AS. See *Kisan Kilol.*

ASAGU. See *Asig.*

ASAIT. Rajasthani poet, who was born at Siddhpur and was an Audiohya Brahmin by caste His *Hansavali* (q.v.) also claimed to be a Gujarati work, was composed in 1370.

ASHA BARHAT (1493-1593). Dingal poet, who was son of Gidha and belonged to the village Bhadras. A well-known poet of the age, he had good relations with many a ruler. He was sent by Rao Maldeo (1531-62) of Jodhpur to persuade and bring back from Jaisalmer the sulky queen Umade, who was annoyed with her husband on seeing the Rao making love to her maid servant Bharmali on the very first night of their marriage; the poet was successful in his mission. He was also commissioned by the Raval of Jaisalmer to bring Bharmali, who had been made over to Bagha of Kotda ; during this mission he became an intimate friend of Bagha. On the death of Umade and Bagha, the poet composed heart-rending verses, famous in Rajasthan.

ASHA GUPTA. Modern scholar, whose works are : *Madhyayugin Hindi Kavi* and *Grierson ke Sahityetihas.*

ASHA PURNA DEVI. Modern fiction writer, whose chief works are : *Pratham Pratishruti, Godhuli, Nepathya Sangit, Jab Prakash hi na Ho, Panchhi Uda Akas* (novels) and *Tuta Shisha* (short story collection).

ASHA SINGH (fl. 17th cent.). One of the court-poets of Guru Govind Singh (q.v.) ; he was a master of Brajbhasha and composed verses in praise of the Guru and wrote devotional poetry in the *Shringar* style.

ASHADH KA EK DIN (A Day in July). Drama (1958) by Mohan Rakesh (q.v.), which describes the imaginary love of Kalidas for Mallika. Kalidas and Mallika love each other and the latter persuades him to go to Ujjain. While Kalidas gets state recognition at Ujjain and is elevated to the status of Governor of Kashmir, Mallika is driven to accept the life of a prostitute. Kalidas comes back to his village and in spite of his knowledge on the fate of his beloved, he marries another girl, Priyangumanjari and leaves the village without meeting Mallika. All these seemingly undignified actions on the part of Kalidas point to an inner conflict, which makes him act in this manner. There is unsuccessful poet, Vilom, whose main concern is to prevent Mallika from getting married to Kalidas : ultimately Vilom gets an opportunity of possessing Mallika only after she adopts a new profession. With *Ashadh ka Ek Din*, "Hindi drama steps out of the boundaries of romanticism".

ASHANT. Modern Bhojpuri poet, who is noted for his stray poems.

ASHI (b. 1844). Perhaps the last Hindi Sufi poet of considerable fame and merit, whose *Dohas*, discovered so far, depicting the meeting of lovers and the pangs of separation, are of high literary merit.

ASHISH SINHA (1943-). Writer, whose *Adamkhor* (The Cannibal), *Is Shahr Men* (In this City ; 1980) and *Badshah Salamat* are short story collections. His novels are : *Kai Laharon ke Bich*, *Ajnabi Indradhanush*, *Samay Bita Hua*, *Suryoday se Pahle* and *Agami Vasant Men*, while *Ek Udas Sham* is his drama.

ASHK. See *Upendra Nath Ashk*.

ASHOK AGRAWAL. Modern fiction writer, whose chief works are : *Vayada Maf Gavah*, *Hissedari* and *Sankari Gali Men*.

ASHOK JERATH. Modern Hindi writer of Jammu-Kashmir, who is noted for his short story collection : *Cherry ke Phul* (The Cherry Blossoms ; 1980), based on the snowy hills of Jammu and Kashmir. He also wrote *Dharti Apni-apni* and a novel : *Na Tutne Vale Pankh* (The Unbreakable Wings).

ASHOK KE PHUL. Collection of essays (1948) of Hazari Prasad Dwivedi (q.v.), which consists of the essays : 'Ashok ke Phul', 'Vasant A Gaya', 'Alochana ka Swatantra Man', 'Bharatiya Sanskriti ki Den', 'Hamari Rashtriya Shiksha Pranali', etc. These essays treat of cultural, literary, educational and other topics and speak of the scholarship and wide study of the author.

ASHOK KUMAR EDALABADKAR. Marathi-speaking modern Hindi poet, whose poems are written on various subjects.

ASHOK PRABHAKAR KAMAT. Marathi-speaking modern Hindi scholar, whose research works are : *Maharashtra ke Nathpanthiya Kaviyon ka Hindi Kavya* and *Hindi aur Maharashtra ka Snehabandh.*

ASHOK RAMCHANDRA KELKAR. Author of *Studies in Hindi-Urdu* (1968).

ASHOK SHUKLA. Writer, whose *Hartal Hari Katha* (1982) on college politics, is a novel.

ASHOK VAJPEYI (1941-). Poet and critic, who is in the Indian Administrative Service. His chief works are : *Shayad ab bhi Sambhavana Hai* (poem ; 1966), *Philhal* (For the Present ; a critical work on modern poetry ; 1970) and *Tisra Sakshya* (criticism).

ASIG (ASIGU). Jain poet and author in Rajasthani of : *Jivdaya Ras* in 53 verses (composed in 1200) on the importance of mercy in living beings, *Chandan Bala Ras* in 35 verses on the incident of giving alms to Lord Mahavir and *Kripan-Grihini Sanvad* in 9 verses forming a dialogue between a husband and a wife about the proper use of money.

ASIYA BANKIDAS. See *Bankidas, Asiya.*

ASIYA DANA (fl. latter half of 18th cent.). Rajasthani poet, whose *Virud Prakas* describes the life of Maharaja Gajsingh (1746—87) of Bikaner.

ASIYA KARAMSI KHINVSAROT (fl. 1543-63). Dingal poet, who got the village Pasunda, as gift from Rana Uday Singh of Mewar for his poetry. His works are : *Marsiya Rao Rajsingh Sirohi Ra, Suja Balecha ra Kavitta* (q.v.) and some *Gits.*

ASKARAN (fl. 1704). Jain poet, whose *Nemichandrika*

delineates beautifully the characters of Neminath, the 22nd Jain Tirthankar and Rajul.

ASTANAND SADASINGH. Modern Hindi dramatist of Mauritius, whose works are : *Avaz*, *Tu-Tu* and *Thuk Diya Bhavishya Par*.

ATHVALE, VI. RA. Marathi-speaking modern Hindi writer, whose chief work is : *Pandit Vishnu Digambar*.

ATIT KE CHALCHITRA. See *Mahadevi Verma*.

ATMA RAM (d. 1759). Rajasthani saint-poet and a follower of Haridas Niranjani Sect, whose stray verses deal with spiritual matters lucidly.

ATMA RAM GAIROLA (1855-1922). Garhwali poet, who was considered one of the pioneers of Garhwali poetry. His Garhwali poems have been published under the title *Garhwali Kavitavali*.

ATMA RAM VISHWANATH (d. 1955). A Maharashtrian, who at the instance of Mahatma Gandhi went to Mauritius in 1912 to edit 'Hindustani' (see *Maganlal Manilal*). He afterwards edited 'Arya Patrika', 'Aryavir Jagriti', 'Aryoday', etc. and though he had leanings towards Arya Samaj, he had cordial relations with all the people there. He knew Marathi, Gujarati, Hindi and English and wrote four important works : *Chhatrapati Shivaji* (1921), *Lakshmibai ki Jivni*, *Mauritius ka Itihas* (1921) and *Hindu Mauritius* (1936). In all, he is said to have written fourteen books. He was also a forceful orator. Almost for 40 years, he furthered the cause of Hindi in Mauritius and then died in Port Louis, the capital of Mauritius, in 1955 at the age of 74.

ATMA RAO DEVKAR (fl. 1900—1920). Marathi-speaking Hindi poet and writer, whose poems lay emphasis on social reform. His novels, mainly detective, are : *Bhayankar Durdasha*, *Trailokya Sundari*, *Maya Marichika*, *Adarsh Mitra*, etc. His short stories generally have been written in the social context. He also composed several Hindi dramas.

AULOVA, RINA ARONOVNA (1927-) Soviet Hindi scholar, who did doctorate in 1973 on 'Hindi ki Shikshan Pranali'. She has prepared texts books in Hindi for teaching Hindi in secondary schools of Russia.

AVADH BIHARI 'SUMAN'. Modern Bhojpuri writer, who is

known for his *Jehal-k-Sanadi*, a collection of ten social short stories.

AVADH NARAYAN LAL (1885-1955). Novelist of Bihar, whose chief work is *Vimata* (The Step-mother ; 1923).

AVADH UPADHYAY (1893-1941). Critic of Balia (Uttar Pradesh), who was noted for his articles on Chhayavad poetry and on Premchand's novels. In his articles on Premchand's novels, he tried to prove that many of them were copied from English works.

AVDHESH KUMAR. Modern poet, whose poems are included in *Chautha Saptak* (q.v.). His poetical work is *Gypsy Larki* (The Gypsy Girl).

AVINASHANAND (1733-82). Gujarati-speaking saint-poet of Swaminarayan Sect, who was initiated by Acharya Ayodhya-prasad Maharaj. His chief work in Hindi is *Chhapaiya Mahatmya*.

AVTAR KRISHNA KAUL. Kashmiri-speaking modern Hindi writer, who is noted for his novelette : *Sarhad aur Pyar* (The Frontier and Love).

AVTAR KRISHNA RAZDAN. Modern Hindi writer of Jammu-Kashmir, who is famous for his *Kashmir men Lalit-Kala* (The Fine Arts of Kashmir).

AXENOV, ANATOLY TIKHONOVICH (1923-). Soviet Hindi scholar, who taught Hindi at the Jawahar Lal Nehru University, New Delhi. He has prepared grammars of Hindi as spoken in the Delhi region.

AYODHYA NATH AVDHESH (b. 1751). Poet of Kashi, whose only work *Shri Durgumukh-Mahotsvopahar* (on the goddess Durga) consisting of 15-16 verses, is extant.

AYODHYA PRASAD, THE LATE. Hindi writer of Fiji, who was noted for his work : *Kisan Sangh ka Itihas* (2 vols.).

AYODHYA PRASAD KHATRI (1857—1905). Writer of Muzaffar-pur, whose *Khari Boli Andolan* (1888) furthered the cause of Khari Boli Movement. He also wrote *Hindi Vyakaran* (Banki-pur, 1877), which was a common grammar for both Hindi and Urdu.

AYODHYA SINGH. Writer, whose *Fasivad* (1980) is a detailed study of Fascism.

AYODHYA SINGH UPADHYAY 'HARIAUDH' (1865—1947). Poet, who was born at Nizamabad in Azamgarh district of Uttar Pradesh. After his retirement from Government service in 1923, he was appointed as Professor of Hindi in the Benares Hindu University. His creative period extended over a long time : in the beginning he wrote in Brajbhasha, but at the instance of Mahavir Prasad Dwivedi (q.v.), he wrote his first Khari Boli epic, *Priya Pravas* (The Sojourn of the Loved ; q.v. ; 1914) exclusively on the model of Sanskrit verse, using Sanskritic diction and vocabulary. Apart from *Priya-Pravas*, his masterpiece, his other chief works are : *Vaidehi Vanvas* (also an epic ; q.v.), *Parijat* (The Celestial Tree), *Karmavir*, *Padmaprasun* (A Lotus Plant), *Kalpalata* (The Celestial Creeper), *Ritu-Mukur* (The Season's Bud), *Kavyopavan* (A Garden of Poetry), *Prem Pushpohar* (A Garland of Love-Flowers), *Premanprapanch* (The Ways of Love), *Premambu-Prashravan* (The Spreading of Water of Love), *Premambu-Varidhi* (The Ocean of Water of Love), *Adhkhila Phul* (The Half-opened Blossom), *Bol-chal* (Conversation), *Rasa-Kalash* (The Pitcher of Juice ; q.v.), *Chokhe Chaupade* (Good Quartrains) and *Chubhte Chaupade* (Sharp and Penetrating Quartrains). In his prose work, sometimes considered as a novel, *Theth Hindi-ka Thath* (The Glory of Pure Hindi), he has sought to demonstrate what the best kind of prose should be like ; *Devbala* is his another novel. He also wrote *Hindi Bhasha aur Sahitya ka Vikas* (The Development of Hindi Language and Literature) and tr. into Hindi some works from English and Persian. He wrote two dramas : *Rukmini-Haran* (The Abduction of Rukmini) and *Pradyumna-Vijay* (The Victory of Pradyumna). He ed. *Kabir Vachnavali* as well.

A hyper-sensitive person, compassion to Hariaudh appears to be the highest virtue and this feeling is also reflected in most of his works. His *Priya-Pravas* is full of excellent descriptions of Nature.

AYUB KHAN 'PREMI' Kashmiri-speaking modern Hindi writer, who has tr. into Hindi verse representative Kashmiri poems under the title *Pratinidhi Kashmiri Kavitayen* (Representative Kashmiri Poems).

AZAM KHAN (fl. *c.* 1730). Riti poet, who was patronized by Muhammad Shah, the Emperor of India. His *Singar Darpan* is a work on *Rasa* and *Nayika-Bhed*.

A[illegible] Written whose *[illegible]* (1980) is a deep study of Fascism.

AYODHYA SINGH UPADHYAY 'HARIAUDH' (1865–1947) Poet who was born at Nizamabad in Azamgarh district of Uttar Pradesh. After his retirement from Government service in 1923, he was appointed as Professor of Hindi in the Benares Hindu University. His creative period extended over a long time. In the beginning he wrote in Brajbhasha, but at the instance of Mahavir Prasad Dwivedi (q.v.), he wrote his first epic in Boli, *Priya Pravas* (The Sojourn of the Loved One, 1914) exclusively on the model of Sanskrit verse, using Sanskritic diction and vocabulary. Apart from *Priya Pravas*, his master-piece, his other chief works are *[illegible]* (1914), an epic [illegible] *[illegible]* (The Celestial Tree), *[illegible]* [illegible] (The [illegible] Creeper), *[illegible]* (The [illegible]), *[illegible]* (A Garland of [illegible]), *[illegible]* (Garland of Love [illegible]), *[illegible]* (The [illegible] of Love), *[illegible]* [illegible] of [illegible] of *[illegible]* (The Ocean or Water of Love), *[illegible]* (The [illegible] and [illegible]), *[illegible]* (Conversation), *[illegible]* (The [illegible]), *[illegible]* [illegible] and *[illegible]*, *[illegible]* (Penetrating [illegible]). In his prose work, sometimes considered as a novel, *[illegible]* (The [illegible] of Pure Hindi), he tried to demonstrate what the [illegible] Hindi prose should be. In *[illegible]* (1907), another novel, he also wrote *[illegible]* [illegible] (The Development of Hindi Language and Literature) and translated into Hindi some works from English and Persian. He wrote two dramas: *[illegible]* (The Abduction of [illegible]) and *[illegible]* (The Victory of Pradyumna). He also edited *[illegible]* as well.

A hyper sensitive person, compassion and humane [illegible] his [illegible] and this feeling is also reflected in his [illegible] which [illegible] is full of excellent [illegible] of [illegible].

AYODHYA [illegible] [illegible] Kashmiri translator into Hindi who [illegible] into Hindi [illegible] Kashmiri poet [illegible] the *[illegible] Kashmiri [illegible]* (Rupa [illegible] Kashmiri Poems).

A[illegible] [illegible] written by [illegible] Shah, the Emperor of India. His *[illegible]* [illegible] is a work on Rama and [illegible].

B

BABA LAL (fl. 1643). Saint-poet of Malwa, whose stray *Padas* are available. He was the preceptor of Prince Dara Shukoh, a son of Emperor Shah Jehan.

BABBAR (fl. 1550). Poet of Tripuri, near Jabbalpur, who was patronized by Raja Karna Kalchuri ; only his stray verses are available.

BABU LAL BHATIA. Modern Malwi writer, who is noted for his farces and short stories.

BABU LAL SHARMA. Writer, whose *Jit men Har aur Har men Jit* is a collection of essays.

BABU RAM ARUN. Modern Hindi poet of Fiji, whose chief work is : *Fiji ki Sundarta.*

BABU RAM SAXENA (1897-). Scholar, who had been Head of the Department of Sanskrit at Allahabad University and Vice-Chancellor of Ravishankar University, Raipur and of Allahabad University. His chief works are : *Avadhi ka Vikas* (Eng. version : *The Evolution of Avadhi*), *Samanya Bhashavigyan* (General Philology), *Dakkhini Hindi* and ed. of *Kirtilata.*

BABU RAO KUNTHEKAR. Kannada-speaking modern Hindi writer, who tr. from Kannada into Hindi the *Padas* of Purandardas as also Shivram Karant's famous Kannada novel *Mareli Mannigai.*

BABU RAO VISHNU PARADKAR (1883-1955). Marathi-speaking Hindi writer, whose essays dealing with religious, social and cultural topics appeared in various magazines. He was also the editor of 'Aj'.

BABU SAHIB CHOUDHARY. Maithili writer, who is noted for his social drama *Kuhes* (1970).

BABUAJI JHA AGYAT. Maithili poet, who was noted for his love lyrics. He was a contemporary of Maharaja Maheshwar Singh (1850-60). His *Rukmini-Parinay*, taken from various Purans, is an epic, which has been published only in 1980.

BABUAJI MISHRA. Modern Maithili scholar, who has edited several Maithili classics.

BACHAN DEV KUMAR. See *Vachan Dev Kumar.*

BACHCHAN. See *Harivansh Rai Bachchan.*

BACHCHAN SINGH (1919-). Noted critic, whose chief works are : *Samkalin Sahitya* : *Alochana ko Chunauti* (Contemporary Literature : Challenge to Criticism), *Alochak aur Alochana* (Critic and Criticism ; 1970), *Adhunik Hindi Sahitya ka Itihas* (History of Modern Hindi Literature ; 1977) and *Hindi Natak.* He had been Professor and Head of the Department of Hindi at Himachal Pradesh University, Shimla.

BACHNESH MISHRA (b. 1875). Poet of Farrukhabad, who was patronized by Maharaja Ramesh Singh of Kalakankar. Bachnesh composed a *Khand-Kavya*, named *Shavari*, which discusses the problem of untouchability.

BADAR (BAHADUR). Rajasthani poet, who was a Mohammedan named Dhadhi. His *Virmayan* (q.v.) composed in the later part of the first half of the 15th century, describes many battles and events connected with the early Rathore chiefs and the Johiyas.

BADI-UZ-ZAMAN. Writer, whose chief novels are : *Ek Chuhe ki Maut* (Death of a Rat ; a satire on bureaucracy ; 1971), *Apurush* (Impotent Person), *Vapsi* and *Chhathatantra.* He has also written short stories, his important stories being 'Pardesi' (The Stranger), 'Ghar' (The Home), 'Chautha Brahman' (The Fourth Brahmin), etc His short stories are collected in *Chautha Brahman* and *Pul Tutate Huye.*

BADRI NARARAN CHAUDHARI 'PREMGHAN' (1855-1922). Critic, writer and poet, who hailed from Mirzapur and was a close friend of Bharatendu Harishchandra (q.v.). He started two literary periodicals, 'Anand Kadambini' and '*Nagari Nirad*'. He was a critic and several important reviews of contemporary publications including that of Shrinivas's *Sanyogita-Swayamvar*, appeared in his papers. His ideal of prose-writing was different from that of Bharatendu, for he turned prose-writing into an art and developed an elaborate alliterative pattern ; his poetry is also permeated with excessive elaboration and ornamentation. His chief dramas are *Bharat Saubhagya* (India's Prosperity), *Virangana-Rahasya* (The Mystery of Amazon), *Prayag-Ramagman* (Arrival in Prayag) and *Kajli Kadambini* (Black Row of Clouds), while his other published works include *Anand Arunoday* (Happy Dawn), *Bharat Badhai* (Homage to India) and *Mangalasha Hardik Dhanyavad* (Heart-felt Thanks for Prosperity) ; *Premghan-Sarvasva* (Complete Premghan) is a collection of his poems.

Premghan's reviews of *Sanyogita Swyamvar* and of Gadadhar Singh's tr. of *Bang Vijeta* are considered generally the starting points for a study of modern Hindi criticism.

BADRI NARAYAN DAS. Modern Maithili novelist, whose chief work is *Chandrakala.*

BADRI NATH BHATT (1891-1934). Dramatist, poet and scholar, who was for some time Professor of Hindi in Lucknow University. His chief works : *Chungi-ki-Umedvari* (Municipal Candidacy ; 1919 ; on the racket of municipal elections), *Labar-Dhon-Dhon* (1926), *Vivah Vigyapan* (Matrimonial Advertisement ; 1927 ; on the aged seeking young brides through newspaper advertisement) and *Miss American* (caricature of Western culture ; 1929) were all successful plays so far humour was concerned ; he wrote also three mythological plays : *Kuruvan-Dahan* (The Wild Fire that Destroyed Kauravs ; 1912), *Prabhas Milan* and *Ven-Charit* and two historical dramas : *Durgavati* and *Chandragupta.* He also wrote a book *Hindi,* treating of Hindi language and its literature.

BADRI NATH JHA, KAVISHEKHAR. Maithili poet, whose *Ekavali Parinay* (q.v. ; 1937-1942), composed under the influence of Sanskrit Mahakavyas, treats of the marriage of Ekavali with Ekvir, the son of king Turvasu of Yadu race. Ekvir meets Yashomati, who tells him of the beauty of her friend, Ekavali, the latter having been abducted by the demon-king Kalketu. Ekvir attacks the demon, rescues the lady and lives happily thereafter with her. Based on the 6th canto of the *Devi Bhagavat,* the epic consists of 15 cantos. He also composed several types of lyrics. See *Giti Ratnavali.*

BADRI NATH KALLA SHASTRI (1931-). Kashmiri-speaking Hindi writer, who is one of the editors of *Kashmiri Bhasha Shabdakosh.* Besides editing the *Manas Darpan,* which is a collection of essays on *Ramcharitmanas,* he has contributed research articles to 'Prakash', 'Shiraja', 'Vitasta', 'Koshur Samachar', etc.

BADRI PRASAD PANCHOLI. Rajasthani writer, whose chief work, *Pani Pali Pal* (1973) is a stage play, based on a plot in the times of the Mahabharat.

BADRI PRASAD SAKARIYA (1896-). Rajasthani scholar, whose chief works are : *Rajasthani Hindi Shabda-Kosh* (with Bhupatiram Sakariya), *Mahakavi Isardas aur Unka Kavya* and *Muhata Nainsi ri Khyat* (4 Pts.) (the last two criticism). He had been Editor of 'Rajasthan Bharati' for several years. He also wrote short stories.

BAGADAWAT. Rajasthani ballad, which deals with the battles of 24 Bagadawat brothers and is sung by Bhopas.

Jaymati (Jailu), the wife of an old Rajput ruler, the Rao of Ran, has a love-affair with Sawai Bhoj (or Bhoja), a handsome Bagadawat brother. In the battle between the Rajputs of the Rao and the Bagadawats, all the 23 Bagadawat brothers, except one Teja, are killed. Later, Bhoja's pregnant wife, Sadhu gives birth to a son named Udaj Rao (Devnaryan). He takes revenge by killing the Rao of Ran. A Bhat of the Bagadawats named Chhochhu, who is also a character of the story, is said to have composed the *Gatha* in 15,000 verses but that is not available. Devnarayan is deemed a god incarnate and is worshipped ; Bhoja is also worshipped. Sung by the Bhopas, the *Gatha* is popular in three forms : the first dealing with the complete story, the second up to the death of Bagadawat brothers and the third with Devnarayan only. Lakshmi Kumari Chundawat has edited the *Gatha* after taking it down from a Bhopa, while K.K. Sharma and Mahendra Bhanawat have respectively edited the second and the third versions. See *Dev Lila Kavya*.

BAGANZ, LUTZ. Modern German scholar, who, though a specialist of Bengali language and literature, has also leanings towards Hindi.

BAGHJI VITHU (fl. between 1450 and 1550). Dingal poet, who composed stray verses and *Gits* for celebrating the victory of Rao Jaitsi of Bikaner over Kamran, a son of Babar.

BAHARI, U.S. Modern scholar, whose chief work is *Topics in Hindi Language* (2 vols.).

BAHAUDDIN BAJHAN, SHEIKH (1387-1505). Gujarati-speaking

poet, whose stray verses are extant in a language akin to Dakkhini Hindi.

BAHL, KALI CHARAN. See *Kali Charan Bahl.*

BAIJ NATH DWIVEDI (b. 1837). Poet, who was son of Dinesh or Shivdin Dwivedi of Tekari (Gaya). He wrote nine Riti works, such as *Gaya-Gadadhar-Vas-Prakash* (on Gaya), *Nakh-Shikh* (description of heroine), *Vam-Vilas*, etc.

BAIJ NATH KEDIYA (1885-1947). Rajasthani writer, who has published *Marwari Git.* He also established a publishing house : 'Hindi Pustak Agency'.

BAIJ NATH PANVAR. Rajasthani writer, whose chief works are *Ladesar* (1970), *Nainan Khutyo Nir* (1977 ; short story collections), *Apano Khas Admi* (one-act plays) and *Gadya-Kavyas.*

BAIJ NATH PRASAD 'BAIJU' (1910-). Popular Bagheli folk-poet, who was born at the village Satgarh in Rewa. His collection of poems : *Baiju ki Suktiyan* (Wise Sayings) treats of the rural life.

BAIJ NATH SINGH 'VINOD'. Modern Hindi writer, whose *Maithili Sahitya* provides information about Maithili literature and culture. He has also published a study of Bhojpuri folk-literature : *Bhojpuri Lok-Sahitya—Ek Adhyayan.*

BAIJU (fl. *c.* 1487-1517). Celebrated musician, who was in the court of Raja Man Singh Tomar of Gwalior. Some of Baiju's *Padas* composed in Brajbhasha are still available.

BAILEY, REV. T. GRAHAM. English Hindi scholar, who was Professor of Hindi in London. His chief works are *Languages of Himalaya Area* (London, 1908), an article on Hindi Grammar (1934) and *Studies in North Indian Languages.*

BAIRISAL. Poet of the Riti School, who was a Brahmabhatt of Asni. He composed *Bhashabharan* (1758), an *Alankar* work in *Dohas.*

BAITAL (b. 1677). Poet who was a Bandijan and attended the court of Vikramsahi. He is celebrated for his *Kundaliyas*, which are replete with worldly wisdom.

BAJE BHAGAT (fl. early 20th cent.). Folk-poet of Sasana

(Haryana), who was a barber by caste. His chief *Sangs* are : *Chandrakiran*, *Jamal* and *Jyani Chor*. Love predominates his *Sangs*, so that Lakhmi Chand called him a 'Bhand' (one who spoke af love without shame).

BAJU (fl. 18th cent. ?). Rajasthani saint-poet of Laldasi Sect, whose *Bhajans* extol faith in God and *Guru* and advocate a simple life.

BAKHNAJI (*c.* 1553-1623). Rajasthani saint-poet of Naraina (Rajasthan), who was said to be a Muslim by birth. A disciple of Dadu (q.v.), his *Sakhis*, classified into 40 *Angas* and 167 *Padas*, deal with the realization of the Absolute Truth through love. His *Bani* has been published and language is simple Rajasthani. He was proficient in music and as such he has composed *Padas* which are meant to be sung.

BAKHSHI. See *Padumlal Punnalal Bakhshi*.

BAKHSHI HANSRAJ 'PREM-SAKHI' (b. 1742). Poet, who was a courtier of Aman Singh, the ruler of Panna. He was a disciple of Vijay Sakhi, a saint of Braj, by whom he was named as "Prem-Sakhi". He composed four works : *Saneh-Sagar* (Ocean of Love ; ed. by Lala Bhagvan Din), *Virah-Vilas* (on separation), *Ray-Chandrika*, *Barahmasa* (description of 12 months ; 1754). The first work runs into nine *Tarangs* and describes Krishna's *Lilas*. The language is simple, flowing and charming.

BAKHSHU (fl. 15th cent.). Celebrated musician, who was in the court of Raja Man Singh Tomar of Gwalior. Bakhshu continued to be patronized by Man Singh's son, Vikramajit but when he died in 1526 in the Battle of Panipat, Bakhshu shifted to Raja Kirat of Kalinjar and thereafter was invited by Bahadur Shah, Sultan of Gujarat, to his court. Some of his *Padas* in Brajbhasha are still available.

BAKHTAVAR SINGH (fl. 1857). Jain poet, who was the author of *Pradyumna-Charit* on the story of Krishna's son, Pradyumna.

BAKHTAVAR SINGH, RAO (1813-1894). Rajasthani poet, who was son of Sukharam but after his father's death was brought up by Thakur Arjun Singh of Basi. In 1852, Bakhtavar was patronized and later on honoured by Maharana Swarup Singh of Udaipur. He continued to enjoy favour from three subsequent Maharanas.

He used to write poems both in Rajasthani and Brajbhasha. Out of his 11 works: *Kehar-Prakash*, *Rasotpatti*, *Swarup-Yash-Prakash*, *Shambhu-Yash-Prakash*, *Sajjan-Yash-Prakash*, *Fateh-Yash-Prakash*, *Sajjan-Chitra-Chandrika*, *Sancharnav*, *Anyokti-Prakash*, *Samant-Yash-Prakash* and *Raginiyon ki Pustak*; the first one, composed in 1879 and also published, is the best of all. Consisting of 1486 metres and written in Rajasthani, it describes the romance of Kamal, a courtesan and her lover, Kesri Singh.

BAKSA (fl. 18th cent. ?). Rajasthani saint-poet of Laldasi Sampraday, whose *Bhajans* extol devotion to God and *Guru* and the desirability of leading a simple life.

BAL BAHARU (fl. 18th cent.). Marathi folk-poet (*Shahir*), who also made compositions in Hindi.

BAL BHADRA MISHRA (fl. *c.* 1580). Poet, who was the elder brother or at least a contemporary of Keshavdas (q.v.) and was an equally erudite Sanskrit scholar. He also enjoyed the patronage of Orchha court. He composed *Nakh-Shikh*, *Balbhadri Vyakaran* (grammar), *Hanumannatak* (drama), *Govardhan Satsai Tika* and *Dushan Vichar* (Evil Thoughts). Among these poems, the first one is his most famous work; it treats of the beauty of the female form, limb by limb, with a view to illustrating the poetic theory of the *Rasas*. Later on, several commentaries were written on this work. He also tr. the *Bhagavata Purana* from Sanskrit into Hindi. Mishra employed far-fetched comparisons and his imagery sometimes becomes tedious; even then in smoothness and liquid flow, his poetry surpasses that of Keshavdas. Mishra's poetry is precursor of the Riti school poetic works.

BAL BHADRA PRASAD DIKSHIT 'PADHIS' (1898-1943). Avadhi folk-poet, whose collection of poems: *Chakallas* (1933) presents a humorous and satiric picture of the contemporary life. He composed other poems, which remain unpublished. See *Ramai Kaka*.

BAL BHADRA THAKUR. Novelist, whose chief works are: *Adityanath* (on the people of Kulu valley), *Muktavali* (on the life and people of Manipur), *Nepal ki Beti* (The Daughter of Nepal; 1959; a description of Nepalese culture) and *Laharon ki Chhati Par* (On the Breast of Waves; 1961).

BAL BHAKTI (fl. 1693). Poet of the Ram-cult, who composed *Neh Prakash* and *Dayal Manjari*.

Baldas (fl. 1630). Hindi poet of the Ram-cult, who composed *Chitra-Bodhan.*

Baldev Das (fl. 17th cent.). Bengali Vaishnav poet, who also composed *Padas* in Brajbuli.

Baldev Mishra, Raj-Pandit. Maithili writer, whose *Raj-Rajeshwari Natak* (1920) and *Rameshoday Natika* (1922) are Kirtaniya dramas. He also edited the songs of Chanda Jha, which were known as *Chandra Padyavali.* A great supporter of the culture and manners of the ancients, he also wanted a few changes and his views are expressed in a balanced and comparatively sober style. His essays are collected in *Sanskriti, Shishu-Shiksha, Ramayan Shiksha* (1939), *Mahabharat Shiksha, Gapp Sapp Vivek* and *Shyamnandan Sahay Vyakhyan Mala.* In oratory, he has no equal to this day in Mithila. He also wrote critical articles.

Baldev Prasad Mishra (1898-1975). Poet, whose chief works are : *Shringar-Shatak* (on love), *Vairagya-Shatak* (on renunciation), *Shyam Shatak* (on Krishna) and *Saket-Sant* (all poetry) ; *Tulsi Darshan* (The Philosophy of Tulsidas) is his well-known research work. He has written historical novels as well. His dramas are : *Mirabai* (1919), *Asadhya Sankalpa* (1925) and *Vasna-Vaibhav.*

Baldev Sharma 'Din'. Garhwali writer, who was the author in 1927 of *Jasi, Rami* and *Bat Gadai,* the refined versions of Garhwali folk-songs.

Baldev Upadhyay. Modern Sanskritist and educationist, whose *Bharatiya Sahityashastra* (The Indian Poetics ; 2 Parts ; 1950) deals with Indian schools and principles of literary criticism.

Baldev Vanshi. Panjabi-speaking Hindi poet and critic, whose *Atmadan* (1982), a long poem, gives a new interpretation of the myth of Ahilya ; according to the *Rigveda,* Ahilya represents night (*ratri*), which is visited by Sun (Indra). His earlier collections of poems are : *Darshak Dirgha* (Visitors' Gallery), *Kala Itihas, Upanagar men Vapsi* (The Return to the Town) and *Andhere ke Bavajud* (Despite the Darkness ; 1978). Baldev Vanshi has been one of the trend setters of thought-poetry in Hindi. His critical works are : *Adhunik Hindi Kavitaon men Vichar* (Ideas in the Modern Hindi Poems ; 1982) and a study of ideas in *Lambi Kavitayen* (Long Poems ; 1982).

BAL GANGADHAR TILAK, LOKMANYA (1856-1920). Marathi-speaking celebrated political leader and scholar, who also wrote some essays in Hindi.

BAL GOVIND JHA. Modern Maithili writer, who is noted for his patriotic drama, *Tripathga.* He has also written some critical works.

BAL KAVI VAIRAGI. Lyrical poet, whose chief works are *Do Tuk* (The Forthright ; 1971), *Ret ke Rishte, Koi to Samjhe* and *Shilvati-Ag*. He has written his autobiography—*Mangte se Minister Tak* (From a Beggar to a Minister). Popular in Kavi Sammelans, he is a Minister in Madhya Pradesh. He has also written a novel : *Kachchh ka Padyatri.*

BALKRISHNA BHATT (1844-1914). Writer, who was a Sanskrit teacher in an Allahabad College. Besides classical languages like Sanskrit and Persian, Bhatt had mastered Hindi, English, Bengali and a few modern Indian languages. He was greatly impressed by Bharatendu Harishchandra's writings and sought to imitate his style. There was hardly a Hindi periodical to which Bhatt did not contribute articles on literary and social subjects and when in 1877 'Hindi Pradip' was started from Allahabad, Bhatt was appointed its firist editor, a place he occupied for full 32 years. His writings usually appeared in this paper ; Bhatt's pithy style, with a good sprinkling of humour tended to make his articles fine literary essays. Historians of Hindi literature have rightly called him the 'Addison' of Hindi. Apart from hundreds of essays and critical articles, Bhatt wrote some dramas : *Jaisa Kam, Vaisa Parinam* (As Deeds, So Results), *Kaliraj ki Sabha* (Kaliraj's Council), *Rail ka Vikat Khel* (The Strange Game of Rail). *Bal Vivah* (Child Marriage), *Veni-Samhar* (based on an episode of the *Mahabharat*), *Damyanti Swayamvar* (1892), *Prithu-Charit* and *Chandrasen* ; he also tr. from Bengali two of Michael Madhusudan Dutt's plays, *Padmavati* and *Sharmishtha.* Among his other works are *Shiksha-Dan* (Donation of Education ; one-act plays), *Sahitya-Suman* (literary essays), *Achar-Vidambana, Bhatt Nibandhavali* (collection of his representative essays), *Sau Ajan ek Sujan* (A Hundred Simpletons and One Wise Man ; a didactic novel), *Nutan Brahmachari* (The New Celibate ; 1886 ; novel) and *Nai Roshni ka Vish* (The Poison of New Light ; farce). He was one of the editors of *Hindi Shabda Sagar* (the first largest Hindi lexicon) and wrote a criticism on Shrinivas's *Sanyogita-Swayamvar.* His essays reveal his profound scholarship and wide knowledge.

Bhatt is considered the first literary critic, who, in 'Hindi

'Pradip' and other journals, discussed the merits and demerits of the works of various writers and their style. In a way, it was his criticism of Bharatendu's writings which attracted Hindi readers and made Hindi writings known widely.

BALKRISHNA JHA. Maithili scholar, who has published in1981 Maithili trs. of T.S. Eliot's three critical essays : 'Tradition and Individual Talent', 'The Function of Criticism' and 'The Frontiers of Criticism'.

BALKRISHNA LAHOTI. Modern Rajasthani writer, who is noted for his drama, *Kanya Bikri* (The Sale of Daughter).

BALKRISHNA NAYAK (fl. 17th cent.). Saint-poet, who was a disciple of Charandas (q.v.). Despite his being a Nirguni saint, he worshipped Vishnu. His chief works, devotional in character, are *Dhyan Manjari* (1669) and *Neh Prakashika* (1692).

BALKRISHNA PILLAI. K.G. Malayalam-speaking modern Hindi writer, who is the author of *Kerala*.

BALKRISHNA RAO, I.C.S. (1913-75). Poet and critic, whose mother tongue was Telugu. His chief works are : *Kaumudi* (The Moonlight ; 1931), *Abhas* (Auto-suggestion ; 1935), *Kavi aur Kavi*, *Rat-biti* (Befallen at Night ; 1954), *Hamari Bat* (Our Point ; 1957) and *Arddha-Shati* (The semi-centenary ; poetical collections) ; *Vikrant Samson* (1957) is a tr. work. He also ed. *Kavya-Bharati* and *Swatantrottara Hindi Sahitya* (Post-Independence Hindi Literature) and tr. Milton's *Aeropagitica* and Aeschylus's play. He was Director-General of All India Radio and Vice-Chancellor of Agra University. He edited 'Madhyam', the literary magazine of Hindi Sahitya Sammelan and organized 'Vichar-gosthis' in Allahabad.

BALKRISHNA SHARMA 'NAVIN' (1898-1960). Poet, who was born at Bhavana in Gwalior, but was educated at Ujjain and Kanpur. He came into contact with Ganesh Shankar Vidyarthi and was influenced by him. His chief works are : *Kumkum* (The Saffron), *Kwasi* (Where are Thou ?), *Rashmirekha* (A Ray of Light), *Apalak* (Wide Awake), *Vinoba-Stavan* (Praise of Vinoha Bhave), *Urmila* (a long poem) and *Ham Vish Payi Janam ke* (poetical collections) ; 'Viplav-gan' and 'Kastvam : Koham' (Who Art Thou, Who am I ?) are his best-known poems. As Kanpur's accredited Congress leader, he was a nationalist and sang full-throated melodies in praise of the Motherland and in support of the freedom struggle. He was a Member of the Parliament. He rose higher as a thinker and invariably soared to philosophic heights. He also wrote some short stories. With Ganesh Shankar Vidyarthi and after Vidyarthi's death, he edited 'Pratap', a weekly.

BALKRISHNA THALAMBIYA. Modern Rajasthani poet, who composed Nature and love poems.

BALKRISHNAN. Malayalam-speaking modern Hindi scholar, who wrote *Hindi-Angrezi-Malayalam Kosh.*

BALMUKUND. Author of *Hindi Kridant Rupon ka Vikas* (1968) and *Hindi Kriya : Swarup aur Vishleshan* (1970).

BALMUKUND CHATURVEDI 'MUKUND'. Modern poet of Mathura, whose *Shrikrishna Kaustubh* describes the story of the *Bhagavata.* He has also composed stray verses.

BALMUKUND GUPTA (1865-1907). Writer, who was born at the village Gudiyana in the district Rohtak of Haryana. Well-versed as he was in Urdu, he preferred to write in the plain and easy manner of Urdu prose writers. His satirical genius gave a pungent quality to his prose as also to his verse. His *Shiv Shambhu ke Chitthe* (1904-1905), a collection of his satirical writings on Lord Curzon as also his later writings, provide a prose-model, which was followed by other writers. He was a writer of repute in Urdu, but at the instance of Pandit Madan Mohan Malviya, he started writing in Hindi.

A journalist of standing, he edited two Urdu papers : 'Akhbare Chunar' and 'Kohenur' and three Hindi papers : 'Hindosthan', 'Hindi Bangvasi' and 'Bharat Mitra'. His essays have been collected in *Gupta Nibandhavali.* His *Shiv Shambhu ke Chitthe* was so popular that when its English version appeared, it was sold in no time.

BALMUKUND GURU (fl. early 20th cent.). Malwi poet, who composed *Machs* (operas) and is considered the propounder of this form.

BALNIL DEVTAM. Poet, whose collections of poems : *Dhup ki Tarah Khila Vartman* (The Present Blossoming like Sunshine) and *Ag Jal Rahi Hai* (The Fire is Burning ; 1980) on the one hand depict love scenes and on the other touch aspects beyond self. He has also published *Ulkapat*, a short story collection.

BALRAM. Modern short story writer, who is the editor of 'Kafila'. His story collection are : *Qalam Huye Hath* (The

Chopped Hands; 1980), *Prati Dhwaniyan* (Echoes) and *Malik ke Mitra* (1984).

BALRAM DAS. Celebrated Oriya poet and author of *Jagmohan Ramayan* or *Dandi Ramayan*. A contemporary of Pratap Rudradev (1479—1535), he also composed some *Padas* in Hindi (Brajboli) as well.

BALRAM PRASAD MISHRA 'DWIJESH' (1872-1959). Poet, who was born at Mishrauliya in the Basti district of Uttar Pradesh. He composed several works on devotion, love and ethics; *Dwijesh Darshan* (1956) is a collection of his poems.

BALRAM VASHISHTH. Modern Hindi writer of Fiji, who is noted for his essays and other writings.

BAL SHAURI REDDY (1928-). Telugu-speaking Hindi novelist, whose chief works are: *Swapna aur Satya* (The Dream and Truth), *Dharti Meri Man* (The Earth—My Mother; both 1968), *Lukuma* (1969; on the sacrifice of Devdasi Lukuma), *Bhagna Simayen* (The Broken Boundaries), *Panchamrit* and *Zindagi ki Rah* (The Path of Life); his works emphasize social service and national unity. He is editor of 'Chanda-Mama'. Madras. His other novels are: *Professor, Barrister, Shabari* (based on an incident of the *Ramayan*), *Prakash aur Parchhain* (The Light and Shadow; on the Vijaynagar Empire), *Duvanal, Ye Basti ye Log, Pratidhwaniyan* (The Echoes; 1980; reportage). He is one of the pioneers of the Sahaj Kahani Movement. *Satya ki Khoj* (The Quest for Truth) is a collection of his one-act plays; *Shubh Nimantran* is his drama.

He revised the *Hindi-Telugu Kosh*, published by the Dakshin Bharat Hindi Prachar Sabha. He tr. into Hindi as *Rudram Devi* (1969) and *Narayan Bhatt* (1971), the Telugu novels of Nori Narsingh Shastri and as *Chandragupta ka Swapna* (1976) the Telugu novel of Satyanarayan. He has also tr. Telugu short stories into Hindi.

BAL SUBRAHMANYAM, G. Telugu-speaking modern Hindi poet, who is noted for his stray poems.

BAL SUBRAHMANYAM, H. Tamil-speaking modern Hindi writer, who has prepared Hindi-self-teaching material for Tamil and Malayalam-speaking people.

BAL SWARUP RAHI. Modern lyricist, whose chief work, *Jo Nitant Meri Hai* (Which is Exclusively Mine) is a collection of songs, which present images similar to those of New Poetry (Nai Kavita).

BALVAN SINGH. Poet of the Riti school, who was son of Raja Chetsingh of Kashi. He composed between 1832 and 1874 a scholarly work, *Chitra Chandrika* on the pattern of a 'Chitrakavya'.

BALVANT RAI SCINDIA (1854-1924). Marathi-speaking poet of the Krishna-cult (Chaitanya Sect), who was son of Maharaja Jiyajirao Scindia. He composed *Dasham-Skandh Bhasha*, *Pada-Mala* and *Smaran Mangal Bhasha*. In addition to these, *Usha* (a drama) is also attributed to him.

BALVANT SINGH (1928-). Panjabi-speaking Hindi wtiter, whose chief works are : *Basi Phul* (The Stale Flowers ; 1967 ; sex-dominated novel), *Raka ki Manzil* (The Destination of Raka ; 1971 ; a novel dealing with the Zulu tribe of Africa), *Chak Piran ka Jassa* (1977 ; a novel, dealing with rural life in Panjab), *Kalekos*, *Mona*, *Sindur ki Talash* (novels), *Meri Priya Kahaniyan* (My Favourite Short Stories), *Chilman* and *Aili ! Aili !* (short story collections).

BALA BAKHSH PALHAWAT BARHAT (1855-1931). Rajasthani poet, who was born at the village Hanuntiya in the then Jaipur State. He had donated a sum of Rs. 7,000 to the Nagari Pracharini Sabha, Kashi for continuous publication of works of Rajasthani bardic poetry. Bala Bakhsh composed some 19 works both in Dingal and Pingal. His chief works are : *Bhupal-Sujas-Vernan*, *Asis-Pachchisi*, *Shok-Shatak*, *Marsiya Thakur Joravsingh Ka*, *Shastra-Saransh*, etc.

BALA DUBE. Writer ; her chief novels : *Bojh* (The Burden) and *Bahurupiye* (Buffoons ; both 1980) depict various facets of contemporary society ; her short story collections are : *Sone ka Indradhanush*, *Galiyan Delhi ki* and *Anjani Itihas Kathayen*.

BALA RAM PATWARI (fl. 1940-1947). Malwi poet, who is noted for his *Kirsani-Kichad*.

BALAK DAS (fl. early 19th cent.). Rajasthani saint-poet of Ram Snehi Sampraday, Khedapa whose *Jan Prabhav Parchi* is a significant poem from the socio-historical point of view.

BALAK RAM YOGESHWAR. Contemporary of Ali Bakhsh (1854-1899) and a folk-poet of Haryana. He composed and staged the *Sangs* : *Purna Bhakta, Raja Gopichand, Shilande, Kunjri, Ramayan*, etc.

BALIN, VICTOR JOSEPHOVICH (1927-). Soviet Hindi scholar, whose research works are : *Hindi Sahitya ka Itihas* and *Madhyayugin evam Adhunik Lekhakon par Shodh*. He has written several articles on Premchand and Bharatendu Harishchandra.

BALLABH. See *Vallabh*.

BALLANTYNE, JAMES R. (1813-1864). English Indologist, who was the author of : *Grammar of the Hindustani with Grammatical Exercises* (1838), *Elements of Hindi and Brajbhasha Grammar* (1839), and *A Grammar of the Hindustani Language with Notices of the Braj and Dakhani Dialects* (London, 1842).

BAN BHATT KI ATMAKATHA (Banbhatt's Autobiography). Novel (1946) by Hazari Prasad Dwivedi (q.v.), which has been written in the autobiographical manner. Its plot has been set in the age of king Harshvardhan. Some of the characters like Ban, Harshvardhan, Krishnavardhan, Shilbhadra, Rajyashri and Jayant Bhatt are historical. The places are all historical but the events and actions are imaginary, though probable according to the conditions of that age.

Ban, who has the habit of wandering from one place to another, once reaches Sthanishwar where he meets Nipunika, an actress, of a dramatic group. It was from her that he comes to know that a certain princess has been imprisoned by the royal family of Maukhri dynasty. With the help of Nipunika, Ban is successful in delivering the princess from the prison. From the princess or Bhattini, Ban comes to know that she is the daughter of Tuvir Milind, a celebrated warrior. Bhattini develops such an intense hatred againt the Sthanishwar royal family that she does not want to remain under the protection of anyone connected with Sthanishwar. For fear of punishment by the Government, Ban and Nipunika along with Bhattini proceed towards Magadh. Facing many a hardship in the way, they at last seek the refuge of Lorik Dev, a noble, connected with the protection of Magadh's Fort. Magadh was about to be invaded by Dasyus and no one except Tuvir Milind could face that onslaught. Bhattini with due respect is invited to Sthanishwar and on this occasion Ban arranges the performance of *Ratnavali*, a drama by Harsh. In this performance, Ban becomes the Raja. In the role of Vasvadatta, when Nipunika places the hand of Ratnavali in the hand of Raja (Ban), she becomes so agitated that she dies. After the funeral rites of Nipunika, when Ban is ordered by the court to proceed to Purushpur, Battini implores Ban to return early but the soul of Ban exclaims that no such meeting would ever be possible.

Dwivedi accepts the conventional view of Ban that he was an irresponsible wicked man, but he recreates his character with psychological insight and has endowed with qualities of boldness, frankness and human sympathy, which transform him into a great scholar and poet—in a convincing manner.

BANADAS (fl. 1833). Poet of the Ram-cult, who was a resident of Ayodhya. He composed some 32 works, including *Ramayan* and *Hanumant-Vijay* (The Victory of Hanuman).

BANANATH (fl. 1st half of 19th cent.). Nath Siddha poet of Jodhpur, whose works *Anubhav Prakash* (consisting of songs to be sung in specified musical tones) and *Parvana* (composed in 1851) are famous in the poetry of Nath tradition. He believes that muttering of the names of Ram or Hari can achieve Siddhi. His language is easy and lucid Rajasthani.

BANARSI DAS (fl. 1638). Jain writer, whose chief works are : *Arddha Kathanak* (The Incomplete Narrative ; the first autobiography in Hindi), *Samay-Sar Natak* (in prose), *Banarsi Paddhati*, *Kalyan Mandir Bhasha* and *Nam Mala* (The Garland of Names). His *Samay-Sar Natak*, though given the name of a Natak, is no drama ; it is a treatise on Jain philosophy in the form of dialogues. All his 75 works, big and small, are collected in *Banarsi Vilas*.

BANARSI DAS CHATURVEDI (1892-1985). Prominent Hindi journalist, who edited the 'Vishal Bharat' for two decades and encouraged young writers and contributors. He is famous for his essays, pen-pictures, biographical sketches and literary assessments ; his published books include *Sansmaran* (Reminiscences ; 1952), *Ganesh Shankar Vidyarthi* (biography), *Hamare Aradhya* (Our Revered Personages ; 1952), *Rekhachitra* (Sketches ; 1953), *Sahitya aur Jivan* (Literature and Life ; 1954) and *Setubandh* (The Adam's Bridged ; 1962). He had a fantastic collection of letters of great men and writers, which he has donated to the National Archives.

BANDAKRISHNA SATYANARAYAN. Telugu-speaking Hindi writer, who is noted for his work : *Acharya Hazariprasvd Dwivedi* (1978).

BANDE NAWAZ GESUDARAZ (1340-1423). Regarded as the first writer of Dakhini (akin to Hindi and Urdu), he wrote three books : two of poetry, *Chakkinama* and *Separa* and one of prose : *Merajnama* or *Miraz-ul-Ashqin.* His subjects, like those of the Sufis of the North, are love stories. His prose work comes very near to the Khari Boli prose.

BANG MAHILA. Daughter of Babu Ramprasanna Ghosh of Mirzapur and wife of Babu Purnachandra, who under the pseudonym of 'Bang Mahila' tr. many Bengali short stories into Hindi. She also wrote original short stories in Hindi, among them was the 'Dulaivali' (The Bride), which was published in 1907 in the 'Saraswati', Allahabad. The 'Dulaivali' is regarded as the first short story in Hindi.

BANITHANIJI. See *Rasik Bihari.*

BANKAVATI (fl. early 18th cent.). Poetess of the Krishna-cult (Nimbark Sect), who was Rani of Maharaja Rajsingh of Krishnagarh. She translated the 11 Skandhas of the *Bhagavata,* which are known by the name of *Brajdasi Bhagavat.*

BANKCHOR KI KATHA. See *Nath Mal.*

BANKIDAS ASIYA, KAVIRAJ (1751-1833). Rajasthani court-poet of Maharaja Mansingh of Jodhpur ; he was a historian and a scholar too. A collection of 27 of his works was published in 3 Parts under the title *Bankidas Granthavali.* He is said to have composed some 42 works. Many of his poems dealing with contemporary social evils are sometimes satirical. Such works are : *Vaisak Varta, Mavadiya Mijaj, Kripan Darpan, Chugal Mukh Chapetika, Vais Varta, Kukavi Battisi, Vidur Battisi, Kayar Bavni,* etc. There are also some poems, which seem to arouse people against the British ; such works, not addressed to any individual, are *Sur Chhattisi, Sih Chhattisi, Vir Vinod, Dhaval Pachchisi,* etc. Other poems of Bankidas, such as *Bhurjal Bhushan, Jehal-Jas-Jadav, Siddhrao Chhattisi, Hamrot Chhattisi, Thakur Rup Singh Raipur ri Jhamal* and *Thalvat Battisi* are historical and include verses describing places and towns. *Niti Maniari, Santosh Bavni, Vachan Vivek Pachchisi, Anyokti-Panchasika,* etc. are didactic in nature and preach about moral behaviour. *Ganga Lahari, Jhamal Radhika Shikh-Nakh* (a small poem on Radha. a theme, rarely touched by a poet), *Moh-Mardan,* etc. are religious poems. His *Khyat* is a collection of stray historical notes in prose and shed a flood of light on the history of Rajputana.

A versatile poet, he was among the earliest to express

nationalistic feelings. His appeal was to both Hindus and Muslims to fight against the British hordes. He had also composed some poems in Brajbhasha, especially in praise of his patron, Maharaja Mansingh.

BANKIDAS GRANTHAVALI. See *Bankidas Asiya.*

BANSHIDHAR SHAIDA. Modern Kannauji poet, who is noted for his Kannauji folk-poems.

BANSIDHARA. See *Dalapatiray-Bansidhar.*

BANSILAL (fl. 1800). Folk-poet of Haryana, who composed the Sangs : *Guru Gugga, Raja Gopichand* and *Raja Nal.*

BANSILAL GUPTA. Modern Hindi writer of Jammu-Kashmir, who is known for his *Dogri Vyakaran.*

BANSILAL SURI, THE LATE. Dogri-speaking Hindi poet, who was noted for his poems marked by new experiments.

BANTI CHALIHA. Assamese-speaking modern Hindi writer, who is famous for her memoirs and reportage.

BANVARI (fl. 1633-1943). Poet. He praised in verse the brave deed of Amar Singh Rathore who, in the Durbar of Emperor Shah Jahan, had killed Salabat Khan, a courtier.

BANVARILAL MISHRA 'SUMAN'. Rajasthani poet, whose chief works are : *Delyan ko Divalo* (1963 ; on the life and deeds of Maharana Pratap ; it starts from the 'Jauhar' of Rani Karma and Panna Dhay's sacrifice of her son in order to save Udaysingh) and *Prem Pradip* (1969).

BAP CHANDRA MAHANT (1928-). Assamese-speaking Hindi critic and poet, whose poetical work is *Desh ki Pukar* (The Call of the Country). He has also written critical and research articles, which have been published in 'Vishwabharati Patrika', 'Rashtrasevak', etc. He has also published a work in Hindi on Bhagavat Dharma in Assam and *Mahapurush Shankardev* and edited the Shankardev Issue of the 'Rashtravani' (Poona). His aim has been to acquaint the Hindi readers with the Assamese literature and culture.

BAPU GAEKWAR (1778-1842). Saint-poet, whose mother tongue was Marathi, but who composed his works in pure Gujarati and *Sadhukkari.* His *Barahmasa* and *Chabkha* in Hindi are popular works. Like Kabir (q.v.), he repudiated the caste system.

BARANNIKOV, ALEXEY PETROVICH (1890-1945). Russian Hindi scholar, who has made Hindi popular in Russia. Besides his works on Hindustani (Urdu and Hindi), on the problems of Hindi, his monumental work is the Russian tr. of Tulsidas's *Ramcharitmanas* in verse, with a long introduction in Russian, which has since been tr. into Hindi. It was mainly due to his efforts that Prem Chand's works have been tr. into Russian. He has written more than 80 works on Hindustani (Hindi-Urdu) and other subjects. He also edited the first Parva of the *Mahabharat.* Barannikov's son is at present continning his father's work in the direction of making Hindi popular in Russia.

BARANNIKOV, PYOTR ALEXIYEVICH (1925-). Soviet Hindi scholar, who has worked on Hindustani (Urdu-Hindi) grammar. He is also the author of *Soviet Sangh ki Lok-Kathayen* (1961), *Bhasha aur Sahitya* (1967) and *Bharat* (Leningrad, 1977). He has also written a number of articles on Hindi language. He is son of Alexey Petrovich Barannikov (q.v.).

BARKATULLAH PREMI, SYED (1660-1720). Muslim poet of Bilgram, whose *Prem Prakash* has been recently published. Its theme is mainly devotional and the language is good Brajbhasha.

BARKHUDAROV, ALEXEY STEPANOVICH (1927-). Soviet Hindi scholar, who is noted for his study on modern literary Hindi. He was one of the compilers of *Hindi-Russian Dictionary* (2 Pts.), consisting of 75,000 words (Moscow, 1971).

BARLINGE, S.S. See *Surendra Barlinge.*

BARNETT, L.D. (1871-1960). English scholar, who was attached with the British Museum, where he prepared a list of Oriental books and Manuscripts. As regards Hindi, he prepared a catalogue of printed books in Hindi, Bihari (including Bhojpuri, Kormali and Maithili) and Pahari in the Library of the British Museum and also wrote reviews of several books published in Hindi.

BARSANE LAL CHATURVEDI (1920-). Humorous poet and writer, whose chief works are : *Hathi ke Pankh* (The Wings of Elephant), *Bure Phanse* (Badly Entangled) and *Bhola Pandit ki Baithak* (The Drawing Room of Bhola Pandit),

Mantriji ke Niji Sachiv ki Diary, *Hansi ke Injection*, *Adhunik Sudama*, *Chacha Chaudhri ke Jhanse*, *Chanakya ke Chele*, *Talash Kale Dhan ki*, *Netaon ki Numaish*, *Musibat Hai* and *Sifarish Puran*, *Hindi Sahitya men Hasya Rasa* (Humour in Hindi Literature ; thesis), *Hindi Hasya aur Hasyakar* (Hindi Humour and Humorists) and *Hasya ki Pravrittiyan* (Propensities of Humour) are his critical works.

BARUJI (fl. 1463). Rajasthani poet, whose stray verses in different popular metres are available.

BARVAI NAYIKABHED. Poem by Rahim (q.v. ; 1553-1626).

The work reveals Rahim's sensitiveness together with descriptions of the various types of heroines. In this work, Rahim has handled with dexterity, the *Barvai* metre, a metrical form pre-eminently suited to the genius of Avadhi. Rahim is considered the originator of this metre.

BARVAI RAMAYAN. Poem by Tulsidas (q.v.) in Avadhi dialect, written in 1612 (?).

It treats of the story of Ram in 69 verses divided in 7 cantos. The work has been composed in the *Barvai* metre, a metre for the first time employed by Rahim (q.v.). The story of Ram is used as a peg to display the poet's skill in the use of metaphor and the nine *Rasas*.

BARZ, R.K. Foreign Hindi scholar of Australian National University, Canberra, who teaches a four-year-course in Hindi for undergraduates and can offer graduate courses when required.

BASANT RAM MAHARAJ (fl. 19th cent.). Sindhi saint-poet of Hyderabad (Sind), who on the pattern of Tulsidas's *Ramayan* composed *Krishnayan*, an epic narrating the life of Krishna in *Dohas* and *Chaupais*. The *Krishnayan* is divided into nine *Dwars* (cantos) and is further sub-divided into *Sopans* or sections. The epic is written in Hindi.

BASANTI LAL BAMB. Modern Malwi writer, who contributed a good deal to the collection of Malwi folk-songs, tales and proverbs.

BASKROVNY, VASILY MATVEYEVITCH (1908-1978). Soviet Hindi scholar, who taught Hindi in the Moscow State

University. He is noted for his *Hindi-Russian Dictionary* (1972) and *Russian-Hindi Dictionary* (1957).

BASTI MAL SOLANKI. Modern Rajasthani poet, who is noted for his patriotic and heroic poems.

BASUKI NATH JHA. Maithili scholar, whose chief critical works are *Vidyapati Kavyalochan* (1979) and *Anushilan Avbodh* (1981 ; a collection of 8 critical essays). He also tr. *Meghaduta* and Parmeshwar Jha's *Yaksha-Samagam-Kavya* (1939) into Maithili.

BATE, REV. J.D. Christian Missionary, who was the author of *A Dictionary of the Hindee Language* (Allahabad, 1875). About the prevalence of Hindi in India, Bate writes that in a vast country like India, there is no language other than Hindi, which is spoken by such a great number of people.

BAUDH-GAN O DOHA. See *Dohakosh.*

BAVARI SAHIBA (fl. 17th cent.). Muslim saint-poetess, who founded the Bavari Panth, which flourished in Delhi. She is famous for her *Savaiya.* Yari Sahib (q.v.) was a famous poet of this Sect.

BAYABAI (fl. 17th cent.). Saint-poetess of Maharashtra, who was follower of Smarth Sect. In addition to her Marathi works, she composed some *Padas* in Hindi.

BEAMES, JOHN (1837-1902). English civil servant, who came to India in 1859 and retired from Indian Civil Service in 1893. In the fied of Comparative Indian Linguistics, he has been compared to Franz Bopp. His works are : *Comparative Grammar of the Modern Indian Languages of India* (3 vols., London, 1872-1879 ; reprint, 1966), *Outlines of Indian Philology with a Map Showing the Distribution of Indian Languages*, Calcutta, 1867, 2nd ed. 1868 ; Urdu tr., Lucknow, 1948), ed. of Henry M. Eliot's *Memoires on the History and Folk-lore and Distribution of Races of North-Western Provinces of India. Being an Amplified Edition of the Original Supplementary Glossary of Indian Terms* (ed. and revised ; 2 vols., London, 1869). He also contributed articles to the 'Journal of the Royal Asiatic Society' as also to 'The Indian Antiquary' on 'Bhojpuri Dialects', 'Chand Bardai's *Prithviraj Raso*', 'A Comparative Dictionary of the Bihari Language', etc.

BECHAN SHARMA PANDEY 'UGRA' (1900-1967). Fiction

writer and dramatist, who was born at Chunar in the Mirzapur district of Uttar Pradesh. His chief works are *Chand Hasinon ke Khatut* (The Letters of some Beauties ; 1927), *Delhi ka Dalal* (The Broker of Delhi ; sex-dominated), *Oudh ke Nawabon ki Rangin Raten* (The Colourful Nights of Nawabs of Oudh), *Sharabi* (Drunkard), *Sarkar Tumhari Ankhon Men* (In Your Eyes, 0 Beloved), *Budhua ki Beti* (The Daughter of Budhua), *Sabzabagh* (Chicanery), *Chocolate*, *Phagun ke Din Char*, *Manushayanand* (novels), *Dozakh ki Ag* (The Fire of Hell), *Indra-Dhanush* (The Rainbow ; short story eollections), etc. ; Ugra weaves out his stories and themes around sex and its attractions and his novels, *Chand Hasinon ke Khatut* is a typical example of this trend of naturalistic realism in Hindi fiction ; he is uninhibited and outspoken. In his drama, *Char Bechare* (The Four Victims ; 1929), he has chosen the editor, the teacher, the reformer and the preacher as his victims ; his pen-pictures of these dignitaries are realistic. His other dramas are : *Mahatma Isa* (on Christ ; it was well-received on its publication in 1922), *Ganga ka Beta* (The Son of Ganga), *Dictator* (1937), *Chumban* (The Kiss ; 1938) and *Avara* (The Wanderer ; 1942). His autobiography *Apni Khabar* (Self-revelation) has acquired fame because of the racy style and frankness of the writer.

Ugra's important short stories are : 'Jallad' (The Hangman), 'Chandni' (The Moonlight), 'Uski Man' (His Mother), 'Kala ka Puraskar' (The Reward of Art), 'Khudaram', 'Kumudini', etc.

'BEDHAB' BANARSI (1895-1968). Humorous poet and writer, whose chief works are : *Bedhab ki Bahak* (The Random Utterances of Bedhab), *Kavya Kamal* (The Lotus of Poetry ; poetical collection ; 1940), *Banarsi Ikka* (The Banarsi Horse-cart), *Gandhi ka Bhut* (The Ghost of Gandhi), *Tanatan* (short story collection) and *Abhineta* (Actor ; drama) ; he has also written some humorous essays. His original name was Krishnadev Prasad Gaur but he wrote under the pseudonym of "Bedhab".

BEER, ROLAND. Modern German Hindi scholar, who, under the tltle : *Surdas Krishnayana* (2 Pts., 1978) has successfully tr. the *Padas* of Surdas into German.

BEKAYEVA, DILARA KAMALOVNA (1939-). Soviet Hindi scholar, who did doctorate on the socio-political novels of the Hindi novelist, Yashpal. He has also written various articles on the various aspects of Yashpal.

BELI KISAN RUKMANI RI. See *Veli Krisan Rukmani Ri.*

BENDER, ERNEST. American Hindi scholar, whose chief works are : *Hindi Grammar and Reader* (1967) and *Introductory Hindi Readings* (1971 ; both pub. by University of Pennsylvania Press, Philadelphia).

BENDIX, EDWARD HERMAN. American Hindi scholar, whose chief work is : *Componential Analysis of General Vocabulary : the semantic structure of a set of verbs in English, Hindi and Japanese* (Ph.D., Columbia, 1965).

BENI (fl. 1643). Poet of the Riti school, who was a Bandijan of Asni. No work composed by him has been traced, but from the many stray *Kavittas* that are extant, it appears that he had written books on *Nakh-Shikh* and *Shadritu* (six seasons).

BENI. See *Veni.*

BENI BANDIJAN (fl. 1792-1823). Poet of the Riti school, who was a resident of Bainti in Raebareli district and was patronized by Maharaja Tikait Ray, Dewan of Nawab Asafuddaula of Lucknow. *Tikait Ray Prakash* (1792), named after his patron, is a work on *Alankars.* His *Rasavilas* (1817) is on *Rasas,* but he is known by his humorous sketches and poems written in a lighter vein, which have been published under the title, *Bhanduva Sangrah* ; in this work the poet has put to ridicule the parsimony of the rich and the niggardliness of the patrons. Beni thus holds his place among the few satirical mediaeval Hindi poets.

BENI DWIJ (b. 1843). Poet of the Riti school, whose stray verses are extant. He was a resident of Kashi.

BENI MADHAV DAS (d. 1642). Writer of Gonda, who was a disciple and constant companion of Tulsidas. He wrote a biography of Tulsidas, entitled *Gosain-Charit* (q.v.).

BENI PRASAD (fl. 1708). Poet of the Riti school, who composed his work, *Rasa-Shringar Samudra.*

BENI PRAVIN (fl. 1807-71). Poet of the Riti school, who was a Kanyakubja Brahmin of Lucknow. In the earlier part of his poetic career, he was patronized by Lallanji, a son of Raja Dayakrishna, the Dewan of Ghaziuddin Haider, the Lucknow ruler. It was at the instance of Lallanji that he composed his famous work, *Navrasa Tarang* (q.v.), a work on which the fame of the poet now mainly rests. On account of its good poetry, the poet is placed somewhere near Matiram (q.v.). Earlier, the poet had written *Shringar Bhushan* (The Embellishment of Love). The third book, the manuscript of which has perished, but was probably a great work, was composed at Bithur to honour Nana Rao, the hero of 1857. It was entitled *Nanarao Prakash* and was written on the model of Keshav Das's *Kavi-Priya*.

BENIPURI. See *Ramvriksh Benipuri*.

BHADANT ANAND KAUSHALAYAN (1905-). Modern Buddhist writer, who has written on the various facets of Buddhist history and philosophy and has interpreted the *Tripitakas* and other Buddhist canonical literature. Apart from his writings on Buddhist religion and philosophy, he has written two travelogues : *Rail-ka Ticket* and *Jo-na-Bhul Saka* (Which I could not Forget). He has translated *Dhammapada* and *Jataka Kathas* in Hindi in many parts. He was a Professor of Buddhist studies in Srilanka.

BHADDARI. See *Dak-Bhaddali, Meghmal-Bhaddari*.

BHADRA DATT SHARMA SHASTRI. Modern poet of Kasganj (Etah district), who is the author of stray poems.

BHADRA SEN (fl. 1618). Rajasthani Jain monk, who composed a romance *Chandan Maliyagiri ri Vat* (q.v.).

BHAGATSINGH HANMATRAO RAJURKAR (1935-). Marathi-speaking Hindi writer, whose chief works are : *Ramkatha ke Patra*) The Characters of Ramkatha ; 1972), *Ramkatha aur Tulsi* (Ramkatha and Tulsidas, 1974 ; both research works), *Chintan Anuchintan* (criticism), *Nayi Kavita : Drishti aur Srishti* and *Bharatiya Kahavat Kosh*. He is at present Head of the Department of Hindi, Marathwada University, Aurangabad.

BHAGIRATH KANORIYA. Author of *Rajasthan Kahavat Kosh* (with Govind Agrawal).

BHAGIRATH MISHRA (1914-). Critic, whose chief works are : *Kavya-Shastra ka Itihas* (The History of Poetics ; 1947), *Hindi Riti Sahitya, Kavya-Shastra* (Poetics), *Mahakavi Tulsidas aur Yuga Sandarbh, Achchhi Hindi Kaise Likhen* (with S. Kapur ; 1963) and *Gandhiji ke Ram tatha anya Nibandh* (essays). He was Head of the Department of Hindi, Poona University and later at Saugar University.

BHAGIRATH THAKUR (fl. 2nd half of 16th cent.). Maithili poet, who was noted for his poems. Patronized by Raja Man Singh of the court of Akbar, he was identified with Bhagirath or Megh Thakur, brother of Maharaja Mahesh Thakur of Mithila.

BHAGVAN DAS (fl. 1st part of 16th cent.). Poet of the Krishna-cult (Chaitanya Sect), who was a prominent disciple of Ramray (q.v.). The number of his extant *Padas* is about one hundred.

BHAGVAN DAS, MAHARAJ (fl. 19th cent.). Sindhi saint-poet of *Sagun* school, whose stray verses in Hindi are available.

BHAGVAN DAS KARVA (1744-1802). Rajasthani saint-poet of Ram Snehi Sampraday, Shahpura, who was initiated by Ramcharan (q.v.) in 1766 at Bhilwara. He had 21 prominent disciples, the traditions of some of them still continues. His *Vani*, equal to about 4,000 *Shlokas* is expressed in popular metres and is in easy Rajasthani. The emphasis is on *Ram-smaran* and Bhakti. Bhagvandas holds a respectable place in the Sampraday.

BHAGVAN DAS KHATRI (fl. 1800). Poet of the Ram-cult, who composed *Maha-Ramayan*.

BHAGVAN DAS NIRANJANI (fl. *c*. middle of 17th cent.). Rajasthani saint-poet and a follower of Haridas Niranjani Sect, who was also a scholar of Vedanta. His available poems : *Amritdhara*, *Kartik Mahatmya* (composed in 1685), *Gita Mahatmya*, *Vairagya Vrind*, *Jaimini Ashwamedh*, *Prem Padarth*, *Adhyatma Ramayan*, *Panchikaran*, *Simhasan Battisi* and a few stray verses are inclined towards Vedanta and *Sagun* Bhakti ; the language is easy.

BHAGVAN DATT GOSWAMI. Modern Rajasthani writer, who is noted for his short stories and sketches.

BHAGVAN DIN 'DIN' (1866—1934). Poet and scholar, who had written both in Brajbhasha and Khari Boli. He was born at the village Barbat in the Fatehpur district of Uttar Pradesh. In 1907, he was appointed a teacher in the Central Hindu College, Kashi. He edited 'Lakshmi'. He used Urdu metrical forms for his verses in honour of old martyrs and heroes. His chief poetical work is *Vir-Panch-Ratna* (heroic poems) ; his stray poems are collected in *Navin Bin* (The New Harp). He also commented upon *Ramchandrika*, *Dohavali*, *Kavitavali* and *Bihari Satsai* (q.v.) and also wrote a novel, *Aghat Ghatna* (Unusual Incident). In the long controversy over the relative greatness of 'Dev' and 'Bihari', Bhagvan Din tried to pull down Dev rather too low. His other works are : *Shringar-Shatak*, *Shringar-Tilak*, *Alankar-Manjusha* and some *Kundaliyas* based on the *Ramayan.*

BHAGVAN 'NAVIN'. Rajasthani writer of Bikaner, whose *Ram Ram Sa* (1982) is a collection of eight shorter stories and nine mini ones.

BHAGVAN SHARAN BHARDVAJ. Modern scholar, whose chief work is *Hindi Jivni Sahitya : Siddhant aur Adhyayan.*

BHAGVAN SINGH. Writer, who is noted for his works : *Fiji Desh aur Log* and *Fiji* (1975). He was High Commissioner for India in Fiji and his ancestors belonged to Fiji.

BHAGVANT RAY KHICHI (fl. 1760). Poet of the Ram-cult, who was ruler of Asothar in Fatehpur district and patronized many a poet. *Shiv Singh Saroj* (q.v.) mentions him as the author of a *Ramayan*, composed in *Kavittas* and completed in seven cantos. This work is not extant, but 50 *Kavittas* extolling Hanuman have been discovered, which might have formed a part of his *Ramayan.* His poetry is forceful and high-spirited.

BHAGVAT MUDIT (*c.* 1593-1663). Poet of the Krishna-cult (Chaitanya Sect), who was son of Madhav Mudit (q.v.) and belonged to Agra. He was of liberal views and wrote his *Rasik Ananya Bhal*, a work describing the 36 devotees of Radhavallabh Sect, in *Doha-Chaupais.* His other work is *Vrindavan Shatak Tika*, which is a tr. in Brajbhasha of Prabodhanand Saraswati's *Shri Vrindavan Mahimamrit.*

BHAGVAT RASIK (fl. 1773-1793). Poet, who was a follower of Tatti Sect and lived in Vrindavan. He was a disciple of Swami Lalit Mohani Das, but abjured all rights to his preceptor's *Gaddi* (religious seat). His *Padas*, *Kundaliyas*, *Chhapays*, etc. are charged with renunciatory spirit on the one hand and are replete with boundless devotion on the other.

BHAGVAT SHARAN UPADHYAY (1910-). Scholar and writer, whose chief works in Hindi are : *Thuntha Am* (The Stump of a Mango Tree ; 1959), *Sanskritik Nibandh* (The Cultural Essays ; both collections of essays), *Samiksha ke Sandarbh* (References of Criticism), *Sahitya aur Kala* (The Literature and Art ; criticism), *Savera* (Dawn ; collection of stories based on the dawn of human civilization), *Sangharsh* (Struggle), *Garjan* (Thunder) and *Itihas par Khun ke Chhinte* (The Blood Stains on History). He is at his best in writing on social, cultural and historical subjects. He has written *Vishwa*

Sahitya (The World Literature), *Vishwa ko Asia ki Den* (The Contribution of Asia to the World), *Kalidas ka Bharat* (India in Kalidasa; also in English) and *Women in Rigved* (in English).

BHAGVAT SWARUP MISHRA. Modern scholar, whose chief work is *Hindi Alochana : Udbhav aur Vikas.*

BHAGVATI CHARAN SHARMA. Modern Garhwali poet, who is noted for his collection of poems : *Hilans.*

BHAGVATI CHARAN VERMA (1903-1982). Novelist and writer, whose chief works are :

Novels : *Chitralekha* (q.v. ; 1934), *Tin Varsh* (Three Years ; 1936 ; on the story of a student who begins with idealism but by a queer combination of circumstances ends up as a rascal), *Tedhe Medhe Raste* (The Meandering Paths ; a political novel depicting the freedom struggle and the Non-Co-operation Movement ; it is the story of a father's three sons, of whom one becomes a Cangressman, the other a Communist and the third a revolutionary), *Akhiri Danv* (The Last Stake ; 1950 ; describing the film world with autobiographical glimpses), *Apne Khilaune* (One's Toys ; 1957 ; a satire on the New Delhi's modern society), *Bhule Bisre Chitra* (The Last and Forgotten Pictures, which won the Sahitya Akademi Award; q v. ; 1959), *Vah Phir Na Ai* (She Did Not Come Again), *Samarthya aur Sima* (Capacity and Limitation), *Thake Panv* (The Tired Feet), *Rekha*, *Patan* (The Fall), *Sidhi Sachchi Baten* (Straight Talks), *Sabhin Nachavat Ram Gosain* (All Dance to the Tune of the Master, Ram ; how everyone dances to the tune of God), *Dhuppal*, *Chanakya*, *Yuvraj Chunda* and *Prashna aur Marichika* (The Question and Mirage). *Chitralekha*, the *magnum opus* of Verma, discusses the problem of sin and virtue through the story of Bijgupta, Kumargiri and the dancing girl, Chitralekha, and comes to the conclusion like Anatole France's *Thais*, that since man has to work under compulsions, he cannot be held responsible for his actions and their consequences.

His other works are *Madhukan* (Honey Drops ; 1932), *Prem Sangit* (Love Music ; 1937), *Manav* (The Man ; 1940), *Ek Din* (Once), *Rangon se Moh* (Fondness for Colours ; 1962), *Meri Kavitayen* (My Poems; all poetry), *Tripathga* (a collection of three radio plays : *Mahakal*, *Karna and Draupadi*), *Rupaya Tumhen Kha Gaya* (Money has Consumed You ; 1955 ; drama), *Bujhta Dipak* (The Extinguishing Lamp), *Vasiyat* (The Will), *Mere Natak* (My Dramas), *Tara* (*Gitinatya*), *Vasvadatta* (Scenario), *Instalment*, *Do Banke* (Two Foppish Persons),

Khilte Phul (The Blooming Flowers), *Rakh aur Chingari* (Ash and Spark), *Meri Kahaniyan* (My Stories), *Morchabandi* (The Entrenchment ; short story collections), *Atit ke Garta Se* (memoirs), *Savinay aur Ek Naraz Kavita* and *Sahitya ke Siddhant tatha Rup* (The Principles and Forms of Literature ; criticism). His important short stories are : 'Prayashchit' (The Penance), 'Mughlon ne Saltanat Bakhsh Di' (The Moghuls Gifted Their Kingdom), 'Instalment', 'Do Banke', etc.

A successful novelist, Verma's approach to life's problems is that of an idealist but he does not turn his back on realities, howsoever sordid they may be. In his stories, he is critical of many customs and prevailing social practices and leaves none in doubt about his thinking. His poems 'Bhainsa Gadi' (The Buffalo Cart) and 'Tram' express the social tyranny and suffocation of the present age.

BHAGVATI DAS BHAIYA (fl. 1679). Jain poet, whose works are : *Chetau Karma Charitra, Shat-Shatottari, Madhubinduk Chaupai, Sua Battisi* and *Panchendriya.* All these poetical works, partly philosophical, have a literary value.

BHAGVATI PRASAD CHANDOLA. Modern Garhwali writer, who is noted for his one-act plays : *Alaso Chhodi Deva.*

BHAGVATI PRASAD DARUKA (fl. early 20th cent.). Rajasthani writer, who was known for his *Bal Vivah Natak, Vriddh Vivah Natak* and *Sithan Sudhar Natak* (all social dramas).

BHAGVATI PRASAD GAUTAM. Writer, whose *Vaktavya Bhutpurva Shikshak Ka* (1980) is a collection of essays.

BHAGVATI PRASAD PANTHARI. Modern Garhwali writer, who had been in the Department of History at Kashi Vidyapith. He has written one-act plays 'Adhah-patan', 'Bhuton ki Khoh', short stories (*Panch Phul*), *Bansuli* (prose poem on the style of Tagore's *Gitanjali*), essays (*Manav Adhikar*), collections of folk-songs, *Garhwali Sahitya ki Bhumika* (Introduction to Garhwali Literature) and *Garhwali ko Agalo Kadam* (Next Step of Garhwali). He also wrote a historical drama : *Kalpi.*

BHAGVATI PRASAD SHUKLA. Modern scholar, whose chief work is *Bagheli Bhasha aur Sahitya* (1971).

BHAGVATI PRASAD VAJPEYI (1899-1973). Fiction writer, who was born at the village Mangalpur of the Kanpur district. His chief works are : *Prem-Path* (The Love Path), *Patita ki Sadhana* (The Sufferings of a Fallen Woman ; 1936), *Do Bahinen*

(The Two Sisters), *Nimantran* (The Invitation), *Gupta Dhan* (Concealed Wealth), *Chalte-chalte* (Casually), *Yatharth se Age* (Beyond Realism), *Vijay-Shri* (Victory), *Pipasa* (Craving), *Unse na Kahna* (Do not Tell Them), *Tutate Bandhan* (The Loosening Bonds), *Vishwas ka Bal*, *Adhura Swarg*, *Chhote Sahib* (novels), *Khali Bottle* (The Empty Bottle), *Pushkarini* (The Lotous Bond), *Utar Chadhav* (The Rise and Fall), *Ek aur Sangharsh* (One More Struggle), *Anagat* (Not Yet Arrived), *Hilor* (The Whim), *Madhupark*, *Bat ek Rishte Ki* (short story collections) and *Chhalna* (Deceipt ; drama).

Vajpeyi's novels, mainly psychological, at times touch the border of obscenity. He is now remembered for his novels *Do Bahinen*, *Chalte-chalte*, *Vishwas ka Bal* and short story collections : *Madhupark*, *Hilor*, *Khali Bottle*. His important short stories, however, are : 'Nindiya Lagi' (The Slumberous Eyes), 'Sidhiyan' (The Stairs), 'Tikuli' (The Spangle on the Forehead), 'Khali Bottle' 'Mithaiwala' (The Sweet-seller), etc.

BHAINRU KAVI (fl. 1771-97). Poet of the Riti school, who was a resident of Khetri Thikana. He wrote *Chhahritu Vilas* (on seasons).

BHAIRAV PRASAD GUPTA (1918-). Writer, whose chief works are : *Shole* (Flames), *Mashal* (The Flaming Torch ; 1951), *Ganga Maiya* (1553 ; also tr. into French ; a challenge against tyranny by two farmers, sons of Ganga Maiya), *Admi aur Zanjiren* (The Man and Chains ; 1956), *Sati Maiya ka Chaura* (The Platform of *Sati Maiya* ; 1959 ; a story of two Hindu-Muslim friends), *Ag aur Ansu*, *Naujavan*, *Dharti*, *Ek Genius ki Prem Katha* (novels), *Manzil* (The Destination), *Bigre Huye Dimagh* (The Loose-tempered), *Sitar ke Tar* (The Strings of Sitar), *Farishta* (The Angel), *Muhabbat ki Rahen* (The Paths of Love). *Mahfil*, *Sapne ka Ant* (The End of the Dream), *Mangli ki Tikuli* and *Balidan ki Kahaniyan* (The Stories of Sacrifice, short story collections). He is a staunch socialist writer, influenced by Marxism.

BHAIYA. See *Bhagvati Das Bhaiya*.

BHAJAN SINGH (fl. early 20th cent.). Garhwali poet, who is noted for his *Singh-nad* (mainly on social reform) and *Khudad Beti*.

BHAKTAMAL (The Garland of Devout Persons). Famous work (1658) by Nabhadas (q.v.).

It describes the lives, spiritual attainments and literary

output of 200 Bhaktas preceding him, in 316 *Chhapay* verses. As one of the source books for all historians of Hindi literature, it was of such great historical significance that in subsequent years, its translations appeared in quite a few regional languages : Bengali, Marathi, Oriya, etc. When dealing with the lives of saints, no referenee has been made to their time. The book is written in a missionary zeal and is above any sectarian bias. Regarded as one of the most difficult works in Braj dialect, the treatment is scanty and a saint is dealt with in one or two stanzas. Priyadas (q.v.), a disciple of Nabhadas, in 1712 wrote a commentary on it.

BHAKTAMAL. See *Pyare Ram.*

BHAKTAMAL. See *Raghavdas.*

BHAKTA NAMAVALI. See *Dhruvdas.*

BHAKTI NATH SINGH THAKUR. Modern Maithili critic, whose *Kala evam Kavyakala Utkarsh* advocates Western principles of literary criticism.

BHAL CHANDRA APTE. Telugu-speaking modern Hindi writer, who is noted for his *Lokmanya* (a biography of Bal Gangadhar Tilak) and *The Hindi Grammar* (written in collaboration with S.R. Shastri).

BHAL CHANDRA RAO TELANG. Scholar and author of *Chhattisgarhi, Halabi, Bhatari Boliyon ka Bhasha Vaigyanik Adhyayan* (1966).

BHALAN (fl. 1488). Gujarati-speaking Vaishnav Hindi poet, who is known for his *Nalakhyan*, which contains several Brajbhasha verses in it. He was an elder contemporary of the celebrated Hindi poet Surdas (q.v.) and was the first to use Hindi along with Gujarati.

BHALE CHANDRA JAYSHETTI. Kannada-speaking modern Hindi writer, who tr. some Kannada poems, U.R. Anantamurti's famous Kannada novel : *Bharatipur*, and his long short story : 'Ghat-Shraddh' and of Alanhalli Krishna's well-known short story 'Aguntak' into Hindi. He also tr. N. Prahlad Rao's essay collection : *Mudhuvrat* from Kannada into Hindi. See *Tippeswami 'Punit'.*

BHAN (fl. 1850). Hindi poet of Cutch Mandvi (Gujarat), whose works are : *Bhan Vilas, Bhan Bavni* and stray verses.

He has laid emphasis on self-realization. The language betrays the influence of Cutch and Gujarat languages.

BHAN KAVI. Poet of the Riti school, who was son of Raja Joravar Singh and was patronized by Raja Ranjor Singh Bundela. His *Narendra-Bhushan* (1788), a work on *Alankars* contains illustrations from *Shringar* as also from other *Rasas*; in this lies freshness of his outlook.

BHAN SINGH SHEKHAWAT. Rajasthani poet, whose *Haldighati ro Gaurav* (1981) eulogizes the valient deeds of Rana Pratap and establishes him as a national hero in the modern sense of the term.

BHANA THAKUR (fl. 18th cent.). Kauravi folk-poet, who had to lose his life for his opposition to king's policy. Knowing that he was destined to meet death, he composed 360 *Kundaliyas* and placed them in a neighbour's house. After his death, when the king read the *Kundaliyas*, he was greatly aggrieved.

BHANDAU VYAS. See *Hammirayan.*

BHANDUVA SANGRAH. See *Beni Bandijan.*

BHANJAN. Maithili poet, who was noted for his lyrics. He was a contemporary of Maharaja Raghav Singh (r. 1704-40).

BHANU DAS (fl. 1498). Saint-poet of Maharashtra, who was great grandfather of Eknath (q.v.). He composed some *Padas* in Hindi as well, where he made no distinction between Ram and Shyam.

BHANU MATI NAGDAN. Mrs. Gujarati-speaking modern Hindi fiction writer of Mauritius, whose chief work is *Minister.*

BHANU NATH JHA. Maithili poet, whose *Prabhavati-Haran*, written under the patronage of Maharaja Maheshwar Singh (r. 1850-1960) and Maharaja Lakshmishwar Singh (r. 1880-1898) is a Kirtaniya form of drama and treats of the abduction of Prabhavati. He was also noted for his love lyrics.

BHANU KAR (fl. 1450-1500). Maithili poet, whose poems are highly Sanskritized. He was the famous author of the Sanskrit work, *Rasa-Manjari.*

BHANVAR. Modern Malwi poet, who is noted for his stray poems.

BHANVAR LAL NAHATA. Rajasthani writer, whose chief work, *Bangi* (1965) contains sketches.

BHANVAR LAL SUTHAR 'BHRAMAR'. Rajasthani writer of Bikaner, whose chief works are : *Tagado* (1972), *Amujo Kad Tanin* (1976 ; both short story collections) and *Bhor Ra Pagaliya* (novel for children). Some of the stories in these collections are common.

BHANVAR PANDEY 'PRAMOD'. Rajasthani poet of Bhilwara, whose *Rupan Bavli* (1978) is a collection of 102 four-line stanzas. It is an erotic poem of sensuous details.

BHANVAR SINGH SAMAUR. Modern Rajasthani poet, who has composed patriotic, heroic and progressive poems.

BHARA MALL (fl. *c.* 1757). Jain poet, whose chief works are : *Shil-Katha*, *Charudatt Charit* and *Sapta Vyasan Charitra* (on seven deadly sins).

BHARAT BHARATI. Poetic work (1912) by Maithili Sharan Gupta (q.v.), which contrasts the glorious heritage of ancient India with the decadent present ; there is also a message for making its future bright. When published, it became extremely popular but the British Government was not very happy about it.

BHARAT BHUSHAN (1931-). Poet whose chief collection of *Gits* is : *Sagar ke Sip* ; *Ram ki Jal-Samadhi* is his long poem.

BHARAT BHUSHAN AGRAWAL (1919-1975). Poet, whose earlier poems were collected in *Tar Saptak* (q.v.) ; his other chief works are : *Chhavi ke Bandhan* (1941 ; The Bonds of Beauty ; a collection of romantic poems), *Jagte Raho* (Keep Awake ; 1945 ; a collection of progressive poems), *Muktimarga* (The Path of Emancipation ; 1947 ; on social consciousness), *0 Aprastut Man* (0 Irrelevant Mind ; 1958), *Ek Utha Hua Hath* (A Hand Upraised ; 1970), *Bahut Baqi Hai*, *Agnilik* (Line of Fire ; poetic drama), *Setu Bandhan*, *Yuga Yuga Ya Panch Minute*, *Tin Kavya Natak* (dramas), *Prasang-Vash* (A critical work) and *Kaghaz ke Phul* (Paper Flowers ; a humorous work). He has written also some one-act plays and a novel, *Lautati Laharon ki Bansuri* (The Flute of the Retreating Waves). His short story collections are : *Adhe-adhe Jism* and *Palayan*. He tr. many plays of Tagore. His posthumous work *Utna Vah Suraj Hai* (That Much is the Sun ; 1978) received a

Sahitya Akademi Award. He was the first, who introduced the limerick form named by him as *Tuktak*. *Lik-Alik* (1980) is a collection of his essays, published posthumously, while his critical work is *Kavi ki Drishti*.

BHARAT DURDASHA. See. *HARISHCHANDRA BHARATENDU*.

BHARAT V. MAURICE. Hindi writer of Fiji, who is noted for his works : *Gali Gali Sita Roye* (1974-75) and *Hay re Zindagi*.

BHARAT VYAS (d. 1982). Modern Rajasthani poet, whose stray verses are very popular. His dramas : *Dhola Marvan* (1949) and *Rangilo Marwari* (Ramu Chanana) were successful on the stage.

BHARAT YAYAVAR. Poet, who is noted for his collection of poems : *Main Hun Yahin Hun*(1983).

BHARATENDU. See *Harishchandra Bharatendu*.

BHARATESHWAR BAHUBALI GHOR. Poem is 48 verses (written around 1168) by Vajra Suri, a Jain poet.

Rishabhdev, the first Jain Tirthankar, before becoming an ascetic, divides his kingdom among his 100 sons. Bharat, the eldest brother, tries to become a 'Chakravarti' and usurps the shares of all the 98 brothers, excepting that of Bahubali, who opposes him openly. Bharat attacks Bahubali but cannot vanquish him. In a duel, Bahubali suffers the blows of Bharat but refuses to retaliate against the elder brother. In a spirit of renunciation, he becomes an ascetic and attains eternal emancipation ; Bharat, after ruling the country, also reaches the state of self-realization.

BHARATESHVAR BAHUBALI RAS. Poem in 203 verses (composed in 1184) by Shalibhadra Suri (q.v.), a Jain poet. As compared to *Bharateshvar Bahubali Ghor* (q.v.), it claims a high place not only in Jain literature but also amongst the heroic poetry of the early period in respect of language and poetic elegance. There are realistic descriptions of warfare and diplomacy and psychological analysis of Bahubali's mind and heart ; for the story see *Bharateshvar Bahubali Ghor*. According to Ganpati Chandra Gupt, Shalibhadra Suri is the first Hind poet and his *Bharateshvar Bahubali Ras* is the first Hindi poem.

BHARATHARI. Bhojpuri folk-tale in songs, which describes how Bharathari renounces this world at the command of his spiritual preceptor and how his wives weep at his departure. Various versions of the Bharathari legend are popular in northern India. It is claimed that this Bharathari and the Sanskrit writer, Bhartrihari are the same person.

BHARATI. See *Devdut Vidyarthi.*

BHARATI. See *Dharma Vir Bharati.*

BHARATI RAMANACHARYA, M.K. Kannada-speaking modern Hindi writer, whose chief work is a story collection : *Gilahari ke Galpa*, for children. He has tr. G. Brahmappa's drama : *Dan Chintamani* from Kannada into Hindi.

BHARATI VADGAMA. Modern Hindi writer of London, whose writings appear in 'Pravasini', London.

BHARATI VIDYARTHI. Malayalam-speaking Hindi writer, who is wife of Devdut Vidyarthi (q.v.). She has tr. Takashi's Malayalam novels into Hindi under the titles of *Do Ser Dhan* (Two Seers of Rice), *Chunauti* (The Challenge)-and *Machhuvare* (The Fishermen).

BHARATIYA (fl. *c.* 1930). Maithili writer, whose chief work, *Jatrak Shubh-Din* is a short story collection.

BHASHA BHUSHAN. Work on *Alankars*, written by Jasvant Singh (q.v.), a Riti poet of the 17th century.

Composed after *Chandralok*, it confines description and illustration of an *Alankar* in a single *Doha*, which has made it popular with students. The number of *Alankars* treated in this work is 108. Several poets wrote commentaries on this, regarding this as a standard work on figures of speech.

BHASHA KAVYA SANGRAH, (A Collection of Hindi Poetry). Work (1873) by Mahesh Datt Shukla, which is a sort of history of Hindi poetry ; in the beginning are the poems and then the life-sketches and times of those poets.

BHASHA YOGA VASISHTH. See *Ram Prasad Niranjani.*

BHASKAR MALL (r. 1694-1702). Ruler of the House of Kantipur (Kathmandu) in Nepal, whose Maithili lyrics are quoted in some collections of *Rags*. These were written in the form of a drama (1702).

BHASKAR SHANKAR JOSHI, PRA. Marathi-speaking modern Hindi dramatist, who is noted for his one-act plays : 'Paglon ki Duniya', 'Shrutika', 'Parivartan', etc.

BHASKAR VISHNU PHADKE (fl. 1900-1940). Marathi-speaking Hindi writer, whose short stories were published in various Hindi magazines.

BHASKARAN NAIR. Malayalam-speaking modern Hindi scholar, who is the author of *Hindi aur Malayalam men Krishna Bhakti Kavya* (The Krishna-cult Poetry in Hindi and Malayalam Poetry) and *Malayalam Sahitya ka Itihas.*

BHATT, BALKRISHNA. See *Balkrishna Bhatt.*

BHATT, S.V. Kannada-speaking modern Hindi critic, who is one of the three editors of *Rashtrakavi Govind Pai : Vyaktitwa aur Krititwa.*

BHATT, UDAYSHANKAR. See *Udayshankar Bhatt.*

BHATT KEDAR (fl. 1168). Poet, whose *Jaychand Prakash* (in praise of Raja Jaychand) is no longer extant.

BHATI, N.S. See *Narayan Singh Bhati.*

BHATTATIRI, P.N. Malayalam-speaking modern Hindi writer, who, along with N.R. Iledam and G. Narayan Pillai has tr. Malayalam poet Shankar Kurup's *Otakhushal* under the title *Bansuri* (The Flute). The Hindi version has been revised by Lakshmichand Jain. He has also tr. Malayalam short stories into Hindi as also Muhammad Bashir's famous Malayalam novel *Balyakal-Sakhi* under the title *Shahzadi.*

BHAUM RAJ BHAMBIRU 'MANGAL'. Rajasthani poet, whose chief work *Mungha Moti* (1944) contains poems on *Niti.*

BHAV NATH JHA. Modern Maithili writer, who is noted for his drama on the poet, Vidyapati. He has also composed good lyrics.

BHAVANI DAS VYAS. Rajasthani poet of Jodhpur, who in his *Ai Anand Vilas* (composed in 1736) narrates lucidly in easy Rajasthani the life of Aiji and the salient features of the *Ai* Panth ; the work consists of 603 verses in different metres and is deemed to be a sacred book in the Panth. See *Aiji.*

BHAVANI DATT THAPLIYAL (fl. early 19th cent.). Garhwali writer, who is famous for his *Jay-Vijay* and *Prahlad* dramas in prose.

BHAVANI DAYAL SANNYASI (1892-1951). Hindi writer of South Africa, who was noted for his *Pravasi ki Atmakatha* (autobiography).

BHAVANI DIN SHUKLA (fl. early 20th cent.). Bagheli poet, who has commented in Bagheli on all the seven cantos of *Valmiki-Ramayana.*

BHAVANI NATH (fl. prior to 1685). Maithili poet, who mentions one Nripdev as his patron. His lyrics were quoted in anthologies.

BHAVANI PRASAD MISHRA (1913-1985). Popular poet of progressive views, who was born in Hoshangabad (Madhya Pradesh). His earlier poems were collected in *Dusra Saptak* (q.v.) ; his other works are : *Git-Farosh* (The Vendor of Songs ; 1956 ; chiefly satirical), *Chakit Hai Dukh* (Sorrow is Puzzled ; 1968), *Buni Hui Rassi* (The Woven Twine) and *Khushbu ka Shilalehk* (The Inscription of Fragrance). His other poetical collections are : *Gandhi Panchshati* (ed. poems on the life of Mahatma Gandhi), *Andheri Kavitayen* (Dark Poems, which received the Sahitya Akademi Award), *Parivartan Jiyen* (1976), *Trikal Sandhya* (poems during Emergency), *Mansarovar Din* (1980 ; a collection of poems), *Sharir Kavita Faslen aur Phul* (1980), *Samprati* (At Present ; a collection of poems ; 1981). *Anam Tum Ate Ho*, *Vyaktigat*, *Idam Na Mam* and *Nili Rekha Tak.* He edited 'Gandhi Marg' and 'Gagananchal' and was Advisor to All India Radio. More influenced by Gandhian thought, there is throughout in his poetry an expression of hope and the higher purpose of life.

BHAVESH (fl. prior to 1685). Maithili poet, who mentions his patron one Damodar, husband of Hrimati and son of Gunishwar. His lyrics were quoted in anthologies.

BHEGO (Meho ; fl. 1st part of 15th cent.). Gujarati-speaking Jain poet, whose *Tirth-Mala Stavan* in Apabhransh-mixed Old Hindi glorifies the Jain pilgrim centres.

BHIKHA (1713-63). Poet-saint of Azamgarh, who was the author of *Ram-Jahaz* (Ram's Ship). Though a disciple of Gulal Sahib, he founded his own sect, named Bhikha.

BHIKHANJI (1726-1803). Jain Rajasthani poet and founder of the Terapanth Sect (Shwetambar), whose main aim was to interpret and make the Jain religious philosophy intelligible to the common man and he adopted the medium of stories for this purpose. Reacting against the laxities of conduct and character in the Jains, he founded his Terapanth Sect in 1760. Giving a new interpretation to the Jain canonical texts, he did not hesitate to say what appeared to him to be logically right. He did not spare Mahavir, the 24th Tirthankar from criticism. His poems are of two types: (1) those which deal with basic and theoretical aspect, like *Nav Padarth*, *Shravak Barah Vrat*; (2) those which are narrative like *Gausala ri Chaupai* (in this he criticises Mahavir), *Uday Raja ro Bakhan* and *Subahukumar ro Bakhan*. The basis of most of these stories is the Jain Agam, but the treatment is his own. In the course of his descriptions, he has given moral precepts in the form of popular sayings.

BHIKHAN SADH (fl. 19th cent.). Rajasthani saint-poet of Laldasi Sect, whose 25 verses including *Harjas* and *Chandrayans* are in exaltation of God and Guru Laldas. His language is Rajasthani with a mixture of Braj.

BHIKHARI DAS 'DAS' (fl. 1728-50). Poet of the Riti school, who was a protege of Hindupati Singh, a brother of Raja Prithwipati Singh of Pratapgarh. His first work, a verse tr. of *Vishnu-purana* (composed in 1728) is not an original work and suffers from traces of immaturity. His other works are: *Rasa Saransh* (1734; though proposing to deal with *Rasas*, it is essentially a book on *Nayikabhed*), *Nam Prakash* (1738; giving a convenient arrangement of the synonyms found in the Sanskrit *Amarakosh*), *Chhandarnav Pingal* (on prosody), *Kavya Nirnay* (a comprehensive book on poetics) and *Shringar Nirnay* (1750; devoted to the treatment of *Shringar Rasa*); it is on the last two books that the great reputation of the poet rests. The other works attributed to him are: *Chhand Prakash* (on prosody), *Shataranj-Shatika* and *Amar-Prakash* (a verse tr. in Hindi).

Das combines scholarship with poetic talent; his chief merits are comprehensiveness, sound judgement and clarity. His books on poetics cover the entire ground and supply the many deficiencies of his predecessors. His verses are free from obscenity and over-statement; the diction is pure and furnishes a good example of literary Brajbhasha at its best. He occupies an important place among the poets of the Riti school.

BHIKHARI MISHRA KAVIRAJ (fl. 15th cent.). Maithili poet, who was noted for his poems in the style of Vidyapati (q.v.).

BHIKHARI THAKUR. Modern Bhojpuri writer, whose *Bidesia*, a folk-drama in verse, has remained very popular and gave rise to creation of several dramas on its pattern. The story of the *Bidesia* runs that a person of Bhojpuri region goes to Bengal in search of his livelihood and remains there for a long time, unmindful of his wife and children left behind. His wife sends her message through a guest, hearing which the husband returns to his village after leaving job.

BHIKHJANJI (fl. 1626). Rajasthani saint-poet of Dadu Sect, who was a Brahmin of Fatehpur and a disciple of Santdas Barah-Hazari. His works, including the ones recently discovered by Hiralal Maheshwari, are : *Sarwang Bavni*, *Nam Mala*, a tr. of *Amarkosh* (525 veres, mainly in *Dohas*), *Dhruv Charitra* (composed in 1623), *Tithi Pandrah*, *Niranjan Stuti*, *Savaiyas* (19) and Sakhis (6 *Dohas*).

His language is mainly fluent Rajasthani. "Profundity of emotion and thought as also lucidity of style are the main characteristics of his poems. His inclination towards the Sagun Bhakti is also noticeable."

BHIKKHU. See *Krishna Chandra Sharma 'Bhikkhu'*.

BHIM. See *Saduyvatsa Vir Prabandh*.

BHIM DATT JHA 'BHIM'. Maithili poet, who was noted for his lyrics. He was a contemporary of Maharaja Lakshmishwar Singh (1878-1898).

BHIM NATH JHA. Maithili poet, whose collections of poems are : *Tridhara* (1968) and *Vina* (1970).

BHIM PANDIYA. Modern Rajasthani poet, who has composed patriotic, heroic and progressive poems.

BHIM PRAKASH. See *Ramdan Lalas*.

BHIM SEN 'NIRMAL'. Telugu-speaking modern Hindi writer, who is noted for his biography : *Mere Liye Mrityu Nahin Haî* and *Hindi-Telugu Kosh* (1976). His research publication is : *Telugu Bhashi Hindi Natak-kar* : *Purushottam Kavi* (Telugu-speaking Hindi dramatist : Purushottam Kavi ; 1967). He has rendered into Hindi five famous folk-tales of Andhra as described by Illindal Saraswati Devi in her Telugu work. He tr. into Hindi the select writings of the Telugu poet, Arudra under the title *Kavishri* : *Arudra* (1970) as also the famous *Ranganath Ramayana* from Telugu into Hindi. Under the titles : *Tirupati Venkat Kachulu* and *Katuri Pingali Kavulu*, he tr. into Hindi prose the select works of the four Telugu poets. He has tr. into Hindi as *Nadi Sundari* (1964), the one-act plays of the Telugu poet, Abburi Ramkrishna Rao and the seven one-act plays of P.V. Venkat Rajmannar as *Rajmannar ke Sat Ekanki* (1966). At present, he is engaged in the tr. of Potana's *Mahabhagavata* into Hindi. He tr. into Hindi Munimanakyam Narasimharao's Telugu novel, *Dikshitulu* (1963) and Dasharathi Rangacharya's Telugu novel as *Ghat ke Devta* (The gods of the Ghat ; 1974). He has also tr. some Telugu short stories into Hindi.

BHIM SEN SHARMA (1854-1917). Disciple of Dayanand Saraswati (q.v.) ; he wrote several books and tracts in support of Dayanand's religious doctrines and preachings. He was a firm believer in chaste Hindi, with no room for Persian or Arabic words. To propagate Hindi and Dayanand's reformist ideas, he started a monthly, called 'Arya Siddhant'.

BHIM SEN TYAGI. Writer, who is noted for his novels : *Nanga Shahr* (1977) and *Kala Gulab* ; his short story collections are : *Zaban* and *Divaren hi Divaren* ; another work is *Admi se Admi Tak* (memoirs).

BHIM SINGH MALIK. Modern scholar, whose chief works are : *Jayasi Kavya ka Sanskritik Adhyayan* and *Haryana Lok-Sahitya* : *Sanskritik Sandarbh*.

BHIM VILAS (1822). Rajasthani poem by Kishanji (q.v.), which describes the life of Maharana Bhim Singh of Mewar and his genealogy. Apart from its historical significance, it is a good poem.

BHIMESHWAR SINGH (fl. *c.* 1940). Maithili writer, who was noted for his short stories.

BHISHMA ANTARVEDI (fl. 1624). Poet, who tr. the *Bhagavad-gita* into *Dohas* and *Chaupais*.

BHISHMA KAVI (fl. *c.* 1400). Versatile Maithili poet, who is famous for his songs in the style of Vidyapati (q.v.). He is also believed to have written two dramas : one on the story of Vatsaraj-Sagarika and the other on the life of Urvashi. He was perhaps a scion of a royal family as he calls himself as 'Kumar' in one of the songs. Bhishma belonged to Morang, a Maithili-speaking district of Nepal.

BHISHMA SAHNI (1915-). Writer, whose chief works are : *Jharokhe* (The Casements), *Kadiyan* (The Links ; 1970), *Tamas* (Darkness ; 1973), *Basanti* (1980 ; on the sufferings of the lower class labourers) (novels), *Shobha-Yatra* (The Procession ; 1981), *Bhagya-Rekha* (Luck-line), *Pahla Path* (The First Lesson), *Patariyan* (The Staves), *Bhatakti Rakh* (The Wandering Ash ; 1966), *Vangchu*, *Nishachar*, *Meri Priya Kahaniyan* (My favourite Short Stories ; 1984), (all short strory collections), *Hanush and Kabir Khada Bazar Men* (Kabir is standing in the Market ; 1981), Madhavi (plays). His novel, *Tamas*, has won the Sahitya Akademi Award. Sahni's important short stories are : 'Chief ki Davat's (The Chief's Dinner), 'Amritsar A Gaya Hai' (This is Amritsar), 'Abhi to Main Javan Hun' (I am Still Young), 'Mauqa Prast' (The Opportunist), 'Indrajal' (Witch-craft), 'Pahla Path', 'Divaswapna' etc. The scene of his drama, *Hanush* is set in Prague of 500 years before, where the hands of a locksmith were cut off so that he could not make another watch of the type he did after 17 years of research. He also edited *Rasta Idhar Hai* (This Way ; 1978), an anthology of poems published for the Progressive Writers Association. His critical work is *Adhunik Hindi Upanyas*.

BHODARAM. Kului song, which describes how Negi Bhodaram marries a prostitute despite the fact that his parents advise him to the contrary. Bhodaram is already married and his wife is a virtuous lady. A Ranger (Forest Officer) is also in love with the prostitute with the result that Bhodaram is put behind the bars.

BHOJ MISHRA (fl. 1720). Court-poet of Raoraja Budh Singh of Bundi, whose *Mishra Shringar* is a Riti work in Brajbhasha.

BHOJA BHAGAT (1784-1852). Saint-poet of Gujarat, who was born in the village Galol of Saurashtra. His work in Hindi goes under the name of *Chabkha*. Like Kabir (q.v.), he believed in denunciation of evils to set the society right. His Hindi is not refined and also betrays the influence of Gujarati.

BHOJAL (fl. 19th cent.). Sindhi saint-poet, whose stray verses in Hindi are available.

BHOLA BHAI PATEL. Modern Gujarati critic, whose research work in Hindi is *Agyey : Ek Adhyayan*.

BHOLA LAL DAS (fl. early 20th cent.). Maithili scholar and editor, who espoused the cause of Maithili. His essays have been collected under *Sansmaran* (1930). His writings have been considered very helpful in awakening the youth of Mithila ; his poem *Yuvak-Sa* is of such a nature. He also wrote critical articles.

BHOLA NATH (fl. 18th cent.). Poet of the Riti school, who was a Kanyakubja Brahmin of Jaipur. Formerly, he was in the court of Raja Surajmal of Bharatpur but later on he came to his native place, Jaipur during the reign of Madho Singh Maharaja. He wrote some 12 works, some of which are : *Lila Prakash*, *Sukh-Nivas*, *Navalanurag*, *Ishqlata*, *Bhagavat Dasamskandh Bhasha*, *Nakhshikh*, *Prem Pachchisi*, *Naishadh Pratham Sarga* (tr.), etc.

BHOLA NATH TIWARI (1923-) Scholar, whose chief works are : *Bhasha-Vigyan*, *Hindi Bhasha ka Saral Vyakaran* (on Hindi grammar), *Hindi Bhasha*, *Abhivyakti Vigyan* (tr.), *Amir Khusro aur Unki Hindi Rachnayen* (Amir Khusro and his Hindi works ; a critical work), *Anuvad Vigyan* (1972), *Shabdon ka Jivan*, *Kaljayi Satya*, *Hindi Muhavara Kosh*, *Hindi Dhwaniyan aur Unka Uchcharan*, *Anuyukta Bhasha Vigyan*, *Bhasha-Vigyan Kosh*, *Hindi ki Arthi Sanrachna* (ed., 1984) and *BrihatHindi Lokokti Kosh* (1985). He is Professor at Delhi University and taught also at Tashkent.

BHOLA RAM BHANDARI (1857-*c.* 1933). Poet of Mathura, who remained *Bhandari* (storekeeper) of the Dwarikadhish Temple, Mathura for 65 years. He composed several poems, including *Holika Varnan*.

BHOMA VITHU (fl. 1828-1948). Rajasthani poet of Deshnok, who was a favourite of Maharaja Ratansingh and his son, Sardarsingh of Bikaner. His works in Dingal are : *Kunvar Sardarsinghji ro Vindotau*, *Maharaj Suratsinghji ra Marsiya*, *Maharaja Ratansinghji ro Rupak*, *Maharaja Ratansinghji ro Rupak*, *Maharaj Kunvar Sardarsinghji ra Kavitta*, *Ratan Vilas* (his best work), *Maharaj Ganpatsinghji ra Kavitta* and stray *Gits*. All his works are of panegyric nature.

BHRAMAR, B.L. See *Bhanvar Lal Suthar 'Bhramar'*.

BHUDHAR DAS (fl. 1732). Jain poet, whose *Parshwa-Puran*, describing the life of Parshwanath, the 23rd Jain Tirthankar, is an epic.

BHUDHAR DAS PALHAWAT, CHARAN (fl. 1st half of 17th cent.). Dingal poet, who wrote poems mostly on contemporary heroes.

and happenings. His *Sekhawaton Rajawaton ki Var* describes a battle between Rao Manohardas of Amarsar (Shekhawati) and Raja Mansingh I of Amer.

BHUJANGACHAR, H.B. (fl. 1935). Kannada-speaking Hindi poet, whose poems were published in the 'Jagriti', a literary magazine. The poems were mainly patriotic in nature.

BHUJBAL (fl. 19th cent.). Bundelkhandi folk-poet, who was noted for his musical poems, called *Phags*.

BHULE BISRE CHITRA (The Lost and Forgotten Pictures). Novel (1959) by Bhagvati Charan Verma (q.v.).

A bulky work, written in five parts, it is the story of four generations of a representative family ranging from the period from 1850 to 1930. The four generations are represented by Munshi Shivlal, Jwala Prasad, Ganga Prasad and Naval.

The most important social event of Indian life is the break-up of the joint family system, for which the openings of service especially of Government service as also other factors are responsible. Circumstances compel even father and sons to live apart. These four generations also represent various stages in the development of national consciousness. Munshi Shivlal, a scribe in the court, stands at the meeting point of feudal and bureaucratic systems, while his son, Jwala Prasad, a Naib Tehsildar, combines the traits of growing bureaucracy and declining feudalism. There is also the depiction of the sexual relations that Jwala Prasad had with Jaidei, the widow of Prabhu Dayal. The third and the fourth parts of the novel describe the luxurious and lascivious life that Ganga Prasad was leading and the death of Jaidei. The last part reveals the death of Jwala Prasad and the advent of Naval.

BHUPATI (Raja Gurudatt Singh ; fl. 1734). Poet of the Riti school, who was the Raja of Amethi. He composed a *Satsai* (1734) in *Dohas* on *Shringar Rasa.* Two other works : *Kanthabhushan* and *Rasaratnakar* have also been written by him. Bhupati highly esteemed poetic talent and patronized Kavindra (q.v.) ; he was a great hero too and killed many a soldier of Saadat Khan, who had besieged his fortress.

BHUPATIRAM SAKARIYA. See *Badri Prasad Sakariya*.

BHUPATKAR, PRA. RA. Marathi-speaking Hindi scholar, who is known for his work, *Hindi aur Marathi ke Aitihasik Natak*.

BHUPATINDRA MALL (r. 1695-1722). Ruler of the House of Bhatgao in Nepal, whose collection of 91 Maithili songs exists in the *Bhashagita*. His other works are: *Nana-Rag-Git-Sangrah*, *Prakirna-Patra*, an elaborate anthology called *Gitmala* and *gits* in the anthologies of others. His songs are devotional, the largest number of them on Shakti. He has written some *Tirhutis* also in the conventional Vidyapati manner. He was, however, more prolific and competent a dramatist than a lyric writer. He used Bengali and Hindi also now and then.

His dramas, which were staged during his reign are: *Madhavanal* (1704), *Gauri-Vivah-Natak* (in 7 Acts), *Muldev-Shashi-Devopakhyan* (1706), *Pashupati-Pradurbhav* (1711); *Gopichandra* (1712), *Usha-Haran* (1713), *Rukmini-Parinay*, *Vidya Vilap*, *Mahabharat* (1702), two unnamed fragments, *Kans-Badh Krishna Charit*, *Kolasur-Badhopakhyan*, *Padmavati-Natak*, *Jalandharopakhyan*, *Jaiminiya-Bharat-Natak*, *Ashwamedh-Natak*, *Manoranjan-Natak*, *Bhasha-Natak*, *Ramayan-Natak* (in 15 Acts), *Mudavati-Haran-Natak*, *Nal-Charit-Mahanatak* and *Sambarasuropakhyan*. The language of some of these plays is mixed Nevari and Bengali. The songs in his dramas are numerous and have a variety unknown to earlier dramatists.

BHUPENDRA NATH RAICHAUDHARY. Assamese-speaking modern Hindi essayist and poet, whose essays and poems have appeared in various magazines and papers. His chief works are: *Bhakti Ratnavali*, *Sankranti ke Bich Yuva Pidhi* (The Youth in Transition) and *Mahapurush Shankardev*.

BHUR SINGH RATHORE. Rajasthani scholar, who has edited and published the classic *Virmayan* (q.v.) under the title *Dhadhi Bhadar and his Writings* (1976). His *Rati Ghati* (1982) is a historical novel dealing with the foundation of the erstwhile state of Bikaner.

BHUSHAN. Celebrated poet, whose real name is unknown. He was the second of the four sons of Ratnakar Tripathi, a Kanyakubja Brahmin, his three brothers being Chintamani, Matiram and Jatashankar alias Nilkanth, all poets. His native place was Tikwanpur in Kanpur district. There is a controversy about the birth and time of Bhushan; according to Ram Chandra Shukla, the year of his birth is 1613, born as he was after Chintamani (b. 1609) and before Matiram (b. *c.* 1617). Shiv Singh Sengar accepts 1681 as his birth year, while according to the Mishrabandhu, 1635 is his birth year; in the former case, it is incredible that he was the brother of Chintamani and Mitiram. He is said to have died in 1715.

Bhushan's first poetical performance was in the court of

Rudra, the Solanki Raja of Chitrakut. Impressed by his poetry Rudra called him as 'Bhushan' ("Jewel among poets"); since then Bhushan became celebrated by his new name.

In search of a generous and noble patron, Bhushan approached many a king: some say that he travelled north and visited the court of Aurangzeb; others opine that he went to south and met Shivaji. At the latter's instance, he recited one of his verses 18 times and got the reward of 18 lakh rupees and 18 villages. Thenceforth he extolled his patron in his work *Shivaraj Bhushan* (q.v.); this work was completed in 7 years after which Bhushan returned home. On his return, he tarried for a while in Panna (Bundelkhand), the capital of Maharaja Chhatrasal, whose political activities were akin to those of Shivaji. Here also Bhushan offered some chosen couplets in praise of Chhatrasal, who was so much moved that he helped with his own shoulder to carry Bhushan in his palanquin on the way. Bhushan, discovering this, alighted from the palanquin and uttered the following verse, which may be rendered into English thus: 'Shall I sing the praises of Shivaji or of Chhatrasal!' In all, Bhushan composed 2 *Dohas* and 8 *Kavittas* in honour of Chhatrasal; these ten verses are contained in the *Chhatrasal Dashak*.

After staying for some time at home, Bhushan set out on a tour through Rajputana, proclaiming the glory of Shivaji. At Kumaon, he recited a verse, at which the ruler offered him a present of one lakh, but which Bhushan declined saying that he had come only to learn whether Shivaji's fame had spread there. Finally, he reached Satara, the capital of Shivaji and remained there till his patron's death in 1680. The poet accompanied him in several battles and the deeds of prowess of the Maratha hero are glorified in his poem, *Shiva Bavni* (q.v.), containing 52 verses.

After Shivaji's death, Bhushan returned home. Again, he wandered here and there in search of a patron to his taste. His last visit was to the court of Maharao Bhav Singh of Bundi from whence he returned disgruntled (see *Matiram*). During this period, Bhushan composed three more works—*Bhushan Ullas*, *Dushan Ullas* and *Bhushan Hazara*, which are not extant.

Bhushan was essentially a poet of Riti period and he composed works on *Alankars*, but his greatness lies not as a rhetorician but as in lifting the poetry from the rut of *Shringar Rasa* into which the poetic creations of his numerous contemporaries tended to fall. His bold voice was a clarion call to arouse the Hindus from the slumber and in Shivaji and Chhatrasal, he found the bulwark of Hinduism. To suit the theme of his poetry, he wrote in the tragic and heroic styles.

The language adopted by him was the same Brajbhasha, but he imported in it Bundelkhandi words as also words of Persian and Arabic origin.

BHUSHAN DWIJ (1580-1650). Assamese poet, whose *Ajamil-Upakhyan Nat* (a drama based on an episode of the *Bhagavat*) is his only work in Hindi (Brajavali).

BHUSNARMATH, R.C. Kannada-speaking modern Hindi dramatist, who is noted for his dramas : *Harlayya Madhuvayya* and *Pyar ki Bhent* (The Offering of Love ; the last one-act play), which display the triumph of love over castes, etc. He and his wife have also tr. from Kannada into Hindi the *Vachans* of Basaveshwar.

BHUSUKAPA (fl. 8th-9th cent.). Vajrayana Siddha-poet ; the language used by him, though Apabhransh, represents the old form of Hindi. See *Dohakosh.*

BHUVAL (fl. 10th cent.). Poet, who tr. the *Bhagavadgita* into *Dohas* and *Chaupais* ; from the language of the work, it appears that the poet belonged to the 17th century.

BHUVAN CHANDRA GOGOI (1887-1940). Assamese patriot and educationist, who established Assam Polytechnic Institution in 1926 in the village Bakta and introduced for the first time Hindi as a subject along with other subjects.

BHUVANESHWAR PRASAD (1910-1957). Dramatist, whose collection of one-act plays appeared under the title of *Caravan* (1935). It contains six one-act plays. The influence of Shaw and Ibsen is evident in these plays. His two other one-act play collections are : *Usar* (Barren ; 1934) *Strike* (strike on the home front) and *Tambe ke Kide* (Insects of Copper ; 1946). He was the first Hindi dramatist to use the sur-realistic or absurd technique.

BHUVANESHWAR PRASAD. Maithili poet, whose chief work is *Maithili Bal Ramayan* (1963).

BHUVANESHWAR PRASAD SHRIVASTAV. Modern Bhojpuri poet, who is noted for his stray poems.

BHUVANESHWAR SINGH 'BHUVAN' (1908-1944). Maithili writer and poet, whose chief work *Visarjan* is a short story collection. His essays, with reformist and revolutionary zeal, are marked with speed and sweeping force. Collections of his poems, which sought to arouse the youth are : *Yugavani*, *Yuvak* and *Udbodhan*. He was the author of *Ashadh* (1936) and *Smriti Kan* (1944), collections of poems, which make a plea for the New Lyric. *Bhuvan Bharati* (1958) is a collection of his complete poems. He also tr. into Maithili *Virahini Brajangana* from Bengali.

BIBHU KUMAR. Modern writer, who is known for his short stories, e.g., 'Yatra : Shav-yatra' (Journey : Funeral Journey).

BIBHUTI ANAND. See *Vibhuti Anand*.

BIDAD SINGH (b. 1840). Rajasthani poet, who was a Jagirdar of Kishenpur village in Alwar State. Writing under the pseudonym of 'Madhav', hundreds of his stray verses are available.

BIHARI. See *Biharilal 'Bihari'*.

BIHARI LAL 'BIHARI' (1603-1663). Great poet of the Riti school ; it is generally accepted that Bihari was born in about 1603 at Basuva Govindpur (Gwalior) and was alive up to 1663. A Mathur Brahmin (Chaturvedi), he studied Sanskrit and Prakrit works at home from his erudite father Keshav Ray. He migrated to Mathura-Vrindavan and married a Brahmin girl. It is said that when he was slighted at his father-in-law's house, he started in search of a patron. He reached Jaipur at the court of Mirza Raja Jay Singh, where he could get no audience of the king, who was so madly infatuated by the charms of his newly-wed young bride that state affairs were neglected and his ministers' effort to entice him out of the harem were all in vain. In some way, a *Doha*, written by Bihari, reached the king, which may be rendered into English as 'Neither pollen, nor honey, nor even the blooming flower/ By the bud is ensnared the bee—blind remains the future'. The couplet served its purpose, the love-sick king came out of the harem, resumed his responsibilities and made Bihari a court-poet. For every couplet that the poet composed, the king offered a guinea. Thus came forth the *Bihari Satsai* (q.v.), i.e., 700 Dohas, though the *Satsai*, now published, contains 726 *Dohas*. Bihari spent the rest of his life as a court-poet in Jaipur. Bihari also read Persian poetry and met Emperor Shahjahan.

On *Satsai* alone, the fame of the poet rests. No poet in Hindi gained reputation on writing so little as Bihari did. The work aptly reveals his vast knowledge of the workings of the human mind and the vicissitudes of erotic emotions. It is also noted for graphic pictures of beauty with utmost economy of words.

Bihari's place in the galaxy of Hindi poets has been a topic of dispute. Some critics place him next only to Surdas and Tulsidas, while others assign this coveted place to Dev. In any case, in his own life time and even today, Bihari is considered one of the most popular Riti poets.

BIHARI SAHIB (fl. 16th cent.). Saint-poet of Cutch, who like Gorakhnath and Kabir, attached utmost importance to spiritual guidance by a *Guru*. He wrote devotional verses; his *Dohas* have been collected in a volume entitled *Pada-Lavani*.

BIHARI SATSAI. Work, containing 700 *Dohas* (couplets) (the published version has 726) of Biharilal (q.v.). The couplets are intended to illustrate figures of rhetoric and other constituents of a poem, each couplet being complete in itself. As the verses do not weave themselves into a yarn, the order of their arrangement can be changed; hence there are different recensions of the *Satsai*. The most famous is that made by Azamshah, the third son of the Emperor Aurangzeb. Based on the Azamshahi recension, is given below outlines of the work.

In the beginning, there are a few miscellaneous verses. Then there are verses on the four types of *Nayaks* (heroes), followed by about 200 verses on *Nayikabhed* (types of heroines). After that, there are verses which illustrate the various constituents of poetic style (*Rasa*), among which verses about 170 deal with *Viyoga* (pangs of love in separation). Then follows *Nakhshikh*, which ends with verses descriptive of six seasons. Next, there are moral apothegms and allusive sayings and a collection of verses, illustrating sentiments appropriate to various occasions. Then follow the verses illustrating the first eight *Rasas*; the *Shringar Rasa* having been dealt with earlier. Most of the *Dohas* are amorous utterances of Radha and Krishna, which are names only to deal with the sensuous relation of the sexes.

The *Dohas* are popular because of their extreme condensation of meaning and the rare pointedness. Each idea presented is shorn of all superfluities and tells much more than meets the eye, with the help of direct and indirect suggestions, associations and contrasts. It is on account of this extreme compression of thought that some 50 commentaries have been written on this work by eminent poets and scholars. As regards pointedness, the couplets have been compared to arrows, outwardly small but going deep.

In elaboration of the poetic art, the *Satsai* is the most remarkable example in Hindi of the rhetoric style in poetry. The language, a mixture of Bundelkhandi and Brajbhasha, is that of ordinary speech but highly refined. But much liberty has been taken with the language : words have been twisted and turned to fit in the pattern of his couplet. Despite these, the *Satsai* remains a cherished treasure of Hindi poetry. The *Satsai* has been tr. into German (by Lothar Lutze) and into English. Dr. Grierson maintained that there is no work like *Bihari Satsai* in any of the European languages.

BIHULA VISHDHARI. Bhojpuri folk-tale in verse, which exists with slight variations in Bengali and Assamese folk-tales. Bihula is so beautiful that several suitors come to woo her but none is successful. She is, however, cursed that on her first wedding night, her husband will die, bitten by a snake. She is married to Bala Lakhandar (Lakshmidhar), son of Chandu Saudagar. She makes every preparation for the safety of her husband but a serpent bites him and he dies. The condition of Bihula has been described pathetically by the anonymous poet. Ultimately, by the devotion of Bihula and with the grace of the goddess Mansa, Lakhandar is brought back to life.

BINDESHWAR MANDAL. Maithili poet, whose *Nutan Kiran* (1968) is a collection of his poems ; one of the poems of this collection became very popular. He also wrote a novel : *Batak Bhet Jingik Geth* (1967).

BINHAI RASO. Long Dingal narrative poem, which is considered the best poem of its author, Mahesdas Rao (q.v.). A historical poem, it describes the three battles fought by the rebel sons of Shah Jahan : Murad, Aurangzeb and Shah Shuja against the imperial armies at Dharmat (Ujjain), Dhaulpur (Shamugarh) and Benares (Bahadurpur), emphasizing the deeds of Gaur heroes in particular. There is a graphic description of the warriors and the events in a forceful language.

BINJHA-SORATH. Rajasthani romance of Binjha-Sorath, of which a manuscript containing 41 verses is dated 1661. Another some 75 verses are found in various other manuscripts. The original verses might have been composed in the early 16th century. It appears from some old *Dohas* that the actual name of the heroine was Sonal. There are also different versions of the tale.

Sorath or Sonal, a very beautiful girl, is first married to a wealthy nomad, Raja Rur, who is invited for gambling by Rao

Khengar of Girnar. The Rao, already charmed by Sorath's beauty, wants to obtain her. Rur loses everything in gambling including Sorath. Binjha, a relation of Khengar, himself falls in love with Sorath, while bringing her to the Rao's palace. He meets Sorath secretly. Once Khengar discovers them in embrace and consequently banishes Binjha (another version is that Rao Khengar seeing Sonal and Binjha in embrace, controls his anger and covers the two with a cloth). Binjha cannot bear separation from Sorath and dies. Sorath, however, manages to come to the funeral of Binjha and there gives up her own life in the hope of union in the next life.

Sorath's longings for her lover, her emotions of grief and sentiments of pathos have been expressed cogently. The poet has also drawn a charming picture of Sorath's beauty.

'BINOO' (1939-1955). Maithili poet, who is noted for his *Ityalam*, a collection of poems, published posthumously.

BIPIN KUMAR AGRAWAL. See *Vipin Kumar Agrawal.*

BIRBAL (fl. 1583). Poet and one of the *Navratnas* (nine gems) of the court of Akbar Formerly, he was under the patronage of Raja Bhagvandas of Jaipur and composed poems under the nom de plume of 'Brahma'. The Raja recommended him to the court of Akbar where by dint of his ability, he found favour with the emperor. Akbar granted him the title 'Kaviray'. Birbal was very generous and was himself a patron of many a scholar and poet of his times, including Keshavdas, Surdas, Gang (qq.v.), etc. No complete work composed by Birbal is extant ; the stray verses. about 200 in number, that are available, reveal him as a poet of a fairly high standard. His favourite themes are devotion (*Bhakti*) and advice addressed to various sections of people to enable them to meet with different situations in life. But Birbal was a man of wit too : numerous jests and remarks attributed to him are current all over the northern India, which speak volumes of his sharp intellect and great presence of mind.

BIRENDRA NARAYAN. Modern writer, whose chief works are : *Surdas* (1961-62 ; a drama on the life of a blind beggar) and *Hindi Drama and Stage* (1981).

BISALDEV RASO. See *Visaldev Raso.*

BISMILLAH, ABDUL. Poet, whose *Chhotey Buton ka Bayan* (1982) is a collection of poems, while *Tuta Hua Pankh* is a collection of his short stories. *Samar Shesh* and *Anguri* are his novels.

BISRAM (fl. early 20th cent.). Bhojpuri poet, who was born in the Azamgarh district of Uttar Pradesh. While still young, his wife died, which kindled his poetic instinct and gave rise to outpourings of his heart in the form of songs, of which some 20 to 25 have so far been discovered.

BIVALKAR, R. VA. Marathi-speaking modern Hindi scholar, whose chief work is : *Rao Gulab Singh aur Unka Hindi Sahitya.*

BLOCH, JULES (d. 1953). French scholar, whose chief works concerning Hindi are : *L' Indo-Aryan* (1934 ; Eng. tr. *Indo-Aryan Languages*) and *La Lang Braj* (The Language Braj). In his *Indo-Aryan Languages*, he has presented the history of modern Indian vernaculars. This work is considered a standard one on the subject.

BLUMHARDT, J.F. Compiler of *Catalogue of Hindustani Printed Books in the Library of the British Museum* (London, 1889).

BODHA (fl. 1747-1803). Poet, who was a Saryupari Brahmin and was born at Rajapur in Banda district. The *Shiv Singh Saroj* mentions the year of his birth as 1747. His full name was Buddhisen but his patron, the ruler of Panna, affectionately called him 'Bodha' and consequently he became popular by that name. He was also a scholar of Sanskrit and Persian.

Bodha was a great love poet ; at the Panna court there was a courtesan, Subhan by name, with whom he fell in love and whose charms he has described in numerous verses. On account of his love for Subhan, he was banished from Panna for six months and his separation from his beloved gave birth to *Virah Vagish* (on pangs of separation from the beloved). *Ishqnama* (on love) is his another work. Despite the fleshy appeal of Bodha's poetry, it acquires a certain force and dignity for its burning passion. The language is Brajbhasha and despite lack of refinement or delicacy, there is music of words and imagery. As a love poet and his disregard for the Riti rules and conventions, he holds his place beside Alam and Ghananand (qq. v.).

BOERNER, BARBARA. Modern German Hindi scholar, who has made a deep and scientific study of Hindi grammar. She at present teaches Hindi grammar through the medium of German.

BRAHMA. See *Birbal*.

BRAHMA DATT. Poet of the Riti school, who was patronized by Babu Dip Narayan Singh, a younger brother of Maharaja Uditnarayan Singh, the ruler of Kashi. *Vidvadvilas* (1803) and *Dip Prakash* (named after his patron ; 1808) are his Riti works.

BRAHMA GOPAL (b. 1535). Poet of the Krishna-cult (Chaitanya Sect), who was son of Radhikanath. His works are : *Ashtayam* and *Shri Hari Lila*. The last work contains *Dohas* and *Padas*, which are written in the name of 'Shri Priyasakhi'.

BRAHMA GOPAL (b. 1744). Poet of the Krishna-cult (Chaitanya Sect), who was son of Radhikanath. His works are : *Shri Yamunashta-Padi* and *Shri Vrindavan Vilas*.

BRAHMA JAY SAGAR (1513-98). Gujarati Jain poet, who was a disciple of Ratnakirti. Of his 12 small works, written in Apabhransh-mixed Old Rajasthani-Gujarati, *Panch-Kalyan Git* and *Chundi Git* are important.

BRAHMA JINDAS (1388-1468). Great Jain scholar and poet, who, besides a dozen poems in Sanskrit, has composed over fifty narrative works, mostly the *Ras* in Hindi and Gujarati mixed Rajasthani. Mainly based on legends popular in the Jain religion, his *Ram Sita Ras* (*Ramayan*) based on *Padma Puran* of Ravishenacharya, is the first major work of its kind.

BRAHMAJIT (fl. last quarter of 16th cent.). Gujarati-speaking Jain poet, whose Hindi works are : *Hanumachcharitra*, *Hansa Git* and *Hansatilak Ras*.

BRAHMA RAY MALL (fl. 1517). Jain poet, who was the author of *Pradyumna Raso* on the story of Krishna's son, Pradyumna.

BRAHMANAND (1771-1831). Saint-poet of Swaminarayan Sect, whose original name was Ladu Barot. Though he was born at Abu, his field of activity was almost the entire Gujarat.

A versatile writer, the number of his works in Gujarati is five, while his Hindi works are : *Upadesh-Ratna Dipak*, *Jhulna*, *Vivek Chintamani*, *Upadesh Chintamani*, *Sampraday Pradip*, *Sumati Prakash*, *Shikshapatri*, *Vartman Vivek*, *Brahma-Vilas*, *Dharmavansh Prakash* and *Niti Prakash*. The language of his works varies from Brajbhasha to Khari Boli, but is influenced by other Hindi dialects.

BRAJ BHUSHAN. Fiction writer, whose *Sonamati* (Gold-Dust)

and *Bhul ka Shul* (The Pain of Oversight ; both 1980) are idealistic novels, while *Kajal ki Kothri* (The Coal-cellar ; 1980) and *Vivek ke Anand se* are his short story collections. He has also published other novels and short story collections ; his dramas are : *Andekhe Chehre* and *Durdarshi.*

BRAJ BIHARI KUMAR. Modern lexicograther, who has prepared some 20 dictionaries of Hindi with Garo, Hill Miri, Mijo, Phom, Kuki, Lotha and other dialects. These dictionaries have been published by Nagaland Bhasha Parishad, Kohima.

BRAJ CHANDRA VALLABHIYA (fl. 19th cent.). Poet of Kashi, who was a contemporary of Bharatendu Harishchandra (q.v.) ; only some stray verses of his are extant.

BRAJ DAS PUJARI (fl. 18th cent.). Poet of the Krishna-cult (Haridasi Sect), whose one *Chhappay* in praise of Viharin Dev (q.v.) is extant.

BRAJ DASI (fl. 1723). Poetess of Rajasthan, whose stray verses on Krishna-cult in Brajbhasha are available.

BRAJ KACHRU. See *Yamuna Kachru.*

BRAJ KI CHAURASI KOS PARIKRAMA KA YATRA-VIVRAN. Manuscript in Brajbhasha, which has been discovered in Venkatgiri (Chittur district) Raj Pustakalaya ; the work is in Telugu characters.

BRAJ KISHORE (b. 1818). Poet of the Krishna-cult (Chaitanya Sect), whose *Seva Prakash* in 101 *Dohas* describes the services to be rendered to Radha-Madhav.

BRAJ KISHORE NIGAM 'AZAD' (1928-). Bagheli folk-poet, who was born in Rewa. His poems are noted for their humour and satire.

BRAJ KISHORE VERMA 'MANIPADMA'. Maithili novelist of Baheda, who has imbibed Mithila folk-lore and poetry. His works, mostly novels are : *Anal-Path, Vidyapati* (1960 ; on the celebrated poet), *Ardhanarishwar* (1967-68), *Lorik-Vijay* (1970 ; on the heroism of the Mithila folk-hero Lorik) and *Naika-Banijara* (1973). It is in the last two novels that he has discovered his true field. He has written a number of short stories. He is the author of a drama *Kanth-Har* (1964) and another drama on Vidyapati. He has tr. into Maithili the famous novel *Kusi Prangnar Chitthi* of the Bengali writer,

Vibhutibhushan Mukhopadhyay on the devastations caused by the river Kosi. He has also made a study of Maithili folk-literature and has successfully adapted folk rhythms and diction to serious poetry.

BRAJ LAL BIYANI. Modern Rajasthani writer, who is famous for his emotional essays.

BRAJ MOHAN JAVALIYA. Modern Rajasthani writer, whose chief work *Al Janjal* (1976) is a collection of historical short stories.

BRAJ MOHAN MATHUR. Modern Rajasthani poet, who has composed Nature poems.

BRAJ MOHAN SHAH. Modern writer, who is noted for his dramas *Trishanku* and *Yuddhaman* (on the ravages of war), *Algojha*, *Shahaye Mat* (The Check-mate), etc. ; *Shri Ramlila* is his poetical work.

BRAJ NANDAN 'KAVIRATNA' (b. 1892). Poet of the Bhavamau village in Raebareilly district, whose several works, including *Vrindavan-Virahini Barvai* and stray verses, etc. are extant.

BRAJ NANDAN SAHAY (1874-1956). Novelist, whose chief works are : *Saundaryopasak* (The Worshipper of Beauty), *Aranyabala* (The Daughter of Forest), *Radha-kant* (Radha's husband ; 1912), *Adarsh Mitra* (The Ideal Friend), *Lal China* (Red China ; 1916) etc. ; his novels may be described as purely descriptive with a display of emotions and imagery here and there. He was noted also for his drama : *Ushangini* (1925).

BRAJ NARAYAN PUROHIT. Rajasthani writer, whose chief works *Atharvan* (1973) and *Vakil Sahib* (1973) are interesting sketches and recollections.

BRAJ NATH BADJENA (1730-1800). Court-poet of Raja Trilochan Mahindra Bahadur of Dhenkanal in Orissa, whose *Gundicha Vijay* is a Hindi composition, describing the car festival of Shri Jagannath.

BRAJ NATH GARG (1941-). Scholar, whose chief works are : *Hindi Bhasha aur Sahitya ka Itihas* and *Sudarshan : Vyaktitwa ewam Krititwa*.

BRAJ PRASAD. Writer, whose chief work is a romantic drama, *Malati Vasant* (1889).

BRAJ RATNA DAS (1890-1966). Writer of Kashi, whose chief works are : *Hindi Natya Sahitya* (Hindi Dramatic Literature ; 1938), *Khari Boli Hindi Sahitya ka Itihas* (A History of Khari Boli Hindi Literature), *Urdu Sahitya ka Itihas* (A History of Urdu Literature) and *Bharatendu Harishchandra* (criticism).

BRAJ VALLABH DEV 'VALLABHSAKHA' (1860-1935). Poet of Mathura, whose chief works are : *Usha-Charit* (on the Usha-Aniruddh episode), *Kadambari*, *Rukmini-Mangal* (Glory of Rukmini), *Vir Abhimanyu*, *Ramashwamedh* (on the Horse-sacrifice of Ram), *Shakuntala*, *Raghuvansh*, *Krishna-Janma* (on the birth of Krishna ; dramas) and *Prem-Pritimala* (The Garland of Love ; in *Dohas*). He himself staged his own dramas. Bharatendu Harishchandra and Shridhar Pathak also knew him.

BRAJ VASI DAS (fl. 1770). Poet of the Krishna-cult, who was a follower of Vallabh Sect. His *Braj Vilas* (The Charms of Braj ; 1770) in *Dohas* and *Chaupais* is a *Prabandh-Kavya*, composed after the fashion of Tulsidas (q.v.). It describes the various *Lilas* of Krishna from his birth to the arrival in Mathura. The story is in the same order as in *Sursagar* (q.v.) ; at places sentiments and words of Surdas (q.v.) have been given the garb of *Chaupais*, as the poet himself admits. The language is pure Braj. The poet also rendered the *Prabodha-chandrodaya*, the Sanskrit drama, into Hindi.

BRAJENDRA KUMAR BHAGAT. Hindi poet of Mauritius, who is noted for his songs. His chief works are : *Madhupark* (1948), *Madhukari*, *Amar Sandesh*, *Hamara Desh*, *Rasarang*, *Gunjan*, *Rasavanti*, *Hindu Gaurav Gan*, *Madhuban*, *Madhumas*, *Madhu-kalash*, *Goswami Tulsidas* and *Madhudip*. He has published short stories and one-act plays (*Adarsh Beti*, *Swatantrata ka Suprabhat*) as also Bhojpuri folk-songs. See *Surya Prasad Mangar Bhagat*.

BRAJESH CHANCHAL. Modern Rajasthani poet, who has composed Nature, patriotic and heroic poems.

BRAJESH MAHAPATRA (b. 1871). Poet of Asni, whose family was honoured by the ruler of Rewa. His chief Riti works are : *Rasang-Nirnay* (on *Rasa*), *Ramesh Ratnakar*, *Vishwanath-Bhushan* *Virah-Vatika*, *Ramayan*, etc.

BRAJESHWAR VERMA. See *Vrajeshwar Verma*.

BRESKOVNI, V. Modern Russian Hindi scholar, who has written a number of articles on Hindi lexicology.

BRETON, PETER. Surgeon in the East India Company, who compiled and published : *Vocabulary of the Names of the Parts of the Human Body and of Medical and Technical Terms in English, Arabic, Persian, Hindi and Sanskrit* (Calcutta, 1825).

BRICE, N. Author of *A Romanized Hindustani and English Dictionary* (Benares, 1880).

BRIGS G.W. European scholar, who is noted for his *Gorakhnath and the Kanphata Jogis* (Calcutta, 1938).

BRIJ LAL RAMDIN. Modern Hindi writer of Mauritius, whose *Parakh* is a short story collection.

BROWNING, DOROTHY ANN. American Hindi scholar, whose chief work is : *Contrastive Callocational analysis with examples from Hindi and English* (Ph. D., Texas at Austin, 1967).

BRYANT, KENNETH EUGENE (1945-). Canadian scholar of Hindi, who is at present Associate Professor in the Department of Asian Studies at the University of British Columbia, Canada. His publications are : *Poems to the Child-God : Structures and Strategies in the Poetry of Surdas* (1978) and *Pada Surdas Ka : The Padas of Surdas in the Fatehpur Manuscript V.S. 1639* (ed. with G.N. Bahura ; including a 20-page introduction by Bryant). Apart from articles, translations and reviews, he is preparing a critical edition of the *Sursagar* (in collaboration with J.S. Hawley of the University of Washington).

BUDDEN, REV. J.H. Author of *Hindi Bhasha ka Vyakaran* (A Grammar of the Hindi Language ; Agra, 1858) ; he also tr. into Hindi Mrs. Sherwood's *Indian Pilgrim* (2nd ed., London, 1861).

BUDDHA SINGH (1685-1739). Brajbhasha poet, who was ruler of Bundi (Rajasthan). After the death of Aurangzeb, there was a war of succession between his two sons : Bahadurshah and Azam ; it was the valour of Buddha Singh that was responsible for installing Bahadur Shah on the throne of Delhi. His *Neh-Tarang* (1727) in 446 metres is a Riti work of its kind.

BUDDHI DHARI SINGH 'RAMAKAR' (1919-). Maithili writer and poet, whose *Prayas* (1946) is a short story collection. His *Sharshayya* (1962) is on the life and teachings of Bhishma during his last days when he was awaiting death on the bed of arrows. He has also written critical articles. His collections of poems are : *Avesh, Amar Bapu* (1949) and *Madhumati* (1958).

BUDDHI LAL. Maithili poet, who was noted for his lyrics. He was a contemporary of Maharaja Raghav Singh (1704-40).

BUDDHI NATH JHA. Modern Maithili poet, who is known for his patriotic poem : *Maithilottejana-Paravar*.

BUDDHI PRAKASH PARIK. Rajasthani poet, who in his poems : *Chuntkya, Chabadka, Tirasa* (all 1964) and *Indar Sun Interview* (1969) points out the poverty and social evils prevalent among the lower middle class people. He has also composed patriotic and heroic poems.

BUDDHI RAS. Rajasthani poem in 65 verses by Shalibhadra Suri (fl. around 1184), a Jain poet. It contains wise sayings and moral teachings for the benefit of the common man. The style of this *Ras* was followed in many subsequent works, e.g., *Sar Sikhaman Ras, Hitshiksha Ras*, etc.

BUDDHI RASO. Rajasthani romance by Jalha (q.v.), the story of which appears to be imaginary.

A young prince of Champavati goes to another country taking with him immense wealth and happens to stay with a young and beautiful courtesan named Jaladhi Tarangini (Putti) for several days. The courtesan falls in love with him and treats the prince as her husband. The prince goes back with a promise to return in the ensuing spring. Atta, another courtesan, wise and old, tries to persuade Putti to continue the usual courtesan's life of seeking wealth, but Putti disregards her suggestions and remains firm in her fidelity. The prince comes back and they live together happy ever afterwards.

The main part of the poem, which is in 137 verses, is in the form of dialogues between the two courtesans. Victory of love over worldly wisdom is the real theme of the dialogues.

The plot is simple and the dialogues are sharp ; the language is Rajasthani with slight impact of Apabhransh. See *Jalha*.

BUDDRUSS, GEORG (1929-). German scholar, who has published several works on the language of Hindukush area. He also specializes in Hindi literature.

BUDHA RAM (fl. early 19th cent.). Rajasthani saint-poet of Ram Snehi Sect, Ren, whose *Vani* consists of stray verses in popular metres.

BUJHAHAN (fl. 1825). Sufi poet, whose *Alifnama*, a small work, treats of Yoga, etc.

BULCKE, CAMILL (1909-1982). Belgian priest, who came to India in 1935. In 1949, he did his doctorate on 'Ramkatha ka Vikas' (The Development of Ram-story) from Allahabad University ; his thesis has been published as *Ramkatha* (Allahabad, 1950). He wrote several articles concerning Ramkatha. He compiled an English-Hindi Dictionary and also wrote a philosophical work, *The Theism of Nyaya-Vaisheshika.* He made a good translation into Hindi of some portions of the *Bible*. He had become an Indian citizen.

BULLA SAHIB (fl. 1763-1768). Saint-poet of Bhurkuda (near Ghazipur), who was the spiritual preceptor of Gulal Sahib. In most of the *Shabdas* composed by him, there is description of 'Surat' and 'Dasham Dwar'.

BUND AUR SAMUDRA (The Drop and the Ocean). Novel (1956) by Amritlal Nagar (q.v.), which depicts the relation between the individual and the society. The author locates his theme in a part of Lucknow, through which he describes the problems, social relations and inconsistencies of Indian life after Independence. It describes how personal and party interests have led to the break-up of social life and disintegration of national life.

BUNNI LAL SINGH. Modern Hindi writer of Nepal, who is noted for his short stories and stray poems.

BURTON PAGE, J. British Hindi scholar, who has written a number of articles, e.g. 'The gender of loan-words in Hindi' (1959).

BUTIYA (fl. first part of 18th cent.). Saint-poet of Gujarat, whose *Padas* were composed in a mixed Hindi-Gujarati language.

BYRSKI, MARIA CRISTOPHER. Modern Polish Hindi scholar, who is Professor of Hindi, Oriental Institute, Warsaw University, Warsaw and has written several articles on ancient dramatic art and modern cinema, Sanskirt drama and Bombay Cinema, etc.

C

CAPPELER. German Indologist and author of *Subhashitmala-German-Hindi Margdarshika.*

CARPENTER, J.E. Author of *The Theology of Tulsidas* (Madras, 1918) ; it was his doctorate thesis from London University.

CERNISOV, V.A. Modern Russian Hindi scholar, who has written a number of articles on Hindi language.

CHACHA. See *Hit Vrindavan Das.*

CHAHUVAN GOGAJI RA CHHAND. See *Barhat Nandan.*

CHAINJI (fl. 17th cent.). Rajasthani saint-poet of Dadu Sect, whose stray verses are available.

CHAINRAM (fl. end of 18th cent. and beginning of 19th cent.). Rajasthani saint-poet of Ram Snehi Sect, Sinthal, whose *Karuna Battisi, Guru Mahima* and a *Dingal Git* are available. His poems reveal the various acts of kindness and compassion of God.

CHAIN RAY (fl. *c.* 1713). Poet of the Krishna-cult (Chaitanya Sect), who was a disciple of Priya Das (q.v.). He is said to have composed *Bhakta Sumirani.*

CHAKRA DHAR BAHUGUNA. Garhwali poet, who was known for his *Mochhang* (1937 ; it was tr. into Gujarati, Marathi, Telugu, etc.) and *Naubat.*

CHAKRA DHAR JHA. Modern Maithili poet, who is famous for his various types of lyrics.

CHAKRAPANI (fl. 18th cent. ?). Maithili poet, whose *Usha-Haran* in more than 200 lines describes the entire episode in the barest outlines, but the story is told excellently. His verses also found respectable place in contemporary anthologies.

CHAKRAVARTI (C.V. Rao). Telugu-speaking Hindi poet, who is noted for his *Pida* (The Pain ; 1959, on the model of Prasad's *Ansu*) and *Shringnad* (heroic poems on the Indo-China Border Conflict). His *Pulkeshin* describes the plots and conspiracies up to the coronation of Maharaj Pulkeshin the Second of the Chalukya dynasty ; *Prasad ki Darshnik Chetna* (The Philosophical Consciousness of Prasad) is his research work.

CHAKRESHWAR BHATTACHARYA (1917-70). Assamese writer, who has written many original essays in Hindi. He has tr. *Banbhatt ki Atmakatha* from Hindi into Assamese and the Assamese novel *Jivanar Batat* into Hindi. He has also rendered many Assamese poems in Hindi.

CHALISANI SUBBARAO. Telugu-speaking modern Hindi dramatist, who is noted for his *Rani Rudramma* (on the victorious exploits of Maharani Rudramma of Kaktiya dynasty) and *Sharatchandra* (biography). His *Sachitra Kahaniyan* (1966) contains stories meant for children. His research publication is *Hindi aur Telugu ke Swatantrata-Purva Aitihasik Upanyason ka Tulnatmak Adhyayan* (Comparative Study of the Historical Novels of Hindi and Telugu before Independence ; 1970).

CHALLA LAKSHMINARAYAN SHASTRI (1903-68). Telugu-speaking Hindi poet, whose *Motiyon ka Har* (The Pearl Necklace) is a collection of 108 songs, published by his son. He also tr. into Telugu the *Bihari Satsai* under the title *Viri Vana* (Rain of Flowers).

CHAMAN LAL SAPRU (1935-). Hindi writer of Kashmir, whose *Santur ke Swar* is a collection of essays. Associated with Government Women College, Srinagar as Head of the Hindi Department, he has ed. 'Kashyap', a monthly magazine. He is also founder-member of Kashmir Hindi Sahitya Sammelan and Jammu-Kashmir Rashtrabhasha Prachar Samiti.

CHAMPAIGN, MAJOR. Author of *How to Learn Hindustani* (London, 1907).

CHANAINI. Bhojpuri folk-tale in verse, which describes the romance of the heroine, Chanaini.

CHANAKYA. See *Dina Nath Pathak*.

CHANAKYANITI. Hindi rendering in verse from the original Sanskrit by an unknown poet of Jammu, which was done in the beginning of the 19th century.

CHANAN (fl. 1483). Rajasthani poet, whose stray verses in different popular metres are available.

CHANCHARIK. Modern Bhojpuri poet, whose *Gram Gitanjali* presents scenes of rural life.

CHAND CHHAND VARNAN KI MAHIMA. See *Gang*.

CHAND KA MUKH TEDHA HAI. See Gajanan Madhav Muktibodh.

CHAND KAVI. Oriya-speaking Hindi poet, whose *Padas* in Hindi (Brajboli) are available. He was a contemporary of Ram Chandra Dev (1578-1607).

CHAND KAVI (fl. 17th cent.). One of the court-poets of Guru Govind Singh (q.v.) ; he was a master of Brajbhasha and composed verses in praise of the Guru ; he also wrote devotional poetry in the *Shringar* style.

CHAND KUNVARI RI VAT. Dingal poem (Script 1765) by Pratap Singh, which describes the romance of an Amaravati Prince and Chand Kunvari, the daughter of a wealthy person there.

CHAND SADH (fl. 18th cent. ?). Rajasthani saint-poet of Laldasi Sect, whose *Bhajans* extol faith in God and Guru and advocate simplicity in life.

CHAND VARDAYI (1126-93). Great Rajasthani poet, who was brought up at Ajmer. A minister and court-poet of Prithwiraj Chauhan, king of Delhi, Chand composed *Prithwiraj Raso* (q.v.), a celebrated Dingal ballad. Tradition goes that before his departure for Ghazni, where he died, the poet entrusted the work of completing the *Raso* to his son, Jalhan. Some scholars including Buhler, however, do not regard the existence of a poet named Chand Vardayi.

CHANDA JHA (1831-1907). Maithili dramatist and poet, whose *Ahalya Charit* (1912) is a *Kirtaniya* form of drama. His *Ramayan* (1898), of which every line was discussed in the court of Maharajadhiraj Lakshmishwar Singh, before this was finally incorporated in the text, is a monumental work. Owing to sweetness of language and style, it became very popular both with the learned and the illiterate. He also composed a large number of lyrics on different topics. The lyrics were collected during his life-time in two small volumes : *Git Saptashati* and *Sangit Sudha* or *Git Sudha*. After the poet's death, Sir Ganga

Nath Jha published a collection of his *Maheshvanis* under the title : *Maheshvani-Sangrah*. The best part of the poet's work consists of his *Maheshvanis* which are remarkable for their simplicity and sincerity ; the poet used to sing daily a new *Maheshvani* to the Lord. He also composed *Muktak* verses. Finally in 1937, several other poems of Chanda Jha were edited by Baldev Mishra and are known as *Chandra Padyavali*. Yet many lyrics could not be compiled. Vishweshar Mishra has collected and edited all of them in *Chandra Rachnavali* (1981). Chanda Jha is regarded as the founder of modern age in Maithili literature.

CHANDAN (fl. 1763-93). Poet of the Riti school, who was a Bandijan of Nahil Puvayan in Shahjahanpur district and was patronized by Raja Kesri Singh of Gaur. He composed *Shringar Sagar* (The Ocean of Love), *Kavyabharan* (Cherishing Poetry ; 1788), *Kallolatarangini*, *Kesri Prakash* (named after his patron), *Chandan-Satsai* (700 couplets), *Pathik Bodh*, *Nakh Shikh*, *Nam Mala* (Dictionary), *Patrika Bodh*, *Tattwa Sangrah*, *Sit Vasant* (a story in verse about the maltreatment with the two princes by their step-mother), *Krishna Kavya* and *Pragya Vilas*. From his works, it appears that the poet did not confine himself within the limits of the Riti poetry, but wrote on other literary topics. He was a Persian poet as well and his *Divan-e-Sandal*, named after his pen name 'Sandal' is extant.

CHANDAN BALA RAS. See *Asig*.

CHANDAN MALIYAGIRI KI VAT. Rajasthani poem, written about 1618 by Bhadrasen, a Jain monk, which describes the romance of Chandan and Maliyagiri.

CHANDIDAN MISHRAN, KAVIRAJA (1791-1835). Brajbhasha poet of Bundi in Rajasthan, whose father Badanji enjoyed respect and patronage at the Bundi court. Chandidan was a great scholar of Sanskrit, Dingal and Pingal and composed in simple language five works : *Sar Sagar*, *Bal Vigrah*, *Vanshabharan*, *Tij-Tarang* and *Virud-Prakas*. Chandidan was father of the famous poet, Suryamall Mishran.

CHANDIDAN SANDU. Modern Rajasthani poet, whose chief poems are : 'Mainakh ro Map' and Dingal *Git* 'Rudo Rajasthan'.

CHANDI PRASAD HRIDAYESH (1891-1927). Fiction writer, who was born in Pilibhit of Uttar Pradesh. His chief works are : *Manorama* (1928), *Mangal Prabhat* (Auspicious Morning ; 1926 ; novels), *Nandan-Nikunj* and *Vanmala* (short story collections) ; he had an ornate style of writing. At the time of his death, he was the editer of 'Chand'.

CHANDRA. Writer, whose chief work is a drama : *Akshayvat* (1983).

CHANDRABAI, B.P. Kannada-speaking modern Hindi writer, who has tr. into Hindi Kuvempu's Kannada drama : *Ambapali.*

CHANDRA BALI PANDEY (1904-58). Scholar and critic, who was born at Sathiyanv village in Azamgarh district of Uttar Pradesh. He was President of the Nagari Pracharini Sabha, Kashi and edited its journal 'Hindi'. He was noted for his research papers on questions relating to language and literature. He has also written an outstanding work on Sufism, *Tasavvuf athva Sufimat*; his other critical work is *Vichar-Vimarsh.*

CHANDRA BHANU SINGH. Modern Maithili poet, who is noted for his lyrics.

CHANDRA BHUSHAN MISHRA. See *Ramai Kaka.*

CHANDRADAN CHARAN. Modern Rajasthani writer, who is the author of *Alakhiya Sampraday* (1964) ; he is also known for his literary articles and reviews.

CHANDRADEV SINGH. Modern Hindi poet of Fiji, whose chief work is *Laghu Jivan.*

CHANDRADEV THAKUR CHANCHRIK, the late. Modern Hindi poet of Nepal, whose chief works are *Shailbala* (epic) and *Madhuyamini.*

CHANDRADHAR SHARMA GULERI (1883-1922) Short story writer and essayist, who is noted for his celebrated short story 'Usne Kaha Tha' (She Had Said So ; 1915 ; since filmed) and other stories : 'Sukhmay Jivan' (The Happy Life) and Buddhu ka-Kanta' ; his short stories are published as *Guleri ki Amar Kahaniyan.* He also wrote articles on old Hindi (*Purani Hindi*) and grammar, which are collected in *Chandradhar Sharma Guleri : Nibandh Ratnavali*, ed. by Shyam Sundar. Das The story 'Usne Kaha Tha' was so popular that for about 40 years after its publication in 1915, no representative collection of short stories appeared in Hindi without the inclusion of this story ; it is also regarded by some critics as the first short story in Hindi. Despite his great learning in Sanskrit, Guleri wrote Hindi naturally and gracefully. He originally belonged to Guler in Kangra (Himachal) but had settled at

Jaipur. He was Head of the Department of Sanskrit at Mayo College, Ajmer.

CHANDRA GOPAL (b. *c.* 1515). Poet of the Krishna-cult (Chaitanya Sect), who was a younger brother of Ramray (q.v.). A great Sanskrit scholar, his works in Brajbhasha are : *Chandra Chaurasi*, *Ashtayam Seva-Sudha*, *Gaurang-Ashtayam*, *Rituvihar* and *Radha-Virah*.

CHANDRAGUPTA. Drama (1931) by Jay Shankar Prasad (q.v.), which presents the life and character of Chandragupta Maurya, who defeated Selecus and ruled over a vast empire. Chanakya here appears to be nobler and more heroic than in Vishakhadatta's Sanskrit drama, *Mudra-Rakshasa*.

CHANDRAGUPTA VIDYALANKAR (1906-85). Writer, whose chief works are : *Chandrakala*, *Vapasi* (Return), *Khule Asman ke Niche Ek Rat* (A Night under a Bare Sky). *Ye Kharchili Biviyan*, *Meri Priya Kahaniyan* (My Favourite Short Stories) short story collections), *Cosmopolitan Club* (one-act plays), *Ashok*, *Reva*, *Dev aur Manav* (Gods and Men) and *Nyaya ki Rat* (Night of Justice ; dramas). In his stories, the narrative and inner feelings are well balanced, one propping and supplementing the other at every crucial turn of the narration. His important short stories are : 'Kam-Kaj', 'Master Sahib', 'Ka, Kha, Ga' (A, B, C), 'Chaubis Ghante' (Twenty-four Hours), 'Ek Saptah' (A Week), etc.

CHANDRAHASAN, A., the late. Malayalam-speaking Hindi writer, who was the first Hindi teacher in Cochin State. He was also appointed in 1963 the Head of the Department of Hindi in the University of Kerala. He retired from the post of Director, Central Hindi Directorate. He was the author of *Hindi-Malayalam-Swabodhini* (Hindi-Malayalam Self-Teacher ; with P.K. Keshavan Nair). He also edited a short-lived Hindi literary magazine 'Arya Kerali'.

CHANDRAKALA (fl. 14th cent.). Maithili poetess, who was described as a daughter-in-law of Vidyapati, perhaps his son Harpati's wife. A solitary Sanskritized *Pada* composed by her has been quoted by Lochan in his *Raga-Tarangini*.

CHANDRAKALA BAI (1866-1908). Rajasthani poetess, who was a maid-servant of Gulab (q.v.). She had learnt the art of composing poems from Gulab and her poems appeared often in the Hindi magazines 'Rasik Mitra' and 'Kavya Sudhakar'.

Her *Karuna-Shatak*, *Padvi Prakash*, *Ramcharitra*, *Mahot-*

sav Prakash, etc. are mainly in Pingal, but her fame rests on her stray verses on *Shringar*.

CHANDRA KANT JHA. Modern Maithili writer, who is the author of various one-act plays, *Balti Club*, *Prayaschitt*, *Parhebak Kharcha*, *Acharya Dron*, etc.

CHANDRA KANT BANDIVADEKAR. Marathi-speaking modern Hindi scholar, whose chief works are : *Agyey ki Kavita : Ek Mulyankan*, *Hindi aur Marathi Upanyason ka Tulnatmak Adhyayan* and *Upanyas : Sthiti aur Gati*.

CHANDRA KANT DEVTALE (1936-). Poet, whose chief works are : *Divaron par Khun Se* (With Blood on Walls). *Lakkarbagga Hans Raha Hai* (The Hyena is Laughing ; 1980), *Roshni ke Maidan ki Taraf* (Towards the Plain of Light ; 1981) and *Bhukhand Tap Raha Hai* (The Region in Scorching Heat ; 1981).

CHANDRA KANT KUSNURKAR. Kannada-speaking Hindi writer, whose chief works are : *Resham ki Gudiya* (The Silken Doll ; 1964 ; a collection of 22 short stories, which has earned an award from the Government of India) and *Mahapurush* (a social drama depicting the hardships which a young unmarried lady has to face). He has tr. U.R. Anantmurti's *Sanskar* and Shrikrishna Alanhalli's *Kadu*, both novels, from Kannada into Hindi. He has also composed Hindi poems.

CHANDRA KANT MEHTA. Gujarati-speaking modern Hindi scholar, whose *Mir Kavya Parampara aur Gujarat ka Agyat Kavi Mir Murad* is a research work.

CHANDRA KANT MUDALIAR. Tamil-speaking Hindi scholar, whose chief work is *Tamil aur Hindi ka Bhakti Sahitya* (Devotional Literature of Tamil and Hindi ; thesis ; 1971).

CHANDRAKANTA. Popular novel (1891) of Devkinandan Khatri (q.v.), which is full of magic and supernatural elements. Vijaygarh Princess Chandrakanta and Naugarh Prince Virendra Singh love each other, but Karur Singh, son of the Minister of Vijaygarh, longs to marry Chandrakanta. After a duel between Virendra Singh and Karur Singh, Chandrakanta is married to Virendra Singh. *Chandrakanta Santati* (1896) written in 6 vols. and 24 Pts. is an extension of the *Chandrakanta*. Thousands of people are said to have learnt Hindi merely to be able to read and enjoy these novels.

CHANDRAKANTA. Kashmiri-speaking modern Hindi fiction writer, whose chief works are : *Baqi Sab Khairiyat Hai*,

Arthantar (novels) and *Ghalat Logon ke Bich* (short story collection).

CHANDRA KIRAN SONRIKSA (1920-). Short story writer ; her chief short story collection *Adam Khor* (*Cannibal*) has been translated into Russian and other foreign languages.

CHANDRA KIRTI (1543-1603). Gujarati-speaking Jain poet, who was a disciple of Rantnakirti. Chandrakirti's *Gaddis* still exist at several places in Gujarat and Rajasthan. Of his works in Gujarati-mixed Rajasthani, *Solah-karan Ras* and *Jay-Kumar Akhyan* are prominent.

CHANDRA KUMAR. Modern writer, whose chief work is *Chhattisgarh ki Lok-Kathayen.*

CHANDRA KUMAR 'SUKUMAR'. Modern Rajasthani poet, who is noted for his stray love poems.

CHANDRA MOHAN RANJIT SINGH. Hindi poet of Surinam, whose *Sangit Prabhakar* (1978) is a poetical collection.

CHANDRA MOHAN RATURI (1880—1920). Garhwali poet, who is considered one of the pioneers of Garhwali poetry. His poems are collected in *Garhwali Kavitavali,* ed. by Tara Datt Gairola.

CHANDRA MUNI (fl. 1023). Jain poet, who was the author of *Puran-Sar* and other commentaries.

CHANDRA NARAYAN MISHRA. Maithili writer, whose *Baladitya* (1980) is a historical novel.

CHANDRA NATH MISHRA 'AMAR'. Maithili writer, whose novels are : *Vir-Kanya* (1950) and *Bidagari* (1963). His short stories are collected in *Jal-Samadhi.* He has written many good one-act plays : *Topi. Niraksharta Nivarak Pathshala, Adhunik Pathya Pranali, Gharaiya Luri, Brahmasthan, Hakim sano Hakim,* etc. He wrote a work (1980), on Murlidhar Jha under the 'Makers of Maithili Literature' series. Along with Ram Dev Jha, he edited *Kavivar Jivan Jha Rachnavali* (1980). He is the author of *Maithili Patrkaritak Itihas* (1981), a history of Maithili journalism. He has written critical articles and lyrics, which are both satirical and conventional. His humorous poems are collected in *Gudgudi* (1945) and *Triphala* (1949). In his poems on *Yugachakra,* published as *Unata Pal,* he has made shrewd and witty observations. His humour is of an accomplished type.

CHANDRA PRAKASH DEVAL. Rajasthani poet, who has composed poems in the style of Nai Kavita. He is noted for *Pagi* (1976), a collection of 28 poems.

CHANDRA PRAKASH SHARMA. Modern Hindi writer of Burma, who has tr. Prem Chand's *Godan* into Burmese. He has also written short stories in Hindi ; his tr. novels : *Ghrina Karti Rho* and *Utpati Shaniputra* are quite popular.

CHANDRA RAJ BANDARI (1902-66). Writer, whose dramas are : *Siddharth Kumar* (1923) and *Samrat Ashok* (1923). He was born at the village Jaitaran in Pali district of Rajasthan but had settled in Bhanpura of Madhya Pradesh.

CHANDRA SAKHI. Braj folk-poetess, who was devoted to the child-form of Krishna. Her songs are popular as far as Bengal ; details about her are not available.

CHANDRA SAKHI (fl. between 1650 and 1725). Malwi poet, whose songs are popular in Braj, Marwar and Kauravi regions.

CHANDRA SAKHI (fl. 1823). Rajasthani poetess, whose songs are quite popular.

CHANDRA SEN KUMAR JAIN (1920-). Writer, whose chief work is : *Oriya aur Bhojpuri Pratyayon ka Tulnatmak Adhyayan* (A Comparative Study of Oriya and Bhojpuri Suffixes ; research). He also tr. Oriya poems into Hindi.

CHANDRA SEN VIRAT. Poet, whose chief poetical collections are : *Dard Kaise Chup Rahe* (How Can Pain be Silent ?), *Mitti Mere Desh Ki* (The Soil of my Country), *Swar ke Sopan* (The Steps of Notes) and *Pile Chaval Dwar Par* (Ceremonial Yellow Rice on the Door ; 1976).

CHANDRA SHARAN. Writer, whose chief work is a drama *Usha-Haran* (The Abduction of Usha ; 1887), on mythological theme.

CHANDRA SHEKHAR DUBE. Modern Malwi writer, who contributed a good deal in the collection of Malwi folk-songs, tales and proverbs. His short story collection in Khari Boli is *Jhulsi Hui Badli.*

CHANDRA SHEKHAR 'JHA' (fl. early 20th cent.). Maithili writer, whose dialogues advocate social reforms.

CHANDRA SHEKHAR PATHAK (1886-1941). Novelist, whose chief works, mainly social, historical and some dealing in magic are : *Prithwiraj*, *Maharana Pratap*, *Napoleon Bonaparte*, *Virangana Rahasya*, *Mayapuri*, *Hemlata*, *Bhim Singh*, *Bhishma Pitamah*, etc. He has copiously used Sanskrit words in his language.

CHANDRA SHEKHAR SINGH. Maithili poet, who was a Minister and brother-in-law of Jagat Prakash Mall (q. v. ; 1644-72), on whose early death, the latter composed an elegy. Moreover, the king calls him 'Mahavir' (great warrior) and declares that there was none so pleasing to him as Chandra Shekhar. Indeed, Chandra Shekhar was more popular and more eminent as a poet than Jagat Prakash himself. It appears his poems, which are preserved in anothologies in Nepal, have been written under the pen name of Chandra Prakash.

CHANDRA SHEKHAR VAJPEYI 'SHEKHAR' (1798-1875). Poet, who was born at Muazzambad in Fatehpur district ; his father Maniram was a famous poet. For several years, Shekhar lived in the locality of Darbhanga ; thereafter he spent six years in the court of Raja Man Singh of Jodhpur and finally settled down at Patiala as the court-poet of Maharaja Karma Singh and later on his son Maharaja Narendra Singh, at whose instance he composed his masterpiece, *Hammir Hath* (q. v.), one of the finest poems of *Vir Rasa* in Hindi. His other works on devotion and Riti type of poetry, etc. are : *Vivek-Vilas*, *Rasik Vinod*, *Haribhakti-Vilas*, *Nakh-Shikh*, *Vrindavan-Shatak*, *Guhapanchashika*, *Tajak Jyotish* and *Madhavi Vasant*.

The poet thrills his readers with the poetry of *Vir Rasa* ; his poetry of *Shringar Rasa* is also sweet and charming. He thus claimed excellence in both the types of poetry and deserves to be ranked with the greatest poets.

CHANDRA SHEKHAR VYAS. Rajasthani poet, whose *Shekhar ka Sortha* (1957) contains *Niti* poems.

CHANDRA SHEKHARAN NAIR, N. Malayalam-speaking modern Hindi poet, who has all along been composing Hindi poems. His *Chiranjiv* eulogizes the heroes of the past, while his poem : *Himalaya Garjta Hai* (The Himalayas Roar) is based on the Chinese aggression on India. He is also the author of three short dramas : *Devyani* (on Puranic theme), *Yuga-Sangam* and *Kurukshetra Jagta Hai* and two short story collections : *Professor aur Rasoiya* (The Professor and the Cook) and *Har ki Jit* (The Defeated one Wins). He has tr Malayalam short stories into Hindi. He also edited for some time the monthly magazine : 'Granthalokam' published from Kerala and wrote *Hindi aur Malayalam ke Do Symbolic Kavi.*

CHANDRA SINGH. Rajasthani poet and prose writer, who is the adopted son of Thakur Harisingh. On his *Vadali* (in 130 *Dohas* ; 1941) in Rajasthani, written on the model of *Meghaduta*, he has been awarded 'Ratnakar-Puraskar' by Nagari Pracharini Sabha, Kashi. His other works are : Lu (104 *Dohas*) on the fierce hot winds that blow during summer in Rajasthan, *Sanjh*, *Sip* (nine pieces of poetic prose ; 1946), *Balsad* and *Kah Mukarni*. In the modern period, portrayal of nature as an object begins with his poems.

CHANDRA SINGH JHALA. Modern Malwi writer, who contributed a good deal in the collection of Malwi folk-songs.

CHADRAVALI. See *Harishchandra Bharatendu.*

CHANDRIKA PRASAD. Modern Hindi poet of Fiji, who is noted for his stray poems.

CHANDSUT ALAM (fl. 1692). Son of Chand, who tr. an Ayurvedic work from Persian into Braj.

CHANDULAL DUBE (1926-). Writer, whose chief works are : *Hindi Natakon ka Rup-Vidhan aur Vastu Vikas* (The Formation and Plot Development of Hindi Drama ; research), *Hindi Rangmanch ka Itihas* (Part I ; A History of Hindi Theatre) and *Hindi Rangmanch aur Natak.*

CHANDU LAL VERMA. Modern Kumaoni poet of Almora, who is noted for *Pyas* (The Thirst), a book on Kumaoni proverbs and *Gits*, some of which are quite popular.

CHANPADE (fl. 1593). Rajasthani poetess, whose stray verses in popular metres are available.

CHARANDAS (1703-82). Saint-poet and propounder of Charandasi or Shuk Sampraday, who was born at Dahra near Alwar. After the death of his father, Murlidhar, his mother Kunjo Devi brought him at the age of seven to her parents in Delhi.

According to Charandas, his Guru was Shukdev, the mythological narrator of the *Shrimad Bhagavata Purana.* Several editions of the collections of Charandas's poems named *Bhaktisagar* have been brought out. His poems go under the titles of 'Varnan' (*Braj Charitra*, *Amarlok Dham*, *Dharma Jahaj*, *Ashtang* Yoga, *Yoga Sandeh Sagar*. *Gyan Swaroday*, *Bhakti*

Padarth, *Brahma Gyan*, etc., 'Ang' (*Gurudev ka*, *Sumiran ka*, *Sant Surma ka*, *Yoga ka*, *Vairagya ka*. etc), '*Lila*' (*Makhan-Chori*, *Matki*, *Dan*, *Kali Nathan*, *Anurag*, *Ras*, *Hori*, *Gopivirah*, *Sanyoga*, *Beni Gunthan*, *Kurukshetra*, *Nasket*, etc.) and miscellaneous *Padas*, *Chhcppays* etc. His poetry is simple but contains a critical synthesis of Yoga, Gyan and Bhakti. Like Kabir (q.v.) he condemned idol-worship.

CHARPAT NATH. Nath Siddha, who, according to Rajjab (q.v.) was born of a Charan woman and as such may be said to belong to Rajasthan. He is said to have been a disciple of Gorakhnath (q.v.) or Balanath. Exposure of defects and vices, and suggestion of remedies are the main notes of his poems. His language is Khari Boli mixed with Rajasthani.

CHARYAPADA (CHARYAGIT). See *Dohakosh*.

CHATRA MOTISAR (1593-1678). Dingal poet, who wrote poems mostly on contemporary heroes and happenings.

CHATTERJI, SUNITI KUMAR (1890-1977). Celebrated Indian linguist, who was Khera Professor at Calcutta University. His chief works are : *Indo-Aryan and Hindi* (Hindi tr. as *Bharatiya Arya Bhasha aur Hindi*), *Rajasthani*, *Language and Linguistic Problems*, *Languages of India*, *Origin and Development of Bengali Language*, *Bengali Phonetic Reader*, etc. He represented India at many international Seminars and was honoured by many foreign Universities.

CHATTUKKUTTI. Malayalam-speaking modern Hindi writer, who has tr. Malayalam poet Kumaran Ashan's poem : *Vin Puvu* as *Jhara Phul* (The Fallen Flower) into Hindi verse.

CHATURANAN (fl. prior to 1685). Maithili poet, whose lyrics have been quoted in anthologies.

CHATURBHUJ. Hindi writer of Panjab in the tradition of Mihrivanu (q.v.), whose *Pothi Chaturbhuj* (1651) is an exposition of the *Vani* of Guru Nanak in a language akin to Braj and Khari Boli.

CHATURBHUJ (fl. 18th cent?). Maithili poet, whose verses found respectable place in contemporary anthologies.

CHATURBHUJ, CHATUR (fl. 1618). Maithili poet, whose large number of *Padas* are extant ; almost every anthology includes his *Padas*. Quite Sanskritized and learned in diction, he could also write in easy and simple language. Shailendra Mohan

Jha has brought out an edition of his *Padas*. His best poem delicately depicts the sentiments of two young damsels while grinding a handmill. He composed devotional *Padas* on Krishna and Shiv. In the Nepal Vir Library, there is a manuscript of a poem in 13 pages, called *Gitgopal* in Maithilakshar, where it is described that he was son of Panditraj Singhdalan Ray, who wrote *Akbar-Nama* in Sanskrit.

CHATURBHUJ DAS (fl. 1493 ?). Poet, who composed *Madhu-Malati*, different from Manjhan's *Madhu-Malati*. It is a romance of Madhu and Malati, who belong to different castes.

CHATURBHUJ DAS. Poet, who was one of the members of the *Ashtachhap* and a disciple of Vitthalnath. He was son of Kumbhandas (fl. 1550 ; q.v.), who was also one of the poets of *Ashtachhap*. He composed *Dwadash Yash*, *Bhakti Pratap*, *Hitju-ko-Mangal* and some stray verses. The main theme of his poetry is a graphic description of the various stages in Krishna's life ; almost every verse that he composed refers to some aspect of *Krishna-Lila*.

CHATURBHJ DAS (c. 1528-c. 1633). Poet of the Krishna-cult (Radhavallabh Sect), whose 12 works are known as *Dwadash Yash* or 12 *Yashs*. His stray verses are also available.

CHATURBHUJ SAHAY (fl. 1620). Rajasthani poet, whose stray verses in popular metres are available.

CHATURBIHARI (b. 1558). Poet of the Krishna-cult (Vallabh Sect), whose *Padas* are available in *Ragsagarodbhav*.

CHATURADAS (fl. 1635). Poet, who tr. Chap. XI of the *Bhagavadgita* into Hindi verse.

CHATURDAS. Poet of the Riti school, who was a resident of Lahore. He was a disciple of Amritray Bhatt. He composed his *Chitra Vilas* (1679) at the instance of his friends.

CHATURDAS (fl. 18th cent.). Poet of the Krishna-cult (Haridasi Sect), whose work is *Chaturdas ki Vani*.

CHATURDAS (fl. end 18th cent.). Rajasthani saint-poet of Ram Snehi Sect, Ren, whose *Vani* consists of stray verses in popular metres.

CHATURSEN SHASTRI (1891-1960). Celebrated fiction writer, who was born in Anupshahar tehsil of Uttar Pradesh. Even at the age of 23, he was considered a famous short story writer. He has published in all about 186 books on various literary genres; abou 30 of his works still remain to be published. The number of his short stories alone is about 450 ; of which 'Dukha Main Kase Kahun Mori Sajni' (To Whom Should I Narrate my Agony) and 'Safed Kauwa' (The White Crow) are considered the best. His short stories have been published in five volumes : *Bahar Bhitar* (Outside and Inside) *Dukhva Main kase Kahun*, *Dharti aur Asman* (The Earth and the Sky), *Soya Hua Shahr* (The Sleeping City) and *Kahani Khatm Ho Gai* (The Tale has Ended).

Shastri has written about 32 novels; his outstanding novels are : *Vaishali ki Nagarvadhu* (The Public Bride of Vaishali ; q.v.), *Somnath* and *Vayam Rakshamah* (We Protect) ; *Vaishali ki Nagarvadhu* is considered his masterpiece. His other novels are : *Atmadah* (Self-immolation), *Hriday ki Pyas* (The Desire of the Heart), *Bagula ke Pankh* (The Wings of a Duck), Goli (on the social life in feudal Rajasthan), *Sona aur Khun* (Gold and Blood) *Hriday ki Parakh* (The Test of Heart), *Amar Abhilasha* (The Eternal Desire), *Narmedh* (Human Sacrifice), *Aparajita* (Durga), *Patthar Yug ke Do But* (Two Images of the Stone Age), *Dharm-putra*, *Haran Nimantran* (Invitation to Abduction ; on the life of Prithwiraj), *Udayasta* (The Rise and Fall), *Sahyadri ki Chattanen* (The Rocks of Sahyadri) *Alamgir*, *Shivaner Kesri*, *Abha*, *Shubhda*, *Nilmani*, etc. *Somnath* describes the famous attack on the Somnath Temple by Mahmud Ghaznavi, giving a new dimension to his character. *Vayam Rakshamah* describes stories of proto-Vedic times, particularly the age of Ravan.

Apart from the short story collections mentioned above, his earlier short story collections were : *Singhgarh-Vijay* (The Victory of Singhgarh), *Akshat* (The Inviolate), *Raj-kan* (The Grains of Dust), *Lala Rukh* (A Red Flower) and *Purnahuti* (The Whole Sacrifice).

Dramas : *Ajit Singh*, *Chhatrasal*, *Dharmraj*, *Sitaram*, *Shriram*, *Pagdhwani* (The Sound of Footsteps) and *Panch Ekanki* (Five one-act plays).

Shastri's other works are : *Antastal* (*Gadyakavya*), *Hindi Sahitya ka Parichay* (Introduction to Hindi Literature), *Hindi Bhasha aur Sahitya ka Itihas* (History of Hindi Language and Literature), *Hindu Rashtra ka Nav-nirman* (Re-construction of Hindu Rashtra), *Kamkala ke Bhed* (on erotics) and *Islam ka Vish Vriksha* (The Poisonous Tree of Islam).

A gifted fiction writer, Chatursen Shastri has written works with historical, psychological and social background.

CHATUR SHIROMANI 'CHATUR ALI' (fl. 1799). Poet of the Krishna-cult (Chaitanya Sect), who was a disciple of Vrindavan Bhattacharya. His works are : *Go-Duhavan. Vanshi-Prashansa* and *Brajlalsa.*

CHATUR SHIROMANI LAL (fl. 17th cent.). Writer, who is noted for his prose work, *Bhavna Sagar.*

CHATUR SINGH MAHARAJ (1880-1929). Rajasthani bhakta-poet and yogi, who was the sixth descendant of Maharaj Baghsingh of Karjali. He was married at the age of 18 but after the death of his wife after 10 years, who had given him by then two daughters, he renounced the world and began to live in a cottage near Sukar village outside Udaipur. His poems are popular in every home of Mewar. He has written 18 books, mostly small in volume, the subject matter of which is yoga, devotion, social incompatibilities, the uplift of women and farmers and removal of social evils, superstitions, etc. His works are : *Bhagavad Gita ki Gitanjali Tika, Parmarath Vichar, Yoga Sutra ki Tika, Sankhya Tattva, Sankhya Karika, Manav Mitra Ram Charitra, Shesh Charitra, Alakh Pachchisi, Tuhi Ashtak, Chatur Chintamani, Mahima Stotra, Chandrashekhar Stotra* (Mewari Tika), *Hanuman Panchak, Saman Battisi, Chatur Prakash, Anubhav Prakash, Balakan ri Pothi* (for children, so that they could learn their mother-tongue) and *Navo Rog. Chatur Vachanamrit* (1979) is a collection of various types of his writings. He has also written on some scriptures.

The unique feature of his works is that he expresses in easy Rajasthani very abstruse and profound thoughts.

CHATURI CHACHA. See *Mukteshwar Tiwari.*

CHATURVEDI, M.G. Author of *A Contrastive Study of Hindi-English Phonology* (1973).

CHATURVEDI, MAKHANLAL. See *Makhanlal Chaturvedi.*

CHAUDHARI, ALURI BAIRAGI. See *Aluri Bairagi Chaudhari.*

CHAUHAN, SHIVDAN SINGH. See *Shivdan Singh Chauhan.*

CHAUHAN, SUBHADRA KUMARI. See *Subhadra Kumari Chauhan.*

CHAUHATH BARHAT (fl. between 1450-1550). Dingal poet, whose stray *Gits* on contemporary rulers and chiefs are available.

CHAUPADA. See *Sant Mavji*.

CHAURAHE PAR KHADE CHAR CHEHRE (Four Faces Standing on the Crossroad). Modern Hindi anthology of verse, which contains representative poems of modern poets of Jammu-Kashmir.

CHAURASI VAISHNAVAN KI VARTA. See *Gokulnath*.

CHAUTHJI. See *Gadan Cholo Mehawat*.

CHAUTHA SAPTAK (Tar Saptak 4 or Fourth Septet). Anthology of Nai Kavita (New Poetry), published in 1979 and ed. by Agyey (q.v.). It contains the select poems of Avdhesh Kumar, Raj Kumar Kumbhaj, Swadesh Bharati, Nand Kishore Acharya, Suman Raje, Shriram Verma and Rajendra Kishore. Each poet is introduced mostly in his own words. See *Tar Saptak*.

CHAVLI SURYANARAYAN MURTI. See *Suryanarayan Murti, Chavali*.

CHEBROLU SHESHGIRI RAO. Telugu-speaking modern Hindi poet, who is noted for his stray poems. He also tr. into Hindi verse a portion of *Andhrapuranam* under the title *Moti-Nath* (1973).

CHELYSHEV, YEVGENI PETROVICH (1921-). Eminent Soviet Hindi scholar, who was awarded the Doctorate of Literature on his thesis 'Adhunik Hindi Kavita ki Parampara aur Vikas'. He has visited India on a number of occasions and his chief works are : *Adhunik Hindi Kavita* (Moscow, 1965), *Hindi Sahitya ka Sankshipt Itihas* (Mowcow, 1968), *Sumitranandan Pant tatha Adhunik Kavita men Parampara aur Navinta* (Sumitranandan Pant and Tradition and Modernity in Modern Hindi Poetry ; 1970), *Adhunik Bharatiya Sahitya* (Moscow, 1981) and *Suryakant Tripathi Nirala* (a critical biography ; 1982). He has also written articles on the problems of modern Indian literature as also essays on Tulsidas, Surdas, Kabir, Bharatendu Harishchandra, Subhadrakumari Chauhan, Nirala, Pant, Muktibodh, Dinkar, Bachchan, Yashpal, Amritlal, Rangey Raghav, etc. He has edited more than 30 works of Indian writers, which have been published from Moscow. In 1967 he was awarded the Nehru Award. He is at present in the Institute of Oriental Studies, U.S.S.R. Academy of Sciences, Moscow.

CHERNYSHEV, VLADIMIR ALEXANDROVICH (1927-). Soviet

Hindi scholar, who got his doctorate in 1958 on 'Adhunik Sahityik Hindi ke Namdhatu'. Apart from his articles on Hindi grammar, language, etc., he has tr. into Russian select short stories and novels of Phanishwarnath Renu, Bhishm Sahni, Markandey, Mohan Rakesh, Rajendra Yadav, Bhagwati Charan Verma, Arigpudi, Shani, Amrit Rai, etc.

CHET RAM (fl. 18th cent.). Saint-poet, who was a disciple of Akhairam (q.v.). He composed *Varuncharitra* on the story of Varun.

CHET RAM (fl. 1833). Poet of the Riti school, who was a grandson of Bholanath (q.v.). He was patronized by Hanumant Singh, the ruler of Shahpura (near Jaipur). His *Rasa Samudra* is a compiled Riti work.

CHETAN NATH JHA. Modern Maithili scholar, who has edited Umapati's *Parijat-Haran*.

CHETAVANI RA CHUNGATYA. See *Kesrisingh Barhat*.

CHHABILE VALLABH GOSWAMI (1920-). Poet of Vrindavan, who is a descendant of Swami Haridas (q.v.). His chief works are : *Brajbhasha Bharati* (on Brajbhasha), *Gandhi Garima* (The Glory of Gandhi) (both poems), *Haridasavataran* (The Advent of Haridas), *Maharas* (dramas) and editing of *Swami Haridas Abhinandan Granth*.

CHHAGAN LAL SHARMA. Modern Rajasthani poet, who has composed stray poems on the bravery of contemporary heroes.

CHHAIL BIHARI DIKSHIT 'KANTAK' (1905-81). Poet, whose *Chalna Hoga* (We Have to Start ; 1981) is a collection of his poems, full of patriotic fervour for building a new India. 'Kantak' was born in Etawah of Uttar Pradesh.

CHHAIL BIHARI GUPTA. Modern poet, whose chief work is *Naya Saptak* (ed.).

CHHAND MAHADEVJI RO. See *Gadan Kesodas*.

CHHATRA KUNVARI BAI (fl. 1768). Princess of Kishengarh State (Rajasthan), whose *Prem Vinod* (Love-sports) describes the divine love of Krishna and Radha.

CHHATRAPATI SINGH. Rajasthani novelist, whose *Trishanku* (1974) depicts the romances of Pavan, the graduate son of a

Zamindar and the conflict in his mind about the rural and urban life.

CHHATRA PRAKASH (The Light of Chhatrasal). Long narrative poem in 150 pages by Lal (q.v.); the text has been published by Nagari Pracharini Sabha, Kashi, but the narrative comes to an abrupt end after 1707 when Aurangzeb's son and successor made peace terms with Raja Chhatrasal of Orchha and sought his help.

Starting with the tracing of the genealogy of the rulers of Orchha, it gives an account of the patriotic and brave deeds of Champat Ray Bundela, the father of his patron. Finally, Chhatrasal's heroic performances and his victories in wars are described in detail. Selecting suitable episodes from the life of his hero, the poet gives at every stage a true idea of the nobility, heroism, and patriotism of Chhatrasal, but while extolling him, he remains faithful to historical facts. The meeting of Chhatrasal with Shivaji as also Chhatrasal's wars maintain the unbroken continuity of the narrative.

Chhatra Prakash has been written in *Dohas* and *Chaupais* and their combination is employed successfully for pure narrative, descriptions, and speeches and dialogues. The diction throughout is simple and natural. Elegance in language is born of beauty of thought and feeling; the language is a mixture of Brajbhasha, Avadhi and Bundelkhandi. The word-pictures are very graphic. The work is one of the richest gems of Hindi poetry. In recent times, it has acquired special importance as a source book of history, throwing much light on the life and times of Chhatrasal. This work gives historical details correctly.

CHHATRASAL. Modern Hindi writer of Jammu-Kashmir, who is noted for his *Tapu ka Admi* (The Man of the Islet), a short story collection.

CHHATRASAL DASHAK. See *Bhushan.*

CHHATRA SINGH KAYASTH. Poet of Ater in the Vateshwar area, who was patronized by Kalyan Singh of Amravati. His *Vijay Muktavali* (1700) describes the story of the *Mahabharat* in an independent *Prabandh-Kavya*.

CHHAUNAJI MAHARAJ (fl. end of 18th cent.). Saint-poet, who was a disciple of Charan Das (q.v.) of Shuk Sampraday. He composed *Shatrup Mukti Gurchele ki Ghoshti* in the form of questions and answers between the disciple and the Guru. As the poet was a native of the area bordering Rajasthan and Braj country, his language is Braj-mixed Rajasthani.

CHHAVI NATH PANDEY. Writer, who was noted for his drama : *Samaj* (The Society ; 1929).

CHHAVI NATH TRIPATHI (1923-). Critic, whose chief works are : *Champu Kavya ka Alochanatmak evam Aitihasik Adhyayan* (Critical and Historical Study of Champu type of Poetry ; research), *Kahani Kala* (The Art of Short Story Writing) and *Hindi Kahaniyon ka Vikas* (The Development of Hindi Short Story).

CHHEDI JHA. Modern Maithili poet, whose *Koili Duti* is a *Khand-Kavya*. He tr. *Gitagovinda* and *Arya Saptashati* into Maithili from Sanskrit original and composed various type of lyrics. His patriotic poems are collected in *Maithili Git Kusumanjali* and *Bandi Jivan*.

CHHIHAL (fl. *c.* 1518). Rajasthani poet, whose extant poems are : *Panch Saheli Git* (1518 ; describing in 65 *Dohas* the pangs of separation of the wives of a gardener, a betel-seller, a cloth-printer, a liquor-seller and a goldsmith from their husbands and their union after some time), *Panthi Git*, *Udar Git*, *Panchendriya Veli* and *Chhihal Bavni* (didactic verses). The language is easy.

CHHIT SWAMI (1515-85). Poet and one of the members of the *Ashtachhap*. He was a family priest of Raja Birbal but on meeting Vitthalnath, he began to detest himself for making religion a profession. By way of expiation, he started writing verses in the worship of Krishna. Apart from the devotion to Krishna, his poetry is charged with the love of sight and scenery of Brajbhumi. He has left behind a few hundred *Padas* and devotional verses. He was so much sentimental that he never took a bath in the Yamuna for fear of contaminating it by his feet ; he either bathed in the water of the well or he rolled himself in the sand of the Yamuna.

CHHITAI VARTA. See *Narayandas*.

CHHITAR MAL (1846-1900). Poet of the Krishna-cult (Chaitanya Sect), who belonged to the village Akbarpur in the Mathura district. He composed a small work, *Shri Harinam Mala*.

CHHOCHHU. See *Bagadawat*.

CHHOGAN LAL JAIN (1924-). Assamese-speaking Hindi writer, who has been associated with the propagation of Hindi in Assam. His works are : *Hanste Hanste Jina* (Living with Laughter ; short story collection), *Insan ki Khoj* (The Search for a Man ; radio play), *Sangharsh* (The Struggle ; drama), a novel and a few works on Hindi language and grammar. He has also tr. some works from Hindi into Assamese and from Assamese into Hindi. He is also the editor and publisher of 'Purva-Jyoti', a weekly.

CHHOTAM (1811-86). Saint-poet of Gujarat, whose original name was Chhotalal Travadi. He was a native of the village Malataj. He composed 40 narrative poems, 35 smaller poems, 400 *Kirtans* and *Sakhis*. He denounced the evils rampant in society and laid emphasis on self-realization.

CHIDAMBARA. See *Sumitra Nandan Pant*.

CHIDON MEN THAHRI BAYAR (Stayed Air in Pine Trees). Modern Hindi anthology of prose-verse, which contains representative pieces of the modern poets and writers.

CHIMANJI. See *Dev Gun Prakash*.

CHIMANJI KAVIYA (1833-87). Rajasthani poet and scholar, who was son of Ludradan and belonged to the village Birai (Shergarh, Jodhpur). He composed 21 poems, the chief ones being : *Sodhayan* (q.v.). *Pragrao Rupag*, *Samman ra Jhulna*, *Ranai Ummed Singh ra Chhand*, *Sodhai Anandsingh ra Marsiya* (historical and heroic), *Harijan Mokhayarthi*. *Pichhmi Pir ra Chhand*, *Guman Bharati ri Vel*, *Ramdev Charit* (devotional), *Jaswant Pingal* and *Bhikha Prastar* (on prosody and rhetoric).

Chimanji contributed to all the trends of the traditional Charan poetry. He remained largely unknown as his works have been published only recently.

CHINTAMANI. Writer, who is noted for his Khari Boli prose work, *Bhasha Pancham Skandha* (Hindi version of the Fifth Book), written in 1696.

CHINTAMANI. See *Ramchandra Shukla*.

CHINTAMANI TRIPATHI (b. 1609). Poet of the Riti school, who was the eldest of the four sons of Ratnakar Tripathi, a Kanakubja Brahmin ; his three brothers were Bhushan, Matiram (qq. v.) and Jata Shankar alias Nilkanth, all poets. Their native place was Tikwanpur in Kanpur district. Chintamani's best known work is *Kavikul-Kalpataru* (The Celestial Tree of Poet's Family ; 1650), which gives a comprehensive treatment of various topics related to poetry. *Shiv Singh Saroj* mentions that Chintamani, for a good time, remained with Makrand Shah Bhonsla, the ruler of Nagpur, on whose name he composed *Chhand-Vichar* (Study of Prosody), a voluminous and elaborate work on prosody. His other works are : *Shringar Manjari* (on *Nayikabhed*), *Kavya Prakash* (on poetics), *Kavya Vivek* and *Ramayan* (in *Kavitta* and other metres). Chintamani was also patronized by Babu Rudra Shahi Solanki, Jaindin Ahmed and the Emperor Shah Jahan. The poet also called himself in his works as 'Manimal'.

Chintamani was an erudite scholar and his works embrace the entire field of poetics. They offer a learned discussion of numerous themes connected with literary creation. His verses, written in Brajbhasha, have an intrinsic value in both form and substance. Moreover, it was after Chintamani that Riti poetry flourished uninterruptedly for full 200 years. While Keshavdas drew his inspiration from earlier Sanskrit rhetoricians (whose canons were not favoured by other Hindi poets), Chintamani followed the later masters Mammat and Vishwanath and had a large following. He described an *Alankar* or a *Rasa* in a couplet and illustrated it by a *Kavitta* or *Savaiya*. On the whole, both as an Acharya and a poet, he holds a distinctive place.

CHINTAMANI UPADHYAY. Modern Malwi writer, who is noted for his farces and short stories. He has also contributed a good deal in the collection of Malwi folk-songs, tales and proverbs.

CHINTAMUNNEE, MOONISHWURLALL. See *Moonishwurlall Chintamunnee*.

CHIRANJIT (1919-). Humorous writer and poet (originally from Panjab), whose chief works are : *Panch Prahsan* (Five Farces), *Gherao*, *Mandir ki Jit*, *Dhol ki Pol* (Boastful Talks), *Rangarang* (Colourful ; collections of one-act plays), *Madhu ki Rat aur Zindagi* and *Kahe Pairudidas* (parodies ; both poems). He was Chief Producer, Drama, All India Radio Headquarters at Delhi.

CHITRALEKHA. Novel (1934) with a historical background by Bhagvati Charan Verma (q.v.), which discusses the problem of sin and virtue through the story of Bijgupta, a rich feudal lord and Kumargiri, a Yogi and Chitralekha (the dancing girl) and comes to the conclusion like Anatole France's *Thais* that since man has to work under compulsions, he cannot be held responsible for his actions and their consequences. The novel has been tr. into many Indian languages as also in English ; it has also been filmed.

CHITRALINGAYYA, M.V. (fl. 1935). Kannada-speaking Hindi poet, whose poems were published in the 'Jagriti', a literary magazine. The poems were mainly patriotic in nature.

CHITRA MAHANT (1936-). Assamese-speaking Hindi writer, who is chiefly an essayist and a critic. By far his chief contribution in Hindi is on Assamese Literature and Litterateurs. He has advanced the cause of Hindi and his essays have been published in 'Rashtrasevak', which he also edited for some time. He has tr. some Assamese poems into Hindi as well.

CHITRAVALI (Portraits). Romance by Usman, Hindi Sufi poet, written in 1613. It describes the love of prince Sujan Kumar of Nepal and the princess Kanvalavati of Sagargarh. The poem is interspersed with mystic suggestions and is written in the manner of *Padmavat* (q.v.) with regard to metre and descriptions.

CHODVARPU RAMSHESHAYYA. See *Ramsheshayya, Chodvarpu.*

CHOKNATHJI (d. 1738). Rajasthani saint-poet of the Jasnathi Sect, whose stray verses and *Sabdas* (about 15) describe Jasnath ji's life and some *Lilas* of Ram and Krishna. He ridiculed the degenerating standards of human behaviour.

CHOUDHRY, RU. GO. Marathi-speaking modern Hindi scholar, whose chief works are : *Hindi Bhasha Bodh* and *Hindi ka Adhyayan evam Adhyapan.*

CHRISTIAN, JOHN (d. 1883). Christian Hindi poet, whose popular work is *Muktavali*, which narrates the life of Christ in verse. A collection of his hymns with those of John Parson was published under the title *A Collection of Hymns for Daily Worship* (4th ed., 1879). A work *John Shatak* or *Satya Shatak* was published from Mirzapur (1861). He also published *Behar Proverbs* (London, 1891).

According to Grierson, he was the only European, who achieved any success as a Hindi writer and the best native scholars admit that many of his hymns are faultless compositions. He has caught the style of those old masters, Vidyapati and Surdas and that the nautch girls all over Bihar sing his songs with having no idea that they are singing Christian songs.

Bharatendu Harishchandra has given specimens of his songs in his work, *Hindi Bhasha.*

CHUNDOJI DADHVADIYA (fl. 1563-68). Rajasthani poet, of whose works : *Nimandha Bandh* (in 33 verses), *Gun Chanak Veli* (41 verses), *Gun Bhakadi*, *Ram Lila* and stray verses, only the first two are available. Both these poems are devotional ; the second in the numerical style starting from ½ to 21. Chundoji was one of the fourteen Charan Bhakta poets mentioned in the *Bhaktamal* (q.v.) of Nabhadas.

CLEMENT MARY, C., THE LATE. Malayalam-speaking Hindi scholar, whose chief work is *Hindi ka Swatantryottar Vicharatmak Gadya* (The Reflective Prose of Hindi after Independence).

COHEN, DAVID. Scholar, who is noted for his article "Hindi 'apana' : a problem in reference assignment".

COLE, PETER. Scholar, who has ed. *Syntax and Semantics* (vol. 8, New York, 1977).

COLEBROOKE, SIR HENRY THOMAS (1765-1836). Indologist, who was Professor of Sanskrit in the College of Fort William. He wrote on Sanskrit and Prakrit languages and was the first to establish a link between the Ancient Indian languages and the modern vernaculars.

COMAN, NINA. Modern Romanian Hindi scholar, who is preparing a tr. of Mircea Eliade's famous novel : *Maitreyi.*

CRAVEN, REV. T. Author of *The Gem Dictionary in English and Hindustani* (Lucknow, 1881) and *The Popular Dictionary, English and Hindustani and Hindustani and English* (Enlarged ed., Lucknow, 1889).

CROOK, WILLIAM. European scholar, whose works are : *Religion and Folklore of Northern India* (3rd ed., 1926) and *Tribes and Castes of North-Western Provinces.*

[illegible] has given a specimen of his songs in [illegible].

Chanand [illegible] Pratishthit poet of whose work [illegible] verses [illegible] only the last [illegible] two [illegible] devanagari [illegible] in the [illegible] of the [illegible] poets [illegible]

CLEMENT MARK [illegible] The Latin [illegible] Hindi [illegible] (Oxford [illegible]

COHEN, DAVID [illegible] Scholar, who is noted for his article 'Hindi [illegible] reference [illegible]'

COLE, [illegible] Scholar, who has [illegible] Syntax and Semantics (vol. 8, New York, 1977).

[illegible] THOMAS [illegible] who was [illegible] in the College of Fort William. He [illegible] and [illegible] and the modern vernaculars.

[illegible] Romanian [illegible] scholar, who is [illegible]

[illegible] author of [illegible] English and Hindi [illegible] Dictionary [illegible] (rev. ed., [illegible]

CROOKE, WILLIAM [illegible] works [illegible] (3rd ed., 1926) and Tribes and Castes of [illegible]

D

Dada Mekaran (1663-1729). Gujarati-speaking saint-poet of Kutch, who was initiated by Gangoji. Known as Kabir of Kutch, he took to Samadhi and died in that state. Like Kabir (q.v.), he opposed orthodoxy in Hindus and Muslims. A social reformer, having no belief in castes, he composed some *Bhajans* in Hindi.

Dadhvadiya, Madhodas. See *Madhodas Dadhvadiya.*

Dadudayal (1543-1603). Founder of the Dadu Panth and a saint-poet, who spiritually belonged to the lineage of Kabir (q.v.). He was born in Ahmedabad but spent greater part of his life in Rajasthan where even now his influence is widespread. It is usually believed that he was a Nagar Brahmin though according to certain traditions, he was a ginner and was thus born a in low caste. He died at Narana near Jaipur.

Dadu is said to have been initiated by Kabir's son, Kamal and there are striking similarities between Dudu and Kabir : both of them proclaimed equality of all men, developed a critical attitude towards orthodoxy, preached against the rigidity of caste system and denounced ritualism ; both of them also led a domestic life and both had counted among their followers : Hindus and Muslims. It was at the age of about thirty that Dadu founded the Brahma Sampraday in Sambhar, which was later on named Dadu Panth, after him In course of time, this Sampraday was divided into four branches based on differences in modes of living, settlement at different places, local reasons and apparel, but there was no difference of basic ideology among them.

Dadu had two sons and two daughters, all of whom in later life made their mark in the religious field. While Dadu was in Amber near Jaipur and was passing his time in religious discussions and recitation of songs, his fame reached Emperor Akbar, who asked him to visit Delhi. The meeting, however, took place at Fatehpur Sikri and the religious discourse is said to have spread over a period of nearly 40 days.

Dadu is said to have composed 5, 000 *Shabadas* but only a portion of them is collected in the *Dahu ki Bani.* His language is Western Hindi with a mixture of Rajasthani. The diction is on the whole more modern and refined than that of Kabir or Nanak ; the *Padas* of Dadu are emotional than those of Kabir. Kshitish Mohan Sen in his Bengali work *Dadu* has dwelt in detail on his philosophical thought.

DAITYARI THAKUR (1516-50). Assamese poet, who was the eldest son of Ram Charan Thakur. His works in Hindi (Brajavali) are : *Nrisingh Yatra, Syamantak Haran* and some stray verses; all these are based on the *Bhagavata* with Sanskrit *Shlokas* in between.

DAK-BHADDALI. Sayings and dialogues of Ghagh and Bhaddari in Rajasthani and Apabhransh, which are current in Rajasthan. These sayings, particularly relating to weather forecasts, were perhaps composed from the 11th to the 13th century.

DAKSHA SAKHI (b. *c.* 1743). Poet of the Krishna cult (Chaitanya Sect), whose small works are : *Mangal Arti, Vyanjanavali, Banvihar Lila*, and *Ashtaklila*.

'DAKSHAN' AHMEDULLAH. See *Ahmedullah 'Dakshan'*.

DAKSHIN KAVYA KUSUMANJALI (1977). Anthology of select poems of some south Indian Hindi poets, which has been edited by Sargu Krishnamurti and Prabhashankar. This contains poems of more than 25 Hindi poets of Karnataka, the prominent being Sargu Krishnamurti, Prabhashankar, Rasik Punnige, Vishnu Hebbar, G.A. Vishweshwar, Maghmitra, Da. Ra. Puranik, S. Keshavmurti, etc.

DAKSHINAMURTI, N.S. Telugu and Kannada-speaking modern Hindi writer, whose research works are : *Hindi tatha Telugu Kahavaton ka Tulnatmak Adhyayan* (Comparative Study of Hindi and Telugu proverbs ; 1966) and *Hindi aur Telugu Krishna-Kavyon ka Tulnatmak Adhyayan* (Comparative Study of Hindi and Telugu Krishna-poems ; 1967). His *Sahitya Sarita* (The Stream of Literature) is a collection of essays on Kannada literature, while *Karnataka aur Uska Sahitya* and *Karnataka Darshan* are his works on Kannada literature and philosophy. His other critical work is : *Surdas aur Potana ke Kavya ka Tulnatmak Adhyayan* (Comparative Study of the

Poetry of Surdas and Potana). *Murtishatak* (1976) is a collection of his 100 poems. *Rashtra ki Vedi Par* (On the Altar of the Country) is a collection of his historical and social one-act plays meant for children. He has also tr. *Pampa Ramayan* from Kannada into Hindi prose as also the Kannada drama *Ratnakar* into Hindi.

DALLA ASIYA (1553-1643). Rajasthani poet, whose stray verses are available.

DALPAT (fl. 1643 1743). Poet of Rajasthan, who was the author of *Khumman Raso* (q.v.). His original name was Dalpat but after he was initiated into Jainism by a Jain monk named Shanti Vijay, his name was changed to Daulat Vijay. Some Scholars regard him to be contemporaneous with Khumman the Second (r. 813-43), but actually he flourished much later. See *Khumman Raso*.

DALPAT RAM (1876-1954). Famous Gujarati poet, who also composed four works in Braj : *Braj Chaturi*, *Gyan Chaturi*, *Purushottam Charitra* and *Shravanakhyan* ; the last is considered his masterpiece in Hindi.

DALPAT RAY (1769-1849). Sindhi saint-poet, who was a disciple of Swami Asardas of Hyderabad (Sind). He composed many verses in Hindi, which unmistakably bear the influence of the Nath Sect.

DALPAT VILAS. Rajasthani historical work, which was composed around 1600, by an anonymous author. It deals with the early life of Dalpat Singh (1564-1613), son of Raja Ray Singh of Bikaner. The available manuscript is incomplete, but it also provides interesting glimpses of the Mughal court. It is a good example of mature Rajasthani prose of the 16th century.

DALPATI RAY-BANSIDHAR (fl. 1735). Two poets of the Riti school, who resided at Ahmedabad. These poets composed the *Alankar Ratnakar* (The Ocean of Alankars ; 1735) at the behest of Maharaja Jagat Singh of Udaipur. The work is largely a commentary on the *Bhasha Bhushan* of Maharaja Jasvant Singh ; the especiality of the work lies in the elaboration of the characteristics of the various figures of speech mentioned in the *Bhasha Bhushan* in a laconic manner, as also the use of prose. Apart from the illustrations abundantly provided by Dalpati Ray and Bansidhar, works of other Hindi poets as well as Sanskrit Acharyas are cited for the elucidation of various figures. The long list of Hindi poets helps in historical research of Hindi poetry.

DAMAU. See *Lakshman Sen Padmavati Katha.*

DAMODAR (fl. 1st half of 17th cent.). Rajasthani poet, whose *Madhavanal Katha* was written in 793 *Dohas.* As in *Madhavanal Kamkandala Chaupai* (q.v.) by Kushal Labh, the poet has quoted Sanshrit *Shlokas* and Prakrit *Gahas.* In order to show the intensity of Madhav's charms, a new incident has been added by Damodar. This is about the miscarriage of the wife of a minister, Manvegi, when she sees Madhav. But for this, the poet follows *Madhavanal Kamkandala Prabandh* (q.v.) by Ganpati Kayasth.

'DAMODAR' ADINATH. See *Adinath 'Damodar'.*

DAMODAR CHAMPATIRAY. Oriya-speaking Hindi (Brajboli) Poet, whose *Shrikrishna-Charit* is a poetical work. He was a contemporary of Ram Chandradev (1570-1609).

DAMODAR DAS. See *Sevakji.*

DAMODAR DAS (fl. 16th cent.). Poet of the Krishna-cult, (Chaitanya Sect), whose *Smaran Mangal* describes the daily life of Radha-Krishna.

DAMODAR DAS HARSANI (b. 1430). A disciple of Vallabhacharya, whose stray *Padas* are available.

DAMODAR JHA (fl. 1st half of 20th cent.). Maithili dramatist and poet, who was noted for his drama, *Gandharva-Vivah.* He tr. into Maithili Ibsen's *Ghosts* as *Bhut ki Chhaya.* His *Kadambari* (a Maithili version in 11 cantos), an epic, has recently (1981) been published. He also wrote *Alankar Kamalakar,* a work on *Alankars* and a critical work, *Pragativad.*

DAMODAR LAL DAS (d. 1981). Maithili poet, whose 21 poems (composed earlier) have been published in 1979 under the title *Nav-Mallika.* It contains songs in praise of the goddess, glory of the country, change of season, etc. His *Shakuntala* composed earlier ; 1981) is in 9 chapters and is a *Khand-Kavya.* He showed an inclination to write humorous verse in his poem *Hamara Virata,* where the speaker is a great coward. His best work is *Prem-Patravali,* of which one part called 'Ghogh Virudavali' alone has been published.

DAMODAR PANDIT (1240-1310). Marathi poet, whose *Bachha*

Haran is based on the 10th canto of the *Bhagavat Puran*. A Sanskrit scholar, he was proficient in music as well. A follower of Mahanubhav Sect, he composed *Chaupadis* and *Padas* in Hindi, which are influenced by Marathi.

DAMODAR PRASAD (1917-78). Malalayam-speaking Hindi writer, whose chief work is *Prasad ki Saral Kathayen* (Easy Stories from Prasad ; 1962).

DAMODAR PRASAD. Modern Rajasthani writer, whose *Top ro Licence* and *Kamran ki Ankhadiyan* are collections of one-act plays.

DAMODAR PRASAD SHARMA. Rajasthani writer, whose chief work *Pretatma ri Prit* (1973) is a short story collection.

DAMODAR PRASAD THAPLIYAL (1923-77), Garhwali writer, who is noted for his one-act plays *Manakhi* and poems.

DAMODAR SHASTRI (fl. 19th cent.). One of the earliest writers in Hindi, who wrote on education, travel, history, etc.

DAMODAR SHASTRI SAPRE(1848-1921). Marathi speaking Hindi dramatist, who wrote seven dramas based on the *Ramayan*. He was one of the earliest writers of modern Hindi drama. He also wrote short stories and essays, which were published in various magazines. *Main Vahi Hun* is an autobiography, while *Meri Purva Digyatra*, *Meri Dakshin Yatra* and *Chittor* are his travelogues. His language is influenced by Marathi.

DAMODAR SINGH. Writer, whose chief work is a romantic drama entitled *Madan-Lekha* (1880).

DAMODAR SOMORI. Modern Hindi writer of Mauritius, who is noted for his short stories.

DAMODAR SWAMI (fl. early 17th cent.). Brajbhasha writer, who wrote his prose work, *Bhakti-Vivechan*.

DAMODARAN USHNI, M.K. (fl. early 20th cent.). Malayalam-speaking Hindi preacher, who was educated at Jwalapur Gurukula, Hardwar. He propagated teaching of Hindi in Tirunelveli (Kerala) and was himself a good teacher.

DANDMUDI MAHIDHAR. Telugu-speaking modern Hindi writer, who is noted for his tr. of Telugu short stories into Hindi ; *Mujhe Gharib Pati Chahiye* is his novel.

DANDMUDI MANJULATA. Telugu-speaking modern Hindi writer, who is noted for her tr. of Telugu short stories into Hindi.

DANDMUDI VENKAT KRISHNARAO. Telugu-speaking modern Hindi writer, whose chief works are : *Shak-karta Shalivahan*, *Stavaniya Shasak Krishnadev Ray* (historical novelletes) and *Chitrangi* (historical short stories).

DANGRE, MU. Marathi-speaking modern Hindi poet, whose poems are written on various subjects.

DANGWAL, AMBA DATT SHARMA. See *Amba Datt Sharma Dangwal.*

DARIYA KHAN (1775-1850). Sindhi Muslim saint-poet, who also composed in Hindi a poetical work : *Brahmaveda* ; this work clearly betrays the influence of the Vedanta philosophy. Dariya Khan was the third son of Rohal (q.v.) and ascended the religious seat after the death of his brother, Ghulam Ali (q.v.).

DARIYA SAHIB (1674-1780). Saint-poet of Dharkandha (Ara), known as 'Biharwale'. Founder of the Dariya Sect, his chief works are : *Dariya-Sagar* (The Ocean of Dariya) and *Gyan Dipak* (The Lamp of Knowledge). He is known among his followers as an incarnation of Kabir (q.v.).

DARIYAV (1676-1758). Rajasthani saint-poet of the Ram Snehi Sect, Ren (Nagore), who was born at Jaitaran. After the death of his father, he came to live at Ren and became the disciple of Premdas (q.v.) in 1712. His place of *Sadhana* was Ren, which is the main seat of his Sect. His extant *Vani* consists of 412 *Sakhis* (*Dohas*) and about 30 *Padas*. The *Sakhis* are classified into such topics, as *Satguru ko*, *Sumiran ko*, *Suratan ko*. The *Vani* reveals his deep devotion and an approach of synthesis towards Nirgun and Sagun types of Bhakti. His language is easy, lively and lucid Rajasthani. Dariyav had 81 chief disciples including women.

DAS. See *Bhikhari Das.*

DASHAM GRANTH (Tenth Granth). See *Govind Singh, Guru.*

DASHAVADHAN THAKUR. Maithili poet, who was perhaps a contemporary of Vidyapati (1350-1440) ; he composed his poems in the style of Vidyapati.

DASHRATH (fl. 17th-18th cent.). Riti poet, whose chief work *Vritt Vichar* deals with prosody.

DASHRATH OJHA (1909-). Writer, whose chief works are: *Hindi Natak : Udbhav aur Vikas* (The Hindi Drama: Origin and Development; thesis; 1954) and *Samiksha Shastra* (On Criticism; 1956). He ed. with Jagdish Chandra Mathur *Ankiya-nat* (one act plays) and also *Hindi Natak Kosh*. He was Reader in Hindi in Delhi University.

DASHRATH RAJ Sindhi-speaking modern Hindi novelist, whose three novels: *Pankhon ki Chhanv* (The Shadows of Wings), *Antim Patra* (The Last Letter) and *Safar aur Sapne* (The Journey and the Dream) have been published. He is known for his research and scholarly works: *Dakkhini Hindi ka Premgatha Kavya* (Love Poetry of Dakkhini Hindi), *Madhyakalin Sufi Sant Kavi Haji Wali Muhammad-krit Premnama* (On *Premnama*), *Sant Rohal ki Rubani* (on Rohal's poetry), *Shah Miranji-krit Khushnama* (on *Khushnama*) and *Khushnaz Vitthal Bipul ki Bani*. He has also written critical essays on Sur, Raskhan, Rasalin, Bachchan, Sumitranandan Pant, etc.

DASO PANT (fl. 16th cent.). Saint-poet of Maharashtra, who was a follower of Datt Sect. There is a good number of compositions made by him in Hindi.

DATA RAM CHAUBEY (fl 19th cent.). Early writer, who wrote more than half a dozen good books on medicine, hygiene and physiology.

DATT (fl. 1773). Poet of the Riti school, who was a resident of Madi in Kanpur district and was patronized by Maharaj Khuman Singh of Charkhari. He composed *Lalityalata*, a good work on *Alankars*.

DATTATREY GANESH NERLEKAR, PRA. Marathi-speaking modern Hindi dramatist, who is noted for his drama: *Mina ki Man*.

DATTU (1772-1844). Hindi poet of Jammu, whose *Vir-Vilas* describes the story of 'Dron-parva' of the *Mahabharat*. His *Braj roj Panchashika* glorifies the Braj country, while *Barahmasa* is the traditional description of the seasons.

DAUD, MULLAH (fl. 1318). Muslim Sufi poet, whose *Chandravati* (Chandayan or Chandabat) is an allegorical romance, no longer extant. Though basically a tale of love, it dealt with the heroic marvels performed by Lorik. See *Loriki.*

DAUDAYAL JOSHI. Modern Rajasthani writer, who is noted for his sketches.

DAULAT. Poet of the Riti school, who composed his *Rasa Prabodh* (on *Nayikabhed*) at Kishengarh in 1789. His another work *Ritu Sukh Sar* (on seasons) was written in 1798 for Savant Singh, a son of Dewan Gopal Singh He also wrote an *Ashtak* and some humorous stray verses. The poet was grandson of Vallabh and son of Sanehi Ram.

DAULAT RAM. Writer of Basva in Madhya Pradesh, who tr. Ravishenacharya's Jain *Padmapuran* in 1761 into Khari Boli prose. It covers over 700 pages and the prose is a good specimen of the language spoken by the people in those days.

DAULAT RAM GUPTA. Chambiyali poet, whose *Him-Tarang* (1935-36) is a collection of folk-songs.

DAULAT VIJAY. Same as *Dalpat* (q.v.).

DAYA BAI (fl. 1743). Rajasthani saint-poetess, who was a disciple of Charandas (q.v.) and was born in a Dhusar family at Dahra near Alwar. She composed two poems : *Daya Bodh* (in 138 verses dealing with *Guru Bhakti*, *Vairagya*, etc.) and *Vinay Malika* (on her devotion and deep faith in God).

DAYAL. Rajasthani poet of Mewar, whose *Rana Raso* (composed between 1680 and 1698) in Pingal describes the history of Mewar from Bapa Raval to Maharana Jaysingh ; the descriptions and especially of the battles of Maharana Kumbha, Maharana Udaysingh, Maharana Pratap and Maharana Amarsingh are in detail and are graphic. His other works are : *Raso ko Ang* and *Akal ko Ang*.

DAYAL. See *Prabhudayal.*

DAYAL ANEMI. Hindi writer of Panjab, who wrote his Vedanta works : *Avagat Ullas* (1675), *Ashtavakra Bhasha* (1679) and a prose tr. of the *Bhagavadgita* (according to the commentary of Shankar ; 1721).

DAYAL ASHA. Sindhi-speaking modern Hindi poet, whose poetical collection : *Tarangen* (The Wavelets ; 1971) is permeated with nationalist and patriotic fervour. His *Sindhi Kaviyon ki Sadhana* (1977) describes the Sindhi-speaking Hindi poets. He has written a biography of Sadhu T.L. Vaswani under the title *Bharat ke Mahapurush Sadhu Vaswani* (1974).

DAYAL DAS (fl. 18th cent.). Poet of the Krishna-cult (Haridasi Sect), whose one *Chhappay* is extant.

DAYALDAS RI KHYAT. See *Sindhayach Dayaldas*.

DAYALUDAS (1759-1825). Rajasthani saint-poet, who was son of Ramdas, the founder of the Ram Snehi Sect, Khedapa and became the next Acharya after his father's death in 1798. He was a householder, like his father. His *Vani* consists of 9 poems, such as *Bhaktamal, Man Pratibodh, Chetan Bodh, Pragat Bodh, Nirnay Bodh, Atma Gyan, Karuna Sagar, Chitavani, Shabha Prakash, Guru Prakaran*, etc. and many verses on different topics, particularly on the Nirgun Bhakti. He also had faith in the Sagun type of Bhakti and his poem, *Karuna Sagar* is a specimen of this. His *Bhaktamal* and *Guru Prakaran* (on the life-story of his Guru-father) are important source books for the literary history and socio-religious trends of the age.

DAYANAND SARASWATI, MAHARSHI (1824-83). Celebrated Vedic scholar, whose prose writings in Hindi gave a fillip to the cause of Hindi. His *magnum opus, Satyarth Prakash* (The Light of Truth ; 1869), originally written in Hindi, became the most popular book of that era. It is generally believed that after Tulsidas's *Ramcharit-manas*, the *Satyarth Prakash* was the most widely-read book among the Hindi-reading Hindus. In his effort to interpret the Vedas and Vedic literature for the benefit of the common man, the Maharshi wrote, both in Sanskrit and Hindi, books which are commentaries on various parts of the Vedas ; the books are : *Rigvedadi-Bhashya-Bhumika, Rigveda Bhashya, Yajurveda Bhashya* and *Gokaruna Nidhi*. Though the Maharshi's mother tongue was Gujarati, he espoused the cause of Hindi.

DAYANAND VERMA (1930-). Writer, whose chief works are *Zindabad* : *Murdabad* (1971 ; a novel describing the suppressed sexual urges of the heroine towards an impotent hero), *Yaun Vyavahar Anushilan* (A Study of Sexual Behaviour), *Ham Sab aur Vah* (All of Us and He ; essays) and *Pashchim ke Tin Rang* (Three Hues of the West ; a travelogue).

DAYA PRAKASH SINHA. Dramatist, who in his two-act drama *Sadar Ap Ka* (Yours Respectfully ; 1980) has exposed the inconsistencies in the contemporary social life. His other dramas are : *Katha ek Kans Ki* (The Story of a Kans), *Itihas Chakra aur oh America*, *Sanjh Savera* and *Hasya Ekanki*.

DAYA PRASAD BANSEDHIYA. Chhattisgarhi poet, whose chief work is *Mahadev ke Bihav* (Songs of the Marriage of Shiv ; 1945).

DAYARAM (1777-1853). Vaishnav poet of Chandod, Gujarat, who was a great devotee of Krishna. It is said that he composed some 41 works and 12,000 *Padas* in Brajbhasha, of which *Sat-Saiya* and *Rasik-Ranjan* are prominent. His language betrays the influence of Gujarati.

DAYARAM (fl. early 19th cent.). Rajasthani saint-poet of Ram Snehi Sect, whose *Vani* consists of stray verses in popular metres.

DAYA SHANKAR ARYA. Rajasthani poet, who composed Nature, patriotic and progressive poems, *e.g.*, 'Admi Sun Pyar Kar Tun' ; his *Maru Minjhar* (1966) is a story in verse.

DAYA SHANKAR DIKSHIT 'DEHATI' (1894-1982). Avadhi folk-poet of Kanpur, whose poems are mostly in *Dohas* and on the the style of Ghagh (q.v.).

DAYAVANTI, B. Telugu-speaking Hindi writer, who has tr. into Hindi Rachkonda Vishwanath Shastri's *Nijam* as *Satya : Ek Dahakta Angara* (1975), Buchchibabu's Telugu novel as *Akhir Jo Bacha* and Kodavatiganti Kutumbrao's Telugu novel as *Kul-Hina*.

DEBRECENI, ARPAD. Modern Hungarian Hindi scholar, whose *Hindi-Hungarian Dictionary* is likely to be published very soon.

DEDAU (fl. 1623). Rajasthani poet, whose stray verses in popular metres are available.

DELEU, JOZEF. Modern Belgian Indologist, who is in the Faculty of Oriental Studies, University of Gent. He has espoused and promoted the cause of Hindi in Belgium.

DELHJI (1433-93). Rajasthani poet, who composed *Katha Ahmani* (q.v.), an *Akhyan Kavya* of 717 verses, dealing with the story of Abhimanyu, a hero of the *Mahabharat*.

DEPAN. Dingal poetess and the wife of Dingal poet, Dalla Asiya (1553-1643) ; her stray verses are available.

DESAI, M.D. Modern Hindi writer, who is the author of *Jain Gurjar Kavio.*

DESALJI RI VACHNIKA. See *Hammirdan Ratanu.*

DEV. See *Devdatt Dev.*

DEV CHANDRA, SHRIMAD (1689-1765). Gujarati-speaking Jain saint-poet, who was initiated into the religious order at an early age of ten. His Hindi works : *Dhyan Chatushpadika*, *Dravya Prakash Agamsar*, *Chaubisi*, *Bisi*, *Sadhu Samasya*, *Dwadash Dodhak*, *Atmahit Shiksha* are in a language, which is influenced by Gujarati and Rajasthani.

DEVDATT 'DEVA' (1674-1767). Great poet of the Riti school, who was a Brahmin, born at Etawah. He was a precocious poet and composed his first poem, *Bhav-Vilas* at the age of 16. He recited this poem and the *Ashtayam* (Description of a day and night) before prince Azamshah, the third son of Emperor Aurangzeb. Though the prince was favourable to Hindu poets and artists, yet he did not seem to have encouraged Dev. In search of a patron, Dev visited Kashmir, Punjab, Bengal, Orissa, Madras, Bombay, Gujarat, Rajputana, Maharashtra and Berar ; hence he had enriched his experience. Wherever he went, he closely observed the women there and described them in his Jati *Vilas*. His patrons were Bhavanidatt Vaishya, Kushalasingh Sengar of Etawah and Raja Udyot Singh Baisa, on whose names he composed *Bhavani Vilas*, *Kushal Vilas* and *Prem Chandrika* respectively, but he seems to have been dissatisfied with each in turn. Perhaps it was his abstruse language which came in his way of finding patrons easily. It was only in his declining years when he seems to have discovered such a patron in Raja Bhogilal (1726), whose generosity he has sung in glowing terms. In 1767, he presented his *Sukh Sagar Tarang*, mainly a compilation from his earlier works, to Akbar Ali Khan, the chief of Pihani, on the occasion of ascending the *Gaddi*. Dev was sensual in his habits and his poetry abounds in lust and lasciviousness ; it was only towards the end of his life, that he was inclined to spiritual life.

Dev was a prolific poet, for there is no other contemporary poet who could compare him in the bulk of his output. Some 72 or 52 works are ascribed to him, of which the following are extant :—

Bhav Vilas (The Delights of Emotions), *Ashtayam* (Description of a day and night), *Bhavani Vilas* (The Delights of Bhavani), *Rasa Vilas* (The Delights of Rasa), *Sukh-Sagar Tarang* (The Wavelets of the Ocean of Happiness), *Sujan Vinod* (The Delights of the Learned), *Rag Ratnakar* (The Ocean of Melody), *Prem Chandrika* (The Love of Moonlight), *Dev Shatak* (a centum, containing the four Darshan Pachchisis—Brahma, Atma, Tattva, Jagat), *Shabda Rasayan* (Medicine of Word), *Vriksha Vilas* (The Description of Trees), *Pavas Vilas* (The Delights of Rainy Season), *Rasananda Lahari* (The Wavelets of Love Charms), *Sumil Vinod* (The Delights of Sumil), *Radhika Vilas* (The Delights of Radhika), *Vairagya Sathak* (a centum on renunciation), *Niti Shatak* (a centum of verses on ethics), *Prem Dipika* (The Lamp of Love), *Jati Vilas* (The Beauties of Castes), *Dev Charitra* (on Krishna), *Kushal Vilas* (The Delights of Kushal Singh), *Prem Tarang* (The Wavelets of Love), *Nakh Shikh Prem-Darshan* (Sight of love born of description of beauty from toe to top), *Krishna Gun Karma Sukhsham Sudan* (Subtle Acceptance of Krishna's Virtues and Deeds and *Nayikabheda* (in Sanskrit). *Sundari Sindur* (Vermilion of Beautiful Women), ed. by Bharatendu Harishchandra, is a collection of 111 best verses of Dev, while *Dev Sudha* (The Elixir of Deva), edited by Mishrabandhus, is a collection of Dev's 271 verses. His important works, however, are : *Bhav Vilas*, *Prem Chandrika* and *Shabda Rasayan*.

Dev's language and his knowledge of poetics are flawless ; in this respect the only poet of this school who can be compared with him is Matiram (q.v.). There was a keen controversy about the place that Dev holds in Hindi poets. While Mishrabandhus and certain other critics tried to give him a place after Tulsidas and Surdas, Ramchandra Shukla and Bhagvan Din tried to pull him down rather too low. The fact, however, remains that Dev is one of the very great poets of Hindi literature and one of the greatest of his age.

DEVDUT VIDYARTHI (1903-72). Native of Bihar, whose original name was Dev Narayan Pande. He was responsible for propagation of Hindi in Kerala ; he himself was a good Hindi writer as also an organizer. He married Bharati, a Keralite ; the latter has tr. several Malayalam novels into Hindi.

DEVGAUR, M. Kannada-speaking modern Hindi writer, who tr into Hindi the Kannada work *Hadideya Dharma*.

DEV GUN PRAKASH. Rajasthani narrative poem of 536 verses, which was composed by Chimanji between 1780 and 1795. While giving captivating descriptions of the battles fought by Rao Devisingh (1763-95) of Sikar against Najaf Kuli Khan at Sirohi and Murtaza Ali at Khatu, it gives an account of the Rao's ancestors from Raja Kuntildev.

DEV KANT JHA. Maithili writer, who has tr. *Dasha Rupaka* from Sanskrit into Maithili in 1979.

DEVKARAN (fl. 1746). Rajasthani poet, who was a Kayasth by caste and was son of Harnath. He was the Dewan of Maharana Jagat Singh the Second of Mewar. His *Varanasi Vilas* (1746) in Pingal consisting of 4052 metres is based on 'Kashikhand' of the *Varah-Puran*; in the beginning of the poem is given a brief history of Mewar.

DEVKARAN BARHAT. Modern Rajasthani poet, whose stray poems in the traditional Charan style are available.

DEV KERALIYA. See *Narayan Dev*.

DEV KISHAN RAJPUROHIT. Modern Rajasthani poet, who is noted for his nationalistic poems. He has also published some folk-tales: *Dant Kathavan* and *Var Judi ro Tap*.

DEV LILA KAVYA. Rajasthani poem by Charan Raghuram Rodhiya, which gives the complete story of the battle of Bagadavat brothers in about 1,000 verses, mixed with prose, called *Vachnika*. See *Bagadavat*.

DEVMAYA PRAPANCH. See *Devdatt Dev*.

DEV NATH MAHARAJ (1754-1821). Saint-poet of Maharashtra, who was born at the village Surji in the district of Amaravati. He was fond of physical exercises and as such worshipped the god Hanuman. It is said that once the god appeared to him in a vision and thereafter he made a pilgrimage of northern India. He composed copiously in Hindi and his language represents a synthesis of Braj and Dakkhini.

DEV NATH PANDEY 'RASAL' (1923-). Poet, whose chief works are: *Dipika* (Taper; songs of love, Nature, etc.), *Bandhavi* (Relationship; dealing with the sad lot of rural people) and *Ritambhara* (songs on various topics).

DEV PRAKASH (1941-70). Writer, whose *Juhi Gandh* (The Fragrance of Jasmine; 1980) is a novel, published posthumously.

DEV RAJ, LALA (1860-1935). Hindi writer of Panjab, who wrote a drama, *Savitri* (1900). He was the founder of Kanya Mahavidyalaya, Jalandhar.

DEVRAJ, NAND KISHORE (1917-). Writer, who was born

in the then Rampur State. He did his doctorate in philosophy and has also written philosophical works. Besides, he has written novels, poetry, criticism, etc. His works are as under :

Novels : *Path ki Khoj* (The Search for a Path ; 1951 ; dealing with the problems of middle class people), *Bahar Bhitar* (Outside and Inside ; 1954), *Rore aur Patthar* (Pebbles and Stones ; 1958), *Ajay ki Diary* (Ajay's Diary ; 1960 ; showing how man and woman supplement each other), *Main, Ve aur Ap* (I, They and You ; 1966 ; in the form of a notebook), *Dohri Ag ki Lapat* (Blaze of the Double Fire), *Bhitar ka Ghav* (The Internal Wound) and *Dusra Sutra*.

Poetry : *Urvashi ne Kaha* (Urvashi thus Said ; 1960), *Itihas Purush* (The Historic Man ; 1965), *Ila aur Amitabh* (based on a romance of mediaeval Europe), *Cleopatra ka Patra Sita ke Nam* (Letter of Cleopatra addressed to Sita ; contrast of Indian and Western civilizations), *Subeh ke Bad* (After Morning ; 1976), *Ahat Atmayen* (The Wounded Souls ; 1979) and *Pranaygit* (a collection of poems).

Criticism : *Chhayavad ka Patan* (The Fall of Chhayavad), *Chhayavad : Utthan-Patan—Punarmulyankan* (The Rise and Fall of Chhayavad : A Re-evaluation), *Sahitya Chinta* (Thoughts on Literature ; 1950), *Adhunik Samiksha* (Modern Criticism; 1954), *Pratikriyayen* (Responses ; 1966) and *Sahitya Samiksha aur Sanskriti Bodh* (Literary Criticism and Cultural Awareness).

A critic with a background of philosophical discipline, he wishes to see literature imbued with an absorbing cultural awareness. He has also written many books in English and Hindi on Indian and Western Philosophy. His chief philosophical works are : *Shankar ka Gyanashastriya Siddhant*, *Sanskriti ka Darshnik Vivechan*, *Bharatiya Darshanshastra ka Itihas*, *Purvi tatha Pashchimi* and *Bharatiya Sanskriti*.

Dev Raj Dinesh (1922-). Poet and dramatist, whose chief works are : *Ullu ke Nam* (Addresses to the Owl), *Pati* (Letters), *Jivan aur Javani* (Life and Youth), *Gandh aur Parag* (Fragrance and Pollen), *Purvaiya ke Nupur* (The Anklets of the East Wind), *Bharat Man ki Lori* (Lullabies of Mother India), *Rishwat ke Anek Dhang* (Various Ways of Bribe ; all poems), *Ravan*, *Bin Bulaye Panch* (Uninvited Arbitrators) and *Manav Pratap* (dramas) ; his works sparkle with humour and satire. His one-act play, 'Samarpan' (Dedication) is a satire on plagiarism.

Dev Raj Upadhyay (1908-81). Writer, whose chief works are : *Adhunik Hindi Katha Sahitya aur Manovigyan* (Modern Narrative Literature and Psychology ; research), *Sahitya ka Manovai-*

gyanik Adhyayan (Psychoanalytical Study of Literature) and *Romantic Sahitya-Shastra* (Romantic Poetics). He was born at the village Babhangavan in Bhojpur district of Bihar and continued to be the President of Bhojpur Zila Sahitya Sammelan'.

DEVRAY NAYAK RI BAT. Dingal work (Script 1790) of an unknown writer, which treats of the romance of Raja Devraj and Princess Naykade.

DEVADAS (d. 1787). Rajasthani saint-poet of Ram Snehi Sampraday, Shahpura, whose stray verses are available.

DEVANAND (fl. in the latter half of 17th and early 18th cent.). Maithili writer, whose *Usha Haran* (on the famous romance of Usha and Aniruddha) is a Kirataniya form of drama. Son of Raghunath and Gunvati Devi, he lived at Parbatpur in south Mithila. The manuscript of Devanand's only play, *Usha-Haran* is very mutilated : the first three pages and some pages in the end are missing.

DEVAU (fl. 1575). Rajasthani poet, whose stray verses in different popular metres are available.

DEVENDRA ISSER. Modern writer, who is noted for his *Kale Gulab ki Salib*, *Kahani ka Ant* (short story collections) and *Cross par Latki Tasvir* (novel). His critical works are : *Sahitya aur Adhunik Yugabodh* and *Sahitya : Mukti aur Sungharsh.*

DEVENDRA JHA. Maithili scholar, whose research work is *Vidyapatik Sringarik Padak Kavya-Shastriya Adhyayan* (1979).

DEVENDRA KIRTI (fl 1665). Jain poet, who composed *Pradyumna Prabandh* on the story of Krishna's son Pradyumna.

DEVENDRA KUMAR JAIN (1924-). Writer, whose chief works are : *Apabhransh Bhasha aur Sahitya* (Apabhransh Language and Literature ; thesis), *Nibandh-kar Gulab Rai* (Gulab Rai the Essayist), *Bhramaragit aur Surdas* and *Swayambhu ke Paum-Chariu ka Hindi Anuvad* (Hindi tr. of Swayambhu's *Paum Chariu*).

DEVENDRA KUMAR SHASTRI. Author of *Aprabhransh Bhasha aur Sahitya ki Shodh Pravrittiyan* ((1972).

DEVENDRA SATYARTHI (1908-). Panjabi and Urdu writer, who has also written in Hindi ; his chief works in Hindi are : *Dharti Gati Hai* (The Earth Sings), *Bajat Ave Dhol*, *Dhire Baho*

Ganga (Let the Ganges Flow Slowly), *Bela Phule Adhirat* (Jasmine Blooms at Midnight), *Jailokgit* (all concerning folksongs), *Bandanvar* (Festoons), *Ek Mulaqat ki Varsh ganth* (Anniversary of a Meeting) (Poetry), *Chattan se Pahle* (Before the Rock ; short story collection), *Ek Yuga Ek Pratik* (One Age, One Image), *Rekhayen Bol Uthin* (The Lines Speak ; sketches), *Kathputli* (The Puppets ; 1953 ; on the story of a dramatist, who is fond of collecting folksongs), *Brahma-putra*, *Dudh-Gachh* (with musical background of the Keralities), *Rath ke Pahiye* (The Wheels of the Chariot ; on the life of Gond tribals) and *Katha Kaho Urvashi* (Let Urvashi Tell the Tale ; 1961 ; story of three generations of a sculptor of Orissa). He is noted as a novelist in Hindi. He also ed. 'Ajkal' (Hindi) for more than a decade. His critical work is *Kala ke Hastakshar*.

DEVENDRA UPADHYAY. Writer, whose *Kai Ek Chehare* (Many Faces ; 1980) is a novel, while *Shahr men Akhiri Din* and *Ek aur Vapasi* (1984) are his short story collections.

DEVESH THAKUR (1933-). Modern fiction writer, whose chief works are : K*anchghar*, *Apna-apna Akash*, *Isiliye* (novels). editing of several volumes (1976 to 1982) of short stories. His critical work is *Adhunik Hindi Sahitya ki Manavtavadi Bhumikayen*.

DEVI DAS (fl. 1570). Vaishya Minister of Rao Lunkaran of Shekhavati, who whole *Rajniti ke Kavitta* (poems on politics) in Braj Bhasha.

DEVI DAYAL CHATURVEDI 'MAST' (1911-). Writer, who ed. 'Saraswati' and was on the editorial staff of 'Bharat', a Hindi daily, published from Allahabad. He has published several novels, poetical collections and stort stories.

DEVI LAL SAGAR. Modern dramatist, whose chief one-act plays are : 'Balidan' (The Sacrifice), 'Bapu', 'Parityakta' (Divorced), 'Chandralok', 'Vir Ballu' (Brave Ballu) and '0 Nila Ghodara Asvar' (0 Rider of the Blue Horse) ; his plays have been successful on the stage and the dramatist has made some experiments in technique.

DEVI LAL SAMAR (1911-81). Rajasthani writer, who has made a notable contribution to the study of Rajasthani *Lilas*. His works are : *Rajasthani Lok-Sangit*, *Rajasthani ke Lokanuranjan*, *Rajasthani Lok-Nritya* and *Rajasthani Lok-Natya*.

DEVI PRASAD, MUNSHI (1847-1923). Rajastani historian, who was born at Jaipur but he settled at Jodhpur, where he held various posts. Apart from official work, he devoted a good time to the study of history. He donated a sum of Rs. 10,000 to Nagari Pracharini Sabha, Kashi, for the publication of works on history. He in all wrote more than 50 works, mostly on history. His biographies of Akbar, Pratap, Mira were written after a good deal of research. His *Marwar ka Itihas* (1895) was written after thorough research.

DEVI PRASAD GUPTA (1936-). Scholar, whose chief works are : *Adhunik Pratinidhi Hindi Mahakavya* (1971), *Swatantryottar Hindi Mahakavya* (1973) and *Sahitya Siddhant aur Samalochana* (1975).

DEVI PRASAD 'PURNA', RAY (1968-1915). Poet of Kanpur, who composed in Brajbhasha. He rendered into Hindi verse the Sanskrit *Meghaduta* under the title, *Dharadhar Dhavan*, which conveyed the sense of the original. In his native city, he had gathered around him a circle of poets who wrote in the decadent Riti style and he himself has written a considerable number of *Kavittas* and *Savaiyas*. His *Chandrkala Bhanukumar Natak* makes a good reading but is not stage-worthy. He wrote poems in Khari Boli also ; his poem Amaltas (*Cassia Fistula*) represents his attitude towards Nature. His long patriotic poem is : *Vasant Viyoga*.

DEVI PRASAD SHARMA (fl. early 20th cent.). Early writer, whose works are : social novels, e.g., *Vidhva Vipatti* (The Woes of Widowhood ; in collaboration with Radha Charan Goswami) and a drama *Bal Vivah* (Child Marriage). He also wrote picaresque novels with magic and supernatural events.

DEVI SHANKAR AVASTHI (1930-66). Writer, whose chief works are : *Vivek ke Rang* (Aspects of Discernment ; 1965 ; ed., containing the best reviews of the literary works of the decade ; prominent among these reviewers are Nemichandra Jain, Kunvar Narayan, Vijay Dev Narayan Sahi and Ashok Vajpeyi), N*ai Kahani* : *Sandarbh aur Prakriti* (New Short Story : Context and Nature), *Rachna aur Alochana* and *Atharahavin Shatabdi ke Brajbhasha Kavya men Premasakti* (Love-attachment in the 18th century Brajbhasha Poetry ; thesis) ; the introductions to these works contain advanced principles of criticism *Kahani Vividha* (Manifold Short Stories) is a work ed. by him.

DEVI SHANKAR PRABHAKAR. Modern scholar and author of *Hariyana : Kahavaten tatha Lok Kathayen*, *Hastinapur ka Singhasan* and *Ganputra*.

DEVKI NANDAN (fl. 1783-1803). Poet of the Riti school, who lived in Makrand Nagar, a village near Kannauj. His father's name was Shashli Shukla. In 1784, Devki Nandan composed *Shringar Chandrika* (The Moonlight of Shringar), which seeks to deal with the *Rasas*, but a part of it is also devoted to the treatment of *Alankars*, which find a separate treatment in *Sarfraz Chandrika* (1800), a work named after his patron, Sarfraz Giri. Later on, the poet shifted to Ruddamau in Hardoi district, where he composed *Avadhut Bhushan*, a work named after his patron, Avadhut Singh. His fourth work is *Nakh-Shikh*. The poet was master of his craft, though he was fond of manipulating words and ideas. His verses, however, do not become obscure and wearisome.

DEVKI NANDAN KHATRI (1861-1913). Celebrated novelist, whose *Chandrakanta* (1891 ; q.v.) and *Chandrakanta Santati* (1896 ; 24 Pts.) became widely famous within a few years of their appearance ; thousands of people are said to have picked up Hindi merely to be able to read and enjoy these novels. Besides these novels, which are his best-known works, Khatri wrote a few other popular novels : *Narendra-Mohini* (1893), *Virendra Vir* (1896), *Kusum Kumari* (1899), *Kajal ki Kothri* (The Howel of Soot ; 1902), *Anuthi Begum* (The Mysterious Begum ; 1905), *Gupta Godana* (The Secret Tattoo ; 1906), *Bhut Nath* (The Lord of Ghosts ; 56 vols. ; 1897), *Naulakha Har* (The Necklace of Nine Lacs) ; the theme of all these novels is romantic love stories touched with magic and supernatural elements. The novels soon captured popular imagination and brought people closer to Hindi. Among the early Hindi novelists, Khatri occupies an important place.

DEVKI NANDAN TRIPATHI (fl. early 20th cent.). Writer, whose chief works are : *Kaliyugi Janeu* (The Sacred Thread of the Kali Era), *Sita-Haran* (The Abducation of Sita) and *Ek-ek-ke Tin-tin* (Each One to Three Each ; all dramas).

DEVOJI (d. 1667). Rajasthani saint-poet of the Jasnathi Sect, whose minor poems *Gun Mala*, *Desunto* (on the secret dwellings of the Pandavas), *Narayan Lila*, *Dharat Puran*, *Suraj Lila*, *Olambo*, *and Sabad* (30 in number) deal with Guru, God, Mother Earth, Bhakti, Niti, etc. The poems, mostly drawn from oral traditions, have their popular appeal.

DEVO SAHIB (fl 1748). Saint-poet of Gujarat, who was born at the village of Hamla in Kutch, where his *Gaddi* still exists. He had a large number of followers ; he and his followers have composed *Padas* and *Kundliyas* in Hindi. Devo's Hindi works are : *Ramsagar*, *Gyan-Kand*, *Harisagar*, *Upasna* Kand, *Krishna-Sagar*, *Karma-Kand*, etc. His language is simple.

DHANANJAY. Critic, whose chief works are : *Prasad ke Aitihasik Natak* (1974 ; thesis) and *Aj ki Hindi Kahani* (Hindi Short Story of Today ; 1969).

DHANANJAY VERMA. Modern fiction writer, whose chief work is *Andhere ke Vartul* ; he has also published *Adhunikta ke Bare men Tin Adhyay* (criticism ; 1984), *Aswad ke Dharatal*, *Hastkshep* and *Andhera Nagar*.

DHANI RAM. Modern Hindi poet of Fiji, who is known for his stray poems.

DHANI RAM 'PREM' (1904-79). Writer, who was noted for his historical drama, *Virangna Panna* (1934). He was born at the village Dariyapur in Aligarh district of Uttar Pradesh and remained in Birmingham for a long time.

DHANNA BHAGAT (fl. 15th cent.). Saint-poet, who sang of Nirgun Brahma. A Jat by caste, he was born perhaps at the village Dhuan in the then Tank State of Rajasthan and was a disciple of Ramanand. His devotional songs are included in many an anthology of Hindi verse. He was so much steeped in Bhakti that many legends have come to be associated with him, ascribing to him almost supernatural powers. According to the *Bhaktamal*, he did not sow seeds in his fields but had a good harvest. Four of his *Padas* are included in the *Granth Sahib* (q.v.).

DHANNA SINGH (fl. 17th cent.). One of the court-poets of Guru Govind Singh (q. v.) ; he was a master of Brajbhasha and composed verses in praise of the Guru and wrote devotional poetry in the Shringar style.

DHANUKCHAND GYANDATT. Modern Hindi poet of Mauritius, whose chief work is *Kavyakali*.

DHANUKHDHARI LAL DAS. Modern Maithili scholar, who tr. the Hindi work, *Bihari Satsai* into Maithili (1936). His *Muktak* poems are collected in *Maithili Saptashati*.

DHANURDHARI. Modern Rajasthani writer, who is noted for his humorous and satirical essays.

DHARMA (fl. 1209). Jain poet, who composed in Rajasthani

the *Jambuswami Chariya* (q.v.) in 41 verses ; Dharma was a pupil of Mahendra Suri.

DHARMA DAS (fl. between 1418 and 1543). Saint-poet of Bandhavgarh in Madhya Pradesh, who was a Vaishya by caste and was one of the chief disciples of Kabir (q v.). To begin with, Dharmadas was an idol worshipper but after his contact with Kabir at Mathura, he changed his allegiance to Nirgun Bhakti. His wife and his eldest son, Chudamanidas, also embraced the faith of Kabirdas. After his *Guru's* death, he was made his sucessor and his *Gaddi* (centre) is in Chhattisgarh. Like Kabir, he wrote on *Virah*. He contributed a good number of *Dohas* dealing principally with devotion and mysticism, as also composed *Holi*, *Basant*, etc. Amongst his many works, *Sukh Nidhan* is the chief one. His language is racy and natural and bears the full imprint of Eastern Hindi. The main feature of his composition is, however, its adaptability to music.

Since Kabir himself did not write anything, Dharmadas collected all the utterances of his *Guru* and thus preserved them for posterity under the title of *Gita-Kavya*.

DHARMADAS (fl. 1643). Poet, who tr. the Sanskrit *Mahabharata* into Hindi verse.

DHARMADAS, SWAMI (fl. 19th cent.). Sindhi saint-poet, whose stray verses in Hindi are available.

DHARMA PAL AKELA. Writer, who is noted for his drama *Dekho Yeh Purush* (See this Man ; 1983).

DHARMA PAL MAINI. Modern scholar, whose chief works are : *Kabir ke Dharmik Vishwas*, *Shri Guru Granth Sahib : Ek Parichay*, *Madhyayugin Nirgun Chetana* and *Guru Govind Singh ke Sahitya men Bharatiya Sanskriti ke Tattwa*.

DHARMA PAL SHASTRI. Writer, who is noted for his *Buddhi ke Vias ki Kahaniyan tatha Upay* (The Stories for the Development of Intellect and Remedies ; 1980).

DHARMA RAJAN, S. Tamil-speaking modern Hindi writer, who is known for his *Tamil aur Hindi ka Tulnatmak Vyakaran* (A Comparative Grammar of Tamil and Hindi), which is a part of his thesis.

DHARMA SHILA DEVI 'SHASHIKALA'. Modern Magahi poetess, who is known for her stray poems.

DHARMA VARDHAN (Dharmsi ; 1643-1726). Jain Rajasthani poet, who, besides his works in Sanskrit, wrote on a variety of subjects. His major narrative poems are : *Shrenik Chaupai*, *Amarsen Vayarsen Chaupai* and *Sur Sundari Ras*. He used a number of popular poetic styles and his stray verses on miscellaneous topics are well-known. He also described the social and political conditions of his time and eulogized heroes like Durgadas and Shivaji.

DHARMAVIR BHARATI (1926-). Poet and writer, who was born and educated at Allahabad. After passing M.A. (Hindi) from Allahabad University and doing teaching there for some time, he came to Bombay in 1956 to edit 'Dharmayuga' and continues up to this day. His chief works are :

Poetry : Poems in *Dusra Saptak*, *Thanda Loha* (Cold Iron ; 1952) *Sat Git Varsh* (Seven Song Years ; 1959), *Deshantar* (Foreign Country) ; *Andha Yuga* (The Blind Age ; 1954 ; q.v. ; a verse play, describing through the medium of the story from the last day of the Mahabharata War to the death of Krishna) and *Kanupriya* (Krishna's Beloved ; 1959 ; a *Prabandh-Kavya*, depicting the love of Krishna and Radha in a new context).

Novels : *Gunahon ka Devta* (The God of Sins ; 1949 ; based on a romantic tale) and *Suraj ka Satvan Ghora* (The Seventh Horse of the Sun ; 1952 ; a description of modern society through the medium of seven stories with dreams for future).

Short Story Collections : *Chand aur Tute Huye Log* (The Moon and the Broken-hearted People ; 1966) and *Band Gali ka Akhiri Makan* (The Last House of the Blind Alley ; 1969). His important stories are : 'Mariz No 7' (Patient No. 7), 'Dhuan' (Smoke), 'Gulki Banno', 'Savitri No. 2', 'Yeh Mere Liye Nahin' (This is Not For Me) and 'Band Gali ka Akhiri Makan'.

Bharati's other works are : *Nadi Pyasi Thi* (The Stream was Athirst ; a collection of five one-act plays), *Avaz ka Nitam* (dramatic monologue), *Nilijhil* (The Blue Lake ; romantic fantasy), *Thele par Himalaya* (The Himalayas on the Cart), *Kahani Ankahani* and *Yashvanti* (Celebrated ; essay collections) and *Manav Mulya aur Sahitya* (Human Values and Literature ; criticism).

Bharati occupies an important place among modern writers.

DHARMA VIR DHURA. Modern Hindi poet of Mauritius, who is known for his stray poems.

DHARMENDRA GUPTA (1933-). Fiction writer, whose chief short story collections are *Chand Romance-hin Kahaniyan* (Some Unromantic Short Stories) and *Dastaken aur Avazen*. He also ed. *Samkalin Jivan Sandarbh aur Premchand* (7 vols. ; 1980 ; these contain articles by Rahi Masoon Raza, Ramakant, Mastram Kapur, etc.). His important short stories are : 'Ek Dhokha Aur' (One More Deception), 'Ek Main Hun' (I am One) and 'Agyat ka Bhay' (The Fear of the Unknown). His novels are : *Nagar Putra Hansta Hai* (The Son of the City Laughs ; 1978) and *Non Tel Lakri* (Salt, Oil, Wood ; 1981). His critical work is *Aj ki Kahani : Sahi Zamin ki Talash.*

DHARMIPITOLA RATANSAR THERO. Modern Hindi writer of Srilanka, who has promoted the cause of Hindi in his country.

DHARNIDAS (b. 1616). Bhojpuri saint-poet of Manjhi Chhapra, who composed *Prem Pragas* or *Prem Prakash* and *Shabda Prakash*, both devotional.

DHARNIDHAR (fl. prior to 1685). Maithili poet, whose lyrics were quoted in anthologies.

DHARNIKANT DEV SHARMA. Assamese-speaking modern Hindi writer, whose *Kamrup Kamakhya* narrates the history of the Kamakhya Tirth.

DHIRA BHAGAT (1749-1832). Saint-poet of Gujarat, who was born in the village Gothda near Sawli. His Hindi works are : *Gyan-Batisi*, *Atmagyan*, *Sat-Var*, *Bar-Mas*, *Kafiya*, *Guru-Shishya-Prashnottari* and other stray verses. He emphasized the purity of mind for realization of Brahma. The language betrays the strong influence of Gujarati, Panjabi and Rajasthani.

DHIRENDRA. See *Dhirenshwar Jha 'Dhirendra'*.

DHIRENDRA ASTHANA Writer, whose chief works are : *Log Hashiye Par* (The People on the Border-line ; 1980 ; a short story collection), *Samay ek Shabda bhar Nahin Hai* (Time is not merely a Word ; 1981) and *Arambh* (Beginning ; 1983 ; novels).

DHIRENDRA MALL. Modern Hindi poet of Nepal, whose chief work is *Yadon ke Khandahar*. He has also written short stories.

DHIRENDRA NATH MISHRA. Maithili writer, whose *Mrigtrishna* (1982) is a short story collection.

DHIRENDRA VARMA (1897-1973). Linguist and essayist, who got D. Litt. from Paris University on his thesis : 'La Lang Braj' written in Paris under the guidance of Jules Bloch. He was Head of the Department of Hindi at Allahabad University and later on as Editor of *Hindi Vishwa Kosh* and then Vice-Chancellor of Jubbalpur University. His chief works are : *Brajbhasha Vyakaran*, *Brajbhasha* (tr. of his thesis), *Hindi Bhasha ka Itihas* (History of Hindi Language), *Madhyadesh*, *Gramin Hindi* (Rural Hindi), *Hindi Sahitya Kosh* (ed.). *Hindi Bhasha ka Vikas* (Development of Hindi Language ; ed.)., *Adhunik Hindi Kavya* (Modern Hindi Poetry), *Hindi Sahitya* (ed., which includes the literatures of Hindi, Urdu, Dakhini, etc.), *Hindi Rashtra*, *Hindi Bhasha aur Lipi* (Hindi Language and Script), *Vichardhara*, *Ashtachhap*, *Sursagar Sar* as also several essays (*Parishad Nibandhavali*) on Hindi language.

Verma is considered the first scholar, who provided a systematic study of Hindi language and he occupies the foremost place among Hindi linguists.

DHIRENSHWAR JHA 'DHIRENDRA'. Maithili novelist, whose chief works are : *Bhorkava* (1965 ; on new light in the life of the lower classes in the villages), *Kado aor Koila* (1969-70 ; on upgrading the life of the lowly and the downtrodden in the cities) and *Thumki Bahu Kamala* (1982). In his short stories, he has presented quite lively pictures of rural life. He has published poems and lyrics as well.

DHOLA. Braj folk-tale, which is popular in Rajasthan, Bhojpur and other places, with slight variations. Raja Nal of Narwar is born in a jungle and he is adopted as a maternal grandson by a rich merchant, who brings Nal and his mother to his house. When Nal grows young, he accompanies the merchant's sons (his maternal uncles) on a foreign voyage for trade, where he meets Motini, who is the daughter of a demon. Nal kills demon and marries Motini but his maternal uncles throw him into the sea. In the sea, Vasuki, the serpent-god becomes his friend. Nal returns to his house and recovers his wife Motini from his adopted maternal uncles. Nal, however, loses in a game of dice and leaves for the jungle in the company of his another wife, Damyanti. They have to face numerous hardships and during this time, Dhola is born. At a very early age, Dhola is married to Maru, but the sufferings of Nal continue. After a long time, things take a turn for good and thereafter Dhola and Maru live happily.

The story, as popular in Rajasthan, considerably varies from the present version. A version includes the story of Kishan Singh, cousin of Dhola.

DHOLA MARU RA DUHA. Celebrated Rajasthani folk-poem by an unknown poet or according to some scholars by Kallol, which was composed in 1473.

Raja Pingal rules over the Pungal country, while Raja Nal rules over Narwar. Pingal is blessed with a daughter named Marvani, while Nal has a son named Dhola. Once there is a famine in Pungal and as a result of this, Pingal goes to Pushkar to stay there for some time. Raja Nal also visits Pushkar on pilgrimage. Both the Rajas develop friendship which culminates in the marriage of 1½ year old Marvani with 3-year old Dhola. On the onset of autumn, both the Rajas leave for their respective captials. As Marvani is a baby, she does not accompany Dhola.

Years pass by and as Dhola grows into a fine young man, his father re-marries him to Malvani, daugther of Raja of Malwa, thinking that Pungal is a far-off country ; this fact that Dhola had already been married to Marvani had been kept concealed to him. When Marvani grows young, her father sends repeated invitations to Dhola to come and take Marvani with him but Malvani contrives in such a way that all the messengers sent by Pingal are killed on the way to Narwar and no message ever reaches Dhola.

Once Marvani sees Dhola in a dream and she begins to pine for him. Simultaneously, a dealer in horses reaches Pungal from Narwar. He informs Pingal of Dhola's marriage with Malvani. Hearing this, Marvani is mad with love and decides to send a message of love through Dhadhis, well-versed in the art of composing and singing songs. She instructs them to be wary of Marvani's men on the way and that they should reach Dhola's palace by any means and deliver her message to him On hearing the tale of Marvani, Dhola immediately starts for Pungal on a horse but is prevented by Malvani from proceeding there. After a few days when Malvani is asleep, Dhola on his favourite camel reaches Pungal. He is accorded a warm reception and after staying there for a week, he starts for Narwar in the company of his bride, Marvani. On one of the halts, where Dhola has to rest for the night, Marvani is bitten by a snake and dies. Dhola weeps bitterly and prepares to burn himself on the funeral pyre of Marvani. But as good luck would have it, Shiv and Parvati in the guise of a Yogi and Yogini pass through that way and bring back Marvani to life.

But another misfortune awaits them. After Dhola and Marvani proceed on their camel for some distance, they are overtaken by Umar, who wants to snatch away Marvani from Dhola. Umar induces Dhola to step down from his camel and share with him Kasumba, a drink mixed with opium. Dhola gets down from his camel but on an indication given to Marvani by one of the ladies of Umar, Marvani by a clever ruse calls Dhola towards her and warns him of the plot of Umar. Dhola and Marvani run away on their camel ; Umar's army pursues them but Dhola is more than a match for them. Dhola and Marvani reach Narwar and live happily thereafter.

One of the most well-known and legendary Rajasthani poems, the remarkable thing about this is that through a simple story, the intense and manifold emotions of love have been expressed in a clear and homely style. The messages of separation by Marvani to Dhola "through human agency of Dhadhis and through the messengers of nature, such as clouds and birds, convey not only the feelings of the departed love but also the physical throb of it. It is essentially human and has, therefore, a universal appeal. The poem is unique among love poems and is rich in local colour."

Owing to the popularity of the theme, many poetic versions and recensions are found, among which the present version and the *Doha-Chaupai* version of Kushal Labh (q.v.) are more popular. The *Duha* version published by the Nagari Pracharini Sabha, Kashi, consisting of 674 verses is a good attempt, though it requires re-editing. With minor variations, the story of Dhola-Maru is also popular in the neighbouring regions of Rajasthan. The version by Kushal Labh retells the legend with certain variations. The marriage of Maru's parents, Raja Pingal and Uma Devadi, is given in a prologue and is an independent tale in itself.

DHOLA MARVANI CHAUPAHI. Dingal poem (1560) by Harraj, which describes the romance of Nalvargarh prince Salha (Dhola) and princess Marav. In Bikaner, four scripts (written in *Dohas*) of this work bearing the title *Dhola Maru ra Duha* are extant. The story is also popular in Braj and Bhojpuri regions with slight variations. Some scholars are of the view that the earliest version of this work was extant in the 11th century as Hemchandra in his *Vyakaran* has quoted certain *Duhas* from it. As it was a popular lay, it changed at several hands. The poets, Kallol and Kushal Labh are considered the authors of some portions of this work.

DHOLAN, RAJA. Bhojpuri version of the Dhola-Maru legend, which is popular in Rajasthan. According to the Bhojpuri folk-tale in verse, Dholan, son of Raja Nal, was married to the daughter Maru of Raja Budh of Pinkalgarh. Dholan goes to other lands and falls in love with Hareva and Pareva, the two young ladies. Ultimately, Dholan meets Maru and they live happily thereafter. See *Dhola Maru ra Duha*.

DHOORUNDHUR, RAMDEO. See *Ramdeo Dhoorundhur.*

DHRUVDAS (fl. 1573-1643). Poet of the Krishna-cult, who became a disciple of Hit Harivansh (q.v.) in a dream. He was born at Deoband in the Saharanpur district of Uttar Pradesh but came to live in Vrindavan at the feet of his Guru. He was a voluminous writer, the number of his works running into 40. His chief works are : *Dhruvdas krit Bani* (Discourses of Dhruvdas), *Siddhant Vichar* (On Principles ; in prose), *Bhakta-Namavali* (Roll of Devotees ; on the pattern of *Bhaktamal* ; q.v.).

DHRUV JAISWAL. Writer, whose *Bahon ka Rin* (The Debt of the Hands ; 1981) and *Jal-kumbhi* are novels.

DHRUV MADHIKARMI. Modern Hindi poet of Nepal, who is noted for his stray poems.

DHRUVSWAMINI. Drama (1933) in 3 Acts by Jayshankar Prasad (q.v.), which makes a contrast between the imbecile Ramgupta and his brave and honourable brother Chandragupta ; the sufferings of Dhruvswamini arouse pity and resentment. The story reveals how Chandragupta is able to save the honour of Dhruvswamini and other ladies by killing the Shak king.

DHUMAN. Rajasthani Charan, whose stray verses are available ; his time is not certain.

DHUMANAND (1795-1867). Gujarati-speaking saint-poet of Swaminarayan Sect, whose *Vasudev Mahatmya* in Hindi glorifies Vasudev and is based on the 'Vishnu-Khand' of the *Skand Puran*. The work is divided into 32 chapters.

DHUMIL (1936-75). Poet, whose chief collection of poems is *Sansad se Sarak Tak* (From the Parliament to the Road ; 1972). He received posthumous award from Sahitya Akademi for his second collection : *Kal Mujhe Sunoge* (1977 ; Tomorrow, You would Listen to Me). His poetry is a combination of emotion, irony and the suffering of the common man caught in social contradictions.

DHUMKETU. Modern Maithili writer and poet, who is noted for his short stories (*Agurvan a anya Katha* ; 1979 ; a collection of nine stories), poems and lyrics. His works in Khari

Boli are : *Mati ki Mahak, Vasmati* (novels), *Anjuri Bhar Rakh* and *Ek thi Shakun Di* (short story collection).

DHUNYAL. Garhwali collection of folk-songs (1954), which was edited by Abodh Bahuguna.

DHURI (1972). Maithili anthology of some of the most expressive modern poems, which represents Bhim Nath Jha, Upendra Doshi, Uday Chandra Jha, Yugabodh, Hans Raj, Dhirendra, Dhumketu, Madhukar, Tara Kant Prakash and Ram Anugrah Jha.

DHURTTA SAMAGAM (The Confluence of the Knaves). Earliest Maithili farce, which was written by Jyotirishwar Kavishekhar (q.v.) around 1324.

A *Sannyasi* (really a fraudulent knave) named Vishwanagar and his disciple Snatak approach a wealthy miser for food, but are directed instead to go to the house of a 'pious' lady, Suratpriya. The lady, though old, is also a knave and she falls in love with the good-looking *Sannayasi*, who also succumbs to her charms. While she starts preparing a good number of things for midday meal for her lover, Snatak goes to meet Anangsena, a courtesan, with whom he is in love ; he is accompanied also by his preceptor. As both of them fight for Anangsena, she commends Asajjati Mishra as the arbitrator ; the arbitrator himself falling in love with the lady, takes her away from both. A barber comes and demands payment from Anangsena for having shaved her private parts. He is also directed to meet Asajjati. As Asajjati gives insufficient payment, he is beaten by the barber, who leaves him with his hands and feet tied. Then Asajjati's friend, Vidushak comes to release him. As the title suggests, it is all an assembly of knaves.

There are in all 20 Maithili songs inserted in it, out of which eight are missing in the extant text.

Jyotirishwar also composed in Sanskrit a farce with a similar title and theme.

DHUSWA SAYAMI (Govind Bahadur Manandhar). Modern Hindi novelist of Nepal, whose works are : *Main Dasi Main Sarai, Ret ki Darar* and *Zalzala*. His novel *Ganki*, written in Newari. has been quite popular and has been tr. into Hindi by Kamta Kamlesh. Dhuswva Sayami has also written poems and short stories.

DHYANDAS (fl. 16th cent.). Rajasthani saint-poet, who was a follower of Haridas Niranjani Sampraday. His poems, *Gun*

Maya Sanvad, Gunadi Bodh and over 100 *Chandrayans* are didactic.

DHYAN MAKHIJA. Modern novelist, whose chief works *Banithani* and *Jethva Ujli* are based on old Rajasthani romances; *Satya-Asatya* is a collection of his short stories.

DHYANANAND, SWAMI (fl. 1830). Gujarati-speaking saint-poet of Swaminarayan Sect, whose chief works in Hindi are: *Harigita* and *Dharmamrit*.

DIAS, D.F.X. Author of *A Vocabulary in Five Languages: English, Portuguese, Goa, Marathi and Hindustani, Printed in the Roman Character* (Satara, 1878).

DIDAR SINGH. Dogri-speaking Hindi writer, whose *Dhundhalke* is a collection of 18 short stories.

DIKSHIT, ANAND PRAKASH. See *Anand Prakash Dikshit*.

DILIP KUMAR BANERJI. Poet, whose chief work *Akela Nahin Main* (1983) is a poetical collection.

DIMASITSA, J.M. Scholar, whose chief work is *Hindi Vyakaran ki Ruprekha* (1966). He also wrote a number of articles on Hindi language.

DIN, AMIYA. See *Amiya Din*.

DIN BANDHU JHA. Modern Maithili scholar, who is known for his Maithili grammar (*Mithilabhasha Vidyotan Dhath*) and lexicon (*Mithilabhasha Shabdakosh*).

DIN DARVESH (fl 1st part of 19th cent.). Hindi poet of Palanpur, Gujarat, who was a blacksmith by profession. He used to manufacture arms for the East India Company when he met an accident. He left his profession and became a disciple of Balgiri of the Nath Sect. His verses betrary the Sufi influence. He and another Din Darvesh (q.v.) may or may not be the same.

DIN DARVESH (*c* 1753-1833). Rajasthani saint-poet, who was born at Gudali (Udaipur Division) and was initiated by Bal Bharati or Bal Guru of Girnar. He used to reside at Kailashpuri or Ekling Temple near Udaipur. Maharana Bhim Singh (1777-1828) held him in high esteem, but after the Maharana's death, he moved over to Kota and was drowned while taking a bath in the Chambal river. His poems dealing with a variety of subjects on Bhakti, are *Din Prakash, Granth Adalanand, Parmarth Prasang, Chitavan Sar, Isar Astut, Raj Chetavani, Bhram Tod, Kakka Battisi, Gagad Nisani, Padas* and stray verses. He has used popular forms such as *Barahmasa, Garabi, Phag*, etc. His language is Rajasthani with slight mixtures of Braj and Khari Boli. He and another Din Darvesh (q.v.) may or may not be the same.

DIN DAYAL GIRI, BABA (1802-1915). Poet, who passed all his life as a mendicant in Kashi. He was a friend of Girdhar Das (q.v.), father of Bharatendu. An erudite Sanskrit scholar as he was, some of his works bear the impress of his learning. But he is primarily known for his *Anyokti Kalpadrum*, a collection of short allegorical poems on a variety of subjects. His other works are : *Anurag Bagh* (1888 ; on the exploits of Krishna), *Vairagya Dinesh* (describing seasons, etc) *Vishwanath Navratna* (on extolling Shankar), *Anyoktimala* and *Drishtant Tarangini* (couplets on worldly wisdom).

A versatile poet, his style is sometimes very simple, while at others it is highly ornate ; invariably, it has a tender grace and mellifluousness. Here and there his poetry has also some metaphysical tendencies.

The Kashi Nagari Pracharini Sabha has published *Din Dayal Giri Granthavali* (1919), edited by Shyam Sundar Das.

DIN DAYAL KUNDAN. Modern Rajasthani novelist, whose chief work is *Gunvar Patho*.

DIN DAYAL OJHA. Rajasthani scholar, who has made significant contribution to the study of Rajasthani folk songs. His poem, 'Manavata ra Akhar' emphasizes the value of human nature. He has also written, mostly for children, short biographies of many national, religious and social leaders in his *Desh ra Gaurav* (1972), *Bharat ra Nirmata* (1972) and *Chhoti Umar Mota Kam* (1972).

DIN DAYALU GUPTA (1903-69). Writer, whose chief works is : *Ashtachhap aur Vallabh Sampraday* (Ashtachhap and Vallabh Sect ; thesis). He was Professor of Hindi in Lucknow University.

DIN GOPAL (fl. 17th-18th centuries). Assamese poet, whose Hindi (Brajavali) works are : *Jarasandh Badh* and *Sita-Haran*, both dramas.

DIN KRISHNADAS (fl. 17th cent.). Oriya-speaking Hindi (Brajboli) poet, whose *Rasa-Kalol* is noted for its sweetness and intensity of love. He also composed some Riti-works as also stray verses.

DIN SUNDARDI (fl. end of 18th cent.). Rajasthani saint-poet of the Vishnoi Sect, whose stray verses are available.

DINA NATH KHATRI. Modern Rajasthani writer, who is noted for his sketches.

DINA NATH PATHAK. Maithili poet, whose *Chanakya* (1965) is the epic of modern Mithila. The poet has conceived Chanakya as the popular leader of the masses in Mithila, who knows how to rouse the spirit of the people for a national cause.

DINESH KHARE. Modern Rajasthani writer, whose *Nuvon Marag*, a collection of one act-plays, treats of social reforms.

DINESH KUMAR JHA. Maithili scholar, whose *Maithili Sahityak Alochanatmak Itihas* (1979) is a critical literary history.

DINESH MISHRA. Rajasthani poet, whose *Bharat Surya* (1965) describes in easy Rajasthani mainly the battle of Haldighati.

DINESH NANDINI DALMIA (1916-). Poetess, who was born in a Vaishya family of Udaipur. She was married to Seth Ramkrishna Dalmia. Her chief works are : *Uravati*, *Parichhaya* (Complete Shadow ; poem), *Iti* (Conclusion ; a collection of her 88 poems) ; *Shabnam* (Dew) *Unmana* (Absent-mindedness), *Sarang* (Cuckoo), *Spandan* (Throbbing), *Sharadiy* (Autumnal), *Mauktikmal* (The Garland of Pearls), *Dupahriya ke Phul* (Flowers of Noontime), *Vanshi Rav* (The Music of the Flute) (prose-poems), *Sharbari* (poems), *Mujhe Maf Karna* (Excuse Me), *Kandil ka Dhuan* and *Aur Suraj Dub Gaya* (novels).

DINESH PATHAK. Writer, whose *Shayad Yah Ant-hin* (Perhaps this is Endless ; 1982) is a short story collection, depicting economic hardships.

DINKAR. See *Ramdhari Singh Dinkar*.

DINKAR SONVALKAR (1933-). Poet, whose chief work is *A se Asabhyata* (S for Savagery; 1972) ; *Pratinidhi Marathi Kavitayen* (Representative Marathi Poems) is a work ed. by him. Three more collections of his poems are : *Ankur ki Kritagyata*, *Pidhiyon ka Darshan* and *Divaron ke Khilaf*.

DINKAR YADAV MARDIKAR (fl. 1850-1900). Marathi-speaking Hindi dramatist, who wrote a drama : *Sudarshan.*

DIPCHAND, PANDIT (fl. last decade of 19th cent.). Famous Haryana folk-poet, who composed and staged the *Sangs* : *Sorath, Sarande Raja Bhoj, Nal-Damayanti, Gopichand Maharaj, Harishchandra, Uttanpad* and *Jyani Chor.* The first *Sang, Sorath,* became so popular that Kutbi, who played the role of Sorath, was weighed in silver by the residents of the village Chalka in district Rohtak. At the time of the First World war, the services of Dipchand were requisitioned by the then British Government for enlisting recruitment to the army and Dipchand's songs in this regard are popular to this day.

DIPCHAND BIHARI. Modern Hindi writer of Mauritius, whose *Sagar Par* is a short story collection. *Swarg men Kya Rakha Hai* and *Masihe Narak Jite Hain* are his novels.

DIPSHIKHA. See *Mahadevi Verma.*

DIPTI KHANDELWAL (1930-). Fiction writer of Hyderabad ; her chief works are : *Vah Tisra* (That Third), *Salib Par* (On the Stone), *Dhup ke Ahsas* (Feelings of Sunshine ; 1977), *Aurat aur Nate, Nariman* (all short story collections), *Priya* (*The Beloved*), *Kohre* and *Pratidhwaniyan* (novels).

DIVAKAR, RAN. RA. Kannada-speaking modern Hindi writer, who has tr. M.R. Shrinivasmurti's Kannada drama, *Nagrik.* Divakar's Kannada work *Antaratmanige* has been tr. into Hindi as *Antaratma* (Conscience).

DIVAKAR BALAJI JOGLEKAR. Marathi-speaking modern Hindi writer, whose chief work is *Shri Smarth Ramdas Charitra.*

DIVAKAR JHA. Modern Maithili writer, whose essays in *Adhunikta* are serious and thoughtful.

DIVIK RAMESH. Poet, whose chief collection of poems is *Khuli Ankhon men Akash* (The Sky in Open Eyes ; 1980) ; he has also edited *Nishedh ke Bad* (After *Nishedh* ; 1981), a collection of poems by 13 poets.

DIVYA. Historical novel (1945) by Yashpal (q.v.), which is one of his major novels. It has been translated into many Indian and foreign languages. It describes the events that took place in Buddhist India of 2nd cent B.C. with the background of the sufferings of a woman.

King Milind defeats the Paurav king of Madra, but when

Milind becomes a Buddhist monk and renounces his kingdom, the nobles, in the absence of an heir to the kingdom, establish an oligarchy in Madra. The people there think that the country belongs to the nobles and they cannot look upon their country as their own. Prestha becomes rich but he cannot be a member of the Council as he belongs to a low caste. His son, Prithu Sen, is given the honour of being declared 'The Finest Swordsman' but he cannot carry on his shoulder princess Divya's palanquin as he is of a low caste. Princess Divya, a beautiful and talented girl of artistic taste, adores Prithu Sen but she cannot love him freely as she belongs to a higher caste. With Prithu's child in her womb, she awaits Prithu's return from the battlefield. He returns wounded but misunderstands Divya's love and consequently falls in love with another girl, Siro. The helpless Divya leaves Madra and wanders from place to place. She suffers great humiliation and is forced to act as a public woman. After becoming a dancer, she returns to Madra, where princess Mallia declares Divya to be her heir but the Brahmins do not allow a prostitute to rule over them. Divya rejects the proposal of Rudradhir, who wishes to marry her as also Prithu Sen's proposal to become a nun as he has become a Buddhist monk. She prefers to marry Marish, whose approach to life resembles Marxism. What Marish says at the end is the sum and substance of the author's philosophy: "Marish cannot keep his beloved in a palace like a queen. He cannot assure her of the eternal happiness of *nirvan*. He feels the joys and sorrows of life. He can exchange experiences of life with her. He is a wanderer on the dusty road of the world. On that path, the man in him meets the woman in Divya. He believes in mutual give-and-take. He can also give her immortality in the form of children born to them."

DIVYA GIRI. Modern Hindi poet of Nepal, who is noted for his stray poems.

DIVYA SINGH, THE FIRST (fl. 18th cent.) Oriya-speaking Hindi (Brajboli) poet, whose *Padas* are available.

DO SAU BAVAN VAISHNAVAN KI VARTA. See *Gokulnath*.

DOHAKOṢH. Collection of *Dohas*, composed by the Siddha poets : Sarahapa, Minapa, Luipa, Shabarpa, Dombiha, Kanhapa, etc. from the 8th to the 12th centuries ; the *Padas*, composed by these Siddhas are collected in *Charyapada* or *Charyagit*.

The manuscript was first discovered in the beginning of this century by Mahamahopadhyay Har Prasad Shastri in Nepal Durbar Library. The *Dohakosh* was edited by M. Shahidullah (Paris, 1928) and by Prabodh Chandra Bagchi (Calcutta, 1939), while the *Charyapada* has been edited by Prabodh Chandra Bagchi under the title *Charyagitikosh* (1956). Many more examples have been brought to light by Rahul Sankrityayan (q.v.). The theme of the *Dohas* is Tantric Yoga-Sadhana, mysticism, religious and philosophical beliefs with ethical strains. The traditional name for the language used is termed 'Sandhya Bhasha', i.e., 'Twilight Tongue', quite close to Apabhransh. See *Sarahapa*.

DOHAVALI Poem by Tulsidas (q.v.) in Avadhi dialect, written in 1583 (?).

In 573 verses (551 *Dohas* and 22 *Sorthas*), it deals with ethical codes, devotion, glorification of Ram and other autobiographical references. The work is partly gleaned from Tulsidas's other works, for only 320 verses are new.

DOI, KYUYA (1916-83). Japanese Hindi scholar, who learnt Hindi in Japan from Mrs. Ratnam, while he was teaching Urdu in 1949 in the Tokyo University of Foreign Studies. After his study in Hindi at Allahabad University for 2 years (1953-54), he tried to get a separate department of Hindi established and he was successful in 1959, when the then existing Department was converted into Bharat-Pakistan Department with 15 seats each for Urdu and Hindi teaching. He prepared *Hindi-Japanese Dictionary*, which is a singular contribution to Hindi studies in Japan. Apart from other articles, in July 1979, Doi wrote an article 'Hindustani, Urdu, Hindi 'which was published in the 'Tsushin' of Tokyo University of Foreign Studies. Doi has also published *Japanese-Hindi Dictionary*, *Japani Bhasha Pravesh*, *Hindi Vartalap*, etc. He had been honoured in 1978 by the Government of India by the award of 'Vishwa Hindi Puraskar'. After his retirement from Tokyo University, Doi taught Hindi in Tokai University, which is a private University. He had been able to prepare a band of Hindi scholars, who now occupy important positions in various Universities.

DOMBIPA (9th cent.). Siddha poet and author of *Dombigitika* and *Yogacharya*.

DONALDSON, SUSAN K. American Hindi scholar, whose chief work is : *On the derivation of Hindi restrictive relating clauses from a Conjoined Source (1973)*.

DONDI, NATALIYA ALEXANDROVNA (1932-). Soviet Hindi scholar, who taught Russian in Delhi. She is noted for the editing of the writings in Hindi of Lenin, Marx, Gorky's *Mother* and the Russian folk-tales.

DOWSON, JOHN. Author of *A Grammar of the Urdu or Hindustani Language* (London, 1872) and *A Classical Dictionary of Hindu Mythology and Religion, Geography, History and Literature* (1879).

DRONVIR KOHLI. Novelist, whose chief works are : *Haveliyon Vale* (The Residents of Mansions ; 1980) and *Chaukhat* ; *Barah Baras Bete* is his short story collection.

D'ROZARIO, P S. Author of *A Dictionay of the Principal Languages in the Bengal Presidency, viz., English, Bengali and Hindustani in the Roman Character* (Calcutta, 1837).

DUBEY, K.N. Author of *Hindi as a Second Language* (3rd ed. 1971).

DUDH NATH SINGH (1936-) Short story writer and poet, whose chief works are : *Sapat Chehare Vala Admi* (A Man with a Flat Face ; 1967), *Sukhant* (Happy Ending ; 1971), *Raktapat* (Bloodshed), *Pahla Kadam* (short story collections), *Nirala ki Atmahanta Astha* (Nirala's faith in Suicide ; critical work ; thesis), *Apni Shatabdi ke Nam* (To our Century) and *Ek aur bhi Admi Hai* (poetical collections) His prominent short stories are : 'Vijeta' (The Victor), 'Dukhant' (The Tragic End), etc.

DUDH NATH UPADHYAY (fl. early 20th cent.). Bhojpuri poet, who was a native of Daya Chhapra village of Balia district. Out of his three works : *Bharti ke Git* (inspiring recruitment in army during the First World War), *Go-Vilap Chhandavali* (on cow slaughter) and *Bhukamp Pachisi*, the first one was very popular.

DUDO ASIYO AMARAVAT (fl. 1528/33-1613). Dingal poet, who was patronized by Rao Sultan of Sirohi. He composed 21 verses in *Kundaliya* metre on Kalla Raimalot of Siwana, who died in a battle with the Mughal army in 1588 ; stray verses on contemporary heroes are also available. His characterization of the hero is natural and genuine.

DUDOJI (d. 1673). Rajasthani poet, whose chief works are *Harchand Puran* and *Prahlad Puran*.

DUDO VISRAL (fl. 1557). Dingal poet, whose *Rathore Ratansingh ri Veli* in 72 verses, describes the battle between Ratansingh of Jaitaran against the Mughal army under the command of Shah Kulikhan in 1557. The poem is noted for maintaining a metaphor of battle and marriage throughout the poem, e.g., the hostile army has been likened to young '*Vish-kanya*' (poisonous maiden) in the role of a bride, while Ratansingh is the bridegroom.

DUGAR, R.K. Rajasthani scholar, whose chief work is *Karanidan Kavia : Vyaktitva aur Krititva* (1978).

DULAH (fl. 1743-68). Poet of the Riti school, who was grandson of Kalidas Trivedi (q.v.) and a son of Udaynath Kavindra (q.v.), both eminent poets, the latter being the poet-laureate at the court of Raja of Amethi. He composed some memorable stray poems and also *Kavi-Kul Kanthabharana* (Neck-ornament of Poet's family), a popular work on *Alankars*. In this work, a single *Kavitta* or *Savaiya* performs the two-fold function of enumerating the features of a particular figure and then illustrating it. This helps in easily memorising the verses. His verses, though meagre in quantity, are of high quality and the name of their author is named along with Dev, Bhikharidas and Matiram (qq.v.).

'*DULAIVALI*' (The Bride ; 1907). Short story, written by Bang Mahila (q.v.), which is taken as one of the earliest short stories and sometimes as the first short story in Hindi.

DULANDAS (fl. *c.* 1770). Saint-poet of Racbareli, who, though a follower of Nirgun Brahma, believed in Krishna Bhakti. He was a disciple of Jagjivan Das.

DULARE LAL BHARGAV (1895-1975). Poet of Lucknow, who was the proprietor of Ganga Pustakmala, which published works of many eminent Hindi writers. He composed *Dulare Dohavali* on the pattern of *Bihari Satsai*.

DULHAI RAM (1794-1824). Rajasthani saint-poet, who was made Acharya of Ram Snehi Sect (see *Ramcharan*) in 1810. His *Vani*, equal to 14,000 *Shlokas*, consists of *Sakhi*, *Chandrayan*, etc. The emphasis in his poems is on Ram Bhakti.

DUNGAR SINGH (fl. 1605). Rajasthani poet, whose stray verses in popular metres are available.

DUNGARSI (fl. 1653). Rajasthani poet, who was a protege of Raoraja Shatrusal of Bundi. The poet was gifted the village

Nainva, which still remains with the descendants of the poet. He was the author of *Shatrusal Raso*, a work in about 500 metres, dealing with the valour and splendour of Shatrusal.

DUNGARSI SADH (fl. 17th cent.). Rajasthani saint-poet of Laldasi Sect, who composed a biography of his Guru Laldas (q.v.), entitled *Shri Laldas Maharaj ki Parichavali* in 580 verses in easy Rajasthani. It is the only old biography of Laldas.

DURAISWAMY, H. Tamil-speaking modern Hindi writer, who is the author of *Nani ki Kahani* (The Stories of Maternal Grandmother) and *Auvaiyar ki Kathayen* (The Tales from Auvaiyar), mainly for children.

DURGA CHARAN PATTANAIK. Oriya-speaking modern Hindi writer, whose chief work is *Meghakrant*.

DURGADAN SINGH GAUR. Modern Rajasthani poet, who has composed Nature, patriotic and progressive poems.

DURGA DAS (fl. end of 18th cent.). Rajasthani saint-poet of the Vishnoi Sect, whose stray verses are available.

DURGA DATT MISHRA (fl. 19th cent. ?). Maithili poet, who tr. from the Sanskrit original the *Durga-Saptashati* into Maithili.

DURGA DATT PANDE. Writer, who composed *Ram Natak* (1924), which was designed for performances lasting many nights, each night portraying a few incidents from Ram's life ; it was meant for Ramlila.

DURGA DHAR JHA. Maithili scholar, whose chief work on Sankhya philosophy is *Sankhya Shastra* (1974).

DURGA DIKSHIT. Marathi-speaking modern Hindi scholar, whose chief works are : *Rasa Siddhant ka Samajik Mulyankan* and *Natak aur Natya Shailiyan*. She has also published poems on various subjects.

DURGA NATH JHA 'SHRISH' (1929-). Maithili critic and poet, whose *Sahitya Vimarsh* advocates Western principles of literary criticism. He has successfully told in verse Puranic tales in *Mahamatsya O Manu* (1961).

DURGA PRASAD KHATRI (1895-1973). Writer, who was noted for his historical novel, *Anangpal*. Son of Devki Nandan Khatri (q.v.), he completed the remaining volumes of *Bhut Nath*

(Lord of Ghosts) and wrote *Lal Panja* (The Red Paw). In his famous novels such as *Rakta Mandal* (The Blood Zone, 1927) and *Kala Chor* (The Black Thief; 1932), there are characters who breathe the spirit of revolution.

DURGA PRASAD SHRESHTH UPENDRA. Modern Hindi novelist of Nepal, whose chief works are : Untalis, *Chandi Ghosh Street*, *Sattare Mausi* (awarded by the Uttar Pradesh Government) and *Soniya*. He has composed poems as well.

DURGA SATTASI. See *Kushal Labh*.

DURGA SHANKAR MISHRA. Modern scholar, who has made studies on the works of Ram Chandra Shukla, Agyey, Nirala, Mahadevi Verma, Niraj and Siyaram Sharan Gupta.

DURGASHANKAR PRASAD SINGH 'NATH' (1896-1971). Bhojpuri scholar, whose chief works are : *Bhojpuri ke Kavi aur Kavya* (The Bhojpuri Poets and their Poetry, 1958) and *Bhojpuri Lok-Giton men Karun-rasa* (research). Nath was born at the village Dalip Pur in Shahabad district of Bihar.

DURGAVATI SINGH. Poetess, who is noted for her works : *Pattiyon ke Bich Se* (From the Midst of Leaves ; 1981) and *Kahin Khulu Akash Nahin* ; *Sidhi-Sadi Yaden* describes her recollections.

DURGESH (fl. 1825). Writer, who composed *Dwaitadwaitavad* ; the work, however, is written in the name of Jay Singh, the Ruler of Rewa.

DURMIL (fl. 18th cent ?). Maithili poet, whose verses found respectable place in contemporary anthologies.

DURSA ADHA (1538-1651). Dingal poet, who was more famous than Sandu Mala (q v) and received gifts from many contemporary rulers and chieftains for his poems. Many stories about his meetings with Bairamkhan and Emperor Akbar are current in Rajasthan, but they lack historicity. His works are : *Virud Chhihattari* (eulogy of Rana Pratap in *Dohas*, though all of them may not be from the pen of Dursa Adha), *Duha Solanki Viramdevji Ra*, *Jhulna Rao Surthan Ra*, *Marsiya Rao Surtan Ra*, *Jhulna Raja Mansingh Kachhwaha Ra*, *Jhulna Ravat Megha Ra*, *Git Raji Shri Rohitasji Ra*, *Jhulna Rao Amarsingh Gajsinghot Ra* (this narrative poem exhibits all the characteristics of Charan heroic and historical poetry and is a classic of this style), *Kirtar Bavni* (52 *Dohas* on the realistic view of life, though some scholars doubt its authorship) and stray verses in different metres on Rana Pratap, Devidas Jaitavat, Hathi Gopaldasot, Nawab Mohabbat Khan, Tog Surtanot, Bhati Bhim, Bhim Amarsinghot, Rao Surtan, etc. and about 120 *Gits* on various contemporary heroes and happenings which have made him very popular.

It is significant that the poet has eulogized persons who opposed each other, such as Rana Pratap and Akbar, Viramdev and Mohabbat Khan, etc. but the poet hails those who opposed the Mughals as saviours of Hinduism and Hindustan, while he does not concede this virtue to others.

DUSHYANT KUMAR (1933-75). Poet and novelist, whose chief works are : *Surya ka Swagat* (Welcome to the Sun), *Avazon ke Ghere* (The Rings of Sounds), *Saye men Dhup* (The Sunshine in the Shade), *Pukarti Dishayen* (Calling Directions), *Ek Kanth Vishpayi* (A Throat which has Drunk Poison ; 1963 ; a poetic drama based on the mythological story of Daksh yagya, depicting the present-day India), *Jalte Hue Van ka Vasant* (The Spring of a Burning Forest ; 1972 ; all poetical collections), *Angan men Ek Vriksh* (A Tree in Yard ; 1969) and *Chhote-chhote Saval* (Short Questions ; novelettes).

DUSRA SAPTAK (The Second Septet). Anthology of Nai Kavita (New Poetry), published in 1951 and edited by Agyey (q.v.). It contains the select poems of Bhavani Prasad Mishra, Shakuntala Mathur, Hari Narayan Vyas, Shamsher Bahadur Singh, Naresh Mehta, Raghuvir Sahay and Dharma Vir Bharati (qq.v.). See *Tar Saptak*.

DWARIKA NATH BHATT (b. 1693). Poet of the Riti school, who was son of Shrikrishna Bhatt Tailang. He was patronized by Maharaja Madho Singh and Maharaja Pratap Singh. His works are : *Madhukar Kalanidhi*, *Vani Vairagya*, *Rag Chandrika*, *Shak Chandrika*, etc.

DWARIKA PRASAD. Modern writer, whose chief work *Ghere ke Bahar* (Outside the Boundary) is a psychological novel, which earned notoriety as it was banned in Bihar ; his second novel *Pahiye* (The Wheels) did not get much recognition. His other novels are : *Ankush* and *Sambandh*. He edited 'Nar-Nari', a magazine on sex.

DWARIKA PRASAD GUPTA. Writer, who wrote a drama, *Agyatvas* (Incognito Stay of the Pandavs in the forest ; 1920).

DWARIKA PRASAD MISHRA (1901-). Poet, who was born at the village Padhri in the Unnao district. His father's name was Ayodhya Prasad Mishra. He has ed. a number of papers and participated in the freedom movement. His *Krishnayan* on the model of *Ramcharitmanas* (q.v.) was composed, while he was in jail ; it deals with the life and deeds of Krishna ; the language of the poem is Avadhi. His other poetical works are : *Anudita* and *Dharma Kshetre Kurukshetre*. He was Chief Minister of Madhya Pradesh. He also translated Ghalib and wrote his autobiography in English.

DWARIKA PRASAD SAXENA. Modern scholar, whose chief works are : *Kamayani men Kavya, Sanskriti aur Darshan, Prasad Darshan, Prasad ka Muktak Kavya* and *Dinkar ka Kavya*.

DWARAKA DAS DADHVADIYA (fl. latter half of 17th cent.). Rajasthani poet, whose *Ajitsinghji ri Davavait* (composed prior to 1669) eulogizes its hero.

DWARKA PRASAD. Writer, who was noted for his one-act plays, *e.g.*, *Admi* (The Man ; 1940).

DWARKA PRASAD. See *Dwarika Prasad*.

DWARKA PRASAD MAURYA. Writer, who wrote a historical drama, *Haidar Ali* (1934).

DWARKA PRASAD TIWARI 'VIPRA' (1908-81). Chhattisgarhi folk-poet, whose chief works are : *Kachhu Kahi* (1935) and *Suraj Git* (1957). He was born in Bilaspur of Madhya Pradesh.

DWIJDEV, MAHARAJA MANSINGH (1823-73). Poet of the Riti school, who was ruler of Ayodhya (the birth place of Ram), though in numerous verses he sang of Radha and Krishna. Both of his works *Shringar-Battisi* (Thirty-two couplets on Shringar) and *Shringar Latika* have been published. He comes at the end of a long chain of poets who for about two centuries had written on *Shringar Rasa*. But his artistic qualities also deserve to be recognised : his poetry is tender and musical ; there is rhythm and the expressions are softest and most appropriate. His poetry gracefully abounds in current maxims and invented epigrams. The description of changing seasons is spontaneous, revealing the poet's own delight, his *Shringar* often merges into *Bhakti*. In short, his poetry is excellent and is rated high by modern critics.

DWIJ HARIDAS (fl. early 16th cent.). Bengali Vaishnav poet, who also composed *Padas* in Brajbuli.

DWIJENDRA NATH MISHRA 'NIRGUN' (1916-). Writer, whose chief works are : *Ye Galiyan Ye Raste* (These Alleys, These Paths ; novel), *Lajvanti, Harungi Nahin* and *Meri Priya Kahaniyan* (My Favourite Short Stories ; short story collections).

DWIREPH. See *Surendra Jha 'Suman'*.

DWIVEDI, HAZARI PRASAD. See *Hazari Prasad Dwivedi.*

DWIVEDI, MAHAVIR PRASAD. See *Mahavir Prasad Dwivedi.*

DWIVEDI, RAM AWADH. Author of *Hindi Literature* (1953) and *Hindi Sahitya ke Vikas ki Ruprekha.*

DYMSHITS, ZALMAN MOVISEYEVICH (1921-). Soviet Hindi scholar, who is Chairman of the Department of Indian Languages in the Moscow State Institute of International Relations. He was awarded the Nehru Award in 1969. His chief works are : *Hindi Vyakaran ki Ruprekha* (1966), *Hindi Vyakaran* (1979), Hindi-Russian and Russian-Hindi dictionaries and *Hindi Pathya Pustak* (3 Pts) and works on Hindi grammar and language. He has written a number of articles on the various problems of Hindi grammar. He has written yet another work on Hindi grammar, which has been tr. by Yogendra Pal from Russian into Hindi as *Hindi Vyakaran* (1983).

E

EASTWICK, LIEUT. E.B. Author of *A Concise Grammar of the Hindustani Language* (London, 1847).

EK APARICHIT AKASH (An Unfamiliar Sky). Hindi anthology of verse, which contains representative poems of modern Jammu-Kashmir poets.

EK TOKRI BHAR MITTI. See *Madhav Rao Sapre.*

EKNATH (1530-99). Celebrated saint-poet of Maharashtra, who had great command on Sanskrit, Marathi and Hindi. Apart from his several works in Marathi, he composed some 200 *Padas* in Hindi. In his Hindi writings, he followed two styles : one of Khari Boli mixed with Braj and the other of Khari Boli mixed with Urdu or Dakkhini.

EKAVALI-PARINAY. See *Badrinath Jha.*

ELIOT, HENRY M. (1808-53). English Indian Civil Service official, who remained for a long time in the service of the Government of India. His works are : *A Glossary of Indian Terms* (Agra, 1855) and *Memoirs on the History, Folklore and Distribution of the Races of the North Western Provinces of India* (1869). See *John Beams.*

ETHERINGTON, REV. WILLIAM. Author of *The Student's Grammar of the Hindi Language* (Benares, 1870), which became quite popular on its publication. In the preface, the author claims that the form of Hindi prevalent in Benares is the one, which is understood by Sikhs, Gujaratis, Marathas and Nepalis. In Hindi, he wrote *Bhasha Bhaskar* (1873), a grammatical work, which was prescribed as a text book ; this work became quite popular and ran in several editions. In 1886 it was published by Nawal Kishore Press. The author was given a prize of Rs. 500 and finally the Government obtained its copyright. The speciality of this work was that it offered illustrations from Hindi works : *Ram charitmanas*, *Shakuntala*, etc.

F

FAIRBANKS, GORDON H. American Hindi scholar and author of *Spoken and Written Hindi* (Ithica, 1966) and *Hindi : A spoken Approach* (with P.B. Pandit, 1965).

FALLON, S.W. (b. 1817). Born at Calcutta, he was Deputy Inspector of Schools around 1865. His *A New Hindustani English Dictionary, with Illustrations from Hindustani Literature and Folklore* (1879) reveals the hard labour put in by the author, since the work is the first of its kind. Fallon had taken words from the peasants, traders, brokers, shoemakers, jugglers, musicians, folk-dramatists, etc. as he believed that the real language is the one that is spoken by the people. He also compiled a *Lokokti Kosh* (Dictionary of Proverbs), which contains proverbs from the rural life of Hindi regions. He also published *A Hindustani-English Law and Commercial Dictionary* (1875-79).

FAQIRBHAI PATEL. Gujarati-speaking modern Hindi scholar, whose *Swatantryottar Hindi aur Gujarati ke Samajik Upanyason ka Tulnatmak Adhyayan* (A Comparative Study of Hindi and Gujarati Social Novels written after Independence) is a research work.

FAQUIR CHAND SHUKLA. Writer, whose *Vishpan* (The Drinking of Poison ; 1982) and *Band Khidkiyon Vala Man* are short story collections.

FAROOQ, ABDUL BASHAR. Assamese-speaking modern Hindi writer, who is noted for his essays.

FATEH SINGH. Modern scholar, who is noted for his *Kamayani Saundarya*.

FATEHKARAN UJAL. Modern Rajasthani poet of Ujlan, Jodhpur, whose *Patra Prabhakar* in Pingal is quite a good poetical work.

FATEH RAM SINDHAYACH (fl. latter half of 18th cent.). Rajasthani poet, whose *Maharaja Gajsingh ro Rupak* describes the life of Maharaja Gajsingh (1846-87) of Bikaner.

FATURA (fl. early 19th cent.). Maithili poet, who took up simple folk-forms and turned them into literary gems. He wrote on the famine of 1880.

FAZIL SHAH (b. 1749). Poet of the court of Pratap Singh, Raja of Chhatarpur, whose *Prem Ratan* (The Gem of Love) is an allegorical romance on the lines of Sufi works. The hero and heroine of his work are Muslims : Nur Shah and Mahemunir.

FERGUSSON, JOHN. Author of *A Dictionary of the Hindostan Language, I. English and Hindostan. II. Hindostan and English. to which is prefixed a Grammar of the Hindostan Language* (London, 1773).

FORBES, DUNCAN. Professor of Oriental Languages and Literature in King's College, London, he was the author of *Hindustani Manual* (1845), *A Dictionary, Hindustani and English: to which is added a reverse part English and Hindustani* (2 Pts., London, 1848 ; revised ed., London, 1866) and *A Grammar of the Hindustani Language, in the Oriental and Roman Character* (London, 1855). The aim of these works was to teach Hindustani to British officers.

FREDERICK PINCOTT (d. 1896). A Briton, who was attracted towards Sanskrit and other Indian languages. He picked up a good knowledge of Hindi and Urdu and after studying their literatures, was convinced that the most suitable language for the people of Northern India was Hindi in Devnagari script. He wrote letters in Hindi prose to eminent Hindi writers and to Bharatendu Harishchandra he wrote his letter in the form of a poem. Pincott wrote two books : *Bal-Dipak* (in 4 Pts. ; it remained a text-book for children in many provinces) and *Victoria Charit* (170-page biography of Queen Victoria). Pincott visited India in 1895 but after one year he died in Lucknow.

FURRELL, J.W. Author of *Hindustani Synonyms—a collection of proximately synonymous words in daily use in the Hindustani Language, etc.* (Calcutta, 1873).

G

Gadadhar Bhatt (fl. 1533). Poet of the Krishna-cult, who was a south Indian Brahmin and was a great scholar of Sanskrit. It is fairly current that he used to recite the Sanskrit *Bhagavata* to Chaitanya. A follower of the Gaudiya Sampraday, he wrote also in Sanskrit and his Hindi verses are of a fairly high order. The number of his Hindi *Padas* is about 100.

Gadadhar Narayan. Novelist, whose *Sanginen Jhuk Gain* (Bayonets Lowered ; 1980) describes the social and political life before the creation of Bangladesh ; there also runs a lovestory.

Gadadhar Singh (1848-98). Writer, who was a contemporary of Bharatendu Harish Chandra (q.v.). He tr. into Hindi *Kadambari* from Sanskrit and *Durgesh Nandini* and *Bang Vijeta* from Bengali and *Othello* from English. He built up a huge Hindi library which he handed over to Kashi Nagari Pracharini Sabha.

Gadan, Aidan. See *Aidan Gadan.*

Gadan Cholo Mahawat (alias Chauthji ; fl. 1st half of 17th cent.). Dingal poet, who wrote poems mostly on contemporary heroes and happenings. His *Sursinghji ri Veli* is in praise of Maharaja Sursingh of Bikaner.

Gadan Gopinath (fl. 1753). Rajasthani poet, whose *Granthraj* (q.v.) in Dingal describes the life of Maharaja Gajsingh (1746-87) of Bikaner. He was highly rewarded by the Maharaja on this work.

Gadan, Kesodas. See *Kesodas Gadan.*

Gadan Pasayat (1400-1487/88). Dingal poet, who was a contemporary of Rathore Rao Ranmall and Jodha of Marwar. His available works are : *Kavitta Rao Ranmall*, *Chundai rai vair main Bhatiyan nai Mariya* (5 verses), *Kavitta Rao Ranmall*,

Nagaur ra dhani Peroz nai Mariya tai samai Ra (7 verses), *Kavitta Rana Mokal main ri Khabar ayan Ra* (5 verses), *Rao Ranmall or Rupak* (71 verses) and *Gun Jodhayan* (75 verses).

The first three poems are stray verses and describe Ranmall's taking vengeance on Bhatis for his father Chunda's death, his killing of Firoz Khan of Nagore in an invasion by Mokal, and his vow and killing of Chacha and Mera, the assassins of Rana Mokal. The last two works are narrative poems and describe the heroic deeds of Rao Ranmall and Rao Jodha. All the poems are of much histori cal value too. Gadan Pasayat was a popular poet.

GADAN SHIVDAS. See *Achaldas Khichi ri Vachnika.*

GADD (fl. 1561-77). Saint-poet of Rajasthan, whose stray verses in Braj are available. Many of his verses are still popular among local people. Gadd was perhaps a protege of Har Ray, Maharaval of Jaisalmer.

GADGIL, M. KE. Marathi-speaking modern Hindi scholar, whose chief work is : *Hindi Ekankiyon men Samajik Jivan ki Abhivyakti.*

GADGIL, N. VI. Marathi-speaking modern Hindi writter, whose chief work is *Sabhashastra* ; he has also published memoirs : *Smritishesh* and *Mere Sansmaran.*

GADHPATI (fl. 1909). Braj folk-poet of Mathura region, who composed a Braj version of the Dhola-Maru romance of Rajasthan. As compared to the language of Madari (q.v.), his style is polished.

GADYANJALI (1961). Hindi prose anthology, published from Jammu-Kashmir, which was edited by V.D. Shastri, Ved Rahi and Prithwinath Pushp. This anthology contains 17 representative prose writings of Jammu-Kashmir writers, which include eight short stories, one one-act play, two pieces of reminiscences and six essays.

GAEFFKE, PETER. Modern German scholar, who has made special study of Hindi Language ; he has writen a number of articles. His chief work is *Untersuchungen zur syntax des Hindi* (1967).

GAGIL. Rajasthani Charan, whose stray verses are available ; his time is not certain.

GAHMARI, GOPALRAM. See *Gopalram Gahmari.*

GAIPO SINDHAYACH 'TUNKARO' (fl. between 1550-1650). Dingal poet, whose stray verses are available in popular metres.

GAJ-GUN RUPAK BANDH. Dingal poem (1301 verses), which was composed by Kesodas Gadan around 1625 in 45 different metres. It describes the battles fought by Maharaja Gajsingh or Jodhpur, as a General of the Mughal Army, against Bhim Sisodiya, commander of the rebel Prince Khurram's army at Hazipur (near Patna) in 1624. The Hazipur battle, which the Maharaja of Jodhpur won, has been described elaborately. The poem is significant for the vivid martial descriptions, *e.g.*, preparation of the army, strategy and march, bloody scenes of the battlefields, etc.

GAJSINGH (fl. 15th cent.). Maithili poet, who was perhaps a contemporary of Vidyapati (q.v.). His poems in the style of Vidyapati, have charm and delicacy in their rhythm. He is also said to have written a drama.

GAJ-UDHAR GRANTH. Rajasthani-devotional poem by Maharaja Ajitsingh (1678-1724) of Jodhpur, which narrates the legend of 'Gaj and Grah' based on the *Bhagavat Puran*, though with minor variations of his own. While the first half of the poem covers the main theme, the second half describes the ten incarnations, origin of the universe, fourteen 'Loks', etc.

GAJANAN MADHAV MUKTIBODH (1917-64). Modernist poet, who was born at Shyampur in the district of Gwalior. After completing his education at Ujjain and Indore, he was appointed a teacher. He made a deep study of Marxist and psychoanalytical literature. His earlier poems are collected in *Tar Saptak* ; his *Chand ka Munh Teddha Hai* (The Moon has a Crooked Face ; 1964) contains over 25 long poems, including poems of the titles, 'Andhere Men' (In Darkness) and 'Chambal ki Ghation Men' (In the Ravines of Chambal). *Bhuri Bhuri Khak Dhul* (Gray Sand Dust ; 1980) contains a collection of his poems. His poetry is born out of a wide experience of struggles in life. His critical prose works are : *Ek Sahityik ki Diary* (The Diary of a Litterateur), *Satya ka Saundarya* (The Beauty of Literature), *Samiksha ki Samasyayen*, *Kamayani : Ek Punarvichar* (Marxist interpretation), *Nayi Kavita ka Atmasangharsh aur anya Nibandh* (Self- struggle of New poetry and other Essays ; 1964), *Satah se Uthta Admi* (The Man Rising above Surface), *Kath ka Sapna* (A Wooden Dream; the last two short story collections), *Vipatra* Anti-character ; an outstanding novel) and *Pakshi aur Dimak* (Birds and White Ants). His complete works *Muktibodh Rachnavali* (6 vols.) edited by Nemi Chandra Jain, are in press.

GAJANAN PUROHIT. Gujarati-speaking modern Hindi scholar, whose *Jayshankar Prasad aur Nhanalal ke Kavya ka Tulnatmak Adhyayan* is a research work.

GAJANAN VERMA. Modern Rajasthani poet, whose *Barahmasa* describes the twelve months of the year, but it is pre-occupied with folk-life and musical tunes. He has also composed many lyrical poems, portraying various aspects of Nature, progressive and love poems. He has also chosen objects of Nature as symbols in expressing progressive ideology.

GALALENG. Rajasthani ballad, which describes the heroism of Galaleng or Gulalsingh, who was killed in the battle of Kadana, during the reigon of Maharaval Ramsingh (1702-29) of Dungarpur. Sung by Jogis, it is said to have been initially composed by one Juita Jogi.

GALLUJI (1827-90). Poet of the Krishna-cult (Chaitanya Sect), who was father of the famous Hindi writer : Radhacharan Goswami (q. v.). He composed poetry under the pen-name of 'Gunmanjari'. His works are : *Shri Radharaman Pada Manjari, Bhagavat Pada Muktavali, Gopal Bhatt Shatak*, etc.

GANAK, SUKAVI. Modern Maithili poet, who is noted for his *Sohars*, particular types of lyrics.

GANDHESHETTI SHRIRAMULU. Telugu-speaking modern Hindi poet, who is noted for his stray poems.

GANESH (fl. end of 18th cent.). Rajasthani poet of Karauli, who was a Chaturvedi Brahmin. He composed *Ras Chandroday, Krishna Bhakti Chandrika Natak, Sabhasurya, Nagar-Shatak* and *Phagun Mahatmya*.

GANESH (fl. 1793-1853). Poet, who was a descendant of Narhari Bandijan (q. v.). He was grandson of Lal Kavi and was patronized by Uditnarayan Singh, the ruler of Kashi. He was the author of three works : *Valmiki Ramayan Shlokarth Prakash* (Hindi rendering of *Valmiki Ramayana* ; consisting of full *Balakanda* and five chapters of *Kishkindhakanda*), *Pradyumna Vijay* (a drama in various metres on the entry of Pradyumna in the demon city of Bajranabhpur and his love-marriage with Prabhavati) and *Hanumat Pachchisi* (25 verses on Hanuman).

GANESH CHAUBE. Modern Bhojpuri scholar of Bihar, who has published a collection of 400 *Bhojpuri Lok-kathas* (folk-tales).

GANESH DATT SARASWAT. Modern scholar, whose chief work is *Hindi Lok Sahitya*.

GANESH LAL VYAS 'USTAD' (1910-65). Rajasthani poet, who tried to awaken socio-political consciousness through compositions and recitation of songs mostly based on the popular folk-tunes and styles. He also composed lyrical poems, portraying various aspects of Nature. A freedom fighter and a crusader against every type of injustice, he wrote patriotic and heroic poems as also progressive poems, *e.g.*, *Gharibon ki Avaz* (1932). Some of his poems have been published in *Jan Kavi Ustad* (1972). He also composed *Nritya Git Rupak*, *Nritya Git*, etc.

GANESH MISHRA (fl. 1588). Poet, who was the author of *Vikram Vilas* (The Delights of Vikram).

GANESH PRASAD DWIVEDI (1900-49). Writer, who was noted for his one-act play collection : *Sohag Bindi* (A mark on the forehead of a woman, whose husband is alive ; 1935).

GANESHPURI (1826-96). Rajasthani poet, who was son of Charan Padma and belonged to the village Charanwas in the Jodhpur State. On receiving rebuff from the celebrated poet, Suryamall (q. v.) that he would not meet Ganeshpuri as he was illiterate, he became a monk and studied at Kashi for 10 years. After return from Kashi, he, at the instance of Maharana Sajjansingh of Mewar, settled in Mewar permanently.

Besides stray verses, his *Vir-Vinod* in Pingal, is very popular in Rajasthan. The work is free rendering of the Karna-Parva of the *Mahabharat*.

GANESH TEKLAL. See *Krishna Sharma*.

GANESHAN, S.N. Tamil-speaking modern Hindi writer, whose chief work is : *Hindi Upanyas Sahitya ka Adhyayan : Pashchatya Upanyas se Tulana Sahit* (A Study of Hindi Novels with Comparison of Western Novels ; 1962 ; Ph. D. thesis), literary essays and a comparative study of Hindi and Tamil grammars. He is at present in the Department of Hindi, Madras University.

GANESHANAND (fl. 1885). Poet of Murarpur (Gaya), who was a Brahmin. His extant works are : *Rituvarnan* (on seasons), *Nayika-Bhed* (on heroines) and stray works.

GANESHWAR JHA. Modern Maithili poet, whose *Devigita* is a *Khandkavya*.

GANG (1533-1617). The foremost poet of Akbar's court, who enjoyed the personal friendship of Rahim (q. v.) and the latter held him in very high esteem. It is quite popular that Rahim presented him with a large sum of 36 lakh rupees. The poet, Bhikharidas (q. v.) ranked Gang with Tulsidas and though Gang may not be as great as Tulsidas, the comparison testifies to the fact that he was a towering personality among the secular and courtly poets of his times. Very little is known about the poet's life and works but various contemporary poets mention repeatedly that he was trampled to death by an elephant owing to the displeasure he had incurred of some peevish ruler (Jahangir ?) or some landlord. Three of Gang's works discovered so far are *Gang-Padavali, Gang-Pachisi* and *Gang-Ratnavali* ; the first book contains 721 *Chhands*, the second only 25 and the third one as many as 1400. But the best-known work of Gang is *Chand Chhand Barnan ki Mahima*, which is a small book in Khari Boli prose ; this makes Gang one of the pioneers of Khari Boli prose.

Gang skilfully wrote poetry both of *Vir* and *Shringar Rasas* ; his poetry is vigorous and polished and the diction is elevated and refined.

GANGA CHARAN TRIPATHI. Scholar, whose chief works are : *Hindi Bhasha aur Vyakaran ka Vyavaharik Gyan* and *Samiksha ke Pratiman* (1985).

GANGADAS (fl. 19th cent. ?). Maithili poet, who tr. the 'Virat-parva' of the *Mahabharata* into Maithili.

GANGADATT SHASTRI 'VINOD' (1924-). Dogri-speaking Hindi writer, whose chief works are : *Hindi Vyakaran* (grammar), *Shanidarshan, Matimanthan* (the last two collections of essays), *Raghunath Gunoday : Ek Samiksha* (research work), *Ullol* (poetical collection) and editing of the manuscripts of Chandidas. He is closely associated with the activities for the promotion of Hindi in Jammu.

GANGA DATT UPRETI. Scholar, who was noted for his *Proverbs and Folk-lore of Kumaon and Garhwal* (1892).

GANGA DATT VINOD. Novelist, whose chief work is *Muskan Hai Kahan* (Where Lies the Smile ? ; 1982).

GANGADHAR (fl. 1850-1900). Marathi-speaking saint-poet, who composed *Padas* in Hindi.

GANGADHAR (fl. 19th cent.). Bundelkhandi folk-poet, who is famous for his poems, called *Phags*.

GANGADHAR MISHRA. Maithili poet, whose chief works are : *Narad-Moh* (1919), *Satya Vratopakhyan* (1921), *Sukanyopakhyan* (1921) and *Sudama-Charit* (1935), all on mythological subjects.

GANGADHAR MISHRA 'JIBU'. Modern Maithili poet, who is noted for his patriotic poem : *Mithilak Vilap* as also for his lyrics.

GANGAI HAR SHUKLA. Modern writer, whose chief works are : *Ji Han, Ji Nahin* (Yes Sir ; No Sir; collection of one-act plays) and *Andhera Chhant Gaya* (Darkness has Gone ; short story collection).

GANGA NATH. Kumaoni Panvada, which describes the romance of Prince Ganganath of Doti and Bhana Joshi, the Brahmin daughter of the village Adauli in Patti Salam.

GANGAPATI SINHA. Modern Maithili writer, who is noted for his critical writings.

GANGA PRASAD AGNIHOTRI. Literary critic, whose essay 'Samalochana' appeared in the 'Nagari Pracharini Patrika' in 1896. Agnihotri favoured Western type of criticism as against the old-style Sanskrit criticism.

GANGA PRASAD DAS (fl. 1850). Poet of Chitrakut, who, though of the Krishna-cult, wrote commentaries in verse and prose on Tulsidas's *Vinay-Patrika*.

GANGA PRASAD GUPTA (1885-1914). Writer, whose historical novels are : *Prithwiraj Chauhan* (1902), *Kunvar Singh Senapati* (Kunvar Singh the Chief Commander ; 1903), *Hammir* (1904), *Nurjahan*, *Poona men Halchal* (Turmoil in Poona) and *Vir Jaimala*.

GANGA PRASAD GUPTA BARSAINYA (1936-). Scholar, whose chief works are : *Chhattisgarh ka Sahitya and Uske Sahityakar* (on Chhattisgarhi Literature) and a study of Hindi one-act plays.

GANGA PRASAD MISHRA. Writer, whose *Zahar Chand Ka* is a novel.

GANGA PRASAD PANDEY 'VASANT' (1918-68). Writer, who was born at Kanchanpur in Satna district of Madhya Pradesh. His chief works are : *Mahapran Nirala* (Nirala's biography) and *Bisvin Shati ki Shreshth-tam Kavya-Kriti Kamayani* (*Kamayani*, the greatest poetical work of the 20th century). His collection of one-act plays is *Sat Shreshth Ekanki.*

GANGA PRASAD SHRIVASTAV. See *Shrivastav, G.P.*

GANGA PRASAD UDAINIYAN. Poet of the Ram-cult, who was the author of *Ramagrah* (Ram's Persistence ; 1787).

GANGA PRASAD VIMAL (1939-). Writer, whose chief works are : *Apne se Alag* (Apart from Self ; 1964), *Tasviren aur Saye* (Pictures and Shades ; 1969), *Kahin Kuchh Aur* (Something Somewhere Else), *Udgam, Marichika* (Mirage ; novels), *Ek aur Vidai* (One More Farewell), *Prashna Chihna* (Question Mark), *Apna Marna* (Self-dying), *Koi Shuruat* (Some Beginning), *Atit men Kuchh* (Something in the Past), *Idhar-Udhar* (Here and There ; 1980), *Bahar-Bhitar, Meri Kahaniyan* (short story collections), *Vijay* (poem), *Samkalin Kahani ka Rachna-Vidhan, Agyey ka Rachna Sansar* (The Formative World of Agyey), *Premchand : Punarmulyankan, Muktibodh ka Sansar, Adhunik Hindi Kahani* (critical works), *Krantikari Samuhgan* (ed. ; a poetical anthology) and *Bodhi Vriksha* (1982 ; collection of poems). He has tr. the Bulgarian poet Lyubomir Levchev's poem as *Shasvat Panchang* (1982). His drama is : *Aj Nahin to Kal.*

GANGA RAM (fl. 1800). Poet, whose *Shabda Brahma* (word-Brahman) is a devotional work.

GANGA RAM GARG (1925-). Writer, who was born at the village Kohand in Karnal district of Haryana. His chief works are : *Sankshipta Oxford Hindi Sahitya Parichayak* (Concise Oxford Companion to Hindi Literature ; a dictionary of Hindi writers, their works, mythological allusions, ancient geographical names, figures of speech, etc, ; 1963) and *Encyclopaedia of Indian Literature* (Sanskrit, Pali, Prakrit & Apabhransh ; 1982 ; in English). He has been associated with Gurukula Kangri Vishwavidyalaya, Hardwar, where he has worked in various capacities as Senior Lecturer, Registrar and Vice-Chancellor.

GANGA RAM PATHIK. Modern Rajasthani poet, who has composed Nature poems.

GANESH GUNJAN. Maithili writer and poet, whose chief work, *Anhar Ijot* (1964) is a short story collection. He brings out the pettiness and greatness in the life of common man and woman. His drama, *Chaubatia Par* (1979) exposes corruption and political hypocrisy, while *Budhi-Badhiya* (1982) is on contemporary life situation. In poetry, apart from his long poem 'Hum Ekta Mithya Parichay', published earlier, on the examination of the modern man, his *Lok Sunu* (1980) is the first collection of his poetry. His one-act plays are : *Lok Natakia* and *Navak Syllabus* (both, 1980). His novel *Pahil Lok* (1982) has proved quite popular. He is one of the editors of 'Katha Disha', a short story magazine.

GANGU HAIBTI (fl. 18th cent.). Marathi folk-poet (*Shahir*), who also made compositions in Hindi.

GAN NATH JHA (fl. 1st half of 20th cent.). Maithili writer, whose chief work is a drama *Bhagvati-Bhakta Natak*. He wrote songs to be sung on the occasion of various ceremonies observed during the worship of the earthen image of Durga in Navratra. He also added seriousness to the songs.

GANPATI BHARAVI (fl. 1778-1803). Poet of the Riti school, who was said to be the Guru of Jaipur ruler. His works are : *Virah Pachisi*, *Priti Manjari*, *Shringar Hazara*, *Navrasa* and *Alankar Sudhanidhi*.

GANPATI CHANDRA BHANDARI. Modern Rajasthani poet, whose chief works are : '*Minakhpani ro kal*', 'Pyaro Marudhar Des' (poems) and *Sihan Jaya Sav* (one-act plays, taking their themes from Rajput history).

GANPATI CHANDRA GUPT (1928-). Critic, whose chief works are : *Hindi Kavya men Shringar Parampara aur Mahakavi Bihari* (Shringar Tradition in Hindi Poetry and the great poet Bihari; thesis), *Sahitya-vigyan ya Sahitya ka Vaigyanik Vivechan* (Litetary history Science or Scientific Study of Literature; research), *Hindi Sahitya : Samasyaen aur Samadhan* (Hindi Literature : Problems and Solutions), *Mahadevi : Naya Mulyankan* (Mahadevi : New Evaluation), *Rasa-Siddhant ka Punarvivechan* (Reconsideration of the Principles of Rasa), *Adikal ki Pramanik Rachanayen* (Authentic Works of the First Age ; 1967) and *Anubhuti ke Swar*. After working as Professor of Hindi at Maharshi Dayanand University, Rohtak he was Vice-Chancellor of Himachal Pradesh University and later of Kurukshetra University.

GANPATI KAYASTH. Rajasthani poet, who was son of Narsa. In 1527, he composed *Madhavanal Kamkandala Prabandh* (q.v.) in an epic style.

GANPATI SWAMI. Modern Rajasthani scholar, who has made significant contribution to the study of Rajasthani folk-songs (*Jin Mata ro Git*, *Tejaji ro Git*, *Pabuji ra Panvada*). His poem 'Murdhar Desh' eulogizes Rajasthan.

GANJAN. Poet of the Riti school, who was a Gujarati Brahmin of Kashi. He was patronized and honoured by Kamar-ud-din, a minister of the Delhi king, on whose name he composed the *Kamar-ud-din Khan Hulas* (1729), a work on *Shringar Rasa*. This work also traces the genealogy of the poet, where in he highly praised the poetic faculties of his great-grandfather, Mukut Ray.

GAPONOVA, GALINA ANDREYEVNA (1925-). Soviet Hindi scholar, who is an editor in the Progressive Publishing House, Moscow. She has edited in Hindi the writings of Gorky, Pushkin, etc.

GARCIN DE TASSY (J.H.) (1794-1878). French scholar, who, while remaining in France acquainted himself with the Hindustani literature. His works on Hindi literature are : *Histoire de la litterature Hindoui et Hindoustanie* (q.v.; 2 Pts., Paris, 1839, 1846 ; 2nd edition in 3 Pts., 1870-81), *Les auterus hindoustanis et leurs ourages D'apres les biographics originales* (Paris, 1868), *Rudiments de la langue Hindoustanic* (1829), *Rudiments de la langue hindoui* (1847) and *Cours d'Hindoustani, Urdu et Hindi Discours d'ouverture* (2 Pts., Paris, 1865). He also made translations of the Shakuntala episode from the *Mahabharata*, the story of Heer-Ranjha from Punjab, *Bagh-o-Bahar*, *Prem Sagar*, etc. as also wrote *Hindi-Hindui Muntakhabat*, a selection of writings from Hindi.

Tassy was the first author to write a history of Hindi and Urdu literatures, when there was not a single history available in Hindi and Urdu.

GARHWALI KAVITAVALI. Collection of Garhwali poems, which were composed during the 19th century.

GATAZLAFF, MARGOT. Modern German Hindi scholar, whose *Grammatischer leitfaden des Hindi* is a standard work for the study of Hindi grammar through the medium of German. Her *Worterbuch Deutsch-Hindi* (German-Hindi Dictionary) contains some 15,000 words.

GAURGAN DAS (fl. 16th cent. ?). Poet of the Krishna-cult (Chaitanya Sect), about whom very little is known. His works are : *Gaurang Bhushan Vilas*, *Shringar Manjavali* (*Purva* and *Uttar*) and *Siddhant Pranali Shakha*.

GAUR KRISHNA (b. c. 1803-*c*. 1843). Poet of the Krishna-cult (Chaitanya Sect), whose stray *Padas* are available.

GAUR VYANVALO. Rajasthani poem in 121 verses, which

was meant to be sung and was composed by Gordhanji (q.v.) in the 18th century.

While treating of the marriage of Gauri or Parvati and Shiv, it introduces an anecdote of Raja Sabairaj of Sabainagari, who wishes to marry Parvati on an invitation sent by her mother in preference to Shiv. Ultimately, Sabairaj is killed and Shiv marries Parvati. The Akhyan depicts folk-customs and traditions then prevalent. The depiction of the mental disposition of Parvati's mother, Chandravati is remarkable.

GAURI DATT PANDEY 'GAURDA'. Modern Kumaoni poet, who has composed poems on social and political subjects.

GAURI DATT SHARMA (1836-1906). Hindi writer of Ludhiana (Panjab), who was noted for his short stories : 'Kahani Takakamani' and 'Devrani Jethani ki Khani', which are mainly didactic in tone. He had ardently served the cause of Hindi in Panjab.

GAURI KANT CHAUDHARI. Maithili writer, whose *Vardan* (1982) is a historical play.

GAURI MISHRA. Modern Maithili writer, who is noted for her short story collection *Thehiayel Mon : Shital Chhahari* ; her stories are full of pathos and pity.

GAURI SHANKAR ARYA. Modern Rajasthani poet, who has composed Nature poems.

GAURI SHANKAR HIRACHAND OJHA (1863-1947). Rajasthani scholar, who is famous for his monumental work on Indian palaeography: *Bharatiya Prachin Lipimala* as also for his scholarly works on Rajputana history (*Rajputana ka Itihas* ; 4 Pts.). Ojha was formerly Head of the Government Archaeological Department in Udaipur but later on was appointed Curator of the Rajputana Museum, Ajmer. He wrote or edited more than a dozen works. He edited Jayanak's *Prithwiraj Vijay Mahakaya* and sought to prove *Prithwiraj Raso* as unauthoritative.

GAURI SHANKAR JHA. Maithili poet, whose Meghnad-Badh (1941) on the killing of Ravan's son, Meghnad, was written under the influence of Michael Madhusudan Dutt's bold experiment of introducing blank verse in modern Indian languages. It is a rendering in Maithili of Dutt's *Meghnad-Badh* in Bengali. He wrote essays, which are serious and thoughtful. He also tr. into Maithili *Bhartriharinirveda from the Sanskrit original.*

GAURI SHANKAR KAMLESH. Modern Rajasthani poet, whose chief poem is 'Manakh Nango Hoto Ja Ryo Che'.

GAURI SHANKAR RAJHANS. Writer, who is noted for his short story collection *Ujli Rekhayen* (The Distinct Lines ; 1980) and novel *Salma*.

GAURI SHANKAR SHARMA. Modern Rajasthani poet, who has contributed to progressive poetry.

GAURI SWAYAMVAR. See *Lal Kavi*.

GAUTAM SWAMI RAS. Rajasthani poem of daily reading among the Jain Shravaks, composed by Upadhyay Vinay Prabh in 1355. A work of poetic beauty, it is mostly rhetorical and the metres are meant to be sung.

GAVARI BAI (1758-1808). Rajasthani saint-poetess, who was born in a Nagar Brahmin family of Dungarpur. A child-widow, she was well-versed in scriptures and was noted for her devotion. Maharaval Shivsingh (1730-85) of Dungarpur built a temple for her. In her last days, she went to Kashi and died there. She is considered an incarnate of Miran Bai. She is said to have composed over 600 *Padas* in easy Rajasthani mixed with Braj and Gujarati, which deal with God and devotion.

GAVRUSHINA, NINA DMITRIYEVNA (1928-). Soviet Hindi scholar, who has written articles on the novels of Jayshankar Prasad, Jainendra Kumar and on the progressive Indian literature.

GAYAPRASAD SHUKLA 'SANEHI' (1883-1972). Poet, who was born at the village Hadha in the Unnao district of Uttar Pradesh. A well known writer of patriotic verse, he changed over to Hindi after having versified in Urdu for many a year. His language was simple, for which reason he was considered a popular poet of his times. His chief collections of poems are : *Prem Pachchisi* (25 verses on Love), *Krishak-Krandan* (The Farmer's Lament), *Rashtriya Vina* (The National Lute), *Trishul Tarang* (Trishul's Fancy) and *Karun-Bharati* (Merciful Saraswati) ; he has written both in Brajbhasha and Khari Boli. He edited a literary periodical 'Sukavi'. He wrote also under the pen-name of 'Trishul'.

GEORGE, JACOB P. Modern scholar, whose chief work is *Adhunik Hindi Gadya aur Gadyakar*.

GEORGE, M. Modern scholar, who is noted for his *Bhakti Andolan aur Sahitya*.

GESUDARRZ. See *Bande Navaz Gesudaraz*.

GHABAN (Embezzlement). Novel (1931) by Prem Chand (q.v.), which narrates the tale of a middle class youth, who has a habit of pretending to be a man of wealth. This habit lands him into trouble as to procure ornaments for his loving wife, he embezzles money from his office. Unable to pay the money back, he runs away to Calcutta. During his absence, his wife discovers the truth, sells the ornaments and clears her husband's embezzled amount. In Calcutta, he is haunted by fear and when the police arrest him in the midst of a political demonstration, he feels that they have found his crime, though, actully no case is pending against him. Taking advantage of the situation, the police officers force him to act as an approver and he betrays a group of revolutionaries by giving false evidence. His wife discovers him in Caluctta and he then realizes that he has nothing to fear and that he should not betray his countrymen.

The novel also exposes the police methods of coercion and of gathering false evidence which are prevalent even today.

GHAGH (b. 1696). Celebrated *Suktikar*, whose utterances in Hindi concerning agriculture are popular throughout northern India. See *Dak-Bhaddali*, *Meghmal-Bhaddri*.

GHANANAND (1673-1739). Poet of the Riti school. A Kayasth by caste, Ghananand was amanuensis (Mirmunshi) of Emperor Muhammad Shah and was born in Delhi. Highly proficient as he was both in poetry and music, the Emperor once insisted on his singing in the court but the latter would not do so until Sujan, a court dancer and his concubine, was not before him. Accordingly, Sujan was summoned and Ghananand began his music. The Emperor was charmed by the music of Ghananand but was displeased with him too, for the poet throughout his singing constantly addressed Sujan, turning his back to the Emperor; hence he was cashiered from service and banished from the city. At the time of his departure, he requested Sujan to accompany him, but she rejected his offer, a professional courtesan as she was. Ghananand was greatly disillusioned, turned a recluse and settled down in Vrindavan where he was admitted to the Vaishnav Order of Nimbark.

The love for Sujan was sublimated and the poet continued writting poetry in praise of Vrindavan and its Lord to the last day of his life. Most of the poems were still addressed to Sujan but the word could stand for Krishna.

There is an interesting story about the poet's death. The Persian king, Nadir Shah sacked Delhi in 1739 and his army reached as far as Mathura in search of wealth. The soldiers demanded from him thrice all his zar (wealth) ; the poet transposed the words in Hindi *raj raj raj* (dust) and since as an ascetic he had no riches to offer, he hurled at them three handfuls of the sacred dust of Vrindavan. The infuriated soldiers mutilated his hand and the poet died with 'Sujan' on his lips. Another version goes that Nadir Shah expressed a desire to hear his music but as he refused to leave Vrindavan, his arms were chopped off and he died.

Some 40 titles have been ascribed to Ghananand; chief among them are *Ghananand Kavitta* (*Kavittas* of Ghananand), *Kripakand Nibandh* (Essays of Sweet Grace), *Viyoga Veli* (The Creeper of Separation), *Prem-Patrika* (Love Letter), *Virah-Lila* (Description of Separation), *Sujan Hit* (For Sujan), *Sujan Sagar* (The Ocean of Sujan), *Kok-Sar* (on erotics), *Ishq-lata* (The Creaper of love, with many Persianisms); *Rasakeli-valli* and *Ghananand Padavali* (Verses of Ghananand) ; *Sujan Sagar* is by far the poet's best known work. His *Virah Lila*, though written in Brajbhasha is in the Persian *Masnavi* metre. In all he wrote 752 verses and 1057 songs.

Setting aside all the stultifying conventions of the Riti school, his poetry follows a natural course. The poet, being a lover both in the mundane and spiritual sense, was subjected to every sort of torture of separation and pined constantly for reunion with his Beloved. This pang is the keynote of his subjective melodious verses. Thus his poetry is characterized by devotion, *Shringar* and emotionalism. Most of his love poetry has been addressed to Sujan. The language he employed is in its purest, maturest and sweetest form and there is natural, easy and smooth flow. He had a peculiar knack of harmonizing ideas and images that usually stand in contrast, and gave to words and phrares new meanings and associations.

Several editions of his works have appeared. Vishwanath Prasad Mishra has published his works under the title *Ghananand*, wherein he has claimed over three dozens of his works as genuine.

Besides Ghananand, there have been two poets bearing the name Anandghan : one is the author of *Padavali* (Verses), *Ishqlata* (Love Creeper) and *Yamuna-Yash* (The Glory of Yamuna) and the other, a Jain, composed two works : *Anandghan Chaubisi* and *Anandghan Bahottari*.

GHANANAND BAHUGUNA. Writer, who was noted for his drama, *Samaj* (The Society ; 1930), it is a problem play which takes up the cause of the widow re-marriage.

GHANARANG DUBE (1819-87), Poet of the Shahabad district

of Bihar, who was honoured by the Ruler of Dumraon. Apart from his *Padas*, his chief work is *Krishna-Ramayan* (describing the story of Ram as narrated by Yashoda to Krishna).

GHANERAO KI GHAZAL. See *Manch*.

GHANNIYA. Kannauji folk-tale, which describes the love of Padmini and Kharaglal.

Raja Gajdhar of Bakesur city is blessed with a daughter, who is christened by the Brahmins as Padmini. In search of a suitable groom for the girl, the Brahmins meet the serpent king Vasuki of Vasavaseli, who suggests and implores that she be engaged to his son, Nagmuniyan. The Brahmins, however do not accept the offer and escape from there. They meet Raja Surajmal of Niba Nibauri, who offers his son Kharaglal as a match for Padmini ; the Tilak ceremony is performed. On the appointed date, the marriage party arrives and is well-received. After the wedding ceremony is over, Nagmuniyan, the serpent, who is hiding in a corner, bites Kharaglal and he dies. Padmini prepares a boat of green bamboos tied with the ropes made of serpents and starts for Kamrup, where her husband becomes alive, but is converted into an animal by the sorceresses, who have developed love for him. It is only after seven years that Kharaglal turns in his true self. Padmini and Kharaglal reach Niba Nibauri and thereafter visit Bakesur. At this place, the bonds af serpents are opened and *yagya* is performed in their honour. The marriage party of Kharaglal again arrives at Bakesur and the marriage celebrations are held with great pomp and show. Padmini and Kharaglal live happily thereafter.

GHANSHYAM DAS (fl. 1653). Bengali Vaishnav poet, who also composed *Padas* in Brajbuli.

GHANSHYAM DAS BIRLA (1891-1983). Noted industrialist, whose works in Hindi are : *Bapu*, *Diary ke Panne*, etc.

GHANASHYAM SETHI. Modern Hindi writer of Jammu-Kashmir, whose *Nagri-Nagri Phira Musafir* is a travelogue.

GHARIB DAS (fl. 1st part of 16th cent.). Poet of the Krishna-cult (Chaitanya Sect), who became a disciple of Ramray (q.v.) and came to live at Vrindavan. He is said to have composed three works : *Shringar-Shatak*, *Anand Shatak* (1523) and *Vrindavan-Shatak*.

GHARIB DAS (b. 1575). Rajasthani saint-poet of the village

Narayan, who was the eldest son of Dadu (q.v.) and ascended the *Gaddi* after the demise of his father. He was a great scholar and a musician too. His works : *Sakhi*, *Pada*, *Anabhai Prabodh*, *Adhyatma Bodh*, etc. are available.

GHARIB DAS (1717-82). Saint-poet, who sang of Nirgun Brahma. A Jat by caste, he was born in village Karonth, near Rohtak, but when he was a kid, he was shifted to Chhudani near Jhajjar. He founded the Gharibdasi Sect but he was a married man, for he believed that a married man with a family can also attain the highest spiritual power if he leads a pious life and adopts the simple way of worship. He wrote nearly 17000 *Padas* ; only one-fourth of them are available now. His poetry is preserved in *Ratan Sagar* (Ocean of Gems), which is recited by Gharibdasis with religious fervour in their homes and Gurudwaras.

GHATAGE, AMRIT MADHAV. See *Amrit Madhav Ghatage*.

GHAZI DAS (fl. 1782-1830). Saint-poet of Chhatisgarh, who was a cobbler by caste. He propagated the doctrines of Satnami Sect in his verses.

GHOTNE, VI. D. Marathi-speaking modern Hindi dramatist, who is noted for his *Mangal ho Tumhara* and *Chandrama*.

GHULAM ALI (1750-1836). Sindhi Muslim saint-poet, who also composed in Hindi a poetical work : *Brahmavichar*, which is influenced by the doctrine of Vedanta. The *Padas* of Ghulam Ali so much resemble those of Kabir (q.v.) that sometimes it becomes difficult to distinguish between them. Gulam Ali occupied the religious seat after the death of his brother Shahu (q.v.).

GHULAM NABI 'RASLIN'. See *Raslin*.

GHULAM RASUL, S. (1922-). Writer, whose chief work is : *Hali tatha Maithilisharan Gupta : Ek Tulna* (Hali and Maithilisharan Gupta : A Comparison). He is Head of the Department of Hindi at Annamalai Univerity.

GILCHRIST, JOHN BORTHWICK (1759-1841). British philologist, who came to India in 1783 as a Medical Officer in the service of the East India Company but soon realized that the Company's officers must know the language of the people if they were to discharge their duties efficiently. He came to the conclusion that the days of oriental languages like Persian and Sanskrit were over and that the growing vernaculars, particularly Hindustani or Hindi, must be encouraged. When the Fort

William College was started in Calcutta in 1800, Dr. Gilchrist was appointed its first Principal. Under his able and sympathetic supervision, a band of Indian scholars was appointed for writing text-books for the use of English officers ; most noteworthy of these scholars were Lallu Lal, Sadasukh Lal, Sadal Mishra and Insha Allah Khan (qq. v.). Gilchrist gave thorough instructions to these men about the real nature of the requirements of the College.

Gilchrist's chief works are : *A Dictionary of English and Hindustani* (in Persian script ; 3 Pts., Calcutta, 1787-96) ; *Appendix to the English and Hindustani Dictionary* (Calcutta, 1800 ; its revised ed. was published from Edinburgh in 1810, in which Roebeck assisted Gilchrist), *A Grammar of the Hindustani Language* (1796-98 ; only Urdu poets have been quoted), *The Stranger's East Indian Guide to Hindustani* (1802 ; it proved very popular), *The Oriental Linguist* (1798 ; an easy and familiar Introduction to the popular language of Hindoostan ; 2nd Ed., Calcutta, 1802), *The Hindi Story-teller of Entertaining Expositor of the Roman, Persian and Nagari Characters* (1802), *The Hindi Directory or Student's Introduction to the Hindustani Language, . . .* (1802), *The Moral Preceptor and Persian Scholar's Shortest Road to the Hindustani Language* (1803), *The Anti-Jargonist* (Calcutta, 1800 ; this is partly an abridgement of *The Oriental Linguist*), *The Oriental Fabulist or Polyglot Translatio nof Aesop's and Other Ancient Fables* (1803), *The Hindi-Roman Orthoepigraphical Ultimatum* (1804 ; revised ed. 1820), *A Collection of Dialogues : English and Hindustani on the Most Familiar and Useful Subjects* and *The Hindi Manual or Casket of India* (Calcutta, 1802 ; in collaboration with Mr. Abdullah Miskin).

GINDARAM VERMA. Modern Rajasthani scholar, whose chief work is *Rajasthani Lokotsav*.

GIRDHAR ASIYA (1633-1718). Rajasthani poet, whose *Sagat Raso* in 943 verses is the only poem, which celebrates the valour of Shakti Singh (younger brother of Rana Pratap), Shakti s son, Achal Singh and grandson Narhari and is of historical value. According to the *Raso*, Shakti Singh joined the imperial court owing to the displeasure of his father, but he did not accept Akbar's proposal to become the ruler of Chittor. He came to inform his people at Chittor about the impending attack by Akbar, but was not allowed to enter the fort. After the battle of Haldighati, Shakti Singh left for Bhainsrodgarh.

GIRDHAR RATHI. Poet, whose *Bahar Bhitar* (Inside and Outside ; 1979) is a collection of short poems about his days of imprisonment (25-6-1975 to 13-2-1977) during the Emergency.

GIRDHARI LAL MALAW. Modern Rajasthani poet, who has contributed to progressive poetry.

GIRDHARI LAL SHASTRI. Rajasthani writer, who is known for his drama, *Pranvir Pratap* (1958).

GIRDHARI LAL THAPLIYAL. Modern Garhwali poet, whose *Navan* is a collection of poems.

GIRDHARI SINGH PARIHAR. Rajasthani poet, whose chief works are : *Mankho* (1964 ; based on mythological reference in the *Mahabharat* and the Purans, it presents Subhadra as the saviour of humanity) and *Jagati Jotan* (1960). He also composed patriotic and heroic poems. His popular poem on Mahatma Gandhi : 'O Char Bhuja ro Vishnu Hai', was included in the anthology *Gandhi Gatha*.

GIRIDHAR DAS (1833-60). Poet, who was father of Bharatendu Harishchandra (q. v.). His real name was Gopalchandra but in poetry his pseudonymns were 'Giridhar Das', 'Giridhar' and 'Giridharan'. Gopalchandra's father, Kale Harshchandra, who was a distinguished rich man of Kashi, died when Gopalchandra was only 11 years old. Gopalchandra, by dint of his self-culture, acquired high proficiency in Hindi and Sanskrit as also made a huge collection of books. The library was named 'Saraswati Bhavan', which the late Dr. Rajendralal Mitra offered to purchase for rupees one lakh. Poets and scholars flocked at the house of Gopalchandra and most of the time was spent in literary discussions.

Bharatendu has given the number of works composed by his father to be 40, but many of them are not traceable. Babu Brajratna Das had seen 18 works, while Babu Radhakrishna Das, basing his information on a note of Bharatendu, has listed 10 additional works. Among the 18 works, the chief ones are *Garg Samhita* (a huge work in *Dohas* and *Chaupais* on the story of Krishna), *Jarasandh-Vadh*, *Bharati-Bhushan*, *Rasa-Ratnakar* and *Grishma-Varnan*. *Garg Samhita* and other religious works are in simple and homely style but the four works, listed above, as also other works in this genre are heavily loaded with figures of speech, which, at times, have been difficult enough to cemprehend. Giridhar Das also composed in 1841 a Natak, *Nahush* (q. v.), which Bharatendu names as the first Hindi drama.

GIRIDHAR GOPAL (1925-). Novelist and poet, whose chief works are : *Chandni ke Khandahar* (The Relics of Moonlight), *Kandil aur Kuhase* (The Lantern and Fog ; 1969 ; both novels), and *Agnima* (a collection of songs).

GIRIDHAR JHA 'VIKAL VISHARAD'. Maithili writer, who is noted for his short stories and novel *Anganak Rekha* (published 1981). He also wrote essays dealing with the problems of art and life.

GIRIDHAR KAVIRAY (b. 1714). Poet, about whom nothing is known, although his *Kundaliyas* are on everybody's lips and many of them have become proverbs. The *Kundaliyas* are probably popular for their directness, rather than for their literary merit. They are born of the experiences of daily life and are full of worldly wisdom. He is supposed to have composed his *Kundaliyas* near about 1743. In his poems, the term *Sai* occurs at many places. Some scholars think these were the compositions of his wife. Almost ten editions—small and big—of his *Kundaliyas* have so far been published.

GIRIDHAR SHARMA 'NAVRATNA' (1881-1961). Hindi writer, was was born at Jhalrapatan in Rajasthan. He was a great scholar of Sanskrit and Hindi and had good knowledge of Prakrit, Bengali, Gujarati, Marathi, etc. He has written some 30 works: 14 in Sanskrit, 12 in Hindi and 4 in Gujarati. His Hindi works are: *Jaya Jayant*, *Rai ka Parvat*, *Prem-Kunj*, *Yuga-Palta*, *Maha-Sudarshan*, *Hindi-Magh-Usha*, *Chitrangad*, *Bhishma-Pratigya*, *Bagvan*, *Gitanjali*, *Phal-Sanchay* and *Guru-Mahima*, which are both in verse and prose. Sharma was well-conversant with works on rhetorics and his poetry is without blemish in this regard.

GIRIJA DATT NAITHANI. Modern Garhwali scholar, whose *Mangal Sangrah* is a collection of folk-songs.

GIRIJA KUMAR MATHUR (1919-). Poet of experimental school, who was born in Ashok Nagar of Madhya Pradesh. After completing his education in Lucknow, he joined the All India Radio and got the opportunity of going abroad. His poems are included in: *Tar Saptak* (earlier poems), collected in *Manjir* (Anklet ; 1941 ; containing romantic poems), *Nash aur Nirman* (Destruction and Construction ; containing progressive and experimental poems), *Dhup ke Dhan* (Paddy in Sunshine ; 1955 ; inspired by social realism), *Shilapankh Chamkile* (Bright Rock-wings ; 1961), *Jo Bandh Nahin Saka* (Who could not be Bound ; 1968), *Bhitari Nadi ki Yatra* (Exploring the Inner Stream ; 1967), *Sakshi Rahe Vartman* (Let the Present Stand Witness ; 1978) and *Chhaya Mat Chhuna Man*. *Prithwi-Kalpa* (The Transformation of Earth) is a poetic drama, using scientific images, *Praja hi Rehne Do* (drama ; on ravages of War) ; *Janma Qaid* (Life Imprisonment) is a collection of his one-act plays, while *Nai Kavita : Simayen aur Sambhavanayen* (New Poetry : Limits and Possibilities ; 1966) is an expression of his advanced views on Modern Hindi poetry. There is a balanced fusion of tradition, realism, aestheticism and modernity in his poetry.

GIRIRAJ BHANVAR. Modern Rajasthani writer, who is noted for his essays.

GIRIRAJ KISHORE (1936-). Writer, whose chief works are : *Log* (The People ; 1966), *Chiriyaghar* (The Zoo), *Yatrayen* (Travels ; 1971), *Jugalbandi* (Coupling), *Do* (Two), *Davedar* (The Claimant), *Yatha Prastavit* (As Proposed ; 1982 ; on bureaucratic red-tapism), *Tisri Satta, Indra Sunen, Parishishta* (all novels), *Char Moti Beab* (Four Pearls Without Lustre), *Paper Weight, Rishta aur anya Kahaniyan* (Relation and Other Short Stories), *Nim ke Phul, Shahr dar Shahr* (From City to City), *Ham Pyar Kar Len* (Let us Love ; 1980), *Jagattarini tatha anya Kahaniyan* (1981) (short story collections), *Nar Medh* (Human Sacrifice), *Ghas aur Ghora* (dramas), *Badshah, Ghulam, Begum* (King, Slave, Queen ; a collection of four one-act plays) and *Samvad Setu* (collection of essays). His prominent short stories are : 'The Paper Weight', 'Rishta', etc.

GIRIRAJ SHARAN AGRAWAL. Writer, whose chief work is *Shodh Sandarbh* (1980 ; written in collaboration with Mina Agrawal).

GIRISH ASTHANA (1920-). Novelist, whose chief works are : *Dhul Bhare Chehre* (Dusty Faces ; 1955) and *Dhup-Chhanhi Rang* (Sunshine-Sunshade Colours ; 2 Pts. ; 1970) ; his novels are painted on the canvas of experiences of the Second World War and the Indian life after attainment of Independence. His collection of short stories is *Kalpataru* (1984).

GIRISH RASTOGI. Modern scholar, whose chief works are : *Adhunik Hindi Natak, Mohan Rakesh aur Natak, Samkalin Hindi Natak-kar, Hindi Natak : Siddhant aur Vivechan* (critical works) and *Rangnath ki Vapasi* (drama).

GIRIVAR DAS VAISHNAV. Chhattisgarhi poet, whose collection of political poems was published under the title : *Chhattisgarhi Suraj* (1935).

GIRJANAN RANGU. Hindi poet of Mauritius, whose *Mauritius men Badh* (1972) is a collection of his poems. He has also written a work : *Prayogatmak Hindi.*

GIRVAR SINGH BHANVAR (fl. 1940-47). Malwi poet, who was noted for his *Keshariya Phag*.

GIT DASHAVTAR (18th cent.?). Maithili poem by Surdas (?), which describes the ten incarnations of Vishnu.

GITAVALI. Poem by Tulsidas (q. v.) in Brajbhasha, which was written perhaps between 1586 and 1593.

It consists of more than 330 *Padas* divided in 7 cantos. On seeing the popularity of Krishna's life written in the form of songs, Tulsidas composed also Ram's story in songs. Ostensibly, it purports to be an eye-witness account of all that happened in Ayodhya and elsewhere. The soul of the work lies in Ram's personal charm and grandeur. Tulsidas's Ram is conceived, however, in certain formal limitation and thus the work lacks sonorousness.

GITI RATNAVALI. Anthology of mediaeval Maithili poems, which was edited by Badrinath Jha (q. v.) ; the work is based on a manuscript.

GITIKA. See *Suryakant Tripathi 'Nirala'*.

GODAN (The Gift of the Cow). Novel (1936) by Premchand (q. v.).

Hori, an ordinary peasant, having only five *Bighas* of land, lives with his wife, Dhaniya, son, Gobar and two daughters : Rupa and Sona. He has an intense desire of having a cow and takes it from Bhola. All the village folk come to see the cow, save Hori's real brothers : Shobha and Hira. When Gobar had gone to fetch the cow from Bhola's house, he saw there Bhola's widow-daughter, Jhuniya and they had fallen in love. Gobar and Jhuniya have several occasions to be alone and Jhuniya becomes pregnant. Once Shobha falls ill and when Hori visits him, Hira, taking advantage of Hori's absence, poisons the cow. Hori himself does not mention this fact to anyone, but Hira flees from the village. The pregnant Jhuniya comes to the house of Hori and Gobar runs away to a neighbouring city where he somehow earns something. Hori incurs a number of debts and he is compelled to work as a labourer, with Sona and Rupa following suit. Gobar returns to the village, has a quarrel with his parents and takes Jhuniya and their child to the city. Hori, on compassionate grounds, has also given shelter to one Siliya of cobbler caste, who is a concubine of Pandit Datadin's son, Matadin. For the marriage of his own daughter Sona, Hori runs into further debt. He feels himself defeated with his relentless fight in life. Gobar works in the sugar mills of one Khanna Sahib and during a strike, he is hit by police. So far Siliya is concerned, ultimately Matadin accepts her and brings her to his house. Along with this story, runs another thread, dealing with urban life. There is one Rai Sahib Amarpal Singh, the Zamindar of the locality, who counts amongst his friends one Onkarnath, the editor of a magazine, Shyambihari Tankha, the insurance agent, B. Mehta, the University Professor, Miss Malati, the Lady Doctor, Khanna Sahib and Mirzaji, who owns a shoe-store. Miss Malati and Mehta have come quite close and treat themselves as friends. Raja Surya Pratap Singh wants to get his daughter married to Rudrapal Singh, the elder son of Rai Sahib Amarpal Singh, but the boy loves Saroj, the elder sister of Malati. The Rai Sahib wants some money for election as also for the marriage of his daughter and he approaches Khanna but the latter gives an evasive reply. The Rai Sahib thus meets frustration from all sides. In the meantime, the financial condition of Hori becomes from bad to worse ; he is compelled to marry his daughter Rupa to a middle-aged but well-to-do peasant, Ramsevak. Gobar returns home and Hori embraces him affectionately. One day, Hori falls a prey to sun-stroke. He is about to meet death and everyone is saying that the ceremony of 'Godan' be performed. Dhaniya places a few coins on the hand of Matadin and says that this is all for the 'Godan' and saying this, she falls on the ground.

Godan, the last novel of Premchand, is the most celebrated one and has been translated into most of the Indian and many European languages. In this work, two different patterns of life, the rural and the urban, are juxtaposed : the excitement and show of city life are contrasted with the sufferings of the poor in the villages. The character of Hori is vital and forceful. Some critics are of the view that this novel shows communist leanings of the writer, but, while it is a fact that Premchand was a man of progressive ideas and wanted exploitation and injustice of all kinds to end and indeed some of the characters of this novel may have said such things, which happen to be in conformity with certain communistic principles, but at the time of writing the novel, the writer did not have Communism in his mind.

The *Godan* has been tr. into English, Russian and other Indian languages.

GOENKA KAMAL KISHORE. See *Kamal Kishore Goenka*.

GOGA. See *Jaharpir*.

GOGADE RUPAK. See *Adha Pahad Khan*.

GOGAJI RA RASAVALA. See *Vithu Meha.*

GOKAKAR, SU. GO. See *Kulkarni, Go. Ra.*

GOKALJI (fl. end of 18th cent.). Rajasthani saint-poet of Vishnoi Sect, whose stray verses are available.

GOKARAN SHARMA. Native of Guyana, who is promoting the cause of Hindi in his country.

GOKUL DAS (b. c. 1743) Poet of the Krishna-cult (Chaitanya Sect, who composed *Bhajan Paddhati*, a devotional work.

GOKULNATH (fl. 16th cent.). Grandson of Vallabhacharya, son of Vitthalnath and author in Brajbhasha prose of *Chaurasi Vaishnavan ki Varta* (Descriptions of the 84 Vaishnavas) and *Do Sau Bavan Vaishnavan ki Varta* (Description of the 252 Vaishnavas). Both these Books contain biographical information about Vallabh's disciples and are written in simple Brajbhasha as spoken in Mathura and Agra ; Gokulnatha's works obtained some status for Brajbhasha prose and for some years writing in prose was quite in vogue.

GOKULNATH, GOPINATH, MANIDEV. Three poets, who, under the patronage of Uditnarayan Singh, the Raja of Kashi, jointly tr. the whole of the Sanskrit *Mahabharata* and its supplement, *Harivansha* into Hindi. This stupendous task, which is unique in Hindi, kept them occupied from 1773 to 1827. Despite its huge size, the work does not show any signs of incoherence ; it sustains interest and poetic excellence throughout. The language too is refined and appropriate to the occasion ; the metres also have been judicially selected. Figures of speech, *e. g.*, alliteration, etc. have been studded at suitable places. Gokulnath also composed other works : *Chet-Chandrika* (on *Alankar*), *Govind Sukhad-Vihar*, *Radha-Krishna Vihar* (on *Rasa*), *Radha-Nakh-Shikh*, *Nam-Ratnamala* (dictionary), *Sitaram-Gunarnav* (tr. of *Adhyatma Ramayana*), *Amarkosh Bhasha* (in Hindi) and *Kavi-Mukh-Mandan* (The Poet's Embellishments). According to Ramchandra Shukla, in the composition of Riti works and *Prabandh*, there is no other poet of equal merit in the whole Riti period other than Gokulnath. Gokulnath was a son of the poet Raghunath (q. v.), while Gopinath was Gokulnath's son. Manidev was a resident of Jahanpur in Bharatpur State and had fled to Kashi owing to the maltreatment of his step-mother. In Kashi he lived with Gokulnath and died in 1863.

GOKUL PRASAD 'BRAJ' (1820-1905). Poet of the Riti school,

who was son of Bhailal. A court-poet of Raja Digvijay Singh of Balrampur, he composed some 15 works, of which *Digvijay Bhushan* is the most important.

GOKULANAND. Maithili writer, whose *Man-Charit Natak*, written under the patronage of Maharaja Madhav Singh (1776-1808) is a Kirtaniya drama.

GOLDWIN. Author of *Dictionary of Mohammedan Law and Bengal Revenue Terms* (Calcutta, 1797).

GOLOK BIHARI DHALDHENKANAL (1921-75). Oriya-speaking Hindi author of *Dhwani Vigyan* (1958). He also tr. many of Premchand's novels into Oriya.

GOLOK CHANDRA VAISHYA. Assamese-speaking modern Hindi writer, who is noted for his essays.

GONDA MAHARAJ (fl. 14th cent.). Saint-poet of Maharashtra, who was son of Namdev (q. v.). He composed a good number of *Padas* in Hindi as well ; the number of his Marathi *Padas* is less than his Hindi *Padas*.

GOP (fl. 17th cent.?). Hindi poet of the Riti school, whose chief works are : *Ramalankar* (on Figures of Speech), *Ramchandra-Bhushan* and *Ramchandra-Bharan*.

GOP. See *Krishnadev Sharansingh, Rao*.

GOP BHATT. (b. *c*. 1843). Poet of Gokul, who belonged to the Krishna-cult (Vallabh Sect). He died at the age of 95 ; several of his *Padas* are extant.

GOPAL. Poet and author of *Rasa-Vilas* (1587), a Brajbhasha work on poetics. This work for the first time mentions the word 'Brajbhasha'.

GOPAL (fl. 18th cent.). Assamese poet, whose Hindi (Brajavali) work is *Bali Chhalan Nat* (on the episode of Bali).

GOPAL ATA (1541-1611). Assamese poet, whose works in Hindi (Brajavali) are two dramas : *Janma-Yatra* (on the birth celebration of Krishna) and *Gopi-Uddhav-Sanvad Nat* (dialogue between Gopis and Uddhav).

GOPAL BHATT (fl. 1550). Bengali Vaishnav poet, who also composed some *Padas* in Brajbuli. Gopal Bhatt remained a celibate throughout his life.

GOPAL BHATT (b. *c.* 1643). Poet of the Krishna-cult (Chaitanya Sect), who belonged to the Braj country. His stray *Padas* are available.

GOPAL CHANDRA DEV 'VRATIBHRATA' (1910-74). Writer, who was noted for his historical drama *Sarja Shivaji* (1937).

GAPAL CHANDRA PRAHRAJ. Oriya-speaking modern writer, whose *Purnachandra Bhasha Kosh* is a dictionary in Sanskrit-Oriya-Hindi-Bengali.

GOPAL DAMODAR TAMASKAR (1889-1950). Marathi-speaking Hindi writer, whose essays dealing with religious, social and cultural topics appeared in various magazines. He also wrote two dramas : *Radha-Madhav* (1922), *Dalip* (1929) and a critical work, *Maulikta*.

GOPAL DAN 'KAVIYA' (1815-85). Rajasthani writer, who was born at the village Udaipura near Sikar. He composed *Lavarasa* (*Kurmavansh-Yash-Puran* ; an eulogy of Kurmavansh), *Shikharvanshotpatti* (Pithi Vartik ; on the origin of the Shikhar dynasty) and *Krishna-Vilas* (The Pleasures of Krishna) and a good number of stray verses. He has adopted that style of Rajasthani, which is quite akin to Brajbhasha. His *Lavarasa* gives a good display of heroic sentiment.

GOPAL DAS (fl. 1648). Gujarati saint-poet, who belonged to Chandod in Gujarat and was Vaishya by caste. Apart from his *Gopal Gita* in Guarati, he also composed some *Padas* in Hindi, which resemble those of Kabir (q.v.).

GOPAL DAS (fl. 1673). Bengali Vaishnav poet, who also composed *Padas* in Brajbuli.

GOPAL DAS (*c.* 1803—*c.* 1873). Poet of the Krishna-cult (Chaitanya Sect), who was son of Khadagram of Vrindavan. He composed poetry under the pen name of 'Gupal Kavi' and of his works, 17 in number, the important one is : *Shri Vrindavan Dhamanuragvali*, which gives complete information about Vrindavan.

GOPAL DAS NIRAJ (1926-). Poet, whose songs are quite popular. His chief collections of songs are : *Nadi Kinare* (On the River Bank), *Antardhwani* (The Inner Voice), *Vibhavari* (Night), *Pran-Git* (The Courageous Songs), *Dard Diya Hai* (on pangs of separation,) *Badar Baras Gaye* (The Clouds Have Burst), *Niraj ki Pati* (Niraj's letter), *Do Git* (Two Songs), *Asavari* (Asavari Songs), *Lahar Pukare* (Wave Calling), *Mukti*

(Liberation), *Git bhi Agit Bhi* (Songs as also unmusical songs), *Likh Likh Bhejat Pati* (Sending Letter after Letter) and *Niraj ke Lokpriya Git* (Popular Songs of Niraj). His lyrics, both in content and form, have considerable literary merit ; they are enjoyable as also thought-provoking. *Sumitranandan Pant : Kal, Kavya aur Darshan* (Sumitranandan Pant : Art, Poetry and Philosophy) is his critical work. He also wrote a novel : *Pyar, Roti our Marghat.* Niraj served as a Lecturer in Hindi at Aligarh for some time, but thereafter joined the film industry.

GOPAL DEV (fl. end 16th and early 17th cent.). Assamese writer, whose only extant play, *Janma-Yatra* depicts the story of Krishna's birth and his subsequent removal to Nand's house; the play is written in Brajavali.

GOPALJI JHA 'GOPESH'. Maithili poet, whose collections of lyrics are : *Sondaik Patra* and *Gumm Bhela Tharih Chhi* (1966).

GOPAL KRISHNA KAUL (1924-). Scholar, whose chief works are : *Natak-kar Ashk, Dinkar : Srishti aur Drishti* and editing of *Kavyadhara.* He had been Senior Producer of Hindi Programme in All India Radio.

GOPAL LAL KHANNA. Modern scholar, whose chief work is *Hindi ka Saral Bhasha-Vigyan* (Easy Philology of Hindi).

GOPAL LAL PRAJAPATI Modern Rajasthani poet, who has composed Nature, patriotic and heroic poems.

GOPAL NAYAK. Celebrated musician, who was a contemporary of Amir Khusro (1253-1325). Some of the *Padas* of Nayak are still available in Brajbhasha.

GOPAL PRASAD MUDGAL. Writer, whose *Lottery* (1980) is a collection of essays.

GOPAL PRASAD VYAS (1916-). Humorous poet and writer, who has also written in Brajbhasha. His chief works are: *Main ne Kaha* (I Said; illustrated), *Kuchh Sach : Kuchh Jhuth* (Some True : Some False), *Aji Suno* (Please Listen), *Gappon ka Khazana* (Treasury of Gossips), *Pancham Swar, Chakachak, Naradji Khabar Layen Hain* (Pts. 1, 2), *Bat Bat men Bat* and *Yatram-Tatram* (Pts. 1, 2). His other works are : *Mohi Braj Bisrat Nahin, Bin Hindi Sab Sun* and ed. of *Swatantrata Rajat Jayanti Abhinandan Granth* (1973). His works are collected in *Rang, Jang aur Vyangya* (Entertainment, Tussle and Satire). He remained on the staff of daily 'Hindustan', New Delhi.

GOPAL RAM. Riti poet, who composed in 1669 his *Rasa Sagar*, a work on *Rasa*.

GOPAL RAM GAHMARI (1866-1946). Early novelist, who was born at the village Gahmar in the Ghazipur district. He has written about 200 works including detective and social novels, historical and social dramas, poems and satires. His chief works are: *Sas Patohu* (The Mother-in-law and the Daughter-in-law), *Bada Bhai* (The Elder Brother), *Naye Babu* (The New Babu), *Double Wife*, *Do Bahan* (Two Sisters), *Devrani Jethani* (Wives of Husband's Younger Brother and Elder Brother), *Tin Patohu* (Three Daughters-in-law), *Chatur Chanchal* (The Wise Unsteady Lady), *Baqi Bebak* (The Balance Paid-up), *Admi Bana* (Has become Humane), *Nanad-Bhaujai* (Husband's sister and Bother's wife), *Amarsingh* (historical), *Desh-dasha* (The Plight of the Country), *Vidyavinod* (Fun with Knowledge), *Babhruvahan* (mythological), *Janmabhumi* (The Motherland), *Ichchha-Shakti* (The Will Power), etc. ; among these are also dramas tr. from Bengali. He is remembered for his detective works, e.g., *Adbhut Lash* (The Strange Corpse), *Begunah ka Khun* (The Murder of the Innocent), *Double Jasus* (Double Detective), *Jasuspar Jasusi* (Detection on the Detective), *Jasus ki Dali*, *Khuni Kaun* ? (Who Was the Murderer ?), *Bekasur ki Phansi* (The Hanging of the Innocent), *Gupta Bhed* (The Hidden Secret), *Sarakti Lash* (The Creeping Corpse), etc. He also edited a detective magazine 'Jasus' (The Detective).

GOPAL SHARAN SINGH (1891-1960). Poet, who, influenced by the Khari Boli slogan, wrote *Madhavi* (The Madhavi Creper ; 1929), *Kadambini* (The Row of Clouds ; 1937), *Sumana* (Flowery ; 1941), *Sanchita* (Collection) and *Jyotishmati* (The Night) ; all these are well-written and are representative of the styel of the Mahavir Prasad Dwivedi era.

GOPAL SINGH NEPALI (1911-63). Poet, whose chief poetical works are: *Pipal* (The Holy Fig Tree), *Hari Ghas* (The Green Grass). *Panchhi* (The Bird), *Umang* (Gusto), *Ragini*, *Panchami* (The Fifth Day), *Rimjhim* (Drizzle) ; *Navin* is a collection of his poems. He was associated for a good time with film industry.

GOPAL UPADHYAY. Dramatist, whose chief works : *Sirf Tumhare Liye* (Only for You) and *Ek Chikh Andhere Ki* (The Cry of Darkness ; both 1980) depict respectively the sad plight of urban and rural woman; *Ek Tukra Itihas* is his novel.

GOPICHAND. Bhojpuri folk-tale in verse, which describes how the legendary Gopichand, the ruler of Rangpur in Bengal, renounces the world and how his wives weep for him. Various versions of the Gopichand legend are popular in northern India, Bengal and Gujarat. Gopichand is regarded as a follower of Gorakhnath (q.v.).

GOPI KRISHNA. Modern Maithili scholar, who has written critical articles.

GOPINATH. See *Gokulnath, Gopinath, Manidev.*

GOPINATHAN, G. Malayalam-speaking Hindi writer, whose chief work is : *Keraliyon ki Hindi ko Den* (The Contribution of Keralites to Hindi ; 1973). He is Professor of Hindi at Calicut Unirersity. He also tr. into Hindi select new poems of Malayalam in free verse.

GOPI SINGH MEHTA. Modern Kumaoni poet, who is famous for his stray poems.

GOPISHWAR (fl. middle of 18th cent.). Maithili poet, who composed hymns on devotional and pseudo-philosophical subjects.

GORA (fl. between 1450-1550). Dingal poet, who composed stray verses and *Gits* in celebrating the victory of Rao Jaitsi of Bikaner over Kamran, a son of Babar. He also composed some verses about Rao Lunkaran, father of Rao Jaitsi, who was later Killed in a battle with Muslims at Narnaul.

GORA BADAL KI BAT. Dingal work by Jatmal (q.v.), which describes the heroic tale of Raja Ratnasen's two warriors : Gora and Badal for rescuing queen Padmavati. It is considered the best work of prose in the 17th century.

GORA BADAL PADMINI CHAUPAI. See *Hemratan Suri.*

GORAKHNATH. Famous Nath Yogi, a disciple of Matsyendranath (q.v.) and a leading exponent of Nath order ; he was counted among the 84 Siddhas, where he was called Gorakshpa. There is a controversy about his time, but it is believed that he lived in the 13th century. The following works, both in verse and prose, have been considered authentic by Pitambar Datt Barthwal : *Sabadi, Pada, Sishya Darsan, Pran Sankali, Narvai Bodh, Atmabodh* (?), *Abhimatra Joga, Pandrah Tithi, Saptavar, Machhindra Gorakh Bodh, Romavali, Gyan Tilak, Gyan Chauntisi* and *Panchmatra* ; other scholars regard *Garakh-Ganesh Goshthi, Mahadev Gorakh Sanvad, Gorakhji Ki Satrah Kala, Gorakh Bodh, Datt-Gorakh Sanvad, Yogeshwar*

Sakhi, Narvai Bodh, Virat Puran, Gorakh Sar, Gorakh-Turk-Samvad and *Gorakh Vani* as his works.

Gorakhnath and his followers rebelled against the immoralities of Vajrayan Siddhas and preached the philosophy of Hathyoga (a Shivaite form of Patanjali's Yoga). Hindu rituals and Hindu articles of faith were discarded and the only religion left to the people was to practise the philosophy of the yogis, too abstruse and abstract for the common people to follow. The literature of Nath Panth, however, provides a chain between the poetry of the Sidddhas and that of Kabir and other Nirgunias.

As regards language, it was Gorakhnath who adopted Brajbhasha, the traditional language of poetry, for prose writing. He made a serious effort to discard all distinctions between the language of prose and poetry.

GORAKHNATH CHAUBE. Modern Bhojpuri writer, who is noted for his social drama, *Ulta Zamana* (The Contrary World), written in a forceful language.

GORAKSH-VIJAY. Maithili drama by Vidyapati (q.v.), which depicts the traditional story of Matsyendranath (the celebrated preceptor of the Yogi Gorakhnath). Two Yogis – Gorakshnath and Kananipad are in search of their preceptor, Matsyendranath, who has become the king of Kadalipur and is engrossed in sensual pleasures. The Yogis are not allowed to enter the palace of Matsyendranath, but when it is announced that they are the dancers, they are permitted to perform their dance. The Yogis in the guise of dancers show excellent poses and sing charming songs, but suddenly they kill the king's son. The King orders the Yogis to be put to death, but as the Yogis revive the dead son, the king's joy knows no bounds. The king recognizes Gorakshnath and also realizes what power he has lost in becoming a king. At the instance of Gorakshnath, Matsyendranath leaves the palace, leaving behind his sad queens. Thus ends the story of the victory of Gorakshnath. See *Harpati*.

GORDHANJI (fl. 18th cent.). Rajasthani poet of Jasnathi tradition, who was a Sinava Rajput of the village Inpalsar (Churu). His *Gaur Vyanvalo* (q.v.) in 121 verses treats of the marriage of Parvati and Shiv.

GORDHAN SINGH SHEKHAWAT. Modern Rajasthani poet, who has composed love poems as also poems in the style of Nai Kavita.

GORYUNOV, VLADIMIR I. Modern Soviet Hindi scholar, whose chief works are : *Russian-Hindi Dictionary* (Moscow, 1957 ; 1375 pages), *Hindi Pathya Pustak* (Pt., 1 ; 1968, pp. 719, Pt. II., pp. 559) and several articles concerning the word 'Jo'.

GOSAIN CHARIT (Biography of Gosain). Biography of Gosain Tulsidas (q.v.), composed by Beni Madhavdas (q.v.) in 1630 ; certain scholars, however, doubt its authenticity.

GOSWAMI, KISHORILAL. See *Kishorilal Goswami.*

GOSWAMI, RADHACHARAN. See *Radhacharan Goswami.*

GOSWAMI TULSIDAS. See *Ramchandra Shukla.*

GOTIYA, AMAN SINGH. See *Aman Singh Gotiya.*

GOVARDHAN NATH SHUKLA (1915-). Writer, whose chief works are *Kavivar Parmanand Das aur Vallabh Sampraday* (The Great Poet Parmanand and the Vallabh Sect), *Survani* and *Mukundamala* (the last in Sanskrit). He has also ed. *Parmanand Sagar* (The Ocean of Parmanand) of the *Ashtachhap* poet, Parmanand Das.

GOVARDHAN PRASAD 'SADAY'. Modern Magahi poet, whose stray poems bear an optimistic strain.

GOVARDHAN SARASWAT (fl. 1854-99). Folk-poet of Haryana, who composed and staged the *Sangs : Mahabharat, Krishna-Lila, Jasvant Singh* and *Dulle.*

GOVARDHAN SHARAN DEV (fl. 18th cent.). Poet of the Krishna-cult (Haridasi Sect), who composed a small *Vani.*

GOVILKAR, M. V. Marathi-speaking modern Hindi scholar, whose chief work is : *Rasik Sundar aur Unka Kavya.*

GOVIND (fl. 15th cent.). Maithili writer, whose *Nal-Charit Natak*, a Kirtaniya form of drama, is based on the familiar story of king Nal's exile. The dialogue is in Sanskrit and Prakrit but the songs are wholly in Maithili. There are poignant scenes in the play, when Damyanti, forsaken by Nal, cries out in distress and the king repents his fault of gambling. Ultimately, the king and the queen are re-united. Govind's verses found respectable place in contemporary anthologies.

GOVIND (fl. end 17th cent.). Poet of the Riti school, whose chief work, *Karnabharan* is on *Alankars.*

GOVIND AGRAWAL. Rajasthani scholar, who has made a study of Rajasthani folk-songs. He has collected over a thousand short folk-tales, of which many have been published in Rajasthani and Hindi. He has also published many Rajasthani proverbs, idioms, riddles, sayings, etc. and has done much work on mediaeval Rajasthani literature. His *Nukti Danan* (1978), a *Gadya-Kavya*. contains poetic prose. See *Bhagirath Kanoriya*.

GOVIND BHATT. Modern Hindi poet of Nepal, who is noted for his work *Buddha*.

GOVIND CHARAN (b. *c.* 1783). Poet of the Krishna-cult (Chaitanya Sect), who hailed from Bengal. His *Ras Panchadhyayi Bhasha* has been composed in a Brajbhasha mixed with Bengali.

GOVIND CHATAK. Garhwali scholar, whose chief works are : *Garhwali Lok Git* (Garhwali folk-songs ; 1956 ; this includes a rendering in Khari Boli), *Garhwal ki Lok Kathayen* (Folk-tales of Garhwal ; 2 vols.), *Garhwal ke Kathatmak Lok-Git*, *Madhya Pahari ka Bhasha Shastriya-Adhyayan*, *Dharti ka Phul*, *Bansuli*, *Bol rai Gain*, *Jangli Phul* (a collection of seven one-act plays), *Kya Gauri Kya Saunli* (eollection of essays, which is based on Garhwali proverbs) and *Git Vasanti* (poems on the pattern of folk-songs). He has also written dramas : *Kala Mukh* (The Blackened Face), *Apne-apne Khunte* and critical works : *Adhunik Natak ka Messiah : Mohan Rakesh* and *Pitambar Das Barthwal ke Shreshth Nibandh*. His short story collection is *Larki aur Per*, while *Brihat Hindi Paryayvachi Kosh* is a dictionary.

GOVIND CHATURVEDI (1912-). Poet, who is son of Navnit Chaturvedi (q.v.). He is noted for his poem : *Brajvani*.

GOVIND CHAUDHARI. Modern Maithili writer, who has written skits entitled *Chumaona*.

GOVIND DAS (b. 1554). Poet of the Krishna-cult, whose chief work is *Ekant Pad* (Lonely Verses).

GOVIND DAS, SETH (1896-1974). Dramatist of Jubbalpur, who had been a prominent Congress leader. His chief dramas are : *Vishwa Prem* (The Love of the World ; 1917), *Kartavya* (Duty; 2 Pts.), *Prakash*, *Ashok*, *Harsh* (historical ; 1935), *Sevapath* (The Path of Service), *Kulinta* (Gentility), *Vikas*, *Shashigupta*, *Prem ya Pap* (Love or Sin ; 1946), *Karna*, *Sher Shah*, *Bada Papi Kaun* ? (Who is a Great Sinner?), *Tyag ya Grahan* (Renunciation or Acquisition ; 1943), *Pakistan*, *Gharibi ya Amiri* (Poverty or Wealthiness), *Ram se Gandhi* (From Ram to Gandhi), *Sukh*

Kismen ? (Where does Happiness Lie ?), *Sneh ya Swarg* (Love or Heaven), *Hinsa aur Ahinsa* (Violence or Non-violence), *Mahatma Gondhi, Bharatendu, Rahim, Bhudan, Santosh Kahan* (Where Lies Contentment ?), *Chatushpath* (a collection of four dramas), *Patit* (The Fallen) ; *Ekadashi* (The Eleventh Day), *Navrasa, Saptarashmi* (The Seven Rays), *Do Natak* (Two Dramas) and *Panchbhut* (The Flve Elements) are his one-act play collections. Most of his plays are written with the political background and the Gandhian ideology. His other chief works are : *Natyakala Mimansa* (criticism: on dramatic art), *Achala, Indumati* (novels), *Prithwiparikrama* (travelogue) and his *autobiography* (3 Pts.).

Some critics do not rate high the works of Govind Das and they think that much of his writing seems to lack inspiration or any genuine inner urge ; this view is, however, not shared by others.

GOVIND DAS JHA (fl. 17th cent.). Maithili poet, who was the greatest successor of Vidyapati and was a contemporary of Maharaja Sundar Thakur (1663/4-1670/1). His brothers : Gangadas, Haridas and Ramdas were all poets. Traditionally, Govind Das is said to have written a work, *Krishna Lila*; perhaps it was the name given to the series of Radha Krishna *Padas*, which are known after him today.

'The poetry of Govind Das has very marked difference from that of Vidyapati. While Vidyapati is sophisticated, piles metaphor upon metaphor, creates courtly atmosphere of joys and sorrows of human life and in general succeeds in entering into the sentiments of men and women through simple and directly sensual images, Govind Das is more concerned with the diction of his poems than with their feelings.'—Jayakanta Mishra : *History of Maithili Literature*, p. 131.

GOVIND DAS KAVIRAJ (1535-1613) Bengali Vaishnav poet, who also composed *Padas* in Brajbuli. Some of his *Padas* are available in *Padakalpataru* (q.v.).

GOVIND DEV (fl. 18th cent.). Saint-poet of the Krishna-cult (Nimbark Sect), who composed *Jayati Chaturdashi.*

GOVIND DWIJ (fl. 18th cent.). Assamese poet, whose only Hindi (Brajavali) work is a drama : *Syamantak-Haran*, available in a manuscript form in the University of Gauhati.

GOVIND GILLABHAI (1848-1924). Poet, hailing from Gujarat. He wrote some 32 works, chief ones being *Niti Vinod* (on polity), *Pavas-Payonidhi, Shelesh-Chandrika* (on puns), *Vishnu-*

Vinay-Pachchisi (25 verses on entreaty to Vishnu).

GOVIND HULAS. Drama (1700 or 1770), recently discovered and since published, which is a free translation of the Sanskrit play, *Vidagdha-Madhava* of Rup Goswami. There is uncertainty of the name of the translator but it is believed that it was translated by Jiv Goswami. The drama portrays the episodes from the life of Radha and Krishna.

GOVIND JHA. Maithili writer, whose chief works are: *Basat* (1969), *Antim Pranam* (1982 ; social dramas), *Mithilak Pratini dhi* (one-act plays) and *Uchchatar Maithili Vyakaran* (1979 ; on higher grammar). He has, in collaboration with Anand Mishra, edited *Varna-Ratnakar* (1980). He also tr. into Maithili *Virangana* from Bengali. As a poet, he is noted for his elegance and harmony.

GOVIND LAL MATHUR. Rajasthani writer, whose *Satrangini* (1955), a collection of one-act plays, treats of social reforms.

GOVIND MALHI. Sindhi-speaking modern Hindi novelist, who is noted for his novel *Chhui Mui* (The Sensitive). He has also edited *Chuni Hui Sindhi Kahaniyan*.

GOVIND MISHRA (1939-). Fiction writer, whose chief works are : *Vah Apna Kata Chehra* (That My Cut-Face), *Lal Pili Zamin* (The Red and Yellow Earth), *Huzur Durbar* (1981), *Naye Purane Man-Bap* (novels), *Antahpur* (Harem ; 1976), *Meri Priya Kahaniyan*, *Khud ke Khilaf* (Against Myself ; 1982), *Dhansu*, *Apahij*, *Khak Itihas* (1984 ; short story collections). His prominent short stories are : 'Apahij' (The Cripple), 'Jantantra' (Democracy), 'Antahpur', etc.

GOVIND NARAYAN MISHRA (1859-1923). Writer, whose prose imitated the involved and elaborate style of *Kadambari*. In his essays and books, he wrote a language which was obviously influenced by Sanskrit. His chief works are *Govind-Nibandhavali* (essays), *Vibhakti Vichar* (on grammar), *Shiksha Sopan* and *Saraswat Sopan*.

GOVIND NARAYAN PATHIK. Modern Hindi poet of Fiji, who is famous for his stray poems.

GOVIND NATH RAJGURU. Scholar, who is noted for his *Gurmukhi Lipi men Hindi Gadya* (Hindi Prose in the Gurmukhi Script ; 1980).

GOVIND PRASAD GHILDIYAL (1870-1922). Writer, who tr.

Shakespeare's *Hamlet* as *Jayant* as also *Othello* into Hindi. He was born at the village Dang in Shrinagar Garhwal of Uttar Pradesh.

GOVIND RAMJI (fl. end of 18th cent.). Rajasthani saint-poet of the Vishnoi Sect, whose stray verses are available.

GOVIND RAO VITTHAL (1890-1966). Chhattisgarhi writer, whose chief work is *Nag-Lila* (1927). He was born in the village Borgaon in Chanda district of Madhya Pradesh.

GOVIND SHARAN DEV (fl. 18th cent.). Saint-poet of the Krishna-cult (Nimbark Sect), whose *Padas* and other verses are preserved at his religious seat in Salemabad (Rajasthan).

GOVIND SHARAN TRIGUNAYAT (1924-). Writer, whose chief works are : *Kabir ki Vichar-Dhara* (Ideas of Kabir), *Kabir aur Jayasi ka Rahasyavad* (Mysticism of Kabir and Jayasi), *Hindi ki Nirgun Kavyadhara aur Uski Darshnik Prishthabhumi* and *Hindi Dashrupak* (tr. from Sanskrit).

GOVIND SHASTRI DUGVEKAR (1883-1961). Marathi-speaking Hindi dramatist, who had a great command of Sanskrit, Marathi and Hindi. He wrote three original dramas : *Sati-Charitra Chandrika*, *Har Har Mahadev*, *Kaldharma* (incomplete) and tr. two other works respectively from Sanskrit and Marathi : *Kalvikagnimitra* and *Subhadraharan*. He also wrote *Vivekanand ki Jivni* and *Kahavat Ratnakar*.

GOVIND SHENAY, V. Malayalam-speaking modern Hindi writer, who has tr. N. Krishna Pillai's Malayalam one-act drama : *Kanyaka* into Hindi. He has also written two satirical works of sketches under the titles of *Mystic Sahib ka Kurta* (The Shirt of Mystic Sahib) and *Age Kaun Haval* (What Would Happen Tomorrow ?).

GOVIND SINGH, GURU (1666-1708). The tenth and the last Guru of the Sikh religion, who was born in Patna, when his father, Guru Tegh Bahadur and Mata Gujari were on tour of the eastern India. He was not only a great poet himself, but did much to encourage Hindi by having in his *Durbar* more than 50 poets, whose writings have lately come to light.

Govind Singh's works have been compiled separately under the title *Dasham Granth* ; with the exception of two, the remaining 12 works are in Hindi. These are : *Akal Stuti* (In Praise of God), *Vichitra Natak* (his autobiography), *Chandi-Charit* (heroic ; in 2 Pts.), *Japu*, *Gyan-Prabodh*, *Chaubis Avtar* (24

Incarnations), *Charitropakhyan*, *Brahmavtar*, *Rudravtar*, *Shastra Nam-Mala*, *Bhagvatiji-ki-Var* (heroic) and stray *Savaiyas*. His *Govind Ramayan* is a work in Braj bhasha, widely read and sung.

The *Dasham Granth* is a voluminous work of 1428 pages and the Hindi works account for more than three-fourth of the volume. Apart from poetry of religious nature, Govind Singh was at his best while writing in *Vira Rasa* and also in *Shringar* and quite one-half of his total output falls under these two categories.

Govind Singh's literary output has a *Puranic* background. As a poet of *Vir Rasa*, he holds a high place among Hindi writers.

GOVIND SWAMI (b. 1505). Poet, who was born at the village Antari in Bharatpur. He was one of the members of the Ashtachhap and a disciple of Vitthalnath. Besides his being a poet, he was a great musician too. Tansen, the celebrated court-musician of Akbar, delighted in his verses and often used to come to him to hear him sing his own compositions. It is said that Akbar himself came to enjoy his compositions. His *Padas* have naturally the special quality of being adaptable to music. He was discovered by Vitthalnath leading the life of a recluse in the Mahaban forest of Govardhan. He was so fond of Brajbhumi that he did not like to go to Heaven if he were to leave his Braj. In his eulogistic descriptions of Braj, he includes sights and scenery too.

GOVIND THAKUR (*c*. 1482-1527). Maithili poet, whose poems show a great felicity of expression and command of the language. He was a scholar of Sanskrit and composed many poems under Kans Narayan's patronage. He is sometimes identified with the author of Sanskrit work, *Kavya-Pradip* or with the author of the Maithili play, *Nal-Charit Nat*.

GOVIND VALLABH PANT. Dramatist and novelist, whose chief works are : *Kanjus ki Khopri* (The Skull of a Miser ; 1923), *Varmala* (The Bridegroom's Garland ; 1925 ; historical drama), *Rajmukut* (1935 ; on the sacrifice of Panna of Chittor), *Angur ki Beti* (1937 ; on the ill effects of wine), *Suhag Bindi*, *Urmila*, *Yayati*, *Antahpur ka Chhidra* (1940), *Sujata*, *Ahankar*, *Tulsidas*, *Panna* (all dramas), *Vishkanya* (a collection of one-act plays); *Parna*, *Maitrey*, *Taron ke Sapne*, *Jal-Samadhi*, *Bala Banjara*, *Kanak Kamal*, *Kohinur ka Haran* and *Madhura* are his chief novels. His short story collections are : *Tin Din* and *Sone ka Devta tatha anya Kahaniyan*. *Varmala* is the story of a girl, Vaishalini, who, despite calamity upon calamity finally succeeds in garlanding Avikshit with the same 'Varmala', which she carried with her for years.

GOWER, G. European scholar, whose chief work is *Himalayan Village* (London, 1938).

GOYAM (GAUTAM). Poet, who added some supplementary material to Chaturbhuj Das's *Madhumalati*. See *Chaturbhuj Das*.

GRAMMATICA HINDOSTANICA. See *Schulzii, Benjamin*.

GRAMMATICA INDOSTANA. A grammar of Hindustani, written in Portuguese (Lisbon, 1778 ; 2nd ed., Lisbon, 1805) ; its author is not known. This is far in advance of Hardley's work.

GRAMYA. See *Sumitra Nandan Pant*.

GRANT, F.N. Author of *The Pocket Hindoostanee Vocabulary* (Calcutta, 1869).

GRANTHRAJ. Rajasthani poem by Gopinath Gadan (q.v.), which describes the life of Maharaja Gajsingh (1746-87) of Bikaner. The poem reveals the poet's deep knowledge of Charan trditional poetry, command over language and mastery over metres. This is considered an important work in Dingal literature.

GRANTH SAHIB (*Adi Granth*). The Scripture of the Sikhs, which was compiled in 1604 by Arjuna Dev, the fifth Guru. Apart from the hymns of Nanak and other Sikh Gurus, it contains hymns of Pre-Nanak saints. The names of the saint-poets and the Sikh Gurus and the number of their hymns included in the *Granth Sahib* are given below :—

1. Jaiyadev, the author of *Gitagovinda* (2 hymns) ; 2. Sheikh Farid, a Sufi, born in 1173 (4 hymns and 130 Shloks) ; 3. Namdev, the Maharashtra saint (60 hymns) ; 4. Trilochan, also from Maharashtra (4 hymns) ; 5. Paramanand (1 hymn) ; 6. Sadna (1 hymn) ; 7. Veni (3 hymns) ; 8. Ramanand (1 hymn) ; 9. Dhanna (4 hymns) ; 10. Pipa (1 hymn) ; 11. Sen (1 hymn) ; 12. Ravidas (41 hymns) ; 13. Kabir (292 hymns).

Sikh Gurus.

1. Nanak (974 hymns including Shloks) ; 2. Angad Dev (62 Shloks) ; 3. Amardas (907 hymns including Shloks) ; 4. Ramdas (679 hymns including Shlokas) ; 5. Arjun Dev (2218 hymns including Shloks) ; 6. Tegh Bahadur (39 hymns and 56 Shloks) ; 7. Govind Singh (1 Shlok).

Other Saints and Bards :

1. Bhikhan (2 hymns) ; 2. Surdas, the famous Hindi poet (2 hymns) ; 3. Sundar (1 poem) ; 4. Mardan (3 Shloks).

Apart from the holy book of the Sikhs, the *Granth* is in the nature of an anthology of religious poetry representing the blending of Hinduism and Islam.

GRANTHI. See *Sumitra Nandan Pant.*

GREAVES, EDWIN (b. 1854). Born in London, he came to India in 1881 as a Christian missionary. He wrote five books in Hindi on religious subjects. He also wrote an article 'Tulsidas ka Jivan Charitra', which was published in 'Nagari Pracharini Patrika'. *A Grammar of Modern Hindi* (Benares, 1896) ran into second edition, which was published in 1908. In 1919, Greaves wrote another work *Hindi Grammar*, which is considered very useful for those who wish to understand Hindi grammar through the medium of English ; it was published by London Missionary Society. He also wrote *Notes on the Grammar of Tulsidas Ramayan* (Calcutta, 1895). He is, however, remembered for his *A Sketch of Hindi Literature*, which was published in 1918 by the Christian Literature Society. After remaining in India almost for 40 years, Greaves returned to London in 1920, but only after he had written another work : *Kashi Nagar* in English. See *Hindi Literature, A Sketch of.*

GREEN, A.O., LIEUT. COL. Author of *A Practical Hindustani Grammar* (2 Pts., Oxford, 1895).

GRIERSON, GEORGE ABRAHAM (1851-1941). Celebrated scholar, who was born in Ireland. He passed the Indian Civil Service examination and came to India in 1871. While holding various official assignments, he wrote and edited a number of works, out of which the very important ones are : *Bihar Peasant's Life* (1885 ; an Encyclopaedia of Bihari rural life), *Seven Grammars of the Dialects and Sub-dialects of the Bihari Language*, *The Modern Vernacular Literature of Hindustan* (the first history of Hindi literature) and his monumental work *Linguistic Survey of India* (11 vols., 1903-28), which was completed in well over 33 years (1894-1927) ; it has become the source of practically all the major research in the field of Indian and General Linguistics. Grierson also wrote essays on Tulsidas (tr. into Hindi as *Tulsidas : Vyakti aur Rachna Sandarbh*), Jayasi, Vidyapati and on various Indian dialects. He collected 82 songs of the poet Vidyapati from various singers. He published about 200 articles on Sanskrit, Prakrit and on other Indian languages and scripts.

His other important works are : *Bihari ka Tulnatmak Kosh* (with Hoernle ; 1889 ; incomplete), *Pishach Language* (1906), *A Manual af Kashmiri Language* (1911), *Kashmiri Kosh* (4 Pts., 1916-32), 'Some Bihari Folk-songs' (1884), 'Some Bhojpuri Folk-songs' (1886), 'Folklore from Eastern Gorakhpur' (1883), 'Two Versions of the Song of Gopichand' (1885), 'The Song of Vijaymal' (1884), 'The Song of Alha's Marriage' (1885), 'A Summary of the Alhakhand' (1885), 'Selected Specimens of the Bihari Language—the Bhojpuri Dialect, the Git Nayak Banjarvar' (1889), 'The Song of Manikchand' (1878) and *The Lay of Alha* (Oxford, 1923).

Highly honoured by the British Government and eminent Universities and loved by Indian scholars, Grierson would always be remembered for the pioneer work that he did in the field of Linguistics.

GRISHINA, ELENA MIKHAILOVNA (1932-). Soviet Hindi scholar, who is an editor in the Progressive Publishing House in Moscow. She has edited in Hindi some writings of Karl Marx, Angles, Lenin, etc.

GROWSE, F.S. English scholar, who edited the manuscript of *Prithwiraj Raso* (1868), which was available in the Agra College Library and wrote articles under the heading 'The Poems of Chand Barday' in the 'Journal of the Royal Asiatic Society, Bengal'. He also tr. into English the *Ramayan of Tulsidas* (1877-80), though the translation remained incomplete.

GUGGA (GOGA). See *Jaharpir*.

GULAB (1830-1901). Rajasthani poet, who was born at Rajgarh in the Alwar State. His patron was Maharao Raja Ramsingh of Bundi, who had granted him two villages and bestowed other honours upon him. He composed 34 poems mainly in Brajbhasha dealing with Ram-Krishna Bhakti as also on poetics, etc., *e.g.*, *Ramashtak*, *Gulab-Kosh*, *Bhushan-Chandrika*, *Brihad-Vanita-Bhushan*, *Krishnalila*, *Ramlila*, *Krishna-Charitra*, etc.

GULAB CHAND NAGAURI. Rajasthani writer, whose chief works are : *Marwari Mausar aur Sagai Janjal* (1923 ; social drama) and short stories : 'Badi Tij' and *Beti ki Bikri tatha Bahu ki Kharidi* (1912).

GULAB KHANDELWAL (1923-). Poet, whose chief works are : *Kavita* (Poetry), *Chandni* (Moonlight), *Bali Nirvas* (mythological), *Kach-Devyani* (*Khand-Kavya*), *Gandhi Bharati* (44 sonnets on the assassination of Mahatma Gandhi), *Ahalya*, *Mere Bharat*, *Mere Swadesh* (patriotic poems), *Sau Gulab Khile* and *Usha* (*Prabandh-Kavya*) ; his language is easy but forceful.

GULAB RAO MAHARAJ (1880-1921). Marathi-speaking saint-poet, who composed *Padas* in Hindi.

GULAB RAI (1887-1963). Critic and essayist, who was born in Etawa. His chief works are : *Navrasa*, *Siddhant aur Adhyayan*, *Kavya ke Rup* (Forms of Poetry), *Hindi Sahitya ka Subodh Itihas* (History of Hindi Literature), *Hindi Natya Vimarsh* (on drama), *Prabandh Prabhakar*, *Man ki Baten* (1954), *Phir Nirasha Kyon*, *Meri Asphaltayen*, *Mere Nibandh* (1955 ; reflective essays), *Hindi Kavya Vimarsh* (on poetry), *Sahitya Samiksha* (on criticism), *Alochak Ramchandra Shukla* (Ramchandra Shukla as Critic ; in collaboration with Vijyendra Snatak) and *Adhyayan aur Aswad* (1957 ; critical essays). In his works, he has applied a synthesis of western and Indian poetics.

GULAB SINGH NIRMALA. Poet of the Nirmala Sect of Nanak Panth, whose *Bhav Rasamrit* (*c.* 1743) contains devotional poems relating to Ram.

GULAL SAHIB (1693-1743). Saint-poet, who was born at Bhurkura in the Ghazipur district. He composed *Barahmasas*, *Hindolas*, *Holis*, *Basants*, *Rekhtas*, *Mangals* and *Artis*, then current forms of poetry, which betray the influence of Kabir. His poetry is replete with love and devotion.

GULERI. See *Chandradhar Sharma Guleri*.

GULHAMID VIGAN. Modern Urdu writer of Mauritius, whose one-act play 'Patni ki Khatir' is written in pure Hindi.

GULSHAN NANDA. Modern popular novelist, whose several novels have been filmed. His chief novels are : *Jhil ke Us Par*, *Chandan*, *Ajnabi*, *Tin Rang*, *Menhdi*, *Vapasi*, *Kali Ghata* and *Jalti Chattan*.

GULYAMOVA, RUNA HOJIYABAROVNA (1939-). Soviet Hindi scholar, who has done doctorate on Vishnu Prabhakar as a writer and dramatist and has also written several articles on the various works of Vishnu Prabhakar.

GUMAN MISHRA (fl. 1743-83). Poet of the Riti school, who was born at Mahoba in Panna State and was patronized by Raja Akbar Ali Khan of Pihani. He is known as the translator from

Sanskrit of Sri Harsha's *Naishadha-Charita* in verse. The translation, on the whole, is successful, though subtleties of meaning in the original defeat the translator. The poet has employed a variety of metres in this work. Guman also composed *Krishna-Chandrika* (1781), a *Prabandh-Kavya* on the devotion to Krishna. On the conventional Riti style, he composed *Chhandavati* (on prosody), *Rasa Nayikabhed*, etc. Guman's poetry is of a fairly high standard.

GUMAN SINGH (1840-1914). Rajasthani Bhakta-poet and Yogi, who was a Jagirdar of Lachhmanpura (Mewar). Mostly spiritual, his poems are : *Moksha Bhavan*, *Manisha Laksha Chandrika*, *Yoga Bhanu Prakashika*, *Gitasar*, *Yogank Shatak*, *Subodhini*, *Ratnasar*, *Tattava Bodh*, *Ram Ratna Mala*, *Lay Yoga Battisi*, *Samaysar Bavni*, *Adwait Bavni*, *Rajniti*, *Shri Ram Gopi Git Ashtak* and *Guman Padavali*.

GUMANI PANT (1790-1846). Kumaoni poet of Kashipur, who, though mainly a Sanskrit poet, has also composed Kumaoni poems : *Phutkal Kavitayen*. His original name was Lok Ratna Pant, but he was called 'Gumani' as he became a court-poet of Raja Guman Singh Dev of Kashipur. His Sanskrit works include *Nitishataka Shatopadesha*, *Ganga Shataka* and *Jnana Bhaishajya Manjari*.

GUMPERZ, JOHN JOSEPH. Scholar, whose chief work is *Conversational Hindi-Urdu* (with June Rumery and others ; 1967).

GUN AGAM. Rajasthani poem by Barhat Isardas (q .v.), in which is eulogized one God, who appears in different forms and in many ways.

GUN BHAKHA CHARITRA. See *Hem Samaur*.

GUN CHHABIIA PRAB. See *Haridas Lalas*.

GUN GOVIND. Rajasthani poem, which was composed by Kalyan Das Rao (q. v.) in 1643. Consisting of 191 Rupaks in 32 metres, besides *Vachnika*, it is a narrative poem dealing with the ten incarnations of Vishnu, particularly the life and deeds of Ram and Krishna ; the poem, however, makes several departures from the prevalent accounts of Ram and Krishna. The poet prophesies that people will discard the study of Persian and go back to Sanskrit.

GUNMAL SHAH DEV KARAN RI. Rajasthani poem, composed by Rao Vena in 1733, which describes the deeds of Shah

Dev Karan, a minister of Mewar in the time of Maharana Sangram Singh II (1710-33).

GUN MANJARI (b. *c.* 1718). Poet of the Krishna-cult (Chaitanya Sect), who lived in Vrindavan. His *Smaran Mangal Bhasha* is a commentary in Brajbhasha on Rup Goswami's *Smaran Mangal.*

GUN NATH JHA. Maithili writer, who is noted for his social dramas : *Kaniya Putara* (1967) and *Pathey.*

GUN NINDA STUTI. Rajasthani poem by Barhat Isardas (q. v.), which ironically censures and commends the numerous deeds of various incarnations of God : Vaman's fraud on Bali and the abduction of Jamvanti by Krishna are two examples. He has also chided God for not having granted a son to Mohammed Sahib and for the death of Hussain.

GUN NIRANJAN PRAN. Rajasthani poem in 45 verses, which was composed by Barhat Asa (q. v.). The work represents a synthesis of Sagun and Nirgun Brahma and oneness of Ram, Krishna and Allah.

GUN RAM VAR NISANI. See *Barhat Narharidas Sanvlot.*

GUN RATNA SURI (fl. 1436). Gujarati-speaking Jain poet, whose *Bharat Bahubali* in Apabhransh-mixed Old Hindi explains the Jain concepts.

GUN SHIV-CHARITT PRAKAS. Rajasthani poem by Natha, which describes the two battles : one of Fatehpur (Shekawati) and the other of Gangrana (near Ajmer) fought by Rao Shivsingh of Sikar (1721-48).

GUNVANT LAL DAS (fl. *c.* 1930). Maithili writer, who was noted for his short stories as also for his Puranic tales in verse, e.g. *Gaj-Grahoddhar* (1914), *Sudarshanopakhyan* (1914-31), *Gangalahari* (1921), *Sukanyopakhyan, Gauri-Parinay-Prabandh* (1921) and *Vratkathas.*

GUN VIJAY VIVAH. Rajasthani poem of about 250 verses, which was composed by Muraridas Barhat in 1718. It narrates the Krishna-Rukmini legend, with minor variations made by the poet himself.

GUNANAND. Maithili poet, who was noted for his lyrics. Son of Jayanand, the poet, he was patronized by Madhav Singh (1776-1808).

GUNANAND DANGWAL. Modern Garhwali poet, who is noted for his stray poems.

GUNANAND JHA. Modern Maithili writer, who is noted for his one-act plays, *Madhu-Yamini*.

GUNJAN. See *Gangesh Gunjan*.

GUPTA, BALMUKUND. See *Balmukund Gupta*.

GUPTA, MAITHILISHARAN. See *Maithilisharan Gupta*.

GUPTA, SIYARAM SHARAN. See *Siyaram Sharan Gupta*.

GUPTANAND MAHARAJ. Malwi saint-poet, whose chief works are *Chaudah Ratna*, *Gupta-Sagar* and *Guptagyan-Gutka* (3rd impression, 1876) ; all these works are devotional.

GUR DIN PANDE. Poet of the Riti school, whose *Bag Manohar* (1803), a Riti work, is written after the manner of *Kavipriya* by Keshavdas (q. v.). While treating of *Rasa*, *Alankar*, *Gun*, etc. it deals with prosody also, an element not touched upon in *Kavipriya*. It is thus an all-embracing work and is thus useful.

GURTI SUBRAHMANYAM. Tamil-speaking modern Hindi scholar, whose chief works are *Hindi Sahitya Samiksha* (A Critical Study of Hindi Literature), *Bisvin Sadi ki Rajnitik Vichardharayen* (The Political Thought of the Twentieth Century) and *Chhatrapati Shivaji*, the latter meant for children.

GURU, KAMTAPRASAD. See *Kamtaprasad Guru*.

GURU BAKHSH LAL (fl. 1864). Poet of Gaya, whose *Kundliya Ramayan* is incomplete.

GURU BHAKTA SINGH 'BHAKTA' (b. 1893). Poet, whose chief works are : *Nurjahan* (1935 ; on Jahangir's love for Nurjahan) and *Vikramaditya* (on the marriage of Chandragupta II with Dhruvdevi and the king's conquests).

GURU DAS, BHAI (1551-1637). Panjabi poet and author of *Gian Ratanavali*, whose 556 verses in Brajbhasha eulogize Guru Nanak. Bhai Gurudas is held in high esteem for his deep devotion to the Guru.

GURU DATT (1894-). Novelist, whose works invariably project certain social and Hindu nationalistic viewpoints. Some of his works are : *Vikramaditya, Sadavatsale Matribhumi, Nirlep, Pushhyamitra* (1980), *Maujmela, Vidhur, Nastik, Basantrag, Kahe Hot Udas* and *Badalte Ayam.* He has written more than 75 novels.

GURU DATT KALASINGH. Modern Hindi poet of Surinam, whose patriotic songs are very popular among the masses.

GURU DATT SINGH (BHUPATI), RAJA. See *Bhupati.*

GURU DAYAL SINGH. Modern poet, whose chief work, *Ravanayan* is an epic ; *Madi ka Diva* is his noval.

GURUNATH JOSHI. Kannada-speaking modern Hindi scholar, whose chief works are : *Kannada Parichay* and a Hindi tr. of Shivram Karant's Kannada novel : *Atidamelai.* He is also the author of *Hindi Kosh* and *Kannada Kosh.*

GURU PRATAP SURAJ. See *Santokh Singh.*

GURURAM PYARE AGNIHOTRI (b. 1915). Bagheli poet, who was born at the village Kari in Satna district of Madhya Pradesh. His chief works are : *Pralap* (poetical collection), *Rani kai Ris* (poems), *Vindhyapradesh ka Itihas, Sohawal Rajya ka Itihas, Kasaunta ke Baghelon ka Itihas* and *Rimahai Boli* on respectively the histories of Vindhyapradesh, Sohawal rule, Baghelas of Kasaunta and the last on grammar.

GWAL KAVI (1792-1867). Poet of the Riti school, who was a Bandijan of Vrindavan and was son of Sevaram. According to his work, *Rasikanand,* he was, however, son of Murlidhar Rao. A contemporary and rival of Padmakar (q.v.), he is reputed to be the author of 50 works, big and small. Of these the important Riti works are : *Rasa-Rang* (on *Rasa*), *Alankar Bhram Bhanjan* (on *Alankar*), *Kavidarpan, Prastar Prakash, Rasikanand* and *Krishnashtak.* His other works, mainly devotional are : *Radha-Madhav-Milan, Radha Ashtak, Yamuna Lahari* (Wavelets of the Yamuna), *Kavi-hriday-Vinod, Guru Pachasa* (50 verses on the Guru), *Balvir Vinod* and *Hammir Hath* (on Hammir).

Next to Senapati, he is the only poet of consequence, who wrote about the seasons. The poet's anxiety for description of seasons is so acute that even the *Yamuna Lahari,* a devotional work, contains classification of the aspects of each season, the activities associated with them, and so on. *Kavi-hriday-Vinod* is the collection of his best poems.

GYANDAS (b. 1530). Bengali Vaishnav poet, who also composed *Padas* in Brajbuli.

GYANDEV AGNIHOTRI (1935-). Dramatist, whose chief works are : *NEFA ki Ek Sham* (An Evening in NEFA; on the Chinese invasion of India), *Shuturmurg* (The Ostrich; 1968; a powerful political satire) and *Mati Jagi Re* (The Soil is Awake).

GYAN DWIP. Allegorical romance by Sheikh Nabi (b. 1620), a Sufi poet.

The poem describes the love-story of Raja Gyan Dwip and Rani Devjani in the style of Sufi poems.

GYANGIRI. See *Lalgiri*.

GYAN HANS ADHIN. Modern Hindi scholar of Surinam, who is noted for his *Hindi-Dutch Dictionary* (1953).

GYANJI, SANT. Rajasthani saint-poet, whose stray verses are available; his time is not certain.

GYAN PRAKASH. Modern short story writer, whose chief short collections are *Andehre ka Silsila* (Chain of Darkness) and *Zahar* (Poison); his stories present a conflict between the individual and the established institutions. His poetical work is *Tafarhin*.

GYAN RAJ GAEKWAR. Marathi-speaking modern Hindi scholar, whose chief work is : *Adhunik Hindi Natkon men Sangharsh Tatwa*.

GYAN RANJAN (1936-). Short story writer, whose chief collections of short stories are : *Fence ke Idhar aur Udhar* (On Either Side of the Fence; 1967), *Yatra* (Journey; 1972) and *Kshanajivi*, his short stories : 'Ghanta' (The Bell), 'Bahirgaman' (The Exile), 'Shesh Ate Hue' etc. are quite popular. His poetical work is : *Is Navann Meri*. He edits 'Pahal', a literary magazine from Jabbalpur.

GYAN SAGAR (fl. 17th cent.). Jain poet, who composed *Sam Pradyumna Ras*, on the story of Krishna's sons : Samb and Pradyumna.

GYAN SAR (1744-1841). Jain Rajasthani poet and scholar, who composed devotional verses and songs. In 1820 he wrote *Chand Chaupai Samalochana* in 413 verses, a criticism on a poem *Chand Raja Chaupai* by Mohan Vijay. Greatly influenced by Anandghan's works, he wrote an annotation *Balavbodh* on the former's *Chaubisi.* His *Mala Pingal* is a work on prosody, while his *Purab Des Varnan* (1973) in Brajbhasha with a slight tinge of Rajasthani, describes the customs and manners of the people of Bengal.

GYAN SHUKLA, MRS. Modern Hindi poetess of Fiji, who is noted for her stray poems.

GYAN SINGH MAN. Panjabi-speaking modern Hindi poet, whose *Nanak Archan* is a poem on Guru Nanak. He has also written novels : *Suna Ambar*, *Dusra Patjhar*, *Jalte Kalash*, etc.

GYAN VIMAL SURI (1637-1725). Gujarati-speaking Jain poet, whose works are : *Prachin Stavan Sangrah* and *Kalyan Mandir Stotra.*

GYANANAND SEMVAL. Garhwali scholar, who was noted for his collection of Garhwali poems : *Jitu Bagadval* (1938), which are refined versions of Garhwali folk-songs.

GYANAPP NAIDU, N. Telugu-speaking Hindi scholar, whose research publication is *Keshav Sahitya men Samaj, Sanskriti aur Darshan* (Society, Culture and Philosophy in the Literature of Keshav; 1978).

GYANENDRA PATI. Poet, whose collection of poems is *Shabda Likhne ke Liye hi yeh Kaghaz Bana Hai* (The Paper has been made for one to write words on it; 1981).

GYANESHWAR (1275-96). Celebrated saint of Maharashtra, who was founder of Varkari Sect. His *Gyaneshwari* is a commentary on the *Bhagavadgita* written in simple Marathi for the common man. In addition to other works in Marathi, he composed some 1,000 stray *Abhangs.* He must have composed *Padas* in Hindi as some of them are extant. This shows that he wished to address non-Marathi speaking people as well.

GYANI DAS. Hindi Writer of Fiji, who was noted for his works : *Hindi Kahaniyan* (1948), *Fiji Galpika*, *Gupta Shaktiyan*, *Bharatiya Upanivesh* and *Mardula.*

GYPSY. Novel (1952) by Ilachandra Joshi (q.v.), which displays fusing of psychoanalytical and social interests through the characters of Ranjan and Maniya, a gypsy girl. It describes the story of an upper class rich man's (Ranjan's) ego and lust and a low-born woman's (Maniya's) sense of self-respect, her mental agony at her helpless surrender to Ranjan's will, her natural jealousy, her anger revengefulness and her courage.

ed by Anandghan's works, he wrote an annotation *Tabbodh* on the former's *Chaubisi*. His *Vala Pingal* is a work on prosody, while his *Purab Des Varnan* (1673) in Brajbhasha with a slight tinge of Rajasthani, describes the customs and manners of the people of Bengal.

GYAN SHUKLA, MRS. Modern Hindi poetess of Fiji, who is noted for her stray poems.

GYAN SINGH MAAN. Panjabi-speaking modern Hindi poet whose *Nanak Archan* is a poem on Guru Nanak. He has also written novels : *Suna Ambar*, *Dharti Pukare*, *Tare Kahan*, etc.

GYAN VIMAL SURI (1637-1725). Gujarati-speaking Jain poet whose works are : *Prachin Stavan Sangrah* and *Adhyatm Mamata Stavan*.

GYANANAND SEMWAL. Garhwali scholar, who was noted for his collection of Garhwali poems : *Jun Bagdindi* (1958), which are refined versions of Garhwali folk-songs.

GYANAPP NAIDU, N. Telugu-speaking Hindi scholar, whose research publication is *Keshav Sahitya men Samaj, Sanskriti aur Darshan* (Society, Culture and Philosophy in the Literature of Keshav; 1978).

GYANENDRA PATI. Poet, whose collection of poems is *Shabda Likhne ke Liye hi yeh Kagaz Bana hai* (The Paper has been made for one to write words on it; 1981).

GYANESHWAR (1275-96). Celebrated saint of Maharashtra, who was founder of Varkari Sect. His *Gyaneshwari* is a commentary on the *Bhagavadgita* written in simple Marathi for the common man. In addition to other works in Marathi, he composed some 1,000 stray *abhangs*. He must have composed *Padas* in Hindi as some of them are extant. They show that he wished to address non-Marathi speaking people as well.

GYANI DAS. Hindi Writer of Fiji, who was noted for his works : *Hindi Sahityakar* (1948), *Fiji Gitanjali*, *Gyan Saptaprabha*, *Pidamita Upanishad* and *Mahrishi*.

GYPSY. Novel (1952) by Ilachandra Joshi (q.v.), which displays fusing of psychoanalytical and social interests through the characters of Ranjan and Maniya, a gypsy girl. It describes the story of an upper-class rich man's (Ranjan's) ego and lust and a low-born woman's (Maniya's) sense of self-respect, her mental agony at her helpless surrender to Ranjan's will, her natural jealousy, her anger, revengefulness and her courage

H

Hacker, Paul (1913-79). German Hindi scholar, whose chief work on Hindi language is : *Zur Funktion einiger Hilfsverbern in modernen Hindi* (Wiesbaden, 1958).

Hackman, Geoffrey James. American Hindi scholar, whose chief work is : *An Integrated analysis of the Hindi tense and aspect System* (Ph. D., Illinois, 1976).

Hafiz (1856-93). Muslim poet of Hardoi district, whose original name was Ifzullah Khan. His works are : *Prem Tarangini*, *Hazara*, *Man Mohini*, *Rasik Sanjivani* and *Navin Sangrah*. He also composed verses on Krishna.

HALA JHALAN RA KUNDLIYA. See *Isardas*.

Hamidullah. Writer, who is known for his dramas, *Uljhi Akritiyan* (Entangled Figures), *Darinde* (The Beasts), *Urvashi ne Kaha* (Urvashi Said), *Ek aur Yuddha* (One More War) and *Khyal Bharmali* (folk-play ; 1981).

Hamilton, N.J. Scholar, whose chief work is *Hindustani for the Tourist* ; a phonetic phrase book for every day use (1965).

Hamir Dan Ratanu (fl. 1st half of the 18th cent.). Rajasthani poet of the village Ghadoi, who was patronized by Maharaval Desalji (1717-51) and his son, Lakhpat of Kachchh. A versatile writer, he was the author of about 175 books of all sorts including those on lexicon, prosody, etc. His chief work, *Desalji ri Vachnika* is a narrative poem, which describes the battle of 1728 between Desalji and Sar Bulandkhan, the Governor of Gujarat. *Pingal Prakash* and *Lakhpat Pingal* are works on prosody ; in the latter the *Gits* are mostly in praise of Lakhpat, the poet's patron. *Hamir Nam Mala*, consisting of 311 verses, is a dictionary of synonyms, particularly of literary Rajasthani words. Most of the works of the poet are in manuscript form.

HAMIR NAM MALA. See *Hamirdan Ratanu*.

HAMMIR HATH. Popular poem of *Vir Rasa* by Chandrashekhar Vajpeyi 'Shekhar' (1798-1875 ; q.v.).

It describes the battle between Raja Hammirdev of Ranthambhor and King Ala-ud-din ; the account given of the battle in this work, however, does not tally with the given in history. According to historical tradition, Hammir was killed in the battlefield, while the poem mentions that Hammir defeated the king but on his return discovering that the desperate ladies had committed suicide, killed himself.

The story of Hammir is old but the treatment is magnificent ; the narrative progresses steadily without any jerk. The story acquires dignity from Hammir, a hero of nobility and courage, in contrast with whom his adversary seems to be petty. The diction and metrical pattern are quite in consonance with the heroic poetry. The readers are thrilled and here lies the especial quality of the poem.

HAMMIR KAVYA. See *Sharngdhar*.

HAMMIR MAHAKAVYA. See *Jay Chandra*.

HAMMIR RASO. Ballad in Dingal by Sharngdhar (fl. 1300) ; it is not available as yet, though 8 verses of it are extant in the *Prakrit-Paingalam*.

It celebrates the dogged valour of Hammir of the royal house of Ranthambhor in his fierce battle with Ala-ud-din, the emperor of Delhi, in which the former meets the heroic death. Some scholars hold that the *Raso* was composed in 1298 by Jajjal, who was a minister, court-poet and commander-in-chief of Hammir.

HAMMIR RASO. See *Jodhraj*.

HAMMIRAYAN. Dingal narrative poem in 327 verses, which was composed by Bhandau Vyas in 1481.

The poem describes the battle between the Chauhan hero, Hammir of Ranthambhor and Ala-ud-din Khalji. The immediate cause of the battle was the refusal of Hammir to hand over to Khalji the two Mangol Mirs, to whom he gave refuge. As the two followers of Hammir : Ranmall and Raipal had betrayed and joined the enemy camp, there was no hope left for victory. Women performed 'Jauhar' (self-immolation), warriors died fighting and Hammir cut off his head with his own hands.

HANDA, R.L. Author of *A History of Hindi Literature* (1978).

HANS JAVAHIR. Allegorical romance by Qasim Shah (b. 1732; q.v.), a Sufi poet, which deals with the love-story of Raja Hans and Rani Javahir.

HANS KUMAR TIWARI (1918-80). Poet, whose chief poems are : *Rimjhim* (Drizzle), *Nirjhar* (Cascade), *Badal* (Cloud), *Anagat* (Not Yet Arrived), *Agyat Bali* (The Unknown Bali) and *Mera Ghar* (My Home). His collection of essays is *Kala*. His most noted work was translations from Bengali. He tr Tagore's songs and verse-plays ; many novels of note like *Aranyak* from Bengali were also translated by him.

HANS RAJ. Maithili writer, who is noted for his short story collection, *Satranja* (1971). His *O Je Kahalani* (1971) depicts in autobiographical form his interviews with eminent litterateurs in an eminently interesting and touching style ; the personality of some of the leading Maithili writers and critics has been made to appear through these interviews. He is also known for his poems and lyrics.

HANSRAJ-BACHCHHRAJ CHAUPAI. See *Vijay Bhadra, Hansavali*.

HANS RAJ RAHBAR. Panjabi-speaking Hindi and Urdu writer, who has written the biographies of Premchand, the novelist as also of Vivekanand. He has written novels : *Pankh-hin Titli* (Wingless Butterfly), *Disha-Hin* (With no Directions ; 1980) and a critical work on progressive literature ; his *Jhuth ki Muskan* is a short story collection.

HANS RAY (fl. 17th cent.). One of the court-poets of Guru Govind Singh (q.v.), his best-known work being *Bharan-Karan* in which he has combined *Vir Rasa* with *Shringar*, with remarkable success. For some of his *Chhands* in *Shringar* the Guru seems to have rewarded him suitably.

HANSAVALI. Rajasthani poem by Asait (q v), which was composed in 1370. Based on the legend of Hansraj Bachchhraj, it consists of 438 verses (mainly *Chaupais*) divided into four parts. It is also claimed to be a Gujarati work.

King Narvahan of Pahithan sees princess Hansavali, daughter of king Sanak Bhram of Patan, in a dream. Narvahan's minister, Mankesar, is successful in getting them married, though the princess is reputed to be a man-hater. Two sons : Bachchhraj and Hansraj are born to them. Once the youth

Hansraj spurns the lustful advances of the principal queen Lilavati, at which the queen conspires to get a death warrant issued against both the brothers. The sentence, however, is not executed and the youths are left in a jungle where they suffer immensely. Bachchhraj falls in love with Chitralekha, daughter of king Sanak Bhram and wins her after many adventures. He is thrown into the sea by his rival Pushpadant in a deceitful manner but is saved. By sheer luck, Hansraj gets the kingdom of Kantinagar which formerly belonged to a king, who died issueless. Bachchhraj joins him there.

The work is noted for its motif, language, antiquity and portrayal of contemporary society.

HANSEN, KATHRYN GAY (1947-). Canadian scholar of Hindi, who is at present Associate Professor in the Department of Asian Studies at the University of British Columbia, Canada. Her publications are : ed. of *Journal of South Asian Literature* (Renu Special Issue, 1982 ; over 250 pages) and *Resonances of Rural Bihar : A Collection of Hindi Short Stories by Phanishwarnath Renu*. Apart from articles and reviews of various works, her special field of research is Renu.

HANUMACHCHHASTRI AYACHIT. Telugu-speaking modern Hindi writer, who is noted for his *Telugu-Hindi Kosh* ; this work gives Telugu words in Devnagari characters.

HANUMAN (d 1879). Poet, who was son of the poet Manidev Bandijan of Kashi. Bharatendu Harishchandra honoured him but he died at the age of 38 ; only his stray verses are now extant.

HANUMANNATAK. See *Balbhadra Mishra, Hridayram*.

HANUMANT RAO, K. 'RAVI'. Kannada-speaking modern Hindi poet, whose *Kavya Rashmiyan* (1964) is a collection of poems.

HANUMANT SINGH DEVDA. Modern Rajasthani poet, whose poems in the traditional Charan style are available. He has also paid poetic homage to the modern heroes, including those, who have sacrificed their lives in fighting against the Chinese attack on India ; he has contributed to progressive poetry as well.

HANUMAYYA, AMBDIPUDI. See *Ambdipudi Hanumayya*.

HAR BAKHSH SINGH (fl. 1850). Poet of the Ram-cult, who was a native of Pratapgarh. He composed *Ramayan-Shatak* and *Ram-Ratnavali*.

HAR CHAND DHUKIYA (1718-1803). Rajasthani poet of the Vishnoi Sect, who wrote narrative poems on mythological themes. His *Laghu Hari Prahlad Charit* in 172 verses, is based on the *Bhagavat Puran* and is in dialogue form.

HARDATT. Writer, who tr. in 1931, the *Kundamala* of Dinnaga, a drama, from Sanskrit into Hindi.

HAR DAYAL. Modern scholar, whose chief works are: *Samkalin Anubhav aur Kavita ki Rachna Prakriya, Hindi Kavita ka Samkalin Paridrishya* and *Adhunik Bodh aur Vidroh.*

HAR DAYALU SINGH (1912-50). Poet, whose chief work, *Daitya Vansh* (The Dynasty of the Demons) is an epic. He was born in a Vaishya family at Mahmudabad in Sitapur district of Uttar Pradesh.

HARDEV. Poet of Vrindavan, who was a contemporary of Gwal (1792-1867). A Vaishya by caste, he wrote a Riti work.

HARDEV BAHRI. Modern lexicographer, whose chief works are : *Brihat Angrezi-Hindi Kosh, Hindi-Angrezi Kosh, Sur Shabda Sagar, Prasad Sahitya Kosh, Hindi : Udbhav, Vikas aur Rup, Shuddha Hindi* and *Gramin Hindi Boliyan.*

HARDEVA SWAMI (fl. early 19th cent.). Famous folk-poet of Gorad (Haryana), whose chief Sangs, which he composed and staged, are : *Hir Ranjha, Jyani Chor* and *Chandrakiran.*

Harjas Ray, Lala (fl. 18th cent. ?). Poet of the Riti school, whose works, *Devadhidev Rachna, Sadhugun Mala* and *Dev Rachna* are devotional, but of Riti type.

HARJI VANIYAL (1688-1788). Rajasthani poet, who was a follower of the Vishnoi Sect, founded by Jambhoji (q.v.). His *Sakhis* treat of the mind, its nature and fickleness and are very impressive.

HAR KRISHNADAS (fl. 18th cent.). Poet of the Krishna-cult (Haridasi Sect), who composed a small *Vani.*

HAR MAHENDRA SINGH BEDI. Panjabi-speaking modern Hindi poet, who is noted for his poetical collection : *Garm Loha.*

HARMAN CHAUHAN. Modern Rajasthani poet, who has composed poems in the style of Nayi Kavita ; *Bhut ke Panv* is his humorous work.

HARNAM SINGH HARNAM. Modern Hindi poet of Fiji, whose chief work is : *Kiski Bhul* ?

HAR NARAYAN. Poet, who was the author of *Madhavanal Kamkandala* (romance) and *Vetal Pachchisi* (a tr. from Sanskrit ; both 1755).

HARNATH (fl. 1603). Rajasthani poet, whose stray verses in popular metres are available.

HARPAL (fl. 1603). Rajasthani poet, whose stray verses in popular metres are available.

HARPATI (fl. 14th cent.). Maithili writer, who was a son of Vidyapati. In Nepal, there is a tradition that it was Vidyapati's son, who wrote the drama, *Goraksh-Vijay*, ascribed to Vidyapati. He is also identified with Harpati, the author of *Vyavahar-Dipak*, a popular work on astrology.

HAR RAY (r. 1561-77). Maharaval of Jaisalmer (Rajasthan), who was a patron of many a poet including Gadd and Kushal Labh (qq v.). The ruler is also said to be the author of *Pingal Shiromani*, a work on Dingal prosody.

HAR SAHAY. Modern Kannauji poet, who is noted for his stray Kannauji folk-poems.

HAR SEVAK MISHRA (fl. 1747). Court-poet of Orchha ruler, who composed *Kamrup Katha Mahakavya* (q.v.).

HAR VANSHLAL SHARMA (1915-). Hindi critic, whose chief works are : *Sur aur Unka Sahitya* (Sur and His Literature ; thesis), *Sur Samiksha* (Criticism of Sur ; 1955), *Bhagavat Dharma, Hindi Sahitya ka Itihas* (*Adikal*) *and Hindi Sahitya ka Iti has* (*Bhaktikal*). He was Head of the Hindi Department in Aligarh University and later Director, Central Hindi Directorate, Delhi.

HARAN. Malayalam-speaking Modern Hindi scholar, who wrote *Hindi-Malayalam Kosh*.

HARDLEY, G. Author of *Grammatical Remarks on the Practical and Vulgar Dialects of the Indostan Language, commonly called Moors . . . The whole calculated for common practice in Bengal* (London, 1772 ; it ran into seven revised editions ; the last ed., London, 1809). He also compiled *A Short Grammar of the Moors Language* (London, 1779).

HARDWARI PRASAD JALAN. Writer, who was noted for his drama : *Gharkat Sum* (1922).

HARE KRISHNA PRADHAN. Oriya-speaking modern Hindi writer, who has tr. Gop Bandhu Das's Oriya poem, *Dharmapada* into Hindi.

HARENDRA NATH BARA (1918-). Assamese-speaking Hindi teacher, whose *Ling Nirnay* in Hindi has been published. He has also written many essays and poems, which are scattered in various magazines : 'Rashtra Bhasha', 'Prachya Bharati', etc.

HARI (Hariji ; d. 1696). Hindi poet and writer of Panjab, who was son of Mihrivanu (q.v.). He is remembered for his three works : *Parmarth Sukhmani Sahasranam* (1646), *Pothi Hariji* (1650) and *Gosati Guru Mihrivanu*, which comment on the *Vani* of Guru Nanak in a language akin to Braj and Khari Boli.

HARIAUDH. See *Ayodhyasingh Upadhyay 'Hariaudh'*.

HARIBHAU UPADHYAY (1893-1972). Prominent political worker of Rajasthan and a writer, who was the author of some 18 works : original as also translations from Marathi, Gujarati, English and Sanskrit. His works as under :

Original : *Swatantrata ki Or* (Towards Independence), *Budbud*, *Swagat*, *Yugadharma* (confiscated), *Hindu Musalman*, *Manan* and *Ahinsa ke Anubhav*.

Translation : *Samrat Ashok*, *Ragini*, *Kabur*, *Bolshevism* (from Marathi), *Jivan Shodhan*, *Mere Jail ke Anubhav*, *Atmakatha* (from Gujarati) , *Congress ka Itihas*, *Meri Kahani* (from English), *Hindi Gita* and *Kritarth Jivan* (from Sanskrit).

Apart from the above, he has written stray articles, poems, etc. numbering several hundreds. He has also edited "Malaw-Mayukh', 'Navjivan', 'Tyagbhumi', 'Rajasthan' and 'Jivan Sahitya'.

Love of the country had inspired him to write his works. Formerly, he wrote in pure Hindi but lately, he started writing Hindustani.

HARICHAND PURAN. See *Jankho Maniyar*.

HARI CHARAN. Poet of the Krishna-cult (Chaitanya Sect), whose *Shri Gopal Bhatt Charit* was composed in 1886.

HARI CHARAN DASS (1709-78). Brajbhasha poet, who was a Brahmin of Kishengarh. He wrote commentaries on *Rasik-Priya* and *Kavi-Priya* by Keshavdas, on *Bihari-Satsai* and on *Bhasha Bhushan* by Maharaja Jasvant Singh, and wrote two original works : *Sabha Prakash* and *Brihatkavi—Vallabh*.

HARIDAS (fl. *c.* 1540-60). Poet of the Krishna-cult, who was founder of the Haridasi Sect or Tatti Sampraday, a sub-sect of the Nimbark Sampraday. A number of well-known devotees like Nagardas, Sarasdas, Navaldas, Maundas and Narharidas joined his sect and flourished as devotees under his preceptorship Besides being a poet, he was a celebrated musician too. Tansen, the court-musician of Akbar, and Baiju were his disciples Besides his *Keli Mal*, containing 108 *Padas* and *Siddhant Padas* consisting of 18, which are the basis of the Sect, there are also stray *Padas*, which are discovered here and there. After Vrindavan, Haridas lived for some time at Nidhuvan. His *Padas* are quite agreeable to be sung in Ragas and Raginis. Tradition goes that Akbar once came to enjoy his songs.

HARIDAS (*c.* 1553-1623). Poet of the Krishna-cult (Chaitanya Sect), who belonged to Vrindavan. It was at his instance that Krishnadas Kaviraj wrote his famous work : *Shri Chaitanya Charitamrit*. His work is *Yuga Prem Rasa Bodhika* ; among his disciples Bhagvatmudit is the most popular.

HARIDAS. Maithili poet, who may be identified with the brother of the famous Maithili poet, Govind Das (*c.* 1643-70). His only extant poem, which is charming and simple, is *Rag-Tarangini*.

HARIDAS (fl. 17th cent). Rajasthani saint-poet of Laldasi Sect, who was known for his scholarship and piety. His works are : *Vivek Gita* (a summary of *Gita* in 515 verses), *Sar Sangrah* (131 verses on the origin, creation and elimination of the universe, etc.), *Atma-Dhyan Joga Sanvad* (131 verses on *Dhyan*, *Jap*, serpent power, etc. in the form of dialogues between him and his Guru, Laldas), *Haridas Premdas Sanvad* (61 verses, dealing with the object of worship), *Bhajans* (500 in number) and stray verses, such as *Rekhta* (24), *Sakhi* (40) and miscellaneous (10). Out of all his works, the *Bhajans*, which are spontaneous and simple expressions of the heart, achieved wide popularity. The language of the *Bhajans* is Rajasthani mixed with Braj, while the dialogues are mostly in Rajasthani.

HARIDAS (fl. end of 18th cent.). Rajasthani saint-poet of

Ram Snehi Sect, Ren, whose *Vani* consists of stray verses in popular metres.

HARIDAS, PANDIT (*b* 1877-78). Bagheli folk-poet, who was born at Gaudh (Rewa). A poor peasant, he composed poems on the daily life of the villagers, which are still remembered by them.

HARIDAS, SANT (fl. 18th cent.). Saint-poet, who was a disciple of Chhaunaji (q.v.). His 18 *Padas*, 18 *Vanis* and 18 *Kavittas* have so far been discovered.

HARIDAS BHAT (fl. 1st half of 17th cent.). Dingal poet, whose works are : *Ajitsingh Charitra* and *Amar Battisi* (1643).

HARIDAS KESARIYA (fl. between 1450-1550). Dingal poet, whose stray *Gits* on contemporary rulers and chiefs are available.

HARIDAS LALAS (fl. 1750). Rajasthani poet, who was son of the Bhakta-poet, Pirdan Lalas (q.v.) and was a resident of the village Judhiya in Marwar. His *Gun Chhabha Prab*, a narrative poem in easy language, is based on the 'Sabha Parva' of the *Mahabharat*.

HARIDAS NIRANJANI (*c.* 1455-1543). Rajasthani saint-poet and propounder of the Haridas Niranjani Sampraday, whose lifetime is said to range from 1417 to 1645, covering over 200 years. A Rajput of the Sankhla clan of village Kapdod (near Didwana), the main seat of his Sect is Didwana. He is said to have been a dacoit but at the instance of a Sadhu, he renounced the world in 1499. Two editions of his poems have been published from Jodhpur and Jaipur, though his poems such as *Byavalo*, *Chalis Padi*, *Chaudah Padi*, *Pandrah Tithi*, *Joga Samadhi*, *Nirpakh Mul Joga*, *Granth Vira Ras*, *Hans Pramodh*, *Granth Man Hath Ko* are also available in a manuscript scribed in 1625, discovered recently. A comparison of the texts of the published works and of those available in the manuscript, shows that while all the poems of Haridas have not been included in the published versions, a few poems included in the published books probably belong to some other Haridas. His poems, quite large in number, consist of *Angas*, *Padas* and stray verses.

Haridas does not believe in the incarnations and idol-worship. Brahma absolute or Brahma bereft of Maya, called Nirakar Niranjan, is worshipped in this Sampraday. Elements of love and Yoga are equally important ; thus Nirgun Bhakti and Yoga are the means of self-realization. But after the 18th century, this Sampraday lost its original character. Temples were built and the worship of the idols of Ram and Krishna began.

The language of Haridas and other poets of his Sect is easy Rajasthani, mixed with Braj and sometimes with Khari Boli.

HARIDASAN PILLAI, V.K. Malayalam-speaking modern Hindi writer, who has written several works for the easy learning of Hindi.

HARIDEV (fl. 1800). Poet of the Krishna-cult (Chaitanya Sect), who was son of Ratiram of Vrindavan. The Mishrabandhu consider his birth year as 1773. Stray verses composed by him are available.

HARIDEV DAS (1778-1807). Rajasthani saint-poet of Ram Snehi Sampraday, Sinthal, who was grandson of Hariram Das (q.v.) and occupied the *Gaddi* of Acharya after him. His poems exalting Guru and *Nam-smaran*, include *Sumiran Bodh*, *Granth Karuna Nidhan*, *Guru Mahima*, *Nam Mahima*, *Gyan Vichar*, *Atma Vichar*, *Gyan Swarup*, *Atma-Krit Brahma Prapti Jan Vichar*, *Padas* and stray verses. He has copiously used *Chhappay* metre.

HARI GHAS PAR KSHAN BHAR. See *Agyey*.

HARIHAR DWIVEDI (fl. early 20th cent.). Famous astrologer of Benares, who was the first to write on astrology and palmistry in Hindi. He wrote also some books on other subjects, mostly non-literary.

HARIHAR SHARMA. Tamil-speaking modern Hindi scholar, whose chief work is *Tamil-Hindi Kosh*.

HARI HARAN USHNITTAN. Malayalam-speaking modern Hindi writer, who has successfully tr. Kumaran Ashan's poetical work : *Sitakavya* (on Sita) into Hindi.

HARIJIT, G.J. (G. JAYSINGHA REDDY). Telugu and Kannada-speaking Hindi writer, whose *Humayun*, a successful historical drama, describes how Rani Karmavati sends *Rakhis* to the Moghul Emperor Humayun and how favourably he responds to her appeal for protection. His other dramas are : *Sambhavami Yugeyuge* (1980) and *Uttar Mrichchhakatik*. His *Rangayan* is a collection of his six historical and social one-act plays.

HARI KANT VIPRA (fl. 1st half of 17th cent.). Assamese poet, whose only Hindi (Brajavali) work is *Syamant-Haran*, a drama.

HARI KINKAR DAS (fl. middle of 19th cent.). Maithili saint-poet, who is known to have written several *Bhajans* in Maithili. A Maithil Brahmin, he travelled to Braj and was a great admirer of *Shrimad-Bhagavata*.

HARI KISAN (early 19th cent.). Rajasthani scholar of Jodhpur, whose chief work *Rupdip Pingal* is a work on metrics.

HARI KRISHNA AVASTHI (1917-). Writer, whose chief works are : *Tulsi : Vyaktitva aur Vichar* (on the personality and ideas of Tulsi), *Goswami Tulsidas : Parivesh, Prerana, Pratiphal* (Goswami Tulsidas : Background, Inspiration, Conclusion) and *Patanjal Yoga-Darshan* (ed.).

HARI KRISHNA DEVSARE. Modern writer, who is noted for his *Bachchon ke Sau Natak* (100 plays for children), *Bachchon ki Sau Kavitayen* (100 poems meant for children), *Bachchon ki Sau Kahaniyan* (100 stories for children), *Bal Sahitya : Rachna aur Samiksha* and *Hindi Bal Sahitya : Ek Adhyayan*.

HARI KRISHNA JAUHAR (1880-1945). Early novelist, who was noted for his novels of magic, mystery and roguery, e.g., *Kusum Lata*, *Mayank Mohini*, *Maya Mahal* (The Enchanted Palace ; 1901), *Kamal Kumari* (1902), *Nirala Naqab Posh* (The Strange Person in the Mask ; 1902) and *Bhayanak Khun* (The Horrible Murder ; 1903).

HARI KRISHNA KAUL (1934-). Hindi writer of Kashmir, whose *Is Hamam Men*, *Arthi* and *Tokri-bhar Dhup* are short story collections. He edited several text-books as also tr. some Kashmiri novels and short stories into Hindi.

HARI KRISHNA PREMI (1908-74). Dramatist and poet, who was born at Guna in the then Gwalior State. He was wedded to nationalism, based on communal unity and religious tolerance. His chief works are : *Svarna Vihan* (The Golden Morning ; 1930), *Rakshabandhan* (1934), *Swapnabhang* (on the life of Dara Shukoh, known for his dedication to Hindu-Muslim unity), *Shapath* (Oath), *Sima-Sanrakshan* (Defence of Boundaries), *Shiva-Sadhana* (on Shivaji), *Ahuti* (Sacrifice), *Mitra* (Friend), *Vishpan* (The Drinking of Poison), *Sanpon ki Srishti* (Creation of Snakes), *Prakash-Stambh* (The Light House), *Amar An* (Eternal Pride), *Pratishodh* (Revenge), *Vida*, *Kirti Stambh*, *Raktadan*, *Patal Vijay* (Conquest of Underworld), *Uddhar* (Deliverance), *Amrit-Putri* (Daughter of Elixir) *Bandhan*

(Bondage), and *Chhaya* (Shadow) ; *Rakshabandhan*, the best of his plays, depicts how the widow of Rana Sanga, Karmavati, sends Rakhi to Humayun with a view to seeking his protection against the ruler of Gujarat and that the gesture works well and paves the way for the author's theme of Hindu-Muslim unity. He has also published several collections of one-act plays (*Matri-Mandir, Rashtra-Mandir, Man Mandir, Nyaya Mandir, Vani Mandir and Badalon ke Par*) and several poetical collections : *Ankhon Men, Anant ke Path Par* (On the Path of Eternity), *Jadugarni* (Sorceress), *Agnigan* (Songs of Fire) and *Ruprekha*. He has made significant contribution to the development of Hindi lyrics. He also edited 'Karmavir' and later he was literary producer at All India Radio, Jalandhar.

HARI MANIK. Modern Hindi poet of Trinidad, who is noted for his stray poems and short stories.

HARI MOHAN. Poet, whose *Nimaili Dhup* (1983) is his first poetical collection.

HARI MOHAN JHA. First great fiction writer of Maithili, whose chief novels are : *Kanyadan* (1930-33 ; a social novel ; reprint 1982), and *Dwiragaman* (on the second marriage ceremony), His chief short story collections are : *Pranamya Devata* (1945), *Rangshala, Ekadashi, Tirth-Yatra* (1953), *Charchari* (1960) and others.

While in his novels, he has created living characters, in his short stories, he has offered healthy criticism of Mithila's life and manners through a small but living world of low comedy.

The greatest modern farce writer of Maithili, his much-praised one-act plays are : *Thop-Sano Top, Relka Jhagra* and *Bauak Dam*. He has written essays, light sketches and skits. His important works are : *Khattar Kaka Tarang* (giving queer interpretation of men and matters), *Chaudhariji ka Chittha* (a collection of essays on social problems similar to *Shiv-Shambhu ka Chittha*) and *Bholababa ka Gapp* (essays, purporting to be the report of a club of gossip-mongers). He has also written humorous pieces on topics : 'Tea Party', etc. Two of his memoirs have been published in 1979 : the first presents a profile of Pandit Janardan Jha 'Jansidan' (his father) and the second that of Babu Lakshmipati Singh.

HARI MOHAN MISHRA. Maithili critic, whose *Adhunik Maithili Kavita* (1980) discusses the modern Maithili Poetry according to the Western literary principles of criticism.

HARINABH (fl. 1683-97). Rajasthani poet, who was patronized by Raja Kesri Singh of Khandela in the then Jaipur State. His *Kesri Singh Samar* in 459 verses describes the valour of Raja Kesri Singh, who was killed in the battle with Aurangzeb's forces in the year 1697.

HARI NANDAN THAKUR 'SAROJ' (fl. early 20th cent.). Maithili writer, who is remembered for his novels and short stories. His short story collections are : *Karnaphul* and *Kaviji-ka-Plat*. He also wrote a drama on the poet, Vidyapati.

HARI NARAYAN (1864-1945). Hindi writer, who was born in the Parik family of the then Jaipur State. A philanthropist, he got constructed schools, temples, etc. Among his chief works are editing of *Mahakavi Gang ke Kavitta*, *Sundar Granthavali*, *Baijnidhi Granthavali* and biographies of Maharaja Mirza Raja Jaysingh and Maharaja Mirza Raja Mansingh.

HARI NARAYAN DATT BARUA (1886-1959). Assamese writer, who has written two essays in Hindi, but his chief contributions are the editing of *Bargit* and *Chitra Bhagavat*.

HARI NARAYAN MAHAVIR. Modern Hindi writer of Mauritius, who is noted for his short stories.

HARI NARAYAN SITA. Modern Hindi poet of Mauritius, whose *Prabhat* is a collection of his poems. See *Pravasi Swar*.

HARI NARAYAN VYAS (1923-). Poet of *Dusra Saptak*, whose poetical collections are : *Mrig aur Trishna* (The Deer and Thirst ; 1968), *Trikon par Suryoday* and *Bargad ke Chikne Patte*.

HARINATH. Maithili poet, who was noted for his lyrics. Patronized by Maharaja Pratap Singh (1761-76), his verses also found respectable place in contemporary anthologies.

HARINATH. Poet of the Riti school, who was a Gujarati Brahmin of Kashi. He wrote his *Alankar Darpan* in 1769.

HARI PINGAL PRABANDH. See *Jogidas Kunariya*.

HARI PRAKASH TYAGI. Novelist, whose chief work is : *Dusra Admi Lao* (Bring Another Man ; 1979).

HARI PRASAD PANDEY. Kannada-speaking modern Hindi poet, whose *Dharti Ambar* (The Earth and the Sky ; 1966) is a collection of poems, displaying the poet's first reaction to the world around him.

HARI PRASAD RISAL MISHRA (fl. 1930). Hindi poet of Mauritius, who is remembered for his songs.

HARI PRASAD 'SUMAN'. Modern Chambiyali writer, who is the author of *Chamba Gata Hai* (a collection of folk-songs) and *Gallan Hoi Bitiyan* (drama).

HARI RAMCHANDRA DIVAKAR (1884-1975). Marathi-speaking modern Hindi scholar, who is noted for his work: *Sant Tukaram.*

HARIRAM DAS (d. 1778). Rajasthani saint-poet and founder of Ram Snehi Sampraday, Sinthal, who was initiated by Jaimaldas (q.v.) in 1743. A householder, like his Guru, his *Vani* consists of *Sakhis* (*Dohas*, 2283), *Doha-Chaupai* (354), *Rekhta* (32), *Padas* (179), *Kavitta*, etc.; *Nisanni* is considered his mature production. Worship of Nirgun Ram and His *Namsmaran* are the pillars of his poems. The language is easy Rajasthani. Among his hundreds of disciples, Biharidas was the leading one and he ascended the *Gaddi* after his death.

HARIRAM DAS (fl. 18th cent). Rajasthani saint-poet and a follower of Haridas Niranjani Sect, who was a versatile scholar. His *Chhand Ratnavali*, *Parmarth Satsai*, *Maharaj Haridas ji ki Parchi* (on the life of Haridas) and many stray verses are noted for their poetic beauty and history.

HARIRAM VYAS (fl. 1565). Poet of the Krishna-cult. who was preceptor of Madhukar Shah, the Orchha ruler. He was the founder of Harivyasi Sect and his chief works are *Vyas ki Bani* (Verses of Vyas) and *Ragmala*.

HARI RAS. Rajasthani poem by Barhat Isardas (q v.), which is regarded as book of recitation of the Vaishnavas. In this work, he raises fundamental questions and answers in his way about *Karma* and *Brahma* and how the Nirakar Brahma originated and how this origin was brought about.

HARI RASU. See *Jaysingh.*

HARI RAY (fl. 1550). Follower of Vallabhacharya, who was prominent Brajbhasha prose writer. His chief works are: *Shri Yamunaji ke Nam, Shri Acharya Mahaprabhu ko Swarup, Shri Acharya Mahaprabhu ki Dwadash Nij Varta* (all in prose) and *Varshotsav* (in verse). His works are concerned with

Vallabhacharya (Mahaprabhu) and sports of Krishna.

HARI SEVAK MISHRA. Poet, who composed in 1744 his *Kamrup Charit* or *Kamrup Katha Mahakavya*, a romance, for the entertainment of Maharajkumar Prithwi Singh of Orchha.

HARI SHANKAR ADESH. Modern Hindi poet of Trinidad, who has written 18 poetical works, one epic, six short story collections, four works on music and one novel. His chief works are : *Shatdal, Akash Ganga, Devalay, Madiralay, Laharon ka Sangit, Devyani, Rajat Jayanti, Nisha ki Bahen, Lakiron ka Khel, Nirasha* and *Rajnigandha*. His wife, Nirmala Adesh is also a good writer, while his daughter Surabhi Adesh writes for children. Harishankar Adesh by his works has popularized Indian music, culture and literature among the masses. He is now settled in Canada.

HARI SHANKAR PARSAI (1924-). Humorous and satirical writer, whose chief works are : *Bhut ke Panv Pichhe* (The Ghosts Have Their Feet Backwise), *Sadachar ka Tabiz* (The Amulet of Good Conduct), *Jaise Unke Din Phire* (As Their Auspicious Days Came), *Rani Nagphani ki Kahani* (The Story of Rani Nagphani), *Vaishnav ki Phislan* (The Slink of a Vaishnav), *Thithurta Hua Gantantra* (Shivering Republic), *Pagdandiyon ka Zamana* (The Age of Shortcuts), *Nithalle ki Diary* (The Diary of an Idler), Aur Ant Men (And at the End ; 1980), *Shikayat Mujhe bhi Hai, Viklang Shraddha ka Daur, Tirchhi Rekhayen, Kag Bhagora, Tat ki Khoj, Do Nak Vale Log* and *Pakhand ka Adhyatma* (1984). Parsai is in line of the master satirists of the 19th century and keeps the common man awake. His popular short stories are : 'Chori ke Vidhayak' (Legislators of Theft), 'Khambe' (Uprooted Poles), 'Bhola Ram ki Atma' (The Soul of Bhola Ram), etc.

HARI SHANKAR PRASAD UPADHYAY. Writer, who wrote a drama, *Bharat Darshan ya Council ke Ummidvar* (See India or Candidates for the Council ; 1921).

HARI SHANKAR SHARMA (1891-1968). Poet, who was son of Nathuram Shankar (q.v.). His chief humorous works are : *Chiriyaghar* (Zoo), *Pinjarapol* (Cow-house), *Matkaram Mishra, Garbar Goshthi* (Disorderly Symposium), *Pakhand Pradarshani* (Exhibition of Hypocrisy ; all poetical collections) ; his other poetical works are : *Ghaspat* (Weeds), *Ramrajya, Krishna-Sandesh, Maharshi Mahima* (The Glory of Maharshi Dayanand) and *Virangana Vaibhav* (Greatness of Amazon).

HARI SINGH (fl. 1849). Hindi poet of Bhavnagar (Gujarat),

who composed stray verses, *Ghazals*, *Lavnis* and a work *Gyan Katari*, containing 28 *Kavitta Savaiyas.*

HARISUR BARHAT (fl. between 1450-1550). Dingal poet, whose stray *Gits* on contemporary rulers and chiefs are available.

HARI VADAN SHARMA. Native of Burma, who is promoting the cause of Hindi in his country. He is the author of *Hindi-Burmese Bodh Navi Hindi.*

HARI VALLABH (fl. 1643). Poet, who wrote a commentary in Hindi verse on the *Bhagavadgita.*

HARI VALLABH (fl. 17th cent. ?). Poet of the Krishna-cult (Chaitanya Sect), whose stray *Padas* are available. He appears to be different from Vishwanath Chakravarti alias 'Harivallabh'.

HARI VALLABH 'HARI'. Modern Rajasthani poet, who has composed patriotic, heroic and progressive poems.

HARIVANSH RAI 'BACHCHAN' (1907-). Poet, who was born in Allahabad. After passing M.A. (English Literature) from the Allahabad University, he got the doctorate on W.B. Yeats from Cambridge University ; his thesis has been published. He entered Government service and in 1952 was nominated to the Rajya Sabha. After the death of his first wife, he gave himself to despair and sang freely of his inner anguish. As a counter-poise to sorrow, his *Madhushala* (Wine-house ; tr., into English ; 1935), *Madhubala* (The Daughter of Wine ; 1936), *Madhukalash* (Wine-pot ; 1937) etc. are the poetical collections written in the bacchanalian and care-free style. With the passing of years, his horizon widened ; the feeling of discontent turned him into a rebel. He revolted against many popular beliefs and conventions but since his poetry is simple, sensuous and impassioned, he continues to be a favourite poet of the younger generation. *Nisha-Nimantaran* (Night invitations ; short elegiac lyrics on the death of his wife ; 1938) and *Ekant Sangit* (Songs of Loneliness ; 1939) are such collections of poems. Finding another partner in life, he leaves despair and his poetry flows along more constructive lines. Works of this phase are *Satrangini* (Seven-coloured). *Halahal* (Deadly Poison), *Milan Yamini* (Night of Union), *Pranay-Patrika* (Love Letter), *Sut ki Mala* (The Garland of the Thread) and *Khadi ke Phul* (The Flowers of Home-spun Cloth ; tributes to Mahatma Gandhi) : his earlier works are : *Akul Antar* (Vexed Interval ; 1943) and *Bengal ka Akal* (The Bengal Famine). His other works are : *Arti aur Angare* (Worship and Embers ; 1958),

Buddha aur Nachghar (Buddha and the Dance Hall ; 1959), *Tribhangima* (1961), *Char Kheme Chaunsath Khunte* (Four Tents and Sixty-four Tent-pins ; 1962), *Do Chattane* (Two Rocks ; 1965), *Kati Pratimaon ki Avaz* (Voice of the Broken Statues) and *Bahut Din Bite* (Long, Long Ago ; 1967) (all poetry). *Jan Gita* is a tr. of the *Bhagavadgita* in *Doha-Chaupai* style. Collections of his works are : *Meri Kavitai ki Adhi Sadi* (Half a Century of My Poetry ; 1981) and *Bachchan Granthavali* (9 vols. ; 1983).

Bachchan's autobiography is published in three parts under the titles : *Kya Bhulun, Kya Yad Karun* (What should I forget and what should I remember ; 1969) *Nid ka Nirman Phir Phir* (The Building of Nest, Again and Again ; 1970) and *Basere se Dur* (Away from Home ; 1982). *Pravasi ki Diary* is a travelogue, while *Tuti-Chhuti Kadiyan* (Broken and Missing Links) and *Naye Purane Jarokhe* (The New and Old Casements) are collections of his essays. Besides the above, he has tr. Shakespeare's *Macbeth* and *Othello* into Hindi verse. He has edited *Hindi ki Pratinidhi Kavitayen—1978* (1978) and with Ajit Kumar has ed. an anthology : *Athven Dashak ki Pratinidhi Shreshth Kavitayen* (Representative Poems of the Eighth Decade ; 1982). *Bachchan ke Vishishta Patra* is a collection of his letters, while *Hindi Patrakarita ke Gaurav* is on Hindi journalism.

HARI VYAS DEV (fl. 1463). Poet of the Krishna-cult (Nimbark Sect), who composed *Mahavani* in five chapters. He also wrote five works in Sanskrit.

HARISH CHANDRA, BHARATENDU (1850-85). Celebrated writer and poet. Born in a rich and illustrious family of Benares, his father Gopalchandra (alias Giridhardas) was a poet of repute. He lost his father when he was ten years old, while his mother had died five years earlier. After private coaching at home, he attended Queen's College for 2 years but left thereafter and was married at the age of 14. Besides knowing Hindi, Sanskrit, Persian and English, he had also acquired a knowledge of Bengali and some other provincial languages. He travelled extensively during his short life span and had contacts with many intellectuals and public workers of his time and was respected equally by the Government and the people. Among the prominent men with whom he had contacts were Keshub Chandra Sen, Ishwarchandra Vidyasagar, Bankim Chandra Chattopadhyay, Navin Chandra Rai and by correspondence with Col. Olcott, Mrs Annie Besant, Frederick Pincott, Garcin de Tassy and George Grierson. He squandered his vast inheritance in the interest of social and literary advancement and he had to suffer later on for his inordinate magnanimity.

During his literary career of 17 years, Bharatendu wrote between 170 to 200 books, edited some 75 works and published three periodicals : 'Kavi-Vachan Sudha', 'Harishchandra Magazine' (later converted to 'Harishchandra Chandrika') and 'Bal-Bodhini'. His chief works are as under :—

Drama : *Satya Harishchandra* (based on the mythological story of Harishchandra), *Prem Jogini* (incomplete), *Chandravali* (1877 ; on the love of Chandravali for Krishna), *Bharat Janani, Bharat Durdasha* (on the degeneration of India), *Nildevi* (on the heroic deed of a Rajput queen ; 1880), *Andher-Nagari* (City of Injustice), *Vaidiki Hinsa Hinsa na Bhavati* (Vedic Slaughter of Animals is no Slaughter ! ; both farces), *Vishasya Vishamaushadham* (Poison is Antidote for Poison), *Madhuri* and *Sati-Pratap* (incomplete ; on the steadfast love of Savitri for Satyavan). In drama, Bharatendu felt the need of providing an alternative to the Parsi Theatre. To ridicule the Parsi dramatic presentation, he wrote *Bandar Sabha* (The Assembly of Monkeys) and to provide a model, he wrote *Chandravali*. His *Pravas* (1868) is no longer extant.

Translated Drama : *Mudrarakshasa, Dhananjaya-Vijaya, Ratnavali* (from Sanskrit), *Karpura Manjari* (from Prakrit), *Pakhand-Vidambana, Vidya Sundar* (from Bengali) and *Durlabh Bandhu* (tr. of Shakespeare's *The Merchant of Venice*).

Poetry : 41 works (all devotional), *Holi, Madhumukul, Prem Phulvari, Prem Pralap, Satsai-Shringar* (on *Shringar*), *Vijiyani-Vijay-Vaijyanti, Bharat Vina, Sumanjali* (patriotic, etc.).

History : *Kashmir-Kusum* (Flowers of Kashmir), *Maharashtra Desh ka Itihas, Agrawalon ki Utpatti, Delhi Durbar Darpan, Badshah Darpan, Udaypuroday, Puravrit-Sangrah* and *Charitavali*.

Akhyan and Essays : (mostly incomplete), *Sulochana, Madalasopakhyan* (both mythological), *Shilvati, Lilavati, Hammir-Hath* (on the dogged valour of Hammir), *Ap Biti Jag Biti* (story), *Parihas Panchak, Parinasini* (both humorous), *Kal Chakra, Natak* (on dramaturgy) and *Ek Kahani-Kuchh Apbiti Kuchh Jagbiti* (autobiography). *Puran Prakash aur Chandra Prabha* is his first social novel ; it may be his original composition or a translation. The essay 'Natak' (1883) is Bharatendu's contribution to Hindi criticism.

Bharatendu developed a new form of Khari Boli prose and at the same time put it to a variety of uses, thus laying the foundation of modern literature. By his writings, he helped to bridge the gulf that had existed for a long time between life and literature. His eminence as a poet was equally great. Brajbhasha acquired a new freshness and charm in his poetry. In Brajbhasha he wrote about Radha and Krishna and in the treatment of this theme succeeded in blending sensuousness with a genuinely devotional attitude. His poetry, written in Khari Boli, sometimes, has a topical interest, serving to express his more modern feelings of patriotism or anxiety for social welfare. He accepted current Urdu and Persian words and his genius in handling them made them a poetical asset.

With Bharatendu, started the modern period of Hindi literature and he can justly be called the Father of Modern Hindi Literature.

The Nagari Pracharini Sabha, Kashi has published his works under the title of *Bharatendu Granthavali* (3 vols.).

HARISH CHANDRA JHA 'HARISH'. Modern Maithili writer, whose chief work, *Chhikka*, a one-act play, is full of humour and wit.

HARISH CHANDRA PRIYADARSHI. Modern Magahi poet, who is noted for his love songs.

HARISH NIGAM. Modern Malwi poet, who is known for his stray poems.

HARISH PATHAK. Poet, whose *Narak ko Kabhi Sharm Nahin Ati* (The Hell Never Feels Ashamed ; 1980) is a collection of revolting poems ; his short story collection is *Saream.*

HARISH SHARMA. Modern scholar, whose chief work is *Bhasha-Vigyan ki Ruprekha.*

HARKH (HARSH) NATH JHA. Maithili poet, whose *Usha-Haran*, *Madhavanand* and *Radha-Krishna-Milan-Lila* are Kirtaniya form of dramas He was patronized by Maharaja Lakshmishwar Singh (r. 1878-98). He is also remembered for his love lyrics.

HARKHA RAM (1746-1804). Rajasthani saint-poet of Nagore, who was made the Acharya of Ram Snehi Sect, Ren after the death of its founder, Dariyav (q v.). Noted for his piety, he composed 17 poems, *Guru Mahima*, *Garbh Chitavani*, *Bhaktamal*, *Shabdabhed Nisani*, *Nam Nisani*, *Karuna Sagar*, *Bhram Vidhwansh*, *Bhram Tor*, *Ajamil ki Parchi*, *Narayan Lila*, *Gyan Samudra*, etc. and many stray verses. Describing both the aspects of Nirgun and Sagun Bhakti, his poetry is touching and impressive.

HARLEY, A.H. Author of *Colloquial Hindustani* (London, 1944 ; rev. ed. 1970).

HAROJI (fl. 18th cent.). Rajasthani saint-poet of Jasnathi Sampraday, whose stray verses and *Sabads* deal with human duties, divine attributes, etc.

HARRIS. Author of *Dictionary* : *English and Hindustani* (Madras, 1790).

HARRIS, RICHARD MARK. American Hindi scholar and author of *A Basic Hindi Reader* (Ithica, 1969) and *Lingua Franca Hindi : A study of Urban Educated Speech* (Ph. D. ; Cornell, 1966).

HARSH NATH Writer, whose chief novels are : *Karmu aur Jagni* (1954 ; with lively description of rural life), *Rakta ke Ansu* (1959 ; description of Suvasi, a lady of character) and *Alag-alag Raste*. He has also written short stories.

HARSH VARDHAN. Malayalam-speaking modern Hindi writer, who has tr. some Malayalam dramas into Hindi.

HARSH VIJAY (fl. 1785). Jain poet, who was the author of *Samb Pradyumna Ras* on the story of Krishna's sons : Samb and Pradyumna.

HARSHAD R. JOSHI. Modern Hindi writer of Kenya, who is noted for his prose works, especially novels.

HARSHAU (fl. 1608). Rajasthani poet, whose stray verses in popular metres are available.

HARSUR ROHDIYO (fl. 2nd half of 14th cent.). Dingal song-writer, who describes Rao Viram's death (in 1383) after killing Johiya Depal ; the accounts given in the songs are historically correct.

HASHIM ALI (fl. 1736). Hindi poet of Gujarat, whose *Divan Husaini* is a collection of 238 elegies Some people are, however, of the view that he belonged to Burhanpur.

HATTI PRAVISHT. Rajasthani Charan, whose stray verses are available ; his time is not certain.

HAWLEY, JOHN STRATTON (1941-). American scholar of

Hindi, who is at present Associate Professor of Asian Languages and Literature (Hindi) in the University of Washington. His publications are : *At Play with Krishna* : *Pilgrimage Dramas from Brindavan* (in association with Shrivats Goswami ; 1981), *The Divine Consort* : *Radha and the Goddesses of India* (with Donna M. Wulff ; 1982 ; ed.), *Krishna, the Butter Thief* (1983) and *Surdas* : *Poet, Singer, Saint* (1984). His field of research is comparative religion and mediaeval Hindi literature and he has written over 30 articles and reviews, all connected with his special field.

He is also Associate Editor for Religion in *Encyclopaedia of South Asia* (1983 ; General ed. Margaret Case).

HAZARI PRASAD DWIVEDI (1907-79). Critic, novelist and essayist, who was born at Dube ka Chhapra in the district of Balia of Bihar. After teaching in Vishwabharati, Shantiniketan, he was Head of the Hindi Department at Benares Hindu University and later at Panjab University, Chandigarh. His chief works are :

Criticism : *Hindi Sahitya ki Bhumika* (Introduction to Hindi Literature ; 1940), *Kabir* (1942), *Hindi Sahitya* (Hindi Literature), *Hindi Sahitya ka Adikal* (The Beginning of Hindi Literature), *Nath Sampraday* (Nath Sect), *Sahaj Sadhana* (The Natural Way of Austerity), *Sur Sahitya* (Literature of Surdas), *Madhyakalin Bodh ka Swarup* (Form of Mediaeval Knowledge), *Prachin Bharat men Kalatmak Vinod* (Artistic Pastimes in Ancient India), *Meghdut* : *Ek Purani Kahani* (*Meghdut* : An Old Story), *Natyashastra ki Bharatiya Parampara aur Dashrupaka* (Indian Tradition of Natyashastra and Dashrupak), *Sahitya ka Marma* (The Essence of Literature ; 1952) *Kalidas ki Lalitya Yojna* (Kalidas's Portrayal of Beauty ; 1965), *Nath Siddhon ki Baniyan* (Works of Nath Siddhas), *Sandesh Rasak*, *Prithwiraj Raso* (The last three edited) and *Sikh Guruon ki Atmakatha* (Works of the Sikh Gurus ; posthumous).

Novels : *Banbhatt ki Atmakatha* (Banbhatt's Autobiography ; 1946 ; q.v.), *Charu Chandralekha* ((1963 ; dealing with the story of Raja Satvahan and Rani Charu Chandralekha), *Punarnava* (1974 ; a description of 4th cent. India) and *Anamdas ka Potha-Ath Raikva-akhyan* (1976; based on a story in *Chhandogya-Upanishad*) ; *Banbhatt ki Atmakatha* deals with the life-story of the famous Sanskrit writer, Banabhatta.

Essay Collections : *Ashok ke Phul* (Blossoms of the Ashok Tree ; 1948), *Vichar aur Vitarka* (Observations and Discussion ; 1949), *Kalpalata* (Heavenly Creeper ; 1951), *Vichar-Vimarsh*

(Considerations), *Vichar Pravah*, *Kutaj* and *Alok-Parva* (Festival of Brightness ; it received Sahitya Akademi Award) ; all these essays display the writer's personality, apart from their valuable contribution to scholarship, research and criticism. His command over language, his deep knowledge and distinctive style mark him out as a leading writer of Hindi prose. He also tr. Tagore's *Rakta Karabi* into Hindi as *Lal Kaner*. *Patra* is a collection of personal letters.

Dwivedi's *Granthavali* (11 vols., 1981) is an edition of his complete works.

Dwivedi occupies a prominent place as a research scholar, a critic, an essayist and a novelist among modern Hindi writers. As a critic, Dwivedi's contribution lies in his enunciation of a synthetic approach.

HAZELGROVE, G.P. Author of *A Vocabulary, English and Hindoostanee* (Bombay, 1865).

HEM KANT MISHRA, CHAUDHARY. Modern Oriya writer, who has tr. *Manushya ke Rup* from Hindi into Oriya.

HEM RAJ SUNDAR. Modern Hindi poet of Mauritius, whose *Chetana* is a collection of his poems.

HEM RATAN SURI (1559-1616). Jain Rajasthani poet, whose fame rests on *Gora Badal Charitra* (or *Gora Badal Padmini Chaupai*). The poet, when narrating this historical event, emphasizes virtues like faith, morality and chastity. The poet describes how Gora and Badal, the brave Rajput warriors, secure the release of Rana Ratansen by defeating Alauddin and the Rana returns to his fort and is re-united with his charming queen, Padmini. The poem consists of 619 verses, mainly *Chaupais*. Hem Ratan's other narrative poems are *Mahipal Chaupai*, *Amar Kumar Chaupai*, *Sita Chaupai* and *Lilavati*.

HEM SAGAR (fl. 1649). Jain Riti poet, who was a disciple of Kalyan Sagar Muniraj. He composed *Chhand Malika*, a work on prosody.

HEM SAMAUR (fl. 1st half 17th cent.). Dingal poet, who wrote poems mostly on contemporary heroes and happenings. His *Gun Bhakha Charitra* describes the battle and victory of Maharaja Gajsingh of Jodhpur against Bhim Sisodiya at Hazipur (Patna). A lexicon, *Hemi Nam Mala* is also ascribed to him, but it is no longer extant.

HEM VIJAY (fl. *c.* 1613). Gujarati-speaking Jain poet, who composed several stray verses in Hindi.

HENRY, JOHN Modern scholar, whose chief work is *Pashchatya Vidvanon ki Hindi Bhasha aur Sahitya ko Den (1800-1900)* (Thesis ; Kurukshetra ; 1963-68).

HETUKAR JHA. Maithili poet, whose *Chetika* is his first collection of poems. *Paristhiti* (1981) is his long poem.

HIMANSHU JOSHI (1935-). Writer, whose chief works are : *Antatah* (Finally), *Manushya-Chihna* (Signs of Man), *Rath-Chakra* (Chariot-wheel), *Himanshu Joshi-ki Vishisht Kahaniyan* (short story collections), *Aranya* (Forest), *Mahasagar* (The Ocean), *Chhaya Mat Chhuna Man* (O Mind, Do not Touch Shadow), *Kagar ki Ag* (Fire on the Edge of the River ; 1977), *Suraj, Tumhare Liye, Samay Sakshi Hai* (Time is Witness ; novels) and *Shreshth Samantar Kahaniyàn* (a short story collection, ed. by him). His important short stories are : 'Abhav' (Destitution), 'Sima ke Kuchh aur Age' (A Little Beyond the Limit), 'Manushya ka Chihna' (The Sign of Man), 'Fasla', etc. *Agni Sambhav* is his humorous work.

HIMANSHU SHRIVASTAV. Novelist, whose chief works are : *Lohe ke Pankh* (The Wings of Iron ; 1958), *Rath ke Pahiye* (The Wheels of Chariot), *Sikandar* (Alexander), *Nanarao Peshwa* (1966 ; based on the story of Nanarao, a leading figure in 1857 War of Independence), *Pichhli Rat ka Andhera* (The Darkness of the Preceding Night : 1980), *Pura Adhura Purush* (The Fully Incomplete Man ; 1982 ; on economic hardships faced by a middle class family), *Ishara* and *Shok Sabha*.

HINDI LITERATURE. A HISTORY OF. A history of Hindi literature (1920), which was written by F.E. Keay.

HINDI LITERATURE, A SKETCH OF. A history of Hindi literature (1917), which was written by Edwin Greaves ; the work consists of 112 pages and divides the Hindi literature in five periods : 800-1400 ; 1400-1580 ; 1580-1700 ; 1700-1800 and 1800 onwards.

HINDI SAHITYA KA ITIHAS. See *Ramchandra Shukla.*

HINDI SAHITYA KA BRIHAT ITIHAS (A Comprehensive History of Hindi Literature), which is in 17 vols. and has been published by the Nagari Pracharini Sabha, Varanasi. It is the largest history of Hindi literature, published so far. Its first volume appeared in 1957.

HINDI SHABDASAGAR. Exhaustive Hindi lexicon (1929), which was completed in seven volumes. It was edited by Shyamsundar Das and in this task he was assisted by Balkrishna Bhatt, Ramchandra Shukla, Amirsingh, Jaganmohan Verma, Bhagvan Din and Ramchandra Verma.

HINGLAJDAN, KAVIYA (1861-1948). Rajasthani poet of the village Sewapura (Jaipur), who was the last great representative of the Charan poetry. Of his many poems, the chief ones are : *Mrigaya Mrigendra* (describing the tiger-hunting by Sher Singh of Kuchaman and an imaginary dialogue between the hunter and the hunted), *Pratyay Payodhar* (on prosody), *Sal Girah Shatak* (on the birth anniversary of Indra Bai, deemed to be a goddess incarnate), *Mehai Mahima* (on the battle between Kamran and Rao Jaitsi of Bikaner and the goddess Karaniji's help to the latter), *Durga Bahattari* (eulogy of Durga), *Akhet Apjas* and *Vanya* (*Banija*) *Raso*, both ironical poems. He also composed stray poems including *Rupsingh Rupak* and eulogies of Karaniji, Indra Bai, Bhavani in Dingal *Gits* and other metres. He is sarcastic about selfish traders and cowards posing as brave warriors. The poet has good command over the language, which is mostly literary.

HIR BHAT (fl. 1st half of 15th cent.). Rajasthani poet, who composed *Man Kutuhal* (q.v.) or *Manvati Vinayavati Prabandh* as a rejoinder to the arrogance of Vilal Kunvari alias Man Kunvari.

HIR KALASH (fl. 1579). Rajasthani writer and author of *Simhasan Battisi* (based on the Sanskrit original).

HIR KAVI (fl. 17th cent.). One of the court-poets of Guru Govind Singh (q.v.), who excelled in Hindi poetry of *Vir Rasa*. He probably saw all the battles with his own eyes and his description of actual fighting in the battlefield, particularly of the last battle of Anandpur, is dignified and is of a very high order. He has also bestowed fulsome praise on Govind Singh's prowess and war-like qualities.

HIRA DAS (1493-1578). Gujarati-speaking saint-poet of Surat (Gujarat), whose Hindi *Padas* are didactic and remind one of the tradition of Kabir (q.v.).

HIRA LAL. Writer, who is noted for his voluminous version (1775) in Brajbhasha prose of Abul Fazl's *Ain-e-Akbari*.

HIRA LAL GUPTA (fl. 1940). Hindi writer of Mauritius, who was known for his Hindi work on Maganlal Manilal (q.v.).

HIRA LAL JHA 'HEM'. Maithili poet, whose chief work *Sita-Charitamrit* (1981) is a collection of poems.

HIRA LAL KAVYOPADHYAY. Chhattisgarhi writer, who was the first to write *Chhattisgarhi Vyakaran* (1890), which was tr. into English by Sir George Grierson the same year. The grammar has since been revised by Lochan Prasad Pandey and has been published by the Madhya Pradesh Government.

HIRA LAL LILADHAR. Modern Hindi dramatist of Mauritius, whose chief work is *Atithi* (The Guest).

HIRA LAL MAHESHWARI. Modern Rajasthani writer, whose chief works are : *Rajasthani Bhasha aur Sahitya* (1960), *Jambhoji, Vishnoi Sampraday aur Sahitya* (2 vols, 1970), *History of Rajasthani Literature* (1980) and *Jambhoji* (1981), the last two published by the Sahitya Akademi.

HIRA NAND SURI. Rajasthani poet and author in 1428 of *Vidyavilas Pavadau* (q v.), a romantic poem of 189 verses.

HIRANMAY (1911-57). Kannada-speaking Hindi poet, whose poems were published in 'Jagriti'. He also started in 1965 'Manasi', a research magazine in collaboration with Na. Nagappa. His other works are : *Hindi aur Kannada men Bhakti Andolan ka Tulnatmak Adhyayan*, *Kannada Sahitya Saurabh*, a translation in Hindi of the Kannada novel : *Choman Dudi* (since filmed) and of a Kannada drama : *Raktakshi*, written by Kuvempu. He tr. some modern Kannada poems into Hindi for the Sahitya Akademi volume : *Bharatiya Kavita*. He also tr. from Kannada into Hindi K.V. Aiyar's novel : *Shantala*. See *Indira Krishnamurti*.

HISLOP, S. European scholar, who wrote *Papers Relating to the Aboriginal Tribes of the Central Provinces* (Nagpur, 1866).

HISTOIRE DE LA LITTERATURE HINDOUE ET HINDOUSTANIE. The first history of Hindi literature, written in French by Garcin de Tassy ; its first part was published in 1839, while the second part was out in 1846. In this work are given the biographies of the poets and the names and details of their works. Its second edition (1871) consisted of three parts and gives in an English alphabetical order the names and works of Hindi and Urdu poets and poetesses ; this edition was completed in 1834 pages. In the 14-page Introduction to this edition, the writer has expressed his views about Hindi language and its literature.

HIT HARIVANSH (1502-52). Poet, who was the founder of Radha Vallabhi Sect or Hit Sampraday, a Sect in which Radha is placed above Krishna as an object of devotion. His father Vyas Mishra was a Gaur Brahmin of Devban (Deoband). When his father with his wife Tararani was on a pilgrimage of Braj, Hit Harivansh was born in the village of Badgaon near Mathura. Many miracles are said to have been taken place at the time of his birth. It is popular among the followers of his Sect that Radha herself initiated him when he was five years old. At 16, he was married to Rukminidevi and had three sons and one daughter. At 32, when his parents were dead, he left Devban all alone and made his way towards Vrindavan. At Chirthawal, he married two daughters—Krishnadasi and Manohardasi of a Brahmin. In Vrindavan, he established his order.

He wrote in Sanskrit the *Radhasudhanidhi* (Radha's Ocean of Elixir ; consisting of 170 verses) and *Yamunashtak*. His principal work is the *Hit Chaurasi* (or *Premlata*). He also wrote some stray verses. *Sphut Vani* describes the principles of his Sect. These works display the erotic side of the Krishna-cult and are full of sensuous imagery. Hit Harivansh was held in very high esteem and exercised great influence on the scholars, poets and devotees of his generation, many of whom paid high tributes to him. The language had been handled so delicately by him that he has been hailed as an "incarnation of Krishna's flute". Hit Vrindavandas and Dhruvdas (q.v.) were the followers of his Sect.

Premdas and Loknath wrote commentaries on the *Hit Chaurasi*. Hariram Vyas composed some poignant verses at Hit Harivansh's death, while Hit Parmanand and Braj Jivandas wrote verses at his nativity. Hit Vrindavandas in his *Hitji-ki-Sahsranamavali* and Chaturbhuj Das in his *Hit-ju-ko-Mangal* eulogised him greatly.

HIT NARAYAN JHA. Modern Maithili scholar, who has written critical articles, applying the Western principles of literary criticism.

HIT TARANGINI. See *Kriparam*.

HIT VRINDAVAN DAS (b. 1695-1710, d. 1793). Poet of the Krishna-cult, who was born in a Gaur Brahmin family. He remained for a long time under the patronage of the brother of Maharaj Nagaridas. Later on he was initiated in the Order of Hit Sampraday or Radhavallabhi Sect, where he is counted one of the chief poets. In his Order, he is popularly known as 'Vrindavan Chacha' and his poetry is termed 'Chachaji-ki-

Vani'. The number of his *Padas* is said to run into 4 lakhs and his works are said to be 158 in number, which include many *Ashtayams*, *Samay-Prabandhs*, *Velis* and two *Sagars*. His published works are : *Lad Sagar*, *Braj Prem-Anand-Sagar*, *Vrindavan Jas Prakash Veli*, *Rasik-Path-Chandrika*, *Kripa Abhilash Veli*, *Jugalsaneh-Patrika*, *Harivansh-Sahsranam*, stray verses, etc. In Chhatarpur, Bharatpur, Kishengarh and Vrindavan, manuscripts of his 80 works are available. In his *Harivansh Sahsranam*, on the pattern of *Bhaktamal* (q.v.), he has given biographical outlines of the devotees of the Radha-vallabh Sect. The *Krishna-Radha-Lilas*, composed by Vrindavan Das are still staged in the Braj country.

HOERNLE, A.F. RUDOLF (1841-1918). Sanskrit scholar, who was Principal of Presidency College, Madras His chief works on Hindi are : *A Grammar of the Eastern Hindi compared with other Guadian Languages* (London, 1880), *Comparative Dictionary of Bihari Language* (Calcutta, Pt. I, 1885 ; Pt. II, 1889 ; in collaboration with G.A. Grierson) and an essay 'Hindi Dhatu Sangrah'.

HOGSON, B H. English scholar, who during 1824-1840 was an Assistant Resident and then Resident in Nepal, where he collected a good number of works in Sanskrit, Pali and Hindi. Five Hindi works compiled by him in manuscript form are preserved in the India Office Library. He also wrote several articles from the year 1835 to 1858 on the adoption of Indian vernaculars as the medium of instruction and on the Comparative Vocabulary of Himalayan Dialects.

HOL RAY (fl. 1585). Poet, who eulogised his patron, Harivansh Ray ; he also composed some verses in praise of Emperor Akbar. He had a meeting with Tulsidas as well.

HOLE TOYD, W.R.M. (fl. early 20th cent.). Author of *Hindustani for Everyday*, which was published from Lahore.

HOM VATI (1902-51). Short story writer of Meerut ; her chief collections of short stories are ; *Nisarg* (Nature ; 1939), *Dharohar* (Trust-money ; 1946), *Swapnabhang* (Shattering of Dream ; 1948) and *Apna Ghar* (Own House ; 1950) ; she had also written stray poems.

HOMEM, P.M. Author of *Novo Vocabularis em Portuguez, Concanim, Ingleze, Hindustani* (Bombay, 1874).

HONAJI (fl. 18th cent.). Marathi folk-poet (*Shahir*), who also made composition in Hindi.

HOOK, PETER EDWIN. American Hindi scholar, whose chief work is : *The Compound Verb in Hindi* (Pennsylvania, 1973).

HRIDAY RAM (fl. probably 17th cent.). Rajasthani saint-poet, whose *Nam Mala* gives a list of disciples of Dadu (q.v.).

HRIDAY RAM BHALLA. Hindi poet of Panjab, who was son of Krishna Das. He composed the *Hanumannatak* in 1623 during the reign of Jahangir on the basis of the Sanskrit *Hanumannataka.* The text reveals, however, that it is a free translation in verse of the Sanskrit play with elaborations and additions by the author. It is one of the important works of the Ram-cult. Hridayram also composed two other dramas : *Rukmini Mangal* and *Sudama-Charit.*

HRIDAYANAND TIWARI 'KUMARESH'. Modern Bhojpuri poet of the Rewati Village in Balia district, whose *Krantidut*, a heroic poem, mentions the atrocities commited by the British rulers on Indians during the Quit India Movement of 1942.

HRIDAYESH (1930-). Writer, whose chief novels are *Kahani Ant-hin* (A Story Without End ; 1972), *Safed Ghora, Kala Savar* (1976) and *Sand* (The Bull ; 1981 ; an attack on the contemporary socio-political system). His short story : 'Gunjlak' (The Coil of the Snake) is quite popular ; *Uttaradhikari* (The Successor ; 1981), *Andheri Gali ka Rasta, Itihas* and *Amar Katha* are his short story collections.

HRISHIKESH CHATURVEDI (1907-70). Brajbhasha poet, whose chief poetical work is *Ramkrishna Kavya* (1943) ; the work describes the stories of both Ram and Krishna.

HUKMICHAND KHIDIYA (fl. 1743-1803). Rajasthani poet, who was noted for the artistic excellence of his Dingal *Gits* on various heroes and events. He had adopted *Nisani* metre. It has become a tradition to memorize his *Gits*. He was patronized by Pratap Singh, the Jaipur ruler.

HULLAR MURADABADI. Modern humorous poet, whose chief work is *Hullar ke Shreshth Hasyavyangya.*

HUNDRAJ LILARAM 'DUKHALAY'. Modern Hindi poet, originally belonging to Sind (now is Pakistan), who, through his poems awakened interest in the Bhudan (Land-gift) Movement of AcharyaVinob a Bhave.

HUNTER, JOSEPH. American Hindi scholar and author of *Basic*

Course in Hindi (Foreign Service Research Institute, America, 1960).

HUNTER, WILLIAM. Author of *Dictionary : Hindustani and English* (2 Pts., Calcutta, 1808), which contains words of Persian-Arabic as also of Hindi-Sanskrit ; the basis of this work was a Hindustani-English Dictionary, prepared for his personal use by Captain Joseph Taylor ; its 2nd ed. was published from London in 1817 and in its 3rd ed. it included words of Dakhini as well. Hunter, while he was Secretary of the Fort William College, was collecting the proverbs being taught in the College, but when he was transferred to Java, he handed over his manuscript to Captain Roebuck (q v.), who continued the work with great enthusiasm. Roebuck also could not complete his assignment before 1819, when he died, with the result that it was H H. Wilson, who gave finishing touches to the *Oriental Proverbial Dictionary* and got it published in 1824. This work was dedicated to John Gilchrist (q.v.).

I

IBBAR RABBI. Poet, whose collection of poems is : *Ghoshna Patra* (The Manifesto ; 1981).

IBERIA, NICOLAE. Modern Romanian Hindi scholar, who teaches Hindi at the Bucharest University, Romania.

IBRAHIM SHARIF (1939-77). Telugu-speaking fiction writer, whose chief works are : *Kai Surajon ke Bich* (In the Midst of Many Suns), *Akhiri Tukra* (short story collections) and *Andhere ke Saye* (The Shadows of Darkness ; novel). His prominent short story is 'Digbhramit' (The Derelict).

ILACHANDRA JOSHI (1902-82). Novelist, who was born in the hill town of Almora. Even before passing the High School examination, he had read the works of Valmiki, Vyas, Shelley, Keats, Tolstoy, Chekhov, etc. He has brought in psycho-analysis as the basic factor in his novels, short stories and other works : the Freudian theory of sex provides the basic key to unravel complexities of human behaviour. Joshi's chief novels are : *Parde ki Rani* (The Queen of the Veil ; 1941), *Sannyasi* (The Recluse ; q.v.), *Pret aur Chhaya* (The Ghost and the Shadow), *Lajja* (Shyness), *Ghrinamayi* (Loathsome), *Nirvasit* (The Exile), *Muktipath* (The Path of Freedom), *Subah ke Bhule* (Lost in the Morning), *Gypsy* (1952 : q.v.), *Jahaz ka Panchhi* (The Bird of the Ship ; q.v. ; 1955), *Rituchakra* (The Cycle of Seasons ; 1968), *Bhut ka Bhavishya* (The Future of the Past ; 1973), *Tyag ka Bhog* and *Kavi ki Preyasi* (The Beloved of the Poet). *Parde ki Rani* is the story of Niranjana, the daughter of a former prostitute and a murderer, who behaves at two levels, her conscious being guided by the modern and liberal education, while her subconsciousness displaying the hidden cumulative impulses, she has inherited from her past through her mother and father.

In Joshi's short stories, the same techniques and presentation patterns are reflected, which characterise his novels. His short story collections are : *Dhup-Rekha* (The Sunshine Line ;

1938), *Diwali aur Holi* (1942), *Romantic Chhaya* (1943), *Ahuti* (Offering ; 1945), *Khandahar ki Atmayen* (The Souls of Ruins ; 1948), *Diary ke Niras Prishth* (The Stale Pages of a Diary ; 1951) and *Katile Phul Lajile Kante* (Thorny Flowers, Shy Thorns ; 1957). Even in his essays, psychonalysis has been given prominence ; his essay collections are : *Sahitya-Sarjana* (Creation of Literature ; 1938), *Vivechana* (Thorough Investigation ; 1943), *Sahitya-Santaran* (Emancipation of Literature ; 1953), *Vishleshan* (Analysis; 1954) and *Sahitya-Chintan* (Reflections on Literature ; 1955).

Joshi's other works are : *Sarat-Vyakti aur Kalakar* (1954), *Ravindranath* (1955) and *Dekha-Parkha* (1957 ; all criticism).

ILEDAM, N.R. See *Bhattatiri, P.N.*

IMAMUDDIN (fl. end of 18th cent.). Muslim poet, who was a resident of Saidanpur in the Barabanki district. His *Alifnama* praises Allah through the medium of Hindi.

INCA, DANIEL. Modern Romanian Hindi scholar, who has tr. into Romanian Premchand's 22 short stories from Hindi.

INDAR SABHA. Drama (1853) by Amanat Ali (1816-58), which was enacted in the court of Wajid Ali Shah, the ruler of Oudh. It is said that the Baradari at Kaiserbagh was especially constructed for the presentation of this opera and Nawab Wajid Ali Shah himself played the role of Indra. Though written in Persian script, it influenced and promoted the Parsi theatre. The drama has a touch of Hindi language throughout.

INDIRA DEVI, MRS. Kannada-speaking Hindi poetess, who was editor of 'Jagriti', a literary journal, published from Mysore. In 1935, she composed quite a good number of Hindi poems, which were published in 'Jagriti' and other magazines.

INDIRA KRISHNAMURTI. Kannada-speaking modern Hindi writer, who along with Dr Hiranmay tr. Shivram Karant's novel *Choman Dudi* from Kannada into Hindi.

INDOKALI. Modern Rajasthani poetess, whose poems in the traditional Charan style are available.

INDRABHANU 'LALIT LADAITI' (fl. 19th cent.). Poet of the Krishna-cult (Chaitanya Sect), whose father hailed from Dera Ghazikhan (now in Pakistan). His *Dampati Vilas*, a voluminous poetical work, is divided into five parts.

INDRADASNAYAKE, MRS. Hindi writer of Srilanka, who has promoted the cause of Hindi in her country through Srilanka Sahitya Sammelan. She has also written a work: *Simhal Dwip ki Loriyan.* She is working in the Department of Modern Languages of the University of Kelaniya near Colombo and the Third World Hindi Conference conferred the 'Saraswati Award' on her.

INDRADEV BHOLA 'INDRA'. Modern Hindi poet of Mauritius, whose *Vardan* is a collection of his poems. He has also written a work *Aj ki Hindi.* See *Pravasi Swar.*

INDRAJIT BHATIA. Writer, whose drama : *Swarg Uncha Kyon* (Why is the Heaven High ? ; 1980) shows how a rich man on the basis of his wealth corrupts society.

INDRAJIT SINGH. Assamese-speaking modern Hindi writer, who is noted for his memoirs and reportage.

INDRAMALL (fl. prior to 1685). Maithili poet, whose lyrics were quoted in Karttik Nath Guru's *Ragmala.*

INDRA NATH CHAUDHURI. Bengali-speaking modern Hindi critic, who has made a comparative study of Hindi and Bengali theoretical criticism ; his chief work is *Adhunik Hindi aur Bangla Kavya Shastra ka Tulnatmak Adhyayan.* He has made a notable contribution towards the analysis and evaluation of modern Hindi literature and also taught Hindi in the Bucharest University, Romania.

INDRA NATH MADAN (1910-84). Critic, whose critical works on novel, short story, criticism, poetry and modern literature are : *Aj ka Hindi Upanyas* (Hindi Novel of To-day), *Hindi Upanyas : Ek Nai Drishti* (Hindi Novel : A New Viewpoint), *Premchand : Ek Vivechan* (on Premchand), *Hindi Kahani : Apni Zabani* (on short story), *Alochana aur Kavya* (Criticism and Poetry), *Adhunik Kavita ka Mulyankan* (Evaluation of Modern Poetry), *Adhunikta aur Hindi Sahitya* (Modernity and Hindi Literature), *Alochana aur Sahitya* (Criticism and Literature), *Kavita aur Kavita, Hindi Alochana : Pahchan aur Parakh, Adhunikta aur Hindi Upanyas* and *Kahani aur Kahani* (the last work ed.) ; *Kuchh Uthle : Kuchh Gahre* is a collection of his humorous essays. *Bhanumati ka Pitara* is his humorous work.

INDRA SINGH RUPAK. See *Sagta Sandu.*

INDRA VIDYAVACHASPATI (1889-1960). Hindi writer, who was

son of Swami Shraddhanand, the founder of Gurukula Kangri. Indra's known works are : *Swarndesh ka Uddhar* (1931 ; a drama), *Atma Balidan*, *Shah Alam ke Ankhen*, *Agni Pariksha*, *Zamindar* and *Sarla ki Bhabhi* (novels). *Samrat Raghu* is a biography of the famous king Raghu, while *Mere Pita* is a work on his father, Swami Shraddhanand. He had been Vice-Chancellor of Gurukula Kangri for about 20 years.

INDRAVATI. Allegorical romance by Nur Muhammad (b. 1745), a Sufi poet.

The poem, modelled on the *Padmavat*, in style, deals with the love-story of prince Raj-Kunvar of Kalinjar and princess Indravati of Agampur.

INDU JAIN (1935-) Poetess, whose chief works are : *Chaunsath Kavitayen* (Sixty-four Poems ; 1964), *Ankh se bhi Chhoti Chiriya* (A Sparrow Smaller than even an Eye ; 1978) and *Ham se Pahle bhi Log Yahan The* (1983). She has published her Hindi poems in English as well. Her collections of essays are *Jhurmut* and *Roznamcha.*

INDU PRAKASH PANDEY (1924-). Critic, whose chief works are *Hindi Literature : Trends and Traits* (1975) and *Hindi ke Anchalik Upanyason men Jivan Satya.* As a folklorist, he has published four books on Avadhi folksongs, tales and proverbs ; he has also done research on Avadhi folksongs and has published *Avadhi Lokgit aur Parampara* (Avadhi Folksongs and Tradition). He has written literary articles, short stories and poems as well. He was the first scholar to write the Hindi text-book (1967) in Romanian. He also taught Hindi at the Bucharest University, Romania.

INSHA ALLAH KHAN (1766-1817). Urdu poet, who, though, born at Murshidabad (Bengal) lived mostly in Delhi where he was attached to the court of Shah Alam II. After the sack of Delhi by Abdali, he shifted to Lucknow, where he was patronized by Nawab of Oudh. Primarly a scholar of Persian and Rekhta, Insha wrote his *Rani Ketki-ki Kahani* (The Story of Rani Ketki) in early Khari Boli prose. Though Insha's prose avoids on the one hand Sanskrit words and on the other Arabic and Persian expressions and makes use of the language of daily speech or *Theth* Hindi, it was too much influenced by the Persian diction. He is one of the early four principal Khari Boli prose writers, others being Sadal Mishra, Lallu Lal and Sadasukh Lal (qq.v.). *Rani Ketki ki Kahani* (between 1800 and 1808) treats of the love of Udaybhan, the son of Raja Suraybhan, and Ketki, the daughter of Raja Jagat Prakash.

IQBAL. See *Adeshwar Rao.*

IQBAL BAHADUR DEVSARE (d. 1985). Novelist, whose chief historical works are : *Orchha ki Nartaki* (The Dancer of Orchha ; based on the romance of the poet Keshav and the dancer), *Shade Oudh* (on the fall of Oudh), *Nawab Bemulk* (The Nawab without any territory), *Begum Hazrat Mahal* (1973), *Tansen, Jane Alam, Parikhana* and *Baba Kahi-Kahi Jat.*

IRAVATI. Incomplete historical novel (1936) by Jayshankar Prasad (q.v.). The story relates to the fall of the Maurya Empire and the rise of the Shung dynasy.

ISAR DAS. See *Ishwar Das.*

ISAR LAL (fl. 19th cent.). Sindhi saint-poet, whose stray verses in Hindi are available.

ISH NATH JHA (1907-65). Maithili writer, who was noted for his dramas *Chini ka Laddu* (1947) and *Ugana* (1956 ; on Vidyapati's attendant, who was Shiv in disguise) ; the former drama has been tr. into Hindi and has been staged several times successfully. He also tr. into Maithili from Sanskrit original : *Shakuntalam* and *Mrichchhakatika.* He has also written humorous character-sketches, e.g., 'Tatai Jha' and 'Dharakhana Jha Ka Nosidani'. *Mala* (1945) is a collection of his lyrics, which has affinity with English poetry.

ISHIDA, HIDEAKI. Modern Japanese Hindi scholar, who, though teaching English in Japan, does research in Hindi. His chief articles in Hindi are on Hindi literature during Emergency, on the novels of Jainendra, etc.

ISHWAR CHANDRA. Sindhi-speaking modern Hindi short story writer, whose stories are often published in magazines. He is noted for his sport story collections : *Na Marne ka Dukh* (No Sorrow for Death ; 1972) and *Andar ka Baunapan.*

ISHWAR CHANDRA VIDYASAGAR (1820-91). Celebrated social reformer of Bengal, who, on his visit to Kashi, stayed at the house of Bharatendu Harishchandra (q.v.). He saw the old manuscripts of *Abhijnan Shakuntalam* at Bharatendu's house. He edited the drama and dedicated it to Bharatendu himself. Vidyasagar also contributed some articles to 'Kavi-Vachan-Sudha', a magazine edited by Bharatendu.

ISHWAR DAS (fl. 1489-1517). Poet, whose *Satyavati ki Katha*

(The Story of Satyavati) is the first love poem. He also wote *Bharat Milap*, a narrative poem.

ISHWAR DAS (ISAR DAS ; 1538-1618). Dingal poet, who was born at the village Bhadras in the then Jodhpur State. Son of Sujaji and Amarbai, he passed 40 years of his life in Jamnagar, where the Raval of Jamnagar granted him nine villages. After staying for some 40 years, he came back to his village and built a cottage on the bank of the river Lunni, where he died.

Ishwar Das was credited with several supernatural powers and many miracles go in his name. In the Charan community, he is almost considered a god : 'Isar Parmesara'. Of his works : *Harirasa*, *Bal-lila*, *Garud-puran*, *Sabha-parva* (of the *Mahabharat*), *Halajhalara Kundaliyan*, *Gun Agam* and *Ras-Kailas* ; *Harirasa* and *Halajhalara Kundaliyan* are more popular. While the *Harirasa* is devotional in character, *Halajhalara* treats of heroism. For his devotional and heroic traits in his poetry, Ishwar Das is quite popular in Rajasthan.

ISHWAR DATT. Modern Hindi writer of Mauritius, whose chief work is *Nayi Kahaniyan*.

ISHWAR JAGA SINGH. Modern Hindi writer of Mauritius, who is noted for his short stories.

ISHWAR LAL. Modern Rajasthani poet of Jhalawar, whose stray verses are available.

ISHWAR LAL DESAI. Gujarati-speaking modern Hindi scholar, whose *Hindi aur Gujarati ki Rashtriya Kavita : Ek Tulnatmak Adhyayan* is a research work.

ISHWAR SINGH. Modern Rajasthani poet, whose hundreds of stray verses in Pingal are available.

ISHWAR SURI. Jain poet, whose chief work is *Lalitang-Charit* (1504).

ISHWARANAND SHARMA. Modern Rajasthani poet, who in his progressive poems, has chosen obejcts of Nature as symbols in expressing progressive ideology.

ISHWARI, M. Malayalam-speaking modern Hindi scholar, whose research work in English is on the Comparative Study of the General Vocabulary of Hindi and Malayalam.

ISHWARI MOHAN KUMARI. Modern Hindi writer of Mauritius, who is known for her short stories.

ISURI (1824-1909). Bundelkhandi folk-poet, who was born at the village Mendki near Mau Ranipur in Jhansi district. He is reputed for his musical poems, called *Phags*.

ITIHAS. See *Ramdan Lalas*.

J

JADA MEHDU (fl. between 1550-1650). Dingal poet, who in his *Sadul-Parmar ro Chhand* (112 verses) has described the heroic deeds of Sadul Parmar, the son of Rawat Maldev. He also composed stray verses including Dingal *Gits* on contemporary heroes and events.

JADAV PRASAD AGARWAL. Author of *Shabdarth Prakash: Adhunik Bhasha Vigyan ki Sabhi Manyataon ka Tarkapurna Khandan* (1974).

JAG BANDHU HARICHANDAN (r. 1740-70). Raja of Athgad in the Ganjam district of Orissa, whose *Padas* in Hindi (Brajboli) are available.

JAGBANDHU MAHAPATRA. Modern Oriya writer, who has tr. *Ramcharitmanas* into Oriya in collaboration with Trinath Mishra.

JAG DEVA SINGH. Author of *A Descriptive Grammar of Bangru* (1970).

JAGADDHAR JADU. Modern Hindi writer of Jammu-Kashmir, who has written *Ap-Biti*, an autobiography.

JAGADVINODA. See *Padmakar Bhatt*.

JAGAJJAY MALL (r. 1702-32). Ruler of the House of Kantipur (Kathmandu) in Nepal, whose Maithili lyrics had been quoted in two *Ragmalas*. He seems to have patronized Maithili language at his court but the *Abhinav Prabodhachandroday* written under him, which is an adaptation of the well-known Sanskrit drama, *Prabodhachandrodaya*, is mixed with Bengali.

JAGANNATH (b. *c.* 1663). Poet of the Krishna-cult (Chaitanya Sect), whose works are: *Guru Charitra* and *Man Battisi va Guru Mahima*.

JAGANNATH DAS (fl. 16th cent.). Bengali Vaishnav poet, who also composed *Padas* in Brajbuli. Some of his *Padas* are available in *Padakalpataru* (q.v.).

JAGANNATH DAS (fl. 16th cent.). Rajasthani saint-poet of Amer, who was initiated by Dadu around 1583. He compiled a selection entitled *Gun Ganj Nama*, which includes *Vanis* of many poets.

JAGANNATT DAS, ATI BADO (fl. 15th-16th cent.). Celebrated Oriya poet, whose *Bhagavat* had a tremendous influence on Oriya life and society. Apart from his poetical writings in Oriya and Bengali, he also composed poems in Hindi (Brajboli).

JAGANNATH DAS 'RATNAKAR' (1866-1932). Poet, who acted as Private Secretary to Raja Pratap Narayan Singh of Ayodhya and later to his widow Rani. Ratnakar was a scholarly man and well-versed in English, Sanskrit, Persian and Urdu in addition to Hindi. He was deeply influenced by Bharatendu's style and language and as such wrote poetry mostly in Brajbhasha. His chief works are : *Harishchandra*, *Gangalahari* (Wavelets of the Ganges), *Kala-Kashi*, *Uddhav Shataka* (1931 ; a dialogue of Uddhav and Gopis on the merits and demerits of *Sagun* and *Nirgun* types of devotion) and *Gangavataran* (1928 ; on the descent of the Ganges), but the last two works gained wide popularity. He tr. into Hindi verse under the title *Samalochanadarsh* Pope's *Essay on Criticism* and wrote *Bihari Ratnakar*, a commentary on *Bihari Satsai*. His language is Sanskritized and he has been scrupulous about the correct use of grammar.

JAGANNATH PRASAD 'BHANU' (1859-1941). Chhattisgarhi poet, whose *Shri Mateshwari Seva ka Gutka* is a collection of songs, addressed to the Devi (the goddess). His chief works in Hindi are : *Chhand Prabhakar* (1894) and *Kavya Prabhakar* (1905). He was honoured by the British Government as also by the Madhya Pradesh Hindi Sahitya Sammelan.

JAGANNATH PRASAD MILIND (1903-). Poet and dramatist, whose chief works are *Ballpath ke Git* (collection of national poems), *Pratap Pratigya* (drama ; 1928) *Samarpan* (1950 : social drama), *Gautam Nand* (1952 ; historical drama), *Tulsidas* (historical drama), *Ashok ki Amar Asha*, *Krantivir Chandrashekhar*, *Jay Swatantra Jantantra* and *Shahid ko Samarpan* (dramas). *Chintan-kan* and *Sanskritik Prashna* are collections of essays. He ed. 'Jivan', a weekly from Gwalior.

JAGANNATH PRASAD SHARMA (1905-). Critic, whose chief works are : *Hindi ki Gadya-Shaili ka Vikas* (thesis ; 1930), *Prasad ke Natakon ka Shastriya Adhyayan* (Classical Study of Prasad's Dramas ; 1952) and *Kahani ka Rachna Vidhan* (Construction of Short Story ; 1953).

JAGANNATH SHARAN (fl. early 20th cent.). Writer, who was noted for his dramas, *Prahlad-Charitamrit* (on Prahlad) and *Kurukshetra* (1928).

JAGANNATH SONI (fl. 18th cent). Rajasthani saint-poet of Ram Snehi Sampraday, Shahpura whose poems in popular Rajasthani are : *Jatharath Bodh* (on Nirgun ideology), *Phul Dol Samadhi* (on the festivity of Phul Dol Samadhi, celebrated every year at Shahpura), *Brahma Samadhi Lin Jog*, *Guru Lila Vilas* (both on the story of Ramcharan, his Guru), *Chaurasi Bol* (listing 84 teachings) and *Binata Lachin Bodh* (or *Binata Bodh*, depicting the characteristics and deeds of various type of women).

JAGANNATH TUPKARI 'BHRING'. Marathi-speaking modern Hindi dramatist, who is the author of *Mitti ki Mahak* and *Amitabh* ; *Pankhuriyan* is his short story collection.

JAGANNATHAN, V.R. Tamil-speaking Hindi scholar, whose *Sur aur Periyalvar ki Kritiyon ka Tulnatmak Adhyayan* (A Comparative Study of the Works of Sur and Periyalvar; thesis ; 1968) discusses the two saint-poets of the Krishna-cult. He is also noted for his essay : 'Hindi aur Tamil ki Saman-Srotiya Bhinnarthi Shabdavali' (on Hindi and Tamil vocabulary).

JAGAN SINGH SENGAR (1903-75). Poet of the Rajnagar village of Sikandararau Tehsil of Aligarh, whose chief works are : *Kisan Satsai* (on farmer), *Murli* (The Flute) and *Jhanki* (The Glimpse).

JAGAT CHANDRA (fl. 1675). Maithili poet, who was devoted to the ruling House of Bhatgao in Nepal. In his *Nana-Rag-Sangrah*, he describes at length how he lived in the court of Jagat Prakash Mall and his two sons : Jitamitra and Ugramall. His songs are collected in two books.

JAGAT PRAKASH MALL (r. 1644-72). The most voluminous writer of Maithili lyrics in Nepal, whose *Padas* are distinguished by directness and simplicity and unadorned beauty. He was a ruler of the dynasty of Bhatgao in Nepal. Among his complete works, the following may be mentioned : *Padya-Samuchchay*, *Git-Sangarh*, *Git-Panchak*, *Gitavali*, *Nanarang-Gitani*

Nanarth-Dev-Devi-Gitam, *Git-Panchakar*, *Prakirna-Patra* and *Daiavataras*. He has not been quoted in the eminent Maithil anthologies but in Nepalese anthologies, he finds invariably a prominent place. On the death of his Minister, a poet, as well as a brother of his dearly-loved queen Annapurna Lakshmi, he wrote an elegy (*Git-Panchakam*) in 8 sections each made of 56 songs. His songs are marked by sincerity of sentiment ; they are devotional on the ten incarnations of Vishnu, Shiv as also on his contemporary poets. Under his active patronage, several poets : Chandrashekhar (his brother-in-law), Vansh Mani Jha and Jagat Chandra seem to have written *Padas*.

The Nepal Durbar Library has eight dramas attributed to him : *Usha Haran* with *Bhanitas* of Jagat Chandra, *Naliya-Natakam* (1670 ; the longest drama, with *Bhanitas* of Chandra Shekhar), *Parijat-Haran*, *Prabhavati-Haran* with *Bhanitas* of Vanshmani, *Malaya-Gandhini* (*1663* ; with *Bhanitas* of Krishna Das), *Madan-Charit Madan-Natak* (1672), *Muldev-Shashidev-Akhyanam* and *Madhav-Malati*, the last two with *Bhanitas* of Jagat Chandra. There is a three-Act drama, *Ramayan-Natak* by Krishnadas, written in Jagat Prakash's name. Some of these dramas seem to have been revised later in the subsequent years under Jagat Prakash Mall's successors. They are invariably in prose as well as verse.

JAGAT RAY (fl. 1680). Poet of the Riti school, who was patronized perhaps by one Himmat Khan, for it was at his instance that he composed his *Chhand Ratnavali*, an important work in seven chapters.

JAGAT SINGH. Poet of the Riti school, who was son of Maharajkumar Digvijay Singh of the village Gonda in the north of the river Saryu. Among his three works : *Sahitya Sudhanidhi* (1805), *Rasa Mrigank* and *Chhand Granth*, the first one, written in 10 chapters, is the most important.

JAGAT VINOD. See *Padmakar Bhatt 'Padmakar'*.

JAGDAMBA PRASAD DIKSHIT. Novelist, whose chief works are : *Murdaghar* (The Morgue ; 1974) and *Kata Hua Asman* (The Mutilated Sky ; 1971 ; a description of the sexual life of the hero and heroine). His first novel deals with the problem of prostitution in the Jhuggis of Bombay.

JAGDAMBA PRASAD MISHRA 'Hitaishi' (1895-1956). Poet of Kanpur, whose chief work, *Vaikali* (The Evening ; 1941) is a poetical collection, containing some charming descriptions of Nature.

JAGDANAND (fl. 1643). Poet of the Krishna-cult, who was the author of *Braj-Parikrama* (on Braj pilgrimage) and *Upakhyan-Sahitya Dasham Skandh* (description of the contents of the tenth canto of the *Bhagavat*).

JAGDEVA KA PAVADA. Rajasthani ballad, which is connected with Devi worship. Jagdeva is a staunch devotee of the mother goddess (Devi) and on demand offers his head, chopping it of with his own hands. The goddes is very pleased and wants to plant back the head on Jagdeva's body. His wife, however, refuses to take back that head. She pleads that what has been given away to the goddess cannot be taken back. Then, by the grace of the goddess, another head comes out of the body of Jagdeva, who becomes alive again.

JAGDISH (fl. prior to 1685). Maithili poet, who was quoted in *Har-Gauri-Vivah* by Bhupatindra Mall. His lyrics exist in anthologies.

JAGDISH BHATT (b. 1723). Poet of the Riti school, who was in the court of Maharaja Pratap Singh. He was a younger brother of Dwarikanath Bhatt (q.v.). His works are : *Kavya Vinod*, *Kishor Sukh Sagar*, *Jagat Niranjan*, *Pada Pankaj*, etc.

JAGDISH CHANDRA. Modern writer of Panjab, whose chief novels are : *Dharti Dhan na Apna* (The Land does not Belong to Anybody), *Kabhi na Chhoren Khet* (Never Leave the Fields), *Mutthi Bhar Kankar* (A Handful of Pebbles), *Adha Pul* (Incomplete Bridge) and *Tunda Lat*. His short story collection is *Pahli Rapat*. He has dealt with the rural life of Panjab.

JAGDISH CHANDRA 'JIT'. Poet, whose *Badalte Bhav* : *Ubharte Swar* (Changing Emotions : Rising Notes ; 1980) is a collection of his poems.

JAGDISH CHANDRA MATHUR (1917-78). Dramatist, who was born in Khurja Tehsil of district Bulandshahr (U.P.). He was interested in dramatic performance from his boyhood and even when he had joined the Indian Civil Service, he continued his interest in drama and achieved fame as a dramatist. He was Director-General of All India Radio and later was Hindi Advisor to the Government of India. His chief works are : *Konark* (on the famous Sun-temple of Orissa ; 1951), *Shardiya* (1960 ; on Hindu-Muslim unity), *Pahla Raja* (1969 ; The First King ; a mythological drama, depicting the present-day India),

Dashrath-Nandan (Son of Dashrath ; mythological work, written in the context of modern India ; all dramas), *Bhor ka Tara* (The Morning Star), *O Mere Sapne* (O My Dreams ; both collections of one act plays), *Bolte Kshan* (Speaking Moments ; essays), *Das Tasviren* (Ten Sketches) and *Jinhon ne Jina Jana* (Those who Understood Life ; essays). He also wrote two puppet plays : *Kunvar Singh ki Tek* and *Gagan Savari* (Air Ride).

JAGDISH CHANDRA PANDEY. Writer, whose *Mahakaleshwar ki Ek Rat* (A Night of Mahakaleshwar ; 1982) and *Dharti aur Ninv* are novels ; his short story collections are : *Kaha Tha Suna Tha* and *Apna-Apna Dukh* (1983).

JAGDISH CHATURVEDI (1933-). Writer, whose chief works are : *Jivan ka Sangharsh* (The Struggle of Life), *Antaral ke do Chhor* (Two Ends of Space), *Andhere ka Admi*, *Pattharon ke Shahr Men Vivart*, *Nihang* (short story collections), *Itihas-Hanta* (The Slayer of History ; collection of poems), *Dubte Itihas ka Gavah* (The Witness of Declining History ; 1980), *Purva Rag* (a collection of adolescent poems ; 1991), *Nishedh* (Denials ; 1970 ; ed. of the representative poems of 11 modern poets) and *Cactus aur Gulab* (The Cactus and Rose ; 1982), a well-edited anthology. He is one of the leading exponents of the *Akavita* (Anti-poetry) in Hindi literature. He has published collections of modern Hindi poetry in English and has also written a drama : *Pili Dopahar*. His critical works are *Adhunik Hindi Kavita* and *Dastavez*.

JAGDISH GUPTA (1924-). Poet, whose collections of poems are : *Nanv ke Panv* (The Legs of a Boat ; 1955), *Shabda-dansh* (Sting of Word ; 1959), *Him Viddha* (Wounded by Snow; 1964), *Yugma* (Couple), *Shambuk* (mythological) and *Chhand-Shati* (in Brajbhasha). From the Chhayavad poetry, he turned to the 'Nai Kavita' (New Poetry). His other poetical works are : *Adim Ekant*, *Kavitantar* and *Gopa Gautam*. Termed as a poet of Nature, he has also written critical works, *Nai Kavita : Swarup aur Samasyaen* (New Poetry : Form and Problems) and *Swachchhandvadi Kavya-Dhara ka Darshnik Vivechan* (Philosophical Treatment of Romantic Poetry). Along with Agyey, he has edited a poetical anthology *Navadha* (1983). He is also a painter and has done good work on 'Pragaitihasik Kala'. He is at present Professor of Hindi at the Allahabad University.

JAGDISH JHA. Maithili writer, whose *Sat Samudra Par* (1966) is a travelogue.

JAGDISH MATHUR. Modern Rajasthani writer, whose *Pitaran*

ro Agaman, a collection of one-act plays, treats of social reforms.

JAGDISH NARAYAN CHAUBE. Modern Magahi poet, whose poems are noted for their imaginative flight, rhythm and spontaneity.

JAGDISH NARAYAN DIPAK (1928-). Maithili poet, who is noted for the collection of his poems, *Arti* (1959).

JAGDISH PRASAD CHATURVEDI. Modern journalist, who is noted for his articles on Fiji, Mauritius and Burma.

JAGDISH PRASAD DWIVEDI (1929-). Bagheli folk-poet, who was born at the village Dhawa in Rewa. His poems are noted for their humour and satire.

JAGDISH SHRIVASTAV. Poet, who is noted for his *Tarikhen* (Days of the Month ; 1978), a poetical collection.

JAGDISH SINGH GAHLOT (1895-1958). Rajasthani scholar, who was born in Jodhpur. His chief works are : *Marwar ke Gramgit* (1919) and *Rajasthani Vatalarth*.

JAGDISH TOMAR. Poet, whose *Kanch ki Divar* (The Glass Wall ; 1980) is a collection of poems.

JAGDISH VAJPEYI. Modern scholar, whose chief work is *Adhunik Brajbhasha Kavya*.

JAGDISHWAR PRASAD YADAV. Modern Magahi writer, whose dramas and one-act plays are quite popular on radio.

JAGGA. See *Khidiya Jagga*.

JAGJIVAN (fl. 1593). Rajasthani saint-poet, who was formerly a Vaishnav but was initiated as a disciple of Dadu (q.v.). His *Vani*, a bulky volume, betrays the influence of Vishnuism. A Brahmin by birth, he was counted among the principal disciples of Dadu.

JAGJIVAN DAS (fl. 16th cent.). Rajasthani saint-poet, who was a disciple of Haridas (q.v.) and a follower of Haridas Niranjani Sampraday. His poems *Chitavani*, *Prem Nam* and a few *Padas* celebrate Niranjan worship.

JAGJIVAN DAS (1670-1761). Saint-poet of Barabanki, whose principal poetic work is *Adhnivas*, which is a collection of religious verses. His other works are : *Gyan-Prakash* (The Light of Knowledge), *Mahapralay* (Deluge) and *Pratham-Granth* (The First Book). He was responsible for re-organizing the Satnami Sect.

JAGJYOTTIRMALL (fl. 1618-33). Maithili poet of Nepal, whose lyrics are found in several anthologies. Besides his many texts on music in Sanskrit, one of his collections of Maithili lyrics is called *Nadotpatti-Mridangetyadibhasha*, which seems to describe the technical matters concerning music. His best work, *Dashavtar-Gitam* is an excellent collection of devotional songs on all the ten incarnations of Vishnu. His songs by and large are devotional.

A great patron of learning and music, he got several important Sanskrit works on music and drama written. His own Maithili dramas are : *Midit-Kuvalayashwar* (1626 ; frequently quoted by scholars for its containing valuable information regarding the Mall dynasty), *Har-Gauri-Vivah* (in 9 Acts ; on the marriage of Shiv and Parvati, but the main emphasis is on acting, dancing and singing) and *Kunj-Vihari-Natak* (on the story of Krishna, Radha and the Gopis).

Jagjyottirmall was a ruler of Bhaktapur and a tributary of Nepal. He invited Vanshmani Jha, a scholar of Mithila to his court to frame laws on houses, lands, castes and dead bodies.

JAG LAL RAMA, the late. Modern Hindi poet of Mauritius, whose *Hriday ki Nidhi* is a collection of his poems.

JAG MOHAN KUMARI, Mrs. Modern Hindi writer of Mauritius, who is noted for her short stories.

JAG MOHAN MISHRA (1928-). Scholar, whose chief works are a collection of new essays and a critical study of Jay Shankar Prasad's *Titli*. He has also written some poetry.

JAG MOHAN SINGH, THAKUR (1857-99). Poet and writer, whose home was in Bundelkhand in the region of Vindhyas but he came in contact with Bharatendu Harishchandra (q.v.) at Varanasi. He was a Sanskrit scholar as also a keen observer of the beauties of nature and the qualities of his prose and verse may be traced chiefly to these two sources. In his prose works, *Shyam Swapna* (a social novel) became most popular, while his poetical works include *Prem-Ratnakar* (*The Ocean of Love*), *Devbani*, *Shyam-Sarojini*, *Manas-Sampatti*, *Ritu-Prakash* and *Shyam-Lata*. His *Shyama Swapna* presents glimpses of rural life and the beauties of the Vindhyas, where the descriptions are vivid.

JAGNIK (fl. 1173). Bard of the court of Parmal (Parmardidev), the Chandela king of Mahoba (Kalinjar) ; he composed a work which is no longer extant. Different versions of songs based on this work are popular in several parts of North India which have been collected under the title of *Alhakhand* (q.v.) by Charles Elliot and George Grierson ; the songs describe the heroic exploits of Parmal's two chieftains—Alha and Udal (Uday Singh).

JAGTANAND DAS (fl. 16th cent.). Poet of the Krishna-cult (Vallabh Sect), who hailed from Thaneshwar (Haryana) and was a disciple of Vallabhacharya. He described the Krishnalilas as mentioned in the *Bhagavat* in about 100 *Kundaliyas*.

JAGTAP, MU. MA. Marathi-speaking modern Hindi writer, whose *Pagdandi* is a short story collection.

JAHANGIR-JAS CHANDRIKA. See *Keshavdas*.

JAHARPIR. A long folk-tale on Jaharpir or Guru Gugga (Goga), who was son of Raja Devray of Bagar and is considered a snake-god. Raja Devray and his Rani Bachhal have no son but as they are blessed by the saint Gorakhnath, Jaharpir is born. Even before his birth, Jaharpir had shown miracles to his parents and maternal grandfather. With the assistance of Nagas and Gorakhnath, Jaharpir marries princess Siriyal. His cousins (sons of the sister of Jaharpir's mother) : Arjan and Sarjan want half of Jaharpir's kingdom, but as he turns down their demand, they with the assistance of a Muslim king, attack Jaharpir. In the battle that ensues, Jaharpir is victorious and he beheads his cousins. Hearing this, Jaharpir's mother refuses to see his face ; at this he slips under earth. The folk-tale is popular in Haryana, Rajasthan and several parts of Uttar Pradesh.

JAHAYRIN, BORIS ALEXZEVICH (1942-). Soviet Hindi scholar, who studied Hindi, Urdu and Sanskrit at the Lucknow University. Apart from his articles on Hindi language, he has written *Hindi Bhasha ke Itihas ka Parichay* (Moscow, 1978).

JAHAZ KA PANCHHI (The Bird of the Ship). Novel (1956) by Ilachandra Joshi (q.v.).

This is the story of an honest and educated young man,

who though poor and unemployed, does not compromise with falsehood and injustice. Struggling with life, he reaches Calcutta and passes through all the hardships of life usual in a metropolitan city. He meets calamity after calamity and like the bird of the ship, he comes back again and again to his plight of suffering and unemployment. At last he meets a rich lady, who falls in love with him but his socialistic idealism does not allow him to adjust with the cultural traditions of an upper class woman. He runs away to Ranchi, where he again meets the woman, who is now ready to renounce everything for him. The hero can now adjust with her and starts his life with her. The author seems to suggest that love between two persons of unequal economic status and different class traditions cannot be stable.

JAI. See *Jay*.

JAINENDRA KUMAR (1905-). Fiction writer, who was born at Kadiaganj in the Aligarh district of Uttar Pradesh but his father died when he was two years old. He joined the national freedom movements and was jailed. His chief works are as under :—

Novel : *Parakh* (The Test ; 1930), *Tapobhumi* (The Penance Grove ; 1936), *Sunita* (q.v.), *Tyagpatra* (The Resignation ; q.v.), *Kalyani*, *Vivart* (Illusion), *Sukhda* (1952), *Vyatit* (The Past), *Jay Vardhan* (1956 ; written in the diary style), *Anantar* (After), *Muktibodh* (The Knowledge of Release ; it received Sahitya Akademi Award) and *Anam Swami* (The Nameless Swami) ; *Sunita* and *Tyagpatra* are considered his best works. Jainendra has introduced a new trend and has given a new technique to Hindi fiction by portraying man and woman's inner thoughts, feelings and complexes and conflicts.

Short Stories : Phansi (The Gallows ; 1929), *Vatayan* (The Window ; 1930), *Nilamdesh ki Rajkanya* (The Princess of the Country of Sapphires), *Ek Rat* (One Night ; 1934), *Do Chidiyan* (Two Sparrows), *Sparddha* (Envy), *Dhruv-yatra* (Journey to the Poles), *Pajeb* (Anklets), *Ek Din* (A Day), *Jay Sandhi* (Victory Alliance) and *Jainendra ki Kahaniyan* (Short Stories of Jainendra ; 10 Pts.) ; his stories, applying the same technique as in his novels, are largely psychological marked by conflict of ideas and a non-conformist approach to social problems. Jainendra's important short stories are : 'Patni' (The Wife), 'Jahnavi', 'Samapti' (The End), 'Khel' (The Play), 'Chor' (The Thief), 'Apna Apna, Bhagya' (One's Own Fate), 'The Gramophone Record', 'Master Sahib', 'Ek Rat' (A Night), 'Pajeb', 'Tatsat' (He Alone is Truth), 'Nilam Desh ki Rajkanya', 'Vigyan-Avigyan' (Science and Non-Science), etc.

Essays : *Jainendra ke Vichar* (The Ideas of Jainendra ; 1937 ; ed. by Prabhakar Machwe), *Jad ki Bat* (The Basic Idea ; 1945), *Purvoday* (The Rise of the East ; 1951), *Sahitya ka Shrey aur Prey*, *Manthan* (Deep Thoughts), *Soch-Vichar* (Reflections), *Kam* (Sexual Love), *Prem aur Parivar* (Love and Family), *Main aur Ve* (I and They) and *Itastatah* ; his essays reflect the thought-current that is prevalent in his novels and short stories.

His other works are *Sahitya Chayan* (1951), *Vichar-Vallari* (both ed. essay collections), *Magdalini* and *Pap aur Prakash* (The Sin and Light ; tr. dramas).

JAISWAL, M.P. Author of *Linguistic Study of Bundeli* (Leiden, 1962).

JAITSI RASO. Dingal poem, which was composed by an anonymous poet between 1534 and 1541. It describes the defeat of Kamran, a son of Babar at the hands of Jaitsi of Bikaner in 1534. See *Vithu Sujo, Rao Jaitsi ro Paghadi Chhand*.

JAJJAL. See *Hammir Raso*.

JAKHU MANIYAR. See *Jankho Maniyar*.

JALAL BUBNAR. Rajasthani romance of Jalal-Bubna, of which about 110 *Dohas* were probably composed during the latter half of the 16th and the early 17th century.

Gahni, the sister of king Mrigatamayachi of Thatta Bhakhar, is married to Kulanhasib, the king of Balakh, with his capital at Gazanipur. Due to the revolt of the Jagirdars, Kulanhasib is killed and Gahni, with her two sons, comes to her brother Mrigatamayachi. Bhanvar, the king of Sindh Samudra, has two daughters, Mumna and Bubna and he wants to give Mumna in marriage to Mrigatamayachi and Bubna to Jalal, one of the two sons of Gahni. But Mrigatamayachi himself wants to marry Bubna, the betrothed of Jalal and has his wish fulfilled by bribing the Kazi. Jalal is thus married to Mumna. But the love of Jalal and Bubna continues and becomes more profound thereafter. Though they often meet secretly, the two cannot come together and die of grief.

In the oral tradition, the tale thus sung is tragic but in the written form, Jalal and Bubna are restored back to life from their graves by Shiv and Parvati ; this conferring new life on Muslim lovers indicates the mutual respect of both the communities in those times.

JALAL GAHNI RI BAT. Dingala poem (Script 1696) by an unknown poet, which describes the romance between Jalal and Gahni ; see *Jalal Bubnar* for a different version of the story.

JALANDHARNATH (Jalandharipa or Hadipa). Nath Siddha, who is said to be the originator of Pav Panth, the seat of which was at Jalore in Rajasthan. This Panth was related at some time to the Vajrayan branch of the Buddhism. It appears to be the impact of Jalandharnath and his Panth that in some Rajasthani poems a faint semblance of the Buddhist traditions, such as the existence and actions of Varahi Devi, are found. The *Ramayan* of Mehoji and *Ram Raso* of Surjan are examples.

JALHA. Rajasthani poet and author of *Buddhi Raso* (q.v.), about whom not much is known. From his style, it appears that he was a Jain poet. The available manuscript of *Buddhi Raso* is dated 1647 and appears to be a copy of some manuscript written earlier. Jalha or Jalhan was also the name of the son of the poet Chand Vardai (the celebrated author of *Prithwiraj Raso*) and this has led some scholars to believe that the author of *Buddhi Raso* and Chand Vardai's son were identical. The *Buddhi Raso* is a romance.

JAILOVA, SHIRIN IRGASHEVNA (1943-). Soviet Hindi scholar, who is a Lecturer in Hindi in the Tashkent State University. She has written several articles on philology.

JAMAL (fl. 1570). Muslim poet of the Krishna-cult, whose *Dohas* in Brajbhasha on Krishna and kindred religious and literary topics are common in Rajasthan, to which state he belonged. He also wrote *Jamal Pachisi*.

JAMBHOJI (1451-1536). Founder of the Vishnoi Sampraday in 1485, whose *Vani*, known as *Sabad Vani* consists of 123 *Sabads*. The language of the *Vani* is unsophisticated Rajasthani, prevalent among the rural people. A Panvar Rajput, born at Pipasar (Nagore), he was son of Lohat and Hansa (Kesar). A celibate, he left his home at the age of 34 and founded his seat at Sambharathal, a high sandy hill near the present village Mukam (Nokha, Bikaner). His was the first Sant Sampraday of the northern India. He admitted both the Hindus and Musalmans to his sect and Sikandar Lodi, the great ruler was enlightened by his preachings. He revived the old Yagya tradition, believed in the incarnations but deprecated idolatry, had compassion for all living beings and asked to observe fast on *Amavasya* (Dark Moon). He was more inclined towards the *Gita* as according to him one should work hard with honesty and sincerity, without desiring the fruit of it. According to him, the object of the human life is to realize the self and to attain *Jivan-Mukti*. He believed in rebirth and *Karma* and warned against ostentation and hypocrisy. He was the propagator of *Sagunonmukh-Nirgun Bhakti*.

JAMBUNATHAN, M.B. Kannada-speaking Hindi writer, whose dramas : *Sati Sharmishtha* and *Danvir Suman* were quite popular in the 'thirties of this century. He got the dramas : *Vir Abhimanyu* and *Bahadur Sundari* of Radheshyam Kathavachak abridged and got them staged. He also wrote *Hindi-Kannada Kosh*, *Urdu Hindi Kosh*, *Hindi Muhavara Kosh* (Dictionary of Hindi Idioms), *Saral Hindi Vyakaran*, etc.

JAMBUSWAMI-CHARIYA. Rajasthani poem (41 verses), composed by Dharma, a Jain poet in 1209.

Jambuswami, on whom many poems have been written, is the son of a wealthy person, Rishabhdatt of Rajgrih, the then capital of Magadh. On the first night of his marriage, he imparts precepts to his eight wives, but his discourse is also heard by a thief, named Prabhav, who, along with his 500 followers, has come to commit a theft in his house. The next morning, Jambuswami, his parents, his eight wives, his 16 in-laws and the 500 thieves take initiation as ascetics from Sudharma, a pupil of Lord Mahavir.

JAMILA ALI JAFRI Modern scholar, whose chief works are *Shodh Sandarbh* : *Naye Ayam* and *Hindi Kavita* : *Islami Sanskriti ke Pariprekshya Men*.

JAMNA PRASAD PACHORIYA. Modern Rajasthani writer, who is noted for his drama, *Nayi Bimani*.

JAMNA PRASAD THADA 'RAHI'. Modern Rajasthani poet, who has composed Nature poems.

JAMUNA, K.A. Tamil-speaking Hindi scholar, whose chief work is *Nalaiyar Divya-Prabandham aur Sursagar men Krishna-katha ka Swarup* (on the story of Krishna in these works ; 1978) ; the research work establishes that the *Bhagavata-Purana* is the source of the Bhakti movement in India. She has written about 50 critical essays, some of them treating of Tamil literature and culture. She has tr. and published in various magazines the poems of many Tamil poets—old and new. She has tr. Akhilan's celebrated novel under the title of *Chitrapriya*. She has tr. into Hindi 20 Tamil short stories under the title : *Katha Bharati* : *Tamil Kahaniyan*, Jaykantan's Tamil short stories under the title of *Yug Sandhi* and Tamil dramas, *e.g.*,

Pammal Sambandh Mudaliyar's as *Apratyashit Ant* (The Unexpected End), Indira Parthasarthi's as *Bhukh* (Hunger) and Jayantan's as *Bhukmari* (The Starvation) and *Zimmedar Kaun ?* (Who is Responsible ?). She has also tr. into Hindi the essays of Kalki, Annadurai, T.P. Meenakshisundaram, etc.

JAN. See *Naimat Khan Jan.*

JAN BEGUM (fl. 18th cent.). Poetess, who was a disciple of Charan Das (q.v.). Her only one work, *Sudama-Charitra* is available.

JAN DAYAL (fl. early 19th cent.). Poet of the Krishna-cult (Chaitanya Sect), who was the author of *Prem Lila.*

JAN DHYAL SHIVANN SHASTRI, THE LATE. Telugu-speaking modern Hindi writer, whose chief works are : *Hindi Vyakaran* and *Hindi-Telugu Kosh* (in collaboration with the late Oruganti Venkateshwar Sharma).

JAN GOPAL RAHORI (fl. early 17th cent.). Rajasthani saint-poet, who was a Vaishya of Fatehpur Sikri. A disciple of Dadu (q.v.), his works : *Dadu Janma Lila Parchi* (on the life of Dadu), *Dhruva Charitra*, *Prahlad Charitra*, *Moh Vivek Sanvad*, *Jad Bharat Charitra*, *Kavya Pran Sanvad*, *Shuk Sanvad*, *Anant Lila*, *Barah Masa*, *Bhent ke Savaiye*, *Padas* and *Sakhis* reveal the influence of Sagun type of Bhakti. The language is mainly Rajasthani.

JAN JASVANT (fl. 16th cent.). Saint-poet of Maharashtra, who composed some *Padas* in Hindi as well. His language is influenced by Marathi.

JAN KAUNRA (fl. 18th cent. ?). Rajasthani saint poet of Laldasi Sampraday, whose *Bhajans* extol devotion towards God and Guru and advocate simplicity of life.

JAN KAVI USTAD. See *Ganeshilal Vyas 'Ustad'.*

JAN RAJ (fl. c. 1776). Poet of the Riti school, who was a Vaishya Agrawal and had settled in Jaipur. His original name was Dhedhraj, but his Guru, pleased with his poetry, called him 'Janraj', by which name he is known. At the instance of his Guru, he composed his exhaustive work, *Kavita Rasa Vinod* in 1776.

JANAK RAJ KISHORISHARAN 'RASIK ALI' (fl. 1740). Muslim poet of the Ram-cult, who was a *Vairagi* of Ayodhya. He composed many a work on devotion, knowledge and on the story of Ram ; some works are in Sanskrit also. So far 24 of his works have come to light. His chief works : *Ashtayam, Sitaram, Siddhant Muktavali, Sitaram Siddhant, Mithila Vihar* and *Ananya-Tarangini* are all connected with the devotion to Ram and Sita. His *Mithila Vihar* treats of Ram's reaching Janakpur. It combines in the description of beauty, the *Riti* skills of poets, who wrote about Radha and Krishna, with intense devotion for Ram.

Janaki Charan (fl. 1820). Poet of the Ram cult, who was a native of Ayodhya ; he was the author of *Prem-Pradhan* and *Siyaram Rasa Manjari*, connected with devotion to Ram and Sita (Siya).

JANAKI MANGAL. Poem by Tulsidas (q.v.) in Avadhi, written in 1586 (?).

The work in 216 verses, describes the marriage of Ram and Sita in accordance with Valmiki's *Ramayana* ; the harangue with Parashuram and the marriages of Ram's other three brothers have also been dealt with.

Janaki Nath Bhan (1924-). Kashmiri-speaking Hindi writer, whose articles have appeared in several literary and other magazines. Besides writing articles on Kashmiri language and literature, he tr. into Hindi and English the *Vakhs* of the Kashmiri poetess Lalleshwari. He has written research articles, short stories, dramas, etc. and has edited the Special Editions on Lalleshwari and Master Zinda Kaul. He has also published a Hindi rendering of Zinda Kaul's poetical collection : *Sumiran*. He has edited a *Hindi-Kashmiri-English Dictionary*.

Janaki Nath Kaul 'Kamal' (1914-). Hindi poet of Kashmir, whose poetry has a spiritual tinge. His poems and religious articles have appeared in 'Koshur Samachar' and other papers ; *Vikshipta Vina* is a collection of his poems. He has also edited the discourses and sermons of his Shivaite preceptor, Lakshman Ju and has published a commentary in Hindi on the Gayatri Mantra.

Janaki Rasik Sharan (fl 1703). Poet of the Ram-cult, who resided at Ayodha. He was the author of the *Avadhi-Sagar* (The Ocean of Avadhi).

Janaki Vallabh Shastri (1916-). Poet, whose chief poetical collections are : *Rup aur Arup* (Beauty and Ugliness ; 1940),

Tir Tarang (Strand Fancies ; 1944 ; collection of 96 songs), *Shipra* (1945 ; it contains also some historical poems), *Megh Git* (Cloud Songs ; 1950 ; description of clouds in various mental states), *Avantika* (1953 ; songs and poems), *Pashani* and *Tamasa*. His *Radha* (1981) is a re-publication of a part of his epic of the same title written about 40 years ago. It contains philosophical ruminations marking a struggle in Krishna's mind as to the choice between love and duty ; in the end he takes the path of duty but only after he has judged the claims of the two in details. Noted for his sweet lyrics, his prose works are *Nirala ke Patra* (Letters of Nirala ; ed) and *Natya Samrat* (criticism).

JANARDAN BHATT (fl. 1678). Poet of the Riti school, whose chief works are : *Durgsingh Shringar* (1678), *Vyavahar Nirnay* (1680) and *Lakshmi Narayan Puja Sar* ; the last work was composed at the instance of Anup Singh, the Maharaja of Bikaner.

JANARDAN JHA 'JANSIDAN' (1872-1958). Maithili novelist and poet, who was born at Kumar Bajipur in Muzaffarpur district of Bihar. His chief works, *Nirdayi Sasu* and *Punarvivah* are social novels ; his *Janaki-Parinay* is a *Khand-Kavya*. *Nitini-bandh* is a collection of his didactic poems.

JANARDAN KALICHARAN. Modern Hindi poet of Mauritius, whose *Prabhat Rashmi* is a collection of his poems. He is also noted for his short stories. See *Pravasi Swar*.

JANARDAN PRASAD JHA 'DWIJ' (1904-64). Poet, whose chief work, *Anubhuti* (Perception) is a poetical collection. He also wrote *Premchand ki Upanyas Kala* (The Art of Premchand the Novelist).

JANARDAN PRATIHAST. Modern Maithili poet, whose *Sita* is an epic.

JANARDAN RAO CHELER. Telugu-speaking modern Hindi scholar, whose publications are *Vrind aur Unka Sahitya* (Vrind and his Literature) and editing of *Vrind Granthavali* (1971).

JANARDAN RAY NAGAR (1908-). Writer of Udaipur, whose chief works are : *Dhruvtara*, *Tiranga Jhanda* (novels), *Adhirat*, *Patit ka Swarga*, *Jivan ka Satya*, *Vish ka Pyala* (dramas) and short stories : *Janardan Ray Nagar ki Kahaniyan* (2 Pts.).

JANARDANAN PILLAI, R. Malayalam-speaking modern Hindi writer, whose chief work is *Pandit Jawaharlal Nehru*.

JANGID, A C., 'SHEKHAWATI'. Rajasthani writer, who is a school teacher. His *Shekhawati ki Anchalik Kahaniyan* (1982) is the first collection of his short stories.

JANKHO MANIYAR. Poet, whose poem *Harichand Puran* (*Pavado*) composed in 1396, is a narrative one, based on the mythological story of Maharaja Harishchandra ; the language of the work is old Hindi, with slight mixtures of Apabhransh and old Rajasthani.

JANMEJAY KA NAG YAGYA. (The Serpent Sacrifice of Janmejay). Drama (1926) by Jayshankar Prasad (q.v.), which is based on a mythological story. The theme is the terrible revenge of Janmejay on the Nags after they had killed his father, Parikshit, the grandson of Arjun.

JASNATHJI (1482-1506). Rajasthani saint-poet and founder of the Jasnathi Sect some time about 1500 at Katariyasar (Bikaner), now its main seat. Like Jambhoji (q.v.), the founder of the Vishnoi Sect, he believes in the daily performance of *Havan* as also in the incarnations. He has followed the Vaishnav ideology and Yoga, rather than the Nath tradition. Jasnathji's *Vani*, in popular Rajasthani, consists of 50 *Sabads*, including *Simbhudhada* and *Kod* and a minor poem, *Gorakh-chhand*. Jasnath's *Agni Nritya* of the Fire Dance is well-known.

JASRAJ. See *Jinharsh*.

JASVANT-JASOBHUSHAN. See *Muraridan*.

JASVANT SINGH, RAJA (1626-78). Poet of the Riti school, who was a ruler of Jodhpur State and had ascended the throne in 1638 after the death of his father, Maharaja Gaj Singh. He had a successful career as a diplomat and warrior and made his mark on the political events of his times. He was a favourite with Shahjahan and supported the Moghuls in many a battle, but when there was a war of succession amongst Sahajahan's sons, he supported Dara. This displeased Aurangzeb and he was despatched to Kabul as Governor, where he died fighting against the Afghans. A poet, a philosopher, and a great patron of letters, he encouraged learning so well that it was said that he drove ignorance out of his kingdom. He was the author of four works : *Aparoksh Siddhant* (The Indirect Principles), *Siddhant Bodh* (The Knowledge of Principles), *Anubhav Prakash* (The Light of Perception), *Siddhant Sar* (The Essence of Principles), *Prabodh chandroday* (on philosophical themes), *Anand Vilas* (Enjoyment of Bliss) and *Bhasha Bhushan* (q.v.) on *Alankars*. The poet's fame chiefly rests on the last work. His *Prabodh-chandroday*, though retains the format of the Sanskrit play, yet really falls in the category of religious treatises in the form of dialogues. He is one of the great scholarly poets and teachers of rhetoric. His skill in versification is creditable, though his works lack poetic elements.

JASVANT SINGH II (fl. *c*. 1799). Poet of the Riti school, who was a Kshatriya Raja of Tervan near Kannauj. He was the author of two works : *Shalihotra* and *Shringar-Shiromani* ; the latter is a great work on *Shringar Rasa*.

JASVANT SINGH BARAIYA. Gujarati-speaking modern Hindi scholar, whose *Sathottari Hindi Gujarati Kavita : Ek Tulnatmak Adhyayan* is a research work.

JATMAL (b. 1624). Jain Sufi poet of Lahore (now in Pakistan), whose two works : *Gora Badal ki Bat* (q.v.) and *Premlata Chaupai* have so far been discovered. The literary merit of Jatmal's poetry is considered to be of just average quality.

JAVAHARLAL, PANDIT (fl. 19th cent.). Sindhi saint-poet of *Sagun* school, whose stray verses in Hindi are available.

JAVAN SINGH (1800-38). Brajbhasha poet, who was son of Maharana Bhimsingh of Mewar. He composed his verses under the pseudonym of Brajraj and his stray verses are collected in *Brajraj Padyavali*.

JAWAHARLAL HANDU (1941-). Kashmiri-speaking Hindi writer, who has published a comparative study of the folksongs of Kashmiri and Khari Boli. He has also published *Kashmiri Lok-Git* (The Folk-songs of Kashmir) and *Lok Sahitya : Swarup evam Sarvekshan*.

JAWAHARLAL RAINA. Kashmiri-speaking modern Hindi writer, who has written Foreword to two Hindi poetical anthologies : *Chaurahe par Bate Chehre* (The Faces Divided on the Cross-road) and *Prismon men Bati Kiranen* (The Rays Divided into Prisms).

JAY BHAGVAN GOYAL. Modern scholar, whose chief works are : *Gurumukhi Lipi men Hindi Sahitya, Guru Pratap Suraj ke Kavya Paksha Ka Adhyayan, Guru Tegh Bahadur : Chintan aur Kala, Madhyayugin Kavya : Naya Mulyankan* and *Ritikal ka Puanrmulyankan*.

JAY BHARAT. Epic (1952) by Maithilisharan Gupta (q.v.),

which re-tells the entire *Mahabharat* story in 47 parts.

JAY CHAND JATI (fl 1st half of the 18th cent.). Jain Rajasthani poet, whose *Mataji ri Vachnika*, composed in 1719, narrates the Durga legend after *Durga Saptashati* with a tinge of local colour. A heroic poem, the poet has reflected upon the prevalent political conditions by designating the army of Shumbh-Nishumbh as that of 'Mlechhas'. The poet has used seven 'Vachnikas' and a variety of metres.

JAY CHAND PRAKASH. See *Kedar*.

JAY CHANDRA (fl. 1403). Jain poet, who was patronized by Tomar Raja Viramdev of Gwalior ; he was the author of *Hammir Mahakavya*, on the heroism of Raja Hammir. See *Hammir Hath*.

JAY CHANDRA RAY (1925-). Critic, whose chief work is : *Acharya Ramchandra Shukla : Siddhant aur Sahitya* (Acharya Ramchandra Shukla : Principles and Literature).

JAY CHANDRA SHARMA. Rajasthani writer, whose *Payal Hansai* (1982) is a collection of one-act plays.

JAY DATT JIUT. Modern Hindi writer of Mauritius, who is noted for his short stories.

JAY DATT JOSHI. Kumaoni writer, whose *Shishubodh* (1914) teaches English grammar through Kumaoni.

JAY DEV (fl. 12th cent.). Saint-poet, whose two *Padas* in Hindi are preserved in the *Granth Sahib* (q.v.). Whether this Jaydev was the same as the author of *Gita Govinda* has not been conclusively proved.

JAY DEV (fl. 18th cent.). Poet of the Krishna-cult (Haridasi Sect), whose two *Padas* under the name of 'Jal-pyauni' are extant.

JAY DEV KULSHRESHTH. Modern scholar, who is known for his *Sufi Mahakavi Jayasi*.

JAY DEV MISHRA. Modern Maithili writer, who has written critical articles.

JAY DEV SWAMI. Maithili saint-poet, who is noted for his *Chaumasa*, wherein the Gopis long for the arrival of Krishna during the rainy season. Nothing is known about his date and life.

JAY DHARI SINGH 'PRABHAKAR'. Modern Maithili critic, whose *Kavya-Mimansa* (2 vols.) presents a synthesis of Eastern and Western principles of literary criticism. He is also noted for his lyrics.

JAYDRATH VADH. See *Maithilisharan Gupta*.

JAY GOPAL KAVIRAJ (1892-1956). Writer, who was known for his drama : *Pashchimi Prabhav* (The Western Influence ; 1930). He was born in Lahore and formerly wrote in Urdu but he was drawn towards Hindi under the influence of Arya Samaj. He also wrote *Dayanand Charitam* and *Satyarth Prakash Kavitamrit*.

JAY GOVIND MISHRA. Modern Maithili scholar, who has made a study of Maithili folk-literature.

JAY KANT MISHRA. Maithili scholar, whose chief work is *History of Maithili Literature* (Sahitya Akademi, 1976).

JAY KRISHNA (fl. prior to 1685). Maithili poet, whose lyrics were quoted in anthologies.

JAY KRISHNADAS. (fl. 19th cent.). Sindhi saint-poet of *Sagun* school whose stray verses in Hindi are available.

JAY KRISHNA VIDYALANKAR. Modern scholar, who has written a number of articles on Hindi language. The subject of his Ph.D. thesis was *Hindi ki Vyakaranik Kotiyon ka Alochanatmak Adhyayan* (1964).

JAYLAL. Poet of the Riti school, who was grandson of the poet, Khus Ram (q.v.). He composed in 1888 his *Ishq Prakashika*, a commentary on *Jalvaye Shahanshah Ishq*.

JAYMALDAS (d. 1753). Rajasthani saint-poet, who was a carpenter of village Sanwatsar (near Sudsar, Bikaner). Initiated by Vaishnav Mahant Charandas (q v.) of Kodamdesar between 1683 and 1688, he stayed at Dulchasar and thence went to Roda (near Nokha, Bikaner) ; his *Gaddis* continued at both the places. In his 47 *Padas*, now available, the emphasis is on *Yoga-Sadhana*.

JAYMALLJI (1708-1796). Jain Rajasthani poet, who was an Acharya of the Sthanakvasi Sect. He composed a number of works, the aim of which was to impart knowledge of the Jain religion and philosophy and to consolidate the faith and to inspire virtues.

'JAYMANGAL'. Modern Maithili poet, who has composed *Maheshvanis* (songs in praise of Mahesh or Shiv).

JAYMANT MISHRA. Modern Maithili poet, who is noted for his lyrics.

JAY NARAYAN KAUSHIK. Modern author of *Hindi-Hariyanvi Uchcharan Bhed* and *Hariyanvi Pratyay*.

JAY NARAYAN MANDAL (1925-1978). Writer, whose chief works are : *Ghunghruon men Qaid* (Imprisoned in Anklets ; 1969 ; a short story collection, designed to present a healthy realism) and *Hindi Sahitya ki Ruparekha* (The Outlines of Hindi Literature).

JAY NARAYAN RAY. Hindi writer of Mauritius, who published a drama *Jivan Sangini* (1941), which was quite a new venture in Mauritius in those days. He is also the author of *Mauritius men Hindi Bhasha ka Sankshipta Itihas.* He edited 'Janta', a weekly paper for several years and wrote articles for English papers.

JAY NATH 'NALIN' (1912-). Writer, whose chief works are : *Hindi Natak-kar* (Hindi Dramatists ; research), *Hindi Nibandh-kar* (Hindi Essayists) and *Kavya Kosh* (Dictionary of Poetry). He has also composed some humorous one-act plays ; *Hathi ke Dant* (Tusks of an Elephant) and *Rang Badrang Hasya Natikayen* are such collections. *Dharti ke Bol* (Tunes of the Soil) is his poetical collection, while *Javani ka Nasha* (Pride of Youth) is a work full of humour.

JAY PRAKASH BHARATI. Novelist, whose chief novel (regional) is *Kohre men Khoye Chandi ke Pahar* (Mountains of Silver lost in Fog ; description of a tribe of Jaunsar Khai, which claims to be the descendants of the Pandavs) ; *Dip se Dip Jale* (Lamp lights Lamp) is a work meant for children. His other fiction works are : *Himalaya ki Pukar*, *Intazar Nahin*, *Hiron ka Har* and *Maitri ke Phul* (1984).

JAYRAM (fl. 1496). Maithili poet, whose lyrics were quoted in anthologies. He may be identified with Jayram Datt of Vanepa, the author of *Pandav-Vijay-Natak* (or *Sabbhaparva-Natak*) in Maithili.

JAY RAMAN, P. Tamil-speaking Hindi poet and writer, whose chief works are : *Dhup ke Shahtir* (The Pillars of the Sunshine ; a collection of poems), a biography of Subrahmanya Bharati, the celebrated Tamil poet, and *Subrahmanya Bharati evam Suryakant Tripathi Nirala ke Kavyon ka Tulnatmak Adhyayan* (A Comparative Study of the Poetry of Bharati and Nirala ; Ph. D. thesis ; 1966) and tr. into Hindi Bharati's poems as : *Kavishri Bharati* as also Na. Parthasarathi's Tamil novel under the title of *Atma ke Rag* (The Songs of the Soul). He has also tr. into Hindi under the title *Purnanuru ki Kathayen* the stories as described in *Purnanuru*, a work of Sangam Age. His other important works are: *Hindi evam Tamil ke Vaishnav Bhakti Sahitya ka Tulnatmak Adhyayan* (A Comparative Study of the Devotional Literature of Hindi and Tamil ; D. Litt. thesis), *Hindi-Tamil Swayam-Shikshak* (Hindi-Tamil Self-Teacher) and critical essays, *e g*., 'Adhunik Tamil Sahitya Sarvekshan' (A Survey of Modern Tamil Literature).

JAY RAMDAS GUPTA (fl. early 20th cent.). Writer, whose historical novels are : *Rang men Bhang* (Disturbance during Merry-making) and *Kashmir Patan* (The Fall of Kashmir). He also wrote some detective novels.

JAYRAM PINDYE (fl. early 17th cent.). Marathi poet, who was born at Nasik in Maharashtra. He was patronized by Shahji Maharaj, the father of Shivaji. He knew some 12 languages including Sanskrit, Prakrit, Braj, Dakkhini, Hindi, etc. Of his *Radhamadhav Vilas Champu*, the first ten cantos are in Sanskrit, while the last canto is in several languages. His other popular work is *Parnalparvat Grahanakhyan*. He had compared his patron with Shahjahan, the Mughal Emperor.

JAYRUP DUBIYAN, THE LATE. Hindi poet of Mauritius, whose *Sudha Kalash* is a collection of his poems.

JAY SAGAR (fl. 1st part of 15th cent.). Gujarati Jain poet, whose *Vayar Swami Guru Ras* was composed at Junagarh. The language of this work is Apabhransh-mixed Hindi-Gujarati.

JAY SHANKAR 'PRASAD' (1889-1937). Celebrated poet, dramatist, novelist and short story writer, who was born in a prosperous Vaishya family of Benares. His education was mostly at home and he acquired intimate knowledge of Sanskrit, English, Bengali, Urdu, Prakrit, Pali, history of Gupta period and Buddhist philosophy. He started writing at the age of fifteen and his early verses in Brajbhasha were collected in a volume, entitled *Chitradhar*. Later he wrote poems in Khari Boli, which are to be found in *Kanan Kusum*

(The Forest Flowers), *Prem Pathik* (Traveller on the Road of Love ; 1913) and *Maharana ka Mahatva* (Importance of the Maharana ; 1914). In 1918, a small collection of his verses was published under the title *Jharna* (Cascade ; its second edition containing a very much larger number of poems appeared in 1927). After 1920, Prasad became one of the champions of *Chhayavad* and his long poem, *Ansu* (Tears ; 1926 ; q.v.) clearly reveals a change in mood and technique ; the poem depicts pangs of separation with the help of imagery, touched here and there with mystic associations. *Lahar* (Ripples), which appeared in 1935, is a collection of stray verses. His last and foremost poetic work, however, is *Kamayani* (1936 ; q.v.), which is an epic poem on a Rigvedic allegory.

As a dramatist, Prasad occupies a unique position. Most of his dramas are historical, but they have didactic and reformist elements in them. His dramas are : *Rajyashri* (1915), *Vishakh* (1921), *Ajatshatru* (1922), *Janmejay-ka-Nag-Yagya* (The Serpent Sacrifice of Janmejay ; 1926), *Skandgupta Vikramaditya* (1928), *Chandragupta* (1931), *Dhruvswamini* (1933) (*qq. v.*) and *Kamna* (Wish ; 1923-24) ; his one-act plays are : *Sajjan* (1910-11 ; mythological), *Kalyani-Parinay* (1912 ; on the marriage of Chandragupta with Cornelia), *Karunalay* (1912 ; verse play ; mythological), *Prayashchit* (Repentance ; 1914 ; on Jaychand) and *Ek Ghunt* (One Mouthful ; 1929 - 30). As true classics, his plays belong to the present age as also to all times.

As a fiction writer, Prasad wrote two social novels : *Kankal* (The Skeleton ; 1929 ; q.v.) and *Titli* (1934 ; q.v.) and one incomplete historical novel *Iravati* (1936 ; q.v.). His novels seek to give realistic pictures of social evils but the purpose is always reformist. His short story collections, which lay stress on certain ideals rather than mere narration, are : *Chhaya* (Shadow), *Chitradhar ki Kahaniyan* (1918), *Pratidhwani* (Echo ; 1926) *Akashdip* (Stars ; 1926), *Andhi* (Storm ; 1931) and *Indrajal* (1936) ; in all he has written 69 short stories. His well-known short stories are : 'Akashdip', 'Puraskar' (Reward), 'Samudra Santaran' (Crossing the Ocean), 'Churivali' (The Bangle Seller), 'Andhi' 'Bisati' (The Pedlar), 'Gunda' (The Scoundrel), 'Madhua', 'Mamta', etc.

Besides, Prasad wrote two Champus : *Urvashi* (1909), *Prem-Rajya* (The Kingdom of Love) and *Karunalay* (The Abode of Mercy ; *Gitinatya*) *Kavya aur Kala* (The Poetry and Art ; essay) and articles in literary magazines : 'Indu', 'Jagran' and 'Hans'. Complete works of Prasad are being published in five volumes as *Shri Jayshankar Prasad Granthavali*, of which the first two volumes have so far been out.

The foremost poet of the modern age, Prasad was the founder of the *Chhayavad* : his *Jharna* and *Ansu* typify in themselves the main traits of *Chhayavad* poetry, while his *Kamayani* brings out his mystic and philosophical approach to life. He had the rare gift of minute observation and was highly sensitive to beauty in all its forms and shapes. A stylist, he set the tune to give a new shape to modern poetic diction. As a dramatist, he is the greatest Hindi playwright, who dived deep into the basic problems of human nature.

Whether in poetry or in drama, Prasad is the most towering personality of the modern age.

JAY SHEKHAR SURI. Jain poet, who was a disciple of Mahendra Suri. His works are : *Prabodh Chintamani* (1405), *Upadesh Chintamani* (in 12,000 *Shlokas*), *Dhammit Charit Mahakavya, Jain Kumar Sambhav* and *Tribhuvan Dipak Prabandh*.

JAYSINGH (fl. early 16th cent). Rajasthani poet, who was probably a Brahmin by caste. His *Hari Raso* devotionally treats of in simple language the attributes of God meant for self-purification.

JAYSINGHA REDDY, G. See *Harijit, G.J.*

JAYACHARYA. See *Jitmalji.*

JAYANAND. Maithili poet, who was noted for his lyrics. He was patronized by Maharaja Madhav Singh (1776-1808).

JAYANTI DEVI. Modern Maithili poetess, who is known for her excellent traditional lyrics, in addition to folk-types and modern types of lyrics.

JAYASI. See *Malik Muhammad Jayasi.*

JAYAT RAM (fl. 1573). Court-poet of Akbar, who commented on the *Bhagavadgita* in Hindi verse.

JAYENDRA. Modern Magahi writer, who is notod for his short stories, written on Marxist lines.

JAYENDRABHAI TRIVEDI, ACHARYA. Modern Gujarati writer of Bhavnagar, who has contributed to the *Hindi Sahitya Kosh*, ed. by Dhirendra Verma.

JEKSA, F A. Modern scholar, whose chief work is *Hindi Bhasha ki Ninv*.

JETHVAI RA SORTHA (*Doha*). Rajasthani story of Jethva-Ujali in about 100 verses, which are found scattered in various manuscripts dating from the 17th century onwards. The original *Sorthas* might have been composed around 1500.

Prince Jethva of Dhumali goes on a horse for hunting but is faced with a severe storm due to which he loses consciousness. The horse takes him to the hut of a Charan (bard), Amara by name. Amara and his young daughter Ujali try hard to revive the young man but as the bard does not have enough clothing to provide warmth to Jethva's body, he asks his daughter to hold Jethva in the warmth of her naked embrace. He tells her that if the young man happens to be of the same caste as theirs, he would give her in marriage to him. Ujali does as she is bid and succeeds in restoring consciousness to Jethva. Jethva assures Ujali that he will marry her. They fall in deep love but on learning that Ujali is a Charan girl, Jethva is perplexed, for marriage between a Rajput and a Charan is traditionally prohibited. Feeling bound by this custom, Jethva abandons the idea of marrying her and leaves for his palace. Ujali does not meet him thereafter.

The verses spoken by Ujali delineate her separation in many ways, imploring Jethva to accept the call of love and meet her. She says that all the waters are one, so are all human beings. She further says, "The high is beyond reach, the low is unaceptable. Mine is a life wasted in this devastating dilemma."

A Gujarati version, with slight linguistic difference, is equally popular in Gujarat.

JHABARMAL SHARMA (1888-1983). Writer of the then Jaipur State, who had been editor of 'Bharat', 'Gyanoday', 'Marwari', 'Calcutta Samachar' and 'Hindu-Sansar'. His chief works are : *Sanbhar ka Itihas*, *Khetri ka Itihas*, *Vivekanand* and *Tilak-Gatha*.

JHAMAL RADHIKA SHIKH-NAKH. See *Bankidas*.

JHANSI KI RANI (The Rani of Jhansi). Novel (1946) by Vrindavanlal Verma (q.v.), which is based on the biography of Lakshmibai the Rani of Jhansi. The plot is divided into four parts : Dawn, Sunrise, Noon and Sunset, and in all the four is shown a gradual development of the queen's life.

JHARNA. See *Jayshankar Prasad*.

JHULNA RAO AMARSINGH GAJSINGHOT RA. See *Dursa Adha.*

JHULNA RAO SURTAN RA. See *Dursa Adha.*

JHUTHA SACH (The False Truth). Novel (1958) written in two volumes by Yashpal (q.v.), which is considered his masterpiece. It describes vividly the suffering of the common people of India and Pakistan before, during and after the partition in 1947. A novel in epic scale, it has been placed with great novels. The refugees who came to India from Pakistan faced their new life of struggle with self-confidence before they establish themselves in a new country. Not only men, women also struggled with a firm resolve to build their future. Thus, while the situation created a feeling of self-confidence and self-respect among men and women, it freed them from the bonds of family life, which resulted in sexual promiscuity. On the one hand, men and women became more active and hardworking, on the other they also became cunning, untruthful, undependable and in some cases anti-social. Side by side, there is the story of the human mind through the characters of Tara, Kanak, Shila, Puri, Gil, Sud, Shobhraj, Chaddha, Asad, etc.

JIALAL HANDU (1927-). Kashmiri-speaking Hindi writer, who holds a doctorate on the comparative study of Kashmiri and Hindi Sufi Poetry. He has also written some research articles.

JIJI DEVI. See *Aiji*.

JIN CHANDRA SURI (fl 17th cent.). Jain poet, who was the author of *Shamb Pradyumna Chaupai*, on the story of Krishna's sons : Samb and Pradyumna.

JINDAL, K.B. Author of *A History of Hindi Literature* (1955).

JINDATT CHARIT. Old Rajasthani poem by Ralha or Rajsingh, composed in 1297. A narrative and romantic poem, it describes in 533 verses the life of Seth Jindatt ; it has been very popular in the Jain community.

JINESHWAR SURI VIVAH VARNAN RAS. See *Som Murti*.

JINHARSH (JASRAJ ; 1628-1722). Jain Rajasthani poet, who composed 74 major poems like *Chandan Malaygiri Chaupai*,

Kusum Shri Mahasati Chaupai, *Vidyavilas Ras*, *Mrigaputra Chaupai* and *Matsyodar Ras*, which are mainly based on the Jain mythology and traditions. Besides, he composed about 350 stray songs and verses on miscellaneous topics on *Dharma*, secularism, etc. Many of his poems, such as *Prem Patrika*, *Dodhak Chhattisi*, *Barahmasa ra Duha*, *Pandrah Tithi ra Duha* and *Nemi Rajmati Git* depict deep emotions of love, longing and separation, in which influence of earlier poets is noticed.

JIN PADMA SURI. See *Thulibhadda Phag*.

JINRAJ SURI (1590-1643). Jain Rajasthani scholar and poet, whose narrative poem *Subhadra Dhanna Chaupai* got much popularity. His other poems are: *Gaj Sukumal Mahamuni Chaupai* and *Ramayan*. His stray songs are eulogies of Tirthankars, Viharmans and descriptions of places of pilgrimage like Shatrunjay and Abu. All his poems are meant to be sung. Jinraj Suri was in the disciple-tradition of Acharya Jin Chandra Suri.

JINVIJAY, MUNI (1888-1976). Celebrated Jain scholar, who was born in a Kshatriya family of Mewar but was initiated into Jainism, his original name being Ranmall. A great scholar of Sanskrit. Pali, Prakrit, Apabhransh, Gujarati, Rajasthani, Hindi, etc., he has edited, compiled and written more than 50 works, which have been appreciated by Indian as well as foreign scholars.

JITAMITRA MALL (r. 1672-96). Ruler of the House of Bhatgao in Nepal, who was greater as a writer of Maithili dramas than as a writer of lyrics. Only a *Dashavtar* collection of lyrics has been noticed, but his poetic power and command over the language is superior to those of Jagat Prakash Mall (q.v.) and others. Under his patronage, four poets are known to have flourished; of these Jagat Chandra deserves special mention. His several dramatic works are: *Kaliya-Mathnopakhyan* (1684; in three Acts), *Madalasa-Haranam* (1687), *Jaiminiya-Bharat-Natakam* (1690), *Gopichandra-Natakam* (1690; in Bengali), *Usha-Haran*, *Nav-Durga-Natakam* (1686), *Sati-Viyog* or *Kumar-Pradurbhav* (with *Bhanitas* of Jagat Chandra), *Baruthini-Haranam* with *Bhanitas* of Dwij Shivhari, *Ramayan-Natak* and an incomplete play, called *Mangal-Mahotsav*. Almost his dramas begin with a benediction to Ardhanarishwar and there is a command over language.

JITENDRA BHATIA (1946-). Short story writer, whose chief short story collections are: *Raktajivi* (Living on Blood) and *Shahadat-Nama* (Evidence Book); *Samay Simant* (Time

Limits) and *Aurat Marad* are his novels. His stories are forceful expression of the sad lot of the common man.

JITENDRA NATH KHAOND (1932-). Assamese-speaking Hindi writer, who has made comparative studies of Hindi and Assamese novels and idioms. His essays have appeared in 'Vishwabharati', 'Rashtrasevak', etc. and he has prepared some text-books as well. He is preparing an Assamese-Hindi-English dictionary.

JITMALJI (JAYACHARYA ; 1803-81). The fourth Acharya of Terapanth (Shwetambar) Sampraday, who was probably the greatest Rajasthani *Katha* writer of the 19th century. He had written a large number of *Kathas*.

JITNARAYAN. Modern Hindi poet of Surinam, whose chief poetical collections are : *Dal Bhat Chatni*, *Hinsa Prasad* and *Jitni Ujjar Joti Utni Gabra Jhalka*. He mainly weaves the web of common man's life in his poems. At present, he lives in Netherlands.

JIV DAYA RAS. See *Asig*.

JIV KANT. Maithili fiction writer, whose chief novels are : *Panipat* (1969 ; portraying the life of an unsuccessful youth, who meets frustration on all sides), *Du Kuhesak Bat* (1968 ; presenting the modern adolescent in a state of indecision and hesitancy) and *Agniban* (an allegory on hunger, frustration and unemployment that has overtaken modern Mithila). His chief short story collection *Eksari Tharki Kadam Tar Re* (1972) presents deep alienation felt by modern man in the new machine age. He has published poems as well : *Nachu He Prithwi* (1971) is a collection of his poems.

JIV NATH (fl. early 13th cent.). Maithili poet, who was noted for his poems in the style of Vidyapati (q.v.). His verses also found respectable place in contemporary anthologies.

JIVCNATH. Modern Maithili poet, whose *Ravan-Vadh*, an epic, desribes the killing of Ravan by Ram.

JIV NATH JHA 'VIDYABHUSHAN' (1910-). Modern Maithili writer, who is noted for his patriotic drama, *Vir Narendra* as also for his tr. of *Shringara-Tilaka* from Sanskit into Maithili. His *Muktak* poems are collected in *Kalpana* (1949).

JIV NATH RAY (fl. early 20th cent.). Maithili writer, whose essays reveal contemporary life in its true colours.

JIVACHH MISHRA. Maithili writer, who tr. portions of the *Ramayana* (1936) from original Sanskrit into Maithili.

JIVAN DAS (d. 1830). Saint-poet of Gujarat, who was known by the name of 'Dasi Jivan'. A follower of Bhim Sahib of Ravibhan Sect, his *Bhajans* and *Padas* enjoy the same respect in his native place Sorath as the work of Mirabai in Rajasthan. He is also called the Raidas of Gujarat.

JIVAN JHA (1848-1912). Maithili dramatist, who under the patronage of the Maithili Raja of Benares (the Kashiraj) wrote dramas on attractive episodes. His *Sattak* variety of dramas are: *Sundar-Sanyog* (1904), *Narmada-Sagar Sattak* (1906), *Maithili-Sattak* (1908) and *Samb-Vati Punarjanma* (on the Puranic story describing the change of sex in a young student in an ancient Gurukula). He was the first to realize the true nature of a modern play and to use Maithili prose copiously. He also wrote some *Maheshvanis*, several types of lyrics and *Muktak* verses.

JIVAN LAL (1813-69). Rajasthani poet, who was a Nagar Brahmin of Bundi. A favourite of Maharao Raja Ramsingh of Bundi, he was Prime Minister of that State for some years and manage the affairs of the State so efficiently that the Raja awarded him liberally.

A scholar of Sanskrit, Persian and Hindi, he composed at the age of 16 *Krishna Khand*, a bulky volume of 12,000 *Shlokas*. His other works in Sanskrit and Hindi are *Usha-Haran, Durgacharitra, Bhagavat-Bhasha, Ramayan, Ganga-Shatak, Avtar-Mala* and *Samhita-Bhashya*.

His poetry is permeated with *Bhakti* and *Shringar*.

JIVANAND THAKUR. Modern Maithili writer, who has tr. into Maithili prose, Bhasa's plays from Sanskrit original.

JIVARAM (fl. 1839). Poet of the Ram-cult (Rasik Sect), who lived at Chiran and Ayodhya. Of his four works: *Rasik Prakash Bhaktamal, Padavali, Shringar-Rasa-Rahasya* and *Ashtayam Vartik*, the first one gives biographical outlines of the Rasik Sect. The work is on the pattern of *Bhaktamal* (q.v.) and is of historical value.

JIVITRAM SAITPAL. Sindhi-speaking modern Hindi poet, whose *Pyasi Dharti* (The Thirsty Earth ; 1972) is a collection of songs permeated with nationalist sentiments. He has published a short story collection: *Ret ke Kagar Par* (On the Edge of Sand ; 1974). He has also edited a literary magazine

'Protsahan', through which he has encouraged young Hindi poets.

JIVIT SINGH (1839-91). Sindhi saint-poet, whose Hindi poems are compiled in *Sindh ki Siddha Mandali.* He belonged to Larkana in Sind (now in Pakistan).

JODH RAJ. Poet, who was a Gaur Brahmin and was son of Balkrishna. At the instance of Raja Chandrabhan Chauhan of Ninvagarh (present Nimran, near Alwar), he composed *Hammir Raso* (1818), describing the famous story of Hammirdev. The language of this work is forceful and events are described in detail. The poet has added a few self-inventive incidents to give a poetic touch and colouring to the work ; thus here historical veracity is welded with poetic excellence. See *Hammir Raso, Hammir Mahakavya, Hammir Hath.*

JODHA AGARSINGH. Rajasthani poet, whose *Pabu Prakash* (5th ed., 1957) describes the deeds and glorious death of Pabuji Rathore, the legendary folk god of Rajasthan. See *Pabuji ka Pavada.*

JOGENDRA SINGH VERMA. Modern scholar, whose chief work is : *Prabhakar Machwe ka Kavya.*

JOGESHWAR TRIPATHI. Oriya-speaking modern Hindi writer, who has tr. Gangadhar Mehar's poem, *Tapaswini* from Oriya into Hindi.

JOGIDAN KAVIYA. Modern Rajasthani poet, who has paid poetic homage to the heroes, who sacrificed their lives in fighting against the Chinese attack on India.

JOGIDAS. Rajasthani poet, whose *Varsalpur Garh Vijay* or *Sujan Raso* (composed about 1712) describes an attack of Maharaja Sujansingh (1700-1746) of Bikaner on the Bhatis of Varsalpur ; the work is important as mention of this attack is found nowhere else. Jogidas's other works are : *Radha Krishnaji ra Duha* and *Vaidyak-Sar.*

JOGIDAS KUNVARIYA (1613- *c.* 83). Rajasthani poet, who was patronized by Maharavat Harisingh (1628-73) of Pratapgarh. On the name of his patron, he composed *Hari-Pingal Prabandh,* a work on metrics ; in the last section is given a genealogical account of his patron and his battles with the Pathans. This work is of a fairly high literary standard. Jogidas's Dingal *Git* on Shivaji Maratha is inspiring.

JOGINDER SINGH KANWAL. Hindi writer and poet of Fiji, whose chief works are : *Savera* (1976 ; a novel, which has earned an award from the U.P. Government), *Dharti Meri Mata* (1978), *Karvat* (1979 ; all novels), *Mera Desh Mere Log* (1974) and *Fiji men Hindi ke Sau Varsh.* As a dramatist, his works are : *Insan Jag Utha* (1959), *Dekho Ve Dip* (1960), *Azadi Ki Kirnen* (1970) and *Hir Ranjha* (1971). His poetical works are : *Alvida, Nav Rashtra Ke Rangin Phulo, Mere Ram, Ek Prem Patra Tere Nam* and *Kaise Hain Ye Shahr ke Log* ? His latest novel is *Sat Samudra Par.* A versatile writer, he is known as 'Prem Chand of Fiji'.

JOGJIT (1687-1783). Rajasthani saint-poet, whose *Lila-Sagar* (composed between 1754-62) in verse is a detailed and authentic biography of his Guru, Charandas (q.v.).

JOGLEKAR, N. CHI. Marathi-speaking modern Hindi poet, whose poems are written on various subjects. He has also written critical works : *Hindi evam Marathi Ke Vaishnav Sahitya Ka Tulnatmak Adhyayan* (A Comparative Study of Marathi and Hindi Vaishnav Literature), *Devnagari Lipi : Swarup, Vikas evam Samasya* (ed., 1962) and *Rashtra Bhasha Vichar Sangrah* (the last two edited).

JOGRAPH, YEVGENY ALEXANDROVICH (1928-). Soviet Hindi scholar, who has done research on Indo-Aryan languages. Apart from a number of articles on Indo-Aryan languages, he has tr. into Russian Indian folk-tales (Leningrad, 1977).

JOHN SAHEB (fl. *c.* 1850). Englishman, who was Manager of a Business Firm in Bihar. After his contact with the Yogi, Lakshminath Goswami, he became a Vaishnav follower and composed hundreds of *Padas* in Hindi, but only a few are extant.

JON, K.J. Malayalam-speaking modern writer, who has tr. Malayalam short stories into Hindi.

JOSHI, G. PU. Marathi-speaking modern Hindi dramatist, who is noted for his work : *Bilvadal,* a collection of one-act plays.

JOSHI, L.D. Modern Rajasthani scholar, whose research work is : *Bagari Boli ka Swarup aur Uska Tulnatmak Adhyayan* (The Form and Comparative Study of Bagari ; 1977).

JOSHI, M.P. See *Mahavir Prasad Joshi.*

JUBKOV, ANATOLI NIKOLAYEVICH (1924-). Soviet Hindi

scholar, who taught Russian through the medium of Hindi at the Lucknow University. He also studied Yoga and was awarded the Diploma in Yoga. Apart from his Russian-Hindi text-books, he has written articles on Hindi personal names. He has also written a dozen articles on Hathayoga. He has tr. into Russian 12 collections of Indian folk-tales as well.

JUGALDAS (fl. 1st part of 16th cent.). Poet of the Krishna-cult (Chaitanya Sect), who became a disciple of Ramray (q.v.) and began to live at Vrindavan. His works are : *Bhaktiyoga* and *Yoga Kalpavalli.*

JWALA DATT SHARMA (1888-1958). Writer, who is remembered for his short stories, *e.g.*, 'Widhwa' (The Widow), 'Milan', etc. He was born at Moradabad in Uttar Pradesh.

JYOTI PUNJ. Rajasthani poet, whose *Sannan na Santa* (1981) is a collection of 76 poems written in the colloquial Bagri dialect. The poems on everyday incidents of life are refreshing.

JYOTIRISHWAR KAVISHEKHAR (*c.* 1280-1340). Earliest Maithili writer, who was son of Dhireshwar Thakur and grandson of Rameshwar Thakur. He was in the court of Karnat king Harsingh Dev (*c.* 1296-1324) and was patronized by his minister Ganeshwar. A high court-official, a Vedic priest, and a scholar of philosophy, he knew many languages and was an expert musician. In Maithili, he is remembered for his two works : *Varna-Ratnakar* (q v.), an extensive compendium of conventional prose descriptions and Maithili *Dhurtt-Samagam* (q.v.), a slightly abbreviated version of his Sanskrit faree of that name.

JYOTISHWAR PATHIK (1940-). Dogri-speaking Hindi poet, whose *Run-jhun* is a poetical collection.

JYOTSNA DEVDHAR. Marathi-speaking modern Hindi writer, who is known for her short story collection : *Antara.*

K

KABIR (1398-1518). Saint-poet and the founder of the Kabir Panth. There is a great controversy about the birth-place, time and caste of Kabir. Tradition goes that he was born to a Brahmin widow by the blessings of Swami Ramanand and to escape slander, the mother exposed the infant near the tank Lahartara, where it was discovered by Niru, a Mohammedan weaver, and his wife Nima ; being issueless, they adopted the infant. Some people believe that Kabir was born at Magahar ; he was married to Loi and had a son named Kamal and a daughter Kamali. By nature, Kabir was religious-minded ; he started his teaching early but could get no following, for he was termed a *Nigura*, i.e., one without a *Guru*. To remove this reproach, he wanted to become the disciple of Ramananda, the celebrated teacher. Fearing that lest he should be rejected, he had recourse to a stratagem. He lied down, early in the morning on the steps of Panchganga Ghat, which Ramanand visited daily, hoping that in the dark, the *Guru* might stumble over him and utter the *mantra* of his Order. The device proved successful and Ramanand pronounced the words "Ram, Ram" as his feet stumbled over Kabir. Kabir claimed that he had been initiated and Ramanand admitted the claim. Kabir travelled widely and remained in the company of saints and *faqirs* There are also Mohammedan followers of Kabir who regard him as the disciple of Sheikh Taqi, the Sufi saint, but the way in which he has addressed Sheikh Taqi in his poetry, there appears to be doubt in it. There are also numerous stories regarding his miraculous escape from the attempts made on his life at the behest of Emperor Sikandar Lodi who was much annoyed by his indictments on the bigotry of Muslims. During his last days, he travelled to Gorakhpur and died in the village of Magahar. It is said that Hindu and Mohammedan followers quarrelled on his obsequial rites but when the coffin was lifted, nothing but flowers were discovered which the two sects shared equally and disposed off according to their own customs.

Though Kabir is considered the author of many popular works, yet the portions compiled in the *Bijak* and the *Granth Sahib* (534 *Padas*) are admitted his authentic works. The *Bijak* is divided into three parts : *Sakhis*, *Shabdas* and *Ramainis*. In Kashi, he remained in the company of learned people and had acquired much. Therefore, despite his being ill-educated, his works are tinged with the Upanishadic and philosophic thought.

Kabir was a man of contented nature ; he was outspoken and fearless in his views. He condemned the caste-barriers and the dogmatism of Hindus and Muslims. His only aim in preaching, however, was that both Hindus and Muslims lead a noble and virtuous life.

Kabir propounded the 'Nirgun' school of Bhakti, which means devotion to a formless God, based on reason, knowledge and also faith. He was influenced by Ramanand, the Vedanta, Nath-panthic Siddhas and Sufis. From Ramanand, he learnt the fundamental principle of Bhakti and the Hindu religion ; he was a great devotee of Ram but for him Ram represented the Infinite Being God. His familiarity with Vedanta, the Upanishads and the other Hindu scriptures can be ascribed to his association with Varanasi. From Namdev and the Nath sect, he learnt a little bit of Yoga, equality between man and man in the sphere of religion and devotion, and the utter futility of rituals and ceremonial ostentation. He stood for devotion to one God as Hindus and Muslims thought of Him, but he did not enjoin idolatry. The contribution of Sheikh Taqi and the Sufis to Kabir's faith was rationalism but as mere reason was not enough, he postulated the relationship of love between man and God ; here also the Sufi influence is discernible. From the Vaishnavites he picked up the doctrine of *ahinsa* and *prapatti* or complete surrender to God. It is for this reason that some critics have suggested that Kabir suffered from confusion of thought and that he had no philosophy of his own.

A fearless critic, when it came to denouncing ostentation and meaningless observances, Kabir spared neither the Hindus nor the Muslims. To him, Truth was not merely a theory or a doctrine, but something to be preached through his works, attacking fearlessly the outward religious observances, idolatry and class distinctions. Though a poet, Kabir was above everything else a religious leader, a un-compromising reformer, who attached the utmost importance to his union with the Supreme Being. His language is Eastern Hindi, but it has words derived from Panjabi, Rajasthani, Khari Boli, Brajbhasha, Persian, etc. Even then, his poetry is of a very high order. Rabindra Nath Tagore has tr. 100 *Padas* of Kabir into English.

KACHRU, YAMUNA. See *Yamuna Kachru.*

KADEKHAN FAQIR (fl. 16th cent.). Muslim poet of the Krishna-cult, who was a dyer by profession. He composed 108 *Kavittas*, which are of a fairly high literary quality. It is fairly current that as he recited his *Kavittas* as a prayer to Krishna, the dead son of his Brahmin friend came back to life.

KAILASH CHANDRA AGRAWAL. Author of *Adhunik Hindi Vyakaran* (1970) ; he has also written a number of articles on Hindi language.

KAILASH CHANDRA BHATIA. Modern scholar, whose chief works are : *Hindi men Akshar tatha Shabda ki Sima* (1970), *Hindi Kavya Bhasha ki Pravrittiyan, Bharatiya Bhashayen* and *Brajbhasha aur Khari Boli ka Tulnatmak Adhyayan.*

KAILASH NATH BHATNAGAR (1906-60). Writer, who was noted for his dramas : *Kunal* (on a son of Emperor Ashok ; 1937) and *Shrivatsa* (mythological ; 1941).

KAILASH SAH. Modern writer, whose *Mrityunjayi* is a short story collection.

KAILASH VAJPEYI (1933-). Poet, whose chief works are : *Sankrant* (The Transference), *Dehant se Hatkar* (Away from Death ; 1967), *Tisra Andhera* (The Third Darkness ; 1972) and *Mahaswapna ka Madhyantar* (The Interval of a Big Dream ; 1980) ; *Adhunik Hindi Kavita men Shilp-vidhan* (Constituting Elements of Modern Hindi Poetry ; 1963) is a critical work. He has integration and intensity but there is a sense of tragic defeat in his poetry. Recently he has turned inward in unravelling mystic psychic experiences. He taught Hindi in Mexico and is Professor at Delhi University.

KAIVALYANAND (1811-86). Assamese poet, whose Hindi (Brajavali) works are : *Kans-Badh*, a drama, and stray verses. In his other two dramas : *Shri Ramchandra-Janma-Natak* and *Amrit-Manthan Natak*, the songs are in Brajavali, though the dialogues are in Sanskrit prose.

KAKA HATHRASI (PRABHU LAL GARG ; 1906-). Popular poet, who has many collections of humorous poems : *Kah Kaka Kaviray*, including a dictionary of rhymings. His latest collections of poems are : *Shreshth Hasya Vyangya Kavitayen*,

Yar Saptak and *Hasant Vasant*, while *Shreshth Hasya Vyangya Ekanki* is a collection of his one-act plays.

KAKA SAHEB KALELKAR (1885-1981). Marathi-speaking modern Hindi writer and a follower of Mahatma Gandhi, who is known for his *Do Am* (drama), *Yugmurti Ravindranath, Sanskriti ke Parivrajak, Gandhi Charitra Kirtan, Smaran Yatra, Qaidi ki Azadi : Uttar Divaren, Namak ke Prabhav se Bapu ki Jhankiyan* (*biographies*), *Yatra ka Anand, Us Par ke Padosi, Himalaya ki Yatra, Jivan Lila* and *Sapta Sarita* (travelogues), *Rashtra Bharati : Hindi ka Mission* and *Hindi ke Janpad Sant*.

KAKKANVAR. Kannada-speaking modern Hindi poet, whose poems are : 'Prabhati' (on morning), 'Uth Jag' and 'Jivan ke liye Jivan Shikshan'. His vocabulary is Sanskritized.

KALACHAND BHAI (fl. 19th cent.). Sindhi saint-poet of *Sagun* school, whose stray verses in Hindi are available.

KALECSENYI, AGNES. Modern Hungarian Hindi scholar, who teaches Hindi in Budapest University. She has prepared a *Hindi-Hungarian Vartalap Pustika*, which is expected to be published very soon. See *Eva Aradi*.

KALI CHARAN BAHL. Scholar, whose chief works are : *A Reference Grammar of Hindi* (Chicago, 1967) and *Studies in the Semantic Structure of Hindi* (1974).

KALIDAS HAZARA. Famous anthology, compiled by the poet, Kalidas Trivedi (q.v.).

It comprises of a thousand poems of 212 poets, representing different periods, from 1424 to 1719. The work has proved very useful in providing material for the history of Hindi poetry.

KALIDAS TRIVEDI (fl. 1688-1719). Poet of the Riti school, who was a Kanyakubja Brahmin of Antarved ; not many details about him are known. Uday Nath Kavindra, the poet, was his son, while Dulah (q v.) was his grandson. It appears that he was present at the time of the siege of Golkunda by Aurangzeb's forces in 1689, since he has left behind descriptions of it. He lived for some time with Jogjit Singh, the ruler of Jambu, for whom he composed the *Varvadhu-Vinod* (The Delights of Bride and Bridegroom ; 1692), a work dealing with heroines, their various classes and categories formed on the basis of their habits, physical features and beauty. A small poem, *Janjiraband* of 32 *Kavittas* was also composed by him.

Another work, that has been traced, is *RadhaMadhav-Budhmilan Vinod* (The Delights of the meeting of Radha and Krishna). But the poet is primarily remembered for his *Kalidas Hazara* (q.v.), which is a compilation of the works of 212 Hindi poets.

KALIKUMAR DAS. Maithili writer, whose chief works are: *Maithili Gitanjali* (Pts. I-III), *Kavya-Kusumanjali* (1930), *Bhishan Anyay* (1923), *Kamala* (1929), *Gangasnan* (1929), *Adla-ka-Badla* (1930) and *Kaminik Jivan* (1927); except the first two, all are short story collections. He also composed songs.

KALINATH JHA. Maithili writer, who is noted for his drama, *Kusum* (1965).

KALINDI DEVI. Modern Maithili poetess, who is known for her excellent traditional lyrics, in addition to folk-types and modern types of lyrics.

KALLOL. Rajasthani poet, who is reputed to be the author of the celebrated folk-poem *Dhola Maru ra Duha* (q.v.). Nothing is known about the poet, except the fact that the poem was composed by him in 1473.

KALURAM USTAD (fl. 1928). Malwi poet, who composed *Machs* (operas) and whose compilations of *Machs* were published around 1928.

KALYAN DAS (d. 1819). Saint-poet of Gujarat, who was a native of the village Unel in Khambhat Taluka. His Hindi works are: *Ajgar-Bodh*, *Kafar-Bodh*, *Sakhis* and stray *Padas*. His language betrays the influence of Arabic and Persian.

KALYANDAS MEHDU JADAWAT (fl. 1st half of 17th cent.). Dingal poet, who wrote poems mostly on contemporary heroes and happenings. His *Rao Ratan ri Veli* describes the battle of Charanardri near Varanasi, which Rao Ratan of Bundi fought on behalf of Emperor Jehangir to suppress the revolt of Prince Khurram.

KALYAN DAS RAO (fl. 1643). Rajasthani poet of village Samela in Mewar and author of *Gun Govind* (q.v.), a poem dealing with the ten incarnations of Vishnu.

KALYAN GAUTAM. Rajasthani poet, whose *Bandhav Ray Bhekh* (1978) tells the moving story of a Rajput husband, who gives a pledge to a moneylender to treat his wife as his sister till he pays off the debt. Based on a folklore, it describes how the couple served a king with a rare devotion to duty and how the queen identified and helped them set free from the bondage.

KALYANJI (fl. 17th cent.). Rajasthani saint-poet of Dadu Sampraday, whose stray verses are available.

KALYAN MAL LODHA (1921-). Writer, whose chief works are : *Maithili Sharan Gupta Abhinandan Granth* (1960 ; ed.), *Balmukund Gupta—Ek Punarmulyankan* (Balmukund Gupta—A Re-evaluation ; 1963 ; ed.), *Kamayani* (1976 ; criticism) and *Premchand : Paricharcha* (ed., 1980). He has also written essays in the epistolary form.

KALYAN PUJARI (b. *c.* 1543). Poet of the Krishna-cult (Radhavallabh Sect), who was initiated by Goswami Vanchandra in 1563. The number of his extant *Padas* is 200, which are available in Vrindavan with Baba Tulsidas. He used to write under the pen names of 'Kali' and 'Kalyan'.

KALYAN RAY (b. 1773). Poet of the Krishna-cult (Chaitanya Sect), who is said to be the author of *Sankalpa Kalpadrum* and *Brajmadhuri*.

KALYAN SAGAR SURI (1576-1661). Gujarati-speaking Jain poet, whose *Visi* had been composed in Hindi.

KALYAN SINGH RAJAWAT. Rajasthani poet, whose *Parbhati* (1979) is a major nature poem. His earlier collection of poems was *Ramatia Mat Tor*. He has also composed patriotic, progressive and love poems and odes.

KALYAN SWAMI (fl. 17th cent.). Saint-poet of Maharashtra, who was a follower of Smarth Sect. In addition to his Marathi works, he composed some Padas in Hindi as well.

KAMAKHYA DEVI. Maithili scholar, who has edited and published in 1982 the stories of 15 prominent short story writers of the post-Independence period. She has also composed some poems.

KAMAKSHI RAO, A.C., the late. Telugu-speaking Hindi writer, whose *Tulnatmak Vyakaran* (Comparative Grammar ; 1963) presents a comparative study of Hindi and Telugu grammars. He also tr. into Hindi verses the famous *Ranganath Ramayan*.

KAMAL CHANDRA BAYAN (1934-). Assamese-speaking Hindi writer, whose memoirs and essays have been published in

'Rashtrasevak', 'Dharmayuga', etc. He has also published several works on Assamese literature and litterateurs.

KAMAL JOSHI (1920-). Fiction writer, whose chief works are: *Badalon ke Bich Dhup* (Sunshine amidst Clouds; short story collection) and *Bahta Tinka* (The Floating Straw; 1954; novel).

KAMAL KANT JHA. Maithili writer, who is noted for his drama, *Ghatakaiti*.

KAMAL KANT PATHAK (1922-). Writer, whose chief works are: *Adhunik Hindi Kavya* (Modern Hindi Poetry; 2 Parts; criticism), *Maithilisharan Gupta: Vyakti aur Kavya* (Maithilisharan Gupta: Personality and Poetry; research work; 1959) and *Rachna aur Alochna* (Creative Work and Criticism; 1968).

KAMAL KESHAR (fl. 1569). Jain poet, who was the author of *Pradyumna-Chaupai* (1569) on the story of Krishna's son, Pradyumna.

KAMAL KISHORE GOENKA. Author of *Premchand Vishwakosh* (Pts. 2; The Encyclopaedia of Premchand; 1981), *Premchand: Kuchh Sansmaran*, *Premchand aur Shatranj ke Khilari* (with Lothar Lutze) and *Prabhakar Machwe: Pratinidhi Rachnayen*.

KAMAL NARAYAN DEV. Assamese-speaking first organizer of Assam Rashtrabhasha Prachar Samiti, who was instrumental in persuading many Assamese-speaking young men for pursuing Hindi studies.

KAMAL SAHITYALANKAR. Modern Garhwali poet, who is noted for his stray poems.

KAMAL SHUKLA. Modern novelist, whose chief works are: *Sisakti Nadi* (The Sobbing Stream), *Ek Ankh ka Parda* (The Veil of one Eye), *Pani ki Divar* (The Wall of the Water), *Tarang* (The Wavelets), *Kranti ke Ankur* (The Sprouts of Revolution), *Chandi ki Rat* (A Silvery Night), *Kachche Dhage aur Zindagi* (Untwisted Threads and Life), *Agnirekha* (The Fire-line), *Pratishodh* (The Revenge), *Naye Log* and *Nadir Shah*. He has written some 40 novels.

KAMALA BAI KIBE (1886-1974). Marathi-speaking modern Hindi writer, whose short stories appeared in various magazines.

KAMALA CHAUDHARI (1908-70). Fiction writer; her chief

works are : *Unmad* (The Frenzy), *Yatra* (The Journey), *Picnic*, *Belpatra* (The Woodapple), *Prasadi Kamandal* (Bowl for Offering ; short story collections), *Pira ki Khoj* (The Search for Pain) and *Desh ki Chinta Men* (Over Concern for the Country) (novels).

KAMALA PRASAD MISHRA. Celebrated Hindi poet of Fiji, who is at present the editor of 'Jay Fiji'. His chief poems are : *Tajmahal*, *Mera Atit*, *Kitna Antar*, *Jivan Marg* , etc. *Kabir ke Dohe* is a selection of Kabir's *Dohas* on ethics. He has been honoured by the Government of India with the award of 'Vishwa Hindi Puraskar'.

KAMALA RATNAM. Modern scholar, who is noted for her work : *Laos mein Ramkatha.*

KAMALA SINGH, MRS. Modern Hindi poetess of Fiji, who is noted for her stray poems.

KAMALUDAS KANDHI. Modern Kannauji poet, who is noted for his Kannauji folk-poems.

KAMAYANI. Celebrated Hindi epic (1936) by Jay Shankar Prasad (q.v.), which is based on a Rigvedic allegory and consists of 15 *Sargas* (*Chinta*, *Asha*, *Shraddha*, *Kam*, *Vasna*, *Lajja*, *Karma*, *Irshya*, *Ida*, *Swapna*, *Sangharsh*, *Nirved*, *Darshan*, *Rahasya* and *Anand*).

In the famous deluge, Manu's ark, propelled by a large fish, reaches the Himalaya's top and Manu gets down. His associations with past glroy and splendour of the gods and his lonely state make him sad. Shraddha, the daughter of a Gandharv king, who is also called Kamayani, enters Manu's life and a son, Manav, is born to them. Finding no exclusive love and attention from Shraddha as also due to her opposition for killing animals in *Yagyas*, Manu deserts her and reaches the kingdom of Ida in the Saraswat region. He manages the affairs of the state in a prudent manner, but as he wishes to have supremacy over Ida, there is a revolt of the people and he is wounded. Seeing all this in a dream, Shraddha repairs to Manu, dresses his wounds but the moment he is fit enough to move, he runs away from Shraddha. Leaving her 12 year old son, Manav in the care of Ida, Shraddha finds Manu and takes him to a place where the light-points of 'desire' 'knowledge' and 'action' are visible ; it is Shraddha or faith that puts them in proper harmony. Manu and Shraddha become celebrated as renowned *Yogis* ; among the people who come to have their *darshan* are Ida and Manav.

In the *Rigveda* Manu has been shown as the primeval man with Shraddha (emotion, faith) and Ida (intellect) as his consorts for the purpose of propagating the human species. "The conflict which develops due to Manu's attraction for both is finally resolved in a harmonious synthesis between emotion and intellect, faith and reality. Shraddha is thus the symbol of heart, Manu of mind and Ida of intellect. Without the harmony all human affairs will remain unbalanced and lead to conflicts... *Kamayani* is thus a poetic testament of Man and its greatness lies in the fact that it has interpreted human personality in a timeless, cosmic frame."

The poet has made use of a mellifluous Sanskritized diction and the entire poem is highly musical. Likewise a continued procession of fresh, vivid, concrete images makes the poem very colourful.

The *Kamayani*, by all accounts, is considered the greatest epic of Khari Boli poetry. It has been tr. into English by Jay Kishan Das, Professor Sahni, Manohar Vandyopadhyay and others.

KAMESHWAR PRASAD 'NAYAN'. Modern Magahi poet, who is noted for his stray poems.

KAMESHWAR RAO, D. Telugu-speaking Hindi writer, whose drama *Badla* (The Revenge ; 1949) is noted for its nationalistic fervour.

KAMLESHWAR SHARAN, SAHAY. Modern scholar, who is known for his work, *Hindi ka Sansmaran Sahitya*.

KAMESHWARI DEVI. Maithili scholar, who has collected and edited *Mithila Sanskar Git* (1980).

KAMLESH BAKHSHI. Fiction writer, whose *Jo Kahungi Sach Kahungi* (I Will Speak Only the Truth ; 1980), a short story collection, depicts the women of the lower strata of society. Her novels are : *Kachche Pakke Raste*, *Surang ke Bahar* and *Anthin Bhatkav*.

KAMLESHWAR (1932-). Writer, whose short story collections are : *Khoi Hui Dishayen* (The Lost Directions ; 1966), *Raja Nirbansiya aur Qasbe ka Admi* (The Issueless King and the Man of the Town ; 1966), *Mans ka Dariya* (The River of Flesh), *Zinda Murde* (The Living Dead ; 1969), *Bayan tatha anya Kahaniyan*, *Kamleshwar ki Shreshth Kahaniyan* (Great Short Stories of Kamleshwar), *Meri Priya Kahaniyan* (My Favourite Short Stories ; 1972) and *Samanantar* (Pt. I). He occupies a prominent place in giving a new direction to the Hindi short story. *Dak Bangla* (on the beauty of Ira), *Kali Andhi* (The Dark Windstorm) *Tisra Admi* (The Third Man), *Badnam Basti* (The Notorious Slum), *Ek Sarak Sattavan Galiyan* (One Road and Fifty-seven Lanes), *Samudra men Khoya Hua Admi* (A Man Lost in the Sea), *Agami Atit* (The Forthcoming Past), *Talash* (The Search), *Phir Bhi* (Even Then), *Vahi Bat* (The Same Talk ; 1980) are his chief novels, while *Adhuri Avaz* (The Incomplete Voice), *Khadiya ka Ghera* and *Charulata* are his dramas ; some of his works have been filmed. His prominent short stories are : 'Asakti' (The Attachment), 'Raja Nirbansiya', 'Talash', 'Ruki Hui Zindagi' (The Suspended Life), 'Nili Jhil' (The Blue Lake), 'Deva ki Man' (Deva's Mother), 'Murdon ki Duniya' (The World of the Dead), 'Mans ka Dariya', 'Bayan' (The Statemeat), 'Khoi Hui Dishaen', 'Delhi men Ek Maut' (A Death in Delhi), etc.

Kamleshwar was Deputy Director, Television, Delhi.

KAMRUP KATHA MAHAKAVYA. Romantic poem by Har Sevak Mishra (fl. 1744), which describes the love story of the Kamrup prince and a princess.

KAMTA KAMLESH (1939-). Writer, whose chief works are : *Vyavaharik Hindi, Prayog evam Vidhi, Uska Nam Vinay Tha* (novel), *Vishwa Hindi ki Yatra* (as co-author), *Mauritius ka Katha-Sahitya, Mauritius ki Hindi Kahaniyan, Mauritius ki Bal Hindi Kahaniyan*, etc. He has also edited a short story collection of Nepalese Hindi writers. See *Dhuswa Saymi*.

KAMTA NATH (1935-). Writer, whose chief works are : *Samudra Tat Par Khulne Vali Khirki* (A Casement Opening on the Sea Coast), *Subah Hone Tak* (Till Morning) ; *Ek aur Hindustan, Tumhare Nam* (novels), *Chhutiyan* (Vacations), *Tisri Sans* (The Third Breath) and *Sab Thik Ho Javega* (short story collections).

KAMTA PRASAD GURU (1875-1947). Celebrated grammarian, who was connected with various Hindi societies. His chief works are : *Hindi Vyakaran* (the first exhaustive and authentic Hindi grammar), *Bhasha Vakya Prithakkaran, Hindi Rachna, Bhaumasur, Vinay-Pachasa* (the last two poems), *Satya Prem* (True Love ; novel) and *Sudarshan* (drama ; 1931). He is known for his *Hindi Vyakaran*, which even now has no equal.

KAN RAJ (fl. 17th cent.). Riti poet, who was the author of *Kavita Rasa Vinoda*.

KAN SINGH BHATI. Modern Rajasthani poet, who has composed Nature poems.

KANAK KUSHAL (fl. 1637). Jain poet of the Riti school, who was a teacher in the Brajbhasha Vidyalaya, established by Maharao Lakhpat Rao of Kachh. He wrote *Rasa Dipika*, a commentary on Sundar Das's *Sundar Shringar*. See *Kunvar Kushal*.

KANAK MANJARI. Romantic poem by Kashiram (fl. 1663), which describes the unsuccessful advances made by Ratanpur Prince towards Kanak Manjari, the wife of Dhandhir Shah, while the husband was away.

KANAK SUNDAR. See *Shiv Chandra.*

KANCHAN LATA SABBARWAL (1918-). Writer, whose chief novels are : *Sneh ke Davedar* (The Claimants of Love ; this represents a successful synthesis of the ideals of the ancient and modern teacher) and *Punaruddhar* (The Redemption) ; *Bhukh* (Hunger), *Pyasi Dharti Sukhe Tal* (Thirsty Soil, Dry Ponds) and *Dhundhli Rekhayen* (Dim Lines) are her short story collections.

KANCHINATH JHA 'KIRAN' (1907-). Maithili writer, whose chief short story collection is : *Iho Chari Khun Kiyek*. His historical drama, *Vijeta Vidyapati* (1972) is reminiscent of mediaeval Mithila, while *Jay-Janmabhumi* is a partiotic play. He has also written many modern one-act plays, based on themes of Mithila's ancient and mediaval history. In poetry, he writes strongly for the down-trodden and the new man and his 'Matik Mahadev' is the expression of modern man's dissatisfaction with old values and old symbols. He has also written a profile of Yatriji, as *Mahakavi Yatriji, Maithili a Ham* (1979). His critical essay : *Alochana : Ek Drishtikon* advocates Western principles of literary critcism His *Sharad Kavita* is a critical work. He composed some *Maheshvanis* as well.

KANGHIKERI. See *Shivmurti Swami.*

KANHA MAHARSHI. Rajasthani poet, whose *Maru Mayank* (*Shri Ramdev Charitra* : 1961) narrates the life and work of Ramdevji Tanvar, one of the famous five folk-gods of Rajasthan, but in this poem he is represented as a social worker. He also composed patriotic and heroic poems.

KANHA RAM. Maithili writer, whose *Gauri-Swayamvar* (1842) is a Kirtaniya drama.

KANHAD DE PRABANDH. Rajasthani poem, composed by Padmanabh, a Nagar Brahmin in 1455.

A narrative poem in about 1,000 verses (or in 1100 according to the poet), it was composed 141 years after the events described therein at the instance of the poet's patron, Akhayraj of Jalore, who was the fifth descendant of Kanhad De. Written in an epic style and divided into four parts, it describes several invasions by Alauddin Khalji on Kanhad De, a Chauhan of Songira branch of Jalore and his nephew Santal of Samiyana. A heroic poem of historical importance, it is a tale of lofty human virtues and benevolent deeds of the Rajput heroes in mediaeval times. The brutality and ruthlessness of invaders and their attempts to get victory by any means stand clear by contrast. It painfully records how prosperous kingdoms fell to ruin through petty conflicts of individual interests and that the Rajputs could not fight in a well-organised way. The portrayal of characters, especially those of Kanhad De, Viram and Firoza is vigorous ; Firoza not only tells of her six previous births, but also about her future one. The poem ends on a note of pathos when Firoza performs Sati to get Viram as her husband in her next birth.

KANHAI KHUNTIA. Oriya-speaking Hindi poet, whose *Padas* in Brajboli (Hindi) are available. He was a contemporary of Chaitanya (1486-1527).

KANHAIYALAL. Writer, who was noted for his drama : *Desh-Dasha* (The Condition of the Country ; 1923).

KANHAIYALAL (fl. 1930). Hindi poet of Mauritius, who was noted for his songs.

KANHAIYALAL DUGAR. Modern Rajasthani poet, whose *Gitan ri Gunjar* is permeated with religious and spiritual fervour. His *Vichar Bavni* (1969) contains poems on *Ni ti*, while his one-act play *Adarsh Vidyarthi* portrays an ideal student.

KANHAIYALAL MISHRA PRABHAKAR (1906-). Writer, whose chief works are : *Zindagi Muskarayi* (Life has Smiled ; 1954), *Baje Payaliya ke Ghunghru* (Anklet Bells are Ringing ; 1957), *Mahke Angan Chahke Dwar* (Fragrant Courtyard, Singing at Gate ; 1963), *Jiyen to Aise Jiyen*, *Kshan Bole Kan Muskaye* and *Mati Ho Gayi Sona* (all essay collections) ; *Akash ke Tare : Dharti ke Phul* is his short story collection, while *Bhule Huye Chahre* (The Forgotten Faces) contains his sketches. He is chiefly remembered for his essays, scintilating with humour and satire.

KANHAIYALAL PODDAR (fl. 20th cent.). Critic, who is noted for his two works on poetics : *Kavyakalpadrum* (in two parts as *Rasa-Manjari* and *Alankar-Manjari*) and *Sanskrit Sahitya ka Itihas*, which is verily a history of Sanskrit poetics.

KANHAIYALAL SAHAL (1911-77). Writer of Rajasthan, who was Principal of Arts College, Pilani. His chief work is : *Rajasthani Kahavaten : Ek Adhyayan* (Rajasthani Proverbs : A Study) ; he has also done much work on Rajasthani *Vat* literature. Along with Patram Gaur (q.v.), he has ed. and published *Chaubol*, which is a Hindi rendering of four Rajasthani *Vats*. His critical works are : *Kamayani-Darshan*, *Keshav Sudha* and *Chintan ke Ayam*. He had also published some poems.

KANHAIYA LAL SETHIYA. Modern Rajasthani poet, whose chief works are : *Ramaniyai ra Sortha* (1940 ; Niti poems), contribution of his poem 'Dharti Dhoran Ri' to an anthology, *Minjhar* (1972 ; in these poems, Nature has been chosen as a medium for philosophical speculation, presentation of ideologies, and solution of human problems), *Liltans* (1974 ; poems born of his experience), contribution to *Phul Kesula Phul* (1976 ; an anthology of lyrics, portraying Nature's various aspects), *Khuli Khirkiyan Chaure Raste*, *Dhar Kunchan Dhar Majalan* (1979 ; offering a deep insight into human existence), the poem 'Patal' or 'Pithal' (in *Minjhar*, 1972 ; it recalls the plight of Rana Pratap in the jungles and the poet Prithwiraj's letter to him). He has also contributed to the patriotic and to the progressive schools of poetry and his 'Minakh' is an example of the latter type of poetry. 'Bikhai ra Ankh men Ansu' (1948) is an elegy, written on the death of Mahatma Gandhi. His poems also reveal the silent changes in the rural life as also in individual life in general. In the field of *Gadya-Kavya*, he occupies a unique position. His *Galgachiya* (1972) consists of 64 pieces of poetic prose, where his ideas, mingled with emotion, have been expressed with utmost brevity and lucidity.

KANHAPA (fl. 840 ?). Vajrayan Siddha poet, who was a great scholar. In his *Dohas*, he has written mostly about the occult and mystic beliefs of his own Tantric cult. See *Dohakosh*.

KANHARJI (fl. 15th cent.). Son of Vallabhacharya, whose stray *Padas* are available.

KANHOJI BARHAT (1443-1523). Rajasthani poet, who wrote devotional verses decrying the prevalent social evils. He was one of the poets of the Vishnoi tradition (see *Jambhoji*), who composed stray verses on miscellaneous topics.

KANIKA TOMAR. Bengali-speaking modern Hindi scholar, who has made a detailed research on Brajbuli literature ; her work is *Brajbhasha aur Brajbuli Sahitya : Tulnatmak Adhyayan* (1964). She is wife of Ram Singh Tomar (q.v.).

KANKAL (The Skeleton). Realistic novel (1929) by Jayshankar Prasad (q v.), which exposes the decadent Indian society in which ignorance, superstition and false values constitute people's mental, social and religious make-up. A purely realistic novel, it presents the evils of society with absolute detachment without the imposition of any values or ideals. It also presents the conflict between the religious and secular trends in the modern age. The novel is crowded with characters like Mangal, Vijay, Ghanti, Latika, Yamuna, Gala, who are the victims of society and suffer due to the curse of cross-breeding.

KANS-NARAYAN LAKSHMINATH (fl. 15th cent. ?). Maithili poet, who was an illustrious name in the post-Vidyapati lyrical poetry. Under his patronage, several poets, Govind, Ramnath and Shridhar seem to have flourished. He was the last king of the Oinivar dynasty of Mithila.

KANTA. Modern poetess, whose chief poetical work is *Samayatit* (The Past Time).

KANTA BHARATI (PANT). Modern novelist, whose works are *Ret ki-Machhli* (The Fish on the Sand) and *Rishton ki Talash* ; she has also published a critical work : *Pant ki Kavya-Bhasha Shaili*.

KANTA NATH PANDEY 'RAJHANS' (1915-72). Writer, who writes under the pseudonym of 'Chonch' (Beak) ; his chief humorous works are ; *Chonch Chalisa*, *Mahakavi Sand* (Bull the Great Poet) and *Gurughantal*.

KANTA PESHIN. Modern Hindi writer of Kashmir, who is noted for her novels, written mainly on traditional lines.

KANTAK Modern Maithili poet, who is noted for his poem *Taregan* (on the stars), meant for children.

KANTI KUMAR. Author of *Chhattisgarhi Boli : Vyakaran aur Kosh* (1969).

KANTI KUMAR BHATT. Gujarati-speaking modern Hindi scholar, whose *Gujarat men Kabir Parampara* is a research work.

KANTI LAL SHAH. Gujarati-speaking modern Hindi scholar, whose *Maharao Lakhpati Singh : Vyaktitva aur Krititva* is a research work.

KANURAM DAS (fl. 16th cent.). Bengali Vaishnav poet, who also composed *Padas* in Brajbuli. Some of his *Padas* are available in *Padakalpataru* (q.v.).

KANVAL, AMARJIT. See *Amarjit Kanval*, Mrs.

KAPIL DEV SINGH. Modern scholar, whose chief work is *Magahi Bhasha aur Sahitya* (Magahi Language and Literature).

KAPIL NATH MISHRA (fl. 1st half of 20th cent.). Chhattisgarhi writer, whose *Khusra Chirai ke Bihav* holds a prominent place in the children's literature of Chhattisgarhi.

KAPIL PRABHAKAR. Maithili writer, who is noted for his drama, *Khattar Kaka Chin-me* (1965).

KAPILESHWAR JHA. Modern Maithili writer, whose chief work is *Dwak Vachanamrit* (Pts. I-IV).

KAPILESHWAR PRASAD. Oriya-speaking modern Hindi writer, who has tr. 40 best short stories of Oriya into Hindi.

KARAMDAS. Rajasthani saint-poet of the Jasnathi Sampraday, who belonged to the village Kharadiyo (Nagore). His *Hari Katha* (composed in 1603) consisting of 116 *Kadis* (a *Kadi* consists of a number of verses) propounds the virtue of noble deeds and Bhakti by taking examples from the *Mahabharat*.

KARAMOJI BHAMBHU (fl. 18th cent.). Rajasthani saint-poet of Jasnathi Sect, whose stray verses and *Sabads* deal with human duties, divine attributes, etc.

KARAN JAYANAND (fl. early 19th cent. ?). Maithili writer, whose *Rukmangad-Natak* is a Kirtaniya drama.

KARAN KAVI (fl. 1803). Poet of the Riti school, who attended the court of Maharaja Hindupati of Panna, a descendant of Chhatrasal. *Sahityarasa* and *Rasakallol* are his Riti works, the former being an exhaustive one. His poetry is sweet and charming.

KARAN MAHESH (fl. prior to 1685). Maithili poet, whose lyrics were quoted in anthologies.

KARAN SHYAM. Maithili poet, who was noted for his *Maheshvanis* and *Nacharis* of exquisite beauty. He was patronized by Maharaja Madhav Singh (1776-1808).

KARANESH. Poet of the Riti school, who was a contemporary of Narhari Bandijan (1505-1610) ; he was the author of *Karnabharan*, *Shruti-Bhushan* and *Bhup Bhushan*, all Riti works, considerably influenced by classical Sanskrit works on poetics and rhetorics.

KARANIDAN, BARHAT. Rajasthani poet, whose chief works are : *Shakuntala* (1974 ; offering a new interpretation to the mythological story), *Shri Rani* Sati (1975 ; how Nirani killed Nawab's son, the slayer of her husband and performed *Sati* near Jhunjhunun), *Jhar Jhar Kantha* and *Admi ro Sing* (1974 ; short stories). He has composed patriotic poems and an elegy on the death of Mahatma Gandhi.

KARANIDAN VIJAYRAMAUT, KAVIYA (1693-1783). Rajasthani court-poet of Maharaja Abhaysingh of Jodhpur, whose *Suraj Prakas* (q.v.) describes the battle of Ahmedabad, which his patron fought against Sar Bulandkhan, the Governor of Gujarat in 1730. The poet's other available works are *Vidad Singar* (138 verses in vigorous style), *Mahri Majej* (128 verses of amorous sentiments and unrestrained love), *Jain Javar* or *Jati Raso* (on Jain *Jatis*), stray verses, *Dohas* and *Gits*. *Abhay Bhushan* and *Maharana Sangramsingh ra Kavitta* are believed to be his compositions but are no longer extant. The poet belonged to the village Shulwara in Mewar.

KARANI RUPAK. See *Ramdan Lalas*.

KARANT, B.V. Kannada-speaking modern Hindi writer, who has tr. Shrirang's drama *Kelu Janamejay* and Girish Karnad's drama *Tughlak* from Kannada into Hindi. These plays have been staged in different parts of India.

KARMABHUMI (The Field of Action). Novel (1932) by Prem Chand (q.v.).

Amarkant, the hero, from the very beginning of his student days, comes under the influence of the national movement, but his father, Samarkant, an ordinary businessman, dissuades his son from joining any political activity. Amarkant's Professor, Shantikumar, however, infuses the spirit of national consciousness among his students and this spirit is aroused further when Munni is harassed by the white soldiers. To take vengeance, Munni kills the white soldiers and in the murder case that follows, Munni is supported by the evidence of Amarkant, Shantikumar, Renukadevi and other characters of the novel. The entire public wants that Munni be acquitted and sensing this public reaction, the judge orders her release ; the public adores her. Meanwhile, Amarkant is blessed with a son, but he has no interest in his wife or the child, as he is drawn towards Sakina, who also loves him. Amarkant reveals his love for Sakina to his father also, but finding no solution of the problem, he leaves for a village, where he resides in a colony of untouchables. He relentlessly engages himself in rural uplift programme ; here he meets Munni and feels attracted towards her. At times, he feels, however, a bit perturbed when he receives letters from Sakina. Amarkant leads the village movement, while his wife, Sukhda is pioneer of the movement in the city. Sukhda brings a remarkable change in the attitude of her father-in-law and spearheads the untouchable movement on a large scale. Several times on the entry of untouchables to the Hindu temples, there are chances of a clash. Shantikumar organizes the untouchables and is wounded in the clash ; he finds Amarkant's sister, Naina drawn towards him. After repeated firings, the people are greatly agitated. Salim, though has sympathies towards the national movement, is selected for the I.C.S. Renukadevi, seeing the national love of her daughter and the son-in-law, Amarkant, creates Sevashram Trust and donates her property worth three to four lakhs ; Naina is married and this breaks the heart of Shantikumar. Salim falls in love with Sakina and the latter assures Sukhda of Amarkant's innocence. Sukhda is in full control of the national movement : a paralysing strike occurs and she is sent to jail. Salim reveals his intention of marrying Sakina, with the result that Amarkant starts forgetting her. His love for Munni also fades. When Amarkant starts a movement against Zamindari abolition, Salim arrests him.

For acquisition of land for the Sevashram Trust, there is a clash with the Municipality ; the stir is led by the aged Pathanin. At the instance of Salim, Amarkant is transferred to Lucknow jail, but for his sympathies towards the national movement, he has to lose his job. Salim joins the revolutionaries and is sent to jail where he meets Amarkant. He also comes to know here that after Salim, Sakina is leading the stir. The aged Pathanin also goes to jail but the movement is now organized by Samarkant, Amarkant's father. Shantikumar and Renukadevi are also arrested and ultimately Naina leads the movement. News reaches that Naina's husband has shot her dead. The martyrdom of Naina ends the movement ; the Sevashram gets the land it desired and all are released from the jail.

The novelist has thrown a flood of light on the various social and political problems of the day.

KARMA CHANDRA GANESH. Modern Hindi poet of Trinidad, who is noted for his stray poems.

KARMANAND, MUNI. See *Anand*.

KARMARKAR, M.C. Marathi-speaking modern Hindi poet, who has written poems on various subjects.

KARNARAJ SHESHGIRI RAO. Telugu-speaking modern Hindi writer, whose *Bhaunron ka Pahad* (The Mountain of Black Bees) is a collection of his four historical one-act plays, which have been successful on the stage. He has also written *Andhra ki Lok-Kthayen* (1955), *Andhra ke Lok-Git* (1974) and *Hindi Nibandh* (essays).

KARNA (KARAN) SINGH (1934-). Former Maharaja of Jammu and Kashmir, who holds a doctorate on the Political Philosophy of Maharshi Aurobindo. His three works in Hindi are : *Prerana ke Morpankh* (tr. of English poems), *Bharatiya Rashtriyata ke Agradut* (on Aurobindo) and *Yugantar ke Kshitij Par* (On the Horizon of a New Era ; collection of essays). His works display a synthesis of philosophy and political science.

KARNA SINGH VERMA. Modern scholar, who is known for his *Kamayani par Vaidik Sahitya ka Prabhav*.

KARNA VIR NAGESHWAR RAO (fl. 1st half 20th cen.). Telugu-speaking Hindi poet, who composed a *Satsai* or 700 verses under the title of *Dalition ki Vinati* on the sad plight of the untouchables. His *Kathamanjari* is a collection of his short stories.

KARNAT. Maithili poet, who was noted for his lyrics. He was a contemporary of Maharaja Lakshmishwar Singh (1878-98).

KARTIK PRASAD KHATRI (1851-1904). Writer, who was a disciple of Bharatendu Harishchandra (q v.). He started two Hindi journals, 'Prem Vilasini' (monthly) and 'Hindi Prakash' (weekly) from Calcutta, which were widely read. He edited the first Hindi dictionary, *Saraswat Dipika* He also tr. three Bengali novels, *Pramila*, *Jaya* and *Madhumalati*.

KARTIK PRASAD VERMA (fl. early 20th cent.). Writer, whose

chief work is a drama, *Usha-Haran* (The Abduction of Usha) on mythological theme.

KARUNABHARAN NATAK. See *Lachhiram*.

KARUNAPATI TRIPATHI. Compiler of *Laghu Hindi Shabdasagar* (1964) and *Laghutar Hindi Shabda Sagar* (1964).

KASHINATH (fl. middle of 16th cent.). Maithili poet, who was noted for his poems in the style of Vidyapati (q v.). He is identified with the author of a Sanskrit work, *Yadu-Vansha-Kavya* or with the author of the Nepalese drama, *Vidya-Vilap*.

KASHI NATH. Marathi-speaking modern Hindi writer, whose chief work is *Buddha Charitra*.

KASHI NATH DAR (1923-). Hindi writer of Kashmir, who taught Hindi and Sanskrit in Srinagar and also edited 'Kashyap', a monthly magazine. He has been associated with various cultural and educational institutions and has edited 'Nilja', a journal of Jammu-Kashmir Rashtrabhasha Prachar, Samiti.

KASHI NATH HALLIKERI. Kannada-speaking modern Hindi writer, who is noted for his *Kannada Sahitya*.

KASHI NATH JHA. Modern Maithili writer, whose essays are serious and thoughtful and attempt to give a reasoned account of some problems of Indian thought. His collection of skits is *Narak Nivaran Relave Kampani*.

KASHI NATH KHATRI (1849-91). Writer of Agra, who was one of Bharatendu Harishchandra's personal friends. He wrote several dramas : *Gram Pathshala* (The Village School), *Nikrisht Naukari* (The Wretched Service), *Tin Aitihasik Rupak* (Three Historical Allegories), *Bal Vidhva*, *Santap Natak* and *Gannaur ki Rani* ; he also tr. six English books into Hindi.

KASHI NATH KISHTO (1884-1947). Hindi writer of Mauritius, who was educated at D.A.V. College, Lahore. He was appointed as a teacher in Vakwa Arya Vidyalaya to teach Hindi. An Arya Samajist missionary, he edited 'Aryavir', a magazine for a long time. He wrote text-books in Hindi for children and a book : *Mauritius ka Bhugol* (The Geography of Mauritius ; 1935). He also taught Hindi in a girls' school.

KASHI NATH MISHRA 'MADHUHP' (1907-). Maithili poet, whose *Radha-Virah* (1969), an epic in 17 cantos, has interpreted

Radha as Bhuvaneshwari, who vows herself to bring about the welfare of the world. The poem is rich in Sanskritized poetic diction and conventional imagery, elaborate in descriptions. His *Vidyapati*, another epic, remains unpublished. His *Prerana Punj* (1980) is the first book of autobiographical recollections in verse, while *Dwadashi* (1979) is a collection of narrative poems. *Bol Bum* (1981) is a collection of 100 poems on Shiv and *Madhup Saptashati* (1982) is a collection of 765 couplets on various gods and goddesses, etc. His earlier collections of poems are : *Apurva Rasgulla* (1940-41), *Jhankar* (1942), *Tatka Jilebi* (1942-4?) and *Shatdal* (1944). He also wrote *Kobar Git* (1946), describing the Kobar ceremony. His drama *Digvijay* (1979) is on the story of Shankaracharya, who propagated his viewpoints throughout the country and scored victories over the scholars of his time.

KASHI NATH SHANKAR KELKAR (1923-79). Marathi speaking Hindi writer, whose chief works are : *Atharahvin Shati ke Hindi Patra* (Hindi Letters of the Eighteenth Century ; thesis) and *Sugam Rashtrabhasha* (Easy Hindi Primers ; 5 Parts). He taught Hindi at S N D.T. University.

KASHI NATH SINGH (1927-). Writer, whose chief works are : *Apna Morcha* (Our Front ; a novel dealing with educational problems ; tr. into Japanese) ; *Chayghar men Mrityu* (Death in a Tea House), *Log Bistaron Par* (People in Beds ; 1968), *Kal ki Phatehal Kahaniyan, Adminama* and *Nayi Tarikh* are his short story collections. His stories 'Sukh' (Happiness) and 'Akhiri Rat' (The Last Night) are popular. He has also written a drama. He is a Marxist and is the younger brother of Dr Namwar Singh.

KASHI NATH THAKUR 'KALESH'. Modern Maithili writer, whose *Maithili Rasa Kanan* is a work on rhetorics.

KASHI NATH VERMA. Writer, who was noted for his drama *Samay* (The Time ; 1917).

KASHI PRASAD SHRIVASTAV. Modern Hindi writer of Nepal, whose chief work is : *Nepal ki Kahaniyan*.

KASHI RAM (fl. 1663). Poet, who was a protege of Nizamat Khan, a Subedar of Aurangzeb ; he was the author of *Kanak Manjari* (q. v.), a love poem.

KASHI RAM KUMUD. Modern Hindi poet of Fiji, whose chief work is : *Prithwiputra*.

KASHYAP. See *Surendra Jha 'Suman'*.

KASIDAS. Magahi poet, who was a priest of Bilari (Patna). A fragment of his stray poems has been discovered recently ; his time is not certain.

KATHA AHMANI. Akhyan Kavya of 717 verses, which was composed by Rajasthani poet, Delhji (q.v.). Meant to be sung in musical modes, it is the only major narrative poem in Rajasthani dealing with the story of Abhimanyu ; the legend has, however, been given the local colouring.

Krishna kills the demon Ahlochan, whose pregnant wife later gives birth to Ahdanav. When Ahdanav grows young, he, in order to take revenge, plans to imprison Krishna in an amulet. Sensing this, Krishna turns Ahdanav into a black-bee and cages it in the amulet. Subhadra, the sister of Krishna, still unmarried, opens the amulet out of curiosity and the bee enters her womb through her mouth. Subhadra is married to Arjun and gives birth to Abhimanyu (in fact Ahdanav, already conceived by her). Abhimanyu, in the Mahabharat War, decides to fight the *Chakravyuh* battle and is killed. The poem depicts Subhadra's vain efforts to prevent Abhimanyu for going to the battlefield ; Abhimayu's death at the hands of the Kauravs ; Uttara's grief ; Arjun's return from the lands of gods, where he had gone to help them in a battle, and later events. Towards the end of the poem, it has been indicated that Abhimanyu's death was intended by Krishna himself as he was Ahdanav incarnate, Krishna's enemy.

KATHA GAJMOKH. See *Surjandas Puniya.*

KATHA HARI GUN. See *Surjandas Puniya.*

KATHA USHA PURAN. See *Surjandas Puniya.*

KAULESHWAR, G.P. Modern Sanskrit scholar of Surinam, who has tr. the *Bhagavadgita* into Hindi.

KAVERI KANT. Modern Rajasthani writer, who is noted for his humorous and satirical essays.

KAVIKUL BODH. See *Udayram Gunga.*

KAVIMALA. Poetical anthology of 75 Hindi poets from the year 1443 to 1643, which was compiled by Tulsi (other than Tulsidas) in 1655.

KAVINDRA, UDAYNATH (b *c.* 1679). Poet of the Riti school, who was son of Kalidas Trivedi (q.v.). For a long time, he remained at the court of Rajas Himmat Singh and Gurudatt Singh of Amethi. His most popular work *Rasachandroday* (1747) is on *Rasa* ; his other works are *Vinod-Chandrika* (1720) and *Jogalila.*

KAVINDRACHARYA SARASWATI (1622-90). Marathi-speaking Hindi poet, who originally belonged to Pratishthan on the bank of the Godavari but had permanently settled in Varanasi. He was a great scholar of Sanskrit and was honoured for it. Apart from his Sanskrit works, such as commentaries on the *Shatapatha Brahmana* and *Rigveda*, he was the author of three Hindi works : *Kavindra Kalpalata, Gyansar* and *Samar Sagar* ; the first Hindi work holds a prominent place on account of its language and style.

With his influence, Kavindracharya was able to get Shahjahan, the Mughal Emperor to waive off the pilgrim tax on Hindus and for this noble act, the poet was acclaimed throughout India.

KAVIPRIYA. Riti work (1601) by Keshav Das (q.v.), which expounds the figures of speech. The first four chapters out of sixteen, deal with the patron's family, poet's family, poetic fallacies and poetic forms, while chapters five to sixteen describe general figures of speech and special figures of speech with appropriate illustrations.

KAVIRATNA. See *Satya Narayan 'Kaviratna'.*

KAVISHRI MALA (Pts. I, II). Works in Hindi, which give accounts of Tamil literature from the Sangam Age to 1960-62. These have been edited by K.M. Shivram Sharma.

KAVITAVALI (*Kavitta Ramayan*). Poem by Tulsidas (q.v.) in Braj, written in 1612 (?). It is considered his last major work, before he died at the age of 80.

The poem consists of 345 verses, predominantly in *Kavitta* metre. Its first half is in the form of an epic description of episodes in Vishnu's life as Ram : his childhood, the trial strength in which he wins his bride, Sita, the abduction of Sita by Ravan and her rescue, while the latter half is contemplative in character and treats mainly the heroism and grandeur of Ram. The work has been tr. into English under the Unesco Series of 'Representative Works of East-West'.

KAVITTA RATNAKAR (The Ocean of Kavittas). Work by

Senapati (q.v.), composed in 1649 ; it consists of 5 Parts.

Part I contains 89 verses, furnishing fine illustrations of Metaphor, Simile and other figures of speech ; Part II has poems depicting erotic side ; Part III is the most important one and consists of poems describing the six seasons ; the verses are very popular and often recited. The penultimate Part tells the story of the *Ramayan*, while the last one is replete with charming natural scenes.

The book contains poetry of various types—rhetorical, erotic, devotional and "nature" and thus commands a very comprehensive range. The poetry throughout is uniformly of a high standard and bears the mark of the poet's grand personality, unmistakable genius, exalted life and character.

KAVITTA SOLANKI JIVRAJ JI RA. See *Ainjan, Barhat.*

KAVIYA, S.K. Rajasthani poet, who has successfully translated Thomas Gray's *Elegy* into Rajasthani (1982).

KAVYA NIRNAY. See *Bhikharidas 'Das'.*

KAVYA VILAS. See *Pratap Sahi.*

KAYAKALPA (The Rejuvenation). Novel (1926) by Prem Chand (q.v.), which in the background of the theory of re-birth portrays the insatiable lust for sex of Rani Devpriya as also of Vishal Singh, who marries Manorama despite his already having three wives. The author also analyses correctly the complicated character of Hindu-Muslim riots from a broad human viewpoint.

Chakradhar, an M.A., wants to do social service, while his faher, Vajradhar likes him to get into Government service. At his father's insistence, Chakradhar becomes a private tutor to Manorama, the daughter of the Dewan of Jagdishpur ; the latter, however, falls in love with him. The widow queen of Jagdishpur, Rani Devpriya leads a luxurious life. One day, a prince, calling himself Devpriya's husband in a former life, reaches there Devpriya entrusts the state to Vishal Singh and goes away with the prince. Vishal Singh's coronation is celebrated on a grand scale, for which people are made to subscribe forcibly. An atmosphere of terror and resentment envelopes the state. When Chakradhar makes a complaint of it to Vishal Singh, he is rebuked. When atrocities are per-petrated in the name of collecting money, the labourers attack the Magistrate and the Police. Chakradhar pacifies the anger of the labourers and saves the situation, though he himself is wounded. He is arrested, tried and imprisoned on the charge of inciting the labourers. Vishal Singh marries Manorama, and on her intervention, Chakradhar is freed.

Chakradhar goes to Agra in connection with the communal riot there. In the riot, one Yashoda Nandan is killed, and Chakradhar's adopted daughter Ahilya is carried off by the Muslims. With the help of a Muslim leader, she is, however, brought back. Chakradhar's parents do not touch her and she lives like an outcaste in the house. Resenting this behaviour, Chakradhar goes to Allahabad with Ahilya. A son is born to him ; he is named Shankhdhar. Getting the news of Manorama's illness, Chakradhar comes back to Jagdishpur. It is now revealed that Ahilya is Vishal Singh's daughter. She gets a portion of the state and begins to lead a life of pleasure, while Chakradhar leads a sad life. Condemning himself for inadvertently killing a villager, Chakradhar goes away from Jagdishpur His son Shankhdhar goes out to search him, and when he comes back after meeting his father, he meets Rani Devpriya. It now transpires that Shankhdhar was Devpriya's husband in a former life. Shankhdhar dies and Devpriya resumes her rule over Jagdishpur, though she is now a sober and virtuous woman.

KAYAM RASO. See *Naimat Khan Jan*.

KAZI MAHMUD (fl. 15th cent). Rajasthani saint-poet, whose *Padas* are still popular in Rajasthan. His *Padas*, 45 in number, are scattered in different manuscripts and they are on mystic experiences and on the transience of life and worldly objects. The language is lucid and easy Rajasthani with a slight mixture of Khari Boli.

KEAY, F.E. Author of *A History of Hindi Literature* (1920), which gives an account of the literatures of Rajasthani, Western Hindi (Braj), Eastern Hindi (Avadhi), Bhojpuri and Maithili. He has also divided the entire literature into four periods as : before 1400 ; between 1400–1550 ; between 1550–1800 and 1800 onwards and discusses in the beginning of each period its chief trends. He got his doctorate from London University on his thesis : *Kabir and His Followers*.

KEDAR (fl 2nd half of 12th cent.). Poet, who was a protego of king Jay Chand of Kannauj ; his *Jay Chand Prakash*, eulogising his patron, is no longer extant.

KEDAR NATH AGARWAL (1911–). Progressive poet of Banda, whose first poem was *Yuga ki Ganga* (1947 ; Ganges of the Ages). His poems : 'Majhi na Bajao Vanshi' (Boatman ! Do not play on Flute) and 'Vasanti Hava' (The Spring Breeze) are collected in *Phul Nahin Rang Bolte Hain* (The Colours and not the Flowers Speak ; 1965) ; 'Ag ka Aina' (The Mirror of Fire ; 1970) is his yet another poem. *Gul Menhdi, Pankh aur Patvar, O Meri Tum* (O Mine You ; 1981), *Mar Pyar ki Thapen* (Give Pats of Love ; 1981), *Kahe Kedar Khari Khari* (1983) and *Jamun Jal Tum* (1984) are his anthologies containing poems about the lower middle class, the rural and urban labour and the peasantry. His poems display a spontaneous, free and forceful description of the beauties of Nature as also of man. *Nind ke Badal* (The Clouds of Sleep), *Lok tatha Alok* (The World and Lustre) and *Yuga ki Ganga* are his earlier three collections of poems, while *Samay Samay Par* (from Time to Time) and *Vivek Vivechan* (1981) contain his essays, interviews, reviews, etc. He won the Soviet Land Nehru Award for his poems.

KEDAR NATH JHA (fl. early 20th cent.). Maithili writer, whose essays discuss the advantages and the disadvantages of the old and the new values of life.

KEDAR NATH LABH. Maithili poet, who first tr. Poddar Ramavtar Arun's Hindi *Khandkavya* : *Ashok-Putra* (1959) into Maithili. Subsequently, he wrote two *Khandkavyas* : *Lakhima Rani* (1960 ; on the beloved of the poet Vidyapati) and *Bharati* ; both portraying great Maithil women, who raised the status of womanhood.

KEDAR NATH MISHRA 'PRABHAT' (1907-). Poet of Ara, whose chief works are : *Kal Dahan* (The Burning of Time ; 1949 ; poetic drama), *Kaikeyi* (1951 ; this *prabandha kavya* depicts Kaikeyi as a true mother), *Tapta Griha* The (Distressed House ; 1954 ; a *prabandh Kavya* based on the story of Bimbsar and Ajatshatru), *Karna* (a long poem on the mythological hero, Karna), *Shubhra* (The Ganges ; lyrical poem), *Betho Mere Pas* (Sit with Me ; sonnets) and *Ritambara* (1957 ; an epic in 15 cantos on the model of *Kamayani* with chief characters as Manu and Shatrupa). His latest poetical work is *Sargant*.

KEDAR NATH SHARMA. Dogri-speaking modern Hindi writer, whose chief works are on Indus Valley Civilization. He has also written travelogues.

REDAR NATH SINGH (1932-). Poet of *Tisra Saptak* (q v.), whose *Abhi Bilkul Abhi* (Here and Now ; 1958), *Zamin Pak Rahi Hai* (The Soil is Getting Ready ; 1980) and *Yahan se Dekho* (1983) are collections of peoms ; *Kalpna aur Chhayavad* (Imagination and Chhayavad) and *Adhunik Hindi Kavita men*

Bimb Vidhan ka Vikas (The Development of Imagery in the Modern Hindi Poetry ; thesis) are his critical works. He is Professor at Jawaharlal Nehru University, New Delhi.

KEDAR NATH VYATHIT. Modern Hindi poet of Nepal, whose poems have been composed on the style of Sumitranandan Pant.

KEHAR PRAKASH. See *Bakhtavar*.

KEHRI (fl. perhaps early 17th cent.). Poet of the Riti school, who composed *Rasik Vilas* on *Nayak-Nayika Bhed*. He was patronized possibly by Rao Shatrusal of Bundi.

KELKAR, KA. SHAN (1923-79). Marathi-speaking Hindi scholar, whose chief work is : *Marathi Shasankalin Atharahvin Shati ke Patra*. He also tr. *Ramcharitmanas into Marathi*.

KELKAR, R. SHAN. Marathi-speaking modern Hindi writer, whose chief works are : *Marathi-Hindi Krishna Kavya ka Tulnatmak Adhyayan* and *Kutte ki Dum* (a collection of essays).

KELLOGG, REV. Samuel Henry (1839-99). American missionary, who was born at West Hampton in New York. He came to India as a Christian missionary in 1872 and taught in the Theological Training School, Allahabad. He was the author of *Light of Asia* and *Light of the World* and preached in the Hindi-speaking areas of India. He is remembered for his *A Grammar of the Hindi Language : in which are treated the Standard Hindi, Braj and the Eastern Hindi of the Ramayan of Tulsidas, also the Colloquial Dialects of Marwar, Kumaon, Avadh, Baghelkhand, Bhojpur, etc.* (Allahabad, 1876 ; 3rd ed. London, 1955 ; reprint 1972). The dialects that have been dealt with are : High Hindi, Kannauji, Braj, Western Rajasthani, Eastern Rajasthani, Garhwali, Kumaoni, Nepali, Old Baiswari, Avadhi, Rewai, Bhojpuri, Magadhi (Magahi) and Maithili. Its revised and enlarged edition appeared as *A Grammar of the Aryan Language of India* in 1893. It goes to the credit of Kellogg that being a foreigner, he was able to cover almost all the dialects of Hindi in his Grammar.

KEMPSON, M. Author of *The Syntax and Idioms of Hindustani* (London, 1890).

KESAR VILAS. See *Shiv Chandra*.

KESHAV. Maithili poet, who was noted for his lyrics. He was patronized by Maharaja Pratap Singh (1761-76). His verses also found respectable place in contemporary anthologies.

KESHAV CHANDRA SAMAL. Oriya-speaking modern Hindi writer, who has tr. Kankucharan Mahanti's Oriya work, *Shasti* into Hindi.

KESHAV CHANDRA VERMA. Writer, whose chief works are: *Kath ka Ullu aur Kabutar* (The Wooden Owl and Pigeon ; 1955 ; a satirical novel), *Ansu ki Machine* (The Machine of Tears ; 1962 ; novel), *Shortcut ki Sanskriti* (The Short-cut Culture ; collection of essays), *Vinapani ke Compound Men* (In the Compound of Vinapani ; poetical collection), *Zyadatar Ghalat* (Mostly Wrong), *Brihannala ka Vaktavya* (The Statement of Brihannala), *Aflatunon ka Shahr* (The City of Snobs), *Murga Chhap Hero* (Hero with the Trademark of Cock) and *Adhunik Hindi Hasya-Vyangya* (Modern Hindi Humour-Satire ; satirical writings). He writes serious poems under the name of 'Keshav Kalidhar'. He works at the All India Radio, Allahabad.

KESHAV DAS. See *Kesodas Gadan*.

KESHAV DAS (1555-1617). Poet, who was son of Kashinath Sanadhya Mishra, author of a work on astrology. His ancestors too were great scholars and renowned poets. His elder brother, Balbhadra Mishra (q.v.) was the author of *Nakh-Shikh*, while his younger brother also composed verses of some merit. On coming of age, he attended the Orchha Durbar, where he spent the major part of his literary career. For a fairly long time, he lived as a protege of Indrajit, the influential younger brother of Maharaja Ram Singh, but after his death he found favour with Vir Singh Dev, whom he honoured by writing one of his two long narrative poems, *Vir Singh Dev Charit*. Keshavdas rendered signal service to the rulers of Orchha for whom (through Birbal's intervention), he obtained the remission of a heavy fine imposed by Akbar, the Moghul Emperor. In return, he was given estates and he lived throughout his life in prosperity and luxury.

Keshavdas is usually regarded as the author of ten books, though only seven of them are really availabe ; these are : *Kavipriya*, *Rasikpriya*, *Vir Singh Dev Charit* (a long narrative poem on war between Vir Singh Dev and Abul Fazl), *Jahangir-Jas-Chandrika* (for paying compliments to Jahangir), *Ratan Bavni* (a collection of 52 *Chhappays*, celebrating the heroism of Ratan, Indrajit's elder brother, who fell on the battlefield fighting, while yet a lad of sixteen), *Vigyan Gita* (a religious work on the model of *Prabodhachandrodaya*) and *Ramchandrika*;

the poet's fame rests, however, on his *Kavipriya* (on *Alankars*), *Rasikpriya* (on *Rasas*), *Ramchandrika* (dealing with the life of Ramchandra), *Nakhshikh* and *Chandamala*. *Kavipriya* was written for initiating Indrajit's favourite woman, Ray Pravin (q.v.) in the art of poetry and poetics, while *Rasikpriya* is a scholarly work. It is due to these two works that Keshav has been looked upon as an *Acharya*, a *Guru* and having founded the school of erotic and scholastic (*Riti*) poetry. His *Ramchandrika* is written in an embellished style and though it is based on the story of Ram, Keshav does not rise above the role of a teacher here also.

As Keshavdas in his works aims at illustrating certain theories and techniques, he uses a difficult language and thus his works are beyond the ken of common readers. It has to be admitted that though a great scholar, Keshav is not equally great as a poet.

The assessment of Keshavdas as a poet has undergone a change in recent years : he is not only deprived of his traditional place after Tulsi and Sur, he is even assigned a place below Dev, Bihari, Matiram, Bhushan and a few others. Even then, he was the first to introduce Brajbhasha in epic form and was also the first to introduce dramatic dialogues in a short epic like *Ramchandrika*. As an Acharya, he enlarged the scope of the analysis of *Riti* and included in *Shringar Rasa* many other emotions not previously included by writers on poetics.

KESHAV DAS (fl. 2nd half of 17th cent.). Gujarati-speaking Jain poet, whose *Keshavdas Bavni* is in Hindi.

KESHAV DAS KAYASTH (fl. 1536). Vaishnav poet of Prabhas Patan (Gujarat), whose *Krishnalila Kavya* in Gujarati contains some stray verses in Brajbhasha.

KESHAV DUBE. Writer, whose *Achchhe Din and Ham men se Ek* (1981) are short story collections.

KESHAV KALIDHAR. Poet, whose chief collection of poems is *Ujjwal Nil Rasa* (1980).

KESHAV MALGAONKAR. Marathi-speaking Hindi writer, whose chief work is *Dhup Chhanh* (1964 ; a collection of 11 short stories).

KESHAV MURTI, S. Kannada-speaking modern Hindi writer, who is known for his short stories and poems.

KESHAV PATHIK. Rajasthani poet of Kapasan (Chittorgarh), whose *Kunpal* (1980) is a collection of poems.

KESHAV PRASAD MISHRA. Modern novelist, whose chief works are : *Kohbar ki Shart* (The Condition of Deity-house), *Dehri ke Arpar* (Across the Threshold), *Gangajal* and *Mahua aur Sanp*.

KESHAV PRASAD SINGH (1927-). Writer, whose chief works are : *Dadupanthi Sahitya ka Samikshatmak Adhyayan* (Critical Study of the Literature of Dadu Sect ; thesis) and *Tulsi Sandarbh Drishti* (on Tulsidas).

KESHAV RAM BHATT (1854-1904). Writer of Maharashtra, who propagated Hindi in Bihar. Inspired by Bharatendu Harishchandra's personality and his ideas during his stay in Benares, he started a weekly paper, 'Bihar Sandesh', which was one of the earliest Hindi papers of Bihar. Bhatt's two social dramas, *Shamshad Sauson* and *Sajjad Sambul* (1877), though of no literary merit, demonstrate Bhatt's zeal for Hindi, although he was better equipped for writing Urdu.

KESHAV RAO PHANSE (fl. 1900-1920). Marathi-speaking Hindi poet, whose poems lay emphasis on social reform.

KESHAV VAMAN PETHE. Marathi writer, who in 1894 wrote *Rashtrabhasha*, which advocated acceptance of Hindi as an all-India language.

KESHAVAN NAIR, P.K. (fl. early 20th cent.). Malayalam writer, who was a great supporter of the cause of Hindi; he was also an eloquent Hindi speaker. He wrote *Dakshin ke Hindi Prachar Andolan ka Itihas* (A History of Hindi Movement in South India ; 1963), *Hindi-Malayalam Swabodhini* (Hindi-Malayalam Self-Teacher) and *Hindi-Malayalam Kosh* (with Chandrahasan ; q v.).

KESHAVAN NAMPUTIRI, V.A. Malayalam-speaking modern Hindi writer, who has tr. Malayalam novels under the titles of *Padosi* (The Neighbour), *Aina* (The Mirror) and *Indulekha*.

KESHAVANAND. Malwi saint-poet, whose chief work is *Tattwagyan Gutka* (1925).

KESHDA MAHANT (1937-). Assamese-speaking Hindi writer, whose essays have appeared in 'Rashtrasevak', 'Hindu Vishwa', etc. She is wife of Bap Chandra Mahant (q v.).

KESHNI PRASAD CHAURASIYA (1930-66). Writer, whose chief

work is a novel : *Chutki Bhar Chandni* (A Pinch of Moonlight). He also ed. a little magazine and wrote some beatnik poems. He committed suicide. He was teaching Hindi at Allahabad University.

KESODAS GADAN (fl. between 1583 and 1644). Noted Dingal poet, who was son of Sadmal Dudavat of village Chhindiyo, which was granted to the latter by Raja Sursingh of Jodhpur in 1596. Kesodas was a favourite of Maharaja Gajsingh of Jodhpur, who granted him the village Sobdavas (Sojat) in 1626. His popularity is mainly due to *Nisani Vivek Var* (q v.), a devotional poem of Nirgun Bhakti. His other works are: *Chhand Mahadevji Ro* (or *Shankar Chhand* ; on Shiv), *Chhand Shri Gorakhnath* (on saint Gorakhnath), *Gaj Gun Rupak Bandh* (q v.), *Rao Amarsinghji ra Duha* (on Amarsingh Rathore), stray verses, *Kavitta*, *Doha* and *Git* on various contemporary persons.

KESODAS GODARA (fl. 1573-79). Rajasthani poet, whose chief Akhyan Kavyas are : *Katha Bhinv-Dusasani* (in 66 verses on Dushasan's death at the hands of Bhim for insulting Draupadi), *Katha Surgarohani* (217 verses on the ascent of the Pandavas to Heaven), *Katha Barhsovani* (550 verses on Pandu's descent to Hell and the Pandava's Swargayagya for salvation) and *Prahlad Charit* (q v. ; on the Prahlad legend). In all these works, the poet has interpreted the legends in terms of the beliefs which were current in his time.

Kesodas Godara belonged to the Vishnoi Sampraday founded by Jambhoji (q.v.). Like his Guru Vilhoji (q.v), he also composed seven *Kathas* : *Bal Lila*, *Uday Atli Ki*, *Sainsai Jokhani Ki*, *Iskandar Ki*, *Jati Talav Ki* and *Loha Pangal Ki*, narrating the life of Jambhoji. His other poems consist of *Sakhis* (19), *Harjas*, *Kavittas* (81), *Savaiyas* (27), *Chandrayan* (85), *Dohas* (120), *Stuti Avtar Ki*, *Das Avtar ka Chhand*, all collections of stray verses on various topics. His *Mriglekh* is a narrative poem, while *Katha Vigatavali* mainly deals with Vishnu and his incarnations. Like Vilhoji, he has also given a few words and phrases used wrongly, giving their right usages.

His poems provide a good deal of material about the contemporary society, particularly the Nath Jogis.

KESRI KUMAR (1919-). Writer, whose chief works are : *Sahitya ke Naye Dharatal*, *Sahitya aur Samiksha* (on theoretical criticism), *Nivedita* (essays), *Naken* ('Prapadya' collection of poems), *Bharatendu aur Unke Natak*, *Prasad aur Unke Natak*, *Sahitya ka Samajvad* (Socialism of Literature) and *Guptaji : Yadhodhara Tak* (research and critical works). He is considered one of the founders of the 'Prapadya' school of Hindi poetry ; he has also written novels and short stories.

KESRI NARAYAN SHUKLA (1916—). Critic of modern Hindi poetry, whose chief works are : *Adhunik Kavyadhara* (Modern Poetry) and *Adhunik Kavyadhara ka Sanskritik Srot* (The Cultural Source of Modern Poetry) and an authentic edition of the letters and essays of Bharatendu Harishchandra ; *Rusi Sahitya* (The Russian Literature) is also one of his chief works. He was Head of the Hindi Department at Lucknow University.

KESRI SINGH BARHAT (1872-1941). Rajasthani poet, who was a revolutionary and nationalist poet. A disciple of Swami Dayanand (q.v.), he kept the flame of nationalism burning against heavy odds. He and his family made tremendous sacrifices for the freedom of the country. Giving the call of awakening in his stray verses, he reminded the princely rulers of their past glories. It was due to his *Chetavani ra Chungatya* (13 *Sorthas*), addressed to Maharana Fatehsingh of Mewar, that the Maharana did not attend the Delhi Durbar in 1903 on an invitation from Lord Curzon.

KESRI SINGH JAITWAT (fl. 1650- *c.*1750). Rajasthani poet, whose *Pankhi Puran* (q.v.) or *Gun Pankhi Pramod* is a collection of stray verses, in which devotional feelings are expressed.

KESRISINGHJI RA JHULNA DOHA VA NISANI. See *Lunkaran, Kaviya.*

KESRI SINGH SAMAR. See *Harinabh.*

KESRI SINGH SONYANA (b. 1870). Dingal poet of Udaipur, who was son of Khemraj Barhat. An extempore poet and a scholar of history, he was the author of *Pratap-Charitra, Rajsingh-Charitra, Durgadas-Charitra, Jasvantsingh Charitra* and *Ruthi Rani.* He was considered to be the poet of *Vir Rasa.*

KETELAAR, JOHN JOSHUA (1659-1716). The first European, who wrote the first Hindustani Grammar in Dutch in the year 1698. Its Latin tr. was published from Leiden in the year 1743. As Ketelaar's business centre was Surat, the Hindi, he used in his Grammar, is as spoken in Surat and has a mixture of Gujarati words.

KEVALPURI (1758-1848). Saint-poet of Gujarat, whose chief work in Hindi is *Guru-Mahima.* Using several metres for his compositions, he had the divine frenzy like that of Kabir (q.v.).

KEVAL RAM (fl. 16th cent.). Poet of the Krishna-cult (Vallabh Sect), whose works are: *Sneh Sagar* (The Ocean of Love), *Gyan Dipak* (The Lamp of Knowledge), *Ratnasagar* (The Ocean of Gems), etc. He was a native of Dera Ghazi Khan, now in Pakistan.

KHADGA (fl. 19th cent.). Poet of Mathura, who was a Brahmin by caste. His verses are included in the *Bhandaua Sangrah* of Kavi Ajan. He had open poetical bouts with Satiya, his aunt.

KHADGA BAHADUR MALL (fl. early 20th cent.). Writer, whose chief works are *Hari Talika Natika*, a cultural drama and *Bharat Arat*.

KHAGESHWAR MAHAPATRA. Modern Oriya writer, who has tr. Shrilal Shukla's *Rag Darbari* from Hindi into Oriya.

KHAGNIYA (fl. 1603). Poetess of Unnao, who is remembered for her riddles.

KHAIR MUHAMMAD SHAH (fl. 18th cent.). Sindhi Muslim saint-poet, who is also noted for his composition of verses in Hindi.

KHANDE RAO MARATHE (fl. 1850-1900). Marathi-speaking Hindi writer, whose essays dealing with religious, social and cultural topics appeared in various magazines.

KHANKHANA, ABDUR RAHIM. See *Abdur Rahim Khankhana*.

KHAPTAR SWAMI, MAHATMA. Modern Hindi scholar of Nepal, whose chief work is *Vichar Vigyan*.

KHATMAL BAISI. The first humorous Hindi poem (1730) in 22 stanzas, written by Alimuhib Khan 'Pritam' (q.v.) on bug.

KHATRI, DEVKINANDAN. See *Devkinandan Khatri*.

KHEMDAS (fl. 1683). Rajasthani saint poet of Dadu Sampraday, who was a disciple of Rajjab (q.v.). His four works in Pingal are: *Karma-Dharma-Sanvad*, *Sukh Sanvad*, *Chitavani Yoga Sangrah* and *Sakhi*.

KHETA RAM (fl. early 19th cent.). Rajasthani saint-poet of Ram Snehi Sampraday, Ren, whose *Vani* consists of stray verses in popular metres.

KHETSI (fl. 1733). Rajasthani poet, who was patronized by Maharaja Abhaysingh of Jodhpur. He was the author in Dingal of *Bhasha Bharat*, a work in 13,000 metres, giving an abridged version of the 18 cantos of the *Mahabharat*.

KHIDIYA BAKHTA (fl. *c.* 1730) Rajasthani court-poet of Maharaja Abhay Singh of Jodhpur, whose *Ahmedabad ra Jhagra ra Kavitta* (in 165 verses) describes the battle at Ahmedabad, which his patron fought against Sar Bulandkhan, the Governor of Gujarat in 1730.

KHIDIYA CHARAN (fl. last half of 15th cent.). Rajasthani poet, who was son of Lumbat and belonged to the village Paghadi in Marwar. A famous poet of his time, he was patronized by Rana Mokal, Rao Jodha and Rao Bika, the founder of the kingdom of Bikaner. He cremated the body of Ranmall and dispersed the ashes in the Ganga. His available works containing stray verses are : *Duha Rao Rinmal Ra* (20verses), *Duha Rao Rindhir Ra* (14), *Duha Satta Bhati Ra* (6), *Bhimoton ke Sorthe* (17), *Git* (1) and *Mataji ra Chhand* (in praise of the goddess Shakti).

With Rao Ranmall, his brother Randhir and his associate Satta Bhati of Jaisalmer also fell fighting in 1438. The first three poems describe their heroic deeds and how they met their ends ; the fourth depicts the fight of Bhimot Rathores, including Bairsal. The *Git* describes the invasion by Rao Bika on Mallukhan of Ajmer, while the last one is composed to celebrate the goddess *Rao Rinmal ra Duha* referred to in the *Vachnika* of Khidiya Jagga is probably by Khidiya Chanan.

KHIDIYA JAGGA. Dingal poet of Rajasthan, who was son of Ratnaji. His descendants live in the village Samalkhera near Sitamau. His narrative poem, *Vachnika Rathore Ratan Singhji Mahesdasaut Ri* or *Ratan Raso* (composed about 1658) describes the battle of Dharmat (Ujjain) between the combined forces of the rebel princes, Aurangzeb and Murad, and the imperial army commanded by Maharaja Jasvant Singh of Jodhpur, and the fall of Rathore Ratan Singh of Ratlam, who fought on after the flight of the commander. The poet has given a graphic description of the army, strategy, elation of the warriors, their fight and fall, and *Sati* by Rajput women. Use of analogies, similes and elegant diction are the characteristics of the poem. The *Vachnika* is also a good example of artistic prose. He also wrote many devotional *Chhappays*, of which about 30 are available. They are in comparatively easy language and show the intensity of his devotion.

KHIM SAHIB (1723-1800). Saint-poet of Gujarat, who was son of Bhan Sahib, the founder of the Bhan Sect. He was initiated by Ravi Sahib (q v.) and spent a greater part of his life in the village Sapar of Kutch. He is also known by the name of 'Dariyayi Pir' and was popular among the ratings working on the ships. His Hindi works are : *Khim-Ravi-Prashnottari*, *Chintamani* and stray verses ; the language betrays the influence of Kutchi and Sorthi.

KHOJI. Modern Chhattisgarhi writer, whose chief work is *Chhattisgarhi Lok-Git* (Chhattisgarhi Folk-songs).

KHUB CHAND (fl. 19th cent.). Bundelkhandi folk-poet, who composed poems, called *Phags*.

KHUMAN (fl. 1773-1823). Poet, who was patronized by Maharaj Vikramsahi, the ruler of Charkhari in Bundelkhand. He composed *Amar Prakash* (1779), *Ashtayam* (1795), *Lakshman-Shatak* (description of the duel between Lakshman and Meghnad in a forceful language ; 1798), *Hanuman Nakh-Shikh*, *Hanuman Panchak*, *Hanuman Pachchisi*, *Niti-Vidhan*, *Samar Sar*, *Nrisingh Charit* (1822) and *Nrisingh-Pachchisi* ; most of them are religious poems in praise of Hanuman and Nrisingh. His pseudonym in poetry was 'Man'.

KHUMMAN RASO. Rajasthani ballad by Dalpat Vijay (fl. 1643-1713). The *Raso*, which has been included by some literary historian in the Early Period (1000-1400 approx.) of Hindi literature, belongs in fact to the 18th century. It was composed about 1712 and the available manuscript, which is incomplete, consists of 3576 verses.

Though entitled *Khumman Raso*, as it deals extensively with Khumman, the poem narrates the history of the rulers of Mewar from Bappa Raval (*A.D* 734) to Maharana Rajsingh (1652-80), who raised a bund at the Jaisamand Lake, and contains two independent poems on Khumman and Padmavati. *Khumman Raso* is divided into eight parts : Pts. 2nd, 3rd and 4th are about Khumman and his marriages and the 6th narrates the Padmini-Alauddin episode. The rest describes mainly the events connected with other rulers.

Khumman marries Ratisundari, the daughter of king of Delhi. Thereafter, he goes for hunting and at Nalwar falls in love with Tilottama, who has been separated from her husband. The Raja of Nalwar marries his daughter Lasa to Khumman. Khumman returns to Chittor with Tilottama and Lasa. Champakdatt, the husband of Tilottama, seeks the help of Emperor Mahmud of Ghazni, who invades Chittor. Khumman, along with Songara Kanhad De and his nephew, Kasmod, fight hard and win the battle.

The parts dealing with Khumman and Padmavati episodes are remarkable for their poetic excellence.

KHUS RAM (fl. 1817-50). Poet of the Riti school, who was son of Daulat. He composed some 20 works, which include *Khus Vilas*, *Rasa Nibandh*, *Alankar Lahari*, *Artis and Ashtaks*, etc.

KHUSHALAN BAI (fl. 18th cent.). Gujarati saint-poetess, who was a disciple of Akhairam (q.v.). In Hindi, she composed two works : *Narsiji ka Bhat* and *Budh Vilas*.

KHUSRO, AMIR (1253-1325). Poet of Patiali (Eta), who was born of a Turk father and an Indian mother ; his full name was Abul Hasan. A disciple of Sheikh Nizamuddin Auliya, the great Sufi saint, from whom he had acquired a liberal outlook on matters, social and religious, he was appointed companion attendant to king Ghiasuddin Balban's son Muhammad. He lived to see eleven kings of three dynasties rule the Sultanate of Delhi and was a court-poet to as many as seven of them. A great scholar of Arabic and Persian, it is said that he composed over 70 works, out of which only 25 are now available. *Khaliq Bari* (Persian-Hindi Dictionary) is his famous work (some scholars, however, are of the opinion that *Khaliq Bari* was not composed by him), while his other chief works are *Nuh Siphihr*, *Hasht Bihisht*, *Majnun Laila* (a romance), *Shirin Khusro*, *Wast-ul-Hayat*, *Nughlak Nama*, *Deval Rani Khizr Khan* (a romance) and *Javahir-in Khusro*.

He wrote poetry in Persian as well as in Hindi ; his wide experience and a cheerful temper are reflected in the *Dohas* (couplets), *Do Sakhuni* (bilingual couplets in Hindi and Persian) and *Pahelis* (riddles) attributed to him. His literary genius was at its best when he composed folk songs, quibbles, riddles and conundrums (*mukaris*) many of which have become household words. In addition to being an eminent poet, he was also a great musician. He had mastered the art of music to an extent as to be able to enrich it by introducing new *Ragas* ; as many as eleven *Ragas* are attributed to him. Khusro's greatest achievement, however, was that he was the first to use Khari Boli and laboured hard to liberate Hindi from the

Prakrit and Apabhransh in the true sense of the word. The element of Brajbhasha in his songs only shows that this form of Hindi derived from Shaurseni Apabhransh was the recognised literary medium all over North India.

Many consider Khusro to be the father of Hindi poetry; in the language which he employed in his poetry, he achieved a happy fusion of Hindi and Urdu words.

KHYALI (fl. 19th cent.). Bundelkhandi folk-poet, who composed his musical poems, called *Phags*.

KIBIRKTSISH, LIDIYA BORISOVNA (1923-). Soviet Hindi scholar, who was a Lecturer in Hindi. Her main field is Urdu but she has also written in Hindi.

KICHAK-BADH. Celebrated Maithili epic in 9 cantos by Tantranath Jha (1938-61), which describes the story of the killing of Kichak by Bhim, during the Pandav's one-year secret sojourn in the palace of Virat, the king of Matsyadesh. The most successful Mahakavya after Chanda Jha's *Ramayan*, its 4th canto is remarkable for its sublime height, when Draupadi is asked to fetch wine from the room of Kichak.

KILHADAS (fl. 15th cent.). Disciple of Krishnadas Payhari (q.v.), who, besides his *Yoga-Sadhana*, was inclined towards Ram Bhakti and this was the reason why he was made the Acharya of Galta *Gaddi*. His poetry is in Braj.

KIRAN. See *Kanchinath Jha 'Kiran'*.

KIRAN JAIN. Modern poetess, whose chief collection of poems, *Swar Parivesh* (The Frontiers of Voice) portrays minutely the various stages and situations in the life of a middle class woman. Her latest collection of poems is : *Yatra aur Yatra*.

KIRAN NAHTA. Rajasthani writer, whose chief work is *Adhunik Rajasthani Sahitya : Prerna Shrot aur Pravrittiyan* (1974). He has also edited in collaboration with M C. Sethia *Dipai Vanro Des* (1980). which contains 28 poems and 13 essays, stories, one-act plays, etc. of modern writers including the new ones.

KIRKPATRIC, W. A contemporary of John Gilchrist; he was the author of *A Vocabulary, Persian, Arabic and English* (London, 1785). At the end of this work, there is given a scheme for preparation of Hindi Grammar and Dictionary, from which it appears that the author had a project to publish it in eight parts, but due to paucity of Nagari printing type, it could not be published, though most of the material had been prepared. He also wrote an article : 'A Comparative Vocabulary of the Language of European Gypsies or Romanical and Colloquial Hindustani'.

KIRTAR BAVNI. See *Dursa Adha.*

KIRTI CHAUDHARI (1935-). Poetess, whose poems are included in the *Tisra Saptak* (q.v.) ; her chief collections of poems are : *Kavitayen* (Poems), *Shikharon par Sanjh* (Evening on Hilltops) and *Khule Huye Asman ke Niche.*

KIRTILATA (The Creeper of Fame). Work by Vidyapati (q.v.), which is in Eastern Avahatth (*i.e*, the latest state of Apabhransh), mixed with Maithili. Written in prose and verse, it is divided into four sections, called *Pallavs.* It describes the regaining of the kingdom of Mithila from the hands of Muslim usurper Aslan by Maharajkumars Virsingh and Kirtisingh (in whose praise the work was composed). The framework of the poem is a dialogue between a *Bhring* (bee) and his wife. There are picturesque and realistic accounts of life in a mediaeval city and in a mediaeval army. The poet sketches the gardens, embankments, ponds, houses, buildings, temples, men and women in the street and even public women. The author appears to have been influenced by Sanskrit prose and erotic Sanskrit poems.

KIRTI NARAYAN MISHRA. Maithili poet of the *Akavitavad* (non-poetic movement), who is noted for his *Simant* (1967) and *Ham Astavan Nahi Likhab* (1979), both collections of poems.

KIRTIPATAKA (The Banner of Fame). Work by Vidyapati (q.v.), written in Avahatth *Dohas* ; it describes the life and love of king Shiv Singh of Mithila Starting with three benedictory verses in Sanskrit praying to Ardhanarishwar form of Shiv in an erotic mood, to Saraswati and to Ganesh, the poet makes a few proud statements about his poetry, sings in praise of Arjun Ray, Jagat Singh and then Tirhut and its rulers. He describes two activities of a king—he should make love and go to war if he has to shine as a king. He says that as Ramchandra was denied the enjoyment of conjugal pleasures because of his separation from Sita, he took another incarnation as Krishna to enjoy the various types of sexual love. Krishna's sexual pleasures and sports or rather of his patron, are described. Then there is an account of a battle in which Maharaja Shiv Singh is shown fighting and killing hundreds of Muslim soldiers and how the enemy was defeated. Ultimately, somehow Shiv Singh seems to have lost his way in the jungles and thereafter he disappears mysteriously.

KISAN KILOL. Rajasthani poem by As, which was composed in 1730. It describes the abduction of Rukmini by Krishna, but its text in the beginning and middle is missing.

KISAN LAL DHOTE. Chattisgarhi poet, whose chief works are: *Ladai ket Git* (The Battle Songs) and *Gita Upadesh* (1954).

KISHAN DAS (fl. 1603). Rajasthani poet, whose stray verses in popular metres are available.

KRISHAN DAS (1688-1768). Rajasthani saint-poet of Ram Snehi Sampraday, Ren, who belonged to the village Tunkla near Ren (Nagore). He was initiated by Dariyav (q.v.) in 1716 and his poems which are in easy Rajasthani, reveal his devotion towards Guru and Ram. He is said to have composed 19 poems, such as *Guru Mahima*, *Bhaktamal*, *Chanak Bodh*, *Nirbhai Dhyan*, *Gyan Udas*, *Sumiran Dhyan*, *Chitavani*, *Samarth Bodh*, *Achal Bodh* and many verses in popular metres.

KISHANJI (Kisna ADHA II ; fl. 1767-1831). Dingal poet, who was a descendant of the famous poet Dursaji (q.v.). He was fully conversant with the Hindi and Sanskrit Riti works. When Colonel Todd was collecting material from Rajputana, Kishanji accompanied and assisted him. Kishanji was patronised by Maharana Bhimsingh of Mewar, on whose name he composed in Pingal *Bhim-Vilas* (1822), describing his patron's genealogy, life and polity. The work is very useful from the historical point of view. The Maharana had granted him the village Bisoda. The poet's another work, *Raghuvar-Jas-Prakash* (q.v. ; 1824) is a work on Dingal prosody. He also composed hundreds of poems and *Gits* on contemporary, heroes, such as Maharana Bhimsingh, Maharajas Mansingh of Jodhpur and Balwant Singh of Ratlam, which are of historical significance.

Kishanji (fl. 1908). Rajasthani Charan, who was patronized by Maharawal Udaysingh of Dungarpur. At the instance of Udaysingh, he composed *Uday Prakash* in 455 metres, which describes the life of his patron.

KISHAN LAL, LALA (1874-1933). Poet of Mathura, of whose many works, only two : *Gajendra-Moksha* (The Liberation of the Elephant-king ; mythological) and *Krishna-Kavitavali* (devotional) are extant. He composed poems under the pen name of Krishna.

KISHAN LAL BHAT (fl. *c.* 1750). Pioneer of the Sang type of folk-drama in Haryana. He composed some Sangs and when these were staged, the hero and the heroine played their role on the stage to the accompaniment of music of the Sarangi and Dholak.

KISHORE. Poet of Mathura, who was a Brahmin and a disciple of Gwal (1792-1867). Several of his *Padas* are still on the lips of the people.

KISHORE DAS (fl. 1st part of 16th cent.). Poet of the Krishna-cult (Chaitanya Sect), who was a native of a place near Chittor. He came under the influence of Ramray (q.v.), became his disciple and began to live at Vrindavan. His available work is : *Kam Kalevar*, which is in *Dohas* and *Savaiyas*.

KISHORE DAS (fl. 1583). Bengali Vaishnav poet, who also composed *Padas* in Brajbuli.

KISHORE DAS (fl. 18th cent.). Poet of the Krishna-cult (Haridasi Sect), whose chief work, *Nijmat Siddhant* (The Principles of My Religion) is written in *Dohas* and *Chaupais*. His one *Pada* on *Ras* is also extant.

KISHORE DAS RAO (BHAT). Dingal poet, who was a younger son of Dasoji and belonged to the village Chikalwas near Udaipur. He was patronized by Maharana Jagatsingh (1627-52) of Udaipur. His narrative poem, *Raj Prakash* (composed around 1658-59) in 132 'Rupaks' containing 377 verses, describes mainly Maharana Rajsingh's attack on and plunder of Malpura and his reception at Udaipur. Besides the genealogy of the Maharana's ancestors and panoramic beauty of Udaipur, descriptions of Rana Pratap's victory over Jehangir and Rajsingh's Malpura attack have exquisite elegance. The poem makes a reference to *Prithwiraj Raso* in the description of Samarsingh.

KISHORE KALPANA KANT. Modern Rajasthanl poet, who started the literary magazine in Rajasthani, entitled *Olamo*. He has composed lyrical poems, portraying various aspeets of Nature, and patriotic and progressive poems. He is also the author of *Dhadavi*, a novel, short stories ('Gitan ro Bavaliyo', etc.) and literary articles and reviews.

KISHORE NATH JHA. Modern Maithili critic, whose *Rasa Nirupan* is a scholarly work on *Rasa*.

KISHORE NEPAL. Modern Hindi writer of Nepal, who is noted for his short stories.

KISHORI DAS (fl. end of 17th cent.). Poet of the Krishna-cult (Chaitanya Sect), who was a Jagirdar of Shyaupur in the then Gwalior State. He came to live in Vrindavan and composed *Padas* concerning the various festivals, which are collected in *Kishoridas ki Bani*.

KISHORI DAS GOSWAMI (*c.* 1623—*c.* 93). Poet of the Krishna-cult (Chaitanya Sect), who was a disciple of Vanshidas Goswami. A lover of musicol poetry, his only one *Pada* of 'Rag Vasant' is extant.

KISHORI DAS VAJPEYI (1898-1981). Famous grammarian of Kankhal (Hardwar), whose chief works are : *Brajbhasha ka Vyakaran*, *Rashtrabhasha ka Pratham Vyakaran*, *Hindi Nirukta* (on Hindi grammar), *Sahitya Nirman*, *Rashtrabhasha ka Itihas*, *Achchhi Hindi*, *Achchhi Hindi ka Namuna*, *Hindi Vartani*, *Shabda-Vishleshan*, *Hindi Shabdanushasan*, *Bharatiya Bhasha-vigyan* and *Sahitya Jivan ke Anubhav aur Sansmaran*. He also wrote a drama, *Sudama* (1939).

KISHORI LAL GOSWAMI (1866-1932). Novelist, who was born and educated at Varanasi. His maternal grandfather, Goswami Krishna Chaitanya was the literary Guru of Bharatendu. Kishorilal confined himself chiefly to novel-writing and he wrote 65 novels, big and small. He also set up his printing press for bringing out a monthly journal, called 'Upanyas' (1895) ; this journal was the sole medium of his literary output and he was able to print all his novels seriatim. His chief works are : *Triveni*, *Anguthi ka Nagina* (The Gem of the Ring), *Punarjanma va Sautia Dah* (Rebirth or Co-Wife's Jealousy), *Prem-mayi*, *Lilavati va Adarsh Sati* (Lilavati or the Ideal Hindu Woman), *Swargiya Kusum* (The Celestial Flower)(social novels), *Chapala*, *Tarun Tapaswini* (Young Ascetic), *Kusum Kumari*, *Razia Begum*, *Rajkumari* (The Princess ; 1902), *Lavanglata va Adarsh Bala* (Lavanglata or The Ideal Girl), *Hirabai*, *Hriday-Harini*, *Ramani* (The Heart Ravisher or the Ideal Woman ; 1909), *Lucknow ki Qabra va Shahi Mahalsara* (The Grave of Lucknow or the Royal Harem) and *Kanak Kusum va Mastani* (Kanak Kusum or The Voluptuous Woman) (historical novels). His magic type of novel is : *Tilismi Shish Mahal* (The Enchanted Palace of Mirrors ; 1905).

Kishorilal's novels made an improvement over their predecessors, though he touched upon social problems and gave a picture of the society of his days. He, however, could not keep up uniformity either in his language or in his style of writing or in the matter of choice of theme. He also wrote dramas, *Mayank-Manjari* (The Creeper of the Moon), *Chaupat Chapet*, *Natya Sambhav*, etc. and wrote several stories ('Gulab-dhara' and 'Indumati', the latter regarded as the first Hindi short story ; 1900, though it is in imitation of Shakespeare's *The Tempest*).

KISHORI SHARAN 'ALI' (1916-) Poet of Vrindavan, whose works are : *Nagari Nakh-Shikh Shatak*, *Ashtayam*, *Hit Harivansh-Yash* and *Ali Urabharan*, all devotional on the glory of Krishna and Hit Harivansh.

KISHUNESH BHAT. Rajasthani poet, who composed in 1774 his *Shatrujit Raysa*, which eulogises the heroism of Maharaja Shatrujit of Datiya.

KISNA ADHA I (d. 1643). Dingal poet, who was son of Dursa Adha (*q.v.*). He composed *Nisani Mahes Dalpatot Ri*, *Nisani Ratan Mahesdasaut Ri*, *Nisani Sahajahan Patisah Ri*, *Rana Jagatsingh ri Veil*, *Bhakhadi Maharaja Gajsingh Ri*, *Gaj Rupak*, *Jhulua Maharao Rajsingh Sirohi* and stray *Gits* on some contemporary heroes ; of these, *Jhulna Maharao Rajsingh Sirohi* and a few *Gits* only are available.

KISNA ADHA II. See *Kishunji*.

KISNAU (fl. latter half of 16th cent). Rajasthani poet, who was probably a Brahmin by caste. His *Mahadev Parvati ri Veli*, consisting of 382 verses, treats of the legends of *Gangavataran* (the descent of the river Ganga) and the marriages of Shiv with Sati and Parvati. The descriptions of Shiv's marriages are charming, but the emotional content is comparatively less.

KISUN. See *Ram Krishna Jha 'Kisun'*.

KLAIMAN, M.H. Modern scholar, whose chief article is 'On post-positioning and related phenomena in Hindi.'

KLEIMAN, ANGELA B. Modern scholar, whose chief article is 'Some aspects of the causative construction in Hindi'.

KOBAYASHI, INSHO. Modern Japanese Hindi scholar, who has done research on Kabir, etc.

KOGA, KATSURO (1935-). Japanese Hindi scholar, who is at present Professor and Head of the Hindi Department in the Osaka University of Foreign Studies, Osaka. He studied

Hindi from 1961 to 1963 in Pilani and Agra and from 1975 to 1976 in Kendriya Hindi Sansthan, New Delhi. He has deep knowledge of History of Hindi prose, folk literature and philology. Apart from his Hindi articles on Tulsidas, Hindi Literature in Japan, Japanese proverbs, etc. he has published *Hindi Textbooks* (Pt. I, 1972 ; Pt. II 1977) and *Hindi-Japanese Shabda Sangrah.* He has also tr. from Hindi the *Ardhkathanak* of Banarsidas, a portion of Rajendra Prasad's *Atmakatha* and Pratapnarayan Mishra's *Lokokti Shatak* (1978) into Japanese.

KOIR SINGH, See *Mani Singh.*

KOLKOTIN, YEVGENI ALEXANDROVICH (1930-). Soviet Hindi scholar, who is an editor in the Progressive Publishing House, Moscow. He has translated into Russian the Hindi poems of Nirala and other poets. He has edited the Hindi versions of the poems of Russian poets as well.

KOMANDURI SHATHKOPACHARYA (1892-1969). Telugu-speaking Hindi scholar, who is noted for his *Telugu-Hindi Kosh.*

KOSTIC, DJORDJE. Author of *A Short Outline of Hindi Phonetics* (with Alokanand Mitter and K.G. Rastogi ; Calcutta, 1975).

KRIPANATH (fl. early 20th cent.). Novelist, whose chief work *Pyas* (Thirst) is a psychological novel.

KRIPA NIVAS (fl. 1786). Poet of the Ram-cult, who originally belonged to South India but came to reside permanently at Ayodhya. His chief works are : *Bhavna Pachchisi, Padavali, Samay Prabandh, Yugal Madhuri Prakash, Janaki Sahasra Nam* and *Lagan Pachchisi.* All these works are devotional in character, praising Ram or Sita. His language is chiefly Braj, though mixed with Panjabi, Rajasthani and Urdu words.

KRIPA RAM. Poet of the Riti school, who composed *Hit Tarangini (1541),* in *Dohas,* which have some poetic excellence of their own. The work treats of the theory of *Rasa* in a lucid manner and is important as a precursor of numerous works of this type composed later on ; it also discusses the types of heroines.

KRIPA RAM (fl. latter half of 18th cent.). Ram-Bhakta poet of the Rasik Sect, founded by Agradas (q.v.). His stray verses in Rajasthani mixed with Braj are available.

KRIPA RAM KHIDIYA (1743-1833). Rajasthani poet, who was a favourite of Raoraja Devisingh of Sikar. His *Rajiyai ra Duha* in 165 couplets on Niti, is addressed to his faithful servant, Rajiya ; hence his name occurs in every couplet. Being issueless, Rajiya was always grief-stricken ; knowing this the poet immortalised him in these couplets. The couplets are wise sayings in a few effective words, popular similes and easy language. His other works are : *Kavitta Chalairay, Chalaknechi, Satrut Varnan* and a treatise on rhetoric with some miscellaneous verses.

KRIPA SHANKAR SINGH. Author of *Bhasha Vigyan aur Bhojpuri* (1973).

KRIPAN GRIHINI SANVAD. See *Asig.*

KRISANJI RI VELI. Rajasthani poem, which was composed by Sankhala Karamsi Runecha about 1540. The available text of the poem, consisting of only 22 verses, which appears to be incomplete, describes the beauty of Rukmini in a very charming manner with effective similes.

KRISANJI RO VYANVALO (*Rukimani Mangal*). Rajasthani *Akhyan Kavya* of about 265 verses (a few manuscripts present a larger recension of the poem, but that is due to addition of the poet's other songs on this legend), which was composed by Padam Bhagat between 1493 and 1500. The work, meant to be sung in popular musical modes, is so popular and held in such high esteem in the western and northern regions of Rajasthan that people term it their *Bhagavat.*

It describes the marriage of Krishna and Rukmini, but here Krishna proceeds to Kundanpur with his brother and army and not alone as in other poems on the legend. He does not abduct Rukmini in a clandestine manner but seizes and seats her in his own chariot and announces his valiant act by blowing the conch-shell. A vivid account of the popular customs and traditions of marriage is given in the poem.

KRISHNA. See *Kishanlal, Lala.*

KRISHNA AGNIHOTRI. Fiction writer ; her chief works are : *Tin ke Ghere* (The Rings of Tin ; 1970), *Galiyare, Napunsak, Virasat, Yahi Banarasi Rang Tha* (1984 ; short story collections), *Tapre Vale, Kumarikayen, Bat Ek Aurat Ki* and *Abhishek* (novels). Her critical work is : *Swatantryottar Hindi Kahani.*

KRISHNA BAHADUR CHANDA. Writer, whose chief work is a drama, *Sarhad* (The Frontier, 1965).

KRISHNA BALDEO VAIDYA (1927-). Fiction writer, whose chief works are : *Bich ka Darvaza* (The Link Door ; 1963), *Mera Dushman* (My Enemy ; 1966), *Dusre Kinare Se* (From the Other Bank ; 1970), *Uske Bad, Vah aur Main* (short story collections) and *Uska Bachpan* (His Childhood ; novelette ; 1956 ; tr. into English as *Steps in Darkness*). His other chief novel is *Guzra Hua Zamana* (The Time Gone-by ; 1981). *Uska Bayan* (His Statement) contains his thoughts. His prominent short stories are : 'Nila Andhera' (The Blue Darkness), 'Trikon' (The Triangle), 'Rin' (The Debt), etc. For the last two decades he lives in U.S.A. and teaches English in New York University.

KRISHNA BHATT DEVRISHI (fl. 1712). Poet of the Riti school, who was a protege of Buddh Singh, Raja of Vindvati. At the instance of his patron, who conferred upon him the title of 'Kavi Kovid Chudamani Sakal Kalanidhi', he composed his *Shringar Maharasa Madhuri* in 15 chapters.

KRISHNA BHAVUK (1940—). Writer, whose chief works are : *Pattharon ke Bich* (Amidst Stones ; 1971), *Ashwamedh, Aj ka Admi* (short story collections), *Panjab Nama* (novel), *Banbhatt ka Sangharsh* (drama) and *Adhunik Hindi Kaviyon ke Shabda Prayog* (Word Experiments of Modern Hindi Poets ; 1970 ; criticism).

KRISHNA BIHARI MISHRA (1890-1958). Critic, whose writings on Dev, Bihari and Matiram (qq.v.) are valuable ; he followed the comparative method of criticism. His fame chiefly rests on his critical work : *Dev aur Bihari.* He also edited a number of works, the chief ones being *Gangabharan, Navras Tarang, Matiram Granthavali* and *Natnagar Vinod.*

KRISHNA CHAITANYA (b. *c.* 1823). Poet of the Krishna-cult (Chaitanya Sect), who wrote under the pen name of 'Nij'. *Shri Radharaman Shringarashtak* is a small work composed by him.

KRISHNA CHANDRA MISHRA. Modern Hindi scholar of Nepal, whose chief work is *Janakpur ka Sant Sahitya.* He has also written research articles on devotional literature. He is at present the Head of the Hindi Department, Tribhuvan University.

KRISHNA CHANDRA SHARMA 'BHIKKHU'. Writer, whose chief works are : *Maut ki Sarai* (The Inn of Death ; 1970 ; based on the French Revolution), *Astangata, Mahashravan Sunen* (Listen Mahashravan), *Ek aur Yayati* (One More Yayati), *Revati* (novels) and *Bela Phule Adhi Rat* (collection of short stories).

KRISHNA DAS (1496 1579 ?). Poet, who was born in the village Chilautara of Gujarat. He came to Mathura at the age of 12 and became Vallabhacharya's disciple the following year. He was one of the members of the *Ashtachhap* and though he belonged to an untouchable caste, he was raised by Vallabhacharya to the pontificate of the temple. He seems to have been a rival of Surdas and Nanddas (qq.v.), though not equal to them in poetical merit. His poetry is, however, graceful and original as his subject would admit. Though more a priest than a poet, he is supposed to be author of three works : *Bhramargit*, *Premtattwa-Nirupan* and *Jugalman-Charit* of erotic verses. His poetry inspired several pupils ; one of them was Agradas (q v.), who was in turn the preceptor of Nabhadas, the author of the *Bhaktamal* (q.v.).

KRISHNA DAS (fl. 1583-1643). Poet of the Krishna-cult (Chaitanya Sect), who was a disciple of Jiv Goswami. He wrote under the pen name of 'Krishna Kavi' and his works are : *Shri Gaur Nam Rasa Champu* and *Laghu Gopal Champu Bhasha*.

KRISHNA DAS (fl. 17th cent.). Poet of the Krishna-cult (Haridasi Sect), who composed *Guru Mangal*. He was a disciple of Nagaridas (q.v.).

KRISHNA DAS. Poet of the Krishna-cult, who was a resident of Mirzapur. His *Madhurya Lahari* (The Sweet Wavelets ; 1796) in 420 pages, describes the story of Krishna in various metres.

KRISHNA DAS, RAI (1892-1980). Writer of Varanasi, who wrote poems, short stories, standard works on fine arts, archaeology and painting. His chief works are : *Bhavuk*, *Brajraj* (both poetical collections), *Chhayapath*, *Sanlap*, *Pravas* (prose poems), *Akhyan*, *Sadhana*, *Sudhanshu*, *Ankhon ki Thah* (short story collections), *Bharatiya Murti Kala* (Indian Sculpture) and *Bharatiya Chitrakala* (Indian Painting). His short stories are artistic expressions of psychological truths seen in social environments His important short stories are : 'Antahpur ka Arambh' (The Origin of the Female Apartments), 'Darpan ka Rahasya' (The Secret of the Mirror), 'Kala aur Kalpana' (Art and Imagination) and 'Kala aur Kritrimta' (Art and Artifice).

KRISHAN DAS KAVIRAJ (1517-73). Bengali Vaishnav poet, who also composed *Padas* in Brajbuli. Some of his *Padas* are available in *Padakalpataru* (q.v.).

KRISHNA DAS PAYHARI (fl. 16th cent.). One of the disciples of Anantanand, who was a Dahima Brahmin of Rajasthan. He was the first to establish the *Gaddi* of Ramanand Sampraday at Galta near Jaipur. A devotee of Ram, he had a number of disciples, who were initiated into the Bhakti cult by him. This seat was formerly under the control of Kanphata Nath Jogis, but Krishnadas by displaying his Yoga-Siddhi outwitted them and occupied it. Two of his disciples, Kilhadas and Agradas were even more famous. From Krishnadas's book, *Rajyoga*, written in Braj, it appears that he was a propagator of the philosophy of Sankhya-Yoga.

KRISHNA DATT. Maithili poet, who composed lyrics. He was patronized by Maharaja Madhav Singh (1776-1808).

KRISHNA, DATT ACHARYA. Telugu-speaking Hindi writer, whose *Aitihasik Kahaniyan* (2 Pts., 1941) and *Swarajya ki Kahaniyan* (1973) are noted for their historical and national content.

KRISHNA DATT PALIWAL. Modern scholar, whose chief works are : *Acharya Ramchandra Shukla ka Chintan Jagat* and *Bhavani Prasad Mishra ka Kavya-Sansar.*

KRISHNA DEV JHARI. Modern scholar, whose chief works are : *Hindi Nirgun Sant Kavya, Ashtachhap aur Nand Das, Ashtachhap aur Parmanand Das* and *Hindi Sahitya men Vibhatsa Rasa.*

KRISHNA DEV PRASAD, THE LATE. Magahi poet and scholar, who may be regarded as the founder of modern Magahi literature. He at first translated works from Sanskrit into Bengali and later composed original Magahi poems, which are full of descriptions of Nature and are based on folk-tunes. His *Magahi Bhasha aur Uska Sahitya* (1953) is a history of Magahi Language and Literature.

KRISHNA DEV SHARANSINGH, RAO 'GOP' (1865-97). Poet, who was connected with the ruling family of Bharatpur. In Kashi, his works : *Prem Sandesh* (The Message of Love), *Man-Charitra* (Life of Man) and *Dohavali* appeared in 'Harishchandra Magazine', 'Harishchandra Chandrika' and Badri Narayan Chaudhari's 'Anand Kadambini', all journals. He also wrote a romantic drama : *Madhuri* (1888).

KRISHNA DEV UPADHYAY. Modern Bhojpuri scholar, whose chief works are : *Bhojpuri Lok-Git* (Pts. I and II ; collections of 701 songs of 40 types), *Bhojpuri aur Uska Sahitya* (Bhojpuri and its Literature), *Bhojpuri Lok-Sahitya ka Adhyayan* (A Study of Bhojpuri Folk-literature), *Bhojpuri Lok-Kathayen* (a collection of 300 folk-tales), *Lok-Sahitya ki Bhumika* (Background of the Folk-literature), *Bhojpuri LokSanskriti ka Adhyayan* (A Study of Bhojpuri folk-culture) and *Avadhi Lok-Git*.

KRISHNA DEVI PANJIKAR (fl. 1920-40). Marathi-speaking Hindi poetess, whose poems were influenced by Chhayavadi Hindi poets.

KRISHNA DIVAKAR. Marathi-speaking modern Hindi writer, whose chief works are: *Maharashtra ka Hindi Lok-Kavya* (Hindi Poetry of Maharashtra ; 1964), *Bhonsla Rajdurbar ke Hindi Kavi* (Hindi Poets of Bhonsla's Court ; 1969), *Hindi Sahitya : Shodh aur Samiksha* and *Kavindracharya Saraswati krit Kavindra-Chandrika*. He has also composed poems on various subjects.

KRISHNA GITAVALI. See *Shrikrishna Gitavali*.

KRISHNA GOPAL. Poet, whose *Jay Dhananjay* (1983) is a *Prabandh-Kavya*.

KRISHNA GOPAL SHARMA. Modern Rajasthani poet, who has composed poems in the style of Nayi Kavita and is also noted for his essays.

KRISHNA GOSWAMI (fl. 1854-99). Folk-poet of Haryana, who composed and staged the *Sangs* : *Dilbar*, *Budhamal*, *Bishno* and *Gulbakavali*.

KRISHNA-JANMA. See *Man Bodh*.

KRISHNA JIVAN LACHHIRAM. See *Lachhiram*.

KRISHNA KALA PATHIK. Modern Hindi poetess of Fiji, who is noted for her stray poems.

KRISHNA KANT MISHRA. Modern Maithili writer, who is noted for his *Atma-Maryada* (one-act plays) and *Maithili Sahityak Itihas*. He has also written critical articles.

KRISHNA KAVI. Poet of the Riti school, who was son of Biharilal (q.v.), the great Hindi poet. His commentary on *Bihari Satsai* was composed during 1728-33. He used the *Savaiya* metre to explain the meanings of *Dohas* ; he also explained the *Kavyangs*.

KRISHNA KUMAR KHULLAR. Modern poet and scholar whose

chief works are : *Bhumi jo Hai Nahin* and *D.H.L awrence ki Kavitayen.*

KRISHNA KUMAR MUKHOPADHYAY. Bengali-speaking Hindi writer, who wrote a drama : *Tulsidas* (1929).

KRISHNA LAL. Brajbhasha Riti poet, who was son of Mahant Mohanlal. He composed *Krishna-Vinod* (1815 ; on *Nayika-Bhed*), *Rasa-Bhushan* (1817 ; on *Alankars*) and wrote a commentary on *Bhaktamal* at the instance of Rathoreji, Rani of Maharao Raja Vishnusingh of Bundi.

KRISHNA LAL BAJAJ. Sindhi-speaking modern Hindi journalist, who had been associated with the Bombay edition of the 'Navbharat Times', a Hindi daily, where his articles appear from time to time.

KRISHNA LAL BIHARI. Modern Hindi poet of Mauritius, whose *Main Hun Kaliyugi Bhagvan* is a collection of his poems ; his *Pahla Kadam* (1960) is a novelette.

KRISHNA MENON. Malayalam-speaking modern Hindi writer, who tr. Sardar Panikkar's Malayalam novel *Kerala Singham* (The Lion of Kerala) into Hindi. He also tr. a Malayalam drama : *Urub* into Hindi under the title *Mitti aur Nari* (The Clay and the Woman).

KRISHNAMURTI. Telugu-speaking modern Hindi poet, whose chief work is : *Kuntal Raso* (a poetical work in the Raso style on the battle of Sultan Tughlak of Delhi and Jambukeshwar).

KRISHNAMURTHI, M.S. Kannada-speaking modern Hindi writer, whose chief works are : *Aparajit* (historical), *Rag Kanada* (1975 ; historical), *Parshuram Ji Behanen* (The Sisters of Parshuram ; social ; 1978) (all novels), a comparative study of Hindi and Kannada literature, *Kavishri Kuvempu* and *Kavishri Bendre* (critical works on the two Kannada poets, who were the Bharatiya Gyanpith Award Winners, with prose translations of their poems). He has written short stories as also tr. some essays and sketches of Siddavvanahalli Krishna Sharma from Kannada into Hindi.

KRISHNAMURTI, N.D. Kannada-speaking modern Hindi writer, who tr. B. Puttaswamayya's Kannada work, *Udayaravi* into Hindi.

KRISHNANAND. Maithili dramatist, whose *Dharma-datt-Charit Natak* was written under the patronage of Mahindra Mall

(1689-94), the ruler of Kantipur (Kathmandu) House of Nepal.

KRISHNANAND GUPTA. Modern Bundelkhandi scholar, whose chief work is *Isuri ki Phagen* (research).

KRISHNAPATI. Maithili poet, who composed lyrics. He was patronized by Maharaja Madhav Singh (1776-1808).

KRISHNA PRASAD SINGH AKHAURI (fl. early 20th cent.). Early novelist, who wrote a historical novel : *Vir Chudamani* (The Brave Chudamani).

KRISHNA RAINA (1940-). Kashmiri-speaking Hindi writer, who holds a doctorate on Hindi and Kashmiri Nirgun-Sant-Kavya (*Hindi aur Kashmiri Nirgun Sant Kavya* : *Tulnatmak Adhyayan*) and has also written research articles and short stories. Her latest work is *Lokanchal aur Sahityanveshan.*

KRISHNA SHANKAR CHIRATE. Marathi-speaking modern Hindi writer, whose short stories have appeared in various magazines.

KRISHNA SHANKAR SHUKLA. Modern critic, who is known for his works : *Keshav ki Kavyakala* (The Poetic Art of Keshav), *Kavivar Ratnakar* and *Adhunik Hindi Sahitya ka Itihas* (The History of Modern Hindi Literature).

KRISHNA SHARMA. Modern Hindi writer of Mauritius, who, in collaboration with Ganesh Teklal, has written *Ramgoolam ki Jivni.*

KRISHNA SOBTI. Fiction writer, whose chief novels are: *Dar se Bichhuri* (Cut off from Branch), *Mitro Marjani* (Depraved Mitro ; 1967 ; it describes Mitro's insatiable lust for sex), *Surajmukhi Andhere Ke* (The Sunflowers of Darkness ; 1972 ; bitter experiences of the heroine after rape) and *Ham Hashmat* (1977) ; *Zindaginama* (The Document of Life ; 1979), a regional novel, is her magnum opus. *Yaron ke Yar—Tin Pahad* and *Badalon ke Ghere* (The Rings of the Clouds) are her short story collections. Her popular short story is 'Sikka Badal Gaya Hai' (The Coin is Changed). The *Surajmukhi Andhere ke* has been tr. into English.

KRISHNAVATI. Poetess, who fl. before 1843 ; she composed *Vivah-Vilas*, describing the marriage of Krishna and Radha.

KRISHNAN KUTTY, K.V. Malayalam-speaking modern Hindi writer, who has written some short dramas (*Laghu Rupak*) in

Hindi. He has also written a critical work : *Swati Tirunal.*

KRISHNAN NAIR, P. Malayalam-speaking modern Hindi scholar, who is the author of *Tribhasha Kosh* (Tri-lingual Dictionary).

KRISHNAN NAMPIYAR. Malayalam-speaking modern writer, who has tr. Malayalam short stories into Hindi.

KSHEM CHANDRA GEORGE. Modern Hindi poet of Trinidad, who is noted for his stray poems.

KSHEM CHANDRA 'SUMAN' (1916-). Poet and writer, whose chief works are : *Mallika* (1943 ; a collection of poems), *Bandi ke Gan* (1945 ; songs), *Kara* (1946), *Nari Tere Rup Anek* (edited poems), *Sahitya Vivechan* (1956), *Adhunik Hindi Sahitya, Adhunik Hindi Kavyitriyon ke Prem Git, Hindi Sahitya aur Uski Pragati* and *Divangat Hindi Sevi* (vol. I, 1981 ; vol. II, 1983).

KSHEM DHARI SINHA. Maithili writer, whose *Nibandh Chandrika* (1963) is a collection of philosophical essays ; he has also written a work on psychology (*Manovigyan*).

KSHEM LATA VOKHLU. Kashmiri-speaking modern Hindi writer, whose two novels : *Kashmir ki Dharti* (The Land of Kashmir) and *Jhil aur Kamal* (The Lake and the Lotus) portray Kashmiri life and culture.

KSHIRSAGAR, BA. G. (fl. 1920-40). Marathi-speaking Hindi novelist, whose works are : *Sunanda* and *Bargad ki Chhanh.* He also wrote short stories under the title : *Kothri ke Chhed.*

KUAN KA MAHANT. Modern Hindi (Maithili) poet of Nepal, whose chief work is *Ram.*

KUBER DAS (1772-1867). Saint-poet of Gujarat, who belonged to the village Sarsa in the Khera district. He was also known by the name of 'Karunasagar'. His works in Hindi are : *Sakarta Bhashya, Sadachar Patrika, Hansla Leva, Vigyansukrit Manidip, Vishwabhram Vishwans, Gyangita, Advait-dvait Narved Chintamani, Vishwabodh Chosra, Gyan-Bhakti-Vairagya-Nirupan, Tithi Granth-Gyan Shiromani, Shikshapatri, Pancham Shasht Ved, Bhav-Timir-Bhaskar, Param Siddhant Pranav Kalpataru, Keval Prakash, Guru-Mahima, Agadh-Bodh, Bhajan-Upasna Vidhi* and stray *Padas.* The language betrays the influence of Gujarati, Arabic and Persian.

KUBER NATH RAY. Writer, whose chief essay collections are :

Priya Nilkanthi, *Rasa Akhetak*, *Gandhmadan*, *Nishad Bansuri*, *Vishad Yoga*, *Kamdhenu* (1980) and *Kirat Nadi men Chandramadhu* (1984).

KUDINOVA, IRINA JARJIVNA (1929-). Soviet Hindi scholar, who is an editor in the Progressive Publishing House in Moscow and has edited some Hindi works of Karl Marx, Lenin, Gorky and others.

KUKTANAND SWAMI (1757-1829). Saint-poet of Swaminarayan Sect, who was a native of Amareli in Gujarat. His Hindi works are : *Guru Chaubis*, *Panch-Ratnam*, *Satsang-Shiromani*, *Kapil Gita*, *Narayan Charitram*, *Vivek Chintamani*, *Bhagavadgita Bhasha*, *Avadhut Gitam*, *Shikshapatri Bhasha*, *Mukund-Bavni*, *Vasudevavtar Charitram*, *Narayan Kavacham*, *Baikunth-Dham Darshanam*, *Gun Vibhag*, *Narayan Gita* and *Utsavamrit* (a collection of *Padas*). On his writings, there appears to be influence of Mira and Kabir (qq.v.).

KUL BHUSHAN (1920-). Short story writer, whose chief short story collections are : *Pagdandi aur Parchhaiyan* (1961), *Lalak* (1967) and *Pani aur Ret ke Kan* (The Water and Grains of Sand).

KULPATI. Maithili poet, who was noted for his lyrics. He was patronized by Maharaja Madhav Singh (1776-1808).

KULPATI MISHRA (fl. 1666-86). Poet of the Riti school, who was born at Agra. He was nephew (sister's son) of Bihari (q v.), the celebrated Hindi poet. His father's name was Parshuram. Mishra was the court-poet of Maharaj Ram Singh (son of Maharaj Jay Singh) of Jaipur, the patron of Bihari. Among his works : *Dron-Parva* (based on the *Mahabharat*), *Yukti-Tarangini* (The Ripples of Skill), *Nakhshikh*, *Sangram-Sar* and *Rasa-Rahasya* (The Mystery of *Rasa*), the last one is the most popular. Mishra was an erudite scholar of Sanskrit literature and poetics and dealt comprehensively with various aspects of literary criticism in his book *Rasa-Rahasya*. The work was composed after the manner of Mammat's *Kavya Prakash* and his views are in accord with those of Mammat, yet at places he has offered his own original criticism. Finding the verse inadequate as a fit medium for discussion of such a subject, he introduced prose. The language he employed is pure Braj, with the inclusion of Prakrit words, here and there.

KULANAND DAS 'NANDAN'. Modern Maithili writer, who is noted for his short stories as also for his essays in *Saphal Jivan* .

KULANAND JHA 'KULESH'. Modern Maithili poet, whose chief work is *Dinmani*, a collection of lyrics.

KULANAND MISHRA. Maithili scholar, whose *Adhunik Maithili Kavita* (1979) is a critical work, while *Khadhi a Khadhi* (1981) is a one-act play.

KULKARNI, GO. RA. Marathi-speaking modern Hindi dramatist, who is noted for his *Kisan Pandit*. He has also written critical works : *Pauranik Kavya : Adhunik Sandarbh* and in collaboration with Su. Go. Gokapar : *Hindi Sahitya men Pratibimbit Vichar Pravah, Adhunik Hindi Kavita* and *Nirala Sahitya : Mulyankan*.

KULKARNI, M. TU. Marathi-speaking modern Hindi writer, whose chief work is : *Shri Smarth Jivan Darshan*.

KUMAR. See *Kalikumar Das 'Kumar'*.

KUMAR GANGANAND SINHA. Maithili writer, whose *Agilahi* (1935) has remained an incomplete novel. He has also written short stories ; his collection of short stories *Bihadi* describes the spirit of revolt among the lower classes of Mithila. His essays with reformist and revolutionary zeal are marked by speed and sweeping force. He also wrote critical articles. His one-act play, *Jivan Sangharsh* deals with modern life and is counted amongst the best plays.

KUMAR-HARAN. Brajavali drama by an unknown Assamese writer, which belongs to the middle of the 18th century.

KUMAR-HRIDAY. Writer, who was noted for his historical drama, *Bhagnavashesh* (The Ruins ; 1936).

KUMAR MANI BHATT. Poet of the Riti school, whom *Shivsingh Saroj* mentions a resident of Gokul. He composed a Riti work : *Rasik Rasal* (The Amorist's Juice ; *c*. 1746), in which he called himself as a son of Harivallabh Shastri. His *Rasika Ranjana* is a Sanskrit work. According to some scholars, he was a native of the village Natyahara of Sagar district and was patronized by some rulers of Bundelkhand.

KUMAR SHIV. Panjabi-speaking modern Hindi poet, who is noted for his poems.

KUMAR VIMAL (1932-). Critic and poet, whose chief works are : *Mulya aur Mimansa* (The Values and Reflections), *Saundarya Shastra ke Tatwa* (The Elements of Aesthetics), *Kavyanushilan* :

Adhunik-Atyadhunik (Deep Study of Poetry : Modern and Ultra-modern), *Chhayavad ka Saundaryashastriya Adhyayan* (The Aesthetic Study of Chhayavad), *Kavya Rachna Prakriya* (all criticism), *Angara* (The Embers), *Ye Umang Anubhav Amrit*, *Ek Samarik Chuppi* (A Strategic Silence), *Rang Khatre men Hai* and *Ek Chhoti si Larai* (A Trivial Conflict ; 1980) (poetical collections).

KUMARENDRA PARASNATH SINGH. Poet, whose chief collection of poems is *Itihas ka Sanvad* (The Dialogue of History ; 1979).

KUMARESH KASHYAP. Maithili poet and journalist, whose *Baital Katha* (1981) is a collection of 7 satirical essays. His *Pratidhwani* (1982) is a collection of foreign poems tr. into Maithili. His real name is Ram Lochan Thakur.

KUMBH KARAN SANDU (fl. *c* 1663 1723). Rajasthani poet, whose works are : *Ratan Raso*, *Jaychand Raso* (no longer extant), *Maharaja Raysinghji ri Satiyon ra Kavitta* (a moving account in 33 verses of the Sati after the death of Rathore Rao Raysingh of Nagore at Med near Sholapur in 1676) and stray verses including *Dohas* and *Gits* on contemporary heroes and events. The first poem, *Ratan Raso* (1675) deals with the battle of Dharmat fought by Shah Jehan's sons for succession.

KUMBHA, MAHARANA (fl. 1433-68). Maharana of Chittor, who was also a poet. His stray verses in different popular metres are available.

KUMBHAN DAS (1468-1583). Poet, who was one of the members of the *Ashtachhap*. A peasant of a village named Jamunamati near Govardhan, he was a Kshatriya by caste and supported his large family by farming. His youngest son, Chaturbhuj Das was also a member of the *Ashtachhap*. Akbar, the great Moghul Emperor, wanted to admit him to his court but he belittled all royal honours and blatantly told him that his muse was at the service of God only. He, however, accepted an invitation from Akbar and visited Fatehpur Sikri, where he recited some of his devotional lyrics Only his stray verses are available, which treat of Krishna's childhood and his love with Gopis.

KUMUD CHANDRA (1588-1630). Gujarati-speaking Jain saint-poet, who was born at Gopur and was a disciple of Rantnakirti (q.v.). Of his 28 works and some stray verses, *Neminath Barahmasa*, *Nemishwar Git*, *Hindolna Git*, *Vanjara Git*, *Desh*

Dharma Git, *Shil Git*, *Parshwanath Git*, *Chintamani Parshwanath Git* are prominent. The language is Braj mixed with Gujarati.

KUMUDISH (fl. prior to 1685). Maithili poet, whose lyrics were quoted in anthologies.

KUNAL. Maithili poet, whose first collection of poems is *Mitak Nam* (1982). He has also tr. into Maithili the Iranian poet, H. Sayeha's poem 'Julus' (1982).

KUNDAN LAL SHAH (fl. *c.* 1925). Writer, who was noted for his *Ramlila Natak*.

KUNJ BIHARI CHAUBE. Modern Chhattisgarhi poet, whose poems portray the exploitation of the peasants and workers of Chhattisgarh region.

KUNJ BIHARI SHARMA. Rajasthani writer, whose sketches, *Batan hi Chalai* (1968) are natural.

KUNTALA KUMARI SAVAT (1901-38). Oriya poetess and novelist, whose *Varmala* is a collection of her Hindi songs. She also edited some Hindi magazines.

KUNTIDEVI AGNIHOTRI (1940-). Bagheli folk-poetess of Rewa, whose stray poems are noted for their sweetness.

KUNVAR BECHAN (1941-). Modern poet, whose chief works are : *Bhitar Sankal Bahar Sankal* (1978 ; collection of *Gits*) and *Shamiyane Kanch Ke* (1983 ; collection of *Ghazals*).

KUNVAR KANT. Maithili novelist, whose chief work is *Sehenta* (1967).

KUNVAR KUSHAL (fl. 1737). Jain poet, who, along with Kanak Kushal (q.v.) was associated with Brajbhasha Vidyalaya, established by Maharao Lakhpat of Kachh. On his patron, he wrote *Lakhpat Pingal* (on prosody), *Lakhpat Jas Sindhu* (on *Alankars*) and *Lakhpat-Manjari* in the form of a dictionary. His most important work, however, is *Parsat Nam-Mala*, a Persian-Brajbhasha Dictionary. On the name of his patron's son, Gohad, he wrote another work on prosody, *Gohad Pingal*.

KUNWAR NARAYAN (1927-). Poet, whose poems are included in *Tisra Saptak* (q.v.) and whose poetical collections are : *Chakravyuh* (A Circular Array of Troops ; 1956) and *Parivesh, Ham Tum* (Boundaries, We and You ; 1961) ;

Atmajayi (1965) is a *Prabandh-Kavya*, based on the Nachiketa story in the *Kathopanishad*. His latest collection of poems is *Apne Samne* (Before Me ; 1980), while *Akaron ke As-Pas* is his short story collection.

KUNVAR SHRI ANUPSINGHJI RI VELI. See *Gadan Virbhan Thakarsiyot*.

KUNVAR SINGH, BABU. Modern Hindi poet of Fiji, who has since 1935 composed a huge collection of 1000 *Bhajans*.

KURUKSHETRA. See *Ramdhari Singh 'Dinkar'*.

KUSHAL DHIR (fl. 1639-71). Rajasthani Jain poet, whose preceptor's name was Kalyan Labh. He wrote three works : a commentary on *Veli Krisan Rukmini Ri* by Prithwiraj, a commentary on *Rasikpriya* by Keshavdas and *Lilavati Raso* (1671) ; the first two works are in prose, while the last work is in verse. The language is Rajasthani, mixed with Gujarati.

KUSHAL LABH (*c*. 1523-93). Jain Rajasthani poet, who wrote on a variety of subjects : popular folk-tales like *Madhavanal Kamkandala Chaupai* (on the romance of Madhavanal and Kamkandala) and *Dhola Marvani Chaupai* ; stories and stray verses like *Agad Datt Ras*, *Pujyavahan Git*, following the Jain traditions, *Durga Satsai* (based on the 'Durga Saptashati' in the *Markandeya Purana* and retelling the Durga legend in simple language) and *Bhavani Chhand* on Devi or Shakti (on prosody), *Pingal Shiromani* (on various metres, including 75 figures of speech and a collection of synonyms of 24 words named *Nam Mala*). The *Pingal Shiromani* is the first work of its kind, where the author has explained the subject through narration of the story of Ram, though it is also ascribed to Kunvar Har Raj of Jaisalmer, whose Guru Kushal Labh was. About Dhola Maru tale, couplets of varying forms were popular. Kushal Labh collected them from various sources, mixed his own *Chaupais* with them and gave the work an artistic form This also explains the differences in forms found in various manuscripts. So far *Madhavanal Kamkandala Chaupai* is concerned, Kushal Labh composed the poem in 1559 to satisfy the curiosity of his crown-prince Har Raj of Jaisalmer. It consists of 662 verses, mostly *Chaupais*, in easy Rajasthani, including some Sanskrit *Shlokas* and Prakrit *Gathas*. The story follows the tale given in Ganpati's *Prabandh*, but Kushal Labh displays originality in giving different stories about the earlier lives of the lovers. See *Ganpati Kayasth*.

KUSHAL MISHRA (fl. 1769). Poet of the Ram-cult, whose chief work is *Ganga Natak* (on the story of the Ganges) ; he belnoged to Agra.

KUSHESHWAR KUMAR. Maithili poet, who was noted for his didactic poems : *Strikartavya* (1924) and *Shikshasopan* (1936).

KUSUM ANSAL. Poetess and writer, who is noted for her *Maun ke Do Pal*, *Dhuen ka Sach* (collection of poems), *Apni-apni Yatra*, *Uski Panchvati*, *Us Tak* (novels) and *Speed-breaker* (collection of short stories).

KUSUM KUMAR. Poetess and dramatist, whose *Trishnankit* (Thirst-marked ; 1980), a collection of poems is noted for simplicity, naturality and straight-forwardness ; her other collection of poems is *Rasta-bhar Jungle*. Her dramas are : *Suno Shaifali* (Listen Shaifali ; 1979), *Sanskar ko Namaskar* (a satire on social reformers), *Dilli Uncha Sunti Hai* (Delhi is Hard of Hearing ; 1982 ; a satire on bureaucracy), *Mada Mitti*, *Om Kranti Kranti* and *Ravanlila*; one of her publications is *Bayan* (The Statement ; 1981) ; *Patte Badalte Hain* is her short story collection. Her critical work is *Hindi Natya Chintan*.

KUTBAN (fl. early 16th cent). Sufi poet of the court of Husain Shah, the king of Jaunpur. A disciple of Sheikh Burhan Chishti, he composed *Mrigavati* (q.v.).

KUTTAN PILLAI. Malayalam-speaking modern Hindi writer, who has tr. Epattachchhan's *Adhyatma Ramayana* into Hindi prose ; the work has been published from Lucknow.

KUTTAN PILLAI, N.P. Telugu-speaking modern Hindi scholar, whose publications are : *Pant Kavya men Bimb-Yojna* (imagism in Pant), *Pant* : *Chhayavadi Vyaktitwa* aur *Krititwa* (1970), *Kerali Vaibhav* (essays on the glory of Kerala), *Adhyayan aur Anusandhan* and *Tulnatmak Vyakaran* (a comparative study of Hindi and Malayalam grammars). Along with Bhimsen Nirmal and Vijayvir Vidyalankar, he has ed. *Dakshin men Ramkatha* (The Story of Ram in South India ; 1974).

KUZIN, VYACHESLAV VLADIMIROVICH (1939-). Soviet Hindi scholar, who is a Lecturer in Hindi in the Patrice Lumumba University. He has done his doctorate on Vidyapati and has written several articles on his poetry.

L

LABDHODAY (1623-93). Jain Rajasthani poet, of whose seven narrative poems, only the four : *Padmini Charit Chaupai* (his chief work, which is on the model of Hemratan's poem and is meant to be sung in different folk tunes and musical modes), *Malay Sundari Chaupai*, *Ratanchud Manichud Chaupai* and *Gunavali Chaupai* are now extant. The first two are written to show the glory of chastity and the other two of charity and other virtues.

LACHHIRAM (fl. *c.* 1715). Poet, whose *Karunabharan Natak*, recently discovered, deals in seven scenes with Krishna's life, his childhood, his pranks with the *Gopis* and the role he played at Kurukshetra. The play, written in excellent Brajbhasha, occupies an important place as being the first *Kavya Natak* in that style of writing. His other chief works are : *Dampati Rang*, *Rag Vichar* and *Gyananand Natak*.

LACHHIRAM BRAHMABHATT (1841-1904). Poet of the Riti school, who was a resident of Almora (Basti). On the names of his patrons including Raja Mansingh of Ayodhya, he wrote Riti works : *Prem-Ratnakar* (The Ocean of Love), *Pratap-Ratnakara*, *Man Singh Ashtak*, *Lakshmishwar Ratnakar*, *Ravan-eshwar-Kalpataru*, *Kamalanand-Kalpataru*, etc. He was a poet of considerable powers and although he belonged to a place away from the main Brajbhasha tract, he knew how to use the dialect.

LADLIDAS (fl. 17th cent. ?). Poet of the Krishna-cult (Chaitanya Sect), whose *Padas* are still sung at the Ladliji-ka Mandir at Barsana.

LAHAR. See *Jayshankar Prasad*.

LAHARI SIDRAM (fl. 18th cent.). Marathi folk-poet (*Shahir*), who also made compositions in Hindi.

LAJJARAM MEHTA, PANDIT (1863-1931). Novelist, who was born

in Bundi (Rajasthan) in a Gujarati Brahmin family. His chief works are: *Dhurt Rasiklal* (Rasiklal the Rascal; 1902), *Swatantra Rama aur Partantra Lakshmi* (Independent Rama and Dependent Lakshmi) and *Adarsh Hindu* (The Ideal Hindu); he has written 13 novels in all, all of them dealing with religion and family life in Indian homes.

LAJPATI, PINGALI. Telugu-speaking Hindi poet, who composed a poetical work in 1929 on the life of Kancharl Gopanna or Ramdas, the famous Ram-devotee of Bhadrachalam. On the advice of his friends, he composed it in Khari Boli and got it published in 1934.

LAKHADAS (fl. early 16th cent.). Poet of the Krishna-cult (Chaitanya Sect), who was a disciple of Ramraj (q.v.). *Shri Vrindavan Kalpadrum* is his poetical work.

LAKHAN CHAND (fl. prior to 1685). Maithili poet, whose lyrics were quoted in anthologies.

LAKHMI CHAND, PANDIT, THE LATE (b. 1903). Celebrated folk-poet of Haryana, who was born at the village Jati in Rohtak district of Haryana. For 4 years, he played a female role in the *Sangs* staged by others, but in 1924, he formed his own troupe. In the initial stages of his career, Lakhmi Chand freed the themes of the '*Sangs*' from religious and puranic subjects to which they had become confined and included in them a blend of love themes and youth, but later on with his contact with Man Singh, he came to realize the importance of religious and Puranic literature. A poet of extraordinary genius, he is claimed to be the greatest *Sangi* of Haryana. People of Haryana held him in high esteeme and called him 'Dada Lakhmi'.

The *Sangs*, he composed and staged are: *Shahi Lakkad-hara, Nautanki, Sarande, Bharthari, Pingla, Chandrahas, Mirabai. Jaimal-Fatta, Anjanadevi, Satyavan Savitri, Harishchandra, Seth Tara Chand, Bija Sorath, Puranmal, Sarvar Nir, Rup Basant, Dharmakaur, Hur Menaka, Shakuntala, Chirharan, Ukha-Aniruddh, Dharu Bhagat, Dharmapal, Shanta Kumari, Taku Tod Balti Phod, Chhore Bagdi, Hir Ranjha, Mahakde-Jyani Chor, Chandrakiran, Jamal, Raghubir Singh, Puranjan-Puranjani* and *Padmavat*.

LAKHPAT PINGAL. See *Hamirdan Ratanu*.

LAKHPAT RAO (fl. *c.* 1750). Maharao of Kachh, who had established a Brajbhasha Vidyalaya. Kanak Kushal and

Kunvar Kushal (qq.v) were associated with this Vidyalaya. The Maharao himself was a poet and his two works : *Shiv Vivah* and *Lakhpati Shringar* have so far been discovered.

LAKKHA BARHAT (fl. between 1550-1650). Rajasthani poet, who was a court-poet of Emperor Akbar. His stray verses in popular metres are available.

LAKSHMAN (fl. 1850). Poet of the Ram-cult, who was a native of Ayodhya ; he wrote *Ram-Ratnavali*.

LAKSHMAN CHOUDHARY 'LALIT'. Maithili scholar, whose research work is *Maithili Sahitya par Pauranik Prabhav* (1979).

LAKSHMAN GOVIND ATHALYE (fl. 1900-1920). Marathi-speaking Hindi writer, whose essays dealing with religious, social and cultural topics appeared in various magazines.

LAKSHMAN JHA. Maithili poet, whose *Ganga* (1966), an epic, is a veritable saga of the Aryan life and culture, while his *Shantidut* treats of the achievements of Jawahar Lal Nehru in the international field.

LAKSHMAN NARAYAN GARDE (1883-1960). Marathi-speaking Hindi writer, whose works are : *Shrikrishna Charitra*, *Gyanesh-war*, *Eknath*, *Tukaram* (biographical), *Lucknow ka Itihas*, *Nakli Professor* and *Miyan ke Kartut*, the last two novels He was a pioneer in the field of journalism. His popular essays are : 'Uddhar ka Marg', 'Matrishakti', 'Dev Danav-Manav-Yuddha', 'Gandhiji aur Satya', etc.

LAKSHMAN PRASAD 'DIN'. Modern Magahi writer, who is noted for his humorous and satirical short stories, poems and for his work, *Bittan Dada*.

LAKSHMAN PRASAD MISHRA. Supporter of Hindi in Italy, who is preparing a 'Hindi-Italian Dictionary' ; in this task he is being assisted by several scholars of Italian Universities. He is also engaged in the tr. of the *Ramcharitmanas* into Italian. He has married an Italian lady and is now an Italian citizen.

LAKSHMAN PRASAD 'MITRA' (b. 1899). Modern Avadhi folk-poet, who has composed *Alha*, *Barahmasa* and *Bhajan-mala* in Avadhi. Influenced by the poetry of Padhis (q.v.), he composed also several poems in Avadhi, e.g., 'Prem-lila', 'Ghus ka Janma' (on bribery), 'Somvari', 'Jagaran Bela', etc He has also written a drama, *Ban Shayya* (based on the *Mahabharat*). 'Mitra' was born in the village Hindora in Sitapur district.

LAKSHMAN SEN PADMAVATI KATHA. *Prabandh-Kavya* (1459) in Rajasthani dialect by Damau, which deals with the love-story of Padmini and Lakshman Sen. It consists of 300 verses, mainly *Doha* and *Chaupai*, divided into three parts. There are also a few Sanskrit *Shlokas* and Prakrit *Gahas*. The story is a mixture of miracles, romance and valour and is important for its record of socio-religious beliefs and antiquity of language.

LAKSHMAN SHASTRI. Malayalam-speaking modern Hindi writer, who has tr. into Hindi and has himself published Toppil Bhasi's Malayalam dramas under the titles of *Utthan* (The Rise) and *Punji* (The Capital). He also tr. into Hindi K. Damodaran's Malayalam novel under the title of *Padmavati*.

LAKSHMAN SINGH. Writer, who was noted for his drama, *Ghulami ka Nasha* (The Intoxication of Slavery ; 1924).

LAKSHMAN SINGH, RAJA (1826-96). Writer, who was one of the founders of modern prose. A resident of Agra, he was awarded the title of 'Raja' by the British Government. He was a poet too and his Hindi tr. of *Shakuntala*, *Raghuvansh* and *Meghdut* are appreciated even today. His other works are : *History of Bulandshahr* (in English, Hindi and Urdu) and *Taziratehind*. His tr. of *Shakuntala* was published from London by Frederick Pincott and was a text-book for I.C.S. examination. Translated in 1863, it was originally in prose. But in the second edition the verses have been translated in verses and prose in prose. The prose is basically Hindi while Brajbhasha has been used for the verse.

Lakshman Singh was a Sanskrit scholar and his poetic diction blends the melody of Sanskrit with the characteristic sweetness of Brajbhasha poetry. As a writer of good prose, his idea of prose was different from that of Raja Shiv Prasad (q.v.). He considered Hindi and Urdu as separate tongues and in his Hindi prose, Urdu expressions have been carefully avoided. To further the cause of Hindi and to popularise his chaste style, he also started a Hindi periodical, 'Praja Hitaishi' from Agra.

LAKSHMAN SINGH 'RASVANT'. Modern Rajasthani poet, who has composed Nature, patriotic and heroic poems.

LAKSHMAYYA SETTY, K. Telugu-speaking Hindi scholar, whose publications are : *Sursagar men Pratik Yojna* (1972) and *Ritikal : Ek Sarvekshan* (1964).

LAKSHMI, S. Tamil-speaking Hindi scholar, whose research work is *Dr. Nagendra ki Saiddhantik evam Vyavaharik Samiksha : Vishleshan aur Mulyankan* (on Dr. Nagendra's role as a critic ; 1971).

Lakshmi Chand Jain (1909-). Writer, whose chief works are : *Kagaz ki Kishtiyan* (The Paper Boats) and *Naye Rang, Naye Dhang* (New Days, New Ways) (essays) ; he has also ed. a novel, *Gyarah Sapnon ka Desh.* His novel is *Antardwandwon Ke Par.* He edited 'Gyanoday' for two decades. He is associated with the editing and managing the publications of the Bharatiya Gyanpith and is the Secretary of the Gyanpith Award Committee.

LAKSHMI DAS (fl. 1676). Jain poet, whose works are : *Yashodhar Charit* (on previous births of Raja Yashodhar) and *Shrenik Charit* (on the life of Raja Shrenik).

LAKSHMI DHAR MALVIYA. Modern Hindi writer, who is now associated with Hindi studies in Japan. He is the author of several novels (*Kisi aur Subah, Dayara, Retghari*) and a short story collection : *Him Ujjas.*

LAKSHMI DHAR VAJPEYI (fl. early 20th cent.). Writer, who tr. Kolhatkar's Marathi drama, *Swami Vivekanand* into Hindi.

LAKSHMI KANT. Modern essayist, whose chief work is *Main ne Kaha* (I Said).

LAKSHMI KANT VERMA (1929-). Socialist poet and writer, whose chief works are : *Atukant* (Without Rhyme), *Tisra Paksh* (The Third Side), *Kanchan Mrig* (collections of poems), *Khali Kursi ki Atma* (The Soul of a Vacant Chair ; 1958), *Ek Kati Hui Zindagi : Ek Kata Hua Kaghaz* (A Life Cut : A Paper Torn ; 1965), *Terra Cotta* (1971 ; on the hypocritical life of New Delhi), *Safed Chehre* (1971), *Tisra Prasang* (The Third Context ; novels), *Roshni Ek Nadi Hai* (Light is a River), *Thahari Hui Zindagi* (The Standing Life ; 1980 ; dramas), *Admi ka Zahar* (Poison of Man ; collection of one-act plays), *Nayi Kavita ke Pratiman* (Patterns of New Poetry ; 1957) and *Naye Pratiman : Purane Nikash* (New Patterns : Old Tests ; both criticism) ; he has written a good number of short stories as well : *Nim ke Phul* is his short story collection.

LAKSHMI KUMARI CHUNDAWAT. Modern Rajasthani scholar and writer, who has made a significant contribution to the study of Rajasthani folk-songs (*Rajasthani Lok-Git*) She has edited the *Gatha* of *Bagadavat* (q.v.) after taking it down from a Bhopa as also edited *Virmayan* (q.v.). She has retold many folk-tales in *Rajasthani Lok-Gatha*, and has also written such stories for children. She is noted for her historical and semi-historical stories : *Manjhal Rat* (1957), *Mumal* (1961), *Gir Uncha Uncha Gadhan* (1960), *Kai Re Chakva Vat* (19 0 and *Amolak Vatan* (1962) ; most of the stories have been written in the Rajasthani *Vat* style, with mixed description of the environment, pleasant and precise diction and powerful expression of emotion. For her one-act play, *Sam Dharma Maji*, she has taken the theme from Rajput history. She has also written essays : *Mewari Phagan*, short stories and *Gadya Kavyas*, e.g., 'Mat Bhom', etc.

LAKSHMIKUTTI AMMA, P. Malayalam-speaking modern Hindi writer, who has written some one-act plays in Hindi as also a work : *Guruvayur*.

LAKSHMI NARAYAN (fl. 1580). Poet of the Krishna-cult, whose chief work is *Prem-Trangini*.

LAKSHMI NARAYAN CHATURVEDI RASAPUNJ. Hindi poet of Mauritius, who was the author of two works : *Rasapunj Kundliyan* (1923) and *Shatabdi Saroj* (1935).

LAKSHMI NARAYAN GUPTA. Author of *Hindi Bhasha aur Sahitya ko Arya Samaj ki Den* (1961-62).

LAKSHMI NARAYAN LAL (1927-). Writer, whose chief works are :—

Novels : *Dharti ki Ankhen* (The Eyes of the Earth ; 1951 ; on the revolt against the feudal age), *Kale Phul ka Paudha* (The Plant with a Black Flower ; 1955), *Baya ka Ghonsla aur Sanp* (Weaverbird's Nest and Snake ; 1958 ; relating to rural life), *Rupa Jiva* (Living on Money ; 1959 ; description of business community), *Badi Champa* : *Chhoti Champa* (1971 ; on the problem of prostitution), *Man Vrindavan* (1966), *Prem : Ek Pavitra Nadi* (Love : A Holy River), *Devina*, *Hara Samudar Gopichandar*, *Shringar*, *Vasant ki Pratiksha* (Wait for Spring) and *Padmini ka Shap*.

Dramas : *Andha Kuan* (The Blind Well ; 1955), *Mada Cactus* (The Mother Cactus ; 1959), *Tin Ankhon Vali Machhali* (A Fish with Three Eyes), *Sundar Rasa*, *Sukha Sarovar* (The Dry Lake ; all the three in 1960), *Natak Tota Maina*, *Raktakamal* (The Red Lotus ; 1962), *Ratrani* (The Night Queen ; 1962), *Darpan* (The Mirror ; 1963), *Suryamukh* (The Sun-view ; 1968), *Kalanki* (The Disgraced), *Mister Abhimanyu* (1971), *Curfew*

(1972), *Narsingh Katha*, *Ek Satya Harishchandra*, *Yaksh Prashna* (The Questions of Yaksh), *Abdullah Divana*, *Vyaktigat* (Personal), *Sabrang Mohbhang*, *Sagun Panchhi* (1977), *Ganga Mati* (1977), *Guru*, *Panch Purush*, *Ramki Ladai*, *Lanka Kand*, *Kajri Van*, *Naya Tamasha*, *etc.*

One-act Play Collections : *Taj Mahal ke Ansu* (The Tears of Taj Mahal), *Parvat ke Pichhe* (Behind the Mountain), *Natak Bahurangi*, *Dusra Darvaza*, *Pratinidhi Ekanki*, *Natak Bahurupi* and *Satrangi*.

His other works are : *Sune Angan Rasa Barse* (Sweetness Falls in a Deserted Courtyard), *Ek Bund Jal* (One Drop of Water), *Ek aur Kahani*, *Daku Aye The* (short story collections), *Parsi Hindi Rangmanch* (Parsi Hindi Theatre ; criticism), *Adhunik Hindi Natak aur Rangmanch* (criticism), *Sat Rang Ekanki* (ed.) and *Jai Prakash* (biography). His short story 'Ram Janaki Road' is quite popular.

In his works, Lakshmi Narayan Lal generally assails modern social and political dogmas.

LAKSHMI NARAYAN MISHRA (1903-). Dramatistand poet, who was born at the Basti village in Azamgarh district. His chief works are : *Sannayasi* (The Recluse ; 1929 how a young man frustrated in love becomes a recluse), *Rakshas ka Mandir* (The Temple of a Demon ; 1931 ; depicting that an unprincipled pleasure-seeker is no better than a rudderless boat), *Rajayoga*, *Sindur ki Holi* (1943 ; exposing the corruption of official class), *Garud-dhwaj* (describing the re-establishment of the Aryan culture after the Shakas), *Ashok*, *Vatsaraj*, *Dashashwamedh*, *Vitasta ki Lahren* (The Waves of Vitasta), *Narad ki Vina* (Narad's Flute), *Mukti ka Rahasya* (The Mystery of Salvation), *Adhi Rat* (The Midnight). *Chakravyuh* (Circular Array of Troops), *Aparajit* (The Invincible), *Saryu-ki Dhar* (The Current of Saryu), *Ganga Dwar*, *Garva ka Shamun* (dramas), *Bhagvan Manu tatha anya Ekanki* (Bhagvan Manu and other One-Act Plays), *Ashok Van* (The Ashok Forest) (collection of one-act plays), *Antarjagat*. *Tapovan* (Penance Forest) (poetical collections), *Vir Gati* (Heroic Death ; poem). *Senapati Karna*, *Sahityik Nibandh* (Literary Essays) and *Dharti ka Hriday* (novel). Mishra's dramas are shadowed by idealism.

LAKSHMI NARAYAN SHASTRI, CHALLA. See *Challa Lakshminarayan Shastri*.

LAKSHMI NARAYAN SINGH 'ISH', the late. Brajbhasha poet of Kashi, whose chief poetical work *Lanka-Dahan* (The Burning of Lanka ; 1950) describes in 9 cantos the burning of Lanka by Hanuman.

LAKSHMI NARAYAN SUDHANSHU (1908-74). Critic, who was born at the village Rupsupar in the Purnea district of Bihar. His chief works are : *Kavya men Abhivyanjanavad* (The Expressionism in Poetry ; 1938), *Jivan ke Tattva aur Kavya ke Siddhant* (The Elements of Life and Principles of Poetry ; 1942), *Vyaktitva ki Jhankiyan* (Glimpses of Personality) and *Sampark Bhasha Hindi* (Hindi as Link Language). In his analysis of the expressionistic theory of art, Sudhanshu seems to sugg est that Croce has steered a middle course between Hegelian idealism and Marxist materialim• Sudhanshu also distinguishes between expressionism and 'Vakrokti', while Ramchandra Shukla considers them one. He has also written novels, short stories and essays. He ed. 'Avantika' and was Chairman of the Bihar Legislative Council.

LAKSHMI NATH DAS (fl. 1st half of the 19th cent.). Assamese poet, whose only drama in Hindi (Brajavali) is *Kumar-Haran Nat* or *Krishna-Vijay*, which treats of the love of Usha and Aniruddh.

LAKSHMI NATH GOSAIN. Maithili saint-poet, whose poems are both in Hindi and Maithili. His Maithil poems are of all kinds, but *Vishnupadas* are certainly his best works. Born in the middle of the 19th century in an orthodox Brahmin family in Bhagalpur district, he had a religious bentof mind from childhood and renounced the world shortly after his marriage. As a poet, Lakshminath had great creative imagi nation and in his home-district, he is still remembered as a-celebrated saint of miraculous powers. He gave new life to vernacular literature by trying to popularise the Vaishnavite faith throughout the length and breadth of Mithila. He contributed copiously to Maithill poetry.

LAKSHMI NATH JHA (fl. 1st half of 20th cent.). Maithili writer, who tr. *Naishada Charita* into Maithili from the original Sanskrit.

LAKSHMI NIWAS BIRLA (b. 1909). Modern Rajasthani writer, whose *Padmani ro Sarap* is a novel. His three other novels in Khari Boli are : *Sultan aur Nihalde*, *Anchal aur Ag* and *Prem ki Devi* ; *Sultan aur Nihalde* is available in English as *Romances of Princess Nihalde* (1968). *Phul aur Kunch* is his short story collection.

LAKSHMIPATI SINGH (d. 1979). Modern Maithili writer, who is noted for his short stories, an autobiography and a *Khand-Kavya* :*Satyavratopakhyan* (1934). He was a journalist, a critic and a poet as well. He also wrote humorous character-sketches in his *Parichayavali*. See *Harimohan Jha.*

LAKSHMI SAGAR VARSHNEY (1914-). Critic, whose chief works are : *Adhunik Hindi Sahitya* (1941), *Fort William College* (1947), *Bharatendu Harishchandra*, *Hindi Sahitya ka Itihas* (History of Hindi Literature ; 1952), *Adhunik Hindi Sahitya ki Bhumika* (1952), *Hindi Sahitya ka Itihas* (tr. from French), *Prachin Hindi Patra Sangrah* (Collection of Old Hindi Letters ; 1959), *Unnisvin Shatabdi* (The Nineteenth Century ; 1962), *Bharatiya Arya Bhasha* (1963 ; Hindi tr. of Jules Bloch's French work), *Pashchimi Alochana Shastra* (Western Criticism ; 1965), *Adhunik Kahani ka Pariparshva* (The Background of Modern Short Story ; 1966), *Bisvin Shatabdi Hindi Sahitya* : *Naye Sandarbh* (Twentieth Century Hindi Literature : New Contexts ; 1966), *Hindi Upanyas* : *Upalabdhiyan* (Hindi Novel : Achievements), *Pariprekshya aur Pratikriyaen* (Contexts and Reactions ; 1972), *Dwitiya Mahayuddhottar Hindi Sahitya ka Itihas* (History of Hindi Literature after World War II ; 1974), *Vividha* (Miscellaneous) and *Itihas aur Sahityetihas.*

He has done a remarkable work in the field of history of Hindi literature and criticism. He was Head of the Department of Hindi at Allahabad University.

LAKSHMI SAKHI (fl. early 20th cent.). Saint-poet, who was born at the Amanaur village in Saran district of Bihar. Son of Munshi Jagmohan Das, his original name was Lakshmidas but as he was a follower of Sakhi Sect, he was invariably called Lakshmi Sakhi. Out of his four works : *Amar Sidhi* (The Immortal Ladder), *Amar Kahani*, *Amar Vilas* and *Amar Pharas*, the first work is the most popular.

LAKSHMI TILAK GANI. See *Shantinath Dev Ras.*

LAKSHMIVATI 'LILA'. Modern Maithili writer, who is noted for her short stories : *Gohnak Sihenta*, dealing with feminine subjects. She has also composed poems.

LAKSHYADHAR PATHAK. Assamese-speaking modern Hindi writer, who has made a comparative study of the tendencies of Hindi and Assamese short stories.

LAL (fl. 1658-1707). Poet of Mau (in Bundelkhand), whose full name was Gorelal Purohit He spent the major part of his life at Orchha as the favourite poet of Maharaj Chhatrasal. The exact years of his birth and death are not known, but he was perhaps present with his patron in many a battle not only as a bard but as a fighter too. He composed three works: *Chhatra Prakash* (q.v.; describing the valour of Raja Chhatrasal), *Vishnu Vilas* and *Rajya Vinod*, but he is famous chiefly as the author of the first. It is due to the *Chhatra Prakash* that Lal is counted among the greatest narrative poets of Hindi (some critics assign him a place next to Tulsidas). Like Bhushan, Lal devoted himself to one of the bravest and most patriotic rulers of his time. Lal is also credited with the authorship of three more works: *Chhatrasal Shatak*, *Chhatra Kirti* and *Chhatra Chhand*.

LAL BALBIR (fl. 19th cent.). Poet of Vrindavan, who was an Agrawal Vaishya. A great devotee of Radhika, his works are: *Braj Vinod Hazara* (on the glory of the Braj country), *Radhashtak* and *Bal-Vinod-Pachisika* (on the sports of the child Krishna).

LAL CHAND (LAKSHODAY). Poet, who was connected with Maharana Jagat Singh of Mewar (1628-52); he composed *Padmini-Charit* on the story of Ratnasen and Padmini. The story here is different from the one mentioned in the *Padmavat* (q.v.).

LAL CHAND GUPTA. Modern scholar, whose chief works are: *Astitwavad: Darshnik tatha Sahityik Bhumika* and *Astitwavad aur Nayi Kahani*.

LAL DAS (fl. 1528). Poet of the Krishna-cult, who was a native of Raebareli; he composed *Haricharitra* (on the life of Krishna) and *Bhagavat Dasham Skandh Bhasha* (Hindi tr. of the 10th canto of the *Bhagavata*).

LAL DAS (1540-1648). Rajasthani saint-poet, who was the propounder of Lal Panth of Laldasi Sampraday. Born at Dholidup near Alwar (Rajasthan) in a poor family of Meo Musalman, his mother's name was Samada, while his father was Chandmal. He finally settled at Nagla, where he remained for 40 years till his death and was buried at Sherpur (Baghera). A householder, he earned his livelihood by manual labour, for he believed that whether a householder or a Sadhu, one should earn one's living by labour and should not go about begging. His sons, Pahada and Kutab, and daughter Sarupa were also noted for their devotion and *Sadhana*.

Although a Muslim, his disciples were both Muslims and Hindus; among his disciples were Haridas, Dungarsi Sadh, Prani Sadh and Bhikhan Sadh, all poets of high merit. The Mahant tradition still continues. *Ram Smaran* and *Kirtan* are the main means of *Sadhana* in this Sect, though Ram is *Nirgun* and *Nirakar*. The followers of this Sect are mostly found in and around Alwar.

No reliable manuscript of Laldas's *Vani* has yet been discovered, although an important collection of poems of Laldas and some other Laldasi poets compiled in 1930 by Dulichand Gupta is available. Over 700 *Sakhis* and 400 *Padas* go in the name of Laldas, though 125 *Sakhis* and 60 *Padas* are definitely his work. His language is Rajasthani, with mixture of Khari Boli and Braj. The poem *Chitavani*, attributed to him, is the work of Laldas of Dadu Sampraday.

LAL DAS (fl. 1643). Poet of the Ram-cult, who composed *Avadh Vilas*, a work dealing with the story of Ram in *Doha* and *Chaupai* metres The work is voluminous, though of common literary importance. Laldas's other work is *Bharatji-ki-Barahmasi*, a description of the 12 months of Bharat.

LAL DAS (fl. 1643). Saint-poet of Alwar and the founder of the Laldasi Sect. His teaching are incorporated in his *Bani*.

LAL DAS. Rajasthani saint-poet, who was in the tradition of Gharibdas (q.v.). He composed his *Nam-Mala* (mentioning the names of 152 disciples of Dadu) and *Chitavani* around 1778.

LAL DAS. Maithili poet, who composed *Rameshwar Ramayan* (1914), named after his patron, Maharajadhiraj Rameshwar Singh (1898-1929). A plain and simple narration of the story of quite a high order, the *Ramayan* emphasises Sita instead of Ram, but as a poetical work it is inferior to Chanda Jha's *Ramayan*. His *Shambhu Vinod Ganesh Khand* and several *Vratkathas* (1909-10) are Puranic tales in verse. Laldas's drama, *Savitri Satyavan*, written some 70 years earlier, has been published in book-form in 1979. His *Janaki Ramayan* (composed earlier) has been published in 1980 ; it represents Sita as 'Adishakti' and the story of Lakshmi, Sita and Radha has been interwoven in one. He also wrote *Virudavalis*.

LAL DAS SAHIB (fl. 1st part of 19th cent.). Hindi poet, who was a disciple of Ravi Sahib and was born at the village Murdhar of Marwar. Dharmdas, Narsinghdas, Ramdas, Mithadas were his prominent disciples. The language of his works is called Sadhukkari Hindi.

LAL GIRI (fl. 19th cent.). Rajasthani saint-poet and propounder of the Alakhiya Sampraday, who was born at the village Sulkhaniya (Churu) in a cobbler family. In his boyhood, he was taken by a Sadhu, perhaps of the Naga branch of Dadu

Sampraday. In 1829, he returned to Bikaner and started preaching. Many became his disciples. He was instrumental in the construction of the famous gigantic well of Bikaner known as Alakh Sagar. Once, when Ratansingh was going to the Lakshminarayan temple, Lalgiri asked the Maharaja to do the *Smaran* of only Alakh, as idol-worship was quite useless. At this, the Maharaja banished him. Consequently, Lalgiri came to Jaipur and remained at Galta till his death.

His available 29 *Shabads* in easy Rajasthani deal with *Nam-Smaran*, illusory nature of the world, condemnation of idol-worship and worship of Alakh alone, the ultimate truth. Hence, the Sampraday was named Alakhiya. The Sampraday was popular in Bikaner and the adjoining regions. His followers mostly came from the backward classes of the society. In this tradition, Gyangiri was a Sadhak poet, whose poem *Alakh Stuti Prakash* (*Alakh Mahima Stuti*) is available.

LAL KAVI. Maithili poet, who is traditionally said to have lived at the court of Maharaja Narendra Singh (1744-61), though the poet does not say anything about himself in his play : *Gauri-Swayamvar*. The play, which is a sort of one-act play, follows the story of Shiv's marriage with Parvati and is the shortest and simplest of all Maithili dramas. It seems that like Umapati's play on Krishna, this play on Shiv set the pattern of a popular Kirtaniya drama. In this drama, Sanskrit and Prakrit are rarely used. The poet was also noted for his *Sohars*, particular types of lyrics.

LALADE (fl. 1583). Rajasthani poetess, whose stray verses in popular metres are available.

LALAKDAS (fl. 1803-23). Poet of Lucknow, who was a weaver by caste and used to roam about with his disciples. His *Satyopakhyan* is a huge narrative work, describing the story of Ram from his birth to his marriage. The language is simple ; the metres used are *Doha* and *Chaupai*. In his narration, he borrowed not only from Hindi poets, but from the Sanskrit ones too.

LALAS, S.R. See *Sita Ram Lalas*.

LALIR (fl. 1551). Poet of Tirhut, who composed *Dangau-Parva*, based on the *Mahabharat*.

LALIT. Maithili novelist, whose chief work *Prithwiputra* (1965) has given a vision and profundity to the poorest classes in rural Mithila. His short story collection *Pratinidhi*

(1964) describes the psychological situation in the life of a man of the lower class.

LALIT KISHORI (fl. 18th cent.). Poet of the Krishna-cult (Haridasi Sect), who composed some 400 *Dohas* and *Padas*.

LALIT KISHORI (1825-73). Poet of the Krishna-cult, whose real name was Shah Kundan Lal. Born in a rich Vaishya Agrawal family of Lucknow, he became a devotee of Krishna. He came to live in Vrindavan, where he got built a marble temple, now known as 'Shahji ka Mandir'. He composed several works : *Rasa-Kalika* (unpublished), *Abhilash Madhuri*, etc. but the theme is always the same. He wrote again and again on *Ashtayam*, an account of how Krishna and Radha spent their days and nights. The poet is often highly sensuous. He composed poems in Khari Boli and Urdu as well.

LALIT KISHORI DAS (fl. 18th cent.). Poet of the Krishna-cult (Haridasi Sect), who was noted for his *Bhaktivatika* (The Garden of Devotion), etc.

LALIT LALAM (The Lonely Jewel). Poem on *Alankar* by Matiram (q.v.), composed any time between 1659 and 1688.

It consists of 444 verses ; about a hundred illustrative verses are in praise of his patron. The work was popular in its age and even now it is the most handy text-book. The illustrative verses are so lucid, precise and yet exhaustive that all the features of an *Alankar* are brought home to the reader. The poetry also is fascinating so that its study of the figures of speech is rendered extremely pleasurable.

LALIT MADHURI (1828-85). Poet of the Krishna-cult, who was a younger brother of Lalit Kishori (q.v.). His real name was Shah Phundan Lal. He belonged to a rich Vaishya Agrawal family of Lucknow, but with his brother Lalit Kishori, he came to live in Vrindavan. He composed *Padas* and *Ghazals*, which are collected in *Abhilash Madhuri*. See *Lalit Kishori*.

LALIT MOHINI (fl. 18th cent.). Poet of the Krishna-cult (Haridasi Sect), who composed *Dohas* and *Padas*.

LALIT PRASAD TRIVEDI 'LALIT' (1831-1901). Writer of Kanpur, on whose *Sumati Manranjan Natak*, Ramlilas, performed even to this day in that zone, are based. His other works are : *Ram Yash Darpan* (drama) and *Digvijay Vinod*.

LALIT SAKHI (b. *c.* 1743). Poet of the Krishna-cult (Chaitanya

Sect), whose works are : *Kahani Rahsi* and *Kunvari-Keli.*

LALIT SEHGAL. Modern writer, whose chief work is a play, *Hatya Ek Akar Ki* (The Murder of a Figure; 1968) on Gandhiji's murder ; it analyses the psychology of a murderer. The play has been tr. into English by Suresh Kohli under the title 'The Verdict'. His other works are : *Vardan, Guphavasi, Nidan, Swapnadip* and *Ek Naye Admi ki Maut.*

LALIT SHUKL. Critic, who is noted for the editing of *Vam Kavita* (Poetry of the Left ; 1978). His other works are : *Dhundhalka, Sojo Lobo* (short story collections), *Dusri Ek Duniya* (novel), *Antargat, Akar* (poetical collections and) *Yuga-Drashta Premchand* (criticism). See *Vishwa Nath Gaur.*

LALITESHWHR JHA. Modern Maithili writer, who is noted for his drama, *Sant Pariksha* (1948) on the life of Sant Sahib Ramdas.

LALJI, MAHAPATRA (b. 1857). Poet of Asni (Fatehpur district). whose works are : *Ashwini Charitra, Shatritu Vinod* (Delights of the Six Seasons), etc.

LALJI MEHDU (fl. between 1450-1550). Dingal poet, whose stray *Gits* on contemporary rulers and chiefs are available.

LALJI RANGKHAN (fl. 1783). Riti poet, who was patronized by Maharaj Sawai Pratap Singh of Jaipur. He composed a work on *Nayak-Nayika Bhed*, the title of which is not available.

LALL (HALL) BHATT. Old Rajasthani poet, who in 10 stray verses has given a graphie description of Rudra Mahalay, built by Siddhraj Jaysingh in Siddhpur in the 12th century.

LALLAN PRASAD VYAS. Modern scholar, whose chief work is *Vishwa Hindi ki Yatra*. He also publishes 'Vishwa Hindi Darshan', a literary magazine.

LALLU LAL (Lalluji Lal ; 1763-1835). Gujarati Brahmin, who was a resident of Agra. He was a scholar of Sanskrit and had picked up both Hindi and Urdu. A teacher at the Government Fort William College, Calcutta, he was instructed by Dr Gilchrist to write suitable text books in Hindi. Accordingly, he wrote *Prem-Sagar* (1803 ; tr. into German), the story of Krishna's early life as described in the Sanskrit *Bhagavata-Purana* This work became immensely popular and was the great model for Hindi prose from the beginning. He also prepared in very good Brajbhaha prose, a rendering of the Sanskrit work,

Hitopadesha, the well-known collection of beast-fables. He tried to eschew all foreign words of Persian and Arabic origin. Although he wrote in Khari Boli prose, his style has been perceptibly influenced by Braj, the language spoken in Agra. His other works are : *Madhava Vilasa* (The Delights of Krishna), *Sabha-Vilas* (both in Braj bhasha verse), *Lal-Chandrika* (a commentary on the *Bihari-satsai*) and *Rajniti* (on polity).

He is one of the early four principal Khari Boli prose writers ; others are : Sadal Mishra, Insha Allah Khan and Sadasukh Lal (qq. v.).

LALMAN BASRAM. Modern Hindi poet of Mauritius, whose *Ravi Ansu* is a collection of his poems.

LALNATHJI (fl. 18th cent.). Rajasthani saint-poet of the Jasnathi Sampraday, whose works *Jiv Samjhotari*, *Varan Vidya*, *Har Ras*, *Harilila*, *Nikalang Puran* (describing the Kalki incarnation), *Suraj Stotra* and stray *Sabads* deal with Bhakti, Karma, Gyan, Yoga, Niti, etc. in various ways.

LAMBERT, HESTER MARJORIE. Author of *Introduction to the Devanagari Script for Students of Sanskrit and Hindi* (Oxford, 1953).

LANG, J. Author of *Eastern Proverbs and Emblems* (London, 1881).

LANKAN DHANI (The Master of Lanka, i. e., Ravan). Rajasthani poem in about 300 verses by Nanuram Sanskarta (q.v.), which was composed in 1976.

Presenting Ravan as a great patriot, scholar and person of lofty character, even the god Shiv hails Ravan as one of the noblest symbols of humanity. Vibhishan has been characterised as a devotee of Ram but a traitor to his homeland. Sacrifice for one's own land has been eulogised. The language is easy Rajasthani.

LEBEDEFF, H. Author of *The Grammar of the Pure and Mixed East Indian Dialects* (London, 1801 ; since ed. and published by Mahadeo Prasad Saha), who came to India in 1785 and learnt Bengali, Hindustani and a bit of Sanskrit in Calcutta, where he used to hold musical concerts. His popularity gave birth to jealousy among Europeans, with the result that he had to leave India in 1797 and returned to London. It was from there that he published his Grammar. He also tr. many English comedies into Bengali and got them staged. His

Grammar gives us a glimpse of that Hindustani, which was spoken in the bazaars of Calcutta.

LEE, IK-MO. Korean Hindi scholar, whose chief work is: A Study of Laryngal source variables, their employment as distinctive cues for the plosive consonants of English, Hindi and Korean, ... (Ph. D., Georgetown, 1971).

LEITNER, DR. Author of *Linguistic Fragments* (1882).

LEKHAN PRATAP 'URGESH'. Modern Bagheli scholar, whose chief work is *Bagheli Lok-Git* (Folk-songs).

LESNY, VINCENC (1882-1953). Czech Indologist, who tr. Ayodhyasingh Upadhyay's Hindi novel *Devbala* into Czech. He was the first Indologist, who apart from the study of Sanskrit, introduced the study of Bengali and Hindi in the Charles University, Prague. He started magazine 'Nava Prachya' or 'Novi Orient' in 1945, which is still continuing and it has published the Czech trs. of the specimens of the works of Prem Chand, Sumitranandan Pant, Harivansh Rai Bachchan, Dinkar, Agyey, Bharat Bhushan Agrawal, Shrikant Verma, etc. He also established a College for the study of Sanskrit, Bengali, Hindi, etc. where students could learn these languages and enjoy the works written in original languages.

LIENHARD, SIEGFRIED. German-speaking modern scholar, who is Professor of Indology at Stockholm University. He has also written on some problems of Hindi grammar and his chief work is *Tempusgebrauch und Aktionsartenbildung in der modernen Hindi* (Stockholm, 1961).

LIKHIS. Modern Avadhi poet, who is noted for his humorous and satirical poems, *e.g.*, 'Ui ko Ahin'.

LILADHAR (fl. 1619). Rajasthani poet, whose stray verses in popular metres are available.

LILADHAR JAGURI. Poet, whose chief poetical collections are: *Natak Jari Hai* (The Drama is Going On), *Rat ab bhi Maujud Hai* (The Night is Still There), *Bachi Hui Prithwi* (1977), *Ghabraye Huye Shabda* (The Perplexed Words; 1981) *Lagbhag Jivan* and *Is Yatra Men*.

LILADHAR JOSHI. Modern Kumaoni writer, who is noted for his tr. into Kumaoni of *Bhagavadgita* from the original Sanskrit.

LILA JYOTI, MRS. Telugu-speaking Hindi scholar, whose research publication is: *Surdas aur Potana: Vatsalya ki Abhivyakti* (Child-love in Surdas and Potana; 1976).

LILY RAY. Maithili writer, whose novel *Patakshep* (1979) describes the Naxalite movement. Her novel *Marichika* (Pt. I 1980, Pt. II 1982) is on the life of 'Rajgharana' to which she belongs. The first part of the novel has been awarded by the Sahitya Akademi.

LINGVA, AITI GRETISH. See *Aiti Gretish Lingva.*

LIPEROVSKI, VLADIMIR PETROVICH (1927—). Soviet Hindi scholar, who has written several works on Hindi grammar, e.g., *Works on Hindi Moods.* He is one of the compilers of the *Hindi-Russian Dictionary* (2 Pts.; 75,000 words). His articles have appeared in several Hindi magazines.

LOCHAN (fl. 17th cent.). Maithili poet and musician, who was the herald of a new age which began with the installation of the House of Khandwa to power. He composed his famous *Raga Tarangini* (The River of Melodies) in Sanskrit, but it contains good portions in Maithili. The work contains stanzas in praise of the kings of Mithila from Mahesh Thakur to Mahinath Thakur under whom Lochan compiled the work for the pleasure of king's brother, Narpati Thakur (1673-90). The *Raga-Tarangini* preserves the works of about 40 poets, 45 *Padas* of Vidyapati and 9 of Lochan himself. A valuable record of the wide-spread poetical activity of the day, it is also an evidence of the greatness of Lochan's musical scholarship. Lochan was the first man to finalize the description and definition of Maithil Ragas and Raginis on the basis of metres and discussed the structure and the prosody of Maithili lyrics.

He considered his own poems in Maithili as important as those of Vidyapati, but his lyrics are distinguished by careful craftsmanship. Sudhakar Jha has brought out an authentic edition of *Raga-Tarangini*, the work has been reprinted in 1981, edited by Shashi Nath Jha.

LOCHAN PRASAD PANDEY (1886-1959). Poet and writer, who was born at Balapur in the Bilaspur district of Uttar Pradesh. His chief works are: *Pravasi* (The Sojourner), *Mewar Gatha* (The Saga of Mewar), *Madhav-Manjari* (The Spring Creeper), *Padya-Pushpanjali* (Verse Anthology; poetry), *Do Mitra* (Two Friends; novel), *Chhatra Durdasha* (Sad Plight of Students), *Gramya-Vivah-Vidhan* (The Ceremony of Village Marriage), *Prem-Prashansa* (The Eulogy of Love) and *Grihasth-Dasha-*

Darpan (The Mirror of Family Life ; dramas). *Bhut ka Mandal* is a collection of his Chhatisgarhi poems.

LOCHAN VIDESHI. Modern Hindi writer of Mauritius, whose chief work is : *Vyavaharik Vyakaran*. He has also written short stories.

LOETZKE, HANNELORE. Modern German Hindi scholar ; she is making a special study of modern Hindi literature in Humboldt University, East Germany.

LOKAYATAN. See *Sumitra Nandan Pant*.

LOKNATH BHARALI (1924-). Assamese-speaking Hindi writer, who is mainly an essayist. His main contribution is *Adhunik Manas ka Sankat* (The Crisis of Modern Man), which has been awarded by the Government of India. He has tr. some works from Assamese into Hindi and has also prepared some text-books.

LOKNATH CHAUBE (fl. 1703). Brajbhasha poet of Bundi, whose *Ras Tarang* and *Harivansh Chaurasi* are Riti works. His wife also composed poems.

LONE, ALI MUHAMMAD. See *Ali Muhammad Lone*.

LORIKI (Lorikayan). Bhojpuri folk-tale in verse, which describes the heroism and marriage of Lorik, a local hero and a god of the Ahirs or milkmen. *Loriki* is apparently a tale of love between Chanda and Lorik. Chanda is married but she has forsaken her husband and has fallen in love with Lorik, who is also married to Maina. Lorik elopes with Chanda, faces many odds and in the end both of them return home. Mullah Daud (q v.) wrote *Chandayan* on this theme.

LUIPA (fl. 9th cent.). Vajrayan Siddh poet, who was preceptor of the Orissa ruler, Darikpa and his minister, Dengipa. The language used by him in his considerable amount of poetry, through Apabhransh, represents the old form of Hindi.

LUMBA BABA (fl. 18th cent. ?) Rajasthani saint-poet, whose *Ai Mata ri Vel* and stray verses are popular in the Ai Panth. See *Aiji*.

LUNKARAN KAVIYA. Dingal poet, whose *Kesrisinghji ra Jhulna, Doha va Nisani* (176 lines) composed about 1663, describes the heroic deeds of Kesrisingh, the son of Maharaja Karansingh of Bikaner, in four engagements—the battles of Dharmat,

Dhaulpur, Ajmer, and the one against Prince Shuja which he fought as a trustworthy warrior of Aurangzeb. The poet has given a chronology of the kings of Delhi, irrespective of the house to which they belong.

LUTZE, LOTHAR. Hindi scholar from West Germany, whose chief work is : *Sahitya* : *Vividh Sandarbh* (The Literature : Various Contexts). He also wrote *Hindi ke Barah Path*, *Hindi as a Second Language* (1970) and tr. *Bihari Satsai* into German.

LYALL, C.J. Author of A *Sketch of the Hindustani Language* (Edinburgh, 1880).

M

Machhandra Nath. Founder of the Nath Sect, who is also known by names : Minapa, Minapal, Minanath, Machhandrapa, Minanath, Matsyendra Nath, etc. In the Tibetan works he is known as Luipa (q.v.). As his name implies, he belonged to a fisherman's family of Kamrup (Assam). The famous Gorakhnath is known to be his disciple. He is also considered to be the founder of 'Yogini' Sect of Kaul-Panth. In his *Yoga Pravah*, Pitambar Dutt Barthwal has hinted at some *Padas* composed by him, while Hazari Prasad Dwivedi in his *Nath Siddhon ki Vaniyan* has quoted stray verses of Minanath. Har Prasad Shastri in his *Baudh-gan O Duha* (q.v.) has discovered many of his *Padas*.

Machida, Kazuhiko. Modern Japanese Hindi scholar, who did M.A. in Hindi from Allahabad University in 1979. Subsequently, he did M.A. from the Tokyo University of Foreign Studies, where he at present teaches. His special field of study is Philology and Poetics.

Machwe. See *Prabhakar Machwe*.

Mada Ram. (fl. early 19th cent.). Rajasthani saint-poet of Ram Snehi Sampraday, Ren, whose *Vani* consists of stray verses in popular metres.

Madan Gopal. Modern writer, whose chief works are : *Qalam ka Mazdur* : *Premchand* (The Labourer of the Pen : Premchand) and *Bharatendu Harishchandra* (both biographies).

Madan Gopal Sharma. Modern Rajasthani poet, who composed lyrical poems, portraying various aspects of Nature and poems on the love of Rajasthan', e.g. 'Dhoran Halo Desh' and 'O rang Rudo Rajasthan'. He also wrote some patriotie and heroic poems and odes. His works in *Khari Boli* are :

Giton ka Banjara and editing of *Marvan tatha anya Gitirupak* and *Mira tatha anya Gitirupak*.

MADAN KUMAR JANI. Gujarati-speaking modern Hindi scholar, whose *Rajasthan evam Gujarat ke Madhyaklin Sant aur Bhakta Kavi* is a research work.

MADAN LAL MADHU. Panjabi-speaking poet of Hindi, whose poems are quite popular in poetical symposia.

MADAN LAL VAISHYA. Modern Rajasthani scholar, who is noted for his *Marwari Git-Mala*.

MADAN MOHAN SIDDHA. Modern Rajasthani writer, who is noted for his drama : *Jaipur ki Jyonar*.

MADAN MOHAN VYAS. Modern Malwi poet, who is noted for his stray poems.

MADAN-SHATAK. Poem (Script 1667-70) by Dam, which describes the romance of Madan Kumar and Champakmala.

MADAN SONI. Editor of *Hona Shru Hona* (1983), a joint collection of poems by four young poets of Bhopal : Dhruva Shukla, Rajendra Dhorapkar, Sanjiv Kshitij and Udayan Bajpai.

MADAN VATSYAYAN (1922-). Poet, whose earlier poems were included in the *Tisra Saptak* (q.v.) ; his poems deal mainly with life in factories and mills.

MADARI (fl. early 19th cent.). Braj folk-poet, who was a native of Lobhan near Mathura. A devotee of the goddess of Nagarkot, he was a Brahmin by caste. On one of his pilgrimages, he heard the Rajasthani version of Dhola-Maru romance. He composed 360 *Pahriyas* on this romance, but at present only 125 are extant. The language of the verses is as spoken in the villages. The work is popular even to this day.

MADARI LAL GUPTA. Novelist, whose *Sakharam* (1924) depicts poverty and its evil effects.

MADHAU DAS. (fl. 1604). Rajasthani saint-poet, who was a disciple of Jagjivanji (q.v.). A resident of Gular (Marwar), his *Sant Gun Sagar Siddhant* consists of 24 *Tarangs* and in many metres describes the life of Dadu.

MADHAU DAS. Mir Munshi of Kishengarh, whose *Shaktl-Bhakti Prakash* (1683) in Pingal is a good religious poem.

MADHAV. Saint-poet of Maharashtra, who was a disciple of Amrit Ray (1698-1753). He also composed some *Padas* in Hindi ; his language is influenced by Brajbhasha.

MADHAV (fl. 18th cent. ?). Maithili poet, whose verses found respeetable place in contemporary anthologies.

MADHAV BHATTACHARYA. Modern Hindi poet of Trinidad, who is noted for his stray poems.

MADHAV DAS (1544-95). Saint-poet of South Gujarat, who was a disciple of Sain Smarth Das and was known by the name of 'Mast-Madhav'. He has left behind in Hindi some 500 *Padas*, 600 *Kundliyas*, etc. From his works, it appears that he had a good knowledge of Hindi, Gujarati, Arabic and Persian.

MADHAV DAS (fl. 1583). Bengali Vaishnav poet, who also composed 2 *Padas* in Brajbuli : one describing the beauty of Radha and the other in adoration of her.

MADHAV DAS (fl. 16th cent.). Saint-poet of Maharashtra, who composed some *Padas* in Hindi as well. His language is influenced by Marathi.

MADHAV DAS CHARAN. Poet of the Ram-cult, who in 1618, composed the *Gunram-Raso* in different metres ; it is a poem, treating of the story of Ram. His *Adhyatma-Ramayan* (1624) is based on the Sanskrit work of that name.

MADHAV DAS DADHVADIYA. See *Madhodas Dadhvadiya*.

MADHAV DAS JAGANNATHI (b. 1483). A devotee of Jagannath ; he belonged to Chaitanya Sect. He visited all the sacred places of Braj. It is said that he translated such large Sanskrit works as the *Mahabharata* and *Itihasa Kathasara Samuchchaya* into Braj, but at present only small works : *Jagannath Mahatmya*, *Raghunath Lila*, *Bal Lila*, a small portion of *Itihasa Kathasara Samuchchaya*, *Narayan Lila*, *Padas*, etc. are extant.

MADHAV DASI. Oriya poetess, who was perhaps born in Puri. A devotee of Chaitanya (1486-1527), some of her *Padas* in Hindi (Brajboli) are extant.

MADHAV DEV (1489-1596). Assamese saint-poet, who was the greatest disciple of Shankardev (q.v.). His Hindi (Brajavali) works are : *Bargit* (songs), stray verses and the dramas : *Arjun Bhanjanyatra, Chirdhara Jhumura, Bhumilotva Jhumura, Pimpara Guchova Jhumura, Bhojan-bihar Jhumura, Brahmamohan Jhumura, Bhushan-Haran Jhumura, Katora Khelova Jhumura* and *Ras Jhumura.* All these works deal mostly with the pranks of Krishna as a child.

MADHAV GHOSH. Contemporary of Chaitanya (1486-1527) and a brother of Vasudev Ghosh (q.v.), who composed *Padas* in Bengali. He also composed a *Pada* in Brajbuli, which describes the love of Radha and Krishna.

MADHAV MUDIT (b. *c.* 1568). Poet of the Krishna-cult (Chaitanya Sect), who was a native of Agra. Though no work of his is extant, it appears that he was a well-known poet. His son Bhagavat Mudit (q.v.) was a famous poet.

MADHAV PRASAD MISHRA (1871-1907). Writer, whose prose style was influenced by Sanskrit. In his essays and books, he excluded all words and expressions that smacked of Urdu. This style was popular in Benares, where Jayshankar Prasad (q.v.) came under its influence. Mishra was the editor of 'Sudarshan', and wrote biographies of Vishuddhanand and of others.

MADHAV RAO, S.V. Telugu-speaking modern Hindi scholar, whose research publication is : *Chatursen Shastri ka Katha-Sahttya* (on fiction of Chatursen Shastri).

MADHAV RAO SAPRE (1871-1926). Marathi-speaking Hindi writer, whose 'Ek Tokri Bhar Mitti' (A Basketful of Earth) is regarded as the first Hindi short story ; it was published in 1901 in 'Chhattisgarh Mitra', a monthly magazine, edited by him. He also wrote essays dealing with religious, social and cultural topics, which appeared in various magazines.

MADHAV SHUKLA (1881-1943). Writer, who is noted for his mythological drama, *Siya-Swyaamvar* (on the marriage of Sita) as also for his nationalist poems. His another mythological drama *Mahabharata* (1915) has dialogues touching the fringes of reality of modern life.

MADHAV YAS PRAKAS. Rajasthani poem, composed by Mansingh Asiya about 1711-14, which describes the battle of

Bandhanwada of 1711, in which Rawat Mahavsingh of Kanaud (Mewar) fought against Ranbazkhan Mewati, the commander of the imperial army, and killed him.

MADHAVANAL KAMKANDALA. Romance, which has been written by atleast four important poets : Ganpati Kayasth, Kushal Labh, Damodar and Alam (qq.v.). The work describes the love-story of Madhavanal and Kamkandala ; *Madhavanal Prabandh Dogdhabandh* also treats of the same theme. See *Madhavanal Kamkandala Chaupai* and *Madhavanal Kamkandala Prabandh.*

MADHAVANAL KAMKANDALA CHAUPAI. Rajasthani poem by Kushal Labh (q.v.), a Jain poet, which was composed in 1559 to satisfy the curiosity of his student, crown-prince Har Raj of Jaisalmer. Consisting of 662 verses, mostly *Chaupais*, in easy Rajasthani, it includes some Sanskrit *Shlokas* and Prakrit *Gahas*. The story follows the tale given in *Madhavanal Kamkandala Prabandh* (q.v.) by Ganpati Kayasth but Kushal Labh displays originality in giving different stories about the earlier lives of the lovers.

MADHAVANAL KAMKANDALA PRABANDH. Romance of Madhavanal and Kamkandala, which has been treated by Ganpati (q.v.). The theme is generally drawn from literary tradition of antiquity or is imaginary. The tale is linked with the Vikram cycle of stories of love and romance.

Madhav, a Brahmin, 'as handsome as the god of love', lives in Pushpavati, where Govindchandra rules. His principal queen, Rudra Mahadevi falls in love with Madhav at first sight and solicits his love but he spurns the offer. The angry queen has him exiled and Madhav goes to Rukmangadpuri, where all the young women of the town fall in love with him. Seeing this, the men requested king Raichand to get rid of Madhav. In order to test intensity of the fascination exercised by Madhav, the king brings him before his queens. Then finding a danger to his own domsetic peace, the king banishes him. After wandering hither and thither, Madhav reaches Kamavati and is successful in getting a respectable place due to his artistic skill in the court of king Kamsen. Once, Kamkandala, a courtesan, is parforming a dance in the court ; a black bee rests on her dress and bits her breast but she continues the performance. Only Madhav notices this and he presents to her the very betel-leaf which was given to him by the king as a mark of honour. This annoys the king and he orders Madhav to leave the city. Before leaving the city, Kamkandala requests him to stay with her for a night and he does so ; both fall in love. Madhav goes to Ujjain and there he writes verses of his agony of separation from Kamkandala on the walls of the temple of Mahakal. King Vikramaditya, who is reputed in relieving the distress of the people, reads the verses and traces Madhav with the help of an old courtesan. Knowing Madhav's love for Kamkadala, Vikram calls upou Kamsen to allow the union of the two lovers but on Kamsen's refusal, he marches on the city. To test the love of Kamkandala, Vikram first tries in vain to win her over for himself and then conveys to her the false information of Madhav's death. She falls dead on hearing this news. Vikram returns and practises a similar ruse on Madhav by telling him that Kamkandala is dead. Madhav too dies. Vikram is mortified to think that he has been instrumental in causing the death of the two lovers. His ghost friend Vaital comes to the king's rescue and restores both the lovers to life. Vikram arranges their marriage and both live happily thereafter.

In this poem, the charm and beauty of both the hero and the heroine have been described in detall. Apart from the depiction of feelings of separation and then union of lovers, the poet has given the previous births of Madhav and Kamkandala. See *Madhvanal Kamkandala Chaupai*, *Madhavanal Katha*.

MADHAVANAL KATHA. See *Damodar*.

MADHODAS DADHVADIA (1553-1621). Rajasthani poet, who was son of Chunda Charan and belonged to the village Balunda-ka-Vas in the then Jodhpur State. His *Ram Raso* (q.v.) composed about 1595 on an epic scale, describes the story of Ram mainly on the basis of *Valmiki Ramayana*. Madhodas's other works are : *Nisani Gajmokh* (a short narrative poem on the theme of 'Gajendra-Moksha' of the *Bhagavat*) and *Haduman* (in praise of god Hanuman).

MADHUBALA JAIN. Modern scholar, who has worked on the similes of *Sursagar*.

MADHUKAR (fl. 1183). Poet, who, in praise of his patron, Jaychand, composed *Jay Mayank Jas Chandrika* ; this work, however, is no longer extant.

MADHUKAR. See *Surendra Jha 'Suman'*.

MADHUKAR GANGADHAR (1934-). Writer from Bihar, whose short story collection : *Garm Gosht* : *Barfili Tasir* contains eight short stories written in the urban background of Purnea region ; his other short story collections are : *Sau ka Note tatha anya Kahaniyan* and *Madhukar Gangadhar ki Kahaniyan* ; *Kavita ki Vapasi* is his poetical collection. His novels are : *Subah Hone Tak* and *Uttar Katha.*

MADHUKAR SINGH (1934-). Writer, whose chief works are : *Pura Sannata* (Complete Silence), *Bhai ka Zakhm* (The Brother's Wound), *Pahla Path*, *Agun Kapad*, *Gardish ke Din*, *Gramya Jivan ki Shreshth Kahaniyan* (ed.) (short story collections), *Sabse Bada Chhal* (The Greatest Deception), *Sonbhadra ki Radha*, *Arjun Zinda Hai* (novels) and *Subah ke Liye* (drama); his works successfully present rural life and the political influences thereon.

MADHUMALATI. An allegorical romance by Manjhan, a Sufi poet (fl. 1504), an incomplete manuscript of which is so far available.

Prince Manohar of Kanesar, while asleep, is placed by nymphs in the bed-chamber of Madhumalati, the princess of Maharas. On waking, both of them fall in love with each other but the nymphs carry the prince back to his palace, when he again falls asleep. The prince sets out on a voyage in quest of Madhumalati ; he rescues Prema, another princess, from the clutches of a demon. It is at the house of Prema that Manohar meets Madhumalati and her mother. Madhumalati's mother persuades her to give up Manohar but when she does not listen to her, she is metamorphosed into a bird. One Tarachand captures the bird ; Madhumalati relates her story of love to Tarachand. He takes the bird to Maharas and the repentant mother restores the bird to her human form. Madhumalati is then married to Manohar. In the allegory, Madhumalati, the heroine, has been likened to Nature in a typical pantheistic way.

The poem embodies a long and intricately-built story of love with mystic implications. It is "remarkable for its literary quality, its tender imagery, the melody of its verse and its portrayal of the beauties of Nature."

Based on the Madhumalati, Nasrati, a Deccani poet, wrote his Gulshane Ishq (The Garden of Love ; 1643).

See *Chaturbhuj Das*.

MADHUP. See *Kashi Nath Mishra 'Madhup'*.

MADHUR ALI. Saint-poet, who was contemporary of Maharaj Raghuraj Singh (r. 1854-80). Some of his letters in verse have been discovered, which give a glimpse of the refinement of Bagheli dialect.

MADHUR SHASTRI. Modern poet, who is noted for his lyrics. He edits 'Srotasvini'.

MADHURACHARYA (fl. end of 17th cent.). Poet of the Ram-cult (Rasik Sect), who, owing to differences with Maharaja Ram Singh of Jaipur, left Galta and came over to Chitrakut. His Sanskrit works are more popular than his Hindi writings. Several of his *Padas* in Brajbhasha bear his pseudonymns : 'Madhurpriya' and 'Madhupritam'. In his 'Sundar Mani Sandarbh', which is a part of his work *Bhagavad-Gun-Darpan*, he defined his Bhakti-cult and tried to establish on the basis of the Vedas, *Valmiki Ramayan*, etc. that the form of worship as enjoined in the Rasik Sect was prevalent in ancient days too.

MADHURI-MADHAVDAS (fl. 16th cent.). Poet of the Krishna-cult (Chaitanya Sect), who was a native of Vrindavan. He wrote his works under the pen-name of 'Madhuri', though his original name was Madhavdas. His works are : *Utkantha Madhuri*, *Vanshivat Madhuri*, *Keli Madhuri*, *Vrindavan Madhuri*, *Dan Madhuri*, *Man Madhuri*, *Hori Madhuri* and *Priyaji ki Badhai*. A work, *Ashtayam* on the *Lilas* of Radha-Krishna is also attributed to him.

MADHUSUDAN (fl. prior to 1685). Maithili poet, whose lyrics were quoted in anthologies.

MADHUSUDAN DAS (fl. early 16th cent.). Poet of the Krishna-cult (Chaitanya Sect), who was a native of Kashi. A disciple of Ramray (q.v.), his devotional works are : *Satsang Pachchisi* and *Prem Darshan*.

MADHUSUDAN DAS (fl. 1782). Poet of the Ram-cult, who was a Chaube of Mathura. At the instance of one Govind Das, he composed his great poetical work, *Ramashwamedh* in 1782 on the pattern of *Ramcharitmanas*. The work describes the events after the return of Ram to Adyodha and can be termed as an appendix to Tulsi's *Ramayan*. The story is based on the *Padma Puran*. From literary points of view, the work equals the *Ramcharitmanas*.

MADHUSUDAN JHA. Modern Maithili writer, whose essays in *Rudhivad O Buddhivad* are serious and thoughtful.

MADHUSUDAN MEHTA. Gujarati-speaking modern Hindi scholar, whose *Adhunik Hindi Gujarati Kavita men Prakriti-Chitran* is a research work.

MADHWA MUNISHWAR (1689-1731). Marathi-speaking saint-poet, who originally belonged to Nasik but afterwards settled at Aurangabad in Maharashtra. It is said that Madhwa-charya himself called him 'Madhwamunishwar' as such. His *Padas*, both in Marathi and Hindi are permeated with sweet-ness as they were sung in *Kirtans*. He was influenced by Sufism and in his Hindi *Padas*, two styles are noticed : the one dominated by Brajbhasha and the other by Dakkhini, consisting of Urdu and Persian words.

MADHWENDRA PURI. Bengali-speaking poet, who in his Brajbuli *Padas* has praised Vrindavan and the sacred places around it. The poet flourished a little before Chaitanya (1486-1527).

MAFATBHAI PATEL. Gujarati-speaking modern Hindi scholar, whose *Hindi ke Manovaigyanik Upanyas : Manovishleshan, Darshan aur Shilp ke Pariprekshya Men* is a research work.

MAGANLAL MANILAL (b. 1881). A native of Baroda (Gujarat), who, at the instance of Mahatma Gandhi went to Mauritius in 1902. He started a daily paper 'Hindustani' in 1908, which was published in Hindi and English. This paper became the spokesman of the sufferings and humiliations to which the people of Mauritius were subjected. He also established a printing press 'Hindustani', which he handed over to Arya Samaj, when he returned to India in 1911. In 1950, when he visited Mauritius, he was accorded a rousing reception.

MAHABHARAT (Hindi version). See *Gokulnath, Gopinath, Manidev*.

MAHADAN BAI. See *Sati Sujas*.

MAHADAN MEHDU (1781-1843). Rajasthani poet, who was noted for his Dingal *Gits*. His *Maharana Bhimsingh ra Jhulna* describes the Pichola Lake and ceremonial procession of Maharana Bhimsingh of Mewar.

MAHADEV PARVATI RI VELI. See *Kisnau.*

MAHADEV PRASAD SINGH. Modern Bhojpuri poet, whose chief narrative works are: *Lorikayan* (on the heroism of Lorik), *Nayakava Banjara* and *Bala Lakhandar* (on the story of Bihula; see *Bihula*).

MAHADEVI VERMA (1907-). Poetess, who was born at Farrukhabad and was educated at Allahabad. She edited 'Chand' for some time from Allahabad. At present she is the Up-Kulpati of Prayag Mahila Vidyapith. She is famous as one of the four great representatives of the *Chhayavad* school. She has made a thorough study of Buddhism and has chosen the path of pessimism and sorrow, both of which are the dominating features of her poetry. Repeatedly she has given expressions to the longings and the pangs of separation which she feels for the invisible object of her adoration; her attitude reminds one of the Sufi devotees. She also resembles Mira; like whom she is anxious to offer her love and worship. Her poetical works, mostly illustrated, are as under:—

Nihar (The Mist; 1930) is a collection of her 47 lyrics (composed between 1924 and 1928), which decidedly are her earliest outpourings.

Rashmi (The Ray of Light; 1932) is a collection of 35 lyrics, in which the pessimism of the poetess is brightened by some hope.

Nirja (The Lotus; 1935), a collection of 58 *Gits*, is a call for struggle against the shortcomings and evils inherent in life. According to her, it is this determined struggle alone, which can engender faith in man and bring him within reach of his salvation.

Sandhyagit (The Evening Songs; 1936) is a collection of 45 lyrics and is rich in emotional context.

Yama is a collection of her poetical collections: *Nihar, Rashmi, Nirja* and *Sandhyagit.*

Dipshikha (The Flame; 1942), a collection of 51 *Gits*, and *Sandhyagit* are both marked by the anguish of the soul pining to free itself from the sorrows of life and to reach a world free from sufferings and pains. The poetess is a skilled painter and the *Dipshikha* bears a background of her paintings. Her other poetical collections are: *Atmtka, Dipgit, Nilambara, Pratham Ayam* and *Parikrama.*

Mahadevi Verma has also written beautiful literary sketches, entitled *Atit ke Chalchitra* (The Cavalcades of the

Past) ; these 11 sketches, in excellent prose, bring out her inner self, her sensibilities, her attachments and her likes and dislikes. *Path ke Sathi* (The Fellow Travellers) and *Smritichitra* are her reminiscences. *Saptaparna* (1960) is a Hindi tr. of Sanskrit portions from Valmiki to Jayadeva. Her other works are : *Shrinkhala ki Kariyan* (The Links of a Chain), *Smriti ki Rekhayen* (Recollections), *Hindi ka Vivechanatmak Gadya* (Critical History of Hindi Prose).

Mahadevi Verma is a woman with deep sensibility which she is able to impart to her lyrics with exceptional success. Her poetry is 'permeated with a sense of pain which she seems to cherish. She would not part with it even after the much-desired union with the Infinite has taken place.'

Her sketches have been translated into English and published in U.S.A. Based on one of her sketches *Chini Pherivala*, a Bengali film 'Nil Akasher Niche' was made. She is winner of the 1983 Jnanpith Award.

MAHADJI SCINDIA (1727-94). Ruler of Gwalior State, who originally hailed from Satara district of Maharashtra. Besides his Marathi works, he also composed *Padas* in Hindi. There is an influence of Braj and Dakkhini on his language.

MAHANAND (fl. 18th cent. ?). Rajasthani saint-poet of Laldasi Sampraday, whose *Bhajans* extol devotion to God and Guru and advocate for leading a simple life.

MAHANAND GANI (fl. 1604). Gujarati-speaking Jain poet, whose *Anjana Sundari Ras* is a Hindi work.

MAHAPATRA, S. Oriya-speaking modern Hindi writer, who has tr. *Oriya Galpamala* into Hindi.

MAHARAJ KRISHNA SANTOSHI. Poet, whose *Is Bar Shayad* (Perhaps this Time ; 1980) is a collection of poems.

MAHARAJA AJIT SINGHNJI KI DAVAVAIT. See *Dwarkadas Dadhvadiya.*

MAHARAJA GAJSIGHJI RAO RUPAK. Dingal poem (1747) of Sinadhayach Fateh Ram (q.v.), which is an eulogy of Maharaja Gajsingh of Bikaner.

MAHARAJA RATANSIGHJI KI DAVAVAIT. See *Sinadhayach Dayaldas.*

MAHARAJA RATANSINGHJI KI KAVITA. Dingal poem of Vithu Bhomau (fl. 1838), which eulogises Maharaja Ratan Singh and his son, Kunvar Sirdar Singh.

MAHARAJA RAYSINGH RI SATIYON RA KAVITTA. See *Kumbhkaran Sandu*.

MAHARAJA SRI SHIVSINGHJI RA KAVITTA. Rajasthani poem of an unknown author in 192 verses, which was composed some time prior to 1790. A powerful poem of much historical importance, it describes the heroic deeds and achievements of Rathore Shivsingh, the ruler of Idar and his loyal warriors ; it includes a genealogy of his ancestors from Rao Sihoji of Marwar onwards.

MAHARANA BHIMSINGH RA JHULNA. See *Mahadan Mehdu*.

MAHATAM SINGH. Native of Guyana, who is promoting the cause of Hindi in his country.

MAHATMYARAM (1825-88). Saint-poet of Gujarat, who was a disciple of Adityaram. He was a native of the village Simdada in the Khera district. A follower of Ram-Kabirya Sect, he composed his Hindi verses in several forms, such as *Ramaini*, *Kafi*, *Rekhta*, *Sakhis*, *Ghazals*, *Lavani*, *Jhulna*, *Kundliyas*, *Garbi*, *Thal*, *Arti*, etc.

MAHAVIR ADHIKARI. Modern writer, whose chief works are *Talash* (The Search), *Manzil se Age* (Beyond Destinations ; novels) and *Lal Bahadur Shastri* (biography). A film was made on one of his novels. He now edits Hindi 'Current'. Previously he wes editor of many Hindi weeklies and dailies from 'Navyug', Delhi to 'Navbharat Times', Bombay.

MAHAVIR JHA 'VIR' (1897-1945). Maithili dramatist, whose chief work *Shambuk-badh* is based on an episode in the life of Ram. He composed poems on traditional themes ; his most beautiful poem, however, proved to be his swan-song.

MAHAVIR MITRA. Modern Hindi poet of Fiji, whose chief works are : *Phag ke Git*, *Prem ke Git and Manav Mitra Vasant* (1962).

MAHAVIR PRASAD DWIVEDI (1864-1938). Celebrated writer, who was born at Daulatpur in the Raibareli district. He went to stay with his father in Bombay where he acquainted himself with Marathi literature. For a number of years, he was in the telegraph section of the railway but resigned his post in protest against the rude behaviour of an English officer. He then edited the Hindi journal 'Saraswati' for 20 years (from 1903 onwards) and turned his office into something of a school for correcting the compositions of his contributors. He was a prolific writer in prose and verse, but many of his works are translations from Sanskrit, English (*Bacon Vichar-Ratnavali*), Marathi and Bengali. His original prose writings have been published under the titles of *Sahitya-Sikar*, *Rasagya-Ranjan*, etc. Dwivedi had a powerful personality and the zeal of a reformer and hence he is rightly regarded as the leader of his own age. He has to be given credit not only for what he himself achieved but also for his ability to inspire and help other writers and poets to create literature. In verse as also in prose, he tried to bring literary expression close to the language of daily speech (Khari Boli), the language as spoken by cultured people in cities. He threw open the columns of the 'Saraswati' to all writers and poets, who would compose in Khari Boli. Among poets, who composed in Khari Boli, the chief contributor was Maithili Sharan Gupta, whose poems started appearing in 'Saraswati' right from 1906. In any case, it was Dwivedi's advocacy and able guidance which put Khari Boli on its feet as the language not only of prose but also of poetry.

MAHAVIR PRASAD JOSHI. Rajasthani poet, whose *Bindraban* (1978) is a narrative poem in 'Sargas' on Krishna's various *Lilas* in Vrindavan He has since published the second part of the story of Krishna as *Mathra* (1982), which deals with the life of Krishna while living at Mathura. He has presented the gist and philosophy of Krishna legend.

MAHBUB (b. 1704). Muslim poet, who has only stray poems to his credit ; some verses describe the return of Krishna with his cows to Vrindavan.

MAHDAISA (1228-1303). Saint-poetess of Maharashtra, who was a disciple of Swami Chakradhar, the founder of the Mahanubhav Sect. She was also known by the name of Mahdamba, Rupai and Umamba. She composed in Marathi *Dhavles*, the songs sung by ladies on the occasion of marriage and wrote two works : *Matriki-Rukmini Swayamvar* and *Garbh-Kand Ovya*. She also composed devotional *Padas* in Hindi but only one or two are extant. Her language appears to be a mixture of Khari Boli and Braj.

MAHENDRA BHALLA (1933-). Fiction writer, whose chief works are : *Ek Pati ke Notes* (The Notes of a Husband ; 1967), *Tin Char Din* (A Few Days), *Dusri Taraf* (The Other Side) and *Pul ki Parchhai* (The Shadow of a Bridge ; 1977).

MAHENDRA BHANAWAT. Rajasthani writer, who has made notable contributions to the study of *Lilas* ; he has also edited a version of *Bagadavat* (q.v.). He is the author of *Lok Natya : Parampara aur Pravrittiyan* (1971) and *Kunkun Kanya* (1982 ; a collection of 6 small one-act plays).

MAHENDRA BHATNAGAR (1926-). Progressive poet with socialist bias, whose chief works are : *Santaran* (The Crossing Over), *Antaral* (Interval), *Jijivisha* (Will to Live), *Taron ke Git* (The Songs of Stars), *Tutati Shrinkhalayen* (The Breaking Chains), *Madhurima* (Sweetness), *Badalte Yuga* (The Changing Times), *Bund Neh ki Dip Hriday Ka* (The Drop of Affection and the Light of Heart ; 1967), *Sanvart* (Existence ; 1972) and *Nai Chetana* (New Consciousness) ; *Kavishri Mahendra Bhatnagar* is a collection of his 40 important poems. His drama is *Ajay Alok*, while *Vikrit Rekhayen Dhundhle Chitra* is a collection of his short stories.

MAHENDRA JHA. Modern Maithili writer, who is noted for his social drama, *Lakshman-Rekha-Khandit* (1970).

MAHENDRA KARTIKEY. Modern poet, whose collections of poems are : *Agami Kal* (Tomorrow ; 1980) and *Kavya Prasang*.

MAHENDRA KUMAR. Scholar, whose chief works are : *Ritikalin Riti Kaviyon ke Kavya Siddhant*, *Matiram : Kavi aur Acharya* and *Hindi Sahitya ka Uttar Madhyakal—Ritikal* (1984). He is at Present Professor and Head of the Department of Hindi at Delhi University.

MAHENDRA MALANGIA. Maithili dramatist, whose drama *Okra Aganak Barahmasa* (1979) is the story of a poor family, where the hero fails to get a proper coffin after his death, while his *Kamala Katak Ram, Lakshman ar Sita* (1981) is an important drama. His two Radio plays are : *Aluk Bori* and *E Janam Ham Vyarth Gamaol* (both 1982), both depicting the wretched conditions of the lower classes.

MAHENDRA NATH PANDEY. Nepali-speaking modern Hindi scholar, who is known for his work, *Hindi Nirgun Kavya aur Nepali Josmani Kavya*.

MAHENDRA PRATAP. Panjabi-speaking modern Hindi poet, whose chief poetical works are : *Sphuling* (Spark) and *Dhwant* (Darkness).

MAHENDRA SHASTRI. Bhojpuri poet of Chhapra in Bihar, whose collections of poems : *Chokha* and *Aj ki Avaz* (The Voice of To-day) treat of social reform, national love and the poverty of the masses.

MAHERAMAN SINGH (1813-52). Hindi poet of Gujarat, who was son of the ruler of Rajkot. He met his death during the reign of his father. He is supposed to have composed *Pravin-Sagar*, a romance on the love of Sagar, the hero and Pravin, the heroine. There are several stories current about the authorship of the work. It is said that Maheraman Singh died before completing this work and it was completed by seven friends including the Limbdi princess Sujan (named Pravin in this work). The work is divided into 84 cantos and betrays the influence of Gujarati, Marathi, Kachchhi, Rajasthani, Braj, Urdu, Panjabi and Sanskrit. The work glorifies love.

MAHESDAS RAO (fl. latter half of 17th cent.). Dingal poet, who was son of Rao Baghji Lakhnaut. He was patronized by Arjun Gaur, a trustworthy officer of Emperor Shah Jehan. His extant works are : *Rao Amarsingh Nagaur ka Saka* (34 verses), *Binhai Raso* (q. v.), *Rana Rajsingh ka Gun Rupak* (58 verses), *Gaudan ki Vanshavali* (on Gaur heroes), *Raja Jaysingh ke Chhappay*, *Raghunath Charit Nav Ras Veli* (q.v.) and *Gits* on some contemporary heroes. All these poems deal with the brave deeds and achievements of their heroes.

MAHESH PRADHAN. Oriya-speaking modern Hindi writer, who taught Hindi for some time in China.

MAHESHRAM JIYAVAN. Modern Hindi poet of Mauritius, who is noted for his stray poems.

MAHESH THAKUR (r. 1557-69). Maharaja of Mithila, who established a new dynasty. A great patron of learning and poetry, he himself was a great scholar of philosophy. After abdicating the throne in about 1569, he passed his remaining life at Varanasi on the banks of the Ganga, where he composed hymns in Maithili on Ganga and Tara.

MAHESH UPADHYAY. Poet, whose *Admi Preshan Hai* (Man is Worried ; 1978) is a collection of his poems.

MRHESHWAR. Writer, whose works are : *Talghar* (novel) and *Sparsh* (short story collection). He is noted for his short stories : 'Koi Ag' (A Fire), 'Dushman' (The Enemy), 'Purvabhas' (Premonition), etc.

MAHAESHWAR MAHANT (1924-). Assamese-speaking Hindi writer, who has contributed much to the advancement of Hindi in Assam. His essays have been published in the 'Rashtrasevak', which he also edited for some years.

MAHESHWARI. Writer, who has tr. into Hindi the Gujarati novel *Chhinnapatra* of Suresh Joshi and the Bengali novel *Dehman* of Narendranath Mitra.

MAHESHWARI, H.L. See *Hira Lal Maheshwari.*

MAHESHWARI SINHA. Modern scholar, whose chief work is : *The Historical Development of Mediaeval Hindi Prosody.*

MAHINATH THAKUR (1559/71--1690/93 ?). Maharaja of Mithila of the dynasty of Khandwa, whose court became the centre of literature and the arts. The Maharaja composed a devotional song in Maithili in praise of Kali on the occasion of departure of his younger brother, Narpati Thakur, for subduing certain turbulent chiefs in Morang (in Nepal). It was in the courts of Mahinath Thakur and Narpati Thakur that the Maithili lyric once again rose to glory. See *Lochan.*

MAHINDRA DWIJ (fl. latter half of the 18th cent.). Assamese poet, whose Hindi (Brajavali) work is *Bodhoday Nat*, a drama in the line of the Sanskrit *Prabodha-Chandrodaya.*

MAHINDRA MALL (r. 1689-94). Ruler of the House of Kantipur (Kathmandu) in Nepal, who succeeded his father, Pratap Mall quite late in his life. There is a complete *Ragmala* containing his Maithili poems. One drama, *Nal-Charit-Natak* (1682) is known to have been written under him.

MAHIP SINGH (1930-). Short story writer, whose chief works are : *Subah ke Phul* (The Morning Flowers), *Ujale ke Ullu* (The Owls of Light), *Gherao*, *Kuchh aur Kitna* (How Much More ?), *Uljhan*, *Kitne Sambandh*, *Shor*, *Meri Priya Kahaniyan* (My Favourite Short Stories; short story collections), 1975 to 1982 *Hindi ki Shreshth Kahaniyan* (ed. in year-wise volumes), and *Yah Bhi Nahin* (Not Even This ; novel, 1976).

His prominent short stories are : 'The Blotting Paper', 'Pani' (Water), 'Pul' (Bridge), 'Pardarshik' (Transparent), 'Kil' (The Nail), etc. There is a selection of his 51 short stories.

He ed. Hindi literary magazine 'Sanchetana' from Delhi. He produced literary programmes on TV and taught Hindi in Japan. He is also the author of a critical work : *Vishnu Prabhakar : Vyaktitwa and Krititwa.*

MAHIPATI (alive between 1611-81). Celebrated saint of Karnataka, who was initiated into the Bhakti-cult by Bhaskar Swami, a great Jogi. He was a great scholar of Kannada, Sanskrit, Marathi, Telugu, Hindi, etc. and he could compose poems in all these languages. His Hindi *Padas* represent a synthesis of *Bhakti*, *Gyan* and *Yoga*.

MAHIPATI (fl. 18th cent. ?). Maithili poet, whose verses found respectable place in contemporary anthologies.

MAHMUD KHAN, HAFIZ (b. 1907). Bagheli folk-poet, who was born in Rewa. His poems in Bagheli are noted for their sweet pricks.

MAILA ANCHAL (The Dirty Region). Novel (1954) by Phanishwar Nath Renu (q.v.), which describes the limitations and potentials of a region with fidelity, subtlety and sympathy. The whole region, with all its beauty and ugliness, its good and evil aspects, appears as a living phenomenon before our eyes. The novel also represents a new technique in Hindi novel.

MAINADE. Rajasthani Pavada, which describes the story of Mainade (Mainavati) and her son, Gopichand. Mainade had been blessed with a son by a boon but on the condition that if Gopichand does not renounce the world after a certain period, he would meet his death. Mainade makes him renounce the world before the appointed time, with the result that Gopichand has become immortal. The story of Gopichand is popular throughout northern India in slightly varying versions.

MAINASAT. Poem (Script 1667-70) by Sadhan, which describes the story of the faithfulness of Rani Maina.

MAISALE, J.G. Kannada-speaking modern Hindi writer, who is the author of *Kannada-Hindi Kosh.*

MAITHIL BHAKTA-PRAKASH. Collection of devotional Maithili and Sanskrit songs, which was compiled by Laliteshwar Singh of Anandpur in 1920.

MAITHIL CHRESTOMATHY. Anthology of mediaeval Maithili poetry, which was compiled by George A. Grierson in 1884.

MAITHILI PRASAD BHARDWAJ. Modern Chambiyali writer, who is noted for his article 'Gallan Hoi Bitiyan' (Himprasth), which sings of an unusual nuptial tale. He also wrote several other articles on folk-literature.

MAITHILISHARAN GUPTA (1886-1964). Celebrated Hindi poet, who was born at Chirgaon in the Jhansi district of Uttar Pradesh. It was through self-study that he acquired a good knowledge of Hindi, Sanskrit, Persian and Bengali. His father, Seth Ramcharan Gupta, was also a poet. Maithilisharan Gupta's poems were first published in 'Saraswati' in 1906, when he came under the influence of Mahavir Prasad Dwivedi (q.v.) and adopted his standards in the Khari Boli. He continued to write poems for the 'Saraswati' as long as Dwivedi was its editor.

Gupta was a prolific writer ; besides writing 43 original works, he also tr. into Hindi nine works from Bengali, Sanskrit and Persian. His chief works are as under :—

Poetry : *Rang men Bhang* (1910), *Jaydrath-Vadh* (1910 ; on the killing of Jaydrath by Arjun), *Bharat Bharati* (1912 ; q.v.), *Padya-Prabandh*, *Kisan* (on the pitiable conditions of Indian farmers), *Vaitalik*, *Shakuntala*, *Patravali*, *Panchvati* 1925 ; q.v.), *Swadeshi-Sangit*, *Hindu*, *Tripathga* (a collection of *Bak-Samhar*, *Van-Vaibhav*, and *Sairandhri*), *Shakti*, *Gurukul* (on the Sikh Gurus), *Vikat Bhat* (on the heroism of a Rajput family), *Jhankar* (mystical poems), *Saket* (his masterpiece ; 1932 ; q.v.), *Yashodhara* (1933 ; q.v.), *Mangal-Ghat*, *Dwapar* (on Krishna), *Siddharaj* (1936), *Nahush* (a mythological poem on the rise, fall and rise again due to one's deeds) *Kunalgit* (1942 ; on Kunal, a son of Ashok), *Kaba aur Karbala* (on Hussain), *Arjan aur Visarjan*, *Vishwa-Vedna*, *Maurya-Vijay*, *Jay-Bharat* (q.v.), *Prithwiputra* and *Vishnu-Priya*.

Drama : *Tilottama* (1916) *Chandrahas* (1916) and *Anagh* 1925 ; verse play).

Translated Works : *Virangana*, *Meghnad-Vadh*, *Palasi-Yuddha*, *Virahini Brajangana* (from Bengali), *Swapna-Vasavadatta* (from Sanskrit ; 1929) *Rubaiyat of Omarkhayyam*. He also wrote a large number of lyrics ; his *Saket* is full of fine lyrical touches.

Proud of the glorious heritage of India, he invoked its spirit so as to create national and social consciousness among Indians. He was the first Hindi poet to have patronized Khari Boli and was its foremost writer. He also revived the epic tradition abandoned since Tulsidas.

In Hindi, he was acclaimed as a national poet. Mahatma Gandhi acknowledged his great contribution to the national cau,e and called him 'Rashtra Kavi' on the occasion of the 50th birth anniversary celebrations of the poet in 1936. He was a nominated Member of Parliament in the Rajya Sabha.

MAKHAN (fl. 18th cent.). Riti poet, whose chief work, *Shrinath Pingal Chhand-Vilas* deals with prosody.

MAKHAN LAL CHATURVEDI (1889-1967). Nationalist poet and writer, who was born at Bavai in the Hoshangabad district of Uttar Pradesh. He served as a teacher, joined the national freedom movement and was jailed. Editor of the weekly, 'Karmavir', Khandwa, he used to write poetry under the pen name of 'Ek Bharatiya Atma'. He was President of the Hindi Sahitya Sammelan.

Chaturvedi's chief works are : *Himkiritini* (Wearing a Snow-Crown ; 1943), *Himtarangini* (Having Snow Wavelets ; 1949), *Mata* (Mother ; 1951 ; a collection of 56 poems, mainly nationalist), *Samarpan* (The Surrender), *Yuga-charan*, *Venu lo Gunje Dhara* (1960), *Bijuri Kajal Anj Rahi* (poetical collections), *Vanvasi* (The Forest Dweller), *Kala ka Anuvad* (The Translation of Art ; short story collections), *Krishnarjun-Yuddha* (a literary drama, which was a grand success on the stage) *Ramanyan-Yuddha*, *Mahabharat* (dramas), *Sahitya-Devata* (prose-poetry), *Chintak ki Lachari*, *Amir Irade : Gharib Irade* (1960 ; essay collections) and *Samay ke Panv* (The Feet of the Time).

An anthology of his unpublished poems : *Dhumra-Valay* has been published in 1981 ; the mood of the most of the poems is happy and serene, though with occasional flashes of the old revolutionary Similarly, *Rangon ki Boli* (The Voice of Colours ; 1982) is a collection of his essays on life, art and literature.

MALATI DIGHE. Marathi-speaking modern Hindi poetess, who has published poems on various subjects.

MALATI JOSHI. Fiction writer ; her works are : *Madhyantar* (The Interval), *Nishkasan* (Explusion ; 1966), *Pashan-Yuga* (The Stone Age), *Patakshep*, *Samarpan ka Sukh*, *Sahcharini*, *Vishwas Gatha*, *Parajay* and *Man na Bhaye Das Bis*.

MALATI PARULKAR. Marathi-speaking modern Hindi poetess, whose poems are written on various subjects ; *Ore Kabira ke Ram* is her poetical collection. She is also the author of a novel *Bali* and a short story collection : *Tum Badi Pagal Ho*. *Ek Arsa Hua* (A Long Time Back ; 1981), *Inni*, *Mukta* and *Jahan Pau Phatne Vali Hai* are her other fiction works.

MALATI SHRIKHAND. Marathi-speaking modern Hindi dramatist, who is the author of *Virangana* and *Dahej*.

MALAYSUNDARI KATHA. Rajasthani poem by Manikya Sundar Suri, which was composed in about 1421.

Mahabal, son of king Surajpal of Prithwisthanpur, sees Malaysundari, the daughter of king Virdhaval of Chandravati sitting in an oriel. Both fall in love and resolve to marry. The prince and the princess are often separated, but are reunited every time ; there are many miraculous episodes as well. The above folk-tale has been very popular, particularly among the Jain poets.

MALCHANDRA SHARMA. Writer, whose *Uday Pravas ki Diary* (1980) is a collection of essays.

MALI, B.L. 'ASHANT'. Rajasthani writer, whose *Kili Kili Kutako* (1978) is a collection of 10 short stories, while *Minakh ra Khoj* is a novel on the abolition of Hindu caste-system. *Bilanio Dado* (1979) is a story for children, where the hero is a dwarf-sized villager, who becomes a leader due to his merits. He has also written other poems for children. His *Dudhiya Dant* (1980) is a long story (novel ?) for children on the theme of untouchability ; *Mati Sun Majak* (1980) is a collection of 15 small essays on corruption, nepotism and other contemporary issues, while *Bolta Akhar* (1981) is a full length drama based on contemporary political situation in the country. *Taran Chai Rat* (1981) contains 11 small essays on the sky, the sun, the moon, etc., while *Hansi ra Sabadaka* (along with M. Sharma) is a book on jokes. *Kachamadi Raju* (1981) is the story of a naughty boy, who at last is reformed. He has also tr. Charles Dickens' *David Copperfield* and *Alice in Wonderland* as *Mayanagari* into Rajasthani.

MALIDAS, BHAT. Rajasthani author of *Davavait Narsingh Das Gaud Ki*, which is a historical work and includes Vanshavali ; his time is not certain.

MALIK MOHAMMED. Tamil-speaking Hindi writer, whose chief works are : *Vaishnav Bhakti Andolan ka Adhyayan* (The Study of Vaishnav Bhakti Movement ; thesis ; 1971), *Amir Khusro : Bhavatmak Ekta ke Agradut* (Amir Khusro : The Harbinger of Emotional Integration) and critical works on Hindi language and literature, e.g., *Rajbhasha Hindi* (Vikas ke Vividh Ayam). He received Nehru Fellowship, Soviet Land Nehru Award and travelled to U.S.S.R. He is Head of the Department of Hindi, Calicut University (Kerala) and is chief of the 'Nagari Ek-lipi-Vistar Parishad'.

MALIK MUHAMMAD JAYASI. Greatest Sufi poet of Hindi, who is said to be born at Ghazipur. According to the poet himself, he was born in A.H. 900 (*c.* A.D. 1493). He had an ugly face and lost one eye on account of smallpox. The poet had, however, considered having one eye as a matter of pride and had compared himself to Shukracharya, the preceptor of the demons. Later on, he shifted to Jayas (Raibarelli) where he passed the major part of his life ; hence he is called 'Jayasi'. He was a disciple of Sheikh Muhiuddin, a Sufi saint, and stands ninth in the hierarchy of Chishti saints. During certain periods of his life, he wandered about like the Sufi mendicants and towards the close of his career, lived in Amethi, the capital of a small principality. There he was much honoured by Raja Ram Singh, who attributed the birth of a son to the prayers of this saint. His tomb is still to be seen at Amethi. In his own life, he was celebrated for piety, devotion and kindliness. He died after 1542 in the reign of Sher Shah.

Jayasi started writing poetry at the age of 30. He composed three famous works : *Padmavat*, *Akhravat* and *Akhiri Kalam* (qq.v.) ; manuscript of another work, *Kanhavat* said to have been composed by Jayasi, has recently been discovered and it has been edited by Parmeshwari Lal Gupta. A learned poet, he has displayed a good knowledge of Hathyoga, chess, astronomy, etc. Despite his being a Mohammadan, Jayasi was very much acquainted with Hindu gods and goddesses and the religion in general. His work is in Avadhi, written in Persian script, later decoded into Nagari and published by Ramchandra Shukla.

MALL DEV, NRIP. Maithili poet of Nepal, whose lyrics are found in *Nepal Padavali* of Vidyapati and *Kansnarayan*

Padavali. He has not been correctly identified, but he appears to have flourished in the 17th century.

MALUKDAS (1574-1682). Saint-poet of Kada (Allahabad), whose *Gaddis* were established even in Nepal and Kabul. He was a follower of Kabir, but he was greatly influenced by Kabir's Guru, Ramanand. He preached equality of all men and was against idol-worship and sham ritualistic religious observances. He was very pious and was tender-hearted. It is said that he used to gather thorns and pebbles from streets daily and throw them aside in order that they may not hurt other passers-by. Emperor Aurangzeb was so much impressed by his ideas that he waived the *Jazia* tax in the area he lived. Malukdas composed *Gyan Bodh* and *Ratnakhan*. His language is easy and smooth. He disregarded all wordly interests and advocated inactivity; some of his utterances are frequently quoted even today. He is said to be the author of *Ramavtar-Lila* also, which some scholars ascribe to another Malukdas.

MALUSHAHI. Kumaoni Panvada, which describes the romance of Raja Malushahi of Katiyuri dnyasty and Rajuli, the exceptionally beautiful daughter of a rich merchant named Shunpati Shauk. The tale is like this that two ladies, a queen and the wife of a businessman, having no issues, go to a temple and receive the blassings of the deity. The queen gets a son, named Malushahi while the other lady gets a daughter, named Rajuli. Rajuli loves Malushahi, but is married to a young man, who tortures her. She escapes, reaches the capital city of Malushahi, enters his sleeping chamber and returns to her mother after placing a letter on Malushahi's couch. On reading the letter, Malushahi as a *Jogi* goes in quest of Rajuli and reaches her place. Rajuli by her magic turns him into a little insect and carfully keeps him in her hair-locks. Later on he is brought back into human form Rajuli's mother poisons Malushahi to death. Seeing all this in a dream, Malushahi's mother takes a large force of *Jogis* of the twelve sects and proceeds to Rajuli's place. Rajuli's mother also instigates Rajuli's husband who also collects a large force. The *Jogi* Guru of Malushahi restores the latter to life and turns him into a parrot, who flies over to Rajuli and informs her of every incident. A fierce battle ensues in which Malushahi is victorious. Malushahi then takes Rajuli to his capital city. This is a very popular ballad in the northern regions of the Hindi area.

MALYAJ (1935-1982). Poet, whose collections of poems: *Zakhm par Dhul* (Dust on the Wound) and *Apne Hone ko*

Aprakashit Karta Hua (Unrevealing the Self-Existence ; 1980) unveil the poet's feelings and perceptions. *Kavita se Sakshatkar* (1979) is on criticism, while *Hanste Hue Mera Akelapan* is a humorous work.

MAMA PRAGDAS (fl. 18th cent.). Poet of the Ram-cult (Rasik Sect), who considered Sita as his sister. He lived in Ayodhya. Several of his *Padas* in Avadhi and Braj are available.

MAMTA KALIYA. Modern short story writer and wife of Ravindra Kaliya (q.v.) ; her chief works are : *Chhutkara* (The Release ; 1969), *Seat No. 6*, *Ek Adad Aurat* (A Single Woman), *Pratidin*, *Ek Qadam Age* (short story collections), *Beghar* (The Houseless ; 1971), *Narak dar-Narak* (From Hell to Hell), *Prem Kahani* (The Love Story ; 1980), and *Larkian* 1983 ; novels). *Ek Qadam Age* (One Step Forward ; ed.) is a collection of 31 short stories of 31 teachers of Rajasthan. Her collection of original poems in English is published by Writers' Workshop, Calcutta.

MAN (fl. 1613-36). Riti poet, who was a disciple of Upadhyay Shiv Nidhan. Among his 11 works, *Bhasha Kavi Rasamanjari* is a work on *Nayak-Nayika Bhed*.

MAN. Riti poet of Bikaner, whose works are : *Saynyogadwatrinshika* (1674), *Kavi Vinod* (Lahore, 1688) and *Kavi Pramod* ; the first work is on erotics, while the remaining two are on Ayurveda.

MAN (MANSINGH ; fl. 1677-83). Jain poet, who was connected with the royal family of Mewar. His *Raj-Vilas* (1680) in 18 cantos describes the heroism of Maharana Rajsingh of Udaipur. He also wrote a commentary on the *Bihari Satsai* in prose.

MAN BODH (d. *c*. 1788). Maithili poet, whose *Krishna-Janma*, a Mahakavya, is an adaptation from *Harivansha* and the *Bhagavata* of the original Sanskrit. It had an universal appeal and is remembered till this day. Grierson first edited ten chapters of it and translated them into English. In 1934, Umesh Mishra edited the complete work in 18 chapters.

The poem, also of linguistic importance, is not limited to Krishna's birth and describes the defeat of Jarasandh, Kans and contains matter dealing with Krishna's childhood. The entire description of Krishna as a child growing in years is a straight-forward narration without any poetic flight or learned imagery and is very popular in Mithila. He was also noted for his *Sohars*, particular types of lyrics.

Man Bodh occupies a prominent place in the history of Maithili literature. He ceased to be tied down by the rigours of Rags and Raginis and other conventions of Vidyapati. He in fact freed Maithili poetry from the learned and sophisticated imagery of Vidyapati and made a distinct bid for simplicity and directness. Other poets followed him.

MAN KAVI. Poet of the Riti school, who was son of Raja Joravar Singh. In 1788, he composed *Narendrabhushan Nagar*, a work on Alankar.

MAN KUMARI, RAO (1905-). Rajasthani poetess of Udaipur, whose Rajasthani poems in traditional Charan style are available. She has also paid poetic homage to the modern heroes, including those, who sacrificed their lives in fighting against the Chinese attack on India.

MAN KUTUHAL (*Manvati-Vinayvati Prabandh*). Rajasthani (mixed with Apabhransh) poem in 114 verses, composed by Hir Bhat in the first half of the 15th century.

Vilal Kunvari (alias Manvati) and Lal Kunvari (alias Vinayvati), the daughters of the ruler of Dungarpur, are married respectively to Rao Gaipa and Nathraj of Toda. Nathraj, an opium addict, is always in a state of intoxication. So, Lal Kunvari somehow manages to elope with Gaipa. Vilal Kunvari, jealous of her sister as co-wife, becomes arrogant, thus making her husband's life miserable. Once the poet Hir Bhat comes to the Rao for some donations and he comes to know the reason of Rao's grief. He tries to bring about a reconciliation between Vilal Kunvari and the Rao by composing the above poem.

MAN MOHAN DAS (fl. 18th cent.). Rajasthani saint-poet of the Charandasi or Shuk Sampraday, whose stray verses are available.

MAN MOHAN DAS. Modern Maithili poet, who is noted for his *Barahmasas* and *Tirhutis*.

MAN MOHAN GAUTAM. Author of *Hindi Bhasha Vigyan* (1971) and *Saral Bhasha Vigyan*.

MAN MOHAN JHA. Maithili writer, who is noted for his short story collections : *Ashrukan* (1949) and *Jhagda* on the love-quarrel.

MAN MOHAN SEHGAL (1932-). Writer, who has made studies of *Granth Sahib*, Sant Poetry, Gurudatt and Jainendra Kumar. His chief works are : *Guru Granth Sahib : Ek Sanskritik Sarvekshan*, *Sant Kavyae ka Darshnik Vishleshan*, *Upanyaskar Gurudatt : Vyaktitva aur Krititva*, *Upanyaskar Jainendrakumar : Mulyankan* and *Panjab ka Hindi Sahitya*. He has also written novels : *Kashmir ki Kasak*, etc.

MAN SINGH, MAHARAJA DWIJDEV. See *Dwijdev*.

MAN SINGH, MAHARAJA (fl. 1599-1614). Courtier of Emperor Akbar, whose Rajasthani stray verses in different popular metres are available.

MAN SINGH, MAHARAJA OF JOPDHUR (1782-1843). Poet, scholar and musicologist, whose poetry in Rajasthani, Braj, Khari Boli, Panjabi and in a mixed form of any two or more of these languages, is varied and extensive. He composed some 60 poems of all sorts, large and small and his poetry mainly deals with the following four subjects :—

On Nath Bhakti and its Philosophy : *Anubhav Manjari*, *Sarupan ra Doha*, *Jalandhar Gyan Sagar* (in Rajasthani), *Jalandharnathji ro Charit Granth*, *Siddha Muktaphal*, *Tej-Manjari*, *Panchavali*, *Nath Kirtan*, *Nath Stotra*, *Jalandharnath ri Nisani*, *Nath Pada-Pushpanjali*, *Shad Chakra Varnan*, etc. (in Rajasthani mixed Braj).

Erotic Works : *Duha Sanyog Shringar*, *Duha Viyog Shringar*, *Shringar Pada*, *Rag-Ratnakar*, *Shringar Shiromani Namvarta Granth* (in prose) in Rajasthani and Rajasthani-mixed Braj.

On Nature : *Udyan Varnan*, *Shadritu Varnan*, etc. (in Rajasthani).

On Ram and Krishna Themes : *Ram Vilas* (incomplete), *Krishna Vilas*, *Rasa-Chandrika* (in Braj).

The number of his *Padas*, which are meant to be sung, on Bhakti and eroticism is very large. Another popular story, *Ratna Hamir ri Varta* in *Vachnika* style, is attributed by some to Mansingh and to Uttamchand Bhandari by others.

His poems are of literary value.

MAN SINGH ASIYA. See *Mahav Yas Prakas*.

MAN SINGH TOMAR (fl. 15th cent.). Ruler of Gwalior, who was a patron of many celebrated musicians including Baiju, Bakhshu, Pande. Man himself was a musician and was the first to sing in the Dhrupad style of music. He composed *Man Kutuhal*, which was translated into Persian by Faqirullah.

MANAGER PANDEY. Modern scholar, whose chief works are : *Krishnakatha ki Parampara aur Surdas ka Kavya* and *Sahitya aur Itihas Drishti.*

MANAK TIWARI 'BANDHU'. Modern Rajasthani poet, who has composed Nature, love, patriotic and progressive poems : 'Label' and 'Mankhar ra Asar'. In his poem ; 'Jalam Bhom', he glorifies Rajasthan.

MANCHHARAM (1770-1833). Dingal poet of Jodhpur, whose father's name was Bakhshiram. He was patronized by Maharaja Mansingh of Jodhpur. His *Raghunath Rupak Gitan Ro* (q. v. ; 1806), a Riti work, describes the story of *Ramayan* by way of illustrations ; the story is mainly based on Tulsidas's *Ramcharitmanas.* The poet's other work *Ghanerao ri Ghazal* describes the town Ghanera of Gaudhvar and the political conditions there.

MANCHITA (fl. 1793). Poet of the Krishna-cult, who was a Brahmin of Mau (Bundelkhand). He composed two works on the story of Krishna : *Surabhi Danlila* and *Krishnayan* ; the first poem describes Krishna's childhood sports, the felling of the Yamalarjun trees, Krishna's charity and even *Nakhshikh. Krishnayan* is composed on the pattern of Tulsidas's *Ramayan* It is in *Dohas* and *Chaupais* and the language is Braj, occasionally mixed with Sanskrit.

MANDA KAMAYYA. See *Shishtu Krishnamurti Shastri.*

MANDAN (fl. 1659). Poet of the Riti school, who was a resident of Jaitpur (Bhundelkhand) and was present in 1659 in the court of Raja Mangad Singh. He composed five works : *Rasa-Ratnavali, Rasa-Vilas* (both on *Rasa*), *Janak Pachisi, Janaki Ju ko Byah* and *Nain-Pachasa* ; many of his stray verses are also extant. His language was natural and flowing. He was a poet of tender feelings.

MANESHWAR BADO. Assamese-speaking modern Hindi writer, who is noted for his essays.

MANGAL (fl. 17th cent.). One of the court-poets of Guru Govind Singh (q. v.) ; his tr. of the Shalya-parva of the

Mahabhcrata into Brajbhasha appears to have been done to the Guru's satisfaction. His *Saral Prashna* describes the chivalry, the generosity and other virtues of the Guru.

MANGAL RAM (fl. 1843). Rajasthani saint-poet, who lived in Dhanni in Udaipur Tehsil of Jaipur. Out of his some 100 works in Pingal, *Sundaroday* is his chief work.

MANGANI RAM JHA (1687-1795). Maithili poet, who was noted for his *Sohars*, particular types of lyrics. He was patronized by Maharaja Madhav Singh (1776-1808).

MANGELAL CHATURVEDI. Rajasthani poet, whose *Maru Bharati* (1952) is a *Niti* poem. He has since published *Krishna Charit* (1982, Pt. I), which is the story of Krishna (based on the *Bhagavat*) upto his victory over Mathura.

MANGE RAM (1906-68). Famous folk-poet of Haryana, who was born at the village Sasna but was brought up by his maternal grandfather Udmi Ram of Panchi village. He was a disciple of the celebrated folk-poet, Lakhmi Chand (q. v.). His *Sangs* were of religious nature and one of the performances was watched even by Pandit Jawahar Lal Nehru. He also established 'Hariyanvi Gandharva Sabha' in 1962, an association of Hariyanvi Sangis. He composed some 40 *Sangs*, of which *Dharu Bhagat* and *Kirsan Janam* were most popular.

MANGLESH DABRAL. Poet, whose *Pahar par Lalten* (The Lantern on the Mount ; 1981) is a collection of poems.

MANGLI SADH (fl. 18th cent. ?) Rajasthani saint-poet of Laldasi Sampraday, whose *Bhajans* extol faith in God and Guru and advocate for leading a simple life.

MANGO RANI. Modern scholar, whose chief works are : *Alochak Pant* and *Wordsworth aur Pant ki Kavya-Chetana*.

MANHAR CHAUHAN (1939-). Writer, whose chief works are : *Hirna Sanvari* (regional novel), *Santulan-Asantulan* (Balance-Unbalance ; 1964), *Surya ka Rakta* (The Blood of the Sun), *Akhiri Safa* (The Last Page), *Samarpan* (novels), *Bis Subahvon ke Bad* (After Twenty Mornings) and *Apni-apni Astha* (short story collections). His chief story is 'Ag' (The Fire). He has in all published 16 novels and has edited several short story collections, *e.g.*, *Pratinidhi Sahsik Kahaniyan* (1984).

MANI, K.S. Malayalam-speaking modern Hindi scholar, whose research work is: *Maithilisharan Gupta aur Vallathol ke Kavya ka Tulnatmak Adhyayan* (A Comparative Study of the Poetry of Maithilisharan Gupta and Vallathol).

MANIDEV. See *Gokulnath, Gopinath, Manidev.*

MANI LAL. See *Maganlal Manilal.*

MANI MADHUKAR. Writer and poet, whose chief works are: *Safed Memne* (The White Lambs; 1971 a regional novel containing some shocking scenes), *Meri Striyan* (My Women; 1981), *Patton ki Biradari* (novels), *Khand Khand Pakhand Parva, Ghas ka Charana, Balram ke Hazar Nam* and *Udti-Hui Nadiyan*(poetical works). His chief short story collections are: *Chuninda Chaudah, Gandh ke Galiyare, He Bhanumati, Pichhla Pahada, Ek Bachan Bahubachan* and *Hava men Akele*. He edited 'Rang-Yoga' in Jodhpur and wrote experimental plays and staged them; his chief dramas being *Ektare ki Ankh* (The Eye of a Monochord; 1980; a description of the inconsistencies in modern age in the background of Kabir's life), *Rasa-Gandharva, Khel Polumpur, Saivaton men Sanvad, Bulbul Sarai* and *Dulari Bai.* He has travelled to Yogoslavia and has ed. 'Anima', 'Ravivar', Calcutta, etc.

MANIPADMA. See *Braj Kishore Verma.*

MANIRAM MISHRA. Poet of the Riti school, who was a resident of Kannauj and was son of Ichchharam Mishra. He composed two works: *Chhand-chhappani* (1772; a work on prosody) and *Anandmangal* (a verse tr. of the 10th skandh of the *Bhagavata*).

MANI SINGH, BHAI (fl. 1718). Hindi poet of Panjab, who was made Granthi of Harmandir, Amritsar after Guru Govind Singh. He wrote *Guru Vilas,* a biography in verse of Guru Govind Singh. Scholars are of the view that Sukkha Singh (fl. 1797) and Koir Singh, the two poets, did not compose *Guru Vilas* of their own, but simply re-wrote the *Guru Vilas*, composed by Mani Singh. The biography is full of miracles performed by the Guru.

MANIK (fl. 1489). Poet, who composed *Baital Pachchisi* (based on the Sanskrit original), which was written at the instance of Sanghai Khemal in the reign of Mansingh Tomar of Garh Gwalior. Manik was a Kayasth of Ayodhya.

MANIK CHAND (fl. 1504-73). Poet of the Krishna-cult (Vallabh Sect), whose *Padas* are available in the *Rag Kalpadrum*, etc.

MANIK PHULSINGH PHUL, Mrs. Modern Hindi poetess of Trinidad, who is noted for her stray poems.

MANIK PRABHU (fl. 17th cent. ?). Founder of the Sakal Sect, who is considered as an incarnation of Guru Dattatrey. His religious seat is at Humnabad, also called Manik Nagar, near Gulbarga. He composed hundreds of *Padas* in Hindi.

MANIKA MOHINI. Modern short writert; her chief short story collections are : *Khatma Hone ke Bad* (After Completion), *Abhi Talash Jari Hai* (The Search is still Going on ; 1976), *Paru ne Kaha Tha* (Paru Had Said ; 1979), *Apna-apna Sach* and *Swapnadansh* (1981). Her latest important short story is 'Asvikrit' (1983). She works for the All India Radio

MANIKYACHANDRA SURI. Jain Rajasthani writer, whose *Prithwichandra Charitra* (*Vagvilas*), composed in 1421, is in prose. Though it tells the romance of Raja Prithwichandra of Paithanpur Patan and Ratnamanjari, the daughter of Raja Somdev of Ayodhya, its main object is a vivid and ornamental depiction of objects and surrounding of seasons, rivers, mountains, horses, elephants, battles, marriages, etc. He also composed *Malaysundari Katha* (q.v.).

MANINDRA KISHORE VERMA. Scholar, whose chief works are : *A Synchronic Comparative Study of the Structure of the Noun Phrase in English and Hindi* (Michigan, 1966), *Hindi and English Sentence and Clause Patterns ; a Study in Systematic Contrastive Analysis* (1968) and *The Structure of the Noun Phrase in English and Hindi* (971). See *Nilsson*.

MANINDRA NATH CHAUDHARY 'RAJKAMAL'. See *Rajkamal Chaudhary*.

MANIYAR SINGH (fl. *c.* 1784). Poet of Kashi, who composed *Mahimna Bhasha* (extolling Parvati or Devi ; 1784), *Hanumat Chhabbisi* and *Sundar-kand*. His language is alliterative, refined and forceful.

MANJARI DAS (fl. 18th cent). Poet of the Krishna-cult, who is noted for his *Padas*.

MANJARI OHALA. Scholar and author of *Topics in Hindi-Urdu Phonology* (1972), *The Abstractness Controversy* ; *Experimental Input from Hindi* (1973), *The Schwa-deletion Rule in Hindi* (1974) and *Aspects of Hindi Phonology* (1983). She is at present working with the School of Humanities and the Arts, San Jose State University, San Jose, California.

MANJHAN (fl. early 16th cent.). Sufi poet, who composed *Madhumalati* (q.v.), an allegorical romance. He is counted among the first three great Sufi poets.

MANJU KESHAVANAND (fl. 1832). Gujarati-speaking saint-poet of Swaminarayan Sect, who was a devotee of Sahajanand. In Hindi, he composed some 4,000 *Pada*s and a work *Aishwarya Prakash*, describing the miracles of his Guru.

MANJULA BHAGAT. Writer ; her chief works are : *Tuta Hua Indradhanush* (The Broken Rainbow ; 1976), *Kya Chhut Gaya* (What is Left Out), *Anaro*, *Begane Ghar Men* (In the House of Others ; 1978), *Tirchhi Bauchhar*, *Khatul* (novels), *Gulmohar ke Guchchhe* (Bunches of Gulmohar), *Atmahatya se Pahle*, *Kitna Chhota Safar*, *Apna-apna Dayara* and *Bavan Patte aur Ek Joker* (short story collections).

MANMATH MATH GUPTA (1908-). Writer, who, as a revolutionary, was associated with the Kakori case. His chief works are : *Krantiyug ke Sansmaran* (Reminiscences of the Revolutionary Period), *Bharatiya Krantikari Andolan ka Itihas* (History of Indian Revolutionary Movement), *Kathakar Premchand* (Premchand as a Fiction Writer), *Pragativad ki Ruprekha* (Outlines of the Progressive Movement ; 1953), *Sahitya, Kala Samiksha* (Estimate of Literature and Art ; 1954), *Bahta Pani* (The Flowing Water ; 1955), *Astin ke Sanp* (The Hidden Enemy), *Kajal ki Kothri*, *Andheri Nagri*, *Dushcharitra*, *Hotel de Taj*, *Adhi rat ke Atithi*, *Sabit Bacha Na Koi* and *Shahid aur Shohde* (the last nine novels) ; he has also written short stories ('Nyay' or Justice, etc.). He edited 'Ajkal' for many years.

MANNAN DWIVEDI (1885-1921). Writer, who is noted for his graceful, rhythmical and chaste prose. His chief works are : *Musalmani Rajya ka Itihas* (The History of Muslim Rule), *Hamara Bhishan Hras* (Our Degradation ; history), *Ramlal* and *Kalyani* (1920 ; social novels). He made appropriate use of Urdu words and phrases along with Sanskrit expressions. He also contributed poems to 'Saraswati' and other monthlies.

He wrote a narrative poem, *Prem* (Love) and a popular book of children's verse, *Vinod*.

MANNU BHANDARI (1931-). Writer, whose chief works are :

Novels : *Ek Inch Muskan* (One-inch Smile ; 1962 ; in collabration with her husband, Rajendra Yadav), *Ap ka Banti* (Your Banti ; 1971 ; on the mental state of a child amidst the straitened relations of the parents), *Mahabhoj* (The Great Feast ; 1979 ; tr. into English), *Kalva* and *Swami*.

Short Story Collections : *Tin Nigahon ki Ek Tasvir* (A Picture of Three Eyes), *Ek Plate Sailab* (A Plate-ful Flood), *Kil aur Kasak*, *Main Har Gai* (I am Defeated), *Yahi Sach Hai* (This is the Truth ; 1972 ; filmed), *Ankhon Dekha Ghunt*, *Trishanku tatha anya Kahaniyan*, *Shreshth Kahaniyan* (Best Short Stories) and *Meri Priya Kahaniyan* (My Favourite Short Stories). Her prominent short stories are 'Yahi Sach Hai', 'Khota Sikka' (The Counterfeit Coin), 'Saza' (The Punishment), 'Kshaya' (Tuberculosis), Rani Ma ka Chabutra' (The Memorial to the Queen-Mother), etc.

Drama. *Bina Divaron ke Ghar* (Houses without Walls ; on the jealousy of a man due to his wife's popularity in society).

She teaches Hindi at Miranda House, Delhi University.

MANOHAR (fl. 1570). Court-poet of Akbar, whose chief work is *Shat-Prashnottari* (100 Questions).

MANOHAR. Poet of the Riti school, who composed *Manohar Manjari* (on *Nayikabhed*) in 1634 (?). He was a native of Mathura.

MANOHAR BANDYOPADHYAY. Bengali-speaking modern Hindi critic, who has made a notable contribution towards the analysis and evaluation of modern Hindi literature in the light of Western criticism. He has also tr. into English Jayshankar Prasad's *Kamayani* (q.v.). *Sune Chaurahe Par* (On a Deserted Crossroad ; 1983), a collection of his poems, reveals the various facets of a single person.

MANOHAR DAS (fl early 16th cent.). Poet of the Krishna-cult (Chaitanya Sect), who was a native of Patna. With his contact with Ramray (q.v.), he became a recluse and came to settle in Vrindavan. He composed some *Padas*.

MANOHAR DAS (fl. around 1828). Poet of the Riti school, who was patronized by one Maharaj Man Singh. He composed his *Jas Abhushan Chandrika*, a work on *Alankars*.

MANOHAR DAS NIRANJANI (fl. latter half of 17th cent.). Rajasthani saint-poet and a follower of Haridas Niranjani Sect, who was a great scholar of Vedanta. His works, *Gyan Manjari*, *Vedanta Paribhasha*, *Shat Prashnottari*, *Gyan Vachan Churnika* (in prose mixed with verse) and *Saptabhumika Gyan Manjari* (1659 ; in verse) treat of Vedanta and allied topics.

MANOHAR KALE. Marathi-speaking modern Hindi writer, who is noted for his *Adhunik Hindi Marathi men Kavyashastriya Adhyayan*, a research work.

MANOHAR LAL GAUR (1918-). Writer, whose chief works are : *Ghanananda aur Ritikal ki Swachchhand Kavyadhara* (research on Ghananand) and *Acharya Kshemendra*.

MANOHAR PRABHAKAR. Modern poet, who has composed lyrical poems, portraying various aspects of Nature ; his poetical collection is *Mahuye Mahak Gaye*. His collection of essays is *Ati Sarvatra Varjyet* (1984).

MANOHAR RAY (b. *c.* 1653). Poet of the Krishna-cult (Chaitanya Sect), who lived in Vrindavan. His works are : *Shri Radharaman Rasa Sagar*, *Sampraday Bodhini* and *Rasik Jivni* ; *Kshanda Giti Chintamani* is a work edited by him.

MANOHAR, S.S. Rajasthani scholar, who has edited *Rajasthani Rasadhara* (1982 ; old and new Rajasthani poetry).

MANOHAR SHARMA. Rajasthani poet and writer, whose chief works are : *Rasa Dhara* (stray poems dealing with Nature), *Aravali ki Atma* (1947), *Gajmoti* (100 verses, where Nature has been viewed with mystic curiosity), *Git Katha* (1947), *Kunjan* (a poem on separated lovers, on the model of *Meghadut*, *Gopi Git* (on Nirgun and Sagun Bhakti in the tradition of *Bhramar Git*), *Marvani* (an allegory, based on the popular romance of Dhola-Maru), *Panchhi* (on the pathetic story of a parrot), *Bapu* (on Mahatma Gandhi's life), *Amarphal* (on the story of Nachiketa as described in the *Katha-Upanishad*), *Antarjami* (a thought-provoking poem, represented as a symbol of modern man) (all published from 1958 to 1960), *Dhoran ro Sangit* (1978 ; short poems, portraying the characters of popular love stories) ; in *Kunjan*, a soldier-king in the Deccan sends a message through the 'Kraunch' bird to his beloved in Bikaner. He has also written short stories (*Kanyadan*, 1971) and some stories depicting the compassion and humanity of the rich and some stories in the style of *Panchatantra* (*Sonal Bhing*; 1976). His *Balbadi* (1981), modelled on the *Panchatantra* is meant for children. He has done much work on *Vat* literature (*Rajasthani Vat Sahitya*: 1976) and on the *Anecdotes of Rajasthan* (1980 ; a collection of about 200 pieces). His play : *Nainsi ro Sako* (1973) takes its theme from Rajput history, while *Rohidai ra Phul* (1973) contains satirical essays. He is among the pioneers in the study of Rajasthani folk-songs. He has published some folk-tales as also sketches, reviews and articles.

MANOHAR SHARMA 'MANJUL'. Rajasthani poet, whose chief work is *Rajasthani Gunj* (Niti poems ; 1959).

MANOHAR SHYAM JOSHI. Writer, whose chief work *Kuru Kuru Swaha* (novel ; 1980) delineates the three facets of the same character in a beautiful manner. His other novels are : *Kasap* and *Uttaradhikarini* ; *Netaji Kahin* is his humarous work. *Baton Baton Men* is his latest work. *Kaise Kissago* (1983) is a collection of his short stories.

MANOHAR VANDYOPADHYAY. See *Manohar Bandopadhyay*.

MANOJ SHANKAR. Poet, whose *Shoshitnama* (1983) is a tirade against Caste-system.

MANORANJAN PRASAD (fl. 1st half of 20th cent.). Bhojpuri poet, whose 'Phirangiya' song on the Non-Co-operation Movement became extremely popular in and around Chhapra, where he was Principal of Rajendra College.

MANORATH RAM (fl. 1st half of 19th cent.). Rajasthani saint-poet of Ram Snehi Sect, Shahpura, whose stray verses are available.

MANSA RAM (fl. 18th cent.). Poet of the Krishna-cult (Haridasi Sect), who composed *Guru Mangal*, in praise of his Guru Lalit Kishori.

MANSA RAM CHANCHAL. Dogri-speaking modern Hindi poet and writer, whose chief works are : *Ashrumal* (The Garland of Tears), *Sushma* (The Excellent Beauty) (poetical collections), *Kisi ne Kaha Tha* (Somebody Had Said ; short story collection) and *Mahapurush* (biographies). He has also edited several papers.

MANSA RAM MODANI (fl. early 18th cent.). Rajasthani saint-poet of Ram Snehi Sampraday, Ren, who belonged to the village Sanju. One of the disciples of Dariyav (q.v.), his *Vani* lays emphasis on *Ram-smaran*, transcience of life, etc.

MANSAROVAR. See *Premchand*.

MANTRESHWAR JHA. Maithili writer and poet whose *Ojha Lekhe Gam Batah* (1979) is a collection of essays, written in a lighter vein. *Anchinhar Gam* (1981), consisting of some 41 poems, mainly satirical, and *Bahasal Ratik Ijot* (1982) are collections of poems.

MANU BHAI PATEL. Gujarati-speaking modern Hindi scholar, whose *Samsamayik Hindi Upanyason men Badalte Hue Mulya aur Unki Prakriyayen* is a research work.

MANU SHARMA. Novelist, whose *Ekling ka Dewan* (1980) is based on history ; his other novels are *Karna ki Atmakatha* and *Marichika* (1984).

MANUJ DEPAVAT. Modern Rajasthani poet, who has composed progressive poems.

MANVATI VINAYVATI PRABANDH. See *Man Kutuhal*.

MAQBUL AHMED. Modern Rajasthani poet, who is noted for his patriotic and heroic poems.

MARKANDEY (1932-). Short story writer, whose chief story collections are : *an-phul* (Betel Leaves and Flowers ; 1954), *Hansa Jai Akela* (Hansa Goes Alone ; 1960), *Bhudan* (The Gift of the Land ; 1961), *Sahaj aur Shubh* (1964), *Mahue ka Ped* (A Mahua Tree), *Mahi* (The Fish) and *Dana Bhusa tatha Anya Kahaniyan* (The Fodder and Other Stories ; 1980) ; *Patthar aur Parchhain* (The Stone and the Shadow) is a collection of his one-act plays. His prominent short story is : 'Hansa Jai Akela'. His last publication *Agnibij* (1981) is a novel.

MARKANDEY PRAVASI. Maithili writer and poet, who is noted for his short stories, poems and the social novels : *Viyan* (1979) and Abhiyan (1980). His 'Gandevo Bhaba' (1979) is a personal type of essay, while in *Agastyayani* (1980), the poet has given a new meaning to the story of saint Agastya and Lopamudra. His biographical novel is *Ham Kalidas* (1982 ; incomplete). Markandey is the pioneer of 'Tadarthvad' (Adhocism) in Maithili.

MARKOVA, DAGMAR. Modern Czech Hindi scholar, whose research articles have been published on modern Hindi literature, especially fiction.

MARSIYA (of Raoraja Bakhtavar Singh). See *Barhat Ummedram Palhavat.*

MARWAR RA PARGANAN RI VIGAT. See *Nainsi.*

MAST RAM KAPUR (1927-). Modern fiction writer, whose chief works are : *Tisari Ankh ka Dard* (The Pain of the Third Eye ; 1979), *Nak ka Doctor* (A Nose Specialist ; 1980) and *Ek Atut Silsila* (novels). He also wrote for children. He is also noted for his humorous writings ; his short story collection is *Gyarah Patte.*

MATAJI RI VACHNIKA. See *Jaychand, Jati.*

MATA PRASAD GUPTA (1909-69). Modern critic and bibliographer, who edited the texts of *Ramcharitmanas*, *Jayasi Granthavali*, *Prithwiraj Raso*, *Visaldev Raso*, *Madhumalati*, etc.; *Qatab Shatak aur Uski Hindui* is his research work. He taught Hindi at Allahabad University and laid down standard in textual research (*Pathanusandhan*). His *Hindi Granth Suchi* is one of the earliest standard bibliographies of Hindi works.

MATAV P.C. Kannada-speaking modern Hindi scholar, whose *Hindi ka Lavani Sahitya* (Lavani Literature of Hindi) is a research work.

MATHUR D.P. Rajasthani poet, whose *Bichhia Bajai* (1979) is a collection of small romantic lyrics.

MATHUR, GIRJAKUMAR. See *Girijakumar Mathur.*

MATHUR, JAGDISH CHANDRA. See *Jagdish Chandra Mathur.*

MATHURA DAS (fl. *c.* 1924). Writer, whose *Rukmini Parinay* (The Marriage of Rukmini) is a *Raslila*, though it is an ordinary play.

MATHURANAND CHOUDHARY. Modern Maithili poet, whose *Kanan Kanya* is an epic, while *Krishak* (1946) is a *Khandkavya* on the plight of a modern peasant. His *Mushak Mahima*, also a *Khandkavya*, comments on the existing literary or cultural aspects of Mithila's life. He also composed good lyrics.

MATHURA PRASAD SHARMA (fl. early 20th cent.). Novelist, who is noted for his historical novel : *Nurjahan*.

MATIRAM (b. *c.* 1617). Poet of the Riti school, who was the third of the four sons of Ratnakar Tripathi, a Kanyakubja Brahmin, his three brothers being Chintamani Tripathi, Bhushan (qq. v.) and Jatashankar alias Nilkanth, all poets. He was born at Tikwanpur in the Kanpur district and had a long span of life. For a number of years, he was the court-poet of Maharaj Bhav Singh of Bundi, to whom he dedicated his *Lalit Lalam* (q. v. ; composed any time between 1659 and 1688), a monumental work on *Alankars*, which contains many verses extolling his patron. At the court, Matiram was highly honoured and lived almost like a prince, but, it is believed, some difference arose between him and the Maharaj over the scant courtesy, which, as the poet thought, had been shown to his brother, Bhushan, when he visited the Bundi court. To keep up the prestige and honour of his brother, Matiram also retired from the court.

Chhand-Sar (or *Vritta Kaumudi*), a book on prosody, was dedicated to Maharaj Shambhunath Solanki, while Matiram's masterpiece, *Rasaraj* (q. v.), on *Rasa*, is without any dedication. His other works are : *Sahitya Sar*, *Lakshana Shringar* and *Matiram Satsai*. Many couplets of the *Satsai* compare favourably with the *Dohas* of Bihari.

The works of Matiram prove that he was well versed in poetics. *Lalit Lalam* and *Rasaraj* were popular during his age and are too even today. But Matiram as a poet is greater than his being an Acharya. The greatest quality of his poetry is that its charm is spontaneous and there is no artificiality of thought or of language. Genuine human experience and expression thereof, which are rare in the Riti age, are to be met here.

MATSYENDRA NATH. See *Machhandra Nath.*

MATSYENDRA SHUKLA. Modern poet, whose collections of poems are : *Andheri Rat ka Suraj* and *Tat ki Laharen* ; *Subah ka Akash* and *Tile par ek Ganv* are his short story collections.

MAVJI, SANT (1714-44). Rajasthani saint-poet, who was an Audichya Brahmin of village Sabla (Dungarpur). He left home at the age of 12 to perform asceticism. He preached devotion to God and service to humanity. His *Vani* called *Chaupada* preaches *Niti* and makes many predictions.

MAYANAND MISHRA. Maithili fiction writer and poet, whose chief novels are : *Bihadi Pat O Pathar* (1960 ; on Tribeni, a widow, who is violently shaken by sexual passion) and *Khola O Chidai* (1965 ; depicting the violence of passion in the life of the heroine, whose husband is impotent). Mayanand's portrayal of sex has the touches of reality, nobility and sublimity. He has also brought to limelight the poetry in the life of the lower classes. *Dishantar* (1965) is a collection of his poems. As a short story writer, his collections are *Bhang ka Lota* (1951 ; funny and humorous skits) and *Agi Mom Pathar*. His art of story narrating grips the reader's attention. He has also written some critical articles.

MAYA RAM (fl. 1761). Jain poet, who composed *Pradyumna Ras* on the story of Krishna's son, Pradyumna.

MAYAN BHATT (MAYAN BAMBH ; fl. 1st half of 15th cent. ?). Rajasthani poet, whose 40 erotic verses in *Kavitta* metre under the title, *Mayan Chhand* are available in different manuscripts. With diction nearly as sweet and delicate as that of *Vasant Vilas* (q.v.), the physical beauty of the woman and amorous feelings, gestures and sports are described in a very charming style.

Mayan Bhatt is also reputed to have composed a number of *Kavittas*, which included Randhaval to break his pledge of not giving alms to any Bhat. This incident is narrated in a Rajasthani story *Randhaval ri Vat* in which some verses of Mayan Bhatt are also included. There is a mention of *Mayan Puran* in Madhavanal-Kamkandala by Ganpati Kayasth ; until this Puran is available, its authorship cannot be ascribed definitely to Mayan.

MAYAN CHHAND. See *Mayan Bhatt.*

MAYAN PURAN. See *Mayan Bhatt.*

MAZUMDAR, D.N. Modern scholar, who is noted for his work : *Folk-songs of Mirzapur.*

McGregor, R.Stuart (1929-). British scholar of Hindi, who is at present in the Faculty of Oriental Studies, University of Cambridge. His publications are: *The Language of Indrajit of Orcha* (Cambridge, 1965), *Exercises in Spoken Hindi* (ed., Cambridge, 1970), *Outline of Hindi Grammar* (Oxford, 1972; 2nd ed., Delhi, 1977), *The Round Dance of Krishna and Uddhav's Message* (London, 1973), *Hindi Literature of the 19th and Early 20th Centuries* (Wiesbaden, 1974), *A New Voice for New Times: the Development of Modern Hindi Literature* (Canberra, 1981; A.L. Basham Lecture), *Hindi Literature from its Beginnings to the 19th Century* (Wiesbaden, 1983) and *Urdu Study Materials for Use with Outline of Hindi Grammar* (1984). His field of research is language and literature, while his work *The Round Dance of Krishna* is a tr. from Nanddas. He presided over the Third World Hindi Conference at Delhi in 1983. Facilities for the study of Hindi Language and Literature up to the degree of Ph.D. exist in the Cambridge University.

Medji Asiya. Rajasthani poet, whose *Pabu Prakash* (1932) describes the deeds and glorious death of Pabuji Rathore, the legendary folk-god of Rajasthan. See *Pabuji ka Pavadas*.

MEGHMAL-BHADDARI. Sayings and dialogues of Ghagh and Bhaddari in Rajasthani and Apabhransh, which are current in Rajasthan. These sayings, particularly relating to weather forecasts, were perhaps composed from the 11th to the 13th century.

MEGHNAD-BADH. See *Gauri Shankar Jha*.

Megh Raj (fl. *c.* 1604). Gujarati-speaking Jain poet, who composed several devotional poems in Hindi.

Megh Raj 'Mukul'. Modern Rajasthani poet, whose chief works are: *Sainani* (q. v.; 1944; a versified story based on a historical event, which was first recited in the Rajasthani Sahitya Sammelan held at Dinajpur and has been recorded also), 'Hiraul', 'An ri Bat', 'Kodamde', 'Chanvari' and 'Rani Padmani' (*Sainani ri Jagi Jot*, 1967; *Kiratyan*, 1968), contribution of lyrics to *Minjhar* (1963), an anthology, which portray Nature's various aspects and 'Dharm ro Marm Gandhi Janvo' (*Gandhi Jivan Jyoti*, 1970). He has also composed patriotic, Nature, love and progressive poems: 'Ghyari men Manakho', 'Mansaur Kumanas' and 'Minakh Bapdo'. He has also chosen objects of Nature as symbols in expressing progressive ideology. His contribution in this field is significant as he continuously wrote on a variety of topics with pointed emphasis and purposeful satire. His collection of poems in Khari Boli is *Git Niruttar*.

MEGH RAJ PRADHAN. Poet, who composed in 1666 his *Mrigavati*, the story of which is partially similar to the story of Kutban's *Mrigavati*. The poet composed his work for Arjun Singh, a son of Raja Sujan Singh of Orchha.

MEHDU KHANGAR (fl. between 1450-1550). Dingal poet, whose stray *Gits* on contemporary rulers and chiefs are available.

MEHOJI (1483-1544). Rajasthani poet, whose *Ramayan* (q.v.) in 261 verses is the earliest Akhyan Kavya in the tradition of Ram-poetry. Composed about 1518, it was meant to be sung in popular musical modes. The poet has created two new characters : Bhoj, a trustworthy companion of Ravan, and Varahi, Ravan's sister, not found in other Akhyans of Ram legend.

MEHRUNNISA PARVEZ (1944-). Writer, whose chief works are : *Ankhon ki Dahliz* (The Threshold of the Eyes), *Korja* (1977), *Uska Ghar* (novels) ; *Adam aur Havva, Antim Chadhai, Ghalat Purush, Phalguni* and *Tahniyon par Dhup* (short story collections). Her prominent short stories are 'Tona' (The Evil Charm) and 'Bade Log'.

MEHTAB (fl. *c.* 1743). Riti poet, who was patronized by Hindupati Singh, a brother of Prithwipati Singh, the Raja of Pratapgarh. He is said to have composed *Nakh-Shikh*, which displays his fondness for figures of speech.

MENO MARENKHA. See *Suryaprasad Vire Shurvir*.

MENON, K.N. Malayalam-speaking modern Hindi writer, who tr. *Harinam Kirtanam*, an old Malayalam poem into Hindi verse.

MERI, B.P. Modern scholar, who has published several articles on Hindi and Malayalam words.

MIHIR. See *Ram Nath Mishra 'Mihir'*.

MIHRIVANU (1580-1640). Earliest commentator of Panjab on *Guruvani*, whose *Pothi Sachukhandu* is the earliest specimen of Khari Boli prose. Besides the life of Guru Nanak, it comments on his *Vani*.

MIKOYAN, SVETLANA ARTEMYEVNA (1939-). Soviet Hindi scholar, who has prepared Linguaphone Courses for the study of Hindi in his country.

MILTNER, VLADIMIR (1933-). Czech Indologist, whose several works have been published from different parts of the world including on Indian cultural history ; his works have enabled the Czech students to appreciate Hindi literature more fully. He is also the author of *Theory of Hindi Syntax* (Hague, 1970) and *Hindi Sentence Structure in the Works of Tulsidas* (1967).

MINA AGRAWAL. See *Giriraj Sharan Agrawal*.

MINAKSHI PURI. Writer, who is noted for her novel, *Jane Pahchane Ajnabi* (Known Strangers ; 1978), *Desh Nikale* and *Sat Phere Adhure*.

MINANATH. See *Machhandranath*.

MINAPA. See *Machhandra Nath*.

MIR ABDUL JALAL (1660-1725). Muslim poet of Bilgram, whose chief Riti works are *Shikh-Nakh* (Description of Top to Toe), *Prem Katha Chaupai* and many *Chhands*.

MIR ABDUL WAHI ZAUQI (fl. 1721). Muslim poet of Bilgram, whose stray verses in Hindi are available ; his Persian work is no longer extant.

MIRA BAI (Miran Bai ; 1498-1547). Rajasthani saint-poetess, whose life and work have been an enigma to the scholars. It is believed that she was the daughter of Rao Ratansi, son of Rathore Rao Duda of Merta and was born in the village Bajoli (near Degana) or Kudki. After the death of her mother in her childhood, she was brought up by Rao Duda. She was married to Kunvar Bhojraj, son of Rana Sanga of Chittor in 1516. Bhojraj died about 1522. Due to her independent nature and preference for the company of saints, Mira is said to have been tortured by her in-laws. She left Chittor about 1531-32 and came to Merta for a short period. Around 1534, she went on pilgrimage and finally remained at Dwarka, where she died.

The following works have been attributed to Mira : *Git Govind ki Tika, Narsiji ro Mahero, Satyabhbmaji nu Rusnun, Rag Sorath, Rag Govind* and *Padas* (*Padavali*). However, the first three do not appear to be her compositions, while the next two are collections of her *Padas*, and not independent works. They are included in the *Padavali.* Thus only the *Padas* are the compositions of Mira.

Mira's fame rests on her *Padas.* So natural and spontaneous is the expression of her emotions and feelings that her *Padas* came to be adopted in Gujarati, Braj and many colloquial speeches, with the result that it has become difficult to determine their original form.

As many as over fifty collections including translations stated to contain her *Padas*, have been published in Hindi, Gujarati, Marathi and translated into Bengali and English ; in English the *Padas* have been tr. by Dr. Raghuvir, Aurobindo, Ram Chandra Tandon and Usha Nilson. At present, about 2,000 *Padas*, [published and unpublished, are available in her name but it appears that only about 250 of them are her own.

"Her Padas reveal deep devotion, Sagun and Nirgun Bhakti of *Kant Bhav*, Yoga, and reflect the state of her Sadhana and life. Self-confidence, unbounded faith in the Lord, love, whether in the state of *Sanyog* (fusion) or *Viyog* (separation), profound and sublime passions, expression of joy, sorrow and trance—all in simple, natural, inimitable and unadorned manner—are the characteristics of her *Padas.* She has revealed the deepest emotions of her heart with spontaneous lucidity in the simplest language. It is for these reasons that she is popular equally with the scholars and the masses. However, she is really the poetess of the people. Traditionally she is deemed to be a devotee of Lord Krishna." —Hiralal Maheshwari : *History of Rajasthani Literature.*

MIRA KI PADAVALI. See *Mira.*

MIRZAKHAN (fl. 20th cent.). Author of *A Grammar of the Braj Bhakha* (Vishwabharati).

MISHRA, BALBHADRA. See *Balbhadra Mishra.*

MISHRA, BHAVANI PRASAD. See *Bhavani Prasad Mishra.*

MISHRA, DWARIKA PRASAD. See *Dwarika Prasad Mishra.*

MISHRA, KRISHNABIHARI. See *Krishnabihari Mishra.*

MISHRA, LAKSHMINARAYAN. See *Lakshminarayan Mishra.*

MISHRA, RAMDAHIN. See *Ramdahin Mishra.*

MISHRA, R.P. Modern scholar, who is noted for his *History of Hindi Literature.*

MISHRA, SHRIPATI. See *Shripati Mishra.*

MISHRA, SUKHDEV. See *Sukhdev Mishra.*

MISHRA, SURATI. See *Surati Mishra.*

MISHRA, VIDAYANIWAS. See *Vidyaniwas Mishra*

MISHRABANDHU. The three Mishra brothers: Ganesh Bihari Mishra (b. 1865), Shyam Bihari Mishra (1872-1947) and Rai Bahadur Shukadev Bihari Mishra (1878-1952), are celebrated in Hindi Literature as 'Mishrabandhu'. All the brothers were highly educated and well-placed in life. They were greatly honoured by the British Government as also by many Universities. It seems they divided among themselves their respective spheres of specialization and after integrating their studies brought out their *Mishrabandhu Vinod* (3 vols.), a comprehensive history of Hindi Literature; the work was based on *Shiv Singh Saroj* and other earlier writings like *Bhaktamal.* This work was followed by *Hindi Navratna,* introducing nine top-ranking Hindi poets to the reading public; when it was published, it aroused much hostile criticism. In the *Sahitya Parijat,* they involved in writing a son of the Mishra brothers as well. They also edited *Dev Granthavali, Bhushan Granthavali* and wrote *Netronmilan, Purva Bharat, Uttar Bharat* (dramas), *Pushpanjali, Sumananjali* (essays), *Padya Pushpanjali* (Poetry), *Virmani* (Gem among the Heroes; 1916-17), *Udayan, Chandragupta Maurya, Pushyamitra, Chandragupta Vikramaditya, Swatantra Bharat* (historical novels), *Dev Sudha,* etc. They wrote in Hindi the histories of Russia and India and also took up the cause of Hindi in various educational institutions and the Universities of Uttar Pradesh, with which they happened to be connected.

MISHABRANDHU VINOD See *Mishrabandhu.*

MISHRA, HRIDAY RAY (fl. 1674). Riti poet of Jaunpur, whose *Rasa Ratnakar* is a work on *Rasa.*

MITHILA-GIT-SANGRAH. Maithili anthology, which is a collection of about 200 songs of Mithila ; it was compiled by Bhola Jha in 1917 (4 Pts.).

MITHILESHWAR. Short story writer, whose chief collections of short stories are : *Meghnad ka Nirnay* (1980), *Gaon ke Log* (The Village Folk ; 1981), *Harihar Kaka aur anya Kahaniyan, Dusra Mahabharat, Babuji, Tiriya Janma, Vigrah Babu, Band Raston ke Bich Chhah Mahilayen* and *Mithileshwar ki Shreshth Kahaniyan* (1984). *Ynddha-Sthal* (The Battlefield ; 1981) is his novel. His important short story is 'Ek aur Hatya' (One More Murder).

MIZOKAMI, TOMIO (1941-). Japanese Hindi scholar, who is at present Assistant Professor in the Bharat-Pakistan Department of the Osaka University of Foreign Studies. He did M.A. and doctorate from Delhi University and studied Hindi at Allahabad and Shantiniketan. His special field of study is Philology and does research on Panjabi and Bengali as well. In Hindi he has written short stories as also articles on the problems and survey of Hindi teaching in Japan. Apart from his articles in Hindi, he has written articles in English and Japanese as well.

MOD NARAYAN. Maithili poet, who was noted for his lyrics. He was patronized by Maharaja Pratap Singh (1761-76).

MOD NATH. Maithili poet, who was noted for his lyrics. He was a contemporary of Maharaja Lakshmishwar Singh (1878-98).

MODSINGH MAHIYARIYA (b. 1861). Rajasthani (Dingal) poet of Marwar, who was a disciple of Ganeshpuri (q.v.). His *Vir Satsai* contains his own 453 *Dohas*, 288 *Dohas* from Suryamall's *Vir Satsai* (left incomplete) and one from Bankidas ; thus the number of *Dohas* exceeds 700. As a poet, Modsingh is, however, not profound in emotion or thought as Suryamall had been, except in a few *Dohas*, but he represents a vanishing link in the tradition of Charan poetry.

MOHAMMED AMIN (fl. 1633). Sufi poet of Gujarat, whose *Yusuf Zulekha* is a popular work. Though the poet called his language as Gujari, yet it is akin to Khari Boli.

MOHAMMED SADDIQUE. Rajasthani poet, who in his *Jujhati Jun* (1979) has portrayed man's struggle for survival ; the collection contains poems composed during the last 25 years. He has also written poems for children.

MOHAN (fl. 1610). Poet of the Krishna-cult, who composed *Kelikallol* (devotional).

MOHAN (fl. 1841). Poet, who was a native of Chitrakut. He composed *Chitrakut Mahatmya* on the glory of Chitrakut.

MOHAN ALOK. Rajasthani poet, whose *Ga Git* (1981) is a collection of songs, which treat of acute poverty of the village folks, the famines and drought conditions. Earlier, he had published 'Dhankhala' or the shooting twigs.

MOHAN AVASTHI (1929-). Poet, whose chief works are: *Mehman ka Mara* (Troubled with Guest), *Bhagvan Makan-pash se Mujh ko Chhudaiye* (O God, Liberate Me from the Snare of the House), *Interview* and *Abhishishapta Maharathi*.

MOHAN BHARDWAJ. Maithili scholar, whose *Natya Sahitya Alochana—Katek Uchit* (1979) tries to find faults with the previously published critique books on dramas. Along with Anand Mishra, he has edited *Kriti Rajkamalak* (1980). He has edited *Smriti Sandhya* (1980), a collection of articles on three important poets : Sitaram Jha, Ram Krishna Jha 'Kisun' and Raj Kamal Choudhary. He has also edited *Swargandha* and other poems of Raj Kamal (1981).

MOHAN CHAND UPRETI. Modern Kumaoni writer, whose chief work is *Kumaoni Lok-Sahitya*.

MOHAN CHOPRA (1929-). Writer whose chief works are: *Subah ke Pahle* (Before Morning), *Ek Chhaya aur Main* (One Shadow and I), *Tuta Hua Admi* (The Broken Man), *Ye Naye Log* (These New People), *Nid se Age* (Beyond the Nest; novels), *Adha Kata Hua Surya* (The Half-cut Sun; short story collection) and *Chattan ka Phul* (The Flower of a Rock; collection of one-act plays).

MOHAN DAS (fl. end of 16th cent.). Bengali Vaishnav poet, who also composed *Padas* in Brajbuli.

MOHAN DAS MEWARI (fl. early 17th cent.). Rajasthani saint-poet, who was a disciple of Dadu (q.v.). His *Nam Mala* gives a list of disciples of Dadu. *Adibodh Siddhant Granth*, a poem consisting of 270 verses, is also attributed to him, though it is regarded the work of his Guru, Dadu.

MOHAN KRISHNA DAR. Kashmiri-speaking modern Hindi writer, who is noted for his works: *Kesar ke Phul* (The Flowers of Saffron), *Sukhe Patte* (The Dry Leaves), *Chanar ke Patte* (The Leaves of Chanar), *Mahan Atma* (The Great Soul) and *Manoram Kashmir* (The Lovely Kashmir), which contain stories, folktales, essays, all depicting culture, art, beauty and archaeological remains of Kashmir. He has also published *Kashmiri ka Lok-Sahitya* (The Folk-literature of Kashmiri).

MOHAN LAL DWIJ. Poet, whose *Pattali* describes the menu served to Krishna's marriage party ; from the language point of view, the work appears to belong to the 18th century.

MOHAN LAL MEHTO 'VIYOGI' (b. 1899). Hindi poet, who was born in Upridih (Gaya). His chief works are : *Achhut* (The Untouchable ; 1925), *Nirmalya* (1926), *Ek Tara* (1927), *Kalpana* (1936 ; all poetical collections) and *Aryavarta* (1943 ; a *Prabandh-Kavya* on the killing of Muhammed Ghori by Prithwiraj Chauhan by a feat of archery). Apart from poetry, he also wrote prose-poems, essays, short stories, novels, etc.

MOHAN LAL MISHRA (fl. 16th cent.). Riti poet, who composed *Shringar-Sagar* (The Ocean of Shringar ; 1559), a work on poetics.

MOHAN LAL PUROHIT. Modern Rajasthani writer, who is noted for his sketches.

MOHAN LAL SHRIVASTAV (1934-). Bagheli folk-poet, who was born at Shahdaul in Madhya Pradesh. He is noted for his originality, love of Nature and depiction of various facets of rural life.

MOHAN LAL VISHNULAL PANDYA (1850-1912). Writer, who was influenced by Bharatendu Harishchandra (q.v.). He was in administrative service and when Bharatendu's 'Harishchandra Chandrika' ran into financial difficulty, Pandya came to his rescue. Of his 12 works dealing mainly with history, the most famous of them is *Raso Sanraksha*, dealing at length with Chand Bardai's *Prithwiraj Raso*. He also wrote a drama, *Prahlad*.

MOHAN NIRASH (1934-). Kashmiri-speaking Hindi poet, whose 35 poems, collected in *Krishna Mera Paryay* (Krishna is My Synonym) have been duly appreciated.

MOHAN, R.P. (fl. 1935). Kannada-speaking Hindi poet, whose poems were published in the 'Jagriti', a literary magazine. The poems were mainly patriotic in nature.

MOHAN RAKESH (1925-72). Pioneer writer, who was born in Amritsar and was educated at Lahore. His chief works are :

Drama : *Ashadh ka Ek Din* (A Day in July ; 1958 ; an imaginary description of the love of Kalidas for Mallika ; q.v.), *Laharon ke Rajhans* (The Swan of the Waves ; 1963 ; on the well-known episode of Nand – Gautam Buddha's brother—and his beautiful wife, Sundari), *Adhe Adhure* (Incomplete Personalities ; q.v. ; story of a family, degraded from middle class ; a daring experimentation in form), *Raten Bitne Tak* and *Pairon Tale ki Zamin* (The Ground Under Feet ; incomplete) ; *Ande ke Chhilke* (The Rinds of Egg) is a collection of his one-act plays.

Novel : *Andhere Band Kamre* (The Dark Closed Rooms ; on the hollowness of Delhi's cultural, political and family life; q.v.), *Na Ane Vala Kal* (The Tomorrow that Never Comes ; 1968 ; on the resignation of a Missionary school teacher on account of his wife), *Antaral* (The Inner Depth ; 1972 ; on suffocation felt by men and women), *Nili Roshni ki Banhen* (The Arms of Blue Light) and *Kanpta Hua Dariya* (The Trembling River).

Short Story Collection : *Insan ke Khandahar* (The Ruins of Man ; 1950), *Naye Badal* (The New Clouds ; 1957), *Janvar aur Janvar* (Animals and Animals ; 1958), *Ek aur Zindagi* (One More Life ; 1961), *Phaulad ka Akash* (The Sky of Steel ; 1966), *Ek Ek Duniya* (Each World ; 1969), *Mohan Rakesh ki Shreshth Kahaniyan* (The Best Short Stories of Mohan Rakesh) ; before his death Mohan Rakesh wanted his short stories to be published in several volumes ; some of which are : *Aj ke Saye* (The Shadows of To-day ; 1967) *Royen Reshe* (1968), *Mile Jule Chehre* (Mixed Faces ; 1969). His important short stories are : 'Ek aur Zindagi', 'Naye Badal', 'Malbe ka Malik' (The Owner of the Debris), 'Paramatma ka Kutta' (God's Dog), 'Ek Thahra Hua Chaku' (A Stayed Knife), etc.

His other works are : *Aine ke Samne* (Before the Mirror ; 1967), *Parivesh* (collection of essays ; 1968), *Rangmanch aur Shabda* (critical), *Kuchh aur Asvikar*, *Vyaktigat* (Diary), *Akhiri Chattan Tak* (To the Last Rock ; travelogue) and tr. of Shudrak's *Mrichchhakatika*.

He is regarded as one of the pioneer writers in the modern Hindi prose.

MOHAN SAPRA. Panjabi-speaking modern Hindi poet, whose chief poetical collection is *Kide* (Worms).

MOHAN SINGH HIRA. Modern Hindi poet of Fiji, whose chief work is : *Prashant ka Bhushan.*

MOHAN SINGH KAVIRAO (1899-1964). Rajasthani poet and scholar, who was great-grandson of the famous poet, Bakhtavarji (q v.). He was born at the village Basi in the Mewar State. He composed poetry both in Dingal and Pingal and has some 17 works to his credit. He has also translated some *Dohas* of Biharilal and some *Padas* of Surdas and Raskhan into Dingal. His chief works are : *Pratap-Yash-Chandroday, Bhupal-Bhushan, Vir Charitra Satsai, Niti Shatak, Durga Bavni, Apni Kathavasi, Kumbha-Kirti Prakash, Mohan Satsai* and *Raghuvansh-Charita.* He has also brought out Rajasthani folk-tales. *Vir Charitra Satsai*, comprising 721 *Dohas* in easy Rajasthani, describes the characters of Maharana Pratap, Durgadas Rathore, Shivaji, Chhatrasal, Govind Singh, etc. The style, however, is traditional.

MOHAN SINGH SENGAR (1914-72). Writer, who was noted for his short stories ; *Dubta Suraj* is a collection of his short stories. He edited 'Naya Samaj', Calcutta successfully for 20 years. He was connected with all India Radio, Delhi.

MOHUN LAL MOHITH (1902-). Hindi writer of Mauritius, who is at present the President of Arya Mahasabha. His chief works are : *Satsang Suman* and *Arya Sabha Mauritius ka Itihas.* A celebrated leader of the Arya Samaj, he came under the influence of Kashinath Kishto (q.v.) and has edited 'Aryavir', 'Arya Patrika' and 'Aryoday'.

MONIER-WILLIAMS, SIR M. (1819-89). Celebrated Indologist, whose works on Hindi are : *An Easy Introduction to Hindi, Rudiments of Hindustani Grammar* (1858), *An Easy Introduction to the Study of Hindustani* (1858), *Hindustani Primer* (London, 1860) and *A Practical Hindustani Grammar* (London, 1862). In the Introduction to his *An Easy Introduction to Hindi,* he has mentioned that one of the causes of Mutiny of 1857 was that English rulers did not fully understand the Indian people and for this he wrote his works on Hindi so that Englishmen could understand the native languages. He also edited *Original Papers, illustrating the History of the Application of the Roman Alphabet to the Languages of India* (London, 1859).

MOONISHWURLAL CHINTAMUNNEE (1935-). Poet and writer of Mauritius, who is Lecturer in the Department of Languages at the Mahatma Gandhi Institute, Mauritius. His poetical collections are : *Pratham Kiran* (1960), *Shantiniketan ki Or*, *Lokpriya Git*, *Nav-Nirman ki Bela* (1972), *Sahmi Sahmi Si Avaz* (1977) and *Ansu ki Anjaliyan* (nearing completion) ; *Mauritius ka Hindi Sahitya tatha anya Nibandh* is a collection of his essays (1977).

MOORE, ROBERT RIPLEY. American Hindi scholar and author of *A Study of Hindi Intonation* (Michigan, 1965).

MORAR SAHIB (1757-1848). Saint-poet of Gujarat, who was a prominent disciple of Ravi Sahib (q.v.). Among his followers were both Hindus and Muslims. His Hindi works are : *Sadguru Virah*, *Guru Mahima*, *Chintamani*, *Barahmasi*, *Dholu* and other stray verses. His language is simple and betrays the influence of Urdu and Gujarati.

MORRIS, J. Author of *English Proverbs, with Hindustani Parallels* (Lahore, 1900).

MOTI. Modern Bhojpuri poet, whose poems *Mahua Bari* and *Ras-Lila* are noted for their sweetness.

MOTI LAL JOTWANI. Sindhi-speaking modern Hindi poet, whose chief works are : *Chand ke Git* (Songs to Moon ; 1961), *Pili Batti Par* (On the Yellow Light ; 1977) and *Ye Log* (These People ; 1980) (the last two novels). He has also edited *Shah Latif ka Kavya* (Poetry of the Sindhi poet, Shah Latif) and has written an essay : *Sindhi Bhasha, Lipi aur Sahitya* (Sindhi Language, Script and Literature ; 1974), His latest poetical collection is *Nim ki Bhumika Alag Hai* (1983).

MOTI LAL KYAMU. Modern Kashmiri dramatist, who is noted for his Hindi one-act plays : *Tin Asangat Ekanki* (Three Incompatible One-act Plays). He has also tr. into Hindi his own Kashmiri drama under the title of *Chhaya* (The Shadow).

MOTI LAL MENARIYA. Modern Rajasthani scholar, who espoused the cause of Rajasthani language and literature and is the author of *Rajasthani Bhasha aur Sahitya* (1948) and *Rajasthan ka Pingal Sahitya* (1952).

MOTI MADHE. Modern Hindi writer of Surinam, whose chief work is : *Sarnami Vyakaran*.

MOTI MADRASI (1931-). Assamese-speaking Hindi writer, whose short stories, mainly humorous, have been published in various magazines and papers.

MOTI RAM (fl. early 19th cent.). Rajasthani saint-poet of Ram Snehi Sampraday, Sinthal, whose *Vani* consists of stray verses in popular metres.

MOTI SAR CHATARI (fl. 1613). Rajasthani poet, whose stray verses in popular metres are available.

MOTI SINGH GADHVI 'MUKTA' (1895-1966). Hindi poet, who was inspired in his poetry by his father and by the Thakurs (Rajas) of Sanand and Dahevan in Gujarat. Of his works: *Mahisagar Lahari*, *Amba Stavan*, *Mukta Bavni*, *Bhaktavatsal*, the last is the most popular, which treats of the lives of Draupadi, Sudama, Vidur, Ambarish, Prahlad, Gajendra, etc. The script is Gujarati and the language is Braj, though influenced by Rajasthani.

MOTI TORAL. Modern Hindi poet of Mauritius, whose chief work is: *Shadi se Abadi Nahin Barbadi*.

MOTIYA RA SORTHA. See *Sandu Raysingh*.

MOTURI SATYANARAYAN. Telugu-speaking modern Hindi writer, who is noted for his *Hindi-Telugu Swabodhini*.

MRIDULA GARG. Writer, whose chief works are: *Vanshaj* (The Descendants), *Tukra Tukra Admi* (1977), *Chittkobra* (The Spotted ; 1979 ; delineation of Richard-Manu relationship on a novel plane), *Anitya* (The Transient ; 1980), *Main aur Main*, *Tum Laut Ao*, *Uske Hisse ki Dhup* (all novels) ; she has also written short stories, the important ones being 'Akash' (The Sky), Ek Chikh ka Intazar' (Wait for a Cry), 'Hari Bindi' (The Green Mark) and 'Subah bhi Andhere se Khali Nahin'. Her chief short story collections are: *Glacier Se*, *Daffodil Jal Rahe Hain*, *Kitni Qaiden* and *Duniya ka Qayada* (1984). She also writes in English.

MRIGAVATI. Poem by Kutban (q.v.), a Sufi Hindi poet (1501), which describes the love of Prince of Chandragiri and Princess Mrigavati of Kanchanpur ; an incomplete copy of the manuscript has recently been discovered.

The prince falls in love with Mrigavati, but one day she flies away. He turns an ascetic and wanders in quest of her ; in his wanderings, he saves Rukmini, another princess, from the clutches of a demon and marries her. After many trials and tribulations, the prince reaches Kanchanpur and finds Mrigavati reigning after the death of her father. He takes her also with him and returns to Chandragiri after twelve years. He is killed by a fall from an elephant and the two queens immolate themselves on their husband's funeral pyre.

Though the entire story runs around a romance, it is allegorical in so far as the unremitting love between the hero and the heroine is supposed to be symbolic of God.

MRIGAVATI. See *Meghraj Pradhan*.

MRIGESH. Modern Avadhi poet of Barabanki, who is noted for his poem 'Kisan Shankar' (on farmers).

MRIGNAYANI. Novel (1950) by Vrindavanlal Varma (q.v.), which is considered his masterpiece.

Man Singh, the Raja of Gwalior, marries Mrignayani, an extremely beautiful and bow-wielding girl of village Rai. He wins many battles and devotes himself to the development of art and culture. The fusion of heroism and art, of personal enjoyment and social service seems to be the ideal of this novel. In the centre, there is the laudable idealism of Man Singh and Mrignayani. There are many digressions, which continue up to the end, e.g., the romance of Atal and Lakhi (across caste barriers), the stories of Sikandar, the Sultan of Delhi, Ghayasuddin, the Sultan of Malwa and Mahmud Bagharra, the Sultan of Gujarat.

MRINAL PANDEY. Short story writer ; her chief story collections are *Darmayan* (Between ; 1977), *Shabdavedhi* (The Sound Target ; 1980) and *Ek Nich Tragedy* (1981) ; she has also written novels : *Viruddha*, *Patarangpur Purana* and dramas : *Maujuda Halat ko Dekhte Huye*, *Jo Ram Rachi Rakha* and *Admi jo Machhuara Nahin Tha* (1984). She also writes in English.

MRITYUNJAY UPADHYAY. Poet, who is noted for his long poem, *Vaishvanar* (1980) ; it is based on an episode of the *Mahabharat* and reveals how the sage Vishwamitra, distracted with hunger, had to steal meat from an untouchable's house.

MUBARAK, SYED MUBARAK ALI BILGRAMI (b. 1583). Muslim poet of the Krishna-cult, who was a scholar of Arabic, Persian and Sanskrit. Of the several works, which he is known to have written in Brajbhasha, his *Alak-shatak*, *Tilak-shatak* and stray verses, are extant. Essentially a poet of female beauty, his favourite *Rasa* is *Shringar*. He is said to have composed 1000 *Dohas* in delineation of only 10 limbs of the heroine and his above two works are part of the *Dohas*.

MUDIYA SWAMI (1851-1928). Hindi poet of Gujarat, who was born at the village Umrala in Saurashtra. His original name was Dayanand. He composed *Bhajans* in a language, which is influenced by Gujarati and Panjabi.

MUDRARAKSHAS (fl. 1900-1920). Marathi-speaking Hindi writer, whose essays dealing with religious, social and cultural topics appeared in various magazines.

MUDRARAKSHAS. Dramatist, who is noted for quaint experiments in poetry and in incongruity on the stage ; his chief dramas are : *Marjiva*, *Tilchatta* (The Cockroach), *Tendua* (The Leopard), *Gufaen* (The Caves ; 1979), *Santola* (1980 ; depicting the murder of Santola by her husband, Professor Saran on the stage), *Yours faithfully* and *Ala Afsar*. He has written stories as well, his collections being *Shabda-Dansh* and *Meri Kahaniyan* (1984). *Ham Sab Mansaram* (All of Us are Mansarams ; 1981), *Mera Nam Tera Nam* and *Bhagora* are his novels. He was working for All India Radio, now free lancing in Lucknow ; he has edited many 'Little Magazines'.

MUHAMMAD AYUB KHAN. Modern scholar, whose chief work is *Nirala ke Kavya men Darshnikta*.

MUHAMMAD HUSSAIN. See *Pollock, W.*

MUHNOT NAINSI. See *Nainsi.*

MUHTA RUGHNATH. Rajasthani poet of the village Balrawa (Jodhpur), whose *Rugh Raso* (q.v.) composed in 1668, treats of the story of Ram.

MUJIB RIZVI. Modern poet, whose *Chhaya ke Bad* is a poetical collection.

MUKAN SINGH. Rajasthani writer, who is noted for *Veli* (*Shiv*, *Bajrang*, *Jasvant Singh*), three booklets, published in 1982. Earlier he had written several works. He had also paid poetic homage to the heroes, who sacrificed their lives in fighting against the Chinese attack on India. He is as expert of Dingal vocabulary, rhetorics and prosody.

MUKTA BAI (fl. 14th cent). Saint-poetess of Maharashtra, who composed in Hindi as well. So far only one *Pada* of hers has been recovered.

MUKTA RAM (d. 1815). Rajasthani saint-poet of Ram Snehi Sect, Shahpura, who was a disciple of Bhagvandas Karva (q.v.). Noted for his Sadhana and Bhakti, his *Vani* is known to equal over 14,000 *Shlokas*, including 20 poems, such as *Guru Stuti*, *Nam Pratap*, *Kakka Battisi*, *Bhakti Mahima*, *Chitavani*, *Gyan Prakash*, *Man Charit*, *Bhakta Virudavali*, *Vichar Bodh* and *Guru Upkar*. The expression is effective and is in easy Rajasthani.

MUKTESHWAR TIWARI 'CHATURI CHACHA'. Modern Bhojpuri writer, whose humorous and satirical writings have been published in two parts as *Chaturi Chacha ki Chatpati Chitthiyan* (Spicy Letters of Chaturi Uncle).

MUKTIBODH. See *Gajanan Madhav Muktibodh*.

MUKUND DAN (1886-1952). Rajasthani poet of Bhuwal, Merta, whose Rajasthani poems in traditional Charan style are available.

MUKUND DWIVEDI. Modern scholar, who has edited the letters of Hazari Prasad Dwivedi.

MUKUND GUGLI (fl. 1651). Gujarati poet of Dwarka, who was an Udichya Brahmin. He is noted for his *Bhaktamal*, a Gujarati work, which describes the lives of Bhaktas or devotees. The lives of Kabir and Gorakhnath (qq.v.) have been described in 'Hindi Gujarati' and Hindi. He composed some Hindi *Padas* as well.

MUKUND JHA. Modern Maithili writer, who is noted for his history of Mithila ; he also composed lyrics, mostly Vishnupadas.

MUKUTDHAR PANDEY (b. 1895). Poet, who inspired by his elder brother, Lochanprasad Pandey, started writing as early as 1909. His poems are collected in *Kanan-Kusum* (The Garden of Flowers).

MULCHAND 'PRANESH'. Modern Rajasthani writer and poet, whose chief works are : *Hiyai Tana Upay* (folk-tale), *Pardeshi ri Goradi* (1965), *Ukalata Antara Shila Sans* (1973), *Chashmadid Gavah* (1980 ; all short story collections) and some poems, with emphasis on human virtues, e.g , 'Avo Apan Admiyat Ugavan'.

MULDAS (1674-1778). Gujarati speaking saint-poet of Amodra in Saurashtra, who was initiated by Lalgiri Maharaj. Popularly known as a 'true saint', he travelled extensively and did not settle at one place. He translated *Bhagavadgita*, *Narad-Gita* and other works into Hindi verse and also composed stray Hindi *Padas*.

MULDAS (fl. end of 18th cent. and beginning of 19th cent.). Rajasthani saint-poet of Ram Snehi Sect, Sinthal, who was born at the village Bamatsar (Bikaner) and lived at Kalu (Bikaner), where he made a Ramdwara, the tradition of which still continues. His *Vani* on Nirgun Bhakti, consists of *Guru Mahima*, *Agam Bodh*, *Brahma Prakash Chetavani*, *Bhaktamal*, etc . about 1400 *Sakhis* (*Dohas*), 47 *Harjas* and some *Chandrayan*, etc. His language is lucid and easy Rajasthani.

MUNNI PRASAD. Modern Magahi writer, who is noted for his social one-act plays.

MUNSHI RAM SHARMA (1901-). Critic, whose chief works are : *Bhramargit Sar*, *Sur Saurabh*, *Surdas ka Kavya Vaibhav*, *Padmavat*, *Prasad ki Kamayani* (all criticism) and *Vaidiki*. His poetical works are : *Virhini* and *Bhagvati Abha*.

MURAD FAQIR (1727-83). Sindhi Muslim saint-poet, who also composed *Prem Gyan* and *Bhajans* in Hindi ; the former work is a rhythmic composition in sweet verses. In his poetry, he lays emphasis on love.

Murad was not only a brother-in-law of Rohal (q.v.), another Sindhi saint-poet, but was also his fellow-pupil. Murad belonged to the village Kotle in Sindh but was troubled by the local Zamindar. Once Murad remarked to Rohal that he was going to curse the Zamindar family, but the latter forbade him to do so and instead advised him to consume himself. Murad lied down covering his body with a sheet and died. His tomb is still visited by people in Kotle.

MURARI DAN (1835-1913). Poet, who was patronized by Maharaja Jasvant Singh the Second, Ruler of Jodhpur. Muraridan was the son of Bharatidan, while his grandfather was Bankidas, the celebrated poet. His *Jasvant-Jasobhushan* is the biggest Alankar work in Hindi and has been completed in 852 pages, while its abridged version, *Jasvant Bhushan* covers 351 pages.

MURARI DAN, KAVIRAJ (1838-1907). Rajasthani poet of Bundi, who was the adopted son of the famous poet, Surajmal (q.v.). He completed the *Vansh Bhaskar*, which was left incomplete by his father. Besides the above, he composed two works : *Dingal Kosh* (primarily a dictionary of synonyms but also dealing with fifteen types of Dingal *Gits*) and *Vansh Samuchchay*. He composed poems in both Pingal and Dingal.

MURARI DAS BARHAT. See *Gun Vijay Vyah*.

MURARI RAM (d. 1833). Rajasthani saint-poet of Ram Snehi Sect, Khedapa, who was a Bhati Rajput and was a disciple of Ramdas (q.v.). His *Vani*, in straight-forward and simple language, consists of *Agyat Bodh*, *Mahimasar Nisani*, *Atmasar*, *Sumiransar*, *Garbh Chetavani*, *Atmaparchi*, *Guru Mahima*, many *Sakhis* and *Harjas*.

MURDON KA TILA (The Mound of the Dead). Historical novel (1948) by Rangey Raghav (q.v.), which describes the civilization and culture of the Mohenjo Daro. The Shreshthis (wealthy people) bought slaves from Iran and treated them like animals. The girl-slaves served them and also satisfied their lust, and yet their life was uncertain like that of a straw floating on a river. The novelist has presented a naked picture of the lust and cruelty of these traders.

MURLI. Rajasthani poet, who was patronized by Rawat Udaybhan of Kotharia in Mewar. At the instance of Udaybhan, he composed *Triya Vinod* (1706 ; q.v.), while his *Ashwamedh-Yagya* (1718) was written at the instance of Maharana Jaysingh of Mewar ; both the works are in Pingal.

MURLIDHAR. See *Shridhar*.

MURLIDHAR JHA, MAHAMAHOPADHYAY (fl. early 20th cent.). Pioneer of the modern Maithili prose, who started the publication of 'Mithila Mod' from Varanasi. His essays bristle with irony and satire. He also wrote editorial notes, monologues and dialogues. In sharpness of criticism, power and vigour of style, his prose has remained unparalleled to this day. See *Chandra Nath Mishra*.

MURLIDHAR KAVI BHUSHAN (fl. 1648-98). Recently discovered Riti poet, whose works are : *Alankar Prakash*, *Chhandohriday* (an exhaustive treatise on prosody) and *Rasa Prakash* (not yet available). He was patronized by Pancham Devisingh, who conferred upon him the title of 'Kavi Bhushan'. Later on he was a protege of Raja Devishah and of Raja Hriday Shah. He is different from the poet Bhushan (q.v.).

MURLIDHAR SHRIVASTAV (1911-). Scholar, whose chief works are : *Yugakavi Dinkar* (1963), *Hindi ke Europiya Vidwan* (European Scholars of Hindi ; 1973), *Madhya Pradesh ki Bhashik Parampara*, *Elements of Hindi Grammar*, *Hindi Dhatukosh* and *Hindi Tadbhav Shastra*.

MURLIDHAR VYAS. Rajasthani writer, whose chief work *Jima Jivanta Chitaram* (1960) gives sketches of professionals, who are fast vanishing due to modernization ; he has also written social short stories (*Varas Ganth* ; 1956) and has published Rajasthani proverbs (*Rajasthani Kahavaten*, 2 vols.) in collaboration with Narottam Das Swami.

MURLI RAM (1475-1800). Rajasthani saint-poet of Ram Snehi Sampraday, who was influenced by Naval Ram Mantri (q.v.) and was initiated in 1768 by Ramcharan (q.v.). He wrote a large number of stray verses and composed nine small books, *Chetavani Sar Bodh*, *Amrit Sar Bodh*, *Nanv Yoga*, *Vaishnav Sar Bodh*, *Grihasth Sar Bodh*, *Guru Mahima Stuti*, *Sadh Parkhya*, etc. concerning the Nirgun Bhakti. There is intensity of feeling and lucidity of expression in his works.

MURTI, ADINARAYAN See *Adinarayan Murti, K.*

MUTTATU, V.K. Malayalam-speaking modern Hindi writer, who has tr. Malayalam poet Vallattol Narayan Menon's several national and romantic poems into Hindi verse. He has also tr. into Hindi C. Madhavan Pillai's Malayalam poem, *Padmarag*, which was serially published in 'Rashtravani', Trivandrum.

MUTTUSWAMI, N.E. Malayalam-speaking modern Hindi writer, who is noted for the preparation of the help-material for students appearing in higher Hindi examinations.

N

NABHA DAS (fl. *c.* 1600). Poet of the Ram-cult, who was a disciple of Agradas (q.v.). According to tradition, he was of the *Dom* (a low) caste. It is said that his parents were very poor and being unable to feed him, left him in a dense forest, from where he was picked up by Agradas, who brought him up. As such, he has been called a Nagar Brahmin of Gwalior or a native of Rambhadrachal of Telang-Godavari area. It was at the instance of his preceptor that he composed his *Bhaktamal*.

Nabhadas composed two *Ashtayams* (one in Avadhi and the other in Braj prose), some verses on devotion to Ram, but his fame chiefly rests on the *Bhaktamal* (q.v.), which describes the lives of 200 saints, both his contemporary and earlier. It is said that Nabhadas had a meeting with Tulsidas.

NABHU LAL (1801-71). Gujarati-speaking saint-poet of Nadiad, who started composing poems at the age of eight. In the beginning he was in Government service but soon got aversion to it. He was very popular due to his attractive personality and melodious voice. He is supposed to have composed 18,000 *Padas* ; his chief works are : *Anubhav Gita*, *Tatwabodh*, *Gurugita*, *Gyan-Parnalika*, *Niralambopanishad*, *Bodh-Ratnavali*, *Gyan-Shodashi*, *Kakko*, *Tithi*, *Mas*, *etc*. His Hindi betrays the influence of Gujarati, Arabic, Persian, Panjabi, Bhojpuri and Khari Boli.

NABI BAKHSH 'FALAK' (1892-1950). Muslim poet of Datiya in Madhya Pradesh, who like Raskhan (q.v.) loved Braj, Brajraj (Krishna) and Brajrani (Radha). He composed stray verses.

NACHIKAT. Maithili writer and poet, who is noted for his popular plays : *Jivan Ekar Nam* (1972) and *Ek Chala Raja* (1973) ; these dramas were written more or less on the lines of translations from Bengali. His collections of poems are: *Kavayo Vedanti* (1966) and *Amritasya Putrah* (1970); he has gone back to the Upanishadic times and seeks to bring a message of peace.

NADI KE DWIP (The Islands in the Stream). Novel (1951) by Agyey (q.v.), in which the characters are mostly introverts.

Bhuvan, the hero, is a scientist but he is emotional and sensitive. He falls in love with Rekha, who, though married, has been living separately from her husband, Hemendra. She conceives and while in that state, her husband sues for divorce. She clears herself through abortion, but finding that Bhuvan has fallen in love with another woman, she proceeds to Calcutta and marries Dr Ramesh Chandra.

It is Agyey's second psychological novel, which is based primarily on sex-life. The author wishes to prove that the individual is an island of a stream, surrounded by the currents in social life, but having an independent identity. Though surrounded by the river, these islands are separate from one another and though separate, are related to the river at some point or the other.

The novel has been tr. into English; its French version is expected soon.

NAFIS AFRIDI. Fiction writer, whose works are: *Ek Thaka Sach* (A Tired Truth; 1981), *Vayada Khilaf* (Of Bad Faith; 1982), *Khule Huye Dariche*, *Phir bhi Akele*, *Dhup ka Dariya*, *Agnikund*, *Apni-apni Simayen* and *Nafis Afridi ki Vishishta Kahaniyan* (1984).

NAG DAMAN. See *Sanya Jhula*.

NAGJI. Poet of Sikar (Rajasthan), who was a contemporary of Maharaja Mansingh 'Dwijdev' (1823-73). Nagji composed *Alankar Panchashikha*, a work on figures of speech.

NAGJI-NAGVANTI. Rajasthani romance of Nagji-Nagvanti or Nagmati, the verses of which, about 50 in number, are available in manuscripts of the 18th century and threafter. The original composition of some of these verses may date back to the 16th century. In some verses, the name of the heroine is given as Sugana.

Nagji falls in love with Nagmati and Nagji's elder brother's wife arranges their marriage in secret. Not knowing of this marriage, Nagmati's father performs her marriage with another man, to whom she was earlier betrotned. Nagji meets Nagmati and finding him married to another person, feels dejected and leaves Nagmati. He commits suicide. When Nagmati comes in search of Nagji, she finds him dead. Then she leaves with her husband for the village of her in-laws. The road passes by the cremation ground where Nagji's body is burning. Unable to bear the separation from Nagji, she gets down from the cart and throws herself on the funeral pyre of Nagji. Thus both are united in death.

The charm of the poem lies in the portrayal of the disappointment that Nagji felt and he preferred death to separation from her.

NAG LAKSHMI. Tamil-speaking Hindi scholar, whose chief work is *Maithilisharan Gupta aur Bharati ka Tulnatmak Adhyayan* (A Comparative Study ; thesis ; 1966).

NAGRAJ SHARMA. Rajasthani poet, whose major poems: *Birkha Binani and Tharo ke Livan Han* (1974) are social and political satires. In collaboration with Ram Niranjan Sharma, he has written humorous one-act plays: *Ram Milai Jodi* (1972) and *Tamarak Tun* (1972). He is also the author of *Ib te Cheto*, a collection of one-act plays, advocating social reform.

NAGA, HIROKI. Modern Japanese Hindi scholar, who teaches Hindi in Asia Africa Language University, a private Institute in Tokyo, with Naresh Mantri, as his associate. Both of them are engaged in research.

NAGAPPA, NA. Kannada-speaking modern Hindi writer, whose chief works are: *Buaji* (a collection of 11 sketches) and *Abhinav Hindi Vyakaran* (grammar ; 1971). He, along with Hiranyam started a literary magazine : 'Manasi' and wrote a number of essays on Hindi grammar. He has tr. some select Kannada poems, Shrirang's drama, *Anadi Anand*, N. Murtirao's essay collection : *Hogaluganasuglu* and V. Sitaramayya's *Pampa Yatra* (travelogue) from Kannada into Hindi as also tr. P.K. Parameshvaran Nair's *History of Malayalam Literature* into Hindi.

NAGAR, AMRIT LAL. See *Amrit Lal Nagar*.

NAGARIDAS (fl. 16th cent.). Poet of Krishna-cult (Haridasi Scct), who composed 100 *Padas*.

NAGARIDAS (1699-1764). Poet, who was born in the royal family of Kishengarh (Rajasthan) and was named Savant Singh. At the age of 13, he stormed Bundi and killed its ruler Jait Singh in the battlefield. He was at the Moghul court in Delhi when his father Raj Singh died in 1747. The Moghul king Ahmed Shah declared him as the successor to the Kishengarh throne, but when Nagaridas returned to his state, he found that his brother had usurped the throne. He returned and with the help of the Marathas regained his throne. But the fratricidal warfare convinced him of the instability of human glory and abdicating in favour of his son, he left for Vrindavan in 1757, where he adopted the pseudonym of 'Nagaridas'. In Vrindavan, he became a devotee of Krishna, and Braj became so dear to him that he could not afford to be away for a single day.

Nagaridas was a prolific writer and some 73 books, e.g., *Brajsar*, *Pada-Prasangmala*, *Ramcharitmala*, *Vairagya-Vallari*, *Jugalbhakti-Vinod* (all devotional) are ascribed to him, but many of them are very short. He also composed *Ishq-Chaman* and some *Kavittas* on rainy season. The themes are generally taken from the lives of Krishna and Radha and their sports in Braj. The poet had a command over Brajbhasha and employed various metres. His *Padas* are good, though his other poems are not of great merit; his works, however, are a good specimen of the contemporary devotional poetry. The Gyan Sagar Press, Bombay has published his works in one omnibus volume, entitled *Nagar Samuchchay*, which includes also the compositions of his wife, Banithaniji (q.v.).

NAGARJUN (1911-). Novelist and poet, whose original name is Vaidyanath Mishra. While in Hindi he writes under the pen name of 'Nagarjun', in Maithili he writes under the name of 'Yatri'. His chief works are as under :

Novel : *Ratinath ki Chachi* (Ratinath's Aunt ; 1948 ; on the life struggle of a Brahmin widow), *Balchanman* (on the miserable struggle of Balchanman, a peasant's son), *Nayi Paudh* (The New Sapling ; 1953), *Baba Batesarnath* (1954 ; story of changes in the four generations in a village), *Duhkhmochan* (1957 ; on Sarvoday fraternity), *Varun ke Bete* (The Sons of the Sea ; 1957 ; on the sad plight of fishermen), *Kumbhipak* (1960 ; a satire), *Hirak Jayanti* (The Diamond Jubilee ; 1961 ; on the weaknesses of leaders), *Ugratara* (1963), *Imaratiya* (1968) aud *Abhinandan* (Felicitation ; 1980). As his novels are set in the Mithila land, they are termed as regional, but they are invariably socialist in colour. Nagarjun has adopted modern techniques of writing and his novels reflect the urges and aspirations of the people. *Jamniya ka Baba* is his short story collection.

Poetical Collection: *Yugadhara* (1953 ; representative collection ; new edn. 1983), *Satrangen Pankhon Vali* (The Feathered One with Seven Colours ; 1959), *Pyasi Pathrai Ankhen* (The Thirsty and Stony Eyes ; 1962), *Chandana*, *Bhasmankur*, *Khichri Viplav Dekha Hamne* (1980), *Tumne Kaha Tha* (You Had Said ; 1980), *Hazar Hazar Bahon Vali* (The Lady with a Thousand Arms ; 1981 ; poems published between 1936 and 1980), *Ratnagarbha* and *Purani Jutiyon ka Chorus*. *Patrahin Nagna Gachh* (1981) is a Hindi adaptation of his Maithili poems as also other poems written over a long period.

He has edited *Gita Govinda*, *Meghaduta* and *Vidyapati ke Git* ; *Annahinam Kriyahinam* (1983) is a collection of his prose writings.

His Maithili novels are : *Paro* (1946 ; on the story of a girl, who shows tender feelings towards her cousin ; the love here appears as a suggestion rather than any serious love affair), *Nav-Turia* (1954) and *Balchanman*. His Maithili poems are : *Budha Var* (satirizing marriage in old age), *Vilap* (a dramatic monologue representing the lamentation of a child-widow), *Kosi-ki-Dhar Men* (death and destructiou caused by the river Kosi), *Goth-Bichani* (on a poor girl gatherer of cow-dung), *Gamak Chitthi* (on the feelings of a husband who has to live apart from his home), *Dvandva* (on the conflict between the old and the new), *Chitra* (1949 ; first collection of poems) and *Patrahin Nagna Gachh* (1981 ; Hindi adaptation of his Maithili poems).

NAGARMAL GOPA. Modern Rajasthani scholar, whose chief work is *Rajasthani Sangit*.

NAGENDRA (1915-). Critic, who was born at the village Atrauli in the Aligarh district of Uttar Pradesh. His chief works are : *Sumitra Nandan Pant* (1938), *Adhunik Hindi Kavita ki Mukhya Pravrittiyan* (Main Tendencies of Modern Hindi Poetry), *Saket : Ek Adhyayan* (a study of *Saket* ; 1940), *Adhunik Hindi Natak* (Modern Hindi Drama), *Dev aur Unki Kavita* (Dev and His Poetry), *Ritikal ki Bhumika* (Background of the Riti-period), *Bharatiya Saundarya-Shastra ki Bhumika* (History of Indian Aesthetics), *Kavya men Udat-tatva*, *Uttar-lekh*, *Vichar aur Anubhuti* (1944), *Vichar aur Vivechan* (1949), *Bharatiya Kavyashastra ki Bhumika* (Background of the Indian Poetics ; 1955), *Kamayani ke Adhyayan ki Samasyayen* (The Problems for the Study of *Kamayani* ; 1963), *Alochak ki*

Astha (1966), *Kavya-Bimb* (*on poetic images* ; 1967), *Nayi Samiksha* : *Naye Sandarbh* (on new criticism) and contexts ; 1971), *Rasa Siddhant* (The Principles of Rasa ; 1964), *Hindi Dhavanyalok* (1952), *Kavyalankar Sutra* (1954), *Vakrokti Jivit* (1955), *Abhinav-Bharati* (1960), *Kavya-Prakash* (1960), tr. of Aristotle's *Poetics* and of the *On the Art of Sublime* by Longinus. He has also ed. critical works on *Prem Chand, Tulsidas, Surdas, Bihari* and *Mailhili Sharan Gupta.*

Nagendra's other works are : *Chetna ke Bimb* (sketches ; 1967), *Yauvan ke Dwar Par* (essay collection), *Astha ke Charan* (larger essay collection), *Shodh aur Siddhant*, *Shaili-Vigyan*, *Tantralok se Yantralok Tak* (1968), *Apravasi ki Yatrayen* (1972 ; both travelogues), *Bharatiya Vangmay* (Indian Literature ; in English and Russian also), *Bharatiya Kavyashastra ki Parampara* (Tradition of Indian Poetics ; both ed.), *Hindi Sahitya ka Itihas* (History of Hindi Literature), *Mithak aur Sahitya* (Myths and Literature ; 1979), *Bharatiya Sahitya Kosh* (Dictionary of Indian Literature ; 1981), *Sahitya ka Samaj Shastra* (The Sociology of Literature ; 1982), *Chintan Anuchintan* and *Mere Priya Nibandh.* He is also the editor of *Hindi Sahitya ka Brihad Itihas.*

Nagendra occupies an important place among modern Hindi critics, conservative and academic. With his profound knowledge of Western literature and a special interest in Indian literature as a unit, he is working out a synthesis between the aesthetic and rhetorical traditions of the East and the West. For his work, *Rasa-Siddhant*, he received the Sahitya Akademi Award. He was Head of the Department of Hindi, Delhi University for more than two decades. He has edited some books in English also.

NAGENDRA KUMAR. Maithili writer, whose chief work, *Sasar-Phani* (1947) is a short story collection ; his *Shyamali* (1981) is a travelogue on his tour to Ireland.

NAGENDRA SINGH. Modern Hindi writer, whose chief work is : *Vindhyachal ka Adhunik Hindi Kavya.*

NAHTA, AGAR CHAHD. See *Agar Chand Nahta.*

NAHTA, K. See *Kiran Nahta.*

NAHUSH. Drama (1841) by Giridhar Das (q.v.), which is in verse. The work is on the mythological story of Nahush. Written on the lines of Sanskrit plays, only one act of the play survives. Bharatendu Harishchandra (q.v.) calls it the first Hindi drama.

NAIM. Poet, whose collections of poems : *Pathrai Ankhen* (The Stony Eyes ; 1980) reveals personal sufferings, failures and disappointments.

NAIMAT KHAN JAN (fl. 1614-64) Rajasthani poet who was the eighth Kayamkhani Nawab of Fatehpur near Sikar, Jaipur. Well-versed in Arabic, Persian and Sanskrit, he was a great scholar of history. His *Kayam Raso* (completed in 1634) is a history of the ruling Kayam dynasty of Gujarat. Though of some literary merit, it is particularly important from the historical point of view. He also oomposed some 75 works in Pingal, many of them being romances, *e.g.*, *Katha Kanakavati*, *Kamlata*, *Gyandip*, *Madhukar Malati*, *Ratnavali*, etc.

NAINSI (1610-70). Rajasthani historian, whose full name was Muhnot Nainsi. An Oswal Mahajan, he was son of Jaimal and had three brothers : Sundardas, Askaran and Narsingh Das, Nainsi by virtue of his being a brave soldier and an able administrator, rose to be the Dewan of Maharaja Jaswant Singh the First of Jodhpur. In 1666, when the Maharaja was at Aurangabad, Nainsi and his brother, Sundardas were with the Maharaja, but as ill luck would have it, the Maharaja was displeased with the brothers and put them behind bars. After two years, the Maharaja imposed a fine of rupees one lakh and released them. As the brothers refused to pay the fine, they were imprisoned again. From Aurangabad Jail, they were transferred to Jodhpur Jail, where the treatment meted out to them was so deplorable, that they stabbed themselves to death.

Nainsi has been called the Abul Fazl of Rajasthan ; his *Muhnot Nainsi ri Khyat*, a historical work, covering more than a thousand pages of large size, treats of the history not only of Rajasthan but also of Gujarat, Kathiawar, Cutchh, Baghelkhand, Bundelkhand and Central India. His second work is a Gazetteer of the Marwar State in 3 Parts, under the title of *Marwar ra Parganan ri Vigat*.

NAKUL RAM MECH. Assamese-speaking modern Hindi writer, who is noted for his memoirs and reportage.

NAL-CHARIT-NATAK. See *Govind*.

NAL-DAMAN. See *Surdas*.

NALHA SINGH BHAT. Rajasthani poet, who was the author of *Vijaypal Raso* (q. v.), a ballad in Dingal. No authoritative account of his life is available but from his *Raso*, it appears that he was Bhat of Sirohiya branch and was patronized by Vijaypal of Vijaygarh (in Krauli), who had gifted to the poet a town named Hindon, other hundred villages, diamonds, elephants, horses, etc. See *Vijaypal Raso.*

NALIN VILOCHAN SHARMA (1916-61). Poet and writer of Bihar, who had poems, novels and short stories to his credit. He was the founder of 'Nakenvad' after the collection of poems by three poets, whose first initials made Na-Ke-Na (Nalin Vilochan Sharma, Kesari, Naresh Kumar). They believed that poems were written not out of emotions, but out of dictionaries (like some French writers). His chief works are *Drishtikon* (Viewpoint ; 1947), *Sahitya ka Itihas-Darshan* (The Philosophical History of Literature), *Mandand* (Criterion; 1963) and *Hindi Rachna Kosh* (with Kesari Kumar ; 1959).

NAMAH, POOJANAND. See *Poojanand Namah.*

NAMDAN BARHAT (fl. latter half of the 16th cent.). Dingal poet, whose *Chahuvan Gogaji ra Chhand* in 57 verses describes the glorious deeds of Gogaji.

NAMDEV (1270-1350). Saint-poet of Maharashtra, who composed some 2,375 *Abhangs* in Marathi. He also composed *Padas* in a large number in Hindi, of which 61 *Padas* are included in the *Granth Sahib* (q.v.). So far four collections of his *Padas* have been published ; there are *Padas* in other collections also, the total number being 300. Of all the saint-poets, who have composed *Padas* in Hindi before him, only the poetry of Namdev is considered of a high mark.

NAMDEV SHRI KRISHNADAS. Rajasthani saint-poet, whose stray verses are available ; his time is not certain.

NAMWAR SINGH (1927-). Marxist critic, whose scholarly works are : *Hindi ke Vikas men Apabhransh ka Yog* (Contribution of Apabhransh towards the Development of Hindi ; research thesis), *Prithwiraj Raso kl Bhasha* (The Language of the *Prithwiraj Raso*), *Purani Rajasthani* (*tr.*) and ed. of *Chintamani.* The works, which distil the quintessence of his critical thought are : *Chhayavad : Itihas aur Alochana* (on Chhayavad), *Adhunik Sahitya ki Pravrittiyan* (The Tendencies of Modern

Literature), *Kahani* : *Nayi Kahani* (on short story), *Kavita ke Naye Pratiman* (on new poetry). *Baqalam Khud* is a collection of his light essays. *Dusri Parampara ki Khoj* (The Discovery of a Second Tradition ; 1982 ; criticism) suggests Hazari Prasad Dwivedi as an enlightened critic and a progressive academician. He has also ed. *Adhunik Rusi Kavitayen.* He edits 'Alochana', a quarterly literary magazine and heads Hindi Department, Jawaharlal Nehru University, New Delhi.

NANAK DAS. Rajasthani saint-poet of Ram Snehi Sampraday, Ren, who was alive in 1717. Noted for his devotion and *Sadhana*, his short poem, *Guru Mahima Sakhis* and *Padas* extol God and Guru.

NANAK, GURU (1469-1538). Founder of the Sikh faith, who was deeply influenced by Kabir's teachings. Born in the village Talwandi, called, Nankana Sahib (now in Pakistan), his father, Kaluchandra Khatri, was a petty trader and he wanted his son to take up the family profession. Nanak, however, had a contemplative bent or mind ; he was married early to Sulakshani and had Shrichand and Lakshmichand as sons.

Nanak sought to convey his message through devotional songs, which are compiled in the *Granth Sahib* (q.v.). These songs are in Panjabi but some of them are in a language akin to Khari Boli and Brajbhasha, now called Hindi. The poetry he has left behind is simple and unsophisticated in content.

Without severing his relations with Hindu culture, Nanak preached monotheism and advocated Hindu Muslim unity.

NANAPPA, C.R. Malayalam-speaking modern writer, who has tr. Malayalam short stories into Hindi.

NAND BHARDWRJ. Rajasthani poet, who composed poems in the style of Nayi Kavita and has also written short stories. His *Daur ar Dayaro* (1981) discusses current trends in contemporary writings ; it also contains reviews of books and interviews with poets and scholars.

NAND DAS (1533-86). Poet, who holds, next to Surdas (q.v.), the highest place as a poet amongst those included in the *Ashtachhap*. *Shivsingh Saroj* mentions his date of birth to be 1528 at the village Soron in the Etah district. Those who regard Soron as the birth-place of Tulsidas, are of the view that Nanddas and Tulsidas were brothers. But it is more likely that the two were fellow-students and received education from the great scholar, Shesh Sanatan of Benares. A story is cureent that Nand Das once invited Tulsidas to Vrindavan. There Tulsidas refused to bow down before the image of Krishna until there was the bow and the arrow, instead of the flute in the hands. For the the time being, the image was metamorphosed and Tulsidas made obeisance to his god, Ram.

The two poets, however, followed different courses. As Tulsidas composed the story of Ram in Hindi, tradition has it that Nadddas translated the entire *Bhagavata* into Hindi. This voluminous work of Nanddas is said to have been dropped in the Yamuna at the instance of Vitthalnath (q.v.), who considered that the religious sanctity of the Sanskrit epic would be lost if rendered into a vernacular

Nanddas is reputed to be the author of 16 books but many do not survive. The works published are : *Raspanchadhyayi* (q.v.), *Bhramar Git*, *Anekarth Manjari*, *Anekarth Nammala*, *Rasamanjari* (on different types of heroines), *Rukmini*, *Uddhav-Shatak*, *Nasiketu Puran* (in prose), etc. The *Raspanchadhyayi* is his best work, though *Bhramargit* is the finest of his short poems. In the *Bhramargits*, there is a debate between the Gopis and Uddhav on the *Sagun* and *Nirgun* ways of worship. Several poets have composed *Bhramargits*, but none with such success as Nanddas. Nanddas's *Bhramargit* is the last word in Hindi on the age-old debate between the *Nirgun* and *Sagun* approaches to God. The Gopis and Uddhav are but instruments for a great philosophical disquisition and from the philosophical point of view, Nanddas even surpasses Surdas.

Not a single word is superfluous in the poetry of Nanddas and each word is so set as to embellish the other. So skilful is his art that a Hindi adage purports to the effect that all other poets are mere smiths before Nanddas, the stone-setter. Nanddas is a pastmaster of alliteration, but his alliteration is not laboured like that of Keshavdas (q.v.). The poetry is full of rich verbal music and the metrical patterns are more regular than in Surdas ; hence the effect is more sustained.

NAND DULARE VAJPEYI (1906-67). Critic, who was born at the village Magrail in the Unnao district. He taught at Benares Hindu University, Varanasi and was Head of the Hindi Department of Saugar University ; he was also appointed as Vice-Chancellor of Vikram University, Ujjain. His chief works are : *Hindi Sahitya—Bisvin Shatabdi* (special study of the inner motives of the 20th century writers in these essays), *Hindi Sahitya ka Sankshipt Itihas* (A Short History of Hindi Literature), *Jayshankar Prasad* (critical essay), *Premchand* (critical work), *Adhunik Sahitya* (1950 ; on the progress of Hindi literature since 1935-36), *Naya Sahitya—Naye Prashna* (New Literature—New Questions ; 1955 ; critical essays), *Kavi Sumitranandan Pant* (critical essay), *Nayi Kavita : Punarmulyankan* (New Poetry : Re-evaluation) *Rasa Siddhant : Naye Sandarbh*, *Kavi Nirala* and *Mahakavi Surdas* (criticism) ; apart from his work *Premchand*, all his writings are collections of essays written from time to time.

Counted as one of the pillars of Hindi criticism, he mainly follows the principles of criticism as laid down by Ramchandra Shukla (q.v.), with, of course, original approach seen in his writings ; for example, Vajpeyi's defence of the *Chhayavad* poets against their not so favourable assessment by Ramchandra Shukla, marks another stage in the development of literary criticism in Hindi. According to Vajpeyi, the critic's first and primary concern is with the study of the work of art and with the enjoyment and appreciation of beauty. In this difficult task, only his profound study, his subtle sense of beauty, his absolute objectivity and his emancipation from pre-conceived principles would come to his help.

NAND KISHORE (fl. 17th-18th cent.). Riti poet, whose chief work, *Pingal Prakash* deals with prosody.

NAND KISHORE (1813-55). Poet of the Krishna-cult (Chaitanya Sect), who was son of Chunnilal. Even at the age of 32, he was renowned for his learning. He was a great Sanskrit scholar and spoke fervently on the *Bhagavata*. He composed many works in Brajbhasha and wrote a commentary in prose on the *Bhagavata*. His stray verses and a small work, *Barahkhadi Mahima* are available.

NAND KISHORE, THE LATE. Hindi poet of Fiji, whose chief works are : *Durgam Path* and *Kisan Mitra*.

NAND KISHORE (fl. 1940-47). Malwi poet, who was noted for his humorous poems, *Pandat Pachchisi* and *Khatmal Battisi* (on bug).

NAND KISHORE ACHARYA. Modern poet, whose poems are included in the *Chautha Saptak* (q.v.) ; *Kise Ghadte Ho* (Whom

Do You Sculpt ?) is his poem. *Jal Hai Jahan* is a collection of his poems.

NAND KISHORE LAL DAS (fl. *c.* 1930). Maithili writer, who was noted for his short stories.

NAND KISHORE NAVAL. Modern scholar, whose chief work is *Hindi Alochana ka Vikas.*

NAND KISHORE PARIK. Modern Rajasthani poet, who has composed Nature poems.

NAND RAM. Rajasthani poet, who was patronized by Maharaja Jagat Singh the Second of Mewar. He composed two works in Pingal : *Shikar-Bhav* (1733 ; on hunting excursions of Maharana Jagat Singh) and *Jag-Vilas* (on the daily routine and splendour of Jagat Singh) ; both the works are of literary and historical value.

NAND RAM (fl. end of 17th cent.). Poet of the Riti school, who, at the instance of his patron, Maharaja Anup Singh of Bikaner, composed his *Alas Bhedani.*

NANDAN (VANDAN) PATHAK (fl. 1849). Poet of Mirzapur, who was patronized by Raja Ishwari Prasad Narayan Singh of Kashi. He was the author of *Manas-Shankavali* (on the removal of doubts about the *Ramcharitmanas*).

NANDESHWAR RAJMEDHI. Assamese-speaking modern Hindi writer, who has made a study of modern Hindi and Assamese poetry in the context of the poetry of Suryakant Tripathi 'Nirala' and Ambikagiri Raichaudhury.

NANDIPATI. Maithili poet, who was by tradition a contemporary of Maharaja Madhav Singh (1776-1808). Son of Krishnapati, who was also a poet, Nandipati, at the end of each Act of his only extant drama, *Shri-Krishna-Kelimala* (q.v.) says that he had twelve names ; probably he bore 'Badari' as his pen name. Nandipati, Umapati and Lal Kavi (qq.v.) made the typical Kirtaniya drama popular and great. Nandipati was also noted for his love lyrics. He and Man Bodh (q.v.) freed Maithili poetry from the learned and sophisticated imagery of Vidyapati and made a distinct bid for simplicity and directness, a departure followed by other poets.

NANDIYE KA PAVADA. Rajasthani Pavada, which describes the heroic deeds of Nandiya, who was son of Budoji (see *Pabuji ka Pavada*); both Pabuji and Budoji laid down their lives in the protection of cows. Before Budoji's wife commits *Sati*, she carries Nandiya in her womb. She cuts across her belly and delivers the babe to be brought up by his maternal grandmother. When Nandiya is 12 years of age, he comes to know of it that his father and uncle (Pabuji) had been killed by Khichi. He becomes a disciple of Gorakhnath and after having his blessings, proceeds to Khichi's town. He kills Khichi and brings his head at the place where his father and uncle were killed. This brave deed of Nandiya is the subject of many a ballad.

NANUJI (fl. 17th cent.). One of the court-poets of Guru Govind Singh (q.v.); he had mastery over Brajbhasha and composed verses in praise of the Guru. He wrote also devotional poetry in the *Shringar* style.

NANU RAM (fl. 1940-47). Malwi poet, who was noted for his stray poems.

NANU RAM SANSKARTA. Rajasthani poet and writer, whose chief works are *Ghar ki Rel* (folk-tales), *Kalyan* (1949; on seasons, including the life of the people in general), *Das Dev* (1955; on ten village gods: five trees and five aspects of Earth), *Samay Vayaro* (1953; in blank verse), *Prakriti Salkado* (100 verses on objects of Nature), *Sankal Sandhan* (1973; story in verse), *Lankan Dhani* (1976; q.v.), *Gopichand* (1977; on the Nath-Siddha Gopichand), *Gyoyi* (1957), *Das Dokh* (1966), *Ghar ki Gay* (1970); three collections of social short stories), descriptive and satiric stories and some patriotic and heroic poems.

NANZHUDEN, K.R. Tamil-speaking Hindi scholar, who is noted for his *Tirumular aur Gorakhnath* (thesis; 1973) and a critical essay: 'Tamil men Siddha Sahitya' (Siddha Literature in Tamil).

NAR NARAYAN RAI. Critic, who has written a work on Lakshminarayan as a dramatist (1980) and has edited *Vaigyanik Ekanki* (Scientific One-act plays), a collection of seven such plays.

NAR NATH BHATTACHARYA (1932-). Assamese-speaking Hindi writer, whose essays have been published in

'Rashtrasevak'. He has tr. into Hindi Banikant Kakati's work on Old Assamese Literature.

NARA, TSUYOSHI. Modern Japanese Hindi scholar, who is at present associated with the Tokyo University of Foreign Studies. His special field of study is historical and comparative study of Indo-Aryan languages, especially Bengali and Hindi.

NARASIMHACHARI, S.T. (1927-). Tamil-speaking Hindi critic, whose chief works are : *Sahityik Abhiruchi aur Samiksha* (Literary Propensity and Criticism ; research), *Prasad ki Kahaniyon ka Pravrittimulak Vishleshan* (on the short stories of Prasad) and *Saundaryatattwa Nirupan* (on aesthetics).

NARASIMHA DAS. Telugu-speaking Hindi writer of Mauritius, whose chief works are : *Shivratri* and *Jyotirlingaradhana*. From 1933 to 1942, he started 'Sanatan Dharmank', a paper in Hindi and French.

NARASIMHA RAO, P.V. Telugu-speaking modern Hindi writer, who has tr. Vishwanath Satyanarayan's famous Telugu novel *Veyi Padagalu* as *Sahasraphan*.

NARAYAN CHITAMBARE (fl. 1920-40). Marathi-speaking Hindi writer, who was noted for his short stories. He also tr. several Marathi works into Hindi.

NARAYAN DAS (fl. 1493). Author of *Chhitai Varta*, a poetical work in a language mixed with Braj, Avadhi and Dingal ; the work deals with the beauty of Chhitai, a princess, whom Allauddin wished to procure for himself.

NARAYAN DAS (fl. 18th cent.). Rajasthani saint-poet of Ram Snehi Sampraday, Sinthal, who belonged to the village Jaitpur (Bikaner) and was initiated by Hariram Das (q.v.) in 1749. His *Vani*, consisting of *Pran Parchai ko Ang*, *Chetavani*, *Harjas*, *Dohas*, etc. deal with Yoga, Guru, *Ram-smaran*, etc. He had 47 main disciples, who like him, were ascetics.

NARAYAN DAS AGRAWAL. Modern Rajastaani writer, who is noted for his dramas : *Mahabharat ko Shri Ganesh* and *Maharana Pratap*.

NARAYAN DAS 'SENGARIYA' (1844-1939). Poet of the Krishna-cult, whose several *Padas* are extant.

NARAYAN DAS SHROTRIYA (fl. 1st half of 16th cent.). Poet of the Krishna-cult (Chaitanya Sect), who was a disciple of Narayan Bhatt. Of his *Padas*, only one is extant.

NARAYAN DATT SHARMA. Modern poet, who has written a narrative poem, which was published in 'Brajbharati'.

NARAYAN DATT SHRIMALI. Modern Rajasthani poet, who has composed poems, portraying various aspects of Nature. He is also the author of satirical stories and one-act plays: *Chiyan Tavado* and *Mati ro Pauredar*. His novel in Khari Boli is *Ek Dali Rajnigandha Ki*.

NARAYAN DEV, P. (fl. early 20th cent.). Malayalam-speaking Hindi teacher, who advocated the cause of Hindi. He was popularly known as 'Dev Keraliya'. He was educated at Lahore and Delhi in the tenets of Arya Samaj. He wrote a Hindi grammar and also composed several poems in Hindi as also a poetical work. He was associated with 'Vishwabharati', a literary magazine published from Kottayam.

NARAYAN GADGIL (fl. 1920-40). Marathi-speaking Hindi novelist, who was noted for his *Ankh-Michauli*.

NARAYAN, K. (fl. 1950). Malayalam-speaking Hindi writer, whose short stories have been published in 'Dharmyuga', 'Sarika', 'Yuga Prabhat', 'Rashtravani', etc. He is regarded as one of the early forceful writers of Hindi short stories in Kerala. A small collection of his short stories has been published from Allahabad. He was a great scholar of psychology, especially of child psychology and was also considered as an authority on music; he edited the special issue of 'Karnataka Sangit'.

NARAYAN KAVI. Poet, who was a disciple of Sardar (fl. 1843). In collaboration with Sardar, he wrote commentaries on *Kavipriya* and *Rasikpriya* of Keshavdas (q v.).

NARYAN, P. Malayalam-speaking modern Hindi poet, who has composed several stray poems.

NARAYAN PAT DESAI. Modern Hindi poet and writer of Mauritius, who is noted for his stray poems and short stories.

NARAYAN PILLAI, G. Malayalam-speaking modern Hindi writer, who has tr. Malayalam poet Shankar Kurup's Malayalam poems under the title *Ek aur Nachiketa* (One More Nachiketa); the Hindi version has been revised by Lakshmi Chand Jain. Narayan Pillai has also tr. from Malayalam into Hindi prose 56 poems of Balamani Amma, which were published with revision by Lakshmi Chand Jain. See *Bhattatiri, P.N.*

NARAYAN RAM ARYA. Modern Kumaoni poet, who is noted for his stray poems.

NARAYAN RAO, J. Telugu-speaking modern Hindi writer, who is noted for his tr. of Telugu short stories into Hindi.

NARAYAN SINGH BHATI. Rajasthani poet, whose chief works are : *Sanjh* (1954 ; in 115 verses on the reaction of the living beings to the evening and on its beauty), *Durgadas* (1956 ; on Durgadas Rathore of Marwar ; in blank verse), *Jivan Dhan Kalap, Param Vir* (1963 ; paying homage to Major Shaitan Singh, who laid down his life in defending the air base at Chushul in Ladhakh during the Chinese attack in 1962), 'Mannas', 'Olun' (1964 ; on the emotions of a newly-married 'virahini' bride in 121 verses), *Miran* (1976 ; a 64-page poem on Mirabai, where the emphasis is on her emotions and poetic circumstances), *Minakh Nai Samjhavanau Dora Hai* and *Barsan ra Digora Dungar Langhiya.* He has also composed love poems and some odes. He is the author also of *Dingal Git Sahitya* (1971) and has edited *Adhunik Rajasthani Kavita* (1981), which contains 8 essays on various aspects of modern Rajasthani poetry, all written by poets and scholars.

NARAYAN SWAMI (1828-1900). Poet of Rawalpindi (now in Pakistan), who came to Vrindavan in 1859. His compositions are collected in *Braj-Bihar.*

NARAYAN VISHNU JOSHI. Marathi-speaking modern Hindi poet and dramatist, whose works are : *Ruponnayan*, *Alok* (poetical), *Jagirdar* and *Vakil Sahib* (dramas).

NARAYANAN, K. Tamil-speaking modern Hindi writer, whose short stories were published in various popular magazines.

NARAYANAN, N.I. (fl. 1950). Malayalam-speaking Hindi writer, who has written works on Hindi grammar. He also tr. into prose Kumaran Ashan's Malayalam poem : 'Vin Puvu' under the title of 'Jhada Phul' and has published a collection of essays : *Nibandh Prabodh* as also research work : *Hindi evam Malayalam ke Natakon par Tulnatmak Adhyayan* (A Comparative Study of Hindi and Malayalam Dramas).

NARENDRA. Writer, who was noted for his drama : *Nich* (The Low ; 1931).

NARENDRA BHANAWAT. Rajasthani writer, whose chief work is : *Rajasthani Veli Sahitya* (1965).

NARENDRA DEV, ACHARYA (1890-1956). Writer and socialist thinker, who was a man of learning and wide scholarship. His *Bhagvan Buddha aur Unka Mat* is an outstanding original work in Hindi on the life, teachings and philosophy of Gautam Buddha. His interpretation of the tenets of Buddhism is part historical and part philosophical. However, both from the point of subject and style, the work is classed among the best works of thought prose in Hindi. It was awarded Sahitya Akademi Award posthumously. He was founder of Kashi Vidyapith, Congress Socialist Party and edited 'Sangharsh' (Lucknow) fortnightly.

NARENDRA KHAJURIA (1933-70). Dogri writer, whose works in Hindi are : *Rasta, Kante aur Hath* (The Path, Thorns and Hand ; drama), *Raste Men* (On the Way ; short story collection) and *Sat Ekanki* (collection of seven one-act plays). One of his Dogri novels has been tr. into Hindi by Dev Ratna Shastri under the title *Nila Ambar Kale Badal* (The Blue Sky and the Black Clouds). He also edited 'Shiraja' for a decade.

NARENDRA KOHLI. Modern fiction writer and satirist, whose chief works are : *Sath Saha Gaya Dukh* (Sorrows Felt Together) and *Atank* (Terror ; novels). His novels based on the story of Ram are : *Diksha*, Sangharsh *ki Or*, *Avsar*, *Prishthabhumi*, *Sakshatkar*, *Abhiyan* and *Yuddha*. *Parinati*, *Namak ka Qaidi*, *Kahani ka Abhav*, *Shuttle*, *Sambandh*, *Drishti Desh men Ekaek* are his short story collections, while *Shambuk ki Hatya* (The Murder of Shambuk) is a drama. His important short stories are : 'The Shuttle', 'Sanchit Bhukh' (The Accumulated Hunger), etc. He has re-interpreted incidents in Indian mythology. He has also written a critical work, *Hindi Upanyas : Srijan aur Siddhant*.

NARENDRA MALL (fl. *c.* 1551). Ruler of Kathmandu, who wrote *Ramayan-Natak* (in 12 Acts) and *Mahabharat-Natak* in Maithili.

NARENDRA MOHAN (1935-). Critic of modern literature and poet, whose chief works are : *Adhunikta aur Samkalin Rachna*, *Adhunik Hindi Kavita men Sandarbh aur Aprastut Vidhan*, *Adhunik Hindi Upanyas* (ed.), *Hindi ki Lambi*

Kavitayen (ed.), *Kahin bhi Kavita Khatma Nahin Hoti* (Poems end Nowhere ; 1978 ; ed. of an anthology of long poems), *Is Hadase Men* (In this Accident ; poetry), *Vichar aur Lahu ke Bich* (1983 ; ed. of a further collection of long poems), *Hindi ki Shreshth Kahaniyan* (ed., 1980), *Premchand ka Katha Sansar* (ed., 1980), *Adhunikta ke Sandarbh men Hindi Kahani* (Hindi Short Story in the Context of Modernity ; 1982 ; a study of short stories from 1950 to 1980), *Kavita ki Vaicharik Bhumika* (criticism), *Sikka Badal Gaya, Bharat Vibhajan* (short story collections), *Samne Hone Par* (When Before Me ; collection of poems ; 1979) and *Ek Agnikand Jagahen Badalta* (1983 ; collection of poems).

NARENDRA NATH DAS. Modern Maithili scholar, who in his *Vidyapati Kavyalok* has applied the method of comparative criticism.

NARENDRA SHARMA (1913-). Poet, who was born in Jahangirpur of Bulandshahr district. After his education at Allahabad, he was associated for some time with film industry and wrote some lyrics for films. Then he became Head of the Vividh Bharati Programme of the All India Radio. His chief works are : *Shul Phul* (The Thorns and Flowers ; 1934), *Karnaphul* (Ear-flowers ; 1936), *Prabhat Pheri* (collection of the poems of the above two works), *Pravasi ke Git* (songs), *Palashvan* (The Forest of Palash), *Mitti aur Phul* (The Clay and the Flowers), *Agnishayya, Hansmala, Kadlivan* (1953), *Draupadi* (a concise version of the *Mahabharat*), *Uttar Jay* (also based on the *Mahabharat* story), *Pyasa Nirjhar* (The Thirsty Spring), *Bahut Rat Gaye* (Late at Night) and *Suvira* ; *Kadvi Mithi Baten* (Bitter Sweet Talks) is his short story collection while *Dukhiyari* is his novel. He is noted for his lyrics and progressive poems.

NARENDRA SINGH BHANDARI. Modern Garhwali scholar, who is noted for his *Snowballs of Garhwal*.

NARENDRA SINGH, RAVAL (1893-1967). Rajasthani historian and a poet of traditional Charan style, who belonged to Jobner. His some 700 *Sorthas* were at first named *Vir Puja Satsai*, but due to addition of more *Sorthas*, the numbet rose to about 1,000. Collectively, they have now been called *Vir Hazara* ; basically the *Vir Hazara* is a historical poem with accent on heroism. The characters described include Karaniji, Ram, Hanuman, Krishna, Rana Pratap, Surajmal Jat, Amarsingh Rathore, Tejoji Jat, etc. His contribution to the almost decaying traditional poetry of Charan style is significant.

NARENDRA SINGH TOMAR (fl. 1940-47). Malwi poet, who was noted for his *Pag-dandi* (The Footpath).

NARENDRA VASHISHTH. Critic, who is noted for his *Shamsher ki Kavita* (The Poetry of Shamsher ; 1980) ; *Salib Par* is a collection of his poems.

NARESH MEHTA (1924-). Writer and poet, whose chief works are as under :—

FICTION. *Dubte Mastul* (The Sinking Masts ; 1954 ; consequences of Ranjana's pride of beauty), *Yah Path Bandhu Tha* (This Path was Friend ; 1962 ; on the story of a shattering family in the background of Indian freedom struggle since 1920), *Dhumketu* : *Ek Shruti, Do Ekant* (1964 ; on the breaking of conjugal life), *Nadi Yashasvi Hai* (The Glorious River ; 1967 ; the second part of *Dhumketu* : *Ek Shruti*), *Pratham Phalgun* (The First Spring ; 1968) *Uttar Katha* (2 Pts.) (all novels), *Tathapi* (1961) and *Ek Samarpit Mahila* (1967) (short story collections).

Poetry : In addition to poems, collected in *Dusra Saptak* (q.v.), *Samay Devta* (Time Deity ; 1948), *Sanshay ki Ek Rat* (portrayal of doubt lurking in Ram's mind before invasion of Lanka), *Banpankhi Suno* (Hark 0 Forest Bird ; 1959) and *Bolne Do Chid Ko* (Let the Pine Tree Speak ; collection of new songs).

Drama : *Subah ke Ghante* (The Morning Bells), *Roti aur Beti* (The Relationship), *Uljhan* (The Complexity), *Damad* (The Son-in-Law), Phaisla (The Judgement) and *Khandit Yatrayen* (The Broken Journeys).

A progressive poet, he has now turned into a mystic and has written *Kavya Ka Vaishnav Vyaktitwa* (criticism) and poems : *Mahaprasthan*, *Pravad Parva*, *Utsava*, *Tum Mera Maun Ho*, *Vagdevi* and *Uttar Gatha* (2 Pts.).

NARESH PANDYA. Gujarati-speaking modern Hindi scholar, whose *Pran Nath Sampraday aur Sahitya* is a research work.

NARAHRI (fl. 18th cent.). Poet of the Krishna-cult (Haridasi Sect), who was noted for his *Narhari Ali ki Vani*.

NARHARI BANDIJAN (1505 1610). Poet of Raebareli, who wielded great influence in the court of Akbar. Patronized by

Humayun, Sher Shah Suri and his son, Islam Shah and Emperor Akbar, it is popular, how Akbar, pleased at a *Chhapay* composed by the poet, banned the practice of cow-slaughter in his kingdom. From all accounts, Narhari was a well-known poet and wielded much influence in the Durbars of contemporary kings. Apart from a few hundred Chhands, he has written on Sita's *Swayamvar*, Gopis' lamentation when separated from their Lord and on the physical charms of Radha and Krishna ; his *Barahmasa* is also remarkable.

NARHARI DAS (1591-1676). Rajasthani poet, who was son of Charan Lakkhaji. He was patronized by Maharaja Gajsingh of Jodhpur, who gifted him the village Tahala. A poet of the Ram-cult, his *Avtar-Charitra*, in 1600 verses treats of the various incarnations of Vishnu ; a major portion deals with Ram. The portion relevant to Ram openly betrays the influence of Tulsidas and Keshavdas (qq. v.). It is said that Narharidas composed also 16 to 17 works, but they are no longer extant ; only the names of six works, which are available, are : *Dasham Skandh Bhasha*, *Ramcharitra Katha*, *Ahilya-Purva-Prasang*, *Vani*, *Narsingh Avtar Katha* and *Amarsinghji ri Duha*.

NARHARI DAS SANVLOT, BARHAT (fl. *c* 1723-63). Rajasthani poet, whose *Gun Ram Var Nisani* narrates the story of Ram in 209 *Nisanis* in a flowing and easy language.

NARHARI DEV, SWAMI (fl. 17th cent.). Poet of the Krishna-cult (Haridasi Sect), who was noted for his small *Vani*.

NARHARI SHASTRI. See *Shishtu Krishnamurti Shastri*.

NARIDAS (fl. 16th cent.). Rajasthani saint-poet of Fatehpur (Shekhawati), who was a disciple of Haridas (q.v.) and a follower of Haridas Niranjani Sampraday. His 1200 *Padas* are didactic in nature.

NARINDAR K. AGGARWAL. Compiler of *A Bibliography of Studies on Hindi Language and Linguistics* (1977). Aggarwal is at present Professor of Library Administration, University of Illinois, Urbana, U.S.A.

NARMADA SHANKAR (1833-86). Famous Gujarati poet, who also composed some stray verses in Braj.

NARROTTAM DAS (fl. 1545). Poet of Badi near Sitapur, who was the author of three works : *Vichar-Mala*, *Dhruv-Charitra* (both no longer extant) and *Sudama-Charitra* (q. v.) ; the last composition has made him popular and has endeared him to the people.

NAROTTAM DAS (fl. 16th cent.). Bengali Vaishnav poet, who also composed *Padas* in Brajbuli. Some of his *Padas* are available in *Padakalpataru* (q.v.).

NAROTTAM DAS SWAMI (1905-81). Noted Rajasthani scholar of Bikaner, whose *Rajasthan ra Duha* has been awarded by the Hindi Sahitya Sammelan, Prayag. He has a also edited *Rajasthan ke Lok-Git*, *Dhola Maru ra Duha*, *Rajiya ra Duha* and has done quite good work on the *Vat* literature of Rajasthan. He has published Rajasthani proverbs, idioms, riddles, sayings, etc. (*Rajasthani Kahavaten*, 2 vols.) and also has written introductions, reviews, articles and comments on important works. He has written history of Rajasthani language and literature (*Rajasthani Sahitya* : *Ek Parichay* ; 1975) as also *Sankshipt Rajasthani Vyakaran* (1960). One of the members of Rajasthani Sahitya Pith, he has espoused the cause of Rajasthani.

NAROTTAM PRASAD NAGAR (1913-68). Writer, whose chief work, *Din ke Tare* (The Stars of the Day) was psychological novel ; he had also written short stories. He edited 'Uchhrinkhal', 'Huns' and other magazines. He was a journalist and a satirist.

NARPATI NALHA. Rajasthani poet of the court of Vigrahraj the Third or the Fourth of Ajmer. Narpati was the author of *Visaldev Raso* (q. v.), a Dingal ballad composed in honour of his royal patron. Scholars differ about his date : according to some he flourished around 1016, while others regard him to have fl. in 1155 or 1156. The hero of the ballad, Vigrahraj the Third rules between 973-999 and on that basis the *Visaldev Raso* was composed in 1016. Thus Narpati has the honour of being the first poet in Hindi. Some scholars, however, are of the view that Narpati was patronized by Vigrahraj the Fourth (r. 1143-53).

NARSA REDDY, K. Telugu-speaking modern Hindi poet, who is noted for his *Yah aur Vah* (This and That).

NARSI (NARSINGH) MEHTA (1413-79) The first saint-poet of Gujarati, who is also said to have composed some *Padas* in Hindi ; a few are extant, though scholars doubt their authenticity.

NARSIJI RO MAHERO. Rajasthani poem, composed by many poets with many variations, which describes the domestic plight of Nani Bai, a married daughter of the famous Bhakta-poet Narsi Mehta (q.v.) and celestial performance of 'Bhat' known as the 'Mahero' episode.

NARSINGH RAY GURU, KAVICHANDRA (fl. 19th cent. ?). Contemporary of Raja Som Nath Singh of Anugul in Dhenkanal district of Orissa, whose *Raja Som Nath Singh* is available in Hindi.

NARUJI (fl. 1603). Rajasthani poet, whose stray verses in popular metres are available.

NARULA, S.S. See *Shamsher Singh Narula*.

NASIKETOPAKHYAN (*Chandravati*). Prose work (1803) by Sadal Mishra (q.v.), which treats of the puranic episode of Maharaja Raghu's daughter, Chandravati and his son, Nasiket in an attractive manner. This work is a landmark in early Khari Boli prose.

NASIR FAQIR (fl. 18th cent.). Sindhi Muslim saint-poet, who was also noted for his composition of stray verses in Hindi.

NATH. See *Gun Shivcharit Prakas*.

NATH (HARINATH). Poet of the Riti school, who was a Gujarati Brahmin of Kashi. He composed *Alankar-Darpan* (The Mirror of the Figures of Speech; 1769), a small work on *Alankars*. In this work, a *Pada* contains many examples.

NATH MAL (fl. 1668). Jain poet, whose *Bankchor ki Katha* (The Story of Bankchor Thief) describes how Bankchor's heart was changed.

NATHMAL, MUNI. Scholar and author of *Hindi Jan-jan ki Bhasha* (1966 ?) and *Bhav aur Anubhav* (Calcutta, 1963).

NATTHAN SINGH. Modern scholar, whose chief work is: *Premchand : Mulyankan aur Mulyankan*.

NATHOJI (fl. 18th cent.). Rajasthani saint-poet of Jasnathi Sect, whose stray verses and *Sabads* deal with human duties, divine attributes, etc.

NATHU DAN (b. 1891). Rajasthani poet, whose stray verses and *Vir Satsai* are available.

NATHU RAM MAHAUR (1885-1959). Poet of Jhansi, whose published works are : *Vir Badhu* (The Brave Bride), *Vir Bala* (The Brave Girl), *Ashrumal*, etc.

NATHU RAM SHANKAR SHARMA (1859-1932). Poet, who was born in Harduaganj of Aligarh district and studied Hindi, Urdu, Persian and Sanskrit. He first used to write in Urdu but under the influence of Arya Samaj and Pratap Narayan Mishra, he began to compose poems in Hindi. He was a popular member of Bharatendu Harishchandra's 'Kavi Samaj' where he recited his own verses. He came to be known as one of the leading Brajbhasha poets ; *Shankar-Sarvasva* is a collection of all his poems, while *Garbh-Ganda-Rahasya* is a *Prabandh Kavya*.

NATHU SADH (fl. 18th cent. ?). Rajasthani saint-poet of Laldasi Sect, whose *Bhajans* extol devotion to God and Guru and advocate simplicity in life.

NATHU SINGH MAHIYARIYA (1891-1975). Rajasthani poet of heroic and nationalist themes in Charan style, who was son of Charan Kesri Singh. His chief works are : *Vir Satsai*, *Gandhi Shatak*, *Hadi Shatak*, *Chunda Shatak*, *Jhala Man Shatak*, *Vir Shatak* and *Kashmir Shatak*. Though he is influenced by the poems of Isardas, Charan Bankidas, Suryamall Mishran and other poets, he is not bound by the stereotyped and conventional pattern and this is the forte of his poetry. He has also eulogised the national heroes of the modern age. From the poetic point of view, his *Vir Satsai* is a very important work.

NATNAGAR (1808-64). Rajasthani poet, who was son of Rajsingh, Ruler of Sitamau. His real name was Ratnasingh but he wrote poems under the pseudonym of Natnagar. A great patron of printing, music and poetry, he himself was a poet of no mean order His *Natnagar Vinod* is a collection of his poems, of both Dingal and Pingal. His poetry is inclined towards Bhakti and *Shringar*.

NATTHAMAL (fl. 19th cent.). Poet of Hathras, whose sayings in Brajbhasha are quite popular in the Mathura region.

NATVAR (fl. 17th cent.). Bengali Vaishnav poet, who also composed *Padas* in Brajbuli.

NAUBAT SINGH. Modern writer, who is noted for his *Vishwadarpan* (an anthology of international poems).

NAUBATI RAY. Modern Kannauji poet, who is noted for his Kannauji folk-poems.

NAVAL DAS (fl. 17th cent.). Poet of the Krishna-cult (Haridasi Sect), who was noted for his small *Vani*.

NAVAL KISHORE DAS. Modern Oriya writer, who has tr. Chatur Sen Shastri's two novels : *Vaishali ki Nagarvadhu* and *Vayam Rakshamah* from Hindi into Oriya.

NAVAL KISHORE 'KANKAR'. Rajasthani writer, whose *Sail Sapata* (1980), a travelogue, is the first of its kind in Rajasthani. A Sanskrit writer of repute, his style in the travelogue reminds one of Dandi and Ban.

NAVAL NATH (fl. 19th cent.). Rajasthani Nath-Siddha poet, whose stray poems lean more towards Vedanta of Shankar.

NAVAL RAM (fl. 19th cent.). Gujarati poet, whose *Akbar Birbal Kavya Tarang* in Gujarati contains many Hindi verses.

NAVAL RAM MANTRI (d. 1785). Rajasthani saint-poet of Bhilwara, who was initiated by Ramcharan (q.v.) of Ram Snehi Sampraday, some time after 1760. Naval Ram Mantri first collected the *Vani* of his own Guru ; his own poems are known by the name of *Naval Sagar*. The emphasis is on *Ram-smaran* and Bhakti and the language is popular Rajasthani.

He also compiled *Sarwang Sar* (q.v.), which contains poems of about 85 poets, some known and some unknown, irrespective of their ideology.

NAVAL SINGH PRADHAN (fl. 1813-69). Poet of Jhansi, who was patronized by Hindupati, the Raja of Samthar. He had special leanings towards devotion and knowledge. He composed some 28 works, the chief ones being : *Raspanchadhyayi*, *Ramchandra-Vilas*, *Rasikranjani*, *Mul Bharat*, *Alha-Ramayan*, *Muldhola*. Most of his works are of small in size and treat of different subjects in different styles.

NAVARUN VERMA (1935-). Assamese-speaking Hindi poet, whose chief poetical works are : *Lachit Barphukan* (nationalist poem), *Sati Jaymati* and *Sindhu-Manthan* (based on a Puranic legend). He has written essays, short stories and novels as well. He has also tr. several Assamese novels, short stories and poems into Hindi.

NAVIN (fl. 1843). Poet, who was a fellow-student of Gwal (q.v.). He was patronized by Maharaja Devendra Singh of Nabha. Navin's works are : *Saras-Rasa*, *Sudhakar*, *Rang-Tarang* and *Neh-Nidan* (The Diagnosis of Love).

NAVIN. See *Balkrishna Sharma 'Navin'*.

NAVIN CHANDRA KALITA (1910-). Assamese-speaking Hindi writer, who wrote many text-books in Hindi for the Assam Hindi Prachar Samiti. He was one of the three young men, who in 1938 were instrumental in propagating Hindi in Assam.

NAVIN CHANDRA MEHTA. Gujarati-speaking modern Hindi scholar, whose *Hindi Gujarati ki Nai Kavita* is a research work.

NAVIN CHANDRA MISHRA. Modern Maithili scholar, who is noted for his critical work : *Pratipada : Ek Adhyayan.*

NAVIN CHANDRA RAY (1838-90). Educationist and reformer, who was a member of the Brahmo Samaj. In Panjab, he rendered services to the cause of Hindi equal to those of Raja Shiv Prasad (q.v.). He started in 1867 the first Hindi journal in Panjab, called 'Gyan Pradayini'. He wrote scores of tracts and pamphlets advocating the cause of Hindi and refuting the arguments of the critics.

NAVNIT CHATURVEDI, KAVINDRA (1858-1932). Poet of Mathura, who was awarded the title of 'Kavindra' by the Raja of Kakrauli. He had a wide reputation and George Grierson came to meet him at his house. Out of his 16 works and 1500 *Padas*, *Prashnottar* (in question-answer form), *Navinotsav* (The New Festival), *Murkh-Shatak* (a centum on fools), *Rahiman-Shatak* (on Rahim), *Kubja-Pachisi* (based on the *Bhramargits*), *Gopi-Prem Piyush Pravah* (on the love of cow-herdesses for Krishna), *Pavas-Pachisi*, *Sneh-Shatak* (devotional) are important.

NAVINT RAM (fl. 1725). Poet of the Riti school, who wrote *Rasa Prakash* on *Rasa*.

NAVRASA TARANG. Poem by Beni Pravin (fl.1807-71).

It treats of the various *Rasas* but as usual the maximum space has been allotted to *Shringar* and its associated themes :

Nayikabhed and *Nakhshikh*. There is an impressive description of the seasons in the work and the diction is pure and chaste.

NAYAKAVA BANJARA. Bhojpuri folk-tale in verse, which was published by Grierson in 1889 ; the version that is available at present was composed by Mahadev Prasad Singh (q.v.). The tale describes the love of husband and wife and their union and separation.

NAYAN RAM, MAHARAJ (fl. 19th cent.). Sindhi saint-poet, whose stray verses in Hindi are available.

NAYAN SUNDAR (1505-56). Gujarati-speaking Jain poet, whose literature in Gujarati is quite ample. There is no specific Hindi work composed by him, but his Gujarati works contain quotations in large number from Sanskrit, Prakrit, Hindi and Urdu works. Some of his works are composed in a mixed Hindi-Gujarati language. His *Nal Damyanti Ras* is an anthology, which contains works of other poets.

NAZIR, SHEIKH (*c*. 1740-*c*. 1820). Poet of Delhi, who came to live in Agra at the time of Ahmedshah Abdali's attack on Delhi. His original name was Sheikh Wali Muhammad. He composed many poems on Krishna's childhood. His works, smaller in character, are : *Kanhaiya-Janma*, *Vanshi*, *Banjara-nama*, *Joginama*, *Hans Nama*, *Adminama*, *Budhapanama*, *Faqiron ki Sada*, etc. His works are met at one place in his *Kulliyate Nazir*.

NAZIR ANANDRAM (fl. 1704). Brajbhasha poet of Rajasthan, whose *Bhagavadgita* is in prose and verse.

NAZIRUDDIN SIDDIQI 'UPAMA' (1896-1942). Bagheli folk-poet, whose chief works are *Upama Bhajanavali* (hymns) and *Bahare Kajli*.

NEGI DAYARI. Kului Panvada, which describes the wisdom of Negi Dayari. The Raja of Nahan invites the Raja of Kulu for a game of dice so that the latter is defeated and the former usurps his kingdom. Negi Dayari, the wise minister of the Kulu ruler, however, saves his Raja from this calamity.

NEHI NAGARIDAS (b. *c*. 1533). Poet of the Krishna-cult (Radhavallabh Sect), who was a Kshatriya of Bundelkhand. After his contact with Chaturbhujdas (q.v.), he came to live in Vrindavan. As he wanted to lead a lonely life, he left Vrindavan for Barsana. His works are : *Siddhant Dohavali* (935 *Dohas*), *Rasa Padavali* (232 *Padas* including stray verses) and *Padavali* (102 *Padas*).

NEM NARAYAN GUPTA (1894-1955). Hindi lover of Mauritius, who was affectionately called by many names, viz., 'Guruji', 'Nemanji', 'Neman Sav', 'Neman Guruji', 'Neman Gupta', etc. He was born in Tripole. For the propagation of Hindi, he almost reached every village of Mauritius and sometimes he remained absent from home for more than a week. He taught Hindi at the Saraswati Kanya Pathshala and it was due to his tireless zeal that several Pathshalas were started in many villages. He was for a chaste and correct Hindi. He organized an annual meeting of the Hindi Sahitya Sammelan in Mauritius in 1941 and an exhibition of Hindi books was held on the occasion. The Library of Hindi Pracharini Sabha is named after him. Despite the fact that he lived a life of absolute poverty, he devoted the whole of his life for the propagation of Hindi. He has rightly been called the first teacher (*Adiguru*) of the Hindi world of Mauritius and the street where he taught Hindi is named after him.

NEM NARAYAN JOSHI (1926-). Writer, whose chief works are : *Sumitranandan Pant ka Navchetana Kavya* (on Pant ; criticism ; 1971) and *Chintan-Anuchintan* (1975 ; essays). He also wrote some sketches.

NEMI BARAHMASA. Rajasthani poem in 16 verses by a Jain poet, Palhan, which was composed in 1233.

The theme of Neminath, the 22nd Tirthankar, and Rajimati (Rajul) has been very popular with the Jain poets. Neminath's marriage is fixed with Rajimati, the daughter of Ugrasen. When the marriage procession reaches Ugrasen's palace, Neminath hears the pathetic cries of captive animals and birds, meant to feed the marriage party. He is moved with pity, renounces the world and reaches Girnar in search of eternal emancipation. Here, Rajimati's pangs of separation in each month of the year beginning from Shravan are described. Contrary to other *Barahmasas*, it ends in the heroine's taking ascetic initiation.

NEMI CHANDRA, KAVI (fl. 1712). Jain poet, whose *Nemishwar Ras*, describing the life of Neminath (the 22nd Jain Tirthankar) in 36 cantos, is an epic.

NEMI CHANDRA JAIN (1918-). Poet of *Tar Saptak* (q.v.), whose chief poetical collection is *Ekant* (The Solitary) ; *Rangmanch* (The Theatre ; 1967), *Adhunik Hindi Natak* (Modern Hindi Drama), *Badalte Pariprekshya* (The Changing Backgrounds) and *Adhure Sakshatkar* (Incomplete Interviews) are his other works containing articles of literary criticism. He has tr. many works from English into Hindi. He was Professor of Drama in the National School of Drama, New Delhi for more than a decade. His latest work is *Paya Patra Tumhara*, which is an edited correspondence between him and Muktibodh (q.v.).

NEMICHANDRIKA. See *Askaran*.

NEMINATH PHAG. Rajasthani poem by Rajshekhar Suri (fl. 14th cent.), which, in its 27 verses, treats of the story of Jain Tirthankar Neminath (for story see *Nemi Barahmasa*). The description of spring, Rajimati's beauty and her pangs of separation are arresting.

NEMISHWAR RAS. See *Nemichandra, Kavi*.

NENE, GO. P. Marathi-speaking modern Hindi scholar, whose chief works are : *Rashtrabhasha ka Andolan* and *Bhasha Samasya ke Kai Ayam*. He is noted also for his short story collection : *Dayre*, a biography of Chhatrapati Shivaji and memoirs : *Sangi Sathi*.

NET RAM (fl. end of 19th cent.). Folk-poet of Haryana, who was disciple of Swami Shankar Das. Originally he was a *Kathavachak* (a religious preacher) but seeing the success of Kishanlal's *Sangs*, he turned a *Sangi* and composed and staged his first Sang : *Sila Sethani*, which became very popular. As his Guru did not want him to be a *Sangi*, he left the stage.

NETI (fl. 1605). Rajasthani poet, whose stray verses in popular metres are available.

NEVAJ (fl. 1680). Poet of the Riti school, who was patronized by Maharaja Chhatrasal of Panna. It is said that he was acquainted with Azam Shah, son of Aurangzeb. His *Shakuntala Upakhyan* was written both in prose and poetry and was received very well. He had good command over the language and had specialized in depicting the inner feelings of the lover and the beloved. He also composed some *Kavittas*, from which it appeared that he was a successful poet and that his language was refined and mature. His description of

Shringar at times led to obscenity. The play, in parts, was published in 1833 by Chandraprabha Yantralay, Benares.

NIHAL CHAND VERMA. Modern Rajasthani scholar, whose chief work is *Marwari Git*.

NIHALDE. Rajasthani *Pavada*, which describes the romance of Nihalde and Sultan, a young Hindu prince. Nihalde goes to a garden for a swing, but rain and finally heavy downpour overtakes her. Sultan, who happens to be there, gives shelter to her ; she, on her part, feels attracted towards him. When she returns home, her mother asks her the cause of the delay and she narrates the whole episode. The *Pavada*, describing the marriage of Nihalde and Sultan, their separation, hardships and finally the union, has been quite popular in Haryana and Rajasthan. It is sung by the Jogis, the language being Rajasthani, mixed with Haryanavi.

NIHAR PATRA. Oriya-speaking modern writer, whose *Oriya-Hindi Kosh* is a pocket dictionary.

NIL MANI MISHRA. Oriya-speaking modern Hindi writer, whose works in Hindi are on Oriya Drama and Stage and on Ram Literature in Orissa.

NIL SAKHI (b. 1724). Poet of the Krishna-cult (Chaitanya Sect), whose original name was Amar Ju. He was born at Satari in Bundelkhand but became a recluse and came to live in Vrindavan. His earlier writings describe the six seasons. His *Bani* consisted of 110 *Padas* but all of them are not available.

NILABH. Modern poet, whose collections of poems are: *Sansmaranarambh* and *Jangal Khamosh Hai*. Son of Upendranath 'Ashk' (q.v.), he works for the Hindi section of B.B.C., London.

NILIMA SINGH. Poetess, whose *Dhup ke Darpan Men* (1983) is her first collection of poems ; her novel is *Swikar Hai Mujhe*.

NILLSON, USHA SAKSENA. Scholar and author of *Intermediate Hindi* ; Structural notes by Maninder K. Verma, with Ramesh Gaur (1967).

NIPAT NIRANJAN (b. 1539). Poet of the Krishna-cult, whose numerous stray verses are available.

NIRAJ. See *Gopaldas Niraj*.

NIRALA. See *Suryakant Tripathi 'Nirala'*.

NIRALA BHARALI. Assamese-speaking modern Hindi writer, who is noted for his memoirs and reportage.

NIRANJAN NATH ACHARYA. Modern Rajasthani writer, whose chief work is *Nahri Jhagdo* (one-act plays) ; he has also composed some patriotic and heroic poems.

NIRANJANI, RAMPRASAD. See *Ramprasad Niranjani*.

'NIRANKUSH'. See *Adya Nath Jha 'Nirankush'*.

NIRANT (1746-1851). Saint-poet, who was born in Karjan Taluka of Gujarat and was initiated by Guru Ramnandi Gokuldas. His *Gaddis* are still extant at Baroda and Padra. He composed stray verses in several metres in Hindi, which are influenced by Gujarati and Urdu.

NIRKHAN JHA 'NIDHI'. Maithili poet, who was noted for his '*Laganis*', a particular form of lyric. He was patronized by Maharaja Narendra Singh (1741-51).

NIRMAL, P.D. Poet, whose *Vidhura* (1983) is a *Prabandh-Kavya*.

NIRMAL DAS (1765-1878). Eminent saint-poet of Surat in Gujarat, whose *Barahmasa* in Hindi is his chief work. His language betrays the influence of Brajbhasha and Gujarati.

NIRMAL KUMAR. Writer, whose *Barf ke Phul* (The Flowers of Snow ; 1982) and *Bela tatha anya Kahaniyan* are short story collections, while *Dhup na Chhanv* is a novel. His dramas are : *Ritujal Neminath*, *Rajkumar Aurangzeb* and *Samrat Aurangzeb*.

NIRMAL VERMA (1929-). Writer, whose chief works are : *Ve Din* (Those Days ; 1964 ; a novel from the existentialist point of view, in which all the cultural and moral values are discarded), *Lal Tin ki Chhat* (The Red Tin-Shed ; 1974 ; novel), *Jalti Jhadi* (The Burning Bush ; 1964), *Pichhli Garmiyon Men* (During the Last Summer), *Parinde* (The Birds ; 1960), *Meri Priya Kahaniyan* (My Favourite Short Stories),

Kavve aur Kala Pani, *Bich Bahas Men* (short story collections), *Tin Ekant* (Three Lonely Persons ; drama), *Shabda aur Smriti* (critical works), *Chidon par Chandni* (The Moonshine on the Pine Tress ; travelogue) and *Kala ka Jokhim* (a collection of essays ; 1981). His other novels are *Ek Chithda Sukh* (Happiness—A Rag ; 1979), *Dusri Duniya* and *Bin Udgam ke Srot*. His important short stories are : 'Parinde', 'Andhere Men' (In Darkness), 'Kavve aur Kala Pani', 'Ek Din ka Mehman', etc.

NIRMAL VINOD (1950-). Dogri-speaking Hindi poet, who is noted for his *Pattharon ka Dariya* (The River of Stones), *Bayar ke Pankhon Men* and *Sakshi Sandhyaon Ke* (poetical collections).

NIRMALA. Novel (1928) by Premchand (q.v.), which is based on a social theme.

Nirmala, the daughter of Udaybhanu Lal, Advocate, is engaged to be married to a son of Bhalchandra Sinha, but after the death of Udaybhanu Lal, the engagement is cancelled as Sinha does not hope now to get a good dowry. Nirmala is thus married to Munshi Totaram, widower with three sons. On account of the age factor, Nirmala is more intimate with young Mansharam, the eldest son of Totaram, rather than with Totaram. This arouses suspicion in the mind of Totaram and he gets Mansharam admitted to the hostel, where he falls sick and dies. Dr. Sinha, who treats Mansharam, is the one who was earlier engaged to Nirmala, and finding an opportunity, Sinha expresses his love to her. When Sinha's wife, Sudha comes to know of it, she scolds him, at which Sinha commits suicide. Totaram's second son also commits suicide when the theft committed by him is brought to light ; the third son turns a *Sadhu* and leaves the house and Totaram goes in search of him. Nirmala, seeing all this, suffers mental torture and passes away. As her dead body is brought to the cremation ground, Totaram comes in time to ignite the funeral pyre.

The novelist has dealt with the problems of dowry system and the marriage of unequal ages.

NIRMALA BAJPEYI. Writer, whose chief works are : *Sukha Sailab* (The Dry Flood ; 1971), *Kanton ke Phul* (novels), *Nahin, Nahin, Vah Roegi Nahin* (No, No, She will not Weep ; 1969 ; a collection of 13 short stories) ; she has also written other works : *Kale Pani ka Sabz Patthar* : *Port Blair* (on Port Blair, the place for life sentence) and *Unmadini*.

NIRMALA BUTANI. Sindhi-speaking modern Hindi journalist, who has been associated with the 'Bal Bharati', New Delhi.

NIRMALA DAR. Kashmiri-speaking modern Hindi writer, whose social novel *Nirjharini aur Patthar* (The Spring and Stone) is written in a chaste language.

NIRMALA DESHPANDE. Marathi-speaking modern Hindi dramatist, who is noted for her *Bhagnamurti* ; she also wrote a novel : *Chingling* and memoirs : *Vinoba ke Sath.*

NIRMALA GARG, MRS. (1954-). Progressive poetess, whose collection of poem is *Abhi Talkh Hai Dhup.*

NIRMALA JAIN. Critic, whose chief works are : *Rasa-Siddhant aur Saundarya-Shastra* : *Tulnatmak Vishleshan* (research), *Adhunik Sahitya* : *Mulya aur Mulyankan* (Modern Literature : Values and Evaluation ; 1980), *Nayi Samiksha ke Pratiman, Hindi Alochana* : *Bisvin Shatabdi, Jainendra ki Sarvashreshth Kahaniyan* (ed.) and a novel *Mutki.*

NIRMALA KULKARNI. Marathi-speaking modern Hindi writer, whose short stories have appeared in various magazines.

NIRMALANAND VATSYAYAN (M. MALLESHWAR RAO). Telugu-speaking modern Hindi poet, who tr. the select poems of Shri in 1970 ; in this task he was assisted by Kamtaprasad Ojha.

NIRUPMA PHUKAN. Assamese-speaking modern Hindi writer, who is noted for her memoirs and reportage.

NIRUPMA SEVATI. Writer, whose chief novels are : *Patjhar ki Avazen* (The Sounds of Autumn ; 1976), *Pratyaghat* (The Counter-Stroke), *Nirantar Sanvad* and Bantata *Hua Admi* ; *Kachche Makan* (The Mud Houses), *Atank Bij, Khamoshi ko Pite Huye* and *Bhid men Gum* are her short story collections. She is a sensitive female writer of psychological vicissitudes.

NISANI GAJMOKH. See *Madhodas Dadhvadiya.*

NISANI RADHIKAJI RI. See *Sanya Jhula.*

NISANI VIVEKVAR. Rajasthani poem by Kesodas Gadan (q.v.), which concerns chiefly with Shankaracharya's Vedanta, though Bhakti and Yoga-Sadhana have also been dealth with. To know the self and to achieve emancipation from the bonds of birth and death is the aim of the poet. The poem, which has been very popular, represents religious synthesis. The language has a good mixture of Khari Boli.

NISHA-NIMANTRAN. See *Harivansh Rai Bachchan*.

NISHCHAL DAS (1781-1863). Saint, who wrote *Vritti-Prabhakar* and *Vichar-Sagar* (a scholarly treatise on Vedanta). A man of great learning, recognised as an authority on Vedanta, he was born in a Jat family of Karhauli village of Haryana. As his father was a follower of Dadu Dayal, young Nishchal was sent to Delhi Dadudwara for education ; he, however, got his higher education at Jalandhar and at Kashi. He wrote also devotional songs, which have been compiled in a collection.

NISHKULANAND (1771-1848). Saint-poet of Gujarat, who was initiated by Swami Sahjanand. He composed some 20 works and 3,000 *Padas* in Hindi, of which the chief ones are : *Purushottam Prakash*, *Yam-Dand*, *Bhakta-Chintamani*, *Arji-Vinay*, *Chihna-Chintamani* and *Hari Vicharan*. His language is simple but has flow and is influenced by Braj.

NITYANAND (fl. 18th cent.). Saint-poet, who belonged to a Brahmin family of Narnaul in Haryana. Inspired by the spiritual power of Gumanidas, he resigned his post as Tehsildar in Bharatpur and became a *Sannyasi*. He spent the rest of his life in Dubal Dhan Majra, near Beri in Haryana. The stray writings of Nityanand describe the entire social life of Haryana during those days.

NITYANAND. Malwi saint-poet, whose chief work is *Nityanand-Vilas* (devotional ; 3rd impression, 1937).

NITYANAND. Short story writer, who is noted for his short story collection *Antim Anuchchhed* (The Last Chapter ; 1980) and a novel *Nile Akash ke Liye*.

NITYANAND PATEL, THE LATE. Gujarati-speaking modern Hindi scholar, whose *Chhayavad ka Punarmulyankan* is a research work. He also did research work on Premchand's novels and his work is : *Premchand ke Upanyas Sahitya men Sanskritik Chetana*.

NITYANAND SHARMA (1921-). Writer, whose chief work is : *Adhunik Hindi Kavya men Pratik Vidhan* (Symbols in Modern Hindi Poetry ; research thesis).

NIZAM-UD-DIN MADNAYAK (1591-1687). Muslim poet of Bilgram, whose chief works in *Shringar* style are : *Nad-Chandrika* and *Madnayak Shringar.*

NRI SINGH RAJPUROHIT. Rajasthani writer, whose chief works are : *Rat Vaso* (1961), *Amar Chunadi* (1969 ; both social short story collections) and other types of short stories, e.g., 'Udik', 'Kalam ri Mar', 'Utar Bhikha Mhari Basi' and 'Kuai Bhang Padi'. He has also published *Katha Bharati* (1978), which is a tr. of 15 stories of other Indian languages. In his *Antas ra Akhar* (edited ; 1980), he discusses many genres in Rajasthani : short story, essay, reportage, poetry, one-act play, sketch, etc.

NRI SINGHACHARYA (1853-96). Hindi poet of Gujarat, who was born at the village Kadod near Surat. From his childhood, he loved loneliness and he had gathered around him a good band of followers owing to his impressive personality. He was the author of 10 works and his language is a mixture of Braj and Khari Boli, with a copious number of Urdu and Persian words.

NRIP PRITINATH (fl. prior to 1685). Maithili poet, whose lyrics are quoted in anthologies.

NUPA BAI (fl. 18th cent.). Rajasthani saint-poetess of the Charandasi Sampraday, whose stray verses are available.

NUR MUHAMMAD (fl. 1744-66). Learned Sufi poet, who was born at Sabarhad in Jaunpur but he settled down at his father-in-law's house at Bhadon in the Azamgarh district. He composed *Indravati* and *Anurag Bansuri* (qq.v.) ; he was a scholar of Persian also.

NUTAN RAKESH. Maithili poet, whose *Akas Tin Lag A* (1981) is a collection of poems.

NYAY SAGAR (fl. 18th cent.). Gujarati-speaking Jain poet, who was a disciple of Dharma Sagar. In Hindi, he composed two *Chaubisis,* which are devotional. His *Mahavir Ragmala,* composed in 36 *Rags* is quite popular.

O

OHALA, MANJARI. See *Manjari Ohala.*

OJHA, GAURISHANKAR HIRACHAND. See *Gaurishankar Hirachand Ojaa.*

OM CHAND HANDA. Modern scholar, who has compiled and edited *Pahari Lok-Git.*

OM GOSWAMI. Modern Hindi writer of Jammu-Kashmir, who is noted for his *Nirvasit* (The Exile) and *Barah Kahaniyan,* short story collections.

OM PRAKASH. Modern writer, whose chief work is *Adhunik Kavi* (with Ram Prakash).

OM PRAKASH BHARDAWAJ. Modern author of *Manak Hindi ka Sanrachnatmak Bhasha Vigyan.*

OM PRAKASH BHATIA. Modern poet, whose works are : *Anam Yuga* and *Satyaj.*

OM PRAKASH GUPTA (1939-). Dogri-speaking Hindi writer, who has published works on Dogri language (*Hindi-Dogri Parsarg, Hindi-Dogri Parpratyay*), a poetical collection : *Sagar ke Tir* (On the Sea Shore) and a collection of one-act plays : *Yuddha aur Shanti* (War and Peace). He has also written : *Thirke Patta Pipal Ka,* a tr. in verse of Dogri folk-songs. *Dogri Lok Git* is his compiled collection of Dogri folk-songs.

OM PRAKASH NIRMAL. Telugu-speaking Hindi writer, whose chief works are : *Baint ke Nishan* (The Marks of a Cane ; 1968), *Khoye Huye Log* (short story collections) and *Bahta*

Pani : *Ramte Jogi* (1969 ; a satirical novel on the life of Mahants with ample rural setting) and *Tin Kamre* : *Ek Dewankhana* (collection of social one-act plays). He edited 'Kalpana' for many years. His important short stories are : 'Baint ke Nishan', 'Jangh se Bahta Khun' (Blood Flowing from the Thigh), etc. He has tr. into Hindi four poetical collections of the Telugu poet, Gunturi Sheshendra Sharma under the titles of *Shesh Jyotsna* (1972), *Meri Dharti Mere Log* (1975), *Dahakta Suraj* (1975) and *Gurilla* (1978).

ONKAR KAUL. Modern Hindi scholar of Kashmir, who got doctorate on the comparative study of Kashmiri and Hindi Ram works (*Hindi and Kashmiri Ramkatha*). He has also written several scholarly articles in Hindi dealing with Kashmiri language and literature.

ONKAR NATH SHRIVASTAV. Modern scholar and author of *Hindi Sahitya* : *Parivartan ke Sau Varsh*.

ONKAR PARIK. Modern Rajasthani poet, who has composed Nature, patriotic, heroic, progressive and love poems. His 'Git Dhiran Viran ri Dharti Ro' is quite popular. Some of his poems have been composed in the style of Nayi Kavita. He has also written some sketches.

ONKAR RAHI. Novelist, whose chief work is *Shav-Yatra* (The Funeral Procession ; 1972 ; based on the division of India in 1947). His other novels are : *Kinare ke Log*, *Sampark* and *Mera Ananya*, while his short story collections are : *Rishtedar* and *Chitra Khinchna Mana Hai*.

ONKARESHWARI (d. 1932). Hindi poetess, whose original name was Lalita Behan. She was born at the village Sisodara near Bhrauch. Her married life was not successful and she became a recluse and was initiated into *Sannyas* by Sagar Maharaj. Like Dhira Bhagat, she uses war phraseology in her religious poetry.

OPA ADHA (*c*. 1752-1843). Rajasthani Bhakta-poet, who was son of Bakhtaji of village Peshwa (Sirohi). He is said to have composed many Dingal *Gits*, but only twenty of them are at present extant. The last great poet of the mythological and religious branch of the Charan poetry, his *Gits* are highly devotional and are full of easy expressions and similes chosen from history and folk life.

ORIENTAL PROVERBIAL DICTIONARY. See *Hunter, William*.

ORKEN (1980). Collection of Bagri (a dialect of Rajasthani) writings, which consists of three parts : the first concerning ancient literature, the second modern prose and the third poems.

ORUGANTI VENKATESHWAR SHARMA (1906-42). Telugu-speaking Hindi writer, whose chief works are : *Adhyatma Yoga tatha Chitt Vikalan* (religious ; 1957) and *Shri Raman Charitamrit* (a biography of Maharshi Raman).

P

PABU PRAKASH. See *Jodha Agarsingh.*

PABU PRAKASH. See *Modiji Asiya.*

PABUJI KA PAVADAS. Rajasthani ballads, which describe the heroism of Rathore Pabuji, who gives up his life in protecting the cows and has been hailed as a folk-deity. Pabuji is fond of horses and mares ; once he has a liking for a mare belonging to Deval Charani. She agrees to give the mare to Pabuji on the condition that when her cows are in danger, he will protect them. Later on when Pabuji's marriage ceremony is being performed, Deval Charani starts weeping for her cows which are being stolen by Jindrao Khichi, the brother-in-law of Pabuji. Leaving the ceremony, Pabu rides his horse and fights bravely against Jindrao but is killed in protecting the cows.

The Pavadas, which are 52 in number, are sung by the Bhopas.

PABUJI KA SORTHA. See *Ramnath Kaviya.*

PADAKALPATARU. Collection of Bengali *Padas* by Vaishnav poets, which was compiled by Vaishnav Das early in the 18th century. It is a collection of 3,101 *Padas* and is divided into 4 chapters. It is in this collection also that many of the *Padas* composed in Brajbuli have been preserved.

PADAVALI. Collection of *Padas* or songs in Maithili, composed by Vidyapati (q.v.). There are mostly love songs, a few devotional songs concerning Shakti, Shiv and Ganga and a very few 'riddles' and 'occasional songs'. The love songs describe the various aspects of love between Radha and Krishna : the dawn of youth, the commencement of Radha's love for Krishna (and that of Krishna for Radha), Radha's beauty, secret meetings, the bridal night, excuses, lovers' quarrels and sports, separation and reunion. The poet describes the beloved in various charming poses, such as, when she has bathed, when she is crossing the river or when she sees her lover, and so on. The language of the *Padavali* is old Maithili, influenced by Brajbhasha. In a way it can be called the old form : 'Brajbuli'. See *Vidyapati.*

PADHIS. See *Balbhadra Dikshit 'Padhis'.*

PADMA BHAGAT. Rajasthani Bhakta poet, whose *Krisanji ro Vyanvalo* (or *Rukmani Mangal* ; q.v.) composed between 1493 and 1500, is so popular and held in such veneration that it is called their *Bhagavat.* The poet also composed many songs on the legend of marriage of Rukmini and Krishna.

PADMA KANT MALVIYA (1908-81). Poet, whose chief works are: *Triveni* (1929), *Pyala* (The Cup ; 1932). *Prem Patra* (Love Letter) and *Rubaiyat Padma.* He was a journalist also.

PADMAKAR BHATT 'PADMAKAR' (17531-833). One of the greatest Hindi poets of the Riti school, who was born at Banda. His father, Mohanlal Bhatt, a Telugu Brahmin, was a profound Sanskrit scholar and a poet, who had been honoured at various courts. Like his father, Padmakar moved from one place to another in quest of patrons and was successful in getting wealth and favours wherever he sought them. His earliest patron was Gosain Anupgiri alias Himmat Bahadur, a brave general serving under the ruler of Lucknow. The poet's *Himmat Bahadur Virudavali,* named after his patron, describes the general's exploits on the field of battle ; the book on the whole is a fine work. It is held by some that earlier the poet had composed *Ram Rasayan,* a rendering of the *Valmiki Ramayana,* in *Doha* and *Chaupai* metres, but as i is a poor stuff, its authenticity is doubtful. After 1799, thet poet went to Satara where Raghunath Rao (Raghoba) rewarded him with an elephant, a lakh of rupees and ten villages. After a short stay, he moved to Jaipur, where he lived for a number of years, enjoying the favours of Maharaja Pratap Singh and his son, Jagat Singh, on whose name he wrote his *magnum opus Jagat Vinod,* a fairly elaborate book dealing with various *Rasas* and *Bhavs* ; the work contains the finest specimens of poetry of the Riti school. Soon after, Padmakar wrote his *Padmabharan in Dohas,* describing and illustrating the various *Alankars.* The poet visited Udaipur, where, at the instance of Maharana Bhim Singh, he wrote *Ghangauria-Varnan,* a description of the Ghangaur Fair. After the death of Bhim Singh, he went to Gwalior, where Maharaja Daulat Rao Scindia honoured him and gave him rich gifts ; it was there at the request of Sardar Udaji, that he rendered the *Hitopadesh* into Hindi. After visiting Bundi Durbar on the way, Padmakar returned to Banda, his native place ; it was there that he wrote his *Prabodh-Pachasa*, a devotional work. When he was old and ill, he moved on to Kanpur to die peacefully on the banks of the Ganges ; his *Ganga Lahari* was composed there.

Padmakar had the wonderful gift of conjuring before the mind's eye concrete images with the help of words and these images are of lovers, their charming sweethearts and of their significant poses and attitudes. He is generally considered to be the last of the Ritikal poets, though during the last years of his life, even his fondness for it had worn off. In his own days, he earned much fame and his glory and influence lasted after him. With the possible exception of Bihari, no other poet left behind him such a trail of admirers and imitators.

PADMA KUMARI, S. Malayalam-speaking modern Hindi writer, who has tr. some Malayalam dramas and short stories into Hindi.

PADMA NABH. Jain poet, whose 52 verses of *Dungar Bavni* (1486) are didactic.

PADMANABH (fl. 15th cent). Rajasthani poet, who was a Nagar Brahmin. At the instance of his patron, Akhayraj of Jalore, who was the fifth descendant of Kanhad De, he composed *Kanhad De Prabandh* (q.v.) in 1455, 141 years after the events described therein.

PADMA SANDU. Dingal poetess and wife of the Dingal poet, Barhat Shankar (1543-1623), whose stray verses are available.

PADMA SINGH SHARMA (1877-1932). Critic and essayist, who was a teacher in Jwalapur Mahavidyalaya and Gurukula Kangri, Hardwar. A scholar of Urdu, Persian, Hindi and Sanskrit, his style is elegant and racy, not so common among Hindi writers. He is famous for his commentary on Bihari's *Satsai*, for his letters to many literary friends (ed. by Benarsi Das Chaturvedi and Hari Shankar Sharma under the title *Padmasingh Sharma ke Patra*) and for his essays in various periodicals : *Padma-Parag* and *Prabandh Manjari* are collections of some of his articles and essays. His *Bihari Satsai-ki Bhumika*, referred to above, is a model of historical and comparative criticism.

Besides his writings, he enriched Hindi by his occasional lectures and addresses to religious and literary gatherings. He also edited several papers, e.g., 'Sahitya', 'Bharatoday', 'Samalochak', etc.

PADMA SINGH SHARMA 'KAMLESH' (1915-74). Modern writer, whose chief works are : *Main Inse Mila* (2 Pts. ; interviews with eminent men of letters), *Hindi Gadya Kavya* (research thesis) and *Nirala* (critical work). He had also published a collection of poems.

PADMA SUDHI. Writer ; her chief novel *Ulte Kante Sidhe Phul* (Obverse Thorns and Straight Flowers ; 1969) deals with education in thelight of students' troubles.

PADMAVAT. Famous allegorical romance (1520-41) by Malik Muhammad Jayasi (q.v.), a Sufi poet.

Gandharvasen, the Raja of Simhal Dwip, has a daughter, Padmavati, renowned for her beauty. He is unable to find a suitable match for her, but he has a very learned parrot, who somehow falls into the hands of Ratnasen, the Raja of Chittor. One day, Ratnasen's queen happens to ask the parrot if he has known any other woman in the world comparable with her in charms and feminine graces. The parrot, Hiraman, at once mentions Padmavati being her better. The jealous queen orders the parrot out of her presence. The king, however, somehow comes to know of the story as narrated by the parrot. It is enough to make Ratnasen restless for the hand of Padmavati.

The Raja, accompanied by the parrot and a number of his devoted followers, reaches the island Simhal, but only after surmounting many a difficulty. Hiraman is able to arrange a meeting between Ratnasen and Padmavati, but at the first glimpse of Padmavati, the Raja faints. Later on, Padmavati exhorts the Raja to storm the palace of Gandharvasen, if he wants her. In the clash, Ratnasen is supported by Shiv, Hanuman and other gods, disguised themselves as *yogis*. It is through the intervention of Shiv that Gandharvasen eventually agrees to his daughter's marriage with Ratnasen. After spending some time there, Ratnasen learns of the woes of his former wife, Nagmati. Ratnasen and Padmavati, laden with riches, set out on their return journey and reach Chittor.

Now begins the second part of the poem. Raghav Chetan, a cashiered astrologer of Ratnasen's court, gives Alauddin, the ruling sovereign of Delhi, an account of Padmavati's beauty. Alauddin, having strong infatuation for Padmavati, attacks Chittor but the beseiged city is able to defend itself for a number of years. Peace proposals are sent to Ratnasen and Allauddin is allowed to enter the fort as a friendly guest. He sees in a mirror the reflection of Padmavati's form and swoons instantaneously. While returning, he treacherously captures Ratnasen and brings him to Delhi.

Ratnasen's friends under the leadership of two celebrated warriors, Gora and Badal dupe Allauddin and rescue the Raja. On his return to Chittor, Ratnasen learns that in his absence King Devpal of Kumbhalner had made overtures to Padmavati. He launches an attack over Kumbhalner and in the war that ensues, both Ratnasen and Devpal are killed. The two queens burn themselves on the pyre along with the dead body of Ratnasen. Alauddin makes another assault on Chittor. He is successful in entering the fort, but finds only heaps of ahses in place of Padmavati.

The first part of the story is culled primarily from the poet's own imagination, but there is much of historical truth in the second part. In the final verses of his work, Jayasi mentions that it is all an allegory. By Chittor, he means the body of man ; by Ratnasen, the soul ; by Padmavati, the Divine Beauty ; by Hiraman, the Guru ; Allauddin is Maya ; Raghav is Satan and Nagmati represents the mundane interests.

Padmavat is a long narrative poem, written in the style of the *Masnavis*. Some of the descriptions constitute a major glory of the poem ; for example, that of the changing seasons and the reactions which they produce in the heart of the forlorn Nagmati, as also the description of the journey to Simhal Dwip.

PADUMAN DAS (fl. *c*. 1684). Poet of the Riti school, whose *Kavya Manjari* in 15 chapters was composed during the reign of Dalel Singh, the ruler of Badmannar.

PADUMLAL PUNNALAL BAKHSHI (1894-1971). Critic and essayist, who was the Editor of 'Saraswati' from 1920 to 1927. His chief works are : *Panchpatra*, *Padbhavan*, *Kuchh*, *Aur Kuchh*, *Mere Priya Nibandh* (My Favourite Essays ; 1964), *Hindi Sahitya Vimarsh* (1923), *Vishwa Sahitya* (1924), *Hindi Kahani Sahitya*, *Hindi Upanyas Sahitya* and *Hindi Sahitya : Ek Aitihasik Samiksha* (Hindi Literature : A Historical Criticism ; 1969). He also tr. Maurice Metterlink's plays as *Prayashchit* and *Unmukti ka Bandhan* (1916).

PADYANJALI (1961). Poetical anthology, published from Jammu-Kashmir, which was edited by Subhash Bhardwaj, Chandrakant Joshi and Prithwinath Pushp. This anthology contains the representative poems of about 3 dozen Jammu-Kashmir Hindi poets for the period 1940-60.

PAHAD KHAN, ADHA (fl. 1723-54). Rajasthani poet, whose *Gogade Rupak* treats of the Rathore-Johiya affairs described in *Virmayan* (q.v.) of Badar Dhadhi ; here also the reader's sympathy remains with Johiya Dalla.

PAHALVAN DAS (b. 1716). Saint-poet of Satnami Sect, whose works include *Upakhyan-Vivek*, *Virah-Sar*, *Arill*, *Guru-Mahatmya* and a large number of stray verses. He was attracted towards *Bhakti* after spending some years in the imperial army as a soldier. His language is refined and his style of writing is quite elegant.

PAHARI. See *Ram Prasad Ghildyal 'Pahari'*.

PAJNES (fl. *c*. 1843). Poet of Panna, about whom very little is known. He is reputed to be the author of *Madhur Priya*, *Nakhshikh* and *Pajnes-Prakash*, of which only the last one is extant. The *Pajnes-Prakash* is a collection of the poet's 127 *Kavitta Savaiyas*. He is nevertheless a popular poet and some of his verses are often quoted. His poetry abounds in words which produce a jarring effect on ears, while his language betrays a mixture of Persian words and expressions.

PALHAN (fl. 1233). Jain poet and author in Rajasthani of *Nemi Barahmasa* (q.v.), composed in 1233 and of *Abu Ras* (in 51 verses on the construction of temples on Mount Abu by ministers Vimal and Vastupal Tejpal).

PALLAV. See *Sumitra Nandan Pant*.

PALMER, E.H. Author of *Simplified Grammar of Hindustani, Persian and Arabic* (London, 1882).

PALTUDAS (fl. 1793). Poet-saint and founder of the Paltudas Sect, who spent the greater part of his life in Ayodhya. In his poetry, he has shown his full acquaintance with the Sufi Sect. He was influenced by Kabir and sang of *Nirgun* Brahma.

PAMMAI GHORANDHAR RI BAT. Dingal prose work (Script 1790), which describes the romance of Raja Ghorandhar and Pammai, the daughter of Kanjoi.

PANCH PANDAV CHARIT RASO. Rajasthani poem of 795 lines, which was composed by Shilbhadra Suri in 1353. It follows the story of the *Mahabharat* but in the end, influenced by the preachings of Nem Muni, the Pandavas embrace Jainism.

PANCH SAHELI. See *Chhihal.*

PANCHVATI. Poem (1925) by Maithili Sharan Gupta (q.v.), which describes the story of Ram, Lakshman and Sita at Panchvati during their exile in forest. The work is noted for its descriptions of the beauties of Nature.

PANCHASAT UPANISHAD BHASHA. Hindi tr. of 50 Upanishads, which was done from the Persian version of the Upanishads prepared by Dara Shukoh. The Hindi tr., however, does not have a racy or clear style and as such has been given a low importance ; its date is not certain.

PANCHOJI (fl. 18th cent.). Rajasthani saint-poet of the Jasnathi Sect, whose stray verses and *Sabads* deal with human duties, divine attributes, etc.

PANDAV YASHENDU CHANDRIKA. See *Swarupdas.*

PANDEY, BECHAN SHARMA 'UGRA'. See *Bechan Sharma Pandey 'Ugra'.*

PANDEY, LOCHANPRASAD. See *Lochanprasad Pandey.*

PANDEY, MUKUTDHAR. See *Mukutdhar Pandey.*

PANDEY, RUPNARAYAN. See *Rupnarayan Pandey.*

PANDEY, SHYAM NARAYAN. See *Shyam Narayan Pandey.*

PANDIT, PRA. S. Marathi-speaking modern Hindi writer, whose chief work is : *Maharshi Karve.*

PANDURANG RAO, A. 'MURLI'. Telugu-speaking modern Hindi poet, whose chief works are : *Kamakshi-Vilas* and other poems scattered in various magazines. He has tr. into Hindi the *Padas* of the celebrated Andhra saint-poet Tyagraju. His *Andhra-Hindi Rupak* (1962) presents a comparative study of Telugu and Hindi dramas. He has also tr. into Hindi the novels of Muppal Ranganayakamma and Balivada Kantarao.

PANGER, N.M. European scholar, who is noted for his work : *The Ocean of Story* (London, 1924-28).

PANJAB RAO JADHAV. Marathi-speaking modern Hindi scholar, whose chief work is : *Hindi Bhasha aur Sahitya ke Adhyayan men Christian Missionarion ka Yogdan* (The Contribution of Christian Missionaries to Hindi Language and Literature ; 1973).

PANKAJ BISHT. Writer, whose *Lekin Darvaza* (1982) is a novel.

PANKAJ SINGH. Poet, whose collection of poems is *Ahaten As-Pas* (1981).

PANKHI PURAN (*Gun Pankhi Pramod*). Rajasthani poem by Kesrisingh Jaitavat (fl. between 1650-1750), which is a collection of stray verses, the largest number of verses being 119 in one of the manuscripts. The verses have been popular in oral tradition and as such there might have been change in their text. Using several devices, the poet imparts human wisdom and arouses religious feelings. This style was later followed by Opa Adha (q.v.).

PANNALAL 'NAYAB' (fl. 1920). Malwi poet, whose *Master Sab ki Anokhi Chhata* is a *Gitinatya* (verse drama).

PANT. See *Sumitranandan Pant*.

PANU KHOLIYA (1939-). Fiction writer ; her collections of short stories are : *Ek Kishti Aur* (One More Boat ; 1967) and *Anna*, while her novels are : *Tute Huye Surya Bimb* and *Sattar Par ke Shikhar*.

PARAS ARORA. Rajasthani poet of Jodhpur, who has composed poems in the style of Nayi Kavita. His novelette *Khulti Ganthan* (1978) tells the story of three raw youths and their girl friends, who prove to be modern and advanced in their thoughts and likings.

PARAS BHAG (*Bhagya ka Paras*). Hindi tr. of a Persian work, *Kimiya-e-Saadat*, written by Imam-al-Ghazali. It describes the Muslim, especially Sufi, philosophy and contains account of the saints and thinkers of Arab countries and Greece. It contains an early specimen of Khari Boli prose.

PARASH RAM (fl. 18th cent.). Marathi folk-poet (*Shahir*), who also made composition in Hindi.

PARDESHI. Writer, whose chief novels are : *Aurat Ek : Chehre Hazar* (Woman One : Faces Thousand ; 1967) and *Jaigarh ka Jogi*. His poetical collections are : *Dard ke Dayre* and *Man ka Mahuk*.

PARESH CHANDRADEV SHARMA (1936-). Assamese-speaking Hindi essayist, whose essays have appeared in 'Rashtrasevak'.

He has tr. Assamese poems into Hindi and has prepared some text-books. He has also edited a Hindi-Assamese dictionary.

PARIHAR, J.S. Rajasthani scholar, whose *Madhyakalin Charan Kavya* (1979) is a research work on mediaeval bardic poetry.

PARIJAT-HARAN. Kirtaniya form of Maithili drama, which was written by Umapati Upadhyay (q.v.). Based on the Purans, with slight variations, it is the only authentic drama of the poet.

Narad presents a Parijat flower to Krishna, which he passes on to Rukmini, the senior queen. Satyabhama, the favourite queen, is angry on this and is pleased only when Krishna promises to bring her not merely one flower, but the entire Parijat tree from Indra's garden. Krishna attacks Indra, carries off the tree and plants it in the courtyard of Satyabhama. Narad now appears and tells Satyabhama that if one's dearest possession is given away under its shadow, one gets undying fruit. Satyabhama, therefore, gives Krishna to him, while Subhadra gives him, her husband, Arjun. Krishna and Arjun thus become Narad's slaves and he puts them up for sale. Satyabhama and Subhadra purchase back their husbands for a cow each, and the play ends with a happy note.

One of the best Maithili plays, it is remarkable for its literary merits and provides a good entertainment. The plot is well-constructed and humour predominates the play. The songs in the play are wholly in Maithili, but Sanskrit verses and Prakrit prose passages are also given. A very popular drama, it made Kirtaniya drama the fashion of the day.

Chetan Nath Jha has edited the *Parijat-Haran* and has written an Introduction to it.

PARIJAT-SAMMAR. Maithili poem by an unknown author, which describes the story of Umapati's famous play, *Parijat-Haran.*

PARIK, S.S. See *Surya Shankar Parik.*

PARIKSHA GURU. See *Shrinivas Das.*

PARIMAL. See *Suryakant Tripathi 'Nirala'.*

PARLIKAR, S.M. Marathi-speaking modern Hindi scholar, whose *Banbhatt ki Atmakatha evam anya Nibandh* is a research work.

PARMAL RASO. Ballad, composed in Dingal, which has

been published by the Nagari Pracharini Sabha in two parts : *Mahoba-Khand* and *Kanvaj-Khand* ; the work, which is completely different from *Alhakhand*, praises kings Parmal (Parmardidev) and Jay Chand of Kannauj. The work may have been written some time in the 12th century.

PARMANAND (1693-1788). Rajasthani saint-poet of the Vishnoi Sect, whose poems consist of 636 *Dohas* and 30 *Kavittas* on 104 religious topics, such as Guru, Sadhu, *Karma*, etc., besides *Harjas*, *Sakhis* and *Visan Astotra*. In easy Rajasthani, he depicts his experiences ; his similes are very effective.

PARMANAND (fl. 1st half of 20th cent.). Maithili poet, who tr. *Kumara-Sambhava* into Maithili from the original Sanskrit.

PARMANAND DAS (*c*. 14931-584). Poet, who was one of the members of the *Ashtachhap* and a disciple of Vallabhacharya. He hailed from Kannauj. From his boyhood he had leanings towards devotion and did not marry. One of his verses made such a deep impression on Vallabhacharya that he readily admitted him to the *Pushti* cult. But even before his initiation, he had his disciples and was called a 'Swami'. He is supposed to be the author of six works : *Parmanand Sagar* (The Ocean of Parmanand; containing 835 verses), *Parmananddas Ji ke Pada*, *Dan Lila*, *Uddhav Lila* (*Performance of Uddhav*), *Dhruv-Charitra* and *Sanskrit Ratna-Mala*. Although he depicted marvellously the childhood of Krishna, his poetry on separation (*Virah*) is considered supreme.

PARMANAND DAS (fl. early 16th cent.). Bengali Vaishnav poet, who also composed *Padas* in Brajbuli.

PARMANAND DAS (fl. 19th cent.). Poet of Kauri village of Shahabad, whose *Barahmasa* and *Kabir-Bhanu-Prakash* (on Kabir) are extant.

PARMANAND DAS (fl. 19th cent. ?). Maithili saint-poet, who was noted for his prayer to Shiv. He was the head of the Makranda Math and originally belonged to the village Harinagar.

PARMANAND DATT 'PARMARTHI' (fl. *c*. 1930). Maithili writer, who was noted for his short stories. He tr. *Harivansha* and *Meghaduta* (1937) into Maithili from the original Sanskrit. He also tried to compose a new kind of *Maheshvanis* where instead of the devotee, Mahesh (Shiv) himself is represented to speak.

PARMANAND PANCHAL (1930-). Writer, whose chief works are : *Hindi ke Muslim Sahityakar* and *Dakkhini Hindi : Vikas aur Itihas*.

PARMANAND SHRIVASTAV. Critic, whose chief works are : *Jainendra aur Unke Upanyas*, *Upanyas ki Yatharth aur Rachnatmak Bhasha* and *Kavikarma aur Kavya Bhasha* (all criticism) ; he has also composed some poems, e.g., *Agli Shatabdi ke Bare Men* (About the Next Century ; 1981 ; a collection of poems) and *Dishantar*.

PARMESHWAR BIHARI. Modern Hindi poet of Mauritius, whose *Abhishap* is a collection of poems.

PARMESHWAR CHHEDI. Modern Hindi poet of Mauritius, who is noted for his stray poems.

PARMESHWAR JHA (fl. early 20th cent.). Maithili novelist, whose *Simantini-Akhyayika* (incomplete) is one of the earliest long narratives. He has also written *Mithila-Tattwa-Vimarsh* (2 vols.).

PARMESHWAR PANIKKAR, K.N. (fl. early 20th cent.). Malayalam-speaking Hindi teacher, who was the first Hindi teacher in Travancore State. He died young but he had a missionary zeal for the propagation of Hindi.

PARMESHWAR PURAN. Rajasthani poem by Pirdan Lalas (fl. 1st half of 18th cent.), in which are mentioned, with deep reverence, the names of many saints, devotees and great men, who followed different religions and beliefs.

PARMESHWARAN, H. Malayalam-speaking modern Hindi writer, who is noted for preparation of help-material for students appearing in higher Hindi examinations. His other work is *Bhashiki*.

PARMESHWARAN PILLAI, K.P. Malayalam-speaking modern Hindi writer, who tr. from Malayalam Pala Narayanan Nair's *Kerala Valarannu* under the title *Kerala Badh Raha Hai* (Kerala is Progressing).

PARMESHWARI DAS (1803-55). Poet of the Ram-cult, who was a native of Kalinjar ; he was the author of *Kavitavali*.

PARMESHWARI LAL GUPTA. Modern scholar, who has edited *Kanhavat*, supposed to be a work of Jayasi.

PARO. See *Yatri*.

PARSHURAM (1767-1839). Rajasthani saint-poet of Ram Snehi Sampraday, Khedapa, who belonged to Bithnok (Bikaner). Initiated by Ramdas (q.v.) at Khedapa in 1788, he travelled widely and ultimately settled in Jodhpur near Sur Sagar. He is considered to be the founder of the Virakta or Tapaswi branch in this tradition and is said to have composed *Sikh Prashna Soran*, *Guru Shishya Sanvad*, *Grih Kup ko Prasang*, *Guru Mahima*, *Atma Bodh*, *Arath Siddhant* and *Sajivan Bodh*, all mainly dealing with divine knowledge and devotion.

PARSHURAM CHATURVEDI (1894-1979). Critic of devotional Hindi poetry, whose *Uttar Bharat ki Sant Parampara* (The Sant Tradition of North India) was acclaimed as a learned treatise on the subject. A top scholar of Sant Sahitya, his other works are : *Sufi Kavya Sangrah* (1951), *Nav Nibandh*, *Madhyakalin Prem Sadhana*, *Sant Kavya* (*Sant Poetry*), *Manas ki Ramkatha*, *Vaishnav Dharm* (1952), *Kabir Sahitya ki Parakh*, *Bharatiya Sahitya-ki Sanskritik Rekhayen* and *Sant Sahitya ke Prerana-Srota* (The Inspirational Sources of Sant Literature). Chaturvedi distinguished himself not only as a writer of scintillating prose but also as a great scholar and deep thinker.

PARSHURAM DEVACHARYA (1520-1600 ?). Gaur Brahmin of village Thikariya, 15 miles from Khandela, (now in Sikar district), who established the main seat of Nimbark Sampraday at Salemabad (Parshurampuri) in Rajasthan. His life-time is still a matter of conjecture : according to one view, it is from 1393 to 1540, while according to the other, it is from 1543 to 1623. The conclusion appears to be that he flourished during the 16th century, most probably from 1520 to 1600. His poetry consists of 2225 *Sakhis* (*Dohas*), 15 *Charit* poems such as *Das Avtar*, *Raghunath*, *Srikrishna* and *Prahlad* and 13 *Lila* poems, such as *Amar Bodh*, *Nam Nidhi*, *Sanch Nishedh*, *Nij Rup*, *Nirvan* and *Hari Lila* and about 600 *Padas*. The *Sakhis* are on 250 miscellaneous topics such as *Pardesi Pritam Ko*, *Virah Agni Ko* and *Hari Bhakti Hin Ko*.

Being the Acharya of the Nimbark Sampraday, he was a devotee of the Sagun Bhakti but many of the *Padas* dealing with the Nirgun Bhakti are equally important.

His language is simple Rajasthani with a mixture of Braj here and there. Some of his expressions have become popular sayings in Rajasthan.

Recently a collection of all of his poems has been published in four volumes, but as other manuscripts of his poems have come to light, a thorough scrutiny is necessary in regard to his poems as also about his life-time.

PARSHWA-PURAN. See *Bhudhar Das.*

PARSON, JOHN. See *Christian, John.*

PARTHASARATHI DABRAL. Poet, whose *Nari-Tirth* (1980) is a *Khand-Kavya* on the life of Kasturba Gandhi, wife of Mahatma Gandhi.

PARTHASARATHI, J. Tamil-speaking Hindi scholar, who is noted for his *Hindi evam Tamil ke Vakya-Vinyas ka Tulnatmak Adhyayan* (A Comparative Study of Sentence Structure of Hindi and Tamil ; thesis ; 1966).

PARTI PARIKATHA. See *Phanishwar Nath Renu.*

PARVATI MANGAL. Poem by Tulsidas (q.v.) in eastern Avadhi dialect, written in 1586 (?).

It describes in 164 verses the renunication of Sati by Shiv, Sati's rebirth as Parvati and their renunion. The work appears to be influenced by the *Kumara Sambhava* of Kalidasa.

PARVATI RANI SINHA. Modern Magahi poetess, who is noted for her stray poems.

PASAYAT GADAN. See *Gadan Pasayat.*

PASHKOVSKAYA, NATALIYA ALEXEYEVNA (1944-). Soviet Hindi scholar, who is a Lecturer in Foreign Languages Institute, Moscow and has published articles on Hindi language.

PATHAK, SHRIDHAR. See *Shridhar Pathak.*

PATNI, AJAY RAJ. See *Ajay Raj Patni.*

PATOLA (fl. 19th cent. ?). Braj folk-poet, who was a native of Agra. He was noted for the composition of his Rajputi *Holis.*

PATRAM GAUR (1913-81). Rajasthani poet and writer, whose chief works are : *Registan* (poem), *Manav aur Prakriti*, *Smarth Guru Ramdas* (drama) and *Rajasthani Muhavare.* Along with Kanhaiyalal Sahal, he has edited and published *Chaubol*, which is a Khari Boli rendering of Rajasthani *Vats.*

PATTAJI ASIYA. See *Surtan Gun Varnan.*

PATTNAIK, AJAY KUMAR. See *Ajay Kumar Pattnaik.*

PAVLOV, VICTOR PAVLOVICH (1935-). Soviet Hindi scholar, who has edited *Hindi-Rusi Bat-Chit ki Pathya-Pustak* (Moscow, 1977), *Hindi-Rusi Pathya Shabdakosh* (Moscow, 1964), *Brihat Rusi-Shabdakosh* (65,000 words; editor and one of the compilers), *Hindi-Rusi Shabdakosh* (2 Pts., 75,000 words ; 1972; one of the compilers and editor) and some texts for learning Russian, meant for foreigners, etc.

PERTOLD, OTAKAR. Czech Hindi scholar, who in 1930 published the first Czech textbook for teaching Hindi. This book was so popular that Hindi was taught for several decades according to it. This book was, however, meant for the study of Hindi in Devnagari script and Urdu in Persian script.

PETRESCU, ION. Modern Romanian Hindi scholar, who taught Hindi in the Bucharest University, Romania. See *Vidya Sagar Dayal.*

PHAHIM (fl. 1607). Poet, who is said to have composed *Dohas.* He was considered as the younger brother of Abul Fazl or Abul Fazl himself.

PHANISHWAR NATH RENU (1921-78). Regional fiction writer, who was born in a village of Purnea district of Bihar. His chief works are as under :—

Novel : *Maila Anchal* (The Dirty Region ; q.v. ; 1954 ; a spectacle of sordid rural life in Purnea district), *Parti Parikatha* (The Tale of the Fallow Land; 1957), *Dirghtapa* (The Woman engaged in a long Penance; 1963; a description of Working Women's Hostel), *Kitne Chaurahe* (How many Crossroads; 1966), *Julus* (The Procession; on the refugees from East Bengal), *Paltu Babu Road* and *Van Tulsi ki Gandh* (a collection of sketches; 1984). His two other works are : *Rinjal Ghanjal* and *Nepali Kranti-Katha.*

Short Story Collection : *Thumri* (1967), *Adim Ratri ki Mahak* (The Fragrance of the First Night), *Agni Khor*, *Ek Shravani Dopahari ki Dhup* and *Phanishwarnath Renu* : *Shreshth Kahaniyan* (ed. by Rajendra Yadav); 'Tisri Qasam' (The Third Oath), 'Rasapriya', 'Lal Pan ki Begum', 'Tin Bindiyan' (Three Marks), etc. are his chief short stories.

The setting of his works has been made in the rural background, with which the author had the emotional attachment. He has also written short stories in Maithili. A special issue on

'Renu' has been published by 'South-East Asia Journal'. See *Hansen, Kathryn Gay*.

PHILIP, V.N. Malayalam-speaking modern Hindi scholar, whose chief work is : *Bhakti Sahitya men Bimb Bhavna* (Imagism in Devotional Literature).

PHILLIPS, COL. A.N. Author of *Hindustani Idioms* (London, 1892).

PHILLO, D.C. Author of *Hindustani Stumbling Blocks* (London, 1909).

PHUL CHAND MANAV. Panjabi-speaking Hindi poet and writer, who is noted for his *Ek hi Jagah* (Only One Place; 1977), a poetical collection and *Anjir*, a short story collection.

PHULLAURI, SHRADDHA RAM. See *Shraddhu Ram Phullauri.*

PIETRZYK, ALFRED HENRY. Scholar, whose chief work is *The Study of Lexical Styles in Hindi.* (1974).

PINCOTT, FREDRICK (b. 1826). Englishman, who wrote *Hindi Manual* to teach Hindi to his countrymen. In his works are included *Bal-Dipk* (4 Pts., prescribed in Bihar as a text-book) and *Victoria Charit* (The Life of Victoria, in 136 pages). He had regular correspondence with eminent Hindi writers of his time, e.g., Bharatendu Harishchandra, Pratap Narain Mishra and Kartik Prasad Khatri. He was a great admirer of Bharatendu, to whom he addressed a *Pada*. He also reviewed a number of books written by Hindi authors and espoused the cause of Hindi. See *Prem Sagar*.

PINGAL PRAKASH. See *Hamirdan Ratanu.*

PINGAL SHIROMANI. See *Kushal Labh.*

PIPA. Saint-poet, who was the ruler of Gagraungarh State. His time is not certain but he might have lived between 1383 and 1453. Formerly, he was a worshipper of the goddess Durga, but later on he was initiated by Ramanand and is said to be one of his twelve famous disciples. He was a great devout; his devotion induced king Shaursen to become his disciple.

His stray *Padas* are available in various manuscripts of different traditions. The earliest one so far available is dated 1625 in which 17 of his *Padas* are written. From a study of *Padas* available in this and other manuscripts, it appears that 25 *Padas* belong to Pipa (including the one in *Granth Sahib*).

Besides, 13 *Sakhis* also go in his name. The *Padas* sing of *Nirgun* Ram Bhakti and of the futility of external practices like pilgrimage. Pipa was so much steeped in Bhakti that many a legend is current around his name.

PIRARAM (fl. early 19th cent.). Rajasthani saint-poet of Ram Snehi Sampraday, Sinthal, who was a Charan of Dadhvadiya branch of village Munjasar (Nokha). He was initiated by Raghunathdas (q.v.) in 1821. His *Vani* dealing with *Nam-Sadhana*, consists of about 400 *Dohas*, *Prakash Bhaskar*, *Guru Mahima* and stray verses.

PIRDAN LALAS (fl. 1st half of 18th cent.). Rajasthani poet, who followed the religious tolerance and synthesis of his 'Bhav Guru' Barhat Isardas (1538-1618). His works : *Narayan Neh*, *Parmeshwar Puran* (q.v.), *Hinglaj Raso*. *Alakh Aradh*, *Ajampa Jap*, *Gyan Charit*, *Patig Pahar* and some Dingal *Gits* reveal his faith in one God, though appearing in many forms. He appears to believe in the ten incarnations of Vishnu and with regard to the cause for incarnation, he followed the *Gita*.

PIRJI (fl. 1583). Rajasthani poet, whose stray verses in different popular metres are available.

PITAMBAR DATT BARTHWAL (1901-44). Scholar, whose chief works are : The *Nirgun School of Hindi Poetry* (in Hindi : *Hindi Kavya ki Nirgun Dhara*) and *Makrand*; his other works are : *Goswami Tulsidas*, *Rupak Rahasya*, *Gorakh-Vani*, *Jayasi-ka Adhyatmavad* and *Yoga Pravah*. Barthwal is noted for his interest in textual analysis and love for a scientific thoroughness.

PITAMBAR DEV (fl. 18th cent.). Poet of the Haridasi Sect under the Krishna-cult, whose chief works are : *Rasa ke Pada*, *Singar ke Pada*, commentary on the *Keli-Mal* of Haridas (in prose), *Guru Mangal*, etc. All of these are devotional works.

PITHODAS (1742-94). Rajasthani saint-poet of Ram Snehi Sampraday, Khedapa, who was disciple of Ramdas (q.v.) and died at Ratlam. His *Vani* consisting of *Behad Bodh*, *Guru Mahima*, *Jugal Granth*, *Padas* and stray verses, is known for lucidity and intensity of emotion.

PLATTS, JOHN T. Professor of Persian in the Oxford University; he was the author of *A Dictionary of Urdu, Classical Hindi and English* (London, 1884), *Hindustani Grammar* and *A Grammar of the Hindustani or Urdu Language*. The Dictionary includes difficult Sanskrit words as well. The significance of this work lies in the fact that it discusses the origin of words.

PODDAR RAMAVTAR ARUN. Writer, whose *Kalidas ki Atmakatha* (The Biography of Kalidas ; 1982) is a novel.

POGHIRE, CICERONE. Modern Romanian Indologist, who was instrumental in getting a Hindi Department founded in the Bucharest University, Romania. He also lectured on Indian culture.

POKHARDAS (d. 1815). Rajasthani saint-poet of Ram Snehi Sampraday, Shahpura, whose stray verses are available.

POLLET, GILBERT. Modern Belgian Indologist, who is in the Faculty of Oriental Studies of the Catholic University of Leuven. He has made a study of the *Bhaktamal* (q.v.).

POLLOCK, W. Author of *Pollock's Pocket Hindustani* (Calcutta, 1900); it was compiled in collaboration with Muhammad Hussain.

POLURI RAMKRISHNAYYA. Telugu-speaking modern Hindi poet, who is noted for his *Shri Charantirthji.*

POOJANAND NEMAH (1943-). Hindi poet of Mauritius, whose poetical collections are : *Subah ki Dhundh*, *Avai* (in press) and *Pattharon ke Niche* (nearing completion); *Akash Ganga* (1970) in an anthology of 18 poems composed by nine poets and edited by him.

POPESCUE, MARIA L. Modern Romanian Hindi scholar, who taught Hindi in the Bucharest University, Romania.

PORIZKA, VINCENC (d. 1982). Modern Czech Hindi scholar, who in 1963 published the second Hindi text book (see *Otakar Pertold*) for teaching of Czech students but apart from Czech, the explanations were given in English also, with the result that it became popular over the continent and soon its second edition had to be published. The work consisting of some 500 pages is entitled *Hindustani-Hindi Languages Course* (Prague, 1972). He also wrote *Hindi Vyakaran* (Prague) and was engaged in compiling a *Hindi-Czech Kosh.*

POSPELOVA, LUDMILA JARYEVNA (1950-). Soviet Hindi scholar, who has written articles on the poetry of Jay Shankar Prasad (q.v.).

PRABHA DEVI. Modern Maithili poetess, who is noted for her stray poems.

PRABHAKAR (fl. 18th cent.). Marathi-folk poet (*Shahir*), who also composed poems in Hindi.

PRABHKAR DWIVEDI. Modern writer, who is noted for his short story collections : *Ikaiyon ke Bich* and *Dhup men Soi Nadi.*

PRABHAKAR JHA. Modern Maithili poet, who is noted for his lyrics.

PRABHAKAR MACHWE (1917-). Poet and writer, whose chief works are :

Poetry : Poems in *Tar Saptak* (1943 ; q.v.), *Swapnabhang* (Dream-break; 1957), *Anukshan* (Every Moment ; 1959), *Tail ki Pakaudiyan* (1962; humorous), *Mepal* (1967) and *Shatdal* (ed. ; 100 select poems of 100 Indian poets).

Novel : *Parantu* (But), *Sancha, Tis-Chalis-Pachas* (Thirty-Forty-Fifty), *Dawbha, Ektara* (Monochord), *Kisliye* ? (For What ?), *Dyut* (Gambling), *Kishore, Jo, Lakshmi Ben, Kahan se Kahan* (From Where to Where), *Dashbhuja, Shabdarekha, Dard ke Paivand* and *Lapata.*

He has also written one-act plays, chief among them being 'Gali ke Mod Par' (On the Turn of the Street); his radio plays are : 'Pagalkhane Men' (In the Lunatic Asylum), 'Panchkanya', 'Parvatshri', 'Raygiri', 'Sankat par Sankat' (Crisis upon Crisis), 'Vadhu Chahiye' (Wanted a Bride) and 'Gandhi ki Rah Par' (On the Path of Gandhi).

Machwe's other works are : *Khargosh ke Sing* (The Horns of a Hare ; humorous essays), *Berang* (a collection of essays), *Vyakti aur Vangmay* (Individual and Literature), *Samiksha ki Samiksha* (Criticism on Criticism), *Jainendra ke Vichar* (The Ideas of Jainendra; ed. 1937), *Santulan* (Balance; criticism), *Hindi aur Marathi ka Nirgun Sant Kavya* (research thesis; 1962), *Marathi aur Uska Sahitya* (on Marathi language and literature), *Gori Nazron men Ham* (1964), *Rus Men* (travelogues), *Bharat aur Asia ka Sahitya* (on Indian and Asian Literature), *Adhunik Hindi Bhasha aur Sahitya* (Modern Hindi Language and Literature; 1971), *Bharatiya Upanyas Kathasar* (I, II) and *Visangati* (essays). Machwe has also written short stories : his important short stories are : 'Girgit' (The Chameleon), 'Vidhayak' (The Legislator), etc.

A prolific writer of encyclopaedic grasp, Machwe's works on history, philosophy, lexicons, edited and translated works as also books in English total 65. He has received Soviet Land Nehru Award for *Tolstov aur Bharat* (tr. 1969). He is considered as an important essayist and critic among modern writers.

Machwe was Secretary of the Sahitya Akademi and is at present Director of Bharatiya Bhasha Parishad, Calcutta.

PRABHAKAR SHROTRIYA. Critic, whose *Sanvad* (*Nayi Kavita, Alochana aur Pratikriya*) examines some eleven *avant gardes* in Hindi poetry since early fifties, including Agyey, Shamsher and Muktibodh. His other works are : *Kavita ki Tisri Ankh, Prasad ka Sahitya* : *Premtatwik Drishti* and *Hindi Kavita ki Pragatishil Bhumika*.

PRABHAS KUMAR CHOUDHARY. Maithili writer, who is noted for his short story collection : *Nav Ghar Uthay Puran Ghar Khasay* and novels : *Navarambh* (1979) and *Raja Pokarime Katek Machhari* (1981 ; on the collapse of a feudal family). He brings out the pettiness and greatness in the life of the common man and woman. He is one of the editors of 'Katha Disha', a short story magazine.

PRABHAT. See *Kedarnath Mishra 'Prabhat'*.

Prabhat, C.L. Modern writer, whose chief works are : *Miranbai, Asvikrit Upalabdhiyan* (research) and criticism of *Samasar Natak* by Raghuram Nagar. His latest critical work is *Pratik aur Pratikvadi Kavya-Mulya* (1984). He is Head of the Department of Hindi, Bombay University.

PRABHAT KUMAR BHATTACHARYA. Modern writer, who is noted for his drama *Kath Mahal* (The Wooden Palace) and a poetical collection : *Ityadi*.

PRABHAT MITTAL. Critic, who is known for the editing of an anthology : *Aj ki Kavita* (Poetry Today; 1978); his short story collection is *Pahli Varsha*.

PRABHAT TRIPATHI. Poet, whose *Nahin Likh Saka Main* (I Could Not Write: 1981) is a collection of personal poems, though not completely devoid of social thought.

PRABHU DAS BHUPATKAR. Marathi-speaking modern Hindi writer, whose *Sone men Sugandh* and *Phagun ke Din Char* are collections of essays. His research work is *Hindi aur Marathi ke Aitihasik Natak*.

PRABHU DAYAL (fl. 1601). Poet, who was the author of *Shashimala Katha*, which describes the love of a man with a Yakshini on the type of love between Pururava and Urvashi.

PRABHU DAYAL MITAL. Modern critic, whose chief works are : *Ashtachhap Parichay, Brajbhasha Sahitya ka Ritusaundarya* (beauty of seasons), *Braj ke Dharma-Sampradayon ka Itihas, Surdas ki Varta, Sur Nirnay, Sur-Saravali, Braj Sahitya* and *Braj ka Sanskritik Itihas* (critical works) : he is a specialist of Brajbhasha poetry and is considered as an authority on the literature of Surdas.

PRABHU JOSHI. Writer, whose *Kis Hath Se* (With Which Hand; 1980) is a short story collection.

PRABHU SADH (fl. 18th cent. ?). Rajasthani saint-poet of Laldasi Sampraday, whose *Bhajans* extol devotion to Ram and Guru and advocate simplicity in life.

PRABODH-CHANDRODAY. See *Jasvant Singh.*

PRABODH NARAYAN CHAUDHARI. Maithili writer, whose *Bichal Phul* (1940) is a short story collection.

PRADHAN GURUDATT. Kannada-speaking modern Hindi critic, whose chief works are : *Urmila* (in Kannada and Hindi) and a tr. of Prabhushankar's drama *Angulimala* from Kannada into Hindi. Both these works are in collaboration with Me. Rajeshvarayya.

PRADIP PANT. Novelist, whose chief works are : *Mahamahim* (His Excellency ; 1980), *Am Admi ka Shav* and *Ek Asambhav Mrityu* ; *Kutte ki Maut* (1984) is his short story collection. *Private Sector ka Vyangyakar* is his humorous work.

PRADYUMNA-CHARIT. Jain poem in 701 verses, which was composed by Sadharu in 1354 ; it narrates the life of Pradyumna, son of Krishna and Rukmini.

PRAHLAD CHARIT. Rajasthani Akhyan Kavya in 596 verses, which was composed by Kesodas Godara (1573-79). Meant to be sung in musical modes, it deals with the Prahlad legend, though the poet has made variations in the story according to the popular beliefs current in his days. This work ranks high among all the poems of Kesodas Godara on account of its poetic excellence and popularity.

Raja Jamghat kills animals indiscriminately and in order to prevent this, all the deer decide to send daily one deer to him. A lame deer, at its turn, makes love to a doe on the way. Both of them go to the Raja who, on seeing their deep love, lets off the deer. The doe has become pregnant but does not give birth to a young one for 18 months. With acute pain, she sits on the way through which Shankar and Parvati are passing. It is only at the repeated entreaties of Parvati that Shankar relieves the doe of her pain and the child comes out. It is Hiranyakashipu, the father of Prahlad.

PRAHLAD RAMSHARAN. Modern Hindi writer of Mauritius, who is known for his *Mauritius ki Lok-Kathayen* and *Dr Sir Seewosagur Ramgoolam ki Rajasthan Yatra*. He has also written short stories.

PRAHLAD RAY, VIPRA (19th cent. ?). Court-poet of Raja Jayant Singh Sambalpur, Orissa, whose *Jay-Chandrika* is a Hindi composition.

PRAHLAD SHARMA GAUR. Modern Rajasthani scholar, who is noted for his *Marwari Git aur Bhajan-Sangrah*.

PRAKASH CHANDRA GUPTA (1908-70). Progressive writer, whose chief works are : *Naya Hindi Sahitya* (New Hindi Literature ; 1939), *Adhunik Hindi Sahitya : Ek Drishti* (Modern Hindi Literature : A Viewpoint ; 1952), *Hindi Sahitya ki Janvadi Parampara* (1953) and *Sahityadhara* (The Stream of Literature ; 1956). He wrote a monograph on Premchand in English for Sahitya Akademi and has tr. Premchand's stories into English. He treats literature as an instrument of social significance and severely censures those literary critics who confine themselves only to an aesthetic category of experience and completely ignore its sociological implications

PRAKASH PARIMAL. Modern Rajasthani poet, who has composed poems in the style of Nayi Kavita.

PRAKASH RAO. Telugu-speaking modern Hindi poet, who is noted for his *Varudhini*, a poetical work.

PRAMOD GANESH LALE. Telugu-speaking Hindi writer, who has rendered into Hindi prose from original Sanskrit : *Shrikrishna Karnamritam* (1971).

PRAMOD SINHA. Writer, whose chief work is a novel : *Uska Shahr* (His City ; 1970).

PRAN CHANDRA CHAUHAN (fl. 1610). Poet of the Ram-cult, who composed *Ramayan Mahanatak*. Giving the story of the *Ramayan* in the verse dialogue form, it is termed as a Natak, otherwise it lacks the dramatic elements.

PRAN NATH (1618-94). Gujarati saint-poet, who was a prominent figure of the Pranami Sect. Born at Nautanpur near Jamnagar, he wrote works under the pseudonyms of Mihir-Raj, Indravati, Mahamati, etc., some of which are feminine names. The saint-poet belonged to Sakhi Sect, in which Radha, the beloved of Krishna, is worshipped. His Hindi works are collected in *Kulzam Swarup*, which is held in very high esteem among the followers of his Sect. He laid emphasis on the worship of Brahma alone and tried to prove that there is no difference between the Veda and the *Koran*. He was the first writer to have used Khari Boli in prose and to have given the name 'Hindustani' to the language, which was a mixture of several languages and dialects. It is said that he was a favourite of Chhatrasal, the ruler of Panna State.

PRAN NATH TRICHHAL. Modern Hindi writer of Jammu-Kashmir, who is noted for his studies in linguistics.

PRANAV KUMAR BANDYOPADHYAY. Bengali-speaking Hindi short story writer and poet, whose chief works are : *Athva* (Or ; 1968), *Ishwar Babu Anupasthit The* (Ishwar Babu was not Present), *Atmaja*, *Pranav Kumar ki Vishishta Kahaniyan* (short story collections), *Murdagadi* (1976), *Naxalbadi* (1978 ; poetical collections), *Kali Kavitayen* (Poems), *December 1979* (travelogue ; 1980), *Ityadi*, *Khabar*, *Vida Bandhu Vida* and *Gopiganj Sanvad* (novels). His works have dealt with the problem of relations between the individual and the society.

PRANESHACHARYA, K. (fl. 1935). Kannada-speaking Hindi poet, whose poems were published in the 'Jagriti', a literary magazine. The poems were mainly patriotic in nature.

PRANI SADH (fl. 17th cent.). Rajasthani saint-poet of Laldasi Sect, whose 40 available *Padas* deal with Nirgun Bhakti and exaltation of God and of the poet's Guru, Laldas.

PRANYESH SHUKLA. Modern poet of Kanpur, whose poems are quite popular in poetical symposia.

PRAPESH KUMAR. Poet, who is noted for his *Shakta Zamin ke Liye* (For a Fertile Soil ; 1982), a collection of poems.

PRASAD GANPAT. Modern Hindi writer of Mauritius, whose *Jivan Pradip* (1966) is a collection of his 14 essays.

PRASHANT VEDALANKAR (1937-). Scholar, whose chief works are : *Rasabhas* (1977) and *Multani aur Hindi* (in press).

PRASHAVATI JHA. Maithili scholar, whose *Maithili Mahakavya men Nari Chitran* (1980) is a research work.

PRASIDDHA NARAYAN SINGH. Modern Bhojpuri poet of Balia, whose poetry is permeated with national fervour. He has also written a treatise on the poets and writers of Balia.

PRATAP BALA (fl. 1833). Rajasthani poetess, whose stray verses in popular metres are available.

PRATAP CHANDER CHUNDAR. Writer, who is noted for his novel : *Job Charnak ki Bibi* (1977) on the tale of Job Charnok of the East India Company, who established Calcutta. His some other works are : *Agnishayya*, *Bhukh*, *Lebdev ki Nayika*, *Swapnabhang* (novels) and *Kathputli* (short story collection).

PRATAP CHANDRA SHARMA. Modern Hindi poet of Fiji, whose chief poetical works are : *Pravasini*, *Bhajanavali* (1947), etc.

PRATAP KUNVARI BAI (*c*. 1816-92). Rajasthani (Pingal) poetess of the Ram-cult, who was born in a Bhat family of the village Jakhan in the then Jodhpur State and was married to Maharaja Mansingh of Jodhpur at the age of sixteen. After the death of the Maharaja in 1843, when she was only 27 years old, she devoted herself to religious duties and worship.

Her works are : *Gyan Sagar*, *Gyan Prakash*, *Pratap Pachchisi*, *Prem Sagar*, *Ramchandra Nam Mahima*, *Ram Gun Sagar*, *Raghubar Sneh Lila*, *Ram Prem Sukh Sagar*, *Ram Sujas Pachchisi*, *Raghunathji ke Kavitta*, *Bhajan Pada Harjas*, *Pratap Vinay*, *Shri Ramchandra Vinay*, *Harjas*, *Gayan*, etc.

PRATAP MALL (1639-89). Ruler of the House of Kantipur (Kathmandu) in Nepal, who was a great Maithili poet. He called himself 'Kavindra' and was more inclined to Sanskritize his diction frequently. Several collections of his independent lyrics, which include Sanskrit lyrics as well, such as, *Gitam Pratap Malliyam*, *Git-Govindam Pratap Mallasya* and *Pratap-Mallavirochit-Gitam* have been noticed as also nine lyrics inscribed in the Taleju Temple. A complete collection of his Maithili lyrics called *Gitmala Bhashatmika* and some lyrics are quoted in an anthology of Rags. Pratap Mall advocated Shakti to be worshipped and ignored Vishnu and Shiv. The famous poet, Vanshmani Jha (q.v.) was originally in his court and wrote his drama under his patronage.

PRATAP NARAYAN. Modern Rajasthani poet of Jaipur, whose stray verses are available.

PRATAP NARAYAN MISHRA (1856-94). Writer, who was born at Kanpur and was influenced by Bharatendu Harishchandra (q.v.). By nature, Mishra was extremely jolly and humorous and all sections of the Kanpur society knew him, some as a singer or versifier, some as one who was ever ready to play the heroine in any drama to be staged and some as a great scholar and editor of the 'Brahmana' monthly, which he founded in 1883. Personal contact with Bharatendu inspired him to write and work for the cause of Hindi. Like Bharatendu, he was keenly interested in the problems of his times and was actuated by reformist zeal. He tried to set things right by referring pointedly and critically and often sarcastically to the questions that were agitating the minds of people in his times. It was by his style which was full of sparkling humour that he attracted new readers towards Hindi. His chief works besides essays are : *Raj Singh*, *Indira*, *Radharani*, *Yugalanguriya* (all. tr. from Bengali), *Sangit Shakuntal* (tr.), *Kali Kautuk*, *Rupak* ; 1874), *Bharat Durdasha*, *Kali-Prabhav*, *Hathi Hammir*, *Gosankat* (dramas), *Juari-Khuari* (The Card Player ; 1876 ; farce) and 7 to 8 works of poetry. His dramas are based on social realism.

Mishra's characteristic humour is present in his poetry as also in his prose. He started the practice of writing short poems on current political and social problems of his time. He wrote mostly in Khari Boli.

PRATAP NARAYAN SHRIVASTAV (1904-78). Novelist, whose chief works are : *Vida* (The Farewell ; 1928 ; portraying city's rich dwellers), *Vijay* (The Victory), *Vikas* (1941), *Bayalis* (1948), *Visarjan* (1950), *Bekasi ka Mazar* (1956 ; dealing with the 1857 revolt), *Vardan*, *Vedna* and *Viragini* (all novels) ; he has portrayed the urban life of the upper middle class people.

PRATAP RUDRADEV (1479-1535). Ruler of Orissa, who was a contemporary of Chaitanya. He was a great scholar of Sanskrit and his works in that language are : *Saraswati-Vilasa*, *Pratapa-Martanda*, etc. In Hindi (Brajboli), some of his *Padas* are extant.

PRATAP SAHI (fl. 1823-53). Poet of the Riti school, who belonged to Bundelkhand. He was the court-poet of the ruler of Charkhari. Apart from his two best known works : *Vyangarth Kaumudi* (1825) and *Kavya Vilas* (1829), he composed a number of other original books and commentaries on *Rasaraj*, *Bihari Satsai* and Balbhadra's *Nakhshikh*. *Vyangarth Kaumudi* gives many examples of *Vyanjana* and is one of the outstanding works of the Dhwani School of Poetics, while *Kavya Vilas* covers a comprehensive ground and treats of poetry in general, its functions, its merits and demerits, etc. As a writer on literary theory, Pratap Sahi occupies his place beside Matiram, Shripati and Bhikharidas (qq.v.). Virtually, in some ways he improves upon earlier writings and deserves a higher place than his predecessors. In sweetness and felicity of expression, he reaches the level of Matiram, while in vividness of imagery he ranks with Padmakar. Both as a poet and a critic, he holds an exalted position.

PRATAP SEHGAL. Poet, whose *Saval ab bhi Maujud Hai* (1983) is his first poetical collection.

PRATAP SINGH, MAHARANA (fl. 1571-96). Celebrated Rajasthani hero, whose stray verses in different popular metres are available.

PRATAP SINGH (1764-1803). Ruler of Jaipur, who ascended the throne in 1776. He had to wage several battles with the Marathas, with the result that his health ran down and he died early. A great patron of poets, scholars and musicians, he got the *Ain-e-Akbari* and *Divan-e-Hafiz* translated into Hindi and was instrumental in getting several works prepared on Astronomy, Ayurved, Music and Dharmashastra. Besides the above, collections were made of his poems under the titles : *Pratap Vir Hazara, Pratap Singh Hazara*, etc.

Pratap Singh, under the pseudonym of Brajnidhi was a great poet and his works in Brajbhasha numbering 23, have been published by the Nagari Pracharini Sabha, Kashi under the title : *Brajnidhi-Granthavali*.

PRATAP SINGH. See *Chand Kunvar ri Vat*.

PRATAP SINGH PAGAL. Modern Hindi poet of Fiji, who is noted for his stray poems.

PRATAP SUDHAKAR. Kannada-speaking modern Hindi writer, who tr. T. Ra. Subbarao's *Hansgite* from Kannade into Hindi ; a Hindi film based on this novel has already been made.

PRATIBHA AGRAWAL. Modern writer, whose chief works are : *Hindi Muhavare, Adhyayan, Sankalan evam Sahityik Prayog, Srijan ka Sukh-Dukh, Kahani Madan Babu Ki*. She has tr. into Hindi some plays of Badal Sarkar, Arthur Miller, Utpal Datt and others ; *Nagarvadhu* is her drama.

PRATIGYA (Solemn Declaration). Novel (1929) by Premchand

(q.v.), which discusses the problems of widows and untouchables ; the novelist here takes the role of a social reformer.

PRAVASI SWAR (1971). A poetical collection, published by Hindi Parishad of Mauritius, which contains 55 poems of 11 poets of Mauritius : 5 poems each of : Brajendra Kumar Bhagat 'Madhukar', Somdatt Bakhori, Ravishankar Kauleshar, Thakurdatt Pandey, Abhimanyu Unnuth 'Shabnam', Janardan Kalicharan 'Sachit', Harinarayan Sita, Moonishwurlall Chintamunnee, Indradev Bhola, Mohanlal Hardayal and Mohanlal Brijmohan. This anthology is a record, presented for the first time, of the progress of Hindi poetry made in Mauritius.

PRAVIN-SAGAR. See *Maheraman Singh*.

PRAY, BRUCE RAYMOND. Scholar, whose chief works are : *Agreement in Hindi-Urdu and its Phonological Implications* (Michigan, 1969) and *Topics in Hindi-Urdu Grammar* (Berkeley, 1970).

PRAYAG DAS BIYANI (fl. between 1598-1623). Rajasthani saint-poet and a follower of Dadu (q.v.), whose 60 *Sakhis* and 20 *Padas* reveal his devotion. He belonged to Didwana near Nagore.

PRAYAG NARAIN TRIPATHI (1919-). Experimentalist poet, whose poems are included in the *Tisra Saptak* (q.v.). After retirement from the All India Radio, he lives in Aurobindo Ashram.

PRAYAG SHUKLA (1940-). Short story writer and poet, whose chief works are : *Akeli Akritiyan* (The Lonely Figures ; 1965), *Iske Bad* (After This), *Vah Antardeshiya* (That Inland ; 1980) (short story collections), *Kavita Sambhav*, *Yeh Ek Din Hai* (This is a Day ; 1980) and *Rat ka Ped* (The Night Tree ; 1981) (collections of poems). He is Sub-editor of 'Dinman'.

PREM CHAND (1880-1936). Celebrated novelist, whose original name was Dhanpat Rai and who was born at Lamhi near Varanasi. His mother died when he was only 8 years old ; he had his second marriage at the age of 25 with Shivrani Devi, a short story writer. For some time, he served as a teacher and then a Sub-Deputy Inspector in the Education Department. In the Non-Co-operatian Movement of 1920, he resigned his service ; he edited 'Maryada' and 'Madhuri' magazines.

He also started his own printing press and edited 'Hans' and 'Jagaran'.

Premchand had already earned a reputation as a writer of fiction in Urdu, before he published his short stories and his first novel, *Seva Sadan*, in Hindi in 1918. His chief works are as under :—

Novel : *Seva Sadan* (Service Home ; 1918 ; q.v.), *Vardan* (The Boon), *Premashram* (The Hermitage of Love ; 1921), *Rangbhumi* (The Theatre ; 1924), *Kayakalpa* (The Rejuvenation ; 1926), *Nirmala* (1927), *Pratigya* (The Solemn Declaration ; 1929), *Ghaban* (The Embezzlement ; 1931), *Karmabhumi* (The Field of Action ; 1932) and *Godan* (The Gift of Cow ; 1936) (qq.v.). His last novel *Mangal Sutra* (The Wedlock Thread ; 1948) is incomplete.

Short Story Collection : *Sapta Saroj*, *Prem Prasun*, *Prem Dwadashi*, *Mansarovar* (a collection of his popular short stories ; 8 Pts.) ; the number of short stories written by him is about 300. His well-known short stories are : 'Panch Parmeshwar' (The Arbitrator as God), 'Budhi Kaka' (The Old Aunt), 'Atmaram', 'Pus ki Rat' (A Winter Night), 'Kafan' (The Shroud), 'Bade Ghar ki Beti' (The Daughter of a High Family), 'Namak ka Darogha' (The Salt Inspector), 'Mantra' (The Spell), 'Nasha' (Intoxication), 'Thakur ka Kuan' (The Thakur's Well), 'Sadgati' (Deliverance), 'Tagada' (A Day in the life of a Debt Collector), 'Idgah', 'Grihdah' (The Family Blaze-up), 'Bade Bhai Sahib' (The Elder Brother), 'Shatranj ke Khiladi' (The Chess Players), etc.

Other Works : *Sangram* (1922), *Karbala* (1924), *Prem-ki Vedi* (1933), *Ruthi Rani* (dramas), *Kuchh Vichar* (critical essays), *Durgadas*, *Mahatma Sheikh Sadi*, *Ramcharcha* (biographies), *Galpa-Ratna*, *Galpa-Samuchchay* (ed. short story collections), *Ahankar*, *Sukhdas*, *Azad Katha*, *Hartal* (1930), *Nyaya* (1931), *Chandi-ki Dibiya* (1931), *Tolstoy-ki Kahaniyan*, *Srishti ka Arambh* (tr. works), etc.

The works of Premchand amply demonstrate the social and political changes effected in his time. His novels give a life-like description of Indian villages, the people's mode of living, their problems, their joys and sorrows ; it equally holds good when the writer describes the complex life of town-dwellers. In his social novels (e.g., *Seva Sadan*, *Premashram*, *Nirmala*, etc.), he comes out as a determined reformer, an uncompromising critic of social evils, like those of child marriage, mal-treatment of widows, prostitution, etc. But Premchand is essentially an idealist and each one of his novels portrays a sphere of human life in order to improve upon it and to raise it higher and higher, for it is his conviction that whereas the soul of literature is idealism, its body is realistic description. In his *Rangbhumi*, *Karmabhumi*, and *Godan*, he has given a vivid description of the freedom struggle India was waging under the leadership of Mahatma Gandhi. By virtue of his wide sympathies, his realistic description of men and things and the vast spectrum of life covered by him, he is rightly called the Father of Hindi Novel.

As a short story writer, Premchand makes even greater appeal than as a novelist. Some of his short stories will go down as gems in Hindi literature. All these stories as also most of his novels, have been tr. into all principal Indian languages as also in some foreign languages.

Since Premchand introduces, portrays and speaks of ordinary men and women, he has tried to use the very language which these people speak in everyday life and with Premchand's background of Urdu, it was not difficult for him to evolve a style, which could command the widest possible intelligibility.

PREM CHAND BHULI. Modern Hindi writer of Mauritius, whose *Chiragh aur Tufan* is a small short story collection.

PREM CHAND RAVAL. Modern Rajasthani poet, who has composed progressive poems.

PREM DAS (1662-1762). Rajasthani saint-poet, who belonged to the village Khinyasar (Bikaner). According to one version, he was initiated by Santdas Gudadpanthi, while according to the other by Balakdas, the disciple of Santdas. His available *Vani*, which lays emphasis on *Ram-smaran*, consists of *Dohas* and *Savaiyas* in popular Rajasthani. Premdas initiated Dariyav (q.v.) in 1712, who founded the Ren (Nagore) branch of Ram Snehi Sampraday.

PREM DAS (fl. 1712). Bengali Vaishnav poet, who also composed *Padas* in Brajbuli.

PREMGHAN. See *Badrinarayan Chaudhari 'Premghan'*.

PREMJI 'PREM'. Rajasthani poet of Kota, whose chief works are : *Chamcho* (1973 ; political satires), *Sanvalo Sanch* (1976 ; a collection of 21 small poems ; the so-called *Ghazals*), *Suraj* (1978 ; a poem of 101 verses on the famous poet, Suryamall Mishran of Bundi) and *Sarvar, Surajaur Sanjhya* (1979 ; a collection of 27 poems of romantic mood). He has edited with three of his associates *Banagi* (1980), which contains 8 prose pieces and 24 poems ; therein is also included *Badi Ghodi* by D.D.S. Gaur. He has composed heroic and patriotic poems as also poems in the style of Nayi Kavita. He has written some powerful short stories as well.

PREM NARAYAN AGRAWAL. Modern Hindi writer of Fiji, whose chief work is *Pravasi*.

PREM NARAYAN TANDON (1915-73). Scholar, who is known for his *Hindi Sevi Sansar, Bisvin Shatabdi ke Purva Hindi Gadya ka Vikas, Braj Bhasha Vyakaran ki Ruprekha* (1962) and *Hindi Sahitya men Hasya Vyangya*. He wrote almost 100 books on Hindi language and literature, mainly for students.

PREM NATH DAR (1914-76). Kashmiri-speaking Hindi writer, who retired as Director (Programme) of All India Radio. *Ghar-ki Bat* (Domestic Scenes) is his one-act plays, while *Kaghaz ka Vasudev* (The Insignificant Vasudev) and *Nili Ankhen* (The Blue Eyes) are his novels. He was an Urdu writer and as such in his Hindi, Urdu idioms are found in quite a good number.

PREM QAIDI. Modern Hindi poet of Nepal, who is noted for his stray poems.

PREM-RATNA. See *Fazil Shah*.

PREM SAGAR. It was first tr. into English by Capt. W. Holings in 1848. It was further tr. by E.B. Eastwick in 1851 under the title *The Ocean of Love* ; this tr. was further revised and published by Frederick Pincott in 1897. It was also tr. into French in 1893. J.F. Burns published *Selection from Prem Sagar* in 1877 with Hindi and English versions. See *Lallu Lal*.

PREM SAKHI (fl. 1734). Poet of the Ram-cult, who composed *Sitaram Nakhshikh, Hori Chhandadi Prabandh* and *Kavittadi Prabandh*.

PREM SHANKAR SINGH. Maithili scholar, whose *Maithili Natak Parichay* (1981) critically describes Maithili dramatists and their works.

PREM SWARUP GUPTA (1927-). Writer, whose chief works are : *Rasagangadhara ka Shastriya Adhyayan, Hindi Vaishnav Sahitya men Rasa Parikalpana* and *Abhinav ka Rasa-Vivechan* (research) ; all on poetics.

PREM YOGI MAN. Modern Hindi poet of Fiji, whose chief work is : *Sath Sal ka Buddha*.

PREMA, V.K. Tamil-speaking Hindi scholar, who is noted for

her *Hindi Kavya men Swapna* (Dream in Hindi Poetry ; thesis ; 1972).

PREMANAND. Modern Hindi writer of Surinam, whose *Pardeshi* is a drama.

PREMANAND, SWAMI (1783-1854). Gujarati-speaking Hindi poet of Swaminarayan Sect, who was a great devotee of Sahajanand. His chief works in Hindi are : *Dhyan Manjari*, *Harinarayan Charitamrit*, *Shikshapatri*, *Vivek-Sar*, etc. In his *Padas*, he has sung of the birth and sports of Krishna.

PREMASHRAM (The Hermitage of Love). Novel (1922) by Prem Chand (q.v.), which describes the sad lot of the poor peasants in the countryside, arising from the tyranny and greed of Zamindars who live as mere parasites.

Gyanshankar, a Zamindar of Lakhanpur, though married, has fallen in love with his widow sister-in-law Gayatri and is ultimately appointed as the Manager of her Estate at Gorakhpur. In the meantime, Gyan Shankar's elder brother, Prem Shankar returns from America ; he gives free advice to the villagers on agricultural and other topics. Gyan Shankar leaves Gorakhpur for Lucknow, where he is followed by Gayatri. When their love reaches the climax, Gyanshankar's wife, Vidyavati cannot bear all this and she passes away. Gayatri also meets her end, when she slips from a hill where she has gone on pilgrimage. There is a complete transformation in the life of Gyanshankar ; Gayatri had adopted Gyanshankar's son, Mayashankar. Premshankar has started a Premashram and Mayashankar is so much impressed by the activities of the Ashram, that he donates his whole property to it. Gyanshankar also wishes to join the Ashram, but feeling shy of his past deeds, he plunges into the Ganges.

Apart from the main story, there are characters, associated with Zamindari system, whose activities are exposed in this novel, but the novelist has discussed at length the problems arising out of the relations between the peasants and the Zamindars.

PREMI (fl. 17th cent.). Kashmiri Sufi poet, whose *Prem Prakash* in Hindi has leanings more towards Khari Boli than Avadhi.

PREMI See *Harikrishna 'Premi'*.

PRICE, WILLIAM. Author of *A New Grammar of Hindoostani Language, with Selection from the Best Authors, to which are added Familiar Phrases in the Proper Character* (London, 1827). He also prepared a *Hindi-English Dictionary* of difficult words of *Prem Sagar* in 1814.

'PRITAM'. See *Ali Muhib Khan 'Pritam'*.

PRITAM DAS (*c*. 1718-97). Gujarati saint-poet, who was next to Akha (q.v.) in popularity. Pritam, belonging to the Barot caste, was born in the village Bawla near Ahmedabad. From his childhood, he enjoyed the company of saints and monks and composed *Bhajans*. When a band of Ramanandi Sadhus reached his village, Pritam also joined their prayers and was ultimately initiated in their Sect by Bhaidas. After 1761, he migrated to the Sandesar village, where his *Gaddi* exists to this day. His Hindi works include *Saras Gita*, *Gyan Prakash*, *Bhagavadgita*, *Prem Prakash* and some *Bhajans*, which he composed before settling down at Sandesar. His poetry is very sweet.

PRITHARANI DE (1938-). Assamese-speaking Hindi critic and essayist, who has made a comparative study of female characters of the fiction of Premchand and Sharat Chandra.

PRITHWI CHAND (fl. prior to 1685). Maithili poet, who refers to a patron called Mallik Dular. His lyrics were quoted in anthologies.

PRITHWI CHANDRA CHARITRA (*Vagvilas*). See *Manikyachandra Suri*.

PRITHWI NATH (fl. *c*. 1450-1550). Celebrated Nath poet, whose four poems : *Sadh Parikhya*, *Niranjan Nirvan*, *Bhakti Vaikunth Jog* and *Sabadi* were known till recently. As a result of further research, as many as 25 more poems and some *Padas* have come to light. Some of these are : *Pran Pachchisi*, *Sikh Sambodh*, *Atma Parchai*, *Gyan Pachchisi*, *Bharam Vidhuns*, *Tat Sangram*, *Man Thamb Sarir Sadhan*, *Mul Padam Mahagyan*, *Solah Kala* and *Solah Tithi*.

The poems of Prithwinath deal with various aspects of Nathism and their language is Khari Boli mixed with Rajasthani and sometimes with Braj.

PRITHWI NATH 'PUSHP' (1917-83). Hindi writer of Jammu and Kashmir, who has edited several works and his research articles have appeared in several magazines and papers. He has edited the magazines : 'Chandroday' and 'Mahavir Dal' and has made a notable contribution to propagation of Hindi.

Under the title *Parmanand Pravah*, he has tr. into Hindi verse a selection of Kashmiri writings of Parmanand.

PRITHWI NATH SHARMA. Writer, whose chief works are: *Duvidha* (Dilemma ; 1938), *Aparadhi* (The Culprit ; 1939), *Sadhu* (A Hermit ; 1944), *Urmila* (1950 ; based on the wife of Lakshman), *Naya Rup* (all dramas), *Vidrup*, *Jyotidan* (novels), *Vivah-Chakra tatha any Kahaniyan* (short story collection) and *Drishti ka Dosh* (one-act plays). His field of specialisation is the world of marriage and human love.

PRITHWI NATH SHARMA 'MADHUP' (1934-). Kashmiri-speaking Hindi poet, whose *Ve Mukhar Kshan* (Those Noisy Moments) is a poetical collection. *Vani Vitasta Ki* is a verse rendering in Hindi of Kashmiri folksongs, while *Kavishri Mala : Parmanand* is on the Jammu-Kashmir poet, Parmanand.

PRITHWI RAJ RASO. Ballad in Dingal by Chand Vardayi (q.v. ; fl. 1126-93). The work describes the battles, marriages and the hunting expeditions of Prithwiraj (1169-1211), king of Delhi and Ajmer. It is an enormous work, consisting of 16,306 pages and is divided into 39 cantos.

Someshwar, the Chauhan king of Ajmer, marries Kamala, the first daughter of Anangapal, the king of Delhi and Prithwiraj is born of this marriage. Anangapal gives his second daughter Sundari in marriage to Vijaypal, the king of Kannauj and from this marriage, Jaychand Rathore is born. When Anangpal adopts Prithviraj as his heir, the kingdoms of Ajmer and Delhi are united. At this, Jaychand feels small and to establish his importance, he decides to perform a *Rajsuy-yagya*, to which all the Rajas except Prithwiraj are invited. To add insult to injury, a golden image of Prithwiraj is installed at the gate of the *Pandal*. On this occasion, Jaychand also organises a *Swayamvar* for his daughter, Sanyogita ; the latter garlands the image of Prithwiraj, thus showing her choice. Prithwiraj abducts Sanyogita but while he is carrying her away to Delhi, he is pursued and attacked by the soldiers of Jaychand. A pitched battle ensues but Prithwiraj is successful in reaching Delhi with his bride.

In the meantime, Shahabuddin Ghori falls in love with Chitrarekha, the wife of one of his own courtiers. The couple escape to Delhi and seek the refuge of Prithwiraj, which according to the Rajput code of honour, he cannot deny. Ghori sends a message to Prithwiraj for the return of the couple but the request is turned down. Shahabuddin makes several onslaughts on the kingdom of Delhi, but all of them are beaten off. During this period, Prithwiraj marries many wives and wages several battles with Rajas. Shahabuddin's chance comes when Prithwiraj has dissipated his military power in fighting against Jaychand and other Rajput Rajas and is sunk deep in pleasurable pursuits. He defeats Prithwiraj and takes him as a captive to his capital. Chand, entrusting the *Raso* to his son Jalhan, also reaches there. One day, when Prithwiraj has been produced in the court to display his feats of archery, he takes a hint from Chand and pierces Shahabuddin's head with his arrow. Thereafter, Chand and Prithwiraj kill each other.

The original manuscript of the *Raso* is not available ; the Nagari Pracharini Sabha, Kashi got it printed on the basis of the manuscript prepared under the patronage of king Amar Singh (fl. *c.* 1583) of Ajmer. The *Raso* is often described as an epic though it does not have all the essential characteristics of an epic. The structure of the poem is loose ; language, though literary, varies considerably from one part to another. It employs, however, all the principal metres—*Kavitta, Chhappay, Duha, Tomar, Shardulvikridit, Sragadhra, Trotak, Arya,* etc., then in use. The principal Rasas are *Vir* and *Shringar*.

For a long time, this work was hailed as the first Hindi epic, but serious doubts have arisen about its authenticity and date as well as about the personality of its composer, Chand Vardayi.

PRITHWI RAJ RATHORE (1549-1600). Rajasthani poet, who was one of the sons of Rao Kalyanmal, the ruler of Bikaner and a grandson of Rao Jaitsi. As such, he was a brother of Rajsingh, the ruler of Bikaner. He was married to Lalade, the daughter of Raval Har Raj of Jaisalmer but after her death, he married her sister, Chanpade. He has been praised for his bravery as also for poetry. His religious devotion has been mentioned in Nabhadas's *Bhaktamal* (q.v.). Most of the time he remained in the court of Akbar and was his court-poet. He despatched a letter to Maharana Pratap, dissuading him from making a truce with Akbar.

Prithwiraj is known for his *Veli Krisan Rukmani Ri* (q.v.), though he composed stray verses, *Dohas* and *Gits,* which eulogize Ram, Krishna, the river Ganga and many heroes. His works are : *Dasam Bhagavat ra Duha* (an epitome of the 10th canto of the *Bhagavat Puran* in 184 *Dohas*), *Ganga Lahari* (in about 80 *Dohas* is praised the river goddess Ganga), *Vasaderavrit* (on Krishna in 165 Dohas), *Dasharathravrit* (praise of Ram in about 65 *Dohas*) and *Sakh ri Git* (containing his short verses).

PRITHWI RAJ SANDU (fl. 18th cent.). Rajasthani court-poet of Maharaja Abhaysingh of Jodhpur, whose *Abhay-Vilas* in sundry metres, describes the life and battles of Maharaja Abhaysingh (r. 1724-49) and also gives his genealogy beginning with Jaychand. The poem mentions dates of salient events and is noted for its racy diction. The available manuscript of the poem is incomplete and from its colophon, it appears that probably the poet himself could not complete it. The poet avoids mentioning the flight of Jasvant Singh from the battlefield of Dharmat.

PRITHWI SINGH AZAD. Modern writer, who is the author of *Yuga-pravartak Sant Guru Ravidas.*

PRIYADAS (fl. 1712). Famous poet of the Ram-cult, who wrote a commentary on the *Bhaktamal* (q.v.), entitled *Bhakta Rasa Bodhini* (1712) in *Kavitta* metre. The commentary is most helpful in understanding the *Bhaktamal*, though at places by a series of disjoined and inexplicit allusions to different legendary events in the saints' lives, he has made his descriptions confused. Priyadas also composed another work, *Ashtayam*, recently discovered, which is one of the earliest specimens of Brajbhasha prose.

PRIYA PRAVAS (The Sojourn of the Loved). Poem (1914) by Ayodhyasingh Upadhyay 'Hariaudh', which is considered as the first epic of Khari Boli. Its diction, vocabulary and metrical form are all Sanskritic, a fact which has made it difficult to be appreciated.

Based on the episode of Krishna's departure from Gokul to Mathura, leaving the Gopikas and Radha suffering the pangs of separation, it places Krishna on a high pedestal as a national hero and social reformer ; even Radha is shown as having dedicated herself to the service of the poor and the downtrodden.

The epic is full of excellent descriptions of Nature : the flowers, the blossoming trees, the streams, sun-rise and moonlit nights. The noet is equally deft in delineating human character and feminine beauty.

PUHUKAR (fl. early half of 16th cent.). Hindu Sufi poet of Mainpuri in Uttar Pradesh, who appeared to have received Jahangir's patronage. His *Rasaratna* (composed in 1616), written in Brajbhasha instead of Avadhi, is an epic poem in 9 cantos, containing 2,800 stanzas; it is an allegorical romance on the love story of Rambhavati and Sursen and is considered to be of great literary value. The language is, however, dominated by erotic flavour.

PUHUPAVATI. Poem of Duhkh Harandas (fl. 1673), which is a love-story of Rajkunvar and Puhupavati.

PULAKIT LAL DAS 'MADHUR'. Maithili poet, who is known for his Khandkavya *Rambha-Shuk-Sanvad* (1936).

PULI BAI. Rajasthani saint-poetess, whose stray verses are available; her time is not certain.

PULLARAO, VAI. Telugu-speaking modern Hindi poet, who is noted for his *Swarnapath* (The Golden Path).

PUND (PUSHYA). Poet, who is mentioned in the *Shivsingh Saroj* as a poet; he flourished in 713 in the court of Raja Man, one of the forefathers of Raja Bhoj. He had written some work in *Dohas* on *Alankar*, but this is no longer extant. He can safely be called the first Hindi poet, as also the pioneer of literary criticism in Hindi.

PURANDAS (1678-1735). Rajasthani saint-poet of Ram Snehi Sampraday, Ren, who was initiated in 1715 by Dariyav (q.v.) and spent his remaining life at Ren. His works, which deal with Ram Bhakti, are *Brahm Prakash*, *Brahm Vilas* and *Vani* under different topics.

PURANDAS (1771-1835). Rajasthani saint-poet of Ram Snehi Sampraday, Khedapa, who was born in the village Malaki in Malwa and was dedicated by his parents to Pithodas (q.v.), who sent him to Khedapa, where Dayaladas (q.v.) initiated him 1781. A householder, Purandas became Acharya in 1828. His *Vani*, giving information about many saint-poets, consists of *Guru Mahima*, *Bhaktamal*, *Janma Lila*, *Sumiran Sar*, *Karuna Chhattisi*, *Shiksha Battisi*, *Padas* and stray verses.

PURAN MALL, KAVIRAJ (fl. prior to 1685). Maithili poet, who may be identified with the grandson of Jagjjyotirmall's daughter. His lyrics were quoted in anthologies.

PURANIK, BA. KE. 'KESHAVTANYA'. Marathi-speaking modern Hindi poet, whose poems are written on various subjects. He is also the author of *Shraddha ka Phal* (The Fruit of Faith).

PURANIK, PRA. D. Marathi-speaking modern *Hindi* scholar, whose chief work is Hindi *Adhyapan Paddhati*.

PURNA, DEVI PRASAD. See *Devi Prasad 'Purna' Ray*.

PURNA SINGH ADHYAPAK (1881-1931). Essayist, who was born in a Sikh family. His essays 'Kanyadan ya Nayanon ki Ganga', 'Pavitrata', 'Acharan ki Sabhyata', 'Mazduri aur Prem' and 'Sachchi Virta' were written in pure Khari Boli. His scanty prose writings show him to be a remarkable stylist. The total number of essays written by him is 8, while 6 of his essays have been printed in *Sardar Purna Singh Adhyapak ke Nibandh.*

PURNA VIRAM. Modern Hindi poet of Nepal, who is noted for his stray poems.

PURNAM SOMSUNDARAM. Tamil-speaking modern Hindi writer, who is noted for his *Tamil aur Uska Sahitya* (Tamil and Its Literature). He has also tr. into Hindi Krishnamurti Kalki's Tamil novel under the title *Chor ki Premika* (The Beloved of a Thief).

PUROHIT, B.N. Rajasthani scholar, who has edited *Rajasthani Gadya Chayanika* (1982), which includes all genres of prose and styles of writing.

PURUSHARTH VATI (fl. early 20th cent.). Hindi writer of Jammu & Kashmir, who was noted for her poetical work, *Antarvedana* (The Inner Anguish), which was published from Lahore.

PURUSHOTTAM ANANG BHIMDEV (1729-76). Raja of Badkhemundi in Orissa, whose Hindi (Brajboli) poems are extant.

PURUSHOTTAM CHAKRAVARTI. Writer, who in his short story collection, *Gulmohur ki Hansi* (The Laughter of Gulmohurs; 1980) describes the inconsistencies in the urban life.

PURUSHOTTAM CHHANGANI. Rajasthani poet and writer of Jaisalmer, whose *Sansan ro Sut* (1978) is a collection of 24 poems. He has also written short stories.

PURUSHOTTAM DAS (fl. early 16th cent.). Bengali Vaishnav poet, who also composed *Padas* in Brajbuli.

PURUSHOTTAM DAS PUROHIT. Modern Rajasthani scholar, whose chief work is *Pushkaranon ka Samajik Git.*

PURUSHOTTAM DOBHAL. Modern Garhwali writer, who is noted for his drama *Bindra* and stray poems.

PURUSHOTTAM KAVI, NADELL (1863-1938). Telugu-speaking writer of Machhlipattnam, who was a great scholar of Telugu and Sanskrit. In Hindi, he composed during 1884-86 no less than 32 plays, out of which 14 plays and some *Bhajans* (hymns) are extant; these have been edited and published by K. Sharada, the grand-daughter of the poet. Most of his plays are based on the *Ramayan*, *Mahabharat*, Purans and history. One play : *Ramdas Charitramu* was published by the poet in Telugu characters. In his childhood, Purushottam lived in Hyderabad and thus got fluency in Dakkhini. The language of his plays is Sanskritized Hindi.

PURUSHOTTAM LAL. Chhattisgarhi folk-poet, whose chief work is *Congress Alha* (1938).

PURUSHOTTAM MENARIYA. Modern Rajasthani scholar, who has made significant contribution to the study of folk-songs (*Rajasthani Lok-Git*).

PURUSHOTTAM 'SAINYA' (b. 1885). Poet of Mathura, whose stray verses are extant.

PUSHPA BUMA. Modern Hindi writer of Mauritius, who is noted for her short stories.

PUSHYA. See *Pund.*

PUTTRAJ GAVAI. Kannada-speaking modern Hindi writer, who tr. the *Basaveshwar Purana* from Kannada into Hindi.

PYARE DAS (fl. 1568). Gujarati-speaking saint-poet, who was a disciple of Madhav Das (q.v.) and ascended the *Gaddi* after his preceptor's death. According to popular beliefs, he was delivered by his Guru from the clutches of Virmati, a prostitute. With his Guru, he settled down in Surat (Gujarat). His Hindi *Padas* describe the pangs of separation from his Lord.

PYARE RAM. Rajasthani saint-poet and a follower of Haridas Niranjani Sect, whose *Bhaktamal*, composed in 1826, gives an account of many saints, chiefly the Niranjanis.

Q

QADIR (fl. 1569). Muslim poet of the Krishna-cult, who was a a resident of Hardoi in Uttar Pradesh. His command over Brajbhasha was exceptionally good; some of his verses are still quoted in literary circles.

QALAM KA SIPAHI. See *Amrit Ray.*

QASIM SHAH (b. 1732). Sufi poet of Dariyabad (Barabanki district), who was the author of the *Hans Javahar* (q.v.), a Sufi allegorical romance.

QAZI ANWAR (1842-1915). Sufi poet of Gujarat, who was son of Qazi Ajamiya of Visnagar. He composed *Bhajans*, *Sakhis*, *Ghazals*, *Garbis*, etc. in Khari Boli, which is influenced by Persian.

QUTUB SATAK. Romantic poem (Script 1573) by an unknown poet, which describes the love-story of Prince Qutub with a Muslim woman, Kishori Sahiba.

Q

QADIR (fl. 1569). Muslim poet of the Krishna-cult, who was a resident of Hardoi in Uttar Pradesh. His command over Brajbhasha was exceptionally good; some of his verses are still quoted in literary circles.

QALAM KA SIPAHI. See *Amrit Rai.*

QASIM SHAH (b. 1732). Sufi poet of Dariyabad (Barabanki district), who was the author of the *Hans Jawahir* (q.v.), a Sufi allegorical romance.

QAZI ANWAR (1[illegible]-191[illegible]). Sufi poet of Gujarat, who was son of Qazi Ajm[illegible] of Visnagar. He composed *Bhajans*, [illegible] *Garbis*, etc., in Khari Boli which is influenced by Persian.

QUTUB SATAK. Romantic poem (Script 1573) by an unknown poet, which describes the love-story of Prince Qutub with a Muslim woman, Kishori Sahiba.

R

RACHNA (fl. 1813). Poet of the Ram-cult, who composed *Satyopakhyan*.

RADHA, KUMARI. Modern Magahi poetess, who is noted for her stray poems.

RADHA CHARAN (fl. 1878). Poet of the Krishna-cult (Chaitanya Sect), who was son of Ladililal. He was the author of *Chaitanya Charit*.

RADHA CHARAN GOSWAMI (1859-1925). Dramatist, who, deeply influenced by Bharatendu Harishchandra's writings in the 'Harishchandra Magazine', also started a monthly from Mathura, called 'Bharatendu'. Goswami was a Brahmo Samajist by faith and influenced by Bharatendu, he took to social reform in Hindu society. Among his dramas : *Sati Chandravali* (on the sad plight of Hindus during the bigoted Auranzeb's reign ; 1890), *Vidhva Vipatti* (The Woes of Widowhood), *Kalpalata*, *Amar Singh Rathore* (1895; historical), *Sudama*, *Tan-Man Dhan Shri Gosainji ke Arpan*, etc., the first two are better known. He also tr. into Hindi three Bengali novels, *Viraj*, *Javitri* and *Mrinmayi*. In 1887, he wrote a novel, *Budhe Munh Muhase* (satire ; tr. from Bengali) and also wrote short stories ('Saudamini', 'Hire ka Mol', etc.). He was connected in one way or the other with Nagari Pracharini Sabha and Hindi Sahitya Sammelan.

RADHA KRISHNA CHAUDHARY. Maithili critic, whose *Mahakavi Lal Das*, a critical work, has been published in 1981 under the Mithilak Bibhuti Series. Earlier his *Sharantidha* (1969), a collection of philosophical essays, makes profound comments on life and letters and embodies a life-time quest for truth. He has also written articles.

RADHA KRISHNA DAS (1865-1907). Writer and poet, who was a cousin of Bharatendu Harishchandra (q.v.) and whose drama,

Sati Pratap was completed by him. Radha Krishna Das's dramas are : *Dukhi Duniya* (The Unhappy World), *Dukhini Bala* (The Unhappy Girl), *Maharani Padmini* (*Padmavati*), *Dharmalap*, and the best of all *Maharana Pratap* or *Rajasthan Kesri* (1887). He turned to history for a serious representation of lofty ideals of nationalism. His other works are *Nihsahay Hindu* (The Help-less Hindus; novel), *Swarnalata* and *Marta Kya na Karta* (the last two novels tr. from Bengali). He also wrote some short stories ('Ramlila', etc.), composed some poems in Khari Boli and Brajbhasha and wrote *Kundlis* on Rahim's *Dohas*.

RADHA KRISHNA JHA 'Bahed'. Modern Maithili writer, who is noted for his short stories as also for his lyrics; he specialises in humorous poetry of the countryside.

RADHA KRISHNA MUDALIAR. Tamil and Kannada-speaking modern Hindi poet, whose *Dyuti-Shruti-Vahini*, a collection of poems, is a unique type of work as it takes five *Padas* each from the 21 languages of India with Hindi rendering.

RADHA NATH RAY. Celebrated modern Oriya poet, who has tr. into Oriya some portions of Tulsidas's *Ramcharitmanas*.

RADHA RAMAN. Maithili poet, whose *Ek Akhi Ganga* (1967), a collection of lyrics, is an exponent of pathetic sentiments.

RADHA VALLABH DAS (fl. end of 16th cent.). Bengali Vaishnav poet, who also composed *Padas* in Brajbuli.

RADHA-VIVAH. See *Kashikant Mishra 'Madhup'*.

RADHE SHYAM KATHAVACHAK (1890-1963). Religious preacher (*Kathavachak*) of Bareilly, whose style of preaching was very attractive. The *Radheshyam Ramayan* became a best-seller of his times. Excerpts from his *Kathas* were also popular in gramophone records. His association with Alfred Theatre Company resulted in his writing dramas, which became very popular. His chief dramas are: *Vir Abhimanyu*, *Usha-Aniruddha*, *Bhakta Prahlad* and *Shrikrishnavtar*.

RADHE SHYAM MISHRA (fl. 1st half of 20th cent.). Writer, who was noted for his drama, *Council ki Memberi* (The Membership of the Council ; 1920).

RADHE SHYAM SHARMA Modern Rajasthani poet, who has composed patriotic and heroic poems.

RADHIKA DAS (b. 1713). Poet of the Krishna-cult (Chaitanya

Sect), who was born in Vrindavan. His *Bhav-Sindhu* (1755) is a small work.

RADHIKADEVI SHRIVASTAV. Modern Bhojpuri writer, who is noted for her humorous short stories.

RADHIKA NATH (b.*c.* 1543). Poet of the Krishna-cult (Chaitanya Sect), who was a disciple of Ramray (q.v.). He composed poems under the pen names of 'Radhapriya', 'Shyama' and 'Makhan'. His works are : *Mahavani, Prem Samput, Radha Rasa Sudhanidhi* and *Rasabindu.* He also wrote a prose work: *Pranalika* in 1583.

RADHIKA RAMAN PRASAD SINGH (1890-1971). Fiction writer, who was born at Suryapura in the Shahbad district of Bihar. His chief works are : *Ram-Rahim* (1936), *Purush aur Nari* (The Man and Woman), *Savani Sabha, Surdas, Tuta Tara* (The Broken Star), *Gandhi Topi* (The Gandhi Cap), *Chumban aur Chanta* (The Kiss and Slap), *Van Jivan va Prem Lahari* (The Forest Life or the Tide of Love) (novels), *Galpa Kusumavali* and *Chuni Kaliyan* (The Select Buds; short story collections); he was one of the early writers of Hindi short stories. His 'Kanon men Kangna' (Bracelet in the Ears) is a poetic story, idealising the reform of character. He founded a Hindi publishing house in Patna.

RAGA-TARANGINI. See *Lochan Kavi.*

RAGHAV DAS. Rajasthani saint-poet, who was a Kshatriya by caste and was a disciple of Prahlad Das. His famous *Bhaktamal* (1660) describes the lives of chief Mahants of Dadu Panth and is very useful. In 1800, Chaturdas wrote a commentary on it in verse.

RAGHAV DAS, BABA (1896-1958). Assamese political worker, whopromoted the cause of Hindi by founding Assam Hindi Prachar Samiti (now known as Assam Rashtrabhasha Prachar Samiti).

RAGHAVACHARYA SHASTRI (1917-). Maithili poet, whose lyrics in *Kranti Git* (1930), *Ban Kusum, Jwalamukhi* (1936) and *Madhukan* (1949), have given the direct impetus to Maithili movement. His *Malladev-Vijay,* a poem, remains unpublished.

RAGHAVAN, T.E.S. Tamil-speaking modern Hindi poet, whose *Kamb,* a collection of poems, deals with contemporary problems.

RAGHAVAN, T.M. Tamil-speaking modern Hindi writer, who is the author of *Bal Ramayan,* a Ramayan for children.

RAGHAVAN NAIR, A.N. (fl. 1950). Malayalam-speaking Hindi writer, who wrote works on Hindi grammar.

RAGHU BIR NARAYAN (fl. 1st half of 20th cent.). Bhojpuri poet, who was born at the village Naya Ganv of Chhapra district in Bihar. His only work is 'Batohiya' song, which became very popular; the song presents a glorious heritage of India.

RAGHU NANDAN. Maithili poet, who was noted for his lyrics. He was a contemporary of Maharaja Lakshmishwar Singh (1878-98). He also composed hymns on devotional and pseudo-philosophical subjects.

RAGHU NANDAN DAS. Maithili poet, whose *Subhadra-Haran* (*c.* 1937-44) in 10 cantos deals with the famous episode of Arjun carrying away Subhadra. His *Bir Balak* (1926), *Khandkavya,* is on the story of Ramchandra's two brave sons, Kush and Lav. He was the author of a drama, *Mithila Natak* as also of a one-act play, 'Dutangad Vyayog' (on Angad's mission to Ravan).

RAGHUNATH (fl. 1733-53). Poet of the Riti school, who was the court-poet of Raja Bariband Singh of Kashi. He composed four works : *Rasik Mohan* (a book on the *Alankars* giving fine illustrations), *Kavya Kaladhar* (treating of the *Nayikabhed* at some length, though the *Rasas* and *Bhavas* have been touched upon), *Jagat Mohan* (describing the daily routine of a sensuous ruler) and *Ishq Mahotsav* (a book of verses in Khari Boli).

RAGHUNATH CHARIT NAV RASA VELI. Rajasthani poem, composed by Maheshdas Rao (1646-98; q.v.) on the story of Ram. A poem of 127 verses, it describes the story up to the return of the marriage party from Janakpur and its reception at Ayodhya. The language is Rajasthani with a mixture of Braj. Shatrughna has been depicted to be talkative and has been shown to have had an argument with Parshuram.

RAGHUNATH DAS (fl. 16th cent.). Bengali Vaishnav poet, who, though, belonged to a lower caste, was held in the highest esteem even by Brahmins. He composed some *Padas* in Brajbuli.

RAGHUNATH DAS. Rajasthani saint-poet and a follower of Haridas Niranjani Sect, whose *Swami Haridasji ki Parchi* (composed about 1773) narrates the life of Haridas (q.v.).

RAGHUNATH DAS (fl. early 19th cent.). Rajasthani saint-poet of Ram Snehi Sampraday, Sinthal, whose *Vani* consists of stray verses in popular metres. He was the fourth Acharya to occupy the *Gaddi* at *Sinthal.*

RAGHUNATH DAS RAM SANEHI, BABA (fl. early 19th cent.). Poet of Ayodhya, whose *Vishram-Sagar* is a verse rendering of scenes and episodes taken from various Purans. It has a popular appeal and is widely read.

RAGUNATH DAYAL. Modern Hindi writer of Mauritius, who is noted for his short stories.

RAGHUNATH MAHAPATRA. Oriya-speaking modern Hindi writer, who is associated with Hindi teaching in Orissa.

RAGHUNATH RUPAK GITAN RO. Rajasthani poem by Manchharam (q.v.), which was composed by him in 1806. A Riti work, it describes the story of *Ramayan* by way of illustrations. The work was popular due to its brevity, clarity and systematic treatment.

Divided into 9 cantos, the first two are of general nature, while the remaining seven cantos deal with 72 types of Dingal *Gits,* the prose styles, *Nisani* and other metres. The illustrative part is in charming narrative poetry and is important in the tradition of Ram-kavyas

RAGHUNATH SHAMBHU RAO KELKAR. Marathi-speaking modern Hindi novelist, whose chief works are : *Tin Murti* and *Tripur-Sundari,* which portray political and social life.

RAGHUNATH SHARMA. Modern Hindi writer of Thailand, who is noted for his promotion of the cause of Hindi in his country through Thai-Bharat Sanskriti Ashram.

RAGHUNATH SINGH, MEHTA. Modern Rajasthani scholar, who is noted for his *Jaisalmeriya Sangit-Ratnakar.*

RAGHURAJ SINGH (1723-79). Poet, who was ruler of Rewa ; his chief works are : *Ram Swayamvar, Rukmini Parinay* (The Marriage of Rukmini), *Anandambu-Nidhi* and *Ramashtayam* (Description of a day and night in Ram's life).

RAGHURAJ SINGH HADA. Rajasthani poet of Jhalawar, whose works are : *Phul Kasula Phul* (1976 ; a collection of one-page 50 poems) and *Hardaul* (1978 ; on the Bundelkhand warrior Hardaul), *An Banchya Akhar* (1970 ; a story in verse) and *Ghughara.* He has also composed some Nature, patriotic, progressive and love poems.

RAGHURAM NAGAR (fl. 1700). Writer of Ahmedabad, whose *Sabha Sar* (1700) is a one-man narration and does not have dialogues. The author calls, however, his work as Natak. The language has a curious mixture of Urdu words.

RAGHURAM ROHADIYA, CHARAN. See *Dev Lila Kavya*.

RAGHUVANSH. Writer, whose chief works are : *Sahitya ka Naya Pariprekshay* (The New Background of Literature ; criticism) and *Tantujal* (1958 ; novel), *Arthahin* (short story collections), *Hindi Sahitya Kosh* (ed., vol. II), *Kavya aur Prakriti* (Poetry and Nature ; research) ; he edited 'Ka-Kha-Ga' for two years, a serious bimonthly from Allahabad. His other works on criticism are : *Adhunikta aur Sarjanshilta* (Modernity and Creativity ; 1980), *Natyakala* and *Samsamyikta aur Adhunik Hindi Kavita*. He was Head of the Department of Hindi, Allahabad University, Allahabad.

RAGHUVAR-JAS PRAKASH. Rajasthani *Lakshan* poetry, which was composed by Kishanji in 1824. Divided into five parts, its first three parts treat of metres, prose styles ; the fourth deals with 91 types of Dingal *Gits*, while the last part explains 12 main types of *Nisani* with their sub-divisions. When dealing with these topics, the poet has exalted Ram and hence the title of the book. The explanations in poetry and prose are lucid.

RAGHUVAR SHARAN (fl. 1850). Poet of the Ram-cult, whose chief works are : *Ram-mantra-Rahasya*, *Janaki ji ko Mangalacharan* and *Bana* (Dulah Ram).

RAGHUVIR CHAUDHARI. Modern Gujarati novelist, whose research work in Hindi is : *Hindi evam Gujarati ke Kriya-Rup*. In Hindi he has published two novels: *Amrita* and *Satah ke Upar Satah ke Niche*.

RAGHUVIR SAHAY (1929-). Poet of *Dusra Saptak* (q.v.), whose chief poetical works are : *Sidhiyon par Dhup Men* (On the Stair in the Sun ; 1959), *Atmahatya ko Viruddha* (Againsit Suicide ; 1967 ; on political subjects), *Hanso, Hanso, Jald Hanso*, *Delhi Mera Pardes* and *Log Bhul Gaye Hain* ; his chief short stories are 'Mere aur Nangi Aurat ke Bich' (Between Me and a Naked Woman) and 'Seb'. As a fiction writer, his work is *Jo Admi Ham Bana Rahen Hain*. "His poems carry a foretaste of the change from the existentialist negation and defeatism of *Nayi Kavita* to the trend of socio-political realism, which was soon to emerge."

RAGHUVIR SHARAN MITRA. Modern novelist and poet, whose chief works are : *Ag aur Pani, Rakta Surya, Sada Sada ke Prashna* (novels), *Jan Nayak* (on Jawahar Lal Nehru), *Bhumija, Virayan* and *Manavendra* (poetical works). He has also written dramas.

RAGHUVIR SHARAN 'VYATHIT'. Modern Hindi writer, who has tr. Malayalam drama of T.N. Gopinathan Nair into Hindi under the title *Pariksha* (The Test).

RAGHUVIR SINGH (1908-). Modern writer, who is Rajkumar of Sitamau and is son of Rathore ruler Sir Ram Singh. A noted historian, his *Malwa men Yugantar* (Malwa in Transition) is a research work. His chief work, *Shesh Smritiyan* is full of vivid memories of the past and gives interesting pictures of life during Muslim rule in India. His other works are : *Saptadip, Jivan-Dhuli, Jivan-Kan* (essay collections) and *Bikhre Phul*.

RAGPAT KESHLIKUMARI. Modern Hindi poetess of Mauritius, whose chief work is *Vinavadini*.

RAHGIR. Modern Bhojpuri poet, who is known for his stray poems.

RAHI KAUNDINYA. Assamese-speaking modern Hindi writer, who is chiefly an essayist, where his essays generally deal with forest tribes of Arunachal. He has also written a book on Khamati literature and society.

RAHI MASOOM RAZA (1927-). Novelist and poet, whose chief novels are : *Adha Ganv* (Half the Village ; 1966 ; concerning Shia Muslims), *Tipi Shukla* (on the Hindu-Muslim relations), *Himmat Jaunpuri* (on the patriotic spirit of Himmat, a Mohammedan), *Os ki Bund* (Dew-drop ; 1970) *Dil Ek Sada Kaghaz* (The Mind is a Plain Paper), *Katra Bi Arzu* (The Mart of Mrs. Arzu ; on Emergency) and *Scene '75*. *Atharah Sau Sattavan* (1857) is his poetical work, while *Main Ek Pherivala* (I am a Hawker) is a collection of his poems ; *Chhote Admi ki Badi Kahani* (The Big Tale of a Small Man) is an autobiography published by him.

RAHIM. See *Abdur Rahim Khankhana*.

RAHIM SATSAI (*Dohavali*). Work by Rahim (q.v. ; 1553-1626), comprising over 700 *Dohas* or couplets.

The *Dohas* of Rahim are born of the rich experience

which their author had during his military, administrative and varied career. They also reveal the ups and downs which Rahim faced during the reign of two monarchs. In this aspect they stand apart from the *Dohas* of Vrinda which embody cumulated wisdom or that of Bihari which deal with the erotic side of life. The *Dohas* are also remarkable for their artistic rounding-off and in this they seem to be precursors of that of Bihari or Padmakar. Rahim is chiefly popular for his *Satsai*.

RAHMAN KHAN (d. 1974). Modern Hindi poet of Surinam, whose *Kundliyas* and *Dohas* have been published under the titles : *Dohavali* (1953) and *Dohe-Kundliya* (1954). Rahman Khan is considered as the first Hindi poet of Surinam.

RAHMATJI (fl. end of 18th cent.). Rajasthani saint-poet of the Vishnoi Sect, whose stray verses are available.

RAHUL SANKRITYAYAN (1893-1963). Writer, who hailed from Azamgarh in Uttar Pradesh and whose original name was Kedarnath Pande. He became a Buddhist scholar of international repute, an Indologist, a fiction writer, a philologist, a historian and a linguist. His autobiography : *Meri Jivan Yatra* (The Journey of My Life ; 5 Pts.) is a book of gripping interest. *Volga se Ganga* (From Volga to Ganga) is a united string of historical short stories ; his novels are *Singh Senapati* (Singh the General ; in the background of ancient Indian republic, propounding Marxian principles), *Jay Yaudhey* (Glory to the Victorious Yaudheys ; dealing with political conditions during the reign of Imperial Guptas), *Madhur Swapna* (The Sweet Dream) and *Vismrit Yatri* (The Forgotton Pilgrim). His other works are *Satmi ke Bachche* (short story collection), *Puratattva Nibandhavali* (essays), *Hindi Kavya Dhara* (The Stream of Hindi Poetry), *Soviet Bhumi* (Soviet Land ; 2 Pts.), *Darshan Digdarshan*, *Tin Natak*, *Ghumakkar Shastra* (on Roving), *Bhago Nahin Badlo* (Do not run away, but change), *Asia ke Durgam Bhumikhandon Men* (In the inaccesible regions of Asia ; travelogue), *Baisvin Sadi* (22nd Century), *Tibbati Vyakaran* (Tibetan Grammar) ; his magnum opus is *Madhya Asia ka Itihas* (History of Central Asia ; 2 vols.) for which he received the Sahitya Akademi Award.

Rahul Sankrityayan made a special study of Siddha literature, which was then extant in Tibet and towards that end made several trips to that country. A writer of progressive views, he was a Professor in Leningrad University as also in Sri Lanka.

He also wrote in Bhojpuri 8 social dramas : *Naiki Duniya*, *Dhunmun Neta*, *Mehrarun ke Durdasa*, *Jonk*, *I Hamar Larai*,

Des Rachchhak, *Japaniya Rachhachh*, *Jarmanava ke Har Nihichay*, which serve as pathfinders for Bhojpuri dramatists. He was also the author in Khari Boli of *Adi Hindi ki Kahaniyan aur Git*, *Himalaya Parichay* and *Kinnar Desh Men* (In the Land of the Kinnars).

RAIDAS (fl. between 1388 and 1518). Saint-poet of Benares, who was one of the 13 disciples of Ramanand. An illiterate and a cobbler by caste, he founded the Raidasi Panth. Humble by nature and too peace-loving to relish criticism of others, he was widely respected as a saint and a religious leader ; several miracles are associated with his name. Unlike Kabir, who was outspoken, Raidas contented himself with preaching his own doctrine without castigating those who held different views. For the most part of his life, Raidas stayed at Varanasi and it is said that the princess of Chittor (Miranbai ?) became his disciple. While his 41 *Padas* have been incorporated in the *Granth Sahib*, his utterances have been collected in *Ravidas-ke Pada* and *Ravidas-ki Bani*. The simple and sincere piety of his poems makes a powerful appeal. *Prahlad Charit* is also regarded his production.

RAINA, S.K. See *Shiban Krishna Raina*.

RAJ BALI PANDEY (1907-71). Writer, whose chief works concerning Hindi literature are : *Hindi men Uchchatar Sahitya* (Higher Literature in Hindi ; 1957) and *Hindi Sahitya ka Brihat Itihas* (A Comprehensive History of Hindi Literature ; Pt. I).

RAJ BHALLA. Modern Hindi writer of Jammu-Kashmir, who is known for her short stories.

RAJ BUDDHIRAJA. Modern novelist, whose chief works are : *Kanyadan*, *Kaveri* and *Ret ka Tila*.

RAJ GOPALAN, N. VI. Tamil-speaking Hindi scholar, whose chief works are : *Tamil aur Hindi ke Kavyashastron ka Tulnatmak Adhyayan* (A Comparative Study of Poetics of Tamil and Hindi ; 1969), *Urdu Sahitya ka Udbhav aur Vikas* (The Origin and Development of Urdu Literature), *Ansu ki Bhav-Bhumi* (on *Ansu*), *Hindi ka Bhashavaigyanik Vyakaran* (on grammar) and *Tamil Sahitya ka Navin Itihas* (A New History of Tamil Literature). He has done *Kamb Ramayan's* Hindi prose rendering in two parts as Kamb Ramayan and has also tr. Nil Padmanabhan's Tamil novels under the titles : *Yatra ka Ant* (The End of the Journey) and *Shayan ki Nagri* (The City of Sleep).

RAJ HIRAMAN. Modern Hindi writer of Mauritius, who is known for his short stories.

RAJ KAMAL CHAUDHARY (1929-67). Writer and poet, whose chief works are : *Machhli Mari Hui* (The Dead Fish ; 1966 ; description of women engaged in lesbianism), *Shahr Tha, Shahr Nahin Tha* (1966), *Ek Anar Ek Bimar* (One Pomegranate One Patient), *Nadi Bahti Thi* (The River Flowed), *Deh-Gatha* (The Body's Tale), *Agni Snan, Suno Brajnari, Bis Runiyon ka Biscope* (all novels), *Swargandha* and *Muktiprasang* (poetical collections) ; Mohan Bhardwaj has edited *Swargandha* and other poems of Rajkamal (1981). He has also written some short stories, chief ones being 'Chhinnamasta', 'Dampatya' (Conjugal), 'Jalte Makan men Kuchh Log' (Some People in a Burning House), 'Pyramid', etc. ; his short story collection is *Machhli-Jal*.

In Maithili, his chief novels are : *Andolan* (published posthumously in 1968 ; portraying his dreams of a happier and fairer world), *Adikatha* (1958 ; here the heroine is of incestuous and voluptuous character) and *Pathar-Phul* (1967). His short story collection *Laka Pag* (1968) reveals contempt of those, who cannot tolerate free sexual behaviour. He believed in free and frank discussion on sex. He died in the prime of his youth.

RAJ KISHORE KAKKAR. Modern scholar, whose chief work is : *Adhunik Hindi Sahitya men Alochana ka Vikas* (1968).

RAJ KISHORE PANDEY (1920-). Writer, whose chief works on histories of literature are : *Hindi Sahitya ka Prarambhik Yuga* (1977), *Dakhini ka Prarambhik Gadya* (1967), *Hindi Sahitya ka Uttar Madhyayuga* (1972) and *Hindi Sahitya ka Ritikal*.

RAJ KUMAR. Assamese-speaking modern Hindi writer, who is noted for his memoirs and reportage.

RAJ KUMAR KUMBHAJ. Poet, whose poems are included in the *Chautha Saptak* (q.v.) ; *Kachche Ghar ke Liye* (For a Kuchcha House ; 1980) is a collection of his poems.

RAJ KUMAR MISHRA. Writer, whose *Darulsafa* (The Hospital ; 1981) is a novel.

RAJ KUNVARI BIBI. Poetess, whose *Prem Ratna* on Krishna devotion was published in 1890 ; its *Padas* are of fairly high literary merit.

RAJ LAKSHMI. Modern Maithili writer, who is noted for her prose works : *Bhagavat Prakash* and *Gaya-Yatra.*

RAJ MOHAN JHA, SRI. Maithili writer, who is known for his short story collections *Ek Adi Ek Ant* (1965) and *Jhuth Sanch.*

RAJ NARAYAN. Modern Hindi poet of Fiji, whose chief works are : *Sagarika, Sagar Manthan* and *Sagar.*

RAJ NARAYAN AGRAWAL. Modern poet, who is noted for his poem *Kubri* (The hunch-backed woman, who loved Krishna).

RAJ NATH PANDEY (1884-1963). Writer, whose chief works are : *Lankadahan* (The Burning of Lanka ; 1940 ; drama), *Vir Navik Mahajanak* (1942; poem), *Ratnamanjari* (Creeper of Gems ; 1951 ; short story collection) and *Pururava-ki Shapath* (The Oath of Pururava ; 1957 ; novel).

RAJ PRAKASH. See *Kishore Das Rao.*

RAJ RUPAK. Rajasthani narrative poem by Ratanu Virbhan Bhojrajaut (q.v.), which is divided into 46 '*Prakashs*' (chapters) and consists of 3317 verses and 25 *Vachnikas.* It describes the battle of Ahmedabad, which Maharaja Abhaysingh of Jodhpur fought against Sar Bulandkhan, Governor of Gujarat in 1730. After a brief mention of the ancestors from Satram to Maharaja Jasvant Singh, a detailed account of Maharajas Ajitsingh and Abhaysingh of Jodhpur is given. The poem, giving a useful account of the Rathore house, is dominated by heroic sentiments and is replete with descriptions of warriors and battles, their abodes at different heavenly places after death, their marriages with celestial damsels, etc. The work is written in a comparatively simple language.

RAJ SAMUDRA (fl. 1590). Jaina poet, who is known for his didactic verses.

RAJ SHEKHAR SURI (fl. 14th cent.). Celebrated author of the Sanskrit *Prabandha-Kosha,* who also composed two well-known Jain poems in Rajasthani : *Neminath Phagu* and *Tribhuvan Dipak Prabandh* (qq.v.).

RAJ SHRI 'SADLHANA'. Modern Rajasthani poetess, whose poems are permeated with religious and spiritual fervour.

RAJ SINGH, MAHARAJA (fl. 1571-1611). Maharaja of Bikaner, whose Rajasthani stray verses in different popular metres are available.

RAJ SINGH (1674-1748). Ruler of Kishengarh State in Rajasthan, whose three works : *Raj Prakash*, *Bahu Vilas* and *Raspay Nayak* in Pingal are available.

RAJABOV, HABIBULLO (1945-). Soviet Hindi scholar, who has done his doctorate on the short stories of Mohan Rakesh (q.v.). His field of specialization is Hindi short stories.

RAJA RAM SHASTRI (1918-). Dramatist, whose chief collections of one-act plays are : *Satlari ka Har* (The Necklace of Seven Strings) and *Shikar* (The Hunt).

RAJAWAT, KALYAN SINGH. See *Kalyan Singh Rajawat*.

RAJENDRA AVASTHI (1930-). Fiction writer, whose chief works are : *Jangal ke Phul* (The Flowers of the Forest), *Suraj Kiran ki Chhanv* (The Shadow of a Sun-ray; 1959), *Utarte Jwar ke Sipiyan* (The Shells of a Receding Tide ; 1968), *Jane Kitni Ankhen* (How Many Eyes ; 1969), *Bahta Hua Pani* (The Flowing Water ; 1971), *Akeli Avaz* (Lonely Voice), *Bimar Shahr* (The Sick City), *Machhli Bazar* (all novels), *Ek Aurat se Interview* (An Interview with a Woman), *Lamsena* and *Ek Rajnigandha Chori* (1984) (short story collections). His prominent short stories are : 'Ek Pyas : Ek Paheli' (A Thirst : A Riddle), 'Lal Jhanda' (The Red Flag), etc. He has also written a drama. He is the editor of 'Kadambini' and 'Kal-chintan' are his editorials.

RAJENDRA DWIVEDI. Modern scholar, who is noted for his *Sahitya Shastra ka Paribhashik Shabdakosh*.

RAJENDRA GAUTAM. Poet, whose *Git Parva Aya Hai* (1983) is a collection of lyrics.

RAJENDRA KISHORE (1922-). Poet, whose chief poetical collection is *Vaiyaktik* (Personal). He is also included in *Chautha Saptak* (q.v.). He has made a good number of experiments in contemporary Hindi poetry. His short story collections are *Mrityukatha* and *Kalpantar* (1984).

RAJENDRA KUMAR SHARMA. Writer, whose chief works are : *Attache Case*, *Parda Uthne se Pahle* (Before the Curtain Rises), *Dip Jalta Rahegu* (The Light would Continue), *Ek se Badh Ek* (Everyone at the Top), *Kalikh aur Lali* (The Black and Red) (collections of one-act plays), *Nauras*, *Ret ki Divar* (The Wall of Sand), *Kayakalpa* (The Rejuvenation; dramas), *Chaurahe Par* (On the Crossroad; 1967), *Sukhe Ansu* and *Ret Hati Hui Nadi* (novels) and *Unke Ghar ka Fasla* (short story collection). He and Suresh Sharma have ed. *Kahani aur Kahani* (1983 ; a collection 12 select short stories of 1983).

RAJENDRA KUMAR YAUDHAY. Modern Magahi poet who influenced by Chhayavadi movement, has composed songs, based on folk-tunes. He has also written *Magahi Bhasha ke Beakaran* (The Grammars of Magahi Language ; 1957).

RAJENDRA PRASAD, DR (1884-1963). The first President of India, whose *Atmakatha* in Hindi is not only of much historical and political importance but has also considerable literary merit. His select Hindi speeches are published by the Government of India. A volume of his writings on culture edited by Nagendra, is also available in Hindi.

RAJENDRA PRASAD SINGH (1930-). Poet, whose chief poetical works are : *Ujli Kasauti* (The Bright Touchstone) and *Ao Khuli Bayar* (Let Open Air Come).

RAJENDRA SHAH (1902-). Gujarati poet, whose *Dhwani*, a collection of songs, contains a poem in Rajasthani.

RAJENDRA SHARMA. Poet, whose chief works are : *Ganga* (1979; *Khand-Kavya*), *Bharat* and *Sheron ne Munh Dhoye*. He has also written novels (*Ek Chand Aur, etc.*) and short stories (*Janam Janam Vishwas*, *Manas Hans*).

RAJENDRA SINGH 'Sudhakar' (1900-43). Rajasthani poet, who was Ruler of Jhalawar. His works are : *Sudhakar Kavya Kala*, *Shankar Shatak*, *Madhushala*, etc.

RAJENDRA UPADHYAY. Poet, whose *Sirf Per Hi nahin Katate Hain* (1983) is a collection of poems.

RAJENDRA YADAV (1929-). Fiction writer, whose chief works are : *Pret Bolte Hain* (on conjugal life, beset with old customs and traditions), *Ukhre Huye Log* (The Displaced Persons; 1957; on the ups and downs of married life), *Kulta*, *Shah aur Mat* (1959 ; a romantic tale in the form of a diary), *Sara Akash* (1960; a revised edition of *Pret Bolte Hain*), *Ek Inch Muskan* (1962; in collaboration with his wife Mannu Bhandari), *Andekhe Anjane Pul* (1963 ; on inferiority complex), *Mantraviddha* (The Spell-bound 1967; all novels), *Abhimanyu ki Atmahatya* (The Suicide of Abhimanyu ; 1950), *Kinare se Kinare Tak*, *Khel-Khilaune*, *Tutna aur anya Kahaniyan*, *Apne Par*, *Jahan Lakshmi Qaid Hai* (Where Lakshmi is Imprisoned), *Meri Priya Kahaniyan* (My Favourite Stories), *Rajendra Yadav ki Shreshth Kahaniyan*, *Dhol aur anya Kahaniyan* (1972),

Chhote-chhote Tajmahal, *Pratiksha*, *Ek Duniya Simanantar*, *Nausihkiya* (short story collections), *Avaz Teri Hai* (Voice is Yours ; poetical collection). *Premchand ki Virasat*, *Atharath Upanyas*, *Kahani* : *Swarup aur Samvedana* (criticism) and *Auron ke Bahane* (1981 ; a collection of essays). His important short stories are : '*Tutna*' (The Break-up), 'Pratiksha' (The Wait), 'Abhimanyu ki Atmahatya', etc.

RAJESH DAYALU. Modern poet of Lucknow, who is the author of *Shyam Rasamayi* (on Krishna), *Rajesh Satsai*, *Gaurang Charitra* (on Chaitanya), *Rajesh Dohavali*, etc.

RAJESH JOSHI. Poet, whose *Ek Din Bolenge Per* (Trees Will Speak One Day ; 1980) is a collection of poems written in a simple and natural style ; his drama is *Jadu Jungle*, while *Somvar aur Unki Kahaniyan* is a short story collection.

RAJESH SHARMA. Modern writer, who is noted for his drama : *Avashyakta Ek Kursi Ki* (Wanted a Chair), which portrays the attempts of different sections of people in finding a chair for themselves. His chief novels are : *Rakhi ki Chunauti* and *Manimay Kundal*.

RAJESHWAR JHA. Maithili writer, who is noted for his drama *Shastrarth* (1967).

RAJESHWAR PRASAD CHATURVEDI. Modern writer, whose chief work is *Braj Lok-Sahitya aur Sanskriti*.

RAJESHWAR PRASAD SINGH (1903-). Fiction writer, whose chief works are : *Admi aur Zindagi* (The Man and Life), *Mrityukiran* (The Ray of Death), *Jangli Phul* (The Wild Flowers; novels), *Nargis ke Phul* and *Sapne aur Sapne* (short story collections).

RAJESHWARAYYA, M. Kannada-speaking modern Hindi critic, whose chief works are : *Urmila* (in Kannada and Hindi), tr. of Prabhushankar's Kannada drama : *Angulimala* into Hindi (both these works are in collaboration with Pradhan Gurudatt) and a tr. of Saint Basveshwar's *Vachans* from Kannada into Hindi. He also edited in Hindi *Kannada ki Shreshth Kahaniyan* (The Best Stories of Kannada), which were published by the Dakshin Bharat Hindi Prachar Sabha. In the *Urmila* is given a comparative study of Kuvempu's *Ramayana-darshanam* and Maithilisharan Gupta's *Saket*. He is Professor and Head of the Department of Hindi, Mysore University.

RAJESHWARI PANDHARI PANDE. See *Yamuna Kachru*.

RAJI SETH. Writer ; her *Tisri Hatheli* (The Third Palm ; 1981) and *Andhe Mor se Age* are short story collections, while *Tatsam* (1983) is her novel.

RAJIV SAXENA (1923-). Progressive poet, whose chief collection of poems is : *Atmanirvasan tatha anya Kavitayen* (Self-exile and other Poems) ; *Paniputri Soma* is his novel.

RAJIYAI RA DUHA. See *Kriparam Khidiya*.

RAJJAB (1567-1689). Rajasthani saint-poet, who was a Pathan of Sanganer (Rajasthan). While proceeding to Amer for marriage, he heard couplets of Dadu (q.v.). He gave up the idea of marriage and became Dadu's disciple. He composed a large number of poems, which include *Sakhi*, *Pada*, *Savaiya*, etc., which reveal his deep love, devotion, intensity of emotion and brilliant way of illustrating a point. The language is mainly Rajasthani. Many of his disciples, such as Chaindas, Ramdas, Khemdas and Kalyandas have admired his poetic genius and asceticism.

Rajjab's anthology *Sarwangi*, consisting of poems of about 65 poets including himself, irrespective of their religion or following, is a reliable source book for our knowledge of many little-known poets and their poems.

RAJJAN TRIVEDI. Modern writer, whose chief works are : *Sangmarmari Manden* (The Marble Lairs), *Nadi Phir Laut Ai* (The River Again Returned), *Triveni ke Tir* (On the Bank of the Triveni), *Ek Basti : Ek Duniya* (One Settlement : One World) (novels), *Andhere ki Parchhaiyan* (The Shadows of Darkness), *Sahama Hua Dhuan* (The Frightened Smoke; short story collections) and *Sahitya Disha* (The Direction of Literature: criticism).

RAJNI PANIKAR (1924-74). Fiction writer; her chief works are: *Mom ke Moti* (Pearls of Wax), *Pyase Badal* (Thirsty Clouds), *Kali Larki* (Dark Girl), *Thokar*, *Badalte Rang aur Duriyan*, *Do Larkiyan* (novels) and *Cigarette ke Tukre* (short story collection). Her works mostly portray the feminist viewpoint.

RAJNI KANT CHAKRAVARTI (1917-). Assamese-speaking Hindi writer, who has been associated with the propagation of Hindi in Assam from the very beginning and was awarded by the 1st World Hindi Conference, Nagpur in 1975. Apart from a dozen of essays in Hindi, he has written three books : *Shri Shri Shankardev*, *Vidyarthi Gandhiji* and *Rashtrabhasha ki Jhanki*; the first two books are for children.

RAJU, P.A. Telugu-speaking Hindi writer, who is noted for his *Chhayavad evam Bhav-vad* (1976).

RAJU SHARMA. Tamil-speaking modern Hindi writer, who is noted for his critical essays, e.g., 'Shaiv Sant-Kavi Nayanmaron ka Sahitya' (The Literature of Shaiv Saint-poet Nayanmars), etc.

RAJURKAR, Bh. H. See *Bhagatsingh Hanmantrao Rajurkar.*

RAJYASHRI. Drama (1915) by Jayshankar Prasad (q.v.), which is based on Kalhan's *Rajatarangini* and other documents.

Rajyashri's husband Grah Varma, the king of Kannauj, is killed by Malaw-king, Devgupta, the latter establishing his control over Kannauj as also on Rajyashri. Rajyashri's elder brother, Rajyavardhan, the prince of Sthaneshwar, accompanied by Narendragupta, the ruler of Gaur country, comes to the aid of his sister. In the meantime, Shanti Bhikshu, in the guise of the dacoit Vikatghosh, gets Rajyashri released from jail. In an encounter, Devgupta is killed, but Narendragupta, for his ulterior motives, gets Rajyavardhan assassinated by Vikatghosh, though in the end, Narendragupta himself is killed. Divakar Mitra, a Buddhist monk, is successful in getting Rajyashri released from the clutches of dacoits, where she had fallen after the assassination of Rajyavardhan, and he gives her shelter in his hermitage. Harshavrdhan, the younger brother of Rajyavardhan, in quest of his sister, Rajyashri, reaches the hermitage when Rajyashri is about to end her life. She is, however, persuaded by her brother not to do so ; both Rajyashri and Harshavardhan embrace Buddhism so that they can devote their lives to the service of humanity at large.

The drama reveals how Rajyashri is able to turn her misfortunes in the prosperity of the country.

RAKESH JAIN. Writer, whose chief work *Manjusha* (ed.; 1980) contains essays of teachers of Rajasthan.

RAKESH VATSA. Writer, who has edited *15 Sakriya Kahaniyan*; the *Sakriya Kahani* is the latest experiment in Hindi short story after *Nai Kahani* and *Samantar Kahani* and is supposed to enlighten the masses; it celebrates the present and seeks to prepare a blueprint for the future. His chief short story collections are *Atirikta* (Extra), *Antim Prajapati*, *Abhiyukta*, *Shruat*, while *Madhuban*, *Jangal ke As Pas* (Near the Jungle; 1982; on man-eater), *Punita* and *Kal ke Liye* are his novels.

RAKHEL SHAH (fl. 18th cent.). Sindhi Muslim saint-poet, who was also noted for his composition of verses in Hindi.

RALHA (RAJ SINGH). See *Jindatt Charit.*

RAM (b. 1646). Poet of the Riti school, who was the author of two works : *Shringar Saurabh* (on *Nayikabhed*) and *Hanuman Natak*. Some of his *Kavittas* are found in *Kalidas Hazara* (q.v.).

RAM ANUGRAH JHA. Modern Maithili poet, who is noted for his poems and lyrics.

RAM ARORA. Modern novelist, whose chief works are *Ritu-shesh* and *Basere*.

RAM AVADH SHARMA (1874-1924). An Arya Samajist of Mauritius, who was sent to D.A.V. College, Lahore for education. He edited 'Hindustani', 'Mauritius Mitra' and later on 'Arya Patrika'. He was the author of *Shishu Vyakaran*, *Bhugol*, etc. in chaste Hindi, which he favoured. He also started a Hindi Pathshala at Port Louis.

RAM AVTAR GUPTA. Modern Hindi poet of Fiji, who is known for his stray poems.

Ram AVTAR TYAGI (1925-). Poet, whose chief poetical collections are : *Sapne Mahak Uthe*, *Gulab aur Babul Van*, *Athvan Swar*, *Mein Delhi Hun* and *Gata Hua Dard* (The Singing Pain; 1981); *Samadhan* is his novel.

RAM AWADH DWIVEDI. See *Dwivedi, Ram Awadh*.

RAM BABU SHARMA. Modern Hindi writer of Hyderabad, who is noted for his researches.

RAM BETA PANDEY 'ADITYA' (1938-). Bagheli folk-poet, who was born at the village Kithara near Satna. His poems are noted for their simple language.

RAM BHADRA JHA (fl. early 20th cent.). Maithili prose writer, whose series of essays in 'Maithil Hit-Sadhan' on the good and the deplorable aspects of the life and character of the people of Mithila occupy an important place in the development of modern Maithili prose.

RAM BHAROSE KAPADI BHRAMAR. Maithili writer of Nepal, who is noted for his one-act play : 'Bharal Khattak Maram' (1981) and poems.

RAM BILAS SHARMA. See *Ram Vilas Sharma*.

RAM CHAITANYA DHIRAJ. Maithili poet, whose *Dwiparna* (1982) is a collection of lyrics.

RAM CHANDRA (fl. 1783). Poet, who composed *Charan Chandrika*, a work in 62 *Kavittas*, on the description of the feet of Parvati; the poem celebrates the divine glory and power of Parvati in a scholarly and high-flown language.

RAM CHANDRA. Rajasthani Charan, whose stray verses are available; his time is not certain.

RAM CHANDRA 'BALAK' (fl. 1656). Jain poet, whose *Sita Charit* (on the life and sufferings of Sita, the spouse of Ram) is almost equivalent to an epic.

RAM CHANDRA CHOUDHARY. Maithili writer, who is noted for his dramas, *Sabhagachik Barad* (1968) and *Piya Mora Balak*. He has also tr. Yogendra Nath's *Mahamati Bidur* from Bengali into Maithili in 1979; this is a work based on the *Vidur-Niti*, so famous in Sanskrit.

RAM CHANDRA DEV, A. Malayalam-speaking modern Hindi scholar, whose research work is : *Tulsi aur Tunchan*. He also wrote *Malayalam Sahitya* : *Ek Sarvekshan* (A Survey of Malayalam Literature).

RAM CHANDRA MISHRA. Modern Maithili writer, whose *Chandrabharan* is the most comprehensive work on *Alankars*.

RAM CHANDRA PRASAD. Scholar, whose chief works are : *Literary Criticism in Hindi* (1976), *Adhunik Hindi Alochana par Pashchatya Prabhav* (Western Influence on Hindi Criticism) and *Shaili*.

RAMCHANDRA RAGHUNATH SARVTE (fl. 1850-1900). Marathi-speaking Hindi dramatist, who was known for his two original dramas : *Pathshala ka ek Drishya* and *Yamraj ka Krodh*. His short stories have also appeared in various magazines.

RAM CHANDRA, SU. Kannada-speaking modern Hindi writer, who has tr. Ashwath's Kannada short stories into Hindi.

RAMCHANDRA SADASHIV ACHREKAR. Marathi-speaking modern Hindi poet, whose 86 poems are collected in *Darshan* ; most of the poems arc invocations to God to remove the bitterness, evils and inequalities in life.

RAM CHANDRA SHARMA. Hindi writer of Fiji, whose chief work is *Fiji Digdarshan* (1936).

RAM CHANDRA SHARMA 'KISHORE'. Modern Magahi poet,

whose poems depict the various stages of the minds of the lover and the beloved.

RAM CHANDRA SHUKLA (1884-1940). Celebrated critic and scholar, who was born at the village Agona in Basti district of Uttar Pradesh. After working as a teacher, he joined the teaching staff of the Benares Hindu University, where he succeeded Babu Shyam Sundar Das (q.v.) as Chairman of the Department of Hindi Studies. Both as a writer and as a teacher, he was held in high esteem and recent Hindi scholars have regarded him as their principal guide.

His work on the history of Hindi literature, *Hindi Sahitya ka Itihas* (1929) was acknowledged the most authentic history of Hindi and its literature ; it displays Shukla's rare capacity for analysis and critical assessment of Hindi writers and certain movements. Shukla had profound scholarship and his critical genius was stupendous and the most striking evidence of this is to be found in his critical essays, *Chintamani* (2 vols.). These essays, together with his works on Tulsidas (*Goswami Tulsidas*), Jayasi and Surdas gave a new orientation to Hindi literary criticism ; Shukla introduced historical, comparative and psychological methods and studied the works of an author in relation to his personality. He was the first to make a scientific study of the theory of *Rasa* and aesthetics, elaborating his point in the light of the works of the Italian philosopher, Croce. Shukla's tr. in Hindi verse of *The Light of Asia* was widely acclaimed for 'its vivid representation of Nature, based on minute observations'. Shukla's prose style is dignified and harmonious and he developed a new kind of Hindi prose, capable of expressing his profound thoughts. His *Gyarah Varsh ka Samay* (Eleven Years' Time ; 1903) is regarded as the first Hindi short story. He has written poems both in Brajbhasha and Khari Boli ; his poetry reveals vivid representation of Nature.

Shukla's other works are : Introductions (*Bhumikas*) to *Jayasi Granthavali*, *Tulsi Granthavali*, *Bhramar Gitsar*, *Rasa-Mimansa* (a collection of essays on *Rasa*, ed. and published after Shukla's death), 'Sahitya', 'Bharatiyon ka Pahrava' (on Indian dress), ed. of *Hindi Shabda Sagar* and of 'Nagari Pracharini Patrika', tr. of one Bengali work (*Shashank*) and of six English works published under the titles of *Vishwaprapanch*, *Adarsh Jivan*, *Rajya-Prabandh-Shiksha*, *Magasthenes ka Bharatvarshiya Varnan*, *Kalpana ka Anand* and stray essays.

Shukla occupies a prominent place among Hindi prose-writers and critics.

RAM CHANDRA SHUKLA 'SARAS' (1903-). Poet of Mau (Banda district), whose *Abhimanyu-Vadh* (The Killing of Abhimanyu) is a *Khand-Kavya*.

RAM CHANDRA SWAMI, S.M. Kannada-speaking modern Hindi writer, who tr. Triveni's two Kannada novels : *Apajay* and *Apaswar* into Hindi. He has also tr. Triveni's select short stories under the title *Triveni Saptak* and of Mastivenkatesh Aiyangar's stories under the title *Shrinivas Ashtak*.

RAM CHANDRA VERMA (1890-1969). Linguist and lexicographer, who was a collaborator of Shyam Sundar Das (q.v.) and was responsible, among other things, for bringing out an authentic Hindi dictionary. His chief works are : *Sankshipta Hindi Shabdasagar* (ed.), *Shiksha aur Deshi Bhashayen*, *Urdu-Hindi Kosh* (1936), *Achchhi Hindi*, *Hindi Prayog*, *Pramanik Hindi Kosh* (1950), *Shabdarth Mimansa* and *Hindi Kosh Rachna* (1955). He had also tr. *Gyaneshwari* from Marathi into Hindi.

RAMCHANDRIKA. See *Keshavdas*.

RAM CHARAN (1719-98). Rajasthani saint-poet and propounder of Ram Snehi Sampraday, Shahpura, who was born in a Bijavargi Vaishya family in the village Soda near Jaipur. He was initiated into Gudar Panth, which he gave up in 1758. In 1760, he came to Bhilwara where he founded the Ram Snehi Samprady. He came to Shahpura in 1769 and remained there till his death. His Sect flourished at Shahpura, which is the main seat of this Sampraday. Of his 12 chief disciples, Naval Ram, Ramjan, Bhagvandas and Ram Pratap were great poets.

Ramcharan's *Vani* is equal to over 36,000 *Anushtup Shlokas* and qualitatively it is equally high. Published under the title *Anbhai Vani*, his *Vani* lays empahsis on *Ram-smaran* and Bhakti. The poems, simple and natural, are in popular Rajasthani, with a slight mixture of Braj and Khari Boli. The *Vani* is considered of encyclopaedic nature with regard to religious poetry. In his works, he has tried to remove the distinction between Sagun and Nirgun forms of devotion.

RAM CHARN DAS (fl. 1769). Poet of the Ram-cult, whose chief works are : *Drishtant Bodhika*, *Kavitavali Ramayan*, *Padavali*, *Ram-Charitra*, *Rasa-Malika*, *Vivek Shatak* and *Virah Shatak*. He was a resident of Ayodhya.

RAM CHARAN THAKUR (1550-1620). Assamese poet, whose

mother was a sister of Madhavdev (q.v.). He has to his credit only one Hindi (Brajavali) drama : *Kans-Badh* (on the slaying of Kans by Krishna).

RAMCHARITMANAS (The Lake of the Life-story of Ram). Epic, which is commonly called the *Tulsikrit Ramayan.* It is the poet's greatest achievement and also, in point of time, probably his first, for it was completed on March 30, 1574.

The life of Ram Chandra, considered as an incarnation of the Supreme, is here dealt with ; the subject is the same as that of the celebrated Sanskrit *Ramayana* of Valmiki, but Tulsidas's *Ramayan* is in no way a tr. of that work. There is an independent story built on the same foundation, but differing from it in the treatment of episodes and in important details. The author himself states that he has taken his account from many different sources and it has been shown that the principal of these, besides Valmiki's work, were the *Adhyatma Ramayana* (a section of the *Brahmanda Purana*), the *Bhushundi Ramayana*, the *Vasishtha Samhita*, and the *Prasanna-Raghava*, attributed to Jayadeva.

The *Ramcharitmanas* is divided into seven books or Kandas, the brief contents of which are as under :—

Bk. I (Bal-Kand or Childhood Section) describes the city of Ayodhya, its ruler Dashrath, who has no sons but when he performs a *Yagya*, his three wives give birth to four sons : Kausalya bears Ram, Sumitra bears Lakshman and Shatrughna, while Kaikeyi bears Bharat.

Years after, Vishwamitra comes to the court of Dashrath and takes with him Ram and Lakshman to slay demons in the Dandak forest, where eventually Tadaka is killed. Vishwamitra also escorts the princes to the court of king Janak of Videh, where Sita's *Swayamvar* is being held. Ram bends the bow and with great rejoicings, the marriage of Ram and Sita is celebrated. Bk. I also includes many Brahmanical myths and legends.

Bk. II (Ayodhya-kand or Ayodhya Section). Dashrath resolves to appoint Ram as heir to the throne but Kaikeyi requests the king that he should banish Ram for fourteen years and appoint her son, Bharat to the throne. Ram, with dutiful Sita and faithful brother, Lakshman, goes into banishment. The king, overwhelmed with sorrow, dies after a few days. Bharat indignantly refuses the succession, sets out with a large retinue to fetch his brother, Ram. In vain are all the entreaties of Bharat ; ultimately, Bharat returns to Ayodhya and acts as Ram's viceger ent.

Bk. III (Aranya-kand or Forest Section). Ravan's sister, Shurpanakha falls in love with Ram, is rejected first by him and then by Lakshman. Full of rage, she is about to swallow Sita, when Lakshman cuts off her ears and nose ; to avenge the insult, she brings his brother Khar with 14,000 demons against Ram, who, however, defeats them all. She then hastens to Lanka and complains to Ravan, its ten-headed ruler, the latter speeds through the air in his golden chariot to the forest. There he transforms his friend, the demon Marich, into a golden deer, which attracts Sita and at her request, is pursued by Ram and Lakshman. In the meantime, Ravan, in the guise of an ascetic, approaches Sita, seizes her and bears her away on his chariot to Lanka. He tries to persuade her to become his consort, but she indignantly spurns his offer.

Bk. IV (Kishkindha-Kand or Kishkindha Section). At the lake Pampa, Ram and Lakshman meet Sugriv, who tells them his sad plight at the hands of his brother, Vali. Ram promises to help Sugriv against Vali, while in return Sugriv promises to aid Ram in the recovery of Sita. Ram kills Vali and Sugriv becomes the king of Kishkindha. Among the councillors of Sugriv, the wisest and most trustworthy is Hanuman. Accompanied by a host of monkeys under the leadership of Sugriv's son, Angad, Hanuman proceeds southwards.

Bk. V (Sundar-Kand or Beautiful Section). Hanuman reaches Lanka and finds Sita in the Ashok grove ; he assures her of Ram's coming to deliver her. Hanuman returns and gives Ram, a message from Sita.

Bk. VI (Yuddha-Kand or Battle Section). Vibhishan, Ravan's brother, denounces Ravan, allies himself with Ram and advises him to get a bridge built up by the monkey-king Nal. The bridge is built in a few days. The city being now besieged, Ravan's army sallies forth and a general battle, as well as many single combats, ensue. Lakshman, Hanuman, Angad and the bear-king Jambavat are on Ram's side, while Ravan's son, Indrajit inflicts serious wounds on Ram and Lakshman, but, through the fragrance of the healing herbs brought by Hanuman from the mount Kailas, the wounds are healed. In one of the combats, when Indrajit is slain by Lakshman, Ravan appears on the battlefield. In a dreadful duel, he falls pierced to the heart and Vibhishan is installed as king of Lanka by Ram.

Bk. VII (Uttar-kand or Last Section). Ram, Lakshman, Sita, accompanied by Hanuman, return to Ayodhya, where Ram is consecreated as king and he reigns gloriously, inaugurating a new golden age for his subjects. After reigning for a long time, Ram ascends to heaven. It may be mentioned that the second banishment of Sita and the killing of Shambuk are not mentioned by Tulsidas in his *Ramayan*.

"The *Manas* has been adjudged as the best Hindi work with devotion as the theme and as one of the best epics in any tongue anywhere. No other book has made such a deep impact on the minds of the people in the North. It has in fact been an integral part of people's lives and their socio-religious make-up these four hundred years. It presents Ram as an ideal man in all respects, as a son, as a brother, as a husband, as a friend, as a warrior and as a king. On the religious and philosophical plane, the story of *Ramcharitmanas* is flawless and of exceptional merit as a piece of literature. .."

The *Ramcharitmans* has been tr. into Russian ; in English, there are many versions of it : by Growse, Hill, Atkins, etc. There are almost 50 commentaries on this work.

RAM CHARIT UPADHYAY (1872-1938). Poet of Azamgarh, whose chief works are : *Rashtrabharati*, *Devdut*, *Devsabha*, *Devi Draupadi*, *Bharat Bhakti* (Kavyas) and *Ramcharit Chintamani* (Prabandh-Kavya). His *Suktis* are collected in *Sukti Muktavali*. The *Ramcharit Chintamani* depicts Ram as a man so that his statesmanship is revealed. He has contributed immensely to the development of Khari Boli as also to the national consciousness.

RAM CHARITRA PANDEY 'ANU' (1919-). Maithili poet, whose poems are collected in *Nakshatra* (1956).

RAM DAHIN MISHRA (1886-1952). Critic, who was born at Pathar in Shahabad district of Bihar. His chief works are : *Kavya Darpan* (1947), *Kavya Vimarsh* (1951), *Kavyalok* and *Kavya men Aprastut-Yojna* ; of these the first one is the most well-known. He was an ardent believer in the superiority of critical genius of the Sanskrit poeticians.

RAMDAN LALAS (1761-1825). Rajasthani poet, who was son of Fatehdan. He was patronized by Maharaja Mansingh of Jodhpur, who had gifted him the village Tolesar. He also remained for some time at the court of Maharana Bhimsingh of Mewar. His works in Dingal are : *Bhim Prakash* (on the grandeur of Mewar in 175 metres), *Karani Rupak* (dealing with the story of the goddess Karaniji) and *Itihas* (a systematic account of the Khichi branch of the Chauhan clan).

RAM DARASH MISHRA (1924-). Poet and writer, whose

chief works are : *Bairing Benam Chitthiyan* (progressive poems), *Pak Gai Hai Dhup* (1968 ; poems), *Samay Devta* (The Time God), Kandhe par Suraj (1977), *Pani ke Prachir* (The Walls of Water; 1961 ; a regional novel), *Jal Tutata Hua* (Waters Breaking ; 1969), *Sukhta Hua Talab* (The Drying Tank ; 1970), *Bich ka Samay* (The (Interval), *Apne Log* (Our People ; 1976), *Akash ki Chhat* (The Ceiling of the Sky ; 1979), *Rat ka Safar* (The Night Journey), *Bina Darvaze ka Makan* (novels), *Khali Ghar* (The Vacant House), *Din-charya* (Daily Routine), *Sarpadansh*, *Vasant ka Ek Din*, *Iksath Kahaniyan* (short story collections), *Hindi Kavita* : *Tin Dashak* (Hindi Poetry : Three Decades), *Aitihasik Upanyaskar* : *Vrindavanlal Verma* (Verma as a historical novelist), *Hindi Alochana ka Itihas* (History of Hindi Criticism), *Hindi Upanyas* (Hindi Novel), *Samiksha* : *Swarup aur Sandarbh* (Criticism : Form and Context ; criticism), *Chhayavad ka Rachnalok* (on Chhayavad ; 1980) and *Hindi ke Anchalik Upanyas*.

Mishra's important short stories are : 'Chitthion ke Bich' (Amidst Letters), 'Man, Sannata aur Bajta Hua Radio' (Mother, Stillness and the Playing Radio), 'Khandahar ki Avaz' (The Voice from the Ruins), 'Sarak' (The Road), 'Ek Aurat, Ek Zindagi' (One Woman, One Life), etc.

RAMDAS (1727-98). Rajasthani saint-poet of Ram Snehi Sect, Khedapa, who was born at the village Bankunkaur. A householder, he was initiated by Hariram Das (q.v.) of Sinthal. He founded the Khedapa Branch in 1763 and though considered to be a branch of Sinthal, it has its separate tradition. His *Vani* consists of over 1,700 *Dohas* on about 90 topics, 72 *Harjas* and 24 poems, such as *Guru Mahima*, *Bhaktamal*, *Chetavani*, *Balbodh*, *Gyan Vivek*, *Amarbodh*, *Nam Mala*, *Atmasar*, *Brahma Jigyasa*, *Atmaveli* and *Niralamb*. His emphasis is on the spiritual life ; the language is lucid and easy Rajasthani.

RAMDAS (1730-1800). Author of Oriya *Bhaktamal*, whose Hindi (Brajboli) *Padas* are available.

RAMDAS GAUR. Writer, who was noted for his drama : *Ishwar Nyay* (The Divine Justice ; 1924).

RAMDAS JHA. Maithili writer, who was the fourth and the youngest brother of Govind Das Jha, the famous successor of Vidyapati and was thus contemporaneous of Maharaja Sundar Thakur (r. 1644-71). Jha was the author of *Anand-Vijay-Natika* (q.v.), a Kirtaniya form of drama.

RAMDAS, SMARTH (1554-1681). Saint-poet of Maharashtra, who was the founder of Smarth Sect. He was the Guru of Chhatrapati Shivaji and his masterpiece, *Dasbodh* has also been tr. into Hindi. He had a good knowledge of Sanskrit, Marathi and Hindi. Besides his Marathi works, he composed several *Padas* in Hindi, which are preserved in the Smarth Vagdevta Mandir of Dhuliya. His Hindi language contains a good number of Arabic and Persian words. He roused the Hindu nation against Muslim domination.

RAM DATT PANT. Modern Kumaoni poet, who is noted for his songs.

RAM DATT SHARMA. Modern Hindi writer of Mauritius, whose dramatic works are : *Bhabhi ki Mamta and Bataun.*

RAM DATTA SANKRITYA. Modern Rajasthani writer, whose chief works are : *Abhalde* (novel) and *Des ro Helo, Jalam Bhom ri Murat* (one-act plays).

RAM DAYAL (fl. 20th cent.). Poet of Lohvan, who was noted for his heroic and humorous poems.

RAM DAYAL RAKESH. Modern Hindi writer of Nepal, who is noted for his short stories and poems.

RAMDEO DHOORUNDHUR (1946-). Hindi writer of Mauritius, whose chief works are : *Chehron ka Admi* (1981), *Chhoti Machhli Bari Machhli* (1983), *Sahme Huye Sach* (1983) and *Apne-apne Dayre* (in press). He has written short stories as well.

RAMDEV, ACHARYA (1934-). Poet, whose chief works are : *Aksharon ka Vidroh* (The Revolt of the Letters of the Alphabet ; 1968) and *Registan se Mahangar Tak* (From Desert to City ; 1980). In his poem 'Nit Rajasthan Jiyo', he has glorified Rajasthan. He has also written satirical short stories.

RAMDEV DWIVEDI. Modern Hindi poet of Nepal, who is noted for his works : *Almast*, *Udayan*, etc.

RAMDEV JHA. Maithili writer and poet, whose *Ek Khira Tna Phak* (1964) is a short story collection, depicting life among the lower classes. He composed *Darbhanga-Varnan* and *Badhi-Varnan*, both in verse as also lyrics. His *Maithili Shaiv Sahitya* (1979) is a research work, while his *Umapati* (1980) has been written under 'Makers of Maithili Literature' series on the famous playwright and poet, Umapati (q.v.). Along with Chandra Nath Mishra 'Amar', he has edited *Kavivar Jivan Jha Rachnavali* (1980).

RAMDEV RAGHUVIR. Modern Hind dramatist of Surinam, who has written more than 20 dramas, of which *Bahu bhi Beti Hai* and *Sainik ke Pita* are very popular on the stage. He directs his own dramas and also takes a role. He has also composed poems, mainly on cultural topics.

RAMDHARI SINGH 'DINKAR' (1908-74). Poet, who was born at Simariya in Monghyr district of Bihar. He was Vice-Chancellor of Bhagalpur University. He was influenced in his own words by *Bharat Bharati* (q.v.) and 1921 Non-co-operation Movement. His chief works are :

Poetry : *Renuka* (Sand Grains ; 1935), *Hunkar* (The Sound of Defiance), *Rasavanti* (Possessed of Love ; 1939), *Sandheni, Dwandgit* (1940), *Kurukshetra* (1946 ; this work, written in the epic style, gives his reflections on the general theme of war and peace and made Dinkar, a poet of all-India fame), *Rashmi-Rathi* (1955 ; on Karna, whom the poet has portrayed as a symbol of suppressed humanity), *Urvashi* (1961 ; on Pururava and Urvashi ; the former is a man of this world fired by burning passion for the divine, while the latter is a celestial nymph thirsting for pleasure of the earth). *Urvashi* is regarded his greatest work, the third canto being more poetic than the rest of the work. *Parshuram ki Pratiksha* (Wait for Parshuram), *Koel aur Kavita* and *Mritt-Tilak* are other epic poems of Dinkar. His other poetical collections are : *Itihas ke Ansu* (Tears of History ; 1951 ; a collection of 10 historical poems), *Dhup aur Dhuan, Hare ko Hari Nam* (For the Defeated, the name of the Lord ; 1970), *Delhi, Nim ke Patte, Nil-Kusum, Pranbhang tatha any Kavitayen* ; *Sanchayita* (A Select Collection) had won him the Gyanpith Award. The *Rashmilok* (1974) is a collection of his two poetical works : *Hare ko Hari Nam* and *Renuka,* composed earlier.

Essay Collection : *Ardhanarishwar, Reti ke Phul, Hamari Sanskritik Ekta* (Our Cultural Unity), *Prasad, Pant aur Maithilisharan* (1958), *Rashtrabhasha aur Rashtriya Sahitya*, *Shuddh Kavita ki Khoj* (In Quest of Pure Poetry ; 1966), *Adhunik Bodh, Chetana ki Shikha* and *Vivah ki Musibaten* ; his earlier work, *Sanskriti ke Char Adhyay* (Four Chapters of Culture) treats of human civilization, divided in four phases, while *Vat Pipal* consists of his meetings with others.

As a poet of robust nationalism, a thinker, a historian and as a writer of lyrics and epic poems, Dinkar occupies a place among the topmost Hindi poets and writers of the post-Independence era.

RAMDUT. See *Shrimant Kumar Vyas*.

RAM GHULAM DWIVEDI (fl. 1813). Poet of the Ram-cult, who was a resident of Mirzapur; he composed *Kavitta Ramayan* and *Vinay Nav Panchak*.

RAM GOPAL (fl. 1800). Poet of the Ram-cult, who composed *Ashtayam*.

RAM GOPAL 'GOPAL'. Poet of Mathura, who was son of Braj Vallabh Dev (1860-1935; q.v.). Several of his stray verses are available.

RAM GOPAL GOYAL. Writer, whose chief works are *Rajasthan ke Premakhyan*: *Parampara aur Pragati* (1969) and *Yuga Dharma* (essays; 1984). He has also written novels and short stories: *Ek Kshan ek Sach*, *Dharti Rahi Pukar*, etc.

RAM GOPAL 'RUDRA'. Modern Magahi poet, whose songs and poems are noted for the groanings of a troubled soul.

RAM GOPAL SHARMA 'NAVAL'. Modern Rajasthani poet, who has composed Nature and love poems.

RAM GYAN PANDEY. Modern Bhojpuri poet, who is known for his stray poems.

RAM HARI (*c*. 1733-*c*. 83). Poet of the Krishna-cult (Chaitanya Sect), whose original name was Hari Ram. He lived in Vrindavan and his works are: *Dhyan Rahsi Vilas*, *Buddhi*, *Sat-Hansi*, *Laghu-Namavali*, *Bodh-Bavni*, *Prem Patri* and *Ras-Pachchisi*.

RAM HARI JOSHI. Modern Hindi poet of Nepal, whose chief work is *Naya Savera*.

RAM IQBAL SINGH 'RAKESH'. Modern Maithili writer, whose chief work, *Maithili Lok-Git* is a collection of Maithili folk-songs, edited by him. He has also published articles on Maithili folk-songs and folk-literature.

RAM JAISWAL. Poet, whose *Bimb-Pratibimb* (Images-Reflections; 1980) is a collection of his poems, having some modernity.

RAM JAN LADDHA (1738-1810). Rajasthani saint-poet of Ram Snehi Sect, Shahpura, who was initiated in 1767 and was the second Acharya to occupy the *Gaddi* in 1798. His *Vani* in *Padas* and other metres is quite large ; his poems are about the Nirgun Bhakti, the main emphasis being on *Ram-smaran* and Bhakti. He has also composed 19 *Granths* (*Updesh Bodh*, *Pratiti Bodh*, *Vairag Bodh*, *Sumiran Bodh*, *Ram Paddhati*, etc) and a commentary on *Drishtant Sagar*. The language is easy Rajasthani.

RAM JASAN PANDIT. Author of *Bhasha Tattwa Bodhini*, an early grammatical work in Hindi, which was prepared around 1860 at the instance of the Government of India.

RAMJI MITRA. Modern writer, who is noted for his short stories, 'Pass-Fail', etc.

RAMJI TASKARI, BABA (fl. 1850-1900). Marathi-speaking saint-poet, who composed *Padas* in Hindi.

RAM JOSHI (fl. 18th cent.). Marathi folk-poet (*Shahir*), who also composed verses in Hindi.

RAM KARAN ASOPA (1857-1943). Rajasthani scholar of Jodhpur, who was son of Baldev and Shringardevi. He was associated for a long time with the History Department of Jodhpur State. His works have contributed to the development of Rajasthani language and literature. His chief works are : *Marwari Vyakaran* (1896 ; the first of its kind in the modern period), two dictionaries of Rajasthani containing 60,000 and 20,000 words respectively (unpublished), *Marwari Pustak* (Pts. I, II, III ; 1960 ; three elementary books for learning Rajasthani, which were prescribed in schools), *Sachitra Bal Bodh* (for beginners in Hindi), *Hindi Vyakaran* (1911 ; nine years before the well-known *Hindi Vyakaran* of Kamtaprasad Guru), translation in Khari Boli of *Bhagavata Purana* and Tulsidas's *Ramayan*, tr. of the *Gita* into Rajasthani prose and editing of *Raj Rupak* by Ratanu Virbhan, ed. of *Suraj Prakash* by Kaviya Karanidan and poems by Asiya Bankidas. An eminent scholar of Charan literature, his history of Marwar (*Marwar ka Mul Itihas*) bears testimony to his scholarship. His epic in Sanskrit, *Rashtrodaya*, consisting of 20,000 *Shlokas*, is the history of the Rathores and is like the *Rajatarangini* of Kalhan. In 1914, he taught Rajasthani language and literature to Dr Tessitori (q.v.).

A scholar of exceptional merit with vision and foresight, he paved the way for systematic study of Rajasthani language and literature in its many aspects.

RAM KATHA. See *Vishwanath 'Vimalesh'*.

RAM KHELAVAN. Modern Hindi writer of Mauritius, who is noted for his short stories : *Dhundhli-Rekhayen*.

RAM KISHORE SHRIVASTAV. Modern scholar, whose chief work is *Hindi Lok-Git*.

RAM KRIPA (*c*. 1723-83). Poet of the Krishna-cult (Chaitanya Sect), who was the author of *Shri Brahmasamhita Digdarshini Tika ki Bhasha* (1.65).

RAM KRISHNA JHA 'KISUN' (d. 1970). Maithili short story writer and poet, whose collected works have been published in the two parts of *Kisun Rachnavali* : the first part containing his available poems including lyrics, is entitled *Kramshah* and the second part containing his available short stories is entitled *Swayamvar* (1982). *Atmanepad* (1963), the book of his poems was published, while he was still alive. His *Maithilik Navin Kavita* (ed.) is an anthology of great lyrics of the New Poets.

RAM KRISHNA SHUKLA 'Shilimukh' (1901-58). Modern critic, who wrote a critical essay : 'Samalochak-Nama'. He laid emphasis on the social function of literary criticism. Apart from his early critical works such as *Sukavi Samiksha*, *Prasad ki Natyakala* (The Dramatic Art of Prasad), *Alochana Samuchchay*, *Adhunik Hindi Kahaniyan*, *Kavya-Jigyasa* and *Shilimukhi*, his major critical output was concerned with the criticism of Premchand's novels. According to Shilimukh, Premchand was more a propagandist than an artist. He was Head of the Department of Hindi-Sanskrit, Maharaja College, Jaipur.

RAM KRISHNA VERMA (1859-1906). Writer of Varanasi, who tr. a number of books from Bengali, Sanskrit, Urdu and English into Hindi and also wrote many original ones including *Krishna Kumari Natak*, *Padmavati Natak*, etc. He also started a printing press and brought out a Hindi monthly, 'Bharat Jivan'. He wrote poetry under the pseudonym of 'Balvir' and 'Vir Kavi' and collection of his poems was titled *Balvir Pachasa*. In Bhojpuri, he wrote *Birha Nayikabhed*.

RAM KUMAR. Writer, whose chief works are : *Husna Bibi tatha anya Kahaniyan* (Husna Bibi and other Stories ; 1959), *Ek Chehra* (A Face), *Ek Lamba Rasta*, *Samudra* (short story collections) and *Europe ke Sketch* (illustrated travelogue). He has also written two novels : *Ghar Bane Ghar Tute* and *Der Saver*.

RAM KUMAR BHRAMAR (1938-). Writer, whose chief works are : *Kachchi Pakki Divaren* (The Crude Walls), *Phansi* (The Hanging), *Kanchghar* (The Glass House), *Tisra Patthar* (The Third Stone), *Faulad ka Admi* (The Man of Steel), *Qaid Avazen* (The Imprisoned Voices), *Sat Rang Sapne*. *Murde* (Dead Bodies), *Gale Gale Pani* (1973), *Tashmahal* (A House of Cards), *Apne-apne Saval*, *Angan* (The Courtyard), *Galiyan* (The Lanes) and *Chaubare* (The Attic ; 1982; the last three are parts of an epic novel) (all novels), *Lau par Rakhi Hui Hatheli* (The Palm on the Flame), *Grastin*, *Katha Yatra* (short story collections) and *Bhasmasur* (1980; a drama, which reveals the inconsistencies in modern political life). His other dramas are : *Khun ki Avaz*, *Vikalpa* and *Tamasha*. His important short story is : 'Lau par Rakhi Hui Hatheli'.

Bhramar is at present engaged in writing a 12-volume novel, based on the *Mahabharat*, of which several parts : *Arambh*, *Ankur*, *Avahan*, *Adhikar*, *Agraj*, *Ahuti* and *Asadhya* have already been published.

RAM KUMAR CHATURVEDI (1926-). Poet, whose chief poetical work is *Nai Pidhi Nai Rahen* (New Generation, New Paths).

RAM KUMAR VERMA (1905-). Dramatist, poet and critic, who was born in the Sagar district of Madhya Pradesh. He retired from the post of the Head of the Hindi Department, Allahabad University. His chief works are :-

Badal ki Mrityu (The Death of a Cloud ; 1930), *Prithwiraj ki Ankhen* (The Eyes of Prithwiraj ; 1935), *Reshmi Tie* (The Silk Tie ; 1941), *Charumitra* (1942 ; also in English), *Vibhuti*, *Sapta-Kiran* (*Seven Rays*), *Sahi Raste*, *Kaumudi Mahotsva*, *Rup Rang* (Beauty; 1948), *Rajat-Rashmi*, *Dipdan*, *Dhruvatarika* (The Pole Star ; 1950), *Rituraj* (The Spring), *Rimjhim*, *Mayur Pankh*, *Indradhanush* (The Rainbow), *Panchjanya*, *Rajni ki Rat*, *Kesar ki Saurabh*, *Juhi ke Phul*, *Mere Shreshth Rang Ekanki* (My Select One-act Plays), *Sarang Swar*, *Agnishikha*, *Sant Tulsidas*, *Itihas ke Swar*, *Bahurangi Natak* (Assorted Plays; 1982), *Samaj ka Swar* (Vyakti), *Samaj ka Swar* (Parivar), *Calendar ka Akhiri Panna*, *Jauhar ki Jyoti*, *Samrat Kanishka*, *Chitra Ekanki*, *Jay Varddhman* (all one-act play collections), *Abhishap*, *Anjali*, *Ruprashi*, *Nishith* (Midnight), *Chitrarekha*, *Chandra-Kiran*, *Vir Hammir*, *Chittor ki Chita* (The Pyre of Chittor), *Gajre Taron Vale*, *Uttarayan*, *Akashganga*, *Eklavya* (an epic based on the *Mahabharata* story (all poetry), *Himhas* (prose-poem), *Hindi Sahitya ka Alochanatmak Itihas* (Critical History of Hindi Literature), *Kabir ka Rahasyavad* (Mysticism of Kabir) and an

English work, *Kabir* (criticism). Apart from his one-act plays, his *Chitrarekha* and *Eklavya* stand prominent works.

Some of Verma's plays are historical but others are motivated by an urge to project the middle class family life and its problems; his plays are stageworthy. As a critic his work on Kabir is considered authoritative.

RAMLAGAN SHIVGOVIND SHARMA. Modern Hindi writer of Mauritius, who is noted for his *Naye Mauritius ke Nirmata Sir Seewosagur Ramgoolam*.

RAM LAKHAN SHASTRI. Modern Hindi poet of Fiji, who is noted for his poems.

RAM LAKHAN SHUKLA (1934-). Writer, whose chief works are : *Sadharanikaran* : *Ek Shastriya Adhyayan*, *Bharatiya Sahityashastra ke Siddhant* (both on poetics), and *Hindi Upanyas Kala* (The Art of Hindi Novels) ; *Pranay Path* and *Mahendraditya* are his novels.

RAM LAKHAN SUKRIT. Modern Hindi writer of Trinidad, who is noted for his short stories.

RAM LAL. Native of Guyana, who is promoting the cause of Hindi in his country.

RAM LAL. Urdu writer, who also writes in Hindi ; his chief novels are: *Mutthi-bhar Dhup* (1972) and *Kohra aur Muskan* (1972), both on conjugal life.

RAM LAL Agnihotri. Writer, who tr. in 1927 Schiller's German drama from its Persian version under the title *Prem Prapanch*.

RAM LAL KHATIK (fl. end of 19th cent.). Folk-poet of Sonipat (Haryana), who was originally a *Kathavachak* (religious preacher), but seeing the success of *Sangs*, he turned a *Sangi*. His popular *Sangs*, which he composed and staged, were ; *Gopichand*, *Shila* and *Puran Bhakta*.

RAM LAL VERMA (fl. 20th cent.). Early novelist, who was known for his magic novel : *Putli Mahal* (The Palace of the Puppet; 1908). His characters show the influence of Urdu poetry and Parsi Theatre.

RAM LALA 'LALA' (1906-75). Poet of Mathura, whose chief works are : *Draupadi Dukul*, *Vikramaditya* and *Mira Devadasi*.

RAM LALA NAHACHHU. A small poem by Tulsidas (q.v.), in Avadhi, written in 1586 (?).

The poem consists of 20 verses supposed to be sung on the occasion of Ram's marriage, otherwise meant for general use on such auspicious occasions (Nahachhu is a certain rite performed during the marriage according to which the bridegroom is shaved, his nails cut, etc.).

RAM LALA SHRIVASTAV 'LALA'. Modern poet of Gorakhpur, who is the author of *Radharaman Vinod* (The Delights of Krishna).

RAM LINGAM. Malayalam-speaking modern Hindi writer, who is noted for preparation of help-material for students appearing in higher Hindi examinations.

RAM LOCHAN THAKUR. See *Kumaresh Kashyap*.

RAM MOHUN ROY, RAJA (1772-1833). Founder of Brahmo Samaj and a great social reformer, who started a paper 'Bangdut' in 1826 from Calcutta, which was published in Hindi, English, Bengali and Persian. He also tr. his *Vedanta-Sar* into Hindi.

RAM MURTI. Mordern Author of *Dhwani Sampraday*.

RAM MURTI TRIPATHI (1929-). Writer, whose chief works are : *Rasa Vimarsh* (1965 ; research), *Lakshman-Shakti aur Uska Hindi Kavya men Prasar*, *Agam aur Tulsi*, *Adhunik Kavyakala aur Darshan*, *Adikalin Hindi Sahitya ki Sanskritik Pithika*, *Rahasyavad* and *Tantra aur Sant* (1975 ; new interpretation). He is Head of the Department of Hindi, Vikram University, Ujjain.

RAM NANDAN. Modern Magahi poet, who is noted for his songs.

RAM NARAYAN JHAU. Modern Hindi writer of Surinam, whose chief works are : *Surinam ke Bharatvanshi* and *Surinam Desh aur Nivasi*.

RAM NARAYAN SHUKLA (1937-68). Modern short story writer, whose chief collection of stories is *Sahara aur anya Kahaniyan*.

RAM NARAYAN UPADHYAY. Writer, who is known for his satirical skits *Bakhshishnama* (The Scroll of Gratuity; 1980) on the upper moneyed-class and for his short story collection : *Janam Janam ke Phere*. His poetical works are : *Man ka Marg Chhoren* and *Man ke Mrigchhaune*.

RAM NARESH PATHAK (1929-). Poet, whose chief poetical works are : *Anama* and *Kwar ki Sanjha*.

RAM NARESH TRIPATHI (1889-1962). Poet, who may well be described as the first Hindi poet of the Indian National Movement. He was born at Koirupur in the Jaunpur district of Uttar Pradesh. Himself an ardent patriot, his three works: *Milan* (The Union; 1918), *Pathik* (The Traveller; 1921) and *Swapna* (Dream; 1929) are long narrative poems, full of patriotic appeal; though not of a very high literary standard, these works made a deep impression on the youth. *Manasi* is a collection of his stray poems. He edited several works under the titles: *Ghagh aur Bhaddari* (on their proverbs), *Hamara Gram-Sahitya* (Our Folk-literature; Pts. I, II, III), *Sohar*, *Gramin Gii* (Folk-songs), *Kavita Kaumudi* (a voluminous poetical collection in 8 vols. covering poets of Hindi, Urdu, Sanskrit, Bengali, etc.), folk-songs, *Marwar ke Manohar Khati*, *Rajasthani Jhilon ke Lok-Git*, etc. He wrote also a drama, *Jayant* (1934), a novel and a commentary in Khari Boli on the *Ramchritmanas*, which became quite popular.

RAM NARESH SHARMA. Writer, whose chief work is a romantic drama, *Simhal-Vijay* (1896).

RAM NATH (fl. middle of 16th cent.). Maithili poet, who was noted for his poem found in the anthology containing popular poems in the court of Kans-Narayan. He also composed hymns on devotional and pseudo-philosophical subjects.

RAM NATH (fl. 1843). Poet of the Ram-cult, whose chief works are: *Rasa-Bhushan*, *Mahabharat Gatha* and *Janaki Pachisi*.

RAM NATH. Writer, whose chief work is a drama, *Savitri Satyavan* (1900) on a mythological theme.

RAM NATH JHA. Modern Maithili scholar, who has distinguished himself in the field of literary history. His numerous studies of the life and biography of Maithili writers of the past have helped in appreciating Maithili literature. His *Prabandh-Sangrah* and *Nibandh-Mala* represent Maithili criticism at its best; chief subjects of his study are Chanda Jha, Govind Das Jha and the Kirtaniya dramatists. He is also the author of *Alayikul-Prakash* in prose.

RAM NATH SHUKLA JYOTISHI (1874-1943). Poet of Ayodhya, whose *Ramchandrodaya-Kavya* has earned the 'Dev Puraskar'.

RAM NATH KAVIYA (1801-79). Rajasthani poet, whose *Pabuji ra Sortha* (32 verses) describes the deeds and glorious death of Pabuji Rathore, the legendary folk-god of Rajasthan (see *Pabuji ka Pavadas*) while *Karuna Bavni* (59 verses) is based on the *Chir-Haran* episode of Draupadi in the 'Sabha-parva' of the *Mahabharat.* He has also composed verses in praise of Karaniji, the Charan goddess, and *Marsiyas* on Suryamall Mishran, Shankardan Samaur and others. His poems were very popular and were frequently repeated and even imitated. Profundity of emotion marks his poems.

RAM NATH MISHRA 'MIHIR'. Maithili poet, whose *Uparag* (1982) is a collection of lyrics; his earlier collection of lyrics was *Madhuri* (1967).

RAM NATH PATHAK 'PRANAYI'. Modern Bhojpuri poet, whose chief collections of poems : *Koiliya* and *Sitar* present pictures of rural life : the scenes of Nature and the oppressed peasantry. His poem 'Sharad' is a good specimen of poetry of Nature.

RAM NATHAN, K. Telugu-speaking modern Hindi scholar, whose research works are : *Hindi-Telugu Vaishnav Bhakti Sahitya* (Vaishnav Devotional Literature of Hindi and Telugu), and *Tulnatmak Anusandhan aur Alochana* (Comparative Study and Criticism).

RAM NIRANJAN SHARMA 'THIMAU'. Rajasthani writer, who is a school-teacher at Pilani. His chief works are : *Bemata ka Ank* (1975 ; satirical short stories) and *Matkachar* (1978 ; a collection of 11 satirical one-act plays). In collaboration with Nagraj Sharma, he is the author of two humorous plays : *Ram Milai Jori* and *Tamarak Tun* (both 1972).

RAM NIVAS SHARMA. Rajasthani writer, whose chief work : *Kal Bhairavi* (1976) is a novel dealing with the tantrik system, which seems to suggest that the sublimity of the sex helps attain the super self. He has written also short stories.

RAM PAL SINGH (1849-1909). Raja of Kalakankar in Uttar Pradesh, who had the distinction of starting a Hindi journal 'Hindosthan' from London in 1889. On his return to India a year later, he converted it into a daily newspaper and it was published from Kalakankar.

RAN PALI BHATI. Rajasthani poet, whose chief work *Char Gatha* (1953) contains stories in verse.

RAM PRAKASH. Writer, who has written two novels : *Pighalte Patthar* and *Bolti Salakhen* ; *Katha Kunj* is his short story collection.

RAM PRAKASH AGRAWAL. Modern scholar, whose chief work is *Valmiki aur Tulsi : Sahityik Mulyankan.*

RAM PRASAD CHAKLAN Modern Rajasthani writer, who is known for his short stories.

RAM PRASAD GHILDYAL 'PAHARI' (1913-). Writer, who is noted for his short stories; his important short stories depicting psychological situation through naked romance are : 'Naya Morcha' (The New Front), 'Rajrani' (The Empress), 'Hiran ki Ankhen' (The Eyes of the Deer), 'Tamasha' (The Carnival), etc. *Sarai* (The Inn) is his psychological novel. He has also edited many literary magazines in Allahabad as also *Hindi ki Kaljayi Kahaniyan.*

RAM PRASAD NIRANJANI. Writer, who was an employee of the Patiala *Durbar*, his job being to recite *Katha* to the Maharani every day. His book, *Bhasha Yoga Vasishth,* written in 1732 shows that Khari Boli had come to have a more or less accepted style in prose even before Lallulal's *Prem Sagar* was written in Khari Boli prose.

RAM PRASAD SINGH 'PUNDRIK'. Poet, whose *Pundrik-Ratnamalika* (1952) contains in the first two parts Khari Boli poems, while the last part is a collection of his Magahi poems.

RAM PRASAD TRIPATHI (1890-1982). Scholar and poet, who was born in Muzaffarnagar and after serving as Professor in the Allahabad University, was appointed as Vice-Chancellor of Saugar University. His several *Padas* in Brajbhasha are extant. He also wrote several works on history.

RAM PRASAD VERMA. Hindi writer of Burma, who is the editor of 'Brahmabhumi'.

RAM PRATAP (d. 1800). Rajasthani saint-poet of Ram Snehi Sampraday (see *Ramcharan*), who composed a large number of poems in different metres and 11 short books, entitled 'Nirupan', such as *Guru Mahima*, *Guru Mahima Sar*, *Guru Sampatti*, *Sumiran Sar*, *Bhakti*, *Kakka Kavya*, *Karni Sar*, *Drishtant Vichar Gudh* and *Kakka Battisi.* The note of renunciation and Ram Bhakti is prominent in his poems, while the language is simple Rajasthani, mixed with a little Braj.

RAM PRIYA SHARAN 'PREMKALI' (fl. *c.* 1703) Poet of the Ram-cult (Rasik Sect), who resided at Janakpur. He was the author of the *Sitayan* or *Sitarampriya* ; the work is on the pattern of the *Ramayan* and is divided into 7 cantos.

RAM RASO. Rajasthani narrative poem in 1034 verses, which was composed by Madhodas Dadhvadiya (q.v.) around 1595. Composed on an epic scale, the poem describes the story of Ram on the basis of *Valmiki Ramayana*, though the poet was influenced by many other works in this field, viz., *Adhyatma Ramayana*, *Ananda Ramayana*, *Vichitra Ramayana*, the *Mahabharata* and the *Bhagavata Purana* ; many folk beliefs and conventions have also been mentioned. There is an idealistic characterization of not only Ram but also of Jatayu, Bali, etc.

RAM RASO. See *Surjandas Puniya.*

RAM RATAN. Modern Hindi poet of Fiji, who is noted for his stray poems.

RAM RATNA RISAL MISHRA, the late. Hindi poet of Mauritius, whose chief poetical collection is : *Bikhre Suman.*

RAM RAY (b. *c.* 1503). Poet of the Chaitanya (Krishna-cult) Sect, who lived in the Radha-Madhav Vatika of Vrindavan. A great Sanskrit scholar, his works are : *Adi Vani* (consisting of 101 *Padas* on the meetings of Krishna and Radha) and *Git Govind Bhasha.*

RAM RUP (1744-90). Rajasthani saint-poet and a follower of Charandasi Sampraday, whose *Muktimarg* (1772), consisting of many poems on Nirgun Bhakti, etc. is held in high esteem. His *Guru Bhakti Prakash* narrates the life of his Guru Charandas (q.v.). He also composed a *Barahmasa.*

RAM RUP DAS (fl. 2nd half of 19th cent.). Maithili saint-poet, who was the founder of the Mari Math at Samastipur. His *Bhajans* are very popular in Mithila.

RAM SAHAY DAS (fl. 1803-23). Poet, who was patronized by Udit Narayan Singh, the Raja of Kashi. He was a resident of Chaubepur (Dist. Benares) and was son of Bhavanidas Kayasth. His *Ram Satsai*, in 700 *Dohas*, is the only book to have been popular among the works composed on the pattern of *Bihari Satsai* (q.v.). Some of its *Dohas* in charming fancy are equal to those of Bihari, but to place the *Ram Satasai* equal to *Bihari Satsai* is not proper. Despite this, *Ram Satsai* is a successful work on *Shringar Rasa.* His other works are : *Vanibhushan* (on *Alankar*), *Vrit-tarangini* (on prosody) and *Kakahara* (on the pattern of *Akharavat* by Jayasi).

RAM SAKHE (fl. 1747). Poet of the Ram-cult (Rasik Sect), who was born in Jaipur. At an early age, he joined the company of wandering monks and visited various places of pilgrimage. Several works have been attributed to him but *Sita Ramchandra Rahasya* and *Nritya Raghav Milan* certainly appear to be his. His language is chiefly Brajbhasha but it betrays the influence of Panjabi, Khari Boli, Avadhi and even Bundeli. He has his religious seats at Rewa and Ayodhya.

RAM SAMUJH PRASAD, the late. Hindi poet of Fiji, whose chief work is : *Jivan kya Hai* ?

RAM SANEHI DAS. Modern Hindi poet of Nepal, who is noted for his *Janaki Charitamrit*.

RAM SATSAI. See *Ram Sahay Das.*

RAM SHANKAR. Modern Hindi poet of Fiji, whose chief work is : *Asha ki Kiranen*.

RAM SHANKAR SHUKLA 'RASAL' (1898-1980). Poet, who was born in Mau (Banda district). He was Head of the Department of Hindi at Gorakhpur University and later on at Jodhpur University. His chief works are : *Ajas Mochan*, *Rasal-Manjari* and *Uddhav-Shatak*.

RAM SHRINGAR GIRI 'VINOD'. Modern Bhojpuri poet, who is noted for his stray poems.

RAM SINGH, SIR (1880-1967). Poet, who was Ruler of Sitamau. His father, Dalel Singh, was a religious-minded man. His *Mohan Vinod*, a collection of Brajbhasha poems, consists of about 400 metres. He also wrote, in collaboration with Suryakaran (q.v.) *Meghmala*, containing 42 sketches resembling the *Gadya Kavya*. The work was written around 1920, but was published in 1979. Ram Singh was also a great Sanskrit scholar.

RAM SINGH (1927-). Poet, whose chief poetical collection is *Samudra-Phen* (Sea-foam).

RAM SINGH, MAHARAJ. Poet of the Riti school, who was the ruler of Narwalgarh State. He composed five works on *Rasa* and *Alankar* : *Rasa Shiromani*, *Yugal Vilas*, *Alankar-Darpan*, *Rasa-Nivas* (1782) and *Rasavinod* (1803). The first work is in *Dohas*.

RAM SINGH SOLANKI. Rajasthani poet, whose *Jan Nayak*

Pratap (1976) in 234 *Sorthas* presents Maharana Pratap as a hero of the people, who fought for freedom and sacrificed everything for the sake of country.

RAM SINGH TANVAR (1902-). Rajasthani scholar, who was among the pioneers in the study of Rajasthani folk-songs and espoused the cause of Rajasthani. He has edited *Veli Krisan Rukmani Ri*, *Dhola Maru ra Duha*, *Chhand Rao Jaitsi Ro*, *Rajasthan ke Lokgit*, etc.

RAM SINGH TOMAR. Modern scholar, whose chief work is *Prakrit aur Apabhransh Sahitya tatha Unka Hindi Sahitya par Prabhav*. He is at present associated with Vishwabharati, Shantiniketan.

RAM SWARUP CHATURVEDI (1931-). Critic, whose chief works are : *Hindi Navlekhan* (The New Writing ; 1960), *Bhasha aur Sanvedana* (1964), *Kavita-Yatra* : *Ratnakar se Raghuvir Sahay* and *Agyey aur Adhunik Rachna ki Samasya*. He declared that modernism is the first important characteristic of the New Writing. Towards foreign influences on Hindi language and literature, he is quite sympathetic and he defends New Writing by considering it, not as a local phenomenon, but as a significant part of a world-wide movement.

RAM SWARUP 'PARESH'. Modern Rajasthani poet, who has composed poems in the style of Nayi Kavita.

RAM VACHAN LAL. Modern Bhojpuri poet, who is noted for his stray poems.

RAM VALLABH (d. 1813). Rajasthani saint-poet of Ram Snehi Sect, Shahpura, whose stray verses are available.

RAM VICHAR PANDEY. Modern Bhojpuri poet of Balia district in Uttar Pradesh, who is known for his collection of poems : *Biniya Bichhiya* and a drama : *Kunvar Singh* on the heroism of Kunvar Singh in the 1857 Mutiny. He has also earned the title of 'Bhojpuri-Ratna' for his excellent poetry in Bhojpuri.

RAM VILAS SHARMA (1912-). Marxist critic and poet, whose chief works are : *Premchand aur Unka Yuga* (Premchand and His Age), *Nirala*, *Bharatendu Harishchandra*, *Pragati aur Parampara* (Progress and Tradition ; 1948), *Pragatishil Sahitya ki Samasyaen* (The Problems of Progressive Literature ; 1954), *Astha aur Saundarya* (1956), *Bhasha, Sahitya aur Sanskriti* (Language, Literature and Culture), *Bharat ki Bhasha Samasya*, *Marxvad aur Prachin Sahitya ka Mulyankan* (Marxism and

Evaluation of Ancient Literature), *Acharya Ramchandra Shukla aur Hindi Alochana*, *Bhasha aur Samaj* (Language and Society), *Swadhinta aur Rashtriya Sahitya* (Independence and National Literature), *Bharatendu Yuga aur Hindi Bhasha ki Vikas-Parampara* (The Age of Bharatendu and the Development of Hindi Language), *Lok Jivan aur Sahitya* (The Common Man and Literature), *Nirala ki Sahityik Sadhna* (The Literary Career of Nirala ; 3 Pts.), *Mahavir Prasad Dwivedi aur Unka Yug* (Dwivedi and His Age), *Mahavir Prasad Dwivedi aur Hindi Navjagaran* (Dwivedi and Hindi Renaissance). *Parampara ka Mulyankan* (The Evaluation of Tradition), *Astitvavad aur Nai Kavita* (Existentialism and New Poetry). *Samkalin Sahitya* (Contemporary Literature), *Bhasha Yuga Bodh aur Kavita* (1981), *Katha Vivechan aur Gadya Shilpa*, *Marxvad aur Pragatishil Sahitya*, *Bharat ke Prachin Bhasha Parivar aur Hindi* (3 Pts., 1981) and *Ghar ki Bat*. Some of his poems are collected in *Tar Saptak* (q.v.), while *Rup Tarang* (The Wave of Beauty ; 1959), *Kavita men Subah*, *Rag Virag* and *Ritugandh* are poetical collections. His work *Nirala ki Sahityik Sadhna* has won him Sahitya Akademy Award. He holds a prominent place among progressive critics.

RAM VRIKSHA BENIPURI (1902-68). Writer, who was born at the village Benipuri in the Muzaffarpur district of Bihar. He started his literary career as a journalist and had edited about a dozen papers. His chief works are : *Laltara* (The Red Star), *Mati ki Murten* (The Clay Idols), *Mil ke Patthar* (The Milestones), *Gehun aur Gulab* (Wheat and Rose), *Qaidi ki Patni* (The Prisoner's Wife), *Chita ka Phul* (sketches, reminiscences, and novels), *Vandevani Vinayakau* (1957 ; collection of essays), *Pairon men Pankh Bandhkar* (1952) and *Udte Chalo, Udte Chalo* (1954 ; both travelogues). He founded 'Nai Dhara', a monthly published from Patna. He is chiefly remembered for his *Mati ki Murten* and *Gehun aur Gulab*. He also wrote a full length play *Ambapali*, portraying the life of the great dancer of Vaishali, who ultimately embraced Buddhism.

RAMADHIN (b. 1884). Poet of Rewa, who was awarded the degree of 'Anyoktyacharya' by the Orchha ruler. He was the author of some eight works and composed 'Sundar-kand' of the *Ramayan* in *Kavittas* at the age of seventeen.

RAMAGYA PRASHNAVALI. Poem by Tulsidas (q.v.), in Avadhi with occasional use of Braj formations, written in 1612 (?).

The work consists of 343 verses, divided into 7 Chaps.,

each of 49 verses. The book is to be used for crystal-gazing; the story of Ram is accidental. Each *Doha* stands for some good or evil and the answer to your question is likewise according as your finger lights on a particular *Doha*.

RAMAKANT. Novelist, whose chief works are *Doshi* (The Culprit; 1979), *Tisra Desh* (The Third Country; 1981) and *Koi aur Bat*. He has published short stories as well; his latest stories are: 'Bhay-mukti' and 'Ghar ki Vitto' (both 1983).

RAMA KANT DWIVEDI 'RAMTA'. Modern Bhojpuri poet, who is known for his stray poems.

RAMAKAR. See *Buddhidhar Singh 'Ramakar'*.

RAMA NAIDU, K. Telugu-speaking modern Hindi writer, who has tr. from Telugu into Hindi Gopichand's novel as *Asmarth ki Jivan-Yatra* (The Life-journey of an Incapacitated) and Balivada Kantarao's novel as *Hara Hua Admi* (A Defeated Man).

RAMANAND (1368-1468). Celebrated saint, who was the preceptor of Kabir, Raidas, Dhanna, Pipa (qq.v.), etc. He was born at Allahabad in a Kanyakubj Brahmin family. *Bhaktamal* gives him as the fourth in Ramanuja's line of disciples. He was an early reformer who did not belive in caste inequities and untouchability. He built a temple and a sect in which all worshippers, irrespective of their castes, could enjoin equally. The Kashi Nagari Pracharini Sabha under the editorship of Hazari Prasad Dwivedi, has published Ramanand's writings in a small book. which include *Ram Raksha* (The Protection by Ram), *Gyan Lila* (The Wonders of the Path of Knowledge), *Hanumanji ki Arti* (Salutation to Hanuman), *Yoga Chintamani* (on Yoga), *Gyan Tilak* (on the Path of Knowledge), *Siddhant Panchmatra* (on principles), *Bhagti Joga* (on devotion), *Ramashtak*, etc. One of his *Padas* has been included in the *Granth Sahib* (q.v.). He occupies a prominent place in both the Sagun and Nirgun Bhakti Movements.

RAMANAND DOSHI (1921-72). Writer and poet, whose chief works are: *Bindu-Bindu Vichar* (Thoughts: Drop by Drop) and *Gile Pankh* (The Wet Feathers; poems). He was editor of 'Kadambini'.

RAMANAND DWIJ (1615-90). Assamese poet, who was the second son of Shriram Ata (q.v.). After the death of his father, he was appointed the Mahant of Kalajhar Vaishnav

Math. So far his 78 songs and one drama : *Prem Kalah Nat* in Hindi (Brajavali) have been published.

RAMANAND JHA 'RAMAN'. Maithili scholar, who has written a critical work in Maithili on modern Maithili poetry (1979) and has also edited *Shyamanand Rachnavali* (1981).

RAMANAND 'RENU'. Maithili fiction writer and poet, whose chief novel *Dudh-Phul* (1967) describes the life of Sakli, who becomes a widow at an early age but refuses to marry so that her young son, Ramesara may not feel lonely and estranged. The work is intensely realistic, human and rich with the rhythm of lower-class life. In his short story collections : *Kachot* (1969) and *Trikon* (1974), he has presented excellent pictures of lower middle classes. His collections of poems are : *Antatah* (1969) and *Okare Nam* (1972).

RAMANAND SAGAR. Writer, whose chief work is a novel, *Aur Insan Mar Gaya* (And the Man Died, 1949). He writes for films in Bombay.

RAMANAND SINGH. Writer, whose chief work is a romantic drama, *Kuvalay Mala* (*c.* 1893).

RAMANAND TIWARI (1919-). Critic, whose chief work is *Satyam, Shivam, Sundaram.*

RAMANAND VASU. Contemporary of Chaitanya (1486-1527), who translated the *Sanskrit Bhagavata* into Bengali. He also composed a *Pada* in Brajbuli, which describes the grandeur and beauty of Radha-Krishna.

RAMA NATH AVASTHI. Modern poet, whose chief poetical works are : *Rat aur Shahnai* (The Night and Clarionet), *Ag aur Parag* (The Fire and Pollen), *Band na Karna Dwar* and *Ab aur Tab.*

RAMA NATH TRIPATHI. Modern writer, who is known for his critical writings and poems ; he has also published a novel *Shankh Sindur.*

RAMA PATI UPADHYAY. Maithili poet, who succeeded in giving a final form to Maithili Kirtaniya drama. He was son of Kavi Krishnapati Jha and was married to the daughter of Thakur Singh, son of Maharaja Narpati Thakur (1692/3-1703/4). His single play, *Rukmini-Parinay* (q.v. ; also called *Rukmini Haran* or *Rukmini-Swayamvar*) was written under the patronage of Maharaja Narendra Singh (1744-61) and staged on the occasion of the Maharaja's Bathing Ceremony in the sacred river, Kamala. The play, based on the Purans, gives an impression of being written in the spirit of a devotee (*Kirtan*) and holds a high place in the history of Kirtaniya drama. Ramapati was also known for his love lyrics.

RAMA SHANKAR SHASTRI. Modern Magahi scholar, whose work *Magahi* (1957) treats of Magahi language.

RAMAI KAKA (1922-). Humorous poet, whose chief works are *Bauchhar* (Showers), *Bhinusar*, Phuhar (Drizzle ; poetical collections) and *Rataundhi* (Night-blindness ; drama). His original name is Chandra Bhushan Trivedi. For many years, he was attached to the All India Radio, Lucknow.

RAMAN BHAI PATEL. Gujarati-speaking modern Hindi scholar, whose *Satven Dashak ke Hindi Upanyas* is a research work.

RAMAN LAL NILKANTH (fl. 19th cent.). Gujarati dramatist, whose Gujarati drama : *Rai no Pravat* contains a Hindi *Doha*. He also edited *Bhavai Sangrah*, a collection of Gujarati folk-dramas ; these folk-dramas contain Hindi *Dohas*, which proves a long tradition of the use of Hindi.

RAMAN LAL PATHAK. Gujarati-speaking modern Hind scholar, whose *Sant Kavi Akha ki Jivni tatha Unki Hindii Kritiyon ka Alochanatmak Adhyayan* is a research work.

RAMAN NAIR, N. Malayalam-speaking modern Hindi writer, who has written several works for the easy learning of Hindi and wrote *Hindi-Malayalam Kosh*. He has made a Hindi version of his Malayalam drama : *Veluttampi Dalava*. His research work is *Hindi tatha Malayalam Bhakti Kavya men Vatsalya Rasa* (Child-love in Hindi and Malayalam Devotional Poetry). He also tr. Malayalam short stories into Hindi.

RAMAULA. Popular ballad of Kumaon and Garhwal region, which contains tales of 17 persons related in some way to Krishna. This ballad brings to life those seven children who were born before Krishna and were put to death by Kansa. Barmi Kanval or Brahma Kumar is one of them. Krishna rubs his body and produces a *bhanvar* or bee and sends a message through it to Brahma Kumar asking him to go to Jaulatal in Tibet and bring *Chausar* from a lady named Motimala. Suraju Kunvar is another brother and the names of other brothers are also given in the list of Naga genealogy of Sem-Mukhem. Krishna is the king of Nagas or Serpents—according to this legend.

Siduva and Viduva are two brothers of Devaki, who by their heroism and magic help Krishna in getting Motimala and Patharmala, who marry Krishna. See *Siduva-Viduva.*

RAMAYAN. Rajasthani Akhyan Kavya in 261 verses by Mehoji (q.v.), which was composed about 1518. The earliest Akhyan Kavya in the tradition of Ram poetry, it was meant to be sung in popular musical modes.

Mehoji has created two new characters : Bhoj, a trustworthy companion of Ravan, and Varahi, Ravan's sister, who are not found in other Akhyans of Ram legend. These two characters might have been current in the popular tradition of the age. Bhoj tells Ravan that Sita is the prettiest woman on the face of the earth and hearing this Ravan decides to abduct Sita. Varahi enquires from a traveller about the welfare of her kith and kin at Lanka, her parental home and she is informed of Ravan's impending doom at the hands of Ram. Some of the scenes are quite enchanting ; for example, Ram in the forest causes a tank to be dug and Sita fetches water in the pair of golden pitchers on her head and with a bowl in her hand. This is a scene dear even today in the north-western parts of Rajasthan.

The poem mentions many popular beliefs and customs and is important from the point of view of poetic excellence, language and style. Most of the story is in dialogues.

RAMAYAN (Maithili). See *Chanda Jha.*

RAMENDRA SHARMA. Assamese-speaking modern Hindi writer, whose memoirs and essays dealing with Assamese culture have appeared in several papers.

RAMESH BAKSHI (1936-). Writer, whose chief works are : *Kisse Upar Kissa* (Story Upon Story ; 1963), *Ek Ghisa Hua Chehra* (A Rubbed Face ; 1963), *Baisakhiyon Vali Imarat* (1966), *Atharah Suraj ke Paudhe* (1965), *Jalta Hua Lava* (The Red Hot Lava ; 1968), *27 Down, Khule Am, Ham Tinke* (novels), *Mez-par Tiki Hui Kahaniyan, Pita-dar-Pita* ; 1971), *Gustakhi Maf, Ek Amurt Taklif, Jinke Makan Dhahte Hain* (short story collections), *Devyani ka Kahna Hai* (Devyani Has Said ; collection of one-act plays), *Kase Hue Tar* (The Tightened Wires), *Tisra Hathi* (The Third Elephant), *Chhote Natak, Vamachar* and *Rupantar*. He also wrote a Malwi drama : *Uma Kaki*. His important short stories in Khari Boli are : 'Shabri', 'Pita-dar-Pita' (Father and Father's Father), etc.

RAMESH BHARDWAJ. Modern scholar, who is known for his work, *Vishwa Bhashaon ka Hindi ko Yogdan.*

RAMESH CHANDRA LAVANIA (1940-). Scholar, whose chief work is : *Hindi Kahani men Jivan Mulya* (1973).

RAMESH CHANDRA MEHROTRA. Author of *Bhashiki ke Das Lekh* (1969).

RAMESH CHANDRA PANDYA. Gujarati-speaking modern Hindi scholar, whose *Hindi Kahani : Vividh Sansthan* is a research work.

RAMESH CHANDRA SHAH. Gujarati-speaking Hindi poet, whose collection of poems is *Harishchandra Ao* (Come Harishchandra ; 1980) ; his *Gobar Ganesh* (1978) and *Shaitan ke Bahane* are novels. *Hindi Gujarati Lokoktiyon aur Muhavaron ka Tulnatmak Adhyayan* is his research work. He has also written a drama : *Mara Jai Khusro.*

RAMESH CHAUDHARI, ARIGPUDI. Telugu-speaking modern Hindi writer, whose chief works are : *Nadi ka Shor* (popular social novel), *Ulti Ganga, Abhishap, Antim Upay, Ye Chhote Bade Log* (novels), *Andhabhikshu* (historical novel), *Jine ki Saza* (The Punishment of Living), *Ek Pahiye ki Gadi, Kala Poshak, Vichitra Nidan* and *Maya Sud Ke* (1984) (short story collections). He has also written a social drama : *Koi-na-Paraya,* folk-tales : *Andhra ki Lok-Kathayen* (The Folk-tales of Andhra ; 1955) and composed poems under the pseudonym of 'Vanjasan'. *Nepathya* is a collection of his stage-worthy one-act plays, while *Bijli aur Barish* (The Lightning and Rain) is a collection of his 14 radio one-act plays. He tr. the famous Telugu novel *Narayanrao* into Hindi.

RAMESH KUMAR SHARMA (1926-). Writer, whose chief works are: *Hindi aur Uske Acharya* (Hindi and its Acharyas; criticism), *Ritikal aur Adhunik Hindi Kavita* (Riti Period and Modern Hindi Poetry) and *Riti Kal ka Punarmulyankan. Vitasta ke Naye Charan* is his poetical collection.

RAMESH KUMAR SHIL. Modern short story writer, whose chief short story collection is *Khirki* (The Window).

RAMESH KUNTAL MEGH. Writer, whose chief works are : *Mithak aur Swapna : Kamayani ki Manassaundarya Samajik Bhumika* (1967), *Tulsi : Adhunik Vatayan Se* (1967), *Madhyayugin Rasa-darshan aur Samkalin Saundarya-Bodh*

(1969), *Adhunikta Bodh aur Adhunikikaran* (1969), *Saundarya-mulya aur Mulyankan* (1975), *Kyonki Samay Ek Shabda Hai* (1975) *Athato Saundarya-jigyasa* (1977) and *Sakshi Hain Saundarya Prashnik* (1980). He is Head of the Hindi Department, G.N.D. University, Amritsar.

RAMESH MATHUR. Modern Hindi scholar, who is looking after the teaching of Hindi in the Kansai University of Foreign Studies in Japan. This University has a good collection of Hindi books.

RAMESH MEHTA (1947-). Dogri-speaking Hindi poet, who is known for his *Khule Kamre Band Dwar* (Open Rooms, Closed Doors), a poetical collection. Under the title *Pratinidhi Kahaniyan* (Representative Short Stories), he has ed. and tr. short stories from Kashmiri and Dogri, while under the title *Kohra aur Dhup* (The Fog and Sunshine), he has edited and tr. Urdu short stories of Jammu-Kashmir. He wrote *Hamara Gaon* (Our Village) for the Song and Drama Division, which was tr. into every Indian language. He has written 18 plays and they proved extremely popular.

RAMESH RANJAK. Poet, whose poetical collections are: *Git Vihag Utra*, *Mitti Bolti Hai* (The Soil Speaks; 1967), *Ramesh Ranjak ke Lok-Git* (The Folk-songs of Ramesh Ranjak; 1978), *Itihas Dubara Likho* and *Harapan Nahin Tutega.*

RAMESH UPADHYAY. Writer, whose chief works are: *Swapnamayl* (The Dreamlike; 1971), *Grih yuddha* (Civil War; 1981; novels), *Nadi ke Sath* (Along with the Stream), *Paidal Andhere Men* (On Foot in Darkness; 1981), *Chaturdik* and *Balav se Pahle* are his short story collections. His important short stories are: 'Julus' (The Procession), 'Upjivi' (The Dependent), 'Astachal' (The Sunset), 'Pani ki Lakir' (The Line of the Water), 'Samtal' (The Even Surface), 'Apne Bich' (Amidst One's Self), etc. His dramas are: *Paper Weight* and *Safai Chalu Hai.*

RAMSHESHAYYA, CHODVARPU. Telugu-speaking modern Hindi writer, who has established his place as a historical dramatist. His chief works are: *Bobbili*, *Rani Mallamma* (both in 3 Acts on the brave story of Rani Mallamma), *Rani Kannaki* (based on the famous Tamil story) and *Grihani* (a social drama). His plays have been very successful on the stage.

RAMESHWAMEDH. See *Madhusudan Das.*

RAMESHWAR. Maithili poet, who was noted for his lyrics. He was a contemporary of Maharaja Raghav Singh (1704-40). His verses found respectable place in contemporary anthologies.

RAMESHWAR DAYAL SHRIMALI. Rajasthani poet, who is a school teacher by profession. His chief works are : *Hadi Rani* (1965 ; in blank verse ; for its story see *Sainani*), *Bavno Himalo* (1971 ; in the traditional form of Dingal *Git*, it describes the ideals for which Mahatma Gandhi fought) and *Mharo Gaon* (1978 ; containing satirical poems on rural life). He has composed progressive poems as also the poems in the style of Nayi Kavita. He has written short stories, e.g., *Salvaten* (1980 ; a collection of short stories).

RAMESHWAR LAL KHANDELWAL 'TARUN' (1919-). Writer, whose chief works are : *Hindi Kavita men Prakriti Chitran* (Nature in Hindi Poetry ; thesis), *Adhunik Hindi Kavita men Prem aur Saundarya* (Love and Beauty in Modern Hindi Poetry), *Hindi Alochana ke Adhar Stambh* (with Suresh Chand Gupta), *Samiksha ke Vatayan*, *Jayshankar Prasad* : *Vastu aur Kala* (criticism) ; *Andhi aur Chandni* (The Windstorm and Moonlight ; 1975) and *Ham Shilpi Santras Ke* are collections of his poems. He was Head, Department of Hindi at Kurukshetra University.

RAMESHWAR PRASAD MISHRA (1925-). Bagheli folk-poet, who was born at the village Bamhauri in the Satna district ; his poems are published in magazines.

RAMESHWAR RAMAYAN. See *Laldas*.

RAMESHWAR SHUKLA 'ANCHAL' (1915-). Poet and writer, who was born at Kishenpur in the Fatehpur district of Uttar Pradesh. He was Principal of Mahakaushal Arts College and a senior teacher in the Jabulpore University. His chief works are :

Poetry : *Madhulika* (1938), *Aparajita*, *Kiranvela*, *Karil*, *Lal Chunar*, *Varshant ke Badal*, *Viram Chihna* (1957), *Pratyush ki Bhatki Kiran Yayavari* and *Anupurva* (all poetical collections) ; in his earlier works, he comes out with his new vision of romanticism and nationalism. His *Varshant ke Badal* (Clouds After Rainy Season) is a tribute to his faith in man and nature. His satirical collection is *Gan-Tantra ki Den* (1980). His *Aparadhita* (1983), a *Prabandh-Kavya*, is on the story of Amba.

His prose works are *Chadhti Dhup* (Rising Sunshine ; 1945, on the problem of marriage), *Nai Imarat* (New Building ; 1946), *Ulka* (1947), *Marupradip* (1951 ; all novels), *Samaj aur Sahitya* (1944), *Rekha-Lekha* (1957 ; both collections of essays) and *Hindi Sahitya Anushilan* (1952 ; criticism).

RAMESHWAR SINGH KASHYAP (1927-). Dramatist, whose chief works are : *Loha Singh*, *Samadhan*, *Bekari ka Ilaj* and *Aparajey Nirala* (The Invincible Nirala) ; he has published some one-act plays as also poems in Bhojpuri.

RAMOLA. See *Ramaula*.

RAMU KHOD (fl. end of 18th cent.). Rajasthani saint-poet of the Vishnoi Sect, whose stray verses are available.

RANAWAT, S.S. Rajasthani poet, whose *Dodhyan Baithi Dekar Boli* (1979) is a collection of 30 poems on the theme of woman, for the poet is of the view that literature will be bankrupt if woman is excluded from it.

RANCHHOD DAS (fl. 18th cent.). Poet of the Krishna-cult (Haridasi Sect), who was noted for his *Padas*.

RANCHHOD DAS, DEWAN (fl. early 19th cent.). Rajasthani scholar, whose *Ran Pingal* (3 Pts.) is a work on metrics.

RANDHAVAL RI VAT. See *Mayan Bhatt*.

RANDHIR LAL SHRIVASTAV. Modern Bhojpuri poet, whose *Barvai Shatak* treats of the folk-life.

RANDHIR UPADHYAY. Gujarati-speaking modern Hindi scholar, whose *Hindi Gujarati Natya Sahitya : Tulnatmak Adhyayan* is a research work.

RANG AVDHUT (1898-1967). Hindi poet of Gujarat, who was born at Godhra. For 30 years, he did spiritual meditation. His works are : *Datt Bavni*, *Padyagita*, *Sangit Gita*, *Shriguru Lilamrit* ; *Avdhuti Mauj* is a collection of his *Bhajans*. He has a good number of followers in Gujarat. On his works and language, he had the unmistakable influence of Sufism.

RANG BHUMI (The Theatre). Novel (1924) by Premchand

(q.v.), which betrays the influence of Gandhian philosophy and of the Satyagraha and Non-Co-operation Movements.

The blind Surdas of Pandepur, Benares, is not prepared to dispose of his land to Christian capitalist, John Sewak for his cigarette factory, but with the influence that John Sewak has with the Municipal Board Chairman, Raja Mahendrakumar, he succeeds in his mission. Sophia, the daughter of John Sewak and of progressive views, wishes to get the land sale-deed annulled by the Magistrate Clarke, but is not successful; the Magistrate is, however, transferred from Benares to Udaipur. During this time, Vinay, brother-in-law of Raja Mahendrakumar, and Sophia come in contact with each other and fall in love, but discovering this affair, Vinay's mother sends him to Udaipur for social service. While advocating for people's cause, Vinay is sent to jail under the orders of Clarke; Sophia also reaches Udaipur and stays with Clarke so that she can get Vinay released but as the people reach Clarke's bungalow in a procession, Sophia is abducted by a revolutionary and carried to a jungle, where she meets Vinay. Vinay and Sophia live together for a year at an unknown place and then reach Benares.

John Sewak's cigarette factory is established but for settling the labour in a colony, the village Pandepur is to be vacated; John Sewak secures orders from Mahendrakumar for the demolition of houses. All the houses have been pulled down, save the hut of Surdas. With malice towards none, Surdas stands silently before his hut and thousands of people come to see this spectacle. People are agitated, but suddenly Surdas is hit by a bullet. He is treated in the hospital, where everyone including Mahendrakumar, John Sewak and Sophia visit him. The people are not fully assured of Vinay's loyalty to the national cause and to prove his love for the country, he commits suicide. Sophia, distressed as she is on this sad event, also plunges into the Ganges and dies.

The novel depicts the ill-effects of industrialisation and how it replaces the simple and charming rural setting; it also simultaneously gives a vivid description of the freedom struggle India was waging under the leadership of Mahatma Gandhi.

RANG NARAYAN PAL VERMA 'RANGPAL', MAHARAJKUMAR (1864-1936). Poet of Hariharpur (Basti district), whose *Padas*, folk-songs as also other works: *Prem Latika*, *Angadarsh*, *Vir Virud*, etc. are available.

RANG NATH SWAMI (fl. 17th cent.). Saint-poet of Maharashtra, who was a follower of Smarth Sect. In addition to his Marathi works, he composed some *Padas* in Hindi.

RANG RELO VITHU. See *Virdas Rohdiyo*.

RANGA, L.N. Rajasthani writer, whose *Hariya Suvatiya* (1981) is a book of four folk-tales meant for children.

RANGAYYA, M. Telugu-speaking Hindi writer, who has tr. the select poems of modern Telugu poets under the title *Telugu Kavya Parimal* (1977).

RANGEY RAGHAV (1923-62). Famous novelist, progressive critic and poet, who was born in Agra. His mother was a Kannada-speaking lady, while his father was Tamil-speaking. His original name was T.N.V. Acharya. His chief works are :

Novel : *Vishad-Math* (The Cloister of Sorrow), *Mere Huzur* (My Lord), *Gharaunde* (Mini Houses), *Sidha-Sada-Rasta* (The Straight Path), *Dayra* (The Circle), etc. (realist), *Akhiri Avaz* (The Last Voice), *Kab tak Pukarun* ? (How Long should I call ? ; 1957), *Dharti Mera Ghar* (The Earth : My House), *Path ka Pap* (The Sin on the Way), *Rai aur Parvat*, etc. (regional), *Yashodhara Jit Gai* (Yashodhara has Won), *Dhuni ka Dhuan* (on Gorakhnath), *Jab Ayegi Kali Ghata* (on Charpatnath), *Lakhma ki Ankhey* (on Vidyapati), *Loi ka Tana* (on Kabir), *Ratna ki Bat* (on Tulsidas), *Meri Bhav Badha Haro* (on Bihari), *Andhere ke Jugnu* (The Glow-worms of Darkness), *Chivar*, *Murdon ka Tila* (The Mound of the Dead), etc. (historical). He has written some 40 novels and some of his other novels are : *Pratidan* (The Counter-Gift), *Ubal* (The Boiling), *Pakshi aur Akash* (The Bird and the Sky), *Kaka*, *Andhi ki Naven* (The Boats of Windstorm), *Bolte Khandahar* (The Speaking Ruins) and *Mahayatra Gatha* ; the *Murdon ka Tila* (q.v.), his *magnum opus* and one of the foremost historical novels of Hindi, is based on the history of Indus Valley as reconstructed on the basis of Mohenjodaro excavations.

Poetry : *Ajey Khandahar* (The Invincible Ruins ; 1948, based on the battle of Stalingrad), *Pighalte Patthar* (The Melting Stones), *Medhavi* (on temporary economic and social problems), *Rah ke Dipak* (The Lamps of the Road ; poetical collection with humanist element), *Panchali* (a *Khand-Kavya* based on the story of Draupadi-Jaydrath) and *Rup Chhaya* (a Prabandh-Kavya). He was an innovative poet, who combined experiments with social realism.

Drama : *Ramanuj* (on the celebrated saint-philosopher Ramanuj), *Virudhak* (relating to the Buddhist period), and one-act plays.

Short Story Collection : *Ek Chhod Ek* ; his important short stories are : 'Gadal' (on a Gujar woman), 'Sanjh ke Shikari', 'Narak', 'Angar na Bujhe', 'Adhuri Murat', 'Devdasi', etc.

Essay collection : *Sangam aur Sangharsh, Bharatiya Sant Parampara aur Samaj, Kavya* and *Kala aur Shastra.*

His critical works are : *Tulsidas ka Kathashilp, Gorakhnath aur Unka Yuga* (Ph. D. thesis from Agra University in 1948) and *Prachin Bharatiya Parampara aur Itihas.*

His other works are : *Tufanon ke Bich* (collection of reportages ; based on 1943-44 Bengal Famine), *Panch Gadhe* (political reportages), *Davedar, Gati ka Satya, Dalal* (reportages on social background) and tr. in Hindi of *Dashakumara Charita.*

RANGI LAL (fl. 17th cent.). Writer, who is noted for his prose work, *Braj-Premanandamrit.*

RANGI LAL. Poet, who was a contemporary of Narayan Swami (1828-1900). He was the author of many works on Krishna's sports and on mythological stories.

RANI KETKI KI KAHANI. See *Insha Allah Khan.*

RANJAN VERMA. Writer, whose chief work, *Album* (1970) is a novel.

RANJHA. Celebrated romance of Heer and Ranjha, which is of Punjab origin, but is also popular in Braj where it is sung mostly by Muslims. In the Braj, version of the story, Ranjha has been shown as blessed and initiated by Gorakhnath.

RANJIT (1937-). Modern poet, whose chief poetical work is *Itihas ka Dard* (The Pangs of History).

RANJIT MALL (r. *c.* 1722-72). Last Ruler of the House of Bhatgao in Nepal, who is known as the compiler of a work on music called, *Sangit-Chudamani,* which contains Maithili lyrics only. His Maithili lyrics collected in anthologies are sincerely devotional. His prose dramas are : *Ram-Charit* (1725), *Krishna-Charit* (1738), *Krishna-Kailas-Yatropakhyan* (1747), *Usha-Haran* (1754 ; in 9 Acts ; staged on the occasion of the repairs of Har Temple), *Indra-Jay-Natak, Mandhatryopakhyan* (1764), *Kolashur-Badhopakhyan* (1766), *Khatvasur-Badhopakhyan* (1767), *Andhakasur-Badhopakhyan* (1768), *Krishna-Charitropakhyan, Madan-Charit, Ramayan-Nataka* (in about 200 pages), *Madhavanal-Kamkandala* (having Bhanitas of Dhanpati), *Nal-Charit* (having Bhanitas of one Ganesh), *Rukmini-Parinay* (in 5 Acts), *Har Gauri-Katha* and several other mythological plays. Most of these dramas were staged to celebrate an auspicious occasion. Some of these dramas are mixed with Bengali ; there is frequent use of prose in these dramas. The plot of *Madhavanal-Kamkandala* is the same as in Rajasthani works, though with slight variations in details.

RANJIT SINGH. Modern scholar, who is noted for his *Sant Nishchaldas : Vyaktitwa aur Krititwa.*

RANKING, G.S.A. *Author of A Guide to Hindustani, specially designed for the use of officers and men serving in India* (Calcutta, 1895).

RAN MALL CHHAND. Rajasthani poem in 70 verses, which was composed by Shridhar Vyas around 1400.

It describes the battle, which Rao Ranmall Rathore of Idar fought against Zafarkhan, the Governor of Gujarat, when the latter invaded Idar in 1398. Ranmall fought fearlessly and bravely and defeated the enemy. Its alliterative diction and vivid description of battle make it a poem of distinction. The first ten verses of this poem are in Sanskrit.

RAN VIR RANGRA (1924-). Scholar, whose chief works are : *Hindi Upanyas men Charitra-Chitran ka Vikas* (The Development of Characterization in Hindi Novels ; 1961), *Srijan ki Manobhumi* (1968), *Sahityik Sakshatkar* (Literary Interviews ; 1978) and *Hindi Upanyas ki Bhumika* (The Background of Hindi Novel ; 1984). He was Director of Central Hindi Directorate, New Delhi.

RAN VIR SINGH, MAHARAJA (r. 1857-85). Ruler of Kashmir, who was instrumental in getting certain works tr. into Hindi and for printing them established a printing press 'Vidyavilas'. The chief works printed at this Press are : *Kirtivilas* by Nilkanth in 1886 ; *Dhananjay Vijay* (1885 ; tr. from Sanskrit), *Ranvir Ratnamala*, *Ranvir Bhasha Prakash* and *Trikuta-Rahasya*. The works, which were written at the instance of the Maharaja but remained so far unpublished are : *Nilkanth ki Vanshavali* (describing the dynasty of the Ruler ; it brings to notice the first specimen of the State's Hindi prose) and Rajendra Prasad's *Naglila* (description of Krishna's deeds in the style of *Chaupais*). The Maharaja also wanted a Hindi magazine 'Jambu Prakash' to be started and had appointed Durga Prasad Mishra as its editor but with the death of the Maharaja, the scheme fell through.

RANVIR SINGH SHAKTAWAT 'RASIK', THAKUR (1909-80). Rajasthani poet, who in his *Pratap Mahakavya* (1973) in Khari Boli eulogizes Rana Pratap in 236 *Dohas*. Earlier, he composed *Narsi-Charit* and stray verses.

RANVIR UPADHYAY. Modern scholar, who is noted for his *Hindi aur Gujarati Natya Sahitya ka Tulnatmak Adhyayan.*

RAO, ADESHWAR. See *Adeshwar Rao, P.*

RAO, BAKHTAVAR. See *Bakhtavar.*

RAO JAITSI CHHAND (*Rao Jaitsi ro Paghadi Chhand*). Dingal poem in 485 verses composed by an unknown author between 1534-41, which describes the defeat of Kamran, the second son of Babar, at the hands of Rao Jaitsi of Bikaner in 1534. The descriptions in this poem are similar to the ones in Vithu Sujo's poem on a similar theme, except that this poem starts from Rao Salkha, the grandfather of Rao Chunda and descriptions relating to Salkha, Viram and Goga are additions to it. The poem is of utmost historical value.

RAO JAITSI RO PAGHADI CHHAND. See *Vithu Sujo.*

RAO RATAN RI VELI. See *Kalyandas Mehdu Jadawat.*

RAO VENA. See *Gunmal Shah Dev Karan Ri.*

RAS BIHARILAL DAS. Maithili novelist, whose *Sumati* (1918) is a didactic novel.

RASA-KALASH (The Pitcher of Rasa). Poem (1931) by Ayodhya Singh Upadhyay 'Hariaudh' (q.v.), which introduces a new point of view into the treatment of the old *Rasa* theme. Written in Brajbhasha in the style of the Riti school of poetry, it describes also *Nayikas* (heroines) devoted to the cause of country and religion.

RASA-RAHASYA. See *Kulpati Mishra.*

RASARAJ (The King of Rasas). Poem on *Rasa* by Matiram (q.v.), a Riti poet, considered to be his masterpiece.

This monumental work, consisting of 426 verses, is without any dedication. Written in the true Riti style, it provides the key to all the *Rasas*. It is a perfect guide and is encyclopaedic in scope so far as the *Rasas* are concerned. After explaining the significance of each *Rasa*, the poet proceeds to furnish suitable illustrations and it is here that he excels himself. For a proper understanding of *Rasas*, there is no better or handier book than the *Rasaraj*. This work reveals Matiram's finest poetry and is one of the classics of Riti poetry.

RASARATNA. See *Puhukar*.

RASA-SIDDHANT. See *Nagendra*.

RASHID AHMED PAHARI. Modern Rajasthani poet, who has composed Nature, patriotic and heroic poems.

RASHMIRATHI. See *Ramdhari Singh 'Dinkar'*.

RASIK (fl. 1574). Poet of the Krishna-cult (Vallabh Sect), whose *Padas* about Krishna's sports are collected in the *Rag Kalpadrum*.

RASIK ALI. See *Janakraj Kishorisharan*.

RASIK BIHARI (d. 1765). Poetess of the Krishna-cult, who composed songs in Brajbhasha and Rajasthani. Besides, she wrote on the cycle of seasons, on Vrindavan and Yamuna. She was the wife of Nagaridas (q.v.) and was also called Banithaniji. Her compositions are included in the *Nagar Samuchchay*.

RASIKDAS (fl. 1593-1643). Poet of the Krishna-cult (Radhavallabh Sect), who was a Kayasth of Bairath ; only his stray *Padas* are available.

RASIKDAS (fl. 1663-1703). Poet of the Krishna-cult (Radhavallabh Sect), who was a disciple of Goswami Dhiridhar and was a native of Bhelsa. He named his poems after 'Lata' and the number of such 'Latas' is 22. Apart from these 'Latas', another work *Rasakadamb Chudamani* (2 Pts.) is available.

RASIKDAS (fl. 1663-1743). Poet of the Krishna-cult (Radhavallabh Sect), whose several *Padas* are quite popular.

RASIKDAS (fl. 1723-93). Poet of the Krishna-cult (Radhavallabh Sect), whose stray *Padas* are available.

RASIKDAS (fl. early 19th cent. ?). Poet of the Krishna-cult (Radhavallabh Sect), who occupied the religious seat of

Chandrasakhi. Chacha Vrindavandas in his 'Vasant Prabandh' has made a reference to him ; so far his works have not come to light.

RASIKDEV (fl. early 18th cent.). Poet of the Krishna-cult (Haridasi Sect), whose chief works are : *Guru Mangal* (1702), *Puja Vilas*, *Kunj Kautuk* (The Sports in a Bower), etc.

RASIK GOVIND (fl. 1793-1833). Poet of the Riti school, who was a resident of Jaipur, but lived in Vrindavan as a follower of Nimbark Sampraday. So far his nine works have been discovered, which are : *Ramayan Suchanika* (describing the story of *Ramayan* in 33 *Dohas*), *Rasik Govindanand Ghan* (1801 ; the author's chief work running into 700-800 pages, on *Rasa*, *Nayak-Nayikabhed*, *Alankar*, *Guna-Dosh, etc.*), *Lachhiman Chandrika* (a treatise on *Lakshanas*, composed at the instance of Lachhiman), *Ashtadesh-bhasha*, *Pingal*, *Samaya-Prabandh*, *Kaliyug Raso* (1808), *Rasik Govind* (1833 ; on *Alankar*) and *Yugal-rasa Madhuri*. The poet has made a detailed treatment of *Kavyangas*. He is the only Acharya in the Riti period, who wrote *Lakshanas* in prose and while explaining *Rasa*, *Alankar*, *Shabda-Shaktis*, quoted Sanskrit rhetoricians also. He can also be termed as the first writer of literary prose in Brajbhasha.

RASIK KISHORI (fl. 18th cent.). Poet of the Krishna-cult (Haridasi Sect), who was known for his *Anand Prabhasika* (on bliss) and *Padas*.

RASIK MOHAN RAY (fl. 16th cent.). Poet of the Krishna-cult (Chaitanya Sect), who was a disciple of Chandragopal (q.v.). His chief work *Rasik Sevak Vani* contains 155 *Kundliyas*. He also composed some *Padas* under the pen name of 'Rasik Sakhi'.

RASIK PRIYA. Riti work (1591) by Keshav Das (q.v.), in which all the nine *Rasas* are illustrated. The first 13 chapters describe in detail the erotic emotion, the hero and heroine, sexual conditions, details of meeting and parting, while in the last three chapters are described other *Rasas*, *Vrittis* and poetic fallacies (*Kavya doshas*).

RASIK PUNNIGE. Kannada-speaking modern Hindi poet, whose poems are collected in *Dakshin Kavya Kusumanjali* (1 77). He also tr. some Kannada songs as also Suryanath Kant's Kannada historical novel *Krishnadev Ray* into Hindi.

RASIK SUMATI (fl. 1728). Poet of the Riti school, who was the author of the *Alankar-Chandroday*, a work on *Alankars*, written after the manner of the Sanskrit work, *Kuvalayananda*. He was a native of Agra and his father's name was Upadhyay Ishwardas.

RASKHAN (1548-1628). Muslim poet of the Krishna-cult, who was a Pathan Sardar, Syed Ibrahim by name and claimed descent from the Pathan rulers of Delhi. He was madly in love with a boy ; he once heard people saying that they should love God as dearly as Ibrahim loves his boy. Ibrahim could not brook this taunt and proceeded to Gokul in search of a preceptor ; there Vitthalnath initiated him into the Vaishnav cult, though not admitting him to the *Ashtachhap*. It is also said that he loved Manini, a lady and due to her behaviour, he left for Vrindavan. Under the nom de plume of Raskhan, he composed verses in honour of Krishna, which are full of devotion and sweetness. He was the author of two small works : *Prem Vatika* (The Garden of Love) composed in 52 *Dohas* and *Sorthas* and *Sujan Raskhan* in 129 *Ghanakshari* and *Savaiyas*. He made a departure from the lyric pattern of Krishnite poets and used *Kavittas* and *Savaiyas*, which became so popular that the name 'Raskhan' came to be termed for them. Though his verses cannot be set to music, they have a verbal melody. Despite the clever use of alliteration, the language is most chaste and unostentatious, which is peculiar to him and to Ghananand (q.v.). His poetry reveals his great love for the Brajbhumi and his yearning to be in Vrindavan, whose very trees, rocks, soil and the birds he envies.

RASALIN, SYED GHULAM NABI (b. 1699). Poet of the Riti school, who resided in the famous village of Bilgram in the Hardoi district. He composed his *Ang Darpan* in 1737, which is a book on *Nakhshikh* ; the work is reputed for its beautiful couplets, some of which are still popular. His other book, *Rasa Prabodh* (1741) is on the theory of *Rasa* and is quite good in its own way. Primarily, Raslin is a poet of Shringar ; he is adept in delineating feminine beauty, but at the same time, he is susceptible to the charms of Nature. In his poetry, there is a touch of versatility. In both of his works, he proceeds with the thoroughness of an *Acharya* to explain the various *Rasas* and the different figures of speech. The fondness he had for the *Dohas* and the skill with which he uses, Rasalin reminds of the great poet Bihari (q.v.). Raslin was a scholar of Arabic and Persian too.

RASNIDHI (fl. 1660). Poet, whose full name was Prithwi Singh and he was a Zamindar of Datiya. His *Ratan Hazara* is composed in *Dohas* on the pattern of *Bihari Satsai* (q.v.) ; at places he has borrowed in his work full sentences from Bihari. Apart from *Ratan Hazara*, he wrote a good number of *Dohas*. Another work, *Arill aur Manjho* has also been discovered. A poet of *Shringar Rasa*, in his *Dohas*, he tried hard to infuse the spirit of Persian poetry.

RASPANCHADHYAYI. Popular poem by Nand Das (fl. *c.* 1568 ; q.v.), one of the members of the *Ashtachhap*.

As its very name implies, the work treats of Krishna's *Ras-Lila* in five chapters, corresponding to the five chapters of the *Bhagavat Puran* on this topic. In Chapter I, Krishna, at the instance of Gopis, agrees to wander in the groves but later on disappears for some time ; in Chapter II, Gopis search Krishna in the groves and ask his whereabouts of creepers and trees. The description in this chapter is very charming and full of pathos. In the following chapter, Gopis entreat Krishna to re-appear ; Chapter IV treats of Krishna's appearance before the Gopis ; the last chapter describes the *Ras-Lila*.

The work is mainly based on the *Bhagavat*. There is a charming description of the sentiments of *Shringar*, *Shant* and *Karun* ; the display of the sentiment Pathos stands unsurpassed in the Hindi literature. There is a full use of alliterations, similes and the metres *Doha* and *Rola*. The flow of language is charming and natural ; the descriptions are so graphic and real that the pictures present themselves before the eyes. There is wonderful setting of verses inasmuch as each verse is a testament to the consummate skill of the poet.

RASPUNJ DAS (fl. 1773). Rajasthani poet, who composed four works : *Prastar Prabhakar*, *Vritt Vinod*, *Chamatkar Chandroday* and *Kavitta Shri Mataji Ra*.

RASRANG (fl. 18th cent.). Poet of the Krishna-cult (Haridasi Sect), whose only one *Pada* is extant.

RASRUP (fl. end of 17th cent.). Poet of the Riti school, whose chief work on Riti is *Tulsi-Bhushan*, a work on *Alankar*.

RASTOGI, D.S. (1926-). Critic, whose chief works are : *Tulnatmak Adhyayan* (1952), *Hindi Sahitya ka Itihas* (1976), *Hindi men Sahityik Nibandh* (1978) and *Bharatiya Kavya Shastra* (1980).

RASVANTI. See *Ramdhari Singh 'Dinkar'*.

RATAN-BAVNI. See *Keshavdas.*

RATAN JANKAR, S.N. Scholar, who was known for his *Folk-songs of Bharatpur* (1939).

RATAN KAVI (b. 1741). Poet of the Riti school, who on the name of his patron, Raja Fateh Shahi of Shrinagar (Garhwal) composed his *Fateh Bhushan*, a work not only on *Alankar*, but on *Lakshana, Dhwani, Rasa*, etc. He composed another work, *Alankar-Darpan* in 1770.

RATAN LAL MEHTA. Modern Malwi scholar, whose chief work is : *Malwi Kahavaten* (Proverbs).

RATAN LAL SHANT (1938-). Kashmiri-speaking Hindi poet, whose *Khoti Kiranen* (The False Rays) is a collection of poems, bearing pessimistic strain. He has also tr. into Hindi verse *Poshimal*, Kashmiri Ghazals of Rasul Mir.

RATAN RASO. See *Kumbharan Sandu.*

RATAN RASO. See *Jaggaji.*

RATAN VILAS. See *Vithu Bhoma.*

RATANU, AKSHAY SINGH. See *Akshay Singh Ratanu.*

RATANU VIRBHAN BHOJRAJAUT (1688-1735). Rajasthani court-poet of Maharaja Abhaysingh of Jodhpur, whose *Raj Rupak* (q.v.) describes the battle of Ahmedabad, which his patron fought against Sar Bulandkhan, the Governor of Gujarat in 1730. His other works are : *Ekakshari Nam-Mala* (a mono-syllabic lexicon), *Bhagavat Prakash* (a poem based on the 10th canto of the *Bhagavat Puran*) and stray verses on several heroes.

RATHAUD RATANSINGH RI VELI. See *Dudo Visral.*

RATHODAN RI VANSAVALI SIHAIJI SUN KALYAN-MALJI TAIN. The earliest Rajasthani Khyat, which was composed around 1573 by an anonymous author. It is a historical work and provides a good example of standard and creative prose.

RATIPATI BHAGAT (fl. late 18th or early 19th cent. ?). Maithili poet, who tr. into Maithili Jayadeva's *Gita-Govinda* from the Sanskrit original. The poem was mostly popular in south

Mithila. Ratipati regarded this work as a Mahakavya, divided into 12 cantos.

RATNA HARI (b. 1791). Poet of the Ram-cult, whose chief devotional works are : *Duradurarth Dohavali*, *Yamak-Damak Dohavali*, *Ram-Rahasya Purvardha*, *Ram-Rahasya Uttarardha* and *Nanak Yash Chandrika*. Formerly he was a follower of Udasi Sampraday of Amritsar but was later converted to Vaishnavism. He also held Guru Nanak in great esteem.

RATNAKAR. See *Jagannath Das 'Ratnakar'*.

RATNA KIRTI BHATTARAK (*c.* 1543-99). Gujarati Jain poet, whom Abhaynandi made his disciple, when impressed by his genius and learning. In 1586, he was awarded the honour of 'Bhattarak' by his Guru. He was very handsome and married many a maiden in a spiritual way. Ratnakirti's disciples have sung several songs in praise of his beauty.

Of his works, 40 *Padas*, *Neminath Phag*, *Neminath Barahmasa*, *Nemishwar Hindolna*, *Nemishwar Ras* are extant. The poet has described the pangs of separation of Rajul. The language is Apabhransh mixed Gujarati-Hindi.

RATNA MAYI DIKSHIT. Malayalam-speaking Hindi writer, who has tr. into Hindi Malayalam poet Vallattol Narayan Menon's poems in the collection : *Bharatiya Kavita* and has written *Kerali Sahitya Darshan* (on literary philosophy).

RATNA PANI . Maithili poet, whose *Usha-Haran* (*c.* 1850 ; q.v.), a Kirtaniya drama, was written under the patronage of Chhatra Singh (1808-39) and Rudra Singh (1839-50). Noted for his lyrics, he also composed hymns on devotional and pseudo-philosophical subjects.

RATNA SHANKAR PRASAD. Modern writer, who is noted for his *Prasad Vangmaya ka Prakkathan.*

RATNA SINGH (of Sitamau). See *Natnagar*.

RATNAI, KAVI (fl. prior to 1685). Maithili poet, whose lyrics are quoted in anthologies. He may be identified with the poet Ratnani or Kavi Ratna ; he mentions Raja Lakhan Chand.

RATNAVALI. Wife of Tulsidas (q.v.), the celebrated Hindi poet, who is said to have written 111 *Dohas*, mainly preaching celibacy and sexual restraint.

RATNO BHAGAT (1874-1944). Hindi poet of Gujarat, who

was born at the village Mamuara near Bhuj and was initiated into *Sannyas* by Atmaram. He holds a good place among the saints of Cutch. The language of his works is unrefined and unpolished.

RAVAN-BADH. See *Jiv Nath Jha.*

RAVERTY, H.G. Author of *Thesaurus of English and Hindustani Technical Terms used in Building and other Useful Arts, etc.* (Hertford, 1859).

RAVI. Modern writer, whose chief works are: *Kya Main Andar A Sakta Hun* ? (May I Come In ? ; collection of essays), *Pyar ke Bandhan* (The Bonds of Love), *Mere Kathaguru ka Kahna Hai* (2 Pts.), *Suraj ka Parda, Uroja ka Asmanjas* (short story collections) and *Tab Yah Mumkin Hai* (novel).

RAVIDAS. See *Raidas.*

RAVI DATT SHUKLA. Bhojpuri writer, whose drama *Devakshar-Charit* (Varanasi, 1884), though written mainly in Khari Boli, had two-three acts written in Bhojpuri. The writer had shown the superiority of the Devnagari Script.

RAVI SAHIB (fl. 1st half of 18th cent.). Gujarati saint-poet, who was a disciple of Bhan Sahib, the founder of the Bhan Sect. He was born at Tanchha village in Amod Taluka of Gujarat in a Vaish family. Among his Hindi works, the chief ones are: *Bodh-Chintamani, Atmalaksha-Chintamani, Ramkunvar-Chintamani, Bhan-Gita. Ravi-Gita, Guru-Mahima, Barahmasa, Rekhta, Kakka* and stray verses. His language betrays a slight influence of Arabic, Persian and Panjabi words.

RAVI SHANKAR KAULESHWAR (1922-). Modern Hindi poet of Mauritius, who is noted for his stray poems and short stories.

RAVI SHANKAR MISHRA. Poet, whose *Suli* (1983) is a *Prabandh-Kavya* ; his another poetical work is *Satyamev Jayate.*

RAVI VERMA. Malayalam-speaking modern Hindi writer, who tr. a Malayalam novel under the title *Dada ka Hathi* (The Grandfather's Elephant) and has also tr. Malayalam short stories into Hindi.

RAVINDRA BHARMAR (1934-). Poet, whose chief poetical works are: *Ravindra Bhramar ke Git* (The Songs of Ravindra

Bhramar) and *Son Machhri Man Basi* ; *Chhayavad* is his critical work.

RAVINDRA KALIYA (1938-). Short story writer, whose chief short story collections are : *Nau Sal Chhoti Patni* (Nine Years Younger Wife ; 1968), *Gharibi Hatao* (Remove Poverty), *Kala Register*, *Gali Kuche* and *Chakaiya Nim* ; *Jalti Nishaniyan* (The Burning Marks) is his novel. *Comrade Mona Lisa* is his latest book of diatribe, lampooning many writers. His important short stories are : 'Nau Sal Chhoti Patni', 'Ek Dari Hui Aurat' (A Frightened Woman), etc. His other novels are : *Khuda Sahi Salamat Hai* (Pt. I) and *Banke Lal*.

RAVINDRA KUMAR. Modern Magahi writer, whose social short stories have been published in the 'Magahi' journal.

RAVINDRA NATH SHRIVASTAV (1936-). Noted linguist, whose chief works are : *Shailivigyan aur Alochana ki Nai Bhumika* (New Background of Stylistic Study and Criticism) and *Samanya Bhasha Vigyan* (General Philology). He is at present Professor of Linguistics in the Delhi University.

RAVINDRA NATH TYAGI (1931-). Poet, whose chief poetical collections are : *Sukhe aur Hare Patte* (Dry and Green Leaves), *Kalpavriksha* (Celestial Tree) and *Akhirkar* ; *Bhittichitra* (Frescoes), *Is Desh ke Log*, *Dhup ki Ghati*, *Bhadra Purush* and *Urdu-Hasya Vyangya* (ed.) are his chief humorous works. His short story collections are : *Sundar Kali*, *Ritu-Varnan* and *Phutkar*.

RAVINDRA VERMA. Writer, whose *Gatha Sheikhchilli* (1981) is the story of a youth, whose idealism is eroded under the influence of acid realities of life. His other novel is *Kissa Tota Sirf Tota*.

RAWAT SARASWAT. Modern Rajasthani writer, who started 'Maru Vani', a monthly magazine from Jaipur in 1953. His works are : *Sampadak ki Maut* (satirical one-act plays) and *Thothi Batan* (essays). He has composed patriotic and heroic poems and has also written reviews and articles. In 1978, he edited *Lakhan*, an anthology of creative writings by teacher-writers of Rajasthan, while in 1982, he edited *Prabandh Parijat*, containing texts from *Visaldev Raso*, *Madhavanal Kamkandala* of Kushal Labh and *Hammirayan* of Bhandau Vyas.

RAY CHAMPATI. A contemporary of Raja Pratap Rudradev (1479-1535) ; he is known in Orissa as 'Vriddh Champati'. He also composed poems in Hindi (Brajboli).

RAY CHAND. Poet of the Ram-cult, who was the author of *Sita-Charitra*, composed in 1656.

RAY MALL PANDE. Poet of the Ram-cult, who was the author of the *Hanuman-Charit* (1639) on the pattern of *Hanumad-bahuk* of Tulsidas (q.v.).

RAY PRAVIN (fl. 16th cent.). Poetess, whose stray verses are available. She considered Keshavdas (q.v.) as her Guru ; as a matter of fact, Keshavdas composed his *Kavipriya* for her. Emperor Akbar was influenced by her poetic gifts and allowed her to stay with Orchha ruler, Indrajit Singh.

RAY RAMANAND PATTNAYAK. Oriya-speaking Hindi (Brajboli) poet, who was commander-in-chief of Shripratap Rudradev (1479-1535). He was a great friend and follower of Chaitanya. Pattnayak's *Padas*, over 100 in number, are considered pieces of high literary merit. His *Padas* are in a language with a mixture of Maithili, Braj, Oriya and Bengali. His *Shrijagannatha Vallabha*, a Sanskrit drama, is a popular Vaishnavite work.

RAY SHEKHAR (Kavi Shekhar ; fl. end of 16th cent.). Bengali Vaishnav poet, who also composed *Padas* in Brajbuli.

RAY SINGH SANDU (1813-78). Rajasthani Bhakta-poet, whose *Motiyai ra Sortha* in about 100 verses deals with Bhakti and *Niti* ; Motiya was a servant of Thakur Naval Singh of Rupnagar, who nursed the poet during his illness and hence all the *Sorthas* are addressed to Motiya.

RENU, SANT (fl. 1661-71). Hindi writer of Panjab, whose chief works are : *Man Prabodh*, *Nanak Vijay*, *Bachan Sangrah* (*Anamai Prakash*), *Udasi Bodh* and *Panch Parmeshwar*; *Nanak Vijay* is an exhaustive biography of Guru Nanak.

REOTI SHARAN SHARMA. Hindi and Urdu dramatist, whose chief works are : *Chiragh ki Lau* (1962 ; based on the story of an honest officer), *Dipshikha*, *Apni Dharti* (1963 ; dealing with Chinese attack on India) (both dramas) and *Ag*, *Rakh aur Roshni* (collection of one-act plays). His plays are often shown on T.V. He has also written novels.

REVATDAN CHARAN. Modern Rajasthani poet, whose progressive poems are noted for their diction, content and emotion. He has chosen objects of Nature as symbols in expressing progressive ideology. He has composed patriotic and heroic poems as well.

REVAT SINGH, THAKUR (b. 1902). Modern Rajasthani poet of Narwar, Kishengarh, who is the author of several works in the traditional Charan style ; his poetry is mature and polished. He has also paid poetic homage to the heroes, who sacrificed their lives in fighting against the Chinese attack on India.

RIDDHI NATH JHA (fl. 1st half of 20th cent.). Maithili writer, who was noted for his drama, *Sati-Pariksha*. His *Shabda-Shakti-Trivenika* (unpublished) advocates Sanskritic principles in evaluating Maithili classics, while according to his *Vishwa-bhushan*, the highest test of literary art is the faithful achievement of *Rasa-Paripak* (fulfilment of the emotional ego). His *Sati-Vibhuti* is a *Khand-Kavya*. He wrote love and devotional lyrics ; his devotional lyrics are collected in *Lakshmivati Gitanjali* (1927). His *Vishweshvar-Champu* (1946) describes the 'Kobar Yatra' ceremony of Raja Bahadur Vishweshvar Singh.

RIPUDAMAN SINGH. Native of Guyana, who is promoting the cause of Hindi in his country.

RISHABH CHARAN JAIN (1911-). Novelist, whose chief works dealing with the life in brothels are : *Delhi ka Vyabhichar*, *Delhi ka Kalank* and *Durachar ke Adde*. His other works are : *Bhai* (The Brother), *Mandir-Dip* (The Lamp of the Temple) and *Satyagrah* (The Passive Resistance).

RISHABH DAS SHRAVAK (fl. 1st part of 17th cent.). Gujarati-speaking Jain poet, who was a disciple of Vijayanand Suri. Of his 43 works only *Kumarpal Ras*, *Shrenik Ras* and *Rohit Ras* are in Old Hindi.

RISHIDEV. Modern Hindi poet of Fiji, who is noted for his stray poems.

RISHIKESH SHAH. Modern Hindi writer of Nepal, whose chief work is : *Nepal Rajnitik Vyavastha evam Par-rashtra Niti*.

RISHINATH (fl. 1733-74). Poet of the Riti school, who was father of Thakur II (q.v.) and great-grandfather of Sevak (q.v.). He belonged to Asni and was patronized by Sadanand, the Dewan of the Raja of Kashi and by Raghuvar Kayasth. He composed his *Alankar-Manjari* (The Creeper of Alankars) in 1744 ; the work is chiefly in *Dohas*.

RITA RANI PALIWAL. Critic, whose chief work is *Rangmanch : Naya Paridrishya* (on theatre ; 1980).

RITURAJ. Poet, whose chief works are : *Angiras, Pul par Pani* (The Water over Bridge ; 1981) and *Abekas* (1981).

ROBIN SHAW PUSHPA. Modern fiction writer, whose chief works are : *Andhe Akash ka Suraj, Dehyatra, Anyay ko Kshama* and *Akrosh*; *Dard ka Sukh* is his drama.

ROBSON, JOHN. Compiler of *Selection of Khyals or Marwari Plays*, with Introduction and Glossary (Beawar, 1866).

ROCHER, LUDO. Author of *Manual of Modern Hindi* or 'Adhunik Hindi Pustak' (Gent, 1958).

RODERMEL, GORDON. American Hindi scholar, whose chief works are : *A Death in Delhi* (a collection of Hindi short stories tr. into English), tr. of Premchand's *Godan* as *Gift of Cow*, tr. of Agyey's *Apne-apne Ajnabi* as *To Each His Stranger* and *Hindi Kahani : Algav ka Darshan* (The Concept of Alienation in Hindi Short Story).

ROEBUCK, THOMAS (1781-1819). English scholar, who was associated with Fort William College. He assisted John Gilchrist in preparation of *British Indian Monitor* and *English-Hindustani Dictionary*. He also compiled *A Laskari Dictionary* or *Anglo-Indian Vocabulary of Terms and Phrases in English and chiefly in the corrupt jargon in use among Laskars or Indian Sailors* (London, 1886). He edited a number of Oriental works and prepared *Annals of the College* from the year 1803 to 1818 on the basis of College Annual Reports. He had a plan to compile his Hindustani Dictionary and had made good progress, but his early death prevented him from completing it. He also compiled a *Lokokti Sangrah*, with English tr., which was later published by H.H. Wilson.

ROHAL (1730-83). Sindhi Muslim saint-poet, who also composed two poetical works : *Manoprabodh, Adhibuddhi-Granth* and some 50 *Shabdas* in Hindi. While the first work consists of 200 *Dohas*, 11 *Kirtan Rahau*, 5 *Savaiyas*, and a *Jhulna*, the second work has 33 *Dohas*, 14 *Savaiyas*, 18 *Chaupais*, 6 *Kavittas*, 2 *Kundaliyas* and *Chhapai* and a stray verse. Like Kabir (q.v.), his poetry is permeated with a longing for a vision of God, who is One. The poet also glorifies and adores his Guru.

ROHIT SINGH MUKTARAM. Modern Hindi writer of Mauritius, who is noted for his short stories.

ROMANOVA, DINA PHILIPOVNA (1928-). Soviet Hindi scholar, who is noted for the editing in Hindi of the select works of Tolstoy, Lenin and Karl Marx.

ROSHAN LAL SURIRVALA. Writer, who is known for his satirical short stories : *Gittalen* (1980) and *Chhoti Bahu*.

ROSY SIVARAN SINGH, MRS. Modern Hindi writer of Trinidad, who is noted for her short stories.

RUDRA. See *Shiv Prasad Mishra 'Rudra'*.

RUDRA DATT SHARMA (1854-1918). Veteran journalist, who edited a large number of journals than anyone else among his contemporaries. An ardent follower of Dayanand Saraswati (q.v.), his chief works are *Apurv Sannyasi* (*Unique Recluse*), *Pakhand Murti*, *Yoga-Darshan Bhashya*, *Swarga-men Mahasabha* (*Great Assembly in Heaven*) and *Swarga-men Subjects Committee* (*Subjects Committee Meeting in Heaven*).

RUDRA DHAR (fl. prior to 1685). Maithili poet, whose lyrics were quoted in anthologies. He may be identified with Rudra Dhar Upadhyay, the author of *Shraddh-Vivek* and several Dharmashastra works in Sanskrit.

RUDRA KASHIKEY. Writer, whose chief works are : *Khushbu Gulab Ki* (novel) and *Bijli* (drama).

RUGH RASO. Rajasthani poem, which was composed by Muhta Rughnath (q.v.) in 1668. It deals with the story of Ram but as the text is incomplete, the story proper starts with the combat between Jatayu and Ravan and includes the happenings after Ram's coronation, Sita's banishment, birth of Lav and creation of Kush from 'Kusha' grass by a Rishi, and boys' heroic deeds. The story goes further and mentions how Bhidsakumbh, the son of Kumbhkaran, obtains a boon from Shiv not to be killed by any womb-born child and seizes Lanka from Vibhishan. Ram's army comes to Vibhishan's rescue and Kush kills Bhidsakumbh. Having known from the Rishi about Sita's child, Ram again accepts Sita and reigns over Ayodhya.

RUKMINI, MRS. Telugu-speaking modern Hindi scholar, whose research publication is *Swatantryottar Hindi aur Telugu Kavita ka Tulnatmak Adhyayan* (Comparative Study of Hindi and Telugu Poetry after Independence).

RUKMINI HARAN. See *Sanya Jhula.*

RUKMINI HARAN. Rajasthani poem in 206 verses, which was composed by Vithal Das between 1643 and 1670. The story deals with the abduction of Rukmini by Krishna, but the accent is on Krishna's character including war preparations at Dwarka before Krishna's march.

RUKMINI-PARINAY. Maithili Kirtaniya play, which was composed by Ramapati Upadhyay (q.v.) ; the play, divided into 6 Acts, is called *Rukmini-Haran* or *Rukmini-Swayamvar.*

The play reveals how Narad induces Krishna to run away with Rukmini, while she goes to worship goddess Gauri. Krishna defeats Rukmini's brother, Rukmi, who wants Rukmini to be married to Shishupal, the king of Chedi. Eventually, Krishna is successful in taking Rukmini to his place and marries her with due formality.

Written in a devotional spirit, the dramatist refutes the charges against Krishna that he had illicit relations with the Gopis ; Krishna's love for Gopis is explained in philosophical terms. The Maithili songs in the play are in the Vidyapati tradition quite conventional and literary. The drama enjoys a high place in the history of Kirtaniya drama.

RUKMINI-SWAYAMVAR. Maithili poem by an unknown author, which describes the story of Rukmini's marriage with Krishna.

RUMERY, JUNE. See *John Joseph Gumperz.*

RUP DAS. Rajasthani saint-poet and a follower of Haridas Niranjani Sect, whose *Sevadas ki Parchi* (composed in 1775) treats of the life of the famous saint-poet, Sevadas (q.v.).

RUP JI. Court-poet of Maharaja Rajsingh of Kishengarh, whose *Rasa-Rup* (1682) is a Riti work on *Nayikabhed.*

RUP KANT THAKUR. Modern Maithili novelist, whose chief work *Momak Nak* is a social satire. His collection of short stories, *Dhukal Kera* (1964) and one-act plays *Vachan Vaishnav* (satirizing people who made themselves popular by false idealism) are full of humour.

RUP NARAYAN DIKSHIT (1936-). Bagheli folk-poet, who

was born in Rewa. His poems are noted for their musical qualities and love of Nature.

RUP NARAYAN JHA 'RAKESH'. Modern Maithili poet, whose poems are noted for creating *Rasa*. He is son of Sitaram Jha (q.v.), a Maithili poet.

RUP NARAYAN PANDEY (1884-1958). Writer and poet, who was born in Lucknow. He was noted for his tr. of dramas from Bengali (of D.L. Roy and others), viz., *Durgadas*, *Us-Par*, *Nurjahan*, *Sita*, *Pashani*, etc. A successful poet, his chief works are : *Parag* (The Pollen ; a collection of poems) and *Van Vaibhav* (The Beauty of the Forest). He also edited 'Madhuri' for a number of years.

RUP RASIK (fl. 15th cent.). Brajbhasha poet of the Nimbark Sect, who at the age of 36 years reached Mathura and became a disciple of Harivyas (q.v.). He composed three works : *Brihadotsav Manimal*, *Harivyas Yashamrit* and *Nityavihar Padavali*.

RUP RASIK (fl. 16th cent.). Hindi writer, who was noted for his prose work, *Lila-Vanshati*.

RUP SAHI. Poet of the Riti school, who was a Kayasth of Panna State. His *Rup Vilas* (1754) in *Dohas*, treats of figures of speech, prosody, *Nayikabhed*, etc.

RUP SAKHI (fl. 18th cent.). Poet of the Ram-cult (Rasik Sampraday), whose stray *Padas* are available. He raised the number of Sita's Sakhis (handmaids) to 700.

RUP SAKHI (fl. 18th cent.). Poet of the Krishna-cult (Haridasi Sect), who was a disciple of Rasik Dev (q.v.). He composed *Padas*, *Kavittas*, etc.

RUSTAMJI (d. 1718). Rajasthani poet, whose *Kisan Vyanvalo* is an *Akhyan Kavya*, meant to be sung.

RUTKOWSKA, TATIANA. Modern Polish Hindi scholar, who is at present in the Oriental Institute at Warsaw University. She has written an article on the progress of Hindi studies in the Warsaw University, Warsaw, Poland.

S

SABAL SINGH CHAUHAN (fl. 1655-1724). Poet, about whom not much is known except that he was a Zamindar in the Etawah district and lived in Delhi with a friend attached to the court of Aurangzeb. He rendered the whole of *Mahabharat* in *Dohas* and *Chaupais* in a leisurely manner between 1661 and 1724. The rendering does not possess much literary merit but is popular with the common man for its simple style. He also tr. into Hindi the *Ritusamhara* and wrote *Rup Vilas* and a work on prosody.

SABHA SAR. See *Raghuram Nagar*.

SACHCHIDANANAD DHUMKETU. Modern novelist, whose chief works are : *Mati ki Mahak* (The Fragrance of the Earth ; a regional novel) and *Jalta Registan* (The Burning Desert).

SACHCHIDANAND HIRANAND VATSYAYAN 'AGYEY'. See *Agyey*.

SACHITRA MARWARI GIT-SANGRAH. Illustrated Marwari collection of folk-songs, which was published in the early 20th century.

SADAIVACHH SAVLINGA RA DUHA. Dingal poem (Script 1653) of an unknown author, which is a love-story of Mungipatan prince Sadaivachh and Savlinga, the daughter of a Minister. See *Sadayvatsa Vir Prabandh*.

SADAL MISHRA (1764-1849). Leading Khari Boli Hindi prose writer, who was born at the village Dhruvdiha in Shahbad district (Bihar). He was a teacher at the Government Fort William College. His *Nasiketopakhyan* (1803 ; q.v.) based on a Puranic legend, is in Hindi prose, but its style has been influenced by the eastern dialects, since Mishra hailed from Bihar. In spite of some literary Brajbhasha forms and Bihari words, this work is also a landmark in early Hindi prose. His other work is *Ramcharit*.

Sadal Mishra is one of the early four principal Khari Boli prose writers, others being Lallu Lal, Insha Allah Khan and Sadasukh Lal (qq.v.).

SADANAND (fl. 17th cent.). Poet of the Krishna-cult (Chaitanya Sect), whose three *Padas* are found in the *Kshanada Giti Chintamani*, written by Manohar Das.

SADANAND, SUKAVI (fl. prior to 1685). Maithili poet, whose lyrics were quoted in anthologies.

SADANAND AVASTHI. Writer, who tr. in 1906 the *Nagananda* of Harsha from Sanskrit into Hindi.

SADANAND MAHADEV PETHE. Marathi-speaking modern Hindi poet, whose poems numbering more than one hundred are scattered in various magazines. His chief poems are : 'Kavita ka Atmanivedan', 'Mridul Mukul', 'Ye Simayen : Ye Rekha-yen', etc.

SADASHIVAN NAIR. Malayalam-speaking modern Hindi writer, who has tr. Nimpiyar's Malayalam poem : *Tullal* into Hindi verse.

SADASUKH LAL, MUNSHI (1746-1824). Leading Hindi prose writer, who was a resident of Delhi and was equally learned in Urdu and Persian. He joined the service of the East India Company in 1793 and was posted at Chunar in Uttar Pradesh. He was taken on the staff of the Fort William College and wrote *Sukhsagar* based on *Vishnu-puran*, which is not avalable in full. But those parts, which are available, establish his repute as a writer of elegant Khari Boli prose. Sadasukh Lal's *Sukhsagar* is in pure Khari Boli style ; it was his Hindi style that met the approval of the East India Company. See *Lallu Lal*, *Sadal Mishra*, *Insha Allah Khan*.

SADAYVATSA VIR PRABANDH. Rajasthani narrative poem in 730 verses, which was composed by Bhim in about 1409 ; it is based on the legend of Sadayvatsa-Savlinga.

According to the legend, which exists in different recensions in Gujarati and Rajasthani, Savlinga, the daughter of king Shalivahan of Pratishthan selects Sadayvatsa, the son of king Prabhuvatsa of Ujjain at a *Swayamvar*. Once Sadayvatsa saves the life of a pregnant Brahmin lady from a royal elephant, which had run amuck. The king, pleased at this, decides to designate Sadayvatsa as his heir-apparent. But the minister later poisons the ears of the king, who orders him into exile.

Savlinga accompanies him. After this are described a series of Sadayvatsa's adventures and miraculous deeds. A few interesting stories have also been interwoven. Ultimately, Sadayvatsa is placed on the throne by his own father.

The poem ranks high amongst the poems of this period in regard to poetic beauty, motif, language and the description of the then society.

SADGURU SHARAN AVASTHI (1901-73). Writer, who was noted for his one-act plays : *Do Ekanki Natak* (1942) and a novel : *Marg ke Gahre Chihna*. His autobiography : *Gahre Pani Paith* (1963) could only be published in 1978.

SADHAN. See *Mainasat*.

SADHARU AGRAWAL (fl. 1354). Poet, whose *Pradyumna-Charit* (q.v. ; on the story of Krishna's son, Pradyumna) is considered the earliest work in Brajbhasha. Sadharu was born in Agroha but he settled in some town named Erachchh, where he composed his work. The *Pradyumna-Charit* has been edited by Chainsukh Das Nyaytirth and Kasturchand Kasliwal.

SADHNA. See *Sadna*.

SADHUCHARAN (*c.* 1693-*c.* 1763). Poet of the Krishna-cult (Chaitanya Sect), whose chief work is : *Rasik Vilas*, sometimes called *Rasik Mangal*.

SADHU KIRTI (fl. 16th cent.). Gujarati-speaking Jain saint-poet, who was a disciple of Amar Manikya. A great scholar of Sanskrit, he was granted the title of 'Upadhyay' by Jin Chandra Suri. Among his Hindi compositions, *Chunadi*, *Ragmala*, *Shatrunjay Stavan*, *Nemirajarshi Chaupai* are prominent. The language is Hindi mixed with Gujarati.

SADHU RAM (d. 1886). Poet of Mathura, who was a Vaishya Agrawal and was a disciple of Gwal (q.v.). Of his many works, a few verses are now extant. It is said that he wrote a poetical work on Gopichand, when the latter became a Yogi.

SADNA (fl. 15th cent.). Saint-poet, who sang of *Nirgun* Brahma. A butcher by caste, his devotional songs are included in many an anthology of Hindi verse. He was so much steeped in Bhakti that many legends have come to be associated with him ascribing to him almost supernatural powers. One of his *Padas* is included in the *Granth Sahib* (q.v.).

SADUL (fl. 1543). Rajasthani poet, whose stray verses in different popular metres are available.

SADUL-PARMAR RO CHHAND. See *Jada Mehdu.*

SAGAN BHAU (fl. 18th cent.). Marathi folk-poet (*Shahir*), who also composed verses in Hindi.

SAGAR MAHARAJ (1882-1945). Gujarati-speaking poet, who was born at Jambusar. His original name was Jagannath Tripathi. His Hindi works, collected in *Divane Sagar* (Pts. I & II) are influenced by mystic love.

SAGAT RASO. See *Girdhar Asiya.*

SAGTA SANDU (fl. latter half of 18th cent.). Rajasthani poet, who was patronized by Thakur Indrasingh Jodha of Khairwa. His *Indrasingh Rupak* in 597 verses describes the battles (including the famous Ahmedabad battle of 1730) fought by the Thakur and his ancestors, as trusted warriors of the Jodhpur army.

SAHAJ RAM (1673-1768). Hindi poet of Panjab, who was initiated into Seva Panth by Seva Ram. About 100 verses of his *Asabariyas* are in Brajbhasha, influenced by Khari Boli.

SAHCHARI SHARAN DEV (b. 1772). Poet of the Krishna-cult (Haridasi Sect), who was noted for his *Lalit Prakash* and *Saras Manjhavali*; the latter work consisting of 140 metres has been praised by Viyogi Hari.

SAHIB RAM DAS. Maithili saint-poet, who was perhaps a contemporary of Maharaja Narendra Singh (1744-61). He was originally a Brahmin of village Kusumali, but was said to have become a Sannyasi and founded the present Math of Pachadhi. A great devotee of Krishna, tradition attributes to him great miraculous powers.

His *Padavali* (1746) consists of 'Vishnupadas', 'Rases', songs in praise of Krishna as well as of Shiv but he devoted special attention to the birth of Krishna, to his killing of Putana, his sports of childhood and youth. In his 'Ras' songs, he expresses his ecstasy. He is also conscious of Vishnu's various incarnations and miracles. He alludes to the stories of Prahlad, Ajamil, Ganika, Kubja, Vyadh, etc. where Vishnu is known to have redeemed the sinners. In one of his most popular songs, he portrays the grief of Ram, when he comes back after killing Marich and finds Sita no more in the hut. His songs, composed in easy and lucid style, are marked for their delightful rhythm. Chanda Jha has paid a compliment to him by imitating his melodies.

SAHITYA LAHARI (The Wavelets of Literature). *Padas* by Surdas (q.v.), which were written about 1550. It is a collection of the *Padas* of Surdas; it includes certain *Padas* of the *Sursagar* as well. Recently, doubts about its authenticity have arisen and some scholars are of the view that the work was composed quite late i.e., around 1743 by some other poet, bearing the name of Surdas.

SAHITYALOCHAN. See *Shyam Sundar Das*.

SAHJANAND (b. 1780). Saint-poet of Ayodhya and the founder of the Swami Narayan Sect; his stray verses are available. The teachings of this Sect are mostly in Gujarati.

SAHJANAND, SWAMI (1889-1950). Socialist Kisan leader, whose autobiography *Mera Jivan Sangharsh* (autobiography) is quite popular. He was born at the village Deva in Ghazipur district of Uttar Pradesh and at the young age of 18, he had become a recluse.

SAHJO BAI (fl. 1743). Rajasthani saint-poetess, who was a disciple of Charandas (q.v.) and was born in a Dhusar family. She composed her *Sahaj-Prakash* in 1743, which extols God, Guru and advocates simplicity in life. The expressions are, natural and easy to follow.

SAHODARA SIV. Modern Hindi writer of Trinidad, who is noted for her short stories and other writings.

SAIFUDDIN SIDDIQI 'SAIFU' (1923-). Bagheli folk-poet, who was born at the village Ramnagar in Rewa and was son of the poet Naziruddin Siddiqi (q.v.). His chief works are : *Saifu-Vinod*, *Shri-Kundan-Kunvari*, *Adarsh Tyagi*, *Bhajanavali* and *Charan-Chihna*.

SAIN. See *Sen*.

SAIN SMARTH DAS (SAMRATH DAS ; 1493-1563). Gujarati-speaking saint-poet of Siddhpur, who was disciple of Lochandas, a saint in the line of Kabir (q.v.). He composed a good number of *Padas*, which in language and style are similar to those of Kabir.

SAINANI. Rajasthani poem (1944) by Meghraj 'Mukul', which is based on a historical episode. The poem has been immensely popular and has since been recorded.

The newly-wed Hadi Rani urges her husband to go to the

battlefield ; he is prepared to go to war but sends a messenger to ask the Rani to give a memento. The bride suspects that the love-lorn warrior might fight only with an attention divided between her and the war. She resolves the suspense by cutting off and presenting her own head as a memento. This lofty sacrifice of the Rani has earned heartfelt homage from the poet.

SAJANOVA, NATALIYA MIKHAILOVNA (1932-). Soveit Hindi scholar, who did doctorate on Bharatendu Harishchandra and is noted for studies on Surdas, Mirabai, Tulsidas, Kabır, Jainendra and the various periods of Hindi literature.

SAKAL DIP SINGH (1930-). Poet, whose chief works are: *Patthar aur Lakiren* (The Stones and Lines ; a poetical collection) and a poem *Akasmik* (Incidentally).

SAKATA, TEIJI. Modern Japanese Hindi scholar, who at present teaches Hindi in a private University : Takushoku University, Tokyo. He is a student of Kyuya Doi (q.v.) and his special field of study is Philology, compilation of folk-literature, history of Hindi literature, etc. on which his articles appear from time to time in various magazines. In collaboration with Otoya Tanaka, he has written : *Bharatiya Sahitya—Dev Yuga se Aj Tak, Ek Sankshipt Parichay* (2nd edition, 1977).

SAKET. Epic (1932) by Maithilisharan Gupta, named after the ancient name of Ayodhya.

The epic, centred around the capital city of Ayodhya, delineates the pangs of separation which Urmila has to suffer after her lord, Lakshman accompanies Ram in the forest for fourteen years. This paticular aspect, which had so far remained neglected, has been successfully touched upon by Gupta. Though based on the story of the *Ramayan*, it has the impact of Gandhism on it at several places. It is considered as the poet's masterpiece. The poet wrote his work after reading Rabindranath Tagore's *Upekshita Urmila.*

SAKHARAM BALKRISHNA SARNAIK (fl. 1850-1900). Marathi-speaking Hindi dramatist, who wrote dramas on Puranic themes ; the dramas are, however, no longer extant.

SAL BEG (fl. 16th cent.). Muslim saint-poet of Orissa, whose *Padas* in Hindi (Brajboli) are available. While his father was Muslim, his mother was an abducted Brahmin lady.

SALVIR. Kumaoni Panvada, which describes the challenge

by a young girl named Rauteli Runa to the heroes : Salvir and his brother Ghoghsal, who lived in Jhanwari Kot.

SAMAN BAI (1825-85). Rajasthani Bhakta-poetess, who was daughter of the poet Ramnath Kaviya and was married to Ramdayal of village Mahmund (Kishengarh, Alwar). Her *Ish Mahima* (106 *Savaiyas*), *Radhika Shariropama* (29 verses), *Shri Krishnopama* (18 verses) and *Pati Patropama* or *Pati Shatak*, of which only six verses are available, in Brajbhasha. In Rajasthani, she is known for her about 70 *Padas*, dealing with marriage of Ram, *Krishna-Lilas* and devotion.

SAMARA RAS. Rajasthani poem by Ambdev Suri, composed in the 14th century. Consisting of 105 verses, it is an important work and gives a vivid and historical description of a pilgrimage to Shatrunjay by Sanghpati Desal and his followers led by Samar Singh.

SAMAS DIN (1433-93). Rajasthani poet, who was one of the saints of the Vishnoi tradition (see *Jambhoji*). He composed stray verses on miscellaneous topics.

SAMAYSAR NATAK. See *Banarsidas*.

SAMAY SUNDAR (1553-1646). Famous Jain poet and scholar, who, besides his Sanskrit works, wrote a large number of works in Rajasthani. About two dozen narrative poems, mostly *Ras* and *Chaupai*, nine collections of verses, known as *Chhattisi* and about 550 songs and stray verses are available. There is a saying that Samay Sundar's songs are as many as the construction works of Rana Kumbha. His narrative poems, *Simhal Sut Pryamelak Ras*, *Champak Seth Chaupai*, *Sitaram Chaupai*, *Nal Damyanti Chaupai*, *Mrigavati Ras*. *Vastupal Tejpal Ras*, etc. are based on folk stories or Jain traditions. His *Satyasiya Dushkal Varnan Chhattisi* gives a heart-rending account of the Famine of 1630.

Through his poems, which are important, he has done a great service to the cultural and religious improvement of the people.

SAMBHAJI (1657-84). Maratha ruler, who was son of Shivaji. Besides his Sanskrit work, *Budha-Bhushana*, his Hindi works are : *Nayikabhed*, *Nakhshikh* and *Sat Satak*. He is also called 'Nripshambhu', 'Shambhuraj', etc.

SAMMAN (fl. 18th-19th cent.). Poet, whose *Dohas* are popular amongst the villagers. He was a Brahmin by caste.

SAMNES. Poet of the Riti school, who was patronized by Jaysingh, Maharaja of Rewa. He composed three works : *Kavya Bhushan*, *Rasik Vilas* (1790) and *Pingal*.

SAMPURNANAND (1890-1969). Sanskrit and Hindi scholar, who was an educationist, a reformer and political thinker. He was also Chief Minister of Uttar Pradesh. His *Samajvad* (Socialism), *Antariksha Yatra* (Space Travel), *Sphut Vichar* (Stray Thoughts), *Brahman-Savdhan* and *Bharatiya Buddhijivi* (Indian Intelligentsia) are a significant contribution to Hindi prose. His language is forceful, elegant and yet simple.

SANADHYA, ABHAY RAM. See *Abhay Ram Sanadhya*.

SANDHAYACH PUNA (fl. between 1550-1650). Dingal poet, who composed a short narrative poem on the battle of Kalindri (Sirohi) of 1574 in 76 verses. He also wrote stray verses including Dingal *Gits* on contemporary heroes and events.

SANDU MALA UDAWAT (*c*. 1533-1623). Dingal poet, who received many gifts and grants from contemporary rulers including Raja Raysingh of Bikaner, Mota Raja Udaisingh of Jodhpur and his son, Sursingh. Considered to be a poet of Jhulna metre, his works are : *Jhulna Maharaj Raysinghji Ra* (298 lines ; on Raja Raysingh), *Jhulna Akbar Patsahji Ra* (describing Akbar's victory over Gujarat in 108 lines), *Jhulna Dewan Shri Pratapsinghji Ra* (302 lines on the battle of Haldighati), *Jhulna Achal Tilokdas Ra* (incomplete; 198 lines), stray poems and 67 *Gits*, *Nisani* and *Kavitta*, etc. on various contemporary and earlier heroes. With description of attributes, achievements and deeds of heroes in a fluent language, the poet has often utilized historic events, hitherto not used by any other poet.

SANDHU RAMA DHARAMSIYOT (fl. between 1550-1650). Dingal poet and author of *Udaysingh ra Veli*. He also wrote stray verses including Dingal *Gits* on contemporary heroes and events.

SANEH-SAGAR. See *Bakhshi Hansraj*.

SANEHI. See *Gayaprasad Shukla 'Sanehi'*.

SANEHI RAM (fl. end of the 19th cent.). Braj folk-poet of Mant in Mathura, who was a farmer by profession. His *Saneh-Lila*, a devotional work, has been published. A great devotee of Krishna, he used to visit the Bankebihari temple at Vrindavan daily and several miracles are associated with his name. He also composed *Bhajans*, *Makhan-Lilas*, *Ras-Lilas* and other verses.

SANGRAM DAS (Sagramdas ; fl. latter half of 18th cent.). Rajasthani saint-poet of Ram Snehi Sect, Shahpura, who was a disciple of Murli Ram (q.v.). His 115 *Kundliyas* on Bhakti, precepts, etc. are in a refined form of popular Rajasthani.

SANGRAM SINGH, MAHARAJA (fl. latter half of 19th cent.). Ruler of Indragarh (Kota), whose Rajasthani poems in the traditional Charan style are available.

SANHAIYA LAL OJHA. Poet of Rajasthan, who is noted for his stray poems in Khari Boli. His novels in Khari Boli are : *Dharma ke Nam Par*, *Sarvanam*, *Sambhavami* (Pts. 1, 2) and *Masum Chandni* : *Kshitij ke Swar* (1984).

SANIDAN (fl. 1652). Rajasthani poet, who was a Charan of Silga Khanp in Mewar State. He composed *Sanmatsar*, an incomplete work in 277 verses, on the science of rain. The work is in the form of dialogue between Shiv and Parvati, Parvati being the questioner.

SANJIV. Writer, whose chief works are : *Kishengarh ke Aheri* (The Hunters of Kishengarh ; 1981), *Circus*, *Rani ki Sarai* (novels), *Tis Sal ka Safarnama* (Travelogue of Thirty Years ; 1981) and *Ap Yahan Hain* (1984 ; short story collections).

SANKHALA KARAMSI RUNECHA. See *Krisanji ri Veli*.

SANKRITYAYAN, RAHUL. See *Rahul Sankrityayan*.

SANNYASI (The Recluse). Novel (1941) by Ilachandra Joshi (q.v.). Nand Kishore, an extremely egoistic character, ruins the lives of many women to satisfy his ego. He neither gets peace himself nor is able to make their life happy and peaceful. Ultimately, he does social service by becoming a sannyasi leader and going to jail.

SANSAR CHAND (1917-). Modern essayist, whose chief works are : *Hindi Kavya men Anyokti* (research), *Sahitya : Anubhuti aur Vivechan*, *Akalan aur Samiksha* (criticism), *Apni Dali ke Kante*, *Baten Ye Jhuthi Hain* (collections of essays), *Bharatiya Kavyashastra ki Bhumika* (Introduction to Indian Poetics), *Sankshipta Bihari* and *Galpa Gaurav*. He was Head of the Department of Hindi at the Jammu University.

SANSKARTA, N.R. See *Nanu Ram Sanskarta*.

SANT DAS (1642-1749). Great Nirgun saint-poet in the tradition of Agradas (q.v.), who had his seat at Dantada (near Shahpura, Bhilwara). He used to wear *Gudad* (tattered garments) and his Sect came to be known as Gudad Panth. His *Vani*, including *Sakhis* (*Dohas*), *Rekhta* and *Padas*, is fairly large. The *Sakhis* are divided into 55 topics and deal with Nirgun Bhakti. He extols God and Guru and condemns all kinds of ostentation. Premdas and Kriparam were his popular disciples.

SANT DAS BARAH-HAZARI (d. 1639). Rajasthani saint-poet and a follower of Dadu (q.v.), who died at Fatehpur (Shekhawati). His *Vani*, named *Alam Ganj*, consisting of 5,000 *Sakhis*, 1442 *Padas*, 613 *Savaiyas* and 3 *Artis*, was first compiled in his life-time in 1631 by his disciple Haridas, the Mahant of Chavdya branch. The poems are equivalent to 12,000 *Anushtup Shlokas* in number and so he came to be known as Barah-Hazari. The *Sakhis* are classified into 27 *Angas* (topics) such as *Guru Mahima Ko*, *Gurdev Ko*, *Sumiran Ko*, *Birah Ko*, *Bairagi Ko*, *Parcha Ko*, etc. Raghavdas in his *Bhaktamal* has praised him for his *Sakhis* and *Padas*. A great Nirgun poet of the age, his treatment is lucid and communicative. His language is mostly popular Rajasthani.

SANT DAS CHHIBER, BHAI (fl. 1777). Hindi poet of Panjab, whose *Janam Sakhi Nanak Shah Ki* is a biography of Guru Nanak. The poet had been influenced by the celebrated poet, Tulsidas (q.v.).

SANT RAM 'ANIL'. Modern Kannauji scholar, whose chief works are : *Kannauji Lok-Sahitya* (Kannauji Folk-Literature) and *Kannauji Lok-Git* (Kannauji Folk-songs).

SANT RAM MAHARAJ (d. 1830). Saint-poet of Gujarat, who was a disciple of Jitamuni in the tradition of Akha (q.v.). There are branches of Sant Ram Mandir at several places in Gujarat and even up to this time, a fair is held on the day he died. His *Guru Bavni*, composed in *Doha* metre, glorifies a meeting between the disciple and the Guru.

SANT RENU. See *Renu, Sant*.

SANTOKH SINGH, BHAI (1888-1943). Sikh writer, whose voluminous work, *Guru Pratap Suraj* in Brajbhasha (though written in Gurumukhi Script), consists of four volumes ; it purports to be the life history of Guru Nanak and other Gurus and a history of the rise and growth of the Sikhs ; it also gives a graphic description of the last battle of Anandpur. A great Hindi and Sanskrit scholar as Santokh Singh was, some of his other works are *Atma-Prakash, Valmiki Ramayan, Nanak-Prakash and Garva Ganjani.*

SANTOSH KUMAR SHRIVASTAV. Modern author of *Bhasha Vigyan aur Hindi Bhasha ka Vikas.*

SANTOSH 'SANTOSH'. Short story writer, whose chief collection of short stories is *Zang* (Rust ; 1970).

SANVAL (fl. 1503). Rajasthani poet, whose stray verses in different popular metres are available.

SANVALDAN ASIYA. Modern Rajasthani poet of Kadiyan, whose chief work is *Mahabharat Rupak.* He also paid poetic homage to several contemporary heroes.

SANVAR DAHIYA. Rajasthani poet and writer of Bikaner, who has composed poems in the style of Nayi Kavita. His *Kal ar Aj Bichchai* (1978) is a book of 23 small progressive poems. He is also the author of *Aswadai Paswadai* (*1975*), *Amujho Kad Tain* and *Dharti Kad Tani Ghumaili* (1980 ; all short story collections).

SANVAT RAM (1733-1806). Rajasthani saint-poet of Ram Snehi Sampraday, Ren, who was a disciple of Nanakram. His *Vani*, equal to about 5,000 *Shlokas*, consists of *Lila Granths* (3), *Prasangs* (7), *Harjas* (42), *Sakhis* (*Dohas*, 1010) and many stray verses. He lays emphasis on *Ram-smaran* and amelioration of human lot.

SANYA JHULA (1575-1646). Rajasthani poet of the village Lilchha, who was the second son of Swamidas. Sanya was a favourite of Rao Kalyanmal Rathore of Idar and was highly honoured by him. A devotee of Krishna, his works are : *Rukmini Haran* (on the abduction of Rukmini by Krishna in, 436 metres), *Nag Daman* (the crushing of Kaliya serpent in the Yamuna ; in 129 metres), *Angad Vishti* (on Angad's mission and the battle between Ram and Ravan), *Nisani Radhikaji Ri* (incomplete ; on the 'Kunj Lila' of Krishna with Radha and Chandravali), *Ran Jang* (on the battle between Rana Pratap and Mughals), *Gun Vasant Lila*, *Ras Lila* and many stray verses. Several other works, viz., *Barahmasa*, *Angad Badsalo*, *Nagdaman Chaupai*, *Nagdaman Chhand*, *Nagdaman Katha* and a *Vat* (story) on *Ras Krida* in Gujarati prose, are also credited to him, but as their manuscripts are no longer extant, nothing definite can be said of their authorship. Picturesque descriptions and captivating dialogues are the characteristics of these poems ; in fact in the matter of witty and eloquent dialogues,

Sanya Jhula stands an unrivalled artist. His *Nisani Radhikaji Ri* is one of the two poems pertaining to Radha during the mediaeval period (see *Bankidas*).

SAPRE, NA. VI. Marathi-speaking modern Hindi dramatist, who is noted for his one-act plays : *Gur ki Chay* and *Jan-Sevak*; his short stories have also appeared in various magazines. *Khik-Khik* is a collection of his essays.

SAPTASATI RA CHHAND. Rajasthani poem in 120 verses, which was composed by Shridhar Vyas (q.v.) in the early 15th century. A heroic poem, it was written in praise of the goddess Shakti and was based on the *Durga-Saptashati*, which is a part of the Sanskrit *Markandeya Purana.* Though not an original poem, it is an important work from the point of view of antiquity of language, style and tradition ; it is also the earliest specimen of mythological poems of the Charan style.

SAR SANGRAH. See *Udayram, Swami.*

SARAHAPA (Sarojvajra ; b. *c.* 750). Earliest of the Siddha poets, who was a Brahmin of Magadh but later became a Buddhist monk and stayed at the University of Nalanda where he was considered a reputed scholar. He ultimately took to Tantra and developed into a Siddha. He is supposed to be the author of 32 books, mostly collections of *Dohas* and songs. His chief works are : *Kavya Koshamrit*, *Dakini-Guhya Vajragiti*, *Doha-kosh* (The Dictionary of Dohas ; the most popular) and *Chittakosh Ajvajragiti.* He and other Siddha poets have written mostly about the occult and mystic beliefs of their own cult or criticized old orthodoxy in a trenchant way. On the basis of researches made by Rahul Sankrityayan, he has been called the first poet of Hindi (see Pund). See *Dohakosh.*

SARAS MADHURI SHARAN (fl. 18th cent.). Rajasthani saint-poet of the Charandasi or Shuk Sampraday, whose stray verses are available.

SARASWATI DEVI. Modern Hindi poetess of Fiji, who is noted for her poems.

SARASWATI RAMNATH, MRS. Tamil-speaking modern Hindi writer, who has presented in Hindi the story of *Kamb Ramayan.* She tr. into Hindi Akhilan's Tamil novel *Pen* under the title *Nari* (The Woman) as also his 12 short stories under the title : *Gopur ka Dip* (The Light of Gopur) and prominent Tamil short stories under the title *Pau Phategi* (It would Dawn). She has tr. from Tamil into Hindi tales from Bharati under the title *Bharati ki Pratik Kathayen.*

SARDAR (fl. 1843). Poet of the Riti school, who was patronized by Ishwari Prasad Singh, Raja of Kashi. His Riti works in verse are : *Vagvilas, Sahitya-Sarasi, Tulsi Bhushan, Shringar-Sangrah, Rag-Ratnakar, Sahitya-Sudhakar, Ramlila Prakash* and *Manhor-Kavya.* He wrote also commentaries on *Bihari Satsai,* on some poems of Surdas and on Keshavdas's *Rasikpriya* and *Kavipriya,* and while they indicate the literary attainments of Sardar, the prose used is rather clumsy and at places ludicrous.

SARGU KRISHNAMURTI (1936-). Kannada and Telugu-speaking Hindi writer, whose chief research works are : *Hindi aur Telugu ki Adhunik Kavita men Manavtavad* (Humanism in Modern Hindi and Telugu Poetry) and *Pamp Ramayan aur Tulsi Ramayan* (both 1976). He has also written short stories for children; his essays are collected in *Prabandh Prabha : Naye Charan* (1977). His *Madhuswapna* (1957) is a collection of his poems, influenced by Maithili Sharan Gupta, Jayshankar Prasad and Sumitranandan Pant. His other poetical works are: *Jwalaketan* (1967 ; collections of his poems) and *Shrikrishna-Gandhi-Charit* (1976; a poem narrating simultaneously the stories of Krishna and Gandhi). See *Dakshin-Kavya Kusumanjali.* He is Professor and Head of the Department of Hindi, Bangalore University.

SARKARIYA, B.P. Rajasthani scholar, who, in collaboration with his son, B.R. Sarkariya, has edited *Dursa Adha Granthavali* (1982). B.P. Sarkariya is also the author of the lexicon : *Rajasthani-Hindi Kosh* (Pt. II), which is a concise dictionary of Rajasthani words explained in Hindi ; it is to consist of three parts of which the second has been published.

SARLA DEVI. Malayalam-speaking modern Hindi scholar, whose research work is : *Maithilisharan Gupta aur Prasad ki Kavya-Kritiyon men Nari* (The Female Role in the Poetry of Gupta and Prasad).

SARNAM SINGH SHARMA 'ARUN' (1917-79). Writer, who was born at a village in Aligarh district of Uttar Pradesh but remained in Jaipur, where he retired as Head of the Department of Hindi, Rajasthan University. His chief works are : *Marwari Bhasha ka Vikas* (Development of Marwari Language), *Rajasthani Bhasha aur Sahitya* (Rajasthani Language and Literature), *Hindi ki Tadbhav Shabdavali* (1968), *Aryabhashaon ke Vikas-*

kram men Apabhransh (1964), *Pali Sahitya aur Samiksha, Hindi Sahitya par Sanskrit Sahitya ka Prabhav* (1964), *Kabir : Vyaktitwa, Krititwa evem Siddhant* (on Kabir; 1966), *Miran Padavali ka Shaili-tatwik Adhyayan, Manas-Vivechan, Acharya Keshavdas, Vimarsh aur Nishkarsh* and *Rasa Siddhant: Punarmulyankan* ; he has also published novels, dramas, one-act plays, short stories, poetry, memoirs, etc.

SAROJ. See *Harinandan Thakur 'Saroj'*.

SAROJ ODHEKAR. Marathi-speaking modern Hindi scholar, whose chief work is : *Adhunik Marathi Sahitya.*

SAROJINI MAHISHI. Kannada-speaking modern Hindi writer, who tr. from Kannada into Hindi a part of Kuvempu's *Ramayana-Darshanam* and D.V. Gundappa's *Mantimman Kagga*, a poetical work.

SAROJNI SHARMA. Modern scholar and author of *Hindi tatha Gujarati ke Aitihasik Upanyason ka Tulnatmak Adhyayan*; she has also ed. *Adhunik Kahani Sangrah* (1984).

SARUP CHAND (fl. early 20th cent.). Folk-poet of Disaurkheri in Haryana, who composed and staged the *Sangs* : *Sarande, Ratnasain, Harishchandra, Padmavat, Mahabharat, Van Parva, Chir Parva, Chir Parva, Bairat Parva, Uttanpad, Jyani Chor* and *Jamal-Gabru.* His *Sangs,* contained *Bhajans, Ragnis, Dohas, Ghazals, Chamole*, etc. to suit the tastes of all sorts of people. He also had a dig over social evils and hypocrisy.

SARUP CHAND BHALLA (fl. 1797). Hindi poet of Panjab, whose *Mahima Prakash* describes the ten Sikh Gurus.

SARUPA BAI. Rajasthani saint-poetess, who was daughter of Naval Ram Mantri (q.v.). She is said to have left her in-laws and was initiated by Ramcharan, the propounder of Ram Snehi Sampraday, Shahpura. She composed in easy Rajasthani devotional *Padas*, which reveal the purity of her heart. She was present at Ramcharan's death in 1798 and composed a '*Marsiya-Pada*'.

SARVADANAND. Writer, whose chief works are : *Mati Khai Janavara* (1960 ; novel, description of Bandana and her incapcitated and sceptic husband) and *Bhnmija* (Sita; drama); he has written short stories as well.

SARVANAM KANHAIYALAL OJHA. Modern novelist, whose chief

works are : *Sindhu Simant* (The Limits of Sindhu), *Tisra Purush* (The Third Man) and *Dharm ke Nam Par* (In the Name of the Righteousness).

SARVANAND CHARAGI. Modern Hindi writer of Jammu-Kashmir, who tr. into Hindi *Lalla Vakyon* from Kashmiri.

SARVANG SAR. Anthology of poems of about 85 Hindi saint-poets, compiled by Rajasthani saint-poet, Naval Ram Mantri (q.v.) some time before 1785. The work, which shows vast learning and wide knowledge of the poet, is useful for literary history and is the only source of supplying specimen poems of many unknown and little known poets. The poets selected are irrespective of their caste, faith or ideology.

SARVANGI. See *Rajjab*.

SARVANJI (fl. 17th cent.). Rajasthani poet, whose *Sit Puran* and *Harkirat Puran* are *Akhyan Kavyas*, meant to be sung.

SARVASUKH SHARAN (fl. 1800). Poet of the Ram-cult, whose devotional works are : *Barahmas-Vinay* and *Tattwabodh*.

SARVESHWAR DAYAL SAXENA (1927-83). Poet of the *Tisra Saptak* (q.v.) and a writer, whose chief works are : *Kath ki Ghantiyan* (The Wooden Bells ; 1959), *Bans ka Pul* (The Bamboo Bridge; 1963), *Ek Suni Nav* (A Deserted Boat; 1966), *Kuano Nadi* (Kuano—the River of Sorrow; 1973), *Garm Havayen* (Hot Winds ; 1968), *Jungle ka Dard* (1976), *Khuntiyon par Tange Log* (People Hanging on Pegs ; 1981), *Andheron ka Hisab*, *Kya Kahkar Pukarun* and *Kavitayen* (2 Pts.) (all poetical collections), *Bakri* (She-goat), *Larai*, *Ab Gharibi Hatao* (Now Remove Poverty ; 1981) (dramas), *Soya Hua Jal* (1959 ; a novel on the shattering values after World War II), *Ure Huye Rang* (The Faded Colours), *Sune Chaukhte* (The Blank Frames) (novels), *Do Laghu Upanyas* (two Novelettes), *Pagal Kutton ka Masiha* (The Messiah of the Mad Dogs ; 1970), *Andhere par Andhera*, *Kachchi Sarak* (short story collections) and *Kuchh Rang*, *Kuchh Gandh* (memoirs). *Nepali Kavitayen* is his edited work.

SARYU PRASAD AGRAWAL (1922-). Writer, whose chief works are : *Akbari Durbar ke Hindi Kavi* (Hindi Poets of the Court of Akbar ; research) and *Bhasha-Vigyan aur Hindi* (Philology and Hindi) ; he has also edited the complete works of Rahim and Gang.

SARYU PRASAD 'KARUN'. Modern Magahi poet, whose poems are noted for descriptions of Nature.

SARYU SINGH 'SUNDAR'. Modern Bhojpuri poet, who is noted for his stray poems.

SATHE, G.N. Marathi-speaking modern Hindi scholar, whose chief work is *Rashtrabhasha ka Adhyapan*.

SATIDAS VYAS (fl. 1676). Riti poet of Bikaner, who composed his *Rasik Aram* during the regin of Anup Singh, the Maharaja of Bikaner.

SATI SUJAS. Rajasthani poem, which was composed by Mahadan Bai in 1843. It describes graphically how queen Devadi, the daughter of Raysingh Devada and other women became *Sati* on the death of Maharaja Mansingh of Jodhpur in 1843.

SATISH JAMALI. Hindi writer of Panjab, who is known for his novels *Pratibaddha*, *Chhappar Tola* and short stories : 'Pratham Purush' (The First Man), 'Pul' (The Bridge), etc. His collection of poems is: *Admi Azad Hai*. His critical works are: *Samkalin Hindi Alochana* and *Hindi Sahitya : Nayi Rachnashilta*.

SATISH JAYASWAL. Modern writer, whose *Jane Kis Bandargah Par* is a short story collection.

SATISH ROHDA. Sindhi-speaking modern Hindi writer, who is known for his *Bhasha*, *Hindi Bhasha* (on Hindi language).

SATISH SHROTRIYA. Modern Malwi writer, who is noted for his farces and short stories.

SATIYA. See *Khadga*.

SATO, TOMOKI. Modern Japanese Hindi scholar, who has done research especially on Kabir.

SATYADEV CHAUDHARI (1921-). Writer, whose *Bharatiya Kavya-Shastra* (Indian Poetics) attempts a re-evaluation of the Riti period.

SATYADEV PARIVRAJAK (1879-1961). Arya Samajist missionary, whose chief works are : *Amriki Digdarshan* (travelogue ; 1911 ; revised ed. as *Amrika-Pravas ki Meri Adbhut Kahani* ; 1958),

Anubhutiyan (1958 ; inspiring poems) and *Anant ki Or* (1958). He became a recluse and had his Ashram 'Satya Gyan Niketan' at Jwalapur, Hardwar.

SATYAKETU. Modern Hindi poet of Trinidad, who is known for his stray poems.

SATYAKETU VIDYALANKAR. Modern writer, who is noted for his historical novel, *Acharya Chanakya*.

SATYANAND PURI, SWAMI. Modern Hindi writer of Thailand, who has prepared *Ramkirti*, a version of the *Ramayan*.

SATYA NARAYAN. Poet, whose *Tum Nahin Kar Sakte* (You Cannot Do It : 1982) is a collection of poems. He has also written a novel : *Prerana* and a short story collection : *Dharti se Jud Kar* (1984 ; ed.).

SATYA NARAYAN 'AMAN'. Rajasthani poet, whose chief works are : *Sisdan* (1961 ; on heroism and sacrifice by Jagdev Panvar, a courtier of Siddhrao Jaysingh of Gujarat), *Chunthiya* (political satires), some patriotic and progressive poems and *Guvad Ri Jayodi* (one-act plays). His poem : 'Mata nai Bandan' glorifies Rajasthan.

SATYA NARAYAN GANGADAS VYAS. Modern Rajasthani writer, who is noted for his psychological and mythological short stories.

SATYA NARAYAN 'KAVIRATNA' (1880-1918). Poet, who was born at the village Sarai in Uttar Pradesh. He was brought up by Baba Raghubar Das of Tajganj (Agra). His married life had not been happy and he was influenced by the ideas of Swami Ramtirth. He kept up the tradition of writing in Brajbhasha, though the language he used was the one in current use. Kaviratna was keenly interested in all contemporary efforts for political and social reform and his *Bhramradut*, written after the well-known poem of Nanddas (q.v.) brings in contemporary material. His poems, sensitive and sincere, are collected in the *Hriday Tarang* (The Ripples of the Heart). He also rendered into Hindi two Sanskrit plays : *Uttara-Ramacharita* and *Malati Madhava* and Macaulay's *Horatius*, which convey the sense of the original. He also wrote panegyrics of Ramtirth, Tilak and Gokhale.

SATYA PAL CHUGH. Poet, whose chief poetical collections are : *Andheri Akrityon ke Par* (Across the Dark Figures ; 1965),

Bhor Kanth, *Vaman ke Charan* (The Footsteps of the Dwarf ; 1980) and *Surya aur Sikri*. His critical works are : *Astha ke Prahari*, *Premchandottar Upanyason ki Shilpa Vidhi* and *Hindi Aitihasik Upanyas*.

SATYA PRAKASH JOSHI. Rajasthani poet, whose chief works are : *Radha* (1960; portraying Radha's boundless love in a new context, when she tries to desist Krishna from devastation in the battle of Mahabharat) and *Bol Bharmali* (1974; an erotic poem on the maid servant of Queen Umade ; see Asa). His 'Olun' is a love poem. He has composed patriotic and progressive poems as also those, which describe in detail the silent changes in individual life in general ; his chief poems being 'Jai Manakha' and 'Dharti ra Diya'. He also composed some odes.

SATYA PRAKASH MILIND. Critic, whose chief work is : *Sahitya Samalochana*. He has also published poems and novels.

SATYA PRAKASH PRAKHAR. Poet, whose *Ag ka Samandar* (The Ocean of Fire ; 1980) is a collection of songs on the style of folksongs.

SATYARTHI. See *Devendra Sayarthi*.

SATYAVATI MALIK. Modern Hindi writer of Jammu & Kashmir, who is noted for her short story collections : *Do Phul* (Two Flowers), *Baisakh ki Rat* (A Night of April) and *Amit Rekhayen* (The Indelible Lines). She has largely remained in Delhi and her writings depict various aspects of female-life.

SATYA VRAT SHARMA. Modern poet, who is noted for his *Mira*, a poetical work.

SATYA VRAT AVASTHI. Modern Avadhi scholar, whose chief work is *Bihag Ragini*.

SATYA VRAT SINGH. Modern Bhojpuri scholar, whose chief work is *Bhojpuri Lok-Gatha* (Folk-tales of Bhojpuri).

SATYEN JOSHI. Modern Rajasthani poet, who has composed lyrical poems, portraying various aspects of Nature, as also love poems. His *Hans Karai Nigrani* (1978) is a collection of 46 small poems, consisting of eulogies of past glories, appreciation of folk-life, erotic songs, didactic verses, etc., the most dominant note, however, being of frustration. He is the author also of a novel *Kanval Puja*, dealing mainly with the battle between Rao Vijayrao of Tanaut and Mahmud of Ghazni; the novel relates to the early history of Jaisalmer. *Rovaniya Das* (1981) contains somewhat nine satirical pen-portraits of simpletons, sexual impotents, women of loose morals, etc.

SATYEN KUMAR. Modern short story writer, whose collections of stories are : *Jahaz*, *Barf tatha anya Kahaniyan* and *Ek Nam Aur tatha anya Kahaniyan.*

SATYENDRA (1907-). Writer, whose chief works are : *Muktiyagya* (on Raja Chhatrasal), *Kunal* (1937), *Vikram ka Atmamedh*, *Prayashchit* (The Expiation ; dramas), *Kala, Kalpana aur Sahitya* (Art, Imagination and Literature), *Hindi Sahitya men Adhunik Pravrittiyan* (Modern Tendencies in Hindi Literature ; collections of literary essays), *Kanchan Mani* (critical essays), *Braj Lok-Sahitya ka Adhyayan* (Study of Braj Folk-literature), *Braj Sahitya ka Itihas* (A History of Braj Literature ; 1967), *Madhyakalin Sahitya ka Lok-tatvik Adhyayan*, *Braj ki Lok Kahaniyan* (on Braj folk-stories), *Braj Lok-Sanskriti* (on Braj folk-culture), *Braj Gram-Sahitya ka Vivaran* (on Braj rural literature), *Jaharpir ya Guru-Gugga* and *Lok-Sahitya Vigyan.*

SATYENDRA NANDAN. Modern Hindi writer of Fiji, who is noted for his short stories and poems.

SATYENDRA SRIVASTAVA. See *Srivastava, S.N.*

SAUBHAGYA SINGH SHEKHAWAT. Rajasthani poet, who has paid poetic homage to the heroes, who sacrificed their lives in fighting against the Chinese attack on India ; he also composed Nature poems. He has done much work on mediaeval Rajasthan *Vat* literature and has published *Vats* and historical short stories. He is the author of *Rajasthani Nibandh Sangrah* (1974), *Rajasthani Sahitya Sampada* (1977) and *Jinmata.*

SAUMYA NARAYANAN. Tamil-speaking modern Hindi writer, who has prepared *Tamil Shikshak*, etc.

SAUNDARVALLI, VAI. Tamil-speaking Hindi scholar, who is known for her *Hindi and Tamil ke Adhunik Gadya ka Vikas* (The Development of Modern Prose of Hindi and Tamil ; Ph.D. thesis ; 1967).

SAVAI SINGH DHAMORA. Modern Rajasthani poet, who has paid poetic homage to the heroes, who sacrificed their lives in fighting against the Chinese attack on India.

SAVITRI SINHA (1922-72). Writer, her chief works are : *Madhyakalin Hindi Kavayitriyan* (Hindi Poetesses of Mediaeval Age ; thesis), *Brajbhasha ke Krishna-bhakti Kavya men Abhivyanjanashilp* and *Anusandhan ka Swarup*. *Mutthiyon men Band Akar* is her poetical collection.

SAWA, EIZO, THE LATE. Modern Japanese Hindi scholar, who taught Urdu at the Osaka University of Foreign Studies. He was a scholar of Persian as well. Apart from his Urdu teaching, on which he had full mastery, he taught *Karmabhumi* of Premchand. It was in 1948 that he published his *Hindi Praveshika*, which is considered as the first work in Devnagari Script published from Japan. He was the author also of *Indobunten*, which treats of Hindi grammar in a comprehensive manner.

SAXENA, K.P. Modern humorous writer, whose chief works are : *Rahiman ki Rail Yatra*, *Shri Gul Sarovar ki Katha*, *Gaz, Foot, Inch* and *Bap re Bap* (the first two fiction works and the other two dramas). His other humorous works are : *Talash Phir ek Columbus Ki* and *Lakhnavi Dhang Se*.

SAYAN JHULA. See *Sanya Jhula*.

SAYILU, B. Telugu-speaking Hindi writer, who is known for his *Hindi Bhasha Shikshan* (on teaching of Hindi ; 1972).

SCHOLEBURG, H.C. Author of *Concise Grammar of the Hindi Language* (Allahabad, 1940) ; the author has made use of the works of Kellogg and Greaves (qq.v.).

SCHULZII, BENJAMIN (1689-1760). Christian missionary, who came to Madras in 1719. As Tamil was spoken in Madras, he had to learn Hindustani for all-India language and wrote the first Hindustani grammar in Latin under the title of *Grammatica Hindostanica* (1745). Schulzii's field of activity was south India and as such the Hindustani he used in his Grammar was the one prevalent in that part of India. The Grammar thus discusses the then current form of Hindi before the advent of Englishmen.

SEN (fl. 1500). Saint-poet, who was a protege of Rajaram, the ruler of Bandhogarh (Rewa). A barber by caste, it is said that once Sen could not present himself for the service of the king ; realizing his predicament God Himself took his form and served the king. Several *Padas* of Sen exist in the *Granth Sahib* (q.v.).

SENANAI (fl. 14th cent.). Saint-poet of Maharashtra or of northern India, who composed some *Padas* in Hindi as well.

SENAPATI (b. *c.* 1589). Poet, who was a Kanyakubja Brahmin and was born in Anupashahr. His father's name was Gangadhar, grandfather's Parashuram and his teacher's Hiramani. The date of his death is not known but he completed his *Kavitta Ratnakar* (q.v.) in 1649 ; his other book is *Kavya Kalpadrum* (The Celestial Tree of Poetry). It appears that he was highly honoured in the Mohammedan court but at the close of his life, he became a recluse and lived at Vrindavan. Even at Vrindavan, he was a devotee of Ram about whom he wrote gloriously. It has come to light recently that Senapati was one of the 52 poets in Guru Govind Singh's *Durbar* and wrote *Guru Shobha* (The Glory of the Guru) which gives Govind Singh's life-history. He also rendered into Hindi the *Chanakya-Niti*.

Senapati is often described as Mahakavi. His poetry (see *Kavitta Ratnakar*) reveals his versatile genius. He had a sensitive mind, quite capable of grasping subtle variations in human emotions and in the beauties of Nature which he expressed in flawless verses of pure Brajbhasha. He was fond of *Kavitta* metre, which he employed with astounding skill. He made masterly use of the various figures of speech.

SENGAR, SHIV SINGH. See *Shiv Singh Sengar*.

SENKEVICH, ALEXANDER NIKOLAYEVICH. (1941-). Soviet Hindi scholar, who did his doctorate on the creative work of Harivansh Rai Bachchan. His special study is on modern Hindi literature and has translated into Russian the verse and prose works of Agyey, Sarveshwar Dayal Saxena, Bachchan, Raghuvir Sahay, Shrikant Verma, Nirala, etc.

SEREBRIYANI, SARGEY DMITRIYEVICH (1946-). Soviet Hindi scholar, who did his doctorate in 1974 on the poetry of Vidyapati. His field of specialization is Modern and Mediaeval Hindi literature.

SETHIA, M.C. See *Kiran Nahta*.

SEV DAS (1640-1741). Rajasthani saint-poet, whose contribution to Sant poetry is remarkable. A follower of Haridas Niranjani Sect, his *Sakhis*, *Padas* and stray verses record his experiences and preachings.

SEVA DAS (fl. 1783). Poet of the Riti school, whose chief

work on figures of speech is : *Raghunath-Alankar*. His other works are : *Gita Mahatmya, Rasa Darpan, Alvalelalji ko Nakhshikh* and *Alvalelalji ko Chhappy*.

SEVADAS KI PARCHI. See *Rupdas*.

SEVA RAM YATRI (1933-). Fiction writer, whose chief works are : *Dusre Chehre, Alag-alag Asvikar, Dharatal, Keval Pita, Silsila* (short story collections on the problems of middle class people), *Darazon men Band Dastavez* (Documents Locked in Drawers), *Lautate Hue* (While Returning), *Tutate Dayare, Pyasi Nadi* and *Bhatka Megh* (1984; novels). His important short stories are : 'Yadon ke Stup' (The Mounds of Memory), 'Dard ke Aine' (The Mirrors of Agony), 'Chor aur Chor' (Thief and Thief), 'Abhay Dan' (The Pledge of Protection), 'Andhere ka Phailav' (The Expanse of Darkness), etc.

SEVA SADAN (Service Home). Novel (1916) by Premchand (q.v.), which seeks to discuss the problem of prostitution and indirectly hints at the evils of dowry and the sham morality of the society.

An honest Police Inspector, Krishna Chandra, in order to meet the dowry expenses for the marriage of his daughter, Suman, accepts bribes and is sentenced to five years' imprisonment. In his absence, Suman is married to a widower Gajadhar Prasad but she is later expelled from the house and has to seek shelter at the house of a prostitute. A social reformer rescues her from there and she is given protection in a Vidhva (widow) Ashram, where she is joined by her younger sister, Shanta, who is left alone after the death of her mother. They have also to leave this place ; Shanta is married to Sadan Singh, with whom she was engaged once and Suman begins to reside with her sister. Suman, however, has to leave Shanta's house too and she meets Swami Gajanand (her former husband, Gajadhar Prasad) and at his instance, she accepts the management of the Seva Sadan, a house meant for the reform of the daughters born of prostitutes.

A social novel, it throws light on many rotten spots in the Indian society.

SEVAK (1815-81). Poet of the Riti school, who was grandson of Thakur I of Asni (q.v.). He lived in Varanasi, where his patron was Babu Harishankar Singh, a rich citizen. The theme of his best-known work, *Vag-Vilas* is *Nayikabhed*, while his other book is *Nakhshikh*, written in *Barvai* metre. Some of Sevak's verses are even recited by lovers of old poetry.

SEVAKJI (*c.* 1520-53). Poet of the Krishna-cult (Radhavallabh Sect), whose original name was Damodardas. He belonged to the village Gadha in Gondwana territory. It is said that he was initiated in dream by Radha. His *Sevak Vani*, based on Hit Harivansh's *Hit Chaurasi* enunciates the principles of the Radhavallabh Sect and is considered as essential among the followers of this Sect for study along with *Hit Chaurasi*. He came to live in Vrindavan but died shortly after his arrival there.

SEVAKENDRA TRIPATHI (b. 1909). Poet, whose chief poetical work *Brajvartika* (1965) gives ample display of the poet's love for the Braj country and its culture.

SHABARPA (SHAVARPA). Siddha poet, who was a disciple of Sarahapa (b. *c.* 750) and preceptor of Luipa. In his works, he has written mostly about the occult and mystic beliefs of his own Tantric cult. His chief works are : *Mahamudra Vajragiti*, *Shungat Drishti*, *Sahajopadesh-Sevadhishthan* and *Shadanga-Yoga*. See *Dohakosh*.

SHABDA RASAYAN. Riti work by Dev (q.v.), which is based on Sanskrit works of poetics. The illustrations of the figures of speech give a glimpse of the poet's unique faculty of imagination.

'SHABNAM'. See *Abhimanyu Unnuth 'Shabnam'*.

SHACHI RANI GURTU. Modern writer ; her chief critical works are : *Vaichariki*, *Mahadevi Verma*, *Sumitranandan Pant*, *Hindi ke Alochak* (The Hindi Critics) and *Gorky aur Premchand* (the last four ed.).

SHACHINDRA PAVAR 'INDRA'. Marathi-speaking modern Hindi dramatist, who is noted for his work : *Rang*, a collection of one-act plays.

SHAH ABDUL ALIM ASHI, MAULANA. See *Ashi*.

SHAH ALI GAMDHANI (fl. latter half of 15th cent.). Sufi poet of Gujarat, whose verses in Dakkhini Hindi were collected by his grandson under the title *Jawahar-ul Asaras*.

SHAHJI MAHARAJ (r. 1684-1712). Telugu-speaking Maratha ruler of Tanjore, who was known as 'Andhra Bhoj'. Apart from his authorship of 21 *Yakshagans* in Telugu, he was the author of several Hindi *Yakshagans*, e.g., *Radha-Bansidhar-*

Vilas Natak (on the separation and union of Radha and Krishna), *Vishwatit Vilas Natak* (on Shiv) and *Panchabhasha Vilas Natak* (with use of five languages : Sanskrit, Hindi, Telugu, Marathi, and Tamil). The language used in these plays is Brajbhasha mixed with Bundelkhandi. His works are preserved in the Saraswati Mahal Library, Tanjore. He is also called by the name of Shahraj, Shahji, Shahbhup, Shahnrip, etc.

SHAHRAJ. See *Shahji Maharaj.*

SHAHU (1747-1815). Sindhi Muslim saint-poet, who also composed in Hindi a poetical work : *Vichar Anubhav* ; he laid emphasis on inner purity instead of observing fasts and going on pilgrimages. Shahu was the eldest son of Rohal (q.v.) and occupied the religious seat after his father's death.

SHAILENDRA MOHAN JHA. Maithili novelist, whose chief works are *Pratima* (1951) and *Madhu-Shravani* (1956 ; on the honey-*vrat* of the newly-wed). He is noted for his short story 'Mrinalak Sut' and his short story collection is *Path Herathi Radha* (1963). He has written good lyrics as also *Braj Boli Sahitya.*

SHAILESH MATIYANI (1931-). Writer, whose chief works are : *Tisra Sukh*, *Atit tatha anya Kahaniyan*, *Hara Hua* (Defeated), *Papmukti tatha anya Kahaniyan*, *Kohra*, *Chil aur any Kahaniyan*, *Jungle men Mangal*, *Pyas aur Patthar*, *Meri Tentis Kahaniyan*, *Bheren aur Gareriya* (all short story collections), *Hauldar* (1960), *Chhote-chhote Pakshi* (Little Birds), *Chauthi Mutthi* (The Fourth Fist ; 1962), *Chitthi Rasan* (The Postman ; 1966), *Boribali se Boribandar Tak* (a description of the people of Bombay), *Savittari* (1980), *Gopuli Gappuran* (1981), *Chand Auraton ka Shahr* (1983), *Ramkali*, *Dere Vale*, *Bavan Pattiyon ka Sangam* (1984) (all regional novels), *Khansi ko Phansi* (collection of one-act plays) and *Janta aur Sahitya* (The People and Literature ; a critical work). His important short stories are : 'Do Dukhon ka ek Sukh' (Two Sorrows Constituting one Joy), 'Bhay' (Fear), etc. In his works, he has described the problems faced by the unprivileged sections of the society.

SHAILESH ZAIDI. Modern scholar, whose chief works are : *Godan : Ek Navya Drishti*, *Tulsi Kavya ki Arbi-Farsi Shabdavali evam Sanskritik Adhyayan*, *Premchand ki Upanyas Yatra : Nav Mulyankan* and *Bilgram ke Musalman Hindi Kavi.*

SHAKESPEARE, JOHN. Author of *A Grammar of the Hindustani*

Language (1813 ; it ran into several editions with subsequent revisions), *An Introduction to Hindustani*, *Muntakhabat Hindi or Selections in Hindustani*, and *A Dictionary-Hindustani and English* (London, 1817), which also ran into 4th edition. In the third edition of the Dictionary, many Dakhini words were included, while in the 4th edition were incorporated words from Urdu poets, Wali, Mir, Taqi, Sauda and others as also from the unpublished manuscript (in several parts) of Dr Harris, who had left it in the India House. This Dictionary also contains many words from Sanskrit.

SHAKIL FAROOQI. Modern Hindi poet, of Pakistan, whose poems appear in Indian magazines and papers from time to time.

SHAKTI DAN KAVIYA. Rajasthani poet, whose poems in the traditional Charan style are available. He has also composed lyrics on Nature's various aspects and has contributed to *Minjhar* (1963), an anthology. His critical work is : *Rajasthani Sahitya ka Anushilan*, while *Phul Saru Pankhdi* (1984) is his short story collection.

SHAKUNT MATHUR (1922-). Poetess of *Dusra Saptak* (q.v.), whose chief poetical collection is *Abhi Aur Kuchh Inka* (Still Something More for Him).

SHAKUNTALA. See *Lakshman Singh*.

SHAKUNTALA UPAKHYAN. See *Nevaj*.

SHALABH SHRIRAM SINGH. Poet, whose poetical collections are : *Kal Subah Hone ke Bad* (After Tomorrow Morning), *Atirikta Purush* (Extra Man ; 1976), *Nigah dar Nigah* and *Rahe Hayat*, *Agnikamal ki Pankhuriyan*, *Phaulad ki Mombatti* and *Andheri Chandni Ujli Chhanv* are his novels.

SHALI SURI. See *Virat Parva*.

SHALI BHADRA SURI. Jain poet and author of *Bharateshvar Bahubali Ras* (composed in 1184 ; q.v.) and of *Buddhiras* (q.v.), both in Rajasthani. According to Ganpati Chandra Gupt, he is the first Hindi poet and his *Bharateshvar Bahubali Ras* is the first Hindi poem.

SHALI BHADRA SURI. See *Panch Pandav Charit-Raso*.

SHALI GRAM VAISHNAV. Garhwali scholar, who was noted for his *Garhwali Pakhana* (1938).

SHALI GRAM VAISHYA (1831-1902). Writer, whose chief works are : *Mordhwaj* (1890), a drama on mythological theme and *Lavanyavati-Sudarshan* (1892), a romantic drama.

SHAMBHAVI DEVI. Modern Maithili short story writer, who is noted for her 'Sodar Sneh' on the love of a sister for her brother. She is also the author of a prose work, *Mithilak Vidushi Mahila* on the learned ladies of Mithila.

SHAMBHU NATH. Critic, whose chief work is *Sahitya aur Sangharsh* (The Literature and Struggle ; 1980 ; on Marxist lines).

SHAMBHU NATH BHATT HALIM. Modern Hindi writer of Jammu-Kashmir, who tr. into Hindi verse *Lalla Vakyon* from Kashmiri, which has been published by the Cultural Academy under the title *Laladyad*.

SHAMBHU NATH JAYASWAL. Modern Magahi writer, who is noted for his humorous one-act plays.

SHAMBHU NATH KAPILDEV. Native of Trinidad, who is promoting the cause of Hindi in his country.

SHAMBHU NATH MISHRA, I (fl. 1749). Poet of the Riti school, who was patronized by Raja Bhagvant Rai Khichi of Asothar in Fatehpur district. He was the author of three Riti works : *Rasakallol*, *Rasatarangini* and *Alankar-Dipak* (chiefly in *Dohas*). There have been two other poets bearing this name : one flourished in 1810 and the other flourished in 1844, but nothing is known about them.

SHAMBHU NATH SHESH (1915-58). Panjabi-speaking Hindi poet, who was one of the pioneers in the field of Hindi *Ghazals* and *Rubais* ; his chief works are : *Unmilika* (The Bloom) and *Suvela* (The Auspicious Time). Some of his poems are collected in the *Kavyadhara*.

SHAMBHU NATH SINGH (1917-). Poet, whose poetical collections are : *Ruprashmi* (The Rays of Beauty ; 1945 ; depicting the poet's fascination for beauty), *Chhayalok* (1946), *Udayachal* (1946), *Manvantar* (1951 ; it contains fourteen long poems), *Divalok* (1953 ; romantic), *Madhyam Main* (1957) and *Khandit Setu* (The Broken Bridge ; 1967). *Samay ki Shila* is a collection of his new songs, while *Dharti aur Akash* (The Earth and Sky) is a drama depicting class-struggle. In the *Navgit Dashak* (3 Pts.) he has edited the new lyrics of new poets.

SHAMIM, A.A. Modern Hindi poet of Fiji, whose chief work is : *Bhala-Anjam.*

SHAMSHER BAHADUR SINGH (1911-). Poet of *Dusra Saptak* (q.v.), whose chief poetical collections are : *Kuchh Kavitayen* (Some Poems ; 1959), *Kuchh aur Kavitayen* (Some More Poems ; 1961), *Chuka Bhi Nahin Hun Main* (I am not yet Exhausted, for which he received Sahitya Akademy Award), *Shamsher* (1971 ; a collection of his poems published between 1952 and 1970), *Itne Pas Apne* (So Near to Me ; 1980), *Bat Bolegi* (The Poetry will Speak Itself ; 1981), *Udita : Abhivyakti ka Sangharsh* and *Ye Akritiyan Tumhari*. His *Kuchh Kavitayen* and *Kuchh aur Kavitayen* have been reprinted in one volume in 1984. There are two main strains apparent in his poetry : socialist and individualistic. *Doab* is a collection of his essays, while *Plot ka March* contains sketches.

SHAMSHER SINGH NARULA. Scholar, whose chief work is *Hindi Bhasha ka Itihas* (History of Hindi Language). His other works are : *Scientific History of the Hindi Language* and *Hindi aur Pradeshik Bhashaon ka Vaigyanik Itihas* (1957). He has also published two novels : *Andhere men Bhatakti Kiran* and *Ek Pankhuri ki Tez Dhar* and a short story collection : *Adhi Rat ka Suraj.*

SHAMTOV, AZAD NASRETDINOVICH (1940-). Soviet Hindi scholar, who is noted for his studies on Dakkhini Hindi, Amir Khusro, etc.

SHANI (1933-). Urdu-speaking Hindi fiction writer, whose full name is Syed Gulsher Ali. His chief works are : *Babul ki Chhanv* (In the Shade of the Babul Tree ; 1950), *Chhote Ghar ka Vidroh* (The Revolt of a Small House ; 1964), *Sanp aur Sidhi* (The Snake and the Ladder), *Ek se Makanon ka Nagar, Biradari tatha anya Kahaniyan, Jahanpanah Jungle, Dali Nahin Phulti, Yuddha* (War), *Meri Priya Kahaniyan* (short story collections), *Kala Jal* (The Black Water), *Pattharon men Band Avaz* (The Locked Voices in Stones), *Kasturi* (Musk), *Nadi aur Sipiyan* (The River and Shells), *Shalvanon ka Dip* (on description of the tribal people of Bastar), *Ek Larki ki Diary* and *Phul Torna Mana Hai* (novels). His *Kala Jal* has been tr. into Russian. His publications have been published in two sets : *Sab Ek Jagah.*

SHANKAR (fl. middle of 18th cent.). Maithili poet, who composed hymns on devotional and pseudo-philosophical subjects.

SHANKAR BAM. Marathi-speaking modern Hindi novelist, whose novelletes for children are quite popular. His chief works are : *Samrat Harsh*, *Samrat Lalitaditya*, *Lohe ka Admi*, *Narmada ki Ladli*, etc. *Gulab ke Phul* is a collection of his one-act plays, while *Kal ke Kampan*, *Khandahar* and *Jhansi ki Rani* are his short story collections. He has also written a biographical work : *Vidrohi ki Beti* and another work *Delhi ki Ramkahani*. His chief novels are : *Man Raksha* and *Sparsh Gandha*.

SHANKAR BARHAT (1543-1623). Rajasthani poet, whose stray verses in popular metres are available.

SHANKAR DAMODAR PARANJPE (fl. 1850-1900). Marathi-speaking Hindi dramatist, who was known for his *Apratim Vaidyaraj*, a farce.

SHANKAR DAN SAMAUR (1824-78). Rajasthani poet of village Bobasar, Sujangarh, who could be called the first great Charan poet of the modern period. He gave a clarion call to the nation against the British, eulogised the heroes who rose against the British rule in 1857 and chided the princely rulers and poets for siding with the British. His stray Dingal *Gits*, *Chhappays* and *Dohas* are on a variety of subjects. Some *Gits* describe contemporary events and heroes such as Thakur Khumman Singh Bidawat Lodhsar, Dungji, Jawaharji, Tantia Tope, who fought against the British rule. His *Gits* in praise of Shakti or Devi are collectively known as *Sagati Sujas*, while *Bhagirathi Mahima* exalts Bhagirathi. His other poems : *Bakhat ro Bayaro*, *Desh Darpan* and *Saket Shatak* in *Doha* metre, depict the prevailing chaotic social, economic and political conditions in the country, ways of the princely rulers, the baneful policies of the British, their oppressive administrative system and the plight of the downtrodden. His place among the nationalist poets is unique, for there are very few poets, who openly raised their voice in revolt against the British rule during the 1857 Mutiny. His language is easy and fluent Rajasthani and he can be called a poet of the people.

SHANKAR DEV (1449-1558). The earliest and perhaps the greatest of the Assamese dramatists, who wrote many Hindi (Brajavali) dramas, of which the following six are extant : *Kaliya Daman* (on the story of Krishna subjugating the Kali-Nag), *Ram Vijay* (on Sita's Swayamvar), *Rukmini-Haran* (on the abduction of Rukmini by Krishna), *Keli-Gopal* (on the amours of Krishna and Gopis), *Parijat-Haran* (on getting celestial tree from Indra's garden) and *Patni-Prasad* (how Krishna helped those wives of Brahmins to have a sight of the gods, who were devoted to Krishna).

SHANKAR LAL (fl. 1854-99). Folk-poet of Haryana, who composed and staged the *Sangs* : *Padmini*, *Bhurabadal*, *Mordhwaj* and *Prahlad*.

SHANKAR LAL (fl. 1940-47). Malwi poet, who was noted for his folk poems.

SHANKAR LAL PUROHIT. Oriya-speaking modern Hindi writer, who has tr. Gopinath Mahanti's Oriya work, *Mati Mathal* into Hindi.

SHANKAR LAL SHARMA (1929-). Assamese-speaking Hindi writer, who is noted for his drama : *Sati Jaymati*. He has tr. some Assamese short storeis into Hindi as well.

SHANKAR LAL YADAV. Modern writer, whose chief work is : *Hariyana Pradesh ka Lok-Sahitya*.

SHANKAR PUNTAMBEKAR. Marathi-speaking modern Hindi dramatist, whose works are : *Shishe ke Tukre* (social) and three collections of one-act plays : *Kalyani*, *Sabse Chhota Admi* and *Mujhe Kaviyon se Bachao*. His novels are : *Huriyali aur Kante*, *Ek Mantri Swarglok Men* and *Kalank Rekha*. He also wrote short stories under the title *Nila Lifafa* ; his essays are collected in *Readymade Kapre*. *Visit Yamraj Ki* is his humorous work. His language is influenced by Marathi.

SHANKAR RAJU NAIDU, S. (1920-). Tamil-speaking Hindi scholar, whose chief works are : *Kamb Ramayan and Tulsi Ramayan* (thesis ; 1956) and the Hindi tr. of the celebrated Tamil classics : *Thirukural* into prose and of *Shilappadikaram* into verse. His *Gitophar* is a collection of poems on nationalism and world peace. He has written about 50 essays in English and Hindi on Tamil literature, culture, etc.

SHANKAR SHARMA PIPASU. Dogri-speaking modern Hindi poet, whose poetical collections are : *Chand* (The Moon) and *Sima ka Panchhi* (A Frontier Bird).

SHANKAR SHESH (1933-81). Dramatist, who is known for his experiments in the dramatic technique. His chief drama : *Are Mayavi Sarovar* (0 Illusive Lake ; 1980) describes the modern social and political life through the medium of an imaginative story of an ancient age. His other dramas are :

Raktabij, *Murtikar*, *Khajuraho ka Shilpi*, *Gharaunda*, *Chehre*, *Ek aur Dronacharya* (One More Dronacharya), *Fandi* (Condemned to Gallows ; both published 1982), *Adhi Rat ke Bad*, *Komal Gandhar*, *Poster* and *Badh ka Pani*. He has published a novel, *Chetana*, a critical work : *Chhattisgarhi ka Bhasha Shastriya Adhyayan* (1973) and a humorous work : *Ratnagarbha*.

SHANKARAYYA SHASTRI, R. Telugu-speaking Hindi writer, who is noted for his *Telugu Bhasha Swabodhini* (Telugu Self-Teacher ; 1966).

SHANTA BHANAWAT. Rajasthani writer, whose *Mahavir ri Olakhan* (1975) is a biography of Mahavir.

SHANTA KUMAR. Writer, who is noted for his *Rajniti ki Shatranj* (The Chess of Politics ; 1982), a memoir. His novels are : *Qaidi*, *Man ke Mit* and *Lajo*, while his short story collection is *Jyotirmayi*. He was Chief Minister of Himachal Pradesh.

SHANTI JOSHI. Writer, whose chief novels are : *Mera Man Banvas Diya Sa* (My Exiled Mind ; 1966), *Udas Panne* (The Cheerless Pages ; 1966 ; written in the first person), *Shunya ki Bahon Men* (In the Arms of Emptiness ; 1969), *Ek aur Bat* (One More Point), *Machhli aur Mara Jal* (The Fish and Dead Water ; both 1971), *Rajul*, *Sanp* ; her other works are : *Mati ki Gandh* (The Smell of Soil ; short story collection) and *Sumitra Nandan Pant* : *Jivan aur Sahitya* (Pant : Life and Literature ; 2 Pts.). She teaches philosophy in Allahabad University.

SHANTI KUMAR NANURAM VYAS. Modern writer, who is noted for his stylish essays and writings on social and cultural subjects. His best work is *Ramayan-kalin Sanskriti* (The Culture in the Age of Ramayana ; 2 vols.).

SHANTI KUMARI. Modern Maithili poetess, who has composed stray poems.

SHANTI LAL BHARDWAJ 'RAKESH'. Modern Rajasthani poet, who has composed Nature poems.

SHANTI MEHROTRA (1926-). Poetess, whose chief works are : *Nishkriti* (The Expiation), *Vida* (The Farewell), *Marichika* (The Mirage), *Rekha*, *Pag-Dhwani* (The Foot-Sounds), *Panch-Pradip*, *Chanakya* and *Khula Akash* : *Mere Pankh* (The Open Sky : My Wings). *Surkhab ker Par* (The

Wings of Ostrich) is her short story collection, while *Dantkatha* is a humorous work. *Thehra Hua Pani* (The Standing Water ; 1980) is her drama. She works as Producer, All India Radio, Allahabad.

SHANTI NATH DEV RAS. Rajasthani poem, which was composed by Lakshmi Tilak Gani, a Jain poet in about 1256. It describes briefly the life of Shantinath, the 16th Tirthankar, and the consecration of the Lord's idols in the temple at Khed in 1201 and at Jalore in 1256 by Jinpati Suri and Jineshwar Suri respectively.

SHANTI PRIYA DWIVEDI (1906-67). Critic, who was born in Varanasi. His chief works are : *Sancharini* (1939), *Yug aur Sahitya* (1941), *Samayiki* (1944), *Dharatal* (1948), *Pratishthan* (1953), *Sakalya* (1955), *Adhan* (1957) and *Vrat aur Vikas* (all essay collections) ; he is regarded as an impressionist critic.

SHANTI SWARUP KUSUM. Poet, whose *Chandrabha* (1983) is a *Prabandh-Kavya.*

SHAPIRO, MICHAEL C. (1946-). American Hindi scholar, who is at present Associate Professor of Asian Languages and Literature (Hindi) in the University of Washington. His publications are : *Aspects of Hindi Abstract Verbal Syntax* (Chicago, 1974), *A Study Guide to Hindi Children's Readers* (vol. 1 ; with Thomas B. Ridgeway ; 1976), *A Three Year Curriculum of Modern Standard Hindi* (with M.K. Verma and Bruce R. Pray ; 1980), *Language and Society in South Asia* (with Harold F. Schiffman ; 1981) and *A Primer of Modern Standard Hindi* (1985). His field of research is Hindi linguistics and he has written about 25 articles and reviews, all connected with Linguistics.

SHARAD DEVDA (1934-). Novelist, whose chief works are : *Tutati Ikaiyan* (The Breaking Units). *College Street ke Naye Masiha* (The New Messiah of College Street ; 1966) and *Patthar ka Lamp-post* (The Stone Lamp-post). He edits 'Anima'.

SHARAD JOSHI. Modern humorous essayist, whose chief works in Hindi are : *Jeep par Swar Illiyan* (The Ants on the Jeep), *Dusri Satah* (The Second Surface), *Tilasma* (The Miracle) ; his dramas (political satires) are : *Andhon ka Hathi* (An Elephant according to the Blind), *Ek Tha Gadha urf Aladad Khan* (There was an Ass named Aladad Khan) published as

Do Vyangya Natak. His short story collections are : *Kisi Bahane* and *Pichhle Dinon*.

SHARADA (fl. 17th cent.). One of the court-poets of Guru Govind Singh (q.v.), he was a master of Brajbhasha and composed an eulogy on the Guru ; he also wrote devotional poetry in the *Shringar* style.

SHARADA DEVI VEDALANKAR. Scholar, whose chief work is *The Development of Hindi Prose Literature in the Early Nineteenth Century* (1800-1856) (Allahabad, 1977).

SHARADA NAND JHA. Modern Maithili writer, who is noted for his drama, *Pherar* on the 'Quit India' movement of 1942 against the British rule.

SHARADA RAO. Writer, whose chief publication is : *Chhoti Malkin* (The Younger Landlady ; 1981).

SHARAN BIHARI GOSWAMI (1930-). Poet, whose chief works are : *Janmabhumi* (The Birth-place) and *Swami Haridas* (criticism).

SHARMA, I.K. Rajasthani scholar, who is Professor of English in Rajasthan University. His *Contemporary Rajasthani Poetry* (1979) is a tr. of the select poems of 20 Rajasthani poets into English.

SHARMA, K.K. Modern Rajasthani scholar, who has edited a version of the *Bagadavat* (q.v.). He is also the author of *Rajasthani Lok-Gatha ka Adhyayan*.

SHARMA, M.B.A.R. Telugu-speaking Hindi writer, who tr. *Kumarashatakam* and *Sumati shatakam* in 1959 from Telugu into Hindi under the titles of *Kumar-Shati* and *Sumati-Shati*.

SHARMA, M.P. Rajasthani scholar, who is noted for his research work : *The Origin and Development of Mewati* (1977).

SHARMA, NARENDRA. See *Narendra Sharma*.

SHARMA, PADMA SINGH. See *Padma Singh Sharma*.

SHARMA, R.C. (1919-). Poet and scholar, whose chief works are : *Nishadhraj*, *Agnipariksha*, *Ashvatthama* (epics) and a cultural study of Sagun Bhakti Kavya of Moghul Times. He is retired Principal of Dayal Singh College, Karnal.

SHARMA, RAM VILAS. See *Ram Vilas Sharma.*

SHARNGADHAR. Celebrated compiler of the Sanskrit anthology, *Sharngadhara Paddhati* (1363), who is also supposed to have composed two poetical works : *Hammir Raso* and *Hammir Kavya* in old Rajasthani or Apabhransh, which treat of the grim battle between Hammir, the Maharana of Ranthambhor and Alauddin ; both these works are no longer extant, but portions thereof are found scatttered in several works, including *Prakrit Pingal.* Sharngadhar was son of Damodar, grandson of Raghav and great-grandson of Hammir Bhupati of Shakambhari country. It is said that he attended the court of Raja Hammir Dev Chauhan of Ramthambhor, of whose valour he sang in his famous work, *Hammir Raso* (q.v.).

SHARANGPANI, SHA. RA. Tamil-speaking modern Hindi writer, whose short stories have been published in various popular magazines. While in Madras, he edited several Hindi magazines ('Dakshini Hindi', 'Dakshin Bharat', 'Hindi Prachar Samachar', etc.) and has also written *Hindi Prachar ka Itihas* (ed , The History of Hindi Movement) and some reportages.

SHASHI BHUSHAN SINGHAL. Modern fiction writer, whose chief works are : *Jani Anjani Rahen* (novel), *Ye Jag Ye Sapne* (short story collection), *Sahityik Shodh ke Ayam, Adhunik Hindi Sahitya* and *Upanyas ka Swarup* (criticism).

SHASHI DHAWAN. Writer, who is noted for the novels *Radha* (1980) and *Shapath.*

SHASHI MALA KATHA. See *Prabhudayal.*

SHASHI NATH CHOUDHURY. Modern Maithili writer, who is noted for his short stories as also critical articles.

SHASHI NATH JHA. Maithili writer, who was noted for his drama, *Kali-Dharm-Prakashika* (1911) and a drama on the life of Udayanacharya. He has made genuine efforts in restoring the original text of Vidyapati's *Padas.*

SHASHI PRABHA SHASTRI. Writer ; her chief works are ; *Jharna* (The Spring), *Pyasa* (The Thirsty), *Amaltas, Naven* (The Boats), *Sidhiyan* (The Stairs), *Parchhaiyon ke Pichhe* (Behind the Shadows ; 1980), *Kyonki* (Because ; 1981),

Karkarekha (novels), *Dhuli Hui Sham* (A Fresh Evening), *Anuttarit* (Without Reply), *Do Kahaniyon ke Bich* (Between the Two Stories ; 1981), *Jod Baqi* (short story collections) and *Hindi ke Pauranik Natakon ke Mul Srot* (Original Sources of Mythological Hindi Dramas ; research). Most of her short stories depict the loosening ties between men and women, e.g., 'Bich ki Kariyan' (The Intermediary Links), 'Ek Dhuli Hui Sham' but these stories also hold up certain values of life.

SHASHI SEHGAL. Critic, whose chief work is *Ghananand ka Rachna Sansar* (The Creative World of Ghananand ; 1980).

SHASHI SHARMA. Poetess, whose *Jangal se Guzarte Huye* (Passing Through the Forest ; 1982) is her first collection of poems.

SHASHI SHEKHAR TOSHKHANI (1935-). Kashmiri-speaking Hindi writer and poet, who got his doctorate on the Kashmiri epic : *Banasur Katha.* His poems have been collected in *Thoda-sa Akash* (A Little Sky) and he has tr. into Hindi some works : (*Lalla Vakyon,* Nund Rishi's *Shruks,* etc.) from Kashmiri. He is also associated with the activities for popularising Hindi in Kashmir.

SHASTRI, S.R. Telugu-speaking modern Hindi writer, who is known for his *The Hindi Grammar* (written in collaboration with Bhalchandra Apte).

SHATRUGHNA PRASAD SHARMA. Modern Magahi writer, who is noted for his social one-act plays.

SHAURI RAJAN, R. Tamil-speaking modern Hindi writer, whose short stories have been published in various magazines ; his chief short stories are : 'Rehearsal', 'Ritibaddha' (The Stereotyped), etc. He has written a number of literary essays on Bhakti Movement in the South, on Ramanujacharya, on Dravids, Dravid Languages, etc. He also wrote two works : *Tamil k i Lok-Kathayen* (The Folk-tales of Tamil) and *Tamil Sanskriti* (Tamil Culture). He has tr. into Hindi Sujata's Tamil novel under the title : *Chaudah Din* (The Fourteen Days) as also Jaykantan's Tamil short stories under the title *Jaykantan ki Kahaniyan* (The Short Stories of Jaykantan). He has tr. T.P. Meenakshisundaram's essay under the title : 'Tamil Sahitya men Jain Dharma' as also S. Shankaran's travelogue to German Democratic Republic.

SHAVARPA. See *Shabarpa.*

SHEIKH. See *Alam-Sheikh*.

SHEIKH NABI (b. 1620). Sufi poet of Jaunpur district, who was the author of *Gyandwip* (q v.), an allegorical romance.

SHEKHAR, R. Telugu-speaking modern Hindi writer, who has tr. from Telugu into Hindi Vishwanath Satyanarayan's famous critical essay as *Shakuntalam ki Abhigyanta.*

SHEKHAR EK JIVNI (Shekhar : A Biography). Novel by Agyey (q.v.), which is considered as autobiographical. The work is an important psycho-analytical study and is remarkable both for the technique of its construction and for its portrayal of subtle, half-conscious motives and urges.

Shekhar, the hero, is a highly accomplished person, an introvert, a bit of philosopher, highly sensitive and self-conscious, yet very serious minded. Towards the evening of his life, he looks back and tries to recollect and assess the happenings of the past five years. In this assessment he scrupulously draws pictures of life as actually lived or it might have been lived. A keen and objective observer Shekhar, in search of truth, delves deep into the sub-consciousness. He is unsparing in analysing things and happenings. Once sure in his mind as to what is right, nothing prevents him from saying so and openly discarding the wrong. The story is fascinating and well-told.

SHEKHAR JOSHI (1934-). Short story writer, whose chief collections of stories are : *Kosi ka Ghatvar* (A Boatman of Kosi ; 1957), *Dajyu*, *Halwaha* (The Ploughman ; 1981) and *Sath ke Log*.

SHEKHAWAT, K.S. Rajasthani scholar, who is Head of the Rajasthani Department in the University of Jodhpur. His *Rajasthani Nibandh* (1981) contains 12 essays on literary and other topics. He also edited *Kunpal* (1982), which is a collection of assorted writings done by school teachers.

SHEKHAWATI. See *A.C. Jangid 'Shekhawati'*.

SHENI-VIJANAND. Rajasthani romance of Sheni-Vijanand in about 80 scattered verses, which are available in different manuscripts and seem to have been written in the 18th century and thereafter. The original verses might have been composed in the 16th century.

When Vijanand, a poor Charan, plays on *Vina*, Sheni, daughter of a wealthy Charan, Veda, listens to him. As both develop love, Vijanand asks for Sheni's hand in marriage. Veda agrees but on this condition that Vija should bring to him within one year 101 buffaloes bearing moon-like white spots all over their black bodies. Vija is unable to fulfil the condition within the stipulated period, while Sheni has taken a vow to marry Vija or remain a virgin. When Vija does not appear at the end of one year, Sheni feels disappointed and she goes to the Himalayas to freeze herself to death there. Vija returns and on learning of Sheni's departure, pursues her. When Vija reaches the Himalayas, he finds her frozen in the snows and on the point of death. He tries to persuade her to return but as nearly the whole of her body has frozen, it is impossible for her to go back with him. Before her death, she asks Vija to play on *Vina* till she breathes her last. Vija does so and sees her die. Vija goes mad and meets death soon after. The poem gives a heart-rending pictures of the pangs of separation in the young heart of Sheni.

SHER ALI, SYED (fl. early 20th cent.). Writer, whose chief work is *Katha Hakikat Ray*.

SHER JANG GARG. Modern poet, some of whose poems are collected in *Tar Saptak* (q.v.) ; *Vyangya ke Mulbhut Prashna* and *Swatantryottar Hindi Kavita men Vyangya* are critical works.

SHER SINGH (fl. early 20th cent.). Writer, who was noted for his detective novels.

SHER SINGH, GYANI. Hindi writer of Punjab, whose *Sri Bir Mrigres Guru Bilas Devtaru* (1911) is a biography of Bir Singh (Guru Dev) in prose. The work, a voluminous one, has been completed in 1914 pages.

SHERRIF, A.G. Scholar, whose collection, *Hindi Folk-songs* was published in 1936 ; its songs are mainly taken from the folk-song collections of Ram Naresh Tripathi, but there are renderings in English of 15 songs by Sheriff. He also tr. some portions of *Padmavat*, Maithilisharan Gupta's 'Prithwiputra' and Siyaram Sharan Gupta's 'Amr itputra' (both long poems) into English.

SHESHMANI PANDEY. Modern poet, whose chief poetical work is *Samapti Par* (Nearing Completion).

SHIBAN KRISHNA RAINA (1942-). Hindi writer of Jammu-Kashmir, who also edited the magazine 'Prakash' from Srinagar. He got his doctorate on his thesis : Comparative Study of Kashmiri and Hindi Proverbs. His other published works are : *Kashmiri Bhasha tatha Sahitya* (Kashmiri Language and Literature), *Pratinidhi Sankalan* : *Kashmiri* (Representative Anthology : Kashmiri) and tr. and transliteration in Hindi of *Kashmiri Ramayan*, *Ramavatar-Charit* and *Lalavakh*.

SHIL. Dramatist and poet, whose chief works are : *Tin Din* : *Tin Ghar* (1961 ; on the stories of three persons for three days), *Kisan* (dramas), *Angrai* (Yawning), *Ek Pag* (One Step), *Uday Path* (The Rising Path) and *Karmavachi Shabda Hai Yah* (poetical collections). His works are collected in *Shil Granthavali*.

SHIL NATH SHABDAMRIT. A collection of Malwi *Padas*, which are popular among the people (1901).

SHIL SAKHI (fl. 18th cent.). Poet of the Krishna-cult (Haridasi Sect), who was noted for his *Acharyon ke Mangal*. He was a disciple of Lalit Kishori (q.v.).

SHILA DEVASYA. Malayalam-speaking modern Hindi scholar, whose research work is : *Premchand aur Takashi* (Premchand and Takashi).

SHILA ROHEKAR. Marathi-speaking modern Hindi writer, whose short stories have appeared in various magazines. She has also published a novel : *Dinant*.

SHILIMUKH. See *Ram Krishna Shukla* '*Shilimukh*'.

SHISHTU KRISHNAMURTI SHASTRI (fl. 1880). Telugu-speaking writer, who tr. into Telugu verse Tulsidas's *Ramcharitmanas* from Hindi. In this stupendous work, he was assisted by Manda Kamayya or Narhari Shastri.

SHISHUNAL SHARIF (1819-89). Kannada poet, who composed hundreds of *Padas* in Kannada and Hindi. He was born in a Muslim family in Dharwar and was appointed a teacher, but he was always occupied with religious ideas. His mystical *Padas*, influenced by folk-songs are sung by people even to this day.

SHITAL PRASAD. Author of *Shabda Prakashika* (Lucknow, 1870), which was prepared at the instance of the Director of Public Instruction. The author was Headmaster of Government School, Unnao.

SHITAL PRASAD TIWARI. Dramatist, whose *Janaki Mangal* was the first play staged in Benares in the year 1862.

SHIV (fl. *c.* 1743). Poet of the Riti school, who composed two works : *Rasik Vilas* (on *Rasa*) and *Alankar Bhushan* (on *Alankar*), but these have not yet been discovered.

SHIV BAKHSH PALHAWAT BARHAT (1844-99). Court-poet of Maharaja Mangal Singh of Alwar, whose *Alwar ki Shatritu Jhamal* in 128 verses in Rajasthani depicts the grandeur of his patron, the beauty of women, hunting and festivals through a description of seasons. His *Vrindavan Shatak* is in Braj, with occasional verses in Pingal. *Alwar Rajya ka Itihas*, in a mixture of Braj, Khari Boli and Urdu, is a history in verse of the Alwar State.

SHIV CHANDRA (fl. 1822). Jain poet, who was the author of *Pradyumna-Prakash* on the story of Krishna's son, Pradyumna.

SHIV CHANDRA BHARATIYA (1853-1915). Writer, who was born in an Agrawal Vaishya family. His ancestors hailed from Jodhpur. A scholar of Sanskrit, Hindi, Marathi and philosophy, he was the author of works in Marathi, Hindi and Rajasthani. A pioneer novelist in Rajasthani, his *Kanak Sundar* (1903) is the first novel for which he used the popular Gujarati term 'Naval Katha'. Dealing with the tale of two families, one orthodox and the other a reformist, the writer upholds the ways of the reformist family. A pioneer in short story also, his short story 'Vishrant Pravasi' was first published in 1904 in a Calcutta Hindi monthly 'Vaishyopakarak'. His *Kesar-Vilas* (1900) may be said to be the first drama in Rajasthani. This and *Phatka Janjal* as also *Budhapa ki Sagai* are about social evils and are motivated by reformist objectives. So far essay is concerned, the earliest form nearer to essay, may be seen in the introductions to his works : *Kanak Sundar*, *Phatka Janjal*, etc.

His other chief works in Rajasthani are : *Motiyon ki Kanthi*, *Vaishya-Prabodh*, *Sangit Mankunwar Natak* and *Bodh Darpan*.

SHIVDAN SINGH CHAUHAN. Marxist critic, whose chief works are : *Pragativad* (Progressivism ; 1946), *Sahitya ki Parakh* (The Test of Literature), *Hindi ka Gadya Sahitya* (Hindi Prose Literature), *Alochana ke Man* (The Criterion of Criticism ; 1958), *Sahitya ki Samasyayen* (The Problems of Literature ; 1959), *Sahityanushilan*. *Alochana : Itihas tatha Siddhant* (Criticism : History and Principles) and *Hindi Sahitya ke Assi Varsh* (Eighty Years of Hindi Literature) ; *Kashmir* :

Desh va Sanskriti is a travelogue. Deeply saturated with the revolutionary ideology of Karl Marx and Friedrich Engels, he endeavours to explain the works of literature with reference to the social context, but at the same time he emphasises that to evaluate the greatness of a work, it is necessary to keep in view its aesthetic experience, its style and its syntactical structure.

SHIVDAS (1443-1513). Rajasthani poet, who was one of the saints of the Vishnoi tradition (see *Jambhoji*). He composed stray verses on miscellaneous topics.

SHIVDAS. See *Achaldas Khichi ri Vachnika.*

SHIVDAS (fl. 1737). Poet of the Riti school, who was perhaps a resident of Agra. His *Rasa Saras* is a work on *Rasa*.

SHIV DATT (fl. early 19th cent. ?). Maithili writer, whose *Parijat-Haran* and *Gauri-Parinay* are Kirtaniya dramas. His *Sita-Haran*, a poem in impure Maithili, describes the marriage of Sita. He is also credited with the authorship of another poem, *Git-Gauri-Swayamvar*, but it is more or less an abridgement of his drama, *Gauri-Parinay* Natak.

SHIV DATT SATI (fl. early 19th cent.). Kumaoni poet, whose chief works are : *Jhabar ke Git* (9 songs), *Ghasyari Natak*, *Prem Sagar* (marriage of Rukmini) and *Gopi-Git* (describing the tragic plight of a young girl, who dies 11 months after widowhood).

SHIV DIN KESRI (1698-1774). Marathi-speaking saint-poet, who belonged to the Nath Sect. In addition to Marathi *Padas*, he composed *Padas* in Hindi, which are dominated by foreign words.

SHIV KARAN (fl. early 19th cent.). Rajasthani saint-poet of Ram Snehi Sampraday, Ren, whose *Vani* consists of stray verses in popular metres.

SHIV MANGAL SINGH 'SUMAN' (1916-). Poet, whose chief works are : *Hillol* (1939), *Jivan ke Gan* (Songs of Life ; 1941), *Pralay-Srijan* (against reactionary forces), *Vindhya-Himalaya*, *Vishwas Badhta hi Gaya*, *Par Ankhen Nahin Bhari*, *Vani ki Vyatha* and *Mitti ki Barat* (Marriage-party of Soil ; the last work has won Sahitya Akademi and Soviet Land Nehru Awards) ; his *Chhayavadottar Kavyadhara* (Post-

Chhayavad Poetry) is a critical work. He is a progressive writer and this element prevails in his poetical works. He has also made a significant contribution to the development of Hindi lyrics.

SHIV MURTI SWAMI. Kannada-speaking modern Hindi writer, whose chief works are: *Rajatotsav Granth* (edited with Siddhanath Pant; treating of Kannada language, literature, dharma, darshan, arts, etc.), Hindi tr. of Jayadevi Tai Ligade's Kannada poems: *Jaygite* and Kuvempu's sketches: *Malenadin Chitragalu* (in collaboration with Kanghikeri).

SHIV NANDAN MISHRA. Writer, who was noted for his drama, *Usha* (1918).

SHIV NANDAN PRASAD (1918-). Writer, whose chief works are: *Matrik Chhandon ka Vikas* (thesis; on prosody), *Hindi Sahitya: Ek Parivritta* and *Pagdandi* (essays).

SHIV NANDAN THAKUR. Modern Maithili scholar, who has made genuine efforts in restoring the original text of Vidyapati's *Padas*.

SHIV NARAYAN (1716-91). Saint-poet of Ghazipur in Uttar Pradesh, who propounded the Shiv Narayani Sect. His *Guru Anyas* (1734) is a collection of his *Padas*.

SHIV NARAYAN DWIVEDI (fl early 20th cent.). Writer, who was noted for his detective novels.

SHIV NARAYAN SINGH 'VISHTH'. Modern Garhwali scholar, who compiled the *Gadhu Sumariyal Panvada*.

SHIV NARAYAN TOSHNIWAL. Rajasthani writer, who was noted for his early short stories: 'Vidya Paramdaivatam' and 'Stri Sikshan ko Onaman' (1916), dealing with social problems.

SHIV NATH (fl. 18th cent. ?). Poet of the Riti school, who was a native of the village Karsi in Barabanki district; only his stray verses have been traced.

SHIV NATH (1917-). Critic, whose chief works are: *Bharatendu-Yugin Nibandh* (on essays), *Hindi Karakon ka Vikas* and *Hindi Bhasha ka Arthatatvik Vikas* (on Hindi language).

SHIV NIRMOHI (1937-). Dogri-speaking Hindi writer, whose

research articles have appeared in several magazines.

SHIV PANDE. Modern Rajasthani poet, who has composed patriotic and heroic poems.

SHIV PRASAD. Poet of the Riti school, who composed his *Rasa Bhushan* in 1812 on the pattern of Yaqub Khan's *Rasa Bhushan*.

SHIV PRASAD. Modern Hindi poet of Fiji, whose chief works are : *Girmit*, *Yagona*, *Siriya*, *Fiji ki Jay* and *Fiji ke Kisan*.

SHIV PRASAD GOYAL (1928-). Scholar, whose chief works are : *Vangmay Vivek* (on criticism ; 1964), *Kavyang Vivek* (1970), *Hindi ke Khand-kavya* (1984) and *Haryana ka Hindi Sahitya : Udbhav aur Vikas* (1984). He is at present Reader, Department of Hindi, Kurukshetra University.

SHIV PRASAD JYOTISHI (fl. 1900). Poet of Mathura, who was the author of *Shakti Charitamrit* (on the goddess Durga, the apostle of Shakti).

SHIV PRASAD MISHRA 'RUDRA' (1911-70). Novelist, whose chief work is : *Bahti Ganga* (The Flowing Ganges ; 1952 ; a colourful description of life in Benares during the last 200 years). He also composed Bhojpuri poems. He edited *Bharatendu Granthavali* as well.

SHIV PRASAD SINGH (1929-). Writer, whose chief works are : *Alag-alag Vaitarni* (Each One's Road to Salvation ; 1968 ; a regional novel), *Gali Age Murti Hai* (The Street Takes a Turn Further ; both novels), *Karmanasha ki Har* (1958), *Inhe Bhi Intazar Hai* (1961), *Murda Sarai* (The Dead Inn ; 1966), *Andhera Hansta Hai*, *Meri Priya Kahaniyan*, *Bheriye* (all short story collections), *Ghatiyan Gunjti Hain* (The Valleys Echo ; drama on the Chinese attack on India), *Shikharon ke Setu*, *Kasturi Mrig* and *Chaturdik* (essay collections). His important short stories are : 'Nanho', 'Murda Sarai', etc.

SHIV PRASAD 'SITARE HIND', RAJA (1823-95). Resident of Varanasi, who rendered devoted service to the British during the Sikh War and, in recognition of which he was appointed Inspector in the Education Department in 1856. He was also awarded the titles of 'Raja' and 'Sitare Hind'. A great scholar of Persian, Urdu and Hindi, he thought that the use of Devnagari script was of fundamental importance in the interest of literary development in the country in general and proper education of the Hindus in particular. In the matter of language, his views had undergone a change. His earlier books such as *Raja Bhoj ka Sapna* (The *Dream* of *Raja Bhoj*), *Vir Singh Vrittant* (The Description of Vir Singh) and *Alsiyon ko Korha* provide specimens of prose free from any excessive Urdu or Persian influence, but his later works, the most typical of which was *Itihas Timiranashak*, furnish proofs of his preference for Urdu and Persian words and phrases. He also wrote *Hindi Grammar* (1875), which was a common grammar for both Hindi and Urdu. His mature view seems to be that Hindi should make use of current words and idioms and should borrow unhesitatingly at the same time from Urdu and Persian which had been the court languages (here he was opposed by Raja Lakshman Singh). To propagate his views, he started a journal from Benares, called 'Benares Akhbar'.

It was due to the Raja's influence and his official position that he succeeded in getting Hindi introduced in schools on the same basis as Urdu, but finding no school text books available in Hindi, he, with the help and co-operation of his friends (Banshidhar, Shrilal and others), was able to write as many as 35 school text-books covering a wide range of subjects. The Raja's other important works are : *Manav Dharma Sar* and *Bhugol Hastamalak*.

SHIV PUJAN SAHAY (1893-1963). Essayist, whose chief work, *Dehati Duniya* (1926) was noted for its style. He edited 'Himalaya' and founded and worked for Bihar Hindi Rashtrabhasha Parishad.

SHIVRAJ BHUSHAN. Poem by Bhushan (q.v.), which is considered his greatest work.

It contains 382 verses and after the fashion of the age, is a work on *Alankars*, but each figure of rhetoric is illustrated by a verse in honour of Shivaji. The illustrations, which are taken not only from *Shringar*, but from other *Rasas* too, are original compositions in which the virtues and achievements of Shivaji are set forth. Some of the *Chhands* are devoted to Rajgarh, the capital of Shivaji's kingdom and present a beautiful picture of its surroundings and forts. The principal theme, is, of course, Shivaji's valour and his successive victories over the Mughal forces. In his inimitable style, the poet describes the terror which Shivaji's fame and chivalry struck in the hearts of the Mughal court and its armies. Opinion varies as to the merits of this work, but it seems certain that the treatment of the *Alankars* is not as satisfactory as in *Lalit Lalam* (q.v.), composed by Matiram, his younger brother.

SHIVRAJ CHHANGANI. Modern Rajasthani poet, who has composed poems in the style of Nayi Kavita. His *Uniyara* and *Olakhan* are character-sketches.

SHIVRAM AIYYAR. Malayalam-speaking modern Hindi writer, who tr. from Malayalam Ullur Parameshwar Aiyyar's *Prem-Sangitam* and *Bhakti-Pradipika* into Hindi.

SHIVRAM SHARMA, K.M. (fl. 1940). Tamil-speaking modern Hindi writer, who has tr. into Hindi from Tamil V.R. Rajan Ayyar's *Kamalambal Charittiram* under the title *Kamalamba ki Katha* (The Story of Kamalamba) as also 11 Tamil short stories in the series of 'Galpa-Sansar Mala'. He also tr. into Hindi some Tamil one-act plays and Tamil sketches as also the essays of Subrahmanya Bharati in the special issues of 'Hans'.

SHIVRAM SHARMA, S.V. Telugu-speaking Hindi scholar, who is noted for his *Hindi Telugu Vyakaranon ka Tulnatmak Adhyayan* (A Comparative Study of Hindi and Telugu Grammars ; 1967).

SHIV RANI PREMCHAND (1889-1976). Wife of the novelist, Premchand (q.v.), who is noted for her work, *Premchand Ghar Men* (Premchand's Private Life) ; the work offers an intimate insight into the man. She has also written short stories.

SHIV RATAN SHASTRI, R. Modern Hindi writer of Surinam, whose chief works are : *Bhakti Prakash, Gyan Prakash, Sandhya Havan*, etc.

SHIV SAGAR MISHRA. Writer, whose chief works are : *Rajtilak* (1961 ; on the coronation of Bimbisar), *Magadh ki Jay, Durdin ki Dhup, Akshat* (1976) and *Kaghaz ka Langar* ; *Vahi Ag Vahi Gangajal, Akhir kab Tak, Kahe Ganv ki Gatha* and *Doctor ka Pratishodh* are his short story collections. His important short stories are : 'Divar par ki Aurat' (The Woman on the Wall), 'Mare Hue Log' (The Dead), etc.

SHIV SAHAY CHATURVEDI. Modern Bundelkhandi scholar, whose chief works are : *Bundelkhand ki Gramya Kahaniyan* (Rural Tales of Bundelkhand), *Gaune ki Bida* (Farewell to the Bride), *Pashan-Nagari* (The Stony-City), *Bundelkhandi Lok-Git* (folk-songs) and *Hamari Lok-Kathayen* (Our Folk-tales).

SHIV SAHAY DAS. Poet of the Riti school, who was a resident of Jaipur. He composed two works : *Shiv Chaupai* (1752) and *Lokoktirasa-Kaumudi* ; the latter work treats of *Nayika-bhed,* basing itself on maxims and proverbs.

SHIV SAHAY PATHAK. Modern scholar, whose chief work is *Hindi Sufi Kavya ka Samagra Anushilan.*

SHIV SATYANARAYAN, K. Telugu-speaking Hindi scholar, who is noted for his *Hindi aur Telugu ke Pratinidhi Kavyon ka Tulnatmak Adhyayan* (A Comparative Study of Representative Hindi and Telugu Poems ; 1974).

SHIV SHAMBHU KE CHITTHE. See *Balmukund Gupta.*

SHIV SHANKAR SHARMA (1921-). Writer, whose chief work is *Bhaktikalin Hindi Sahitya men Yoga-Bhavna* (1971 ; research work).

SHIV SINGH CHOYAL. Modern Rajasthani scholar, who has made a significant contribution to the study of folk-songs.

SHIV SINGH SAROJ. An exhaustive history of Hindi literature (1878), written by Shiv Singh Sengar (q.v.). It contains an account of about 1,000 poets and occupies an important place in histories of Hindi Literature ; the work is based on old accounts and anthologies.

SHIV SINGH SENGAR (1833-78). Writer of Kantha, who wrote his celebrated work, *Shiv Singh Saroj* (q.v.), the first history of Hindi literature (1878) ; he also tr. into Hindi prose two Sanskrit works : *Brahmottara-Khanda* and *Shiva-Purana.*

SHIV SWARUP SHARMA 'ACHAL'. Rajasthani writer, whose chief work is *Rajasthani Gadya Sahitya* (1961).

SHIVA (fl. between 1450 and 1550). Dingal poet, who composed stray verses and *Gits* in celebrating the victory of Rao Jaitsi of Bikaner over Kamran, a son of Babar.

SHIVA BAVNI. Poem by Bhushan (q.v.), a poet of the Riti school, which consists of 52 verses and describes the deeds of bravery of Shivaji. A work of national pride, Bhushan comes out in these stanzas as a great poet of Hindudom. No doubt he uses aggressive language, but he balances it with a constructive thought and a good deal of historical truth. Some critics regard this work of a higher literary standard than even that of *Shivraj Bhushan.*

SHIVAJI (1630-80). Celebrated Maratha ruler, who was a patron of arts and letters. No work composed by him in Sanskrit or Marathi has been traced so far, but one Hindi *Pada* composed by him has been traced.

SHIVANANDA (fl. 1821). Poet of the Ram-cult, who was the author of *Shriramdhyan-Manjari*, a devotional work.

SHIVANAND BHAT. Malayalam-speaking modern Hindi writer, who is noted for preparation of help-material for students appearing in higher Hindi examinations.

SHIVANAND NAUTIYAL. Modern Garhwali poet, who is known for his stray poems.

SHIVANI, GAURA PANT (1923-). Novelist, whose chief works are : *Chaudah Phere* (on the liberation of women), *Krishnakali* (description of a woman struggling against society), *Bhairavi* (miseries suffered by a woman on account of her beauty), *Mayapuri* and *Vivartta* ; *Aparadhini* (1971) contains five stories, while, *Swayamsiddha* and *Kishunali* are her chief short story collections. Shivani's essay collection is *Vatayan*, while *Gainda* contains a novelette and two short stories. *Meri Priya Kahaniyan* are her favourite short stories.

SHOBH NATH (SHOBH). Poet of the Riti school, who was patronized by Madhav Singh, the ruler of Jaipur. Up to 1768, he was at Jaipur, where he composed two works : *Madhav Jayati* and *Chhand Shiromani* ; the first work describes the battle between Madhav Singh of Jaipur and Jawahar Singh of Bharatpur at Mandwa in 1767. The *Chhand Shiromani* was composed in 1768 for Raja Prithwi Singh, son of Raja Madhav Singh. Another work, *Naval Rasa Chandroduya*, was composed by Shobh in 1761 at the instance of Naval Singh of Bharatpur. Some scholars are of the view that Shobhnath and Shobh were different poets.

SHOBHA. Modern Hindi poetess of Trinidad, who is known for her stray poems.

SHOBHA CHAND JAMMAD. Rajasthani writer, whose *Vriddha Vivah Vidushan* (1930), a one-act play, advocates social reform.

SHOBHAN LAL (b. 1854). Poet of the Krishna-cult (Chaitanya Sect), whose *Radha Pada Ashtak* is a small work.

SHOBHNA DASHRATH. Modern Hindi writer of Mauritius, who is known for her short stories.

SHRADDHA RAM PHULLAURI (1837-81). Staunch supporter of Hindi in Panjab, who advocated a style free from Urdu and Persian influences. A prolific writer, a preacher and a *Katha-Vachak*, his chief works covering theological and metaphysical topics are : *Satyamrit-Pravah* (1864), *Atma Chikitsa Tatwa Dipak*, *Dharma Raksha*, *Shatopadesh* (a collection of *Dohas*), *Upadesh-Sangrah*, *Bhagyavati* (The Fortunate Woman ; 1877 ; social novel) and a 1400-page autobiography (not extant). Moving from place to place, he spoke on the greatness of the Hindu religion and always ended with an appeal in favour of Hindi. His learning and the high standard set by him in prose writings were of great help to Hindi. Some scholars regard his *Bhagyavati* as the first original novel in Hindi. He wrote a number of books in Urdu and Panjabi also.

SHRAVAN KUMAR (1931-). Fiction writer, whose chief works are : *Zahar* (Poison), *Andhere ki Ankhen* (The Eyes of Darkness), *Data ka Shukra Hai* (God Be Thanked ; 1980), *Kampti Avaz* (short story collections), *Yatra* and *Pret* (The Evil Spirit ; novels). His drama is *Sonar Bangla*. In English, he has published *Hindi Short Story* in a pocket book edition.

SHRI BHATT (fl. 1350-1450). Poet of the Krishna-cult (Nimbark Sect), who was the author of *Yugal-Shatak* or *Adi Vani*, which is considered as the first work of this Sect.

SHRI BHATT (fl. 1565). Poet of the Krishn a-cult, who was the author of the *Yugal-Shatak* (a centum of verses on Radha-Krishna).

SHRI BHAVANI SHANKAR RO GUN SHIV PURAN. Rajasthani poem by Aidan Gadan (fl. latter half of 17th cent.), which is based on the *Shiv Puran* and narrates all the popular legends concerning Shiv. The description of Shiv's marriage with Parvati is by far the most charming.

SHRI CHAND RAY. Rajasthani writer, who was noted for his early short stories in the mid-forties.

SHRI CHANDRA AGNIHOTRI. Novelist, whose chief work is *Nayi Bisat* (1980), a novel.

SHRI CHANDRA JAIN. Modern Bagheli scholar, whose chief works are : *Vindhyapradesh ke Lok-Git*, *Vindhyabhumi ki*

Lok-Kathayen, *Vindhyapradesh ke Adivasiyon ke Lok-Git* and *Bundelkhand ke Lok-Kavi*, respectively on folk-songs, folk-tales, folk-songs of aborgines and the folk-poets.

SHRIDHAR (fl. between 15th and 16th centuries). Maithili writer, whose *Vidya-Vinod-Natak-Tantra* is preserved in Nepal National Library, Kathmandu.

SHRIDHAR (Murlidhar ; b.*c.* 1680). Poet of the Riti school, who was a Brahmin of Prayag. His *Jangnama*, describing the battle between Farrukh Saiyar and Jahandar, has been published. His other works are : *Nayikabhed* and *Chitrakavya*.

SHRIDHAR Menon, M. Malayalam-speaking modern Hindi poet, who has several poems to his credit. He also tr. Vallattol's Malayalam poems into Hindi, which have been published by the Rashtrabhasha Prachar Samiti, Wardha, under the Series 'Kavishri'.

SHARIDHAR PATHAK (1858-1928). Poet, who was born at Jondhri in the Agra district of Uttar Pradesh. Beginning with the tr. of Goldsmith's *Traveller* and *Deserted Village* under the titles : *Shrant Pathik* and *Ujar Gaon* respectively, he wrote original poems in both Khari Boli and Brajbhasha, though more in the former. His *Ekantvasi* (The Recluse ; a verse tr. of Goldsmith's *Hermit* ; 1887) was written in Khari Boli and with every successive poem, he improved his style as would be evident from *Kashmir Sushama* (Charming Beauty of Kashmir), which is his best poem. Departing from the traditional treatment of Nature, Shridhar Pathak described the beauties of Nature for enjoyment in solitude. The poet also used new types of verse and manipulated his lines so as to create new schemes. His songs, permeated with national fervour, are collected in *Bharat Git*. His other works are : *Jagat Sachai Sar* (original) and *Ritu-Sanhar* (tr.). Shridhar Pathak used Khari Boli for sustained poeticwriting and was a precursor of the romantic trend which flowered in the early part of the 20th century.

SHRIDHAR PRASAD MISHRA. Modern Magahi poet, whose chief folk-poems are *Girija-Girish Charit*, *Uma-Shankar-Vivah-Kirtan* (both on the marriage of Shiv and Parvati), *Lanka-Dahan* (the burning of Lanka), *Gandhi-Virah-Lahari* (on Gandhi) and *Ram-Van-Gaman* (Ram's exile to the forest).

SHRIDHAR SINGH (1931-). Writer, whose chief works relating to Tulsidas and his literature are : *Ramcharitmanas ka Katha-Shilp* (1959 ; criticism), *Tulsidas ki Karayitri Pratibha ka Adhyayan* (1967 ; research), *Tulsi-Sahitya ki Paribhashik Shabdavali* (1973) and *Hindi Kahani ke Pratiman.*

SHRIDHAR VYAS (fl. early 15th cent.). Noted Rajasthani poet, who contributed to the heroic and religious poetry. A contemporary of Raja Ranmall Rathore of Idar, his poems are : *Ranmall Chhand, Saptsati ra Chhand* (qq.v.) and *Kavitta Bhagavat* or *Bhagavat Dasham Skandh* (in 127 verses ; incomplete; based on the 10th canto of the *Bhagavata Purana*).

SHRI GOPAL JAIN. Rajasthani poet, whose *Kalchetana* (1982) is a philosophic poem, advocating the inevitable birth of the perfect human being.

SHRI Gopal VEDANTASHASTRI. Bengali-speaking modern Hindi writer, who prepared Hindi-Bengali dictionary.

SHRI HATHIJI (fl. 1780). Poet, who was a follower of Radhavallabh Sect founded by Hit Harivansh. His *Radhasudha-Shatak* (1780) in praise of Radha contains 11 *Dohas* and 103 *Kavittas.* In this work, the poet has laid great emphasis on the artistic aspect ; it was also in good favour with Bharatendu Harishchandra.

SHRIKANT GANAK. Maithili poet, whose *Shri Krishna-Janma-Rahasya*, written some time after Maharaja Narendra Singh (1744-60), is a Kirtaniya form of drama and treats of the birth-mystery of Krishna.

SHRIKANT JOSHI. Modern poet, whose chief poetical collections are : *Prashna Kaun Todega* ? (Who Shall Break Question ?), *Kisi bhi Tarikh Ko* and *Bhatka Megh.* He edited a work of essays on Makhanlal Chaturvedi.

SHRIKANT SHASTRI. Modern Magahi writer, who edited 'Magahi' monthly journal for a long time. He has collected Magahi Proverbs and has also written a drama, *Naya Ganv.* His one-act plays on radio are also quite popular. He at first tr. works into Magahi from English and Bengali and later on composed Magahi poems and songs, which are noted for their experimental content.

SHRIKANT VERMA (1931-). Poet and writer, whose chief works are : *Bhatka Megh* (A Wandering Cloud ; 1959), *Maya Darpan* (The Mirror of Illusion ; 1967), *Dinarambh* (Beginning of Day), *Jalsaghar* (all poetical collections), *Dusri Bar* (A Second Time ; 1968 ; novel), *Jhari* (Bush), *Sanvad*

(Dialogue), *Bhir*, *Prasang* and *Dusre ke Pair* (short story collections). In his poems, he has made a severe attack on social incongruities and there is a broader sweep of social realism. He was editor of 'Dinman'. His latest work is *Bisvini Shatabdi ke Andhere Men.* He is a nominated Member of the Parliament.

SHRI KRISHNA BHATT TAILANG (b. 1668). Poet of the Riti school, who was son of Lakshman Bhatt Tailang. He was patronized by Raoraja Budh Singh of Bundi, but Maharaja Sawai Jaysingh brought him from there to his own court at Jaipur, where the title of 'Kavi Kala Nidhi' was conferred upon him. He composed some 13 works : *Alankar Kalanidhi*, *Nakhshikh Varnan*, *Shringar Rasa Madhuri*, *Jaysingh Gun Sarita*, *Ramchandrodaya*, etc. He is different from Krishna Bhatt Devrishi.

SHRI KRISHNA CHAITANYA GOSWAMI (fl. 1850). Poet of the Riti school, who was highly respected by Bharatendu Harishchandra, Raja Shivprasad, etc. He was initiated into Radharamani Sampraday. He composed *Uktijukti Rasa Kaumudi*, an exhaustive Riti work.

SHRI KRISHNA CHANDRA BAITLI. Sindhi-speaking modern Hindi writer, who is noted for his *Sindhi Bhasha ka Parichay* (Introduction to Sindhi Language).

SHRI KRISHNA DAS (fl. 18th cent.). Poet of the Krishna-cult (Haridasi Sect), who was noted for his *Padas* in praise of his Guru Govardhan Dev.

SHRI-KRISHNA GITAVALI (Songs for Krishna). Short poem by Tulsidas (q.v.) in Braj, written in 1571 (?).

It consists of 61 *Padas*, describing certain episodes from Krishna's life. When this work was composed, Tulsidas must have been under the influence of the Krishna-cult. Some of its *Padas* are met with in the *Sursagar* (q.v.).

SHRI-KRISHNA-KELIMALA. Maithili Kirtaniya drama, which was composed by Nandipati (q.v.).

The drama begins with a long prose benediction in praise of Krishna, the celebration of whose sports forms the subject-matter of this play. It has very few Sanskrit and Prakrit passages ; the songs in Maithili form the major portion of the play. The superhuman character of Krishna is stressed now and then. The work is considered as the most effective vernacular play of Mithila.

SHRI KRISHNA LAL, THE LATE. Writer, who was noted for his *Adhunik Hindi Sahitya ka Vikas, 1900-1925* (The Development of Modern Hindi Literature, 1900-1925).

SHRI KRISHNA MISHRA (1918-). Maithili critic and poet, who has discussed in prose the contribution of Harimohan Jha (q.v.) to the comic muse. He has published two volumes of poems : *Meruprabha* and *Agradut* ; he wrote mostly in free verse.

SHRI KRISHNAMURTI. Tamil-speaking modern Hindi scholar, who with Vishnupriya, has compiled *Lifco Hindi-Tamil Kosh*, etc.

SHRI-KRISHNA-PRYANANAM-NATAK. Maithili drama by an unknown Assamese writer, which belongs to the time of King Pramatt Singh (r. 1745-51). It contains speeches in Sanskrit, but the songs are in Assamese and Brajbuli.

SHRI KRISHNA THAKUR. Maithili writer, whose chief work, *Chandrabhaga* (1885) is a short story collection.

SHRILAL (fl. 1st part of 19th cent.). Poet of the Krishna-cult (Chaitanya Sect), who was preceptor of Shah Biharilal, a famous rich man of Lucknow. He is said to be the author of an *Ashtayam.*

SHRILAL. Author of a Hindi gramatical work, *Bhasha Chandroday* (1856) ; the author was a native of Bihar. The work was written at the instance of the Director of Public Instruction.

SHRILAL MISHRA. Modern Rajasthani writer, who is noted for his literary articles and reviews.

SHRILAL NATHMAL JOSHI. Rajasthani writer, whose chief works are : *Abhai Patki* (1956 ; a novel on the problem of Hindu widowhood), *Dhoran ro Dhori* (1968 ; a novel on the famous scholar, Tessitori, who was a man of inexhaustible energy), *Ek Binani do Bin* (1973 ; rendering in prose of Tennyson's poem *Enoch Arden*), *Paranyodi Kanvari* (1974 ; short stories) , plays on social evils, *Sach Bolyan Kiyan Par Padai* (essays), *Sabadka* (1960 ; a collection of sketches) and *Apana Bapuji* (1969 ; an autobiography of Mahatma Gandhi). A reformist and idealist, his works bear the impact of his views.

SHRILAL SHUKLA (1925-). Novelist, whose chief works are : *Rag Darbari* (The Darbari's Tune ; 1967 ; a popular work on the portrayal of new problems poised before Independent India), *Suni Ghati ka Suraj* (The Sun of a Desolate Valley ; 1957), *Admi ka Zahar*, *Simayen Tutati Hain* (The Traditons are Breaking), *Makan* and *Agyatvas* ; *Angad ka Panv* and *Yahan se Vahan* are his humorous works. *Yah Ghar Mera Nahin* is a collection of his short stories.

SHRIMALI, R.D. See *Rameshwar Dayal Shrimali.*

SHRIMANT KUMAR VYAS. Rajasthani poet, whose *Ramdut* (1966) presents a compact and comprehensive picture of Hanuman and is the only Rajasthani poem of its type. His 'Olyundi' is a love poem. He has also composed patriotic, heroic and progressive poems and has written one-act plays : *Chananau*.

SHRIMANT PATHAK. Modern Maithili poet, who is noted for his lyrics.

SHRI NARAYAN AGRAWAL. Rajasthani idealist novelist, whose *Champa* (1925) deals with the problem of marriage in old age.

SHRI NARAYAN CHATURVEDI Modern poet and writer, who had been editor of 'Vishvabharati Series of Books' and of 'Saraswati'. Two poetical collections of his have been published under the titles of *Ratnadip* and *Jivankan* under the name of Shridhar, while *Rajbhavan ki Cigarette-dani* contains his mature satirical writings under the pseudonym of Vinod Sharma.

SHRI NATH MODI. Rajasthani writer, whose 'Gaon Sudhar ya Goma Jat' (1931), a one-act play, treats of social reform.

SHRI NATH SHARMA (fl. 2nd half of 18th cent.). Courtier of Raval Mulraj of Jaisalmer, who was a great scholar and poet of Sanskrit, Hindi and Dingal. He was the author of four Riti works : *Mulraj-Kavya*, *Anyokti Manjusha*, *Lolimbraj* and *Mul-Vilas* in Pingal.

SHRINGAR SHAT. Rajasthani poem in 105 verses of an unknown author, which was composed around 1350. An erotic poem, as its name indicates, it describes in varying syllabic metres also the characteristics of a heroine and the six seasons beginning with the Spring. The pangs of separation and amorous enjoyment during the various seasons are expressed in lucid language.

SHRINIVAS. Poet of the Riti school, whose *Rasa Sagar* was composed in 1693.

SHRINIVAS BALAJI HARDIKAR. Marathi-speaking modern Hindi writer, who is known for his works : *Shivaji*, *Nana Phadnawis*, *Nana Sahib Peshwa* and *Rani Lakshmibai* and historical works : *Attharah Sau Sattavan* and *1857 ki Chingariyan*.

SHRINIVAS BATRA. Modern scholar and author of *Hindi tatha Farsi Sufi Kavya ka Tulnatmak Adhyayan*.

SHRINIVAS DAS (1850-97). Writer, who was born at Mathura but lived in Delhi. A contemporary and friend of Bharatendu Harishchandra (q.v.), he wrote a number of dramas, which became immediately popular after publication ; his better-known dramas are : *Prahlad Charitra* (1888 ; mythological), *Tapti-Samvaran* (1883 ; mythological), *Randhir aur Premmohini* (1880 ; a drama influenced by *Romeo and Julliet*) and *Sanyogita-Swayamvar* (1886 ; on the elopement of Sanyogita by Prithwiraj).

Shrinivas is, however, best known for his *Pariksha Guru* (Trial as Teacher ; 1882), a social novel, portraying the life of a middle-class trader. It is an original novel, the first of its kind in Hindi and is counted among the earliest Hindi novels.

Shrinivas's prose is racy and at places he uses a language which reads like simple Hindi prose of today.

SHRINIVAS JAGDATT (1910-58). Hindi lover of Mauritius, who was educated in England and was instrumental in getting the courses of Hindi Pracharini Sabha started in 1946 ; the topper in these examinations is now awarded the 'Jagdatt Puraskar'. He also gave a helping hand in establishing the 'Gita Mahamandal', 'Mauritius Seva Sangh', 'Mauritius-Indo Association' and starting a paper 'Mauritius Times'. He looked after more than 50 sittings where Hindi was taught and wrote articles for the 'Advance' and 'Mauritius Times'. He came to India for recruitment of teachers for teaching Hindi to higher classes in Mauritius but he fell ill and died in India.

SHRINIVAS JOSHI (fl. 1950). Malwi writer, whose chief works are : *Vah re Pattha Bhari Kari* (a novel on the story of a fat Brahmin (Panda), who got the opportunity of a world tour) and several short stories.

SHRINIVAS MALL, RAKA (r. 1657-1701). Ruler of the House of Lalitpur (or Patan) in Nepal, who was a great patron of music and dancing. His Maithili songs are found in the *Raga-Tarangini* and *Ragamala*. He extended the period of dancing in Karttik. A Maithili drama, *Lalit-Kuvalyashav* is known to have been written under his patronage.

SHRINIVAS MUNDRA. Marathi-speaking modern Hindi poet, whose poems are written on various subjects.

SHRINIVAS UDGATA. Oriya-speaking modern Hindi writer, who has tr. Surendra Mahanti's *Nil Shaile* into Hindi. He has also tr. Bhagvati Charan Verma's *Chitralekha* and Hazari Prasad Dwivedi's *Banbhatt ki Atmakatha* from Hindi into Oriya.

SHRINIVASACHARI, V. Telugu-speaking modern Hindi scholar, whose research publication is *Premchand evam Telugu ke Yugin Upanyaskar* (Premcand and his Contemporary Telugu Novelists).

SHRINIVASACHARYA, KA. SHRI. Tamil-speaking modern Hindi writer, who is noted for his critical essays, mainly on Tamil epics and modern Tamil literature. He has also edited some special issues of Hindi magazines : 'Galpa-Sansar Mala', 'Hans', etc.

SHRINIVASAN. Tamil-speaking modern Hindi writer, whose short stories have been published in various popular magazines.

SHRINIVASI. Modern poet of Surinam, whose several poetical collections in Dutch, Spanish and English have been published. His *Anjali* is a collection of poems composed in Hindi or Sarnami.

SHRIPAD JOSHI. Marathi-speaking modern Hindi writer, whose chief works are : *Vir Shivaji*, *Maharashtra ke Samaj Sudharak* and *Gandhiji : Ek Jhalak*. See *Go. P. Nene*.

SHRIPAL SINGH 'KSHEM'. Modern poet, whose chief poetical collections are : *Jivan Teri*, *Nilam Jyoti* and *Sangharsh* (The Struggle).

SHRIPATI (fl. 18th cent.). Maithili poet, whose verses found respectable place in contemporary anthologies.

SHRIPATI MISHRA. Poet of the Riti school, who was a Kanyakubja Brahmin of Kalpi. He was the author of several Riti works : *Kavya Saroj* (1720), *Kalpadrum*, *Rasa-Sagar*,

Anupras-Vinod, *Vikram Vilas*, *Saroj Latika* and *Alankar Ganga* ; of these the first one is the most popular and comprehensive. A poet known for his versatility and poetic gifts, his works cover almost every aspect of poetics ; his treatment of these themes is erudite and thorough.

SHRI RAJ MOHAN JHA. See *Raj Mohan Jha, Shri*.

SHRI RAM ATA (fl. 16th-17th centuries). Assamese poet, who was appointed Mahant of Kalajhar Vaishnav Math after the death of Gopal Ata (q.v.). Of his Hindi (Brajavali) works, some are stray verses and a drama. Birinchi Kumar Barua has published his 19 songs, while *Subhadra Haran*, the drama, written in Assamese characters, has been published under 'Ankmala' edited by Satyendra Nath.

SHRI RAMCHANDRANDU, P. Telugu-speaking Hindi writer, who is noted for his *Hindi-Telugu Vyakaran* (grammar ; 1953).

SHRI RAM NAGAR. Gujarati-speaking modern Hindi scholar, whose chief works are : *Hindi ki Prayogshil Kavita aur Uske Prerana Srot* and *Gujarati Santon ki Hindi Vani* (ed.).

SHRI RAM SHARMA. Modern Hindi writer of Hyderabad, who is noted for his research in Dakkhini language and literature. His works are : *Dakkhini Hindi ka Udbhav aur Vikas* (1964) and *Dakkhini Hindi ka Sahitya* (1972). He also rendered into Hindi the radio version of C. Narayan Reddy's famous one-act play as *Ramappa ka Mandir*, with the assistance of Iriventi Krishnamurti.

SHRI RAM SHARMA (1912-). Writer, whose works on hunting are : *Pranon ka Sauda* (Bargain for Life), *Shikar*, *Bolti Pratima* and *Jungle ke Jiv* (The Creatures of Jungle).

SHRI RAM SHARMA. Modern Hindi poet of Fiji, who is noted for his stray poems.

SHRI RAM SHARMA 'ARUN'. Writer, who is known for his novels : *Panghat ka Patthar* (The Slab of the Quay) and *Tat Dub Gaya* (The Bank is Submerged ; both 1982).

SHRI RAM VERMA. Poet, whose poems are included in the *Chautha Saptak* (q.v.) ; *Kalpatra* (The Chronicle Capsule ; 1980) and *Shabdon ki Shatabdi* are his poetical collections. His 'Gali ka Parivesh' (1958) is a long poem.

SHRI RAM YADAV. Modern Kannauji poet, who is noted for his Kannauji folk-poems.

SHRIVASTAV, G.P. (1891-1976). Humorous writer, who was born at Chhapra in the Saran district of Bihar. His full name is Ganga Prasad Shrivastav. His chief works are : *Ulatpher* (1918), *Dumdar Admi* (The Man with a Tail ; 1919), *Gadbad-Jhala*, *Mardani Aurat* (The Manly Woman ; 1920), *Bhul-Chuk* (Errors or Omissions ; 1920), *Kursi-Man* and *Sahitya ka Saput* (humorous plays) ; he has also written novels and short stories which are also humorous in character. He was greatly influenced by the French writer, Moliere.

SHUBH CHANDRA BHATTARK (1516-56). Gujarati-speaking Jain poet, who was a disciple of Vijay Kirti and was honoured by the Jain and non-Jain communities. He had a good knowledge of Sanskrit, Prakrit, Apabhransh, Hindi and Gujarati and his works, which are 14 in number, have been composed in Gujarati-mixed Hindi. The works are : *Adhyatma Tarangini* (a commentary on Amritchandra's *Samay-Sar Kalash*), a commentary on *Swami Kirtikeyanupreksha*, *Chandana Charit*, *Pandav Puran*, *Trividhividyadhar*, *Tatwasar Doha*, *Mahavir Chhand*, *Vijay-Kirti Chhand*, *Guru Chhand*, *Neminath Chhand*, *Chatuvinshati Stuti*, *Kshetrapal Git*, *Ashtahnika Git* and stray verses.

SHUBHA VERMA. Writer, who is noted for her novels : *Free Lancer* (1981) and *Mohtarma* (1984).

SHUBHANKAR THAKUR, MAHARAJA (r. 1557?-1570/1). Ruler of Mithila of the Khandvalakul dynasty, who wrote several works in Maithili on acting and dancing.

SHUKHRAM DAS LUHAR (1701-65). Rajasthani saint-poet of Ram Snehi Sampraday, Ren, who belonged to the village Harsur. His poems, dealing with Nirgun Bhakti are : *Bhakta Vansavali*, *Chintamani*, *Chanak Bodh*, *Bharam Tod*, *Vichar Bodh*, *Gyan Dipak*, *Gyan Sar*, *Atma Bodh*, *Anbhai Bodh*, *Vichar Nisani*, *Dhyan Mul*, etc. and stray verses in popular metres. His poems are mature and deeply moving.

SHUKLA, RAMCHANDRA. See *Ramchandra Shukla*.

SHUKLAL PRASAD PANDEY (fl. 1st half of 20th cent.). Chhattisgarhi poet, whose chief poem is *Giyan*.

SHUKRARAJ SHASTRI, THE LATE. Modern Hindi scholar of

Nepal, who had commented in Hindi on the *Brahmasutra Shankara Bhashya*.

SHYAM BIHARI DAS 'NAVIN'. Maithili poet, whose *Godhuli* (1943) is a *Khandkavya*.

SHYAM BIHARI TIWARI 'DEHATI'. Modern Bhojpuri poet of Betiya district in Bihar, whose collection of poems: *Dehati Dulki* (3 Pts.) presents pictures of rural life.

SHYAM CHARAN DUBE. Scholar, who is noted for his *Field Songs of Chhattisgarh.*

SHYAM DAS (fl. 17th cent.). Bengali Vaishnav poet, who also composed *Padas* in Brajbuli.

SHYAM GOVIND. Poet, whose chief collection of poems is *Samay Teri Kavitayen* (1983).

SHYAM LAL BHARATI (alias U Bati). Modern Hindi writer of Burma, whose chief work is *Hindi Shikshavali.*

SHYAM LAL CHATURVEDI. Chhattisgarhi folk-poet, whose chief work is *Ram Banvas* (1954).

SHYAM LAL SHARMA. Dogri-speaking Hindi writer, whose chief work is on Prem Nath Dogra. He has edited 'Shiraja' and 'Brahmavani' as also other Hindi works. He has published *Dogri Lok-Kathayen tatha Kashmiri Lok-Kathayen* (Dogri and Kashmiri Folk-tales).

SHYAM MAHARSHI. Rajasthani poet of Dungargarh, whose *Ukalati Okal* (1978) is a collection of poems. He also edited *Athvain Dashak ri Pragatishil Kavita* (1981), which is an anthology of 50 poems of 23 progressive poets of the Eighties.

SHYAM NANDAN KISHORE (1932-). Critic and poet, whose chief works are: *Adhunik Mahakavyon ka Shilp-Vidhan* (on modern epics; 1965, criticism), *Hindi Sahitya: Shodhatmak Nishkarsh, Jivan Sahitya evam Sanskriti* (both essay collections), *Vibhavari* (Starry Night), *Git Adhure Hain* (Songs are Incomplete) and *Suraj Naya Purani Dharti* (New Sun, Old Earth; poetical collections).

SHYAM NANDAN SHASTRI. Modern Magahi poet, whose poems are influenced by *Rahasyavadi* movement.

SHYAM NARAYAN MISHRA 'SHYAM'. Modern poet, whose chief poetical work is *Nishwas* (The Breathing Out).

SHYAM NARAYAN PANDE (1910-). Heroic poet, who was born at Dumraon in the Azamgarh district. He composed *Haldighati* (1941 ; an epic dealing with the famous Haldighati Battle between Rana Pratap and Akbar's forces) and *Jauhar* (ceremonial self-immolation of women). His critical work is *Brajras Lila* : *Srot aur Siddhant*.

SHYAM PARMAR (1924-77). Poet and writer of Malwa, whose chief works are : *Malwi Lok-Sahitya* (research), *Malwi Lok-Git* (1942), *Malwi aur Uska Sahitya*, *Malwi ki Lok-Kathayen* (a collection of 15 folk-tales ; 1955), *Lok-Dharmi Natya-Parampara* (on the tradition of folk-drama), *Bharatiya Lok-Sahitya* (on Indian folk-literature), *Akavita aur Kala Sandarbh* (on Anti-Poetry) and *Morjhal* (a novel on the Bhils of Malwa). He was one of the leading exponents of the 'Akavita' (Anti-poetry) in Hindi literature. His poetical collection is : *Kavitayen Kavita ke Bahar*.

SHYAM SEVAK (b. 1891). Poet of Mauganj (Rewa), whose chief works are : *Prem-Faujdari* (The Quarrel of Love), *Gyan Manjari* (The Creeper of Knowledge), *Kirti Muktavali*, etc.

SHYAM SUNDAR (fl. 16th cent.). Saint-poet of Maharashtra, who composed some *Padas* in Hindi as well. His language is influenced by Marathi.

SHYAM SUNDAR DAS, BABU (1875-1945). Celebrated writer, who was one of the founders of Nagari Pracharini Sabha and a pioneer of Hindi movement. He was Head of the Department of Hindi in the Benares Hindu University and taught students, who were later on the best scholars of those days. His literary activity covered a wide field : research, editing and writing of original works and for this he was awarded by Benares Hindu University honorary degrees of 'Sahitya Vachaspati' and D. Litt. He was the first successful lexicographer, having prepared the first dependable Hindi dictionary (*Hindi Shabda Sagar*) and compiled a lexicon of scientific and technical terms (*Vaigyanik Kosh*). He also wrote a detailed history of Hindi language and literature, *Hindi Bhasha aur Sahitya* and books on literary theory and philosophy : *Sahityalochan* (1927) and *Bhasha Vigyan*. His other prominent works are : *Rupak Rahasya*, *Bhasha Rahasya* and annual research reports of Hindi manuscripts. Besides, he wrote on the lives and works of contemporary authors, on Tulsidas (*Goswami Tulsidas*) and on Indian dramaturgy. During his whole life, he contributed numerous notes and articles to monthlies. He also ed. a number of works, including *Prithwiraj Raso*, *Ramcharitmanas*, *Hammir Raso*, *Chhatra-Prakash*, *Parmal Raso*, *Dindayal Giri Granthavali* and wrote his biography. In his early career, he wrote *An Elementary Grammar of Hindi and Urdu* (1906), on the model of modern English grammars.

SHYAM SUNDAR GHOSH (1934-). Bengali-speaking modern Hindi writer and poet, whose chief works are : *Nayi Kavita ka Swarup-Vikas*, *Bachchan ka Parvarti Kavya* (criticism) and *Nav-Lekhan : Samasyayen aur Sandarbh*. His other works are : *Naye Shishu ka Janma* (poetical collection), *Madhumaya* (songs; 1951), *Sham aur Urvashi* (The Evening and Urvashi ; short story collection), *Bhadrakali* (novel) and some satirical pieces. *Vyangya Kya Vyangya Kyon* is on satire.

SHYAM SUNDAR VAIDYA (fl. early 20th cent.). Early novelist, who is noted for his historical novel : *Panjab Patan* (The Downfall of the Panjab) and a drama : *Vriddhavastha Vivah* (The Old Age Marriage).

SHYAM VIMAL. Poet and novelist who is noted for his *Ritu Samhar* and *Itna jo Mila* (1983), poetical collections and novels : *Naven Apni-apni* and *Ghalat Sahi Ghadiyan*.

SHYAM VYAS (1929-). Writer, whose chief novel, *Ek Pyasa Talab* (A Thirsty Tank ; 1968) describes the sex-hunger of Chanda ; *Saundarya aur Sanp* (The Beauty and Snake ; 1980) is his essay collection. He has also written short stories, his collection being *Gali Bairagi* and *Jalta Hua Makan*.

SHYAM CHARAN MISHRA. Modern Hindi writer of Burma, whose chief works are : *Burma—Aj aur Kal*, *Burma ka Itihas*, *Samajvadi Burma* and *Pravasi* (novel).

SHYAMA DEVI. Modern Maithili poetess, who is noted for her excellent traditional lyrics, in addition to folk and modern types of lyrics.

SHYAMA KANT PATHAK (1898-1943). Writer, who was noted for his historical drama, *Bundel Kesri* (1934). He was born in Jabalpur and was a famous astrologer.

SHYAMAL DAS DADHIVADIYA, KAVIRAJA (1837-94). Rajasthani historian and poet, who was patronized and highly honoured by Maharaja Sajjan Singh of Mewar. He was awarded the title of 'Kaisar-e-Hind' by the British Government.

Kaviraja Shyamaldas was persuaded by Maharana Shambhu Singh to write an elaborate and detailed history of Mewar. His *Vir Vinod*, a monumental work on the history of Rajasthan, was begun in 1871 and was completed in 1892 in the reign of Maharana Fateh Singh. The Mewar State spent in those days 1 lakh rupees for collecting material for this work and though it was published, Maharana Fateh Singh prohibited its circulation. It was only later on that it was offered for sale. This work is considered as a standard history not only of Mewar, but also of Jaipur, Jodhpur, Jaisalmer, etc. The work is divided in two parts and consists of 2,700 pages of royal 4-page size. In its prose, Shyamaldas has made copious use of Arabic and Persian words and though the script is Devnagari, it appears almost Urdu prose.

SHYAMANAND JHA. Maithili writer, whose *Jivan Bhumi* (1979) is a summary tr. of Pearl S. Buck's world famous book, *The Good Earth*. He is also noted for his short stories, one-act plays, essays and poems. In his *Beng-ki Rashtriya Sabha*, he presents an excellent parallel to Chaucer's *The Parliament of Fowls*. He also edited in the 'twenties an anthology of patriotic poetry, entitled *Maithili Sandesh*.

SIDDHA GOPAL (fl. 1st part of 20th cent.). Kannada-speaking Hindi writer, who wrote *Kannada Sahitya*. He was one of those protagonists of Hindi, who propagated Hindi around 1925.

SIDDHALING PATTANSHETTI 'SAGAR'. Kannada-speaking Hindi poet, whose poems are chiefly collected in the 2nd part of the *Shail aur Sagar* (The Mountain and the Ocean ; 1963). His *Adhunik Hindi aur Kannada Kavya* (Modern Hindi and Kannada Poetry) is a critical work containing 7 essays on Hindi and Kannada poets and literary genres. He has also tr. some Kannada poems into Hindi. He was one of the three editors of *Rashtrakavi Govind Pai—Vyaktitva aur Krititva*.

SIDDHALINGESH (1378-1428). Virshaiv saint of Karnataka, who was born at the village Badhwal near Solapur. He was a disciple of Siddhanagesh, the Virshaiv saint but as he was influenced by Sufism, he considered Nasiruddin Chiragh also as his preceptor. He was the first to compose *Padas* in Dakkhini Hindi.

SIDDHA NATH KUMAR (1927-). Writer, whose chief works

are : *Srishti ki Sanjh aur anya Natak* (a collection of five *Giti-Natyas*, dealing with current problems), *Rasta Band Hai*, *Rang aur Rup* (collection of one-act plays, in which radio technique has been used), *Radio Varta-Shilpa* and *Radio Natya Shilpa* (both dealing with radio technique). His latest critical work is *Hindi Ekanki ki Shilpa-vidhi ka Vikas*.

SIDDHA NATH MADHAV AGARKAR (1891-1945). Marathi-speaking Hindi poet, whose poems laid emphasis on social reform and were also influenced by the Chhayavadi poets. He also wrote short stories and essays, which were published in various magazines.

SIDDHA NATH PANT (fl. early 20th cent.). Kannada-speaking Hindi writer, who propagated Hindi in Karnataka. His *Hindi-Kannada Swayambodhini* (Hindi-Kannada Self-Teacher) proved quite useful for learning Hindi in rural areas. See *Shivmurti Swami*.

SIDDHA SEN (fl. 1499). Rajasthani poet and author of *Vikram Panchdand Chaupai*.

SIDDHESH (1938-). Short story writer, whose collections of short stories are : *Do Lambi Kahaniyan aur Paro* (Two Long Stories and Paro), *Anam-Sangrah*, *Arthhin Vaha Mein* and *Anupasthit Shahr* (Absent City).

SIDDHESHWAR MAHARAJ. Saint-poet of Maharashtra, who was a disciple of Amrit Ray (1698-1753). He also composed *Padas* in Hindi ; his language is influenced by Dakkhini.

SIDDHESHWAR VARMA (1887-1985). Celebrated linguist, whose *Prachin Bharatiya Vaiyakaranon ke Dhwanyatmak Vicharon ka Vivechanatmak Adhyayan* is a Hindi rendering of his *Critical Studies in the Phonetic Observations of Indian Grammarians*. His other work is *Dictionary of Technical Terms in Hindi*.

SIDDHI NARSINGH DEV (r. 1620-57). Ruler of the House of Lalitpur (or Patan) in Nepal, who seems to have been a prolific Maithili poet as an entire *Padavali* is known after him. A drama, *Harishchandramrityam* (1651), on the story of Raja Harishchandra, is known to have been written under his patronage by a poet, called Damodar. His poems are found in almost every anthology including *Kans-Narayan Padavali*, *Raga-Tarangini*, *Ragmala* and *Bhasha-Git-Sangrah*. He is also reputed to have founded the tradition of a song and drama festival at Patan called 'Karttik Nach'.

SIDDIQUI, AHMAD H. Author of *The Syntax and Symantics of Questions in English, Hindi and Urdu : a Study in Applied Linguistics* (1977).

SIDUVA-VIDUVA. Kumaoni Ramaula, which describes the extraordinary happenings in the lives of two leading merchants, Siduva and Viduva, who were considered the younger brothers, brothers-in-law or sons-in-law of Krishna. They were reputed for playing upon their flutes and could bring anyone under their sway. When they played upon their instruments, nymphs from Indra's heaven used to come to perform their dance. Once the life-breath of Siduva was imprisoned in a casket by the nymphs of Indra, so that they could hear the flute permanently. Krishna came and rescued Siduva. See *Ramaula*.

SIMHASAN BATTISI. See *Hir Kalash*.

SIMMI HARSHITA. Writer ; her collection of short stories *Dharashayi* (1980) mainly deals with the sorrows of woman ; her another collection of short stories is *Kamre men Band Abhas*.

SINDHAYACH CHAUBHUJA (fl. 1st half of 15th cent.). Rajasthani poet, whose Dingal *Git* treats of the death of Ranmall in Chittor in 1438. Although Ranmall was tied to a cot while asleep and then attacked, he killed many persons in that state before he met his end.

SINDHAYACH DAYALDAS (1798-1891). Rajasthani author of *Maharaj Ratansinghji ki Dav avait*, which consists of verses and passages of rhymed prose. His *Dayaldas ri Khyat* is a history of Rathores, particularly of the Bikaner family ; it is a significant contribution to history, culture and literature. His two other books, *Desh Darpan* and *Aryakhyan Kalpadrum* are also notable contributions to history.

SINDHAYACH FATEHRAM. See *Maharaj Gajsinghji Rao Rupak*.

SINDHAYACH HORDAN (fl. early 19th cent.). Rajasthani scholar of Mogda, whose *Chhand Divakar* is a work on metrics.

SINDHU BHINGARKAR. Marathi-speaking modern Hindi poet, whose poems are written on various subjects. He has also written a critical work : *Jainendra ke Upanyason men Nari-Chitran.*

SINDUR KI HOLI. See *Lakshmi Narayan Mishra.*

SINGA (fl. 17th cent. ?). Malwi saint-poet, whose songs are popular among peasants.

SITA CHARIT. See *Ram Chandra 'Balak'.*

SITA DEVI. Assamese-speaking modern Hindi writer, who is noted for her memoirs and essays. She has tr. an Assamese novel into Hindi and has also prepared some Hindi text-books.

SITA DEVI. Modern Kauravi scholar, whose chief work is *Dhulidhusarita Maniyan.*

SITA KULKARNI. Marathi-speaking modern Hindi poetess, who has published poems on various subjects.

SITA RAM 'BHUP' (1858-1937). Writer of Ayodhya, who enriched Hindi prose through translations. Beginning from *Kumarasambhava*, he tr. *Meghaduta*, *Raghuvansha*, *Ritusamhara*, *Uttara-Ramacharita*, *Malati-Madhava*, *Mrichhakatika*, *Nagananda*, *Mahavira-Charitam*, *Malavikagnimitra*, *Hitopadesha*, *Praja Kartavya* and some of Shakespeare's plays. His translations of Kalidasa's works are even today looked upon as the best in Hindi. Mahavir Prasad Dwivedi had, however, in an article, criticised his translation of Kalidasa's plays. He also composed poems in Brajbhasha and Khari Boli.

SITA RAM CHATURVEDI. Modern scholar, whose chief works are : *Vagvigyan*, *Mahaprabhu Shrimadvallabhacharya aur Pushtimarg*, *Mahakavi Surdas*, *Shaili aur Kaushal* and *Bhashaki Shiksha : Uski Samasyayen, Samadhan aur Shikshan Vidhiyan.*

SITA RAM GURJAR (fl. 1850-1900). Marathi-speaking saint-poet, who composed *Padas* in Hindi.

SITA RAM JHA. Maithili poet, who is known for his epic, *Amba-Charit* (1956) and stray poems. He composed several types of lyrics and a large number of *Muktak* poems and collected them in several volumes : *Shiksha-Sudha* (didactic), *Lok-Lakshan* and *Upadeshakshamala.* His *Lok-Lakshan* contains epigrammatic summaries of various kinds of distinctions that are made among men and women. His satirical poems are : *Padhua-Charitra* and *Purvapar Vyavahar* (1920-34). His *Bharat Bhraman* (1979) is a travelogue. He has also written *Alankar-Darpan* on *Alankar* and *Chhandolankar-Manjusha* on prosody and rhetorics.

SITA RAM LALAS. Rajasthani writer, whose chief works are : *Rajasthani Sabad Kos* (Rajasthani-Hindi Dictionary ; 9 vols., 1962-79 ; containing about 2,00,000 words) and *Rajasthani Vyakaran* (1954).

SITA RAM MAHAPATRA. Marathi-speaking modern Hindi scholar, whose chief works are : *Uktivilas* and *Sant Eknath aur Unka Hindi Kavya.*

SITA RAM MAHARSHI. Modern Rajasthani poet, who composed Nature, patriotic and heroic poems. His *Machhali Man Mahro* is a collection of poems of tender emotions, while his *Prit Pid ri Pal* (1971) is in 101 verses. He is the author also of two novels : *Kun Samajhai Chanvari ra Kaul* (1976) and *Laladi Ek Pherun Gamagi*, dealing with the marital maladjustments.

SITA RAM MURTI, MRS. Hindi writer of Hong Kong, who has contributed to the cause of Hindi in that country. She teaches Hindi to those students, who are desirous of learning it.

SITA RAMAYYA, G. Telugu-speaking Hindi poet, whose *Mulyankan* (Evaluation ; 1976) is based on the famous Telugu poem *Parijat-Haranmu* on the love of Krishna and his wife, Satyabhama.

SITAL (fl. 18th cent.). Poet of Shahbad, who was a follower of Haridas Sect. A great scholar of Sanskrit and Persian, he was the author of *Gulzar-Chaman* (4 Pts.) ; his poetry had given good impetus to Khari Boli poetry.

SIYARAM SHARAN GUPTA (1895-1964). Poet and writer, who was younger brother of Maithili Sharan Gupta (q.v.). He was greatly influenced by Gandhian teachings and the national movement. His chief works are : *Ardra* (1928), *Durvadal*, *Vishad*, *Pathey*. *Mrinmayi*, *Bapu* (1938 ; patriotic poems), *Unmukta* (in defence of non-violence), *Noakhali* (on opposition to Noakhali massacre), *Nakul* (1947 ; based on the *Mahabharat*), *Jai Hind*, *Atmotsarga* (a poem in praise of Ganesh Shankar Vidyarthi, who sacrificed his life for the sake of Hindu-Muslim unity), 'Amritputra', *Anath*, *Gopika* (all poems or poetical collections), *God* (The Lap ; 1932), *Nari* (The Woman), *Antim Akanksha* (The Last Desire ; 1934) (novels), *Punyaparva* (drama) ; has is also written short stories (*Manushi*) and essays ; 'Bail ki Bikri' (The Sale of a Bullock) is his popular short story.

The element of sobriety and a wide humanitarian approach have coloured all his writings.

SIYA SAKHI (Gopal Das ; fl. 1st half of 18th cent.). Gaur Brahmin poet of Badagaon (Jhunjhunun) in Rajasthan, who followed the Rasik Sect, originated by Agradas (q.v.). His stray verses in Rajasthani are available.

SKANDGUPTA. Drama (1929) by Jayshankar Prasad (q.v.).

Skandgupta, the son of king Kumargupta by his elder queen Devki, goes to the help of Malwa king in the hope that Parnadatt, with all the armies, will protect Magadh from the onslaughts of Pushyamitra. Purugupta, son of Kumargupta by his younger queen, Anantdevi, ignores the affairs of the state; moreover Anantdevi wants her son to succeed the Magadh throne. A conspiracy is hatched by Anantdevi for the assassination of Devki, but at the nick of time, Skandgupta saves his mother and both of them proceed to Ujjayini ; in the meantime Skand ascends the throne. Vijaya, who is in love with Skandgupta, arranges in such a way that Devsena her rival, is sacrificed in a cemetry, but on the timely arrival of Skandgupta, she is saved ; feeling frustration in love, Vijaya commits suicide. Anantdevi, in collusion with Huns, attacks Skandgupta ; Bhatarka, Skand's commander, betrays and in the war Skand's army is washed away from the sudden burst of a dam. Skand, with the treasure left by Vijaya organizes his army and finally vanquishes the Huns. Skand wins ; he makes Purugupta the crown prince and declares that he will remain unmarried throughout his life.

This drama is considered as the masterpiece of the dramatist : the hero of the drama frees the land for a time from the menace of Hun invasions, and in him Prasad has presented a truly noble character, brave and wise, with a sense of duty and capacity for self-sacrifice.

SMEKEL, ODOLENE (1928-). Czech Hindi scholar, who is the author of *Hindi Vartalap* (Prague, 1968), *Hindi Reader* (1968), *Hindi Verbal Basis* (1970-71), *Hindi Kriya Padbandh* (1970-71) and *Hindi Glossary* (1971), all for the teaching of Hindi. He has done research and written essays especially on rural and regional novels. He has tr. into Czech Premchand's Godan (1957), Indian Folk-tales (1967, 1974) and an anthology of modern Hindi poetry in 1975, in which the select poems of some 25 Hindi poets have been included. His *Tere Dan Kiye Git* (The Songs Gifted by You ; 1982) is a collection of original Hindi poems. The poems are sensuous, simple and sentimental and represent a commendable attempt by a foreigner. His latest poetical works are : *Kamal ko Lekar Chal* and *Swati Bund.* For the last decade, he is Head of the Indology Department in the Charles University, Prague.

SMITA DATYE. Marathi-speaking modern Hindi poetess, who has published poems on various subjects.

SMITH, RICHARD RHODES. Scholar, whose chief work is *Awadhi/Kanauji Transition Phenomena and their Correlates : a Study in Dialect Geography* (Ph.D., Cornell, 1974).

SNEHMAYI CHAUDHRI. Poetess, whose poetical collections are : *Ekaki Donon*, *Pura Ghalat Path* (Completely Wrong Lesson ; 1976) and *Apne Khilaf* (Against Oneself ; 1981).

SOBHAN SADH (fl. 17th cent.). Rajasthani saint-poet of Laldasi Sampraday, whose 40 stray verses deal with God and Guru Bhakti, while his *Yagya Bakhan*, a small poem, narrates some important events in Laldas's life.

SOBHOJI SONI (fl. 18th cent.). Rajasthani saint-poet of Jasnathi Sampraday, whose stray verses and *Sabads* deal with human duties, divine attributes, etc.

SODA BARHAT JAMNAJI (fl. between 1450-1550). Rajasthani poet, whose stray *Gits* on contemporary rulers and chiefs are available. In a Dingal *Git*, he consoled Rana Sanga after his defeat in the battle of Khanwa in 1526 at the hands of Babar.

SODHAYAN. Rajasthani historical narrative poem by Chimanji Kaviya (q.v.), which deals with the heroic deeds of Rajputs of the Sodha branch of the Parmar clan, who mostly inhabited the Dhat and Parkar regions of Sind (now in Pakistan). It is the only poem of its kind.

SOHAN LAL DWIVEDI (1907-). Poet, who was not only influenced by the nationalist movement but was also an active Congressman and a participant in the freedom struggle. He is also distinguished as a writer for children and the youth ; his chief works are : *Bhairavi*, *Vasavadatta* (1942), *Kunal* (1942 ; on the story of Kunal, a son of Ashok), *Pujagit*, *Chitra*, *Vasanti*, *Yugadhar*, *Prabhati*, *Vishpan*, *Puja ke Swar*, *Sevagram*, *Shishu-Bharati* (1949), *Balcharati* (1953), *Chetana* (1954), *Jay Bharat Jay* and *Sanjivni* ;*Bachon-ke-Bapu* *Chacha Nehru*, etc. are works meant for children. In 1956, *Jay Gandhi* (Victory to Gandhi) was published, which consists of his nationalist poems. His other poetical works are : *Gandhyan* and *Muktigandha*.

SOHANI RI VAT. Dingal romance in prose (Script 1790) by an unknown author, which is a love story between Sohani and Maliyar.

SOLANTSEVA, NINA IVANOVNA (1923-). Soviet Hindi scholar, who is noted for her studies on the principles of Hindi-Russian translation, Hindi dictionaries and on text-books. She has also prepared a Russian-Hindi dictionary.

SOM DATT. Writer, who tr. into Hindi the poems of the famous Turkish poet under the title *Nazim Hikmat ki Kavitayen* (The Poems of Nizam Hikmat ; 1981), who gave voice to the struggling oppressed mankind across the boundaries of nations. Som Datt's collection of poems is *Kismen Arbon Hain.*

SOM DATT Bakhori (1921-). Hindi poet of Mauritius, whose first collection of poems appeared in 1967 ; his second poetical collection : *Bich men Bahti Dhara* appeared in 1971. *Ganga ki Pukar* is a travelogue on his visit to India. He has also written short stories, dramas, essays and *Hinai Sahtiya Farichay.* His latest poetical collection is *Sanp Bhi Sanpera Bhi.* He was honoured by the Government of India in 1979 with the award of 'Vishwa Hindi Puraskar'.

SOM DEV. Maithili novelist, whose chief works are : *Chano Dai* (1959 ; on sexual problem) and *Brahm-Pishach* (1964 ; about modern blackmarketeers). He has publised poems (*Kaldhwani*; 1965 ; a collection of poems) and short stories. He has also written a masterly and elaborate survey of lyric poetry from 1940 to 1960.

SOM MURTI (fl. *c.* 1274). Jain poet, whose chief works in Rajasthani are : *Jineshwar Suri Vivah Varnana Ras* (an allegory, describing the marriage of Jineshwar Suri and Sanyam Shri, the initiation which he took and the act of his becoming a disciple at Khed). *Jin Prabodh Suri Charchari*, *Guravali Relua* and *Jin Prabodh Suri Bolika.*

SOM NATH (b. 1687-1702). Poet of the Riti school, who was a Mathur Brahmin and was patronized by Pratap Singh, the yongest son of Badan Singh, the ruler of Bharatpur State. His best known work *Rasapiyush-Nidhi* (1737) contains a very learned and fair discussion of the many topics on the art of poetic composition ; the work is comprehensive and scholarly and can equal the works of Shripati and Bhikhari Das (qq.v.). Somnath's poetry has a natural grace and makes a pleasant reading, being unburdened with his scholarship. He also tr. *Simhasana Battisi* in prose, under the title *Sujan-Vilas* (1750), wrote *Madhav Vinod Natak* (1752) after *Malati Madhava*, *Krishna Lilavati* and *Panchadhyayi* (1743). His *Shringar Vilas* is not an independent work, but is a part of his *Rasapiyush-Nidhi.* These works prove that he was aversatile genius.

SOM NATH GUPTA (1905-). Writer, whose chief works are : *Hindi Natya Sahitya ka Itihas* (History of Hindi Dramatic Literature ; 1950) and *Parsi Theatre : Udbhav aur Vikas*.

SOM SHEKHAR 'SOM' (1938-). Scholar, whose articles in Kannada and Hindi have appeared from time to time in several magazines. His chief work is *Hindi aur Kannada ki Saman Shabdavali ka Bhashavaigyanik Adhyayan* (1972). He is at present Visiting Hindi Professor, Berlin, East Germany.

SOMA VIRA (1932-). Fiction writer ; her chief works are : *Do Ankhen Vale Chehre* (1968 ; on the description of Indian youths settled in Amcrica), *Dharti ki Beti* (The Daughter of Soil), *Parchhaiyon ke Prashna* (all short story collections), *Tinni* (novel) and *Sathi Hath Badhana* (collection of one-act plays).

SOMESHWAR DAS (1928-). Assamese-speaking Hindi writer, whose *Adarsh Asamiya-Hindi Shabdakosh* is an Assamese-Hindi Dictionary. He has also published some essays.

SOMESHWAR SHARMA, VAI. Telugu-speaking modern Hindi writer, whose *Shri Venkatachal Mahatmya* glorifies Balaji of Tirupati.

SONA LAL NEMDHARI. Modern Hindi writer of Mauritius, who is noted for his short stories.

SORATH RA DUHA. Dingal romance (Script 1653) of an unknown author, which contains *Dohas* of the love of Bijo and Sorath ; another copy of this (Script 1765) is known as *Bija Sorath ri Bat*. See *Binjha-Sorath*.

SORATHI. Bhojpuri folk-tale in verse, which describes how Sorathi, immediately after her birth was placed by her parents in a cradle and flown in a river. She was picked up by a boatsman, who brought her up and got her married. The description by an unknown poet, is lively, especially the romance of Sorathi. See *Binjha-Sorath*.

SOUMITRA MOHAN (1938-). Panjabi-speaking modernist Hindi poet, whose chief work, *Chaku se Khelte Hue* (Toying with Knife) is a poetical collection ; his long poem, entitled 'Luqman Ali' reminds the reader of surrealism in its structure. *Luqman Ali aur any Kavitayen* appeared in 1978.

SOUTHWORTH, FRANKLIN CHESTER. Scholar, whose chief work is *The Student's Hindi-Urdu Reference Manual* (1971).

SRIJANA SAMARTH. Rajasthani writer, whose works for children are : *Lakhtakio* (tr. from English), *Rusi Tabaran Men* (tr.) and *Chauboli* (tr. from English ; all 1982).

SRIVASTAVA, M. Modern scholar, whose chief work is *The Elements of Hindi Grammar*.

SRIVASTAVA, S.N. (1935-). Hindi scholar and poet, who is at present in the Faculty of Oriental Studies, University of Cambridge, England. His works are : *Jal-Tarang* (1952), *Ek Kiran ek Phul* (One Ray, one Flower ; 1960), *Sthir Yatrayen* (Permanent Travels; 1979), *Misez Jons aur vah Gali* (Mrs. Jones and that Lane ; 1983) (all poems), *The Development of Western Medicine in South India* (1870-1914) and *The Ladies of the Raj* (the last two forthcoming).

STERIAN, CORNEL. Modern Romanian Hindi scholar, who has tr. into Romanian Vishnu Narlikar's two scientific short stories : 'Dhumketu' and 'Aksha'.

STRELTSOVA. YELYENA IVANOVNA (1927-). Soviet Hindi scholar, who was a Lecturer in Hindi and is at present an editor in the Progressive Publication House, Moscow. She is noted for editing the Hindi versions of the select works of Karl Marx, Chekhov and other writers.

SUBAL CHANDRA THAKUR (fl. 1607). Bengali Vaishnav poet, who also composed *Padas* in Brajbuli.

SUBAL SHYAM (fl. early 18th cent.). Poet of the Krishna-cult (Chaitanya Sect), who lived permanently in Vrindavan. His original name was 'Benikrishna'. His *Shri Chaitanya Charit-amrit* is a tr. in Braj of the original written in Bengali.

SUBBALAKSHMI. Kannada-speaking modern Hindi writer, who tr. from Kannada into Hindi Niranjan's novel : *Vimochanai* ; the novel has since been tr. into Russian as well.

SUBBARAO 'HARIKISHORE', B.V. Telugu-speaking Hindi poet, whose chief works are : *Mrinalini* (1959 ; a poem on an imaginary theme but with mythological background), *Hampi ke Khandahar* (The Ruins of Hampi ; 1965), *Rehsmi Kurta* (The Silk Shirt), *Bharatshri*, *Pranay* (1955) and *Meri Kavya-Sadhana* (all poetical collections). *Ufan* is his social novel, while his short stories : *Kathaguchchh* (1957 ; 6 Pts.), *Katha Bharati*, *Rashtra ke Pujari* are meant for children. He has also written *Siddhahast*, a biography.

SUBBULAKSHMI, T.V. Tamil-speaking Hindi scholar, who is noted for her *Tamil aur Hindi Sahitya men Rashtriya Chetana* (The National Consciousness in Tamil and Hindi Literature ; thesis ; 1973) and *Dr Nagendra ki Sahitya-Sadhana* (The Literary Career of Nagendra).

SUBHADRA. Writer, who is noted for her novels *Ghalat Jagah* (The Wrong Place ; 1981), *Sanjh ke Palash* and *Ajanmi Atma ki Bahen* (1984).

SUBHADRA JHA. Maithili essayist, whose chief essays, written in the form of letters are : 'Kutuhalak Ant', 'Andher Nagari', 'Gamak Panch' (1979), etc. His chief work is *Formation of the Maithili Language* (London, 1958), while *Hamara Prabas* (1947) is a travelogue. He has made genuine efforts to restore the original text of Vidyapati's *Padas* and has tr. Vidyapati's *Padas* into English prose.

SUBHADRA KUMARI CHAUHAN (1904-47). Nationalits poetess, who was born in Allahabad. After education, she was married to Thakur Lakshman Singh, an Advocate of Nawalpur. She also participated in the national freedom movement. She was the author of her celebrated poem, *Jhansi ki Rani* (The Queen of Jhansi ; 1926); her other works are : *Mukul* (Bud ; 1931), *Tridhara* (poetical collections), *Sabha ka Khel* (poems for children), *Unmadini* (novel) and *Bikhre Moti* (The Scattered Pearls ; 1932; short story collection). She had also written some essays.

SUBHADRA KUMARI PATHYA. Modern Maithili poetess, who has composed stray good poems.

SUBHASH BHARDWAJ. Dogri-speaking modern Hindi poet, whose chief works are : *Tandav* (Shiv's Dance), *Ret ka Sagar* (The Ocean of Sand ; poetical collections) and *Gadyanjali* (a prose anthology).

SUBRAMANIYAM. Tamil-speaking modern Hindi scholar, whose work is *Bharatendu aur Bharati ke Kavya ka Tulnatmak Adhyayan* (A Comparative Study of the Poetry of Bharatendu and Bharati ; thesis).

SUBRAHMANYAM 'VISHNUPRIYA'. Tamil-speaking modern Hindi poet, whose *Anamika* is a collection of love poems.

SUDAMA (fl. 17th cent.). One of the court-poets of Guru Govind Singh (q.v.) ; he was a master of Brajbhasha and composed an eulogy on the Guru. He also wrote devotionl poetry in the *Shringar* style.

SUDAMA-CAHRITRA. Poem by Narottam Das (q.v.; fl. 1545).

It describes the meeting of two old friends—Krishna and his poor school-fellow Sudama. The poet in the guise of Sudama has delineated those indolent persons who cast a garb of asceticism and renunciation on their lethargy. Sudama's wife has unbraced the heart of Sudama in clear terms. To show the greatness of the character of Krishna is the object of this little poem. The flow of the verse is smooth and graceful, the diction is simple, pure and appropriate and the work is of a high literary merit. The poem occupies a very high place in Hindi poems and is recited up to our own times.

SUDAMA-CHARITRA (18th cent. ?). Maithili poem of an anonymous author, which describes the story of Sudama, a poor Brahmin, who was raised from abject poverty to affluence by Krishna.

SUDAN (fl. 1763). Poet, who was born at Mathura in a Chaube family. He moved to Bharatpur where he was a court poet of Raja Sujan Singh alias Suraj Mal. On the name of his patron, Sudan wrote in Pingal the *Sujan-Charitra* (q.v.) or *Sujan-Vilas*, a *Prabandh Kavya,* written in the heroic style.

SUDARSHAN (1896-1967). Short story writer and dramatist, whose original name was Badrinath Bhatt and who was born in Sialkot (now in Pakistan). His chief works are : *Tirth-Yatra* (Pilgrimage), *Suprabhat* (Good Morning), *Panghat*, *Sudarshan Sudha*, *Sudarshan Suman*, *Anguthi ka Muqadma* (The Case of a Ring), *Pushpalata*, *Sudarshan ki Shreshth Kahaniyan* (The Best Stories of Sudarshan ; all short story collections), *Anjana* (1923 ; mythological drama on Hanuman's mother), *Dayanand* (1917), *Honorary Magistrate* (humorous drama ; 1929), *Bhagya Chakra* (Irony of Fate), *Sikandar* (historical drama), *Dhup-chhanh* (all dramas), *Prem Pujarin*, *Parivartan* and *Mitha Ped Kadva Phal* (Sweet Tree : Bitter Fruit ; novels). Sudarshan's famous short stories are : 'Har-ki Jit' (Defeat Turned into Victory), 'Adarsh Badla' (The Ideal Revenge), 'Album', 'Ashirvad' (The Benediction), 'Rajputani ka Prayashchit' (The Penance of a Rajput Woman), etc.; he has in all left 12 collections of short stories, published between 1919 and 1940. He wrote one-act plays as also for films for some time. His short stories have been tr. into English, Russian, Japanese and other languages. He was also the author of a good deal of literature for children.

SUDARSHAN CHOPRA (1929-78). Writer, whose chief novels are : *Pratinayika* (Vaillainess), *Sammohan* (Fascination), *Simant* (The End of Limit) and *Sannata* (Listlessness) ; he had also written short stories, his collection being *Sarak Durghatna*. His dramas are : *Apni Pahchan* and *Kala Pahad*.

SUDARSHAN MAJITHIYA (1932-). Writer, whose chief novels are : *Lohe ki Lashen* (The Dead Bodies of Iron ; 1969), *Ukhri Hui Andhi*, *Topon ke Saye Men* and *Kaghzi Sultan*. His other humorous works are : *Telephone ki Ghanti Se*, *Disco Culture* and *Meri Shreshth Vyangy Rachnayen*.

SUDARSHAN NARANG. Writer, whose chief works are : *Ek Tha Keshoram* (There Was a Keshoram ; novel), *Mahanagar ki Kahaniyan* (ed.) and *Shav-Yatra* (drama). His short story collections are : *Itna Bada Pul*, *Sirf ek Akash*, *Ham Shakla*, *Katha Madhyam* and *Ganga Ghat* (1984).

SUDHA ARORA (1946-). Writer ; her chief short story collections are : *Baghair Tarashe Hue* (Without Trimming) and *Yuddha-Viram* (Cease-fire).

SUDHA GUPTA. Modern scholar and author of *Swatantryottar Hindi Kavya*.

SUDHA GUPTA. Modern scholar, whose chief work is on the characterization of Sita through the ages. She has also written some poems.

SUDHA KALRA. Author of *Hindi Vakya Vinyas* (1971).

SUDHA KANT MISHRA. Modern Maithili poet, whose *Tista Kavita* is a collection of modernist poems.

SUDHA PATEL. Gujarati-speaking modern Hindi scholar, whose *Harivansh Rai Bachchan : Vyaktitva aur Krititva* is a research work.

SUDHAKAR. Kannada-speaking modern Hindi writer, who has tr. Kuvempu's Kannada drama *Shmshan Kurukshetra* into Hindi.

SUDHAKAR DWIVEDI (1860-1910). Writer, who, along with George Grierson, wrote a commentary on the *Padmavat*. Dwivedi's other works are : *Tulsi Sudhakar*, *Naya Sangrah*, *Manas Patrika*, *Hindi Vaigyanik Kosh*, *Ganit* and several works on astronomy.

SUDHAKAR KALVADE. Marathi-speaking modern Hindi scholar, whose chief works are : *Adhunik Hindi Kavita men Rashtriya Bhavna* and *Sahitya Shastra.*

SUDHAKAR PANDEY. Modern scholar, whose chief works are : *Manas Anushilan* (ed.), *Hindi Sahitya, Hindi Sahitya aur Sahityakar, Adhunik Hindi Sahitya* : *Mulya aur Manyatayen, Kavya Prabhakar* and *Hindi Sahitya ka Parishkar* (Dwivedi Kal : vol. IX of *Hindi Sahitya ka Brihat Itihas*). As convenor of the Brihat Itihas Upasamiti, he has brought out *Hindi Sahitya ka Brihat Itihas* in 16 volumes.

SUDHANSHU. See *Lakshmi Narayan Sudhanshu.*

SUDHANSHU CHATURVEDI. Modern Hindi writer, who has tr. from Malayalam into Hindi Kainikkara Padmanabh Pillai's famous drama : *Veluttampi Dalava* as also C.N. Shrikanthan Nair's *Kanchan Sita.*

SUDHANSHU SHEKHAR CHOUDHARY (1922-). Maithili writer, whose chief works are : *Tar Patta Upar Patta* (1961 ; a novel on sexual theme), *Hath-Tutta Kursi* (one-act plays) and *Sandarbh* (a collection of 30 literary essays). He has written short stories, critical articles as also poems.

SUDHINDRA (1915-). Poet and critic, who was born at Khairabad near Kota. His chief poetical works are : *Shankhnad, Mere Git, Pralay-Vina, Jauhar* and *Amritlekha,* while *Hindi Kavita men Yugantar* is his thesis. He also wrote *Sahitya Samikshanjali.* He tr. *Gitanjali* into Hindi, edited 'Tyagbhumi' with Haribhau Upadhyay and later 'Jivan Sahitya'.

SUDIP. Writer, whose *Sadhusingh Parchari* (1980) is a novelette; his other novel is *Nid* (Nest). His *Ant-hin* is a short story collection.

SUHAG KE NUPUR. See *Amrit Lal Nagar.*

SUJA BALECHA RA KAVITTA. Dingal poem in 61 verses by Asiya Karamsi Khinvsarot (q.v.), which describes the heroic deeds in three battles of an otherwise little known hero, Suja Balecha, son of Samant Singh. He fought for Rana Udaysingh and Rao Maldev of Jodhpur and was killed in the battle of Harmada in 1556.

SUJAN CHARITRA (*Sujan Vilas*). *Prabandh-Kavya* by Sudan

(q.v.), which narrates the exploits and the prowess of Sujan Singh alias Surajmal, the ruler of Bharatpur. It treats of the seven battles during 1745-53 ; it has been published by the Nagari Pracharini Sabha and runs into 234 pages and yet appears to be incomplete.

The work is divided into seven 'Jangs' or battles which serve as cantos and employs various metres. Jang I describes routing of the armies of Asad Khan, the commander-in-chief of king Ahmed Shah by Surajmal and conquering of Mewar, Mandogarh, etc. ; Jang II on the defeat of the Marathas ; Jang III treats of the defeat of Salabat Khan, the royal commander-in-chief ; IV on the attack on Pathans ; V on the defeat of Rao Bahadur Singh of Ghashare ; VI describes the plunder of the bazaars of Delhi in collaboration with Mansur Jang ; the last Jang describes Surajmal's preparations for battle against Marathas and the royal army. The accounts are historically accurate and are based on personal knowledge, rather than on mere imagination ; the poet at places indulges in exaggeration in describing the qualities and achievements of his hero.

In the beginning of the work, Sudan pays homage to the poets preceding him, but the ten verses of the prologue have resulted only in a bibliography of 175 names. He excels in describing preparations for battles, rather than in describing battles themselves. Seeing the army formations preparing for assault, he draws inventories. At places, he goes on enumerating the different varieties of horses in a cavalry regiment, or men of different races in an infantry division, or the implements and weapons of warfare with an artillery force. There is also no purity of language ; words of Panjabi and Khari Boli origin are interspersed with Brajbhasha. These defects as also his love of alliteration detract from the literary value of the work but some of his verses are free from these faults and contain spirited and heroic descriptions.

SUJANHIT. See *Ghananand.*

SUJAN RASO. See *Jogidas.*

SUJAN SINGH (fl. 1733). Poet, who was born in the royal family of Krauli. His *Sujan-Vilas*, a Riti work, is quite popular.

SUJAN SINGH RAWAT. Modern Rajasthani poet of Bhagwanpur, whose *Gajendra-Moksha* and stray verses are available.

SUJO (fl. 1534-41). Rajasthani poet, who was son of Nagraj

and was also a contemporary of Rao Bika and Rao Lunkaran. Rao Jaitsi granted him the village Khileriyo. Sujo's *Rao Jaitsi ro Paghadi Chhand* describes the defeat of Kamran (the second son of Emperor Babar) at the hands of Rao Jaitsi of Bikaner in 1534.

The poet first describes the achievements of the ancestors of the Rao Chunda, Ranmall, Jodha, Bika, Lunkaran and then those of Jaitsi. Kamran, after conquering Bhatner, reaches the outskirts of Bikaner. Leaving his trusted soldiers inside the fort for an opportunity to attack, the Rao and his selected warriors attack the enemy at the dead of night. The Mughals cannot withstand the attack and flee from the battle ; the Rao is victorious. The poem is of utmost historical value.

SUKH DEV MISHRA (fl. 1663-1703). Poet of the Riti school, who was born at Kampil and was educated at Varanasi. He enjoyed patronage of several personages : Raja Bhagwant Rai Khichi of Asothar in Fatehpur district, Rao Mardan Singh of Daundiyakhere and Fazl Ali Shah, a minister of Aurangzeb. At last he became the court-poet of Raja Devisingh of Murarmau, at whose persistence, he settled with his family at Daulatpur in Raibareli district, where his descendants still reside. Raja Jay Singh Gaur honoured him with the title of 'Kaviraj'. Mishra was the author of seven Riti works : *Vritta-Vichar*, *Rasa-Ratnakar*, *Chhand-Vichar*, *Fazl Ali Prakash*, *Rasarnav* (The Ocean of Rasa), *Shringar-Lata*, *Adhyatma Prakash* and *Dashrath Ray*. His best-known works, *Fazl Ali Prakash* and *Rasarnav* are devoted to an exposition of *Shringar* and contain some of the finest illustrations of this *Rasa* ; the treatment of prosody is particularly elaborate and successful. As a poet, Mishra seems to have been more successful than his contemporary, Kulpati Mishra (q.v.).

SUKH RAM (fl. 1940-47). Malwi poet, whose chief work is *Lalitadevi na Vyav* (The Marriage of Lalitadevi).

SUKH SAMPATIRAY BHANDARI (b. 1895). Rajasthani scholar, who was born at Jaitaran village in the then Jodhpur State. A great scholar of Sanskrit, Marathi and Gujarati, he had edited 'Shri Venkateshwar Samachar', etc. He was the author of some 20 works on various subjects, the chief ones being *Bharat ke Deshi Rajya* and *English-Hindi Scientific Dictionary*.

SUKH VIR SINGH GAHLOT. Modern Rajasthani scholar, who is noted for his *Rajasthani Krishi Kahavaten*.

SUKKHA SINGH. See *Mani Singh*.

SUKHI RAM (fl. early 20th cent.?). Popular Kauravi folk-poet, who was born at the village Syana in the Mahendragarh district of Haryana Pradesh. A Brahmin by caste, he was noted for his *Bhajans*.

SULTAN MAMA. Modern Malwi poet, who is noted for his stray poems.

SUMAN RAJE. Poetess, whose poems are included in the *Chautha Saptak* (q.v.) and *Bodh Kavitayen*. Her critical works are : *Sahityetihas* and *Sahityetihas Sanrachna aur Swarup*.

SUMAN VASISHTH. Poetess, whose *Abhi Abhi Nikle Hain Pankh* (The Feathers Have Grown Just Now ; 1979) is her first collection ; her poems are mostly about her family and her husband's poet-friends.

SUMANESH JOSHI. Modern Rajasthani poet, who tried to awaken socio-political consciousness through compositions and recitation of songs mostly based on the popular folk-tunes and styles. He has also composed patriotic and progressive poems.

SUMATI AIYER. Tamil-speaking modern Hindi writer, whose short stories have been published in various popular Hindi magazines ; *Ghatnachakra* is her collection of stories.

SUMATI HANS (fl. 1634). Rajasthani poet, who was the author of *Vinod Rasa*.

SUMATI TALUKDAR (1930). Assamese-speaking Hindi writer, who is noted for her essays and memoirs, published in the 'Rashtrasevak'. She has also tr. several works from Assamese into Hindi, the chief one being *Sahitya-Kala* by Nilmani.

SUMATINDRAN. Tamil-speaking modern Hindi poet, who is counted among the forceful progressive poets. His collection of poems, *Ek Pal ki Yad Men* (In the Memory of a Moment) contains poems of national fervour as also of social inequalities. Some of his poems are available in the collection : *Naye Git, Naye Swar* edited by Nand Kumar and in *Hindi ke Lokpriya Kavi*.

SUMER SINGH SHEKHAWAT. Rajasthani poet, whose *Meghmal* (1964 ; appears to be influenced by Kalidasa's *Meghaduta* in 108 verses depicts the beauty of the dense clouds in the rainy season. His other publication is *Marumangal* (1982), which contains one long poem and 31 smaller ones ; the longer poem, consisting of over 200 stanzas, is the name of the title.

SUMITRA KUMARI SINHA (1915-). Poetess, whose chief *Git* collections are : *Vihag*, *Asha-Parva*, *Panthini* and *Bolo ke Devta* ; her poems give a display of the variant moods of love. She has written short stories as also poem in Avadhi.

SUMITRA NANDAN PANT (1900-78). Chhayavadi poet, who was born at Kausani, a beauty spot of great fascination in Almora ; it was from his very childhood that he imbibed a deep love for Nature which is so clearly reflected in his poetry. He had education at Benares and Allahabad. *Uchchhvas* (Sighs) was his first poem. His poetical works are as under :—

Vina (The Lute ; 1918) is a collection of earlier poems, which bear testimony to the keenness of the poet's observation, the intensity of his feelings, and the new poetic diction and form ; traces of Tagore's influences are present.

Granthi (The Knot ; 1920) is a small narrative poem, dealing with the theme of love ; the various states of mind associated with love are beautifully depicted.

Pallav (The Sprout ; 1927) presents all the main features of Chhayavad poetry and the poems here made the poet famous ; Pant comes out as a mature poet and a master lyricist. It contains famous poems as 'Parivartan' (The Change), 'Ansu' (The Tears), 'Badal' (The Cloud), etc. The language is full of musical and pictorial effects and is wonderfully suggestive. Nature in all her beauty and variety is represented in the light of the changing thoughts and moods that she inspires. Some of the poems are full of mystic suggestions.

Gunjan (Buzzing ; 1932) and *Yugant* (End of the Age ; 1936). The poet's concern now is not so much with *Sundaram* or the beautiful as with *Shivam* or the common good. The change becomes more pronounced in *Yugant*.

Yugavani (The Voice of the Age ; 1939). The poet is attracted, for a while, by Communist ideology and becomes an ardent supporter of anti-imperialist struggle going on in India and elsewhere.

Gramya (Rurality ; 1940). From the urban life, the poet shifts his interest to the rural scene dotted with teeming millions ; rural life with its wants and difficulties is vividly presented. The poet dreams of a classless society, in which all will be equal, socially and economically. Pant, though fascinated by Marx, never became a Marxist in the true sense ; he drew his inspiration from Vivekanand, Dayanand, Ramakrishna Paramahans, Rabindranath Tagore and Mahatma Gandhi. After 1944, there is again a change in Pant.

Swarna-Kirana (The Gold-ray), *Swarna-Dhuli* (The Gold-dust), *Uttara* and *Manasi* (Worship in Mind ; 1944 onwards). The poet was influenced by the philosophy of Aurobindo and sought realization of eternal verities in the inner consciousness. There is a corresponding change in his diction, the old technique of Chhayavad seemed to be partly coming back.

Shilpi (The Artist; 1952), *Atima* (1955), and *Kala aur Budha Chand* (The Art and Old Moon ; a Sahitya Akademi Award winner).

Lokayatan (1964) earned the Soviet Land Nehru Award and was hailed as one of the most outstanding epic of the post-Independence era. Here Pant emerges as a thinker, a philosopher, a teacher and a humanist. He preaches that life, individual and collective, should be reconstructed for the evolution of mankind to a higher level. Here Aurobindo's influence on Pant is quite evident. At the same time, he decries economic inequality and considers that the real test of scientific progress is that it should establish a just and equitable order.

Chidambaram is Pant's latest collection ; most of the poems included in it are thought-provoking. These poems were selected by the poet himself out of his writings of the post-*Yugant* period. The collection has earned the Gyanpith Award in 1968. Its English tr. has been published by the Bharatiya Gyanpith.

Pant's other poetical works are *Muktiyagya, Satyakam, Gandhvithi* and *Git-Agit* (1977).

Other works : *Jyotsna* (Moonlight ; 1934), *Pari* (Fariy), *Krida, Rani, Rajat-shikhar* (The Silvery Summit ; dramas), *Har* (Garland ; novel), Hindi tr. of *Omar Khayyam's Rubaiyat, Panch Kahaniyan, Khadi ke Phul* (The Flowers of Khadi ; a poem on the assassination of Mahatma Gandhi), *Sath Varsh—Ek Rekhankan* (Sixty Years—A Sketch ; 1960 ; autobiography) and *Gadyapath* (criticism).

Sumitra Nandan Pant Granthavali has been published in 7 volumes.

Gifted with great poetic powers as he is, his lyrics will stand comparison with the creations of the greatest poets of the world. It was the love of Nature that burst forth in his earlier verses and Nature remained his guiding principle until he developed interest in the destiny of man as a member of society. The poet is without an equal in the use of graceful language ; no other poet has succeeded in endowing Khari

Boli with so much sweetness, tenderness and suggestiveness as Pant.

SUNDAR (fl. 1631). Poet of the Riti school, who was a native of Gwalior. He was the author of *Sundar Singar* (on poetics); two other works: *Barahmasa* and *Simhasan Battisi* are also ascribed to him. He had earned the titles of 'Kaviraj' and then 'Mahakaviraj' from Emperor Shahjahan.

SUNDAR (fl. 17th cent.). One of the court-poets of Guru Govind Singh (q.v.); he was a master of Brajbhasha and composed a eulogy of the Guru. He also wrote devotional poetry in the *Shringar* style.

SUNDAR. Hindi poet of Jammu, who was a contemporary of Dattu (1772-1844). He had composed 'Virat-parva' of the *Mahabharat* in *Dohas*, *Savaiyas* and other metres.

SUNDAR DAS (1596-1689). Saint-poet of Dyausa near Jaipur, who was a Khandelwal Mahajan. His father's name was Chokha, while his mother's was Sati. He became Dadu's disciple at the age of six. For thirty years, he made a thorough study of scriptures in Benares. A linguist, he had a command over Hindi, Panjabi, Gujarati, Marwari, Sanskrit and Persian languages and thus was well-versed in almost all the languages prevalent at the time in the north-west of India. He had travelled the whole of northern India and had direct contact with the people speaking different languages. His principal works are: *Sundar-Vilas*, *Dashon Dishaon ke Savaiya*, *Gyan Samudra* (The Ocean of Knowledge) and *Sundardas ke Pada* (The Padas). He was the only scholar-poet in the whole range of Hindi *Nirgun* poetry. Familiar with rhetoric, the metres which he chiefly employed were *Kavitta* and *Savaiya*. He also wrote *Chitra-Kavya*, *Chhatra-Kavya*, *Nag-Bandh*, etc. and made full use of figures of speech. His works are literary and sonorous; diction is refined. His *Suktis* are popular in all the *Rasas* save *Shringar*.

SUNDAR JHA SHASTRI. Modern Hindi poet of Nepal, who is noted for his work *Parvashta*.

SUNDAR (SUNDARI) KUNVARIBAI (1734-*c.* 96). Poetess of Nimbark Sect, who was daughter of Maharaja Rajsingh of Kishengarh in Rajasthan and was a sister of Nagaridas, the famous Bhakta-poet. Due to the war of successon among her brothers, she could be married only at the age of 31 to Prince Balvant Singh of Raghaugarh. She composed 11 works

(*Neh-Nidhi*, *Mitra-Shiksha*, etc.) in Brajbhasha mostly on Krishna devotion. Her poetry is permeated with love and devotion.

STNDAR LAL GARG. Modern Rajasthani writer, who is noted for his short story collection : *Panphul* and the novel : *Abhagini*.

SUNDAR LAL SHARMA. Chhattisgarhi writer, whose *Dan-Lila* (1924) became so popular in Chhattisgarh region that several works in its style such as *Nag-Lila* and *Bhut-Lila* were written.

SUNDAR REDDY, G. (1919-). Telugu-speaking Hindi writer, whose chief works are : *Hindi aur Telugu—Ek Tulnatmak Adhyayan* (A Comparative Study of Hindi and Telugu ; 1966 ; research), *Shodh aur Bodh* (ed., 1974), *Hindi Sahitya ke Vikas men Dakshin ka Yogdan* (Contribution of South in the Development of Hindi Literature ; ed., 1975), *Hindi tatha Dravid Bhashaon ke Samanrupi Bhinnarth Shabda* (as co-writer) and *Dakshin ki Bhashayen aur Unka Sahitya* (Languages of the South and their Literature). His essay collections are : *Sahitya aur Samaj* (1954), *Mere Vichar* (1960) and *Vaichariki* (1971).

SUNDAR SAKHI (fl. 18th cent.). Poet of the Krishna-cult (Haridasi Sect), who is noted for his *Padas*, dealing with the marriage of Krishna and Radha.

SUNDARAM (1907-). Gujarati poet, whose spiritual realization has found expression sometimes through the medium of Hindi poems. His three to four Hindi poems have been published.

SUNDARAM, NA. Tamil-speaking modern Hindi scholar, whose chief work *Mira aur Andal ka Tulnatmak Adhyayan* (A Comparative Study of Mira and Andal ; 1971) discusses the two devotees of Krishna. He has also tr. into Hindi the poems of Subrahmanya Bharati's poems under the title : *Subrahmanya Bharati ki Rashtriya Kavitayen* (The National Poems of Bharati) as also Varadrajan's Tamil novel under the title : *Koyale ka Tukra* (A Piece of Coal).

SUNDARI UTTAMCHANDANI. Sindhi-speaking modern Hindi novelist, who is noted for her novel, *Rekha*.

SUNIL KAUSHIK. Writer, whose short story collection : *Band Darvaze* (The Closed Doors ; 1980) mainly deals with family ties ; his other short story collections are *Nim ki Pattiyan* and *Andhere ka Sailab.*

SUNITA. Novel (1936) by Jainendra Kumar (q.v.), which is considered to be one of his major novels.

Shrikant lives with his wife Sunita and though she is beautiful and accomplished, he does not feel fulfilled in his life. One day, he brings home his revolutionary friend, Hari Prasann and asks his wife to look after him. Attracted towards Sunita, Hari Prasann insists on her joining the revolutionary movement and though she does not like the proposal, she goes with him into the forest, where he declares his love for her and wants to have her. Sunita gets extremely agitated and starts taking off her clothes. But as soon as she does so, he retracts. He takes Sunita home and then disappears and Sunita resumes her happy married life with her husband.

The psychoanalytical powers of the author find their proper expression in this novel.

SUNITA BAI. Malayalam-speaking modern Hindi scholar, whose chief work is *Dwapar—Ek Vishleshan* (The Analytical Study of Dwapar).

SUNITA JAIN. Poetess, whose chief collections of poems are : *Ho Jane do Mukta* (Let Me be Free ; 1978), *Kaunsa Akash* (Which Sky ? ; 1979) and *Ek aur Din* (One more Day ; 1983). As a fiction writer, her works are *Bindu. Ham Safar, Ham Mohre Din Rat Ke* and *Itne Barson Bad.* She has published her Hindi poems and short stories in English as well.

SUR CHAND (fl. 1583). Rajasthani poet, whose stray verses in popular metres are available.

SUR DAS (1478-1583). Celebrated poet of the Krishna-cult and the greatest one of the *Ashtachhap.* In popularity, he is almost equal to that of Tulsidas (q.v.), the greatest Hindi poet. He was born in the village Sihi, two miles from Ballabhgarh (not far from Delhi). His father, Ramdas was a Saraswat Brahmin, though this view is contradicted by Dhirendra Verma. At the age of eight, Surdas accompanied his parents on a pilgrimage to Mathura ; from there he did not return and his parents had to leave him in the guardianship of a mendicant. He settled himself at Gaughat on the road that linked up Mathura and Agra. There on the banks of the Yamuna he led the life of an ascetic devotee with a number of disciples. He met Vallabhacharya in 1509-10 at Gaughat, who asked him to sing about the *Lilas* (Divine Sports) of Lord Krishna. He composed new songs every-day and sang them in the temple of Shrinath. He is said to have composed 1,00,000 *Padas* but all that is extant is available in *Sur Sagar*. There Surdas spent the rest of his life and died in the village Parsauli at the foot of the Govardhan.

In the *Sahitya Lahari* (The Wavelets of Literature), Surdas mentions that he was a Brahmabhatt and a direct descendant of Chand Vardai, the author of the *Prithwiraj Raso* (q.v.). Some scholars regard this fact as interpolation by some poet of a later date. He also mentions that he was the youngest of seven brothers ; the first six fell in battles against Muslims but the youngest was spared for his being born blind. Surdas wandered about alone and one day fell into a well from which, it is said, he was taken out on the 7th day by Krishna himself. Krishna granted him eye-sight and the devotee feasted his eyes with the beatific vision. But he prayed to Krishna that he might again lose his sight since he preferred not to see anything else. It is also popular that in his youth, he fell in love with a damsel and regarding this to be the fault of his eyes, he branded them. But it is almost definite that he was not born blind since the dainty touches of colour and the apt descriptions of natural scenes cannot come from the mind of a born-blind.

Surdas is reputed to be the author of 5 works but his fame as a poet mainly depends on his monumental work, *Sur-Sagar* (The Ocean of Surdas ; q.v.). His other two great works are *Sursagar Saravali* (Essence of *Sursagar*) and *Sahitya Lahari* (qq.v.) ; his *Nal-Damayanti* and *Vyahala* have not yet been discovered. He has also written some *Drishtikuts* that are like puzzles to be solved by the ingenious.

The scope of Surdas's poetry is limited, for it is preoccupied only with the childhood and youthful love of Krishna. In this Surdas differs from Tulsidas, whose hero, Ram lives a full life. But in its own limited range, the poetry of Surdas is full of endless variety. The infancy of Krishna, the pranks of his childhood are described very minutely and no effort is spared in bringing out the sweetness and waggishness of early years. Similarly, the love of Krishna and Gopis, their love chase, the Ras on the banks of Yamuna in the moonlit nights and particularly the love of Radha and Krishna are protrayed in charming verses. But Surdas is a pastmaster in depicting the pangs of separation which the Gopis felt when Krishna migrated to Mathura. When Krishna sent Uddhav to console the Gopis, he was overwhelmed by the Gopis with queries, taunts and pleasantries. The debate between the Gopis and Uddhav on the *Sagun* and *Nirgun* modes of worship is embodied in the *Bhramargit*. The verses of separation reveal Surdas at his best.

Surdas wrote in literary Brajbhasha and seems to have transformed it into something noble and graceful. He avoids colloquial forms and by adding expressions from Sanskrit or even Avadhi gives dignity to Brajbhasha. Surdas chose certain episodes from Krishna's life and composed at length on them to illustrate the philosophy of the "Path of Divine Grace". In the field of child pyschology, Surdas stands unsurpassed. There are also elaborate descriptions of the beauty of Krishna and Radha to the minutest details right from the toe-nail to the tuft of hair on the top. The two *Rasas*. which Surdas depicted with great success and mastery are the *Vatsalya* and *Shringar*. Surdas's genius is essentially lyrical and as a lyrical poet he is in the line of Jayadev and Vidyapati, with whom he is common in depicting a sensuous love of beauty and excessive melodiousness.

Surdas's *Padas* have appeared in selections in Russian.

SUR DAS. Sufi poet, who composed his *Nal-Daman*, discovered recently. He was son of Gobardhan Das and originally belonged to Kalanaur in Gurdaspur district but had settled in Lucknow. His *Nal-Daman*, composed in 1657, is based on the story of Nal and Damyanti as narrated in the *Mahabharat*. The work has been edited and published by Hindi Vidyapith, Agra University.

SUR DAS MADAN MOHAN (fl. 1543). Poet of the Krishna-cult (Chaitanya Sect), whose collections of stray verses are extant. He is said to have spent a sum of 13 lakh rupees of Government in the service of the monks and then came to reside at Vrindavan as a devotee of Krishna.

SUR DATT. Riti poet of Kashi, who at the instance of Krishna Chandra, son of Ray Manohar of Amarsar (Shekhawati), composed in 1659 his *Rasik Hulas*, a work on *Rasa*.

SUR KISHORE (fl. 1703-4). Poet of the Ram-cult (Rasik Sect), who was born in Jaipur. When his Guru, Madhuracharya (q.v.) left Galta for Chitrakut, he himself made his departure for Sikar. He considered Sita as his daughter and finally settled in Mithila, where he established a seat of the Rasik Sect. He composed *Mithila Vilas*, of which *Mithila Mahatmya* is a portion.

SUR SAGAR (The Ocean of Surdas). Work by Surdas (q.v.), composed in *c.* 1530, which, according to tradition, had a hundred and a quarter thousand verses. The number of verses in existence is, however, 4,132. The work, like the

Bhagavat-purana, on which it is based, is divided into 12 Skandhs.

Sursagar, in its present form, is a reproduction of the contents of the *Bhagavata-purana*, but the two agree only in the barest outline ; the author enlarging or compressing, omitting or adding as suits his purpose. Though all the 24 incarnations of Vishnu, as mentioned in the *Bhagavata*, have been described here, more than three-fourth of the space is given to Krishna. The 10th canto, treating of the story of Krishna, is larger than all the rest of the cantos put together and even then it does not contain a full life-portrait of Krishna. One thousand verses are on Krishna's childhood ; the rest are on Krishna's amours with Gopis and in Krishna's absence, their pangs of separation. Surdas thus only chose certain episodes from the life of Krishna and wrote copiously on them to illustrate the philosophy of the "Path of Divine Grace".

As a matter of fact, *Sursagar* is a collection of *Padas*, which were sung at the time of *Kirtans* in the Shrinath Mandir. Several versions of the work are available, but the one published by the Nagari Pracharini Sabha, Kashi is considered authentic.

SUR SAGAR SARAVALI (Essence of *Sursagar*). Work by Surdas (q.v.). composed in *c.* 1550. It covers briefly and in a more discursive manner the same ground as the *Sursagar* (q.v.).

SUR SINGHJI RI VELI. See *Gadan Cholo Mehawat.*

SURAJ. Hindi poet of Surinam, whose *Meri Avaz* (1982) is a poetical collection.

SURAJ BHAN. Writer, whose chief novel : *Khemkaran ki Lal Rekha* (The Bloody Battle-front of Khemkaran ; 1970) describes the bravery of Vinod in the Indo-Pakistan War.

SURAJ BHAN SINGH (1936-). Scholar, who has published *Hindi Bhasha ki Pathyapustak* (2 Pts., 1980, 1981) for use in Romania. He also taught Hindi in Bucharest University, Romania. His earlier publication was *Bilingual Conversational Guide Hindi-English* (1973).

SURAJ MAL. See *Suryamall Mishran.*

SURAJ PRAKAS. Rajasthani narrative poem by Karanidan Vijayramaut (q.v.), which consists of 7,500 couplets. It describes the battle of Ahmedabad, which Maharaja Abhaysingh of Jodhpur fought against Sar Bulandkhan, the Governor of Gujarat in 1730. About half of the poem is devoted to an account of Rathore dynasty linking it on mythological and historical basis with the story of Ram as narrated in Valmiki's epic. The poem is dominated by heroic sentiments and is replete with descriptions of warriors and battles, their abodes at different heavenly places after death, their marriages with celestial damsels, etc. A classical poem of the Charan style, it is encyclopaedic in nature.

SURAJ RAM PANDIT. Poet, whose *Jaimini Puran Bhasha* (1748), composed in *Dohas* and *Chaupais* and running into 36 chapters, treats of the stories of Yudhishthir's *Rajsuya-Yagya, Ramayan*, abandonment of Sita, battle of Lav-Kush, Mayurdhwaj, Chandrahas, etc.

SURAJ SHARAN SHARMA 'SARJUJAN' (fl. 1904-28). Poet of Kanpur, who was the author of two works : *Piyapany* and *Rumal-Shatak* (a *centum* of verses on handkerchief).

SURAJ SOLANKI. Modern Rajasthani poet, whose chief work is *Juni Vatan*.

SURAT-BAHAR (fl. 1832). Two Sufi poets (Surat and Bahar) of Hyderabad, Sind (now in Pakistan), who jointly composed poems on Krishna.

SURAT RAM (d. 1818). Rajasthani saint-poet of Ram Snehi Sampraday, Shahpura, whose stray verses are available.

SURATI MISHRA. Poet of the Riti school, who was a Kanyakubja Brahmin of Agra. He was the author of *Alankar-Mala* (1709) and *Amar Chandrika* (a commentary on *Bihari Satsai* ; 1734). He had access to a nobleman, named Nasarulla Khan and to the court of Muhammad Shah. He wrote commentaries on *Kavipriya* and *Rasikpriya* too ; all his commentaries are in Brajbhasha prose. He also tr. into Brajbhasha prose *Vetala Panchavinshati* ; his other Riti works are : *Rasaratna Mala, Saras Rasa, Rasa Grahak Chandrika, Nakhshikh, Kavya Siddhant* and *Rasa Ratnakar*. The *Alankar-Mala* is composed after the fashion of *Bhasha Bhushna* (q.v.). None of his works is extant ; Ramchandra Shukla in his *Hindi Sahitya ka Itihas* has quoted a *Padya*, which displays his refined literary taste.

SURENDRA. Novelist, whose chief work is *Vasnamayi* (Full of Passions ; 1967), a novel.

SURENDRA ANCHAL. Modern Rajasthani writer, whose *Ragat*

ek Minakh Ro, a collection of one-act plays, treats of social reforms. His short story collection in Khari Boli is *Tukre-Tukre*.

Surenra Arora (1940-), Writer, whose chief works are: *Admi, Abnus, Kali Roshni* (short story collections) and *Akahani* (Anti-story ; 1967).

Surendra Barlinge (1919-). Scholar, whose Marathi work has been tr. into Hindi by Manohar Kale as : *Saundarya-Tattva aur Kavya Siddhant* (1963). He had been Professor and Head of the Department of Philosophy, University of Poona, Pune.

Surendra Doshi. Gujarati-speaking modern Hindi scholar, whose *Bhagvati Prasad Vajpeyi ka Katha Sahitya* is a research work.

Surendra Jha 'Suman' (1910-). Maithili writer and poet, who, under the pseudonyms of 'Kashyap', 'Madhukar' and 'Dwireph' has published short story collections : *Kala-ka Puruskar, Madhushravani* and *Brihaspati-ka Shekh*. He has also ed. *Kathamukhi*, a short story selection. His epic *Uttara* on the wife of Arjun's son, Abhimanyu (based on the *Mahabharat*) and *Alankar Shastra* have been published during 1980. His *Chandicharyya* (1963), a *Khandkavya*, is on the deeds of Durga, while *Ritu Shringar* (1964) is virtually based on Kalidasa's poem, *Ritu-Samhara*. His collections of poems are : *Pratipada, Saon Bhadon, Archana* (1950) and *Payaswini* (1969). He has also written critical articles.

Surendra Kumar Tiwari. Writer, whose chief works are : *Ek aur Raja* (One More King ; drama ; 1980), *Isi Shahr Men* (In this very City ; 1982) and *Mil ka Pahla Patthar* (short story collections).

Surendra Nath Verma. Modern Hindi writer of Mauritius, who is noted for his *Pravasi Sahitya* (ed.).

Surendra Pal (1932-). Writer, whose chief work *Lok-Laj Khoi* (Without Care for Public Opinion ; 1963) is a novel.

Surendra Pandey. Modern Bhojpuri poet, who is known for his stray poems.

Surendra Prasad 'Tarun'. Modern Magahi poet, whose

poems are noted for descriptions of Nature.

SURENDRA VERMA. Dramatist, whose chief plays are : *Draupadi*, *Setubandh* (Construction of the Bridge), *Nayak, Khalnayak, Vidushak* (The Hero, the Villain and the Clown), *Surya ki Antim Kiran se Surya ki Pahali Kiran Tak* (From the last Ray of the Sun to the first Ray of the Sun), *Athvan Sarg* (The Eighth Canto), *Nind Kyon Rat Bhar Nahin Ati, Tin Natak, Chhote Saiyad Bade Saiyad* (Younger Saiyad Elder Saiyad) ; *Pyar ki Baten tatha anya Kahaniyan* (Love Talks and Other Stories) and *Kitna Sundar Joda* are his short story collections, while *Aswikrit Surya* (1976) is a poetical collection. *Andhere se Pare* is his novel.

SURESH. Panjabi-speaking modern Hindi poet, whose chief poetical works are : *Ankur* (A Sprout) and *Praval* (Corals).

SURESH CHAND GUPTA (1933-). Writer, whose chief works are : *Adhunik Hindi Kaviyon ke Kavya-Siddhant* and *Hindi Sahitya ka Itihas* (History of Hindi Literature ; ed. with Nagendra).

SURESH CHANDRA TRIVEDI (1931-). Gujarati-speaking modern Hindi scholar, whose chief works are : *Gujarati Sahitya ka Navin Itihas, Gujarati Santon ki Hindi Vani* (ed.) and *Auchitya Siddhant aur Hindi ka Riti-Kavya* (research). He is at present working in the Sardar Patel Vishwavidyalaya, Vallabh Vidyanagar.

SURESH DUBE 'SARAS'. Modern Magahi poet, whose songs are inspired by the folk-life and culture.

SURESH KUMAR. Modern scholar, whose chief works are : *Shaili Vigyan* and *Shaili Vigyan aur Premchand ki Bhasha*.

SURESH NANDA. Oriya-speaking modern Hindi writer, whose works are available in Hindi as well as Oriya.

SURESH NIRAV. Writer, who has ed. *Athwen Dashak ki Vyangya Kavita* (The Satirical Poetry of the Eighth Decade ; 1980) ; the compilation contains poems of Lakshmimal Sindhavi, Sher Jang Garg, Dinkar Sonvalkar, Manik Verma, Sarojini Pritam, etc.

SURESH PRASAD SINHA. Modern Magahi writer, who is noted for his short stories.

SURESH RAMBARAN. Modern Hindi writer of Mauritius, who

is known for his work *Chacha Ramgoolam ke Sansmaran.*

SURESH RITUPARNA (1948-). Poet, whose collection of poems is *Akeli Gauraiya Dekh* (See 0 Lonely Girl ; 1980).

SURESH SETH. Writer, whose *Sonjuhi Bimar Hai* (Sonjuhi is Ill ; 1980) is a collection of five one-act radio plays. His novel is *Shahr Vahi Hai*, while his short story collection is *Jina Marna.*

SURESH SHARMA. See *Rajendra Kumar Sharma.*

SURESH SINHA (1940-73). Writer, whose chief novels are : *Ek aur Ajnabi* (One More Stranger ; 1961), *Subah Andhere Path Par* (1967 ; on the clash of values of two generations), *Pattharon ka Shahr* (City of Stones ; 1971 ; description of the changing life of a middle class family) ; *Nai Kahani ki Mul Sanvedana* is another work on short story (criticism), published by him. His important short story is 'Halat' (The Plight), his collection of stories being *Kai Avazon ke Bich.* On novel, he wrote a critical work, *Hindi Upanyas.*

SURJAN DAS PUNIYA (1583-1691). Rajasthani saint-poet of the village Bhiyansar (Phalaudi), who was renowned for his deep learning and saintliness. He is known as a poet of the *Chhappay* metre, for he composed some 400 *Chhappays* mostly devotional. His narrative poems are : *Katha Hari Gun* (192 verses in praise of God in various ways), *Katha Usha Puran* (232 verses, describing the romance of Usha and Aniruddha ; here the legendary battle between Krishna and Shiv is described as between a Kshatriya and a Yogi). *Katha Gajmokh* (69 verses, on the liberation of *Gaj* from the clutches of *Grah*) and *Ram Raso* (176 verses ; on the story of Ram, beginning from Shurpanakha's marriage proposal to Ram in exile). In the last poem, a few incidents are unusual : for example, Hanuman disguises himself as a he-cat, while searching for Sita in Lanka and that Lakshman swoons twice, first from the bite of a snake sent by Varahi Devi from 'Patal' after the death of Mahiravan and the second by a hit from Ravan.

A follower of the Vishnoi Sect, his *Katha Chetan, Chitavani* and *Dharm-Chari* are religious poems, recommending good deeds to get rid of the cycle of re-birth. *Katha Autar Ki* and *Katha Prasiddha* narrate in brief the story of Jambhoji, the founder of the Vishnoi Sect. *Gyan Mahatam* and *Gyan Tilk* are allegories, where the body is likened to a fort and different instincts have been presented as human characters. His other poems on miscellaneous topics are *Sakhis, Dingal Gits, Harjas,*

Sakhi Ang Chetan, Das Avtar Duha, Asmedh Jag ka Duha, Chhand, Kaviita, Kavitta-Bavni, Savaiya, etc.

A representative poet of the 17th century, his poetry, in easy and literary Rajasthani, is an attempt towards the elevation of humanity to higher planes of consciousness. He has also contributed to all the major trends of Rajasthani poetry.

SURJAN PAROHI. Modern Hindi poet of Surinam, whose *Mohini* (1975) is a collection of poems. Popular among poetial symposia, he writes in a satirical vein as also glorifies the rich cultural heritage.

SURJAN SINGH SHEKHAWAT. Modern Rajasthani poet, who has paid poetic homage to the heroes, who sacrificed their lives in fighting against the Chinese attack on India.

SUROVA, YELYENA YURYEVNA (1951-). Soviet Hindi scholar, whose chief study is on Gurudatt's novels.

SURTAN GUN VARNAN. Rajasthani poem, which was composed by Pattaji Asiya in 1715. It describes the deeds of Rawat Chauhan Surtansingh of Bedala (Mewar).

SURYA BALA. Writer, who is noted for her fiction works : *Subah ke Intazar Tak* (Wait Till Morning ; 1980), *Dishahin Main* and *Indradhanush Zubeda ke Nam.*

SURYA DEV SIVRAT. Modern Hindi poet and writer of Mauritius, who is noted for his poems and short stories.

SURYA KANT (d. 1983). Hindi and Sanskrit writer, whose chief works in Hindi are : *Hindi Sahitya ka Vivechanatmak Itihas* (Descriptive History of Hindi Literature ; 1931), *Hindi Sahitya ki Ruparekha* (Outlines of Hindi Literature) and *Sahitya Mimansa.*

SURYA KANT JHA 'KAMAL'. Maithili poet, whose *Tapaswi* (1948) is a patriotic *Khandkavya.*

SURYA KANT TRIPATHI 'NIRALA' (1896-1961). Celebrated *Chhayavadi* Hindi poet, who was born in Mednipur (Bengal) and is said to have written his first poem in Bengali at the age of 9. Nirala's forefathers had migrated to Bengal, but his wife hailed from Uttar Pradesh and she persuaded him to write in Hindi. Besides English and Sanskrit, Nirala acquired a good knowledge of Bengali literature. His early acquaintance with Advaita philosophy and his knowledge of Bengali literature have profoundly affected the quality of his poetry. He also ed. the 'Matwala' from Calcutta and the 'Samanvaya', a magazine published by Ramakrishna Mission.

Nirala, as his pen-name suggests, combined in his personality almost irreconcilable elements. He had the cold logic of a philosopher but the fathomless faith of a mystic. In his personal life, he was spartan, yet he melted before the suffering of even a scoundrel. Despite his mysticism, he was always conscious of the sordid realities of Indian surroundings and always fought for the underdog.

Nirala was at once a poet, a seer, a singer and a warrior. Throughout his life, he had to struggle with himself, his surroundings, his fate and his struggle with a hostile and uncharitable world. For about two decades, Hindi critics and litterateurs mocked him for his free and unconventional ways and indeed Nirala was nothing if not a rebel and non-conformist.

For the first time, Nirala introduced into Hindi free and unrhymed verse. These free verse lines were bound by rhythm and nothing else, so that they moved with much greater freedom than was admitted by rules of the classical prosody. His *Juhi ki Kali* (1916) was composed in this style. Acknowledged as one of the pioneers of the *Chhayavad* school in Hindi poetry, he never forgot humanity, which was struggling against the tyranny of man, Nature and fate. Even while doting on Nature, he sang passionately of freedom, truth and justice. He could write in terse and apparently abstruse language, but has also written some of the most lucid and charming poems on village life, on seasons, on flowers and such homely subjects, which have enchanted the rustic, the labourer, the village maiden and the school lad alike.

Apart from works of poetry, Nirala has written in prose. His chief works are as under :

Poetry : *Anamika* (Without Name) ; the first small collection of verses, which earned for him the wrath of many who were intolerant of any departure from the beaten track ; it contains important poems : 'Samrat Ashtam Edward ke Prati' (on abdication of Edward VIII in favour of love), 'Saroj Smriti' (after the death of his wife Saroj), 'Ram ki Shaktipuja' ; it later appeared in 1937 in an enlarged edition, *Parimal* (The Fragrance ; 1929 ; considered as the best collection), *Gitika* (1936 ; compilation of musical songs), *Tulsidas* (a beautiful poem on the saint), *Kukurmutta* (Mushroom ; 1942 ; progressive poems), *Anima* (Minuteness), *Vela* (Time), *Naye*

Patte (New Leaves ; 1946), *Archana* (Worship ; 1952), *Apara* (Worldly Wisdom), *Aradhana* (Devotion ; 1960), *Gitgunj*, *Sandhya Kakli*, etc. His most outstanding achievement is *Ram ki Shakti Puja* (1936), a long poem in less than 300 lines, which could be compared with the best in any poetry. A collection of his unpublished poems : *Asankalit Kavitayen* has been published in 1981, though these had appeared in different periodicals from time to time. But they (with the exception of two poems from his first anthology *Anamika*) have been published in this anthology for the first time.

Novels : *Apsara* (The Nymph), *Alaka*, *Prabhavati*, *Nirupama*, *Uchchhrinkhal*, *Choti ki Pakad*, *Kale Karname* (Black Deeds) and *Chameli* ; all these novels display revolt against decadent social traditions.

Other Works : *Lili*, *Sakhi*, *Chaturi Chamar*, *Sukul ki Bibi* (short story collections), *Kulli Bhat* (almost an autobiography), *Billesur Bakariha* (Billesur, the Goatherd ; 1945 ; sketches), *Prabandh-Padya*, *Prabandh-Pratibha*, *Prabandh-Parichaya*, *Ravindra-Kavita-Kanan*, *Chayan*, *Chabuk*, *Sangrah* (critical essay collections), *Rana Pratap*, *Bhim*. *Prahlad*, *Dhruv*, *Shakuntala* (biographies) and *Panchvati Prasang* (Incident at Panchvati, poetic play).

Translations : *Mahabharat*, *Shri Ramakrishna-Vachanamrit* (4 Pts.), *Parivrajak Swami Vivekanand ke Bhashan*, *Devi Chaudhrani*, *Anand Math* , *Chandrashekhar*, *Krishnakant ka Will*, *Durgesh Nandini*, *Rajni*, *Yugalanguliya*, *Radharani*, *Tulsi Ramayan's Tika* and *Vatsyayana Kamasutra*. Nirala's letters have been edited by Janaki Vallabh Shastri under the title : *Nirala ke Patra* (Letters of Nirala).

Nirala's complete works have been published as *Nirala Rachnavali* (8 vols.).

SURYA KARAN PARIK (1902-39). Rajasthani writer, who was Vice-Principal of Birla College, Pilani. He edited *Veli Kisan Rukmani Ri*, *Dhola Maru ra Duha*, *Chhand Rao Jaitsi Ri*, etc. A pioneer in the study of Rajasthani folk-songs, he edited *Rajasthan ke Lokgit* (2 vols.) and *Rajasthan ke Gram Git* and did much work on Rajasthani *Vat* literature. His *Bolavan* or *Pratigya Purti*, a one-act play, depicts the Rajput trait of keeping a pledge even at the cost of life. He espoused the cause of Rajasthani and had worked on mediaeval Rajasthani literature. See *Ramsingh*.

SURYA KUMAR JOSHI (1920-80). Novelist, whose chief work : *Digambari* (1957) describes the unusual sex-hunger of Sadasha; his other novel is *Surya Grahan*.

SURYA MALL MISHRAN (Suraj Mal ; 1815-68). Rajasthani poet, who is considered to be the last great scholar and poet of the Charan style in the modern times. Born in Bundi, he was son of Chandidan. He had six wives, but could get no son from any one of them. Accordingly, he adopted Muraridan (q.v.) as his son. At the instance of his patron, Maharao Ramsingh of Bundi (1811-89), Suryamall started writing the *Vansh Bhaskar* (q.v.) in 1840, which is encyclopaedic in character ; it describes the history of the Bundi State and is considered the *Mahabharat* of Rajasthani. The next great work of the poet is *Vir Satsai* (q.v.), which was composed during and after the 1857 Mutiny ; the poet's implicit intention seems to have been to arouse the dormant Rajput chivalry. *Ram Ranjat* (145 verses) and *Balvant Vilas* (584 verses) are the poet's narrative poems on Maharao Ramsingh of Bundi and Raja Balvant Singh of Bhinay respectively. *Ram Ranjat* was composed in 1825, when Suryamall was a ten-year lad. His *Dhatu Rupavali* is a work of no great merit. *Chhandomayukh* on metrics and *Sati Raso*, also attributed to him, are not extant.

Regarded as the greatest Dingal poet of *Vir Rasa*, Suryamall had a great impact on contemporary Rajasthani poetry.

SURYA NARAYAN, G. Telugu-speaking Hindi scholar, who is noted for his *Hindi-Telugu Kosh* (Dictionary; 1950).

SURYA NARAYAN, RAPARTI. Telugu-speaking Hindi poet, whose chief works are : *Yojangandha* (1961) and *Tarkeshwar Mahima* (incomplete).

SURYA NARAYAN 'BHANU', P. Telugu-speaking modern Hindi poet, whose *Rup Rag* is influenced by the philosophy of Abhinavgupta. He has also tr. the famous Telugu poems under the titles : *Adhunik Telugu Kavyadhara* (Modern Telugu Poetry) and *Telugu ke Lok-priya Kavi* (The Popular Poets of Telugu ; 1972).

SURYA NARYAN MURTI, CHAVALI, THE LATE. Telugu-speaking modern Hindi poet and dramatist, who is the author of *Sati Urmila* (1961) on the neglected Urmila, the wife of Lakshman. His dramatical works are : *Mahanash ki Or* (Towards Complete Annihilation ; on the story of the Pandavas), *Satyamev Jayate* (on Raja Harishchandra) and *Samjhauta* (The Truce ; a social drama). His research publication is *Hindi aur Telugu ke Madhyakalin Ram Sahityon ka Tulnatmak*

Adhyayan (A Comparative Study of Mediaeval Ram literature of Hindi and Telugu ; 1975).

SURYA NARAYAN VYAS. Modern Malwi poet, who tr. *Meghaduta* from Sanskrit original into Malwi.

SURYA NATH GOP. Modern Hindi writer of Nepal, who is noted for his essays.

SURYA PAL (alias Hind Lal). Modern Hindi poet of Fiji, who has composed some 500-600 *Phag* poems.

SURYA PRAKASH VIDYALANKAR (1946-). Scholar, whose chief work on modern Hindi poetry is : *Saptak-Tray—Adhunikta aur Parampara* (Saptak-Tray—Modernity and Tradition ; 1980). He has also made a rendering in Hindi verse of *Sankhya Karika* from the original Sanskrit.

SURYA PRASAD MANGAR BHAGAT. Modern Hindi scholar of Mauritius, who has been Secretary of the Hindi Pracharini Sabha, Mauritius. He also edited 'Janta' and 'Jan Jivan' for years. His family members, particularly Girdhari Bhagat, Lekhman Bhagat, Ramlal Bhagat and Brajendra Bhagat during the last 60 years have been instrumental in promoting the cause of Hindi Pracharini Sabha.

SURYA PRASAD VIRE SHURVIR. Modern Hindi writer of Surinam, whose chief work is : *Nadipur ki Kahani.* Shurvir and Meno Marenkha have written a long short story : *Lakshmi ka Desh.* Shurvir is the Secretary of the Surinam Hindi Parishad.

SURYA SHANKAR PARIK. Rajasthani poet of Bikaner, whose chief works are : *Dharti* (1976 ; award-winning volume of poetry on the rural Rajasthan life), *Siddha Jasnathji ro Sirloko* (1977 ; a biography of Sant Jasnathji in 354 verses), *Siddha Raj* (a versified story of Rustamji, an ascetic of Jasnathi Sect) and many patriotic, heroic, Nature and progressive poems : 'Disat ra Minakh', etc. He has also edited the text of *Siddha Charit*.

SUSHIL JHA. Maithili writer, who has tr. Ganganath Jha's *Autobiography* from English into Maithili (1980). His novel *Gambali* (1982) is the story of a village lady, who liberates herself from the bondage of caste.

SUSHIL KALRA. Writer, who is noted for his satirical writings :

Chamche ka Dhakkan (The Lid of a Spoon ; 1980) and *Nikka Nimana* (1984).

SUSHIL KUMAR. Modern scholar, who is the author of *Himachal ke Hindi Sahitya ka Itihas* ; he has also written short stories.

SUTHRA DAS. Saint-poet of Allahabad and the founder of the Suthra Sect. He was a disciple of Malukdas (1574-1682) and was the author of *Maluk-Parichay* (Introduction to Malukdas).

SUZUKI, YOSHIAKI. Modern Japanese Hindi scholar, who is the editor of 'Jwalamukh', a literary magazine in Hindi, published from Japan. He has also done research, especially on *Sursagar*.

SVETKOV, YURI VASILYEVICH (1928-). Soviet Hindi scholar, who did his doctorate in 1971 on the poetry of Surdas. His field of specialization is the poetry of Surdas, Tulsidas, Rahim, Vidyapati, Bachchan, Sumitranandan Pant, etc.

SWADESH BHARATI. Poet, whose poems are included in the *Chautha Saptak* (q.v.) ; 'O Kavita' (O Poetry) and 'O Calcutta' (O Calcutta) are his poems. He has also written a novel, *Auratnama*.

SWAMI, N.D. See *Narottam Das Swami*.

SWAMI HARIDASJI KI PARCHI. See *Raghunath Das*.

SWAPNESHWAR DAS. Modern Oriya writer, who has tr. Jayshankar Prasad's *Kamayani* from Hindi into Oriya.

SWARNA-DHULI. See *Sumitra Nandan Pant*.

SWARNA-KIRAN. See *Sumitra Nandan Pant*.

SWARNA LATA AGRAWAL. Modern Rajasthani scholar, who has made significant contribution to the study of folk-songs. Her chief work is *Rajasthani Lok-Git*. She has also written a novel : *Bikhre Suman*.

SWARNA MAHANT. Assamese-speaking modern Hindi writer, who is noted for his memoirs and reportages.

SWARUP DAS (1801-63). Rajasthani poet, who was a follower of Dadu Sect and was a scholar of Sanskrit, Rajasthani, Pingal and Hindu Religion. Son of Charan Mishridan, he enjoyed respect in the courts of the Rajas of Ratlam and Sitamau; Crown Prince Ratnasingh of Sitamau held the poet in the highest esteem.

Out of his twelve works, *Hrinnayananjan*, *Rasa Ratnakar*, *Pakhand Khandan*, *Varnarth Manjari*, *Drishtant Dipika*, *Vritti Bodh*, *Chijjad Bodh Patrika*, *Sukshmopadesh*, *Tark Prabandh*, *Sadharanopadesh*, *Avivek Paddhati* and *Pandav Yashendu Chandrika* or *Ukti Chandrika*, the last one is the best and most popular. It is mainly a summary in verse of the *Mahabharat* in 16 sections, mostly in Braj mixed with Rajasthani.

SWATI TIRUNAL RAMVARMA (1813-49). State official of Travancore State in Kerala, who was an able administrator and a lover of arts. He was also called 'Garbh Shriman'. He composed *Gits* not only in Malayalam, his mother tongue, but in Sanskrit, Marathi and Hindi as well. The number of songs he composed in Hindi is 37 and they are on Krishna, Ram, Shankar, Devi, etc. The language is influenced by Braj. His songs are popular to this day among the singers of the south India.

SYAMANT-HARAN. Maithili drama, which represents how Krishna takes away the jewel known as Syamant Mani after subjugating Jambuvan, and ultimately marries Jambuvati, the latter's daughter. The drama was written by an unknown Assamese writer, a disciple of Shankardev.

SYED PAHAR (fl. 1883). Muslim poet of Kashi, who composed *Rasa Ratnabhar*, An Ayurved work. In the beginning of his work, he has made an obeisance to Alakh Niranjan and Mohammed.

T

TAHAL SINGH. Hindi writer of Panjab, whose *Alankar Sagar Sudha* (1733) is a Riti work, discussing figures of speech.

TAHIR (TAHAR). See *Ahmed*.

TAHKAM. One of the Hindi court-poets of Guru Govind Singh (1666-1708); he composed *Jaiminiya Ashwamedh* and *Amar Kosh*.

TAJ (fl. 1644). Muslim poetess of the Krishna-cult, whose love for Krishna is reminiscent of Mirabai's devotion. Her verses, 200 in number, have almost the same depth, fire and sharpness : she dotes on Krishna and yearns for him. Her language is a mixture of Brajbhasha, Panjabi, Urdu, Khari Boli and Sanskrit.

TAKAHASHI, AKIRA (1953-). Japanese Hindi scholar, who is at present Lecturer in the Hindi Department of Osaka University of Foreign Studies, Osaka. His chief work is : *Mulla Wajhi-Krit Sabrasa ki Dakkhini ka Bhasha-Vishleshan* (1983).

TAMASKAR, GO DA. Marathi-speaking modern Hindi writer, who is noted for his biography : *Shivaji* and *Brihad Marathi-Hindi Shabdakosh* and *Brihad Hindi-Marathi Shabdakosh* (the last two in collaboration with Shriphad Joshi).

TAMIL SAHITYA. A collection of articles by scholars of various periods of Tamil literature, which has been published by the Dakshin Bharat Hindi Prachar Sabha, Madras.

TANAKA, OTOYA. Modern Japanese Hindi scholar, who, in collaboration with Teiji Sakata, has written : *Bharatiya Sahitya—Dev Yug se Aj Tak, Ek Sankshipta Parichay* (2nd edition, 1977).

TANAKA, TOSHIO. Modern Japanese Hindi scholar, who is at present Head of the Hindi Studies in the Tokyo University of

Foreign Studies. He studied Hindi at the Delhi University from 1965 to 1976. His special field of study is modern Hindi literature and he has written articles on Agyey, Ugra, Hindi literature at the time of India's partition, Rahi Masoom Raza, Munshi Navalkishore, Yashpal, Rahul Sankrityayan, Hazari Prasad Dwivedi, etc.

TANGAPPAN, E. Tamil-speaking modern Hindi writer, who is the author of *Vir Pandiya Kattbomman*, a biography meant for children.

TANKMANI AMMA. Malayalam-speaking modern Hindi writer, whose research work is *Malayalam ke Khand-Kavya*.

TANSEN (fl. 16th cent.). A *Nava-ratna* (one of the nine gems) of Akbar's court, who was a celebrated musician. In Hindi, some *Padas* have been ascribed to him.

TANTRA NATH JHA (1909-). Maithili poet, whose *Kichak-Badh* (q.v.; 1938-61), written under the influence of Michael Madhusudan's bold experiment of introducing blank verse, treats of the killing of Kichak by Bhim; the work is based on the *Mahabharat*. His *Ekanki-Chayanika* is a collection of one-act plays. His humour is of a subtle and sophisticated type and his plays are quite popular on the stage. His essay entitled *Hamara Theng* tries to imitate the genial smile and frolicsome humour of Charles Lamb in Maithili prose. His lyrics have been collected in *Namasya* (1968) and *Mangal Panchashik* (1974).

TAR SAPTAK (The Sharp Septet). Anthology of *Nai Kavita*, published in 1943 and edited by Agyey (q.v.). It contains select poems of Agyey, Gajanan Muktibodh, Nemichand, Bharat Bhushan Agrawal, Prabhakar Machwe, Girija Kumar Mathur and Ram Vilas Sharma. According to these poets, the poet's foremost task is to look for self-fulfilment and develop his own personality and the quest for personality led the writers of *Nai Kavita* to call themselves Experimentalists. These poets have made experiments not only with forms and metres, words and phrases but also with subject. Poets of this school have completely freed themselves of the limitations of metre and language ; as regards subject, the ugliest and the most beautiful objects have similar, almost equal, poetic potentiality. The new poet 'is a stark realist and believing in a liberated personlity as he does, he is anxious to seek direct avenues for expression of so-called suppressed urges.

of man lying embeded in the sub-consciouness. And in his attempt to do so, he often takes pride in consciously breaking up the bonds of restraint enjoined by tradition and culture. Obviously, under the Freudian influence, he has given pictures of love, which are mostly fleshy and sensual in a language that would often appear to the puritan bordering on the indelicate, if not obscene'. See *Dusra Saptak*, *Tisra Saptak*, *Chautha Saptak*.

TARA BEHAN SANT. Gujarati-speaking modern Hindi scholar, whose *Hindi ki Gadya Lekhikayen* is a research work.

TARA CHAND OJHA. Modern Rajasthani scholar, whose chief work is *Marwari Stri-Git Sangrah*.

TARA CHAND VYAS (fl. 18th cent. ?). Rajasthani poet of Bilada, who in his *Ai Ugra Prakash* tells in a lucid and easy Rajasthani the story of Aiji (q.v.), with a brief history of the Ai Panth.

TARA CHARAN JHA. Modern Maithili scholar, who is noted for his work, *Prachin O Arvachin Vidwan*.

TARA DATT GAIROLA. Garhwali poet, who composed a *Khand-Kavya Sadei* (1924) on the style of folk-songs of 'Sadei'. His *Phyunli Ranteli* and *Jhumailo* are refined versions of folk-songs and have been quite popular. He was the author in prose of *Himalayan Folk-lore* (1935), which is a collection of Garhwali heroic tales.

TARA KANT PRAKASH. Modern Maithili poet, who is noted for his poems and lyrics.

TARA NATH. Kannada-speaking Hindi writer, whose drama: *Dinbandhu Kabir* (1926) was staged before Mahatma Gandhi. Tara Nath was a great scholar of Karnataka and his drama greatly advanced the cause of Hindi as several dramas were written on the model of his drama.

TARA PANDE (1914-). Poetess, whose chief works are: *Sikar* (Drizzle), *Shuk Pik*, *Venuki* (Flute Pipe), *Antarangini*, *Abha* (Lustre), *Pavas* (Rainy Season); *Vallaki* (Lute), *Bhav Gandha* (poetical collections) and *Utsarga* (short story collection); her love feeling is tender, soft and touching.

TARA VISHNU DAYAL SINGH USHA, MRS. Modern Hindi poetess of Trinidad, who is noted for her stray poems.

TARINI CHARAN DAS. Oriya-speaking modern Hindi writer, whose chief works are : *Kala aur Sahitya* (Art and Literature ; criticism), some poems and essays.

TARINI CHARAN MITRA. Bengali scholar, who was Head Munshi of the Hindustani Department of Fort William College from 1810 to 1830. He edited *Vaital Pachisi* and got it published.

TARKESHWAR BHARATI. Modern Magahi writer, who is noted for his short stories.

TARUN AZAD DEKA (1929-). Assamese-speaking Hindi writer, who is known for his dramas, broadcast from various centres of All India Radio. His chief dramas are : *Kavach* (The Armour ; awarded by the Government of India), *Insan*, (The Man). *Kamrup*, *Mirabai*, *Rani Durgavati*, *Rukmini*. He has tr. hundreds of Assamese dramas into Hindi. He has also written in Hindi a history of Assam.

TARUN PRABH SURI. Jain Rajasthani writer, whose *Shadavashyak Balavbodh* (1354) provides good examples of creative and mature prose.

TATA KRISHNA GAIROLA (fl. early 20th cent.). Garhwali poet, who is noted for his *Premi Pathik*, a *Khand-Kavya*, based on love and marriage.

TATWAVETTA (Tikamdas; fl. early 16th cent.). Rajasthani saint-poet, who is said to be a disciple of Parshuram Dev Acharya. His main seat was at Jaitaran (Pali) and continues up to this time. There he founded the Gopal Dwara, where a collection of his poems called *Tatwavettaji ki Vani* is said to have been preserved in the manuscript form. In another manuscript at Udaipur, *Tatwavetta ra Savaiya,* about 198 *Chhappays* are available. The works treat of mythological and religious topics. The language is Rajasthani mixed with Braj.

TAU HARYANVI. Modern Haryanvi folk-poet, who is noted for his *Tau ke Tir*.

TAYLOR, CAPT. J. Author of *A Dictionary—Hindoostanee and English* (2 vols., Calcutta, 1808).

TEDHE MEDHE RASTE. See *Bhagvati Charan Verma*.

TEG ALI (fl. early 20th cent.). Poet of Varanasi, who was the author of *Badmash Darpan* (The Mirror of a Rogue) in Western Bhojpuri.

TEJ K. BHATIA. Modern scholar, who has written several articles on the scope of negation in Hindi.

TEJ NATH JHA. Modern Maithili writer, whose essays are serious and thoughtful and attempt to give a reasoned account of some problems of Indian thought.

TEJ SINGH JODHA. Rajasthani poet, whose chief work is *Olun ri Olyan* (1970 ; 157 verses) ; he has also composed poems in the style of Nayi Kavita.

TEJA LOK KAVYA. Rajasthani ballad, which describes the heroism of Tejoji, a Jat of Dholya branch of village Kharual (Nagore), who gave up his life for the protection of cows and for the sake of his word. He is worshipped as a folk-deity. *Tejaji* is another such ballad.

TEJAJI. See *Teja Lok Kavya*.

TEJOJI CHARAN (1423-1518). Rajasthani poet, who wrote devotional verses, decrying the prevalent social evils. He was one of the saints of the Vishnoi tradition, who composed stray verses on miscellaneous topics.

TEKHAN (fl. 17th cent). One of the court-poets of Guru Govind Singh (q.v.) ; he was a Hindi and Sanskrit scholar. He rendered into Hindi the *Ashvamedh parva* of the *Mahabharata*, but as he was a soldier, he is at his best when describing battle scenes or giving expression to the sentiment of war.

TELANG, BHAL CHANDRA RAO. See *Bhal Chandra Rao Telang*.

TEMDAS (fl. end of 18th cent.). Rajasthani saint-poet of Ram Snehi Sampraday, Ren, whose *Vani* consists of stray verses in popular metres.

TESSITORI, LUGI PIO (1887-1919). Scholar of Italy, who did his doctorate from the Florence University on the 'Comparative Study of *Ramcharitmans* and *Valmiki Ramayan*' in 1910; this was published in 1911. His *Notes on the Grammar of the Old Western Rajasthani with special reference to Apabhransh and Gujarati and Marwari* were published in the 'Indian Antiquary', Calcutta (1914-16). He prepared three *Descriptive Cata-*

logues of Bardic and Historical Manuscripts : (1) Prose Chronicles of Jodhpur (1917), (2) of Bikaner (1918) and (3) Bardic Poetry, Bikaner (1918). He prepared four *Reports on the Bardic and Historical Survey of Rajputana* (with several appendices; 1916-19), which were published in the 'Journal of Royal Asiatic Society, Calcutta'. He edited the poems : *Veli Krisan Rukmani Ri* (1919) by Prithwiraj Rathore, *Vachnika Rathore Ratansinghji Ri* (1917) by Khidiya Jagga and *Chhand Rau Jaitasi Rau* by Vithu Sujo Nagarajot.

Tessitori came to India in 1914 and continued his work till his death in 1919 at Bikaner. Shrilal Nathmal Joshi in his *Dhoran ro Dhori* (1968) presents Tessitory as a man of inexhaustible energy and lofty ideals.

TEUNRA, BHAI (fl. 19th cent.). Sindhi saint-poet of Sagun school, whose stray verses in Hindi are available.

TEZA, E. Author of *Dei Primi studi sulle lingue indostaniche. Alle note di G.A. Grierson nota del socio* (Rome, 1895).

THAKUR. There have been three Hindi poets of this name; their poems too are sometimes inextricably mixed up. For further details, see *Thakur I*, *Thakur II*, and *Thakur Bundelkhandi*.

THAKUR I, OF ASNI (fl. 1643). Poet ; little is known about him except that some stray verses composed by him are extant.

THAKUR II, of ASNI (fl. *c.* 1803). Poet, who was son of Rishinath (q.v.) and the grandfather of Sevak (q.v.). He was patronized by Devakinandan, a relative of the Raja of Kashi. He composed *Satsai Barnarth* (1804), a commentary on Bihari's *Satsai*. He named his commentary as *Devakinandan Tika*, also on the name of his patron. His poetry is charming and there is a flow in description.

THAKUR BUNDELKHANDI (1766-1823). Poet, whose family belonged originally to Oudh but his father settled down in Bundelkhand where Thakur was born at Orchha. Thakur's full name was Thakurdas. After Thakur's education, he lived in the court of Raja Parichhit of Jaitpur, where he was much honoured. Bhagvan Din edited his poems under the title of *Thakur-Thasak*, but it also contains poems of the other two Thakurs. There are also a number of stray poems by the poet.

Thakur had an independent character and his poetry reveals his strong character. He is also essentially a lover and his emotions are powerful and their expression is direct and forceful. He criticised poetry written in conventional style and advocated freedom in poetic treatment ; his own poetry bears the stamp of his principles. Thakur was quite popular in his life-time, largely because of his simple style and the variety of themes. He occasionally went to the Durbar of Himmat Bahadur of Banda, where he had poetic skirmishes with Padmakar (q.v.).

THAKUR DAS (Thakuriya ; fl. 17th cent.). Rajasthani saint-poet of Laldasi Sampraday, whose *Bhajans* extol devotion to Ram and Guru and advocate a simple life.

THAKUR DAS, MAHARAJ (fl. 19th cent.). Sindhi saint-poet of *Sagun* school, whose stray verses in Hindi are available.

THAKUR DATT PANDEY. Hindi poet of Mauritius, whose collections of poems are : *Nisha* and *Shraddhanjali* (for children); his *Dipavali* is a poem. *Panch Ekanki aur Ek Sapna* is a collection of his one-act plays.

THAKUR, K.N (fl. *c.* 1930). Maithili writer, whose chief work, *Darde-dil-ka Saukh* is a short story collection.

THAKUR PRASAD SINGH (1924-). Poet, whose *Mahamanav* (Great Man), a *Prabandh-Kavya*, is based on the life of Mahatma Gandhi; *Vanshi aur Badal* is a collection of his songs, wherein he has derived inspiration and joy from Nature. He has also written some satirical essays, short stories and a novel: *Adim*.

THAKKURSI (fl. 1523-26). Poet, whose, *Panchendriya Bel*, a didactic work, has been written in *Dohas*.

THAN KAVI. Poet of the Riti school, whose full name was Than Ray. He was son of a sister of Chandan (q.v.), a Hindi poet and lived in Daundiyakhere in the Raebareli district of Uttar Pradesh. His *Dalel Prakash* (1801), a Riti work, is named after Dalel Singh, a rich man of Chandra Vaiswara ; it is a work of high merit.

THEBAN, LAURENTIU. Modern Romanian Hindi scholar, who taught Hindi in the Bucharest University, Romania.

THIEL-HORSTMANN, MONIKA (1941-), German scholar of Hindi, who is at present Professor of Indian Studies, Rheinische

Friedrich-Wilhelms-Universitat, Bonn. Her publications are : *Sadani : A Bhojpuri Dialect in Chhotanagpur* (Bihar) (Wiesbaden, 1969), *Sadani-Lieder. Studien zu einer nordindischen Volkslied-Literatur* (Wiesbaden, 1978), *Crossing the Ocean af Existence. Braj Religious Poetry from Rajasthan. A Reader* (Wiesbaden, 1983), ed. of *Bhakti in Current Research* (Proceedings of the Second International Conference on Early Devotional Literature in New Indo-Aryan Languages ; Berlin, 1983). Author of over a dozen articles, including on Dadu, her field of research is Middle Hindi and Bhakti Literature of Dadupanth.

THIMM, C.A. Author of *Hindustani Self-taught* (London, 1902).

THOMPSON, REV. J.T. Author of *A Dictionary in Oordoo and English, etc*, (Serampore, 1838) and *Hindi and English Dictionary* (Delhi, 1856). Thompson was of the view that the Arabian Hindoostanee, which has grown up at Calcutta under the fostering care of Government and is spoken by the Moonshees of the College of Fort William and the Moulvees and students of the Mohammedan College, is quite a different language from that which prevails in any other part of India.

THULIBHADDA (*Sthulibhadra*) *PHAG*. Rajasthani poem by Jin Padma Suri, which was composed in 1333. A small poem of 27 verses, it is based on a critical incident in the Jain ascetic Sthulibhadra's life.

Sthulibhadra, son of a minister named Shaktar of king Nand of Magadh, falls in love with a beautiful courtesan Koshya and remains with her for 12 long years. In the meantime, due to court intrigues, his innocent father is killed, but the son cannot meet the dying father. This proves to be a turning point in his life. He decides to renounce the world and takes initiation from Acharya Sambhuti Vijay. To test his self-restraint, he spends four months at the house of Koshya but with all her allurements, he subdues his passions. Ultimately, she is also initiated and follows him.

TIKA RAM SHARMA. Modern Garhwali poet, who is noted for his collections of poems : *Garh Ganjar Vatika* and *Maletha ki Kul*.

TIKKANEN, BERTIL (1949-). Modern Finnish Hindi scholar, who is a part-time Lecturer in Hindi-Urdu in the Helsinki University. He has already tr. Prem Chand's *Godan* into French and is at present preparing a Finnish version of it. He has also prepared Hindi-Urdu grammars in Finnish.

TIPPANACHARYA (fl. 18th cent.). Kannada-speaking Hindi poet, who was a follower of Madhva Sect. Besides his two works in Kannada, his third work is composed in five languages. His *Shrikrishna Lila* contains 20 Hindi verses in various metres.

TIPPESWAMI 'PUNIT'. Kannada-speaking modern Hindi critic, whose *Samagam* is a collection of his 11 critical and comparative studies. The 5 essays on comparative studies treat of the Kannada and Hindi poets, e.g., Purandardas, Tulsidas, Surdas, Kabir, Allamprabhu, etc., while the remaining essays treat of modern Kannada literature. He has tr. some Kannada poems and with Bhalchandra Jayshetti tr. U.R. Anantamurti's novel, *Bharatipur* into Hindi. He also tr. into Hindi the Kannada stories of U.R. Anantmurti, Krishna Alanhalli and K.P. Purnachandra 'Tejaswi', some Kannada essays and sketches of Ha. Ma. Nayak, H S.K. and M. Ramarao.

TIRTH RAM (fl. early 16th cent.). Poet of the Krishna-cult (Chaitanya Sect), who was a Brahmin of Marwar. Under the influence of Ramay (q.v.), he left his home and came to settle in Vrindavan. His works are : *Dravya-Dosh, Tyag-Turni, Shri Harilila, Rasikacharya Charcha* and *Brajvas.*

TISRA SAPTAK (Tar Saptak 3 or the Third Septet). Anthology of Nai Kavita, published in 1959 and edited by Agyey (q.v.). It contains select poems of Prayag Narain Tripathi, Madan Vatsyayan, Kedar Nath Singh, Kunwar Narain, Vijaydev Narain Sahi, Sarweshwar Dayal Saxena and Kirti Chaudhari. See *Tar Saptak.*

TITLI. Novel (1934) by Jayshankar Prasad (q.v.), which presents a realistic picture of farmers' lives and the problems and conflicts faced by them. The author projects the basic pull of the conjugal life in the perspective of Indian and Western conjugal lives.

Mudhuban, representative of a great family, now in distress, owns only the ruins of Sherkot. Baba Ramnath teaches among others Madhuban and Titli, an orphan, brought up by the Baba. Madhuban's widowed sister wants Titli to be married to Indradev, but she fails and Titli is married to Madhuban. Indradev, the ruler of Dhampur State, goes to England and brings with him Shella, who was the daughter of Warley, a very cruel indigo planter in India. Indradev wishes to marry Shella but his mother is opposed to the proposal.

At the instigation of the Tehsildar of Dhampur State, it is proposed to levy land revenue on the land gifted to Ramnath

Indradev is, however, liberal in outlook and a bank and a hospital are established in Sherkot. The Tehsildar, Chaube and other officials perpetrate atrocities on the poor. In the end, Indradev almost renounces all his authority. Shella gradually extricates herself from their circle. She loves Indradev but she cannot make him her own as she is likely to lose her freedom. A distance develops between them and Shella, willingly or unwilling, is inclined towards Watson. To maintain her freedom, she opens a hospital and a bank, but she feels some kind of void within herself.

Titli, though an ordinary girl, blooms into a woman, whose qualities are enviable. After getting a son, she turns into a full mature woman. Madhuban deserts her and she suffers pangs of separation as also economic hardships, but her self-respect does not allow her to ask anyone for help. Titli is thus a living symbol of Indian womanhood.

TIWARI, BHOLA NATH. See *Bhola Nath Tiwari.*

TIWARI, UDAY NARAYAN. See *Uday Narayan Tiwari.*

TOD, JAMES, COLONEL. Author of *Annals and Antiquities of Rajasthan* (1829), which is a monumental history of Rajasthan. The valour and glorious life of Rajput warriors and their women described in this work, inculcated a spirit of national pride among the Indian people.

TODAR MAL (fl. 16th cent.). A *Nav-Ratna* (one of the nine gems) of Akbar's court, who, besides, being a Hindi writer, was a great patron of Hindi. Some stray verses, ascribed to him, are available.

TOSHNIDHI (fl. *c.* 1735). Poet of the Riti school, who lived in the village Shringverpur (Singraur) in Allahabad district. He composed the *Sudhanidhi* (1734), a book of more than 500 verses, dealing with *Rasa* and *Bhav.* His other two works are *Vinãy-Shatak* and *Nakhshikh.* Toshnidhi's poetry is of high order and some of his verses are often quoted and recited. His mind is sensitive but his descriptions sometimes are highly exaggerated.

TOTA RAM VERMA (1847-1902). Writer of Aligarh, who set up a big printing press for bringing out his Hindi weekly, 'Bharat Bandhu'. He knew Sanskrit, English, Marathi, Gujarati and Bengali languages and tr. good many works from them, notably *Katokritant* (from English *Cato*) and Valmiki's *Ramayana* (from

Sanskrit ; incomplete). His other works are : *Kirtiketu* (drama) and *Stri-Subobhini.* He founded at Aligarh the Bhasha Sanvardhini Sabha, which did commendable work for propagating the Hindi language and the Devnagari script in Urdu-ridden western Uttar Pradesh. Totaram came under Dayanand's influence and was of reformist ideas.

TOTA RAM SANADHYA (1876-1948). Celebrated writer of Fiji, who was born at the village Hirango near Firozabad in Uttar Pradesh. Due to abject poverty, he left home at the age of 17 and was sent to Fiji as a coolie. The first five years of his life were spent under the oppressive and brutal treatment of British officers. He was in direct correspondence with Mahatma Gandhi about the sad plight of the 'coolies' in Fiji. He was noted for his works : *Fiji Dwip men Mere Ikkis Varsh*, *Bhut Lane ki Katha* and *Fiji ki Samasya.* His first work was so popular that its Gujarati, Marathi and Bengali translations appeared very soon. Its English tr. was done by C.F. Andrews and he himself took it to Fiji. His fourth book : *Fiji men Mainne Kya Dekha* remains unpublished. Mahatma Gandhi paid tributes on his wife's death in 1932 as also on his death in 1948.

TRIBHUVAN DIPAK PRABANDH. Rajasthani poem by a Jain poet, Rajshekhar Suri (fl. 14th cent.), which is an allegory. In this narrative poem, which is in lucid style, different instincts have been presented as various human characters and ultimately the good ones have victory over the vicious ones. The poem is interspersed with verses.

The Soul Sovereign (*Atma*) trapped by a young beautiful woman Illusion (*Maya*) is made a prisoner in the body-city (*Kayanagari*). His minister, Mind (*Man*) becomes all-powerful. He marries two women, Attachment (*Pravritti*) and Liberation (*Nivritti*) and has two sons, Ḍelusion (*Moh*) and Wisdom (*Vivek*) from them respectively. Delusion captures the city but his step-brother Wisdom, with the help of his two wives, Restraint (*Samyamshri*) and Good Sense (*Sumati*), defeats him and re-thrones the Soul Sovereign.

TRIBHUVAN SINGH. Writer, who is noted for his *Adhunik Hindi Sahitya Nibandh* (Modern Hindi Literary Essays ; 1982).

TRIKAM DAS (fl. 1734). Vaishnav poet of Junagarh, Gujarat, whose Hindi works are *Dakor-Lila*, *Rukmini-Haran* and some 160 stray *Padas.* He had a good command over Brajbhasha.

TRILOCHAN (b. 1267). Saint-poet of Maharashtra, who had

close relations with Namdev (q.v.). Three of Trilochan's *Padas* are included in the *Granth Sahib* (q.v.).

TRILOCHAN PANDEY. Modern scholar, where chief work is *Kumaoni Lok Sahitya ki Prishthbhumi.*

TRILOCHAN SHASTRI (1917-). Poet, whose chief poetical collections are : *Dharti* (The Earth), *Gulab aur Bulbul* (The Rose and the Nightingale; a collection of his Ghazals), *Digant* (The Horizon ; 1957 ; a collection of his sonnets). *Tap ke Taye Huye Din* (The Melted Days ; 1980) and *Shabda* (Words ; 1980), etc. His *Us Janpad ka Kavi Hun* (I am a Poet of that Region ; 1981) contains his sonnets written over a span of 30 years, though very few of them were published earlier.

TRILOK GOYAL. Modern poet, who has composed lyrical poems, portraying various aspects of Nature ; he also composed patriotic, heroic and love poems. His poems have been collected in *Trilok Goyal ki Kavitayen.*

TRILOK NATH MISHRA (fl. 1st half of 20th cent.). Maithili dramatist, who was noted for his *Jimut-Vahan-Natak.*

TRILOK SHARMA. Modern Rajasthani poet, who has composed progressive poems.

TRILOKI NARAYAN DIKSHIT (1920-76). Modern writer, whose chief works are : *Avadhi aur Uska Sahitya* (Avadhi and its Literature) and *Hindi Sant Sahitya.*

TRILOKI NATH GANJU (1931-). Kashmiri-speaking Hindi writer, who holds a doctorate on the Origin and Development of Kashmiri Language (written in Hindi). His articles also appear in the 'Prakash', 'Kashyap', 'Vitasta', etc. He has tried to establish that Kashmiri language is derived from the Vedic Sanskrit.

TRINATH MISHRA. See *Jagbandhu Mahapatra.*

TRIPATHI, RAM NARESH. See *Ram Naresh Tripathi.*

TRIPTI NARAYAN LAL. Maithili writer, who is noted for his social drama, *Sappat* (1967).

TRISHUK (1983). Anothology, which contains the poems of

three young poets : Vasant Pandey, Kamini Bhatnagar and Ashwini.

TRIVEDI, KALIDAS. See *Kalidas Trivedi.*

TRIVIKRAMANAND (1759-1819). Saint-poet of Gujarat, who was a native of Jambsur and was initiated by Raghavanand. He had a good knowledge of Braj, Urdu, Sanskrit, Hindi and Gujarati ; his stray verses are available.

TRIYA VINOD. Poem (1706) of Murli (q.v.), which describes the imaginary romance of a characterless lady.

TRUBNIKOVA, SVETLANA VICTOROVNA (1936-). Soviet Hindi scholar, whose field of specialization is the poetry of Dinkar and is noted for tr. into Russian the stories and novels of Yashpal, Amritlal Nagar, etc.

TSEHRA, IRONA, MRS. Modern German Hindi scholar, who has edited *Moderne Hindi Lyrik*, an anthology of Hindi lyrics.

TUKARAM (1598-1649). Saint-poet of Maharashtra, who composed some 100 *Padas* in Hindi as well ; some of his Hindi *Abhangs* have been discovered along with Marathi *Abhangs.* His Hindi is influenced by Marathi.

TUKDOJI MAHARAJ, SANT (1909-68). Marathi-speaking Hindi saint-poet, whose poems are in line of the traditional religious poetry but at the same time are permeated with modern national and social life. His *Gram Gita* is an important work.

TUL PATI SINGH (fl. early 20th cent.). Maithili novelist, whose *Madan-Raj-Charit Upanyas* (incomplete) is one of the earliest long narratives.

TULSI ACHARYA (1914-). Ninth Acharya of Tarapanth (Shwetambar) Sect and a Rajasthani poet, who has revived the tradition of *Charit Kavya* by composing in Rajasthani *Manak Mahima, Dalim Charitra, Kalu Yashovilas* (in over 500 pages) and *Magan Charitra.* They deal with the lives, works and preachings respectively of Manak Gani, Dal Gani, Kalu Gani (the 6th, 7th and 8th Acharyas) and Muni Maganlal of Terapanth. The language is is easy and the style simple.

TULSIDAS. The greatest Hindi poet, whose *magnum opus* is *Ramcharitmanas* (q.v.). According to Dr Grierson and the

Manas-Mayank (an old commentary on the *Ramcharitmanas*), Tulsidas was born in 1532 but the *Gosain Charitra* places this date as 1497. Yet, according to another work, the *Shiv Singh Saroj*, he was born in about 1526. The *Tulsi Charitra* and the *Shiv Singh Saroj* mention Tulsi's birth-place as Rajapur in the Banda district in Uttar Pradesh. Ram Naresh Tripathi is, however, of the view that Tulsi was born at Shukarkshetra (Soron) near Chitrakut. It is now believed that Tulsi was born in Soron and later on he shifted to Rajapur. The Banda Gazetteer also states that Rajapur was founded by Tulsidas, the saint of Soron. Moreover, the descendants of Nanddas, the brother (?) of Tulsidas, reside to this day in the village of Soron. Tulsi's original name was Rambola (so called, because the first word he uttered in his infancy was Ram); his father's name was Atma Ram and mother's Hulsi. Born in a Saryupari family, his mother died when he was very young and his father handed him over to the maid-servant, Muniya, regarding him as an inauspicious child. Muniya took him to her father-in-law's house but when Tulsi was five years old, Muniya also died. A message was sent to Atmaram in Rajapur to bring the child back but he refused to own the child. Baba Narharidas, who happened to pass by Muniya's village, Haripur, took pity on the vagrant child and took him away with him. The child was christened 'Tulsidas'. Here Tulsidas received his first lessons in the devotion to Ram from his preceptor. When Tulsi grew older, he was taken by Narharidas to the Panchganga Ghat at Benares and was introduced to the great scholar, Shesh Sanatan. Shesh Sanatan accepted him as his disciple and taught him the Vedas and the Purans. After 15 years, the teacher died and Tulsidas returned to Rajapur. On his return to Rajapur, he found his house in a dilapidated condition. Any way, at Rajapur, he began to preach the *Bhakti* of Ram. Dinbandhu Pathak, who lived in a village across the Yamuna, was very much impressed by the scholarship of Tulsidas and married his daughter, Ratnavali to him. Ratnavali was very charming and beautiful and Tulsidas was much enamoured of her. Once, when Ratnavali had gone to her father's house, Tulsidas felt the pangs of separation terribly and with a view to meeting her, swam across the Yamuna in its full spate at the dead of night. It is said that Ratnavali scolded him for his extreme infatuation for her, so that he renounced mundane interests and dedicated himself exclusively to the devotion to Ram. After his disillusionment, he took up his abode at Benares. There he spent the greater part of his life, visiting frequently Ayodhya, Mathura, Vridavan, Kurukshetra, Chitrakut, Prayag, Jagannathpuri, Rameshwaram, etc. He made his pilgrimage as far as to Badarikashram, Kailas and Manasarovar. It is said that he met Surdas and Mira (qq.v.), and that at Mathura-Vrindavan, he had a meeting with his brother Nanddas (q.v.). In his vagrancy, he is said to have met his wife but nothing could lead him astray from his path. He commenced writing the *Ramcharitmanas* at Ayodhya, but a fairly large portion of the poem was composed at Benares. He died at Benares near the confluence of the Ganges and Asi in 1623.

37 formal works have been attributed to Tulsidas in the Inquiry Report of the Nagari Pracharini Sabha, Kashi. Twelve of these have been regarded as authentic and have been published by the aforesaid Sabha, entitled as "Tulsi Granthavali". Ram Ghulam Dwivedi has also regarded these 12 works composed by Tulsidas ; these are : *Ramcharitmanas* (*Lake of Rama's Deeds*). *Ramlala Nahachhu*, *Vairagya Sandipini*, *Barvai Ramayan*, *Parvati Mangal*, *Janaki Mangal*, *Ramagya Prashnavali*, *Dohavali*, *Hanuman Bahuk*, *Kavitavali*, *Gitavali*, *Shrikrishna Gitavali and Vinaypatrika* (qq. v.). The *Shiv Singh Saroj* mentions, however, 10 more works as authentic ; out of these, some are not even extant. The *Hanuman Bahuk*, according to Ram Ghulam, has been considered as forming a part of *Kavitavali*. Some scholars consider certain portions of *Ram-Satsai* as genuinely composed by Tulsidas. His chief works, however, are : *Ramcharitmanas* and several other compositions based on *Ramayana* (like *Gitavali*, *Kavitavali* and *Vinay Patrika*).

Nabhadas and Beni Madhavdas, two of Tulsidas's contemporaries, wrote his biographical sketches in their *Bhaktamal* and *Gasain Charita*; Priyadas prepared a glossary of the enigmatic verses of the *Bhaktamal* in 1712. Another account of Tulsidas can be found in the *Tulsi Charit* of Raghubardas, whose time is uncertain. All these biographies contain much apocryphal matter and furnish scanty information about the poet's life.

Tulsidas tried the various modes and forms of poetic compositions that were in vogue in his times. He transformed the colloquial Avadhi used by Jayasi with something more dignified and refined. Likewise, Brajbhasha acquired distinction when used by him. He skilfully employed *Kavitta*, *Savaiya*, *Doha* and *Chaupai* metres and tried his hands at *Chhappai* and *Barvai*. According to Mishra Bandhu, Tulsidas was "endowed with keen perception, a great sweep, power of sustained effort, strong common sense, insight into human nature, complete mastery over the language, forceful expression, admirable flow and grace, subtle wit and humour, deep religious fervour in widest range of observation. His characters are alive. His similes, metaphors, *Utprekshas*, eulogies of Ram, description of nature, are without parallel, especially in his *Ayodhya-kand*. His works are easily understood, yet full of deep significance and beauty, piously religious in their import, yet touching every aspect of life's values. Tens of thousands of Hindus read the *Ramayan* daily and constantly turn to his other works." Tulsidas is free from any intolerance or traces of conflict between different ideologies. He seeks to reconcile in his poetry the Ram-cult and Shiv-cult, the rival paths of *Karma* and *Gyan*, the asceticism and domestic life.

Tulsidas's chief message is devotion to Ram : *Janm Janm Rati Ram Pada.*

Tulsidas has been translated into French, Russian, Italian German and English (three translations by Hill, Growse and Atkins are in English alone).

TULSIDAS. Riti poet, who composed in 1654 his *Rasa Kallol*, a work on *Rasa*.

TULSIDAS. Poem (1938) by Suryakant Tripathi 'Nirala' (q.v.) on the famous Hindi poet Tulsidas, which describes how he engaged himself in creative activity after he had burnt his sexual desire at the scolding of his wife, Ratnavali. The poet seems to suggest that sexual abstinence is necessary for creative activity.

TULSIDAS BHATIA. Modern writer, who is noted for his drama *Maryada* (Limits of Propriety).

TULSI JAYRAMAN, MRS. Tamil-speaking modern Hindi poetess, whose some 35 poems are scattered in various magazines ; her chief poems are 'Hindi ki Bindi', 'Pratiksha' (Wait) and 'Sagar ki Laharen' (The Waves of Ocean). Along with P. Jayraman, she has written the biography of Subrahmanya Bharati for children.

TULSI RAM SHARMA 'DINESH' (1896-1956). Poet, who was born at Kaisu in Bhiwani district of Haryana. His chief works are : *Purushottam Mahakavya*, *Shyam Satsai* and *Mangal men Dangal* (drama).

TULSI SAHIB (b. 1788). Learned poet-saint and founder of the Ava Panth. He spent his whole life in Hathras (near Aligarh) and considered himself as an incarnation of Tulsidas, the celebrated author of the *Ramcharitmanas* Among his devotional works : *Ghat Ramayan*, *Shabdavali* and *Ratnasagar*, the second one is the most popular.

TULSIDAS (fl. 16th cent.). Rajasthani saint-poet, who was a

follower of Haridas Niranjani Sampraday. A contemporary of Haridas (q.v.) himself, he and Sevadas (q.v.) are well-known for the large number of their compositions. Tulsi's poems consist of *Sakhis* divided into 200 topics, 461 *Padas* (on mystic experiences) and stray verses on miscellaneous topics concerning the Nirgun Bhakti. His expression is natural and the language easy.

TWEEDIE, J. Author of *Hindustani as It Ought to be Spoken* (Calcutta, 1890).

TWENTY-ONE VAISHNAV HYMNS. Maithili anthology, which is a collection of some of the less known mediaeval poems, dealing with Krishna legend. It was compiled by George A. Grierson in 1884.

TYAGPATRA (The Resignation). Novel (1937) by Jainendra Kumar (q.v.).

Mrinal, born in a rich family, loses her parents when she is a baby. Her elder brother becomes her guardian and she gets all the love in the family. Like a spoilt child, she makes many mischiefs in the school and then falls in love with the brother of her friend, Shila. Her sister-in-law gives her a beating and she is married to a middle aged man, but when her husband hears of her previous affair with Shila's brother, he turns her out of the house. She suffers immensely and at last finds peace in death. It is a psychological novel with a social relevance.

TYDALL, W.S.C. American Hindi scholar and author of *Hindustani Conversation Grammar* (New York, 1960).

U

UBHADEV KA GAUNA. Kannauji Panvada, which describes the love of Jiva and Ubhadev.

Jiva is married at an early age to Ubhadev, but even when the 'Gauna' (the departure of a mature bride for her husband's house) ceremony is not performed for 12 years, Jiva, at the taunting of her brother's wife, sends a message through a Brahmin to her husband. Ubhadev rides a mare to meet Jiva and the 'Gauna' ceremony is performed. On their return journey to Jaminigarh, Ray Pammar of Jarauli, who bears animosity towards Ubhadev, asks for his mare but the latter turns down the demand. A fierce duel follows in which Ubhadev is killed. As Jiva prepares herself for Sati in which she is to be burnt on the funeral pyre of her dead husband, Shiv and Parvati reach there and seeing the plight of Jiva, revive her dead husband. Both Ubhadev and Jiva live happily thereafter. The beauty of Jiva has also been described by the poet. The work is very popular among Ahirs.

UCHIDA, NORIHIKO. Modern Japanese Hindi scholar, who was associated with Osaka University of Foreign Studies, Osaka from 1960 to 1963 ; earlier, he had taught Japanese at Delhi and Jawahar Lal Nehru Universities. Apart from his works in English and in German on Hindi Dhwanis, his popular work is *Hindi Phonology.*

UDAY. Modern Magahi writer, who is noted for his social one-act plays.

UDAY BHAN MISHRA (1939-). Poet, whose chief work is : *Sirph Ek Gulab ke Liye* (Only for a Rose).

UDAY BHANU HANS. Poet, whose *Rubais* and songs are quite popular in poetical symposia. His works are : *Shankh aur Shahnai* and *Haryana Gaurav Gatha.*

UDAY BHANU SINGH (1917-). Critic, whose chief works are : *Tulsi-Darshan Mimansa* (on Tulsi's philosophy) and *Mahavir Prasad Dwivedi aur Unka Yuga* (Dwivedi and His Age).

UDAY CHAND. Jain Riti poet, who was patronized by Raja Karnasut Anup Singh of Vikrampur or Bikaner. His works are : *Anup Rasal* (on *Rasa* and *Alankar* ; 1671 ; named after his patron), *Panditya Darpana* (in Sanskrit ; 1677) and *Bikaner Ghazal.*

UDAY CHANDRA JHA. Modern Maithili poet, who is noted for his poems and lyrics.

UDAY DHARMA (fl. *c.* 13th cent.). Jain poet, who was pupil of Ratnasen Suri. He was the author in Rajasthani of *Uvaeshmal Kahanay Chhappay*, a didactic work in 81 *Chhappays.*

UDAY NARAYAN TIWARI (1903-84). Linguist, who was formerly Head of the Department of Hindi Linguistics, Jabbulpur University. His chief works are : *Bhojpuri Bhasha aur Sahitya* (Bhojpuri Language and Literature, 1954), *Hindi Bhasha ka Udgam aur Vikas* (The Origin and Development of Hindi Language), *Bhasha Shastra ki Ruprekha* (The Outlines of Philology), *Hindi Bhasha tatha Sahitya*, *Panini ke Uttaradhikari* (The Successors of Panini ; 1971), *Hindi aur Hindi ki Boliyan* (Hindi and its Dialects) and *Bharat ka Bhasha Sarvekshan* (Hindi tr. of Grierson's 1st vol. of *Linguistic Survey of India*). He had also written on Bhojpuri idioms, proverbs and on the origin and development of Bhojpuri language.

UDAY PRAKASH Poet, whose collection of poems : *Suno Karigar* (Listen Worker ; 1980) deals with the lower strata of society : labourer, postman, etc.

UDAY RAJ (Udo ; 1574-1619). Gujarati-speaking Jain saint-poet, who was a disciple of Bhav Harsh. His works in Rajasthani-Braj are : *Magan Chhattisi*, *Gun Bavni* (*1609*), *Vaidya Virhini Prabandh*, *Chaubis Jin Savaie* aad 500 *Dohas.*

UDAY RAJ SINGH. Modern writer, who is noted for his novel : *Andhere ke Viruddh* (Against Darkness).

UDAY RAJ UJAL (1885-1967). Scholar of Rajasthani Charan literature and a good poet of the traditional style, the main note of his poetry is love for Rajasthan, its glory, language and literature. He praised the heroes of yore and admired the freedom fighters of his times. The metres he used most, are *Sortha*, *Doha*, Dingal *Git* and *Chhappay*. His chief works are :

Dhudsar, *Marwar ra Vir Dudh Prakash*, *Matribhasha Dohavali*, *Bhaniyai ra Duha*, *Swaraj Shatak*, *Ujwal Shatak*, *Tej Shatak*, *Sarvoday Shatak*, *Shram Shatak*, *Sati Shatak*, *Jagirdaran rai Avgunan ra Duha*, *Gandhi ra Duha*, *Vigyan ra Duha*, and *Bhasha Shatak* In some of his verses, he has praised the Rajasthani poet, Kesarisingh Barhat (q.v.) as also the heroes, who sacrificed their lives in fighting against the Chinese attack on India.

UDAY RAM SWAMI (fl. latter half of 19th cent. and early 20th cent.). Rajasthani poet and a follower of Haridas Niranjani Sect, whose *Sar Sangrah* is an important anthology of the poems of many poets, mainly of the Niranjani tradition and includes his own compositions as well.

UDAY RAM GUNGA. Rajasthani poet, who was a resident of village Thabukada. He was a contemporary of Maharaja Mansingh (1782-1843) of Jodhpur and was a favourite poet of Raja Bharmal of Kachchh Bhuj and his son, Desalji II. His *Kavikul Bodh*, divided into ten *Tarangs*, deals with *Gits*, their types, Dingal, Pingal, *Nam Malas*, synonyms, 84 types of Dingal *Gits*, etc. In his illustrations, the poet praises Desalji, his patron.

UDAY SHANKAR BHATT (1898-1966). Dramatist, poet and novelist, who was born at Etawah in Uttar Pradesh. His ancestors had settled in Karnawas in Bulandshahr district. He was educated at home in Sanskrit, where his father used to compose and recite poems in poetical symposia. He taught in a number of colleges at Lahore. Finally, he was appointed Adviser and Director in the All India Radio. His chief works are :

Drama : *Kamala*, *Antahin-Ant* (The Endless End ; 1938), *Vidrohani Amba* (Rebel Amba ; social), *Naya Samaj*, *Parvati*, *Muktidut*, *Dahar athva Sindh Patan* (Dahar or the Fall of Sind), *Shak-Vijay*, *Chandragupta Maurya* (1931), *Vikramaditya* (1933) (historical), *Matsyagandha* (1937), *Radha* (1941), *Ashok Vandini*, *Vishwamitra* (poetic plays), *Sagar-Vijay*, *Adim-Yuga* (mythological), *Ekla Chalo Re*, *Kalidas* (radio plays). *Samasya ka Ant*, *Dhumshikha*, *Krantikari*, *Astoday*, *Stri ka Hriday* (The Heart of a Woman ; 1942), *Parde ke Pichhe* (Behind the Curtain ; 1950), *Andhkar aur Prakash* (1952), *Asur Sundari*, *Javani aur Chhah Ekanki*, *Aj ka Admi*, *Abhinav Ekanki Natak* and *Sat Prahasan* (collections of one-act plays) and *Kumarsambhnv* (on the problem of ethics and art). In his dramas, Bhatt has dealt with man-woman relationship in which his sympathy is with woman, whatever her calling ; he is essentially a reformist and his characters are not guilty of preaching what they do not practise.

Poetry: *Takshashila* (1931), *Raka* (Full Moon Night), *Manasi* (Worship in Mind), *Visarjan*, *Yuga-Dip*, *Yatharth aur Kalpana* (Realism and Imagination), *Vijay-Path*, *Antardarshan* (1958), *Ityadi*, *Mujh mein jo Shesh Hai* and *Purvapar* (Eastern and Western); in many of his poems included in *Manasi*, he has questioned the validity of spiritual values which have encouraged man to exploit his fellow beings with the convenient use of destiny and fatalism ; some of his poems are influenced by progressive trends, *e g*., Realism and Idealism.

Novel: *Vah Jo Main-ne Dekha* (What I Have Seen ; 3 Pts.), *Naya Mod* (The New Turn), *Sagar, Lahren aur Manushya* (The Sea, the Waves and the Man ; 1956 ; story of fishermen in Bombay), *Lok Parlok* (This World and the Other World; 1958), *Shesh Ashesh* (The Remainder and the Whole ; 1960 ; on the life of Sannyasis), *Doctor Shephali*, *Do Adhyay* (Two Chapters) and *Ek Nid Do Panchhi* (One Nest, Two Birds) ; *Sahitya ke Swar* (Aspects of Literature) is a work on criticism.

Bhatt's works are a fine blend of his faith in ancient Indian culture and his fascination for new ideas.

UDAY SINGH, MAHARANA (fl. 1537-71). Rajasthani ruler, whose stray verses in different popular metres are available.

UDAY SINGH BHATNAGAR. Modern poet of Rajasthan, who has composed stray poems in Khari Boli.

UDAY VIR SHARMA. Rajasthani poet, whose *Damphi* (1973) describes the cold wave and its terrible effects on Nature and on living beings. His *Sunto* (1981) narrates the various phases of the cyclonic rain in the desert and its deadly effect on the peasantry, crops, birds, beasts, plants, etc. *Bat men Hunkaro* (1981) is a book of folk-tales, of which two are translations from Russian and Ukrarian tales. *Kirtyan ro Jhumko* (1982) is a collection of 90 shorter stories, most of them in the style of fables ; they are intended to convey some subtle ideas or philosophy of life in the form of fiction, while *Contribution of Shekhawati Region to Hindi and Rajasthani Literature* (1982) lists a number of works of this region in Hindi and Rajasthani written during 1600-1900 V.S. or 1543-1843.

UDDHAV DAS (fl. 17th-18th cent.). Oriya-speaking Hindi (Brajboli) poet, whose commentary on *Gita Govinda* is a charming work. His language is polished and refined.

UDDHAV-SHATAK. See *Jagannath Das 'Ratnakar'*.

UDHO DAS (fl. 17th cent.). Saint-poet, who sang of *Nirgun*

Brahma and was founder of the famous Satnami Sect. He was born at Narnaul in Haryana some time after Dadu Dayal and was in fact the head of the Haryana centre of the sect, which had been founded by Jagjivandas in Oudh. This sect had a number of encounters with Aurangzeb. Udho Das's followers, though small in number, recite his *Vani*. His devotional songs are simple but are steeped in Bhakti and are popular in Haryana even today.

UDOJI ADING (1761-1816). Rajasthani poet of the Vishnoi Sampraday, who wrote narrative poems on mythological themes. His works : *Prahlad Charit* (in 348 verses), *Vishnu Charit* (110 verses), *Kakka Charit* (37 verses), *Lur* and stray verses reveal his intensity of feelings and deep devotion.

UDOJI NAIN (1448-1536). Rajasthani saint-poet of the Vishnoi tradition (see Jambhoji), whose *Sakhis*, *Harjas*, *Kavittas* and *Garbh-Chitvani* are available. He expresses his spiritual experiences lucidly and clearly.

UGRA. See *Bechan Sharma Pandey 'Ugra'*.

UJIYARE. Poet of the Riti school, who was a native of Vrindavan and was son of Naval Shah. His *Jugal Rasa Prakash* (1780) was written for Jugal Kishore, Dewan of Hathras, while *Rasa-Chandrika* was written for Daulat Ram of Jaipur ; in reality, both these works are the same.

UJIYARE LAL 'LALITESH'. Modern poet of Bharthana village in Etawah district, whose chief works are on Gandhi and the heroism of Ravan (*Dashanan Digvijay*).

ULFAT SINGH CHAUHAN 'NIRBHAY' (1899-1980) Poet of the Agra district in Uttar Pradesh, whose chief works are : *Kisan Satsai* (on farmers), *Kisanon ki Pukar* (The Call of the Farmers ; 1924) and *Nirbhay Niti Sangrah* (1975).

ULHA CHAI (ALIAS U PARGU). Native of Burma, who is promoting the cause of Hindi in his country. He has also tr. the Sanskrit work, *Saundarananda* into Burmese, which has won him an award from the Burmese Government.

ULTSIFEROV, DONE NATALIYA (1932-). Soviet Hindi scholar, who is at present an editor in the Progressive Publishing House, Moscow. She has edited the Hindi versions of the works of Karl Marx, Angeles, Lenin, Tolstoy, Gorky, etc.

ULTSIFEROV, OLEG (1932-). Soviet Hindi scholar, who is at

present Reader in Hindi in the Institute of International Relations, Moscow. He has also been awarded the Nehru Award. He has written *Hindi Bhasha ki Pathaypustak* (3 Pts.) and on Hindi grammar (*Hindi men Kriya*). He has also translated into Russian *Nirmala* and *Ghaban* of Prem Chand and *Kab tak Pukarun* of Rangey Raghav, all novels. He has in all written ten books and a good number of articles.

UMA BUDHRAM. Modern Hindi poetess of Trinidad, who is noted for her stray poems.

UMACHANDRAN. Modern Tamil writer, whose short stories in Hindi have been published in various magazines ; he has also written numerous radio one-act plays. He has tr. into Hindi his Tamil novel *Mullum Malrum* under the title : *Kanta aur Kali* (The Thorn and the Bud) and another novel *Muyu* under the title of *Kahin Unche* (Even Higher).

UMA KANT GUPTA. Scholar, whose works are : *Saptak Kavya Parampara aur Chautha Saptak* (1981) and *Nayi Kavita ke Prabandh Kavya* (1984).

UMA KANT MALVIYA. Lyric poet, whose chief collections of lyrics are *Subah Rakta Palash Ki* (1976) and *Abhishapta Amarbeli* ; *Sahitya Mahodadhi ka Chayan* (1984) is his humorous work.

UMA NATH JHA. Modern Maithili writer, who is noted for his chief short story collections : *Rekhachitra* and *Adh Ghanta*. His critical work, *Alochana : Samkalin Pravriti* advocates Western principles of literary criticism.

UMA PATI SHASTRI. Kannada-speaking modern Hindi writer, who tr. Akka Mahadevi's select *Vachans* from Kanada into Hindi ; Akka Mahadevi is regarded as 'Mira' of Kannada.

UMA PATI UPADHYAY. Greatest of mediaeval Kirtaniya dramatist, whose *Parijat Haran* (q.v.) in Maithili seems to have been written for a non-Maithil court. Some people believe that he was the founder of the Kirtaniya drama in Mithila and that he used to sing and dance before Krishna's image.

Umapati has been placed in two widely-different periods, as there are several persons who are known to have borne this name. It appears that Umapati was an older contemporary of Gokulnath Upadhyay and that he lived during the regins of Maharaja Narpati Thakur (1692/3-1703/4) and Maharaja Raghav Singh (1704-40) and wrote his drama under the patronage of Bundelkhand chief, Hindupati. Ram Dev Jha, who has written a book in 1980 on Umapati, is of the view that his period was between 1570-1670.

Umapati's play gained wide popularity and indeed it made Kirtaniya drama the fashion of the day.

UMA RANI, K. Tamil-speaking Hindi scholar, who is noted for her *Dakshin ke Hindi Sahitya ka Alochanatmak Itihas* (A Critical History of Hindi Literature in South India ; thesis ; 1972).

UMA SHANKAR. Novelist, whose chief works are : *Kaveri ke Kinare* (On the Bank of the Kaveri ; 1959) and *Bhuvan Vijayam* (1963 ; dealing with Krishnadev Ray of Vijaynagar).

UMA SHANKAR DWIVEDI. Modern Rajasthani poet, whose stray verses on *Vir Rasa* are available.

UMADE BHATIYANI RA KAVITTA. Dingal poem in 14 verses by Asha Barhat (q.v.), which describes the vow of Bhatiyani Rani of Rao Malde of Jodhpur, that she would not speak with her husband throughout her life, for she was annoyed with her husband since the very first night of their marriage on seeing the Rao making love to her maid-servant Bharmali, but later on as she learnt of the death of her husband, she consigned herself to flames. See *Asha Barhat*.

UMARDAN LALAS (1852-1903). Rajasthani poet, who was born in the Dhadharwara village of the then Jodhpur State. After the death of his parents in childhood, he became a disciple of Mangiram of the Ram Snehi Sect of the Khedapa tradition. He came in contact with Swami Dayanand (q.v.) and was influenced by his teachings. His *Umar-Kavya*, a collection of his poems, realistically portrays the prevailing social conditions and advocates social reforms. His satires on social evils are sharp and uncompromising and occasionally the language becomes crude, though the descriptions are charming and the language is easy Rajasthani. His poetry is popular among the uneducated masses.

UMESH MISHRA, MAHAMAHOPADHYAY (1895-1967). Maithili writer, who started his critical writing during the early years of the 20th century under the auspices of Murlidhar Jha (q.v.), the editor of 'Mithilamod'. He tr. the Sanskrit *Sahitya-Darpan* into Maithili, edited many works (of Man Bodh, etc.) and laid down the scientific lines of studying Maithili classics. His other works are : *Bharatiya Darshan, Vidyapati Thakur* and *Maithili Sanskriti aur Sabhyata.* Critics of the present generation have been most widely inspired by his writings. He had shown how both traditional and modern principles could be utilized to produce the best results.

In the field of essay writing, he wrote essays on duty, the art of thieving, the method of religious debates, on the outward descriptions of men or the inward descriptions of the mind during an aesthetic experience. In the essays, he shows himself eminently to be a creative critic of life and literature.

UMESH SHARMA. Writer, whose *Taral Pashan* (The Liquid Stones ; 1980) is a collection of short stories.

UMESH SHASTRI. Modern scholar, whose chief work is *Hindi Gadya Sahitya ka Vikas Kram* (1984) ; *Rupray* is his novel.

UMMEDRAM PALHAWAT BARHAT (1743-1821). Rajasthani poet, who was patronized by Raoraja Bakhtavar Singh of Alwar. His chief works: *Brahma Kavach*, *Vani Bhushan*, *Bhasha Chanakya*, *Bhasha Rajniti* and *Satyopadesh* are in Braj, while the *Marsiya* in Rajasthani was composed after the death of Raoraja Bakhtavar Singh of Alwar in 1814. The intensity of Queen Musi's grief and her *Sati* with the dead body of the Raoraja have been touchingly described by the poet. He wrote commentaries on *Bihari Satsai* and on Keshavdas's *Kavipriya*.

UMMED SINGH KHINDASAR, KUNVAR. Rajasthani poet, whose *Maharana ri Olyun* (1956) describes in easy Rajasthani mainly the battle of Haldighati.

UMRAO SINGH PANDE (b. 1902). Modern poet of Mainpuri, who is noted for his *Padas* in devotion to Krishna.

UNNUTH, ABHIMANYU. See *Abhimanyu Unnuth*.

UPADHYAY, BHAGWAT SHARAN. See *Bhagwat Sharan Upadhyay*.

UPENDRA DOSHI. Modern Maithili poet, who is noted for his poems and lyrics.

UPENDRA NATH ASHK (1910-). Dramatist, fiction writer and poet, who was born in a middle class Brahmin family of Jalandhar. He passed the Ll. B. examination in 1936 and the same year his wife died. His chief works are :—

Drama : *Jay-Prajay* (Victory-Defeat ; 1937), *Swarg ki Jhalak* (The Glimpse of Paradise ; 1938 ; expression of unhappiness with 'modern' girls who pursue social and outdoor activities at the cost of peace and happiness of the home), *Chhatha Beta* (The Sixth Son ; 1940 ; a psychological play on the problem of a retired father), *Qaid* (Prison ; 1945), *Udan* (The Flight ; 1946 ; on man-woman relationship), *Bhanwar* (Whirlpool ; 1950), *Alag-alag Raste* (Separate Paths), *Paintare, Abhishipta, Bade Khiladi, Kshitij ke Par*, and *Anjo Didi* (Anjo, the Elder Sister ; 1955). By virtue of his ability to mirror actual life, particularly the life in middle and lower middle class families, Ashk has given a new direction to Hindi drama.

One-act Play Collection : *Charvahe* (Shepherds ; 1947), *Devtaon ki Chhaya Men, Tufan se Pahile, Adi Marg, Andhi Gali ke Ath Ekanki, Parda Uthao, Parda Girao* (Raise the Curtain, Lower the Curtain ; 1951 ; humorous), *Sahib ko Zukam Hai, Pachchis Shreshth Ekanki, Mere Shreshth Ekanki, Naye Rang Ekanki*, etc. Ashk, while depicting middle class here as well, has succeeded by his keen observation in imparting to his one-act plays the literary quality with realistic touches.

Novel : *Sitaron ke Khel* (1938 ; romantic), *Girti Divaren* (The Crumbling Walls ; 1948 ; a novel, in which Chetan, the hero, his drunkard father, his kind-hearted mother, his innocent wife, his charming sister-in-law and the villainous Viadya all act and behave naturally), *Garma Rakh* (Hot Ahses), *Badi-badi Ankhen* (Big Eyes ; 1954 ; description of the corruption prevalent in Institutions), *Patthar-al-Patthar* (1957 ; on surrender to the Will of God), *Shahr men Ghumta Aina* (The Mirror, Moving Round the City ; 1963, *Ek Nanhin Kandil* ; Pts. 2 and 3 of the epic novel of which *Girti Divaren* is the first part), *Bandho na Nav us Thanv* (1973 ; 2 Pts), *His Excellency*, and *Nimisha* (Blink ; 1976) ; all his novels draw true pictures of life, especially of middle class families.

Ashk has also written about 200 short stories ; his narratives, written in a lucid and racy style, are problem-oriented and marked by a reformist bias. His short story collections are : *Kahani Lekhika aur Jhelum ke Sat Pul, Ye Raje Ye Rishi, Chacha Ramdita, Ubal aur anya Kahaniyan, Akash-chari, Kale Sahab, Chhinte, Judai ki Sham ka Git, Palang, Pinjra, Baingan ka Paudha, Chauntis Kahaniyan, Ashk ki Sarvashreshth Kahaniyan, Sattar Shreshth Kahaniyan*, etc. His important short stories are : 'Dachi', 'Akash-chari' (The Rover in the Sky), 'Kankda ka Teli' (The Oilman of Kankda), 'Kale Sahib', 'Nasur (The Cancer), 'Ankur' (The Sprout), 'Daliye', 'Khali Dibba' (The Empty Tin), 'Ek Udasin Sham' (A Melancholy Evening), etc.

Besides, he has written mainly progressive poems (*Urmiyan, Prat Pradip, Khoya Hua Prabhamandal, Adrishya Nadi, Chandni Rat aur Ajgar, Dip Jalega, Bargad ki Beti, Sarkon men Dhale Saye*), essays, and reminiscences and has tr. some foreign works into Hindi. *Anveshan ki Sah-Yatra, Amne Samne, Upanyaskar aur Mulyankan, Kahani ke Ird Gird, Girti Divaren : Drishti-prati-Drishti*, etc. are his critical works.

UPENDRA NATH JHA 'VYAS'. Maithili fiction writer and poet, whose chief novels are : *Kumar* (1946) and *Dui Patra* (1969). His chief short story collections are *Vidambana*, *Debu* and *Bakri* ; as a short story writer, Vyas holds a high place, for in his stories, he presents those facts of life, which though insignificant, matter so much to the common man's everyday existence. His short story 'Rusal Jamay' (The Sulky Son-in-law) gave a new direction to Maithili short story writing. His *Sannyasi* (1948), written in blank verse, is on the story of a man, who becomes an ascetic and leaves for the Himalayas but on realizing the importance of a healthy house-holder's life, returns home only to find his wife on death-bed, while *Patan* (1969) is on the story of Nahush's fall from heaven. His *Vidyapati-ka Avsan* has been composed in an elegant style. He has also tr. *Gita* and *Omar Khayyam's Rubaiyat*.

UPENDRA THAKUR. Maithili scholar of history, whose *Mithilak Itihas* (1980) is a history of Mithila from ancient times till Muslim invasion.

UPENDRA THAKUR 'MOHAN' (1913-). Maithili poet, whose chief works are : *Phuldali* (1940 ; a collection of lyrics) and *Apahnuti-Manjari*, a collection of his *Muktak* poems.

URDAM CHAUBE. Poet, who was a contemporary and rival of Gwal (1792-1867) ; a few of his verses are now available.

URMIL SATYABHUSHAN. Poetess, whose *Kasturi Gandh* (1983) is a collection of poems.

URMILA NIRKHI Marathi-speaking modern Hindi poetess, who has published poems on various subjects.

URVASHI. See *Ramdhari Singh 'Dinkar'*.

USHA DEVI MITRA (1897-1966). Bengali-speaking Hindi fiction writer, whose chief works are : *Piya* (1927), *Jivan ki Muskan* (The Laughter of Life ; 1939), *Pathchari* (1940), *Bachan ka Mol, Nashta Nid, Sohini* (novels), *Sandhya Purabi, Nim Chameli, Megh Malhar, Picnic, Rat ki Rani and Ragini* (short story collections). She presented Indian women in high ideal settings.

USHA-HARAN (The Abduction of Usha). Maithili Kirtaniya drama, which was composed by Ratnapani (q v.). Representing a very scholarly and dignified kind of the fully evolved vernacular Kirtaniya play, there are now and then some Sanskrit songs and dialogues interspersed with vernacular passage.

Gauri grants to Usha, the daughter of Banasur, the king of Shonitpur, the boon of getting a desirable husband in a dream. Usha sees a person and enjoys company with him. Her friend, Chitralekha, helps her in identifying that person as Aniruddh, the grandson of Krishna. While conveying her message of love to Aniruddh, Chitralekha meets Narad, who with his magic brings Aniruddh himself to the chamber of Usha. They engage in love sports but are detected by the gate-keepers. Banasur arrests Aniruddh but on the advice of his Dewan, does not kill him. Narad goes to Dwarika and informs Krishna of Aniruddh's whereabouts. Krishna with his army attacks Shonitpur and defeats Banasur ; the latter seeks the aid of Shiv. There is a great battle between the two parties : one led by Krishna and the other by Shiv. Though Shiv refrains from rendering active help, yet Shiv's son, Karttikey comes to the aid of Banasur but is drawn away from the battle when Gauri intervenes. Thereupon Banasur realizes the might of Krishna and accepts his defeat. Krishna arranges for the marriage of the couple——Aniruddh and Usha. Krishna restores the kingdom to Banasur's people and comes back to Dwarika along the newly-wed couple.

USHA PRIYAMVADA. Modern fiction writer, whose chief novels are : *Pachpan Khambhe, Lal Divaren* (Fifty-five Pillars and Red Walls ; 1961 ; description of the suffocation of the heroine in 55 pillars and red walls of the hostel) and *Rukogi Nahin Radhika* ? (Will You not Stop, Radhika ? ; 1967 ; Radhika here represents the revolt of the woman, who, though unmarried, welcomes sex and wine) ; her short story collections : *Phir Vasant Aya* (Spring Came Again), *Zindagi aur Gulab ke Phul* (Life and Roses ; 1961), *Ek Koi Dusra* (Any Other ; 1966), *Kitna Bada Jhuth* (How Great Falsehood ; 1972 ; revealing the consequences of recklessly accepting new values by the modern woman) and *Shesh Yatra* (1984 ; on the story of a woman, who has been forsaken by her husband in a foreign country). Her prominent short stories are : 'Zindagi aur Gulab ke Phul', 'The Return', etc.

USHA SHARMA, MRS. Modern Hindi writer of Nepal, who is noted for her short stories.

USHA BARUA. Modern writer ; her *Sien Nadi ki Laharen* is a novel.

USHA VYAS. Modern Hindi writer of Kashmir, who is noted for her novels, written on new lines.

USMAN (b. 1613). Hindi Sufi poet of Ghazipur, who was the author of *Chitravali* (q. v.), an allegorical romance. The poet was son of Sheikh Husain and was a disciple of Haji Baba. Among Hindi Sufi poets, he holds a place next to Jayasi (q.v.).

USMAN (fl. early 19th cent.). Sindhi Muslim saint-poet, who was also noted for his composition of verses in Hindi.

USMANOVA, LALA HAMDMOVNA (1940-). Soviet Hindi scholar, whose field of study is modern Hindi literature, especially the works of Upendranath Ashk.

UTTAM CHAND BHANDARI (fl. 1803). Contemporary of Maharaja Mansingh of Jodhpur, who was the author of 4 to 5 works, of which *Alankar-Ashay* is the best of all. See *Mansingh, Maharaja of Jodhpur*.

UTTAM KUMAR CHARIT CHAUPAI. See *Vinay Chandra*.

UTTAM NATH (fl. 19th cent.). Rajasthani Nath Siddha poet, whose poetry leans towards Vedanta of Shankar.

UTTAM PARMAR. Writer, whose novel *Shraddha* (Faith ; 1980) deals with tragic element along with the love-story. His other novels are : *Maryada*, *Sukhda*, *Apeksha* and *Sanskar* (1984).

UTTAM RAM SHUKLA 'NAGAR' (b. 1910). Poet of Mathura, who is a great scholar of Sanskrit, Ayurveda, Jyotish, Music etc. In his work, he has presented the whole of the Indian *Sangit-shastra* (Indian music).

UVAESHMAL KAHANAY CHHAPPAY. See *Uday Dharma*.

V

VACHAN DEV KUMAR (1934-). Writer, whose chief works are : *Tulsi ke Bhaktyatmak Git : Visheshtah Vinay-Patrika* (Devotional Songs of Tulsi : Vinay Patrika in Particular), *Ramcharitmanas men Alankar Yojna* (Plan of Figures of speech in the Ramcharitmanas ; both research works), *Tulsi Vividh Sandarbhon Men, Lehhak aur Parivesh, Chintan ki Mudrayen, Chintan ke Dhage* The (Strands of Thought) and *Saket : Vichar aur Vishleshan* (*criticism*) His poetical collections are : *Vrit Ek Bindu Anek, O Ajanma Suno* and *Kavitayen Bemausam Ki.*

VACHASPATI PATHAK (1905-80). Writer, who was noted for his short stories ; he was influenced by the short stories of Jayshankar Prasad (q.v.). His short story collections are : *Ikkis Kahaniyan, Achchhi Kahaniyan, Dwadashi and Pradip.* He also wrote a critical work : *Prasad, Nirala, Pant, Mahadevi ki Shreshth Rachnayen.*

VACHNIKA RATHAUD RATAN SINGHJI MAHESDASAUTRI. See *Khidiya Jagga.*

VADICHANDRA (fl. 1594-97). Gujarati Jain poet, whose *Yashodhar Charit* and *Shripal Akhyan* are in Hindi.

VAGVILAS. See *Manikyachandra Suri.*

VAIDEHI VANVAS (The Forest Exile of Sita). Epic (1940) by Ayodhya Singh Upadhyay 'Hariaudh' (q.v.).

Though based on the *Uttar-Kand* of the *Ramayan*, it departs from the original in the sense that Sita is told about the people's feelings about her character before she decides voluntarily to go to the forest the second time. As compared to *Priya Pravas* (q.v.), the diction and vocabulary are less Sanskritized and it is also full of descriptions of Nature.

VAIDYA, KRISHNA BALDEO. See *Krishna Baldeo Vaidya.*

VAIDYA NATH (fl. early 19th cent. ?). Maithili poet, whose *Bhasha Chamatkar* (incomplete) translates the stories of the *Mahabharat* and the Purans in simple Maithili verses. The work has been composed in *Dohas* and other short metres.

VAIDYA NATH MISHRA. See *Nagarjun*.

VAIDYA NATH MISHRA 'VIDYASINDHU'. Modern Maithili writer, whose chief works are : *Katha-Sangrah* (simple stories) and *Galp Sapp-ka-Kharihan* (humorous stories).

VAIKUNTH NATH MANI SHUKLA (fl. 17th cent.). Writer, who was an employee of the Orchha Durbar ; he was noted for his two books in Brajbhasha prose, e.g., *Agahan Mahatmya* and *Vaishakh Mahatmya*.

VAIRAGYA SANDIPINI (Kindling of Renunciation). Poem by Tulsidas (q.v.) in Avadhi, written between 1582-1612.

The work in 62 verses, describes the characteristics of saints ; it betrays the influence of Vairagi cult on Tulsidas. Some scholars doubt the authorship of this work by Tulsidas.

VAISHALI KI NAGARVADHU (The Public Bride of Vaishali). Historical novel (1948) by Chatursen Shastri (q.v.), which is considered his masterpiece. It portrays life in the Vajjian Republic of Vaishali around 600 B.C. in which the most beautiful girl of the Republic was not allowed to marry, but it was incumbent upon her to entertain and cater to recreation of all people in accordance with clearly-defined state regulations. Ambapali, the heroine, caters to the recreation of the youth of Vaishali but at the same time asserts the dignity of womanhood ; she keeps her body untouched. The author has depicted different religious, social and political conditions and situations of contemporary life, through which a live picture of the whole age appears before our eyes.

VAISHAMPAYAN, G R. Marathi-speaking modern Hindi scholar, who is the author of *Marathi se Hindi Shabda Sangrah*.

VAISHNAV DAS. See *Padakalpataru*.

VAISHNAV DAS 'RASJANI' (fl. 18th cent.). Poet of the Krishna-cult (Chaitanya Sect), who was grandson of Priyadas (q.v.) and lived in Vrindavan. His works are : *Bhaktamal Mahatmya*, *Bhakta Urvasi*, *Bhagavat Bhasha*, *Git Govind Bhasha*, *Bhakti Ratnavali Bhasha and* stray *Padas*.

VAJID. See *Vajind.*

VAJIND (fl. probably between 1550 and 1650). Rajasthani saint-poet, who was a Pathan and a disciple of Dadu (q v.). Of his many poems, *Chandrayans* or the '*Arillas*' (metrical compositions), about 135 in number, are didactic in character and are by far the most important for universality of their appeal ; some of them have become popular sayings.

VAJPEYI, BHAGVATI PRASAD. See *Bhagvati Prasad Vajpeyi.*

VAJPEYI, KISHORIDAS See *Kishoridas Vajpeyi.*

VAJPEYI, NAND DULARE. See *Nand Dulare Vajpeyi.*

VAJRA MATTI 'MAGHMITRA'. Kannada-speaking modern Hindi poet, whose chief collections of poems are : *Mitti ke Phul* (The Flowers of Clay) and *Agnipath* (The Fire-path ; 1971). The poems are sometimes patriotic or revolutionary with deep sympathy for the downtrodden.

VAJRA SURI. Jain poet, whose Rajasthani poem *Bharateshwar Bahubali Ghor* (composed in 1168 ; q.v.) in 48 verses describes the battle between Bharat and Bahubali.

VALLABH (fl. early 18th cent.). Court-poet of Maharaja Rajsingh of Kishengarh, who was son of Vrind (q.v.). He composed two Riti works : *Vallabh-Vilas* and *Vallabh-Muktavali* in Pingal.

VALLABH DAS (fl. 1583). Bengali Vaishnav poet, who also composed *Padas* in Brajbuli.

VALLABH DEV. Writer, whose *Tulsi-krit Ramayan* was an easy rendering in 1572 of Tulsidas's *Ramcharitmanas.*

VALLABH DOBHAL. Modern fiction writer, whose chief works are : *Meri Shreshth Kahaniyan* (Pts. I, II) and *Tibbet ki Beti* (novel).

VALLABH JHA (1906-40). Maithili writer, who was noted for his short stories as also for the tr. of *Ritusamhara*, Bhartrihari's *Nitishataka* ; *Chanakya-Shataka* and *Drishtanta-Shataka* from Sanskrit. He also composed poems in Maithili, which were inspired by Sanskritic conventions.

VALLABH SIDDHARTH. Short story writer, whose chief collections of stories are : *Mahapurushon ki Vapsi* (The Return of the

Great Men ; 1969), *Band Darvaze* (The Closed Doors ; 1970), *Blackout* and *Shesh Prasang*.

VALMIKI TRIPATHI. Novelist, whose chief works are : *Vikalang* (1960 ; on the heroic life of Rana Sangram Singh), *Satta aur Sangharsh* (1963), *Durabhisandhi* (1970), *Jay-Vijay*, *Ek aur Begum* and *Philhal*.

VAMAN RAMDASI (fl. 17th cent). Saint-poet of Maharashtra, who was a follower of Smarth Sect. In addition to his Marathi works, he composed some *Padas* in Hindi as well.

VAN OLPHEN, HERMAN HENDRIK. Scholar, whose chief work is *The Structure of the Hindi Verb Phrase* (Texas at Austin, 1970).

VANIRA GIRI. Modern Hindi writer of Nepal, who is noted for his short stories and stray poems.

VANMALI DAS. Oriya-speaking modern Hindi writer, who prepared Hindi text-books for Orissa schools. He has been associated with Utkal Rashtrabhasha Prachar Samiti.

VANSH BHASKAR. Rajasthani poetical work by Suryamall Mishran (q.v.), which is a history of Bundi State in verse. The poet started writing this in 1840 at the instance of Maharao Ramsingh of Bundi (1811-89).

Written in the *Champu* form and in a variety of metres and pieces, it is a monumental work of its own type and is encyclopaedic in character. It is not only the history of ancestors of his patron, but is a veritable store-house of information about other clans of the Rajput royal houses, historical events, anecdotes, etc. Though the basic linguistic structure of this work is Pingal, Sanskrit, Prakrit, Apabhransh and Dingal words have also been used at places. The descriptions of armies, heroes, townships, social customs and festivals, which abound in the work are enchanting and are of considerable historical value.

Left incomplete, the work was completed by his son, Muraridan (q.v.).

VANSH MANI JHA. Maithili scholar, who flourished in the court of Pratap Mall Dev (1639-89), the ruler of Kantipur (Kathmandu) in Nepal. Son of Ram Chandra Jha, he composed at the court of Jagjjyotirmall of Bhaktapur, several works on music, such as *Sangit-Bhaskar* (1631). He was the author also of two Maithili dramas : *Git-Digambar* (1655 ; in 4

Acts on the story of Shiv's enticement by Parvati) and *Mudit-Madalasa.*

VANSHI DHAR PANDEY. Chhattisgarhi writer, whose short story, 'Hiru ke Kahini' (1926) introduced the trend of prose-writing in Chhattisgarhi.

VANSHI DHAR SHUKLA (1904-80). Avadhi folk-poet, who was born at the village Manyaura in Lakhimpur district. A born critic of individual, society, country, administration and religion, his poems are noted for their humour and satire. He also collected 450 Avadhi riddles, 500 folk-songs and 4,500 Avadhi words, but all his poems including the collections emain unpublished.

VANSHI DHAR VIDYALANKAR (1900-66). Hindi writer of Hyderabad, who was noted for his poems and critical essays. His chief works are : *Mere Phul* (poetical work), *Bala Pada* (*Git*) and *Sahitya* (Hindi tr. of Rabindra Nath Tagore's essays). He edited 'Kalpana', Hyderabad for a number of years and was Head of the Department of Hindi and Sanskrit, Osmania University, Hyderabad.

VANSHI VADAN (b. 1498). Bengali Vaishnav poet, who composed a *Pada* in Brajbuli on the sports of cowherd boy Krishna and the Gopis.

VANSHI VALLABH MISHRA (fl. end of 18th cent.). Oriya-speaking Hindi (Brajboli) poet, whose *Padas* are available.

VARANASI RAMMURTI 'RENU'. Telugu-speaking Hindi poet, whose *Vihog Git* (1951) is a colleetion of songs. His *Sahityik Adan Pradan* (1972) is a collection of critical essays. He tr. into Hindi verse the four select incidents from Potana's *Mahabhagavata* (1963) as also G. Jashua's message poem *Gabbilamu* under the title *Chamgadad* (The Bat ; 1965).

VARANNIKOV. See *Barannikov*.

VARMALA. See *Govind Vallabh Pant*.

VARNA-RATNAKAR (The Ocean of Descriptions). Maithili prose work in 156 pages of manuscript, which is divided in seven chapters or 'waves'. Written by Jyotirishwar Kavi-shekhar (q.v.), it is an encyclopaedic work of life and culture of mediaeval India in general and of Mithila in particular.

The work describes jewels, clothes, fine stuffs, tents,

gambling houses, doctors, astrologers, the fort, the lower castes, the hero, the heroine and her friends, kinds of heroines and the prostitutes, the pimp, the court, the palace of the king, his bathroom, shampoos, food, love and sleep, the various seasons of the year, the royal family, hunting, war, forests, mountains, hermitages, poetry, music, dancing, graveyards, deserts, seas, holy places, rivers, boats, etc. With profusion of details, it includes descriptions of almost all the things worth describing in human life.

This book seems to have guided the genius of Vidyapati.

VARSALPUR GARH VIJAY. See *Jogidas*.

VARTIKA AGRAWAL. Writer, whose chief work, *Shesh Phir* (1984) is a short story collection.

VASANT RAMKRISHNA DEV, PRA. Marathi-speaking modern Hindi poet, whose poems are collected in *Dikhti Nahin Apni hi Chhanh*, which has earned an award from the Government of India. He is also the author of a drama : *Sarja Shivaji*.

VASANT VILAS PHAGU. Rajasthani poem of an anonymous author, which is available in two versions : containing 52 verses and 84 or 86 verses. The work has been brought out in several editions. After each couplet, a Sanskrit or Prakrit verse depicting similar emotion is given. Composed some time around 1350, it describes the spring season and its amorous sports, the absolute command and influence of Cupid, the agony of separation, the delightful re-union of the spouses and women's physical charms. A popular poem, it was meant to be sung.

VASANTA, S. Tamil-speaking Hindi scholar, who is noted for her *Adhunik Hindi Kavita men Duruhata* (1975) on the difficulty of understanding modern Hindi poetry.

VASTO VISHWAMBHAR (fl. 1774). Gujarati saint-poet of the village Sakarpur in Khambat, who composed *Sakhis* in Hindi and Gujarati; in Hindi he wrote 2641 *Sakhis*, *Gurugita*, *Mangal-Kavyas* and *Padas*.

VASU B. PUTRAN. Kannada-speaking modern Hindi writer, who tr. S.L. Bherappa's Kannada work *Vanshvriksha* into Hindi.

VASUDEV (b. 1853). Poet of the Krishna-cult (Chaitanya Sect), who was born in Vrindavan. In Brajbhasha his work is *Pranalika*, while in Sanskrit his work is *Shri Radha-Madhava Utsava Pranalika.*

VASUDEV ATHALYE (fl. 1920-40). Marathi-speaking Hindi novelist, whose chief work is *Mangal-Path.*

VASUDEV GHOSH. Contemporary of Chaitanya (1486-1527). who composed *Padas* in Bengali. His *Padas* in praise of Chaitanya are the best of their kind and they generally form the *Gaur Chandrika* or the prelude to the songs of Radha and Krishna in all the collections of Vaishnav *Padas.* He also composed *Padas* in Brajbuli in praise of Chaitanya.

VASUDEV NANDAN. Modern author of *Hindi Bhasha: Samasyaen aur Samadhan.*

VASUDEV, P.G. Malayalam-speaking modern Hindi writer whose works are : *Jivanmala, Bachchon ke Kunchan, Bachchon ke Chattampi* (for children). He tr. C.J. Thomas's Malayalam drama under the title of *Vah Phir A Raha Hai* (He is Coming Back) and T.N. Gopinathan Nayar's as *Gitanand.* He also tr. some Malayalam short stories into Hindi.

VASUDEV SHARAN AGRAWAL (1904-66). Eminent scholar of Indian culture and literature, who was born at Pilakhua in Ghaziabad district of Uttar Pradesh. His chief works are : *Prithvi Putra* (1949), *Mata Bhumi* (The Motherland), *Kala aur Sanskriti* (Art and Culture ; 1952 ; both collections of essays) and commentaries on Jayasi's *Padmavat* and Vidyapati's *Kirtilata.* His other important works are : *Paninikalin Bharat* (India as Known to Panini) and *Bharat Savitri* (interpreting the happenings of the *Ramayan* and *Mahabharat* period in a lucid manner). He died at Kashi.

VASUDEV VISHNOODAYAL (1906-) Hindi writer of Mauritius, who has also written in English and French. His Hindi works are : *Sainik, Mauritius ke Yuddh men Bharatiya Yoddha, Mauritius ka Parichay, Kuchh Mahatvapurna Granth, Gita ka Adbhut Sandesh* and *Veda Bhagvan Bole.* He has also written hundreds of articles, many of which are collected in *Vishnoodayal Rachnavali, Vishnoodayal Lekhavali* (3 Pts.) and *Vishnoodayal Nibandhavali.* He has also tr. into Hindi two works from French.

VASUDEVAN PILLAI, K. (fl. early 20th cent.). Malayalam-speaking Hindi teacher, who was a great protagonist of Hindi in Trivandrum. He had a large number of follower-students.

He had sacrificed his all for the sake of Hindi. He was the author of *Hindi-Malayalam Swabodhini* (Hindi-Malayalam Self-Teacher).

VASUDHA MANE. Marathi-speaking modern Hindi poetess, whose poems are written on various subjects.

VAUDEVIL, CHARLOTTE. French Hindi scholar, who has made a French tr. of Kabir's poetry and has done research on 'Tulsi Ramayan ke Adhyatmik Srot'.

VAZ, A. Author of *The Marine Officer's Hindustani Interpreter* (Bombay, 1879).

VED PRAKASH AMITABH. Poet, whose *Vasant ke Intazar Men* (1983) is his first collection of poems.

VED PRAKASH SHASTRI. Modern scholar, whose chief works are : *Sur ki Maulikta* and *Hindi Gadya ko Dakkhin ki Den.*

VED PRAKASH VATUK. Poet, whose *Naye Abhilekh ka Suraj* (The Sun of New Writing ; 1982) and *Kalpana ke Pankh Pakar* are his chief collections of poems.

VED RAHI. Dogri-speaking Hindi short story writer, whose collections are : *Sima ka Patthar* (Milestone ; 1962), *Tutate Vriksh* (The Breaking Trees), *Nai Paudh* (New Generation ; 1965) and *Darar* (The Rift ; 1971). He is now associated with film industry.

VED VYAS. Modern Rajasthani poet, who has composed progressive and love poems ; *Parikrama* is a collection of his essays.

VEDANAND JHA. Modern Maithili scholar and poet, who has written *Alankritibodh*, a work on Alankars. His *Muktak* poems are collected in *Ratnabatua.*

VELI KRISAN RUKMANI RI. Celebrated Rajasthani poem by Prithwiraj Rathore (1548-1600), which consists of 304 verses and was composed in 1580.

Based mainly on the *Bhagavat Puran*, it describes the childhood and youth of Rukmini, the proposal of her marriage with Shishupal, Rukmini's love for Krishna and her letter to the latter ; the meeting of Krishna and Rukmini in the temple, abduction of Rukmini, Krishna's battle with Shishupal and with Rukmini's brother, Rukmi and their defeat, Krishna's departure for Dwarika with Rukmini, the union of Krishna and Rukmini, description of six seasons, birth of Pradyumna, and then description of Aniruddha, the son of Pradyumna, etc.

An erotic love poem, it culminates in Bhakti. More than a dozen annotations in Sanskrit, Braj and Rajasthani were written by scholars in the mediaeval period. And in modern times, more than half a dozen editions of the *Veli* have been brought out. A fine blend of the elements of devotional and Riti schools of Hindi poetry in Rajasthan, it has been given the status of the Fifth Veda.

VEMURI RADHAKRISHNA MURTI. Telugu-speaking modern Hindi poet, whose *Nagarjun Sagar* has been composed on the style of Telugu folk-songs. His *Telugu ke Adhunik Kavi* (Modern Telugu Poets ; 1963) is a collection of essays on the 16 modern Telugu poets.

VENI (fl. before 1543-1606). Saint-poet, whose three *Padas* are included in the *Granth Sahib* (q.v.).

VENIDATT GOSAIN. Sanskrit saint-poet and scholar, who was patronized by Madhav Singh (1776-1808). He composed some erotic verses, despite his being a saint, in Maithili also and was also known for his lyrics.

VENI MADHAV. Modern Hindi writer of Mauritius, whose chief work is : *Hindi Praveshika*. He is also noted for his short stories.

VENKAT KRISHNA AYYANGAR. Tamil-speaking modern Hindi writer, who is noted for his critical essays on the lives and literatures of Vaishnav Alvar Saints.

VENKAT KRISHNARAO, DANDMUDI. See *Dandmudi Venkat Krishnarao*.

VENKAT KRISHNA, MU. GO. Tamil-speaking modern Hindi writer, who has tr. into Hindi from original Tamil *Tirukural* under the title *Uttar-veda* and of the *Shilppaddikaram* under the title : *Nupur-Kavya* (The Lay of the Anklet).

VENKATRAM SHASTRI, PIDPARTI. Telugu-speaking modern Hindi writer, who is noted for his articles on linguistics.

VENKATRAMAN RAO, VAI. Telugu-speaking Hindi scholar, whose research publications are : *Teulgu aur Hindi Lokoktiyan*

(Telugu and Hindi Proverbs ; 1971) and *Ritikalin Kavya ki Sanskritik Prishthbhumi* (The Cultural Background of Riti-period Poetry).

VENKATARAMAYYA, K.S. (fl. 1935). Kannada-speaking Hindi poet, whose poems were published in the 'Jagriti', a literary magazine. The poems were mainly patriotic in nature.

VENKATESHWAR RAO, KANAKMEDAL. Telugu-speaking Hindi poet, who is noted for his *Mahavir Balchandra* (1954), a long narrative poem on the heroism of Balchandra, a boy, in the battle of Palnadu.

VENKATESHWARAN, N. (fl. early 20th cent.). Malayalam-speaking Hindi writer, who was one of the early advocates of Hindi in Kerala. He was a good Hindi teacher and the number of his students was quite good. He was also the author of *Kerala Vaibhav* (The Glory of Kerala), *Kerala Sanskrit* (The Kerala Culture) and *Kerala ke Hindi Kavi : Garbh Shriman* (Garbh Shriman : Kerala's Hindi Poet).

VENU GOPAL RAO. Poet, whose collection of poems : *Hawayen Chup Nahin Rehtin* (The Winds do not remain Silent ; 1980) reveals in a simple and natural language the contemporary life ; his other poetical collections are : *Chattanon ka Jal Git* and *Ve Hath Hote Hain*. He has published a novel, *House Surgeon*.

VERMA, BHAGVATI CHARAN. See *Bhagvati Charan Verma.*

VERMA, DHIRENDRA. See *Dhirendra Verma.*

VERMA, MANINDRA KISHORE. See *Manindra Kishore Verma.*

VERMA, RAM KUMAR. See *Ram Kumar Verma.*

VERMA, S.B. Modern writer, who is known for his work : *Japani Kavitayen*.

VERMA, VRAJESHWAR. See *Vrajeshwar Verma.*

VERMA, VRINDAVANLAL. See *Vrindavanlal Verma.*

VERRIER, ELWIN, THE LATE. Scholar, who was noted for his *Folk-tales of Mahakoshal* (1944), *Folk-songs of Chhattisgarh* (1946), *Songs of the Forest* (1935 ; along with Shyam Rao Hiwale), etc.

VIBHUTI ANAND. Maithili writer and poet, whose chief works are : *Pravesh* (1979 ; collection of his short stories), *Sungait Ekta Gamak Katha* (1980 ; a short novel on the exploitation of poor people by selfish politicians), *Utha Rahal Ghosh Timir* (1981 ; a collection of *Ghazals*) and a critical work on Lalit (q.v.), entitled *Shri Lalit a Hunak Katha-Yatra* (1981). His two novels are *Gam Sungait* and *Parajit-Aparajit* (both 1982).

VICARION, PENJONO. Author of *Grammatica Italiana Indostan* (1874) ; being in Italian, it could not become popular.

VICHCHHAND CHARAN PATNNAIK (1901-). Oriya-speaking Hindi writer, who tr. *Ramcharitmanas* and *Vinay Patrika* (qq. v.) into Oriya.

VICHITRA NARAYAN DATT BARUA (1902-). Assamese-speaking Hindi writer, whose original works are *Shabda-Sangrah* and *Assam Gaurav* (on historical characters of Assam). He has also published the Hindi version of Ram Saraswati's *Bhim-Charit* from Assamese.

VICHITRA NATAK. See *Govind Singh, Guru*.

VIDHU. Modern Maithili poet, whose *Sitayan* is an epic.

VIDHU BHUSHAN DASGUPTA. Bengali-speaking modern Hindi writer, who prepared school text-books for propagation of Hindi in non-Hindi speaking areas.

VIDYA BHASKAR ARUN. Panjabi-speaking modern Hindi poet, who is noted for his poems : *Saya aur Savera* (The Shadow and the Morning).

VIDYA DHAR PANDIT (fl. prior to 1685). Maithili poet, whose lyrics are quoted in the present Karttik Nach-Guru's *Ragmala*.

VIDYA DHAR SHUKLA. Modern Hindi writer of Thailand, who is noted for his promotion of the cause of Hindi in his country.

VIDYA DHAR SHUKLA. Modern scholar, whose chief work is *Hindi Alochana aur Aj ki Kahani*.

VIDYA DHARI DEVI. Modern Rajasthani scholar, who is noted for her *Asli Marwari Git-Sangrah*.

VIDYA NATH GUPTA (1923-). Dogri-speaking Hindi poet and scholar, who is noted for his two works : *Mere Git Adhure*

Hain (My Songs are Incomplete) and *Hindi Kavita men Rashtriya Bhavna* (The National Feeling in Hindi Poetry).

VIDYA NATH RAY. Modern Maithili writer, who is noted for a drama on the poet, Vidyapati.

VIDYA NIDHI (fl. 18th cent.), Poet of the Krishna-cult (Haridasi Sect), who is known for his *Padas* in praise of his Guru Govardhan Dev.

VIDYA NIWAS MISHRA (1926-). Essayist, whose chief works are : *Chitvan ki Chhanh* (1953), *Tum Chandan Ham Pani* (1957), *Angan ka Panchhi* : *Banjara Man*, *Mere Ram ka Mukut Bhig Raha Hai*, *Kantile Taron ke Ar-Par*, *Parampara Bandhan Nahin*, *Kaun Tu Phulav Binanihari*, *Angad ki Niyati*, *Lago Rang Hari* (collections of essays), *Ritivigyan* (criticism), *Bharatiya Chintan ke Kuchh Paksha*, *Hindi Shabda- Sampada*, *Asmita ke Liye* and *Sahitya ka Prayojan*. In his essays, Mishra has tried to unify the Indian literature and culture with the daily life of the people. His collection of poems is : *Pani ki Pukar*. With Robert Nethan, he has published *Modern Hindi Poetry*.

VIDYAPATI (1368-1475). Celebrated Hindi and Sanskrit poet of Mithila, who was grandson of Jaydatt, son of Ganpati and a court-poet of three Mithila kings, Kirti Singh, Dev Singh (fl. 1413), Shiv Singh and of Vishwas Devi, queen of Padma Singh. His *Padavali* (q.v.) is in Maithili, while *Kirtilata* and *Kirtipataka* (qq.v.) are in Avahatta, a mixture of Maithili and Apabhransh. His *Goraksha Vijay* (q.v.) is in the form of a drama, consisting of dialogues in Sanskrit and Prakrit as well as some 25 *Padas* in Maithili ; the drama was composed for the purpose of being presented on the stage on the occasion of *Kalipuja* during the short reign of Shiv Singh, to whom the poet was a close friend and guide.

Vidyapati's claim to a high place in Hindi literature is mostly based on the popularity of the *Padavali*, where *Shringar* is used as a medium of devotion. It prepared the ground for the Vaishnavites and may be said to have inspired the poets of the *Bhakti* era and also of *Riti Kal*. The *Padavali* is also noted for its lyrical quality as also for its enchanting melodiousness The theme which Vidyapati chose for his lyrics, namely love of Krishna and Radha, proved to be irresistible for poets coming after him. His lyrics on the the life of Radha and Krishna became a craze in Bengal and Orissa, where young poets began to emulate Vidyapati and write lyrics using his diction, metre and even vocabulary. His songs are equally popular among the Hindi-speaking people.

The *Padavali* has been rendered into English by a distinguished Bengali as Shri Aurobindo.

Vidypati's *Goraksha Vijay* gives artistic expression to a sound philosophy of life, striking a golden mean between restraint and erotic abandon, a happy balance between *Yoga* and *Bhoga*.

Known throughout Bihar, the land of his birth, as 'Maithil Kokil' or Mithila's nightingale, Vidyapati was the first to use to good effect Maithili, with an admixture of Apabhransh, the common man's language in that region, as the medium of poetry.

Vidyapati is also the author of several works in Sanskrit, *e.g.*, *Bhu-parikrama*, *Purushapariksha*, etc.

VIDYAPATI THAKUR. Maithili writer, who has tr. his father, Shivnandan Thakur's Hindi book *Mahakavi Vidyapati* into Maithili (1979) in an edited form.

VIDYA SAGAR DAYAL. Scholar, who prepared 'Hindi Bhasha Course' in Romania and in collaboration with Ion Petrescu published *Hindi-Romanian Shabdakosh* and *Romanian-Hindi Shabdakosh* (1978). He also taught Hindi in the Bucharest University, Romania.

VIDYA VATI KOKIL (1914-). Poetess, whose chief poetical collections are : *Ankurita*, *Suhagin* (1952), *Punarmilan* (1956) and *Saptak* (Septet, containg tr of some of Aurobindo's poems). Her works deal mainly with filial love, devotion, daily life, etc.

VIDYA-VILAP. First Maithili drama, which was composed in 1720 by Bhupatindra Mall (q.v.), the ruler of the Bhatgao House in Nepal.

Vidyavati, the daughter of king Vir Singh of Ujjain, is a very talented girl and she has taken a vow to marry that person who can defeat her in discussion. Many a prince come to try their luck but go disappointed. Her father grows anxious and sends his court-poet to invite prince Sundar of Kanchi, who is reported to be a learned man. Prince Sundar, also hearing of Vidyavati's beauty and accomplishments, wishes to woo her. He comes to Ujjain without anybody's knowledge and puts up his residence at the house of the garland-girl of the king. After developing intimacy with her, the prince tells her his mind and seeks her help in the affair. She contrives to bring both of them together and from the first sight, they become enamoured of each other. The king and queen, however, come to know of their clandestine meetings and the lovers are caught. Sundar is brought before the king and sentenced to the punishment of a thief. But subsequently, the court-poet, who had gone to Kanchi, returns and tells the king that the captive is no other than prince Sundar, the son of king Gunsindhu. Upon this, the king immediately releases him from captivity and unites him with his daughter in marriage.

The play, in 7 Acts, owes its charm to references to everyday life in Mithila.

VIDYA VILAS PAVADAU. Rajasthani poem of 189 verses, composed by Hiranand Suri in 1428 on the basis of the story of Murkhchatt or Vinaychatt.

Dhansagar is turned out of the house by his father, Dhanvah, a wealthy merchant, for saying that he would be king of Ujjain. He comes to Shripur and joins a school where a prince, princess Sahagsundari and Lachchhinivas, a son of the minister, are also studying. Dhansagar is stupid but humble and is, therefore, nicknamed Murkhchatt for his stupidity and Vinaychatt for his humility. The princess wants to marry Lachchhinivas but the prince likes her to marry Vinaychatt. Lachchhinivas fixes a rendezvous with the princess but on her reaching the appointed spot, she is fraudently married to Vinaychatt. After the marriage, the couple ride to Ujjain on the back of a camel and it is only at day-break that she discovers to her utter disappointment that the man to whom she is married is not the prince but Vinaychatt. Earlier, Vinaychatt had been blessed by the goddess of learning and now being an accomplished scholar, he comes to acquire the name of Vidyavilas. After many adventures, he ultimately becomes king of Ujjain.

The poem, meant to be sung, mentions musical modes and notes as also describes the royal court, trade and commerce, feuds over females and methods of reception, etc.

VIHARI VALLABH (fl. 18th cent.). Poet of the Krishna-cult (Haridasi Sect), who was a disciple of Bhagvat Rasik (q.v.). He composed many works including *Sakhi Sukh Sar Siddhant* (on principles), *Bhagvat Sakhi Prashansa* (devotional), etc.

VIHARIN DEV (fl. 16th cent.). Poet of the Krishna-cult (Haridasi Sect), who composed 700 *Dohas* and several *Padas*, all providing a theoretical basis of the Sect.

VIJ BAPAT. Marathi-speaking modern Hindi writer, whose

chief work is *Prasadottar Natya Sahitya.* He also tr. into Hindi the Marathi drama *Barrister* (1980) written by Jayvant Dalvi.

VIJAL VIJOGAN RI KATHA. Dingal romance (Script 1769), written by an unknown writer.

VIJAP. The first collection of three Akavitavadi poets : 'Vimal' (Gangaprasad), 'Jagdish' (Chaturvedi) and (Shyam) Parmar, which was published in 1967. These poets consider Progressivism as out-moded and look upon the sophisticated diction of Experimentalists (of Nai Kavita) as a mere escape from the grim task of self-identification. These poets reject outright all old institutions, though they have faith in man and his ability to live his own life, unmindful of the traditions. The Akavitavadi poets favour the rugged but natural idiom, which certainly has brought some freshness by stripping poetry of all pretensions.

VIJAY BHADRA. Jain Rajasthani poet, who composed in 1354 the earliest versified folk-tale, the *Hansraj-Bachchhraj Chaupai* See *Hansavali.*

VIJAY CHAUHAN (1930-). Progressive short story writer, whose chief collections are : *Ek Butshikan ka Janma* (The Birth of an Iconoclast) and *Dharma Kshetre Kurukshetra* ; her *Yuddha ki Qimat* (The price of War) contains Soviet stories.

VIJAY DAN DETHA. Modern Rajasthani fiction writer, who has converted a folk-tale into modern fiction in his navel *Tido Rao.* On the style of folk-tales, he has published a dozen volumes in his series *Batan ri Phulvari.* His short story collections in Khari Boli are : *Duvidha aur anya Kahaniyan* and *Uljhan.*

VIJAY DEV NARAIN SAHI, the late (b. 1924). Poet of the *Tisra Saptak* (q.v.), whose chief works : *Machhalighar* (Aquarium) and *Sakhi* are poetical collections. His *Jayasi* (1983) is a critical work.

VIJAY KAPUR. Poet, whose *Taragrah Tapte Huye* (The Burning Stars ;1982) is a collection of poems.

VIJAY MAL. Bhojpuri folk-tale in verse, which describes the heroism of Kunvar Vijayi. At present, the folk-tale, which exists under the title *Kunvar Vijayi,* was composed by Mahadev Prasad Singh.

VIJAY MOHAN SINGH. Critic, whose *Aj ki Kahani* (1983) is a

collection of his articles and reviews pertaining to Hindi short story.

VIJAY NARAIN MISHRA SAHITYALANKAR 'PRAVASI'. Maithili poet, whose *Annapurna* (1974) is a collection of poems.

VIJAY NILAM. Modern Hindi writer of Kashmir, who is noted for her novels, written mainly on traditional lines.

VIJAY PAL RASO. Ballad in Dingal by Nalha Singh Bhat; it celebrates the heroic battles of Vijaypal of Vijaygarh (Karauli). The work is incomplete: consisting of only 42 metres and is of some literary value. The time mentioned by the poet of Vijaypal's battles is 1036 but the language of the *Raso* reveals that it was composed some time in the 16th-17th centuries. It appears that its real author added the fictitious name of Nalha Singh Bhat to it to give the version an old garb.

VIJAY PAL SINGH. Writer, whose chief works on Keshavdas are : *Keshav-Sudha* (1969), *Keshav aur Unka Sahitya*, *Keshav ka Acharyatva*, *Keshav ki Kavya-Chetana* and *Keshavdas* (1970). He has also edited *Ritikavya Sangrah*.

VIJAY RAGHAV REDDY. Telugu-speaking Hindi writer, who is noted for his *Saman Srot aur Bhinn Vartani ki Shabdavali* (Hindi-Oriya ; 1974) and *Saman Srot aur Bhinn Vartani ki Shabdavali* (Hindi-Assamese ; 1976). He has also tr. Telugu short stories into Hindi.

VIJAY SHANKAR MALL. Modern scholar, whose chief work is : *Hindi Kavya men Pragativad*.

VIJAYAN, P.V. Malayalam-speaking modern Hindi poet, in whose satirical poetical collection : *Kathya aur Tathya* (Fiction and Fact), the poem 'Adhunik Eklavya' (The Modern Eklavya) is quite popular.

VIJAYANAND (fl. 19th cent.). Poet, who was a friend of Babu Ramkrishna Verma, the editor of 'Bharat-Jivan'. His stray verses are available.

VIJENDRA KUMAR. Poet, whose chief works are : *Tras* (Awe), *Chait ki Lal Tahni* (The Red Branch of March ; 1982) and *Ye Akritiyan Tumhari* (collection of poems).

VIJHARAI AHIR RI BAT. Dingal romance (Script 1790), which is written by an unknown author.

VIJYENDRA SNATAK (1914-). Writer, whose chief works are : *Radhavallabh Sampraday* : *Siddhant aur Sahitya* (research on Radhavallabh Sect ; 1957), *Kamayani-Darshan* (The Philosophy of *Kamayani*), *Alochak Ramchandra Shukla* (Ramchandra Shukla the Critic), *Mahakavi Prasad, Chintan ke Kshan* (thoughtful essays on modern topics), *Hindi Gadya* : *Udbhav aur Vikas* (Hindi Prose: Origin and Development), *Hindi Sahitya aur Uski Pragati* (Hindi Literature and its Progress), *Adhunik Hindi Sahitya* (Modern Hindi Literature), *Hindi Sahitya ka Sankshipta Itihas* (Concise History of Hindi Literature), *Anusandhan ki Prakriya* (The Methodology of Research) and *Vimarsh ke Kshan*. He was Head of the Hindi Department at Delhi University.

VIKRAM PANCHDAND CHAUPAI. See *Siddhasen*.

VILAS GUPTE. Marathi-speaking modern Hindi fiction writer, whose *Raja Nanga Hai* is a short story collection ; his other publication is *Akhiri Hathiyar*.

VILHOJI (1532-1616). Rajasthani saint-poet, who provided a firm footing to the Vishnoi Sampraday (see *Jambhoji*) by his deeds and writings. His seven Kathas : *Dhadabandh, Autarpat, Gugaliyai Ki, Phulhoji Ki, Draunpur Ki, Jaisalmer Ki* and *Jhordan Ki* describe episodes in the life of Jambhoji, the founder of his Sampraday. His other works on miscellaneous topics are : *Katha Gyanchari, Sach-Akhari Vigatavali* (providing a list of many words and phrases used in a 'wrong' sense), *Visan Chhattisi, Harjas, Sakhi, Chhappay* and *Duha* ; the *Sakhis* and *Harjas* are meant to be sung in various musical tunes. His poems are full of emotion and express his deep devotion.

VILINATHAN, RA. Tamil-speaking modern Hindi writer, who is noted for his critical essays : 'Tamil Sahitya par Hindi ka Prabhav' (The Influence of Tamil Literature on Hindi), etc. and *Balopyogi Kathayen* stories meant for children. He tr. from Tamil into Hindi Krishnamurti Kalki's novels under the titles of *Parthiv ka Sapna* (The Dream of Parthiv), *Laharon ki Avaz* (The Sound of Waves), *Shaulaimalai ki Rajkumari* (The Princess of Shaulaimalai), of Jagshirpiyan's novel as *Bahar ka Admi* (The Outsider) and *Chidambaram*. of Subrahmanyam's novel as *Hriday-nad* (The Heart-beat). On the model of the celebrated Tamil epic, *Shilppaddikaram*, he has written a novel in Hindi under the title *Nupur-gatha*. He tr. into Hindi Janakiraman's Tamil dramas as *Masterji* and B.S. Ramiya's as *Kasauti* (The Touchstone). He also tr. Ra Ganpati's biography of Shankaracharya under the title *Jay Jay Shankar* (Victory of Shankar).

VIMAL, GANGAPRASAD. See *Gangaprasad Vimal.*

VIMAL MITRA. Modern novelist, whose chief novels are: *Main, Sahib Bibi Ghulam, Rajabadal, Parastri, Vishay Vish Nahin, Chakar Gatha, Gavah No. 3, Kharidi Kaudiyon ke Mol* (2 Pts.), *Ve Donon aur Vah, Kaun* and *Vivahita* (1984). He has written so far some 40 novels. His short stories have been published as *Vimal Mitra ki Shreshth Kahaniyan* (2 Pts.).

VIMAL SAHASRABUDDHE. Marathi-speaking modern Hindi scholar, whose chief work is: *Hindi Upanyason men Nari ka Manovaigyanik Vishleshan.*

VIMALA LUTHRA. Modern writer, whose chief one-act plays are: 'Munne ka Namkaran', 'Pritibhoj', 'Dhobi ka Agaman', 'Line Clear', 'Tansen' and 'Pachpan ka Pher'; her plays bear the impact of English one-act plays.

VIMALA RAINA. Kashmiri-speaking Hindi writer; her chief works are: *Tin Yuga* (1958; a drama describing three generations of a family), *Ahen aur Muskan* (Sighs and Smiles; collection of one-act plays), *Pyasa Pani* (Thirsty Water), *Forget Me Not* (novels), *Ham Tum aur Ve* (We, You and They) and *Bujhe Dip* (Extinguished Lamps; short story collections).

VIMLESH. See *Vishwanath Sharma 'Vimlesh'.*

VINAY (1937-). Poet, whose chief poetical work, *Ek Purush Aur* (One More Man) gives a new interpretation to the mythical story of Urvashi and Vishwamitra; *Dusra Rag* (Another Melody; 1976), *Kai Antaral* (1980) and *Punarvas ka Dand* are his poetical collections, while *Adi Vidrohi* (The First Rebel; 1980) is his drama based on an episode in the *Mahabharat* regarding the demon, Bak. His another drama is *Vikalpa* His critical works are: *Samkalin Kahani: Samantar Kahani* and *Samkalin Hindi Natak aur Rangmanch.* His short story collection is *Pravesh.*

VINAY CHANDRA (fl. 1668-1712). Jain Rajasthani poet, who composed verses mostly numerical like *Chaubisi* and *Bisi*, to express his devotional fervour. His major narrative poem, *Uttam Kumar Charit Chaupai*, describes the love and adventures of Uttam Kumar, son of Raja Makardhwaj of Benares, and his becoming a Jain ascetic in the end. Most of its verses as also his stray poems are meant to be sung in the popular folk-tunes. Idioms and expressions from common man's life are prominent characteristics of his poems.

VINAY DUBE Poet, whose collection of poems are *Mahamahim Chup Hain* (His Excellency is Silent ; 1980) and *Sapnon men ata hai Rakshas* (1983).

VINAY GOPAL JHA. Maithili writer, who has tr. Saradchandra Dev Sharma's *Turask Upanyashak* from Bengali into Maithili as *Turask Katha* (1979).

VINAY MOHAN SHARMA (1905-). Critic whose chief works are : *Bhule Git* (1944 ; poetical collection), *Kavi Prasad : Ansu tatha anya Kritiyan* (1945), *Hindi Git-Govind* (1945 ; Hindi tr. of Jayadeva's *Gitagovinda*), *Drishtikon* (1950), *Sahityavalokan* (1953), *Sahitya, Shodh, Samiksha* (1958 ; all the three collections of critical essays), *Hindi ko Marathi Santon ki Den* (Contribution of Marathi Saints to Hindi ; 1957), *Hindi ka Vyavaharik Rup* and *Rekhayen aur Rang* (1967 ; collection of sketches). The main trend of his criticism is academic, as he has been a teacher in his career. His real name is Shukdev Prasad Tiwari and his poetic name is 'Veeratma'.

VINAY PATRIKA (*Vinayavali* or The Book of Prayers). Poem by Tulsidas (q.v.) in Braj, written perhaps between 1579 and 1581.

Consisting of 279 verses, it is a prayer to Ram and as it is difficult to approach Him directly, Tulsi has sought the help of Ganesh, Surya, Shiv, Devi, Ganga, Yamuna, Kashi, Chitrakut, Hanuman, Lakshman, Bharat, etc. The book opens with a hymn on Ganesh and the following verse is in the worship of god Surya ; verses 3-16 praise Shiv and Durga. The remaining part of the book is dedicated to the worship of Vishnu, whose incarnation is Ram. It is in this work that the poet has the occasion to write about himself. The verses have been written in 21 forms of Rags and Raginis ; the book is replete with the sentiment '*Shant*' and is full of devotion.

In comparison with other works of Tulsidas, the *Vinay Patrika* is more difficult to understand but 'it is in some respects his finest work and displays very deep religious feelings.' Its elevated descriptions sometimes excel those of *Ramcharitmanas*. There are several commentaries on this work and it has been tr. into English as well under the 'Unesco Series of Representative Works of East-West'.

VINAY PRABH. See *Gautam Swami Ras*.

VINAYAK RAO KORTKAR. Marathi-speaking modern Hindi writer, whose short stories have appeared in various magazines.

VINAYAK RAO VIDYALANKAR (1896-1962). Telugu-speaking Hindi writer of Hyderabad, whose chief works are *Chabuk* (1951 ; a collection of his satirical short stories), a short biography of Mahatma Gandhi (1948) and *Rashtrapati Lincoln* (1951).

VINDHYACHAL TRIPATHI. Telugu-speaking Hindi scholar, whose *Gulab ki Tahani* (The Branch of a Rose ; 1960) is a collection of his short stories.

VINDHYA NATH JHA. Modern Maithili poet, who has composed some *Maheshvanis* (songs in praise of Mahesh or Shiv) and lyrics. He has incorporated a serious element in lyrics.

VINDHYESHWAR PRASAD TRIPATHI. Writer, whose chief work is a drama, *Mithilesh Kumari* (Sita ; 1889).

VINOD BHARDWAJ. Poet, whose collections of Poems are : *Pichha aur anya Kavitayen* (The Chase and Other Poems) and *Jalta Makan* (The Burning House ; 1980).

VINOD CHANDRA PANDEY. Modern poet, whose chief works are : *Suryast*, *Vikalpa Krishnapuksha*, *Shishir Patra*, *Pranay Pragit* and *Rashtravani*.

VINOD KUMAR SHUKLA. Poet, whose collection of poems is : *Vah Admi Naya Garam Kot Pahan kar Chala Gaya Vichar ki Tarah* (That Man has Left with a Warm Coat like a Thought ; 1981). He has also written a novel : *Naukar ki Kamiz*.

VINOD RAS. See *Sumati Hans*.

VINOD RASTOGI (1923-). Dramatist, whose chief works *Azadi ke Bad* (After Independence), *Hath* (The Hand), *Barf ki Minar* (The Tower of Snow) and *Bhagirath ke Bete* (The Sons of Bhagirath) ; *Purush ka Pap* (The Sin of Man) and *Qasam Quran Ki* (The Oath by Quran) are his chief one-act play collections.

VINOD SHANKAR VYAS (1904-66). Short story writer, whose chief works are : *Tulika* (1928), *Bhuli Bat*, *Dhup Dip* (all short story collections), *Madhukari* (2 Pts., a compilation of selected short stories of prominent writers) and *Kahani Kala* (in collaboration with Gyan Chandra). He followed the emotional style of story-writing and as such his stories come under the category of the stories of Jayshankar Prasad (q.v.).

VINOD SHARMA. Poet, whose *Kavita Ek Khidki Hai* (The

Poetry is a Window ; 1980) is a collection of poems on the inconsistencies in the modern city-life.

VINOD SOMANI HANS. Modern Rajasthani poet, whose chief poems are : 'Jivanai ro Maram' and 'Minakh Jun' ; his *Rang men Bhang* is a collection of satirical one-act plays.

VINODILAL (fl. 1685). Jain poet, who was the author of *Rajul Pachchisi*, *Nemi-Byah* (*Vivah*), *Neminath Mangal* and *Nemi-Rajul-Barahmasa Sanvad*, all dealing with the story of Neminath, the 22nd Jain Tirthankar and Rajul, his wife.

VINSON, J. Author of *Manuel de la langue Hindostani-Urdu et Hindi, etc.* (Paris, 1899).

VINYA, K. Marathi-speaking modern Hindi poetess, who has published poems on various subjects.

VIPIN KUMAR AGRAWAL. Dramatist, who has written short plays of contemporay sensibility ; these are collected in *Tin Apahaj* (Three Cripples ; 1963) and *Khoye Huye Admi ki Khoj* (The Search of a Lost Man ; 1980). *Is Dharti Par* (On this Earth ; 1981) and *Nange Pair* are collections of his poems, while *Biti Ap Biti Ap* is his novel. His critical work is : *Adhunikta ke Pehlu*.

VIPRA. Modern Bhojpuri poet, who is noted for his stray poems.

VIPRA NAGARIDAS (fl. 1775). Poet, who tr. the *Bhagavata Purana* into Brajbhasha. He was a disciple of Charan Das (q.v.) of Shuk Sampraday.

VIR. Poet of the Riti school, who was a Kayasth of Delhi. He composed *Krishna-Chandrika* (1722), a work on *Rasa* and *Nayikabhed*.

VIRAJ. Writer, whose historical novel, *Nepaleshwar* (The King of Nepal ; 1973) is based on the description of Nepal from 1775 to 1857.

VIRANJI KUNVARI (fl. 1848). Poetess, who was daughter of Thakur Sitalsingh of Devara (Varanasi). Her *Sati-Vilas* on chaste wives is extant.

VIRAT PARVA. Rajasthani poem in 183 stanzas, which was composed by Shali Suri before 1421. Narrating the story of the 'Virat Parva' of the *Mahabharat* in his own way, the poet has used Sanskrit syllabic metres.

VIRATA KI PADMINI (The Padmini of Virata). Novel (1936) by Vrindavanlal Verma (q.v.), which is a historical romance.

A Dangi of Palar has an extremely beautiful girl, Kumud and the people look upon her as the incarnation of Devi Uma, the consort of Shiv. In the meantime, Kumud and Kunjar meet each other and are lost in romantic dreams. Alim Din tries to gain Kumud and he attacks Virata. In the battle Kunjar is killed and Kumud sacrifices her life by drowning herself. There are, however, many episodic stories in the novel.

VIRBHAN (fl. 1603). Saint-poet of Narnaul in Haryana and the founder of the Sadh or Satnami Sect, which in 1672 took to revolt. The forces of Aurangzeb suppressed it and made this sect powerless; the number of Satnamis killed was about 2,000. Stray verses of the saint are extant with the followers of the sect.

VIRBHAN (1688-1735). Dingal poet, who was the author of *Rajrupak* (1749), a work, describing the battle in 1730 between Abhay Singh, Ruler of Jodhpur and Sarbaland Khan, Subedar of Ahmedabad in which the latter was defeated. The work is divided into 46 cantos.

VIRBHAN THAKARSIYOT GADAN (fl. latter half of 17th cent.). Rajasthani poet, whose *Kunvar Shri Anupsinghji ri Veli* (composed prior to 1669) describes the deeds of his hero.

VIR CHAND (fl. last quarter of 16th cent.). Gujarati-speaking Jain poet, whose chief works in Hindi are: *Vir-Vilas Phagu*, *Jambuswami Beli* and *Neminath Ras*.

VIR CHARITRA SATSAI. See *Mohansingh, Kavirao*.

VIR DAS ROHDIYO (alias Rengrelo Vithu; *c.* 1520-1608). Dingal poet, of whose satirical verses only a few are extant.

VIR NARAYAN. Maithili poet of Nepal, who is noted for his lyrics in the tradition of Vidyapati. He may be identified with the poet, who is reported to have composed an anonymous drama on the life of Krishna under Tribhuvan Mall alias Trailokyamall (1572-85/86).

VIR SATSAI. Rajasthani work in Pingal, which was composed by Suryamall Mishran (q.v.). Though, as its name indicates, it should have contained 700 *Dohas*, it is incomplete and at present consists of 288 *Dohas* only. Composed during and after the 1857 Mutiny, the sentiments expressed in the *Dohas* do not pertain to any particular individual but are intended to arouse the Rajput heroic spirit. He voiced the lofty ideals of mediaeval Rajput chivalry, expressed mostly through the medium of brave women so that the contemporary and future generations may adopt the high ideals.

VIR SATSAI. See *Nathusingh Mahiyariya.*

VIR SINGH DEV CHARITA. See *Keshavdas.*

VIR VINOD. See *Shyamaldas Dadhivadiya.*

VIRENDRA KUMAR BARSUWALA (1930-). Scholar, whose chief works are : *Vidyapati* and *Yashodhara Kavya Sandarbh.*

VIRENDRA KUMAR JAIN (1916-). Poet, whose chief poetical works are : *Anagata ki Ankhen* (The Eyes of one not arrived ; 1959), *Yatna ka Surya* (The Sun of Agony ; 1966) and *Shunya Purush aur Vastuen* (1972) ; he has also published a novel, *Muktidut* (The Angel of Liberty) and a short story collection : *Ek aur Nilanjana* (One More Nilanjana). He is the pioneer of Sanatan Suryodayi Kavita Movement. He has written a huge novel on Mahavir—*Anuttara Yogi* (4 Pts.) and another novel *Anatit* (1984). He edits 'Navneet'.

VIRENDRA MEDHIRATH Writer, who has edited *Kahani ke Aspas* (Near the Short Story ; 1979), which is a collection of a dozen short stories, presenting a variety of themes ; the stories are thought-provoking *Mitti par Nange Panv* is a collection of his short stories.

VIRENDRA MISHRA (1928-). Lyricist, whose chief works are : *Gitam*, *Lekhni Bela* and *Aviral Chal Madhuvanti* (1967). His critical works are : *Ekanki : Udbhav aur Vikas* and *Brajbhasha Gadya Sahitya ka Itihas* (1984), while *Avoz A Rahi Hai* is his drama.

VIRENDRA PRASAD SINGH 'VIPLAV'. Modern Magahi writer, who is noted for his social one-act plays.

VIRENDRA VIDYAVACHASPATI (1909-79). Scholar, whose chief work is : *Apabhransh Bhasha ka Adhyayan.*

VIRMAYAN. Dingal poem by Badar, Bahadur or Bhadar, a Mohammedan Dhadhi, composed in the first half of the 15th century.

The poem describes in 285 verses many battles and events connected with the early Rathore chiefs (Jaitmal, Mallinath, Viramdev, all sons of Rao Salakha; Jagmal, the son of Mallinath; Chunda and Goga, the sons of Viramdev) and the Johiyas (Dalla, the chief of the clan, his brothers and other relatives) from a little earlier than 1374 to 1402, when Mallinath became the ruler of Mahewa and Khed and Goga was killed by the Johiyas Major events revovle, however, around the deeds of Viram and Johiyas and are linked in a chain of action and reaction.

An important source of Rathore history in the 14th century, here the Rajput feudal society has emerged with all its grandeur and weaknesses The poem was so popular that later many of its lines became proverbial.

The poem has been written in the *Nisani* metre and hence is also called *Nisani Virman Ri.*

VIRUD CHHIHATTARI. See *Dursa Adha.*

VIRUD PRAKAS. See *Asiya Dana.*

VISALDEV RASO. Ballad in Dingal by Narpati Nalha (q.v.; fl. *c.* 1215), which consists of 2,000 verses and is divided into four cantos. Three different editions of *Visaldev Raso* have been published.

Bhojraj Parmar of Dhara (r. 1010-50) despatches a trusted Brahmin for finding out a suitable match for his charming daughter, Rajmati The Brahmin ultimately chooses Visaldev (Vigrahraj the Fourth, r. *c.* 155) of Ajmer, who agrees to marry Rajmati. With a large retinue, the king reaches Dhara; the takes place and Visaldev gets several kingdoms and fabulous riches from his father-in-law as presents The king returns to Ajmer and lives happily for some time with his newly-wed wife. The wife and the husband, however, fall out one day in the course of a casual talk. Considering his rich dowry, the king grows puffed and tells his consort that he is the greatest monarch. Rajmati thereupon remarks that he should not swell with pride as there are several kings greater than he: for instance, there is the king of Orissa in whose kingdom mines bring forth gems and diamonds while his Sambhar lake produces only salt. This remark pierced the heart of Visaldev, who makes up his mind to set out for Orissa to collect diamonds. Despite the entreaties of his young wife and the persuasion of his relatives, the king leaves for Orissa where he spends twelve long years. In his absence, the young wife is very sad and her pangs of separation are narrated at length in the poem. At the instance of Rajmati, the Raja of Orissa intervenes and Visaldev returns home with presents of gems and diamonds from the king of Orissa. Visaldev invites his father-in-law to Ajmer and with him Rajmati goes to Dhara for a brief sojourn. Visaldev soon brings her back to Ajmer and the couple live thereafter happily.

There is much controversy about the date of this work, for Visaldev lived more than a century after the Bhojraj. The theme of the poem is not war but love and interest of the poem lies in its numerous descriptions. The language is Dingal, with addition of Pingal and a few words of Persian origin.

VISHAKH. Drama (1921) by Jayshankar Prasad (q.v.), which is based on Kalhana's *Rajtarangini*. It describes the love of Vishakh for Chandralekha, the daughter of Sushrava, a noble of the court of Nardev, the king of Kashmir.

VISHNEVSKYA, NATALIYA ALANDROVNA (1929-). Soviet Hindi scholar, who has done her doctorate on the Origin and Development of Hindi One-act Plays. She has also written 40 articles connected with research and translation.

VISHNU CHANDRA SHARMA. Modern poet, whose chief poetical works are: *Akash Vibhajit Hai* (The Sky is Divided) and *Antrang*. He has also published a novel, *Mudrarakshas*.

VISHNU DAS (fl. early 16th cent.). Poet of the Krishna-cult (Chaitanya Sect), who was a Vaishya Agrawal of Agra. After his contact with Ramraj (q.v.), he became a recluse and came to Vrindavan. His *Vairagya Vigyan* contains 100 *Savaiyas*.

VISHNU DAS (fl. 16th cent.). Poet of the Krishna-cult (Vallabh Sect), whose several *Padas* are extant.

VISHNU DAS (fl. 1850-1900). Marathi-speaking saint-poet, who composed *Padas* in Hindi.

VISHNU DAS, GOSWAMI (fl. 1435). Poet, who composed *Pandu Charit* or *Mahabharat Katha* (available only 5 Parvas), *Rukmini Mangal*, *Swargarohan* (all based on the *Mahabharat*), *Sneh Lila* and *Vishnupadas*. It appears that he was patronized by Dungrendra Singh Tomar, the ruler of Gopachal (Gwalior). Vishnu Das was the pioneer in the sense that after him many works based on the story of the *Mahabharat*, the abduction of

Rukmini and *Bhramragit* (an extension of *Sneh Lila*) came to be written in Brajbhasha by subsequent poets.

VISHNU DATT MADHU 'CHANDRA'. Hindi poet of Mauritius, whose first poetical collection appeared in 1966. His two other poetical works are : *Hasya Vatika* and *Mauritius Bharati* (ed.). He also wrote two novels : *Phat Gai Dharti* and *Rashtra Rashmi*.

VISHNU DATT RAKESH (1941-). Scholar, whose chief works are : *Tulnatmak Sahityashastra*, a critical work on Kulpati Mishra, a history of Nirgun literature of northern India, several works on Riti poetry and the editing of Pant's *Satyakam*.

VISHNU GOVIND SHARMA (fl. early 20th cent.). Writer, who is noted for his drama, *Karna*.

VISHNU GOVIND SHIRODKAR (fl. 1850-1900). Marathi-speaking Hindi dramatist, who wrote dramas on Puranic themes ; the dramas are, however, no longer extant.

VISHNU KHARE. Poet, whose collection of poems : *Khud Apni Ankh Se* (With His Own Eyes ; 1978) builds up a cumulative effect out of day-to-day insignifances ; his another poetical collection is *Yah Chaku Samay*.

VISHNU NAGAR. Poet, whose chief work is *Talab men Dubi Larkiyan* (Girls Immersed in a Tank ; 1980) is a collection of poems ; *Aj ka Din* (Today ; 1981) and *Khandit Puja* are collections of his short stories.

VISHNU PRABHAKAR 1912-). Writer, whose chief works are *Dhalti Rat* (1951), *Tat ke Bandhan* (Bonds of the Shore), *Swapnamayi* (1956), *Darpan ka Vyakti* (The Man in the Mirror), *Koi To* (Some One ; 1980), *Nishikant* (novels), *Dharti ab bhi Ghum Rahi Hai*, *Meri Tentis Kahaniyan*, *Sangharsh ke Bad* (1953), *Meri Priya Kahaniyan* (My Favourite Short Stories), *Pul Tutne se Pahle*, *Apki Kripa Hai* (It is Your Kindness ; 1982) (short story collections), *Samadhi*, *Doctor*, *Yuge-Yuge Kranti*, *Tutate Parivesh*, *Hori*, *Navprabhat*, *Gandhar ki Bhikshuni* (1982), *Sunanda*, *Bandini*, *Kuhasa aur Kiran*, *Main bhi Manav Hun*, *Shwet Kamal* (dramas), *Prakash aur Parchhain*, *Insan* (*Man*), *Man ka Beta*, *Barah Ekanki*, *Kya Vah Doshi Tha* ? (Was He a Culprit ?), *Das Baje Rat*, *Uncha Parvat Gahra Sagar*. *Ye Rekhayen Ye Dayare*, *Mere Shreshth Rang Ekanki* (My Chief One-act Plays), *Naye Ekanki* (collections of one-act plays), etc., *Awara Masih* (Vagrant Messiah ; biography of Sharatchandra),

Sardar Vallabh Bhai Patel (biography) ; he has also written sketches, memoirs and reportage (*Kuchh Shabda : Kuchh Rekhayen, Hanste Nirjhar : Dahakti Bhatti, Adi aur Ant, Jyoti Punj Himalaya*) and *Kya Khoya Kya Paya* (essays on literary subjects). His important short stories are: 'Dharti ab bhi Ghum Rahi Hai' (The Earth Still Revolves), 'Grihasthi' (The Householder), 'Rehman ka Beta' (Rehman's Son), 'Judge ka Faisla' (The Award of the Judge), 'Agam Pravah' (The Impassable Tide), etc.

Vishnu Prabhakar's works display a fine blend of idealism and realism.

VISHNU PRASAD JANI. Gujarati-speaking modern Hindi scholar, whose *Gujarati Sahitya ka Navin Itihas* (in collaboration with Suresh Chandra Trivedi) is a research publication.

VISHNU PURI (1425-1500 ?). Maithili poet, who was noted for his devotional lyrics A Vaishnav Sannyasi, he was liberal enough to have composed *Padas* on Shiv as well. He was the author of the Sanskrit *Bhaktiratnavali*.

VISHNU SINGH (b 1773). Poet of the Riti school, who was Raja of Bundi. He wrote some ten thousand *Kavittas* and *Savaiyas*.

VISHNU SINGH MALL (fl. *c.* 1737). Ruler of the House of Lalitpur (or Patan) in Nepal, whose Maithili lyrics are preserved in an anthology of *Rags*. He was the great-grandson of Shrinivas Mall. He was the author of *Usha-Haran Natak* or *Krishna-Charitra* (a long one-act play) preserved in the National Library of Nepal.

VISHWAMBHAR DATT UNIYAL (fl. early 20th cent.). Garhwali writer, who was noted for his one-act plays : 'Vasanti' and 'Char Gailya'.

VISHWAMBHAR DWIJ (fl. 18th cent.). Assamese poet, whose Hindi (Brajavali) works are two dramas : *Shat-Skandh Ravan-Badh* (based on *Adbhut Ramayan*) and *Prabhas-Yatra* (based on Ram Saraswati's Assamese version of the *Mahabharat*).

VISHWAMBHAR MANAV (1912-80). Critic, who was born at Dibai in Bulandshahr district of Uttar Pradesh. His chief works are : a commentary on *Kamayani, Sumitra Nandan Pant, Kavya ka Devta Nirala, Mahadevi ki Rahasya-Sadhana, Hindi Sahtlya ka Sarvekshan, Khari Boli ke Gaurav Granth* (all criticism), *Pile Gulab ki Atma, Kaveri* (novels) and *Lahar aur Chattan* (a collection of one-act plays).

VISHWAMBHAR NATH JIJJA (fl. 1st half of 20th cent.) Writer, who was known for his historical novel, *Turk Taruni* (The Turk Lass) and short stories.

VISHWAMBHAR NATH SHARMA KAUSHIK (1891-1946). Fiction writer, whose chief works are : *Manimala* (1919), *Chitrashala* (2 Pts , 1924), *Kallol* (1933) (short story collections), *Man* (The Mother ; 1929), *Bhikharini* (The Beggar Woman ; 1929) ; the theme of both the novels is social, though they are mediocre in structure) and *Sangharsh* (novel). His prominent short stories are : 'Tai' (The Aunt), '*Pap ka Phal*' Fruit of Sin), 'Raksha Bandhan', 'Kritagyata' (Gratefulness) and 'Mata ka Hriday' (A Motherer's Heart). Besides the above, he wrote a mythological drama, entitled *Bhishma*.

VISHWAMBHAR NATH UPADHYAY (1925-). Writer, whose chief works are : *Bharatiya Kavya Shastra ka Adhyayan* (*Marxvad ke Alok Men*), *Hindi ki Darshnik Prishthabhumi* (The Philosophical Background of Hindi), *Surdas aur Unka Bhramargit*, *Adhuni k Hindi Kavita* (Modern Hindi Poetey), *Samkalin Kavita ki Bhumika* (Background of Contemporary Poetry), *Samkalin Sahitya aur Siddhant* (Contemporary Literature and Principles), *Jalte aur Ubalte Prashna*, *Bindu Pratibindu* : *Samkalin Alochana* (all criticism), *Pakshadhar* (1971), *Richh*, *Jag Machchhandar Gorakh Aya* (1984 ; novels), *Kabandh* (Torso ; 1978), a poetical work and *Kavi ki Niyati* (drama).

VISHWAMBHARAN, T.N. Malayalam-speaking modern Hindi scholar, whose research work is : *Kahani* : *Swar aur Swarup* (on short story).

VISHWAMITRA, J., THE LATE. Telugu-speaking Hindi writer, who is noted for his *Telugu aur Hindi Dhwaniyon ka Tulnatmak Adhyayan* (A Comparative Study of Telugu and Hindi *Dhwanis* ; 1974).

VISHWANATH. Rajasthani poet, whose humorous collections of poems are : *Lyo Hanslyo* and *Khari Maskhari* (1981 ; 50 poems concerned with current problems of corruption, nepotism, etc).

VISHWANATH AIYYAR, E. (1920-). Malayalam-speaking scholar, who is the author of *Vigyan Yogini*, *Swatantra Hindi Bodhini* (Self Teacher) and *Malayalam-Hindi Kosh*. His other important works are ; *Nibandhopahar* (a collection of essays),

Shahr So Raha Hai (literary essays, written in the cultural background of Kerala; 1975), *Kerala ke Pratham Hindi Gitkar* (The First Song-writers of Kerala), *Adhunik Hindi Kavya tatha Malayalam Kavya* (Modern Hindi and Malayalam Poetry ; 1970) and *Prachin Kavi Keshavdas.* He also tr. Malayalam short stories, poems and novels, the last under the titles of *Jo Jina Bhul Gai*, *Jaden* and *Adhi Ghadi.*

VISHWANATH GAUR (1921-81). Writer of Kanpur, whose chief work is : *Adhunik Hindi Kavya men Rahasyavad* (Mysticism in Modern Hindi Poetry ; 1955 ; criticism) ; with Lalit Shukl, he has published *Ayam*, a poetical work.

VISHWANATH JHA 'BALAJI'. Maithili poet, whose *Natika* (1839), a Kirtaniya drama, was written under the patronage of Rameshwar Singh. He was also noted for his lyrics.

VISHWANATH JHA 'VISHPAYI'. Modern Maithili poet, who is noted for his lyrics.

VISHWANATH PRASAD. Modern Bhojpuri scholar, who has made a study of the phonetic elements of Bhojpuri.

VISHWANATH PRASAD MISHRA (1906-82). Critic, who was born in Varanasi. His chief works are : *Vangmay Vimarsh*, *Bihari ki Vagvibhuti* (on Bihari), *Hindi Sahitya ka Atit* (The Past of the Hindi Literature) and *Hindi ka Samayik Sahitya* (Contemporary Hindi Literature) ; he has also edited the text of *Ramcharitmanas* (Kashiraj edition) as also the works of Keshavdas, Ghananand, Raskhan, Padmakar, Bhikharidas, Bhushan, etc. The tradition of scholarship in Hindi textual criticism was well maintained by him. He held many important posts including Head of the Department of Hindi, Magadh Vishwavidyalaya, Gaya.

VISHWANATH PRASAD SHUKLA. Modern scholar, whose chief work is *Ramkrishna Kavyottar Hindi Sagun Bhakti Kavya.*

VISHWANATH PRASAD TIWARI. Writer, who is noted for his critical works : *Agyey*, *Adhunik Hindi Kavita—Prasad se Agyey Tak* (1977), *Chhayavadottar Hindi Gadya Sahitya*, *Hazari Prasad Dwivedi* and *Samkalin Hindi Kavita* ; *Sath Chalte Huye* is his poetical collection.

VISHWANATH SHARMA 'VIMLESH'. Rajasthani poet, whose chief works are : *Ram Katha* (1966 ; on the story of Ram from his birth to coronation at Ayodhya in easy Rajasthani), *Nav Rasa Men Rasa Hasya* (1973 ; humorous and satirical poems),

Janta ko Durbar (1977 ; collection of 48 poems as reaction to Emergency imposed in 1975 and *Janta ki Sarkar* (1982), a collection of satirical poems. He has also composed patriotic poems as also poems on Nature.

VISHWANATH SHUKLA. Modern scholar, whose chief work is *Hindi Krishna-bhakti Kavya par Shrimad Bhagavat ka Prabhav.*

VISHWANATH SINGH, MAHARAJ (1789-1856). Poet, who was the ruler of Rewa State and who patronized many a poet. He composed 32 or 46 works in all. Among his works, *Ramayan, Anand Raghunandan* (drama), *Gita Raghunandan Pramanik, Kabir Bijak ki Tika, Vinay Patrika Tika, Param-tattwa*, etc., the *Anand Raghunandan* (q.v.) stands supreme ; some scholars regard this as the first Hindi drama. Despite the fact that he was a poet of the Ram-cult, he had great regard for *Nirgun* poetry. His two works : *Param-Dharma-Nirnay* and *Vishwanath Prakash* (*Amrit-Sagar*) are in Bagheli. His commentary on *Kabir Bijak* under the title *Pakhand Khandini* bears a testimony of his scholarship.

VISHWNATH TRIPATHI. Poet, whose collection of poems is *Jaisa Kah Saka* (As I Could Say ; 1980) ; his critical work is *Hindi Alochana*.

VISHWANATH VAISHAMPAYAN. Marathi-speaking modern Hindi writer, whose chief work is : *Amar Shahid Chandra-shekhar Azad.*

VISHWESHAR MISHRA. Maithili scholar, who has edited all the songs of Chanda Jha under the title *Chanda Rachnavali* (1981).

VISHWESHWAR NATH PATHAK. Writer, whose chief work is a romantic drama, *Lavang-Lata* (The Clove-Creeper ; 1885).

VISHWESHWAR NATH REU (1890-1966). Writer of Jodhpur, whose chief works are : *Bharat ke Prachin Rajvansh, Marwar ka Itihas, Raja Bhoj* and *Rashtrakuton ka Itihas.*

VITHAL DAS. See *Rukmini Haran.*

VITHU BHOMAU. See *Maharaj Ratan Singh ri Kavita.*

VITHU MEHA (fl latter half of 16th cent.) Dingal poet, who was granted the village Khedi by Rao Maldev of Jodhpur. His works are *Gogaji ra Rasavala, Pabuji ra Chhand, Karaniji ra Chhand* (on the glorious deeds of Gogaji, Pabuji and Karaniji respectively), *Bhati Somsi Ratanavat ro Chhand*,

Kavitta Chauhan Karamsi, *Sanvaldas Ra*, *Chandaji ri Vel* and verses on Kumpa Mehrajot.

VITHU SUJO. See *Sujo*.

VITHU SURA (fl. between 1450-1550). Rajasthani poet, whose stray *Gits* on contemporary rulers and chiefs are available.

VITTHALANATH (b. 1485). Son and disciple of Vallabhacharya; his chief works in Hindi are : *Shringar Rasa Mandan* (in prose), *Yamunashtak* (tr. from Sanskrit) and *Navratna Satik* (in Brajbhasha prose). He established the order *Ashtachhap* and did a lot for the propagation of Brajbhasha in verse as also in prose.

VIVEK NATH (fl. 19th cent.). Rajasthani Nath Siddha poet, whose poetry leans towards Vedanta of Shankar.

VIVEKANAND SHARMA (1939-). Fiji Hindi writer, who did M.A. from Delhi University. He was awarded the doctorate on his thesis : 'Cultural Contribution of Tulsi to Fiji'. He had been Youth and Sports Minister in the Fiji Government. He has edited 'Prashant Samachar' and 'Udayachal'. His chief works are : *Prashant ki Laharen* (2 Pts.), *Manavta Karah Uthi*, *Fiji ke Pradhan-mantri*, *Fiji Ke Ganv men Bharatiya Kisan*, *Fiji ke Bharatiya Parva*, *Prarthana Pustak*, *Havan Pustika*, *Vedic Prarthana*, *Ramayan Arti* and *Fiji men Sanatan Dharma ke Sau Sal*.

VIVEKI RAY (1927-). Writer, whose chief works are : *Phir Baitalva Dalkar* (essay collection), *Hindi Upanyas : Uttar Shati ki Uplabdhiyan* (Criticism), *Babul* (The Acacia *Tree*), *Purush Puran* (The Story of Man), *Lok-Rin* (The Public Debt), *Shwet Patra* and *Sona Mati* (1984 ; novels). He is noted for his essays. He has also written short stories as 'Nayi Katha' (New Story), 'Rambabu B.D.O se Mile' (Rambabu met the B.D.O.). His short story collections are : *Ganga Jahaz*, *Bete ki Bikri*, *Nayi Koel*, *Kalatit*, *Viveki Ray ki Shreshth Kahaniyan* (1984) and *Meri Shreshth Vyangya Rachnayen* (satirical writings).

VIYOGI, MOHANLAL MEHTO. See *Mohanlal Mehto 'Viyogi'*.

VIYOGI HARI (1896-). Poet and writer, who was born in a Brahmin family of Chhatarpur State. In the beginning, he was non-dualist, but after his contact with Maharani Kamalakumari 'Yugalpriya' of Chhatarpur State, he became a dualist and a devotee of Krishna. His contact with Purushottam Das Tandon inspired him towards literary creation, while

Mahatma Gandhi's influence made him a social reformer. His chief works are : *Antarnad*, *Vir Satsai* (1927 ; 700 couplets in praise of ancient and modern heroes), *Kavi Kirtan*, *Anurag Vatika*, *Prem Pathik* (poems), *Chhadmayogini*, *Vir Hardaul*, *Prabuddha Yamun* (dramas), *Mera Jivan Pravah* (My Life Stream ; autobiography) and *Tulsi Sudhasar* (criticism). His *Vir Satsai* in Brajbhasha holds a prominent place in his writings. He has also made a notable contribution to the development of Hindi prose poems.

VRAJBHAR DIKSHIT (fl. 1603). A follower of Vallabhacharya, who wrote a commentary in Brajbhasha prose on *Vallabhakhyat*.

VRAJESHWAR VARMA (1913-). Writer, whose chief works are : *Surdas* (1946 ; research work), *Sur Mimansa* (1953), *Hindi Sahitya Kosh* (ed.), *Hindi Sahitya* (ed.) *Bhartiya Bhashaon ka Bhasha Shastriya Adhyayan* (ed. with N.V. Rajagopalan ; 1965) and *Mahakavi Sur* : *Ek Punishchintan*. He has also ed. 'Hindi Anushilan', 'Alochana' and 'Gaveshana'.

VRIND (1643-1723). Poet of Merta in Rajasthan, whose ancestors belonged to Bikaner. His mother's name was Kaushalya, while his father was Rupji. When Vrind was 10 years old, he was sent to Kashi for education. On his return from there, he was honoured by Maharaja Jaswant Singh of Jodhpur. It was at the instance of the Maharaja of Jodhpur that he was introduced to Aurangzeb. Aurangzeb appointed him as his court-poet and tutor to his son, Ba hadur Shah and grandson, Azimushshan. When Azimushshan was appointed the Governor of Bengal and Orissa, he took Vrind with him. In 1707, Maharaja Rajsingh of Kishengarh took Vrind to his court and he settled there, where he died in 1723. His descendants still reside in Kishengarh.

Although he has written on *Shringar Rasa* and his two works : *Shringar Shiksha* (1691) and *Bhav-Panchashika* are devoted to this *Rasa*, he is popular as the author of the *Vrind-Satsai*, a compilation of 713 couplets ; each embodying some worldly experience. The expression is pithy but Vrind's work belongs essentially to the literature of knowledge. Besides stray verses in Dingal and Pingal, his other works are : *Yamak Satsai* (700 *Dohas*), *Vachnika* (1705; on the heroism of Raja Rupsingh of Kishengarh), *Satyaswarup* (1707; on the bravery of Maharaja Rajsingh of Kishengarh), *Pavan Pachisi*, *Samet Sikhar Chhand*, *Hitopadeshashtak*, *Bharat Katha* and *Hitopadesh*.

VRIND-SATSAI. See *Vrind*.

VRINDAVAN CHANDRA (*c.* 1673-1743). Poet of the Krishna-cult (Chaitanya Sect), whose only work in Brajbhasha is *Ashtayam.* He was also a Sanskrit scholar and wrote commentaries on some Sanskrit works.

VRINDAVAN DAS (*b.* 1507). Bengali Vaishnav poet, who composed *Chaitanya Bhagavat* on the life of Chaitanya. He also composed 4 *Padas* in Brajbuli : two on Chaitanya Mahaprabhu and two on the *Lila* of Radha and Krishna.

VRINDAVAN DAS. See *Hit Vrindavan Das.*

VRINDAVAN DAS (*c.* 1718-*c.* 83). Poet of the Krishna-cult (Chaitanya Sect), who belonged to the Braj country. He composed three small works : *Bhakta-Namavali, Prembhakti Chandrika* and *Vilap Kusumanjali* : all trs., the first two from Bengali and the last from Sanskrit. He also composed some stray *Padas* in praise of Chaitanya.

VRINDAVAN DEV (fl. 16th cent.). Saint-poet of the Krishna-cult (Nimbark Sect), who was born in a Gaur Brahmin family of Rajasthan. He composed *Padas* only, which are collected in *Krishnamrit Ganga* (The Stream of Elixir of Krishna).

VRINDAVAN LAL VARMA (1889-1969). Novelist and dramatist, who was born at the village Mauranipur in the Jhansi district of Uttar Pradesh. While still in the 9th class, he wrote three short dramas and sent them to Indian Press, Allahabad for which he was given a prize. Thereafter he wrote *Mahatma Buddha ka Jivancharitra* and tr. Shakespeare's *Tempest* into Hindi. In 1909, he wrote *Senapati Udal,* a drama, which was confiscated by the then British Government. Varma's great grandfather was a Diwan of Jhansi State and was killed while fighting for the Rani ki Jhansi. He had great attachment wlth Bundelkhand and many of his works are woven around the history of that region.

His chief novels are : *Garh Kundar* (The Fort of Kundar ; 1929 ; description of Bundelkhand in the 14th century), *Kundali Chakra, Virata ki Padmini* (The Padmini of Virata ; q.v.), *Jhansi ki Rani* (The Queen of Jhansi; q.v.; 1946), *Kachnar, Mrignayani* (The Fawn-eyed), *Ahalyabai* (1954), *Madhoji Scindhia, Bhuvan-Vikram, Ramgarh ki Rani, Musahibju* (The Courtier ; all historical novels), *Prem ki Bhent* (The Offering of Love), *Achal Mera Koi, Amar Bel* (The Ivy), *Lagan* (The Engagement), *Sangam* (The Meeting), *Kabhi na Kabhi* (Sooner or Later), *Tute Kante* (The Broken Thorns), *Uday Kiran, Pratyagat* (The Return) (social novels) ; *Mrignayani* (q.v.), considered to be his *magnum opus*, describes the artistic achievement and heroic deeds of the heroine.

Varma has also written short stories and some dramas, his chief works being *Purva ki Or* (Towards the East), *Hans Mayur* (on the re-establishment of Aryan culture after Shaks), *Lalit Vikram, Rakhi ki Laj, Pile Hath, Jhansi ki Rani, Kevat* (on un-principled defection in the present-day politics), *Bans ki Phans* (on a social theme) and *Dhire-Dhire* (Little by Little). He has published 7 collections of the short stories, the chief ones being *Sharnagat* and *Kalakar ka Dand* (The Punishment of an Artist). He has also two so-far unpublished novels : *Rana Sanga* and *Chhatrasal.*

In his mastery of historical details and in the presentation and portrayal of events, Varma occupies an important place among historical novelists.

VRISHBHAN KUNVARI (fl. 1728-47). Poetess of the Krishna-cult, who was the queen of Orchha ruler. Her chief works on devotion are : *Bhakti-Virudavali, Aurang-Chandrika* and *Danlila.*

VYANGARTH KAUMUDI. See *Pratap Sahi.*

VYAS, AMBIKA DATT. See *Ambika Datt Vyas.*

VYAS, R.K. Rajasthani writer, whose *Mhara to Girdhar Gopal* (1982) is a full length drama on Mira (q.v.), the saint-poetess.

VYAS, R S. Rajasthani scholar, whose *Rajasthani Gadya Sahitya ka Samikshatmak evam Vikasatmak Itihas* (1979) is a critical history of the development of Rajasthani prose literature ; it is a research work.

VYATHIT HRIDAY. Modern fiction writer, whose chief novels are *Yamuna Tire* and *Suryaputra.* He has also written dramas, short stories ((*Dahej ka Dagh*) and several books for children. His critical work is : *Braj ke Sidhha Sant.*

W

WAJAHI (fl. 1580-1650). One of thc foremost writers of Dakhini, whose *Sabrasa* is considered the best-known prose work in Dakhini ; it is a philosophical and allegorical love-story covering about 300 pages. His earlier work, *Qutub Mushtri* is a romance.

WALI (*d.* 1707). Sufi poet of Aurangabad or Ahmedabad (Gujarat), whose full name was Wali Mohammad. Several of his verses are in Dakhini Hindi.

WATERFIELD, W. European scholar, who was noted for his *The Lay of Alha* (Oxford, 1923).

WENDER, E. American Hindi scholar and author of *Hindi Grammar with Reader* (Philadelphia, 1968).

WHALE, PAUL. Author of *Hindi Etymologies* (1904).

WIDEMANN, DIETHELM. Modern German scholar, who, as Director of School of Asian Studies, Humboldt University, East Germany, has promoted the study of Hindi in his country.

W

Wajhi (fl. 1580-1650). One of the foremost writers of Dakhini, whose Sabras is considered the best-known prose work in Dakhini; it is a philosophical and allegorical [illegible] story covering about 300 pages. His earlier work, *Qutb Mushtari*, is a romance.

Wali (d. 1707). Sufi poet of Aurangabad or Ahmedabad (Gujarat), whose full name was Wali Mohammad. Several of his verses are in Dakhini Hindi.

W[illegible], W. European scholar who was noted for his *The [illegible] of Man* (Oxford, 1913).

W[illegible], J. American Hindi scholar and author of *Hindi Grammar with Reader* (Philadelphia, 1958).

W[illegible], Paul. Author of *Hindi Etymologies* (1904).

W[illegible], Dr. Peter. Modern German scholar who as Director of School of Asian Studies, Humboldt University, East Germany, has promoted the study of Hindi in that country.

Y

Yadunandan Das (fl. 1607). Bengali Vaishnav poet, who also composed *Padas* in Brajbuli.

Yadunandan Das (fl. 1st half of 20th cent.). Maithili poet, who tr. *Kumarasambhava* into Maithili from the original Sanskrit.

Yadunandan Jha 'Pralayankar' (fl. *c.* 1930). Maithili writer, who was noted for his short stories.

Yadunandan Sharma (fl. 1930). Hindi poet of Mauritius, who was noted for his songs.

Yadunath Jha 'Yaduvar'. Modern Maithili poet, whose chief work is the editing in the 'Twenties of *Maithili Gitanjali*, an anthology of patriotic poetry. His *Muktak* poems are collected in *Anyokti Shatak*.

Yadupati. A contemporary of Raja Narsingh Dev (r. 1605-35) of Orissa ; he has eulogised his patron Narsingh Dev in Hindi (Brajboli).

Yaduvansh Lal Chandra. Modern Hindi poet of Nepal, whose chief works are : *Pushpanjali* and *Sudha*.

Yadvendra Sharma 'Chandra'. Novelist, whose chief works are : *Itvar*, *Sannyasi aur Sundari* (A Recluse and a Beautiful Woman), *Dhuli aur Narttan*, *Simant Bijgupta* (an extension of the story of *Chitralekha* by Bhagvati Charan Verma), *Airavati* (completion of the incomplete novel of the same name by Jayshankar Prasad), *Panthhin*, *Dharti ki Pir*, *Chhan-Annadata*, *Chehre Mat Utaro* (1979 ; a realistic novel), *Talaq-dar-Talaq* (Divorce upon Divorce ; 1980), *Agnipath*. *Apna Atit* and *Sapna* (1984). He has also published several collections of short stories, *e.g.*, *Meri Priya Kahaniyan* (1984). In Rajasthani, his works are : *Hun Gori Kin Piv Ri* (1970 ; a popular novel on the life of a potter's widow), *Jog Sanjog* (on inter-caste marriage), *Tas ro Ghar* (1973 ; a forceful drama on contemporary life) and *Devta* (one-act plays).

YAGYA DATT SHARMA (1916-). Writer, whose novel *Insan* has been written in the background of communal riots ; his other chief novels are : *Shilanyas*, *Swapna Khil Utha*, *Gomti ke Kinare* and *Rangshala*. His novels, *Badalti Rahen*, *Jhuniya ki Shadi*, *Insaf*, *Parivar*, *Bap-Beti*, *Antim Charan*, *Mahal aur Makan*, etc. reveal the post-Independence consciousness. He has written about 40 novels.

YAGYA NARAYAN SHASTRI, PASUMARTI. Telugu author of *Andhra Nat Prakashika* (1920), which mentions that in the early stages of Telugu drama, there were composed many Hindi plays, which were also staged.

YAMA. See *Mahadevi Verma*.

YAMUNA DAS (fl. *c*. 1700). Poet, who was author of the *Git Raghunandan*, a work based on the Sanskrit *Gita Govinda* of Jayadeva.

YAMUNA KACHRU. Scholar and author of *An Introduction to Hindi Syntax* (1966), *Studies in Hindi Linguistics* (with Braj Kachru ; ed. 1968), *Papers on Hindi Syntax* (ed. 1971), *Hindi Rupatantratmak Vyakaran ke Kuchh Prakaran* (1973), *Hindi ka Samayik Vyakaran* and *Intermediate Hindi* (2 Pts. ; 1983 ; with Rajeshwari Pandhari Pande), which is a selection of teaching material for teaching Hindi as a second or foreign language. She has also published a good number of articles on Hindi language and grammar. She is at present Professor of Linguistics and English in the University of Illinois, Urbana-Champaign, America

YAMUNA PRASAD SHARMA 'JWALA'. Modern Magahi poet, who is noted for his stray poems.

YAMUNA SHEWDE. Marathi-speaking modern Hindi fiction writer, whose short stories have appeared in various magazines. She has also written two novels : *Jivan Sangit* and *Purnahuti*

YAQUB KHAN. Poet of the Riti school, whose *Rasa Bhushan* was composed in 1718. He is said to have composed another work, *Hazara*.

YARAMKOVA, SVETLANA NIKOLYEVNA (1937-). Soviet Hindi

scholar, who did her doctorate on the works of Subhadra Kumari Chauhan. She has written several articles on the works of Subhadra Kumari Chauhan and Maithili Sharan Gupta.

YARI SAHIB (1668-1723) Muslim saint-poet, who lived at Delhi, where his Samadhi lies. His *Kavittas, Jhulnas* and *Sakhians* are very popular ; like Kabir, he made full use of images. He was a follower of Bavari Panth.

YASH GULATI. Critic, whose chief work is *Kavita aur Sangharsh Chetana* (1980).

YASH PAL (1903-76). Novelist, who was born in Ferozepur Cantt. His mother wanted him to be an Arya Samajist preacher and as such he was educated at Gurukula Kangri, Hardwar. At the Gurukula, he was fired with patriotic zeal. After his study at the National College, Lahore, he was introduced to the revolutionaries like Bhagat Singh, Sukhdev and others He was sent to jail in 1932 but was released in 1938. Again in 1941, he was jailed. He was a leftist and a revolutionary by conviction ; his earliest novels *Dada Comrade* (The Leader Comrade ; 1941), *Desh Drohi* (The Traitor), *Party Comrade*, etc. present pictures of socialist and communist ideology. His other chief works are : *Do Duniya* (Two Worlds), *Manushya-ke-Rup* (The Faces of Man ; 1949 ; partly social and partly political ; on the life-struggle of Soma, a hill woman), *Divya* (1954 ; q.v. ; a historical novel, which demonstrates that a learned Brahmin and a staunch Buddhist are both amenable to the charms of feminine beauty), *Amita* (1956 ; historical), *Jhutha Sach* (False Truth ; q.v. ; a novel in two parts on an epic scale in the background of partition of India in 1947), *Chhattis Ghante* (Thirty-six Hours ; 1963 ; this shows that love and marriage are dependent on physical bonds rather than of souls), *Kyon Phanse* ? (Why Got Involved ; 1968), *Meri Teri Uski Bat* (Between You, Me and Him ; based on the social and political life of the pre- and post- Independence India), *Dharma-yuddha* (The Holy War), *Pucca Qadam, Zulaikha* and *Apsara ka Shap*.

Yash Pal's short story collections are : *Pinjre ki Udan* (The Flight of the Cage), *Vo Duniya* (That World), *Gyandan* (The Imparting of Knowledge), *Abhishapta* (The Cursed), *Tark ka Tufan* (The Storm of Logic), *Bhasmavrit Chingari, Phulo ka Kurta* (Phulo's Long Shirt), *Bhairavi, Uttama ki Man* (Uttama's Mother), *Sach Bolne ki Bhul* (To Forget the Speaking of the Truth) and *Tumne Kyon Kaha Tha ki Main Sundar Hun* ? (Why did you say that you are Beautiful ?), *Uttaradhikari, Chitra ka*

Shirshak, *Khachchar aur Admi*, *Bhukh ke Tin Din*, *Bibiji Kahti Hain Mera Chehra Robila Hai* and *Lamp Shade* ; in some of his stories, he comes out as one obsessed with his political ideology. He has in all written about 200 short stories. His important short stories are : 'Sag' (The Vegetable), 'Admi ka Bachcha' (The Son of Man), 'Parlok' (The Other World), 'Karma-phal' (The Fruit of Action), 'Phulo ka Kurta', 'Pativrata' (The Chaste Wife), 'Pratishtha ka Bojh' (The Burden of Respectability', 'Gyan-dan', 'Dharm Raksha' (The Protection of Dharm), 'Parda' (The Veil), 'Kala Admi' (The Black Man), 'Char Anna' (The Four Annas), 'Makril', etc. A collection of his short stories in English has been published from America.

Yash Pal's other works are : *Dekha, Socha, Samjha, Bat Bat Men Bat*, *Marxvad*, *Gandhivad ki Shav-Pariksha* (The Post-mortem of Gandhism), *Chakkar Club*, *Ram-Rajya ki Katha* (political essays), *Nyay ka Sangharsh* (The Struggle for Justice ; essay collections), *Nashe-Nashe ki Bat* (drama) and *Simhalokan* (A Retrospect ; autobiography in 3 parts). *Lohe ki Diwar ke Donon Or* (1953) and *Rah Biti* (1956) are his travelogues.

YASHPAL, ADARSH KUMARI. See *Adarsh Kumari Yashpal*.

YASH PAL JAIN. Modern short story writer, whose chief short story collections are : *Dayare aur Insan*, *As Bandh Gai* and *Triveni Sangam*.

YASHODA NANDAN (b. 1771). Poet of the Riti school, whose *Barvai Nayikabhed*, a small work on the types of heroines, is considered of equal merit as that of Rahim's work, bearing an identical name Yashoda Nandan's work has 62 *Barvais*, 9 in Sanskrit and 53 in pure Avadhi.

YASHODA NATH JHA. Maithili critic, whose *Yatri Kavya Vivechan* (1980) discusses the Maithili contribution of Nagarjun to Maithili and Hindi poetry ; Yatri is the pen-name of Nagarjun (q v.) in Maithili.

YASHODHAR NAV-KAVISHEKHAR (1493-1531). Maithili poet, whose poems in the style of Vidyapati's *Padas* are extant.

YASHODHARA. Poetical work (1932) by Maithili Sharan Gupta (q.v.), which treats of the life of Yashodhara, the wife of Gautam Buddha The poet has successfully depicted the mental state of Yashodhara when hes ays that while she has milk and affection for her son, Rahul, her eyes are sad with tears for losing her lord, who has said good-bye to her without saying any word to her.

YASHORAJ KHAN (fl. 1493-1519). Bengali poet, who was patronized by Hussain Shah, the Gaur Sultan. A *Pada* composed by him in Brajbuli is available.

YASHOVIJAY UPADHYAY (1623-76). Gujarati-speaking Jain saint-poet, who is said to have composed 300 works in Sanskrit, Gujarati and Hindi. Of his Hindi works only five to six books and some stray verses are extant ; his works are : *Anandghan Ashtapadi* (in praise of Anandghan), *Dikpat Chaurasi Bol*, *Samadhi-Shatak* (tr.), *Samata-Shatak* and *Jas-Vilas*. He was well-versed in Indian philosophy.

YASHVANT-YASHOBHUSHAN. See *Muraridan*.

YATES, WILLIAM. Author of *Introduction to the Hindustani Language* (Calcutta, 1827), the first part of which contains Hindustani Grammar. It ran into several editions ; the National Library, Calcutta has its 1843 edition. He also compiled *A Dictionary, Hindustani and English* (Calcutta, 1847).

YATRI. See *Nagarjun*.

YATRI, Se. Ra. See *Seva Ram Yatri*.

YELIZARENKOVA, TATYANA YAKOVLEVNA (1929-). Soviet Hindi scholar, who has published 7 works and some 90 articles. Her field of specialization is Indo-Aryan languages and Ancient Indian Literature. She has written several works on Hindi grammar as well.

YEREMIYAN, LARISA VARSHAMOVNA (1938-). Soviet Hindi scholar, whose research work is on the progressive Indian writers. He has also written on Prem Chand, Yashpal, Hazari Prasad Dwivedi and on Marxist literature.

YOG CHANDRA MUNI (fl. 12th cent.) Celebrated Jain poet, whose *Yogasar*, written in *Dohas*, is a religious work, in which Hindi appears to take its definite form.

YOG NARENDRA MALL (fl 1633-55). Maithili poet of Nepal, whose only poetical work appears to have been used in a *Ragmala*, which contains *Padas* only by Vidyapati and Jagatjjay Mall. A Sanskrit drama on the *Mahabharat* is also attributed to him.

YOGANAND JHA. Maithili writer, whose chief novels are: *Bhal-Manus* (1944) and *Pavitra* (1967). His *Bhal-Manus* has aroused much attention on account of caste-prejudices in the marriage of the Kulin community. *Am Khaeba ka Muh* and *Sannyasi* are his short story collections, while *Munika Matibhram* on the story of Sukanya, is a great one-act play. His another one-act play is *Antim Ramcharit*. He has also tr. into Maithili Mahatma Gandhi's *Autobiography* (1982).

YOGENDRA BAKHSHI. Panjabi-speaking modern Hindi scholar and author of *Hindi tatha Panjabi Upanyason ka Tulnatmak Adhyayan*.

YOGENDRA NATH SINHA. Modern writer, whose regional novel, *Van ke Man Men* (In the Forest's Mind) describes the life of the Ho tribe.

YOGESH CHANDRA BHARGAVA. Writer, who is noted for his novels, *Jwala* (The Fire ; 1980) and *Patjhar ka Ant*.

YOGESH GUPTA (1931-). Fiction writer, whose chief novels are : *Upsanhar* (Conclusion ; 1980), *Swapna Dansh* (The Dream Sting ; 1982) and *Patthar par Khinchi Lakiren* (1984). He has also published short story collections : *Abrak ke Phul*, *Tuta Hua Kona* and *Un Do Shahron ki Tarah* (1984).

YOGESHWAR JHA. Maithili poet, whose *Nor* (1979), a *Khand-Kavya*, describes the devastations caused by the river Kosi. His *Arya* is a collection of *Muktaks* dealing with modern subjects written in *Arya* metre,

YOGESHWAR PRASAD SINGH 'YOGESH'. Modern Magahi poet, who is noted for his humorous and satirical poems.

YOGINDRA PURI MAHANT (fl. early 20th cent). Garhwali poet, who is noted for his collection of poems : *Phul Kundi*, treating of religion, ethics, social reform, Nature and the sorrows of women.

YUGAL KISHORE DWIVEDI (fl. 1940-47). Malwi poet, who is noted for his *Yugal Ninad*.

YUGANT. See *Sumitra Nandan Pant*.

YUGBODH. Modern Maithili poet, who is known for his poems and lyrics.

YUGESHWAR. Author of *Magahi Bhasha* (1969).

YUGVANI. See *Sumitra Nandan Pant*.

YUKTIBHADRA DIKSHIT (1927-). Avadhi folk-poet, who is son of the late Padhis (q.v.) and was born at the Ambarpur village in Sitapur district. Attached to the All India Radio, Allahabad, he has written 150 poems, 15 tales in verse and over 150 dramas and has collected over 1,000 folk-songs, but most of his works remain unpublished. *Ghar ki Beti* is his published drama.

Z

ZAHIR QURESHI. Poet, whose chief work is *Ek Tukra Dhup* (A Patch of Sunshine ; 1979), a poetical collection.

ZAHUR KHAN. Rajasthani scholar, whose chief work is *Rajasthani Sanskriti ra Chitram* (1981), which gives picture-glimpses of Rajasthani culture. The work is the first of its kind.

ZAIDI, N.H. Author of *A Reader of Nine Short Stories Arranged in Order of Difficulties for Second-year Students* (Honolulu, 1965).

ZINDA KAUL. Hindi writer of Jammu and Kashmir, who is noted for his work *Patrapushpa* (A Little Offering).

ZUTSHI, S.K. Kashmiri-speaking modern Hindi writer, whose first novel *Rakh ka Dher* (A Heap of Ashes) represents the revolutionary fervour of the new generation.

List of Foreign Authors

FIJI

Author Index, With Surnames First

E

F

G

J

K

L

N

O

Q

R

W

Y

Z